Lecture Notes in Computer Science 13276

More information about this series at https://link.springer.com/bookseries/558

Orr Dunkelman · Stefan Dziembowski (Eds.)

Advances in Cryptology – EUROCRYPT 2022

41st Annual International Conference on the Theory
and Applications of Cryptographic Techniques
Trondheim, Norway, May 30 – June 3, 2022
Proceedings, Part II

 Springer

Editors
Orr Dunkelman ⓘ
University of Haifa
Haifa, Haifa, Israel

Stefan Dziembowski ⓘ
University of Warsaw
Warsaw, Poland

ISSN 0302-9743   ISSN 1611-3349 (electronic)
Lecture Notes in Computer Science
ISBN 978-3-031-07084-6   ISBN 978-3-031-07085-3 (eBook)
https://doi.org/10.1007/978-3-031-07085-3

This Springer imprint is published by the registered company Springer Nature Switzerland AG
The registered company address is: Gewerbestrasse 11, 6330 Cham, Switzerland

Preface

The 41st Annual International Conference on the Theory and Applications of Cryptographic Techniques, Eurocrypt 2022, was held in Trondheim, Norway. Breaking tradition, the conference started on the evening of Monday, May 30, and ended at noon on Friday, June 3, 2022. Eurocrypt is one of the three flagship conferences of the International Association for Cryptologic Research (IACR), which sponsors the event. Colin Boyd (NTNU, Norway) was the general chair of Eurocrypt 2022 who took care of all the local arrangements.

The 372 anonymous submissions we received in the IACR HotCRP system were each reviewed by at least three of the 70 Program Committee members (who were allowed at most two submissions). We used a rebuttal round for all submissions. After a lengthy and thorough review process, 85 submissions were selected for publication. The revised versions of these submissions can be found in these three-volume proceedings.

In addition to these papers, the committee selected the "EpiGRAM: Practical Garbled RAM" by David Heath, Vladimir Kolesnikov, and Rafail Ostrovsky for the best paper award. Two more papers — "On Building Fine-Grained One-Way Functions from Strong Average-Case Hardness" and "Quantum Algorithms for Variants of Average-Case Lattice Problems via Filtering" received an invitation to the Journal of Cryptology. Together with presentions of the 85 accepted papers, the program included two invited talks: The IACR distinguished lecture, carried by Ingrid Verbauwhede, on "Hardware: an essential partner to cryptography", and "Symmetric Cryptography for Long Term Security" by María Naya-Plasancia.

We would like to take this opportunity to thank numerous people. First of all, the authors of all submitted papers, whether they were accepted or rejected. The Program Committee members who read, commented, and debated the papers generating more than 4,500 comments(!) in addition to a large volume of email communications. The review process also relied on 368 subreviewers (some of which submitted more than one subreivew). We cannot thank you all enough for your hard work.

A few individuals were extremely helpful in running the review process. First and foremost, Kevin McCurley, who configured, solved, answered, re-answered, supported, and did all in his (great) power to help with the IACR system. Wkdqn Brx! We are also extremely grateful to Gaëtan Leurent for offering his wonderful tool to make paper assignment an easy task. The wisdom and experience dispensed by Anne Canteaut, Itai Dinur, Bart Preneel, and François-Xavier Standaert are also noteworthy and helped usher the conference into a safe haven. Finally, we wish to thank the area chairs—Sonia Belaïd, Carmit Hazay, Thomas Peyrin, Nigel Smart, and Martijn Stam. You made our work manageable.

Finally, we thank all the people who were involved in the program of Eurocrypt 2022: the rump session chairs, the session chairs, the speakers, and all the technical support staff in Trondheim. We would also like to mention the various sponsors and thank them for the generous support. We wish to thank the continuous support of the Cryptography Research Fund for supporting student speakers.

May 2022

Orr Dunkelman
Stefan Dziembowski

Organization

**The 41st Annual International Conference on the Theory
and Applications of Cryptographic Techniques (Eurocrypt 2022)**

Sponsored by the *International Association for Cryptologic Research*
Trondheim, Norway
May 30 – June 3, 2022

General Chair

Colin Boyd   NTNU, Norway

Program Chairs

Orr Dunkelman   University of Haifa, Israel
Stefan Dziembowski   University of Warsaw, Poland

Program Committee

Masayuki Abe   NTT Laboratories, Japan
Shashank Agrawal   Western Digital Research, USA
Joël Alwen   AWS Wickr, Austria
Marshall Ball   New York University, USA
Gustavo Banegas   Inria and Institut Polytechnique de Paris, France
Paulo Barreto   University of Washington Tacoma, USA
Sonia Belaïd   CryptoExperts, France
Jean-François Biasse   University of South Florida, USA
Begül Bilgin   Rambus Cryptography Research, The Netherlands
Alex Biryukov   University of Luxembourg, Luxembourg
Olivier Blazy   Ecole Polytechnique, France
Billy Bob Brumley   Tampere University, Finland
Chitchanok Chuengsatiansup   University of Adelaide, Australia
Michele Ciampi   University of Edinburgh, UK
Ran Cohen   IDC Herzliya, Israel
Henry Corrigan-Gibbs   Massachusetts Institute of Technology, USA
Cas Cremers   CISPA Helmholtz Center for Information
                               Security, Germany
Dana Dachman-Soled   University of Maryland, USA
Jean Paul Degabriele   TU Darmstadt, Germany
Itai Dinur   Ben-Gurion University, Israel

Meltem Sönmez Turan	National Institute of Standards and Technology, USA
Daniele Venturi	Sapienza University of Rome, Italy
Ivan Visconti	University of Salerno, Italy
Gaoli Wang	East China Normal University, China
Stefan Wolf	University of Italian Switzerland, Switzerland
Sophia Yakoubov	Aarhus University, Denmark
Avishay Yanai	VMware Research, Israel
Bo-Yin Yang	Academia Sinica, Taiwan
Arkady Yerukhimovich	George Washington University, USA
Yu Yu	Shanghai Jiao Tong University, China
Mark Zhandry	NTT Research and Princeton University, USA

Subreviewers

Behzad Abdolmaleki
Ittai Abraham
Damiano Abram
Anasuya Acharya
Alexandre Adomnicai
Amit Agarwal
Shweta Agrawal
Thomas Agrikola
Akshima
Navid Alamati
Alejandro Cabrera Aldaya
Bar Alon
Miguel Ambrona
Hiroaki Anada
Diego F. Aranha
Victor Arribas
Tomer Ashur
Gennaro Avitabile
Matilda Backendal
Saikrishna Badrinarayanan
Shi Bai
Ero Balsa
Augustin Bariant
James Bartusek
Balthazar Bauer
Carsten Baum
Ämin Baumeler
Arthur Beckers
Charles Bédard

Christof Beierle
Pascal Bemmann
Fabrice Benhamouda
Francesco Berti
Tim Beyne
Rishabh Bhadauria
Adithya Bhat
Sai Lakshmi Bhavana Obbattu
Alexander Bienstock
Erica Blum
Jan Bobolz
Xavier Bonnetain
Cecilia Boschini
Raphael Bost
Vincenzo Botta
Katharina Boudgoust
Christina Boura
Zvika Brakerski
Luís Brandão
Lennart Braun
Jacqueline Brendel
Gianluca Brian
Anne Broadbent
Marek Broll
Christopher Brzuska
Chloe Cachet
Matteo Campanelli
Federico Canale
Anne Canteaut

Ignacio Cascudo

Andre Chailloux

Nishanth Chandran

Donghoon Chang

Binyi Chen

Shan Chen

Weikeng Chen

Yilei Chen

Jung Hee Cheon

Jesus-Javier Chi-Dominguez

Seung Geol Choi

Wutichai Chongchitmate

Arka Rai Choudhuri

Sherman S. M. Chow

Jeremy Clark

Xavier Coiteux-Roy

Andrea Coladangelo

Nan Cui

Benjamin R. Curtis

Jan Czajkowski

Jan-Pieter D'Anvers

Hila Dahari

Thinh Dang

Quang Dao

Poulami Das

Pratish Datta

Bernardo David

Gareth T. Davies

Hannah Davis

Lauren De Meyer

Gabrielle De Micheli

Elke De Mulder

Luke Demarest

Julien Devevey

Siemen Dhooghe

Denis Diemert

Jintai Ding

Jack Doerner

Xiaoyang Dong

Nico Döttling

Benjamin Dowling

Yang Du

Leo Ducas

Julien Duman

Betul Durak

Oğuzhan Ersoy

Andreas Erwig

Daniel Escudero

Muhammed F. Esgin

Saba Eskandarian

Prastudy Fauzi

Patrick Felke

Thibauld Feneuil

Peter Fenteany

Diodato Ferraioli

Marc Fischlin

Nils Fleischhacker

Cody Freitag

Daniele Friolo

Tommaso Gagliardoni

Steven D. Galbraith

Pierre Galissant

Chaya Ganesh

Cesar Pereida García

Romain Gay

Kai Gellert

Craig Gentry

Marilyn George

Hossein Ghodosi

Satrajit Ghosh

Jan Gilcher

Aarushi Goel

Eli Goldin

Junqing Gong

Dov Gordon

Jérôme Govinden

Lorenzo Grassi

Johann Großschädl

Jiaxin Guan

Daniel Guenther

Milos Gujic

Qian Guo

Cyril Guyot

Mohammad Hajiabadi

Ariel Hamlin

Shuai Han

Abida Haque

Patrick Harasser

Dominik Hartmann

Phil Hebborn

Alexandra Henzinger
Javier Herranz
Julia Hesse
Justin Holmgren
Akinori Hosoyamada
Kai Hu
Andreas Hülsing
Shih-Han Hung
Vincenzo Iovino
Joseph Jaeger
Aayush Jain
Christian Janson
Samuel Jaques
Stanislaw Jarecki
Corentin Jeudy
Zhengzhong Jin
Daniel Jost
Saqib Kakvi
Vukašin Karadžić
Angshuman Karmakar
Shuichi Katsumata
Jonathan Katz
Mahimna Kelkar
Nathan Keller
John Kelsey
Mustafa Khairallah
Hamidreza Amini Khorasgani
Dongwoo Kim
Miran Kim
Elena Kirshanova
Fuyuki Kitagawa
Michael Klooß
Sebastian Kolby
Lukas Kölsch
Yashvanth Kondi
David Kretzler
Veronika Kuchta
Marie-Sarah Lacharité
Yi-Fu Lai
Baptiste Lambin
Mario Larangeira
Rio LaVigne
Quoc-Huy Le
Jooyoung Lee
Julia Len

Antonin Leroux
Hanjun Li
Jianwei Li
Yiming Li
Xiao Liang
Damien Ligier
Chengyu Lin
Dongxi Liu
Jiahui Liu
Linsheng Liu
Qipeng Liu
Xiangyu Liu
Chen-Da Liu Zhang
Julian Loss
Vadim Lyubashevsky
Lin Lyu
You Lyu
Fermi Ma
Varun Madathil
Akash Madhusudan
Bernardo Magri
Monosij Maitra
Nikolaos Makriyannis
Mary Maller
Giorgia Marson
Christian Matt
Noam Mazor
Nikolas Melissaris
Bart Mennink
Antonis Michalas
Brice Minaud
Kazuhiko Minematsu
Alberto Montina
Amir Moradi
Marta Mularczyk
Varun Narayanan
Jade Nardi
Patrick Neumann
Ruth Ng
Hai H. Nguyen
Kirill Nikitin
Ryo Nishimaki
Anca Nitulescu
Ariel Nof
Julian Nowakowski

Adam O'Neill

Maciej Obremski

Eran Omri

Maximilian Orlt

Bijeeta Pal

Jiaxin Pan

Omer Paneth

Lorenz Panny

Dimitrios Papadopoulos

Jeongeun Park

Anat Paskin-Cherniavsky

Sikhar Patranabis

Marcin Pawłowski

Hilder Pereira

Ray Perlner

Clara Pernot

Léo Perrin

Giuseppe Persiano

Edoardo Persichetti

Albrecht Petzoldt

Duong Hieu Phan

Krzysztof Pietrzak

Jeroen Pijnenburg

Rachel Player

Antigoni Polychroniadou

Willy Quach

Anaïs Querol

Srinivasan Raghuraman

Adrián Ranea

Simon Rastikian

Divya Ravi

Francesco Regazzoni

Maryam Rezapour

Mir Ali Rezazadeh Baee

Siavash Riahi

Joao Ribeiro

Vincent Rijmen

Bhaskar Roberts

Francisco Rodriguez-Henríquez

Paul Rösler

Arnab Roy

Iftekhar Salam

Paolo Santini

Roozbeh Sarenche

Yu Sasaki

Matteo Scarlata

Tobias Schmalz

Mahdi Sedaghat

Vladimir Sedlacek

Nicolas Sendrier

Jae Hong Seo

Srinath Setty

Yaobin Shen

Sina Shiehian

Omri Shmueli

Janno Siim

Jad Silbak

Leonie Simpson

Rohit Sinha

Daniel Slamanig

Fang Song

Yongsoo Song

Damien Stehle

Ron Steinfeld

Noah Stephens-Davidowitz

Christoph Striecks

Fatih Sulak

Chao Sun

Ling Sun

Siwei Sun

Koutarou Suzuki

Katsuyuki Takashima

Hervé Tale Kalachi

Quan Quan Tan

Yi Tang

Je Sen Teh

Cihangir Tezcan

Aishwarya Thiruvengadam

Orfeas Thyfronitis

Mehdi Tibouchi

Ni Trieu

Yiannis Tselekounis

Michael Tunstall

Nicola Tuveri

Nirvan Tyagi

Sohaib ul Hassan

Wessel van Woerden

Kerem Varc

Prashant Vasudevan

Damien Vergnaud

Jorge L. Villar
Giuseppe Vitto
Sameer Wagh
Hendrik Waldner
Alexandre Wallet
Ming Wan
Xiao Wang
Yuyu Wang
Zhedong Wang
Hoeteck Wee
Mor Weiss
Weiqiang Wen
Daniel Wichs
Mathias Wolf
Lennert Wouters
Michał Wroński
David Wu
Yusai Wu
Keita Xagawa
Yu Xia

Zejun Xiang
Tiancheng Xie
Shota Yamada
Takashi Yamakawa
Lisa Yang
Kevin Yeo
Eylon Yogev
Kazuki Yoneyama
Yusuke Yoshida
William Youmans
Alexandros Zacharakis
Michał Zając
Arantxa Zapico
Greg Zaverucha
Shang Zehua
Tina Zhang
Wentao Zhang
Yinuo Zhang
Yu Zhou
Cong Zuo

Contents – Part II

Cryptographic Primitives

Real-World Systems

Cryptographic Protocols

Single-Server Private Information Retrieval with Sublinear Amortized Time

Henry Corrigan-Gibbs[1], Alexandra Henzinger[1]([✉]), and Dmitry Kogan[2]

[1] MIT, Cambridge, MA, USA
{henrycg,ahenz}@csail.mit.edu
[2] Fordefi, Tel Aviv, Israel
dkogan@cs.stanford.edu

Abstract. We construct new private-information-retrieval protocols in the single-server setting. Our schemes allow a client to privately fetch a sequence of database records from a server, while the server answers each query in average time sublinear in the database size. Specifically, we introduce the first single-server private-information-retrieval schemes that have sublinear amortized server time, require sublinear additional storage, and allow the client to make her queries adaptively. Our protocols rely only on standard cryptographic assumptions (decision Diffie-Hellman, quadratic residuosity, learning with errors, etc.). They work by having the client first fetch a small "hint" about the database contents from the server. Generating this hint requires server time linear in the database size. Thereafter, the client can use the hint to make a bounded number of adaptive queries to the server, which the server answers in sublinear time—yielding sublinear amortized cost. Finally, we give lower bounds proving that our most efficient scheme is optimal with respect to the trade-off it achieves between server online time and client storage.

1 Introduction

A private-information-retrieval protocol [34,35] allows a client to fetch a record from a database server without revealing which record she has fetched. In the simplest setting of private information retrieval, the server holds an n-bit database, the client holds an index $i \in \{1, \ldots, n\}$, and the client's goal is to recover the i-th database bit while hiding her index i from the server.

Fast protocols for private information retrieval (PIR) would have an array of applications. Using PIR, a student could fetch a book from a digital library without revealing to the library which book she fetched. Or, she could stream a movie without revealing which movie she streamed. Or, she could read an online news article without revealing which article she read. More broadly, PIR is at the heart of a number of systems for metadata-hiding messaging [7,32], privacy-preserving advertising [8,60,70,88], private file-sharing [40], private e-commerce [66], private media-consumption [62], and privacy-friendly web browsing [72].

Unfortunately, the *computational cost* of private information retrieval is a barrier to its use in practice. In particular, to respond to each client's query,

O. Dunkelman and S. Dziembowski (Eds.): EUROCRYPT 2022, LNCS 13276, pp. 3–33, 2022.
https://doi.org/10.1007/978-3-031-07085-3_1

Beimel, Ishai, and Malkin [14] showed that the running time of a PIR server must be at least linear in the size of the database. This linear-server-time lower bound holds even if the client communicates with many non-colluding database replicas. So, for a client to privately fetch a single book from a digital library, the library's servers would have to do work proportional to the total length of all of the books in the library, which is costly both in theory and in practice.

Towards reducing the server-side cost of PIR, a number of prior works [7, 39, 64, 68, 79] observe that clients in many applications of PIR will make a sequence of queries to the same database. For example, a student may browse many books in a library; a web browser makes many domain name system (DNS) queries on each page load [80]; a mail client may check all incoming URLs against a database of known phishing websites [16, 72]; or, an antivirus software may check the hashes of executed files against known malware [72]. The lower bound of Beimel, Ishai, and Malkin [14] only implies that a PIR server will take linear time to respond to the client's very first PIR query. This leaves open the possibility of reducing the server-side cost for subsequent queries. In other words, in the multi-query setting, we can hope for the *amortized* server-side time per query to be sublinear in the database size.

Indeed, there exist an array of techniques for constructing PIR schemes with sublinear amortized server-side cost. Yet, prior PIR schemes achieving sublinear amortized time come with limitations that make them cumbersome to use in practice. Schemes that require multiple non-colluding servers [39, 72, 89] demand careful coordination between many business entities, which is a major practical annoyance [4, 15, 81, 90]. In addition, the security of these schemes is relatively brittle, since it relies on an adversary not being able to compromise multiple servers, rather than on cryptographic hardness. Recent offline/online PIR schemes [39, 72, 89] require, in the single-server setting, the server to perform a linear-time preprocessing step *for each query*. Thus, these schemes cannot have sublinear amortized time. Batch-PIR schemes [7, 64, 68, 79], which require the client to make all of her queries at once, in a single non-adaptive batch, do not apply to many natural applications (e.g., digital library, web browsing), in which the client decides over time which elements she wants to query.

The world of private-information-retrieval is thus in an undesirable state: the practical applications are compelling, but existing schemes cannot satisfy the deployment demands (single server, adaptive queries, small storage, based on implementable primitives) while avoiding very large server-side costs.

1.1 Our Results

This paper aims to advance the state of the art in private information retrieval by introducing the first PIR schemes that simultaneously offer a number of important properties for use in practice: they require only a single database server, they have sublinear amortized server time, they allow the client to issue its database queries adaptively, and they require extra storage sublinear in the database size (Fig. 1). Our schemes further rely only on standard cryptographic primitives and incur no additional server-side (per client) storage, making them attractive even

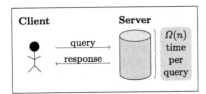 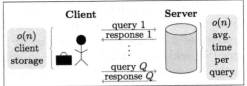

(a) Standard single-server PIR [74].   (b) *This work*: Single-server, many-query PIR with sublinear amortized time and storage.

Fig. 1. Comparison of single-server PIR models, on database size n.

when many clients query a single database. One limitation of our schemes is that they require more client-side storage and computation than standard PIR schemes, though we give lower bounds showing that some of these costs are inherent to achieving sublinear amortized server time. While the schemes in this paper may not yet be concretely efficient enough to use in practice, they demonstrate that sublinear-amortized-time single-server PIR is theoretically feasible. We hope that future work pushes PIR even closer to practice.

Specifically, in this paper we construct two new families of PIR schemes:

Single-Server PIR with Sublinear Amortized Time from Linearly Homomorphic Encryption. First, we show in Theorem 16 that any one of a variety of standard assumptions—including quadratic residuosity, decision Diffie-Hellman, decision composite residuosity, and learning with errors—suffices to construct single-server PIR schemes with sublinear amortized time. In particular, on database size n, if the client makes at least $n^{1/4}$ adaptive queries, our schemes have: amortized server time $n^{3/4}$, amortized communication complexity $n^{1/2}$, client storage $n^{3/4}$, and amortized client time $n^{1/2}$. (When describing protocol costs in this section, we hide both $\log n$ factors and polynomials in the security parameter.) More generally, the existence of linearly homomorphic encryption with sufficiently compact ciphertexts and standard single-server PIR with polylogarithmic communication together imply the existence of our PIR schemes. Our client-side costs are much larger than those required for standard stateless PIR—which needs no client storage and requires client time polylogarithmic in the database size. Our schemes thus reduce server-side costs at some expense to the client.

Single-Server PIR with Sublinear Amortized Time and an Optimal Storage/ Online-Time Trade-Off from Fully Homomorphic Encryption. Next, we show in Theorem 19 that under the stronger assumption that fully homomorphic encryption exists, we can construct PIR schemes with even lower amortized server time and client storage. In particular, we construct a PIR scheme that on database size n, and as long as the client makes at least $n^{1/2}$ queries, has amortized server time $n^{1/2}$, amortized communication complexity $n^{1/2}$, client storage $n^{1/2}$, and amortized client time $n^{1/2}$. (In contrast, from linearly homomorphic encryption, we get schemes with larger server time and client storage $n^{3/4}$.)

Lower Bounds on Multi-query PIR. Finally, we give new lower bounds on PIR schemes in the amortized (i.e., multi-query) setting. We give one lower bound against PIR schemes that allow the client to make its queries adaptively, and another against schemes that require the client to make its queries in a non-adaptive batch. In the *adaptive* setting, we show in Theorem 21 that any multi-query PIR scheme on database size n in which: the client stores S bits between queries, the server stores the database in its original form, and the server runs in amortized online time T, it must be that $ST \geq n$. This lower bound implies that our fully-homomorphic-encryption-based PIR scheme achieves the optimal trade-off (up to $\log n$ factors and polynomials in the security parameter) between online server time and client storage, when the servers store the database in unmodified form.

In Theorem 23, we show that a similar lower bound holds, even if the client makes all of its queries in a single *batch* and if the client is able to store some precomputed information about the database contents. In particular, if the client stores at most S bits of information, the client makes a batch of Q non-adaptive queries, the server stores the database in its original form, and the server runs in amortized time T per query, it must hold that $ST + QT \geq n$. This generalizes the bound of Beimel, Ishai, and Malkin [13], who prove this result for the case $S = 0$. Our bound implies that when:

- $S < Q$, existing batch PIR schemes [68] achieve optimal amortized time even in the setting in which the client can obtain some preprocessed advice about the database contents, and
- $S > Q$, our new fully-homomorphic-encryption-based PIR scheme achieves optimal amortized time,

up to $\log n$ factors and polynomials in the security parameter.

1.2 Overview of Techniques

We construct our new PIR schemes in two steps. First, we construct a new sort of *two*-server PIR scheme. Second, we use cryptographic assumptions to "compile" the two-server scheme into a single-server scheme.

Step 1: Two-server offline/online PIR with a single-server online phase. In the first step (Sect. 3), we design a new type of *two*-server offline/online PIR scheme [39]. The communication pattern of the two-server schemes we construct is as follows:

1. *Offline phase.* In a setup phase, the client sends a setup request to the first server (the "offline server"). The offline server runs in time at least linear in the database size and returns to the client a "hint" about the database state. The hint has size sublinear in the length of the database.
2. *Online phases (runs once for each of Q queries).* Whenever the client wants to make a PIR query, it uses its hint to issue a query to the second server (the "online server"). The online server produces an answer to the query in time sublinear in the database size and returns its answer to the client. The total communication in this step is sublinear in the database size.

The client can run the online phase Q times—for some parameter Q determined by the PIR scheme—using the same hint and without communicating with the offline server. After Q queries, the client discards its hint and reruns the offline setup phase from scratch.

Prior offline/online PIR schemes [39] require the client to communicate with *both* servers in the online phases, whenever the client makes multiple queries with the same hint. (If the client only ever makes a single query, the client can communicate with only one server in the online phase, but then the scheme cannot achieve sublinear amortized time.) In contrast, our schemes crucially allow the client to only communicate with a single server (the online server) in the online phase. Unlike schemes for private stateful information retrieval [83], the online phase in our scheme runs in sublinear time.

To build our two-server offline/online PIR scheme, we give a generic technique for "compiling" a two-server PIR scheme that supports a *single* query with sublinear online time into one that supports *multiple* queries with sublinear online time. Plugging the existing single-query offline/online PIR schemes with sublinear online time [39,89] into this compiler completes the two-server construction.

Provided that the offline server time is $\widetilde{O}(n)$ and the number of supported queries is at least n^ϵ, for constant $\epsilon > 0$, this two-server scheme already allows adaptive queries and has sublinear total amortized time and sublinear client storage. The only limitation is that it requires two non-colluding servers.

Step 2: Converting a two-server scheme to a one-server scheme. The last step (Sects. 4 and 5) is to convert the two-server PIR scheme into a one-server scheme. Following Corrigan-Gibbs and Kogan [39], we have the client encrypt the hint request that she sends to the offline server using a fully homomorphic encryption scheme. (As we discuss in Sect. 4, Aiello, Bhatt, Ostrovsky, and Rajagopalan [2] proposed a similar technique for converting multi-prover proof systems to single-prover proof systems, formalizing the approach of Biehl, Meyer, and Wetzel [18].) The offline server can then homomorphically answer the client's hint request in the offline phase while learning nothing about it. At this point, the client can execute both the offline and online phases with the same server, which completes the construction.

To construct the PIR schemes from weaker assumptions (linearly homomorphic encryption), we exploit the linearity of the underlying two-server PIR scheme. In particular, we show that the hint that the client downloads from the offline server corresponds to a client-specified linear function applied to the database. With a careful balancing of parameters and application of linearly homomorphic encryption and standard single-server PIR, we show that the client can obtain this linear function without revealing it to the database server.

The construction of our most asymptotically efficient PIR scheme, which appears in Sect. 5, implicitly follows essentially the same two-step strategy. The only difference is that achieving the improved efficiency requires us to design a new two-server offline/online PIR scheme for multiple queries from scratch. The offline phase of this scheme requires the server to compute non-linear functions of the client query—and thus requires fully homomorphic encryption—but the online time of the scheme is lower, which is the source of efficiency improvements.

Lower Bounds. Our first lower bound (Theorem 21) relates the number S of bits of information the client stores between queries and the amortized online time T of the PIR server, for PIR schemes in which the server stores the database in unmodified form. In particular, we show that $ST = \widetilde{\Omega}(n)$. To prove this lower bound, we show that if there is a single-server PIR scheme with client storage S and amortized online T, there exists a two-server offline/online PIR scheme for a single query with hint size S and online time T. Then, applying existing lower bounds on such schemes [39] completes the proof.

Our second lower bound (Theorem 23) considers the setting in which the client makes a batch of queries at once. We prove this result using an incompressibility argument [3,41–43,50,95], showing that the existence of a better-than-expected PIR scheme would yield a better-than-possible compression algorithm. (As we discuss in the full version [38], it is not clear whether it is possible to derive the same bound from the elegant and more modern "presampling" method [36,37,92]).

1.3 Related Work

Multi-server PIR. Chor, Goldreich, Kushilevitz, and Sudan [35] introduced private information retrieval and gave the first protocols, which were in the multi-server information-theoretic setting and achieved communication $O(n^{1/3})$. A sequence of works [5,11,12,21,22,33,46,49,55,96] then improved the communication complexity of PIR, and today's PIR schemes can achieve sub-polynomial communication complexity in the information-theoretic setting [46] and logarithmic communication complexity in the computational setting [22]. Multi-server PIR schemes are more efficient, both in terms of communication and computation, than single-server schemes. However, the security of multi-server PIR relies on non-collusion between the servers, which can be hard to guarantee in practice.

Single-Server PIR. Kushilevitz and Ostrovsky [74] presented the first single-server PIR schemes, based on linearly homomorphic encryption. A sequence of works then improved the communication complexity of single-server PIR, and showed how to construct PIR schemes with polylogarithmic communication from a wide range of public-key assumptions, such as the ϕ-hiding assumption [28,53], the decisional composite-residuosity assumption [30,77], the decisional Diffie-Hellman assumption [45], and the quadratic-residuosity assumption [45].

Recent works [1,4,6,52,81] have used lattice-based encryption schemes to improve the concrete efficiency of single-server PIR, in terms of both communication and computation. The goal is to get the most efficient single-server PIR schemes subject to the linear-server-time lower bound. These techniques are complementary to ours, and applying lattice-based optimizations to our setting could improve the concrete efficiency of our protocols.

Computational Overhead of PIR. All early PIR protocols required the servers to perform work linear in the database size when responding to a query.

Table 1. A comparison of single-server, many-query PIR schemes. We present the per-query, asymptotic costs of each scheme, on a database of size n, where each of m clients makes many PIR queries and at most $\hat{m}$ clients may be corrupted. We omit poly-logarithmic factors in n and m, along with polynomial factors in the security parameter. For lower bounds, we denote the extra client storage by S. We use ϵ as an arbitrarily small, positive constant. We amortize the costs over the number of queries that minimizes the per-query costs. For each scheme, the table indicates:
– the additional cryptographic assumptions made beyond single-server PIR with poly-logarithmic communication,
– the number of queries (per client) over which we amortize,
– whether the client makes her queries adaptively or as a batch,
– the *amortized* number of bits communicated per query,
– the *amortized* client and server time per query, and
– the additional number of bits stored by the client and the server between queries.
For schemes in the offline/online model, the communication and computation costs are taken to be the sum of the offline costs, amortized over the number of queries supported by a single offline phase, and the online costs. The extra server storage does not include the n-bit database, stored by the server. The extra client storage does not include the indices queried, even if these indices are queried as a batch.

Scheme (extra assumptions)	Per-client queries	Adaptive?	Per-query comm.	Per-query time Client	Per-query time Server	Extra storage Client	Extra storage Server
Batch PIR [68,64,6]	Q	×	1	1	$\frac{n}{Q}$	0	0
Stateful PIR [83]	$n^{1/2}$	✓	$n^{1/2}$	n	n †	$n^{1/2}$	0
Single-query single-server PIR							
Standard [74,28]	1	✓	1	1	n	0	0
Offline/online [39] (LHE)	1	✓	$n^{2/3}$	$n^{2/3}$	n	$n^{2/3}$	0
Offline/online [39] (FHE)	1	✓	$n^{1/2}$	$n^{1/2}$	n	$n^{1/2}$	0
Download entire DB	$n^{1-\epsilon}$	✓	n^{ϵ}	n^{ϵ}	n^{ϵ}	n	0
Doubly-efficient PIR							
Secret key (OLDC) [29,25]	$n^{1-\epsilon}$	✓	n^{ϵ}	n^{ϵ}	n^{ϵ}	1	mn
Public key (OLDC+VBB) [25]	1*	✓	n^{ϵ}	n^{ϵ}	n^{ϵ}	0	n
Private anonymous data access							
Read-only [63] (FHE)	1*	✓	$\hat{m}$	$\hat{m}$	$\hat{m}$	$\hat{m}$	$\hat{m}n^{1+\epsilon}$
This work							
Theorem 16 (LHE)	$n^{1/4}$	✓	$n^{1/2}$	$n^{1/2}$	$n^{3/4}$	$n^{3/4}$	0
Theorem 19 (FHE)	$n^{1/2}$	✓	$n^{1/2}$	$n^{1/2}$	$n^{1/2}$	$n^{1/2}$	0
Lower bounds, for Q queries, *on schemes storing the database in its original form*							
Standard PIR [14]	Q	×	–	–	$\geq \frac{n}{Q}$	–	–
This work (Theorem 21)	Q	✓	–	–	$\geq \frac{n}{S}$	S	0
This work (Theorem 23)	Q	×	–	–	$\geq \frac{n}{S+Q}$	S	0

† The number of public-key operations is $n^{1/2}$.

* This number of per-client queries assumes that the total number of clients, m, grows sufficiently large.

Beimel, Ishai, and Malkin [14] showed that this is inherent, giving an $\Omega(n)$ lower bound on the server time. Their lower bound applies to both multi-server and single-server schemes with either information-theoretic or computational security.

Many lines of work have sought to construct PIR schemes with lower computational costs, which circumvent the above linear lower bound (Table 1):

- *PIR with preprocessing* denotes a class of schemes in which the server(s) store the database in encoded form [13,14,94], which allows them to respond to queries in time sublinear in the database size. The first such schemes targeted the multi-server setting. Recent work [25,29] applies oblivious locally decodable codes [19,23,24] to construct single-server PIR schemes with sublinear server time, after a one-time database preprocessing step. However, these schemes require extra server-side storage per client that is linear in the database size. While an idealized form of program obfuscation [9] can be used to drastically reduce this storage [25], the lack of concretely efficient candidate constructions for program obfuscation rules out the use of these schemes for the time being. In contrast, the single-server schemes in this paper require only standard assumptions.

  "Offline/online PIR" schemes use a different type of preprocessing: the client and server run a one-time linear-complexity offline setup process, during which the client downloads and stores information about the database. After that, the client can make queries to the database, and the server can respond in sublinear time. Previous works [39,72,89] mostly focus on the two-server setting, where they achieve sublinear amortized time. In the single-server setting, previous offline/online PIR schemes [39] allow for only a single online query after each execution of the offline phase. As a result, in the single-server setting, the cost of each query is still linear in the database size.

  Finally, Lipmaa [78] constructs single-server PIR with slighly sublinear time by encoding the database as a branching program that is obliviously evaluated in $O(\frac{n}{\log n})$ operations. The schemes in this work achieve significantly lower amortized time, yet require the client to make multiple queries.

- *Make queries in a non-adaptive batch:* When the client knows the entire sequence of database queries she will make in advance, the client and server can use "batch PIR" schemes [6,7,31,61,64,65,68] to achieve sublinear amortized server time. The multi-server scheme of Lueks and Goldberg [79] allows the servers to simultaneously process a batch of queries from different clients, and achieves sublinear per-query time. Our schemes require only one server and achieve sublinear amortized time, even given a single client making her queries in an adaptive sequence.

- *Download and store the entire database:* If the client has enough storage space, she can keep a local copy of the entire database. The server pays a linear cost to ship the database to the client, but the client can answer subsequent database queries on her own with no server work. In contrast, the schemes in this paper avoid having to store the entire database at the client.

– *Settle on a sublinear number of public-key operations:* Private stateful information retrieval [83] schemes improve the concrete efficiency of single-server PIR by having the server do a sublinear number of public-key operations for each query. Such schemes [81,83] still require a linear number of symmetric key and plaintext operations for each query. In contrast, the schemes in this paper require sublinear amortized work of any kind, per query.

Communication Lower Bounds on PIR. A series of works give bounds on the communication required for multi-server PIR [56,93]. Single-server PIR constructions match the trivial $\log n$ lower bound (up to polylogarithmic factors).

Lower Bounds for PIR with Preprocessing. Beimel, Ishai, and Malkin [13] proved that if a server can store an S-bit hint and run in amortized time T, then it must hold that $ST \geq n$. Persiano and Yeo [84] recently improved this lower bound to $ST \geq n \log n$ in the single-server case. In this paper, we are interested in offline/online PIR schemes, in which the client stores a hint and the server stores the database in unmodified form.

Lower Bounds on Oblivious RAM. Recent work proves strong limits on the performance of oblivious-RAM [58] schemes [26,69,73,75,76]. These schemes allow the server to maintain per-client state; in our setting of PIR, the server is stateless. The PIR setting thus requires different lower-bound approaches [13].

2   Background

Notation. We write the set of positive integers as $\mathbb{N}$. For an integer $n \in \mathbb{N}$, we write $[n] = \{1, \ldots, n\}$ and we write the empty set as $\emptyset$. We ignore issues of integrality, and treat numbers such as $n^{1/2}$ and n/k as integers. We use $\mathrm{poly}(\cdot)$ to denote a fixed polynomial in its argument. We use the standard Landau notation $O(\cdot)$ and $\Omega(\cdot)$ for asymptotics. When the big-O contains multiple variables, such as $f(n) = O(n/S)$, all variables other than n are implicit functions of n (which is the database size when it is not made explicit). The notation $\widetilde{O}(f(n))$ hides polylogarithmic factors in the parameter n, and $\widetilde{O}_\lambda(\cdot)$ hides $\mathrm{poly}(\log n, \lambda)$ factors. For a finite set $\mathcal{X}$, $x \xleftarrow{\mathbb{R}} \mathcal{X}$ denotes an independent and uniformly random draw from $\mathcal{X}$. When unspecified, we take all logarithms base two.

   We work in the RAM model, with word size logarithmic in the input length (i.e., database size n) and polynomial in the security parameter λ. We give running times up to $\mathrm{poly}(\log n, \lambda)$ factors, which makes our results relatively independent of the specifics of the computational model. An "efficient algorithm" is one that runs in probabilistic polynomial time in its inputs and in λ.

2.1   Standard Definitions

We begin by defining the standard cryptographic primitives that this work uses.

Pseudorandom Permutations. We use the standard notion of pseudorandom permutations [57]. On security parameter $\lambda \in \mathbb{N}$, a domain size $n \in \mathbb{N}$, and a key space $\mathcal{K}_\lambda$, we denote a pseudorandom permutation by $\mathsf{PRP} : \mathcal{K}_\lambda \times [n] \to [n]$.

Definition 1 (Linearly homomorphic encryption). Let $(\mathsf{Gen}, \mathsf{Enc}, \mathsf{Dec})$ be a public-key encryption scheme. The scheme is *linearly homomorphic* if, for every keypair $(\mathsf{sk}, \mathsf{pk})$ that Gen outputs,

- the message space is a group $(\mathcal{M}_{\mathsf{pk}}, +)$,
- the ciphertext space is a group $(\mathcal{C}_{\mathsf{pk}}, \cdot)$, and
- for every pair of messages $m_0, m_1 \in \mathcal{M}_{\mathsf{pk}}$, it holds that

$$\mathsf{Dec}(\mathsf{sk}, \mathsf{Enc}(\mathsf{pk}, m_0) \cdot \mathsf{Enc}(\mathsf{pk}, m_1) \in \mathcal{C}_{\mathsf{pk}}) = \mathsf{Dec}(\mathsf{sk}, \mathsf{Enc}(\mathsf{pk}, m_0 + m_1 \in \mathcal{M}_{\mathsf{pk}})).$$

Definition 2 (Gate-by-gate fully homomorphic encryption). We use $(\mathsf{FHE.Gen}, \mathsf{FHE.Enc}, \mathsf{FHE.Dec}, \mathsf{FHE.Eval})$ to denote a symmetric-key fully homomorphic encryption scheme [51]. We say a scheme is a *gate-by-gate* fully homomorphic encryption scheme if the homomorphic evaluation routine $\mathsf{FHE.Eval}$ on a circuit of size $|C|$ and security parameter λ runs in time $|C| \cdot \mathsf{poly}(\log |C|, \lambda)$. Standard fully homomorphic encryption schemes are gate-by-gate [27,51,54].

2.2 Definition of Offline/Online PIR

Throughout, we present our new single-server PIR schemes in an offline/online model [39,83]. That is, the client first interacts with the server in an offline phase to obtain a succinct "hint" about the database contents. This hint allows the client to make many queries in a subsequent online phase. Provided that the server-side cost is low enough in both phases, the server's total amortized time (including the cost of both phases) will be sublinear in the database size.

We now give definitions for one- and two-server offline/online PIR schemes that support many adaptive queries. Our definition of offline/online PIR differs from that of prior work in one important way [39,72]. In our definition, in the two-server setting, the client may only communicate with a *single* server in the online phase. Prior two-server offline/online PIR schemes [39,72] allow the client to communicate with *both* servers in the online phase.

Definition 3 (Offline/online PIR for adaptive queries). An *offline/online PIR scheme for adaptive queries* is a tuple of polynomial-time algorithms:

- $\mathsf{HintQuery}(1^\lambda, n) \to (\mathsf{ck}, q)$, a randomized algorithm that takes in a security parameter λ and a database length $n \in \mathbb{N}$, and outputs a client key ck and a hint request q,
- $\mathsf{HintAnswer}(D, q) \to a$, a deterministic algorithm that takes in a database $D \in \{0,1\}^n$ and a hint request q, and outputs a hint answer a,
- $\mathsf{HintReconstruct}(\mathsf{ck}, a) \to h$, a deterministic algorithm that takes in a client key ck and a hint answer a, and outputs a hint h,
- $\mathsf{Query}(\mathsf{ck}, i) \to (\mathsf{ck}', \mathsf{st}, q)$, a randomized algorithm that takes in a client key ck and an index $i \in [n]$, and outputs an updated client key ck', a client query state st, and a query q,
- $\mathsf{Answer}^D(q) \to a$, a deterministic algorithm that takes in a query q, and gets access to an oracle that:

Experiment 4 (Correctness). Parameterized by a PIR scheme Π, security parameter $\lambda \in \mathbb{N}$, number of queries $Q \in \mathbb{N}$, database size $n \in \mathbb{N}$, database $D \in \{0,1\}^n$, and query sequence $(i_1, \ldots, i_Q) \in [n]^Q$.

– Compute:

$$(\mathsf{ck}, q) \leftarrow \Pi.\mathsf{HintQuery}(1^\lambda, n)$$
$$a \leftarrow \Pi.\mathsf{HintAnswer}(D, q)$$
$$h \leftarrow \Pi.\mathsf{HintReconstruct}(\mathsf{ck}, a)$$

– For $t = 1, \ldots, Q$, compute:

$$(\mathsf{ck}, \mathsf{st}, q) \leftarrow \Pi.\mathsf{Query}(\mathsf{ck}, i_t)$$
$$a \leftarrow \Pi.\mathsf{Answer}^D(q)$$
$$(h, v_i) \leftarrow \Pi.\mathsf{Reconstruct}(\mathsf{st}, h, a)$$

– Output "1" if $v_t = D_{i_t}$ for all $t \in [Q]$. Output "0" otherwise.

Experiment 5 (Security). Parameterized by an adversary $\mathcal{A}$, PIR scheme Π, number of servers $k \in \{1, 2\}$, security parameter $\lambda \in \mathbb{N}$, number of queries $Q \in \mathbb{N}$, database size $n \in \mathbb{N}$, and bit $b \in \{0, 1\}$.

– Compute:

$$(\mathsf{ck}, q) \leftarrow \Pi.\mathsf{HintQuery}(1^\lambda, n)$$

If $k = 1$: // *Single-server security*

$$\mathsf{st} \leftarrow \mathcal{A}(1^\lambda, q)$$

Else: // *Two-server security*

$$\mathsf{st} \leftarrow \mathcal{A}(1^\lambda)$$

– For $t = 1, \ldots, Q$, compute:

$$(\mathsf{st}, i_0, i_1) \leftarrow \mathcal{A}(\mathsf{st})$$
$$(\mathsf{ck}, \_, q) \leftarrow \Pi.\mathsf{Query}(\mathsf{ck}, i_b)$$
$$\mathsf{st} \leftarrow \mathcal{A}(\mathsf{st}, q)$$

– Output $b' \leftarrow \mathcal{A}(\mathsf{st})$.

- takes as input an index $j \in [n]$, and
- returns the j-th bit of the database $D_j \in \{0, 1\}$,

and outputs an answer string a, and

– Reconstruct$(\mathsf{st}, h, a) \rightarrow (h', D_i)$, a deterministic algorithm that takes in a query state st, a hint h, and an answer string a, and outputs an updated hint h' and a database bit D_i.

In a deployment, (HintQuery, HintAnswer, HintReconstruct) are executed in the offline phase, while (Query, Answer, Reconstruct) are executed in each online phase. Furthermore, we say that the PIR scheme *supports Q adaptive queries* if it satisfies the following notions of (1) correctness and (2) security for Q queries:

Correctness for Q Queries. We require that if a client and a server correctly execute the protocol, the client can recover any Q database records of its choosing, even if the client chooses these records adaptively. Formally, a multi-query offline/online PIR scheme Π satisfies *correctness for Q queries* if for every $\lambda, n \in \mathbb{N}$, $D \in \{0, 1\}^n$, and every $(i_1, \ldots, i_Q) \in [n]^Q$, Experiment 4 outputs "1" with probability $1 - \mathsf{negl}(\lambda)$.

Security for Q Queries. We require that an adversarial (malicious) server "learns nothing" about which sequence of database records the client is fetching, even if the adversary can adaptively choose these indices. In the single-server setting, where the same server runs both the offline and online phase, the adversary is first given the hint request. In the two-server setting, where a separate server runs the offline phase, the adversary only sees the online queries. (This is sufficient, as an adversarial offline server trivially learns nothing about the client's queries since the hint request does not depend on these queries.)

Formally, for an adversary $\mathcal{A}$, multi-query offline/online PIR scheme Π, number of servers $k \in \{1, 2\}$, security parameter $\lambda \in \mathbb{N}$, database size $n \in \mathbb{N}$, and bit $b \in \{0, 1\}$, let $W_{\mathcal{A}, k, \lambda, Q, n, b}$ be the event that Experiment 5 outputs "1" when parameterized with these values. We define the Q-query PIR advantage of $\mathcal{A}$:

$$\mathsf{PIRAdv}_k[\mathcal{A}, \Pi](\lambda, n) := \left| \Pr[W_{\mathcal{A}, k, \lambda, Q, n, 0}] - \Pr[W_{\mathcal{A}, k, \lambda, Q, n, 1}] \right|.$$

We say that a multi-query offline/online PIR scheme Π is k-server secure if, for all efficient algorithms $\mathcal{A}$, all polynomially bounded functions $n(\lambda)$, and all $\lambda \in \mathbb{N}$, $\mathsf{PIRAdv}_k[\mathcal{A}, \Pi](\lambda, n(\lambda)) \leq \mathsf{negl}(\lambda)$.

Definition 6 (Sublinear amortized time). We say that an offline/online PIR scheme has *sublinear amortized time* if there exists a number of queries. $Q \in \mathbb{N}$ such that the total server time required to run the offline and online phases for Q queries on a database of size n is $o(Qn)$. More formally, for every choice of the security parameter $\lambda \in \mathbb{N}$, database size $n \in \mathbb{N}$, and query sequence $(i_1, \ldots, i_Q) \in [n]^Q$, the total running time of HintAnswer (executed once) and Answer (executed Q times) in Experiment 4 must be $o(Qn)$.

Remark 7 (Handling an unbounded number of queries). A scheme with sublinear amortized time for some number of queries $Q \in \mathbb{N}$ immediately implies a scheme with sublinear amortized time for any larger number of queries, including a number that is a-priori unbounded. One can obtain such a scheme by "restarting" the scheme every Q queries and rerunning the offline phase from scratch. The amortized costs remain the same.

Remark 8 (Malicious security). In our definition (Definition 3), following prior work [39], the client's queries do not depend on the server's answers to prior queries. In this way, our PIR schemes naturally protect client privacy against a malicious server—the server learns the same information about the client's queries whether or not the server executes the protocol faithfully.

Remark 9 (Correctness failures). Our definition does not require that correctness holds if the client makes a sequence of queries that is correlated with the randomness it used to generate the hint request. A stronger correctness definition would guarantee correctness in all cases (i.e., with probability one). Strengthening our PIR schemes to provide this form of correctness represents an interesting challenge for future work.

Remark 10 (Handling database changes). In many natural applications of private information retrieval, the database contents change often. Naïvely, whenever the database contents change, the client and server would need to rerun the costly hint-generation process. In the limit—when the entire contents of the database changes between a client's queries—rerunning the hint-generation step is inherently required. When the database changes more slowly, prior work on offline/online PIR [72], building on much earlier work in dynamic data structures [17], shows how to update the client's hint at modest cost. In particular, when a constant number of database rows change between each pair of client queries, the scheme's costs do not change, up to factors in the security parameter and logarithmic in the database size. These techniques from prior work apply directly to our setting, so we do not discuss them further.

3 Two-Server PIR with a Single-Server Online Phase and Sublinear Amortized Time

In this section, we give a generic construction that converts a two-server offline/online PIR scheme that supports *a single query* into a two-server offline/online PIR scheme that supports *any number of adaptive queries*. The transformation has three useful properties:

1. If the original PIR scheme has linear offline server time, then the resulting multi-query scheme has linear offline server time as well.
2. If the original PIR scheme has sublinear online server time, then the resulting multi-query scheme has sublinear online server time as well.
3. During the online phase—when the client is making its sequence of adaptive queries—the client only communicates with one of the servers. (In contrast, prior two-server PIR schemes with sublinear amortized time [39,72] require the client to communicate with *both* servers in the online phase.)

After presenting the generic transformation (Lemma 11) in this section, we instantiate this transformation in Sect. 4 and use it to construct single-server PIR schemes with sublinear amortized time.

Lemma 11 (The Compiler Lemma). *Let Π be a two-server offline/online PIR scheme that supports a single query. Then, for any database size $n \in \mathbb{N}$, security parameter $\lambda \in \mathbb{N}$, and number of queries $Q < n$, Construction 15, when instantiated with a secure pseudorandom permutation, is a two-server offline/online PIR scheme that supports Q adaptive queries and whose offline and online phases have communication, computation, and client storage costs dominated by running $O(\lambda Q)$ instances of Π, each on a database of size n/Q.*

To prove the lemma, we must show that the scheme of Construction 15 satisfies the claimed efficiency properties, along with correctness and security. Efficiency follows by construction. We give the full correctness and security arguments in the full version of this paper [38].

Remark 12. In the PIR scheme implied by Lemma 11, the online-phase upload communication (from the client to server) is in fact only as large as the upload communication required for running a *single* instance of the underlying PIR scheme Π on a database of size n/Q.

Before giving the construction that proves Lemma 11, we describe the idea behind our approach. We take inspiration from the work of Ishai, Kushilevitz,

Ostrovsky, and Sahai [68], who construct "batch" PIR schemes, in which the client can issue a batch of Q queries at once, and the server can respond to all Q queries in time $\tilde{O}(n)$. (In contrast, answering Q queries using a non-batch PIR scheme requires server time $\Omega(Qn)$.) The crucial difference between our PIR schemes and prior work on batch PIR is that our schemes allow the client to make its Q queries adaptively, rather than in a single batch all at once.

Our idea is to first permute the database according to a pseudorandom permutation and then partition the n database records into Q chunks, each of size n/Q. The key observation is that, if the client makes Q adaptive queries, it is extremely unlikely that the client will ever need to query any chunk more than λ times. In particular, by a balls-in-bins argument, the probability, taken over the random key of the pseudorandom permutation, that any chunk receives more than λ queries is negligible in λ.

Then, given a two-server offline/online PIR scheme Π for a *single query*, we construct a two-server offline/online PIR scheme for many queries as follows:

- *Offline phase.* The client and the offline server run the offline phase of Π on each of the Q database chunks λ times. For each of the Q database chunks, the client then holds λ client keys and hints.
- *Online phase.* Whenever the client wants to make a database query, it identifies the chunk in which its desired database record falls. The client finds an unused client key for that chunk and runs the online phase of Π for that chunk to produce a query. The client sends the query to the online server, who answers that query with respect to each of the Q database chunks. Using the online server's answers, the client can reconstruct its database record of interest. Crucially, the client's query does not reveal to the server the chunk in which its desired database record falls. Finally, the client then deletes the client key and hint that it used for this query.

The formal description of our protocol appears in Construction 15.

Remark 13. Construction 15 uses a pseudorandom permutation (PRP) to permute and partition the database. The client then reveals the PRP key it used for this partitioning to the server. Crucially, the security of our construction does *not* rely on the pseudorandomness of the PRP. The PRP security property only appears in the correctness argument of our scheme (which we give in the full version of this paper [38]). So, revealing the PRP key to the server in this way has no effect on the security of the scheme.

Remark 14 (Reducing online download). In the online phase of Construction 15, the online server's answer to the client consists of a vector of Q answers $a = ((a)_1, \ldots, (a)_Q)$. The client uses only one of these answers $(a)_{j^*}$. To reduce download cost, the client and server can run a single-server PIR protocol, where the server's input is the database a of Q answers and the client's input is the index $j^* \in [Q]$ of it's desired answer. This reduces the client's online download cost by a factor of Q, at the cost of requiring the server to perform $O_\lambda(Q)$ public-key operations in the online phase.

Construction 15 (Two-server offline/online PIR for Q adaptive queries with a single-server online phase). The scheme uses a single-query two-server offline/online PIR scheme Π and a pseudorandom permutation $\mathsf{PRP} : \mathcal{K}_\lambda \times [n] \to [n]$. The scheme is parameterized by a maximum number of queries $Q = Q(n) < n$.

I. Offline phase. ──────────────────────────────────

$\mathsf{HintQuery}(1^\lambda, n) \to (\mathsf{ck}, q)$.

1. For $j \in [Q]$ and $\ell \in [\lambda]$: $((\hat{\mathsf{ck}})_{j\ell}, (\hat{q})_{j\ell}) \leftarrow \Pi.\mathsf{HintQuery}(1^\lambda, n/Q)$.
2. Sample $k \stackrel{\mathrm{R}}{\leftarrow} \mathcal{K}_\lambda$, set $\mathsf{ck} \leftarrow (k, \hat{\mathsf{ck}}, \emptyset)$, and set $q \leftarrow (k, \hat{q})$.
3. Return (ck, q).

$\mathsf{HintAnswer}(D, q) \to a$.

1. Parse $(k, \hat{q}) \leftarrow q$.
2. // *Permute the database according to* $\mathsf{PRP}(k, \cdot)$ *and divide it into* Q *chunks.*
   For $j \in [Q]$: $C_j \leftarrow (D_{\mathsf{PRP}(k,(j-1)(n/Q)+1)} \| \ldots \| D_{\mathsf{PRP}(k,(j+1)(n/Q))}) \in \{0,1\}^{n/Q}$.
3. For $j \in [Q]$ and $\ell \in [\lambda]$: $(a)_{j\ell} \leftarrow \Pi.\mathsf{HintAnswer}(C_j, (\hat{q})_{j\ell})$.
4. Return a.

$\mathsf{HintReconstruct}(\mathsf{ck}, a) \to h$.

1. Parse $(k, \hat{\mathsf{ck}}, \mathsf{queried}) \leftarrow \mathsf{ck}$.
2. For $j \in [Q]$ and $\ell \in [\lambda]$: $(\hat{h})_{j\ell} \leftarrow \Pi.\mathsf{HintReconstruct}((\hat{\mathsf{ck}})_{j\ell}, (a)_{j\ell})$.
3. Set $\mathsf{cache} \leftarrow \{\}$. // *An empty map (associative array) data structure.*
4. Return $h = (\hat{h}, \mathsf{cache})$.

II. Online phase. ──────────────────────────────────

$\mathsf{Query}(\mathsf{ck}, i) \to (\mathsf{ck}', \mathsf{st}, q)$.

1. Parse $(k, \hat{\mathsf{ck}}, \mathsf{queried}) \leftarrow \mathsf{ck}$.
2. Find (the unique) $i^* \in [n/Q]$ and $j^* \in [Q]$ so that $\mathsf{PRP}(k, i) = (j^* - 1)(n/Q) + i^*$.
3. Find $\ell^* \in [\lambda]$ such that $(\mathsf{ck})_{j^*\ell^*} \neq \bot$.
   - If no such ℓ^* exists or $i \in \mathsf{queried}$, sample $i^* \stackrel{\mathrm{R}}{\leftarrow} [n/Q]$ and choose a random $j^* \in [Q]$ and $\ell^* \in [\lambda]$ out of those for which $(\mathsf{ck})_{j^*\ell^*} \neq \bot$.
4. Let $(\_, \mathsf{st}', q') \leftarrow \Pi.\mathsf{Query}((\hat{\mathsf{ck}})_{j^*\ell^*}, i^*)$.
5. Let $(\hat{\mathsf{ck}})_{j^*\ell^*} \leftarrow \bot$, let $\mathsf{st} \leftarrow (\mathsf{st}', i, j^*, \ell^*)$, let $q \leftarrow (k, q')$, and let $\mathsf{ck}' \leftarrow (k, \hat{\mathsf{ck}}, \mathsf{queried} \cup \{i\})$.
6. Return $(\mathsf{ck}', \mathsf{st}, q)$.

$\mathsf{Answer}^D(q) \to a$.

1. Parse $(k, q') \leftarrow q$.
2. For $j \in [Q]$: $(a)_j \leftarrow \Pi.\mathsf{Answer}^{\mathcal{O}_j}(q')$, where $\mathcal{O}_j(x) := D_{\mathsf{PRP}(k,(j-1)(n/Q)+x)}$.
3. Return a.

$\mathsf{Reconstruct}(\mathsf{st}, h, a) \to (h', D_i)$.

1. Parse $(\mathsf{st}', i, j^*, \ell^*) \leftarrow \mathsf{st}$ and parse $(\hat{h}, \mathsf{cache}) \leftarrow h$.
2. If $\mathsf{cache}[i]$ is not set, let $\mathsf{cache}[i] \leftarrow \Pi.\mathsf{Reconstruct}(\mathsf{st}', (\hat{h})_{j^*\ell^*}, (a)_{j^*})$.
3. Set $D_i \leftarrow \mathsf{cache}[i]$. Set $h' \leftarrow (\hat{h}, \mathsf{cache})$.
4. Return (h', D_i).

4 Single-Server PIR with Sublinear Amortized Time from DCR, QR, DDH, or LWE

In this section, we use the general transformation of Sect. 3 to construct the first single-server PIR schemes with sublinear amortized total time and sublinear extra storage, allowing the client to make her queries adaptively.

These constructions work in two steps:

- First, we use the Compiler Lemma (Lemma 11) to convert a two-server offline/online PIR scheme for a single query into a two-server offline/online PIR scheme for *multiple adaptive queries*, in which the client only communicates with a single server in the online phase.
- Next, we use linearly homomorphic encryption and single-server PIR to allow the client and server to run the offline phase of the two-server scheme without leaking any information to the server. At this point, we can execute the functionality of both servers in the two-server scheme using just a single server. In other words, we have constructed a single-server offline/online PIR scheme that supports multiple adaptive queries.

The idea of using homomorphic encryption to run a two-server protocol on a single server arose first, to our knowledge, in the domain of multi-prover interactive proofs. Aiello, Bhatt, Ostrovsky, and Rajagopalan [2] formalized this general approach, which was initially proposed by Biehl, Meyer, and Wetzel [18]. Subsequent work demonstrated that compiling multi-prover proof systems to single-prover systems requires care [44,47,48,71,91] (in particular it requires the underlying proof system to be sound against "no-signaling" provers [91]). Corrigan-Gibbs and Kogan [39] used homomorphic encryption to convert a two-server PIR scheme to a single-server offline/online PIR scheme that supports a *single* query in sublinear online time. Our contribution is to construct a single-server PIR scheme that supports multiple, adaptive queries and that thus achieves *sublinear amortized total time*.

We now show that any one of a variety of cryptographic assumptions—the Decision Composite Residuosity assumption [77,82], the Quadratic Residuosity assumption [59], the Decision Diffie-Hellman assumption [20], or the Learning with Errors assumption [87]—suffices for constructing single-server PIR with sublinear amortized time:

Theorem 16 (Single-server PIR with sublinear amortized time). *Under the DCR, LWE, QR, or DDH assumptions, there exists a single-server offline/online PIR scheme that, on database size n, security parameter λ, and as long as the client makes at least $n^{1/4}$ adaptive queries, has*

- *amortized communication $\widetilde{O}_\lambda(n^{1/2})$,*
- *amortized server time $\widetilde{O}_\lambda(n^{3/4})$,*
- *amortized client time $\widetilde{O}_\lambda(n^{1/2})$, and*
- *client storage $\widetilde{O}_\lambda(n^{3/4})$.*

The proof of Theorem 16 will make use of the following two-server offline/online PIR scheme which is implicit in prior work.

Lemma 17 (Implicit in Theorem 20 of CK20 [39]). *There is a two-server offline/online PIR scheme (with information-theoretic security) that supports a single query on database size n such that, in the offline phase:*

- *the client uploads a vector $q \in \{0,1\}^n$ to the offline server,*
- *the offline server computes the inner product of the database with all n cyclic shifts of the query vector q (in $\widetilde{O}(n)$ time using a fast Fourier transform),*
- *the client downloads $\widetilde{O}(\sqrt{n})$ bits of the resulting matrix-vector product*

and, in the online phase:

- *the client uploads $\widetilde{O}(\sqrt{n})$ bits to the online server,*
- *the online server runs in time $\widetilde{O}(\sqrt{n})$, and*
- *the client downloads one bit.*

Proof of Theorem 16. The proof works in two main steps. First, we use Lemma 11 to "compile" the single-query two-server PIR scheme of Lemma 17 into a multi-query two-server PIR scheme. Second, we use linearly homomorphic encryption—following the work of Corrigan-Gibbs and Kogan [39] in the single-query setting—to allow a single server to implement the role of both servers.

Step 1: A stepping-stone two-server scheme. We first construct a two-server offline/online PIR scheme that: (a) supports multiple queries, (b) has sublinear online time, and (c) requires only one server in the online phase. To do so, we use the Compiler Lemma (Lemma 11) to convert the two-server PIR scheme of Lemma 17 into a two-server PIR scheme satisfying these three goals.

In particular, Lemma 11 and Lemma 17 together imply a two-server offline/online PIR scheme that supports any number of queries $Q < n$, and whose offline and online phases consist of running $O(\lambda Q)$ instances of the PIR scheme of Lemma 17 on databases of size n/Q. The resulting scheme then has the following structure in the offline phase:

- the client uploads $\widetilde{O}_\lambda(Q)$ bit vectors to the offline server, each of size n/Q,
- the offline server applies a length-preserving linear function to each vector (in quasi-linear time, as in the Lemma 17 scheme),
- the client downloads a total of $\widetilde{O}_\lambda(\sqrt{Qn})$ bits from the vectors that the server computes.

And in the online phase,

- the client uploads $\widetilde{O}_\lambda(\sqrt{Qn})$ bits to the online server,
- the online server runs in time $\widetilde{O}_\lambda(\sqrt{Qn})$, and
- the client downloads $\widetilde{O}_\lambda(Q)$ bits.

This scheme requires the existence of one-way functions.

As desired, this scheme supports multiple queries, has sublinear online time (whenever $Q \ll n$), and requires only one server in the online phase. The offline upload cost and the client time of the scheme are $\widetilde{\Omega}_\lambda(n)$—linear in the database size, but we remove this limitation later on.

Step 2: Using homomorphic encryption to run the two-server scheme on one server. Next, we show that the client can fetch the information it needs to complete the offline phase of the Step-1 scheme without revealing any information to the server. In the Step-1 scheme, the offline server's work consists of evaluating a client-supplied linear function over the database and can thus be performed under linearly homomorphic encryption. For this step, we will need a linearly homomorphic encryption scheme with ciphertexts of size $\widetilde{O}_\lambda(1)$, along with a single-server PIR scheme with communication cost and client time $\widetilde{O}_\lambda(1)$. The existence of both primitives follows from the Decision Composite Residue (DCR) assumptions [77,82] and the Learning with Errors (LWE) assumption [87]. Recent work of Döttling, Garg, Ishai, Malavolta, Mour, and Ostrovsky [45] shows that the Quadratic Residuosity (QR) assumption [59] and decision Diffie-Hellman (DDH) assumption [20] also imply these primitives.

In particular, the client first samples a random encryption key for a linearly homomorphic encryption scheme. Then the client executes the offline phase as follows:

- The client encrypts each component of its $\widetilde{O}_\lambda(Q)$ bit vectors using the linearly homomorphic encryption scheme. The client sends these vectors to the server.
- Under encryption, the server applies the length-preserving linear function to each encrypted vector. As in the Step-1 scheme, this computation takes $\widetilde{O}_\lambda(n)$ time using an FFT on the encrypted values.
- The client uses a single-server PIR scheme [74], to fetch a total of $\widetilde{O}_\lambda(\sqrt{Qn})$ components of the ciphertext vectors that the server has computed. Since modern single-server PIR schemes have communication cost $\widetilde{O}_\lambda(1)$, this step requires communication and client time $\widetilde{O}_\lambda(\sqrt{Qn})$. Using batch PIR [7,64,68], the server can answer this set of queries in time $\widetilde{O}_\lambda(n)$.

Finally, the client decrypts the resulting ciphertexts to recover exactly the same information that it obtained at the end of the offline phase of the two-server scheme. At this point, the offline phase has upload $\widetilde{O}_\lambda(n)$, server time $\widetilde{O}_\lambda(n)$, client time $\widetilde{O}_\lambda(n)$, and download $\widetilde{O}_\lambda(\sqrt{Qn})$. The online phase has upload $\widetilde{O}_\lambda(\sqrt{Qn})$ bits, server time $\widetilde{O}(\sqrt{Qn})$, client time $\widetilde{O}_\lambda(\sqrt{Qn} + Q)$, and download $\widetilde{O}_\lambda(Q)$.

Final Rebalancing. We complete the proof by reducing the offline upload cost using the standard rebalancing idea [34, Section 4.3]. In particular, we divide the database into k chunks, of size $n' = n/k$, for a parameter k chosen later.

Now, the offline phase has upload $\widetilde{O}_\lambda(n/k)$, server time $\widetilde{O}_\lambda(n)$, client time $\widetilde{O}_\lambda(n/k + \sqrt{Qnk})$, and download $k \cdot \widetilde{O}_\lambda(\sqrt{Qn/k})$ and the online phase has upload $\widetilde{O}_\lambda(\sqrt{Qn/k})$ bits, server time $k \cdot \widetilde{O}(\sqrt{Qn/k})$, client time $\widetilde{O}_\lambda(\sqrt{Qn/k} + Qk)$ and download $k \cdot \widetilde{O}_\lambda(Q)$. We choose Q and k to balance the following costs, ignoring poly$(\lambda, \log n)$ factors:

- the amortized offline time: n/Q, and
- the online server time: $\sqrt{kQn}$.

To do so, we choose $k = \frac{n}{Q^3}$ and $Q \leq n^{1/3}$. This yields a PIR scheme with amortized server time $\widetilde{O}_\lambda(n/Q)$, amortized client time $\widetilde{O}_\lambda(Q^2 + n/Q^2)$ and amortized communication $\widetilde{O}_\lambda(Q^2 + n/Q^2)$. The client storage is equal to the (non-amortized) offline download cost, which is $\widetilde{O}_\lambda(n/Q)$.

Finally, to construct the scheme of Theorem 16, we chose $Q = n^{1/4}$ to minimize the offline upload. This causes the amortized server time and the client storage to become $\widetilde{O}_\lambda(n^{3/4})$, while the amortized client time and the amortized communication are both $\widetilde{O}_\lambda(n^{1/2})$.

Efficiency. The efficiency claims follow immediately from the construction.

Security. The security argument closely follows that of prior work on single-server offline/online PIR [39]. More formally, the server's view in an interaction with a client consists of (1) the client's encrypted bit vectors sent in the offline phase, (2) the client's standard single-server PIR queries sent in the offline phase, (3) the messages that the client sends in the online phase. To prove security, we can construct a sequence of hybrid distributions that move from the world in which the client queries a sequence of database indexes $I_0 = (i_{0,1}, i_{0,1}, \ldots, i_{0,Q})$ to the world in which the client queries a different sequence $I_1 = (i_{1,1}, i_{1,1}, \ldots, i_{1,Q})$. The steps of the argument are:

- replace the encrypted bit vectors with encryptions of zeros, using the semantic security of the encryption scheme,
- replace the client's standard single-server PIR query with a query to a fixed database row, using the security of the underlying single-server PIR scheme,
- swap query sequence I_0 with query sequence I_1, using the security of the underlying two-server offline/online PIR scheme,
- swap the client's standard single-server PIR query and encrypted bit vectors back again, using the security of these primitives.   □

Remark 18 (Single-server PIR with $\widetilde{O}_\lambda(n^{2/3})$ amortized time and communication). With an alternate rebalancing (taking Q to be $n^{1/3}$), we can build a single-server offline/online PIR scheme that, as long as the client makes at least $n^{1/3}$ adaptive queries, has amortized communication $\widetilde{O}_\lambda(n^{2/3})$, amortized server time $\widetilde{O}_\lambda(n^{2/3})$, amortized client time $\widetilde{O}_\lambda(n^{2/3})$, and client storage $\widetilde{O}_\lambda(n^{2/3})$. This PIR scheme has better amortized server time than that of Theorem 16, at the cost of requiring a client upload linear in n in the offline phase. (However, the *amortized* communication of this scheme is still sublinear in n.)

5   Single-Server PIR with Optimal Amortized Time and Storage from Fully Homomorphic Encryption

In this section, we construct a single-server many-query offline/online PIR scheme directly, rather than through a generic transformation. Assuming fully homomorphic encryption (Definition 2), our scheme achieves the optimal tradeoff between amortized server time and client storage, up to polylogarithmic factors. This fills a gap left open by the protocols of Sect. 4 and demonstrates that the lower bound we give in Sect. 6 is tight. We prove the following result:

Theorem 19 (Single-server PIR with optimal amortized time and storage from fully homomorphic encryption). *Assuming gate-by-gate fully homomorphic encryption (Definition 2), there exists a single-server offline/online PIR scheme that, on security parameter $\lambda \in \mathbb{N}$, database size $n \in \mathbb{N}$, and maximum number of queries $Q < n$, supports Q adaptive queries with:*

- *amortized server time $\tilde{O}_\lambda(n/Q)$,*
- *client-side storage $\tilde{O}_\lambda(Q)$,*
- *amortized communication $\tilde{O}_\lambda(n/Q)$, and*
- *amortized client time $\tilde{O}_\lambda(Q + n/Q)$.*

This new scheme achieves amortized server time better than we could expect from any protocol derived from the generic compiler of Sect. 3, given current state-of-the-art offline/online PIR protocols. To answer each query, that compiler executes the online phase of a PIR scheme on Q database chunks, each of size n/Q. Similar to the compiler of Sect. 3, the PIR scheme here works by splitting the database into random chunks, so that the client's distinct adaptive queries fall into distinct chunks with high probability. However, the new PIR scheme in this section keeps the mapping of database rows to chunks *secret* from the server. (In contrast, in the scheme of Sect. 3, the client reveals to the server the mapping of database rows to chunks.) By keeping the mapping of database rows to chunks secret, in the online phase of this scheme, the server only has to compute over the contents a single chunk. In this way, we achieve lower computation than the schemes of Sect. 4, which execute an online phase for each database chunk.

In this section, we sketch the ideas behind the PIR scheme that proves Theorem 19; a complete proof appears in the full version of this paper [38].

Proof idea for Theorem 19. At a very high level, the PIR scheme that we construct works as follows:

1. In an offline phase, the client chooses small, random subsets $S_1, \ldots, S_m \subseteq [n]$. For each subset, the client privately fetches from the server the parity of the database bits indexed by the set.
2. When the client wants to fetch database record i in the online phase, it finds a subset $S \in \{S_1, \ldots, S_m\}$ such that $i \in S$. Then, the client *usually* asks the server for the parity of the database bits indexed by $S \setminus \{i\}$. The parity of the database bits indexed by S and $S \setminus \{i\}$ give the client enough

information to recover the value of the ith database record, D_i. Then, the client re-randomizes the set S it just used.

In more detail, our PIR scheme operates as follows: in the offline phase, the client samples $(\lambda+1)\cdot Q$ random subsets of $[n]$, each of size n/Q. We refer to the first λQ sets as the "primary" sets and to the remaining Q sets as the "backup" sets. For each set S, the client retrieves the parity of the database bits the set indexes, i.e., $\sum_{j\in S} D_j$ mod 2, from the server, while keeping the set contents hidden using encryption. For each backup set S, the client additionally chooses a random member of the set S and privately retrieves the database value indexed by that element, via a batch PIR protocol [7,64,68].

With high probability over the client's random choice of sets, whenever the client wants to fetch the i-th database record, the client holds a primary set that contains i. Again with good probability, the client then asks the server for the parity of the database bits indexed by the punctured set $S\setminus\{i\}$, with which she can reconstruct the desired database value D_i. Finally, the client must refresh her state, as using the same S to query for another index i' could leak (i, i') to the server and thus break security. To achieve this, the client discards S and promotes the next available backup set, S_b, to become a new primary set. If S_b does not already contain i, the client modifies S_b by deleting the set element whose database value she knows and inserting i; the client recomputes the parity of this new set using the value of D_i she has just retrieved. With this mechanism, the distribution of the client's primary sets remains random, ensuring that her online queries are independent.

There are two failure events in this scheme: it is possible that (a) none of the primary sets contain the index queried, i, or that (b) the client sends the server a set other than $S\setminus\{i\}$, as decided by a coin flip (to avoid always sending a query set that does not contain i). We drive down the probability of either failure event to $\mathrm{negl}(\lambda)$, by repeating the offline and online phases λ times. Then, by construction, this scheme satisfies correctness for Q queries. Intuitively, the scheme is secure because (a) the use of encryption and batch PIR in the offline phase prevents the server from learning the contents of the presampled sets, and (b) the client's online queries are indistinguishable from uniformly random subsets of $[n]$ of size $n/Q - 1$, as proved in the full version of this paper [38].

We now discuss the PIR scheme's efficiency.

Communication and Storage. The client can succinctly represent her presampled sets with only logarithmic-size keys by leveraging pseudorandomness. Then, in the offline phase, she exchanges only $\widetilde{O}_\lambda(Q)$ bits with the server to communicate the (encrypted) descriptions and parities of $O_\lambda(Q)$ randomly sampled sets. The client additionally retrieves the database values of Q indices—one from each backup set—in $\widetilde{O}_\lambda(Q)$ communication with batch PIR. The client stores her presampled sets and her state between queries in $\widetilde{O}_\lambda(Q)$ bits. In each online phase, the client must however hide whether she inserted an index into her query set (and, if so, which index she inserted). Therefore, the client explicitly lists all elements in the punctured set she is querying for (instead of using pseudorandomness) and thus exchanges $\widetilde{O}_\lambda(n/Q)$ bits with the server.

Computation. In the offline phase, the client retrieves the encrypted parities of the database bits indexed by each of $O_\lambda(Q)$ encrypted sets of size n/Q. In the full version of this paper [38], we present a Boolean circuit that computes the parities of the database bits of s subsets of $[n]$, each of size ℓ, in $\widetilde{O}(s \cdot \ell + n)$ gates. Our circuit is inspired by circuits for private set intersection [67,85,86] and makes use of sorting networks [10]. The server can execute the offline phase in $\widetilde{O}_\lambda(n)$ time by running the above circuit under a gate-by-fate fully homomorphic encryption scheme. Further, the offline server can respond to the client's batch PIR query in $\widetilde{O}_\lambda(n)$ time. In each online phase, the server must complete $O_\lambda(n/Q)$ work per query, as it computes the parity of a punctured set containing $n/Q - 1$ elements. Thus, each query requires $\widetilde{O}_\lambda(n/Q)$ amortized total server time.

As for the client, in the offline phase, she generates $\mathcal{O}_\lambda(Q)$ random sets. Using pseudorandomness to represent each set, the time to generate these sets without expanding them is $\widetilde{O}_\lambda(Q)$. Also in the offline phase, the client runs a batch PIR protocol with the server to recover Q database values, requiring at most $\widetilde{O}_\lambda(Q)$ client time. In the online phase, the client first has to find a primary set that contains the index $i \in [n]$ she wants to read. By generating each set using a pseudorandom permutation, she can efficiently test whether each set contains i by inverting the permutation in time $\widetilde{O}_\lambda(1)$. Testing all $\mathcal{O}_\lambda(Q)$ primary sets takes the client time $\widetilde{O}_\lambda(Q)$. When she finds a succinctly-represented primary set that contains i, the client expands the set in time $\widetilde{O}_\lambda(n/Q)$ to build her online query. Finally, promoting a backup set to become a new primary set and, if necessary, replacing a set element by i takes time $\widetilde{O}_\lambda(1)$. We conclude that the client's amortized, per-query time is $\widetilde{O}_\lambda(Q + n/Q)$.

6   Lower Bounds

In this section, we present lower bounds for multi-query offline/online PIR schemes in which the server stores the database in its original form—that is, the server does not preprocess or encode the database. (If preprocessing is allowed, candidate single-server PIR schemes using program obfuscation can circumvent our lower bounds [25].)

Remark 20 (Generalization to multi-server PIR). While we present and prove these lower bounds in the single-server setting, both lower bounds hold for protocols with any constant number of servers. With multiple servers, T bounds the database bits probed per query by any online server.

6.1   Lower Bound for Adaptive Schemes

First, we give a new lower bound on the product of the (a) client storage and (b) online time of any single-server, offline/online PIR scheme for many adaptive queries. Specifically, we show that in any adaptive, multi-query, offline/online PIR scheme, where the client stores S bits between queries and the server responds to each query in amortized time T, it must hold that $ST = \widetilde{\Omega}(n)$.

This new lower bound matches the best adaptive multi-query scheme in the two-server setting [39, Section 4] and it matches our new scheme (Sect. 5) in the single-server setting, up to polylogarithmic factors.

In the following, we say that a single-server PIR scheme for Q adaptive queries probes T database bits per query *on average* if, for every sequence of Q indices and *every choice of the client's randomness*, the server makes at most QT total probes to the database in the process of answering all Q queries.

Theorem 21 (Lower bound for adaptive schemes). *Consider a computationally secure, single-server PIR scheme for many adaptive queries, such that, on security parameter $\lambda \in \mathbb{N}$ and database size $n \in \mathbb{N}$,*

- *the server stores the database in its original form,*
- *the client stores at most S bits between consecutive queries, and*
- *the server probes T database bits per query on average.*

Then, for polynomially bounded $n = n(\lambda)$ and large enough λ, it holds that $(S + 1) \cdot (T + 1) \geq \widetilde{\Omega}(n)$.

We give a complete proof of Theorem 21 in the full version of this paper [38]. Our proof invokes the following lower bound from prior work, which shows that for any *single-query* offline/online PIR scheme, either the offline communication or the online server time must be large:

Theorem 22 ([39, Section 6]). *Consider a computationally secure, single-query, offline/online PIR scheme such that, on security parameter $\lambda \in \mathbb{N}$ and database size $n \in \mathbb{N}$,*

- *the server stores the database in its original form,*
- *the client downloads C bits in the offline phase,*
- *the server probes T bits of the database to process each online query, and*
- *the client recovers its index of interest with probability at least $\epsilon \geq 1/2 + \Omega(1)$.*

Then, for polynomially bounded $n = n(\lambda)$, it holds that $(C + 1) \cdot (T + 1) \geq \widetilde{\Omega}(n)$.

Proof idea for Theorem 21. We show that any *multi-query* PIR scheme with small client storage implies a *single-query* offline/online PIR scheme with small offline communication. In more detail, the reduction works as follows:

1. First, we show that, for any *many-query* PIR scheme Π as in the theorem statement, there must exist a query sequence that satisfies the following condition: if the client makes PIR queries to each of the indices in this sequence one at a time, and then makes any subsequent PIR query, the server answers this last query with at most T database probes in expectation. We call such a query sequence a *good* query sequence.
2. Then, we build a *single-query* PIR scheme using Π and any fixed, good query sequence for Π. In an offline phase, we first let the PIR server run Π's offline phase, and then run as many iterations of Π's online phase as needed to query

for each index in the good query sequence. At this point, the server sends its intermediate state from running Π to the client. In an online phase, the client then runs one iteration of Π's online phase, using the intermediate state it received from the server, to query for its index of interest.

By construction, this single-query scheme requires S bits of offline download, and at most T database probes in expectation in the online phase. Correctness and security follow from the correctness and security of Π.

3. Finally, we modify the above single-query scheme to make $O(T)$ online database probes in the worst case, rather than in expectation.

Applying Theorem 22 to this single-query scheme then gives the bound on the client storage S and the running time T of the PIR scheme.   □

6.2   Lower Bound for Batch PIR with Advice

The lower bound of section Sect. 6.1 rules out PIR schemes with small client storage and small amortized server online time in the adaptive setting. In this section, we ask whether it is possible to do better if the client makes all of its queries in a *single non-adaptive batch*. In particular, we consider schemes for "batch PIR with advice," in which a client obtains—via out-of-band means or via an offline phase—S bits of preprocessed advice about the database contents (before she knows which indices she wants to query). Then, the client makes a batch of Q non-adaptive queries, and the server makes at most T database probes per query (i.e., at most QT probes per batch). We show that $ST + QT = \widetilde{\Omega}(n)$.

For simplicity, we state the theorem in terms of batch PIR with advice, which we formally define in the full version of this paper [38]. This PIR model is in fact identical to single-server, multi-query, offline/online PIR, in which the client makes its queries non-adaptively, up to some syntactic differences.

Theorem 23 (Lower bound for batch PIR with advice). *Consider a computationally secure, single-server batch-PIR-with-advice scheme such that, on security parameter $\lambda \in \mathbb{N}$, database size $n \in \mathbb{N}$, and batch size $Q \in [n]$,*

- *the server stores the database in its original form,*
- *the client downloads S bits of advice, and*
- *the server probes at most QT database bits to answer a batch of Q queries.*

Then, for polynomially bounded $n = n(\lambda)$ and large enough λ, it holds that $ST + QT \geq \widetilde{\Omega}(n)$.

Theorem 23 shows that it is impossible to get additional speedups from PIR schemes that both (a) have the client store information, as in the offline/online PIR model, and (b) jointly process a batch of queries, as in the batch PIR model. An alternative interpretation of Theorem 23 suggests that adaptivity can "come for free" in the single-server setting: it requires no more online server time than standard batch PIR, as long as the client has at least $O(Q)$ storage.

We formally prove Theorem 23 in the full version of this paper [38].

Proof idea for Theorem 23. We prove this theorem via an incompressibility argument [3,41–43,50,95], by demonstrating that any batch PIR with advice scheme that defies this lower bound could be used to compress the database it is run on—thus, such a PIR scheme cannot exist. We make this argument in steps:

1. First, we define the multi-query Box Problem, an extension of Yao's Box Problem [95] in which the players iteratively open many boxes. Informally, the multi-query Box Problem encodes a game involving two players and an n-bit string $D = (D_1, \ldots, D_n)$:
   - Initially, the first player examines D and produces an S-bit advice string to be passed to the second player.
   - Then, the second player is given the S-bit advice string and a set of Q indices $\{i_1, \ldots, i_Q\}$. The player's goal is to output $(D_{i_1}, \ldots, D_{i_Q}) \in \{0,1\}^Q$. To solve this task, the second player may read at most QT bits of D. When the player reads a bit of D whose index lies in the challenge set $\{i_1, \ldots, i_Q\}$, we say that the player's query is a "violation" and we require that the player make at most V violations.

   The two players win the game if the second player recovers $(D_{i_1}, \ldots, D_{i_Q})$. We say that a strategy ϵ-solves the multi-query Box Problem if it allows the players to win with probability at least ϵ.

2. With an incompressibility argument, we prove that any strategy that ϵ-solves the multi-query Box Problem with a large enough Q and a small enough V must satisfy that $ST + QT = \tilde{\Omega}(\epsilon n)$.

3. We show that an efficient batch-PIR-with-advice scheme for Q queries, with advice length S and per-query online time T, gives a good solution to the multi-query Box Problem. More specifically, given any such PIR scheme, we devise the following strategy for the multi-query Box Problem:
   - Both players treat the n-bit input string D as a database, that the first player examines and that the second player must recover at Q points.
   - Initially, the first player computes and outputs the S-bit advice string that the batch-PIR-with-advice scheme would have produced on this database.
   - Then, the second player takes in the S-bit advice string and Q database indices to retrieve. The second player retrieves these Q database values by executing the batch PIR scheme with the advice—probing at most QT database indices in total, across all Q queries.

   In this construction, the second player probes each index in the challenge set with low probability. (Otherwise, the PIR scheme would leak which values the player is reading from what indices are probed.) We show that this strategy $(1/2 - \text{negl}(\lambda))$-solves the multi-query Box Problem with at most $2Q^2T/n$ violations. The bounds on any algorithm that solves the multi-query Box Problem must also apply to the PIR scheme, giving that $ST + QT = \tilde{\Omega}(n)$. □

7   Conclusion

We construct new single-server PIR schemes that have sublinear amortized total server time. A number of related problems remain open:

- Is it possible to match the performance of our PIR scheme based on fully homomorphic encryption (Sect. 5) while using simpler assumptions?
- Can we construct single-server PIR schemes for many adaptive queries that achieve optimal $\widetilde{O}_\lambda(1)$ communication, $\widetilde{O}_\lambda(n^{1/2})$ amortized server time, and $\widetilde{O}_\lambda(n^{1/2})$ client storage? Our scheme from Sect. 5 has larger communication $\widetilde{O}_\lambda(n^{1/2})$. One approach would be to design puncturable pseudorandom sets [39,89] with short descriptions that support both insertions and deletions.
- Our lower bounds in Sect. 6 only apply to PIR schemes in which the server stores the database in unencoded form. Can we beat these bounds by having the server store the database in some encoded form [14]?

Acknowledgements. We thank David Wu and Yuval Ishai for reading an early draft of this work and for their helpful suggestions on how to improve it. We thank Yevgeniy Dodis, Siyao Guo, and Sandro Coretti for answering questions about presampling. We deeply appreciate the support and technical advice that Dan Boneh gave on this project from the very start. Part of this work was done when the third author was a student at Stanford University. This work was supported in part by the National Science Foundation (Award CNS-2054869), a gift from Google, a Facebook Research Award, and the Fintech@CSAIL Initiative, as well as the National Science Foundation Graduate Research Fellowship under Grant No. 1745302 and an EECS Great Educators Fellowship.

References

1. Aguilar-Melchor, C., Barrier, J., Fousse, L., Killijian, M.O.: XPIR: private information retrieval for everyone. PoPETs **2**, 155–174 (2016)
2. Aiello, W., Bhatt, S., Ostrovsky, R., Rajagopalan, S.R.: Fast verification of any remote procedure call: short witness-indistinguishable one-round proofs for NP. In: Montanari, U., Rolim, J.D.P., Welzl, E. (eds.) ICALP 2000. LNCS, vol. 1853, pp. 463–474. Springer, Heidelberg (2000). https://doi.org/10.1007/3-540-45022-X_39
3. Akshima, Cash, D., Drucker, A., Wee, H.: Time-space tradeoffs and short collisions in Merkle-Damgård hash functions. In: Micciancio, D., Ristenpart, T. (eds.) CRYPTO 2020. LNCS, vol. 12170, pp. 157–186. Springer, Heidelberg (2020). https://doi.org/10.1007/978-3-030-56784-2_6
4. Ali, A., et al.: Communication–computation trade-offs in PIR. In: USENIX Security, pp. 1811–1828. USENIX Association (2021)
5. Ambainis, A.: Upper bound on the communication complexity of private information retrieval. In: Degano, P., Gorrieri, R., Marchetti-Spaccamela, A. (eds.) ICALP 1997. LNCS, vol. 1256, pp. 401–407. Springer, Heidelberg (1997). https://doi.org/10.1007/3-540-63165-8_196
6. Angel, S., Chen, H., Laine, K., Setty, S.T.V.: PIR with compressed queries and amortized query processing. In: S&P (2018)
7. Angel, S., Setty, S.: Unobservable communication over fully untrusted infrastructure. In: SOSP, pp. 551–569 (2016)
8. Backes, M., Kate, A., Maffei, M., Pecina, K.: ObliviAd: provably secure and practical online behavioral advertising. In: S&P (2012)
9. Barak, B., et al.: On the (im)possibility of obfuscating programs. In: Kilian, J. (ed.) CRYPTO 2001. LNCS, vol. 2139, pp. 1–18. Springer, Heidelberg (2001). https://doi.org/10.1007/3-540-44647-8_1

10. Batcher, K.E.: Sorting networks and their applications. In: AFIPS, p. 307–314. Association for Computing Machinery (1968)
11. Beimel, A., Ishai, Y.: Information-theoretic private information retrieval: a unified construction. In: Orejas, F., Spirakis, P.G., van Leeuwen, J. (eds.) ICALP 2001. LNCS, vol. 2076, pp. 912–926. Springer, Heidelberg (2001). https://doi.org/10.1007/3-540-48224-5_74
12. Beimel, A., Ishai, Y., Kushilevitz, E., Raymond, J.: Breaking the $O(n^{1/(2k-1)})$ barrier for information-theoretic private information retrieval. In: FOCS, pp. 261–270. IEEE Computer Society (2002)
13. Beimel, A., Ishai, Y., Malkin, T.: Reducing the servers computation in private information retrieval: PIR with preprocessing. In: Bellare, M. (ed.) CRYPTO 2000. LNCS, vol. 1880, pp. 55–73. Springer, Heidelberg (2000). https://doi.org/10.1007/3-540-44598-6_4
14. Beimel, A., Ishai, Y., Malkin, T.: Reducing the servers' computation in private information retrieval: PIR with preprocessing. J. Cryptol. **17**, 125–151 (2004)
15. Bell, J.H., Bonawitz, K.A., Gascón, A., Lepoint, T., Raykova, M.: Secure single-server aggregation with (poly) logarithmic overhead. In: CCS (2020)
16. Bell, S., Komisarczuk, P.: An analysis of phishing blacklists: Google Safe Browsing, OpenPhish, and PhishTank. In: ACSW (2020)
17. Bentley, J.L., Saxe, J.B.: Decomposable searching problems I: static-to-dynamic transformation. J. Algorithms **1**, 301–358 (1980)
18. Biehl, I., Meyer, B., Wetzel, S.: Ensuring the integrity of agent-based computations by short proofs. In: Rothermel, K., Hohl, F. (eds.) MA 1998. LNCS, vol. 1477, pp. 183–194. Springer, Heidelberg (1998). https://doi.org/10.1007/BFb0057658
19. Blackwell, K., Wootters, M.: A note on the permuted puzzles toy conjecture. arXiv preprint arXiv:2108.07885 (2021)
20. Boneh, D.: The decision Diffie-Hellman problem. In: Buhler, J.P. (ed.) ANTS 1998. LNCS, vol. 1423, pp. 48–63. Springer, Heidelberg (1998). https://doi.org/10.1007/BFb0054851
21. Boyle, E., Gilboa, N., Ishai, Y.: Function secret sharing. In: Oswald, E., Fischlin, M. (eds.) EUROCRYPT 2015. LNCS, vol. 9057, pp. 337–367. Springer, Heidelberg (2015). https://doi.org/10.1007/978-3-662-46803-6_12
22. Boyle, E., Gilboa, N., Ishai, Y.: Function secret sharing: improvements and extensions. In: CCS, pp. 1292–1303. ACM (2016)
23. Boyle, E., Holmgren, J., Ma, F., Weiss, M.: On the security of doubly efficient PIR. Cryptology ePrint Archive, Report 2021/1113 (2021)
24. Boyle, E., Holmgren, J., Weiss, M.: Permuted puzzles and cryptographic hardness. In: Hofheinz, D., Rosen, A. (eds.) TCC 2019. LNCS, vol. 11892, pp. 465–493. Springer, Cham (2019). https://doi.org/10.1007/978-3-030-36033-7_18
25. Boyle, E., Ishai, Y., Pass, R., Wootters, M.: Can we access a database both locally and privately? In: Kalai, Y., Reyzin, L. (eds.) TCC 2017. LNCS, vol. 10678, pp. 662–693. Springer, Cham (2017). https://doi.org/10.1007/978-3-319-70503-3_22
26. Boyle, E., Naor, M.: Is there an oblivious RAM lower bound? In: ITCS (2016)
27. Brakerski, Z., Vaikuntanathan, V.: Fully homomorphic encryption from ring-LWE and security for key dependent messages. In: Rogaway, P. (ed.) CRYPTO 2011. LNCS, vol. 6841, pp. 505–524. Springer, Heidelberg (2011). https://doi.org/10.1007/978-3-642-22792-9_29
28. Cachin, C., Micali, S., Stadler, M.: Computationally private information retrieval with polylogarithmic communication. In: Stern, J. (ed.) EUROCRYPT 1999. LNCS, vol. 1592, pp. 402–414. Springer, Heidelberg (1999). https://doi.org/10.1007/3-540-48910-X_28

29. Canetti, R., Holmgren, J., Richelson, S.: Towards doubly efficient private informa-tion retrieval. In: Kalai, Y., Reyzin, L. (eds.) TCC 2017. LNCS, vol. 10678, pp. 694–726. Springer, Cham (2017). https://doi.org/10.1007/978-3-319-70503-3_23

30. Chang, Y.-C.: Single database private information retrieval with logarithmic com-munication. In: Wang, H., Pieprzyk, J., Varadharajan, V. (eds.) ACISP 2004. LNCS, vol. 3108, pp. 50–61. Springer, Heidelberg (2004). https://doi.org/10.1007/978-3-540-27800-9_5

31. Chen, H., Huang, Z., Laine, K., Rindal, P.: Labeled PSI from fully homomorphic encryption with malicious security. In: CCS, pp. 1223–1237 (2018)

32. Cheng, R., et al.: Talek: private group messaging with hidden access patterns. In: ACSAC, pp. 84–99. ACM (2020)

33. Chor, B., Gilboa, N.: Computationally private information retrieval (extended abstract). In: STOC, pp. 304–313. ACM (1997)

34. Chor, B., Goldreich, O., Kushilevitz, E., Sudan, M.: Private information retrieval. In: FOCS, pp. 41–50. IEEE Computer Society (1995)

35. Chor, B., Goldreich, O., Kushilevitz, E., Sudan, M.: Private information retrieval. J. ACM **45**, 965–981 (1998)

36. Coretti, S., Dodis, Y., Guo, S.: Non-uniform bounds in the random-permutation, ideal-cipher, and generic-group models. In: Shacham, H., Boldyreva, A. (eds.) CRYPTO 2018. LNCS, vol. 10991, pp. 693–721. Springer, Cham (2018). https://doi.org/10.1007/978-3-319-96884-1_23

37. Coretti, S., Dodis, Y., Guo, S., Steinberger, J.: Random oracles and non-uniformity. In: Nielsen, J.B., Rijmen, V. (eds.) EUROCRYPT 2018. LNCS, vol. 10820, pp. 227–258. Springer, Cham (2018). https://doi.org/10.1007/978-3-319-78381-9_9

38. Corrigan-Gibbs, H., Henzinger, A., Kogan, D.: Single-server private informa-tion retrieval with sublinear amortized time. Cryptology ePrint Archive, Report 2022/081 (2022)

39. Corrigan-Gibbs, H., Kogan, D.: Private information retrieval with sublinear online time. In: Canteaut, A., Ishai, Y. (eds.) EUROCRYPT 2020. LNCS, vol. 12105, pp. 44–75. Springer, Cham (2020). https://doi.org/10.1007/978-3-030-45721-1_3

40. Dauterman, E., Feng, E., Luo, E., Popa, R.A., Stoica, I.: DORY: an encrypted search system with distributed trust. In: OSDI, pp. 1101–1119. USENIX Associa-tion (2020)

41. De, A., Trevisan, L., Tulsiani, M.: Time space tradeoffs for attacks against one-way functions and PRGs. In: Rabin, T. (ed.) CRYPTO 2010. LNCS, vol. 6223, pp. 649–665. Springer, Heidelberg (2010). https://doi.org/10.1007/978-3-642-14623-7_35

42. Dodis, Y., Guo, S., Katz, J.: Fixing cracks in the concrete: random oracles with auxiliary input, revisited. In: Coron, J.-S., Nielsen, J.B. (eds.) EUROCRYPT 2017. LNCS, vol. 10211, pp. 473–495. Springer, Cham (2017). https://doi.org/10.1007/978-3-319-56614-6_16

43. Dodis, Y., Haitner, I., Tentes, A.: On the instantiability of hash-and-sign RSA signatures. In: Cramer, R. (ed.) TCC 2012. LNCS, vol. 7194, pp. 112–132. Springer, Heidelberg (2012). https://doi.org/10.1007/978-3-642-28914-9_7

44. Dodis, Y., Halevi, S., Rothblum, R.D., Wichs, D.: Spooky encryption and its appli-cations. In: Robshaw, M., Katz, J. (eds.) CRYPTO 2016. LNCS, vol. 9816, pp. 93–122. Springer, Heidelberg (2016). https://doi.org/10.1007/978-3-662-53015-3_4

45. Döttling, N., Garg, S., Ishai, Y., Malavolta, G., Mour, T., Ostrovsky, R.: Trapdoor hash functions and their applications. In: Boldyreva, A., Micciancio, D. (eds.) CRYPTO 2019. LNCS, vol. 11694, pp. 3–32. Springer, Cham (2019). https://doi.org/10.1007/978-3-030-26954-8_1

46. Dvir, Z., Gopi, S.: 2-server PIR with subpolynomial communication. J. ACM **63**, 1–15 (2016)
47. Dwork, C., Langberg, M., Naor, M., Nissim, K., Reingold, O.: Succinct proofs for NP and Spooky interactions (2004)
48. Dwork, C., Naor, M., Rothblum, G.N.: Spooky interaction and its discontents: compilers for succinct two-message argument systems. In: Robshaw, M., Katz, J. (eds.) CRYPTO 2016. LNCS, vol. 9816, pp. 123–145. Springer, Heidelberg (2016). https://doi.org/10.1007/978-3-662-53015-3_5
49. Efremenko, K.: 3-query locally decodable codes of subexponential length. SIAM J. Comput. **41**, 1694–1703 (2012)
50. Gennaro, R., Trevisan, L.: Lower bounds on the efficiency of generic cryptographic constructions. In: FOCS, pp. 305–313 (2000)
51. Gentry, C.: A fully homomorphic encryption scheme. Ph.D. thesis, Stanford University (2009)
52. Gentry, C., Halevi, S.: Compressible FHE with applications to PIR. In: Hofheinz, D., Rosen, A. (eds.) TCC 2019. LNCS, vol. 11892, pp. 438–464. Springer, Cham (2019). https://doi.org/10.1007/978-3-030-36033-7_17
53. Gentry, C., Ramzan, Z.: Single-database private information retrieval with constant communication rate. In: Caires, L., Italiano, G.F., Monteiro, L., Palamidessi, C., Yung, M. (eds.) ICALP 2005. LNCS, vol. 3580, pp. 803–815. Springer, Heidelberg (2005). https://doi.org/10.1007/11523468_65
54. Gentry, C., Sahai, A., Waters, B.: Homomorphic encryption from learning with errors: conceptually-simpler, asymptotically-faster, attribute-based. In: Canetti, R., Garay, J.A. (eds.) CRYPTO 2013. LNCS, vol. 8042, pp. 75–92. Springer, Heidelberg (2013). https://doi.org/10.1007/978-3-642-40041-4_5
55. Gilboa, N., Ishai, Y.: Distributed point functions and their applications. In: Nguyen, P.Q., Oswald, E. (eds.) EUROCRYPT 2014. LNCS, vol. 8441, pp. 640–658. Springer, Heidelberg (2014). https://doi.org/10.1007/978-3-642-55220-5_35
56. Goldreich, O., Karloff, H., Schulman, L., Trevisan, L.: Lower bounds for linear locally decodable codes and private information retrieval. In: CCC (2002)
57. Goldreich, O.: Foundations of Cryptography. Cambridge University Press, Cambridge (2001)
58. Goldreich, O., Ostrovsky, R.: Software protection and simulation on oblivious RAMs. J. ACM **43**, 431–473 (1996)
59. Goldwasser, S., Micali, S.: Probabilistic encryption. J. Comput. Syst. Sci. **28**, 270–299 (1984)
60. Green, M., Ladd, W., Miers, I.: A protocol for privately reporting ad impressions at scale. In: CCS, pp. 1591–1601. ACM (2016)
61. Groth, J., Kiayias, A., Lipmaa, H.: Multi-query computationally-private information retrieval with constant communication rate. In: Nguyen, P.Q., Pointcheval, D. (eds.) PKC 2010. LNCS, vol. 6056, pp. 107–123. Springer, Heidelberg (2010). https://doi.org/10.1007/978-3-642-13013-7_7
62. Gupta, T., Crooks, N., Mulhern, W., Setty, S., Alvisi, L., Walfish, M.: Scalable and private media consumption with Popcorn. In: NSDI, pp. 91–107 (2016)
63. Hamlin, A., Ostrovsky, R., Weiss, M., Wichs, D.: Private anonymous data access. In: Ishai, Y., Rijmen, V. (eds.) EUROCRYPT 2019. LNCS, vol. 11477, pp. 244–273. Springer, Cham (2019). https://doi.org/10.1007/978-3-030-17656-3_9
64. Henry, R.: Polynomial batch codes for efficient IT-PIR. PoPETs (2016)
65. Henry, R., Huang, Y., Goldberg, I.: One (block) size fits all: PIR and SPIR with variable-length records via multi-block queries. In: NDSS. The Internet Society (2013)

66. Henry, R., Olumofin, F.G., Goldberg, I.: Practical PIR for electronic commerce. In: CCS, pp. 677–690. ACM (2011)

67. Huang, Y., Evans, D., Katz, J.: Private set intersection: are garbled circuits better than custom protocols? In: NDSS. The Internet Society (2012)

68. Ishai, Y., Kushilevitz, E., Ostrovsky, R., Sahai, A.: Batch codes and their applications. In: STOC, pp. 262–271. ACM (2004)

69. Jacob, R., Larsen, K.G., Nielsen, J.B.: Lower bounds for oblivious data structures. In: SODA, pp. 2439–2447. SIAM (2019)

70. Juels, A.: Targeted advertising ... and privacy too. In: Naccache, D. (ed.) CT-RSA 2001. LNCS, vol. 2020, pp. 408–424. Springer, Heidelberg (2001). https://doi.org/10.1007/3-540-45353-9_30

71. Kalai, Y.T., Raz, R., Rothblum, R.D.: How to delegate computations: the power of no-signaling proofs. In: STOC, pp. 485–494 (2014)

72. Kogan, D., Corrigan-Gibbs, H.: Private blocklist lookups with Checklist. In: USENIX Security (2021)

73. Komargodski, I., Lin, W.-K.: A logarithmic lower bound for oblivious RAM (for all parameters). In: Malkin, T., Peikert, C. (eds.) CRYPTO 2021. LNCS, vol. 12828, pp. 579–609. Springer, Cham (2021). https://doi.org/10.1007/978-3-030-84259-8_20

74. Kushilevitz, E., Ostrovsky, R.: Replication is not needed: single database, computationally-private information retrieval. In: FOCS, pp. 364–373. IEEE (1997)

75. Larsen, K.G., Nielsen, J.B.: Yes, there is an oblivious RAM lower bound! In: Shacham, H., Boldyreva, A. (eds.) CRYPTO 2018. LNCS, vol. 10992, pp. 523–542. Springer, Cham (2018). https://doi.org/10.1007/978-3-319-96881-0_18

76. Larsen, K.G., Simkin, M., Yeo, K.: Lower bounds for multi-server oblivious RAMs. In: Pass, R., Pietrzak, K. (eds.) TCC 2020. LNCS, vol. 12550, pp. 486–503. Springer, Cham (2020). https://doi.org/10.1007/978-3-030-64375-1_17

77. Lipmaa, H.: An oblivious transfer protocol with log-squared communication. In: Zhou, J., Lopez, J., Deng, R.H., Bao, F. (eds.) ISC 2005. LNCS, vol. 3650, pp. 314–328. Springer, Heidelberg (2005). https://doi.org/10.1007/11556992_23

78. Lipmaa, H.: First CPIR protocol with data-dependent computation. In: Lee, D., Hong, S. (eds.) ICISC 2009. LNCS, vol. 5984, pp. 193–210. Springer, Heidelberg (2010). https://doi.org/10.1007/978-3-642-14423-3_14

79. Lueks, W., Goldberg, I.: Sublinear scaling for multi-client private information retrieval. In: Böhme, R., Okamoto, T. (eds.) FC 2015. LNCS, vol. 8975, pp. 168–186. Springer, Heidelberg (2015). https://doi.org/10.1007/978-3-662-47854-7_10

80. Mockapetris, P.: Domain names - concepts and facilities. RFC 1034 (1987). http://www.rfc-editor.org/rfc/rfc1034.txt

81. Mughees, M.H., Chen, H., Ren, L.: OnionPIR: response efficient single-server PIR. In: CCS (2021)

82. Paillier, P.: Public-key cryptosystems based on composite degree residuosity classes. In: Stern, J. (ed.) EUROCRYPT 1999. LNCS, vol. 1592, pp. 223–238. Springer, Heidelberg (1999). https://doi.org/10.1007/3-540-48910-X_16

83. Patel, S., Persiano, G., Yeo, K.: Private stateful information retrieval. In: CCS, pp. 1002–1019 (2018)

84. Persiano, G., Yeo, K.: Limits of preprocessing for single-server PIR. In: SODA (2022)

85. Pinkas, B., Schneider, T., Zohner, M.: Faster private set intersection based on OT extension. In: USENIX Security, pp. 797–812. USENIX Association, San Diego (2014)

86. Pinkas, B., Schneider, T., Zohner, M.: Scalable private set intersection based on OT extension. ACM Trans. Priv. Secur. **21**, 1–35 (2018)

87. Regev, O.: On lattices, learning with errors, random linear codes, and cryptography. J. ACM **56**, 1–40 (2009)

88. Servan-Schreiber, S., Hogan, K., Devadas, S.: AdVeil: a private targeted-advertising ecosystem. Cryptology ePrint Archive, Report 2021/1032 (2021)

89. Shi, E., Aqeel, W., Chandrasekaran, B., Maggs, B.: Puncturable pseudorandom sets and private information retrieval with near-optimal online bandwidth and time. In: Malkin, T., Peikert, C. (eds.) CRYPTO 2021. LNCS, vol. 12828, pp. 641–669. Springer, Cham (2021). https://doi.org/10.1007/978-3-030-84259-8_22

90. Stark, E.M.: Splitting up trust, 14 September 2021. https://emilymstark.com/2021/09/14/splitting-up-trust.html

91. Tauman Kalai, Y., Raz, R., Rothblum, R.D.: Delegation for bounded space. In: STOC, pp. 565–574 (2013)

92. Unruh, D.: Random oracles and auxiliary input. In: Menezes, A. (ed.) CRYPTO 2007. LNCS, vol. 4622, pp. 205–223. Springer, Heidelberg (2007). https://doi.org/10.1007/978-3-540-74143-5_12

93. Wehner, S., de Wolf, R.: Improved lower bounds for locally decodable codes and private information retrieval. In: Caires, L., Italiano, G.F., Monteiro, L., Palamidessi, C., Yung, M. (eds.) ICALP 2005. LNCS, vol. 3580, pp. 1424–1436. Springer, Heidelberg (2005). https://doi.org/10.1007/11523468_115

94. Woodruff, D., Yekhanin, S.: A geometric approach to information-theoretic private information retrieval. In: CCC. IEEE (2005)

95. Yao, A.: Coherent functions and program checkers. In: STOC (1990)

96. Yekhanin, S.: Towards 3-query locally decodable codes of subexponential length. J. ACM **55**, 1–16 (2008)

Anamorphic Encryption: Private Communication Against a Dictator

Giuseppe Persiano[1], Duong Hieu Phan[2], and Moti Yung[3,4(✉)]

[1] Università di Salerno, Salerno, Italy
giuper@gmail.com
[2] Telecom Paris, Institut Polytechnique de Paris, Paris, France
hieu.phan@telecom-paris.fr
[3] Google LLC, New York, NY, USA
motiyung@gmail.com
[4] Columbia University, New York City, USA

Abstract. Cryptosystems have been developed over the years under the typical prevalent setting which assumes that the receiver's key is kept secure from the adversary, and that the choice of the message to be sent is freely performed by the sender and is kept secure from the adversary as well. Under these fundamental and basic operational assumptions, modern Cryptography has flourished over the last half a century or so, with amazing achievements: New systems (including public-key Cryptography), beautiful and useful models (including security definitions such as semantic security), and new primitives (such as zero-knowledge proofs) have been developed. Furthermore, these fundamental achievements have been translated into actual working systems, and span many of the daily human activities over the Internet.

However, in recent years, there is an overgrowing pressure from many governments to allow the government itself access to keys and messages of encryption systems (under various names: escrow encryption, emergency access, communication decency acts, etc.). Numerous non-direct arguments against such policies have been raised, such as "the bad guys can utilize other encryption system" so all other cryptosystems have to be declared illegal, or that "allowing the government access is an ill-advised policy since it creates a natural weak systems security point, which may attract others (to masquerade as the government)." It has remained a fundamental open issue, though, to show directly that the above mentioned efforts by a government (called here "a dictator" for brevity) which mandate breaking of the basic operational assumption (and disallowing other cryptosystems), is, in fact, a futile exercise. This is a direct technical point which needs to be made and has not been made to date.

In this work, as a technical demonstration of the futility of the dictator's demands, we invent the notion of *"Anamorphic Encryption"* which shows that even if the dictator gets the keys and the messages used in the system (before anything is sent) and no other system is allowed, there is a covert way within the context of **well established public-key cryptosystems** for an entity to immediately (with no latency) send piggybacked secure messages which are, in spite of the stringent dictator

O. Dunkelman and S. Dziembowski (Eds.): EUROCRYPT 2022, LNCS 13276, pp. 34–63, 2022.
https://doi.org/10.1007/978-3-031-07085-3_2

conditions, hidden from the dictator itself! We feel that this may be an important direct technical argument against the nature of governments' attempts to police the use of strong cryptographic systems, and we hope to stimulate further works in this direction.

1 Introduction

Cryptography, like most scientific fields, has a profound impact on our Society, and even more so as it touches upon one of the most basic human rights, the right to privacy. The threats to privacy posed by the increased reliance on electronic forms of communication has been very well identified (see, for example, [DL]) and there has been a very vigorous debate between technologists and politicians about the ways of limiting the power of encryption as a safeguard to privacy (see the discussion on escrow systems below). One of the beneficial effects of the debate has been the increased awareness of the need to protect our privacy; this is witnessed by the growing use of end to end encryption (E2E encryption) in, for example, messaging apps [MP16, Wha20].

Cryptography "rearranges power" [Rog15] and it obviously attracts the attention of the institutions and individuals that hold the same power that Cryptography threatens to rearrange. Among these power holding institutions, our main concerns involve the institutions that have the power to undermine the two assumptions on which Cryptography relies. As we argue below these assumptions, which have long gone overlooked (or implicit), are rather different in nature from the usual cryptographic assumptions (e.g., about the computing power of parties). More precisely, the security guarantees offered by Cryptography even for its most basic and classic setting, two-party private communication [Sha49], rely on two implicit and fundamental assumptions, one regarding the sender and one regarding the receiver, that can be challenged by exactly those parties whose power Cryptography threatens to limit. When these assumptions are challenged, all privacy guarantees are void (this holds for symmetric [Fei73] as well as for public key [DH76, RSA78, GM84] systems).

Concretely, it is assumed that the encryption and the decryption processes are conducted freely and privately by the sender and the receiver, respectively. Specifically, on the receiver's side, a message, once encrypted, is considered private based on the assumption that the receiver's (Bob's) private key (regardless of where it resides) is not compromised. In fact, relying solely on the key not being compromised and not on other obscurities is known as the Kerckhoffs principle and was already formulated in 1883 [Ker83]. On the sender's side, in turn, it is concretely assumed that the sender (Alice) is free to pick the message to be sent.

Indeed, if Alice is not free to pick the message to be sent, we can hardly talk of communication "from Alice to Bob." Similarly, if Bob's secret key is compromised (and the key is the only source of secrecy), we cannot consider the communication to be private. In other words, Cryptography currently implements *private communication* assuming that encryption takes as input a message freely chosen by Alice and that, among all other parties, only Bob has access to the key necessary for decryption. We call these two assumptions the *sender-freedom assumption* and the *receiver-privacy assumption*, respectively.

Both assumptions are realistic for normal settings, and thus, it is not a big surprise that the majority of symmetric and asymmetric encryption systems have been developed under them, and it is so natural that these are implicit in the modeling. Yet, these assumptions fail to exist in a dictator-led country where law enforcement agencies have the (legal) power to get the private key of citizens to be surrendered upon request (thus undermining the receiver-privacy assumption). Furthermore, in a dictatorship, individuals can be forced by the authorities to encrypt and send some adversary selected (e.g., wrong) statements (thus undermining the sender-freedom assumption). Note that while we characterize the above as a dictator-led country, it is quite prevalent around the world today for governments (of all types) to ask for at least some of the above powers when discussing encryption!

Let us now discuss the two assumptions more in depth.

The Receiver-Privacy Assumption. Achieving security without having to rely on this assumption asks us to consider the classical cryptographic problem of two parties that wish to privately communicate in the presence of an adversary that has the ability to eavesdrop on all communication between the two parties *and* the power to request the receiver's secret key[1]. At first sight, achieving privacy against such an adversary seems like an impossible task since, by definition, the secret key allows for the decryption of any ciphertext and, once an adversary has gained access to the secret key, nothing can stop it from decrypting the ciphertexts.

Before giving an intuitive idea of how we plan to approach this seemingly impossible problem, we want to elaborate on the security threat that we address and how it puts further constraints on the solution space. As mentioned before, this setting models adversaries of the scale of a nation state whose government has the "legal" power to force citizens to reveal their secret keys. In such a setting, it is expected that a citizen would abide by the request as any refusal could be considered as evidence that the communication was unlawful (or be considered such in the eyes of the adversary/government); in fact, the citizens may wish (as an advantage in an hostile environment) to be able to prove the benign nature of their messages. As we shall see, addressing the needs of privacy in the presence of such a powerful adversary in an effective way cannot be achieved by introducing *new* constructions that would immediately be ruled as illegal, but rather by showing that *existing* constructions can be adapted to support the new need. Indeed, for its own nature, the deployment itself of countermeasures must be hidden from the adversary as a government has the legal means and the power to make it illegal.

The Sender-Freedom Assumption. This assumption posits that the sender Alice is free to choose which message to encrypt; without this assumption, the meaning of *communication* originating from Alice is lost. It is not difficult to imagine a setting in which someone is under duress to send a ciphertext with a fake message. Specifically, the sender might be forced to produce a ciphertext ct for a given message m, the *forced* message, with respect to a given public key fPK,

---

[1] This is masterly described in xkcd comic 538 (see https://xkcd.com/538).

the *forced* public key. In addition the adversary will want to see the coin tosses R used to produce ct so as to be able to check that $\text{ct} = \text{Enc}(\text{fPK}, m; R)$. Is there a way for the sender to satisfy the adversary but still send a message other than m to some other party? Clearly, if the adversary has the power to pick the message m and the randomness to be used, then the sender has no maneuvering space. This would be equivalent to the adversary holding Alice's cellphone and using it to send messages on Alice's behalf; clearly (with no freedom to choose anything) nothing can be done to prevent this (which is a, de facto, impersonation of Alice). Instead, we do not consider impersonation, but rather consider the setting in which the more remote adversary does select the message to be sent, lets Alice compute the ciphertext ct and later on Alice is required to exhibit the coin tosses used to compute ct; i.e., the adversary does not completely control the cryptographic device as in an impersonation attack, it allows strong cryptography as well, but forces a valid explanation for the ciphertext for messages it chooses, including possibly some one-way hash post-processing of truly random bits to produce the random bits used in encryption, to prevent, e.g., some meaningful message being part of the randomness used for systems that encrypt over a message and randomness, and issues of this sort.

Again, in authoritarian regimes, under threats, dissidents are often forced to send false statements to public and international newspapers. In this situation, an international human rights organization (HR) that is not under the control of the dictator can release its public key. When dissidents in a country ruled by a dictator are forced by the authority to send false statements to an international newspaper, say AP News under the public key of AP News, dissidents can obey that request while being able to add hidden messages to HR, for example saying that what they are saying is false, as an additional protection.

Normative Prescriptions. One may ask: most of Cryptography is based on computational assumptions and this has not slowed down its deployment in real-world applications; why should we be worried by two extra assumptions? Let us pause and ask ourselves why we believe in the assumptions we use to design cryptographic schemes. The assumed hardness of computational problems reflects our current intuition about and understanding of Nature (and thus, its representation within mathematical models): randomness, one-way functions, and trapdoor functions do exist in our current understanding of Nature. On the other hand, let us look at the receiver-privacy assumption. Why do we believe that users will not be forced to reveal their private key? Essentially because there is a *normative prescription*[2] by which forcing someone to do something against its will is a punishable crime. In other words, society attaches a punishment to anybody who violates the receiver-privacy assumption. The same holds for the sender-freedom assumption. However normative prescriptions are not laws of Nature (not inherent to the way things are!) and they can be modified by a new social/normative re-order. And this is exactly what a dictator will do. On the other hand, quite

---

[2] We do not use the term "law" to mark the conceptual difference from "law of Nature."

obviously, no dictator will ever be able to make a one-way function efficiently invertible or will be able to predict a random bit[3].

Indeed Cryptography can be seen as an effort to replace assumptions based on normative prescriptions with milder assumptions leveraging our understanding of Nature and, more specifically, of Computational Complexity (combined with Information Theory) and/or of Computing Architectures. A primary example of this effort is the concept of Secure Multiparty Computation (aka Private Function Evaluation). If we accept assumptions based on normative prescriptions, then we can identify some individual to act as *a trusted third party* (TTP); that is, the TTP receives the private inputs and returns the value of the function to be computed. A law (a normative prescription) will describe the expected behavior of the TTP and identify the penalties for not following the prescription. On the other hand, the field of Secure multi-party computation [Yao86, GMW87] has shown how to achieve the same without relying on normative prescriptions regarding the TTP (replacing it with reliance on computational complexity assumptions and/or architectural separation and isolation of computing elements).

2   Related Works

Having presented the crux of our notion, let us examine related works and notions dealing with other aspects of violations of the two implicit normative assumptions above.

Key-Escrow. The availability and proliferation of E2E encryption for smartphone messaging applications (see [MP16, ACD19, Wha20] for two of the most widely used applications and for some of the formal treatment of the Cryptography on which they are based) has renewed the debate between law enforcement and government security agencies, and technologists. Actually, the debate goes back to at almost 30 years ago when the Internet became mainstream (early 1990s). The following quote is from [Dak96]:

Presently, anyone can obtain encryption devices for voice or data transmissions. Unfortunately, this group may include criminals, terrorists and drug dealers. Law enforcement groups believe this could soon create a devastating problem because these authorities commonly rely on electronic surveillance, also known as "wiretapping", as a tool for fighting crime. That is, if criminals can use advanced encryption technology in their transmissions, electronic surveillance techniques could be rendered useless because of law enforcement's inability to decode the message.

Much research in Cryptography has focused on methods to make the strong privacy guarantees offered by encryption ineffective under very specific and well identified situations. An early prototypical and pioneering example of this kind of work is the concept of a *Fair Cryptosystem* by Micali [Mic] that was one of the first to consider the possibility of targeted revocation of the privacy offered

---

[3] In "The Game-Players of Titan", a novel by Philip K. Dick, randomness is the only weapon humans can use against silicon-based telepath aliens from Titan, called *vugs*.

by encryption. Roughly speaking, this was achieved by sharing the secret key among a number of parties (the majority of which is assumed to be honest, say) and each would reveal its share, so as to allow reconstruction, only if a court order to that effect would be produced. In 1993 (essentially at the same time of Fair Cryptosystems), the US government put forth *The Clipper* proposal [Cli] by which all strong encryption systems had to retain a copy of keys necessary to decrypt information with a trusted third party who would turn over keys to law enforcement upon proper legal authorization. The Clipper chip was attempting to bind the ability to identify the key of the sender to facilitate government access and the ability to decrypt. The proposal had a flaws involving a too small authentication field [Bla94] and, actually, the binding was shown to be broken so as to bypass the mechanism [FY93]. All the above systems employed either trusted hardware or other trusted elements (trustees) added to the Public-Key Infrastructure setting. An open question at the time was to construct a "software only" escrow, employing the existing trusted point of the certification authority within the existing public key infrastructure as a handle (see [YY98]).

Given general security concerns, the report by Abelson et al. [AAB+97] (see also [AAB+15]) identifies the major threats of such a *key-escrow* system (primarily, the availability of an access method to the user's encrypted data which is not under the user own responsibility). The possibility that a key-escrow system could be abused by law-enforcement agency to violate the privacy of the users and to conduct large scale surveillance, which is our main concern in this paper, and was identified in the first report [AAB+97] that looked into the privacy issues arising from the Clipper chip and from other key-escrow mechanisms. We note that, obviously, the same concerns and more hold if weak Cryptography, which can be broken with enough feasible resources, is mandated in our modern time and with available public computational resources, such Cryptography simply does not work.

The main approach taken by cryptographers to address the above important point regarding escrow has been to construct systems relying on cryptographic tools (mathematical assumptions) that will make it impossible for governments to infringe on the privacy of the individuals and the guarantees made relying on a combination of normative assumptions as well as on cryptographic primitives. For example, the guarantee offered by a Fair Cryptosystem rely on the cryptographic strength of the secret-sharing primitives and on the normative prescription that the majority of shareholders will only act upon a request from the recognized authority, which, in turn, relies on the assumption that share holder are honest and uncoercible. From our point of view it is natural to ask: What if the authority is a dictator, and thus normative prescriptions have no effect?

Along these lines, the very recent work of Green et al. [GKVL] offers the most complete approach by formally defining the desired properties for a *law enforcement access system* and putting forth the notion of an *abuse-resistant law enforcement access system (ARLEAS)*. In addition, they gave a feasibility result using standard cryptographic techniques. Most systems, including

ARLEAS [GKVL], consider three types of parties: *users*, that employ encryption to exchange messages; *law enforcement*, that need to access encrypted messages produced by users; *judiciary*, that grants or denies authorizations to the access requests of the law enforcement. Note that such a system does not offer any protection against dictatorial states. First of all, in most dictatorships the judiciary is not an independent power thus making the abuse-resistant property nothing more than a wish. Actually, a key-escrow system makes it even easier for a dictator to violate the privacy of the users as it is enough to nominate themselves, as dictators tend to do, to be the judiciary and law enforcement. Even more importantly, note that all such systems still rely on the receiver-privacy and sender-freedom assumptions.

The main technical objective of our work is to show that one can achieve privacy in communication using existing cryptographic systems even in the presence of a dictator without relying on any normative prescription.

Deniable Encryption. The concept of *Deniable Encryption*, put forth by Canetti et al. [CDNO97], might seem to be relevant to our setting. A deniable encryption scheme allows the sender to generate *fake* coin tosses that make the ciphertext looks like an encryption of another, innocent, cleartext. So whenever the sender is requested to open a ciphertext by surrendering the coin tosses, he can just generate fake coin tosses and thus effectively conceal the real plaintext. However, an assumption in deniable encryption is that the adversary has the power to approach the sender *after* the ciphertext was transmitted. It was mentioned in [CDNO97] that deniability is impossible in the context of direct physical access, where "Eve [the adversary] approaches Alice [the sender] *before* the transmission and requires Alice [the sender] to send specific messages". It was clearly stated in the original paper [CDNO97] that "Certainly, if Alice [the sender] must hand Eve [the adversary] the *real* cleartext and random bits then no protection is possible". Hence, while deniability is an important property, it does not solve the issue of facing a dictator.

Kleptography. The concept of having a cryptosystem inside another cryptosystem was used in Kleptography [YYa, YY97, YYb]. However, the goal in Kleptography is to attack the cryptosystem owner by using inside an implementation (or a specification) a method to leak exclusively to an adversary. This goal is in fact, not to help against an adversary, but to covertly introduce an adversary, and is a tool to help a dictator!. In some sense it can be used as an implicit key escrow, and in some formal sense it negated the US government plan to distribute cryptography in black-box hardware devices. Due to Snowden revelations, in fact, an Elliptic Curve variant of the repeated DH kleptogram in the above works was deployed in the Dual-EC pseudorandom generator standard, as was verified in [CNE+14]. As a response, nowadays, the cryptographic community is working on systems and architectures which can mitigate such system subversion attacks (see [BPR, RTYZ, RTYZ17]).

Steganography and "Chaffing and Winnowing". The other tool to send secret messages with is steganography, where a message is concealed within another message (exploiting some redundancy in the message structure and style). This is always possible, but systems of this nature are hard to deploy widely and systematically as part of an established large scale computing base in a situation it is not allowed (by the dictator).

In a response to the US government possibly restricting encryption systems while allowing authentication method as part of its cryptographic export control, Rivest proposed in 1998 the "chaffing and winnowing" system [Riv]. This system shows how sharing a MAC key for authentication is turned into a method for sending concealed message (in some steganographic sense). This clearly demonstrated that the separation of cryptography for authentication and cryptography for confidentiality, proposed by the possible export regulation, is quite artificial, and gave a way to bypass key escrow using authentication keys which were not proposed to be part of escrow encryption schemes at the time. Note that in our scenario of the dictator, the dictator can certainly ask for a MAC (authentication) key as well and get the concealed message itself.

PublicKey Steganography and Subvertable Backdoored Encryption. von Ahn and Hopper [vAH04] were the first to study steganographic public key and key exchange. Their constructions rely on the existence of a public random string that cannot be tampered or chosen by the dictator. The work of Horel et al. [HPRV19] removes this assumptions by showing that steganographic key exchange can be achieved without resorting to public information. The key exchange is used then in conjunction with the *rejection sampling technique* (see Sect. 5.1).

Comparing our model with the one of [HPRV19], we note that our model assumes the parties have originally shared (private and thus un-tampered by dictator) information. This, importantly, allows for *zero-latency* communication hidden from the dictator. In Sect. 5.3 nevertheless, we show how to combine [HPRV19] with our construction thus sacrificing zero-latency and dispensing with the need of shared information. Comparing, in turn, one of our main solutions (see Sect. 5.3) with the one of Horel et al. [HPRV19] we note that, for a ciphertext carrying λ bits, rejection sampling allows to transmit $O(\log \lambda)$ extra bits whereas our construction carries λ thus achieving *bandwidth rate* of 1 (as opposed to $(\log \lambda)/\lambda$). Such a bandwidth rate is rare in steganographic systems in general. Our second result in Sect. 6 also achieves zero latency, and does not need the parties to share a private key.

3   Our Approach

In this section, we would like to give a taste of our approach, and present a generic but limited solution that shows its feasibility. For concreteness, we consider the receiver's side.

As we have already observed, there is no hope for preventing an adversary that is in possession of the secret key from decrypting a ciphertext. In turn, one might think of ciphertexts that carry two messages and a different key is needed for each of them. When asked for the secret key, the receiver might release only one of the two keys, thus protecting one of the messages. But then, if the adversary knows that there are two keys, why should he be happy to receive just one key? Because we will make sure that the adversary *believes* that there is no second key! Roughly speaking, we would like to have an encryption scheme for which it is possible to generate a public key with one secret key or, alternatively, to generate a public key that has *two* associated secret keys. More precisely, the technical core of our proposed solution consists of the concept of an *Anamorphic Encryption* scheme, a special encryption scheme whose public keys can be generated in one of two possible modes: *normal* or *anamorphic*.

- A *Normal* public key is associated with a *Normal* secret key and it can be used for the normal encryption functionality: the sender encrypts the message m using the public key, and the receiver decrypts the ciphertext using the secret key. An adversarial authority (i.e., the dictator) that is in possession of a ciphertext can (legally) force the receiver to surrender the secret key and thus gain access to the message.
- An *Anamorphic*[4] public key instead is associated with two secret keys: a *normal* secret key and a *double* secret key. A ciphertext ct produced with an anamorphic public key carries two messages: the *normal* message m_0, that can be obtained by decrypting ct using the normal secret key; and the *anamorphic* message m_1, only visible to parties that have the *double* secret key. When requested to surrender his secret key to allow inspection of the ciphertexts, the owner of an anamorphic public key will pretend that the key is normal and reveal the normal secret key. Thus, the dictator will gain access only to the normal message m_0 and the special message m_1 is kept private.

Normal public keys can be used by receivers who do not expect their secret keys to be requested by the adversarial authority. Actually, these users need not even know about anamorphic public keys and their operations will not be affected in any way. Anamorphic public keys could instead be generated by someone who has reasons to believe that the dictator will want to get the information he has received; for example, an investigative reporter or an opposition leader. As an example, consider an investigative reporter Bob who wants to communicate in a private way with his informant, Alice. Bob sets up his public key as an anamorphic key and gives Alice the double secret key. Note that Bob publishes his anamorphic public key for everybody to use. However, when Alice has some sensitive information for Bob, she uses the double key obtained from Bob to produce an anamorphic ciphertext carrying two messages: m_0 is set equal to some innocent looking message (for example, a general question about the work of the reporter; recall that in a dictatorship Alice does not even have a free choice

---

[4] The adjective *Anamorphic* is used to denote a drawing with a distorted projection that appears normal when viewed from a particular point or with a suitable mirror or lens. Similarly, an anamorphic ciphertext will reveal a different plaintext when decrypted with a suitable key.

of this message), and message m_1 will instead contain the sensitive information that Alice wishes to communicate to Bob. Should Bob be requested to surrender his secret key, he will pretend that his public key is just a normal public key and will reveal the normal secret key. In this way the adversary will be able to read message m_0 (the innocent message containing no sensitive information) and will gain no access to the potentially incriminating message m_1.

Clearly, for this to work the following conditions must be satisfied:

- a pair of anamorphic public and secret keys must be indistinguishable from a normal corresponding pair; and
- the ciphertexts produced using an anamorphic public key must be indistinguishable from those produced by a normal public key.

In addition, we are interested in performance parameters: We would like the system to have *zero-latency* in the sense that the anamorphic system is ready to be used whenever the normal system is ready. Additionally, we are interested in system where the anamorphic *bandwidth rate* (i.e., number of anomorphic bit transmitted divided by the number of normal bits transmitted) is high (whenever and as much as possible).

A Simple Solution that Does Not Work. At first, one might think that constructing an Anamorphic Encryption scheme is not difficult and indeed it is possible to turn any encryption scheme $\mathcal{E}$ into a Anamorphic Encryption AME in the following rather straightforward way by adding redundancy to the ciphertext. The normal encryption process of AME consists of computing a ciphertext ct according to $\mathcal{E}$ and then outputting $(\mathtt{ct}, R)$, where R is a randomly selected string. During the decryption process of AME with the normal secret key, the random string R is ignored and the message is obtained by decrypting ct according to $\mathcal{E}$. Thus, a normal pair of public and secret key for AME is simply a pair of keys from $\mathcal{E}$. An anamorphic public key instead is associated also with the secret key K of a symmetric encryption scheme $\mathcal{E}'$ with pseudorandom ciphertexts (e.g., it is a pseudorandom permutation). During the anamorphic encryption process, ciphertext ct is an encryption of m_0 according to $\mathcal{E}$ and the random string R that is appended to ct is an encryption of m_1 with respect to $\mathcal{E}'$ computed using key K that, thus, plays the role of the double key. Note that the public keys are identical and, by the pseudorandomness properties of the ciphertexts of $\mathcal{E}'$, a normal ciphertext, in which R is truly random, is indistinguishable from an anamorphic ciphertext in which R is a ciphertext of $\mathcal{E}'$.

So, the question is: do we have a satisfactory solutions? Hardly so! The mere fact of using a standard encryption scheme and augmenting each ciphertext with a random string is suspicious and, moreover, a user not interested in sending hidden messages has no incentive to append a random string to the ciphertext just to attract the attention of the dictator. Rather we are interested in showing that *existing* encryption schemes can be used, in the form in which they have been originally designed, to provide a second channel that is secure also with respect to an adversary that has access to the secret key of the receiver. In practice, this will not raise any suspicion since all ciphertexts will be from a standard encryption scheme or will be indistinguishable from them. In addition, no extra action (like generating and appending a random string to each ciphertext) is required from the normal users who can actually be completely unaware of the special mode of operation.

In other words the question we ask is not

Can we construct an Anamorphic Encryption scheme?

but rather:

Is any of the existing encryption schemes also Anamorphic?

A positive answer to this question will constitute technical evidence of the futility of the efforts of governments around the world (dictatorships and democracies) to control encryption.

Our Main Technical Contributions. The rest of this paper consists of identifying encryption schemes that appear in the literature which address the two limitations we identified above.

- **Receiver's side.** We show that the Naor-Yung paradigm for CCA secure encryption from CPA secure encryption gives receiver-Anamorphic Encryption schemes (see Definition 1) with a *bandwidth rate* of 1. That is, each ciphertext for λ plaintext bits carries λ additional bits that are hidden from the dictator. Moreover, as in the public key model, communication hidden from the dictator can start with *zero latency*.
- **Sender's side.** We show that a lattice based cryptosystems from the literature [Reg05, GPV08] are sender-Anamorphic Encryption (see Definition 3) and they also achieve hidden communication with *zero latency*. In addition, they do not require the sender and receiver to share any secret (just that there is an additional receiver in the system), thus, enhancing their practicality.

Given these, one can conclude that the "Crypto Wars" which consists of attacks on the free use of strong cryptography (involving requirements to give keys of such cryptographic schemes to the dictator) are possibly futile. One may then conclude that dictators should mandate only weak cryptography! But, due to earlier battles, we are already know that disallowing strong Cryptography is totally unhelpful to and imposes limits on the development of advanced information technology systems, implying dire consequences to the economy and to society.

Roadmap. In Sect. 4, we put forth the concept of a Receiver-Anamorphic Encryption and give a formal notion of security. In Sect. 5.3, we show that the Naor-Yung paradigm [NY90] gives Receiver-Anamorphic Encryption with *zero latency and bandwidth rate 1*. In Sect. 6, we define the concept of an Sender-Anamorphic Encryption that can be used to obtain private communication when the sender-freedom assumption does not hold. We show that lattice-based cryptosystems have this property (and give some evidence that other public key cryptosystems are not Sender-Anamorphic Encryption). The scheme is *zero-latency* as well.

4   Receiver-Anamorphic Encryption

In this section we present the concept of a *Receiver-Anamorphic Encryption scheme* that provides private communication without relying on the receiver-privacy assumption (while in Sect. 6 we will present the concept of a *Sender-Anamorphic Encryption scheme*).

A *Receiver-Anamorphic Encryption* scheme (a Receiver-AM scheme) consists of two encryption schemes: the *normal* scheme (KG, Enc, Dec) and the *anamorphic* scheme (aKG, aEnc, aDec). It can be deployed as normal scheme in which case Bob runs the (real) key generation algorithm KG to obtain a pair of keys (PK, SK) and, as usual, publishes PK. When Alice wishes to send message m, she produces ciphertext ct by running the (real) encryption algorithm Enc by using PK and m. When ct is received by Bob, it is decrypted by running the (real) decryption algorithm Dec and using SK. Thus, when deployed as normal a Receiver-AM is just a regular public-key encryption scheme. If the dictator comes for the secret key, Bob surrenders SK. We are interested in Receiver-AM schemes in which the normal scheme is an *established* and *already used* cryptosystem.

Bob deploys the scheme as anamorphic when he wants to protect the confidentiality of the communication with Alice even in the event that he is forced to surrender his secret decryption key to the dictator. In this case, Bob runs the *anamorphic* key generation algorithm aKG that returns a pair of anamorphic public-secret keys (aPK, aSK) along with a special key, dkey, called the *double key*. As usual, Bob publishes aPK and keeps aSK private but dkey is shared with Alice. If asked, Bob will surrender aSK to the dictator. The pair (aPK, aSK) is a fully functional pair of keys: if a message m is encrypted by using Enc and aPK, it can be decrypted by Dec on input aSK. Key dkey is instead used by Alice to send Bob messages that remain confidential even if aSK is compromised. Specifically, whenever Alice has a message m_1 that must remain confidential, she picks an innocent looking message m_0 and encrypts (m_0, m_1) using the anamorphic encryption algorithm aEnc with dkey. The ciphertext ct produced by aEnc has the property that it returns m_0 when decrypted with the normal decryption algorithm Dec and with key aSK; whereas it returns m_1 when decrypted by running the anamorphic decryption algorithm aDec on input the double key dkey. In other words, the authority will obtain m_0 and Bob will obtain m_1. Clearly, the ciphertext produced by Alice must indistinguishable from a ciphertext of m_1 produced using Enc even to an adversary that has access to aSK.

We stress again that Alice and Bob share a key, dkey, in order to achieve privacy without having to rely on the secret-key assumption.

4.1   Syntax

In this section we formally define the concept of a Receiver-Anamorphic Encryption scheme. Then in Sect. 4.3 we will present the corresponding security notion.

Definition 1. *An encryption scheme* AME = (AME.KG, AME.Enc, AME.Dec) *is a* Receiver-Anamorphic Encryption *(or, simply, a Receiver-AM) if there exists* *an* anamorphic *triplet* aAME = (AME.aKG, AME.aEnc, AME.aDec) *with the following syntax*

- AME.aKG *takes as input the security parameter* 1^λ *and returns an* anamorphic *public key* aPK, *an* anamorphic *secret key* aSK *and a* double key dkey.
- AME.aEnc *takes as input the double key* dkey *and two messages* m_0 *and* m_1 *and returns an* anamorphic *ciphertext* act.
- AME.aDec *takes as input the double key* dkey *and an anamorphic ciphertext* act, *computed by running* AME.aEnc *on input* dkey *and messages* m_0 *and* m_1, *and returns message* m_1.

As we have seen previously, a Receiver-AM scheme can be deployed as normal or as anamorphic. When Bob deploys the Receiver-AM scheme as anamorphic, Alice (or any other user that has received dkey from Bob) can use aEnc to produce ciphertexts. However, Bob cannot instruct all users to use aEnc as that would be like admitting that he has deployed the scheme as anamorphic; in other words users that are unaware that the scheme has been deployed as anamorphic will use Enc. It is thus crucial that the encryption-decryption functionality does not break for these users, despite using the normal encryption algorithm with an anamorphic public key. Indeed, the fact that ciphertexts generated by the normal encryption algorithm cannot be decrypted could be a strong evidence, if not a proof, that the public key is anamorphic.

Next, we formally identify the four different modes of operations that arise from mixing normal, and anamorphic algorithms and keys and then in Sect. 4.3 we present our security notion.

4.2 Modes of Operation

A Receiver-AM scheme AME naturally defines the following four modes of operation, each corresponding to a different scenario. Of these four modes, one uses the normal keys and three use anamorphic keys. The security definition (see Definition 4) will require that, roughly speaking, the the *normal* and the *fully anamorphic* mode be indistinguishable. This is sufficient to prove that all of them are indeed pairwise indistinguishable.

1. The *fully anamorphic encryption* mode is used when Bob deploys the scheme as anamorphic and Alice uses dkey to send Bob a private message. This mode is associated with the triplet of algorithms $\mathsf{fAME}_{\hat{m}} = (\mathsf{AME.aKG}_3, \mathsf{AME.aEnc}_{1,\hat{m}}, \mathsf{AME.aDec})$ where, for every message $\hat{m}$,
   - $\mathsf{AME.aKG}_3(1^\lambda)$ is the algorithm that runs $\mathsf{AME.aKG}(1^\lambda)$ obtaining (aPK, aSK, dkey) and returns dkey. Note that the index in aKG_3 denotes the components of the triplet generated by aKG that is selected to appear in the output.
   - $\mathsf{AME.aEnc}_{1,\hat{m}}(\mathsf{aPK}, m)$ is the algorithm that returns AME.aEnc(aPK, $\hat{m}, m$). Note that index 1 in $\mathsf{AME.aEnc}_{1,\hat{m}}$ denotes that message $\hat{m}$ will be passed as first message to algorithm aEnc.
   Note that $\mathsf{fAME}_{\hat{m}}$ is, for every $\hat{m}$, a symmetric encryption scheme (Fig. 1).

	Key Gen.	Encryption	Decryption
Fully Anamorphic	aKG	aEnc	aDec
Anamorphic with Normal Dec	aKG	aEnc	Dec
Anamorphic with Normal Enc	aKG	Enc	Dec
Normal	KG	Enc	Dec

Fig. 1. The four modes of operation of an anamorphic encryption scheme. The *fully anamorphic mode* is used by Bob to communicate privately with Alice. The *anamorphic mode with normal decryption* is used by Bob when the dictator requests the decryption of an anamorphic ciphertext sent by Alice. The *anamorphic mode with normal encryption* is used by Charlie, unaware that Bob has an anamorphic key, to send a message to Bob. The *normal mode* is used by Charlie that sets up his key in normal mode to receive messages from other users. The normal mode offers no privacy guarantee against the dictator.

2. The *anamorphic with normal decryption* mode is used when Bob deploys the scheme as anamorphic (and thus the public key is generated using algorithm AME.aKG), the ciphertext ct is produced by Alice by running the anamorphic encryption algorithm AME.aEnc on input (m_0, m_1) and the double key dkey, and the ciphertext is decrypted by the dictator by running the normal encryption algorithm AME.Dec on input aSK.

   More formally, the mode is associated with the triplet $andAME_{\hat{m}} = (aKG_{1,2}, aEnc_{2,\hat{m}}, Dec)$, where, for every $\hat{m}$,
   – $andAME.aEnc_{2,\hat{m}}(aPK, m)$ is the algorithm that returns AME.aEnc(aPK, $m, \hat{m}$). Note that the index 2 in AME.aEnc$_{2,\hat{m}}$ denotes that message $\hat{m}$ will be passed as second message to algorithm aEnc.

3. The *anamorphic with normal encryption* mode is used when Bob deploys the scheme as anamorphic (and thus the anamorphic public key aPK is used as public key) and a sender encrypts messages using the normal encryption algorithm AME.Enc. The ciphertexts produced in this way can be read by the dictator that has the secret key aSK associated with aPK by running the normal decryption algorithm AME.Dec.

   More formally, the mode is associated with the triplet $aneAME = (aKG_{1,2}, Enc, Dec)$, where
   – $aKG_{1,2}(1^\lambda)$ is the algorithm that runs AME.aKG(1^λ), obtaining (aPK, aSK, dkey), and returns the pair (aPK, aSK). Note that the indices in aKG$_{1,2}$ denote the components of the triplet generated by aKG that are selected to appear in the output.

4. The *normal* mode of operation is associated to the triple of algorithms $nAME = (AME.KG, AME.Enc, AME.Dec)$ and it corresponds to the scenario in which the scheme is deployed and used in normal mode; that is, the keys are generated by running KG, the ciphertexts are constructed by running Enc and decrypted by running Dec.

4.3 Security Notion

We are now ready to define the notion of a *Secure Receiver-AM* scheme. As we shall see, the security notion posits that no PPT dictator can distinguish whether the Receiver-AM scheme is in normal mode or in fully anamorphic mode. In other words, it is indistinguishable whether nAME or fAME$\hat{m}$, for message $\hat{m}$, is being used. We first make two interesting remarks:

- No explicit security requirement is made for the security of the fully anamorphic mode; in other words, it is not explicitly required that Alice's secret message m_1 is actually secret.
- No explicit security and functional requirement regarding the partial anamorphic modes of operation, anamorphic with normal encryption and anamorphic with normal decryption, is made.

The requirements in both bullets above are clearly desirable: first, we would like Alice's secret message to be kept secure from the authorities; and we do not want the authority to be able to distinguish whether the normal mode or one of the other anamorphic modes is being used. As we shall see, the security notion of Definition 2 is sufficient for the requirements in the two bullets above. Let us now proceed more formally and define the following two games involving a dictator $\mathcal{D}$.

$\mathsf{NormalGame}_{\mathsf{AME},\mathcal{D}}(\lambda)$

1. Set $(\mathsf{PK}, \mathsf{SK}) \leftarrow \mathsf{AME.KG}(1^\lambda)$ and send $(\mathsf{PK}, \mathsf{SK})$ to $\mathcal{D}$.
2. For $i = 1, \ldots, \mathsf{poly}(\lambda)$:
   - $\mathcal{D}$ issues query (m_0^i, m_1^i) and receives $\mathtt{ct} = \mathsf{AME.Enc}(\mathsf{PK}, m_0^i)$.
3. Return $\mathcal{D}$'s output.

$\mathsf{FullyAGame}_{\mathsf{AME},\mathcal{D}}(\lambda)$

1. Set $(\mathsf{aPK}, \mathsf{aSK}, \mathsf{dkey}) \leftarrow \mathsf{AME.aKG}(1^\lambda)$ and send $(\mathsf{aPK}, \mathsf{aSK})$ to $\mathcal{D}$.
2. For $i = 1, \ldots, \mathsf{poly}(\lambda)$:
   - $\mathcal{D}$ issues query (m_0^i, m_1^i) and receives $\mathtt{ct} = \mathsf{AME.aEnc}(\mathsf{dkey}, m_0^i, m_1^i)$.
3. Return $\mathcal{D}$'s output.

Note that in $\mathsf{NormalGame}$ the key is normal (that is, output by KG) and the i-th ciphertext is an encryption of m_0^i computed using Enc. In other words, $\mathcal{D}$ interacts with the scheme in normal mode. On the other hand, in $\mathsf{FullyAGame}$ the key is output by aKG and the i-th ciphertext carries both messages m_0^i and m_1^i. In other words, $\mathcal{D}$ with the scheme in fully anamorphic mode. Note that in both cases, $\mathcal{D}$ is given the public key and the *associated secret key*.

More formally, we denote by $p_{\mathsf{AME},\mathcal{D}}^{\mathsf{NormalGame}}(\lambda)$ (respectively, $p_{\mathsf{AME},\mathcal{D}}^{\mathsf{FullyAGame}}(\lambda)$) the probability that $\mathsf{NormalGame}_{\mathsf{AME},\mathcal{D}}(\lambda)$ (respectively, $\mathsf{FullyAGame}_{\mathsf{AME},\mathcal{D}}(\lambda)$) outputs 1 and we introduce the following definition.

Definition 2. *A* Receiver-AM *scheme* AME = (KG, Enc, Dec) *with anamorphic triplet* (aKG, aEnc, aDec) *is a Secure Receiver-AM scheme if*

1. AME *is an IND-CPA scheme;*
2. *for every message* $\hat{m}$, $\mathsf{fAME}_{\hat{m}}$ *is a symmetric encryption scheme;*
3. *for all PPT dictators* $\mathcal{D}$,

$$\left| p_{\mathsf{AME},\mathcal{D}}^{\mathsf{NormalGame}}(\lambda) - p_{\mathsf{AME},\mathcal{D}}^{\mathsf{FullyAGame}}(\lambda) \right| \leq \mathsf{negl}(\lambda).$$

In the rest of this section, we prove that the fully anamorphic mode (used by Alice and Bob to communicate privately) is an IND-CPA private key encryption scheme, thus addressing the observation in the first bullet above. We start in Sect. 4.4 by proving that the anamorphic modes with normal encryption is indistinguishable from the fully anamorphic mode and from the normal mode. We then build on this to prove the security of the fully anamorphic mode in Sect. 4.5. We will address the observation in the second bullet in the final version of the paper.

4.4 Properties of the Anamorphic Mode with Normal Encryption

We start by defining game $\mathsf{aneGame}_{\mathsf{AME},\mathcal{A}}$, for a Secure Receiver-AM AME and a PPT adversary $\mathcal{A}$. As usual, we denote by $p_{\mathsf{AME},\mathcal{A}}^{\mathsf{aneGame}}(\lambda)$ the probability that $\mathsf{aneGame}_{\mathsf{AME},\mathcal{A}}(\lambda)$ outputs 1. Game $\mathsf{aneGame}$ describes the Anamorphic Mode with Normal Encryption.

$\mathsf{aneGame}_{\mathsf{AME},\mathcal{A}}(\lambda)$

1. Set (aPK, aSK, dkey) $\leftarrow$ AME.aKG(1^λ) and send (aPK, aSK) to $\mathcal{A}$.
2. For $i = 1, \ldots, \mathsf{poly}(\lambda)$:
   - $\mathcal{A}$ issues query (m_0^i, m_1^i) and receives ct = AME.Enc(aPK, m_0^i).
3. Return $\mathcal{A}$'s output.

We note that $\mathcal{A}$ issues encryption queries (m_0^i, m_1^i) and that, clearly, $\mathcal{A}$ can also use the keys in its possession to encrypt and decrypt ciphertexts of its choice. The next lemma proves that $\mathsf{aneGame}$ is indistinguishable from $\mathsf{NormalGame}$ thus yielding that the Normal Mode is indistinguishable from the Anamorphic Mode with Normal Encryption.

Lemma 1. *Let* AME *be a Secure Receiver-AM scheme. Then for all PPT adversaries* $\mathcal{A}$, *we have*

$$\left| p_{\mathsf{AME},\mathcal{A}}^{\mathsf{NormalGame}}(\lambda) - p_{\mathsf{AME},\mathcal{A}}^{\mathsf{aneGame}}(\lambda) \right| \leq \mathsf{negl}(\lambda).$$

Proof. Suppose that there exists an adversary $\mathcal{A}$ that distinguishes $\mathsf{aneGame}$ from $\mathsf{NormalGame}$. We will use $\mathcal{A}$ to construct a dictator $\mathcal{D}$ that distinguishes $\mathsf{NormalGame}$ from $\mathsf{FullyAGame}$, thus violating the security of AME. $\mathcal{D}$ receives the challenge pair of keys (PK*, SK*) and runs $\mathcal{A}$ on input (PK*, SK*). For each query (m_0^i, m_1^i) issued by $\mathcal{A}$, $\mathcal{D}$ replies by returning Enc(PK*, m_0^i). When $\mathcal{A}$ stops and returns b, $\mathcal{D}$ outputs b. This terminates the description of $\mathcal{D}$. Note that $\mathcal{D}$ issues no encryption query.

Now observe that if $\mathcal{D}$ is playing FullyAGame then $(\mathsf{PK}^\star, \mathsf{SK}^\star)$ are output by aKG and thus $\mathcal{D}$ is simulating aneGame for $\mathcal{A}$. On the other hand, if $\mathcal{D}$ is playing NormalGame then $(\mathsf{PK}^\star, \mathsf{SK}^\star)$ are output by KG and thus $\mathcal{D}$ is simulating NormalGame for $\mathcal{A}$. This concludes the proof. □

Transitivity of indistinguishability gives the following lemma.

Lemma 2. *Let* AME *be a Secure Receiver-AM scheme. Then for all PPT adversaries* $\mathcal{A}$, *we have*

$$\left| p_{\mathsf{AME},\mathcal{A}}^{\mathsf{FullyAGame}}(\lambda) - p_{\mathsf{AME},\mathcal{A}}^{\mathsf{aneGame}}(\lambda) \right| \leq \mathsf{negl}(\lambda).$$

4.5 Security of the Fully Anamorphic Mode

We are now ready to prove that the fully anamorphic mode of a *Secure Receiver-AM* scheme is IND-CPA even for an adversary that has access to $(\mathsf{aPK}, \mathsf{aSK})$ but not to dkey.

Let us start by formally defining the notion of IND-CPA security of the fully anamorphic mode of a *Secure Receiver-AM* scheme. For $\eta = 0, 1$, message $\hat{m}$, and stateful PPT adversary $\mathcal{A}$, we define game $\mathsf{IndCPA}_{\mathsf{AME},\mathcal{A},\hat{m}}^{\eta}$ as follows.

$\mathsf{IndCPA}_{\mathsf{AME},\mathcal{A},\hat{m}}^{\eta}(\lambda)$

1. Set $(\mathsf{aPK}, \mathsf{aSK}, \mathsf{dkey}) \leftarrow \mathsf{AME.aKG}(1^\lambda)$.
2. $(m_1^0, m_1^1) \leftarrow \mathcal{A}^{\mathsf{aEnc}(\mathsf{dkey},\hat{m},\cdot)}(\mathsf{aPK}, \mathsf{aSK})$.
3. Compute $\mathsf{ct} \leftarrow \mathsf{aEnc}(\mathsf{dkey}, \hat{m}, m_1^\eta)$.
4. $b \leftarrow \mathcal{A}^{\mathsf{aEnc}(\mathsf{dkey},\hat{m},\cdot)}(\mathsf{ct})$.

We denote by $\mathsf{pcpa}_{\mathsf{AME},\mathcal{A},\hat{m}}^{\eta}$ the probability that, in game $\mathsf{IndCPA}_{\mathsf{AME},\mathcal{A},\hat{m}}^{\eta}$, adversary $\mathcal{A}$ outputs 1. We will prove the following theorem.

Theorem 1. *If* AME *is a Secure Receiver-AM scheme, then, for every message* $\hat{m}$, $\mathsf{fAME}_{\hat{m}}$ *is IND-CPA secure. That is, for all PPT adversaries* $\mathcal{A}$ *and every* $\hat{m}$

$$\left| \mathsf{pcpa}_{\mathsf{AME},\mathcal{A},\hat{m}}^0(1^\lambda) - \mathsf{pcpa}_{\mathsf{AME},\mathcal{A},\hat{m}}^1(1^\lambda) \right| \leq \mathsf{negl}(\lambda).$$

To prove the theorem above, we consider, for $\eta = 0, 1$, the hybrid game $H_{\mathsf{AME},\mathcal{A},\hat{m}}^{\eta}$, in which all $\mathcal{A}$'s oracle calls to $\mathsf{aEnc}(\mathsf{dkey}, \hat{m}, \cdot)$ in IndCPA^{η} are replaced with calls to $\mathsf{Enc}(\mathsf{aPK}, \hat{m})$ and the challenge ciphertext ct at Line 3 of IndCPA^{η} is computed as $\mathsf{ct} \leftarrow \mathsf{Enc}(\mathsf{aPK}, \hat{m})$. We denote by $\mathsf{hcpa}_{\mathsf{AME},\mathcal{A},\hat{m}}^{\eta}(1^\lambda)$ the probability that $\mathcal{A}$ outputs 1 in $H_{\mathsf{AME},\mathcal{A},\hat{m}}^{\eta}$ with security parameter λ.

We have the following lemma whose proof relies on Lemma 2 above.

Lemma 3. *If* AME *is a Secure Receiver-AM then, for* $\eta = 0, 1$, *we have*

$$\left| \mathsf{pcpa}_{\mathsf{AME},\mathcal{A},\hat{m}}^{\eta}(1^\lambda) - \mathsf{hcpa}_{\mathsf{AME},\mathcal{A},\hat{m}}^{\eta}(1^\lambda) \right| \leq \mathsf{negl}(\lambda).$$

Proof. For the sake of contradiction, assume there exists an adversary $\mathcal{A}$ that violates the lemma. We then construct an efficient dictator $\mathcal{D}$ that distinguishes aneGame and FullyAGame thus contradicting Lemma 2.

$\mathcal{D}$ receives the pair (aPK, aSK) computed by aKG and has access to an encryption oracle $\mathcal{O}(\cdot, \cdot)$. $\mathcal{D}$ runs $\mathcal{A}$ on input (aPK, aSK) and when $\mathcal{A}$ issues a query for m, $\mathcal{D}$ returns $\mathcal{O}(\hat{m}, m)$. Similarly, when $\mathcal{A}$ outputs the pair of messages (m_1^0, m_1^1), $\mathcal{D}$ returns $\mathcal{O}(\hat{m}, m_1^\eta)$. At the end, $\mathcal{D}$ returns $\mathcal{A}$'s output.

If $\mathcal{D}$ is playing game aneGame then $\mathcal{O}(\hat{m}, m)$ returns $\mathsf{Enc}(\mathsf{aPK}, \hat{m})$. Therefore ct is computed as $\mathtt{ct} \leftarrow \mathsf{Enc}(\mathsf{aPK}, \hat{m})$. This implies that $\mathcal{D}$ simulates $H_{\mathcal{A}, \mathsf{AME}, \hat{m}}^\eta$ for $\mathcal{A}$. On the other hand, if $\mathcal{D}$ is playing FullyAGame then $\mathcal{O}(\hat{m}, m)$ returns $\mathsf{aEnc}(\mathsf{dkey}, \hat{m}, m)$. Therefore ct is computed as $\mathtt{ct} \leftarrow \mathsf{Enc}(\mathsf{aPK}, \hat{m}, m_1^\eta)$ and $\mathcal{D}$ simulates $\mathsf{IndCPA}_{\mathcal{A}, \mathsf{AME}, \hat{m}}^\eta(1^\lambda)$ for $\mathcal{A}$. This concludes the proof of the lemma. $\square$

We are now ready to prove Theorem 1.

Proof of Theorem 1. The theorem follows from Lemma 3 and from the observation that game $H_{\mathcal{A}, \mathsf{AME}, \hat{m}}^\eta$ is independent from η and thus

$$\mathsf{hcpa}_{\mathcal{A}, \mathsf{AME}, \hat{m}}^0(1^\lambda) = \mathsf{hcpa}_{\mathcal{A}, \mathsf{AME}, \hat{m}}^1(1^\lambda).$$

$\square$

5   Constructions

In this section we present two constructions of AM schemes. We first review the simple construction for a $(\log \lambda)$-bit AM scheme discussed in the Introduction and then, in Sect. 5.2, we present a construction for $\mathtt{poly}(\lambda)$ bits.

5.1   Rejection Sampling

In this section we present our first construction 1bit, a simple cryptosystem that gives guarantees even if the secret-key assumption and the sender-freedom assumption do not hold. It is based on the *rejection sampling* technique inspired by the *biased-ciphertext attack* of [BPR] and it is used also by Horel et al. [HPRV19]. We review it here just to give a first example of a Receiver-Anamorphic Encryption. We note that the objective of the biased-ciphertext attack is to *subvert* an encryption scheme so that the private key can be leaked without the legitimate owner noticing any abnormal behaviour and it is interesting to note that this technique can be used to setup a dictator setting, as shown in [BPR], as well as for the opposite of objective, as we show below.

The normal triplet of 1bit is any IND-CPA secure encryption scheme $\mathcal{E} = (\mathsf{KG}, \mathsf{Enc}, \mathsf{Dec})$ and the anamorphic triplet is defined as follows:

– 1bit.aKG, on input the security parameter 1^λ, runs the key generation algorithm KG of $\mathcal{E}$ obtaining (PK, SK) and random seed K for PRF F. The anamorphic public key is $\mathsf{aPK} = \mathsf{PK}$, the anamorphic secret key is $\mathsf{aSK} = \mathsf{SK}$ and the double key $\mathtt{dkey} = (\mathsf{PK}, K)$.

- 1bit.aEnc takes as input the double key $\mathsf{dkey} = (\mathsf{PK}, K)$ and two messages m_0 and $m_1 \in \{0,1\}$. Algorithm 1bit.aEnc samples ciphertexts $\mathsf{ctEnc}(\mathsf{PK}, m_0)$ and the anamorphic ciphertext act is set equal to the first ct such that $F(K, \mathsf{ct}) = m_1$.
- 1bit.aDec takes as input act and dkey and returns $m_1 = F(K, \mathsf{act})$.

Note that 1bit can be extended to l-bit of hidden plaintexts at the cost of pushing the expect encryption time to $O(2^l)$. Therefore $l = O(\log \lambda)$ hidden bits per ciphertext will keep encryption polynomial and it gives a bandwidth rate of $O((\log \lambda)/\lambda)$. To prove that 1bit is a Secure Anamorphic Encryption we observe that the anamorphic keys have the same distribution as the normal keys. In addition the only difference between the normal ciphertext ct and the anamorphic ciphertext act is that the former is randomly distributed over the set of ciphertexts for PK and m_0 whereas act is randomly chosen over the set of ciphertexts for $\mathsf{aPK} = \mathsf{PK}$ and m_0 such that $F(K, \mathsf{act}) = m_1$. From the pseudorandomness of F and the fact that K is randomly chosen and hidden from the adversary $\mathcal{A}$, we can conclude that 1bit is secure.

Theorem 2. *If F is a PRF and $\mathcal{E}$ is an IND-CPA Encryption scheme then 1bit is a Secure Anamorphic Encryption.*

We also observe that the sender of 1bit, should she be forced to encrypt a given message m and reveal the coin tosses used, can still send a secret bit of her choice to Bob. In other words, the security of 1bit does not rely on the sender-freedom assumption. In Sect. 6, we will show that this can be achieved by encryption schemes based on lattice hardness assumptions without the sender and receiver having to share a key beforehand.

5.2   The Naor-Yung Transform

In this section we describe the Naor-Yung transform [NY90] (see also [Sah99]) that, when applied to an IND-CPA public-key cryptosystem $\mathcal{E}$ and a simulation sound NIZK Π for a specific polynomial-time relation $\mathsf{EqMsg}_{\mathcal{E}}$, gives a CCA public-key cryptosystem NYE. The formal definitions of the concepts used in the construction (IND-CPA, simulation sound NIK) are omitted in this version and can be found in the extended version.

The polynomial time relation $\mathsf{EqMsg}_{\mathcal{E}}$ is defined by setting the witness for instance $((\mathsf{PK}_0, \mathsf{ct}_0), (\mathsf{PK}_1, \mathsf{ct}_1))$ to be the triplet (r_0, r_1, m) of two coin tosses and one message m such that

$$\mathsf{ct}_0 = \mathsf{Enc}(\mathsf{PK}_0, m; r_0) \text{ and } \mathsf{ct}_1 = \mathsf{Enc}(\mathsf{PK}_0, m; r_1).$$

The key generation algorithm $\mathsf{NYE.KG}$ constructs the public key $\mathsf{NYE.PK} = (\mathsf{PK}_0, \mathsf{PK}_1, \Sigma)$ as consisting of two random and independently chosen public keys PK_0 and PK_1 of $\mathcal{E}$ and of a random string Σ. The secret key $\mathsf{NYE.SK} = (\mathsf{SK}_0)$ associated with $\mathsf{NYE.PK}$ consists solely of the secret key SK_0 associated with PK_0.

To encrypt message m, the encryption algorithm $\mathsf{NYE.Enc}$ first computes ciphertexts $\mathsf{ct}_0 = \mathsf{Enc}(\mathsf{PK}_0, m; r_0)$ and $\mathsf{ct}_1 = \mathsf{Enc}(\mathsf{PK}_1, m; r_1)$, using random and independent coin tosses r_0 and r_1. Then, it runs the prover's algorithm of Π to produce a proof π that ct_0 and ct_1 encrypt the same message. More precisely, the prover's algorithm of Π is run on input instance $((PK_0, ct_0), (PK_1, ct_1))$ and witness (r_0, r_1, m) using Σ found in NYE.PK as reference string. The ciphertext PK is finally set to (ct_0, ct_1, π).

The decryption algorithm NYE.Dec, on input ciphertext $ct = (ct_0, ct_1, \pi)$, runs the verifier algorithm of Π to check π and, if successful, outputs m obtained by decrypting ct_0 using SK_0.

5.3   The NY Transform Gives Receive-AM Encryption

In this section we describe $Receiver - AM$ scheme NY with bandwidth rate 1 that is derived from NYE. The normal triplet of NY consists of the triple (NYE.KG, NYE.Enc, NYE.Dec) described in the previous section. Next we define the anamorphic triplet (NYE.aKG, NYE.aEnc, NYE.aDec).

- The anamorphic key generation algorithm NYE.aKG constructs the anamorphic public key NYE.aPK $= (PK_0, PK_1, \Sigma)$ as consisting of two random and independently chosen public keys PK_0 and PK_1 of $\mathcal{E}$; the string Σ instead is obtained by running simulator $S_0(1^\lambda)$ that returns the pair (Σ, aux). The secret key aSK $= (SK_0)$ is set equal to the secret key associated with PK_0 whereas the double key is set equal to dkey $= (PK_0, PK_1, SK_1, aux)$.
- The anamorphic encryption algorithm NYE.aEnc takes as input the dkey and two messages m_0 and m_1 and starts constructing the anamorphic ciphertext by computing $ct_0 = Enc(PK_0, m_0)$ and $ct_1 = Enc(PK_1, m_1)$. The proof π is constructed by running the simulator S_1 on input instance $((PK_0, ct_0), (PK_1, ct_1))$ and auxiliary information aux. Note that m_0 and m_1 are two messages of the same length and thus the construction has a bandwidth rate of 1
- The anamorphic decryption algorithm NYE.aDec takes an anamorphic ciphertext act $= (ct_0, ct_1, \pi)$ and uses SK_1 found in dkey to decrypt ct_1 to obtain m_1.

We next prove that the anamorphic encryption scheme NY is secure according to Definition 4; that is, that games NormalGame and FullyAGame are indistinguishable. To do so, we consider the hybrid game aneG and will show that aneG and NormalGame are indistinguishable by the security properties of the NIZK and that aneG and FullyAGame are indistinguishable by the security of the encryption scheme $\mathcal{E}$. This implies that that NormalGame and FullyAGame are indistinguishable thus satisfying Definition 4. Let us now proceed more formally by instantiating game NormalGame$_{NY}$. We remind the reader that $p_{NY,\mathcal{A}}^{NormalGame}(\lambda)$ denote the probability that adversary $\mathcal{A}$ outputs 1 in game NormalGame$_{NY,\mathcal{A}}$. Next we define game aneG$_{NY}$ that differs from NormalGame$_{NY}$ in the way in which the public key and ciphertexts ct_i, replies to $\mathcal{A}$'s queries, are computed. Specifically, the reference string Σ, that is part of the public key, and the proof π^i, that is part of the i-th ciphertext ct^i, are computed by running the simulator. We define $p_{NY,\mathcal{A}}^{aneG}(\lambda)$ to be the probability that adversary $\mathcal{A}$ outputs 1 in game $aneG_{NY,\mathcal{A}}$.

$NormalGame_{NY,\mathcal{A}}(\lambda)$

1. Set $(PK_0, SK_0), (PK_1, SK_1) \leftarrow \mathcal{E}.KG(1^\lambda)$.
2. Set $\Sigma \leftarrow \{0,1\}^\lambda$.
3. Send $PK = (PK_0, PK_1, \Sigma)$ and $SK = (SK_0)$ to $\mathcal{A}$.
4. For $i = 1, \ldots, poly(\lambda)$:
   $\mathcal{A}$ issues query (m_0^i, m_1^i) and receives ct^i computed as follows:
   - Set $ct_0^i = Enc(PK_0, m_0^i; r_0^i)$.
   - Set $ct_1^i = Enc(PK_1, m_0^i; r_1^i)$.
   - Set $\pi^i \leftarrow Prover(((PK_0, ct_0^i), (PK_1, ct_1^i)), (r_0^i, r_1^i), \Sigma)$.
   - Set $ct^i = (ct_0^i, ct_1^i, \pi^i)$.
5. $\mathcal{A}$ outputs $b \in \{0, 1\}$.

$aneG_{NY,\mathcal{A}}(\lambda)$

1. Set $(PK_0, SK_0), (PK_1, SK_1) \leftarrow \mathcal{E}.KG(1^\lambda)$.
2. Set $(\Sigma, aux) \leftarrow S_0(1^\lambda)$ and $dkey = (PK_0, PK_1, SK_1, aux)$.
3. Send $PK = (PK_0, PK_1, \Sigma)$ and $SK = (SK_0)$ to $\mathcal{A}$.
4. For $i = 1, \ldots, poly(\lambda)$:
   $\mathcal{A}$ issues query (m_0^i, m_1^i) and receives ct^i computed as follows:
   - Set $ct_0^i = Enc(PK_0, m_0^i; r_0^i)$.
   - Set $ct_1^i = Enc(PK_1, m_0^i; r_1^i)$.
   - Set $\pi^i \leftarrow S_1(((PK_0, ct_0^i), (PK_1, ct_1^i)), aux)$.
   - Set $ct^i = (ct_0^i, ct_1^i, \pi^i)$.
5. $\mathcal{A}$ outputs $b \in \{0, 1\}$.

Lemma 4. *If* $\Pi = (Prover, Verifier)$ *is a NIZK then for all PPT adversaries* $\mathcal{A}$

$$\left| p_{NY,\mathcal{A}}^{aneG}(\lambda) - p_{NY,\mathcal{A}}^{NormalGame}(\lambda) \right| < negl(\lambda).$$

Proof. Suppose, for the sake of contradiction, that there exists a PPT $\mathcal{A}$ for which

$$\left| p_{NY,\mathcal{A}}^{aneG}(\lambda) - p_{NY,\mathcal{A}}^{NormalGame}(\lambda) \right| \geq 1/poly(\lambda).$$

Then we construct an adversary $\mathcal{B}$ that receives a string Σ and has access to an oracle $\mathcal{O}$ that returns proofs and that breaks the zero-knowledge property of Π.

1. $\mathcal{B}(\Sigma)$ sets $(PK_0, SK_0), (PK_1, SK_1) \leftarrow \mathcal{E}.KG(1^\lambda)$.
2. $\mathcal{B}$ receives Σ and starts $\mathcal{A}$ on input $PK = (PK_0, PK_1, \Sigma)$ and $SK = (SK_0)$.
3. For $i = 1, \ldots, poly(\lambda)$
   (a) $\mathcal{B}$ receives query (m_0^i, m_1^i) from $\mathcal{A}$.
   (b) $\mathcal{B}$ sets $ct_0^i = Enc(PK_0, m_0^i; r_0^i)$.
   (c) $\mathcal{B}$ sets $ct_1^i = Enc(PK_1, m_0^i; r_1^i)$.

(d) $\mathcal{B}$ invokes the oracle $\mathcal{O}$ on input instance $((\mathsf{PK}_0, \mathsf{ct}_0^i), (\mathsf{PK}_1, \mathsf{ct}_1^i))$ and witness $(r_0^i, r_1^)$ and receives proof π^i.

(e) $\mathcal{B}$ returns $\mathsf{ct}^i = (\mathsf{ct}_0^i, \mathsf{ct}_1^i, \pi^i)$ to $\mathcal{A}$.

4. $\mathcal{B}$ returns $\mathcal{A}$'s output.

Now observe that if $\mathcal{B}$ is playing experiment RealZK, then Σ is randomly chosen from $\{0,1\}^\lambda$ and $\mathcal{O} = $ Prover and therefore $\mathcal{A}$'s view is the same as in NormalGame. On the other hand, if $\mathcal{B}$ is playing experiment IdealZK then Σ is output by S_0 and $\mathcal{O} = $ Oracle and therefore $\mathcal{A}$'s view is the same as in aneG. Since we assumed that $\mathcal{A}$ distinguishes between NormalGame and aneG then we can conclude that $\mathcal{B}$ breaks the Zero-Knowledge property of Π.   □

Next we instantiate the anamorphic security game FullyAGame$_{\mathsf{NY}}$. We remind the reader that $p_{\mathsf{NY},\mathcal{A}}^{\mathsf{FullyAGame}}(\lambda)$ denote the probability that adversary $\mathcal{A}$ outputs 1 in game FullyAGame$_{\mathsf{NY},\mathcal{A}}$.

FullyAGame$_{\mathsf{NY},\mathcal{A}}(\lambda)$

1. Set $(\mathsf{PK}_0, \mathsf{SK}_0), (\mathsf{PK}_1, \mathsf{SK}_1) \leftarrow \mathcal{E}.\mathsf{KG}(1^\lambda)$.
2. Set $(\Sigma, \mathsf{aux}) \leftarrow S_0(1^\lambda)$ and $\mathsf{dkey} = (\mathsf{PK}_0, \mathsf{PK}_1, \mathsf{SK}_1, \mathsf{aux})$.
3. Send $\mathsf{PK} = (\mathsf{PK}_0, \mathsf{PK}_1, \Sigma)$ and $\mathsf{SK} = (\mathsf{SK}_0)$ to $\mathcal{A}$.
4. For $i = 1, \ldots, \mathsf{poly}(\lambda)$:
   $\mathcal{A}$ issues query (m_0^i, m_1^i) and receives ct^i computed as follows:
   - Set $\mathsf{ct}_0^i = \mathsf{Enc}(\mathsf{PK}_0, m_0^i; r_0^i)$.
   - Set $\mathsf{ct}_1^i = \mathsf{Enc}(\mathsf{PK}_1, m_1^i; r_1^i)$.
   - Set $\pi^i \leftarrow S_1(((\mathsf{PK}_0, \mathsf{ct}_0^i), (\mathsf{PK}_1, \mathsf{ct}_1^i)), \mathsf{aux})$.
   - Set $\mathsf{ct}^i = (\mathsf{ct}_0^i, \mathsf{ct}_1^i, \pi^i)$.
5. $\mathcal{A}$ outputs $b \in \{0,1\}$.

We have the following lemma.

Lemma 5. *If $\mathcal{E}$ is an IND-CPA secure encryption scheme then for all PPT adversaries $\mathcal{A}$*

$$\left| p_{\mathsf{NY},\mathcal{A}}^{\mathsf{aneG}}(\lambda) - p_{\mathsf{NY},\mathcal{A}}^{\mathsf{FullyAGame}}(\lambda) \right| < \mathsf{negl}(\lambda).$$

Proof. Suppose, for the sake of contradiction, that there exists a PPT $\mathcal{A}$ for which

$$\left| p_{\mathsf{NY},\mathcal{A}}^{\mathsf{aneG}}(\lambda) - p_{\mathsf{NY},\mathcal{A}}^{\mathsf{FullyAGame}}(\lambda) \right| \geq 1/\mathsf{poly}(\lambda).$$

Then we construct an adversary $\mathcal{B}$ that receives a public key PK and has an encryption oracle $\mathcal{O}(\mathsf{PK}, \cdot, \cdot)$ that returns a ciphertext.

1. $\mathcal{B}(\mathsf{PK})$ sets $(\mathsf{PK}_0, \mathsf{SK}_0)$ and $\mathsf{PK}_1 = \mathsf{PK}$.
2. $\mathcal{B}$ sets $(\Sigma, \mathsf{aux}) \leftarrow S_0(1^\lambda)$ and runs $\mathcal{A}$ on input $\mathsf{PK} = (\mathsf{PK}_0, \mathsf{PK}_1, \Sigma)$ and $\mathsf{SK} = (\mathsf{SK}_0)$.
3. For $i = 1, \ldots, \mathsf{poly}(\lambda)$:
   $\mathcal{A}$ issues query (m_0^i, m_1^i) and receives ct^i computed as follows:
   - $\mathcal{B}$ sets $\mathsf{ct}_0^i = \mathsf{Enc}(\mathsf{PK}_0, m_0^i; r_0^i)$;

- $\mathcal{B}$ sets $\mathtt{ct}_1^i = \mathcal{O}(\mathtt{PK}, m_0^i, m_1^i)$;
- $\mathcal{B}$ sets $\pi^i \leftarrow S_1(((\mathtt{PK}_0, \mathtt{ct}_0^i), (\mathtt{PK}_1, \mathtt{ct}_1^i)), \mathtt{aux})$.
- $\mathcal{B}$ sets $\mathtt{ct}^i = (\mathtt{ct}_0^i, \mathtt{ct}_1^i, \pi^i)$.
4. $\mathcal{B}$ returns $\mathcal{A}$'s output.

Now observe that if $\mathcal{B}$ is playing the $\mathsf{IndCPA}_{\mathcal{E}}^0$ game then $\mathcal{O}(\mathtt{PK}, m_0, m_1) = \mathsf{Oracle}^0(\mathtt{PK}, m_0, m_1)$ returns an encryption of m_0 and therefore $\mathcal{A}$'s view is exactly as in $\mathsf{aneG_{NY}}$. On the other hand, if $\mathcal{B}$ is playing the $\mathsf{IndCPA}_{\mathcal{E}}^0$ game then $\mathcal{O}(\mathtt{PK}, m_0, m_1) = \mathsf{Oracle}^1(\mathtt{PK}, m_0, m_1)$ returns an encryption of m_1 and therefore $\mathcal{A}$'s view is exactly as in $\mathsf{FullyAGame_{NY}}$. Since we assumed that $\mathcal{A}$ distinguishes between $\mathsf{aneG_{NY}}$ and $\mathsf{FullyAGame_{NY}}$, we can conclude that $\mathcal{B}$ breaks the IND-CPA security of $\mathcal{E}$. □

Bootstrapping the NY *Construction.* In the description of the anamorphic triplet for the NY construction we have assumed that the sender and the receiver have a safe way to exchange dkey. This is a reasonable assumption for most applications as it is expected that the dictator is able to monitor online communication but it will be difficult to monitor a physical exchange. We next briefly note how to use the bootstrap technique of Horel et al. [HPRV19] in combination with the NY construction. Note that the result scheme does not enjoy the zero-latency property. Observe that dkey consists of $(\mathtt{PK}_0, \mathtt{PK}_1, \mathtt{SK1}, \mathtt{aux})$. However $\mathtt{PK}_0$ and $\mathtt{PK}_1$ are public and $\mathtt{SK1}$ is not used by the sender and it is only used by the receiver to decrypt the message. Therefore, it is enough for the two parties to share the random string used by simulator S_0 to generate aux and this can be achieved by using the two-step bootstrap procedure of Horel et al. [HPRV19].

6   Sender-Anamorphic Encryption

In this section we address the sender-freedom assumption. In the introduction, and more formally in Sect. 5.1, we presented a simple cryptosystem whose security does not rely on the sender-freedom assumption. Specifically, Alice, fearing that she might be forced by the authorities to send a fake message, sets up a private shared key K with Bob that allows to produce, for every adversarially chosen message $\mathtt{m}_0$, a ciphertext $\mathtt{ct}$ carrying $\mathtt{m}_0$ and the coin tosses used to produce $\mathtt{ct}$ such that, when decrypted with K, $\mathtt{ct}$ gives a one-bit message $\mathtt{m}_1$ for Bob to receive privately. The main drawback of this setting is that Alice and Bob must interact in advance to share the key K and this is not always possible: Alice might not know of Bob when she first sets up her public key or might not have a way of securely sending K to Bob.

Next, we show that prior communication between Alice and Bob is not necessary and formalize the concept of a Sender-Anamorphic Encryption in this context. It seems again impossible (seems like decryption is not well defined?). However, the existence of other receivers and public channels save the day!

Specifically, when Alice is forced by the authorities to send the *forced* message $\mathtt{m}_0$ to Carol using Carol's public key $\mathtt{fPK}$ as the *forced* receiving public key, Alice might decide to embed a duplicate message $\mathtt{m}_1$ in the ciphertext that is revealed when the ciphertext is decrypted with Bob's key; that is, the secret key associated with the *duplicate* public key dPK. We stress again that dPK, Bob's public key, is generated by Bob without even knowing that one day he might receive a message from Alice and no secret is shared between Alice and Bob. To do so, we equip Alice with a special coin-toss faking algorithm fRandom that on input the *forced* public key fPK, the *duplicate* public key dPK, the *forced* message m_0, and the *duplicate* message m_1 outputs coin tosses to produce a ciphertext ct that gives m_0 or m_1 depending on whether it is decrypted with the secret key associated with the forced public key or with the secret key associated with the duplicate public key.

We next present formal definition for *Sender-Anamorphic Encryption*. Our definition is tailored for the no-shared secret setting that we have described. Similarly to the receiver side, it could be possible to define the notion of Sender-Anamorphic Encryption also for the case in which sender and receiver share a secret.

Definition 3. *We say that a public-key encryption scheme $\mathcal{E} = (\mathsf{KG}, \mathsf{Enc}, \mathsf{Dec})$ is a* Sender-Anamorphic Encryption scheme *(Sender-AM) if there exists a coin-toss faking algorithm* fRandom *that, on input the* forced *public key* fPK, *and the* forced *message* m_0, *and the* duplicate *public key* dPK *and the duplicate message* m_1, *outputs the faking coin tosses* $R^\star = \mathsf{fRandom}(\mathsf{fPK}, m_0, \mathsf{dPK}, m_1)$ *such that*

- *Let* $\mathsf{ct} = \mathsf{Enc}(\mathsf{fPK}, m_0; R^\star)$ *be the ciphertext computed using the faking coin tosses; then* $\mathsf{Dec}(\mathsf{dSK}, \mathsf{ct}) = m_1$, *except with negligible probability. The probability is taken over the coin tosses of* fRandom *and the coin tosses used to generate* fPK *and* dPK.

To define the concept of a Secure Sender-Anamorphic Encryption we introduce two experiments. In both experiments, the adversary receives one public key fPK and gives polynomially many pairs of forced and duplicate message and for each pair receives as a reply a ciphertext for the first message and the random coin tosses used to produce it. In the real experiment, the ciphertext is produced by Alice that uses random coin tosses output by fRandom with respect to randomly chosen duplicate key. We require the real experiment to be indistinguishable from the ideal experiment in which there is only one public key and the forced message is encrypted by using truly random coin tosses.

$\mathsf{Ideal}_{\mathcal{E}, \mathcal{A}}(\lambda)$

1. Set $(\mathsf{fPK}, \mathsf{fSK}) \leftarrow \mathsf{KG}(1^\lambda)$ and send fPK to $\mathcal{A}$.
2. For $i = 1, \ldots, \mathsf{poly}(\lambda)$:
   - $\mathcal{A}$ issues query (m_0^i, m_1^i) and receives $\mathsf{ct} = \mathsf{Enc}(\mathsf{fPK}, m_0^i; R^i)$, where R_i are randomly chosen coin tosses.
3. $\mathcal{A}$ outputs $b \in \{0, 1\}$.

$\mathsf{Real}_{\mathcal{E},\mathcal{A}}^{\mathsf{fRandom}}(\lambda)$

1. Set $(\mathsf{fPK}, \mathsf{fSK}) \leftarrow \mathsf{KG}(1^\lambda)$ and send fPK to $\mathcal{A}$.
2. Set $(\mathsf{dPK}, \mathsf{dSK}) \leftarrow \mathsf{KG}(1^\lambda)$.
3. For $i = 1, \ldots, \mathsf{poly}(\lambda)$:
   - $\mathcal{A}$ issues query $(\mathsf{m}_0^i, \mathsf{m}_1^i)$ and receives $\mathsf{ct} = \mathsf{Enc}(\mathsf{fPK}, \mathsf{m}_0^i; R^i)$, where $R^i = \mathsf{fRandom}(\mathsf{fPK}, \mathsf{m}_0^i, \mathsf{dPK}, \mathsf{m}_1^i)$.
4. $\mathcal{A}$ outputs $b \in \{0, 1\}$.

We denote by $p_{\mathcal{E},\mathcal{A}}^{\mathsf{Ideal}}(\lambda)$ (respectively, $p_{\mathcal{E},\mathcal{A}}^{\mathsf{Real}}(\lambda)$) the probability that $\mathsf{Ideal}_{\mathcal{E},\mathcal{A}}$ (respectively, $\mathsf{Real}_{\mathcal{E},\mathcal{A}}$) outputs 1 and present the following definition.

Definition 4. *A Sender-AM scheme* $\mathcal{E} = (\mathsf{KG}, \mathsf{Enc}, \mathsf{Dec})$ *with coin-toss faking algorithm* $\mathsf{fRandom}$ *is a SSender-AM scheme if*

1. *$\mathcal{E}$ is an IND-CPA scheme;*
2. *for all PPT adversaries $\mathcal{A}$,*

$$\left| p_{\mathcal{E},\mathcal{A}}^{\mathsf{Ideal}}(\lambda) - p_{\mathcal{E},\mathcal{A}}^{\mathsf{Real}}(\lambda) \right| \leq \mathsf{negl}(\lambda).$$

Difficulties in Achieving Sender-AM with No Shared Key. Not every standard encryption can be used as AM with no shared key. In order to embed a secret message in a ciphertext for public key fPK a valid ciphertext for Bob's public key PK, it must be the case that ciphertext is a valid ciphertext for both keys. From this point of view, the schemes with redundancy (in particular, with validity check in the decryption) seem difficult to employ because a ciphertext for Bob should probably be an invalid ciphertext to Carlos. Almost all known CCA encryption with redundancy (like the one based on the Naor-Yung transform) cannot be used in this context.

But the lack of redundancy is not sufficient for a scheme to be used as AM with no shared key. For the schemes that do not have the property of common randomness, we do not know how to add secret messages to ciphertexts. For example, in Goldwasser-Micali cryptosystem [GM84], the very first semantically secure encryption, two users generate two independent moduli N_0 and N_1 and the secret key of one system is independent of the other one. Therefore, given a ciphertext ct for N_0, without the knowledge of the factorization of N_1, it is hard to decide whether this ciphertext is a quadratic residue modulo N_1. As a result, Alice does not know the underlying plaintext for the ciphertext ct with respect to Bob's key. Consequently, this gives evidence that it seems impossible for Alice, in the no-shared-key model, to embed a secret message to a ciphertext in the Goldwasser-Micali cryptosystem. We next identify a set of sufficient conditions for AM with no shared key and then we describe some encryption schemes from the literature that satisfy the conditions.

6.1 Sufficient Conditions for Sender-AM with No Shared Key

In this section, we introduce three sufficient conditions for a one-bit cryptosystem $\mathcal{E} = (\mathsf{KG}, \mathsf{Enc}, \mathsf{Dec})$ to be Sender-AM with no shared key.

1. *Common randomness property.* Public key encryption scheme $\mathcal{E}$ satisfies the common randomness property if:
   for every two public keys PK_0 and PK_1 output by KG and for every ciphertext ct produced using public key PK_0 and coin tosses R there exists a message m such that $\mathsf{ct} = \mathsf{Enc}(\mathsf{PK}_1, m; R)$; that is, ct is a ciphertext also for public key PK_1 with the *same* coin tosses R.
   For example, the Elgamal encryption-s over a public group satisfies this common randomness property.

2. *Message recovery from randomness.* A public key encryption scheme $\mathcal{E}$ satisfies the common randomness property if:
   it is possible to recover the plaintext carried by a ciphertext ct from the randomness R used to produce it and the public key PK.

3. *Equal Distribution of Plaintexts.* A one-bit public key encryption scheme satisfies the property of equal distribution of plaintexts if the following properties are verified:
   - all public keys share the same ciphertext space;
   - for a ciphertext ct in the common ciphertext space and for a random key pair $(\mathsf{PK}, \mathsf{SK})$ as sampled by the key generation algorithm, ct is the ciphertext of the bit 0 with a probability $\frac{1}{2}$.

We now show that, if a one-bit public key encryption satisfies the above three properties, it is a Sender-AM with no shared key.

Theorem 3. *If an IND-CPA secure one-bit public key encryption scheme satisfies the three properties of common randomness, message recovery from randomness, and equal distribution of plaintexts, then it is a Sender-AM scheme with no shared key.*

Proof. Let $\mathcal{E} = (\mathsf{KG}, \mathsf{Enc}, \mathsf{Dec})$ be an IND-CPA secure scheme and define $\mathsf{fRandom}(\mathsf{fPK}, m_0, \mathsf{dPK}, m_1)$ as follows:

1. Randomly choose coin tosses R;
2. Compute $\mathsf{ct} = \mathsf{Enc}(\mathsf{fPK}, m_0; R)$;
3. By the property of common randomness, ct is also a ciphertext according to dPK and it is computed using the same coin tosses R.
4. By the property of message recovery from randomness, message m' carried by ct w.r.t. to dPK can be computed; that is $\mathsf{Enc}(\mathsf{dPK}, m'; R)$ is equal to ct.
5. If $m' = m_1$ then return (ct, R) and halt; otherwise, go back to Step 1.

The $\mathsf{fRandom}$ defined above satisfies Definition 3. Indeed, the correctness is directly verified. Now observe that the coin tosses R selected at step 1 of $\mathsf{fRandom}$ have probability $1/2$ of being the output in the last step, over the choices of random dPK, by the equal distribution of plaintexts. As dPK is uniformly distributed (and unknown) to the adversary, the adversary cannot distinguish the outputted coin tosses with a real randomness. □

6.2 Constructions Based on LWE Encryption Schemes

Theorem 4. *The LWE Encryption and the Dual LWE Encryption are each a Sender-AM scheme with no shared key.*

Proof. A detailed exposition of LWE Encryption, Dual LWE Encryption can be found in [Reg05, GPV08]. We recall here a quick description of these schemes and their properties assuring that they are AM schemes with no shared key.

We first recall the LWE encryption [Reg05] in Fig. 2. It is parameterized by some $r \leq \omega(\sqrt{\log m})$, which specifies the discrete Gaussian distribution $D_{\mathbb{Z}^m, r}$ over the integer lattice $\mathbb{Z}^m$ from which the secret keys are chosen.

Setup: The system is characterized by m, q and a probability distribution χ on $\mathbb{Z}_q^n$. All users share a common matrix $\mathbf{A} \in \mathbb{Z}_q^{nm}$ chosen uniformly at random, which is the index of the function $f_{\mathbf{A}}(\mathbf{e}) = \mathbf{A}\mathbf{e} \mod q$.

Key Generation:

- Choose $s \in \mathbb{Z}_q^n$ uniformly at random. The private key is s.
- Choose error vector $\mathbf{e} \leftarrow D_{\mathbb{Z}^m, r}$. The public key consists of $(\mathbf{A}, \mathbf{b} = f_{\mathbf{A}}(\mathbf{s}) + \mathbf{e})$

Encryption: The encryption of a bit $x \in \{0, 1\}$ is done by choosing a random subset S of $[m]$ and then defining the ciphertext of x as $(\sum_{i \in S} \mathbf{a}_i, x\lfloor \frac{q}{2} \rfloor + \sum_{i \in S} b_i)$

Decryption: The decryption of $(\mathbf{a}, b)$ is 0 if $b - \langle \mathbf{a}, \mathbf{s} \rangle$ is closer to 0 than to $\lfloor \frac{q}{2} \rfloor$ modulo q, and 1 otherwise.

Fig. 2. LWE public-key encryption

- From the ciphertext $(\mathbf{a}, b)$, we see that, for any user, the implicit random input is the same. This satisfies the property of common randomness.
- From the random input and the public-key, one can get the plaintext. This satisfies the property of message recovery from randomness.
- For a ciphertext $(\mathbf{a}, b)$, with a public key that is returned from the key generation, the vector $\boldsymbol{b}$ is indistinguishable from a randomly chosen vector in $\mathbb{Z}_q^n$, the underlying plaintext is thus 0 with probability $\frac{1}{2}$. This satisfies the property of equal distribution of plaintexts.

We now recall the Dual LWE encryption [GPV08] in Fig. 3. It is parameterized by two integers m, q and a probability distribution χ on $\mathbb{Z}_q$. We show that it supports AM in the similar way as in the case of the LWE encryption:

- From the ciphertext $(\mathbf{p}, c)$, we see that, for any user, the implicit random input is the same. This gives the property of common randomness.
- From the random input and the public-key, one can get the plaintext. This satisfies the property of message recovery from randomness.

– For a ciphertext $(\mathbf{p}, c)$, with a public key that is returned from the key generation, the vector $\mathbf{u}^T\mathbf{s}$ is indistinguishable from a randomly chosen vector in $\mathbb{Z}_q$, the underlying plaintext is thus 0 with probability $\frac{1}{2}$. This satisfies the property of equal distribution of plaintexts.   □

Setup: all users share a common matrix $\mathbf{A} \in \mathbb{Z}_q^{nm}$ chosen uniformly at random, which is the index of the function $f_\mathbf{A}(\mathbf{e}) = \mathbf{A}\mathbf{e} \mod q$.

Key Generation:
  – Choose an error vector $\mathbf{e} \leftarrow D_{\mathbb{Z}^m, r}$ which is the secret key.
  – The public key is the syndrome $\mathbf{u} = f_\mathbf{A}(\mathbf{e})$.

Encryption: to encrypt a bit $b \in \{0, 1\}$, choose $\mathbf{s} \in \mathbb{Z}_q^n$ uniformly and $\mathbf{p} = \mathbf{A}^T\mathbf{s} + \mathbf{x} \in \mathbb{Z}_q^m$, where $\mathbf{x} \in \chi^m$. Output the ciphertext $(\mathbf{p}; c = \mathbf{u}^T\mathbf{s} + x + b\lfloor \frac{q}{2} \rfloor) \in \mathbb{Z}_q^m \times \mathbb{Z}_q$, where $x \leftarrow \chi$.

Decryption: Compute $z = c - \mathbf{e}^T\mathbf{p} \in \mathbb{Z}_q$. Output 0 if z is closer to 0 than to $\lfloor \frac{q}{2} \rfloor \mod q$, otherwise output 1.

Fig. 3. Dual LWE public-key encryption

7 Conclusion

This is the first and most likely not the last work on Anamorphic Encryption as our framework does not cover all the schemes. In this first work, we have shown the anamorphic property for some standard encryptions with specific properties. This does not mean that it is impossible for schemes without these properties. It is also reasonable to wonder what would happen if the dictator can ban these schemes from being used. However, in this way, the dictator will always need to run after our research and this will force the dictator to assure that his children will get a PhD in Cryptography.

Of course, we leave it to others to determine, based on policy, law, and other societal aspects beyond pure technology, whether our results are aiming toward being the final nail in the coffin of governments control of the use of strong cryptographic systems. Our meta-conjecture (and induced policy implication) is that *for any standard scheme, there is a technical demonstration (perhaps employing Anamorphism+stego+klepto) of the futility of the dictator's demands.*

Acknowledgments. We thank all anonymous reviewers for insightful feedback. Duong Hieu Phan was partially supported by the ANR ALAMBIC (ANR16-CE39-0006). Part of this work was done while Giuseppe Persiano was visiting Google NY.

References

[AAB+97] Abelson, H., et al.: The risks of key recovery, key escrow, and trusted third-party encryption (1997). https://doi.org/10.7916/D8GM8F2W

[AAB+15] Abelson, H., et al.: Keys under doormats: mandating insecurity by requiring government access to all data and communications (2015). https://doi.org/10.7916/D8H41R9K

[ACD19] Alwen, J., Coretti, S., Dodis, Y.: The double ratchet: security notions, proofs, and modularization for the signal protocol. In: Ishai, Y., Rijmen, V. (eds.) EUROCRYPT 2019. LNCS, vol. 11476, pp. 129–158. Springer, Cham (2019). https://doi.org/10.1007/978-3-030-17653-2_5

[Bla94] Blaze, M.: Protocol failure in the escrowed encryption standard. In: CCS 1994, pp. 59–67 (1994)

[BPR] Bellare, M., Paterson, K.G., Rogaway, P.: Security of symmetric encryption against mass surveillance. In: Garay, J.A., Gennaro, R. (eds.) CRYPTO 2014. LNCS, vol. 8616, pp. 1–19. Springer, Heidelberg (2014). https://doi.org/10.1007/978-3-662-44371-2_1

[CDNO97] Canetti, R., Dwork, C., Naor, M., Ostrovsky, R.: Deniable encryption. In: Kaliski, B.S. (ed.) CRYPTO 1997. LNCS, vol. 1294, pp. 90–104. Springer, Heidelberg (1997). https://doi.org/10.1007/BFb0052229

[Cli] Statement by the Press Secretary, The White House, 16 April 1993. Reprinted in David Banisar (ed.) Cryptography and Privacy Sourcebook (1994)

[CNE+14] Checkoway, S., et al.: On the practical exploitability of dual EC in TLS implementations. In: USENIX Security Symposium, pp. 319–335 (2014)

[Dak96] Dakoff, H.S.: The clipper chip proposal: deciphering the unfounded fears that are wrongfully derailing its implementation. J. Marshall L. Rev. **29**, 475 (1996)

[DH76] Diffie, W., Hellman, M.E.: New directions in cryptography. IEEE Trans. Inf. Theory **22**, 644–654 (1976)

[DL] Diffie, W., Landau, S.: Privacy on the Line. The Politics of Wiretapping and Encryption

[Fei73] Feistel, H.: Cryptography and computer privacy. Sci. Am. **228**(5), 15–23 (1973)

[FY93] Frankel, Y., Yung, M.: Escrow encryption systems visited: attacks, analysis and designs. In: Coppersmith, D. (ed.) CRYPTO 1995. LNCS, vol. 963, pp. 222–235. Springer, Heidelberg (1995). https://doi.org/10.1007/3-540-44750-4_18

[GKVL] Green, M., Kaptchuk, G., Van Laer, G.: Abuse resistant law enforcement access systems. In: Canteaut, A., Standaert, F.-X. (eds.) EUROCRYPT 2021. LNCS, vol. 12698, pp. 553–583. Springer, Cham (2021). https://doi.org/10.1007/978-3-030-77883-5_19

[GM84] Goldwasser, S., Micali, S.: Probabilistic encryption. J. Comput. Syst. Sci. **2**, 270–299 (1984)

[GMW87] Goldreich, O., Micali, S., Wigderson, A.: How to play any mental game. In: STOC 1987, pp. 218–229 (1987)

[GPV08] Gentry, C., Peikert, C., Vaikuntanathan, V.: Trapdoors for hard lattices and new cryptographic constructions. In: STOC 2008, pp. 197–206 (2008)

[HPRV19] Horel, T., Park, S., Richelson, S., Vaikuntanathan, V.: How to subvert backdoored encryption: Security against adversaries that decrypt all ciphertexts. In: 10th ITCS, pp. 1–20 (2019)

[Ker83] Kerckhoffs, A.: La Cryptographie Militaire. Journal des sciences militaires (1883)

[Mic]   Micali, S.: Fair public-key cryptosystems. In: Brickell, E.F. (ed.) CRYPTO 1992. LNCS, vol. 740, pp. 113–138. Springer, Heidelberg (1993). https://doi.org/10.1007/3-540-48071-4_9

[MP16]   Marlinspike, M., Perrin, T.: The double ratchet algorithm, November 2016. https://whispersystems.org/docs/specifications/doubleratchet/doubleratchet.pdf

[NY90]   Naor, M., Yung, M.: Public-key cryptosystems provably secure against chosen ciphertext attacks. In: STOC 1990, pp. 427–437 (1990)

[Reg05]   Regev, O.: On lattices, learning with errors, random linear codes, and cryptography. In: STOC 2005, pp. 84–93 (2005)

[Riv]   Rivest, R.L.: Chaffing and Winnowing: Confidentiality without Encryption. MIT Lab for Computer Science, 18 March 1998. http://people.csail.mit.edu/rivest/chaffing-980701.txt. Accessed 1 July 1998

[Rog15]   Rogaway, P.: The Moral Character of Cryptographic Work. ePrint 2015/1162 (2015). https://ia.cr/2015/1162

[RSA78]   Rivest, R.L., Shamir, A., Adleman, L.: A method for obtaining digital signatures and public-key cryptosystems. Commun. ACM **21** (1978)

[RTYZ]   Russell, A., Tang, Q., Yung, M., Zhou, H.-S.: Cliptography: clipping the power of kleptographic attacks. In: Cheon, J.H., Takagi, T. (eds.) ASIACRYPT 2016. LNCS, vol. 10032, pp. 34–64. Springer, Heidelberg (2016). https://doi.org/10.1007/978-3-662-53890-6_2

[RTYZ17] Russell, A., Tang, Q., Yung, M., Zhou, H.-S.: Generic semantic security against a kleptographic adversary. In: CCS 2017, pp. 907–922 (2017)

[Sah99]   Sahai, A.: Non-malleable non-interactive zero knowledge and adaptive chosen-ciphertext security. In: FOCS 1999, p. 543 (1999)

[Sha49]   Shannon, C.E.: Communication theory of secrecy systems. Bell Syst. Tech. J. **28**(4), 656–715 (1949)

[vAH04]   von Ahn, L., Hopper, N.J.: Public-key steganography. In: Cachin, C., Camenisch, J.L. (eds.) EUROCRYPT 2004. LNCS, vol. 3027, pp. 323–341. Springer, Heidelberg (2004). https://doi.org/10.1007/978-3-540-24676-3_20

[Wha20]   WhatsApp. WhatsApp Encryption Overview, October 2020

[Yao86]   Yao, A.C.-C.: How to generate and exchange secrets. In: FOCS 1986, pp. 162–167 (1986)

[YYa]   Young, A., Yung, M.: The dark side of "Black-Box" cryptography or: should we trust capstone? In: Koblitz, N. (ed.) CRYPTO 1996. LNCS, vol. 1109, pp. 89–103. Springer, Heidelberg (1996). https://doi.org/10.1007/3-540-68697-5_8

[YYb]   Young, A., Yung, M.: The prevalence of kleptographic attacks on discrete-log based cryptosystems. In: Kaliski, B.S. (ed.) CRYPTO 1997. LNCS, vol. 1294, pp. 264–276. Springer, Heidelberg (1997). https://doi.org/10.1007/BFb0052241

[YY97]   Young, A., Yung, M.: Kleptography: using cryptography against cryptography. In: Fumy, W. (ed.) EUROCRYPT 1997. LNCS, vol. 1233, pp. 62–74. Springer, Heidelberg (1997). https://doi.org/10.1007/3-540-69053-0_6

[YY98]   Young, A., Yung, M.: Auto-recoverable auto-certifiable cryptosystems. In: Nyberg, K. (ed.) EUROCRYPT 1998. LNCS, vol. 1403, pp. 17–31. Springer, Heidelberg (1998). https://doi.org/10.1007/BFb0054114

A PCP Theorem for Interactive Proofs and Applications

Gal Arnon[1]([⊠]), Alessandro Chiesa[2], and Eylon Yogev[3]

[1] Weizmann Institute, Rehovot, Israel
gal.arnon@weizmann.ac.il
[2] EPFL, Lausanne, Switzerland
alessandro.chiesa@epfl.ch
[3] Bar-Ilan University, Ramat Gan, Israel
eylon.yogev@biu.ac.il

Abstract. The celebrated PCP Theorem states that any language in NP can be decided via a verifier that reads $O(1)$ bits from a polynomially long proof. Interactive oracle proofs (IOP), a generalization of PCPs, allow the verifier to interact with the prover for multiple rounds while reading a small number of bits from each prover message. While PCPs are relatively well understood, the power captured by IOPs (beyond NP) has yet to be fully explored.

We present a generalization of the PCP theorem for interactive languages. We show that any language decidable by a $k(n)$-round IP has a $k(n)$-round public-coin IOP, where the verifier makes its decision by reading only $O(1)$ bits from each (polynomially long) prover message and $O(1)$ bits from each of its own (random) messages to the prover.

Our result and the underlying techniques have several applications. We get a new hardness of approximation result for a stochastic satisfiability problem, we show IOP-to-IOP transformations that previously were known to hold only for IPs, and we formulate a new notion of PCPs (index-decodable PCPs) that enables us to obtain a commit-and-prove SNARK in the random oracle model for nondeterministic computations.

Keywords: Interactive proofs · Probabilistically checkable proofs · Interactive oracle proofs

G. Arnon—Supported in part by a grant from the Israel Science Foundation (no. 2686/20) and by the Simons Foundation Collaboration on the Theory of Algorithmic Fairness.

A. Chiesa—Funded by the Ethereum Foundation.

E. Yogev—Part of this project was performed when Eylon Yogev was in Tel Aviv University where he was funded by the ISF grants 484/18, 1789/19, Len Blavatnik and the Blavatnik Foundation, and The Blavatnik Interdisciplinary Cyber Research Center at Tel Aviv University.

O. Dunkelman and S. Dziembowski (Eds.): EUROCRYPT 2022, LNCS 13276, pp. 64–94, 2022.
https://doi.org/10.1007/978-3-031-07085-3_3

1   Introduction

Probabilistic proofs play a central role in complexity theory and cryptography. In the past decades, probabilistic proofs have become powerful and versatile tools in these fields, leading to breakthroughs in zero-knowledge, delegation of computation, hardness of approximation, and other areas.

As an example, interactive proofs (IPs) [40] allow proof-verification to be randomized and interactive, which seemingly confers them much more power than their deterministic (and non-interactive) counterparts. In a k-round IP, a probabilistic polynomial-time verifier exchanges k messages with an all-powerful prover and then accepts or rejects; IP[k] is the class of languages decidable via a k-round interactive proof. Seminal results characterize the power of IPs (IP[poly(n)] = PSPACE) [48,54] and also achieve zero-knowledge [38,40].

The development of IPs, in turn, led to probabilistically checkable proofs (PCPs) [4,36], where a probabilistic polynomial-time verifier has query access to a proof string. Here PCP[r, q] denotes the class of languages decidable by a PCP verifier that uses at most r bits of randomness and queries at most q bits of the proof string. A line of works culminated in the PCP Theorem [1,2], which can be stated as NP = PCP[$O(\log n), O(1)$]; that is, every language in NP can be decided, with constant soundness error, by probabilistically examining only a constant number of bits in a polynomially long proof.

These advances in probabilistic proofs have reshaped theoretical computer science.

Interactive Oracle Proofs. More recently, researchers formulated *interactive oracle proofs* (IOPs) [12,52], a model of probabilistic proof that combines aspects of the IP and PCP models. A k-round IOP is a k-round IP where the verifier has PCP-like access to each prover message: the prover and verifier interact for k rounds, and after the interaction the verifier probabilistically reads a small number of bits from each prover message and decides to accept or reject based on the examined locations. The randomness used in the final phase is called *decision randomness* (which we distinguish from the random messages that the verifier sends to the prover during the interaction).

Recent work has constructed highly-efficient IOPs [7–11,13,18–21,26,53]. While the shortest PCPs known to date have quasi-linear length [16,30], IOPs can achieve linear proof length and fast provers. These developments are at the heart of recent constructions of non-interactive succinct arguments (SNARGs), and have facilitated their deployment in numerous real-world systems. IOPs are also used to construct IPs for delegating computation [52].

IOPs Beyond NP? Most research regarding IOPs has focused on understanding IOPs for languages in NP (and more generally various forms of non-deterministic computations) while using the additional rounds of interaction to achieve better efficiency compared to PCPs for those languages.

However, the power of IOPs for languages beyond NP is not well understood. We do know that IPs can express all languages in PSPACE for sufficiently large round complexity [48,54]; moreover more rounds lead to more languages because, under plausible complexity assumptions, it holds that IP[k] $\not\subseteq$ IP[o(k)] (while restricting to polynomial communication complexity) [39]. But what can we say about the power of IOPs *with small query complexity (over the binary alphabet)*?[1] Not much is known about the power of general k-round IOPs, which leads us to ask:

> *What languages have a* k-*round IOP where the verifier decides by reading* $O(1)$ *bits from each prover message and from each verifier message?*

1.1   Main Results

We answer the above question by showing that (informally) the power of IOPs with k rounds where the verifier reads $O(1)$ bits from each communication round (both prover and verifier messages) is the same as if the verifier reads the entire protocol transcript (as in an IP). This can be seen as extending the PCP Theorem to interactive proofs, interpreted as *"you can be convinced by a conversation while barely listening (even to yourself)"*.

To achieve this, our main result is a transformation from IPs to IOPs: we transform any IP into a corresponding IOP where the verifier reads $O(1)$ bits from each communication round and uses a total of $O(\log n)$ bits of decision randomness.[2] The round complexity is preserved, and other parameters are preserved up to polynomial factors. (A round is a verifier message followed by a prover message; after the interaction, the verifier's decision is probabilistic).

Theorem 1 (IP $\rightarrow$ IOP). *Let L be a language with a public-coin IP with* k *rounds and constant soundness error. Then L has an IOP with* k *rounds, constant soundness error, where the verifier decides by using* $O(\log n)$ *bits of decision randomness and reading* $O(1)$ *bits from each prover message and each verifier message. All other parameters are polynomially related.*

Prior Work on IOPs Beyond NP. The PCP Theorem can be viewed as a "half-round" IOP with query complexity $O(1)$ and decision randomness $O(\log n)$ for NP. For languages above NP, prior works imply certain facts about k-round IOPs for extreme settings of k.

– For languages that have a public-coin IP with k $= 1$ round (a verifier message followed by a prover message), Drucker [33] proves a hardness of approximation result in the terminology of CSPs. His result can be re-interpreted showing that these languages have a one-round IOP where the verifier reads $O(1)$ bits from each message and decides (using $O(\log n)$ bits of decision randomness). However, Drucker's result does not extend to arbitrary many rounds.[3]

---

[1] An IP is an IOP where the verifier has large query complexity over the binary alphabet.

[2] After the interaction, the verifier uses $O(\log n)$ random bits to decide which locations to read from all k rounds.

[3] Round reduction [5] can reduce the number of rounds from any k to 1 with a blow-up in communication that is exponential in k. This does not work when k is super constant; see Sect. 2.2 for further discussion.

- When k can be polynomially large, we observe that constant-query IOPs for PSPACE can be obtained from [27, 28],[4] which in turn provides such an IOP for every language having an IP. Other analogues of PCP have been given (e.g., [43] applies to the polynomial hierarchy, [32] is also for PSPACE) but they do not seem to translate to IOPs.
- For general k, one can use the fact that AM[k] $\subseteq$ NEXP, and obtain a PCP where the prover sends a single *exponentially-long* message from which the (polynomial-time) verifier reads $O(1)$ bits. However, this does not help if we require the prover to send messages of *polynomial length*.

See Fig. 1 for a table summarizing these results and ours.

	complexity class	model	proof length	alphabet	query complexity	round complexity
[14]	NEXP	PCP	$\exp(|x|)$	$\{0,1\}$	$O(1)$	1
[28]	PSPACE	IOP	$\text{poly}(|x|)$	$\{0,1\}$	$O(1)$	$\text{poly}(|x|)$
implied by [14]	AM[k]	PCP	$\exp(|x|)$	$\{0,1\}$	$O(1)$	1
[3, 40]	AM[k]	IP	k	$\{0,1\}^{\text{poly}(|x|)}$	1 per round	k
[this work]	AM[k]	IOP	$\text{poly}(|x|)$	$\{0,1\}$	$O(1)$ per round	k
[33]	AM	IOP	$\text{poly}(|x|)$	$\{0,1\}$	$O(1)$	1
[1, 2]	NP	PCP	$\text{poly}(|x|)$	$\{0,1\}$	$O(1)$	1

Fig. 1. Classes captured by different types of probabilistic proofs (in the regime of constant soundness error). Here, x denotes the instance whose membership in the language the verifier is deciding. Here, AM stands for two-message public-coin protocols (a verifier random message followed by a prover message), and AM[k] is a k-round public-coin protocol.

Hardness of Approximation for Stochastic Satisfiability. We use Theorem 1 to prove the hardness of approximating the value of an instance of the *stochastic satisfiability* (SSAT) problem, which we now informally define.

SSAT is a variant of TQBF (true quantified boolean formulas) where the formula is in 3CNF and the variables are quantified by alternating existential quantifiers and *random* quantifiers (the value of the quantified variable is chosen uniformly at random). A formula ϕ is in the language SSAT if the probability that there is a setting of the existential variables that cause ϕ to be satisfied is greater than $1/2$. The *value* of an SSAT instance ϕ is the expected number of satisfied clauses in ϕ if the existential variables are chosen to maximize the

---

[4] Their result shows that PSPACE has what is known as a *probabilistically checkable debate system*. In their system, one prover plays a uniform random strategy. Thus one can naturally translate the debate system into an IOP.

number of satisfied clauses in ϕ. We denote by k-SSAT the SSAT problem when there are k alternations between existential and random quantifiers.

SSAT can be viewed as a restricted "game against nature" [51] where all parties are binary, and "nature's" moves are made uniformly at random. Variations of SSAT are related to areas of research in artificial intelligence, specifically planning and reasoning under uncertainty [47]. Previous research on SSAT has studied complexity-theoretical aspects [28,33,34] and SAT-solvers for it (e.g., [45,47,49]).

Our result on the hardness of approximation for k-SSAT is as follows.

Theorem 2. *For every* k, *it is* AM[k]*-complete to distinguish whether a* k-SSAT *instance has value* 1 *or value at most* $1 - \frac{1}{O(k)}$.

We compare Theorem 2 with prior ones about k-SSAT. For $k = 1$, our result matches that of [33] who showed that the value of 1-SSAT is AM[1]-hard to approximate up to a constant factor. Condon, Feigenbaum, Lund, and Shor [28] show that there exists a constant $c > 1$ such that for every language L in IP = PSPACE, one can reduce an instance x to a poly($|x|$)-SSAT instance ϕ such that if $x \in L$ then the value of ϕ is 1, and otherwise the value of ϕ is $1/c$. The approaches used in both prior works do not seem to extend to other values of k.

This state of affairs motives the following natural question:

How hard is it to approximate the value of k-SSAT *to a constant factor independent of* k*?*

While PCPs have well-known applications to the hardness of approximation of numerous NP problems, no similar connection between IOPs and hardness of approximation was known. (Indeed, this possibility was raised as an open problem in prior work.) The works of Drucker [33] and Condon et al. [28] can be reinterpreted as giving such results for stochastic satisfiability problems. In this paper we make this connection explicit and extend their results.

Transformations for IOPs. We obtain IOP analogues of classical IP theorems, as a corollary of Theorem 1. We show IOP-to-IOP transformations, with small query complexity, and achieve classical results that were known for IPs, including: a private-coin to public-coin transformation (in the style of [41]); a round reduction technique (in the style of [5]); and a method to obtain perfect completeness (in the style of [37]). A graphic of this corollary is displayed in Fig. 2.

Corollary 1. *Let L be a language with a k-round IOP with polynomial proof length over a binary alphabet. Then the following holds:*

1. **private-coins to public-coins:** *L has a $O(k)$-round public-coin IOP;*
2. **round reduction:** *for every constant $c \le$ k, L has a k/c-round IOP;*
3. **perfect completeness:** *L has a perfectly complete k-round IOP.*

All resulting IOPs have polynomial proof length and $O(1)$ per-round query complexity over a binary alphabet; all other parameters are polynomially related to the original IOP.

Similar to the case with IPs, one can combine these transformations to get all properties at once. In particular, one can transform any IOP to be public-coin and have perfect completeness while preserving the round complexity.

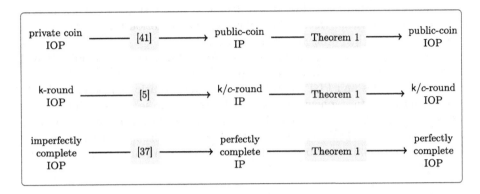

Fig. 2. Corollary 1 provides IOP analogues of classical IP theorems.

1.2   A Cryptographic Application to SNARKs

A building block that underlies Theorem 1 is a new notion of PCP that we call *index-decodable PCPs*. We informally describe this object in Sect. 1.2 below (and postpone the definition and a comparison with other PCP notions to Sect. 2.3). Moreover, we prove that index-decodable PCPs are a useful tool beyond the aforementioned application to Theorem 1, by establishing a generic transformation from index-decodable PCPs to commit-and-prove SNARKs. We discuss these SNARKs and our result in Sect. 1.2 below (and postpone further discussion to Sect. 2.6).

Index-Decodable PCPs. An index-decodable PCP can be seen as a PCP on *maliciously encoded data*. The prover wishes to convince the verifier about a statement that involves k data segments $i[1], \ldots, i[k]$ and an instance x, for example, that it knows a witness w such that $(i[1], \ldots, i[k], x, w) \in R$ for some relation R. The prover outputs a PCP string Π for this statement. The verifier receives as input only the instance x, and is given query access to an *encoding* of each data segment $i[i]$ and query access to the PCP string Π. This means that the verifier has query access to a total of $k + 1$ oracles.

The definition of an index-decodable PCP, to be useful, needs to take into account several delicate points (which, in fact, are crucial for our proof of Theorem 1).

First, the encoding of each data segment must be computed independently of other data segments and even the instance. (Though the PCP string Π can depend on all data segments and the instance).

Second, the verifier is not guaranteed that the k data oracles are valid encodings, in the sense that "security" is required to hold even against malicious provers that have full control of all k + 1 oracles (not just the PCP string oracle). In other words, we wish to formulate a security notion that is meaningful even for data that has been maliciously encoded.

The security notion that we use is *decodability*. Informally, we require that if the verifier accepts with high-enough probability a given set of (possibly malicious) data oracles and PCP string, then each data oracle can be individually decoded into a data segment and the PCP string can be decoded into a witness such that, collectively, all the data segments, the instance, and the witness form a true statement. We stress that the decoder algorithms must run on each data oracle separately from other data oracles and the instance (similarly as the encoder).

Commit-and-Prove SNARKs. A *commit-and-prove SNARK* (CaP-SNARK) is a SNARK that enables proving statements about previously committed data, and commitments can be reused across different statements. CaP-SNARKs have been studied in a line of work [17,22,29,35,46], where constructions have been achieved assuming specific computational assumptions (e.g., knowledge of exponent assumptions) and usually with the added property of zero-knowledge.

We show how to use index-decodable PCPs to unconditionally achieve CaP-SNARKs in the random oracle model (ROM);[5] in more detail we need the index-decodable PCP to have efficient indexing/decoding and certain proximity properties. Our transformation can be seen as an index-decodable PCP analogue of the Micali construction of SNARKs in the ROM from PCPs [50].

Theorem 3. *There is a transformation that takes as input an index-decodable PCP (that has an efficient indexer and decoder and satisfies certain proximity properties) for a relation R with proof length l and query complexity q, and outputs a CaP-SNARK in the ROM for R with argument size $O_\lambda(q \cdot \log l)$. (Here λ is the output size of the random oracle.)*

We obtain a concrete construction of a CaP-SNARK in the ROM (for non-deterministic computations) by applying the above theorem to our construction of an index-decodable PCP system.

We conclude by noting that the ROM supports several well-known constructions of succinct arguments that can be heuristically instantiated via lightweight

---

[5] In this model, all parties (honest and malicious) receive query access to the same random function.

cryptographic hash functions, are plausibly post-quantum secure [25], and have led to realizations that are useful in practice. It is plausible that our construction can be shown to have these benefits as well—we leave this, and constructing zero-knowledge CaP-SNARKs in the ROM, to future work.

2   Techniques

We summarize the main ideas underlying our results.

We begin by discussing the question of transforming IPs to IOPs. In Sect. 2.1, we describe a solution in [33] that works for a single round and explain why it is challenging to extend it for multiple rounds. Then, we describe our transformation for many rounds in two steps. First, in Sect. 2.2, we describe how to make a verifier query each of its random messages at few locations. Next, in Sect. 2.3, we define our new notion of *index-decodable PCPs* and, in Sect. 2.4, describe how to use these to make the verifier query each prover message at few locations (without affecting the first step). In Sect. 2.5, we explain how to construct index-decodable PCPs with good parameters.

We conclude by describing applications of our results and constructions: (i) in Sect. 2.6, we construct commit-and-prove SNARKs in the random oracle model from index-decodable PCPs; and (ii) in Sect. 2.7, we show that Theorem 1 has implications on the hardness of approximating the value of certain stochastic problems.

Throughout, we call *interaction randomness* (or verifier random messages) the randomness sent by the verifier to the prover during the interaction, and *decision randomness* the randomness used by the verifier in the post-interaction decision stage.

2.1   Towards Transforming IPs to IOPs

We discuss the problem of transforming IPs into IOPs. We begin by describing a solution in [33] that transforms a single-round IP into a single-round IOP. Following that, we describe the challenges of extending this approach to work for multi-round IPs.

The Case of a Single-Round IP. The case of a single-round was settled by Drucker [33], whose work implies a transformation from a public-coin single-round IP to a single-round IOP where the verifier reads $O(1)$ bits from the communication transcript (here consisting of the prover message and the verifier message). His construction uses as building blocks the randomness-efficient amplification technique of [6] and *PCPs of proximity* (PCPPs) [15,31].[6] We give a high-level overview of his construction.

---

[6] A PCPP is a PCP system where the verifier has oracle access to its input in addition to the prover's proof; the soundness guarantee is that if the input is *far* (in Hamming distance) from any input in the language, then the verifier accepts with small probability.

In a public-coin single-round IP, given a common input instance x, the verifier $\mathbf{V}_{\mathsf{IP}}$ sends randomness ρ, the prover $\mathbf{P}_{\mathsf{IP}}$ sends a message a, and the verifier $\mathbf{V}_{\mathsf{IP}}$ decides whether to accept by applying a predicate to (x, ρ, a). Consider the non-deterministic machine M such that $M(x, \rho) = 1$ if and only if there exists a such that $\mathbf{V}_{\mathsf{IP}}$ accepts (x, ρ, a). The constructed IOP works as follows:

1. the IOP verifier sends $\mathbf{V}_{\mathsf{IP}}$'s randomness ρ;
2. the IOP prover computes $\mathbf{P}_{\mathsf{IP}}$'s message a and produces a PCPP string Π for the claim "$M(x, \rho) = 1$";
3. the IOP verifier checks Π using the PCPP verifier with explicit inputs M and x and implicit input ρ.

This IOP is sound if the underlying IP is "randomness-robust", which means that if x is not in the language then with high probability over ρ it holds that ρ is *far* from any accepting input for $M(x, \cdot)$. Drucker achieves this property by using an amplification technique in [6] that achieves soundness error $2^{-|\rho|}$ while using $O(|\rho|)$ random bits (standard amplification would, when starting with a constant-soundness protocol, result in $\omega(|\rho|)$ random bits). Thus, with high probability, ρ is not only a "good" random string (which holds for any single-round IP) but also is δ-far from any "bad" random string, for some small constant $\delta > 0$. This follows since the ball of radius δ around any bad random string has size $2^{\delta'|\rho|}$, for some small constant δ' that depends only on δ.

Challenges of Extending the Single-Round Approach to Multi-round IPs. We wish to obtain a similarly efficient transformation for a public-coin k-round IP where $k = \mathrm{poly}(n)$.

One possible approach would be to reduce the number of rounds of the given IP from k to 1 and then apply the transformation for single-round IPs. The round reduction of Babai and Moran [5] shows that any public-coin k-round IP can be transformed into a one-round IP where efficiency parameters grow by $n^{O(k)}$. This transformation, however, is not efficient for super-constant values of k. Moreover, it is undesirable even when k is constant because the transformation overhead is not a fixed polynomial (the exponent depends on k rather than being a fixed constant).

Therefore, we seek an approach that directly applies to a multi-round IP. Unfortunately, Drucker's approach for one-round IPs does not generalize to multiple-round IPs for several reasons. First, the corresponding machine $M(x, \rho_1, \ldots, \rho_k)$ (which accepts if and only if there exist prover messages $a_1, \ldots, a_k$ such that $\mathbf{V}_{\mathsf{IP}}$ accepts $(x, \rho_1, a_1, \ldots, \rho_k, a_k)$) does not capture the soundness of the interactive proof because it fails to capture interaction (a protocol may be sound according to the IP definition and, yet, for every x and $\rho_1, \ldots, \rho_k$ it could be that $M(x, \rho_1, \ldots, \rho_k) = 1$). Moreover, it is not clear how to perform a randomness-efficient amplification for multiple rounds that makes the protocol sufficiently "randomness robust" for the use of a PCPP. The main reason is that to get soundness error 2^{-m} (as in [33]), the techniques of [6] add $O(m)$ bits *per round*, which is too much when the protocol has many rounds (see Sect. 2.2 for a more detailed discussion on why this approach fails for many rounds).

We give a different solution that circumvents this step and works for any number of rounds. Our transformation from k-round IP to an IOP in two stages. In the first stage, we transform the IP into one in which the verifier reads only $O(1)$ bits from each random message it sends. In the second stage, we transform the IP into an IOP with $O(1)$ per-round query complexity, simultaneously for each prover message and each verifier message. We achieve this via a new notion of PCPs that we call *index-decodable PCPs*, and we describe in Sect. 2.3. First, we explain how to achieve the property that the verifier reads $O(1)$ bits from each of its random messages to the prover.

2.2 Local Access to Randomness

We transform a public-coin IP $(\mathbf{P}_{\mathsf{IP}}, \mathbf{V}_{\mathsf{IP}})$ into an IP $(\mathbf{P}'_{\mathsf{IP}}, \mathbf{V}'_{\mathsf{IP}})$ whose verifier (i) reads $O(1)$ bits from each of its random messages to the prover, and (ii) has logarithmic decision randomness (the randomness used by the verifier in the post-interaction decision stage). For now, the verifier reads in full every message received from the prover, and only later we discuss how to reduce the query complexity to prover messages while preserving the query complexity to the verifier random messages.

One-Round Public-Coin Proofs. In order to describe our ideas we begin with the simple case of one-round public-coin interactive proofs. Recall from Sect. 2.1 that this case is solved in [33], but we nevertheless first describe our alternative approach for this case and after that we will discuss the multiple-round case.

A Strawman Protocol. Recall that in a one-round public-coin IP the verifier sends a uniformly random message, the prover replies with some answer, and the verifier uses both of these messages to decide whether to accept. An idea to allow the verifier to not read in full its own random message would be for the prover to send the received random message back to the verifier, and the verifier to use this latter and test consistency with its own randomness. Given an instance $\mathbb{x}$: $\mathbf{V}'_{\mathsf{IP}}$ sends $\mathbf{V}_{\mathsf{IP}}$'s random message $\rho \in \{0,1\}^r$; $\mathbf{P}'_{\mathsf{IP}}$ replies with $\rho' := \rho$ and the message $a := \mathbf{P}_{\mathsf{IP}}(\mathbb{x}, \rho)$; and $\mathbf{V}'_{\mathsf{IP}}$ checks that ρ and ρ' agree on a random location and that $\mathbf{V}_{\mathsf{IP}}(\mathbb{x}, \rho', a) = 1$.

This new IP is complete, and its verifier queries its random message at one location to conduct the consistency test. However, the protocol might not be sound, as we explain. Suppose that $\mathbb{x} \notin L$. Let r be the length of ρ, let β be the soundness error of the original IP, and let ν_r be the volume of the Hamming sphere of radius $r/3$ in $\{0,1\}^r$. A choice of verifier message ρ is *bad* if there exists a such that $\mathbf{V}_{\mathsf{IP}}(\mathbb{x}, \rho, a) = 1$. By the soundness guarantee of $\mathbf{V}_{\mathsf{IP}}$, the fraction of bad choices of random verifier messages is at most β. A choice of verifier message ρ is *ball-bad* if there exist a bad ρ' that is $1/3$-close to ρ. By the union bound, the fraction of ball-bad coins is at most $\gamma = \beta \cdot \nu_r$.

Let E be the event over the choice of ρ that the prover sends ρ' that is $1/3$-far from ρ.

- Conditioned on E occurring, $\mathbf{V}'_{\mathsf{IP}}$ rejects with probability at least 1/3 (whenever $\mathbf{V}'_{\mathsf{IP}}$ chooses a location on which ρ and ρ' disagree).
- Conditioned on E not occurring, $\mathbf{P}'_{\mathsf{IP}}$ cannot send any ρ' and a such that $\mathbf{V}_{\mathsf{IP}}(\mathbb{x}, \rho', a) = 1$ unless ρ is ball-bad, and so $\mathbf{V}'_{\mathsf{IP}}$ rejects with probability at least $1 - \gamma$.

Therefore, for the new IP to be sound, we need $\gamma = \beta \cdot \nu_{\mathsf{r}}$ to be small. Notice that $\nu_{\mathsf{r}} = 2^{c \cdot \mathsf{r}}$ (for some constant $0 < c < 1$) depends on r but not on β. Thus we need to achieve $\log 1/\beta > c \cdot \mathsf{r}$. As in Drucker's transformation, this can be done using the randomness-efficient soundness amplification of [6], *but we deliberately take a different approach that will generalize for multiple rounds.*

Shrinking γ Using Extractors. Let Ext be an extractor with output length r, seed length $O(\log 1/\beta)$, and error β;[7] such extractors are constructed in [42]. Suppose that the prover and verifier have access to a sample z from a source D with high min-entropy. Consider the following IP: $\mathbf{V}'_{\mathsf{IP}}$ sends s; $\mathbf{P}'_{\mathsf{IP}}$ replies with $s' := s$ and $a := \mathbf{P}_{\mathsf{IP}}(\mathbb{x}, \mathsf{Ext}(z, s'))$; $\mathbf{V}'_{\mathsf{IP}}$ checks that s and s' agree on a random location and that $\mathbf{V}_{\mathsf{IP}}(\mathbb{x}, \mathsf{Ext}(z, s'), a) = 1$.

At most a 2β-fraction of the seeds s are such that there exists a such that $\mathbf{V}_{\mathsf{IP}}(\mathbb{x}, \mathsf{Ext}(z, s), a) = 1$, because Ext is an extractor with error β and D is a distribution with high min-entropy. By an identical argument to the one done previously, either $\mathbf{P}'_{\mathsf{IP}}$ sends s' that is far from s and so $\mathbf{V}'_{\mathsf{IP}}$ rejects with constant probability, or $\mathbf{V}'_{\mathsf{IP}}$ rejects with probability at least $\gamma = 2\beta \cdot \nu_{\mathsf{r}'}$ where $\mathsf{r}' = |s| = O(\log 1/\beta)$. Thus we have that $\gamma = 2 \cdot \beta^{1-c}$, which is a constant fraction for small enough values of β (which can be achieved with standard parallel repetition).

Generating a Source of High Min-Entropy. We describe how the prover and verifier can agree on a sample from a high-entropy source by leveraging the following observation: if z is a uniformly random string and z' is an arbitrary string that is close in Hamming distance to z, then z' has high min-entropy. Thus we can sample via similar ideas as above: $\mathbf{V}'_{\mathsf{IP}}$ samples and sends z; $\mathbf{P}'_{\mathsf{IP}}$ replies with $z' := z$; and $\mathbf{V}'_{\mathsf{IP}}$ checks that z and z' agree on a random location. (So $\mathbf{V}'_{\mathsf{IP}}$ reads one bit of its random message z.) If, with constant probability over z, $\mathbf{P}'_{\mathsf{IP}}$ sends z' that is far from z, then $\mathbf{V}'_{\mathsf{IP}}$ rejects with constant probability. Otherwise, we show that z' has high min-entropy because with high probability it agrees with z on most of its locations.

Putting it All Together. Let $(\mathbf{P}_{\mathsf{IP}}, \mathbf{V}_{\mathsf{IP}})$ be a public-coin single-round IP with soundness error β and randomness complexity r, and let Ext be an extractor with output length r, seed length $O(\log 1/\beta)$, and error β. The new IP $(\mathbf{P}'_{\mathsf{IP}}, \mathbf{V}'_{\mathsf{IP}})$ is as follows.

- *Sample high min-entropy source:* $\mathbf{V}'_{\mathsf{IP}}$ sends z and $\mathbf{P}'_{\mathsf{IP}}$ replies with $z' := z$.
- *Sample extractor seed:* $\mathbf{V}'_{\mathsf{IP}}$ sends s and $\mathbf{P}'_{\mathsf{IP}}$ replies with $s' := s$.

---

[7] A function $\mathsf{Ext} \colon \{0,1\}^n \times \{0,1\}^d \to \{0,1\}^m$ is a (k, ε)-extractor if, for every random variable X over $\{0,1\}^n$ with min-entropy at least k, the statistical distance between $\mathsf{Ext}(X, U_d)$ and U_m is at most ε.

- *Prover message:* $\mathbf{P}'_{\mathsf{IP}}$ sends $a := \mathbf{P}_{\mathsf{IP}}(\mathbb{x}, \mathsf{Ext}(z', s'))$.
- *Verification:* $\mathbf{V}'_{\mathsf{IP}}$ checks that z and z' agree on a random location, s and s' agree on a random location, and $\mathbf{V}_{\mathsf{IP}}(\mathbb{x}, \mathsf{Ext}(z', s'), a) = 1$.

Extending to Multiple Rounds. In order to extend the previously described protocol to multiple rounds, we leverage the notion of *round-by-round soundness*. An IP for a language L has round-by-round soundness error β_{rbr} if there exists a "state" function such that: (i) for $\mathbb{x} \notin L$, the starting state is "doomed"; (ii) for every doomed state and next message that a malicious prover might send, with probability β_{rbr} over the verifier's next message, the protocol state will remain doomed; (iii) if at the end of interaction the state is doomed then the verifier rejects.

In the analysis of the one-round case there was an event (called *bad*) over the IP verifier's random message ρ such that if this event does not occur then the prover has no accepting strategy. This event can be replaced, in the round-by-round case, by the event that, in a given round, the verifier chooses randomness where the transcript remains doomed. This idea leads to a natural extension of the one-round protocol described in Sect. 2.2 to the multi-round case, which is our final protocol.

Let $(\mathbf{P}_{\mathsf{IP}}, \mathbf{V}_{\mathsf{IP}})$ be a public-coin k-round IP with round-by-round soundness error β_{rbr} and randomness complexity r, and Ext an extractor with output length r, seed length $O(\log 1/\beta_{\mathrm{rbr}})$, and error β_{rbr}.

- For each round $j \in [\mathsf{k}]$ of the original IP:
  1. *Sample high min-entropy source:* $\mathbf{V}'_{\mathsf{IP}}$ sends z_j and $\mathbf{P}'_{\mathsf{IP}}$ replies with $z'_j := z_j$.
  2. *Sample extractor seed:* $\mathbf{V}'_{\mathsf{IP}}$ sends s_j and $\mathbf{P}'_{\mathsf{IP}}$ replies with $s'_j := s_j$.
  3. *Prover message:* $\mathbf{P}'_{\mathsf{IP}}$ sends $a_j := \mathbf{P}_{\mathsf{IP}}(\mathbb{x}, \rho_1, \ldots, \rho_j)$ where $\rho_i := \mathsf{Ext}(z_i, s_i)$.
- $\mathbf{V}'_{\mathsf{IP}}$ accepts if and only if the following tests pass:
  1. Choose a random location and, for every $j \in [\mathsf{k}]$, test that z_j and z'_j agree on this location.
  2. Choose a random location and, for every $j \in [\mathsf{k}]$, test that s_j and s'_j agree on this location.
  3. For every $j \in [\mathsf{k}]$, compute $\rho_j := \mathsf{Ext}(z'_j, s'_j)$. Check that $\mathbf{V}_{\mathsf{IP}}(\mathbb{x}, \rho_1, a_1, \ldots, \rho_{\mathsf{k}}, a_{\mathsf{k}}) = 1$.

The soundness analysis of this protocol is similar to the one-round case. Suppose that $\mathbb{x} \notin L$. Then the empty transcript is "doomed". By an analysis similar to the one-round case, except where we set "bad" verifier messages to be ones where the transcript state switches from doomed to not doomed, if a round begins with a doomed transcript then except with probability $\gamma = 2 \cdot \beta_{\mathrm{rbr}}^{1-c}$ (for some constant c) the transcript in the next round is also doomed. Thus, by a union bound, the probability that the transcript ends up doomed, and as a result the verifier rejects, is at least $1 - 2 \cdot \mathsf{k} \cdot \beta_{\mathrm{rbr}}^{1-c}$. As shown in [23] round-by-round soundness error can be reduced via parallel repetition, albeit at a lower rate than regular soundness error. Thus, by doing enough parallel repetition before applying our transformation, the round-by-round soundness error β_{rbr} can be reduced enough so that the verifier rejects with constant probability.

The above protocol has $2k_{\mathsf{IP}}$ rounds. The verifier reads 1 bit from each of its random messages, and has $O(\log |\mathbb{x}|)$ bits of decision randomness (to sample random locations for testing consistency between each z'_j and z_j and between each s'_j and s_j). To achieve k_{IP} rounds, we first apply the round reduction of [5] on the original IP to reduce to $k_{\mathsf{IP}}/2$ rounds, and then apply our transformation.

Why Randomness-Efficient Soundness Amplification is Insufficient. We briefly sketch why applying randomness-efficient soundness amplification in the style of [6] is insufficient in the multi-round case, even if we were to consider round-by-round soundness. Recall that we wish for $\beta_{\mathrm{rbr}} \cdot 2^{\Theta(r)}$ to be small, where β_{rbr} is the round-by-round soundness of the protocol and r is the number of random bits sent by the verifier in a single round. Bellare, Goldreich and Goldwasser [6] show that, starting with constant soundness and randomness r, one can achieve soundness error 2^{-m} using $r' = O(r + m)$ random bits; they do this via m parallel repetitions where the randomness between repetitions is shared in a clever way. Using parallel repetition, achieving round-by-round soundness error 2^{-m} requires m/k repetitions (see [23]). Thus, even if we were to show that the transformation of [6] reduces round-by-round soundness error at the same rate as standard parallel repetition (as it does for standard soundness), in order to get round-by-round soundness error 2^{-m}, we would need $r' = O(r + m \cdot k)$ bits of randomness. This would achieve $\beta_{\mathrm{rbr}} \cdot 2^{\Theta(r')} = 2^{-m} \cdot 2^{\Theta(r+mk)}$, which, for super-constant values of k, is greater than 1 regardless of r.

2.3   Index-Decodable PCPs

We introduce *index-decodable PCPs*, a notion of PCP that works on *multi-indexed relations*. A multi-indexed relation R is a set of tuples $(\mathbb{i}[1], \dots, \mathbb{i}[k], \mathbb{x}, \mathbb{w})$ where $(\mathbb{i}[1], \dots, \mathbb{i}[k])$ is the index vector, $\mathbb{x}$ the instance, and $\mathbb{w}$ the witness. As seen in the following definition, an index-decodable PCP treats the index vector $(\mathbb{i}[1], \dots, \mathbb{i}[k])$ and the instance $\mathbb{x}$ differently, which is why they are not "merged" into an instance $\mathbb{x}' = (\mathbb{i}[1], \dots, \mathbb{i}[k], \mathbb{x})$ (and why we do not consider standard relations).

Definition 1. *An **index-decodable PCP** for a multi-indexed relation $R = \{ (\mathbb{i}[1], \dots, \mathbb{i}[k], \mathbb{x}, \mathbb{w}) \}$ is a tuple of algorithms $(\mathbf{I}_{\mathsf{PCP}}, \mathbf{P}_{\mathsf{PCP}}, \mathbf{V}_{\mathsf{PCP}}, \mathbf{iD}_{\mathsf{PCP}}, \mathbf{wD}_{\mathsf{PCP}})$, where $\mathbf{I}_{\mathsf{PCP}}$ is the (honest) indexer, $\mathbf{P}_{\mathsf{PCP}}$ the (honest) prover, $\mathbf{V}_{\mathsf{PCP}}$ the verifier, $\mathbf{iD}_{\mathsf{PCP}}$ the index decoder, and $\mathbf{wD}_{\mathsf{PCP}}$ the witness decoder. The system has (perfect completeness and) decodability bound κ_{PCP} if the following conditions hold.*

- **Completeness.** *For every $(\mathbb{i}[1], \dots, \mathbb{i}[k], \mathbb{x}, \mathbb{w}) \in R$,*

$$
\Pr_{\rho} \left[\mathbf{V}_{\mathsf{PCP}}^{\pi_1, \dots, \pi_k, \Pi}(\mathbb{x}; \rho) = 1 \;\middle|\; \begin{array}{r} \pi_1 \leftarrow \mathbf{I}_{\mathsf{PCP}}(\mathbb{i}[1]) \\ \vdots \\ \pi_k \leftarrow \mathbf{I}_{\mathsf{PCP}}(\mathbb{i}[k]) \\ \Pi \leftarrow \mathbf{P}_{\mathsf{PCP}}(\mathbb{i}[1], \dots, \mathbb{i}[k], \mathbb{x}, \mathbb{w}) \end{array} \right] = 1.
$$

– **Decodability.** *For every* $\mathbb{x}$, *indexer proofs* $\tilde{\pi}_1, \ldots, \tilde{\pi}_k$, *and malicious prover proof* $\tilde{\Pi}$, *if*

$$\Pr_{\rho}\left[\mathbf{V}_{\mathsf{PCP}}^{\tilde{\pi}_1, \ldots, \tilde{\pi}_k, \tilde{\Pi}}(\mathbb{x}; \rho) = 1 \right] > \kappa_{\mathsf{PCP}}(|\mathbb{x}|)$$

then $\left(\mathbf{iD}_{\mathsf{PCP}}(\tilde{\pi}_1), \ldots, \mathbf{iD}_{\mathsf{PCP}}(\tilde{\pi}_k), \mathbb{x}, \mathbf{wD}_{\mathsf{PCP}}(\tilde{\Pi}) \right) \in R$.

The indexer $\mathbf{I}_{\mathsf{PCP}}$ separately encodes each index, independent of indices and the instance, to obtain a corresponding *indexer proof*. The prover $\mathbf{P}_{\mathsf{PCP}}$ gets all the data as input (index vector, instance, and witness) and outputs a *prover proof*. The verifier $\mathbf{V}_{\mathsf{PCP}}$ gets the instance as input and has query access to $k + 1$ oracles (k indexer proofs and 1 prover proof), and outputs a bit.

The decodability condition warrants some discussion. The usual soundness condition of a PCP for a standard relation R has the following form: "if $\mathbf{V}_{\mathsf{PCP}}^{\tilde{\Pi}}(\mathbb{x})$ accepts with high-enough probability then there exists a witness $\mathbb{w}$ such that $(\mathbb{x}, \mathbb{w}) \in R$". For a multi-indexed relation it could be that for any given instance $\mathbb{x}$ there exist indexes $\mathbb{i}[1], \ldots, \mathbb{i}[k]$ and a witness $\mathbb{w}$ such that $(\mathbb{i}[1], \ldots, \mathbb{i}[k], \mathbb{x}, \mathbb{w}) \in R$. Since we do not trust the indexer's outputs, a soundness condition is not meaningful.

Instead, the decodability condition that we consider has the following form: "if $\mathbf{V}_{\mathsf{PCP}}^{\tilde{\pi}_1, \ldots, \tilde{\pi}_k, \tilde{\Pi}}(\mathbb{x})$ accepts with high-enough probability then $(\mathbb{i}[1], \ldots, \mathbb{i}[k], \mathbb{x}, \mathbb{w}) \in R$ where $\mathbb{i}[1], \ldots, \mathbb{i}[k]$ and $\mathbb{w}$ are the decoded indices and witness respectively found in $\tilde{\pi}_1, \ldots, \tilde{\pi}_k$ and $\tilde{\Pi}$". It is crucial that the index decoder receives as input the relevant indexer proof but not also the instance, or else the decodability condition would be trivially satisfied (the index decoder could output the relevant index of the lexicographically first index vector putting the instance in the relation). This ensures that the proofs collectively convince the verifier not only that there exists an index vector and witness that place the instance in the relation, but that the prover encoded a witness that, along with index vector obtainable from the index oracles via the index decoder, places the instance in the relation.

We do not require the indexer or the decoders to be efficient. However, in some applications, it is useful to have an efficient indexer and decoders, and indeed we construct an index-decodable PCP with an efficient indexer and decoders.

Remark 1 (comparison with holography). We compare index-decodable PCPs and holographic PCPs, which also work for indexed relations (see [24] and references therein). In both cases, an indexer produces an encoding of the index (independent of the instance). However, there are key differences between the two: (i) in an index-decodable PCP the indexer works separately on each entry of the index vector, while in a holographic PCP there is a single index; moreover, (ii) in a holographic PCP the indexer is trusted in the sense that security is required to hold only when the verifier has oracle access to the honest indexer's output, but in an index-decodable PCP, the indexer is **not trusted** in the sense that the malicious prover can choose encodings for all of the indices. *Both differences are essential properties for our transformation of IPs into IOPs.*

We construct a binary index-decodable PCPs with $O(1)$ query complexity per oracle.

Theorem 4. *Any multi-indexed relation* $R = \{(i[1], \ldots, i[k], x, w)\}$ *to which membership can be verified in nondeterministic time* T *has a non-adaptive index-decodable PCP with the following parameters:*

Index-Decodable PCP for $(i[1], \ldots, i[k], x, w) \in R$	
Indexer proof length (per proof)	$O(|i[i]|)$
Prover proof length	$\text{poly}(T)$
Alphabet size	2
Queries per oracle	$O(1)$
Randomness	$O(\log |x|)$
Decodability bound	$O(1)$
Indexer running time	$\tilde{O}(|i[i]|)$
Prover running time	$\text{poly}(T)$
Verifier running time	$\text{poly}(|x|, k, \log T)$
Index decoding running	$\tilde{O}(|i[i]|)$
Witness decoding time	$\text{poly}(T)$

Our construction achieves optimal parameters similar to the PCP theorem: it has $O(1)$ query complexity (per oracle) over a binary alphabet, and the randomness complexity is logarithmic, *independent* of the number of indexes k. Achieving small randomness complexity is challenging and useful. First, it facilitates proof composition (where a prover writes a proof for every possible random string), which is common when constructing zero-knowledge PCPs (e.g., [44]). Second, small randomness complexity is necessary for our hardness of approximation results (see Sect. 2.7).

A similar notion is (implicitly) considered in [1] but their construction does not achieve the parameters we obtain in Theorem 4 (most crucially, they do not achieve small randomness).

2.4   Local Access to Prover Messages

We show how to transform an IP into an IOP by eliminating the need of the verifier to read more than a few bits of each prover message. This transformation preserves the number of bits read by the verifier to its own interaction randomness. Thus, combining it with the transformation described in Sect. 2.2, this completes the proof (overview) of Theorem 1.

We transform any public-coin IP into an IOP by using an index-decodable PCP. In a public-coin k-round IP, the prover $\mathbf{P}_{\text{IP}}$ and verifier $\mathbf{V}_{\text{IP}}$ receive as input an instance x and then, in each round i, the verifier $\mathbf{V}_{\text{IP}}$ sends randomness ρ_i and the prover replies with a message $a_i \leftarrow \mathbf{P}_{\text{IP}}(x, \rho_1, \ldots, \rho_i)$; after the interaction, the verifier $\mathbf{V}_{\text{IP}}$ runs an efficient probabilistic algorithm with decision randomness ρ_{dc} on the transcript $(\mathbf{x}, \rho_1, a_1, \ldots, \rho_k, a_k)$ to decide whether to accept or reject.

The IP verifier $\mathbf{V}_{\text{IP}}$ defines a multi-indexed relation $R(\mathbf{V}_{\text{IP}})$ consisting of tuples

$$\Big(\mathbf{i}[1], \ldots, \mathbf{i}[k], \mathbf{x}', \mathbf{w}\Big) = \Big(a_1, \ldots, a_k, (\mathbf{x}, \rho_1, \ldots, \rho_k, \rho_{\text{dc}}), \perp\Big)$$

such that the IP verifier $\mathbf{V}_{\text{IP}}$ accepts the instance $\mathbf{x}$, transcript $(\rho_1, a_1, \ldots, \rho_k, a_k)$, and decision randomness ρ_{dc}. (Here we do not rely on witnesses although the definition of index-decodable PCPs supports this.)

From IP to IOP. Let $(\mathbf{I}_{\text{PCP}}, \mathbf{P}_{\text{PCP}}, \mathbf{V}_{\text{PCP}}, \mathbf{iD}_{\text{PCP}}, \mathbf{wD}_{\text{PCP}})$ be an index-decodable PCP for the relation $R(\mathbf{V}_{\text{IP}})$. We construct the IOP as follows. The IOP prover and IOP verifier receive an instance $\mathbf{x}$. In round $i \in [k]$, the IOP verifier sends randomness ρ_i (just like the IP verifier $\mathbf{V}_{\text{IP}}$) and the (honest) IOP prover sends the indexer proof $\pi_i := \mathbf{I}_{\text{PCP}}(a_i)$ where $a_i \leftarrow \mathbf{P}_{\text{IP}}(\mathbf{x}, \rho_1, \ldots, \rho_i)$. In a final additional message (which can be sent at the same time as the last indexer proof π_k), the IOP prover sends $\varPi := \{\varPi_{\rho_{\text{dc}}}\}_{\rho_{\text{dc}}}$ where, for every possible choice of decision randomness ρ_{dc}, $\varPi_{\rho_{\text{dc}}}$ is an index-decodable PCP prover proof to the fact that $(a_1, \ldots, a_k, (\mathbf{x}, \rho_1, \ldots, \rho_k, \rho_{\text{dc}}), \perp) \in R(\mathbf{V}_{\text{IP}})$. After the interaction, the IOP verifier samples IP decision randomness ρ_{dc} and checks that $\mathbf{V}_{\text{PCP}}^{\tilde{\pi}_1, \ldots, \tilde{\pi}_k, \tilde{\varPi}_{\rho_{\text{dc}}}}(\mathbf{x}, \rho_1, \ldots, \rho_k, \rho_{\text{dc}}) = 1$.

Proof Sketch. Completeness follows straightforwardly from the construction. We now sketch a proof of soundness. Letting L be the language decided by $(\mathbf{P}_{\text{IP}}, \mathbf{V}_{\text{IP}})$, fix an instance $\mathbf{x} \notin L$ and a malicious IOP prover $\tilde{\mathbf{P}}_{\text{IOP}}$. Given interaction randomness $\rho_1, \ldots, \rho_k$, consider the messages $\tilde{\pi}_1, \ldots, \tilde{\pi}_k$ output by $\tilde{\mathbf{P}}_{\text{IOP}}$ in the relevant rounds ($\tilde{\pi}_i$ depends on $\rho_1, \ldots, \rho_i$) and the message $\tilde{\varPi} = \{\tilde{\varPi}_{\rho_{\text{dc}}}\}_{\rho_{\text{dc}}}$ output by $\tilde{\mathbf{P}}_{\text{IOP}}$ in the last round (this message depends on $\rho_1, \ldots, \rho_k$). We consider two complementary options of events over the IOP verifier's randomness $(\rho_1, \ldots, \rho_k, \rho_{\text{dc}})$.

1. With high probability the proofs $\tilde{\pi}_1, \ldots, \tilde{\pi}_k$ and $\tilde{\varPi}_{\rho_{\text{dc}}}$ generated while interacting with $\tilde{\mathbf{P}}_{\text{IOP}}$ using randomness $\rho_1, \ldots, \rho_k$ and ρ_{dc} are such that

$$\Big(\mathbf{iD}_{\text{PCP}}(\tilde{\pi}_1), \ldots, \mathbf{iD}_{\text{PCP}}(\tilde{\pi}_k), (\mathbf{x}, \rho_1, \ldots, \rho_k, \rho_{\text{dc}}), \perp\Big) \notin R(\mathbf{V}_{\text{IP}}).$$

If this is true, then, by the decodability property of the index-decodable PCP, the IOP verifier must reject with high probability over the choice of randomness for $\mathbf{V}_{\text{PCP}}$.

2. With high probability the proofs $\tilde{\pi}_1, \ldots, \tilde{\pi}_k$ and $\tilde{\varPi}_{\rho_{\text{dc}}}$ generated while interacting with $\tilde{\mathbf{P}}_{\text{IOP}}$ using randomness $\rho_1, \ldots, \rho_k$ and ρ_{dc} are such that

$$\Big(\mathbf{iD}_{\text{PCP}}(\tilde{\pi}_1), \ldots, \mathbf{iD}_{\text{PCP}}(\tilde{\pi}_k), (\mathbf{x}, \rho_1, \ldots, \rho_k, \rho_{\text{dc}}), \perp\Big) \in R(\mathbf{V}_{\text{IP}}).$$

We prove that this case cannot occur by showing that it contradicts the soundness of the original IP. Suppose towards contradiction that the above is true. We use $\tilde{\mathbf{P}}_{\text{IOP}}$ and the index decoder of the index-decodable PCP, $\mathbf{iD}_{\text{PCP}}$, to construct a malicious IP prover for the original IP as follows.

In round i, the transcript $(\rho_1, a_1, \ldots, \rho_{i-1}, a_{i-1})$ has already been set during previous interaction. The IP verifier sends randomness ρ_i. The IP prover sends $a_i := \mathbf{iD}_{\mathsf{PCP}}(\tilde{\pi}_i)$ to the IP verifier, where $\tilde{\pi}_i := \hat{\mathbf{P}}_{\mathsf{IOP}}(\rho_1, \ldots, \rho_i)$. Recall that $\left(\mathbf{D}_{\mathsf{PCP}}(\tilde{\pi}_1), \ldots, \mathbf{D}_{\mathsf{PCP}}(\tilde{\pi}_k), (\mathbb{x}, \rho_1, \ldots, \rho_k, \rho_{dc}), \bot\right) \in R(\mathbf{V}_{\mathsf{IP}})$ if and only if the IP verifier accepts given instance $\mathbb{x}$, randomness $(\rho_1, \ldots, \rho_k, \rho_{dc})$, and prover messages $\mathbf{D}_{\mathsf{PCP}}(\tilde{\pi}_1), \ldots, \mathbf{D}_{\mathsf{PCP}}(\tilde{\pi}_k)$, which is precisely what the IP prover supplies it with. Since the event that $\left(\mathbf{D}_{\mathsf{PCP}}(\tilde{\pi}_1), \ldots, \mathbf{D}_{\mathsf{PCP}}(\tilde{\pi}_k), (\mathbb{x}, \rho_1, \ldots, \rho_k, \rho_{dc}), \bot\right) \in R(\mathbf{V}_{\mathsf{IP}})$ happens with high probability, this implies that with high probability the IP verifier will accept, contradicting soundness of the original IP. Here we crucially used the fact that the decoder $\mathbf{D}_{\mathsf{PCP}}$ does not depend on the instance of the index-decodable PCP (which consists of $\mathbb{x}$ and all of the IP verifier's randomness $\rho_1, \ldots, \rho_k, \rho_{dc}$) or on the other indexer messages.

The resulting IOP has k rounds, exactly as in the original IP. The IOP verifier uses as much randomness as the original IP verifier with the addition of the randomness used by the index-decodable PCP. The query complexity is that of the underlying verifier of the index-decodable PCP. The proof length and alphabet are the same as those of the index-decodable PCP.

Preserving Local Access to Randomness. The transformation described above can be modified to preserve the query complexity of the verifier to its own interaction randomness if the verifier is non-adaptive with respect to its queries to its random messages (i.e., the choice of bits that it reads depends only on $\mathbb{x}$ and ρ_{dc}). We can redefine the multi-indexed relation $R(\mathbf{V}_{\mathsf{IP}})$ to have as explicit inputs the instance $\mathbb{x}$, decision randomness ρ_{dc}, and the bits of $\rho_1, \ldots, \rho_k$ that the verifier needs to read to decide whether to accept or reject (rather than the entire interaction randomness strings). In more detail, suppose that the verifier reads q bits from its own interaction randomness. Then the new multi-indexed relation consists of tuples:

$$\left(\mathbb{i}[1], \ldots, \mathbb{i}[k], \mathbb{x}', \mathbb{w}\right) = \left(a_1, \ldots, a_k, (\mathbb{x}, b_1, \ldots, b_q, \rho_{dc}), \bot\right)$$

such that given decision randomness ρ_{dc} the IP verifier $\mathbf{V}_{\mathsf{IP}}$ accepts given instance $\mathbb{x}$, decision randomness ρ_{dc}, prover messages $(a_1, \ldots, a_k)$, and $(b_1, \ldots, b_q)$ as answers to its q queries to $\rho_1, \ldots, \rho_k$.

Given a multi-indexed PCP for this relation, the IP to IOP transformation is identical to the one described above, except that after the interaction, the IOP verifier samples IP decision randomness, queries its own interaction randomness to get answers $b_1, \ldots, b_q$, and these replace $\rho_1, \ldots, \rho_k$ as explicit inputs to the index-decodable PCP verifier $\mathbf{V}_{\mathsf{PCP}}$.

2.5   Constructing Index-Decodable PCPs

We describe how to construct index-decodable PCPs: in Sect. 2.5 we outline a randomness-efficient index-decodable PCP that makes $O(1)$ queries to each of its oracles, where the indexer proofs are over the binary alphabet and the prover proof is over a large alphabet; then in Sect. 2.5 we use proof composition to reduce the alphabet size of the latter.

Basic Construction from PCPPs. We outline a construction of an index-decodable PCP with $O(1)$ query complexity to each indexer proof and to the prover proof, and where the prover proof is over a large alphabet (of size 2^k). For a later proof composition while preserving polynomial proof length, here we additionally require that the verifier has logarithmic randomness complexity.

Building Blocks. In our construction we rely on variants of PCPPs. Recall that a PCPP is a PCP system where the verifier has oracle access to its input in addition to the prover's proof; the soundness guarantee is that if the input is *far* (in Hamming distance) from any input in the language, then the verifier accepts with small probability.

We use PCPPs that are *multi-input* and *oblivious*. We explain each of these properties.

- A PCPP is multi-input if the verifier has oracle access to multiple (oracle) inputs. The soundness guarantee is that, for every vector of inputs that satisfy the machine in question, if at least one input oracle is far from the respective satisfying input, then the verifier accepts with small probability.
- A (non-adaptive) PCPP is oblivious for a family of nondeterministic machines $\mathcal{M} = \{M_i\}_{i \in [k]}$ if the queries made by the verifier to its oracles depend only on $\mathcal{M}$ and its randomness. In particular they do not depend on i. This property will be used later to facilitate bundling queries. We will have k PCPs, each with a different M_i, but the verifier will use the same randomness in each test. Since the PCPPs are oblivious, this means that the verifier makes the same queries for every test. Thus we can group together the k proofs into a single proof with larger alphabet and maintain good query complexity on this proof. This property is important in order to achieve our final parameters.

See the full version of this paper for formal definitions for the above notions, and how to obtain them from standard PCPPs. Henceforth, all PCPPs that we use will be over the binary alphabet and have constant proximity, constant soundness error, constant query complexity, and logarithmic randomness complexity.

The Construction. We construct an index-decodable PCP for a multi-indexed relation $R = \{(\mathtt{i}[1], \dots, \mathtt{i}[k], \mathtt{x}, \mathtt{w})\}$ whose membership can be verified efficiently.

The indexer encodes each index via an error-correcting code with (constant) relative distance greater than the (constant) proximity parameter of the PCPP used later. The prover uses PCPPs to prove that there exist indexes and a witness that put the given instance in the relation and adds consistency checks to prove that the indices are consistent with those encoded by the indexer. The verifier checks each of these claims. The index decoder decodes the indexer proofs using the same code.

In slightly more detail, the index-decodable PCP is as follows.

- $\mathbf{I}_{\mathsf{PCP}}(\mathtt{i}[i])$: Encode the index $\mathtt{i}[i]$ as π_i using an error-correcting code.
- $\mathbf{P}_{\mathsf{PCP}}(\mathtt{i}[1], \dots, \mathtt{i}[k], \mathtt{x}, \mathtt{w})$:

1. *Encoding the indexes.* Compute Π_*, an encoding of the string $(\mathring{\imath}[1], \ldots, \mathring{\imath}[k], w)$.

2. *Membership of encoding.* Compute a PCPP string Π_{mem} for the claim that $M_*(x, \Pi_*) = 1$ where M_* checks that Π_* is a valid encoding of indexes and a witness that put x in R.

3. *Consistency of encoding.* For every $j \in [k]$, compute a PCPP string Π_j for the claim that $M_j(\pi_j, \Pi_*) = 1$ where M_j checks that π_j and Π_* are valid encodings and that the string $\mathring{\imath}[j]$ encoded within π_j is equal to the matching string encoded within Π_*.

4. Output $(\Pi_*, \Pi_{\mathsf{mem}}, \Pi_{\mathring{\imath}})$ where $\Pi_{\mathring{\imath}}$ are the proofs $\Pi_1, \ldots, \Pi_k$ "bundled" together into symbols of k bits such that $\Pi_{\mathring{\imath}}[q] = (\Pi_1[q], \ldots, \Pi_k[q])$.

- $\mathbf{V}_{\mathsf{PCP}}^{\tilde{\pi}_1, \ldots, \tilde{\pi}_k, (\tilde{\Pi}_*, \tilde{\Pi}_{\mathsf{mem}}, \tilde{\Pi}_{\mathring{\imath}})}(x)$: Check that all the tests below pass.

  1. *Membership.* Run the PCPP verifier on the claim that $M_*(x, \tilde{\Pi}_*) = 1$ using proof oracle $\tilde{\Pi}_{\mathsf{mem}}$.

  2. *Consistency.* For every $j \in [k]$, run the PCPP verifier on the claim that $M_j(\tilde{\pi}_j, \tilde{\Pi}_*) = 1$ using proof oracle $\tilde{\Pi}_j$. These k tests are run *with the same randomness*. Since the PCPP is oblivious and randomness is shared, the queries made by the PCPP verifier in each test are identical, and so each query can be made by reading the appropriate k-bit symbols from $\tilde{\Pi}_{\mathring{\imath}}$.

- $\mathbf{iD}_{\mathsf{PCP}}(\tilde{\pi}_j)$: output the codeword closest to $\tilde{\pi}_j$ in the error-correcting code.

- $\mathbf{wD}_{\mathsf{PCP}}(\tilde{\Pi}_*, \tilde{\Pi}_{\mathsf{mem}}, \tilde{\Pi}_{\mathring{\imath}})$: Let $(\tilde{\mathring{\imath}}[1], \ldots, \tilde{\mathring{\imath}}[k], \tilde{w})$ be the codeword closest to $\tilde{\Pi}_*$ in the error-correcting code and output $\tilde{w}$.

Completeness follows straightforwardly from the construction. We now sketch decodability.

Decodability. Fix an instance x, indexer proofs $\tilde{\pi}_1, \ldots, \tilde{\pi}_k$, and prover proof $(\tilde{\Pi}_*, \tilde{\Pi}_{\mathsf{mem}}, \tilde{\Pi}_{\mathring{\imath}})$. Suppose that the verifier accepts with high-enough probability. We argue that this implies that there exists w such that $(\mathbf{iD}_{\mathsf{PCP}}(\tilde{\pi}_1), \ldots, \mathbf{iD}_{\mathsf{PCP}}(\tilde{\pi}_k), x, \mathbf{wD}_{\mathsf{PCP}}(\tilde{\Pi})) \in R$. Specifically, we argue that $\tilde{\Pi}_*$ encodes indices $\tilde{\mathring{\imath}}[1], \ldots, \tilde{\mathring{\imath}}[k]$ and witness $\tilde{w}$ that place x in R and, additionally, each $\tilde{\pi}_j$ is an encoding of $\tilde{\mathring{\imath}}[j]$. This completes the proof of decodability because $\mathbf{iD}_{\mathsf{PCP}}$ decodes each $\tilde{\pi}_j$ to $\tilde{\mathring{\imath}}[j]$, and these strings together with $\tilde{w}$ put x in the multi-indexed relation R.

Let δ_{PCPP} be the PCPP's proximity and δ_{ECC} the code's (relative) distance; recall that $\delta_{\mathsf{PCPP}} \leq \delta_{\mathsf{ECC}}$.

- *Membership:* We claim that there exist strings $\tilde{\mathring{\imath}}[1], \ldots, \tilde{\mathring{\imath}}[k]$ and $\tilde{w}$ that place x in R and whose encoding has Hamming distance at most δ_{PCPP} from $\tilde{\Pi}_*$; since $\delta_{\mathsf{PCPP}} \leq \delta_{\mathsf{ECC}}$, this implies that $\tilde{\Pi}_*$ decodes to $(\tilde{\mathring{\imath}}[1], \ldots, \tilde{\mathring{\imath}}[k], \tilde{w})$. Suppose towards contradiction that there are no such strings. In other words, for every codeword $\hat{\Pi}_*$ that is close in Hamming distance to $\tilde{\Pi}_*$ we have that $M_{*,x}(x, \hat{\Pi}_*) = 0$. As a result the PCPP verifier must reject with high probability, which contradicts our assumption that $\mathbf{V}_{\mathsf{PCP}}$ (which runs the PCPP verifier) *accepts* with high probability.

– *Consistency*: We claim that there exist strings $\tilde{\mathtt{i}}[1], \dots, \tilde{\mathtt{i}}[k]$ and $\tilde{w}$ such that their collective encoding is close to $\tilde{\varPi}_*$ and that, for every $j \in [k]$, $\tilde{\pi}_j$ is close to the encoding of $\tilde{\mathtt{i}}[j]$. As before, since the proximity parameter of the PCPP is smaller than the distance of the code, this implies that $\tilde{\varPi}_*$ decodes to $(\tilde{\mathtt{i}}[1], \dots, \tilde{\mathtt{i}}[k], \tilde{w})$ and that $\tilde{\pi}_j$ decodes to $\tilde{\mathtt{i}}[j]$. Suppose towards contradiction that for some $j \in [k]$ the above condition does not hold: for every $\hat{\pi}_j$ and $\widehat{\varPi}$ such that $\hat{\pi}_j$ is close to $\tilde{\pi}_j$ and $\widehat{\varPi}_*$ is close to $\tilde{\varPi}_*$ it holds that $M_j(\hat{\pi}_j, \widehat{\varPi}_*) = 0$. By the soundness of the (*multi-input*) PCPP, the PCPP verifier must reject with high probability, which contradicts our assumption that $\mathbf{V}_{\text{PCP}}$ (which runs the PCPP verifier) *accepts* with high probability.

Complexity Measures. The above construction is an index-decodable PCP with polynomial-length proofs and where the verifier makes $O(1)$ queries to each indexer proof and makes $O(1)$ queries to the prover proof. Moreover, the prover proof has alphabet size 2^k since the prover bundles the PCPP consistency test proofs into k-bit symbols; this bundling is possible because the verifier shares randomness between all of the (oblivious) PCPPs in the consistency test. Since the PCPPs are oblivious to the index i, and they share randomness, they all must make the same queries to their oracles. The verifier uses $O(\log |\mathbf{x}|)$ bits of randomness: $O(\log |\mathbf{x}|)$ for the membership test, and $O(\log |\mathbf{x}|)$ for all k consistency tests combined.

Achieving Constant Query Complexity over a Binary Alphabet. We

describe how to achieve an index-decodable PCP with constant query complexity per proof over the binary alphabet. The main tool is proof composition. In order to apply proof composition, we define and construct a robust variant of index-decodable PCPs.

Proof Composition. Proof composition is a technique to lower the query complexity of PCPs [2] and IOPs [9]. In proof composition, an "inner" PCP is used to prove that a random execution of the "outer" PCP would have accepted. The inner PCP needs to be a PCPP, which is a PCP system where the verifier has oracle access to its input in addition to the prover's proof, and the soundness guarantee is that if the input is *far* from any input in the language, then the verifier accepts with small probability. To match this, the outer PCP must be *robust*, which means that the soundness guarantee ensures that when the instance is not in the language then not only is a random local view of the verifier rejecting but it is also far (in Hamming distance) from any accepting local view.

Typically the robust outer PCP has small proof length but large query complexity, while the inner PCPP has small query complexity but possibly a large proof length. Composition yields a PCP with small query complexity and small proof length.

We observe that proof composition *preserves decodability*: if the outer PCP in the composition is index-decodable, then the composed PCP is index-decodable. This is because the composition operation does not change the outer PCP proof and only adds a verification layer to show that the outer verifier accepts.

We thus apply proof composition as follows: the outer PCP is a robust variant of the index-decodable PCP from Sect. 2.5; and the inner PCP is a standard PCPP with polynomial proof length. This will complete the proof sketch of Theorem 4.

Defining Robust Index-Decodable PCPs. Our goal is to perform proof composition where the outer PCP is index-decodable. As mentioned above, this requires the PCP to be robust. Our starting point is the index-decodable PCP from Sect. 2.5. This PCP does have large query complexity over the binary alphabet ($O(k)$ queries to the prover proof). However, the fact that its queries to the prover proof are already bundled into a constant number of locations over an alphabet of size 2^k implies that we do not have to worry about a "generic" query bundling step and instead only have to perform a (tailored) robustification step prior to composition. Accordingly, the robustness definition below focuses on the prover proof, and so is the corresponding construction described after.

Definition 2. *A* non-adaptive[8] *index-decodable PCP* $(\mathbf{I}_{\mathsf{PCP}}, \mathbf{P}_{\mathsf{PCP}}, (\mathbf{V}^{\mathsf{qry}}_{\mathsf{PCP}}, \mathbf{V}^{\mathsf{dc}}_{\mathsf{PCP}}), \mathbf{iD}_{\mathsf{PCP}}, \mathbf{wD}_{\mathsf{PCP}})$ *for a multi-indexed relation* R *is* **prover-robustly index-decodable** *with decodability bound* κ_{PCP} *and robustness* σ_{PCP} *if for every* $\mathbb{x}$ *and proofs* $\tilde{\mathbf{\Pi}}_i = (\tilde{\pi}_1, \dots, \tilde{\pi}_k)$ *and* $\tilde{\Pi}$ *if*

$$\Pr_\rho \left[\exists A' \ s.t. \ \mathbf{V}^{\mathsf{dc}}_{\mathsf{PCP}}(\mathbb{x}, \rho, \tilde{\mathbf{\Pi}}_i[Q_i], A') = 1 \wedge \Delta(A', A) \le \sigma_{\mathsf{PCP}}(|\mathbb{x}|) \ \middle| \ \begin{matrix} (Q_i, Q_*) \leftarrow \mathbf{V}^{\mathsf{qry}}_{\mathsf{PCP}}(\mathbb{x}, \rho) \\ A := \{ \ \tilde{\Pi}[q] \mid q \in Q_* \ \} \end{matrix} \right] > \kappa_{\mathsf{PCP}}(|\mathbb{x}|)$$

then $(\mathbf{iD}_{\mathsf{PCP}}(\tilde{\pi}_1), \dots, \mathbf{iD}_{\mathsf{PCP}}(\tilde{\pi}_k), \mathbb{x}, \mathbf{wD}_{\mathsf{PCP}}(\tilde{\Pi})) \in R$. *Above* Q_i *and* Q_* *are the queries made to the indexer proofs the prover proof respectively and* $\Delta(A', A)$ *is the relative distance between* A' *and* A.

In other words, if $(\mathbf{iD}_{\mathsf{PCP}}(\tilde{\pi}_1), \dots, \mathbf{iD}_{\mathsf{PCP}}(\tilde{\pi}_k), \mathbb{x}, \mathbf{wD}_{\mathsf{PCP}}(\tilde{\Pi})) \notin R$ then with high probability not only will the verifier reject but also any set of answers *from the prover proof* that are close in Hamming distance to the real set of answers will also be rejecting.

Robustification. We outline how we transform the index-decodable PCP constructed in Sect. 2.5 into a *robust* index-decodable PCP. The techniques follow the robustification step in [15]. The transformation preserves the verifier's randomness complexity $O(\log |\mathbb{x}|)$, which facilitates using this modified PCP as the outer PCP in proof composition.

We apply an error-correcting code separately to each symbol of the prover proof. When the verifier wants to read a symbol from this proof, it reads the codeword encoding the symbol, decodes it, and then continues. It reads the indexer proofs as in the original PCP. This makes the PCP robust because if a few bits of the codeword representing a symbol are corrupted, then it will still be decoded to the same value. The robustness, however, degrades with the

---

[8] A PCP verifier is non-adaptive if it can be split into two algorithms: $\mathbf{V}^{\mathsf{qry}}_{\mathsf{PCP}}$ chooses which locations to query without accessing its oracles; and $\mathbf{V}^{\mathsf{dc}}_{\mathsf{PCP}}$ receives the results of the queries and decides whether to accept or reject.

number of queries. If the relative distance of the error-correcting code is δ and the original verifier reads q symbols from the prover proof, then the resulting PCP will have robustness $O(\delta/q)$.

Indeed, let $c_1, \ldots, c_q$ be the codewords read by the new PCP verifier from the prover proof, and let $a_1, \ldots, a_q$ be such that a_i is the decoding of c_i. In order to change the decoding into some other set of strings $a'_1, \ldots, a'_q$ that, when received by the verifier, may induce a different decision than $a_1, \ldots, a_q$, it suffices (in the worst case) to change a single codeword to decode to a different value. Since the relative distance of the code is δ, to do this, one must change at least a δ-fraction of the bits of a single codeword, c_i. A δ-fraction of a single codeword is a δ/q-fraction of the whole string of q codewords, $c_1, \ldots, c_q$.

In sum, to achieve constant robustness, *we need to begin with an index-decodable PCP with a small number of queries to the prover proof*, but possibly with a large alphabet. It is for this reason that we required this property in Sect. 2.5.

2.6   Commit-and Prove SNARKs from Index-Decodable PCPs

We outline the proof of Theorem 3 by showing how to generically transform an index-decodable PCP into a commit-and-prove SNARK. First, we review the Micali transformation from PCPs to SNARGs. Then, we define commit-and-prove SNARKs and explain the challenges in constructing them. Finally, we outline how we overcome these challenges in our construction.

Review: The Micali Construction. The SNARG prover uses the random oracle to Merkle hash the (long) PCP string into a (short) Merkle root that acts as a commitment; then, the SNARG prover uses the random oracle to derive randomness for the PCP verifier's queries; finally, the SNARG prover outputs an argument string that includes the Merkle root, answers to the PCP verifier's queries, and Merkle authentication paths for each of those answers (acting as local openings to the commitment). The SNARG verifier re-derives the PCP verifier's queries from the Merkle root and runs the PCP verifier with the provided answers, ensuring that each answer is authenticated.

The security analysis roughly works as follows. Fix a malicious prover that makes at most t queries to the random oracle and convinces the SNARG verifier to accept with probability δ. First, one argues that the malicious prover does not find any collisions or inversions for the random oracle except with probability $\mu := O(\frac{t^2}{2^\lambda})$. Next, one argues that there is an algorithm that, given the malicious prover, finds a PCP string that makes the PCP verifier accept with probability at least $\frac{1}{t} \cdot (\delta - \mu)$. This enables to establish soundness of the SNARG (if the PCP has soundness error β_{PCP} then for instances not in the language it must be that $\frac{1}{t} \cdot (\delta - \mu) \leq \beta_{\mathsf{PCP}}$ and thus that the SNARG has soundness error $t \cdot \beta_{\mathsf{PCP}} + \mu$) and also to establish knowledge soundness of the SNARG (if the PCP has knowledge error κ_{PCP} then the PCP extractor works provided that $\frac{1}{t} \cdot (\delta - \mu) \geq \kappa_{\mathsf{PCP}}$ and thus the SNARG is a SNARK with knowledge error $t \cdot \kappa_{\mathsf{PCP}} + \mu$).

The aforementioned algorithm that finds the PCP string is known as *Valiant's extractor* (it was used implicitly in [55] and formally defined and analyzed in [12]). Given the query/answer transcript of the malicious prover to the random oracle, Valiant's extractor finds the partial PCP string that the malicious prover "had in mind" when producing the SNARG: any location that the malicious prover could open is part of the partial PCP string (and has a unique value as we conditioned on the prover finding no collisions); conversely, any location that is not part of the partial PCP string is one for which the malicious prover could not generate a valid local opening. Crucially, the malicious prover, in order to cause the SNARG verifier to accept, must generate randomness by applying the random oracle to the Merkle root, and answering the corresponding PCP queries with authenticated answers. Hence the partial PCP string output by Valiant's extractor causes the PCP verifier to accept with the same probability as the malicious prover, up to (i) the additive loss μ due to conditioning on no inversions and collisions, and (ii) the multiplicative loss of t due to the fact that the malicious prover can generate up to t different options of randomness for the PCP verifier and then choose among them which to use for the output SNARG. Overall, while Valiant's extractor *cannot* generate an entire PCP string, it finds "enough" of a PCP string to mimic the malicious prover, and so the PCP string's undefined locations can be set arbitrarily.

Commit-and-Prove SNARK. A CaP-SNARK (in the ROM) for an indexed relation $R = \{(\mathbb{i}, \mathbb{x}, \mathbb{w})\}$ is a tuple $\mathsf{ARG} = (\mathbf{C}, \mathbf{P}, \mathbf{V})$ of deterministic polynomial-time oracle machines, where $\mathbf{C} = (\mathsf{Com}, \mathsf{Check})$ is a succinct commitment scheme,[9] that works as follows. The committer sends a short commitment $\mathsf{cm} := \mathbf{C}.\mathsf{Com}(\mathbb{i})$ to the verifier. Subsequently, the prover sends a short proof $\mathsf{pf} := \mathbf{P}(\mathbb{i}, \mathbb{x}, \mathbb{w})$ attesting that it knows a witness $\mathbb{w}$ such that $(\mathbb{i}, \mathbb{x}, \mathbb{w}) \in R$ and $\mathbb{i}$ is the index committed in cm. The verifier $\mathbf{V}$ receives $(\mathsf{cm}, \mathbb{x}, \mathsf{pf})$ and decides whether to accept the prover's claim. Completeness states that, if all parties act honestly, the verifier always accepts.

The security requirement of a CaP-SNARK is *(straight-line) knowledge soundness*. Informally, knowledge soundness says that if a query-bounded malicious prover convinces the verifier to accept the tuple $(\mathsf{cm}, \mathbb{x}, \mathsf{pf})$ with large enough probability, then the prover "knows" an index $\mathbb{i}$ opening cm and a witness $\mathbb{w}$ such that $(\mathbb{i}, \mathbb{x}, \mathbb{w}) \in R$. In more detail, we say that $\mathsf{ARG} = (\mathbf{C}, \mathbf{P}, \mathbf{V})$ has knowledge error ϵ if there exists a deterministic polynomial-time machine $\mathbf{E}$ (the extractor) such that for every $\lambda \in \mathbb{N}$, $n \in \mathbb{N}$, and deterministic t-query (malicious) prover $\tilde{\mathbf{P}}$,

$$\Pr\left[\begin{array}{c} \mathbf{V}^\zeta(\mathsf{cm}, \mathbb{x}, \mathsf{pf}) = 1 \wedge |\mathbb{x}| = n \wedge \\ \left((\mathbb{i}, \mathbb{x}, \mathbb{w}) \notin R \vee \mathbf{C}.\mathsf{Check}^\zeta(\mathsf{cm}, \mathbb{i}, \mathsf{op}) = 0\right) \end{array} \middle| \begin{array}{c} \zeta \leftarrow \mathcal{U}(\lambda) \\ (\mathsf{cm}, \mathbb{x}, \mathsf{pf}; \mathsf{tr}) := \tilde{\mathbf{P}}^\zeta \\ (\mathbb{i}, \mathsf{op}, \mathbb{w}) := \mathbf{E}(\mathsf{cm}, \mathbb{x}, \mathsf{pf}, \mathsf{tr}) \end{array}\right] \leq \epsilon(\lambda, n, t),$$

---

[9] A pair of algorithms $\mathbf{C} = (\mathsf{Com}, \mathsf{Check})$ is a succinct commitment scheme if: (1) it is hard for every query-bounded adversary to find two different messages that pass verification for the same commitment string; and (2) the commitment of a message of length n with security parameter λ has length $\mathrm{poly}(\lambda, \log n)$.

where $\mathcal{U}(\lambda)$ is the uniform distribution over functions $\zeta \colon \{0,1\}^* \to \{0,1\}^\lambda$ and $\mathsf{tr} := (j_1, a_1, \ldots, j_t, a_t)$ are the query/answer pairs made by $\tilde{\mathbf{P}}$ to its oracle.

First Construction Attempt. At first glance, constructing CaP-SNARKs using index-decodable PCPs seems like a straightforward variation of Micali's construction of SNARGs from PCPs.

- **C.Com**: Apply the ID-PCP indexer $\mathbf{I}_{\mathsf{PCP}}$ to the index $\mathfrak{i}$ and output the Merkle root $\mathsf{rt}_\mathfrak{i}$ of its output.
- **C.Check**: Given a Merkle root $\mathsf{rt}_\mathfrak{i}$ and index $\mathfrak{i}$, check that $\mathbf{C}.\mathsf{Com}(\mathfrak{i}) = \mathsf{rt}_\mathfrak{i}$.
- **P**: Compute the ID-PCP prover proof and a corresponding Merkle root; then use the random oracle to derive randomness for the ID-PCP verifier's queries; finally, output an argument string pf that includes the Merkle root, answers to the verifier's queries, and authentication paths for each answer relative to the appropriate Merkle root (for the indexer proof or for the prover proof).
- **V**: Re-derive the ID-PCP verifier's queries from the Merkle root and run the ID-PCP verifier with the provided answers, ensuring that each answer is authenticated.

The main issue with this strawman construction is that we need to handle malicious provers that have a *partial tree* in their query trace. Consider a malicious prover that, for some $(\mathfrak{i}, \mathbf{x}, \mathbf{w}) \in R$, computes honestly the indexer proof for $\mathfrak{i}$ as $\pi := \mathbf{I}_{\mathsf{PCP}}(\mathfrak{i})$ and then generates as its "commitment" a Merkle tree root $\mathsf{rt}_\mathfrak{i}$ obtained by computing a partial Merkle tree that ignores a small number of locations of π (i.e., for a small number of locations it begins deriving the tree from a level other than the leaves). While this malicious prover cannot open this small number of locations of π, it can still open all other locations of π. Next, the malicious prover generates honestly an argument string pf, opening the required locations of π from $\mathsf{rt}_\mathfrak{i}$. This malicious prover makes the argument verifier accept (w.h.p.) since the ID-PCP verifier queries the small subset of locations that the prover cannot open with small probability.

However, the only way to find a string π' that (honestly) hashes to rt is to find inversions in the random oracle, which is infeasible. Thus, there is no efficient extractor that, given rt and all of the queries that the prover made, outputs $\mathfrak{i}'$ whose indexer proof hashes to rt.

Solving the Problem via Proximity. We solve the above difficulty by modifying the commitment scheme $\mathbf{C} = (\mathsf{Com}, \mathsf{Check})$ and requiring more properties from the underlying index-decodable PCP.

- **C.Com**: Compute $\pi := \mathbf{I}_{\mathsf{PCP}}(\mathfrak{i})$ (apply the ID-PCP indexer to the index $\mathfrak{i}$) and output the commitment $\mathsf{cm} := \mathsf{rt}_\mathfrak{i}$ that equals the Merkle hash of π and output the opening information op that consists of the list of authentication paths for each entry in π.
- **C.Check**: Given a commitment $\mathsf{cm} = \mathsf{rt}_\mathfrak{i}$, index $\mathfrak{i}$, and opening information op, check that op is a list of valid authentication paths for a number of entries that is above a certain threshold, and that the partial string specified by them decodes into $\mathfrak{i}$ (when setting the unspecified values arbitrarily).

Now **C.Check** allows *partial* specification of the string under the Merkle root, so to preserve the binding property of the commitment scheme we require that $(\mathbf{I}_{\text{PCP}}, \mathbf{iD}_{\text{PCP}})$ is an error correcting code. *The threshold of the number of authentication paths required is related to the distance of this code.*

In the security analysis, Valiant's extractor finds a partial PCP string that makes the ID-PCP verifier accept with probability related to the SNARG prover's convincing probability, as well as authentication paths for each entry of that partial PCP string. To ensure that the number of authenticated entries is large enough to pass the threshold in **C.Check**, we add another requirement: if $\tilde{\pi}$ and $\tilde{\Pi}$ make the ID-PCP verifier accept an instance $\mathbb{x}$ with probability larger than the decodability bound then $\tilde{\pi}$ is close to a codeword of the code $(\mathbf{I}_{\text{PCP}}, \mathbf{iD}_{\text{PCP}})$ (in addition to the fact that the decodings of $\tilde{\pi}$ and $\tilde{\Pi}$ put $\mathbb{x}$ in the relation as is the case in the definition considered so far).

Our construction of index-decodable PCP supports these new requirements.

From an Index-Decodable PCP to a CaP-SNARK. Let $(\mathbf{I}_{\text{PCP}}, \mathbf{P}_{\text{PCP}}, \mathbf{V}_{\text{PCP}}, \mathbf{iD}_{\text{PCP}}, \mathbf{wD}_{\text{PCP}})$ be an index-decodable PCP system where $(\mathbf{I}_{\text{PCP}}, \mathbf{iD}_{\text{PCP}})$ is an error correcting code with relative distance δ and where indexer proofs are guaranteed to be $\delta/8$-close to valid codewords (when $\mathbf{V}_{\text{PCP}}$ accepts above the decodability bound). We construct a CaP-SNARK $\mathsf{ARG} = (\mathbf{C}, \mathbf{P}, \mathbf{V})$ as follows.

- **C.Com:** Given as input an index $\mathbb{i}$, compute the indexer proof $\pi := \mathbf{I}_{\text{PCP}}(\mathbb{i})$, compute the Merkle root $\mathsf{rt}_{\mathbb{i}}$ of a Merkle tree on π (using the random oracle as the hash function), and output the commitment $\mathsf{cm} := \mathsf{rt}_{\mathbb{i}}$ and the opening op containing all authentication paths.
- **C.Check:** Given as input a commitment $\mathsf{cm} := \mathsf{rt}_{\mathbb{i}}$, an index $\mathbb{i}$, and an opening op containing authentication paths, do the following:
  - check that op contains a list of authenticated entries relative to the Merkle root $\mathsf{rt}_{\mathbb{i}}$;
  - check that op represents at least a $(1 - \frac{\delta}{8})$-fraction of all possible entries for a string under $\mathsf{rt}_{\mathbb{i}}$;
  - let π be the string induced by the authenticated entries in op, setting arbitrarily other entries;
  - check that $\mathbf{I}_{\text{PCP}}(\mathbb{i})$ is $\delta/4$-close to π.
- **P:** Given as input $(\mathbb{i}, \mathbb{x}, \mathbb{w})$, do the following:
  - compute the commitment $\mathsf{rt}_{\mathbb{i}}$ to the index $\mathbb{i}$ as the committer does;
  - compute the PCP string $\Pi := \mathbf{P}_{\text{PCP}}(\mathbb{i}, \mathbb{x}, \mathbb{w})$;
  - compute the Merkle root rt_{w} of a Merkle tree on Π;
  - apply the random oracle to the string $(\mathsf{rt}_{\mathbb{i}} || \mathbb{x} || \mathsf{rt}_{\mathsf{w}})$ to derive randomness for the index-decodable PCP verifier $\mathbf{V}_{\text{PCP}}$, and compute the answers to the verifier's queries to both π and Π;
  - collect authentication paths from the Merkle trees for each answer; and
  - output a proof pf containing rt_{w}, query answers for π and Π and their authentication paths.
- **V:** Check the authentication paths, re-derive randomness, and run the index-decodable PCP verifier with this randomness and given these answers.

The tuple $\mathbf{C} = (\mathsf{Com}, \mathsf{Check})$ is a binding commitment scheme, as we now explain. Consider an attacker that outputs $\mathsf{cm} := \mathsf{rt}$, two distinct messages m, m', and two openings $\mathsf{op} := S$ and $\mathsf{op}' := S'$ such that $\mathbf{C}.\mathsf{Check}^\zeta(\check{\mathsf{cm}}, \mathsf{m}, \mathsf{op}) = 1$ and $\mathbf{C}.\mathsf{Check}^\zeta(\check{\mathsf{cm}}, \mathsf{m}', \mathsf{op}') = 1$. Condition on the attacker not finding collisions or inversions of the random oracle ζ (as this is true with high probability). Since S and S' each pass the checks in $\mathbf{C}.\mathsf{Check}$, each set covers at least $(1 - \delta/8)$ of the possible openings for a string. Therefore, their intersection covers at least $(1 - \delta/4)$ of the possible openings. Since there are no collisions or inversions, S and S' agree on all of these locations. Thus, letting π and π' be the strings defined using S and S' respectively (as computed by $\mathbf{C}.\mathsf{Check}$), we have that $\Delta(\pi, \pi') \leq \delta/4$. Additionally, we have that that $\Delta(\mathbf{I}_{\mathsf{PCP}}(\mathsf{m}), \pi) \leq \delta/4$ and $\Delta(\mathbf{I}_{\mathsf{PCP}}(\mathsf{m}'), \pi') \leq \delta/4$ since $\mathbf{C}.\mathsf{Check}$ accepts the commitments to m and m', and this is one of the checks it does. Putting all of this together, we have that $\Delta(\mathbf{I}_{\mathsf{PCP}}(\mathsf{m}), \mathbf{I}_{\mathsf{PCP}}(\mathsf{m}')) \leq \delta/2$ which implies that $\mathsf{m} = \mathsf{m}'$ since $\delta/2$ is the unique decoding distance.

Completeness of the CaP-SNARK is straightforward. Below we outline the extractor $\mathbf{E}$, which receives as input a commitment $\mathsf{cm} := \mathsf{rt}_i$, an argument string pf (containing the commitment rt_w, query answers for π and Π, and corresponding authentication paths with respect to rt_i and rt_w), and the list tr of query/answer pairs made by the malicious prover $\tilde{\mathbf{P}}$ to the random oracle.

> Use Valiant's extractor to compute the set S_i of all valid local openings of rt_i that the prover could generate and similarly extract S_w from rt_w. Let $\tilde{\pi}$ be the string whose entries are defined by the local openings generated by rt_i (and whose undefined entries are set arbitrarily to 0). Let $\tilde{\Pi}$ be defined similarly from the openings of rt_w. Compute the index $i := \mathbf{iD}_{\mathsf{PCP}}(\tilde{\pi})$ and the witness $\mathsf{w} := \mathbf{wD}_{\mathsf{PCP}}(\tilde{\Pi})$, and set $\mathsf{op} := S_i$. Output $(i, \mathsf{op}, \mathsf{w})$.

We show the following lemma. See the full version of this paper for a proof.

Lemma 1. *Let κ_{PCP} be the decodability bound of the index-decodable PCP, $t \in \mathbb{N}$ be a bound on the number of queries made by a malicious prover $\tilde{\mathbf{P}}$, and $\lambda \in \mathbb{N}$ be a security parameter. Then the knowledge extractor $\mathbf{E}$ above has knowledge error $t \cdot \kappa_{\mathsf{PCP}} + O(\frac{t^2}{2^\lambda})$.*

2.7 Hardness of Approximation

We outline our proof of Theorem 2 (it is AM[k]-complete to decide if an instance of k-SSAT has value 1 or at most $1 - \frac{1}{O(k)}$). See Sect. 1.1 for definitions.

First we explain how an AM[k] protocol can distinguish whether a k-SSAT instance has value 1 or value $1 - \frac{1}{O(k)}$. On input a k-SSAT instance ϕ, the prover and verifier take turns giving values to the variables: the verifier sends random bits $\rho_{1,1}, \ldots, \rho_{1,\ell}$, the prover answers with $a_{1,1}, \ldots, a_{1,\ell}$, the verifier sends $\rho_{2,1}, \ldots, \rho_{2,\ell}$, and so on until all of the variables of ϕ are given values. The verifier then accepts if and only if all of the clauses of ϕ are satisfied. For completeness, if ϕ has value 1, then for any choice of verifier messages there exists some strategy for the prover that will make the verifier accept. For soundness, when the value of ϕ is at most $1 - \frac{1}{O(k)}$, no matter what strategy the prover uses, the probability that the verifier accepts is at most $1 - \frac{1}{O(k)}$ (which can be made constant using parallel repetition).

Next we show that, for every language $L \in \mathsf{AM}[k]$, a given instance x can be reduced in deterministic polynomial time to a k-SSAT formula ϕ such that:

- if $x \in L$ then the value of ϕ is 1;
- if $x \notin L$ then the value of ϕ is at most $1 - \frac{1}{O(k)}$.

By Theorem 1, L has a k-round public-coin IOP with a non-adaptive verifier, polynomial proof length, and logarithmic decision randomness where the IOP verifier reads $q = O(k)$ bits of its interaction with the IOP prover. We stress that in the following proof it is crucial that Theorem 1 achieves an IOP with both logarithmic decision randomness complexity and small query complexity to both the prover and verifier messages.

Let $\mathbf{V}_{\rho_{dc}}$ be the circuit that computes the decision bit of the verifier given as input the q answers to the q queries made by the IOP verifier, for the instance x and decision randomness ρ_{dc}. By carefully following the proof of Theorem 1, we know that the IOP verifier's decision is the conjunction of $O(k)$ computations, each of which takes $O(1)$ bits as input. Therefore $d := |\mathbf{V}_{\rho_{dc}}| = O(k)$.

Via the Cook–Levin theorem we efficiently transform $\mathbf{V}_{\rho_{dc}}$ into a 3CNF formula $\phi_{\rho_{dc}} : \{0,1\}^{q+O(d)} \to \{0,1\}$ of size $O(d)$ the satisfies the following for every $b_1, \ldots, b_q \in \{0,1\}$:

- if $\mathbf{V}_{\rho_{dc}}(b_1, \ldots, b_q) = 1$ then $\exists z_1, \ldots, z_{O(d)} \in \{0,1\}$ $\phi_{\rho_{dc}}(b_1, \ldots, b_q, z_1, \ldots, z_{O(d)}) = 1$;
- if $\mathbf{V}_{\rho_{dc}}(b_1, \ldots, b_q) = 0$ then $\forall z_1, \ldots, z_{O(d)} \in \{0,1\}$ $\phi_{\rho_{dc}}(b_1, \ldots, b_q, z_1, \ldots, z_{O(d)}) = 0$.

Next we describe the k-SSAT instance ϕ. The variables of ϕ correspond to messages in the IOP as follows. For each $i \in [k]$, the random variables $\rho_{i,1}, \ldots, \rho_{i,r}$ represent the verifier's message in round i and the existential variables $a_{i,1}, \ldots, a_{i,l}$ represent the prover's message in round i. To the final set of existential variables we add additional variables $z_{\rho_{dc},1} \ldots, z_{\rho_{dc},O(d)}$ for every $\rho_{dc} \in \{0,1\}^{O(\log |x|)}$, matching the additional variables added when reducing the boolean circuit $\mathbf{V}_{\rho_{dc}}$ to the boolean formula $\phi_{\rho_{dc}}$. The k-SSAT instance ϕ is the conjunction of the formulas $\phi_{\rho_{dc}}$ for every $\rho_{dc} \in \{0,1\}^{O(\log |x|)}$ where each $\phi_{\rho_{dc}}$ has as its variables the variables matching the locations in the IOP transcript that the IOP verifier queries given x and ρ_{dc}, and additionally the variables added by converting $\mathbf{V}_{\rho_{dc}}$ into a formula, $z_{\rho_{dc},1} \ldots, z_{\rho_{dc},O(d)}$.

By perfect completeness of the IOP, if $x \in L$ then there is a prover strategy such that, no matter what randomness is chosen by the verifier, every $\mathbf{V}_{\rho_{dc}}$ is simultaneously satisfied, and hence so are the formulas $\phi_{\rho_{dc}}$, implying that the value of ϕ is 1.

By soundness of the IOP, if $x \notin L$ then (in expectation) at most a constant fraction of the circuits $\{\mathbf{V}_{\rho_{dc}}\}_{\rho_{dc} \in \{0,1\}^{O(\log |x|)}}$ are simultaneously satisfiable, and thus this is also true for the formulas $\{\phi_{\rho_{dc}}\}_{\rho_{dc} \in \{0,1\}^{O(\log |x|)}}$. Every formula $\phi_{\rho_{dc}}$

that is not satisfied has at least one of its $O(d)$ clauses not satisfied. Thus, the value of ϕ is at most $1 - \frac{1}{O(d)} = 1 - \frac{1}{O(k)}$.

References

1. Arora, S., Lund, C., Motwani, R., Sudan, M., Szegedy, M.: Proof verification and the hardness of approximation problems. J. ACM **45**(3), 501–555 (1998)
2. Arora, S., Safra, S.: Probabilistic checking of proofs: a new characterization of NP. J. ACM **45**(1), 70–122 (1998). Preliminary version in FOCS 1992
3. Babai, L.: Trading group theory for randomness. In: Proceedings of the 17th Annual ACM Symposium on Theory of Computing, STOC 1985, pp. 421–429 (1985)
4. Babai, L., Fortnow, L., Levin, L.A., Szegedy, M.: Checking computations in poly-logarithmic time. In: Proceedings of the 23rd Annual ACM Symposium on Theory of Computing, STOC 1991, pp. 21–32 (1991)
5. Babai, L., Moran, S.: Arthur-merlin games: a randomized proof system, and a hierarchy of complexity classes. J. Comput. Syst. Sci. **36**(2), 254–276 (1988)
6. Bellare, M., Goldreich, O., Goldwasser, S.: Randomness in interactive proofs. In: Proceedings of the 31st Annual Symposium on Foundations of Computer Science, FOCS 1990, pp. 563–572 (1990)
7. Ben-Sasson, E., Bentov, I., Horesh, Y., Riabzev, M.: Fast Reed-Solomon interactive oracle proofs of proximity. In: Proceedings of the 45th International Colloquium on Automata, Languages and Programming, ICALP 2018, pp. 14:1–14:17 (2018)
8. Ben-Sasson, E., Bentov, I., Horesh, Y., Riabzev, M.: Scalable zero knowledge with no trusted setup. In: Boldyreva, A., Micciancio, D. (eds.) CRYPTO 2019. LNCS, vol. 11694, pp. 701–732. Springer, Cham (2019). https://doi.org/10.1007/978-3-030-26954-8_23
9. Ben-Sasson, E., Chiesa, A., Gabizon, A., Riabzev, M., Spooner, N.: Interactive oracle proofs with constant rate and query complexity. In: Proceedings of the 44th International Colloquium on Automata, Languages and Programming, ICALP 2017, pp. 40:1–40:15 (2017)
10. Ben-Sasson, E., Chiesa, A., Goldberg, L., Gur, T., Riabzev, M., Spooner, N.: Linear-size constant-query IOPs for delegating computation. In: Hofheinz, D., Rosen, A. (eds.) TCC 2019. LNCS, vol. 11892, pp. 494–521. Springer, Cham (2019). https://doi.org/10.1007/978-3-030-36033-7_19
11. Ben-Sasson, E., Chiesa, A., Riabzev, M., Spooner, N., Virza, M., Ward, N.P.: Aurora: transparent succinct arguments for R1CS. In: Ishai, Y., Rijmen, V. (eds.) EUROCRYPT 2019. LNCS, vol. 11476, pp. 103–128. Springer, Cham (2019). https://doi.org/10.1007/978-3-030-17653-2_4
12. Ben-Sasson, E., Chiesa, A., Spooner, N.: Interactive oracle proofs. In: Hirt, M., Smith, A. (eds.) TCC 2016. LNCS, vol. 9986, pp. 31–60. Springer, Heidelberg (2016). https://doi.org/10.1007/978-3-662-53644-5_2
13. Ben-Sasson, E., Goldberg, L., Kopparty, S., Saraf, S.: DEEP-FRI: sampling outside the box improves soundness. In: Proceedings of the 11th Innovations in Theoretical Computer Science Conference, ITCS 2020, pp. 5:1–5:32 (2020)
14. Ben-Sasson, E., Goldreich, O., Harsha, P., Sudan, M., Vadhan, S.: Short PCPs verifiable in polylogarithmic time. In: Proceedings of the 20th Annual IEEE Conference on Computational Complexity, CCC 2005, pp. 120–134 (2005)

15. Ben-Sasson, E., Goldreich, O., Harsha, P., Sudan, M., Vadhan, S.P.: Robust PCPs of proximity, shorter PCPs, and applications to coding. SIAM J. Comput. **36**(4), 889–974 (2006)

16. Ben-Sasson, E., Sudan, M.: Short PCPs with polylog query complexity. SIAM J. Comput. **38**(2), 551–607 (2008)

17. Benarroch, D., et al.: Proposal: commit-and-prove zero-knowledge proof systems and extensions (2021). https://docs.zkproof.org/pages/standards/accepted-workshop4/proposal-commit.pdf

18. Bootle, J., Cerulli, A., Ghadafi, E., Groth, J., Hajiabadi, M., Jakobsen, S.K.: Linear-time zero-knowledge proofs for arithmetic circuit satisfiability. In: Takagi, T., Peyrin, T. (eds.) ASIACRYPT 2017. LNCS, vol. 10626, pp. 336–365. Springer, Cham (2017). https://doi.org/10.1007/978-3-319-70700-6_12

19. Bootle, J., Chiesa, A., Groth, J.: Linear-time arguments with sublinear verification from tensor codes. In: Pass, R., Pietrzak, K. (eds.) TCC 2020. LNCS, vol. 12551, pp. 19–46. Springer, Cham (2020). https://doi.org/10.1007/978-3-030-64378-2_2

20. Bootle, J., Chiesa, A., Liu, S.: Zero-knowledge IOPs with linear-time prover and polylogarithmic-time verifier. Cryptology ePrint Archive, Report 2020/1527 (2020)

21. Bordage, S., Nardi, J.: Interactive oracle proofs of proximity to algebraic geometry codes. arXiv cs/2011.04295 (2021)

22. Campanelli, M., Fiore, D., Querol, A.: LegoSNARK: modular design and composition of succinct zero-knowledge proofs. In: Proceedings of the 26th Conference on Computer and Communications Security, CCS 2019, pp. 2075–2092 (2019)

23. Canetti, R., Chen, Y., Holmgren, J., Lombardi, A., Rothblum, G.N., Rothblum, R.D.: Fiat-Shamir from simpler assumptions. Cryptology ePrint Archive, Report 2018/1004 (2018)

24. Chiesa, A., Hu, Y., Maller, M., Mishra, P., Vesely, N., Ward, N.: Marlin: preprocessing zkSNARKs with universal and updatable SRS. In: Canteaut, A., Ishai, Y. (eds.) EUROCRYPT 2020. LNCS, vol. 12105, pp. 738–768. Springer, Cham (2020). https://doi.org/10.1007/978-3-030-45721-1_26

25. Chiesa, A., Manohar, P., Spooner, N.: Succinct arguments in the quantum random oracle model. In: Hofheinz, D., Rosen, A. (eds.) TCC 2019. LNCS, vol. 11892, pp. 1–29. Springer, Cham (2019). https://doi.org/10.1007/978-3-030-36033-7_1

26. Chiesa, A., Ojha, D., Spooner, N.: FRACTAL: post-quantum and transparent recursive proofs from holography. In: Canteaut, A., Ishai, Y. (eds.) EUROCRYPT 2020. LNCS, vol. 12105, pp. 769–793. Springer, Cham (2020). https://doi.org/10.1007/978-3-030-45721-1_27

27. Condon, A., Feigenbaum, J., Lund, C., Shor, P.W.: Probabilistically checkable debate systems and nonapproximability of PSPACE-hard functions. Chicago J. Theor. Comput. Sci. **1995** (1995)

28. Condon, A., Feigenbaum, J., Lund, C., Shor, P.W.: Random debaters and the hardness of approximating stochastic functions. SIAM J. Comput. **26**(2), 369–400 (1997)

29. Costello, C., et al.: Geppetto: versatile verifiable computation. In: Proceedings of the 36th IEEE Symposium on Security and Privacy, S&P 2015, pp. 250–273 (2015)

30. Dinur, I.: The PCP theorem by gap amplification. J. ACM **54**(3), 12 (2007)

31. Dinur, I., Reingold, O.: Assignment testers: towards a combinatorial proof of the PCP theorem. In: Proceedings of the 45th Annual IEEE Symposium on Foundations of Computer Science, FOCS 2004, pp. 155–164 (2004)

32. Drucker, A.: Efficient probabilistically checkable debates. In: Goldberg, L.A., Jansen, K., Ravi, R., Rolim, J.D.P. (eds.) APPROX/RANDOM-2011. LNCS, vol. 6845, pp. 519–529. Springer, Heidelberg (2011). https://doi.org/10.1007/978-3-642-22935-0_44

33. Drucker, A.: A PCP characterization of AM. In: Aceto, L., Henzinger, M., Sgall, J. (eds.) ICALP 2011. LNCS, vol. 6755, pp. 581–592. Springer, Heidelberg (2011). https://doi.org/10.1007/978-3-642-22006-7_49

34. Drucker, A.: An improved exponential-time approximation algorithm for fully-alternating games against nature. In: Proceedings of the 61st Annual IEEE Symposium on Foundations of Computer Science, FOCS 2020, pp. 1081–1090 (2020)

35. Escala, A., Groth, J.: Fine-tuning Groth-Sahai proofs. In: Krawczyk, H. (ed.) PKC 2014. LNCS, vol. 8383, pp. 630–649. Springer, Heidelberg (2014). https://doi.org/10.1007/978-3-642-54631-0_36

36. Feige, U., Goldwasser, S., Lovász, L., Safra, S., Szegedy, M.: Interactive proofs and the hardness of approximating cliques. J. ACM 43(2), 268–292 (1996). Preliminary version in FOCS 1991

37. Fürer, M., Goldreich, O., Mansour, Y., Sipser, M., Zachos, S.: On completeness and soundness in interactive proof systems. Adv. Comput. Res. 5, 429–442 (1989)

38. Goldreich, O., Micali, S., Wigderson, A.: Proofs that yield nothing but their validity or all languages in NP have zero-knowledge proof systems. J. ACM 38(3), 691–729 (1991). Preliminary version appeared in FOCS 1986

39. Goldreich, O., Vadhan, S., Wigderson, A.: On interactive proofs with a laconic prover. Comput. Complex. 11(1/2), 1–53 (2002)

40. Goldwasser, S., Micali, S., Rackoff, C.: The knowledge complexity of interactive proof systems. SIAM J. Comput. 18(1), 186–208 (1989). Preliminary version appeared in STOC 1985

41. Goldwasser, S., Sipser, M.: Private coins versus public coins in interactive proof systems. In: Proceedings of the 18th Annual ACM Symposium on Theory of Computing, STOC 1986, pp. 59–68 (1986)

42. Guruswami, V., Umans, C., Vadhan, S.P.: Unbalanced expanders and randomness extractors from Parvaresh-Vardy codes. J. ACM 56(4), 20:1–20:34 (2009)

43. Haviv, I., Regev, O., Ta-Shma, A.: On the hardness of satisfiability with bounded occurrences in the polynomial-time hierarchy. Theory Comput. 3(1), 45–60 (2007)

44. Ishai, Y., Weiss, M.: Probabilistically checkable proofs of proximity with zero-knowledge. In: Lindell, Y. (ed.) TCC 2014. LNCS, vol. 8349, pp. 121–145. Springer, Heidelberg (2014). https://doi.org/10.1007/978-3-642-54242-8_6

45. Lee, N., Wang, Y., Jiang, J.R.: Solving stochastic Boolean satisfiability under random-exist quantification. In: Proceedings of the 26th International Joint Conference on Artificial Intelligence, IJCAI 2017, pp. 688–694 (2017)

46. Lipmaa, H.: Prover-efficient commit-and-prove zero-knowledge SNARKs. Int. J. Appl. Cryptogr. 3(4), 344–362 (2017)

47. Littman, M.L., Majercik, S.M., Pitassi, T.: Stochastic Boolean satisfiability. J. Autom. Reason. 27(3), 251–296 (2001)

48. Lund, C., Fortnow, L., Karloff, H.J., Nisan, N.: Algebraic methods for interactive proof systems. J. ACM 39(4), 859–868 (1992)

49. Majercik, S.M.: APPSSAT: approximate probabilistic planning using stochastic satisfiability. Int. J. Approximate Reasoning 45(2), 402–419 (2007)

50. Micali, S.: Computationally sound proofs. SIAM J. Comput. 30(4), 1253–1298 (2000). Preliminary version appeared in FOCS 1994

51. Papadimitriou, C.H.: Games against nature (extended abstract). In: 24th Annual ACM Symposium on Theory of Computing, STOC 1983, pp. 446–450 (1983)

52. Reingold, O., Rothblum, R., Rothblum, G.: Constant-round interactive proofs for delegating computation. In: Proceedings of the 48th ACM Symposium on the Theory of Computing, STOC 2016, pp. 49–62 (2016)
53. Ron-Zewi, N., Rothblum, R.: Local proofs approaching the witness length. In: Proceedings of the 61st Annual IEEE Symposium on Foundations of Computer Science, FOCS 2020, pp. 846–857 (2020)
54. Shamir, A.: IP = PSPACE. J. ACM **39**(4), 869–877 (1992)
55. Valiant, P.: Incrementally verifiable computation or proofs of knowledge imply time/space efficiency. In: Canetti, R. (ed.) TCC 2008. LNCS, vol. 4948, pp. 1–18. Springer, Heidelberg (2008). https://doi.org/10.1007/978-3-540-78524-8_1

Group Signatures and More
from Isogenies and Lattices: Generic,
Simple, and Efficient

Ward Beullens[1,2] , Samuel Dobson[3] , Shuichi Katsumata[4(✉)] ,
Yi-Fu Lai[3] , and Federico Pintore[5]

[1] imec-COSIC, KU Leuven, Leuven, Belgium
[2] IBM Research, Zurich, Switzerland
wbe@zurich.ibm.com
[3] University of Auckland, Auckland, New Zealand
ylai276@aucklanduni.ac.nz
[4] National Institute of Advanced Industrial Science and Technology (AIST),
Tokyo, Japan
shuichi.katsumata@aist.go.jp
[5] Department of Mathematics, University of Bari, Bari, Italy
federico.pintore@uniba.it

Abstract. We construct an efficient dynamic group signature (or more
generally an accountable ring signature) from isogeny and lattice assumptions. Our group signature is based on a simple generic construction that
can be instantiated by cryptographically hard group actions such as the
CSIDH group action or an MLWE-based group action. The signature is
of size $O(\log N)$, where N is the number of users in the group. Our idea
builds on the recent efficient OR-proof by Beullens, Katsumata, and Pintore (Asiacrypt'20), where we efficiently add a proof of valid ciphertext
to their OR-proof and further show that the resulting non-interactive
zero-knowledge proof system is *online extractable*.

Our group signatures satisfy more ideal security properties compared to previously known constructions, while simultaneously having
an attractive signature size. The signature size of our isogeny-based construction is an order of magnitude smaller than all previously known
post-quantum group signatures (e.g., 6.6 KB for 64 members). In comparison, our lattice-based construction has a larger signature size (e.g.,
either 126 KB or 89 KB for 64 members depending on the satisfied
security property). However, since the $O(\cdot)$-notation hides a very small
constant factor, it remains small even for very large group sizes, say 2^{20}.

1 Introduction

Group signature schemes, introduced by Chaum and van Heyst [22], allow authorized members of a group to individually sign on behalf of the group while the
specific identity of the signer remains anonymous. However, should the need

© International Association for Cryptologic Research 2022
O. Dunkelman and S. Dziembowski (Eds.): EUROCRYPT 2022, LNCS 13276, pp. 95–126, 2022.
https://doi.org/10.1007/978-3-031-07085-3_4

arise, a special entity called the group manager (or sometimes the tracing authority) can trace the signature to the signer, thus holding the group members accountable for their signatures. Group signatures have been an active area of academic research for the past three decades, and have also been gathering practical attention due to the recent real-world deployment of variants of group signatures such as directed anonymous attestation (DAA) [15] and enhanced privacy ID (EPID) [16].

Currently, there are versatile constructions of *efficient* group signatures from *classical* assumptions, e.g., [3,9,10,23,26,27,38,40,48,49]. In this work, when we argue the efficiency of a group signature, we focus on one of the quintessential metrics: the signature size. We require it to be smaller than $c \cdot \log N$ bits, where N is the group size and c is some explicit small polynomial in the security parameter. In their seminal work, Bellare, Micciancio, and Warinschi [4] provided a generic construction of a group signature with signature size $O(1)$ from any signature scheme, public-key encryption scheme, and general non-interactive zero-knowledge (NIZK) proof system. Unfortunately, this only provides an asymptotic feasibility result, and thus one of the main focuses of subsequent works, including ours, has been to construct a concretely efficient group signature.

In contrast to the classical setting, constructing efficient group signatures from any *post-quantum* assumptions has been elusive. Since the first lattice-based construction by Gordon, Katz, and Vaikuntanathan [39], there has been a rich line of subsequent works on lattice-based (and one code-based) group signatures, including but not limited to [33,41,45,47,50]. However, these results remained purely asymptotic. It was not until recently that efficient lattice-based group signatures appeared [14,25,31,32]. In [31], Esgin et al. report a signature size of 12KB and 19KB for a group size of $N = 2^6$ and 2^{10}, respectively—several orders of magnitude better than prior constructions.[1] These rapid improvements in efficiency for lattices originate in the recent progress of lattice-based NIZK proof systems for useful languages [2,13,29,30,51,52,58], most of which rely heavily on the properties of special structured lattices. Thus, it seems impossible to import similar techniques to other post-quantum assumptions or to standard non-structured lattices. For instance, constructing efficient group signatures from isogenies—one of the promising alternative post-quantum tools to lattices—still seems out of reach using current techniques. This brings us to the main question of this work:

Can we construct an efficient group signature secure from isogenies? Moreover, can we have a generic construction that can be instantiated from versatile assumptions, including those based on less structured lattices?

In addition, as we discuss in more detail later, we notice that all works regarding efficient post-quantum group signatures [14,25,31,32,42] do not satisfy the ideal security properties (which are by now considered standard) formalized by Bootle et al. [11]. Thus, we are also interested in the following question:

---

[1] We note that their signature size grows by $\log^t N$ for a small constant $t > 1$ rather than simply by $\log N$. .

Can we construct efficient post-quantum group signatures satisfying the ideal security properties formalized by Bootle et al. [11]?

To address these questions, in this work we focus on *accountable ring signatures* [57]. An accountable ring signature offers the flexibility of choosing the group of users when creating a signature (like a ring signature [55]), while also enforcing accountability by including one of the openers in the group (like a group signature). Although research on accountable ring signatures is still limited [12,32,44,46,57], we advocate that they are as relevant and interesting as group and ring signatures. As shown by Bootle et al. [12], accountable ring signatures imply group and ring signatures by naturally limiting or downgrading their functionality. Thus, an efficient post-quantum solution to an accountable ring signature implies solutions for *both* secure (dynamic) group signatures [5] and ring signatures, making it an attractive target to focus on.

Finally, as an independent interest, we are also concerned with *tightly*-secure constructions. To the best of our knowledge, all prior efficient post-quantum secure group and ring signatures are in the random oracle model and have a very loose reduction loss. In typical security proofs, given an adversary with advantage ϵ that breaks some security property of the group signature, we can only construct an adversary with advantage at most $(N^2Q)^{-1} \cdot \epsilon^2$ against the underlying hard problem, where Q is the number of random oracle queries and N is the number of users in the system. If we aim for 128-bit security (i.e., $\epsilon = 2^{-128}$), and set for example $(N, Q) = (2^{10}, 2^{50})$, then we need at least 326-bits of security for the hard problem. When aiming for a provably-secure construction, the parameters must be set much larger to compensate for this significant reduction loss, which then leads to a less efficient scheme. This is especially unattractive in the isogeny setting since only the smallest among the CSIDH parameters [20] enjoys properties suitable to achieve concrete efficiency [8].

1.1   Our Contribution

In this work, we construct an efficient accountable ring signature based on isogenies and lattices. This in particular implies the first efficient isogeny-based group signature. Our generic construction departs from known general feasibility results such as [4] and builds on primitives that can be efficiently instantiated. Unlike previous efficient post-quantum group signatures, our scheme satisfies all the desired properties provided by Bootle et al. [11] including *dynamicity* and *fully (CCA) anonymity*: the former states that the group members can be added and revoked dynamically and are not fixed on setup; the later states that anonymity holds even in the presence of an adversary that sees the signing keys of all honest users, who is additionally granted access to an opening oracle. We also satisfy the ideal variant of *non-frameability* and *traceability* [11], where the former is captured by *unforgeability* in the context of accountable ring signature. Roughly, this ensures that arbitrary collusion among members, even with the help of a corrupted group manager, cannot falsely open a signature to an honest user.

Our accountable ring signature schemes are realized in three steps. We first provide a generic construction of an accountable ring signature from simple cryptographic primitives such as a public-key encryption (PKE) scheme and an accompanying NIZK for a specific language. We then show an efficient instantiation of these primitives based on a group action that satisfies certain cryptographic properties. Finally, we instantiate the group action by either the CSIDH group action or the MLWE-based group action. Our generic construction builds on the recent efficient OR-proofs for isogeny and lattice-based hard languages by Beullens, Katsumata, and Pintore [7], which were used to construct ring signatures. The most technical part of this work is to efficiently add a proof of valid ciphertext to their OR-proof and proving full anonymity, which done naively would incur an exponential security loss. At the core of our construction is an efficient *online-extractable* OR-proof that allows to also prove validity of a ciphertext.

Moreover, thanks to the online extractability, our construction achieves a much tighter reduction loss compared to prior accountable ring signatures (and also group and ring signatures). It suffices to assume that the underlying post-quantum hard problem cannot be solved with advantage more than $N^{-1} \cdot \epsilon$ rather than $(N^2Q)^{-1} \cdot \epsilon^2$ as in prior works whose proofs rely on the forking lemma [34,54]. Working with the above example, we only lose 10-bits rather than 198-bits of security. We further show how to remove N^{-1} using the Katz-Wang technique [43] along with some techniques unique to our NIZK. As a side product, we obtain a tightly-secure and efficient isogeny and lattice-based ring signatures, improving upon those by Beullens et al. [7] which have a loose security reduction.

Comparison to Prior Work. To the best of our knowledge, Esgin et al. [31,32] are the only other work that (implicitly) provide an efficient post-quantum accountable ring signature.[2] Since the efficiency of an accountable ring signature is equivalent to those of the group signature obtained through limiting the functionality of the accountable ring signature, we chose to compare the efficiency of our scheme with other state-of-the-art post-quantum group signatures. Table 1 includes a comparison of the signature size and the different notions of security it satisfies. The first two schemes satisfy all the desired security properties of a dynamic group signature formalized by Bootle et al. [11]. Our scheme is the only one to achieve full CCA anonymity. Esgin et al. [31] achieves full CPA anonymity, where anonymity is broken once an adversary is given access to an opening oracle; in practice, this means that if a specific signature is once opened to some user, then any signature ever signed by that particular user will lose anonymity. Here, "full" means that the signing key of all the users may be exposed to the adversary. In contrast, Katz, Kolesnikov, and Wang [42] satisfies *selfless* CCA anonymity. While their scheme supports opening oracles, anonymity no longer holds if the signing key used to sign the signature is exposed to the adversary. Moreover, our scheme is the only one that also achieves the ideal variant of non-frameability and traceability [5,11] (illustrated in the "Manager Accountability"

---

[2] To be precise, they consider a weaker variant of standard accountable ring signature where no Judge algorithm is considered.

Table 1. Comparison of the signature size (KB) of some concretely efficient post-quantum group signature schemes. The first three rows are our scheme. Manager accountability states whether the (possibly malicious) group manager is accountable when opening a signature to some user. Namely, it is "Yes" when even a malicious group manager cannot falsely accuse an honest user of signing a signature that it hasn't signed.

	N					Hardness	Security	Anonymity	Manager
	2	2^5	2^6	2^{10}	2^{21}	Assumption	Level		Accountable
Isogeny	3.6	6.0	6.6	9.0	15.5	CSIDH-512	*	CCA	Yes
Lattice	124	126	126	129	134	MSIS/MLWE	NIST 2	CCA	Yes
Lattice	86	88	89	91	96	MSIS/MLWE	NIST 2	CCA	No
ESZ [31]	/	12	/	19	/	MSIS/MLWE	NIST 2	CPA	No
KKW [42]	/	/	280	418	/	LowMC	NIST 5	selfless-CCA	No

*128 bits of classical security and 60 bits of quantum security [53].

column). The two schemes [31,42] assume the group manager honestly executes the opening algorithm and that everyone trusts the output. Put differently, a malicious group manager can frame any honest members in the group by simply replacing the output of the opening algorithm. In contrast, our scheme remains secure even against malicious group managers since the validity of the output of the opening algorithm is verifiable. That is, even the group manager is held *accountable* in our group signature.

Not only our group signatures satisfy more ideal security properties compared to previous constructions, Table 1 shows that our signature size remains competitive. Our isogeny-based group signature based on CSIDH provides the smallest signature size among all post-quantum group signatures, which is $0.6 \log_2(N) + 3$ KB. In contrast, our lattice signature is larger; the scheme in the second (resp. third) row has signature size $0.5 \log_2(N) + 123.5$ KB (resp. $0.5 \log_2(N) + 85.9$ KB). It is smaller compared to [42], while larger compared to [31]. Compared to the two constructions, our signature size grows much slower with the group size N (see also Footnote 1) and also satisfies stronger security. We thus leave it as an interesting open problem to lower the constants in our construction.

1.2 Technical Overview

An accountable ring signature is like a standard ring signature where the ring R also includes an arbitrary opener public key opk of the signer's choice when creating a signature σ. The signature σ remains anonymous for anybody who does not know the corresponding opener secret key osk, while the designated opener can use osk to trace the user who created σ. A ring signature can be thought of as an accountable ring signature where opk = ⊥, while a group signature can be thought as an accountable ring signature where there is only a single opener.

General Approach. Our generic construction of an accountable ring signature follows the well-known template of the encrypt-then-prove approach to construct a group signature [17]. The high-level idea is simple. The signer encrypts its verification key vk (or another unique identifier) using the opener's public key opk for a PKE scheme and provides a NIZK proof for the following three facts: the ciphertext ct encrypts vk via opk; vk is included in the ring R; and that it knows a secret key sk corresponding to vk. To trace the signer, the opener simply decrypts ct to recover vk. Notice that the NIZK proof implicitly defines a verifiable encryption scheme [18,19] since it is proving that ct is a valid encryption for some message vk in R. Below, although our construction can be based on any cryptographically-hard group action, we mainly focus on isogenies for simplicity.

One of the difficulties in instantiating this template using isogeny-based cryptography is that we do not have an efficient verifiable encryption scheme for an appropriate PKE scheme. To achieve full anonymity, most of the efficient group signatures, e.g., [25,26,38,40,48,49], use an IND-CCA secure PKE as a building block and construct an efficient NIZK that proves validity of the ciphertext. Full anonymity stipulates that an adversary cannot de-anonymize a signature even if it is provided with an opening oracle, which traces the signatures submitted by the adversary. Roughly, by using an IND-CCA secure PKE as a building block, the reduction can simulate the opening oracle by using the decapsulation oracle provided by the IND-CCA game, rather than the opener's secret key. In the classical setting, constructing such an efficient IND-CCA secure verifiable encryption scheme is possible using the Cramer-Shoup PKE [24] that offers a rich algebraic structure. Unfortunately, in the isogeny setting, although we know how to construct an IND-CCA secure PKE based on the Fujisaki-Okamoto transform [37], it seems quite difficult to provide an accompanying verifiable encryption scheme as the construction internally uses a hash function modeled as a random oracle. Another approach is to rely on the weaker IND-CPA secure PKE but to use a stronger NIZK satisfying *online-extractability* [35]. At a high level, the reduction can use the online-extractor to extract the witness in the ciphertext ct instead of relying on the decapsulation oracle.[3] However, it turns out that even this approach is still non-trivial since we do not have any efficient verifiable encryption scheme for existing isogeny-based PKEs, let alone an accompanying online-extractable NIZK. For instance, most isogeny-based IND-CPA secure PKEs are based on the *hashed* version of ElGamal, and to the best of our knowledge, there are no efficient verifiable encryption schemes for hashed ElGamal.

Verifiable Encryption Scheme for a Limited Class of PKE. In this work, we observe that in the context of accountable ring signatures and group signatures, we do not require the full decryption capability of a standard PKE. Observe that decryption is only used by the opener and that it *knows* the ciphertext ct must be an encryption of one of the verification keys included in the ring (or group) R. Therefore, given a ciphertext ct, we only require a mechanism to check if ct encrypts a particular message M, rather than being able to decrypt an arbitrary unknown message. Specifically, the opener can simply run through

---

[3] Note that extractability via rewinding is insufficient for full anonymity as it will cause an exponential reduction loss when trying to extract the witness from adaptively chosen signatures [6].

all the verification keys $vk \in R$ to figure out which vk was encrypted in ct. This allows us to use a simple IND-CPA secure PKE with limited decryption capability based on the CSIDH group action: Let $E_0 \in \mathcal{E}\ell\ell_p(\mathcal{O}, \pi)$ be a fixed and public elliptic curve. The public key is $pk = (E_0, E := s \star E_0)$, where $sk = s$ is sampled uniformly at random from the class group $\mathcal{C}\ell(\mathcal{O})$. To encrypt a message $M \in \mathcal{C}\ell(\mathcal{O})$, we sample $r \leftarrow \mathcal{C}\ell(\mathcal{O})$ and set $ct = (ct_0 := r \star E_0, ct_1 := M \star (r \star E))$. To check if ct decrypts to M', we check whether ct_1 is equal to $M' \star (sk \star ct_0)$. Note that in general we cannot decrypt when M is unknown since we cannot cancel out $sk \star ct_0$ from ct_1. Now, observe that proving ct encrypts $M \in \mathcal{C}\ell(\mathcal{O})$ is easy since there is a simple sigma protocol for the Diffie-Hellman-like statement $(ct_0, (-M) \star ct_1) = (r \star E_0, r \star E)$, where r is the witness, e.g., [28]. Although this comes closer to what we want, this simple sigma protocol is not yet sufficient since the prover must reveal the message M to run it. Specifically, it proves that ct is an encryption of M, while what we want to prove is that ct is an encryption of *some* $M \in R$. In the context of accountable ring signature and group signature, this amounts to the signer being able to hide its verification key $vk \in R$.

Constructing NIZK *for Accountable Ring Signature.* Let us move forward to the intermediate goal of constructing a (non-online-extractable) NIZK proof system for the following three facts: the ciphertext ct encrypts vk via pk; vk is included in the ring R; and that the prover knows a secret key sk corresponding to vk. Recently, Beullens, Katsumata, and Pintore [7] proposed an efficient sigma protocol (and a non-online-extractable NIZK via the Fiat-Shamir transform) for proving the last two facts, which in particular constitutes an efficient OR-proof. We show how to glue the above "weak" verifiable encryption scheme with their OR-proof.

We first review a variant of the OR-sigma protocol in [7] with proof size $O(N)$, where N is the size of the ring. Assume each user $i \in [N]$ in the ring holds $vk_i = (E_0, E_i := s_i \star E_0) \in \mathcal{E}\ell\ell_p(\mathcal{O}, \pi)^2$ and $sk_i = s_i \in \mathcal{C}\ell(\mathcal{O})$. To prove $vk_I \in R$ and that it knows sk_I, the prover first sample $s' \leftarrow \mathcal{C}\ell(\mathcal{O})$ and sets $R_i = s' \star E_i$ for $i \in [N]$. It also samples randomness $rand_i$ and creates commitments $(C_i = \mathsf{Com}(R_i, rand_i))_{i \in [N]}$, where this commitment is simply instantiated by a random oracle. It finally samples a random permutation ϕ over $[N]$ and sends a permuted tuple $(C_{\phi(i)} = \mathsf{Com}(R_i, rand_i))_{i \in [N]}$. The verifier samples a random bit $b \in \{0, 1\}$. If $b = 0$, the prover returns all the randomness $(s', (rand_i)_{i \in [N]}, \phi)$ used to create the first message. The verifier then checks if the first message sent by the prover is consistent with this randomness. Otherwise, if $b = 1$, the prover returns $(I'', rand'', s'') := (\phi(I), rand_I, s' + s_I)$. The verifier then checks if $C_{I''} = \mathsf{Com}(s'' \star E_0, rand'')$ holds. Notice that if the prover is honest, then $s'' \star E_0 = s' \star E_I$ as desired. It is easy to check it is honest-verifier zero-knowledge. The transcript when $b = 0$ is independent of the witness, while the transcript when $b = 1$ can be simulated if the commitment scheme is hiding. Moreover, special soundness can be checked by noticing that given s'' and s', we can extract some (i^*, s^*) such that $(E_0, E_{i^*} = s^* \star E_0) \in R$. A full-fledged OR-sigma protocol with proof size $O(N)$ is then obtained by running this protocol λ-times in parallel, where λ denotes the security parameter. [7] showed several simple optimization techniques to compress the proof size from $O(N)$ to $O(\log N)$, but we first explain our main idea below.

We add our "weakly decryptable" PKE to this OR-sigma protocol. Since our PKE only handles messages in $\mathcal{C}\ell(\mathcal{O})$, the prover with $\mathsf{vk}_I \in \mathsf{R}$ encrypts the index $I \in [N]$ rather than vk_I, where we assume the verification keys in the ring R are ordered lexicographically.[4] The statement now consists of the ring R and the ciphertext $\mathsf{ct} = (\mathsf{ct}_0 := r \star E_0, \mathsf{ct}_1 = I \star (r \star E))$, where (E_0, E) is the opener's public key opk. Recall the opener can decrypt ct with knowledge of the ring R by brute-force searching for an $i \in [N]$ such that $\mathsf{ct}_1 = i \star (\mathsf{osk} \star \mathsf{ct}_0)$. Now, to prove vk_I is an entry in R and that it knows sk_I, the prover samples $s' \leftarrow \mathcal{C}\ell(\mathcal{O})$ and sets $R_i = s' \star E_i$ for $i \in [N]$ as before. It then further samples $r' \leftarrow \mathcal{C}\ell(\mathcal{O})$ and prepares $\mathsf{ct}'_i = (r' \star \mathsf{ct}_0, (-i) \star (r' \star \mathsf{ct}_1))$ for all $i \in [N]$. Observe that ct'_i is an encryption of the message $(I - i)$ using randomness $(r' + r)$. Specifically, ct'_i is of the form $((r' + r) \star E_0, (r' + r) \star E)$, which admits a natural sigma protocol as explained above. Finally, the prover samples randomness rand_i and a random permutation ϕ over $[N]$, and sends the randomly permuted commitments $(\mathsf{C}_{\phi(i)} = \mathsf{Com}(R_i \| \mathsf{ct}'_i, \mathsf{rand}_i))_{i \in [N]}$. The verifier samples a random bit $b \in \{0, 1\}$. If $b = 0$, then similarly to the above OR-sigma protocol, the prover simply returns all the randomness and the verifier checks the consistency of the first message. Otherwise, if $b = 1$, the prover returns $(I'', \mathsf{rand}'', s'', r'') := (\phi(I), \mathsf{rand}_I, s' + s_I, r' + r)$. The verifier checks if $\mathsf{C}_{I''} = \mathsf{Com}(s'' \star E_0 \| (r'' \star E_0, r'' \star E), \mathsf{rand}'')$ holds. Correctness and honest-verifier zero-knowledge holds essentially for the same reason as the above OR-sigma protocol. More importantly, special soundness holds as well. Intuitively, since the opening to $b = 0$ forces the cheating prover to commit to the proper (vk_i, i)-pair, a cheating prover cannot encrypt an index I' and prove that it has sk_I corresponding to vk_I for a different $I \neq I'$.

To compile our sigma protocol into an NIZK, we apply the Fiat-Shamir transform. Moreover, we apply similar optimization techniques used in [7] to compress the proof size from $O(N)$ to $O(\log N)$. Roughly, the prover additionally uses a pseudorandom generator to generate the randomness (i.e., $s', r', \phi, (\mathsf{rand}_i)_{i \in [N]}$). Then, in case $b = 0$, the prover needs to reply only with the seed of size $O(1)$. The prover also uses a Merkle tree to accumulate $(\mathsf{C}_{\phi(i)})_{i \in [N]}$ and sends the root value in the first message. It then only opens to the path necessary for verification when $b = 1$. This has a positive side-effect that we no longer require a permutation ϕ since the path hides the index if we use a slightly tweaked variant of the standard Merkle tree. Finally, we take advantage of the asymmetry in the prover's response size for $b = 0$ and $b = 1$, which are $O(1)$ and $O(\log N)$, respectively. Namely, we imbalance the challenge space so that the prover opens to more 0 than 1, while still maintaining negligible soundness error.

Adding Online-Extractability. To build an accountable ring signature or group signature, we require the above NIZK to be (multi-proof) *online-extractable*. This is a strengthening of standard proof of knowledge (PoK) that roughly states that the knowledge extractor, who can see what the adversary queries to the random oracle, is able to directly extract witnesses from the proofs output by

---

[4] The choice of what to encrypt is rather arbitrary. The same idea works if for instance we hash vk into $\mathcal{C}\ell(\mathcal{O})$ and view the digest as the message.

the adversary. The OR-proof by [7], which our NIZK builds on, was only shown to satisfy the standard PoK, which bases on a *rewinding* extractor.

One simple way to add online-extractability to our NIZK is to apply the Unruh transform [56]. Namely, we can modify the prover to add two more commitments $h_0 = \mathsf{Com}(s'\|r', \mathsf{rand}_0)$ and $h_1 = \mathsf{Com}(s''\|r'', \mathsf{rand}_1)$ in the first message, where Com is instantiated by the random oracle. Then, if $b = 0$ (resp. $b = 1$), the prover further opens to h_0 (resp. h_1). Recall that if the reduction obtains both (s', r') and (s'', r''), then it can invoke the extractor provided by the underlying sigma protocol to extract some (i^*, s^*) such that $(E_0, E_{i^*} = s^* \star E_0) \in \mathsf{R}$. Therefore, for the cheating adversary to fool the reduction, it must guess the bit b and create h_b correctly while creating h_{1-b} arbitrary. Intuitively, if we have λ-repetition of the sigma protocol, then the cheating prover cannot possibly guess all the challenge bits correctly. Therefore, there must be some challenge where it created h_0 and h_1 honestly. For that challenge bit, the reduction algorithm can then retrieve the corresponding inputs $(s'\|r', \mathsf{rand}_0)$ and $(s''\|r'', \mathsf{rand}_1)$ from simply observing the random oracle, and then, run the extractor to obtain the witness.

This idea works but it comes with an extra two hashes per one execution of the binary-challenge sigma protocol. Although it may sound insignificant in an asymptotic sense, these hashes add up when we execute the sigma protocol many times, and it makes it difficult to apply some of the optimization tricks. Concretely, when we apply this change to the isogeny-based ring signature by Beullen et al. [7], the signature grows by roughly a factor of 2 to 3.

In this work, we show that we can in fact prove online-extractability *without* making any modification to the aforementioned NIZK. Our main observations are the following: if the prover uses a seed to generate the randomness used in the first message via a random oracle, then the online extractor can observe $(s', r', \phi, (\mathsf{rand}_i)_{i \in [N]})$; and the prover must respond to some execution of the binary-challenge sigma protocol where the challenge bit is 1. The first implies that the seed implicitly acts as a type of commitment to (s', r'). The second implies the prover returns a response that includes (s'', r''). Specifically, our online extractor only looks at all the responses for the rounds where the challenge bit was 1, and checks the random oracle for any seed that leads to the commitment provided in the first message of the sigma protocol. If such seed is found, then it succeeds in extracting a witness. The intuition is simple but it turns out that the formal proof is technically more complicated due to the several optimizations performed on the basic sigma protocol to achieve proof size $O(\log N)$.

Generalizing with Group Actions. Although we have been explaining our generic construction using the CSIDH group action, it is not unique to them. It works equally well for any group action that naturally induces a PKE. Specifically, we instantiate the above idea also by the MLWE group action defined roughly as $\star : R_q^{n+m} \times R_q^m : (\mathbf{s}, \mathbf{e}) \star \mathbf{t} \to \mathbf{A} \star \mathbf{s} + \mathbf{e} + \mathbf{t}$, where $R_q = \mathbb{Z}_q[X]/(X^d + 1)$. Since CSIDH and MLWE induce a PKE with slightly different algebraic structures, we introduce a *group-action-based* PKE defined by two group actions to formally capture both instances. This abstraction may be of an independent interest since at first glance, isogeny-based and lattice-based PKEs seem to rely on different algebraic structures. Finally, one interesting feature unique to our generic construction is that since our sigma protocol is rather combinatorial in nature, we can for instance use CSIDH for the user's public key vk and mix it with an MLWE-based PKE for the opener' public key opk. The practical impact of such mixture is that we can achieve stronger bit-security for anonymity (due to MLWE) while keeping the user's public key and signature small (due to CSIDH).

Achieving Tight Reduction. Since the proofs do not rely on the forking lemma [34, 54] to extract witnesses from the forged proofs, our construction achieves a tighter reduction compared to prior works on efficient group signatures. However, we still lose a factor $1/N$ in the proof of unforgeability, which may vary from $1/2$ to $1/2^{20}$.[5] Recall N is the size of the group in group signatures but it is the size of all the users enrolled in the system for accountable ring signatures, which may be far larger than the size of the ring. The main reason for this loss was because the reduction needs to guess one user's verification key used by the adversary to create its forgery and to embed the hard problem into it.

A well known technique to obtain a tight proof is to rely on the Katz-Wang technique [43] along with the generic OR-composition of sigma protocols, and rely on a multi-instance version of the hard problem (which are believed to be as difficult as the single-instance version for specific hard problems). Namely, we modify the scheme to assign two verification keys $(vk^{(1)}, vk^{(2)})$ to each user. The users will only hold one signing key $sk^{(b)}$ for $b \in \{1, 2\}$ corresponding to the verification key $vk^{(b)}$. The user can honestly run the aforementioned sigma protocol where the statement includes $vk^{(b)}$, and a simulated sigma protocol using the ZK-simulator where the statement includes $vk^{(3-b)}$. We can then use the sequential OR-proof technique as presented in [1,36] to bridge these two sigma protocols so that it hides the b.[6]

While this generic transform works, it unfortunately doubles the signature size, which may outweigh the motivation for having a tight reduction. In this work, we present a novel and far cheaper technique tailored to our sigma protocol. The signature size overhead is a mere 512B for our concrete lattice-based instantiation. The key observation is that we can view the set of all users' verification key $(vk^{(1)}, vk^{(2)})$ as a ring of size $2N$, rather than a ring of size N where each ring element consists of two verification keys. This observation itself is not yet sufficient since recall that we typically must encrypt some information bound to the signer for traceability, e.g., encrypt the position/index of vk in R, and it is no longer clear what to encrypt when we have two verification keys in the ring. Luckily, it turns out that our sigma protocol can be easily modified with no loss in efficiency to overcome this apparent issue. Details are provided in Sect. 5.3.

---

[5] We note that we also have some independent looseness in the anonymity proof since we rely on the "multi-challenge" IND-CPA security from our PKE. This is handled in a standard way, and this is also why we only achieve a truly tight group signature from lattices and not from isogenies.

[6] We note that it seems difficult to use the parallel OR-proof for our sigma protocol since the challenge space is structured.

2   Preliminaries

Due to page limitation, the notation we use is defined in the full version of the paper, as are the standard primitives such as relaxed sigma protocol in the random oracle model and PKE. We instantiate several standard cryptographic primitives, such as pseudorandom number generators (i.e., Expand) and commitment schemes, by hash functions modeled as a random oracle $\mathcal{O}$. With abuse of notation, we may occasionally write for example $\mathcal{O}(\mathsf{Expand} \parallel \cdot)$ instead of $\mathsf{Expand}(\cdot)$ to make the usage of the random oracle explicit. Finally, we denote by $\mathcal{A}^{\mathcal{O}}$ an algorithm $\mathcal{A}$ that has black-box access to $\mathcal{O}$, and we may occasionally omit the superscript $\mathcal{O}$ for simplicity when the meaning is clear from context.

2.1   Non-interactive Zero-Knowledge Proofs of Knowledge in the ROM

We consider non-interactive zero-knowledge proof of knowledge protocols (or simply NIZK (proof system)) in the ROM. Below, we define a variant where the proof is generated with respect to a label. Although syntactically different, such NIZK is analogous to the notion of signature of knowledge [21].

Definition 1 (NIZK Proof System). *Let* L *denote a label space, where checking membership can be done efficiently. A non-interactive zero-knowledge (NIZK) proof system* Π_{NIZK} *for the relations* R *and* $\tilde{R}$ *such that* $R \subseteq \tilde{R}$ *(which are implicitly parameterized by* λ*) consists of oracle-calling PPT algorithms* (Prove, Verify) *defined as follows:*

$\mathsf{Prove}^{\mathcal{O}}(\mathsf{lbl}, \mathsf{X}, \mathsf{W}) \to \pi/\bot$: *On input a label* $\mathsf{lbl} \in \mathsf{L}$*, a statement and witness pair* $(\mathsf{X}, \mathsf{W}) \in R$*, it outputs a proof* π *or a special symbol* $\bot$ *denoting abort.*

$\mathsf{Verify}^{\mathcal{O}}(\mathsf{lbl}, \mathsf{X}, \pi) \to \top/\bot$: *On input a label* $\mathsf{lbl} \in \mathsf{L}$*, a statement* X*, and a proof* π*, it outputs either* $\top$ *(accept) or* $\bot$ *(reject).*

We omit the standard notions of correctness, zero-knowledge, and statistical soundness to the full version of the paper. Below, we define one of the core property we require from NIZK to construct our ARS.

Definition 2 (Multi-Proof Online Extractability). *A* NIZK *proof system* Π_{NIZK} *is (multi-proof) online extractable if there exists a PPT extractor* OnlineExtract *such that for any (possibly computationally-unbounded) adversary* $\mathcal{A}$ *making at most polynomially-many queries has at most a negligible advantage in the following game played against a challenger (with access to a random oracle* $\mathcal{O}$*).*

(i) The challenger prepares empty lists $L_{\mathcal{O}}$ *and* L_P*, and sets* flag *to 0.*

(ii) $\mathcal{A}$ *can make random-oracle, prove, and extract queries an arbitrary polynomial number of times:*

- (hash, x): *The challenger updates* $L_\mathcal{O} \leftarrow L_\mathcal{O} \cup \{x, \mathcal{O}(x)\}$ *and returns* $\mathcal{O}(x)$. *We assume below that* $\mathcal{A}$ *runs the verification algorithm after receiving a proof from the prover oracle and before submitting a proof to the extract oracle.*[7]
- (prove, lbl, X, W): *The challenger returns* $\perp$ *if* lbl $\notin$ L *or* (X, W) $\notin$ R. *Otherwise, it returns* $\pi \leftarrow$ Prove$^\mathcal{O}$(lbl, X, W) *and updates* $L_P \leftarrow L_P \cup \{$lbl, X, $\pi\}$.
- (extract, lbl, X, π): *The challenger checks if* Verify$^\mathcal{O}$(lbl, X, π) $= \top$ *and* (lbl, X, π) $\notin L_P$, *and returns* $\perp$ *if not. Otherwise, it runs* W $\leftarrow$ OnlineExtract$^\mathcal{O}$(lbl, X, π, $L_\mathcal{O}$) *and checks if* (X, W) $\notin \tilde{R}$, *and returns* $\perp$ *if yes and sets* flag $= 1$. *Otherwise, if all checks pass, it returns* W.

(iii) *At some point* $\mathcal{A}$ *outputs 1 to indicate that it is finished with the game. We say* $\mathcal{A}$ *wins if* flag $= 1$. *The advantage of* $\mathcal{A}$ *is defined as* Adv$^{\mathsf{OE}}_{\Pi_{\mathsf{NIZK}}}(\mathcal{A}) = \Pr[\mathcal{A}$ *wins] where the probability is also taken over the randomness used by the random oracle.*

Note, importantly, that OnlineExtract is not given access to the queries Prove$^\mathcal{O}$ makes directly to $\mathcal{O}$. Thus, OnlineExtract is not guaranteed to return a valid witness W when called with any output of the Prove oracle. The requirement that (lbl, X, π) $\notin L_P$ ensures that this does not allow the adversary to trivially win the game, and in particular by extension ensures that modifying the label lbl should invalidate any proof obtained from the Prove oracle. When L $= \{\perp\}$, then it is a standard NIZK.

2.2 Accountable Ring Signatures

We provide the definition of accountable ring signatures (ARSs), following the formalization introduced by Bootle et al. [12].

Definition 3 (Accountable Ring Signature). *An accountable ring signature* Π_{ARS} *consists of PPT algorithms* (Setup, OKGen, UKGen, Sign, Verify, Open, Judge) *defined as follows:*

Setup(1^λ) $\rightarrow$ pp : *On input a security parameter* 1^λ, *it returns a public parameter* pp *(sometimes implicitly) used by the scheme. We assume* pp *defines openers' public-key space* $\mathcal{K}_{\mathsf{opk}}$ *and users' verification-key space* $\mathcal{K}_{\mathsf{vk}}$, *with efficient algorithms to decide membership.*

OKGen(pp) $\rightarrow$ (opk, osk) : *On input a public parameter* pp, *it outputs a pair of public and secret keys* (opk, osk) *for an* opener.

UKGen(pp) $\rightarrow$ (vk, sk) : *On input a public parameter* pp, *it outputs a pair of verification and signing keys* (vk, sk) *for a user.*

Sign(opk, sk, R, M) $\rightarrow \sigma$: *On input an opener's public key* opk, *a signing key* sk, *a list of verification keys, i.e., a ring,* R $= \{$vk$_1, \ldots,$ vk$_N\}$, *and a message* M, *it outputs a signature* σ.

---

[7] This is w.l.o.g., and guarantees that the list $L_\mathcal{O}$ is updated with the input/output required to verify the proof $\mathcal{A}$ receives or sends.

Verify(opk, R, M, σ) $\rightarrow$ $\top/\bot$: *On input an opener's public key* opk, *a ring* R = $\{vk_1, \ldots, vk_N\}$, *a message* M, *and a signature* σ, *it (deterministically) outputs either* $\top$ *(accept) or* $\bot$ *(reject).*

Open(osk, R, M, σ) $\rightarrow$ (vk, π)$/\bot$: *On input an opener's secret key* osk, *a ring* R = $\{vk_1, \ldots, vk_N\}$, *a message* M, *a signature* σ, *it (deterministically) outputs either a pair of verification key* vk *and a proof* π *that the owner of* vk *produced the signature, or* $\bot$.

Judge(opk, R, vk, M, σ, π) $\rightarrow$ $\top/\bot$: *On input an opener's public key* opk, *a ring* R = $\{vk_1, \ldots, vk_N\}$, *a verification key* vk, *a message* M, *a signature* σ, *and a proof* π, *it (deterministically) outputs either* $\top$ *(accept) or* $\bot$ *(reject). We assume without loss of generality that* Judge(opk, R, vk, M, σ, π) *outputs* $\bot$ *if* Verify(opk, R, M, σ) *outputs* $\bot$.

An accountable ring signature is required to satisfy the following properties: correctness, anonymity, traceability, unforgeability, and tracing soundness.

First, we require correctness to hold even if the ring contains maliciously-generated user keys or the signature has been produced for a maliciously-generated opener key. Note that the correctness guarantee for the open and judge algorithms are defined implicitly in the subsequent security definitions.

Definition 4 (Correctness). *An accountable ring signature* Π_{ARS} *is correct if, for all* $\lambda \in \mathbb{N}$, *any PPT adversary* $\mathcal{A}$ *has at most a negligible advantage in* λ *in the following game played against a challenger.*

(i) The challenger runs pp $\leftarrow$ Setup(1^λ) *and generates a user key* (vk, sk) $\leftarrow$ UKGen(pp). *It then provides* (pp, vk, sk) *to* $\mathcal{A}$.

(ii) $\mathcal{A}$ *outputs an opener's public key, a ring, and a message tuple* (opk, R, M) *to the challenger.*

(iii) The challenger runs $\sigma \leftarrow$ Sign(opk, sk, R, M). *We say* $\mathcal{A}$ *wins if*
- opk $\in \mathcal{K}_{\mathsf{opk}}$, R $\subseteq \mathcal{K}_{\mathsf{vk}}$, *and* vk $\in$ R,
- Verify(opk, R, M, σ) = $\bot$.

The advantage of $\mathcal{A}$ *is defined as* $\mathsf{Adv}^{\mathsf{Correct}}_{\Pi_{\mathsf{ARS}}}(\mathcal{A}) = \Pr[\mathcal{A}\ wins]$.

Anonymity requires that a signature does not leak any information on who signed it. We consider the standard type of anonymity notion where the adversary gets to choose the signing key used to generate the signature. Moreover, we allow the adversary to make (non-trivial) opening queries that reveal who signed the messages. This notion is often called *full (CCA)* anonymity [4,11] to differentiate between weaker notions of anonymity such as *selfless* anonymity that restricts the adversary from exposing the signing key used to sign the signature or *CPA* anonymity where the adversary is restricted from querying the open oracle.

Definition 5 (Anonymity). *An accountable ring signature* Π_{ARS} *is (CCA) anonymous (against full key exposure) if, for all* $\lambda \in \mathbb{N}$, *any PPT adversary* $\mathcal{A}$ *has at most a negligible advantage in the following game played against a challenger.*

(i) *The challenger runs* pp $\leftarrow$ Setup(1^λ) *and generates an opener key* (opk, osk) $\leftarrow$ OKGen(pp). *It also prepares an empty list* Q_{sign} *and samples a random bit* $b \leftarrow \{0,1\}$.

(ii) *The challenger provides* (pp, opk) *to* $\mathcal{A}$.

(iii) $\mathcal{A}$ *can make signing and opening queries an arbitrary polynomial number of times:*

- (sign, R, M, sk_0, sk_1): *The challenger runs* $\sigma_i \leftarrow$ Sign(opk, sk_i, R, M) *for* $i \in \{0,1\}$ *and returns* $\perp$ *if* Verify(opk, R, M, σ_i) = $\perp$ *for either of* $i \in \{0,1\}$. *Otherwise, it updates* $Q_{\text{sign}} \leftarrow Q_{\text{sign}} \cup \{(R, M, \sigma_b)\}$ *and returns* σ_b.
- (open, R, M, σ): *The challenger returns* $\perp$ *if* (R, M, σ) $\in Q_{\text{sign}}$. *Otherwise, it returns*
  Open(osk, R, M, σ).

(iv) $\mathcal{A}$ *outputs a guess* b^*. *We say* $\mathcal{A}$ *wins if* $b^* = b$.

The advantage of $\mathcal{A}$ *is defined as* $\text{Adv}_{\Pi_{\text{ARS}}}^{\text{Anon}}(\mathcal{A}) = |\Pr[\mathcal{A} \text{ wins}] - 1/2|$.

Unforgeability considers two types of forgeries. The first captures the natural notion of unforgeability where an adversary cannot forge a signature for a ring of honest users, i.e., a ring of users for which it does not know any of the corresponding secret keys. The second captures the fact that an adversary cannot accuse an honest user of producing a signature even if the ring contains malicious users and the opener is malicious.

Definition 6 (Unforgeability). *An accountable ring signature scheme* Π_{ARS} *is unforgeable (with respect to insider corruption) if, for all* $\lambda \in \mathbb{N}$, *any PPT adversary* $\mathcal{A}$ *has at most negligible advantage in the following game played against a challenger.*

(i) *The challenger runs* pp $\leftarrow$ Setup(1^λ) *and initializes an empty keyed dictionary* $D_{\text{UKey}}[\cdot]$ *and three empty sets* Q_{UKey}, Q_{sign} *and* Q_{cor}. *It provides* pp *to* $\mathcal{A}$.

(ii) $\mathcal{A}$ *can make user key generation, signing, and corruption queries an arbitrary polynomial number of times:*

- (ukeygen): *The challenger runs* (vk, sk) $\leftarrow$ UKGen(pp). *If* $D_{\text{UKey}}[\text{vk}] \neq \perp$, *then it returns* $\perp$. *Otherwise, it updates* $D_{\text{UKey}}[\text{vk}] = $ sk *and* $Q_{\text{UKey}} \leftarrow Q_{\text{UKey}} \cup \{\text{vk}\}$, *and returns* vk.
- (sign, opk, vk, R, M): *The challenger returns* $\perp$ *if* vk $\notin Q_{\text{UKey}} \cap R$. *Otherwise, it runs* $\sigma \leftarrow$ Sign(opk, $D_{\text{UKey}}[\text{vk}]$, R, M). *The challenger updates* $Q_{\text{sign}} \leftarrow Q_{\text{sign}} \cup \{(\text{opk}, \text{vk}, R, M, \sigma)\}$ *and returns* σ.
- (corrupt, vk): *The challenger returns* $\perp$ *if* vk $\notin Q_{\text{UKey}}$. *Otherwise, it updates* $Q_{\text{cor}} \leftarrow Q_{\text{cor}} \cup \{\text{vk}\}$ *and returns* $D_{\text{UKey}}[\text{vk}]$.

(iv) $\mathcal{A}$ *outputs* (opk, vk, R, M, σ, π). *We say* $\mathcal{A}$ *wins if*

- (opk, $*$, R, M, σ) $\notin Q_{\text{sign}}$, R $\subseteq Q_{\text{UKey}} \backslash Q_{\text{cor}}$,
- Verify(opk, R, M, σ) = $\top$,

or

- (opk, vk, R, M, σ) $\notin Q_{\text{sign}}$, vk $\in Q_{\text{UKey}} \backslash Q_{\text{cor}}$,
- Judge(opk, R, vk, M, σ, π) = $\top$.

The advantage of $\mathcal{A}$ is defined as $\mathsf{Adv}^{\mathsf{Unf}}_{\Pi_{\mathsf{ARS}}}(\mathcal{A}) = \Pr[\mathcal{A}\ wins]$.

Traceability requires that any opener key pair $(\mathsf{opk}, \mathsf{osk})$ in the range of the opener key-generation algorithm can open a valid signature σ to some user vk along with a proof valid π. This ensures that any opener can trace the user and produce a proof for its decision. Below, rather than assuming an efficient algorithm that checks set membership $(\mathsf{opk}, \mathsf{osk}) \in \mathsf{OKGen}(\mathsf{pp})$, we simply ask the adversary to output the randomness used to generate $(\mathsf{opk}, \mathsf{osk})$. Note that this definition contains the prior definitions where opk was assumed to be uniquely defined and efficiently computable from osk [12].

Definition 7 (Traceability). *An accountable ring signature scheme Π_{ARS} is traceable if, for all $\lambda \in \mathbb{N}$, any PPT adversary $\mathcal{A}$ has at most negligible advantage in the following game played against a challenger.*

(i)   The challenger runs $\mathsf{pp} \leftarrow \mathsf{Setup}(1^\lambda)$ *and provides* pp *to $\mathcal{A}$.*
(ii) $\mathcal{A}$ returns a randomness, a ring, a message, and a signature tuple $(\mathsf{rr}, \mathsf{R}, \mathsf{M}, \sigma)$. *We say $\mathcal{A}$ wins if*
   - $\mathsf{Verify}(\mathsf{opk}, \mathsf{R}, \mathsf{M}, \sigma) = \top$, *where* $(\mathsf{opk}, \mathsf{osk}) \leftarrow \mathsf{OKGen}(\mathsf{pp}; \mathsf{rr})$, *and*
   - $\mathsf{Judge}(\mathsf{opk}, \mathsf{R}, \mathsf{vk}, \mathsf{M}, \sigma, \pi) = \bot$, *where* $(\mathsf{vk}, \pi) \leftarrow \mathsf{Open}(\mathsf{osk}, \mathsf{R}, \mathsf{M}, \sigma)$.

The advantage of $\mathcal{A}$ is defined as $\mathsf{Adv}^{\mathsf{Tra}}_{\Pi_{\mathsf{ARS}}}(\mathcal{A}) = \Pr[\mathcal{A}\ wins]$.

Finally, tracing soundness requires that a signature cannot trace to two different users in the ring. This must hold even if all the users in the ring and the opener are corrupt.

Definition 8 (Tracing Soundness). *An accountable ring signature scheme Π_{ARS} is traceable sound if, for all $\lambda \in \mathbb{N}$, any PPT adversary $\mathcal{A}$ has at most negligible advantage in the following game played against a challenger.*

(i)   The challenger runs $\mathsf{pp} \leftarrow \mathsf{Setup}(1^\lambda)$ *and provides* pp *to $\mathcal{A}$.*
(ii) $\mathcal{A}$ returns an opener's public key, a ring, a message, a signature, and two verification keys and proofs $(\mathsf{opk}, \mathsf{R}, \mathsf{M}, \sigma, \{(\mathsf{vk}_b, \pi_b)\}_{b \in \{0,1\}})$. *We say $\mathcal{A}$ wins if*
   - $\mathsf{vk}_0 \neq \mathsf{vk}_1$,
   - $\mathsf{Judge}(\mathsf{opk}, \mathsf{R}, \mathsf{vk}_0, \mathsf{M}, \sigma, \pi_0) = \top$,
   - $\mathsf{Judge}(\mathsf{opk}, \mathsf{R}, \mathsf{vk}_1, \mathsf{M}, \sigma, \pi_1) = \top$.

The advantage of $\mathcal{A}$ is defined as $\mathsf{Adv}^{\mathsf{TraS}}_{\Pi_{\mathsf{ARS}}}(\mathcal{A}) = \Pr[\mathcal{A}\ wins]$.

3   Generic Construction of Accountable Ring Signature and Dynamic Group Signature

In this section, we present novel generic frameworks for accountable ring signature, dynamic group signature, and their tightly secure variants. Firstly, we introduce a generic construction of an accountable ring signature in Sect. 3.1. Constructing a dynamic group signature immediately follows by limiting the functionality of accountable ring signature. Our construction achieves a tighter reduction compared to prior works on efficient group signatures as it does not rely on the forking lemma [34,54]. However, since we still lose a factor of $1/N$ in the reduction, we finally show how to modify our construction to be truly tight using the Katz-Wang technique [43] in Sect. 3.3.

3.1 Generic Construction of Accountable Ring Signature

In this subsection, we present our generic construction of an accountable ring signature scheme. Before diving in the details we give a brief overview of our generic construction. The setup is as follows. The opening authorities generate a PKE key-pair, denoted as $(\mathsf{opk}, \mathsf{osk})$ to indicate that they are the opener's keys, and publish the opening public key opk. The users generate an element (x, w) in a hard relation R, and publish the statement x as verification key, and keep the witness w as secret signing key. A signature for our ARS scheme for a ring $R = \{\mathsf{x}_1, \ldots, \mathsf{x}_N\}$ consists of a ciphertext ct, and a NIZK proof that: 1) The ciphertext is an encryption of an index $I \in [N]$ under an opener public key opk, and 2) that the signer knows a witness w corresponding to the I-th statement x_I in the ring R. The second property ensures that the signature is unforgeable, and the first property ensures that the opener (who has the secret key opk) can decrypt the ciphertext to find out who the real signer is. To convince others that a signature was produced by the I-th member of the ring, the opener uses a second NIZK proof to prove that he knows an opener secret key osk that is consistent with opk, and such that $\mathsf{Dec}(\mathsf{osk}, \mathsf{ct}) = I$. If the opener could find a second secret key osk', consistent with opk and such that ct decrypts to $I' \neq I$ under osk', then the opener could frame I' for signing a signature, which breaks the tracing soundness of the signature scheme. To prevent this we require the PKE to satisfy a strong correctness property, which says that an encryption of I will always decrypt to I, even if the encryption randomness and decryption key are invalid (in some specific, controlled way). More formally we define the following special correctness notion for a PKE scheme.

Definition 9 ($(\mathcal{R}', \mathcal{KR}')$-correctness). *Consider a public-key encryption scheme $\Pi_{\mathsf{PKE}} = (\mathsf{Setup}, \mathsf{KeyGen}, \mathsf{Enc}, \mathsf{Dec})$, with $\mathcal{R}$ the set containing all possible randomness used by Enc and $\mathcal{KR}$ the binary relation that contains all the key pairs $(\mathsf{pk}, \mathsf{sk})$ that can be generated by running KeyGen. Let $\mathcal{R}'$ be a set containing $\mathcal{R}$, and $\mathcal{KR}'$ a relation containing $\mathcal{KR}$. Then we say that Π_{PKE} is $(\mathcal{R}', \mathcal{KR}')$-correct if, for all $\lambda \in \mathbb{N}$, and for all but a negligible fraction of $\mathsf{pp} \in \mathsf{Setup}(1^\lambda)$, we have for all $(\mathsf{pk}, \mathsf{sk}) \in \mathcal{KR}'$, for all messages m in the plaintext space $\mathcal{M}$, and all $r \in \mathcal{R}'$ that $\mathsf{Dec}(\mathsf{sk}, \mathsf{Enc}(\mathsf{pk}, m; r)) = m$.*

Our generic construction of an accountable ring signature scheme $\Pi_{\mathsf{ARS}} = (\mathsf{ARS.Setup}, \mathsf{ARS.OKGen}, \mathsf{ARS.UKGen}, \mathsf{ARS.Sign}, \mathsf{ARS.Verify}, \mathsf{ARS.Open}, \mathsf{ARS.Judge})$, provide in Fig. 1, is based on the following building blocks:

- A hard-instance generator contains a setup algorithm RelSetup that, on input a security parameter λ, outputs a description pp of a pair of binary relations $R_{\mathsf{pp}} \subseteq \tilde{R}_{\mathsf{pp}}$, and an instance generator IGen for those pairs of relations. That is, RelSetup and IGen are PPT algorithms such that $\Pr[(\mathsf{x}, \mathsf{w}) \in R_{\mathsf{pp}} \mid \mathsf{pp} \leftarrow \mathsf{RelSetup}(1^\lambda); (\mathsf{x}, \mathsf{w}) \leftarrow \mathsf{IGen}(\mathsf{pp})] = 1$, and such that if we define the advantage of an adversary $\mathcal{A}$ against $(\mathsf{RelSetup}, \mathsf{IGen})$ as

$$\mathsf{Adv}^{\mathsf{Hard}}_{\mathsf{RelSetup},\mathsf{IGen}}(\mathcal{A}) = \Pr\left[(\mathsf{x},\mathsf{w}') \in \tilde{R}_{\mathsf{pp}} \,\middle|\, \begin{array}{l} \mathsf{pp} \leftarrow \mathsf{RelSetup}(1^\lambda) \\ (\mathsf{x},\mathsf{w}) \leftarrow \mathsf{IGen}(\mathsf{pp}) \\ \mathsf{w}' \leftarrow \mathcal{A}(\mathsf{pp},\mathsf{x}) \end{array}\right],$$

then $\mathsf{Adv}^{\mathsf{Hard}}_{\mathsf{RelSetup},\mathsf{IGen}}(\mathcal{A})$ is a negligible function of λ for every PPT adversary $\mathcal{A}$.

- A public-key encryption scheme $\Pi_{\mathsf{PKE}} = (\mathsf{PKE.Setup}, \mathsf{KeyGen}, \mathsf{Enc}, \mathsf{Dec})$ with multi-challenge IND-CPA security, and with $(\mathcal{R}', \mathcal{KR}')$-correctness for some relaxed randomness set $\mathcal{R}'$ and some relaxed key relation $\mathcal{KR}'$. The message space of the encryption scheme contains a set of indices $[N]$ for any polynomially large $N \in \mathbb{N}$.

- A multi-proof online extractable NIZK proof system with labels $\Pi_{\mathsf{NIZK,lbl}} = (\mathsf{NIZK.Setup}_{\mathsf{lbl}}, \mathsf{NIZK.Prove}_{\mathsf{lbl}}, \mathsf{NIZK.Verify}_{\mathsf{lbl}})$ for the relations

$$R_{\mathsf{sig}} = \left\{ \big((\{\mathsf{x}_i\}_{i\in[N]}, \mathsf{pk}, \mathsf{ct}), (I, \mathsf{w}, r)\big) \,\middle|\, (\mathsf{x}_I, \mathsf{w}) \in R_{\mathsf{pp}} \wedge \mathsf{ct} = \mathsf{Enc}(\mathsf{pk}, I; r) \right\}$$

$$\tilde{R}_{\mathsf{sig}} = \left\{ \big((\{\mathsf{x}_i\}_{i\in[N]}, \mathsf{pk}, \mathsf{ct}), (I, \mathsf{w}, r)\big) \,\middle|\, (\mathsf{x}_I, \mathsf{w}) \in \tilde{R}_{\mathsf{pp}} \wedge \mathsf{ct} = \mathsf{Enc}(\mathsf{pk}, I; r) \right\}.$$

To be precise, we need to also include the public parameters output by RelSetup and PKE.Setup in the statement. We omit them for better readability.

- A statistically sound NIZK proof system (without labels) $\Pi_{\mathsf{NIZK}} = (\mathsf{NIZK.Setup}, \mathsf{NIZK.Prove}, \mathsf{NIZK.Verify})$ for the relations

$$R_{\mathsf{open}} = \{((\mathsf{pk}, \mathsf{ct}, I), \mathsf{sk}) \mid (\mathsf{pk}, \mathsf{sk}) \in \mathcal{KR} \wedge \mathsf{Dec}(\mathsf{sk}, \mathsf{ct}) = I\}$$

$$\tilde{R}_{\mathsf{open}} = \{((\mathsf{pk}, \mathsf{ct}, I), \mathsf{sk}) \mid (\mathsf{pk}, \mathsf{sk}) \in \mathcal{KR}' \wedge \mathsf{Dec}(\mathsf{sk}, \mathsf{ct}) = I\}.$$

Similarly to above, we omit the public parameter output by PKE.Setup in the statement. We emphasize that Π_{NIZK} does not need to be online extractable.

Due to page limitation, we refer to the full version of this paper for the correctness and security of our accountable ring signature scheme Π_{ARS}.

3.2 Accountable Ring Signature to Dynamic Group Signature

Accountable ring signatures are known to trivially imply dynamic group signatures [11,12]. A formal treatment is provided by Bootle et al. [11]. We remark that the transformation provided in [11] retains the same level of security provided by the underlying accountable ring signature. That is, all reductions between unforgeability, full-anonymity and traceability are tight. For completeness, we provide more details on group signatures and the transform in the full version of this paper.

ARS.Setup(1^λ)

1: $pp_1 \leftarrow RelSetup(1^\lambda)$
2: $pp_2 \leftarrow PKE.Setup(1^\lambda)$
3: **return** $pp = (pp_1, pp_2)$

ARS.OKGen(pp)

1: $(pk, sk) \leftarrow KeyGen(pp_2)$
2: **return** $(opk := pk, osk := sk)$

ARS.UKGen(pp)

1: $(x, w) \leftarrow IGen(pp_1)$
2: **return** $(vk := x, sk := w)$

ARS.Sign(opk, sk, R, M)

1: $\{x_i\}_{i\in[N]} \leftarrow R$
2: **if** $\nexists I : (x_I, sk) \in R_{pp_1}$ **then**
3:     **return** $\perp$.
4: $r \xleftarrow{\$} \mathcal{R}$
5: $ct = Enc(opk, I; r)$
6: $\pi_{sign} \quad\quad\quad\quad\quad\quad\quad\quad \leftarrow$
    $NIZK.Prove_{lbl}(M, (R, opk, ct), (I, sk, r))$
7: **return** $\sigma := (ct, \pi_{sign})$

ARS.Verify(opk, R, M, σ)

1: $(ct, \pi_{sign}) \leftarrow \sigma$
2: **return** $NIZK.Verify_{lbl}(M, (R, opk, ct), \pi_{sign})$

ARS.Judge(opk, R, vk, M, σ, π_{open})

1: $(ct, \pi_{sign}) \leftarrow \sigma$
2: **if** $\nexists I : vk = R_I$ **then**
3:     **return** $\perp$.
4: $b_0 \leftarrow ARS.Verify(opk, R, M, \sigma)$
5: $b_1 \leftarrow NIZK.Verify((opk, ct, I), \pi_{open})$
6: **return** $b_0 \wedge b_1$

ARS.Open(osk, R, M, σ)

1: **if** $ARS.Verify(opk, R, M, \sigma) = \perp$
    then
2:     **return** $\perp$
3: $(ct, \pi_{sign}) \leftarrow \sigma$
4: $I \leftarrow Dec(osk, ct)$
5: $\pi_{open} \leftarrow NIZK.Prove((opk, ct, I), osk)$
6: **return** $\pi := (R_I, \pi_{open})$

Fig. 1. Generic construction of an accountable ring signature Π_{ARS} obtained from a hard instance generator (RelSetup, IGen), a public-key encryption algorithm (PKE.Setup, KeyGen, Enc, Dec) satisfying some suitable security and correctness properties, a NIZK with labels $\Pi_{NIZK,lbl}$ for R_{sig}, and a NIZK without labels Π_{NIZK} for R_{open}. The public parameter pp is provided to all algorithms where we may omit them for readability.

3.3 Tightly Secure Variant

Observe the only source of loose reduction in the previous section was in the unforgeability proof (see the full version of this paper), where we assume each building blocks, i.e., NIZK and PKE, are tightly reduced to concrete hardness assumptions. In this subsection, we present a modification of the construction in Fig. 1 to obtain a tight reduction in the unforgeability proof by using the Katz-Wang method [43]. The main difference is that we rely on a multi-proof online extractable NIZK proof system with labels for the following family of relations:

$$R_{sig}^{Tight} = \left\{ \left((pp, \{x_i^{(j)}\}_{(i,j)\in[N]\times[2]}, pk, ct), (I, b, w, r)\right) \, \middle| \, \begin{array}{l} (I, r) \in [N] \times \mathcal{R} \wedge \\ (x_I^{(b)}, w) \in R_{pp} \wedge \\ ct = Enc(pk, I; r) \end{array} \right\}$$

$$\tilde{R}_{sig}^{Tight} = \left\{ \left((pp, \{x_i^{(j)}\}_{(i,j)\in[N]\times[2]}, pk, ct), (I, b, w, r)\right) \, \middle| \, \begin{array}{l} (I, r) \in [N] \times \mathcal{R}' \wedge \\ (x_I^{(b)}, w) \in \tilde{R}_{pp} \wedge \\ ct = Enc(pk, I; r) \end{array} \right\} .$$

We show in Sect. 5.3 that we can obtain such a NIZK efficiently by slightly tweaking our NIZK for R_{sig}. The high level idea of how to use the Katz-Wang technique along with our NIZK for $R_{\text{sig}}^{\text{Tight}}$ is provided in the technical overview. Due to page limitation, we provide the full detail in the full version of this paper.

4   Group-Action-Based Hard Instance Generators and PKEs

In this section, we introduce group-action-based hard instance generators (HIGs) and group-action-based PKEs. These are classes of HIGs and PKEs, that derive their security from cryptographic group actions, and which have some specific internal structure. We define these concepts because, as we will see in Sects. 5 and 6, if we instantiate our generic accountable ring signature construction with a group-action-based HIG and a group-action-based PKE, then we can construct a very efficient multi-proof online extractable NIZK for the R_{sig} relation. We provide concrete instantiations of group-action-based HIGs and PKEs from lattices and isogenies in Sect. 7.

4.1   Group-Action-Based Hard Instance Generator

We consider a special class of hard instance generators naturally induced by cryptographic hard actions.

Definition 10 (Group-Action-based Hard Instance Generator). *A group-action-based hard instance generator, GA-HIG in short, is a pair of efficient algorithms* (RelSetup, IGen) *with the following properties:*

– *On input a security parameter λ,* RelSetup *outputs* $\mathsf{pp} = (G, S_1, S_2, \delta, X_0, \mathcal{X}, \star)$ *such that: G is an additive group whose elements can be represented uniquely, $S_1 \subseteq S_2$ are symmetric subsets of G, such that membership in S_1 and S_2 can be decided efficiently, and such that the group law can be computed efficiently for elements in $S_1 \cup S_2$. Moreover, the intersection $S_3 = \cap_{g \in S_1} g + S_2$ has cardinality $\delta |S_2|$ and membership of S_3 can be decided efficiently. $\star$ is an action $\star : G \times \mathcal{X} \to \mathcal{X}$ of G on a set $\mathcal{X}$ that contains the element X_0. $\star$ can be evaluated efficiently on elements of $S_1 \cup S_2$. These parameters describe an NP-relation $R_{\mathsf{pp}} = \{(X, s) \mid s \in S_1 : s \star X_0 = X\}$, and a relaxed NP-relation $\tilde{R}_{\mathsf{pp}} = \{(X, s) \mid s \in S_2 + S_3 : s \star X_0 = X\}.$*
– *On input* pp*,* IGen *samples an element s from S_1 and outputs $(s \star X_0, s) \in R_{\mathsf{pp}}.$*
– (RelSetup, IGen) *is a hard instance generator as defined in Sect. 3.*

4.2   Group-Action-Based PKE

We also consider group actions provided with a corresponding public-key encryption scheme, as specified in the following definition.

Definition 11 (Group-action-based PKE). *A* group-action-based public-key encryption scheme, GA-PKE *in short, is a public-key encryption scheme* $\Pi_{\mathsf{GA\text{-}PKE}} = (\mathsf{Setup}, \mathsf{KeyGen}, \mathsf{Enc}, \mathsf{Dec})$ *with the following properties:*

$\mathsf{Setup}(1^\lambda) \to \mathsf{pp}$: *On input a security parameter* 1^λ, *it returns the public parameter* $\mathsf{pp} = (G, G_\mathsf{M}, \mathcal{X}, S_1, S_2, \delta, D_\mathcal{X}, \star_\mathsf{M}, \mathcal{M})$ *(sometimes implicitly) used by the scheme. Here,* G, G_M *are additive groups,* S_1, S_2 *two symmetric subsets of* G, $\mathcal{X}$ *a finite set,* δ *a real number in* $[0, 1]$, $D_\mathcal{X}$ *a distribution over a set of group actions* $\star_\mathsf{pk} : G \times \mathcal{X} \to \mathcal{X}$ *and elements in* $\mathcal{X}$, $\star_\mathsf{M} : G_\mathsf{M} \times \mathcal{X} \to \mathcal{X}$ *a group action,* $\mathcal{M} \subseteq G_\mathsf{M}$ *a message space. For any polynomially large* $N \in \mathbb{N}$, *we assume that there exists a feasible and invertible embedding* τ *from the set of index* $[N]$ *into the message space* $\mathcal{M}$. *For simplicity, we will write* $\tau(i) \star_\mathcal{M} X$, $\mathsf{Enc}(\mathsf{pk}, \tau(i))$ *as* $i \star_\mathsf{M} X$, $\mathsf{Enc}(\mathsf{pk}, i)$ *respectively without causing confusion.*

$\mathsf{KeyGen}(\mathsf{pp}) \to (\mathsf{pk}, \mathsf{sk})$: *On input a public parameter* pp, *it returns a public key* pk *and a secret key* sk. *We assume* $\mathsf{pk} = (\star_\mathsf{pk}, X_\mathsf{pk})$ *to be drawn from* $D_\mathcal{X}$, *where* $\star_\mathsf{pk} : G \times \mathcal{X} \to \mathcal{X}$ *is a group action and* $X_\mathsf{pk} \in \mathcal{X}$, *and* $\mathsf{sk} \in G$. *We also assume* pk *includes* pp *w.l.o.g.*

$\mathsf{Enc}(\mathsf{pk}, \mathsf{M}; r) \to \mathsf{ct}$: *On input a public key* $\mathsf{pk} = (\star_\mathsf{pk}, X_\mathsf{pk})$ *and a message* $\mathsf{M} \in \mathcal{M}$, *it returns a ciphertext* ct. *We assume* ct *is generated as* $\mathsf{M} \star_\mathsf{M} (r \star_\mathsf{pk} X_\mathsf{pk}) \in \mathcal{X}$, *where the encryption randomness is sampled as* $r \xleftarrow{\$} S_1$.

$\mathsf{Dec}(\mathsf{sk}, \mathsf{ct}) \to \mathsf{M}$: *On input a secret key* sk *and a ciphertext* ct, *it (deterministically) returns a message* $\mathsf{M} \in \mathcal{M}$.

In addition, we assume the following properties hold for the group actions defined by pp.

1. *There exists a positive-valued polynomial* T *such that for all* $\lambda \in \mathbb{N}$, $\mathsf{pp} \in \mathsf{Setup}(1^\lambda)$, *and* $(\mathsf{pk}, \mathsf{sk}) \in \mathsf{KeyGen}(\mathsf{pp})$, *one can efficiently compute* $g \star_\mathsf{pk} X$ *for all* $g \in S_1 \cup S_2$ *and all* $X \in \mathcal{X}$ *in time at most* $T(\lambda)$, *sample uniformly from* S_1 *and* S_2, *and represent elements of* G *and* $\mathcal{X}$ *uniquely. It is also efficient to compute the action* $\star_\mathsf{M}$ *for every possible input.*

2. *The intersection* S_3 *of the sets* $S_2 + g$, *with* g *varying in* S_1, *is such that its cardinality is equal to* $\delta |S_2|$. *Furthermore, it is efficient to check whether an element* $g \in G$ *belongs to* S_3.

We further require a group-action-based PKE to satisfy standard correctness and decryption efficiency.

Definition 12 (Correctness and Decryption Efficiency). *We say a group-action-based* PKE $\Pi_{\mathsf{GA\text{-}PKE}}$ *is correct if for all* $\lambda \in \mathbb{N}$, *and for all but a negligible fraction of* $\mathsf{pp} \in \mathsf{Setup}(1^\lambda)$, *we have* $\mathsf{Dec}(\mathsf{sk}, \mathsf{Enc}(\mathsf{pk}, \mathsf{M})) = \mathsf{M}$ *for all* $(\mathsf{pk}, \mathsf{sk}) \in \mathsf{KeyGen}(\mathsf{pp})$ *and* $\mathsf{M} \in \mathcal{M}$. *Moreover, we require* Dec *to run in* $\mathsf{poly}(\lambda)$ *for a fixed polynomial function* poly *and for all possible inputs.*

As we show in Sect. 3.1, in order to construct an accountable ring signature, a group-action-based PKE is also required to be (multi-challenge) IND-CPA secure and $(\mathcal{R}', \mathcal{KR}')$-correct for some relaxed randomness set $\mathcal{R}'$ and some relaxed key relation $\mathcal{KR}'$ (Definition 9).

5   Sigma Protocol for a "Traceable" OR Relation

In this section, we present an efficient sigma protocol for the relation R_{sig} introduced in Sect. 3.1, using group-action-based HIG and a group-action-based PKE from the previous section. Recall this relation was used to define the multi-proof online extractable NIZK with labels Π_{NIZK}, which allowed an OR proof along with a proof of opening to a ciphertext. Looking ahead, in Sect. 6, we show that our sigma protocol can be turned into a multi-proof online extractable NIZK using the Fiat-Shamir transform. This is in contrast to the common application of Fiat-Shamir transform that only provides a proof of knowledge via the rewinding argument [34,54]. We note that we do not focus on the other NIZK for the relation R_{open} in Sect. 3.1 since they can be obtained easily from prior works.

We call the sigma protocol we present in this section as a *traceable* OR sigma protocol since it allows to trace the prover. This section is structured as follows. Firstly, we introduce a *base* traceable OR sigma protocol $\Pi_{\Sigma}^{\text{base}}$ for the relation R_{sig} with proof size $O(\log N)$ but with a binary challenge space. Secondly, we amplify the soundness of the sigma protocol by performing parallel repetitions. Here, instead of applying λ-parallel repetitions naively, we optimize it using three approaches developed in [7] to obtain our *main* traceable OR sigma protocol $\Pi_{\Sigma}^{\text{tOR}}$. Finally, we show a sigma protocol for the "tight" relation $R_{\text{sig}}^{\text{Tight}}$ introduced in Sect. 3.3.

5.1   From a Group-Action-Based HIG and PKE to Base Traceable or Sigma Protocol

In this section, we present a *base* OR sigma protocol for the relation R_{sig} with a binary challenge space from which the main OR sigma protocol will be deduced.

Parameters and Binary Relation. The sigma protocol is based on a group-action-based HIG and PKE. Let $\text{pp}_1 = (G, \mathcal{X}, S_1, S_2, \delta_x, \star, X_0)$ and $\text{pp}_2 = (\overline{G}, \overline{G}_T, \mathcal{Y}, \overline{S}_1, \overline{S}_2, \delta_y, D_y, \star_{\text{M}}, \mathcal{M})$ be public parameters in the image of RelSetup and PKE.Setup, respectively. Moreover, let $(\text{pk}, \text{sk}) \in \text{KeyGen}(\text{pp}_2)$. The relation R_{sig} in Sect. 3.1 can be equivalently rewritten as follows:

$$R_{\text{sig}} = \left\{ \left((\{X_i\}_{i \in [N]}, \text{pk}, \text{ct}), (I, s, r) \right) \;\middle|\; \begin{array}{c} (I, s, r) \in [N] \times S_1 \times \overline{S}_1 \wedge \\ X_I = s \star X_0 \wedge \text{ct} = \text{Enc}(\text{pk}, I; r) \end{array} \right\} .$$

Recall that by definition of GA-PKE (Definition 11), the ciphertext ct is restricted to the simple form $I \star_{\text{M}} (r \star_{\text{pk}} Y_{\text{pk}}) \in \mathcal{Y}$, where $r \in \overline{S}_1 \subseteq \overline{G}$.

Sigma Protocol for R_{sig}. We now sketch the base traceable OR sigma protocol $\Pi_{\Sigma}^{\text{base}}$. A prover with witness $(I, s, r) \in [N] \times S_1 \times \overline{S}_1$ first samples $(s', r') \xleftarrow{\$} S_2 \times \overline{S}_2$, and $(\{\text{bits}_i\}_{i \in [N]}) \leftarrow \{0,1\}^{\lambda N}$. Then, it computes commitments

$$\mathsf{C}_i = \mathcal{O}(\text{Com} \parallel s' \star X_i \parallel r' \star_{\text{pk}} (-i \star_{\text{M}} \text{ct}) \parallel \text{bits}_i) \quad \forall i \in [N],$$

and builds a Merkle tree with $(\mathsf{C}_1, \ldots, \mathsf{C}_N)$ as its leaves, obtaining root. Here, notice $r' \star_{\text{pk}} (-i \star_{\text{M}} \text{ct}) = r' \star_{\text{pk}} (-i + I) \star_{\text{M}} (r \star_{\text{pk}} Y_{\text{pk}})$ is simply $(r' + r) \star_{\text{pk}} Y_{\text{pk}}$

when $i = I$. Then, the prover sends com = root to the verifier as the commitment of the sigma protocol. The verifier, in turn, responds with a uniform challenge chall $\in \{0, 1\}$.

If the challenge bit chall is 0, then the prover sends (s', r') and the commitment randomness $\{\text{bits}_i\}_{i \in [N]}$. That is, all the randomness it generated in the first round. The verifier then can reconstruct the Merkle tree and verify that the root of the obtained tree is equal to root.

If the challenge bit chall is equal to 1, then the prover computes $s'' = s' + s$, $r'' = r' + r$. The prover aborts the protocol if $s'' \notin S_3$ or $r'' \notin \overline{S}_3$. The first event will occur with probability $(1 - \delta_x)$ and, similarly, the second event will occur with probability $(1 - \delta_y)$. Otherwise, the prover sends (r'', s'') together with the path connecting C_I to root in the Merkle tree, and the corresponding commitment randomness bits$_I$ to the verifier. The verifier computes $\widetilde{C}_I = \mathcal{O}(\text{Com} \parallel s'' \star X_0 \parallel r'' \star_{\text{pk}} Y_{\text{pk}} \parallel \text{bits}_I)$ and uses the received path to reconstruct $\widetilde{\text{root}}$ of the Merkle tree. The verifier checks whether $\widetilde{\text{root}} = \text{root}$.

To reduce the communication cost, a pseudorandom number generator (PRG) Expand can be run over a uniform seed seed $\in \{0, 1\}^\lambda$ to produce the group elements s', r' and all commitment randomness values $\text{bits}_1, \ldots, \text{bits}_N$ (part of the response for chall $= 0$). As a consequence, if the challenge bit is 0, the prover responds with seed so that the verifier can generate $(s', r', \text{bits}_1, \cdots, \text{bits}_N)$ with the PRG Expand. The response corresponding to the challenge bit chall $= 1$ remains unchanged. We instantiate the PRG by a random oracle $\mathcal{O}(\text{Expand} \parallel \cdot)$. Looking ahead, using a PRG not only provides efficiency, but it proves to be essential when proving multi-proof online extractability when compiled into a NIZK. Roughly, the seed binds the cheating prover from using arbitrary $(s', r', \text{bits}_1, \cdots, \text{bits}_N)$ and the random oracle allows for efficient extraction. Finally, we instantiate the collision-resistant hash function $\mathcal{H}_{\text{Coll}}(\cdot)$ used in our Merkle tree by a random oracle $\mathcal{O}(\text{Coll} \parallel \cdot)$.

A formal description of Π_Σ^{base} is provided in Fig. 2. The full detail on its correctness and security is provided in the full version of this paper.

5.2 From Base to Main Traceable or Sigma Protocol

In this section, we expand the challenge space of Π_Σ^{base} to make the soundness error negligibly small. Such expansion is straightforward if we run the OR sigma protocol in parallel λ-times. However, we show how to do much better by incorporating the three optimizations developed in [7] explained in the technical overview. As the way we apply these optimizations follows [7] closely, we leave the details of our main traceable OR sigma protocol, denoted by Π_Σ^{tOR}, to the full version of this paper.

5.3 Base Sigma Protocol for the "Tight" Relation $R_{\text{sig}}^{\text{Tight}}$

In this section, we show how to slightly tweak our base sigma protocol for the relation R_{sig} to obtain a sigma protocol for the "tight" relation $R_{\text{sig}}^{\text{Tight}}$ (see Sect. 3.3).

---

round 1: $P_1'^{\mathcal{O}}((\{X_i\}_{i\in[N]}, \mathsf{pk}, \mathsf{ct}), (I, s, r))$

1: $\mathsf{seed} \xleftarrow{\$} \{0,1\}^\lambda$
2: $(s', r', \mathsf{bits}_1, \cdots, \mathsf{bits}_N) \leftarrow \mathcal{O}(\mathsf{Expand} \parallel \mathsf{seed})$ ▷ Sample $(s', r') \in S_2 \times \overline{S}_2$ and
   $\mathsf{bits} \in \{0,1\}^\lambda$
3: **for** i from 1 to N **do**
4:     $(T_i, \mathsf{ct}_i) \leftarrow (s' \star X_i, r' \star_{\mathsf{pk}} (-i \star_{\mathsf{M}} \mathsf{ct}))$
5:     $\mathsf{C}_i \leftarrow \mathcal{O}(\mathsf{Com} \parallel T_i \parallel \mathsf{ct}_i \parallel \mathsf{bits}_i)$ ▷ Create commitments $\mathsf{C}_i \in \{0,1\}^{2\lambda}$
6: $(\mathsf{root}, \mathsf{tree}) \leftarrow \mathsf{MerkleTree}(\mathsf{C}_1, \cdots, \mathsf{C}_N)$
7: Prover sends $\mathsf{com} \leftarrow \mathsf{root}$ to Verifier.

round 2: $V_1'(\mathsf{com})$

1: $c \xleftarrow{\$} \{0,1\}$
2: Verifier sends $\mathsf{chall} \leftarrow c$ to Prover.

round 3: $P_2'((I, s, r), \mathsf{chall})$

1: $c \leftarrow \mathsf{chall}$
2: **if** $c = 1$ **then**
3:     $(s'', r'') \leftarrow (s' + s, r' + r)$
4:     **if** $s'' \notin S_3$ or $r'' \notin \overline{S}_3$ **then**
5:         P aborts the protocol.
6:     $\mathsf{path} \leftarrow \mathsf{getMerklePath}(\mathsf{tree}, I)$
7:     $\mathsf{resp} \leftarrow (s'', r'', \mathsf{path}, \mathsf{bits}_I)$
8: **else**
9:     $\mathsf{resp} \leftarrow \mathsf{seed}$
10: Prover sends resp to Verifier

Verification: $V_2'^{\mathcal{O}}(\mathsf{com}, \mathsf{chall}, \mathsf{resp})$

1: $(\mathsf{root}, c) \leftarrow (\mathsf{com}, \mathsf{chall})$
2: **if** $c = 1$ **then**
3:     $(s'', r'', \mathsf{path}, \mathsf{bits}) \leftarrow \mathsf{resp}$
4:     **if** $s'' \notin S_3$ or $r'' \notin \overline{S}_3$ **then**
5:         V outputs reject.
6:     $(\widetilde{T}, \widetilde{\mathsf{ct}}) \leftarrow (s'' \star X_0, r'' \star_{\mathsf{pk}} Y_{\mathsf{pk}})$
7:     $\widetilde{\mathsf{C}} \leftarrow \mathcal{O}(\mathsf{Com} \parallel \widetilde{T} \parallel \widetilde{\mathsf{ct}} \parallel \mathsf{bits})$
8:     $\widetilde{\mathsf{root}} \leftarrow \mathsf{ReconstructRoot}(\widetilde{\mathsf{C}}, \mathsf{path})$
9:     Verifier accepts only if $\widetilde{\mathsf{root}} = \mathsf{root}$.
10: **else**
11:     Repeat **round 1** with $\mathsf{seed} \leftarrow \mathsf{resp}$.
12:     Output accept if the computation
    results in root, and reject otherwise.

Fig. 2. Construction of the base traceable OR sigma protocol $\Pi_\Sigma^{\mathsf{base}} = (P' = (P_1', P_2'), V' = (V_1', V_2'))$ for the relation R_{sig}. Informally, $O(\mathsf{Expand}\|\cdot)$ and $O(\mathsf{Com}\|\cdot)$ are a PRG and a commitment scheme instantiated by the random oracle, respectively.

This can then be used to construct the desired NIZK for $R_{\mathsf{sig}}^{\mathsf{Tight}}$ required for our tightly secure accountable ring signature construction (see the full version of this paper).

As explained in the technical overview, we can use the sigma protocol for R_{sig} along with the sequential OR-proof [36] to construct a sigma protocol for the "tight" relation $R_{\mathsf{sig}}^{\mathsf{Tight}}$. Unfortunately, this approach requires to double the proof size. Instead, we present a small tweak to our sigma protocol for R_{sig} to directly support statements in $R_{\mathsf{sig}}^{\mathsf{Tight}}$. Concretely, we use the same Merkle tree to commit to the $2N$ instances $\{X_i^{(j)}\}_{(i,j)\in[N]\times[2]}$ and for each $X_i^{(1)}$ and $X_i^{(2)}$, we encrypt the *same* index i. The main observation is that when the prover opens to the challenge bit 1 (which is the only case that depends on the witness), the path does no leak which $X_i^{(1)}$ and $X_i^{(2)}$ it opened to, and hence hides $b \in [2]$.

Notice the only increase in the size of the response is due to the path. Since the accumulated commitment only grows from N to $2N$, the overhead in the size of the path is merely 2λ bits. By using the unbalanced challenge space $C_{M,K}$ for the optimized parallel repetition, which consists of M-bit strings of Hamming weight K, the additional cost is only $2K\lambda$ where we typically set K to be a small constant (e.g., $K \leq 20$ for our concrete instantiation). This is much more efficient than the generic approach that doubles the proof size. More details are provided in the full version of this paper.

6   Multi-proof Online Extractable NIZK from Sigma Protocol Π_Σ^{tOR}

In this section, we show that applying the Fiat-Shamir transform to our traceable OR sigma protocol Π_Σ^{tOR} from the previous section results in a multi-proof online extractable NIZK with labels $\Pi_{\text{NIZK,lbl}}$. The construction of our $\Pi_{\text{NIZK,lbl}}$ for the relation R_{sig} is provide in Fig. 3.[8] We assume the output of $\mathcal{O}(\text{FS} \| \cdot)$ is an M-bit string of Hamming weight K, i.e., the image is the challenge set $C_{M,K}$.

$\text{Prove}^{\mathcal{O}}(\text{lbl}, (\{X_i\}_{i\in[N]}, \text{pk}, \text{ct}), (I, s_I, r))$

1: $\text{resp} := \bot$
2: **while** $\text{resp} = \bot$ **do**
3:     $\text{com} \leftarrow P_1^{\mathcal{O}}((\{X_i\}_{i\in[N]}, \text{pk}, \text{ct}), (I, s_I, r))$
4:     $\text{chall} \leftarrow \mathcal{O}(\text{FS} \| \text{lbl} \| (\{X_i\}_{i\in[N]}, \text{pk}, \text{ct}) \| \text{com})$
5:     $\text{resp} \leftarrow P_2^{\mathcal{O}}((I, s_I, r), \text{chall})$
6: **return** $\pi \leftarrow (\text{com}, \text{chall}, \text{resp})$

$\text{Verify}^{\mathcal{O}}(\text{lbl}, (\{X_i\}_{i\in[N]}, \text{pk}, \text{ct}), \pi)$

1: $(\text{com}, \text{chall}, \text{resp}) \leftarrow \pi$
2: **if** $\text{accept} \leftarrow V_2^{\mathcal{O}}(\text{com}, \text{chall}, \text{resp}) \wedge \text{chall} = \mathcal{O}(\text{FS} \| \text{lbl} \| (\{X_i\}_{i\in[N]}, \text{pk}, \text{ct}) \| \text{com})$
   then
3:     **return** $\top$
4: **else**
5:     **return** $\bot$

Fig. 3. A multi-proof online extractable NIZK with labels $\Pi_{\text{NIZK,lbl}}$ for the relation R_{sig} obtained by applying the Fiat-Shamir transform to the traceable OR sigma protocol $\Pi_\Sigma^{\text{tOR}} = (P = (P_1, P_2), V = (V_1, V_2))$ defined in the full version of this paper.

Correctness of $\Pi_{\text{NIZK,lbl}}$ for the relation R_{sig} follows directly from the correctness of the underlying traceable OR sigma protocol Π_Σ^{tOR}. We show in the full version of this paper hat $\Pi_{\text{NIZK,lbl}}$ is multi-proof online extractable and zero-knowledge. We highlight that while we show special soundness for Π_Σ^{tOR} with

---

[8] An astute reader may notice that the prover is only *expected* polynomial time. We can always assign an upper bound on the runtime of the prover, but did not do so for better readability. In practice, for concrete choices of the parameter, the number of repetition never exceeds, say 10.

respect to the relaxed relation $\tilde{R}'_{\text{sig}}$ (see the full version), $\Pi_{\text{NIZK,lbl}}$ is multi-proof online extractable with respect to the relaxed relation $\tilde{R}_{\text{sig}}$ originally considered in Sect. 3.1 for the generic construction of accountable ring signature. At a high level, we upper bound the probability that a cheating prover finds a collision in the random oracle, which was the only difference between $\tilde{R}_{\text{sig}}$ and $\tilde{R}'_{\text{sig}}$. This subtle difference makes the resulting NIZK more handy to use as a building block, since we can ignore the edge case where the extractor accidentally extracts a collision in the random oracle. Due to page limitation, the proof of zero-knowledge is provided in the full version of the paper. Below, we provide the proof of the multi-proof online extractability. Formally, we have the following.

Theorem 13. *The* NIZK *with labels* $\Pi_{\text{NIZK,lbl}}$ *in Fig. 3 is multi-proof online extractable for the family of relations* R_{sig} *and* $\tilde{R}_{\text{sig}}$ *considered in Sect. 3.1, where* R_{sig} *was formally redefined using notations related to group actions in Sect. 5.1 and* $\tilde{R}_{\text{sig}}$ *is formally redefined as follows:*

$$\tilde{R}_{\text{sig}} = \left\{ ((\{X_i\}_{i\in[N]}, \text{pk}, \text{ct}), \text{W}) \;\middle|\; \begin{array}{c} \text{W} = (I, s, r) \in [N] \times (S_2 + S_3) \times (\overline{S}_2 + \overline{S}_3) \\ \wedge\ X_I = s \star X_0 \wedge \text{ct} = \text{Enc}(\text{pk}, I; r) \end{array} \right\}.$$

More precisely, for any (possibly computationally-unbounded) adversary $\mathcal{A}$ *making at most* Q *queries to the random oracle and* T *queries to the extract oracle, we have*

$$\text{Adv}^{\text{OE}}_{\Pi_{\text{NIZK,lbl}}}(\mathcal{A}) \leq T \cdot \left(Q^2/2^{2\lambda-2} + (M \cdot Q)/2^\lambda + 1/|C_{M,K}| \right),$$

where $C_{M,K}$ *is the challenge space (or equivalently the output space of* $\mathcal{O}(\text{FS} \| \cdot)$*).*

Proof. We begin the proof by providing the description of the online extractor OnlineExtract. Below, it is given as input $(\text{lbl}, \text{X}, \pi, L_{\mathcal{O}})$, where π is guaranteed to be valid by definition.

1. It parses $(\{X_i\}_{i\in[N]}, \text{pk}, \text{ct}) \leftarrow \text{X}$, $(\overline{\text{com}}, \overline{\text{chall}}, \overline{\text{resp}}) \leftarrow \pi$, $((\text{salt}, \text{com}_1, \cdots, \text{com}_M), \mathbf{c} = (c_1, \cdots, c_M)) \leftarrow (\overline{\text{com}}, \overline{\text{chall}})$, $(\text{seeds}_{\text{internal}}, \{\text{resp}_j\}_{j\ \text{s.t.}\ c_j=1}) \leftarrow \overline{\text{resp}}$, and $\text{root}_j \leftarrow \text{com}_j$ for $j \in [M]$.[9]
2. For $j \in [M]$ such that $c_j = 1$, it proceeds as follows:
   (a) It parses $(s''_j, r''_j, \text{path}_j) \leftarrow \text{resp}_j$.
   (b) For every $((\text{salt} \| j \| \text{Expand} \| \text{seed}), (s', r', \text{bits}_1, \cdots, \text{bits}_N)) \in L_{\mathcal{O}}$, where $\text{salt} \| j \| \text{Expand}$ is fixed, it proceeds as follows:
      i. It sets $(s, r) = (s''_j - s', r''_j - r')$ and checks if $(s, r) \in (S_2 + S_3) \times (\overline{S}_2 + \overline{S}_3)$.
      ii. It then checks if there exists $I \in [N]$ such that $X_I = s \star X_0$ and $\text{ct} = \text{Enc}(\text{pk}, I; r)$.
      iii. If all the check above passes, it returns $\text{W} = (I, s, r)$.
3. If it finds no witness W of the above form, then it returns $\text{W} = \bot$.

---

[9] Throughout the proof, we use overlines for $(\overline{\text{com}}, \overline{\text{chall}}, \overline{\text{resp}})$ to indicate that it is a transcript of of Π^{tOR}_Σ. We use resp_i without overlines to indicate elements of $\overline{\text{resp}}$.

We analyze the probability of $\mathcal{A}$ winning the multi-proof online extractability game with the above online extractor OnlineExtract. Below, P' and V' are the prover and verifier of the base traceable OR sigma protocol $\Pi_\Sigma^{\mathsf{base}}$ in Fig. 2.

- We say a tuple $\mathsf{input}_{\mathsf{base}} = (\mathsf{X}, \mathsf{salt}, j, \mathsf{com}, \mathsf{chall}, \mathsf{resp})$ is valid if the following properties hold:
  - $\mathsf{chall} = 1$;
  - $V_2'^{\mathcal{O}(\mathsf{salt}\|j\|\cdot)}(\mathsf{com}, \mathsf{chall}, \mathsf{resp})$ outputs accept (i.e., it is a valid transcript for $\Pi_\Sigma^{\mathsf{base}}$ with challenge 1);
  - there exists $(\mathsf{seed}, s', r', \mathsf{bits}_1, \cdots, \mathsf{bits}_N)$ such that $((\mathsf{salt} \| j \| \mathsf{Expand} \| \mathsf{seed}), (s', r', \mathsf{bits}_1, \cdots, \mathsf{bits}_N)) \in L_{\mathcal{O}}$, and if we execute $P_1'^{\mathcal{O}(\mathsf{salt}\|j\|\cdot)}$ with randomness seed, it produces com. Here, we use the fact that $P_1'^{\mathcal{O}(\mathsf{salt}\|j\|\cdot)}$ can be executed without the witness. By correctness of $\Pi_\Sigma^{\mathsf{base}}$, this implies that $(\mathsf{com}, 0, \mathsf{seed})$ is a valid transcript.
- We say a tuple $\mathsf{input}_{\mathsf{base}} = (\mathsf{X}, \mathsf{salt}, j, \mathsf{com}, \mathsf{chall}, \mathsf{resp})$ is invalid if $\mathsf{chall} = 1$, $V_2'^{\mathcal{O}(\mathsf{salt}\|j\|\cdot)}(\mathsf{com}, \mathsf{chall}, \mathsf{resp})$ outputs accept, but it is not valid.

Observe that if $\mathsf{input}_{\mathsf{base}}$ is valid, then the online extractor can recover a valid transcript $(\mathsf{com}, 0, \mathsf{seed})$ from $\mathsf{input}_{\mathsf{base}}$. Then, it can (informally) extract a witness by combining it with $(\mathsf{com}, 1, \mathsf{resp})$ and using the extractor from $\Pi_\Sigma^{\mathsf{base}}$ constructed in the full version of this paper. In contrast, if $\mathsf{input}_{\mathsf{base}}$ is invalid, then intuitively, no adversary would be able to prepare a valid response $\mathsf{resp} = \mathsf{seed}$ for the challenge $\mathsf{chall} = 0$ since $L_{\mathcal{O}}$ (i.e., the random oracle query the adversary makes) does not contain a valid response. However, to make this claim formal, we need to also take into account the fact that the adversary may learn non-trivial information about $\mathsf{resp} = \mathsf{seed}$ via the proof output by the prove query. That is, when the challenger runs $P^{\mathcal{O}}$, the adversary may learn non-trivial input/output pairs without directly querying the random oracle itself. In this case, even though no useful information is stored in $L_{\mathcal{O}}$, the adversary may still be able to forge a proof.

We formally show in Lemma 14 below that if an adversary $\mathcal{A}$ submits an extract query on a valid input $(\mathsf{lbl}, \mathsf{X}, \pi)$, then a valid $\mathsf{input}_{\mathsf{base}}$ must be included in π (i.e., it cannot consist of $\mathsf{input}_{\mathsf{base}}$ that are all invalid). This allows us to argue that the online extractor will be able to recover two valid transcripts with overwhelming probability, which then further allows the online extractor to extract the witness by running the extractor for the special soundness of the base traceable OR sigma protocol $\Pi_\Sigma^{\mathsf{base}}$. Due to page limitation, the proof is provide in the full version of this paper.

Lemma 14. *Assume an adversary $\mathcal{A}$ submits a total of T extract queries of the form $\{(\mathsf{lbl}_k, \mathsf{X}_k, \pi_k)\}_{k \in [T]}$, where every π_k is a valid proof including the same salt and satisfies $(\mathsf{lbl}_k, \mathsf{X}_k, \pi_k) \notin L_P$. Let $\{(\mathsf{com}_{k,j}, \mathsf{chall}_{k,j}, \mathsf{resp}_{k,j})\}_{j \in [M]}$ be the transcript of the base traceable OR sigma protocol $\Pi_\Sigma^{\mathsf{base}}$ that the verification algorithm reconstructs when verifying π_k (see the full version of the paper). Then, with probability at least $1 - T \cdot \left(Q_{\mathsf{salt}}/2^{2\lambda-1} + (M \cdot Q_{\mathsf{salt}})/2^\lambda + 1/|C_{M,K}|\right)$, for all $k \in T$ there exists at least one $j \in [M]$ such that $\mathsf{input}_{\mathsf{base}} = (\mathsf{X}_k, \mathsf{salt}, j, \mathsf{com}_{k,j}, \mathsf{chall}_{k,j} = 1, \mathsf{resp}_{k,j})$ is valid.*

We are now prepared to analyze the probability that $\mathcal{A}$ wins the multi-proof online extractability game with the aforementioned online extractor OnlineExtract. By Lemma 14, if $\mathcal{A}$ makes at most T extract queries, then by a simple union bound and using the inequality $\sum_i Q_{\mathsf{salt}_i} \leq Q$, with probability at least $1 - T \cdot \left((2Q)/2^{2\lambda} + (M \cdot Q)/2^\lambda + 1/|C_{M,K}| \right)$, all the input$_{\mathsf{base}}$ included in the queried proof are valid. Then, by the definition of valid and the description of OnlineExtract, OnlineExtract is able to extract two valid transcripts for all T proofs queried by $\mathcal{A}$. As shown in the full version of the paper, OnlineExtract either succeeds in extracting a witness $\mathsf{W} = (I, s, r) \in [N] \times (S_2 + S_3) \times (\overline{S}_2 + \overline{S}_3)$ or a witness that consists of a collision in $\mathcal{O}(\mathsf{salt} \| j \| \mathsf{Coll} \| \cdot)$ or $\mathcal{O}(\mathsf{salt} \| j \| \mathsf{Com} \| \cdot)$ for some $j \in [M]$. Hence, with all but probability $Q^2/2^{2\lambda}$, OnlineExtract succeeds in extracting a witness $\mathsf{W} = (I, s, r)$ as desired, conditioned on all the input$_{\mathsf{base}}$ included in the queried proof are valid. Collecting the bounds, we arrive at our statement.

7   Instantiations

We instantiate the building blocks required for our generic construction of an accountable ring signature scheme presented in Sect. 3 via isogenies based on CSIDH group action and lattices. Specifically, we instantiate a group-action-based HIG and PKE, and the corresponding NIZKs for the relations R_{sig} and R_{open} from the CSIDH group action and the MLWE group action. We use well-known PKEs based on isogenies and lattices as the basis for the group-action-based PKE. Due to page limitation, the details are provided in the full version of this paper.

We finish by providing details on how we arrive at the concrete parameters presented in Table 1. For our isogeny based instantiation, we chose an HIG and a PKE based on the CSIDH-512 group action. The structure of this class group has been computed, which allows for more efficient proofs. We chose the challenge space as string of length $M = 855$ with Hamming weight $K = 19$. Most of the signature is independent of N, and contains a fixed number of curves and class group elements as well as some overhead from the generic construction such as a hash value, the internal nodes in the seed tree, and commitment randomness to open the commitments. The only reason the signature size increases with N is that the signature contains a fixed amount of paths in a Merkle tree of depth $\log_2 N$. This makes for a very mild dependence on N.

For the lattice based instantiations, we use $M = 1749, K = 16$. Our HIG is based on the NIST security level 2 parameter set from the (Round 3) NIST submission Dilithium. Our PKE uses the Lindner-Peikert framework, where we are forced to use MLWE parameters with a large modulus ($q \approx 2^{49}$) to achieve the $(\mathcal{R}', \mathcal{KR}')$-correctness requirement. For the instantiation without manager accountability, we only need $(\mathcal{R}', \mathcal{KR}')$-correctness which allows us to use smaller parameters ($q \approx 2^{30}$). We use an optimization due to Bai and Galbraith to reduce the size of the proofs (and therefore the size of the signature). Similar to the isogeny instantiation, the signature size depends very mildly on N because N

only affects the length of some paths in the signature. For precise parameters we refer to the full version of this paper. Finally, we can use Sect. 5.3 to obtain a tightly secure scheme. Since $K = 16$, the overhead compared to the non-tight scheme is a mere 512B.

Acknowledgements. Yi-Fu Lai was supported by the Ministry for Business, Innovation and Employment in New Zealand. Shuichi Katsumata was supported by JST CREST Grant Number JPMJCR19F6, Japan. This work was supported by CyberSecurity Research Flanders with reference number VR20192203, and in part by the Research Council KU Leuven grant C14/18/067 on Cryptanalysis of post-quantum cryptography. Ward Beullens is funded by FWO Junior Postdoc- toral Fellowship 1S95620N.

References

1. Abe, M., Ohkubo, M., Suzuki, K.: 1-out-of-n signatures from a variety of keys. In: Zheng, Y. (ed.) ASIACRYPT 2002. LNCS, vol. 2501, pp. 415–432. Springer, Heidelberg (2002). https://doi.org/10.1007/3-540-36178-2_26

2. Attema, T., Lyubashevsky, V., Seiler, G.: Practical product proofs for lattice commitments. In: Micciancio, D., Ristenpart, T. (eds.) CRYPTO 2020. LNCS, vol. 12171, pp. 470–499. Springer, Cham (2020). https://doi.org/10.1007/978-3-030-56880-1_17

3. Backes, M., Hanzlik, L., Schneider-Bensch, J.: Membership privacy for fully dynamic group signatures. In: ACM CCS 2019, pp. 2181–2198 (2019)

4. Bellare, M., Micciancio, D., Warinschi, B.: Foundations of group signatures: formal definitions, simplified requirements, and a construction based on general assumptions. In: Biham, E. (ed.) EUROCRYPT 2003. LNCS, vol. 2656, pp. 614–629. Springer, Heidelberg (2003). https://doi.org/10.1007/3-540-39200-9_38

5. Bellare, M., Shi, H., Zhang, C.: Foundations of group signatures: the case of dynamic groups. In: Menezes, A. (ed.) CT-RSA 2005. LNCS, vol. 3376, pp. 136–153. Springer, Heidelberg (2005). https://doi.org/10.1007/978-3-540-30574-3_11

6. Bernhard, D., Fischlin, M., Warinschi, B.: Adaptive proofs of knowledge in the random oracle model. In: Katz, J. (ed.) PKC 2015. LNCS, vol. 9020, pp. 629–649. Springer, Heidelberg (2015). https://doi.org/10.1007/978-3-662-46447-2_28

7. Beullens, W., Katsumata, S., Pintore, F.: Calamari and Falafl: logarithmic (linkable) ring signatures from isogenies and lattices. In: Moriai, S., Wang, H. (eds.) ASIACRYPT 2020. LNCS, vol. 12492, pp. 464–492. Springer, Cham (2020). https://doi.org/10.1007/978-3-030-64834-3_16

8. Beullens, W., Kleinjung, T., Vercauteren, F.: CSI-FiSh: efficient isogeny based signatures through class group computations. In: Galbraith, S.D., Moriai, S. (eds.) ASIACRYPT 2019. LNCS, vol. 11921, pp. 227–247. Springer, Cham (2019). https://doi.org/10.1007/978-3-030-34578-5_9

9. Bichsel, P., Camenisch, J., Neven, G., Smart, N.P., Warinschi, B.: Get shorty via group signatures without encryption. In: Garay, J.A., De Prisco, R. (eds.) SCN 2010. LNCS, vol. 6280, pp. 381–398. Springer, Heidelberg (2010). https://doi.org/10.1007/978-3-642-15317-4_24

10. Boneh, D., Boyen, X., Shacham, H.: Short group signatures. In: Franklin, M. (ed.) CRYPTO 2004. LNCS, vol. 3152, pp. 41–55. Springer, Heidelberg (2004). https://doi.org/10.1007/978-3-540-28628-8_3

11. Bootle, J., Cerulli, A., Chaidos, P., Ghadafi, E., Groth, J.: Foundations of fully dynamic group signatures. In: Manulis, M., Sadeghi, A.-R., Schneider, S. (eds.) ACNS 2016. LNCS, vol. 9696, pp. 117–136. Springer, Cham (2016). https://doi.org/10.1007/978-3-319-39555-5_7

12. Bootle, J., Cerulli, A., Chaidos, P., Ghadafi, E., Groth, J., Petit, C.: Short accountable ring signatures based on DDH. In: Pernul, G., Ryan, P.Y.A., Weippl, E. (eds.) ESORICS 2015. LNCS, vol. 9326, pp. 243–265. Springer, Cham (2015). https://doi.org/10.1007/978-3-319-24174-6_13

13. Bootle, J., Lyubashevsky, V., Seiler, G.: Algebraic techniques for short(er) exact lattice-based zero-knowledge proofs. In: Boldyreva, A., Micciancio, D. (eds.) CRYPTO 2019. LNCS, vol. 11692, pp. 176–202. Springer, Cham (2019). https://doi.org/10.1007/978-3-030-26948-7_7

14. Boschini, C., Camenisch, J., Neven, G.: Floppy-sized group signatures from lattices. In: Preneel, B., Vercauteren, F. (eds.) ACNS 2018. LNCS, vol. 10892, pp. 163–182. Springer, Cham (2018). https://doi.org/10.1007/978-3-319-93387-0_9

15. Brickell, E.F., Camenisch, J., Chen, L.: Direct anonymous attestation. In: ACM CCS 2004, pp. 132–145 (2004)

16. Brickell, E., Li, J.: Enhanced privacy ID: a direct anonymous attestation scheme with enhanced revocation capabilities. In: Proceedings of the 2007 ACM Workshop on Privacy in Electronic Society, pp. 21–30 (2007)

17. Camenisch, J.: Efficient and generalized group signatures. In: Fumy, W. (ed.) EUROCRYPT 1997. LNCS, vol. 1233, pp. 465–479. Springer, Heidelberg (1997). https://doi.org/10.1007/3-540-69053-0_32

18. Camenisch, J., Damgård, I.: Verifiable encryption, group encryption, and their applications to separable group signatures and signature sharing schemes. In: Okamoto, T. (ed.) ASIACRYPT 2000. LNCS, vol. 1976, pp. 331–345. Springer, Heidelberg (2000). https://doi.org/10.1007/3-540-44448-3_25

19. Camenisch, J., Shoup, V.: Practical verifiable encryption and decryption of discrete logarithms. In: Boneh, D. (ed.) CRYPTO 2003. LNCS, vol. 2729, pp. 126–144. Springer, Heidelberg (2003). https://doi.org/10.1007/978-3-540-45146-4_8

20. Castryck, W., Lange, T., Martindale, C., Panny, L., Renes, J.: CSIDH: an efficient post-quantum commutative group action. In: Peyrin, T., Galbraith, S. (eds.) ASIACRYPT 2018. LNCS, vol. 11274, pp. 395–427. Springer, Cham (2018). https://doi.org/10.1007/978-3-030-03332-3_15

21. Chase, M., Lysyanskaya, A.: On signatures of knowledge. In: Dwork, C. (ed.) CRYPTO 2006. LNCS, vol. 4117, pp. 78–96. Springer, Heidelberg (2006). https://doi.org/10.1007/11818175_5

22. Chaum, D., van Heyst, E.: Group signatures. In: Davies, D.W. (ed.) EUROCRYPT 1991. LNCS, vol. 547, pp. 257–265. Springer, Heidelberg (1991). https://doi.org/10.1007/3-540-46416-6_22

23. Clarisse, R., Sanders, O.: Group signature without random oracles from randomizable signatures. In: Nguyen, K., Wu, W., Lam, K.Y., Wang, H. (eds.) ProvSec 2020. LNCS, vol. 12505, pp. 3–23. Springer, Cham (2020). https://doi.org/10.1007/978-3-030-62576-4_1

24. Cramer, R., Shoup, V.: A practical public key cryptosystem provably secure against adaptive chosen ciphertext attack. In: Krawczyk, H. (ed.) CRYPTO 1998. LNCS, vol. 1462, pp. 13–25. Springer, Heidelberg (1998). https://doi.org/10.1007/BFb0055717

25. del Pino, R., Lyubashevsky, V., Seiler, G.: Lattice-based group signatures and zero-knowledge proofs of automorphism stability. In: ACM CCS 2018, pp. 574–591 (2018)

26. Delerablée, C., Pointcheval, D.: Dynamic fully anonymous short group signatures. In: Nguyen, P.Q. (ed.) VIETCRYPT 2006. LNCS, vol. 4341, pp. 193–210. Springer, Heidelberg (2006). https://doi.org/10.1007/11958239_13

27. Derler, D., Slamanig, D.: Highly-efficient fully-anonymous dynamic group signatures. In: ASIACCS 2018, pp. 551–565 (2018)

28. El Kaafarani, A., Katsumata, S., Pintore, F.: Lossy CSI-FiSh: efficient signature scheme with tight reduction to decisional CSIDH-512. In: Kiayias, A., Kohlweiss, M., Wallden, P., Zikas, V. (eds.) PKC 2020. LNCS, vol. 12111, pp. 157–186. Springer, Cham (2020). https://doi.org/10.1007/978-3-030-45388-6_6

29. Esgin, M.F., Nguyen, N.K., Seiler, G.: Practical exact proofs from lattices: new techniques to exploit fully-splitting rings. In: Moriai, S., Wang, H. (eds.) ASIACRYPT 2020. LNCS, vol. 12492, pp. 259–288. Springer, Cham (2020). https://doi.org/10.1007/978-3-030-64834-3_9

30. Esgin, M.F., Steinfeld, R., Liu, J.K., Liu, D.: Lattice-based zero-knowledge proofs: new techniques for shorter and faster constructions and applications. In: Boldyreva, A., Micciancio, D. (eds.) CRYPTO 2019. LNCS, vol. 11692, pp. 115–146. Springer, Cham (2019). https://doi.org/10.1007/978-3-030-26948-7_5

31. Esgin, M.F., Steinfeld, R., Zhao, R.K.: Matrict+: more efficient post-quantum private blockchain payments. Cryptology ePrint Archive, Report 2021/545

32. Esgin, M.F., Zhao, R.K., Steinfeld, R., Liu, J.K., Liu, D.: MatRiCT: efficient, scalable and post-quantum blockchain confidential transactions protocol. In: ACM CCS 2019, pp. 567–584 (2019)

33. Ezerman, M.F., Lee, H.T., Ling, S., Nguyen, K., Wang, H.: A provably secure group signature scheme from code-based assumptions. In: Iwata, T., Cheon, J.H. (eds.) ASIACRYPT 2015. LNCS, vol. 9452, pp. 260–285. Springer, Heidelberg (2015). https://doi.org/10.1007/978-3-662-48797-6_12

34. Fiat, A., Shamir, A.: How to prove yourself: practical solutions to identification and signature problems. In: Odlyzko, A.M. (ed.) CRYPTO 1986. LNCS, vol. 263, pp. 186–194. Springer, Heidelberg (1987). https://doi.org/10.1007/3-540-47721-7_12

35. Fischlin, M.: Communication-efficient non-interactive proofs of knowledge with online extractors. In: Shoup, V. (ed.) CRYPTO 2005. LNCS, vol. 3621, pp. 152–168. Springer, Heidelberg (2005). https://doi.org/10.1007/11535218_10

36. Fischlin, M., Harasser, P., Janson, C.: Signatures from sequential-OR proofs. In: Canteaut, A., Ishai, Y. (eds.) EUROCRYPT 2020. LNCS, vol. 12107, pp. 212–244. Springer, Cham (2020). https://doi.org/10.1007/978-3-030-45727-3_8

37. Fujisaki, E., Okamoto, T.: Secure integration of asymmetric and symmetric encryption schemes. In: Wiener, M. (ed.) CRYPTO 1999. LNCS, vol. 1666, pp. 537–554. Springer, Heidelberg (1999). https://doi.org/10.1007/3-540-48405-1_34

38. Furukawa, J., Imai, H.: An efficient group signature scheme from bilinear maps. IEICE Trans. Fundam. Electron. Commun. Comput. Sci. 89(5), 1328–1338 (2006)

39. Gordon, S.D., Katz, J., Vaikuntanathan, V.: A group signature scheme from lattice assumptions. In: Abe, M. (ed.) ASIACRYPT 2010. LNCS, vol. 6477, pp. 395–412. Springer, Heidelberg (2010). https://doi.org/10.1007/978-3-642-17373-8_23

40. Groth, J.: Fully anonymous group signatures without random oracles. In: Kurosawa, K. (ed.) ASIACRYPT 2007. LNCS, vol. 4833, pp. 164–180. Springer, Heidelberg (2007). https://doi.org/10.1007/978-3-540-76900-2_10

41. Katsumata, S., Yamada, S.: Group signatures without NIZK: from lattices in the standard model. In: Ishai, Y., Rijmen, V. (eds.) EUROCRYPT 2019. LNCS, vol. 11478, pp. 312–344. Springer, Cham (2019). https://doi.org/10.1007/978-3-030-17659-4_11

42. Katz, J., Kolesnikov, V., Wang, X.: Improved non-interactive zero knowledge with applications to post-quantum signatures. In: ACM CCS 2018, pp. 525–537 (2018)
43. Katz, J., Wang, N.: Efficiency improvements for signature schemes with tight security reductions. In: ACM CCS 2003, pp. 155–164 (2003)
44. Kumawat, S., Paul, S.: A new constant-size accountable ring signature scheme without random oracles. In: Chen, X., Lin, D., Yung, M. (eds.) Inscrypt 2017. LNCS, vol. 10726, pp. 157–179. Springer, Cham (2018). https://doi.org/10.1007/978-3-319-75160-3_11
45. Laguillaumie, F., Langlois, A., Libert, B., Stehlé, D.: Lattice-based group signatures with logarithmic signature size. In: Sako, K., Sarkar, P. (eds.) ASIACRYPT 2013. LNCS, vol. 8270, pp. 41–61. Springer, Heidelberg (2013). https://doi.org/10.1007/978-3-642-42045-0_3
46. Lai, R.W.F., Zhang, T., Chow, S.S.M., Schröder, D.: Efficient sanitizable signatures without random oracles. In: Askoxylakis, I., Ioannidis, S., Katsikas, S., Meadows, C. (eds.) ESORICS 2016. LNCS, vol. 9878, pp. 363–380. Springer, Cham (2016). https://doi.org/10.1007/978-3-319-45744-4_18
47. Libert, B., Ling, S., Nguyen, K., Wang, H.: Zero-knowledge arguments for lattice-based accumulators: logarithmic-size ring signatures and group signatures without trapdoors. In: Fischlin, M., Coron, J.-S. (eds.) EUROCRYPT 2016. LNCS, vol. 9666, pp. 1–31. Springer, Heidelberg (2016). https://doi.org/10.1007/978-3-662-49896-5_1
48. Libert, B., Mouhartem, F., Peters, T., Yung, M.: Practical "signatures with efficient protocols" from simple assumptions. In: ASIACCS 2016, pp. 511–522 (2016)
49. Libert, B., Peters, T., Yung, M.: Short group signatures via structure-preserving signatures: standard model security from simple assumptions. In: Gennaro, R., Robshaw, M. (eds.) CRYPTO 2015. LNCS, vol. 9216, pp. 296–316. Springer, Heidelberg (2015). https://doi.org/10.1007/978-3-662-48000-7_15
50. Ling, S., Nguyen, K., Wang, H., Xu, Y.: Constant-size group signatures from lattices. In: Abdalla, M., Dahab, R. (eds.) PKC 2018. LNCS, vol. 10770, pp. 58–88. Springer, Cham (2018). https://doi.org/10.1007/978-3-319-76581-5_3
51. Lyubashevsky, V., Nguyen, N.K., Seiler, G.: Practical lattice-based zero-knowledge proofs for integer relations. In: ACM CCS 2020, pp. 1051–1070 (2020)
52. Lyubashevsky, V., Nguyen, N.K., Seiler, G.: SMILE: set membership from ideal lattices with applications to ring signatures and confidential transactions. In: Malkin, T., Peikert, C. (eds.) CRYPTO 2021. LNCS, vol. 12826, pp. 611–640. Springer, Cham (2021). https://doi.org/10.1007/978-3-030-84245-1_21
53. Peikert, C.: He gives C-Sieves on the CSIDH. In: Canteaut, A., Ishai, Y. (eds.) EUROCRYPT 2020. LNCS, vol. 12106, pp. 463–492. Springer, Cham (2020). https://doi.org/10.1007/978-3-030-45724-2_16
54. Pointcheval, D., Stern, J.: Security arguments for digital signatures and blind signatures. J. Cryptol. **13**(3), 361–396 (2000)
55. Rivest, R.L., Shamir, A., Tauman, Y.: How to leak a secret. In: Boyd, C. (ed.) ASIACRYPT 2001. LNCS, vol. 2248, pp. 552–565. Springer, Heidelberg (2001). https://doi.org/10.1007/3-540-45682-1_32
56. Unruh, D.: Non-interactive zero-knowledge proofs in the quantum random oracle model. In: Oswald, E., Fischlin, M. (eds.) EUROCRYPT 2015. LNCS, vol. 9057, pp. 755–784. Springer, Heidelberg (2015). https://doi.org/10.1007/978-3-662-46803-6_25

57. Xu, S., Yung, M.: Accountable ring signatures: a smart card approach. In: Quisquater, J.-J., Paradinas, P., Deswarte, Y., El Kalam, A.A. (eds.) CARDIS 2004. IIFIP, vol. 153, pp. 271–286. Springer, Boston (2004). https://doi.org/10.1007/1-4020-8147-2_18

58. Yang, R., Au, M.H., Zhang, Z., Xu, Q., Yu, Z., Whyte, W.: Efficient lattice-based zero-knowledge arguments with standard soundness: construction and applications. In: Boldyreva, A., Micciancio, D. (eds.) CRYPTO 2019. LNCS, vol. 11692, pp. 147–175. Springer, Cham (2019). https://doi.org/10.1007/978-3-030-26948-7_6

Asymmetric PAKE with Low Computation *and* communication

Bruno Freitas Dos Santos[1], Yanqi Gu[1], Stanislaw Jarecki[1(✉)], and Hugo Krawczyk[2]

[1] University of California, Irvine, USA
{brunof,yanqig1,sjarecki}@uci.edu
[2] Algorand Foundation, New York, USA

Abstract. In Crypto'21 Gu, Jarecki, and Krawczyk [25] showed an *asymmetric* password authenticated key exchange protocol (aPAKE) whose computational cost matches (symmetric) password authenticated key exchange (PAKE) and plain (i.e. unauthenticated) key exchange (KE). However, this minimal-cost aPAKE did not match prior aPAKE's in round complexity, using 4 rounds assuming the client initiates compared to 2 rounds in an aPAKE of Bradley et al. [13].

In this paper we show two aPAKE protocols (but not *strong* aPAKEs like [13,30]), which achieve optimal computational cost *and* optimal round complexity. Our protocols can be seen as variants of the *Encrypted Key Exchange* (EKE) compiler of Bellovin and Merritt [7], which creates password-authenticated key exchange by password-encrypting messages in a key exchange protocol. Whereas Bellovin and Merritt used this method to construct a PAKE by applying password-encryption to KE messages, we construct an aPAKE by password-encrypting messages of a *unilaterally authenticated* Key Exchange (ua-KE). We present two versions of this compiler. The first uses *salted* password hash and takes 2 rounds if the server initiates. The second uses unsalted password hash and takes a single simultaneous flow, thus *simultaneously matching the minimal computational cost and the minimal round complexity of PAKE and KE*.

We analyze our aPAKE protocols assuming an Ideal Cipher (IC) on a group, and we analyze them as modular constructions from ua-KE realized via a universally composable Authenticated Key Exchange where the server uses *one-time keys* (otk-AKE). We also show that one-pass variants of 3DH and HMQV securely realize otk-AKE in the ROM. Interestingly, the two resulting concrete aPAKE's use the exact same protocol messages as variants of EKE, and the only difference between the symmetric PAKE (EKE) and asymmetric PAKE (our protocols) is in the key derivation equation.

1 Introduction

Password authenticated key exchange (PAKE) lets two parties establish a secure shared session key if and only if they hold the same (possibly low-entropy) password. The *asymmetric* password authenticated key exchange protocols (aPAKE)

© International Association for Cryptologic Research 2022
O. Dunkelman and S. Dziembowski (Eds.): EUROCRYPT 2022, LNCS 13276, pp. 127–156, 2022.
https://doi.org/10.1007/978-3-031-07085-3_5

is a client-server variant of such protocol where the input to the server party is a one-way function of the password, a.k.a., a *password hash*, and the protocol establishes a shared key iff the client's input is a preimage of the server's input. Both PAKE's and aPAKE's have been extensively studied in the crypto literature, starting from respectively [7] and [29], but recently there has been a renewed interest in aPAKE's due to the weaknesses of current password authentication methods and to the ongoing PAKE standardization effort of the Internet Engineering Task Force [39]. Perhaps the most striking vulnerabilities of the current PKI-based "password-over-TLS" authentication practice, where the client sends its password over a TLS connection to the server, are that it enables phishing attacks against clients who establish a TLS connection with the wrong party, and that it discloses password cleartexts on the server, exposing them to server-side attacks. (To see why the latter might be a problem consider that even security-conscious companies were known to accidentally store large quantities of plaintext passwords [1,2]).

The recent work of Gu, Jarecki, and Krawczyk [25] considered minimal-cost aPAKE's, and they showed an aPAKE protocol *KHAPE* which nearly matches the computational cost of unauthenticated key exchange (KE), namely Diffie-Hellman (uDH), which is 1fb+1vb exp per party (i.e., 1 fixed-base and 1 variable-base exponentiation). The KE cost is a lower-bound for both PAKE and aPAKE because aPAKE $\Rightarrow$ PAKE $\Rightarrow$ KE. However, the minimal-cost aPAKE protocol of [25] is not close to KE in round complexity. Indeed, the aPAKE of [25] takes 3 rounds assuming the server initiates the protocol, while uDH takes a single simultaneous flow, where each party sends a single protocol message without waiting for the counterparty. Note that this minimal round complexity is achieved by minimal-cost universally composable (UC) PAKE's, including EKE [6,7,37], SPAKE2 [3,4], and TBPEKE [3,38].[1]

Our Contributions. We show that cost-optimal aPAKE does not have to come at the expense of round complexity. We do so with two new aPAKE constructions, called OKAPE and aEKE, which are generic compilers that construct aPAKE's from any key-hiding *one-time-key* Authenticated Key Exchange (*otkAKE*). Both constructions use the Random Oracle Model (ROM) and an Ideal Cipher (IC) on message spaces formed by otkAKE public keys, and in the case of aEKE also on the space(s) of otkAKE protocol messages. We define the notion of key-hiding otkAKE as a relaxation of the UC key-hiding AKE of [25], and we show that it is realized by "one-pass" variants of 3DH and HMQV which were shown as UC key-hiding AKEs in [25].

The two compilers instantiated with one-pass HMQV produce two concrete aPAKE schemes which we call OKAPE-HMQV and aEKE-HMQV. Both protocols have close to optimal computational cost of 1fb+1vb exp for the client and 1fb+1mvb exp for the server, where mvb stands for multi-exponentiation with two bases. Moreover, protocol aEKE-HMQV needs only a single simultaneous flow

---

[1] Abdalla et al. [3] show that SPAKE2 [4] and TBPEKE [38] realize a relaxed version of the UC PAKE functionality of Canetti et al. [15].

of communication, hence aEKE-HMQV matches the lowest cost KE and PAKE protocols in both computation and round complexity.

Protocol OKAPE requires 2 communication rounds if the server initiates the protocol, and 3 if the client does. However, protocol aEKE uses *unsalted* password hashes, whereas OKAPE supports *(publicly) salted* password hashes, which have several security and operational benefits over unsalted ones (see Note 1 below). Note that every aPAKE can be generically transformed to support a publicly salted hash if the server first sends the salt to the client and the two parties run aPAKE on the password appended by the salt. However, among prior UC aPAKE's that use unsalted password hashes [24,28,32,41], only the aPAKE of Jutla and Roy [32] and Hwang et al. [28] match the round complexity of OKAPE-HMQV after this transformation, but they do not match its computational cost: The PAKE-to-aPAKE compiler of [28] instantiatied with a minimal-cost PAKE has a total computational cost of 3fb+3vb exps, i.e. 50% more than uDH, while the aPAKE of [32] is significantly more expensive, in particular because it uses bilinear maps. This generic transformation can also be applied to aEKE-HMQV, and the resulting protocol would match both the rounds and exponentiation count of OKAPE-HMQV, but OKAPE-HMQV uses only one ideal cipher operation per party whereas aEKE-HMQV uses two, hence the latter is preferable if the cost of IC on a group is not negligible.

The only prior UC aPAKE's that natively support salted hashes with 3 or fewer communication rounds is the 3-round protocol OPAQUE of Jarecki et al. [30,31] and the 2-round CKEM-based protocol of Bradley et al. [13]. Both of these protocols have at least 2 times higher computational costs than uDH. However, both [30] and [13] provide *strong* aPAKEs (saPAKE), where the salt in the password hash is private, whereas OKAPE supports publicly salted hash and aEKE supports only unsalted hash, see Note 1 below.

In Table 1 we compare efficiency and security properties of prior UC aPAKE's and the concrete protocols we propose. Note that all schemes which achieve explicit authentication for only one party can also achieve it for the other using one additional key confirmation flow. Note also that any single-flow aPAKE can be transformed so it achieves explicit authentication for both parties in 3 flows, regardless of which party starts. In the table we do not include aPAKE schemes which were not proven in UC models so far, including VPAKE [8] or PAK-X [12], but both schemes are slightly costlier than e.g. KC-SPAKE2+ [41], see e.g. [13] for exact cost comparisons.

Main Idea: Encrypted Key Exchange Paradigm for aPAKE. Our protocols are compilers which build aPAKE's from any key-hiding otkAKE, i.e. an AKE where one party uses a one-time key. In both protocols server S picks a one-time public key pair (b, B) and sends the public key B encrypted under a password hash h to client C, who decrypts it under a hash of its password pw. C also has a long-term private key a derived as a password hash as well, i.e. $(h, a) = H(pw)$, and S holds the corresponding public key A together with h in the password file for this client. The two parties then run a *key-hiding* otkAKE on respective inputs (a, B) and (b, A), but here the two compilers diverge: In

Table 1. Comparison of UC aPAKE schemes, with our schemes marked [*]: (1) f, v denote resp. fixed-base and variable-base exponentiation, two-base multi-exponentiation is counted as 1.2v, O(1) stands for significantly larger costs including bilinear maps; (2) x(C) and x(S) denote x rounds if respectively client starts or server starts, while "1" denotes a single-flow protocol; (3) EA column lists the parties that explicitly authenticate their counterparty at protocol termination. OPAQUE-HMQV appeared in [30], but above we give optimized performances characteristics due to [31].

scheme	client[1]	server[1]	rounds[2]	salting	EA[3]	assump.	model
aEKE-HMQV [*]	1f+1.2v	1f+1.2v	1	none	none	gapDH	RO/IC
Jutla-Roy [32]	O(1)	O(1)	1	none	none	XDH	RO
KC-SPAKE2+ [41]	2f+2v	2f+2v	3(C)	none	C+S	CDH	RO
OKAPE-HMQV [*]	1f+1.2v	1f+1.2v	2(S)	public	S	gapDH	RO/IC
Hwang [28] +EKE [7]	2f+1v	1f+2.2v	2(S)	public	S	CDH	RO/IC
KHAPE-HMQV [25]	1f+1.2v	1f+1.2v	3(S)	public	C+S	gapDH	RO/IC
CKEM-saPAKE [13]	10f+1v	2f+2v	2(C)	private	C	sDH, DDH	RO
OPAQUE-HMQV [31]	2f+2.2v	1f+2.2v	3(C)	private	C+S	OM-DH	RO

OKAPE the otkAKE subprotocol is executed in a black-box way, and it is followed by explicit key confirmation message from C to S, whereas in aEKE each otkAKE subprotocol message is encrypted under the password hash by its sender and decrypted under the password hash by its receiver, and no key confirmation message is needed for security. The protocols are shown secure if password-encryption is implemented with an Ideal Cipher on the appropriate message domain, which consists of one-time public keys and/or protocol messages of the underlying otkAKE. Finally, the aEKE compiler requires the key-hiding otkAKE to satisfy a *random transcript* property, i.e. that protocol messages are indistinguishable from uniform over their message spaces.

Note that in both protocols S and C start on resp. inputs A and a and run the following subprotocol: (1) S picks a one-time key pair (b, B) and sends B to C, and (2) the two run otkAKE on resp. (a, B) and (b, A). This subprotocol forms an Authenticated Key Exchange with *unilateral authentication* (ua-KE), where C is authenticated to S but not vice versa. Viewed in this way, protocol aEKE can be seen as an application of the same paradigm as the *Encrypted Key Exchange (EKE)* of Bellovin and Merritt [7]. EKE is a compiler which constructs a (symmetric) PAKE from any random-transcript KE: Each party runs the underlying KE but encrypts protocol messages using a password as a key. This creates a UC PAKE if the encryption is an IC on the KE protocol message space [6,37]. Protocol aEKE utilizes the exact same methodology of IC-encryption of KE protocol messages with a password (or its hash), but applied to ua-KE instead of KE, and we show that this creates a UC *asymmetric* PAKE.

If an EKE is applied to a single simultaneous flow, i.e. 1-round, KE like uDH, it creates 1-round PAKE. In the same way our aEKE compiler creates 1-round aPAKE given a 1-round ua-KE. On the other hand, if EKE instantiated with uDH is executed sequentially then the responder party can send its DH message without IC-encrypting it under the password if it attaches a key confirmation message the response [6,7]. The same trade-off is done by OKAPE compared to aEKE: OKAPE forgoes on IC-encryption of C's ua-KE message but requires C to send a key confirmation message instead.

$$C(pw) \qquad\qquad S(pw)$$
$$h \leftarrow H(pw) \qquad\qquad h \leftarrow H(pw)$$

$$\underrightarrow{IC.E_h(g^x)} \qquad \underleftarrow{IC.E_h(g^b)}$$

$$k = g^{xb}$$

(a) EKE.v1: simultaneous flow

$$C(pw) \qquad\qquad S(h, A)$$
$$(h, a) \leftarrow H(pw) \qquad\qquad [\,A = g^a\,]$$

$$\underrightarrow{IC.E_h(g^x)} \qquad \underleftarrow{IC.E_h(g^b)}$$

$$k = g^{(x+d\cdot a)b} \text{ for } d = H'(\text{trans})$$

(b) aEKE-HMQV

$$C(pw) \qquad\qquad S(pw)$$
$$h \leftarrow H(pw) \qquad\qquad h \leftarrow H(pw)$$

$$\underleftarrow{IC.E_h(g^b)}$$
$$\underrightarrow{g^x, \ \mathsf{prf}(k, 1)}$$

$$k = g^{xb}$$

(c) EKE.v2: sequential, with initiator S

$$C(pw) \qquad\qquad S(h, A)$$
$$(h, a) \leftarrow H(pw) \qquad\qquad [\,A = g^a\,]$$

$$\underleftarrow{IC.E_h(g^b)}$$
$$\underrightarrow{g^x, \ \mathsf{prf}(k, 1)}$$

$$k = g^{(x+d\cdot a)b} \text{ for } d = H'(\text{trans})$$

(d) OKAPE-HMQV

Fig. 1. Symmetric PAKE: *EKE* (a, c) vs. our asymmetric PAKE's (b, d) (Color figure online)

These parallels are easy to see if the one-pass HMQV instantiations of aEKE and OKAPE are put side-by-side the two variants of EKE instantiated with uDH as KE, see Fig. 1.[2] Since both EKE and our protocols are compilers, resp. from KE and ua-KE, we highlight the underlying uDH instantiation of KE and the one-pass HMQV instantiation of ua-KE in these figures in blue. The choice of variable names g^x and g^b in the Diffie-Hellman key agreement comes from one-pass HMQV, where g^a and g^b are resp. the permanent public key of C and the one-time public key of S, while g^x is the Diffie-Hellman contribution of C. Intuitively, a corresponding g^y contribution of S is not needed because the *ephemeral* key g^b already plays this role.

The security of our aPAKEs holds for essentially the same reasons as the security of EKE: (1) security against passive attackers holds regardless of pw by the passive security of the underlying (ua-)KE; (2) if encryption is an ideal cipher then any ciphertext sent by an attacker to C decrypts to a random group element $B' = g^{b'}$ on all passwords except the one used by an attacker in encryption, so an attack on such sessions would be an attack on a passively observed otkAKE instance; (3) the attacker can encrypt a chosen g^b value under a single password, but in the IC model the simulator can observe this and extract a unique password

---

[2] Actual protocols diverge from Fig. 1 in some technicalities, e.g. session key derivation uses a hash of k, but crucially H inputs include a *salt* in OKAPE-HMQV and server/user identifiers in aEKE-HMQV: We come back to this last point below.

guess which the attacker tests in such protocol instance; (4) same arguments work regarding attacks on S in aEKE, while in OKAPE the client's key confirmation message commits the attacker to a session key, which implies a single input pair (a, B) for which this session key is correct, which in turn commits to a single password from which (a, B) are derived.

Although our protocols can be seen as applications of EKE compiler to ua-KE, we analyze them as compilers from otkAKE for several reasons: First, otkAKE is a simpler notion which can be realized with a single protocol flow; Second, otkAKE yields ua-KE (see above) while the converse is not clear; Third, setting the boundary around otkAKE lets us treat it as a black box in OKAPE compiler, because S's one time key g^b, which is the only part that OKAPE wraps using IC encryption is an input to otkAKE, and not its protocol message. In aEKE the otkAKE subprotocol is not used as a black-box, because its protocol messages are IC-encrypted, and this compiler is secure only if otkAKE has a random-transcript property. We prove aEKE secure only for otkAKE realized with a single-flow protocol, which includes both our otkAKE instantiations, i.e. one-pass 3DH and HMQV. Although we believe that this compiler works for multi-round protocols as well, we show it only for single-round otkAKE to limit the complexities in the security argument, which arise from the non-black-box use of otkAKE in this compiler.

Similarities to OPAQUE and KHAPE. Our protocols are also closely related to saPAKE protocol OPAQUE [30] and aPAKE protocol KHAPE [25]. Both of these protocols were compilers from AKE (the OPAQUE protocol in addition uses an Oblivious PRF), where passwords are used to encrypt the client's private key a and the server's public key B, the corresponding keys A and b are held in a password file held by S for this client C, and the key establishment comes from AKE run on these inputs. Protocol KHAPE can be seen as a variant of OPAQUE without the Oblivious PRF. In that case security degrades from saPAKE to aPAKE, but the resulting aPAKE can have minimal cost (i.e. $\approx$ KE) if C's AKE inputs (a, B) are delivered from S to C in an envelope, IC-encrypted under the password, and if the AKE protocol is *key-hiding*, i.e. even an active attacker cannot tell what keys (sk_P, pk_{CP}) an attacked party P assumes except if the attacker knows the corresponding pair (pk_P, sk_{CP}). The reason the KHAPE compiler needs the key-hiding property of AKE is to avoid off-line attacks, because if each password decrypts the envelope sent to the client into some pair (a', B'), there must be no way to test which pair corresponds to either the client or the server keys unless via an active attack which tests at most one of these choices.

Our compilers OKAPE and aEKE are *refinements of the KHAPE compiler*: First, instead of permanent envelope in the password file that encrypts (and authenticates) a permanent server public key g^b, we ask the server to create one-time key per each execution, and IC-encrypt it under a password hash stored in the password file. Replacing key-hiding AKE with key-hiding one-time-key AKE reduces complexity because it can be instantiated with a single C-to-S message. In addition, the IC encryption with subsequent otkAKE together implement implicit S-to-C authentication: If the attacker does not encrypt $B = g^b$ under C's password then C will decrypt it into a random key $B' = g^{b'}$, for which the attacker cannot compute the corresponding session key because it does not know b'. This lets us eliminate the S-to-C key confirmation message in KHAPE and leads to OKAPE. If in addition C's AKE message is IC-encrypted under a password hash then we eliminate also the C-to-S key confirmation message in KHAPE and we get the aEKE protocol, an aPAKE which is non-interactive *and* has optimal computation cost.

Note 1: Salted and Unsalted Password Hashes vs. Round Complexity. The UC aPAKE model of Gentry et al. [24] does not enforce salting of password hashes, which allows their precomputation and an immediate look-up once the server storage is breached. By contrast, Jarecki et al. [30] proposed a UC *strong* aPAKE model (saPAKE), where each password file includes a random and *private* salt value s, and the password hash involves this salt and cannot be precomputed without it. Our protocols aEKE and OKAPE are just aPAKEs, not saPAKEs, but they can support *public* salting of the password hash, which has security advantages over unsalted hash. Looking more closely, the aPAKE model of [24] enforces that a single real-world offline dictionary attack test corresponds not only to a single password guess pw^* but also a single tuple (S, uid) where S is an identifier of a server S and uid is a *userID* with which S associates a password file. (This can be seen in command (OfflineTestPwd, S, uid, pw^*) to the aPAKE functionality of [24], included in Fig. 9 in Sect. A.) This means that a password hash in UC aPAKE, at least as defined by [24], cannot be implemented e.g. simply as $h = H(pw)$ but in the very least as $h = H(S, uid, pw)$, so that a single H computation corresponds to a single password guess pw and a single account (S, *uid*). This is indeed how we implement the RO hash in protocol aEKE, see Sect. 4.

However, such implementation has some negative implications, stemming from the fact that C has to know values (S, uid) in the protocol. (This is reflected in the aPAKE functionality realized by protocol aEKE, see Appendix A.) Tying such application-layer values in a cryptographic protocol can be problematic. For example, in some applications it might be fine to equate S with e.g. the server's domain name, but it would be then impossible to modify it, since all users would have to reinitialize and recompute their password hashes. An alternative generic implementation is to use (semi) *public salts* as follows: S can associate each uid account with a random salt s, set the password hash as $h = H(pw|s)$, attach s in the first S-to-C aPAKE message, and the two parties can then run an *unsalted* aPAKE on a modified password $pw' = pw|s$. Since each s is associated with a unique (S, uid) pair, each H computation still corresponds to a unique (S, uid, pw) tuple, but C does not need values (S, uid) within the aPAKE protocol, and password hashes do not have to change with changes to identifiers S or uid. Moreover, if the aPAKE protocol runs over a TLS connection then an adversary can find s only via an online interaction with S, and it needs to know the user ID string uid for S to retrieve the uid-indexed password file and send s out. Even better, if clients update the (s, h) values at each login, then value s the adversary compromises for some user will be obsolete after that user authenticates to S.

However, this implementation requires interaction. Since S sends the first message in OKAPE, attaching s to S's message does not influence the round complexity of OKAPE, and this is indeed how we implement password hashes in that protocol, see Sect. 3. Every unsalted aPAKE can be transformed to *publicly salted* in this way, but for many aPAKEs, including aEKE, this would imply additional communication rounds.

Note 2: Implicit and Explicit Authentication vs. Round Complexity. Note that our round-minimal aPAKE protocol aEKE does not have explicit entity authentication, i.e. each party computes a key and the security implies that only a party with proper credentials can compute that key as well, but they do not get a confirmation that their counterparty can compute the same key and thus is indeed the party they meant to establish a connection with. Key confirmation can be added to any KE protocol, but it adds a round of communication. Likewise, our three-round (if C initializes) aPAKE protocol OKAPE has only C-to-S entity authentication, and adding S-to-C entity authentication would make it a four-round protocol. Therefore the round-reduction advantage of OKAPE over protocol KHAPE of [25] will benefit only those applications where C can use the session key without waiting for S's key confirmation message.

Note 3: Current Costs of Ideal Cipher on Groups. Just like EKE [6,7], our protocols rely on an ideal cipher on group elements. Implementing an ideal cipher on elliptic curve groups, which are of most interest for current aPAKE proposals, is non-trivial and current techniques for implementing them incur non-negligible costs in computation and sometimes in bandwidth expansion as well. We discuss several implementation options for group IC in Sect. 6, but to give an example, using the Elligator2 method [9] each IC operation can cost $\approx$10–15% of 1vb exp and it requires resampling of the encrypted random group element with probability $1/2$. Thus we can estimate the total computational cost of OKAPE-HMQV with this IC implementation as (expected) 2fb+1.15vb for S and 1fb+1.15vb for C, and of aEKE-HMQV as 2fb+1.30vb per each party. However, the overhead of IC might be significantly smaller in the case of other settings of interest, like lattice cryptosystems.

Organization. In Sect. 2, we define key-hiding one-time-key AKE as a UC notion, and we show that 2DH and one-pass HMQV both securely realize this notion under the Gap DH assumption in ROM. In Sect. 3 and Sect. 4, we show our two compilers from otkAKE to asymmetric PAKE, namely OKAPE and aEKE. In Sect. 5 we describe two concrete aPAKE protocol proposals, OKAPE-HMQV and aEKE-HMQV, which instantiate OKAPE and aEKE with one-pass HMQV as the otkAKE. In Sect. 6 we discuss possible implementation choices of an ideal cipher encryption on elliptic curve groups. Finally, in Appendix A we include our definition(s) of the UC aPAKE model, and in Appendix B we include the overview of the security proof for protocol OKAPE. For space constraint reasons we defer all security proofs to the full version [23], including an extension which instantiates otkAKE based on SKEME [34], which allows for aPAKE construction based solely on KEM.

2   Key-Hiding One-Time-Key AKE

We define key-hiding *one-time-key* Authenticated Key Exchange (otkAKE), as an asymmetric variant of the universally composable key-hiding AKE defined in [25]. We denote the otkAKE functionality $\mathcal{F}_{\text{otkAKE}}$ and we include it in Fig. 2. An AKE functionality allows parties to generate public key pairs (this is modeled by environment query Init to the functionality). These keys can be compromised, modeled by adversarial query Compromise. However, this is the key difference between our (key-hiding) otkAKE functionality and the (key-hiding) AKE functionality of [25], here we distinguish two types of keys, the long-term keys which can be compromised by the adversary, and the ephemeral keys which cannot. We arbitrarily call the first type "client keys" and the second "server keys" because this is how we will use an otkAKE protocol in the context of our otkAKE-to-aPAKE compilers in Sect. 3 and 4, i.e. clients will use long-term keys and servers will use ephemeral keys in both of these applications of otkAKE.

As in [25], any party P holding a key pair indexed by the public key pk_P, whether a long-term one or an ephemeral one, can start a session using such key, and using also some key pk_{CP} as the public key of the counterparty that P expends on this session. This is modeled by the environment's command (NewSession, sid, CP, role, pk_P, pk_{CP}) to P, where sid is the unique session identifier, CP is the supposed identifier of the counterparty, and role is either cl or sr, defining if P is supposed to run the long-term-key party or the ephemeral-key party. (As we can see below, the protocols realizing this functionality can be asymmetric, so parties act differently based on that role bit). As in [25], the functionality marks this session as initially fresh, creates an appropriate session record and picks a random function R_P^{sid} (whose meaning we will explain shortly). Crucially the functionality only sends (NewSession, sid, P, CP, role) to the adversary, i.e. the adversary only learns which party P wants to authenticate, which party CP they intend to communicate with, what session identifier sid they use, and whether they play the client and the server role, but the adversary does *not* learn the *keys* this party uses, neither their own key pk_P nor the key pk_{CP} this party expects of its counterparty. This, exactly as in [25], models the *key-hiding* property of the AKE's which are required in our AKE-to-aPAKE compiler constructions.

Next, if an adversary actively attacks session P^{sid}, as opposed to passively observing its interaction with some other session CP^{sid}, this is modeled by the adversarial query Interfere, and its effect is that session P^{sid} is marked as interfered. The consequence of this marking comes in when the session terminates (i.e. if the adversary delivers all messages this party expects) and outputs

---

PK stores all public keys created in Init; CPK stores all compromised keys;
PK_P^{cl} stores P's permanent public keys; PK_P^{sr} stores P's ephemeral public keys;

Keys: Initialization and Attacks

On (Init, role) from P:

If role $\in \{\mathtt{cl}, \mathtt{sr}\}$ send (Init, P, role) to $\mathcal{A}$, let $\mathcal{A}$ specify pk s.t. $pk \notin PK$, add pk to PK and PK_P^{role}, and output (Init, pk) to P. If P is corrupt then add pk to CPK.

On (Compromise, P, pk) from $\mathcal{A}$: [*this query must be approved by the environment*]
If $pk \in PK_P^{cl}$ then add pk to CPK.

Login Sessions: Initialization and Attacks

On (NewSession, sid, CP, role, pk_P, pk_{CP}) from P:

If $pk_P \in PK_P^{role}$ and there is no prior session record $\langle \mathsf{sid}, \mathsf{P}, \cdot, \cdot, \cdot, \cdot, \cdot \rangle$ then:
 - create session record $\langle \mathsf{sid}, \mathsf{P}, \mathsf{CP}, pk_P, pk_{CP}, \mathsf{role}, \bot \rangle$ marked fresh;
 - if role = cl and $pk_{CP}^{sr} \notin PK_{CP}^{sr}$ then re-label this record as interfered;
 - initialize random function $R_P^{sid} : \{0,1\}^3 \to \{0,1\}^\kappa$;
 - send (NewSession, sid, P, CP, role) to $\mathcal{A}$.

On (Interfere, sid, P) from $\mathcal{A}$:

If there is session $\langle \mathsf{sid}, \mathsf{P}, \cdot, \cdot, \cdot, \cdot, \bot \rangle$ marked fresh then change it to interfered.

Login Sessions: Key Establishment

On (NewKey, sid, P, α) from $\mathcal{A}$:

If $\exists$ session record rec $= \langle \mathsf{sid}, \mathsf{P}, \mathsf{CP}, pk_P, pk_{CP}, \mathsf{role}, \bot \rangle$ then:
 - if rec is marked fresh: If $\exists$ record $\langle \mathsf{sid}, \mathsf{CP}, \mathsf{P}, pk_{CP}, pk_P, \mathsf{role}', k' \rangle$ marked fresh s.t. role' $\neq$ role and $k' \neq \bot$ then set $k \leftarrow k'$, else pick $k \leftarrow_R \{0,1\}^\kappa$;
 - if rec is marked interfered then set $k \leftarrow R_P^{sid}(pk_P, pk_{CP}, \alpha)$;
 - update rec to $\langle \mathsf{sid}, \mathsf{P}, \mathsf{CP}, pk_P, pk_{CP}, \mathsf{role}, k \rangle$ and output (NewKey, sid, k) to P.

Session-Key Query

On (SessionKey, sid, P, pk, pk', α) from $\mathcal{A}$:

If $\exists$ record $\langle \mathsf{sid}, \mathsf{P}, \cdot, \cdot, \cdot, \cdot, \cdot \rangle$ and $pk' \notin (PK \setminus CPK)$ then send $R_P^{sid}(pk, pk', \alpha)$ to $\mathcal{A}$.

Fig. 2. $\mathcal{F}_{\mathsf{otkAKE}}$: functionality for key-hiding one-time key AKE

---

a key, which is modeled by adversarial query NewKey. Namely, if a session is fresh, i.e. it was not actively attacked, then the functionality picks its output session key k as a random string. In other words, this key is secure because there is no interface which allows the adversary to get any information about it. If the adversary passively connects two sessions, e.g. P^{sid} and CP^{sid}, by honestly exchanging their messages, then $\mathcal{F}_{\mathsf{otkAKE}}$ will notice at the NewKey processing that there are two sessions (P, sid, CP, pk_P, pk_{CP}, role) (CP, sid, P, pk_P', pk_{CP}', role') that run on matching keys, i.e. $pk_{CP} = pk_P'$ and $pk_{CP}' = pk_P$, and complementary roles, i.e. role $\neq$ role$'$, then $\mathcal{F}_{\mathsf{otkAKE}}$ sets the key of the session that terminates last as a copy of the one that terminated first. This is indeed as it should be: If two parties run AKE on matching inputs and keys and their messages are delivered without interference they should output the same key.

However, if session $\mathsf{P}^{\mathsf{sid}}$ has been actively attacked, hence it is marked interfered, the session key k output by $\mathsf{P}^{\mathsf{sid}}$ is determined by the random function $R_{\mathsf{P}}^{\mathsf{sid}}$. Specifically, the key will be assigned as the value of $R_{\mathsf{P}}^{\mathsf{sid}}$ on a tuple of three inputs: (1) P's own key pk_{P}, (2) the counterparty's key pk_{CP} which P assumes, and (3) the protocol transcript α which w.l.o.g. is determined by the adversary on this session. This is a non-standard way of modeling KE functionalities, but it suffices for our applications and it allows for inexpensive and communication-minimal implementations as we exhibit with protocols 2DH and one-pass HMQV below. The intuition is that this assures that for any protocol transcript the adversary chooses, each key pair $(pk_{\mathsf{P}}, pk_{\mathsf{CP}})$ which P can use corresponds to an independent session key output of P. Some of these keys can be computed by the adversary via interface SessionKey: The adversary can use it to compute the key P would output on a given transcript α and a given pair $(pk_{\mathsf{P}}, pk_{\mathsf{CP}}) = (pk, pk')$ but only if pk' is either compromised or it is an adversarial key, hence w.l.o.g. we assume the adversary knows the corresponding secret key.

Here is also where our key-hiding one-time-key AKE diverges from the key-hiding AKE notion of [25]: If session $\mathsf{P}^{\mathsf{sid}}$ runs with a client-role then its session key output is guaranteed secure if their assumed counterparty's key pk_{CP} is indeed an ephemeral key of the intended counterparty. Since such keys cannot be compromised, a SessionKey query with $pk' = pk_{\mathsf{CP}}$ will fail the criterion that pk' is compromised or adversarial, hence the adversary has *no interface to learn* P*'s output session key*. However, if the environment (i.e. the higher-level application, like either of our compilers, which utilizes the otkAKE subprotocol) asks $\mathsf{P}^{\mathsf{sid}}$ to run on pk_{CP} which is *not* an ephemeral key of the intended counterparty then $\mathcal{F}_{\mathsf{otkAKE}}$ treats such session as automatically attacked, and marks it interfered. Such session's output key will be computed as $k \leftarrow R_{\mathsf{P}}^{\mathsf{sid}}(pk_{\mathsf{P}}, pk_{\mathsf{CP}}, \alpha)$, and whether or not the adversary can recompute this key via the SessionKey interface depends on whether this (potentially non-ephemeral) key pk_{CP} is compromised or adversarial.

The security of our otkAKE protocols, 2DH and one-pass HMQV, are based on hardness of Gap CDH problem. Recall that Gap CDH is defined as follows: Let g generates a cyclic group $\mathbb{G}$ of prime order p. The Computational Diffie-Hellman (CDH) assumption on $\mathbb{G}$ states that given $(X, Y) = (g^x, g^y)$ for $(x, y) \leftarrow_{\mathsf{R}} (\mathbb{Z}_p)^2$ it's hard to find $\mathsf{cdh}_g(X, Y) = g^{xy}$. The Gap CDH assumption states that CDH is hard even if adversary has access to a Decisional Diffie-Hellman oracle ddh_g, which on input (A, B, C) returns 1 if $C = \mathsf{cdh}_g(A, B)$ and 0 otherwise.

2.1   2DH as Key-Hiding One-Time-Key AKE

We show that key-hiding one-time-key AKE can be instantiated with a "one-pass" variant of the 3DH AKE protocol. 3DH is an implicitly authenticated key exchange used as the basis of the X3DH protocol [36] that underlies the Signal encrypted communication application. 3DH consists of a plain Diffie-Hellman exchange which is authenticated by combining the ephemeral and long-term key of both peers. Specifically, if (a, A) and (b, B) are the long-term key pairs of two communicating parties C and S, and (x, X) and (y, Y) are their ephemeral DH values, then 3DH computes the session key as a hash of the *triple* of Diffie-Hellman values, (g^{xb}, g^{ay}, g^{xy}).

---

group $\mathbb{G}$ of prime order p with generator g
hash function $\mathsf{H} : \{0, 1\}^* \to \{0, 1\}^\kappa$

$\underline{\mathsf{P}_1 \text{ on } (\mathsf{Init}, \mathtt{cl})}$
$a \leftarrow_\mathrm{R} \mathbb{Z}_p,\ A \leftarrow g^a$
store $sk = a$ tagged by $pk = A$
output $pk = A$

$\underline{\mathsf{P}_2 \text{ on } (\mathsf{Init}, \mathtt{sr})}$
$b \leftarrow_\mathrm{R} \mathbb{Z}_p,\ B \leftarrow g^b$
store $sk = b$ tagged by $pk = B$
output $pk = B$

$\underline{\mathsf{P}_1 \text{ on } (\mathsf{NewSession}, \mathsf{sid}, \mathsf{CP}_1, \mathtt{cl}, A, B)}$
retrieve $sk = a$ tagged by $pk = A$
$x \leftarrow_\mathrm{R} \mathbb{Z}_p,\ X \leftarrow g^x$

$\underline{\mathsf{P}_2 \text{ on } (\mathsf{NewSession}, \mathsf{sid}, \mathsf{CP}_2, \mathtt{sr}, B, A)}$
retrieve $sk = b$ tagged by $pk = B$
(abort if key B is not ephemeral)

$$\xrightarrow{\quad X \quad}$$

$\sigma_{\mathtt{cl}} \leftarrow B^x \| B^a$
$k_{\mathtt{cl}} \leftarrow \mathsf{H}(\mathsf{sid}, \mathsf{P}_1, \mathsf{CP}_1, X, \sigma_{\mathtt{cl}})$
output $k_{\mathtt{cl}}$

$\sigma_{\mathtt{sr}} \leftarrow X^b \| A^b$
$k_{\mathtt{sr}} \leftarrow \mathsf{H}(\mathsf{sid}, \mathsf{CP}_2, \mathsf{P}_2, X, \sigma_{\mathtt{sr}})$
output $k_{\mathtt{sr}}$

Fig. 3. otkAKE protocol $2DH$

This protocol was shown to realize the key-hiding AKE functionality in [25], and here we show that a one-pass version of this protocol, which we call *2DH*, realizes the key-hiding one-time-key AKE functionality $\mathcal{F}_{\mathsf{otkAKE}}$ defined above. In this modified setting key (b, B) is a one-time key of party S, and hence it can play a double-role as S authenticator *and* its ephemeral DH contribution. Therefore the only additional ephemeral key needed is the (x, X) value provided by C, and 2DH will compute the session key as a (hash of) the *pair* of DH values, (g^{xb}, g^{ab}). See Fig. 3 were we describe the 2DH protocol in more detail. In that figure we assume that both C's key (a, A) and S's key (b, B) were created prior to protocol execution, but we note that S's key must be a one-time, i.e. ephemeral, key, so in practice it should be created just before the protocol starts and erased once the protocol executes.

We capture the security property of 2DH in the following theorem:

Theorem 1. *Protocol 2DH shown in Fig. 3 realizes functionality* $\mathcal{F}_{\text{otkAKE}}$, *assuming that the Gap CDH assumption holds on group* $\mathbb{G}$ *and* H *is a random oracle.*

The proof of the above theorem is a close variant of the proof given in [25] that 3DH realizes the key-hiding AKE functionality (where both parties use permanent keys). For the reason of space constraints we include this proof in the full version of the paper [23].

2.2 One-Pass HMQV as Key-Hiding One-Time-Key AKE

Similiarly to the case of 3DH, we show that a one-pass version of the HMQV protocol [26,35] realizes functionality $\mathcal{F}_{\text{otkAKE}}$ under the same Gap CDH assumption in ROM. HMQV is a significantly more efficient AKE protocol compared to 3DH because it replaces 3 variable-base exponentiations with 1 multi-exponentiation with two bases. Just like 3DH, HMQV involves both the ephemeral sessions secrets (x, y) and the long-term keys (a, b), and computes session key using a DH-like formula $g^{(x+da)\cdot(y+eb)}$ where d and e are derived via an RO hash of the ephemeral DH contributions, resp. $X = g^x$ and $Y = g^y$.

---

group $\mathbb{G}$ of prime order p with generator g
hash functions $\mathsf{H} : \{0,1\}^* \rightarrow \{0,1\}^\kappa$, $\mathsf{H}' : \{0,1\}^* \rightarrow \mathbb{Z}_p$

P_1 on $\mathsf{Init, cl}$	P_2 on $\mathsf{Init, sr}$
$a \leftarrow_{\mathsf{R}} \mathbb{Z}_p, A \leftarrow g^a$	$b \leftarrow_{\mathsf{R}} \mathbb{Z}_p, B \leftarrow g^b$
store $sk = a$ tagged by $pk = A$	store $sk = b$ tagged by $pk = B$
output $pk = A$	output $pk = B$

P_1 on $(\mathsf{NewSession, sid, CP}_1, \mathsf{cl}, A, B)$	P_2 on $(\mathsf{NewSession, sid, CP}_2, \mathsf{sr}, B, A)$
retrieve $sk = a$ tagged by $pk = A$	retrieve $sk = b$ tagged by $pk = B$
$x \leftarrow_{\mathsf{R}} \mathbb{Z}_p, X \leftarrow g^x$	(abort if key B is not ephemeral)

$$\xrightarrow{\quad X \quad}$$

$d_{\mathsf{cl}} \leftarrow \mathsf{H}'(\mathsf{sid}, \mathsf{P}_1, \mathsf{CP}_1, X)$	$d_{\mathsf{sr}} \leftarrow \mathsf{H}'(\mathsf{sid}, \mathsf{CP}_2, \mathsf{P}_2, X)$
$\sigma_{\mathsf{cl}} \leftarrow B^{x+d_{\mathsf{cl}} \cdot a}$	$\sigma_{\mathsf{sr}} \leftarrow (X \cdot A^{d_{\mathsf{sr}}})^b$

$k_{\mathsf{cl}} \leftarrow \mathsf{H}(\mathsf{sid}, \mathsf{P}_1, \mathsf{CP}_1, X, \sigma_{\mathsf{cl}})$	$k_{\mathsf{sr}} \leftarrow \mathsf{H}(\mathsf{sid}, \mathsf{CP}_2, \mathsf{P}_2, X, \sigma_{\mathsf{sr}})$
output k_{cl}	output k_{sr}

Fig. 4. otkAKE protocol One-Pass HMQV

Gu et al. [25] showed that HMQV realizes the same key-hiding AKE functionality as 3DH, and here we show that a one-pass HMQV realizes the key-hiding *one-time-key* AKE functionality $\mathcal{F}_{\text{otkAKE}}$. Just like in 2DH, in one-pass HMQV pair (b, B) is a one-time key of party S, which effectively plays the role of both server's public key and its ephemeral DH contribution. Hence just as 2DH, the only ephemeral DH contribution needed is pair (x, X) provided by C, and the session key can be derived as $g^{(x+a)\cdot b}$. The full protocol is shown in Fig. 4. As in 2DH we assume that the client and server keys are created before protocol execution, but that the server's key must be a one-time key which is used once and erased afterwards.

We capture the security of one-pass HMQV in the following theorem:

Theorem 2. *Protocol One-Pass HMQV shown in Fig 4 realizes* $\mathcal{F}_{\text{otkAKE}}$ *if the Gap CDH assumption holds on group* $\mathbb{G}$ *and* H *is a random oracle.*

The proof of theorem 2 follows the template of the proof for the corresponding theorem on 2DH security, i.e. Theorem 1. It is also a variant of the similar proof shown in [25] which showed that the full HMQV realizes the permanent-key variant of the key-hiding functionality $\mathcal{F}_{\text{otkAKE}}$ defined therein. Because of space constraints, we defer this proof to the full version of the paper [23].

3   Protocol **OKAPE**: Asymmetric PAKE Construction #1

In this section we show how any UC key-hiding one-time-key AKE protocol can be converted into a UC aPAKE, with very small communication and computational overhead. We call this otkAKE-to-aPAKE compiler **OKAPE**, which stands for One-time-Key Asymetric PakE, and we present it in Fig. 5. As we discussed in the introduction, protocol **OKAPE** is similar to protocol KHAPE of [25] which is a compiler that creates an aPAKE from any UC key-hiding AKE where both parties use permanent keys. As in KHAPE, the password file which the server S stores and the password which the client C enters into the protocol, allow them to derive AKE inputs (a, B) for C and (b, A) for S, where (a, A) is effectively a client's password-authenticated public key pair and (b, B) is a server's password-authenticated public key pair, and the authenticated key agreement then consists of executing a key-hiding AKE on the above inputs. (The AKE must be key-hiding or otherwise an attacker could link the keys used by either party to a password they used to derive them).

Protocol otkAKE follows the same general strategy but it differs from KHAPE in (1) how these keys are derived from the client's password and the server's password file, (2) in the type of key-hiding AKE it requires, and (3) whether or not the AKE must be followed by key confirmation messages sent be both parties. In KHAPE the server-side AKE inputs (b, A) were part of the server's password file, and the client-side AKE inputs (a, B) were password-encrypted using an ideal cipher in an envelope $e = \text{IC.E}_{pw}(a, B)$ stored in the password file and sent from S to C in each protocol instance. Finally, since both public keys were long-term keys, the protocol required each party to send a key-confirmation message and C needed to send its confirmation before S did or otherwise the protocol would be subject to an offline dictionary attack. The first modification made by **OKAPE** is that the client's private key a is derived directly as a password hash, and does not need to be encrypted in envelope e. Secondly, there is no permanent server's key (b, B). Instead S generates a *one-time* key pair (b, B) at

---

Building blocks: (1) one-time-key Authenticated Key Exchange otkAKE; (2) ideal cipher $(\mathsf{IC^*.E}, \mathsf{IC^*.D})$ on space PK of otkAKE public keys; (3) RO hash function $\mathsf{H} : \{0,1\}^* \to \{0,1\}^\kappa \times \{0,1\}^\kappa$; (4) pseudorandom function prf.

Password File Initialization on S's input $(\mathsf{StorePwdFile}, \mathsf{uid}, pw)$:

S picks $s \leftarrow_{\mathrm{R}} \{0,1\}^\kappa$, sets $(h, a) \leftarrow \mathsf{H}(pw, s)$, S generates otkAKE public key A corresponding to a, stores $\mathsf{file}[\mathsf{uid}, \mathsf{S}] \leftarrow (A, h, s)$, and discards all other values

C on $(\mathsf{CltSession}, \mathsf{sid}, \mathsf{S}, pw)$		S on $(\mathsf{SvrSession}, \mathsf{sid}, \mathsf{C}, \mathsf{uid})$
		$(A, h, s) \leftarrow \mathsf{file}[\mathsf{uid}, \mathsf{S}]$
$(h, a) \leftarrow \mathsf{H}(pw, s)$	$\xleftarrow{\;e = \mathsf{IC^*.E}(h, B), s\;}$	$(b, B) \leftarrow \mathsf{Key.Gen}$
$B \leftarrow \mathsf{IC^*.D}(h, e)$		
$\xrightarrow{\;(\mathsf{sid}, \mathsf{S}, \mathtt{cl}, a, B)\;}$		$\xleftarrow{\;(\mathsf{sid}, \mathsf{C}, \mathtt{sr}, b, A)\;}$
	$\boxed{\text{otkAKE}}$	
$\xleftarrow{\;k_{\mathtt{cl}}\;}$		$\xrightarrow{\;k_{\mathtt{sr}}\;}$
$\tau \leftarrow \mathsf{prf}(k_{\mathtt{cl}}, 1)$	$\xrightarrow{\quad\tau\quad}$	$K_{\mathtt{sr}} \leftarrow \perp$ if $\tau \neq \mathsf{prf}(k_{\mathtt{sr}}, 1)$
$K_{\mathtt{cl}} \leftarrow \mathsf{prf}(k_{\mathtt{cl}}, 0)$		else $K_{\mathtt{sr}} \leftarrow \mathsf{prf}(k_{\mathtt{sr}}, 0)$
output $K_{\mathtt{cl}}$		output $K_{\mathtt{sr}}$

Fig. 5. Protocol OKAPE: compiler from key-hiding otkAKE to aPAKE

each protocol instance, and authenticates-and-encrypts its public key B under a password by sending to C an envelope $e = \mathsf{IC.E}_h(B)$ where h is a password hash stored in the password file. Since B is now a one-time key, we can replace key-hiding AKE used in KHAPE with a key-hiding one-time-key AKE, which as we saw in Sect. 2 can be realized with cheaper subprotocols.

More importantly, the IC-encryption of the one-time key B followed by computing the otkAKE session key output by C given input B, implies implicit password-authentication under a unique password: By the properties of the ideal cipher a ciphertext e commits the sender to a single choice of key h (and hence password pw from which h is derived) used to create this ciphertext on a plaintext B chosen by the sender. Hence there can be at most one key h (and thus at most one password pw) s.t. envelope e decrypts to a key B for which the sender knows the corresponding secret key b, and thus can complete the otkAKE protocol ran by C on the key B it decrypts from e. Whereas the protocol still requires a key confirmation by C (otherwise a malicious C could stage an offline dictionary attack once it learned S's session key), the fact that the envelope already implicitly authenticates S implies that it no longer needs a subsequent key confirmation by S.

The main appeal of OKAPE compared to the KHAPE construction in [25] comes from the last implication, i.e. from the fact that we achieve security without the explicit key confirmation from S. If the OKAPE subprotocol is instantiated with either of the two key-hiding otkAKE protocols of Sect. 2, the result is a 2-round aPAKE protocol if S is an initiator and a 3-round protocol if C is an initiator (such concrete instantiation is shown in Fig. 7 in Sect. 5). Lastly, because S starts the protocol, protocol OKAPE can use (publicly) *salted* password hash at no extra cost to such instantiations: A random salt value s can be part of the password file, the password hash can be defined as $H(pw, s)$, and s can be delivered from S to C in S's first protocol message, together with envelope e.

This round-complexity improvement is "purchased" at the cost of two trade-offs. First, in OKAPE server S is only implicitly authenticated to C, and if C requires an explicit authentication of S before C uses its session key then the round reduction no longer applies. Secondly, OKAPE can be slightly more computationally expensive than KHAPE because S needs to generate envelope e on-line, which adds an ideal cipher encryption operation to the protocol cost, and current ideal cipher implementations for e.g. elliptic curve group elements have small but non-negligible costs (see Sect. 6).

One additional caveat in protocol OKAPE is that because we want C to derive its AKE private key a from a password hash, we must assume that OKAPE generates private keys from uniformly random bitstrings. This is true about any public key generator if that bitstring is treated as the randomness of the key generator algorithm. For some public key cryptosystems, e.g. RSA, this would be a rather impractical representation of the private key, but in the cryptosystems based on Diffie-Hellman in prime-order groups this randomness can be simply equated with the private key.

Theorem 3. *Protocol* OKAPE *realizes the UC aPAKE functionality $\mathcal{F}_{\text{aPAKE-cEA}}$ if the AKE protocol realizes functionality $\mathcal{F}_{\text{otkAKE}}$, assuming that* prf *is a secure PRF and* IC* *is an ideal cipher over the space of* otkAKE *ephemeral public keys.*

Functionality $\mathcal{F}_{\text{aPAKE-cEA}}$ is a standard UC aPAKE functionality extended by client-to-server entity authentication. The functionality $\mathcal{F}_{\text{aPAKE-cEA}}$ we use is a modification of the UC aPAKE functionality given by [24], but with some refinements we adopt from [25]. We include this functionality in Appendix A. We provide an abridged version of the proof of Theorem 3 in Appendix B. It describes our simulation strategy and contains the formal definition of our two-part simulator. For a full version, including the intermediary games and (negligible) bounds between the real and ideal-world interaction, we refer the reader to the full proof in the Appendix of [23].

4   Protocol aEKE: Asymmetric PAKE Construction #2

In Fig. 6 we present an asymmetric PAKE protocol that we name *asymmetric encrypted key exchange* (aEKE). It is a close variant of the otkAKE-to-aPAKE compiler OKAPE described in Fig. 5 in Sect. 3. The password file stored by the server also contains client's public key A and a password hash h (which are now split into two values h_0, h_1), the server again picks a one-time-key B and sends it over to the client IC-encrypted under the partial password hash h_0, the client

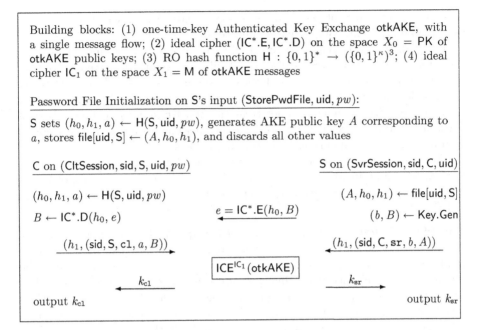

Building blocks: (1) one-time-key Authenticated Key Exchange otkAKE, with a single message flow; (2) ideal cipher $(\mathsf{IC}^*.\mathsf{E}, \mathsf{IC}^*.\mathsf{D})$ on the space $X_0 = \mathsf{PK}$ of otkAKE public keys; (3) RO hash function $\mathsf{H} : \{0,1\}^* \rightarrow (\{0,1\}^\kappa)^3$; (4) ideal cipher IC_1 on the space $X_1 = \mathsf{M}$ of otkAKE messages

Password File Initialization on S's input $(\mathsf{StorePwdFile}, \mathsf{uid}, pw)$:

S sets $(h_0, h_1, a) \leftarrow \mathsf{H}(\mathsf{S}, \mathsf{uid}, pw)$, generates AKE public key A corresponding to a, stores $\mathsf{file}[\mathsf{uid}, \mathsf{S}] \leftarrow (A, h_0, h_1)$, and discards all other values

C on $(\mathsf{CltSession}, \mathsf{sid}, \mathsf{S}, \mathsf{uid}, pw)$ S on $(\mathsf{SvrSession}, \mathsf{sid}, \mathsf{C}, \mathsf{uid})$

$(h_0, h_1, a) \leftarrow \mathsf{H}(\mathsf{S}, \mathsf{uid}, pw)$ $(A, h_0, h_1) \leftarrow \mathsf{file}[\mathsf{uid}, \mathsf{S}]$

$B \leftarrow \mathsf{IC}^*.\mathsf{D}(h_0, e)$ $e = \mathsf{IC}^*.\mathsf{E}(h_0, B)$ $(b, B) \leftarrow \mathsf{Key.Gen}$

$(h_1, (\mathsf{sid}, \mathsf{S}, \mathsf{cl}, a, B))$ $(h_1, (\mathsf{sid}, \mathsf{C}, \mathsf{sr}, b, A))$

$\boxed{\mathsf{ICE}^{\mathsf{IC}_1}(\mathsf{otkAKE})}$

k_{cl} k_{sr}

output k_{cl} output k_{sr}

Fig. 6. Protocol aEKE: EKE-style compiler from key-hiding otkAKE to aPAKE

derives its private key a via a password hash as well, and the client and server perform otkAKE on the same respective inputs (a, B) and (b, A).

However, the two compilers differ in three important aspects: First, subprotocol otkAKE is not executed as a black box, but it is "IC-encrypted" using the second part h_1 of the password hash as the key. We describe what IC-encrypted protocol is more formally below, but intuitively an *IC-encrypted protocol Π* means that the two parties execute the protocol Π but they use the ideal cipher to encrypt each outgoing message and decrypt each incoming message. The second difference is that the protocol no longer needs C-to-S key confirmation for its security, as was required by protocol OKAPE, which allows for further reduction of round complexity in concrete instantiations.

Lastly, we eliminate the salt value s from the input of the password hash. This last change is done chiefly so that our concrete instantiation of this compiler produces a protocol which requires only a single **simultaneous** flow between the two parties. This will be true as long as the otkAKE subprotocol involves only one message, from C to S, and moreover this message can be generated prior to client learning input B which C derives from the envelope received from S. Note that this is true for our two otkAKE instantiations, namely one-pass HMQV and 2DH. Note that the protocol can be salted in a generic way, i.e. by S storing a salt and sending it to C before the protocol starts, but this would add a S-to-C round of interaction to the protocol (in particular C will need the salt value to generate h_1 and encrypt its protocol message under it), at which point aEKE would loose its round-complexity advantage over OKAPE.

In Fig. 6, and in the security analysis of protocol aEKE, we assume a restricted case of a *single-flow* (C-to-S) realization of subprotocol otkAKE. We believe that the compiler works for multi-round otkAKE subprotocols as well, but dropping this restriction would make the security argument significantly more complex since our security argument cannot treat the otkAKE subprotocol entirely as a black box, and must explicitly process ideal cipher encryption and decryption of each message in the underlying otkAKE subprotocol.

We stress that, as described in the introduction, even though we drop salting in aEKE our functionality requires that offline password tests correspond to a unique choice of pair (S, uid), and we enforce this by setting the password hash as $H(S, uid, pw)$.

The *Ideal-Cipher-Encrypted* Protocol Compiler. The *IC-encrypted* protocol compiler, denoted ICE, takes an ideal cipher IC and any two-party protocol Π and creates a new protocol $\Pi' = \mathsf{ICE}^{\mathsf{IC}}(\Pi)$, which proceeds by running the original protocol Π and encrypting each of its outgoing messages using the ideal cipher IC and decrypting any incoming messages using the same cipher. More specifically, the input of P to protocol Π' is $x' = (k, x)$ where k is a key of an ideal cipher IC and x is P's input in protocol Π. P then runs protocol Π on x, and whenever Π creates an outgoing message $\mathsf{msg_{out}}$ then P encrypts it as $\mathsf{ciph_{out}} \leftarrow \mathsf{IC.E}(k, \mathsf{msg_{out}})$ and sends out ciphertext $\mathsf{ciph_{out}}$ instead of the original message $\mathsf{msg_{out}}$. Because P's counterparty is assumed to follow the same protocol, party P parses its incoming message as a ciphertext $\mathsf{ciph_{in}}$, decrypts it as $\mathsf{msg_{in}} \leftarrow \mathsf{IC.D}(k, \mathsf{ciph_{in}})$, and passes $\mathsf{msg_{in}}$ as an incoming message to protocol Π. Whenever Π terminates with some output this is also the output of protocol Π'.

Observe that the ICE compiler generalizes the Encrypted Key Exchange (EKE) construction of Bellovin and Meritt [7]. The EKE protocol can be seen as protocol $\mathsf{EKE} = \mathsf{ICE}^{\mathsf{IC}}(\mathsf{KE})$, where KE is an unauthenticated Key Exchange, and the password (or its hash) is used as the ideal cipher key. Protocol aEKE is created using exactly the same compiler but applied to otkAKE instead of KE, and it results in asymmetric PAKE instead of symmetric PAKE.

Below we define random-transcript property for single-flow protocol Π. Clearly both 2DH and one-pass HMQV satisfy this property.

Definition 1 *[random transcript single-flow protocol].* *Let* M *be the message space of a single-flow protocol* Π. *We say that protocol* Π *has a* random transcript *property if for any input* x *of* Π, *the message* m *which* Π *generates on* x *is indistinguishable from a message uniformly sampled from* M, *i.e. for any PPT adversary* $\mathcal{A}$ *and any* x, *there is a negligible function* negl *such that:*

$$|\Pr[\mathcal{A}(m_0 \leftarrow \Pi(x)) = 1] - \Pr[\mathcal{A}(m_1 \leftarrow_R M) = 1]| \leq \mathsf{negl}(\kappa)$$

Theorem 4. *Protocol* aEKE *realizes the UC aPAKE functionality* $\mathcal{F}_{\mathsf{aPAKE}}$ *if the* otkAKE *protocol realizes functionality* $\mathcal{F}_{\mathsf{otkAKE}}$ *and (1)* otkAKE *protocol uses a single client-to-server message, (2)* otkAKE *protocol has the random-transcript property, (3)* IC^* *is an ideal cipher over message space of* otkAKE *public keys, (4)* IC_1 *is an ideal cipher over message space* M *of the single-flow* otkAKE.

Because of space constraints the proof of Theorem 4 is deferred to the full version of the paper [23].

5   Concrete aPAKE Protocol Instantiations

We include two concrete aPAKE protocols we call OKAPE-HMQV and aEKE-HMQV. Protocol OKAPE-HMQV, shown in Fig. 7, is an instantiation of protocol OKAPE from Sect. 3 with one-pass-HMQV as the key-hiding otkAKE (shown in Sect. 2.2). Protocol aEKE-HMQV, shown in Fig. 8, is an instantiation of aEKE from Sect. 4 with the same one-pass-HMQV. Both of these protocols were shown in a simplified form in Fig. 1 in the introduction, but here we show both protocols with all details.

Building blocks: (1) group $\mathbb{G}$ of prime order p with generator g; (2) ideal cipher $(\mathsf{IC}^*.\mathsf{E}, \mathsf{IC}^*.\mathsf{D})$ on space of $\mathbb{G}$; (3) RO hash functions $\mathsf{H}, \mathsf{H}', \mathsf{H}''$ with ranges resp. $\{0,1\}^\kappa \times \mathbb{Z}_p$, $\mathbb{Z}_p$, and $\{0,1\}^\kappa$; (4) pseudorandom function prf.

Password File Initialization on S's input $(\mathsf{StorePwdFile}, \mathsf{uid}, pw)$:

S picks $s \leftarrow_{\mathrm{R}} \{0,1\}^\kappa$, sets $(h, a) \leftarrow \mathsf{H}(pw, s)$, S generates AKE public key $A \leftarrow g^a$, stores $\mathsf{file}[\mathsf{uid}, \mathsf{S}] \leftarrow (A, h, s)$, and discards all other values

C on $(\mathsf{CltSession}, \mathsf{sid}, \mathsf{S}, pw)$		S on $(\mathsf{SvrSession}, \mathsf{sid}, \mathsf{C}, \mathsf{uid})$
$x \leftarrow_{\mathrm{R}} \mathbb{Z}_p,\ X \leftarrow g^x$	$\xleftarrow{\ e = \mathsf{IC}^*.\mathsf{E}(h, B),\ s\ }$	$(A, h, s) \leftarrow \mathsf{file}[\mathsf{uid}, \mathsf{S}]$
$(h, a) \leftarrow \mathsf{H}(pw, s)$		$b \leftarrow_{\mathrm{R}} \mathbb{Z}_p,\ B \leftarrow g^b$
$B \leftarrow \mathsf{IC}^*.\mathsf{D}(h, e)$		
$d_{\mathsf{C}} \leftarrow \mathsf{H}'(\mathsf{sid}, \mathsf{C}, \mathsf{S}, X)$	$\xrightarrow{\quad X \quad}$	$d_{\mathsf{S}} \leftarrow \mathsf{H}'(\mathsf{sid}, \mathsf{C}, \mathsf{S}, X)$
$\sigma_{\mathsf{C}} \leftarrow B^{x + d_{\mathsf{C}} \cdot a}$		$\sigma_{\mathsf{S}} \leftarrow (X \cdot A^{d_{\mathsf{S}}})^b$
$k_{\mathrm{cl}} \leftarrow \mathsf{H}''(\mathsf{sid}, \mathsf{C}, \mathsf{S}, X, \sigma_{\mathsf{C}})$		$k_{\mathrm{sr}} \leftarrow \mathsf{H}''(\mathsf{sid}, \mathsf{C}, \mathsf{S}, X, \sigma_{\mathsf{S}})$
$\tau \leftarrow \mathsf{prf}(k_{\mathrm{cl}}, 1)$	$\xrightarrow{\quad \tau \quad}$	$K_{\mathrm{sr}} \leftarrow \perp$ if $\tau \neq \mathsf{prf}(k_{\mathrm{sr}}, 1)$
$K_{\mathrm{cl}} \leftarrow \mathsf{prf}(k_{\mathrm{cl}}, 0)$		else $K_{\mathrm{sr}} \leftarrow \mathsf{prf}(k_{\mathrm{sr}}, 0)$
output K_{cl}		output K_{sr}

Fig. 7. OKAPE with one-pass-HMQV: concrete aPAKE protocol OKAPE-HMQV

Protocol OKAPE-HMQV has 2 flows if the server initiates (and 3 if the client does), while protocol aEKE-HMQV is non-interactive, i.e. each party can

Building blocks: (1) group $\mathbb{G}$ of prime order p with generator g; (2) ideal cipher $(\mathsf{IC}^*.\mathsf{E}, \mathsf{IC}^*.\mathsf{D})$ on space of $\mathbb{G}$; (3) RO hash functions $\mathsf{H}, \mathsf{H}', \mathsf{H}''$ with ranges resp. $(\{0,1\}^\kappa)^3$, $\mathbb{Z}_p$, and $\{0,1\}^\kappa$

Password File Initialization on S's input (StorePwdFile, uid, pw):

S sets $(h_1, h_2, a) \leftarrow \mathsf{H}(\mathsf{S}, \mathsf{uid}, pw)$, S generates AKE public key $A \leftarrow g^a$, stores file[uid, S] $\leftarrow (A, h_1, h_2)$, and discards all other values

C on (CltSession, sid, S, uid, pw)	S on (SvrSession, sid, C, uid)
$(h_1, h_2, a) \leftarrow \mathsf{H}(\mathsf{S}, \mathsf{uid}, pw)$	$(A, h_1, h_2) \leftarrow$ file[uid, S]
$x \leftarrow_{\mathrm{R}} \mathbb{Z}_p,\ X \leftarrow g^x$	$b \leftarrow_{\mathrm{R}} \mathbb{Z}_p,\ B \leftarrow g^b$

$$f = \mathsf{IC}^*.\mathsf{E}(h_2, X) \longrightarrow$$
$$\longleftarrow e = \mathsf{IC}^*.\mathsf{E}(h_1, B)$$

$B \leftarrow \mathsf{IC}^*.\mathsf{D}(h_1, e)$	$X \leftarrow \mathsf{IC}^*.\mathsf{D}(h_2, f)$
$d_\mathsf{C} \leftarrow \mathsf{H}'(\mathsf{sid}, \mathsf{C}, \mathsf{S}, X)$	$d_\mathsf{S} \leftarrow \mathsf{H}'(\mathsf{sid}, \mathsf{C}, \mathsf{S}, X)$
$\sigma_\mathsf{C} \leftarrow B^{x + d_\mathsf{C} \cdot a}$	$\sigma_\mathsf{S} \leftarrow (X \cdot A^{d_\mathsf{S}})^b$
$k_{\mathrm{cl}} \leftarrow \mathsf{H}''(\mathsf{sid}, \mathsf{C}, \mathsf{S}, X, \sigma_\mathsf{C})$	$k_{\mathrm{sr}} \leftarrow \mathsf{H}''(\mathsf{sid}, \mathsf{C}, \mathsf{S}, X, \sigma_\mathsf{S})$
output k_{cl}	output k_{sr}

Fig. 8. aEKE with one-pass-HMQV: concrete aPAKE protocol aEKE-HMQV

send its message without waiting for the counterparty. Note that in both protocols each party uses only 1 fixed-base exponentiation plus 1 variable-base (multi)exponentiation. In OKAPE-HMQV each party performs one ideal cipher operation: S performs encryption and C decryption, while in protocol aEKE-HMQV each party performs 1 encryption and 1 decryption.

The communication costs are as in Diffie-Hellman key exchange, with one-sided key confirmation and a κ-bit salt value in the case of protocol OKAPE-HMQV. (Recall that OKAPE is a *salted* aPAKE while aEKE is an *unsalted* aPAKE.) Depending on the implementation of an Ideal Cipher encryption on group $\mathbb{G}$, the ciphertext e encrypting B, and in the case of aEKE-HMQV also ciphertext f encrypting X, can introduce additional bandwidth overhead of $\Omega(\kappa)$ bits, and they may also impose non-trivial computational costs on operations $\mathsf{IC}^*.\mathsf{E}$ and $\mathsf{IC}^*.\mathsf{D}$ as well, see Sect. 6.

6   Curve Encodings and Ideal Cipher

Quasi Bijections. Protocols OKAPE and aEKE use an Ideal Cipher (IC) on values related to a key-hiding otkAKE subprotocol with which these compiler constructions are instantiated. These values are the server's otkAKE one-time public key B, and in the case of aEKE these are also otkAKE protocol messages. However, since in Sect. 4 we restrict our claims about aEKE only to the case when subprotocol otkAKE is a single-flow protocol, the IC encryption will be applied only to the client's single otkAKE message. In both instantiations of otkAKE we exhibit, i.e. 2DH and one-pass HMQV shown in Sects. 2.1 and 2.2, the server's public key B is a group element and so is the client' single protocol message X. Hence we need the ideal cipher on a message space which is group $\mathbb{G}$ used in these otkAKE instantiations.

We use the same methodology for implementing an ideal cipher on a group as in [25]. We briefly summarize it here and we refer for more details to [25]. We assume that we have an ideal cipher $\mathsf{IC} = (\mathsf{IC.E}, \mathsf{IC.D})$ which works over fixed-length bitstrings, i.e. space $\{0,1\}^n$ for some n.[3] Then, an ideal cipher on $\mathbb{G}$ can be implemented by encoding plaintext $m \in \mathbb{G}$ as a bitstring of length n, and then apply the ideal cipher IC to the resulting bitstring. The encoding map : $\mathbb{G} \to \{0,1\}^n$ must be *injective*, i.e. 1-1, so that there exists an (efficient) inverse map $\mathsf{map}^{-1} : \{0,1\}^n \to \mathbb{G}$. The encoding must also be *surjective* (or close) so that every bitstring decodes into a group element, so that e.g. if e is an encryption of $g \in \mathbb{G}$ under key k, the decryption of e under key $k' \neq k$ returns another element in $\mathbb{G}$. If $\mathbb{G}$ is an elliptic curve then we only know examples of *randomized* encodings which satisfy these properties. Formally we define a randomized encoding which is close to a bijection as in [25]:

Definition 2 [25]. *A randomized ε-quasi bijection* map *with domain A, randomness space $R = \{0,1\}^\rho$ and range B consists of two efficient algorithms* map $: A \times R \to B$ *and* $\mathsf{map}^{-1} : B \to A$ *with the following properties:*

1. map^{-1} *is deterministic and for all $a \in A, r \in R, \mathsf{map}^{-1}(\mathsf{map}(a,r)) = a$;*
2. map *maps the uniform distribution on $A \times R$ to a distribution on B that is (statistically) ε-close to uniform.*

We say that map is a *quasi bijection* without specifying ε when it is an ε-quasi bijection for negligible ε. Given such encoding a (randomized) ideal cipher $\mathsf{IC}^* = (\mathsf{IC}^*.\mathsf{E}, \mathsf{IC}^*.\mathsf{D})$ on $\mathbb{G}$ can be implemented as $\mathsf{IC}^*.\mathsf{E}(k,m) = \mathsf{IC.E}(k, \mathsf{map}(m;r))$ for random r and $\mathsf{IC}^*.\mathsf{D}(k,c) = \mathsf{map}^{-1}(\mathsf{IC.D}(k,c))$. However, rather than define a new notion of randomized ideal cipher, in protocols OKAPE and aEKE we assume that the ideal cipher on $\mathbb{G}$ is implemented using the above construction IC^* and we argue directly based on the properties of quasi-bijective encoding map and the bitstring ideal cipher IC.

Elliptic Curve Encodings. There are many well-studied quasi-bijective encodings for elliptic curves in the literature (cf. [9,14,22,40,42]). We briefly introduce two representative examples and refer to [25] for more details. The **Elligator-squared** method [33,42] applies to most elliptic curves and implements quasi bijection for the whole group $\mathbb{G}$ of prime order q. It encodes curve points $m \in \mathbb{G}$ as pair of field elements $(u,v) \in \mathbb{Z}_q^2$ using a deterministic function $f : \mathbb{Z}_q \to \mathbb{G}$ s.t. $\mathsf{map}^{-1}(u,v) = m$ iff $m = f(u) + f(v)$. Since u,v are field elements, a further

---

[3] For $n = 128$ one can assume that e.g. AES is an ideal cipher, while for larger values one has to use domain-extension techniques, e.g. [16,17,20,27] or direct constructions, e.g. [5,10,11,18,19,21].

quasi bijection is needed to represent such pair as a bitstring unless q is close to a power of 2. The performance of map^{-1} used in IC*.D depends on function f whose cost is typically dominated by 1 base-field exponentiation, which costs $\approx$10–15% of a scalar multiplication (a.k.a. a "variable-base exponentiation" in $\mathbb{G}$). The randomized map map used in IC*.E can cost e.g. 3 base-field exponentiations on some curves [42]. The **Elligator2** method [9] is more restrictive, and defines an injective mapping from *half* of the domain $\mathbb{G}$ to integer range $[0, (q - 1)/2]$. The advantages of Ellligator2 is that it uses a single field element to represent a group element (thus reducing bandwidth), and that both directions of the map are very efficient, each costing about 1 base-field exponentiation. The disadvantage is that message $m \in \mathbb{G}$ (i.e. S's message B or C's message X) has to be resampled until it lies in the Elligator2 domain.[4] Finally, in a recent work of McQuoid et al. [37] show a "one-time" variant of a randomized ideal cipher on a group, called *Programmable Once Public Function* (**POPF**) therein, which utilizes a single RO-indistinguishable hash onto group $\mathbb{G}$ in both encryption and decryption directions, and as McQuoid et al. show suffices as a replacement for an ideal cipher in the proof that EKE realizes UC PAKE functionality [37]. Because of the similarities between our aPAKE's and EKE, the same POPF notion could suffice in the context of our aPAKEs as well, leading to another method for instantiating the group ideal cipher IC*, but we leave formal verification that this is the case to future work.

A   Universally Composable Asymmetric PAKE Model

We include for reference the UC aPAKE definition in the form of a functionality $\mathcal{F}_{\mathsf{aPAKE}}$, shown in Fig. 9. This functionality is largely as it was originally defined by Gentry, Mackenzie, and Ramzan [24], but it adopts few notational modifications introduced by Gu et al. [25]. These include naming what amounts to user accounts explicitly as uid instead of generic-sounding sid, using sid instead of ssid as a session-identifier for on-line authentication attempts, and using only pairs (S, uid) to identify server password files and not (S, U, uid) tuples as in [24].

Because in this paper we differentiate between unsalted and (publicly) salted aPAKE's, an explicit support for unsalted aPAKE's is reflected in aPAKE functionality $\mathcal{F}_{\mathsf{aPAKE}}$ by introducing a slight modification in the functionality of [25]. These modifications are highlighted in Fig. 9, and they all concern a client-side usage of the user account field uid. As we mention in the introduction, the round-minimal protocol aEKE is *unsalted*, and to enforce the aPAKE contract defined by [24], which is that a single real-world offline dictionary attack operation must correspond not only to a single password guess but also to a unique user password file, identified by a unique pair (S, uid), the client must get as environment's inputs both the server identifier S *and* the user account identifier uid.

---

[4] We should note that a cost-saving implementation which walks through *consecutive* values e.g. $X_i = g^{x+i}$ for $i = 0, 1, \ldots$ to find X_i which is the Elligator2 domain, and encrypts that X_i under a password, would leak information about the password if the adversary learns the length of this walk from timing information.

Password Registration

- On (StorePwdFile, uid, pw) from S create record ⟨file, S, uid, pw⟩ marked fresh.

Stealing Password Data   [*these queries must be approved by the environment*]

- On (StealPwdFile, S, uid) from $\mathcal{A}$, if there is no record ⟨file, S, uid, pw⟩, return "no password file". Otherwise mark this record compromised, and if there is a record ⟨offline, S, uid, pw⟩ then send pw to $\mathcal{A}$.
- On (OfflineTestPwd, S, uid, pw^*) from $\mathcal{A}$, then do:
  - If ∃ record ⟨file, S, uid, pw⟩ marked compromised, do the following:
    If $pw^* = pw$ then return "correct guess" to $\mathcal{A}$ else return "wrong guess."
  - Else record ⟨offline, S, uid, pw^*⟩

Password Authentication

- On (CltSession, sid, S, uid , pw) from C, if there is no record ⟨sid, C, ...⟩ then save ⟨sid, C, S, uid , pw, cl⟩ marked fresh, send (CltSession, sid, C, S, uid) to $\mathcal{A}$.
- On (SvrSession, sid, C, uid) from S, if there is no record ⟨sid, S, ...⟩ then retrieve record ⟨file, S, uid, pw⟩, and if it exists then save ⟨sid, S, C, uid , pw, sr⟩ marked fresh and send (SvrSession, sid, S, C, uid) to $\mathcal{A}$.

Active Session Attacks

- On (TestPwd, sid, P, uid , pw^*) from $\mathcal{A}$, if ∃ record ⟨sid, P, P′, uid , pw, role⟩ marked fresh, then do: If $pw^* = pw$ then mark it compromised and return "correct guess" to $\mathcal{A}$; else mark it interrupted and return "wrong guess."
- On (Impersonate, sid, C, S, uid) from $\mathcal{A}$, if ∃ record rec = ⟨sid, C, S, uid , pw, cl⟩ marked fresh, then do: If ∃ record ⟨file, S, uid, pw⟩ marked compromised then mark rec compromised and return "correct guess" to $\mathcal{A}$; else mark it interrupted and return "wrong guess."

Key Generation and Authentication

- On (NewKey, sid, P, K^*) from $\mathcal{A}$, if ∃ record rec = ⟨sid, P, P′, uid , pw, role⟩ not marked completed, then do:
  1. If rec is marked compromised set $K \leftarrow K^*$;
  2. Else if rec is fresh and there is record ⟨sid, P′, P, uid , pw, role′⟩ for role′ ≠ role and $\mathcal{F}_{\mathsf{aPAKE}}$ sent (sid, $K′$) to P′ when this record was fresh, set $K \leftarrow K′$;
  3. Else set $K \leftarrow_{\mathrm{R}} \{0,1\}^{\ell}$.
  Finally, mark rec as completed and send output (sid, K) to P.

Note: Modifications from $\mathcal{F}_{\mathsf{aPAKE}}$ defined in [25] are marked like this *. They consist of assuming input* uid *in* CltSession *and* TestPwd *and enforcing* uid-*equality between client and server sessions in* NewKey *processing.*

Fig. 9. $\mathcal{F}_{\mathsf{aPAKE}}$: asymmetric PAKE functionality adapted from [25]

Queries StorePwdFile from S, StealPwdFile or OfflineTestPwd from $\mathcal{A}$, CltSession from C, SvrSession from S, and TestPwd or Impersonate from $\mathcal{A}$, functionality $\mathcal{F}_{\mathsf{aPAKE\text{-}cEA}}$ acts as $\mathcal{F}_{\mathsf{aPAKE}}$ of Figure 9, *except* it omits all parts marked uid (i.e. it does not require uid input for C and does not enforce uid-equality for C and S).

Below we mark like this parts of NewKey processing which differ from $\mathcal{F}_{\mathsf{aPAKE}}$.

Key Generation and Authentication

- On (NewKey, sid, P, K^*) from $\mathcal{A}$, if there is a record rec = $\langle$sid, P, P', pw, role$\rangle$ not marked completed, then do:
  1. If rec is marked compromised set $K \leftarrow K^*$;
  2. Else if rec is fresh , role = sr, and there is record $\langle$sid, P', P, pw, cl $\rangle$ s.t. $\mathcal{F}_{\mathsf{aPAKE\text{-}cEA}}$ sent (sid, K') to P' when this record was fresh, set $K \leftarrow K'$;
  3. Else if role = cl set $K \leftarrow_{\mathrm{R}} \{0,1\}^{\ell}$, and if role = sr set $K \leftarrow \perp$.

  Finally, mark rec as completed and send output (sid, K) to P.

Fig. 10. $\mathcal{F}_{\mathsf{aPAKE\text{-}cEA}}$: asymmetric PAKE with explicit C-to-S authentication

This is reflected in including uid in the inputs to CltSession command in Fig. 9. However, since the client now performs computation on a fixed uid, honest client and server sessions will not agree on the same output key unless they run not only on the same password pw but also on the same uid. Hence the NewKey processing now includes uid-equality enforcement. Finally, for the same reason, an online password test TestPwd must specify the uid field in addition to password guess pw^*.

Functionality $\mathcal{F}_{\mathsf{aPAKE}}$ currently allows both the server and the client sessions to leak the account identifier uid input to the adversary. The server-side leakage of this information was inherent (although not immediate to observe) in the original aPAKE functionality of [24], and it was adopted by subsequent works, including e.g. [25,30]. Now, however, we also introduce client-side leakage of the same information. The uid has to be transmitted from the client to the server before the protocol starts, but it is not clear that the cryptographic protocol should leak it. We leave plugging this leakage and/or verifying whether it is necessary in known aPAKEs, including ours, to future work.

Client-to-Server Entity Authentication. Since our protocol OKAPE shown includes client-to-server authentication (it is *not* optional, and the protocol is insecure without it), it realizes an aPAKE functionality amended by client-to-server entity authentication. We use $\mathcal{F}_{\mathsf{aPAKE\text{-}cEA}}$ to denote the variant of aPAKE functionality with uni-directional client-to-server entity authentication, and we include it in Fig. 10. Since protocol OKAPE is a *salted* aPAKE, it does not need the uid input on the client side, so the $\mathcal{F}_{\mathsf{aPAKE\text{-}cEA}}$ functionality in Fig. 10 incorporates all the code of functionality $\mathcal{F}_{\mathsf{aPAKE}}$ but without the uid-related modifications. To simplify NewKey processing functionality $\mathcal{F}_{\mathsf{aPAKE\text{-}cEA}}$ in Fig. 10 assumes that the client party terminates first, so if two honest parties are connected then the client party computes its session key output first, and it is always the server party which can potentially get the same key copied by the functionality. One could define it more generally but we expect that in most aPAKE protocols with unilateral client-to-server explicit authentication the server will indeed be the last party to terminate.

B   Simulator for Proof of Theorem 3

Because of space constraints, we refer the reader to [23] for a complete proof of Theorem 3, and provide here an abridged version containing only the overall proof strategy and the description of the simulator.

To prove the theorem we need to construct a simulator, denoted SIM, such that the environment's view of the real-world security game, i.e. an interaction between the adversary $\mathcal{A}$ (whom we consider as a subprocedure of the environment $\mathcal{Z}$) and honest parties following protocol OKAPE, is indistinguishable from the environment's view in the ideal-world interaction between $\mathcal{A}$, SIM, and the functionality $\mathcal{F}_{\mathsf{aPAKE\text{-}cEA}}$.

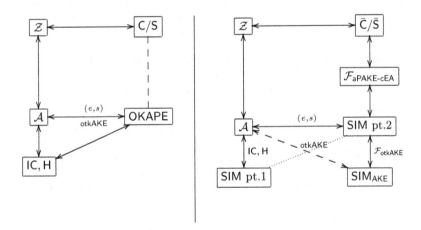

Fig. 11. Real-world (left) vs. simulation (right) for protocol OKAPE

Simulator Construction. We show an overview of our simulation strategy in Fig 11, which gives the top-level view of the real world execution compared to the ideal world execution which involves the simulator SIM shown in Figs. 12 and 13 as well as the simulator $\mathsf{SIM}_{\mathsf{AKE}}$ for the otkAKE subprotocol. The description of simulator SIM is split into two parts as follows: Fig. 12 contains the SIM pt.1 part of the diagram in Fig 11, i.e. it deals with adversary's ideal cipher and hash queries, and in addition with the compromise of password files. Figure 13 contains the SIM pt.2 part of the diagram in Fig 11 dealing with on-line aPAKE sessions. We rely on the fact that protocol otkAKE realizes functionality $\mathcal{F}_{\mathsf{otkAKE}}$, so we can assume that there exists a simulator $\mathsf{SIM}_{\mathsf{AKE}}$ which exhibits this UC-security of otkAKE. Our simulator SIM uses simulator $\mathsf{SIM_{AKE}}$ as a sub-procedure. Namely, SIM hands over to $\mathsf{SIM_{AKE}}$ the simulation of all C-side and S-side AKE instances where parties run on either honestly generated or adversarial AKE keys. SIM employs $\mathsf{SIM_{AKE}}$ to generate such keys - in H queries, password file compromise and in IC decryption queries - see Fig. 12, and then it hands off to $\mathsf{SIM_{AKE}}$ the handling of all AKE instances that run on such keys, see Fig. 13.

Initialization

Initialize simulator $\mathsf{SIM_{AKE}}$, empty tables $\mathsf{T_{IC}}$ and $\mathsf{T_H}$, empty lists PK, CPK

Notation: $\mathsf{T}_{IC}^h.X' = \{x' \mid \exists y \ (h, x', y) \in \mathsf{T_{IC}}\}$, $\mathsf{T}_{IC}^h.Y = \{y \mid \exists x' \ (h, x', y) \in \mathsf{T_{IC}}\}$.

Convention: First call to SvrSession or StealPwdFile for $(\mathsf{S}, \mathsf{uid})$ sets $s_\mathsf{S}^\mathsf{uid} \leftarrow_\mathsf{R} \{0,1\}^\kappa$.

On query (pw, s) to random oracle H

send back (h, a) if $\exists \ \langle (pw, s), (h, a) \rangle \in \mathsf{T_H}$, otherwise do:

1. If $s \neq s_\mathsf{S}^\mathsf{uid}$ for all $(\mathsf{S}, \mathsf{uid})$ then $h \leftarrow_\mathsf{R} \{0,1\}^\kappa$, init. key A via (Init, clts, cl) call to $\mathsf{SIM_{AKE}}$, send (Compromise, A) to $\mathsf{SIM_{AKE}}$, define a as $\mathsf{SIM_{AKE}}$'s response, add A to CPK

2. If $s = s_\mathsf{S}^\mathsf{uid}$ for some $(\mathsf{S}, \mathsf{uid})$ send (OfflineTestPwd, $\mathsf{S}, \mathsf{uid}, pw$) to $\mathcal{F}_\mathsf{aPAKE\text{-}cEA}$ and:
   (a) if $\mathcal{F}_\mathsf{aPAKE\text{-}cEA}$ sends "correct guess" then set $A \leftarrow A_\mathsf{S}^\mathsf{uid}$ and $h \leftarrow h_\mathsf{S}^\mathsf{uid}$
   (b) else inititalize key A via call (Init, clts, cl) to $\mathsf{SIM_{AKE}}$, add A to PK, pick $h \leftarrow \{0,1\}^\kappa$
   In either case send (Compromise, A) to $\mathsf{SIM_{AKE}}$, define a as $\mathsf{SIM_{AKE}}$'s response, add A to CPK, set $\mathsf{info}_\mathsf{S}^\mathsf{uid}(pw) \leftarrow (A, h)$

In all cases add $\langle (pw, s), (h, a) \rangle$ to $\mathsf{T_H}$ and send back (h, a)

Ideal Cipher IC queries

  - On query (h, x') to IC.E, send back y if $(h, x', y) \in \mathsf{T_{IC}}$, otherwise pick $y \leftarrow_\mathsf{R} Y \setminus \mathsf{T}_{IC}^h.Y$, add (h, x', y) to $\mathsf{T_{IC}}$, and send back y

  - On query (h, y) to IC.D, send back x' if $(h, x', y) \in \mathsf{T_{IC}}$. Otherwise if there exists $(\mathsf{S}, \mathsf{uid})$ and (A, pw) such that $y = e_{\mathsf{S}, \mathsf{uid}}^\mathsf{sid}$ and $\mathsf{info}_\mathsf{S}^\mathsf{uid}(pw) = (A, h)$ then set $\mathsf{id} = \mathsf{S}$, else set $\mathsf{id} = \mathsf{null}$. Initialize key B via call (Init, id, sr) to $\mathsf{SIM_{AKE}}$ and add B to PK. Set $x' \leftarrow_\mathsf{R} \mathsf{map}(B)$, add (h, x', y) to $\mathsf{T_{IC}}$ and send back x'

Stealing Password Data

On $\mathcal{Z}$'s permission to do so send (StealPwdFile, S, uid) to $\mathcal{F}_\mathsf{aPAKE\text{-}cEA}$. If $\mathcal{F}_\mathsf{aPAKE\text{-}cEA}$ sends "no password file," pass it to $\mathcal{A}$, otherwise do the following:

1. if $\mathcal{F}_\mathsf{aPAKE\text{-}cEA}$ returns pw, set $(A, h) \leftarrow \mathsf{info}_\mathsf{S}^\mathsf{uid}(pw)$
2. else init. A via call (Init, clts, cl) to $\mathsf{SIM_{AKE}}$, add A to PK, pick $h \leftarrow \{0,1\}^\kappa$

Set $(A_\mathsf{S}^\mathsf{uid}, h_\mathsf{S}^\mathsf{uid}) \leftarrow (A, h)$, return file[uid, S] $\leftarrow (A_\mathsf{S}^\mathsf{uid}, h_\mathsf{S}^\mathsf{uid}, s_\mathsf{S}^\mathsf{uid})$ to $\mathcal{A}$.

Fig. 12. Simulator SIM showing that protocol OKAPE$\mathcal{F}_\mathsf{aPAKE\text{-}cEA}$: part 1

Starting AKE sessions

On $(\mathsf{SvrSession}, \mathsf{sid}, \mathsf{S}, \mathsf{C}, \mathsf{uid})$ from $\mathcal{F}_{\mathsf{aPAKE\text{-}cEA}}$, initialize random function $R_\mathsf{S}^\mathsf{sid}$: $(\{0,1\}^*)^3 \to \{0,1\}^\kappa$, pick $e_{\mathsf{S},\mathsf{uid}}^\mathsf{sid} \leftarrow_\mathsf{R} Y$, set $\mathsf{flag}(\mathsf{S}^\mathsf{sid}) \leftarrow \mathsf{hbc}$, send $(e_{\mathsf{S},\mathsf{uid}}^\mathsf{sid}, s_\mathsf{S}^\mathsf{uid})$ to $\mathcal{A}$ as a message from S^sid, and send $(\mathsf{NewSession}, \mathsf{sid}, \mathsf{S}, \mathsf{C}, \mathtt{sr})$ to $\mathsf{SIM}_\mathsf{AKE}$

On $(\mathsf{CltSession}, \mathsf{sid}, \mathsf{C}, \mathsf{S})$ from $\mathcal{F}_{\mathsf{aPAKE\text{-}cEA}}$ and message (e', s') sent by $\mathcal{A}$ to C^sid, initialize random function $R_\mathsf{C}^\mathsf{sid} : (\{0,1\}^*)^3 \to \{0,1\}^\kappa$, and:

1. If $\exists$ uid s.t. $(e', s') = (e_{\mathsf{S},\mathsf{uid}}^\mathsf{sid}, s_\mathsf{S}^\mathsf{uid})$, set $\mathsf{flag}(\mathsf{C}^\mathsf{sid}) \leftarrow \mathsf{hbc}_\mathsf{S}^\mathsf{uid}$, go to 5.

2. If $\exists x', \mathsf{uid}$ s.t. $s' = s_\mathsf{S}^\mathsf{uid}$ and e' was output by IC.E on $(h_\mathsf{S}^\mathsf{uid}, x')$, send $(\mathsf{Impersonate}, \mathsf{sid}, \mathsf{C}, \mathsf{S}, \mathsf{uid})$ to $\mathcal{F}_{\mathsf{aPAKE\text{-}cEA}}$ and:
   (a) If $\mathcal{F}_{\mathsf{aPAKE\text{-}cEA}}$ returns "correct guess", $\mathsf{flag}(\mathsf{C}^\mathsf{sid}) \leftarrow (\mathsf{act}_\mathsf{S}^\mathsf{uid}, A_\mathsf{S}^\mathsf{uid}, \mathsf{map}^{-1}(x'))$
   (b) If it returns "wrong guess", set $\mathsf{flag}(\mathsf{C}^\mathsf{sid}) \leftarrow \mathsf{rnd}$.
   Either case, go to 5.

3. If $\exists (x', h, a, pw)$ s.t. e' was output by IC.E on (h, x') and $\langle (pw, s'), (h, a) \rangle \in \mathsf{T_H}$ (SIM aborts if tuple not unique), send $(\mathsf{TestPwd}, \mathsf{sid}, \mathsf{C}, pw)$ to $\mathcal{F}_{\mathsf{aPAKE\text{-}cEA}}$ and:
   (a) If $\mathcal{F}_{\mathsf{aPAKE\text{-}cEA}}$ returns "correct guess", $\mathsf{flag}(\mathsf{C}^\mathsf{sid}) \leftarrow (\mathsf{act}_\mathsf{S}^\mathsf{uid}, A, \mathsf{map}^{-1}(x'))$ where A is the public key generated from a.
   (b) If it returns "wrong guess", set $\mathsf{flag}(\mathsf{C}^\mathsf{sid}) \leftarrow \mathsf{rnd}$.
   Either case, go to 5.

4. In all other cases set $\mathsf{flag}(\mathsf{C}^\mathsf{sid}) \leftarrow \mathsf{rnd}$, go to 5.

5. Send $(\mathsf{NewSession}, \mathsf{sid}, \mathsf{C}, \mathsf{S}, \mathtt{cl})$ to $\mathsf{SIM}_\mathsf{AKE}$

Responding to $\mathsf{SIM}_\mathsf{AKE}$ messages to $\mathcal{F}_{\mathsf{otkAKE}}$ emulated by SIM

SIM passes otkAKE protocol messages between $\mathsf{SIM}_\mathsf{AKE}$ and $\mathcal{A}$, but when $\mathsf{SIM}_\mathsf{AKE}$ outputs queries to (what $\mathsf{SIM}_\mathsf{AKE}$ thinks is) $\mathcal{F}_{\mathsf{otkAKE}}$, SIM reacts as follows:

If $\mathsf{SIM}_\mathsf{AKE}$ outputs $(\mathsf{Interfere}, \mathsf{sid}, \mathsf{S})$ set $\mathsf{flag}(\mathsf{S}^\mathsf{sid}) \leftarrow \mathsf{act}$

If $\mathsf{SIM}_\mathsf{AKE}$ outputs $(\mathsf{Interfere}, \mathsf{sid}, \mathsf{C})$ and $\mathsf{flag}(\mathsf{C}^\mathsf{sid}) = \mathsf{hbc}_\mathsf{S}^\mathsf{uid}$ then set $\mathsf{flag}(\mathsf{C}^\mathsf{sid}) \leftarrow \mathsf{rnd}$

If $\mathsf{SIM}_\mathsf{AKE}$ outputs $(\mathsf{NewKey}, \mathsf{sid}, \mathsf{C}, \alpha)$:
1. If $\mathsf{flag}(\mathsf{C}^\mathsf{sid}) = (\mathsf{act}_\mathsf{S}^\mathsf{uid}, A, B)$ then $k \leftarrow R_\mathsf{C}^\mathsf{sid}(A, B, \alpha)$, output $\tau \leftarrow \mathsf{prf}(k, 1)$ and send $(\mathsf{NewKey}, \mathsf{sid}, \mathsf{C}, \mathsf{prf}(k, 0))$ to $\mathcal{F}_{\mathsf{aPAKE\text{-}cEA}}$
2. Else output $\tau \leftarrow_\mathsf{R} \{0,1\}^\kappa$ and send $(\mathsf{NewKey}, \mathsf{sid}, \mathsf{C}, \perp)$ to $\mathcal{F}_{\mathsf{aPAKE\text{-}cEA}}$

If $\mathsf{SIM}_\mathsf{AKE}$ outputs $(\mathsf{NewKey}, \mathsf{sid}, \mathsf{S}, \alpha)$ and $\mathcal{A}$ sends τ' to S^sid:
1. If $\mathsf{flag}(\mathsf{S}^\mathsf{sid}) = \mathsf{hbc}$ and τ' was generated by SIM for C^sid s.t. $\mathsf{flag}(\mathsf{C}^\mathsf{sid}) = \mathsf{hbc}_\mathsf{S}^\mathsf{uid}$, then send $(\mathsf{NewKey}, \mathsf{sid}, \mathsf{S}, \perp)$ to $\mathcal{F}_{\mathsf{aPAKE\text{-}cEA}}$
2. If $\mathsf{flag}(\mathsf{S}^\mathsf{sid}) = \mathsf{act}$ and $\exists (pw, B)$ s.t. $\tau' = \mathsf{prf}(k, 1)$ for $k = R_\mathsf{S}^\mathsf{sid}(B, A, \alpha)$ where $(A, h) = \mathsf{info}_\mathsf{S}^\mathsf{uid}(pw)$ and $(h, \mathsf{map}(B), e_{\mathsf{S},\mathsf{uid}}^\mathsf{sid}) \in \mathsf{T_{IC}}$ (SIM aborts if tuple not unique), send $(\mathsf{TestPwd}, \mathsf{sid}, \mathsf{S}, pw)$ and $(\mathsf{NewKey}, \mathsf{sid}, \mathsf{S}, \mathsf{prf}(k, 0))$ to $\mathcal{F}_{\mathsf{aPAKE\text{-}cEA}}$
3. In any other case send $(\mathsf{TestPwd}, \mathsf{sid}, \mathsf{S}, \perp)$ and $(\mathsf{NewKey}, \mathsf{sid}, \mathsf{S}, \perp)$ to $\mathcal{F}_{\mathsf{aPAKE\text{-}cEA}}$

If $\mathsf{SIM}_\mathsf{AKE}$ outputs $(\mathsf{SessionKey}, \mathsf{sid}, \mathsf{P}, pk, pk', \alpha)$:
   If $pk' \notin (PK \setminus CPK)$ send $R_\mathsf{P}^\mathsf{sid}(pk, pk', \alpha)$ to $\mathcal{A}$

Fig. 13. Simulator SIM showing that protocol OKAPE realizes $\mathcal{F}_{\mathsf{aPAKE\text{-}cEA}}$: part 2

References

1. Facebook stored hundreds of millions of passwords in plain text. https://www.theverge.com/2019/3/21/18275837/facebook-plain-text-password-storage-hundreds-millions-users

2. Google stored some passwords in plain text for fourteen years. https://www.theverge.com/2019/5/21/18634842/google-passwords-plain-text-g-suite-fourteen-years

3. Abdalla, M., Barbosa, M., Bradley, T., Jarecki, S., Katz, J., Xu, J.: Universally composable relaxed password authenticated key exchange. In: Micciancio, D., Ristenpart, T. (eds.) CRYPTO 2020. LNCS, vol. 12170, pp. 278–307. Springer, Cham (2020). https://doi.org/10.1007/978-3-030-56784-2_10

4. Abdalla, M., Pointcheval, D.: Simple password-based encrypted key exchange protocols. In: Menezes, A. (ed.) CT-RSA 2005. LNCS, vol. 3376, pp. 191–208. Springer, Heidelberg (2005). https://doi.org/10.1007/978-3-540-30574-3_14

5. Andreeva, E., Bogdanov, A., Dodis, Y., Mennink, B., Steinberger, J.P.: On the indifferentiability of key-alternating ciphers. In: Canetti, R., Garay, J.A. (eds.) CRYPTO 2013. LNCS, vol. 8042, pp. 531–550. Springer, Heidelberg (2013). https://doi.org/10.1007/978-3-642-40041-4_29

6. Bellare, M., Pointcheval, D., Rogaway, P.: Authenticated key exchange secure against dictionary attacks. In: Preneel, B. (ed.) EUROCRYPT 2000. LNCS, vol. 1807, pp. 139–155. Springer, Heidelberg (2000). https://doi.org/10.1007/3-540-45539-6_11

7. Bellovin, S.M., Merritt, M.: Encrypted key exchange: password-based protocols secure against dictionary attacks. In: IEEE Computer Society Symposium on Research in Security and Privacy - S&P 1992, pp. 72–84. IEEE (1992)

8. Benhamouda, F., Pointcheval, D.: Verifier-based password-authenticated key exchange: new models and constructions. IACR Cryptology ePrint Archive 2013:833 (2013)

9. Bernstein, D.J., Hamburg, M., Krasnova, A., Lange, T.: Elligator: elliptic-curve points indistinguishable from uniform random strings. In: ACM Conference on Computer and Communications Security - CCS 2013 (2013)

10. Bernstein, D.J., et al.: Gimli: a cross-platform permutation. Cryptology ePrint Archive, Report 2017/630 (2017). http://eprint.iacr.org/2017/630

11. Bertoni, G., Daemen, J., Peeters, M., Van Assche, G.: Keccak. In: Johansson, T., Nguyen, P.Q. (eds.) EUROCRYPT 2013. LNCS, vol. 7881, pp. 313–314. Springer, Heidelberg (2013). https://doi.org/10.1007/978-3-642-38348-9_19

12. Boyko, V., MacKenzie, P., Patel, S.: Provably secure password-authenticated key exchange using Diffie-Hellman. In: Preneel, B. (ed.) EUROCRYPT 2000. LNCS, vol. 1807, pp. 156–171. Springer, Heidelberg (2000). https://doi.org/10.1007/3-540-45539-6_12

13. Bradley, T., Jarecki, S., Xu, J.: Strong asymmetric PAKE based on trapdoor CKEM. In: Boldyreva, A., Micciancio, D. (eds.) CRYPTO 2019. LNCS, vol. 11694, pp. 798–825. Springer, Cham (2019). https://doi.org/10.1007/978-3-030-26954-8_26

14. Brier, E., Coron, J.-S., Icart, T., Madore, D., Randriam, H., Tibouchi, M.: Efficient indifferentiable hashing into ordinary elliptic curves. In: Rabin, T. (ed.) CRYPTO 2010. LNCS, vol. 6223, pp. 237–254. Springer, Heidelberg (2010). https://doi.org/10.1007/978-3-642-14623-7_13

15. Canetti, R., Halevi, S., Katz, J., Lindell, Y., MacKenzie, P.: Universally composable password-based key exchange. In: Cramer, R. (ed.) EUROCRYPT 2005. LNCS, vol. 3494, pp. 404–421. Springer, Heidelberg (2005). https://doi.org/10.1007/11426639_24

16. Coron, J.-S., Dodis, Y., Mandal, A., Seurin, Y.: A domain extender for the ideal cipher. In: Micciancio, D. (ed.) TCC 2010. LNCS, vol. 5978, pp. 273–289. Springer, Heidelberg (2010). https://doi.org/10.1007/978-3-642-11799-2_17

17. Dachman-Soled, D., Katz, J., Thiruvengadam, A.: 10-round Feistel is indifferentiable from an ideal cipher. In: Fischlin, M., Coron, J.-S. (eds.) EUROCRYPT 2016. LNCS, vol. 9666, pp. 649–678. Springer, Heidelberg (2016). https://doi.org/10.1007/978-3-662-49896-5_23

18. Daemen, J., Hoffert, S., Assche, G.V., Keer, R.V.: The design of Xoodoo and Xoofff. **2018**, 1–38 (2018)

19. Dai, Y., Seurin, Y., Steinberger, J., Thiruvengadam, A.: Indifferentiability of iterated Even-Mansour ciphers with non-idealized key-schedules: five rounds are necessary and sufficient. In: Katz, J., Shacham, H. (eds.) CRYPTO 2017. LNCS, vol. 10403, pp. 524–555. Springer, Cham (2017). https://doi.org/10.1007/978-3-319-63697-9_18

20. Dai, Y., Steinberger, J.: Indifferentiability of 8-round Feistel networks. In: Robshaw, M., Katz, J. (eds.) CRYPTO 2016. LNCS, vol. 9814, pp. 95–120. Springer, Heidelberg (2016). https://doi.org/10.1007/978-3-662-53018-4_4

21. Dodis, Y., Stam, M., Steinberger, J., Liu, T.: Indifferentiability of confusion-diffusion networks. In: Fischlin, M., Coron, J.-S. (eds.) EUROCRYPT 2016. LNCS, vol. 9666, pp. 679–704. Springer, Heidelberg (2016). https://doi.org/10.1007/978-3-662-49896-5_24

22. Fouque, P.-A., Joux, A., Tibouchi, M.: Injective encodings to elliptic curves. In: Boyd, C., Simpson, L. (eds.) ACISP 2013. LNCS, vol. 7959, pp. 203–218. Springer, Heidelberg (2013). https://doi.org/10.1007/978-3-642-39059-3_14

23. Freitas Dos Santos, B., Gu, Y., Jarecki, S., Krawczyk, H.: Asymmetric PAKE with low computation and communication. IACR Cryptology ePrint Archive, 2022 (2022). https://ia.cr/2022

24. Gentry, C., MacKenzie, P., Ramzan, Z.: A method for making password-based key exchange resilient to server compromise. In: Dwork, C. (ed.) CRYPTO 2006. LNCS, vol. 4117, pp. 142–159. Springer, Heidelberg (2006). https://doi.org/10.1007/11818175_9

25. Gu, Y., Jarecki, S., Krawczyk, H.: KHAPE: asymmetric PAKE from key-hiding key exchange. In: Malkin, T., Peikert, C. (eds.) CRYPTO 2021. LNCS, vol. 12828, pp. 701–730. Springer, Cham (2021). https://doi.org/10.1007/978-3-030-84259-8_24, https://ia.cr/2021/873

26. Halevi, S., Krawczyk, H.: One-pass HMQV and asymmetric key-wrapping. In: Catalano, D., Fazio, N., Gennaro, R., Nicolosi, A. (eds.) PKC 2011. LNCS, vol. 6571, pp. 317–334. Springer, Heidelberg (2011). https://doi.org/10.1007/978-3-642-19379-8_20

27. Holenstein, T., Künzler, R., Tessaro, S.: The equivalence of the random oracle model and the ideal cipher model, revisited. In: STOC 2011 (2011)

28. Hwang, J.Y., Jarecki, S., Kwon, T., Lee, J., Shin, J.S., Xu, J.: Round-reduced modular construction of asymmetric password-authenticated key exchange. In: Catalano, D., De Prisco, R. (eds.) SCN 2018. LNCS, vol. 11035, pp. 485–504. Springer, Cham (2018). https://doi.org/10.1007/978-3-319-98113-0_26

29. Jablon, D.P.: Extended password key exchange protocols immune to dictionary attacks. In: 6th IEEE International Workshops on Enabling Technologies: Infrastructure for Collaborative Enterprises (WETICE 1997), pp. 248–255, Cambridge, MA, USA, 18–20 June 1997. IEEE Computer Society (1997)

30. Jarecki, S., Krawczyk, H., Xu, J.: OPAQUE: an asymmetric PAKE protocol secure against pre-computation attacks. In: Nielsen, J.B., Rijmen, V. (eds.) EUROCRYPT 2018. LNCS, vol. 10822, pp. 456–486. Springer, Cham (2018). https://doi.org/10.1007/978-3-319-78372-7_15

31. Jarecki, S., Krawczyk, H., Xu, J.: On the (in)security of the Diffie-Hellman oblivious PRF with multiplicative blinding. In: Garay, J.A. (ed.) PKC 2021. LNCS, vol. 12711, pp. 380–409. Springer, Cham (2021). https://doi.org/10.1007/978-3-030-75248-4_14

32. Jutla, C.S., Roy, A.: Smooth NIZK arguments. In: Beimel, A., Dziembowski, S. (eds.) TCC 2018. LNCS, vol. 11239, pp. 235–262. Springer, Cham (2018). https://doi.org/10.1007/978-3-030-03807-6_9

33. Kim, T., Tibouchi, M.: Invalid curve attacks in a GLS setting. In: Tanaka, K., Suga, Y. (eds.) IWSEC 2015. LNCS, vol. 9241, pp. 41–55. Springer, Cham (2015). https://doi.org/10.1007/978-3-319-22425-1_3

34. Krawczyk, H.: SKEME: a versatile secure key exchange mechanism for internet. In: 1996 Internet Society Symposium on Network and Distributed System Security (NDSS), pp. 114–127 (1996)

35. Krawczyk, H.: HMQV: a high-performance secure Diffie-Hellman protocol. In: Shoup, V. (ed.) CRYPTO 2005. LNCS, vol. 3621, pp. 546–566. Springer, Heidelberg (2005). https://doi.org/10.1007/11535218_33

36. Marlinspike, M., Perrin, T.: The X3DH key agreement protocol (2016). https://signal.org/docs/specifications/x3dh/

37. McQuoid, I., Rosulek, M., Roy, L.: Minimal symmetric PAKE and 1-out-of-n OT from programmable-once public functions. In: Ligatti, J., Ou, X., Katz, J., Vigna, G. (eds.) CCS 2020: 2020 ACM SIGSAC Conference on Computer and Communications Security, Virtual Event, USA, 9–13 November 2020. https://eprint.iacr.org/2020/1043

38. Pointcheval, D., Wang, G.: VTBPEKE: verifier-based two-basis password exponential key exchange. In: ASIACCS 2017, pp. 301–312. ACM Press (2017)

39. Schmidt, J.: Requirements for password-authenticated key agreement (PAKE) schemes, April 2017. https://tools.ietf.org/html/rfc8125

40. Shallue, A., van de Woestijne, C.E.: Construction of rational points on elliptic curves over finite fields. In: Hess, F., Pauli, S., Pohst, M. (eds.) ANTS 2006. LNCS, vol. 4076, pp. 510–524. Springer, Heidelberg (2006). https://doi.org/10.1007/11792086_36

41. Shoup, V.: Security analysis of SPAKE2+. IACR Cryptol. ePrint Arch. **2020**, 313 (2020)

42. Tibouchi, M.: Elligator squared: uniform points on elliptic curves of prime order as uniform random strings. In: Christin, N., Safavi-Naini, R. (eds.) FC 2014. LNCS, vol. 8437, pp. 139–156. Springer, Heidelberg (2014). https://doi.org/10.1007/978-3-662-45472-5_10

Batch-OT with Optimal Rate

Zvika Brakerski[1], Pedro Branco[2(✉)], Nico Döttling[3], and Sihang Pu[3(✉)]

[1] Weizmann Institute of Science, Rehovot, Israel
[2] IT, IST - University of Lisbon, Lisbon, Portugal
`pedrodemelobranco@gmail.com`
[3] CISPA Helmholtz Center for Information Security, Saarbrücken, Germany
`sihang.pu@gmail.com`

Abstract. We show that it is possible to perform n independent copies of 1-out-of-2 oblivious transfer in two messages, where the communication complexity of the receiver and sender (each) is $n(1 + o(1))$ for sufficiently large n. Note that this matches the information-theoretic lower bound. Prior to this work, this was only achievable by using the heavy machinery of rate-1 fully homomorphic encryption (Rate-1 FHE, Brakerski et al., TCC 2019).

To achieve rate-1 both on the receiver's and sender's end, we use the LPN assumption, with slightly sub-constant noise rate $1/m^\epsilon$ for any $\epsilon > 0$ together with either the DDH, QR or LWE assumptions. In terms of efficiency, our protocols only rely on linear homomorphism, as opposed to the FHE-based solution which inherently requires an expensive "bootstrapping" operation. We believe that in terms of efficiency we compare favorably to existing batch-OT protocols, while achieving superior communication complexity. We show similar results for Oblivious Linear Evaluation (OLE).

For our DDH-based solution we develop a new technique that may be of independent interest. We show that it is possible to "emulate" the binary group $\mathbb{Z}_2$ (or any other small-order group) inside a prime-order group $\mathbb{Z}_p$ in a *function-private manner*. That is, $\mathbb{Z}_2$ operations are mapped to $\mathbb{Z}_p$ operations such that the outcome of the latter do not reveal additional information beyond the $\mathbb{Z}_2$ outcome. Our encoding technique uses the discrete Gaussian distribution, which to our knowledge was not done before in the context of DDH.

1 Introduction

Oblivious Transfer (OT) [20,34] is one of the most basic cryptographic primitives. In the simple 1-out-of-2 OT, a receiver holds a bit $b \in \{0, 1\}$ and a sender holds two bits x_0, x_1. In the end of the protocol, the receiver should learn x_b, but nothing about x_{1-b}, and the sender should learn nothing about the value of b. In most applications, one OT is not enough and one is required to perform many OT operations in parallel. We let n denote the number of parallel executions. Various techniques have been developed to address this task of *batch-OT* [5,6,29]. For the most part, they involve a preprocessing "offline" phase where

© International Association for Cryptologic Research 2022
O. Dunkelman and S. Dziembowski (Eds.): EUROCRYPT 2022, LNCS 13276, pp. 157–186, 2022.
https://doi.org/10.1007/978-3-031-07085-3_6

the parties generate random OT correlations.[1] Given such correlations, executing the OT protocol in the so-called "online phase" is computationally very simple. This approach is very useful for purposes of computational efficiency, since the offline phase can be carried out even before the actual inputs of the computation are known. However, in terms of communication complexity, there is an inherent cost, even just in the online phase, of n receiver bits and $2n$ sender bits. In contrast, the insecure implementation only requires n bits to be sent from each party in a two-message protocol: the receiver sends its input, and the sender returns all of the appropriate x_b values. As always in cryptography, we wish to understand what is the "cost of privacy", namely can we approach the information theoretic minimum without losing privacy. Note that we can only hope to achieve this for a sufficiently large n, due to the security parameter overhead.[2]

In prior work, Döttling et al. [19] showed that if the same receiver bit is used for multiple OT instances, then the sender's response can be compressed to $n(1+o(1))$, achieving an optimal amortized rate. This was shown under a variety of computational assumptions: Decisional Diffie-Hellman (DDH), Quadratic Residuosity (QR), or Learning with Errors (LWE). It was also shown by Brakerski et al. [10] and by Gentry and Halevi [23] that fully homomorphic encryption (FHE) can achieve optimal communication complexity, which in particular implies that under the LWE assumption, optimal rate batch-OT is achievable. However, the FHE-based protocol inherently requires the use of a computationally exorbitant "bootstrapping" mechanism in order to compress the receiver's message.

1.1   Our Contribution

We show that optimal-rate[3] batch-OT can be achieved from various computational assumptions, and without giving up on computational efficiency. In particular, we require the LPN assumption with a small-inverse-polynomial noise[4], in addition to one of the assumptions DDH, QR or LWE. In terms of computational cost, our protocol does not require heavy operations such as bootstrapping and relies on linear homomorphism only. We believe that in terms of overall cost it compares favorably even with random-OT based methods. All of our results are in the semi-honest (honest-but-curious) setting.

We further extend our results to the task of Oblivious Linear Evaluation (OLE) [12,14,24,30], where the sender holds a linear function over a ring and

---

[1] That is, a protocol in which the receiver obtains b, x_b and the sender obtains x_0, x_1, where b, x_0, x_1 are all (pseudo-)randomly sampled.

[2] In more detail, since 2-message OT implies a public-key encryption scheme, the messages must have length that relates to the security parameter of the underlying computation assumption. This is the case even for single-bit OT.

[3] Achieving optimal rate (or any rate above $1/2$) seems to involve a "phase-transition" and should be viewed as more than a "constant factor" improvement. For example, OT beyond this threshold implies the existence of lossy trapdoor functions (see discussion in [19], Sect. 6.3). Therefore one could expect such a protocol to inherently be heavier on public-key operations.

[4] This is still a regime where LPN alone is not known to imply public-key encryption.

the receiver holds an input for the function, and we wish for the receiver to learn the output on its input and nothing more, and the sender learns nothing as usual. OLE has been shown to be useful in various settings [14,27].

Our techniques rely mostly on linear homomorphism, namely on the ability to evaluate linear functions on encrypted data (see Sect. 2 below). Notably, we require a linearly homomorphic scheme over $\mathbb{Z}_2$ (more generally $\mathbb{Z}_q$ for OLE) where the evaluation is *function-private*. Namely, the output ciphertext should not reveal any information about the linear function that was evaluated. This was not known to be achievable from DDH prior to this work, and we introduce a new technique that we believe may be of independent interest. The reason for this is that DDH works "natively" over the group $\mathbb{Z}_p$ where p is a super-polynomially large prime. Furthermore, we only have access to the $\mathbb{Z}_p$ elements in the exponent of a group generator g. Indeed, one can encode $0 \to g^0, 1 \to g^1$, and linear $\mathbb{Z}_2$ homomorphism will follow in the sense that after applying a linear function in the exponent, we obtain g^x, where $x \pmod 2$ is the desired $\mathbb{Z}_2$ output. This creates two obstacles: first we need to be able to efficiently map $g^x \to x$, which means that x must come from a polynomially-bounded domain, and second that recovering x reveals more information than just $x \pmod 2$. We develop a new method to resolve this issue using *discrete Gaussian variables*. A technique that was used in the context of the LWE assumption but to the best of our knowledge not for DDH. We view this as an additional contribution of this work, which may find additional applications. In particular we show that it can be used to enhance the key-dependent-message security properties of the well-known encryption scheme [3].

For more details on all of our contributions, see the technical overview in Sect. 2.

1.2 Related Work

The communication complexity of OT has been extensively studied throughout the decades. Here we present a brief overlook of previous works.

OT from Pseudorandom Correlations. A recent line of research studies the feasibility of efficiently extending OTs in a *silent* manner [5,6]. In these works, a setup phase is performed to distributed some *shares* between the parties. These shares can later be expanded into random OT correlations. In the most efficient scheme [5] the setup phase can be performed in just two rounds assuming just a pseudorandom generator and an OT scheme. Using this scheme for performing the setup together with the standard transformations form random OT to chosen-input OT, [5] shows that n independent instances of OT for s-bit strings can be performed with communication complexity $(2s + 1)n + o(n)$. For bit OT, this yields a communication complexity $3n + o(n)$ bits.

Download Rate-1 OT. We say that an OT protocol has download rate 1 if the rate of the sender's message is asymptotically close to 1. OT protocols with download rate 1 were presented in [15,19,21]. However, these protocols do not achieve upload rate 1, that is, the rate of the receiver's message is far from being 1. Moreover, it is not clear how we can extend these protocols to achieve upload rate 1.

Using Rate-1 FHE. As mentioned before, optimal-rate OT can be achieved using the recent scheme for rate-1 fully homomorphic encryption (FHE) of [10,23] together with (semi-honest) circuit-privacy techniques for FHE (e.g. [4]). However this can only be instantiated using LWE.

Laconic OT. Laconic OT [1,16,28,33] is a flavor of two-round OT where the first message sent by the receiver is sublinear (ideally polylogarithmically) in the size of its input. However, by a simple information-theoretical argument, the sender's message has size at least as large as the size of the sender's input. Note that, if this is not the case, then we would have an OT protocol with asymptotically better communication than an insecure OT protocol.

2 Technical Overview

2.1 Oblivious Transfer from Homomorphic Encryption

Our starting point is a textbook construction of oblivious transfer from simple homomorphic encryption schemes, such as ElGamal. For a cryptographic group $\mathbb{G} = \langle g \rangle$ of prime order p, recall that an ElGamal public key is of the form $\mathsf{pk} = (g, h = g^x) \in \mathbb{G}^2$, where $x \overset{\$}{\leftarrow} \mathbb{Z}_p$ is the secret key. Ciphertexts are of the form $c = (c_1, c_2) = (g^r, h^r \cdot g^b)$, where $r \overset{\$}{\leftarrow} \mathbb{Z}_p$ is uniformly random and $b \in \{0,1\}$ is the encrypted message. Given such a ciphertext c, the public key pk and two bits $m_0, m_1 \in \{0,1\}$, anyone can homomorphically compute a new ciphertext c' which is distributed identically to a fresh encryption of m_b, by *homomorphically evaluating* the linear function $f(x) = (1-x) \cdot m_0 + x \cdot m_1 = (m_1 - m_0) \cdot x + m_0$ on the ciphertext c and rerandomizing the resulting ciphertext. Note that if $b \in \{0,1\}$ is a bit, then it holds that $f(b) = m_b$. This homomorphic evaluation can be achieved by computing

$$c_1' \leftarrow g^{r^*} \cdot c_1^{m_1 - m_0}$$
$$c_2' \leftarrow h^{r^*} \cdot c_2^{m_1 - m_0} \cdot g^{m_0},$$

where $r^* \overset{\$}{\leftarrow} \mathbb{Z}_p$ is chosen uniformly random. Note that it holds that

$$c_1' = g^{r^* + r \cdot (m_1 - m_0)}$$
$$c_2' = h^{r^* + r \cdot (m_1 - m_0)} \cdot g^{(m_1 - m_0) \cdot b + m_0} = h^{r^* + r \cdot (m_1 - m_0)} \cdot g^{m_b}.$$

Since $r^* \overset{\$}{\leftarrow} \mathbb{Z}_p$ is chosen uniformly random, it holds that $r' = r^* + r \cdot (m_1 - m_0)$ is distributed uniformly random and we can conclude that $c' = (c_1', c_2')$ is distributed identical to a fresh encryption of m_b. Since c' does not reveal more than the function value $f(b) = m_b$, we call the above homomorphic evaluation procedure function private.

This immediately implies an OT protocol: An OT-receiver holding a choice-bit $b \in \{0,1\}$ generates a pair (pk, sk) of ElGamal public and secret keys, encrypts the bit b under pk and sends the resulting ciphertext to the OT-sender. The OT-sender, holding messages m_0, m_1, homomorphically computes a ciphertext c' encrypting m_b and sends c' back to the OT-receiver, who decrypts c' to m_b. Security against semi-honest senders follows from the IND-CPA security of ElGamal, whereas security against semi-honest receivers follows from the function privacy property established above.

2.2 Download-Rate Optimal String OT

While the above OT protocol is simple and efficient, it suffers from a very poor communication rate. While the receiver's message encrypts just a single bit, he needs to send 4 group elements, whereas the sender sends 2 group elements, each of size $\mathsf{poly}(\lambda)$.

Döttling et al. [19] proposed a compression technique for *batched ElGamal ciphertexts* based on the share-conversion technique of [7]. A batched ElGamal ciphertext is of the form $\mathbf{c} = (c_0, c_1, \ldots, c_\ell) = (g^r, h_1^r \cdot g^{b_1}, \ldots, h_\ell^r \cdot g^{b_\ell})$, where $\mathsf{pk} = (g, h_1, \ldots, h_\ell)$ is the corresponding public key and $\mathsf{sk} = (s_1, \ldots, s_\ell)$ with $h_i = g^{s_i}$ is the secret key. The compression technique of [19] keeps c_0 compresses each of the $c_1, \ldots, c_\ell$ into just a single bit. The idea is instead of sending each $c_i \in \mathbb{G}$ (for $i \geq 1$) in full, to first compute the distance d to the next pseudorandom *break-point* in $\mathbb{G}$, and then only send its parity $d \bmod 2$. The break points $\mathcal{P} \subseteq \mathbb{G}$ are the set of all points $h \in \mathbb{G}$ satisfying $\mathsf{PRF}_K(h) = 0^t$, where $\mathsf{PRF} : \mathbb{G} \to \{0,1\}^t$ is a pseudorandom function with a range of size $2^t = \mathsf{poly}(\lambda)$. Thus, the distance $d = d(c_i)$ of a group element c_i to the nearest break point is the smallest non-negative d such that $c_i \cdot g^d \in \mathcal{P}$. Given that neither c_i nor $c_i \cdot g^{-1}$ is a breakpoint, we can recover the bit b_i from $c_0 = g^r$, $\beta_{=}d(c_i) \bmod 2$ and the secret key component s_i. It was shown in [9] that for a given ciphertext $c = (c_0, c_1, \ldots, c_\ell)$, the PRF-key K can be (efficiently) chosen such that all c_i are good, in the sense that neither c_i nor $c_i \cdot g^{-1}$ is a breakpoint. This ensures that a receiver can recover the $b_1, \ldots, b_\ell$ from $c' = (K, c_0, \beta_1, \ldots, \beta_\ell)$, where $\beta_i = d(c_i) \bmod 2$. Since all the β_i are bits, such a compressed ciphertext only has additive size-overhead consisting of K, c_0. For a sufficiently large ℓ, this fixed overhead becomes insignificant and the ciphertext rate approaches 1.

The compressed batched ElGamal we've outlined leads to a batch bit-oblivious transfer protocol with *download-rate 1*: The receiver generates a key-pair pk, sk for batched ElGamal, and encrypts his choice-bits $b_1, \ldots, b_\ell$ into

$$\mathbf{c}_1 = \mathsf{Enc}_{\mathsf{pk}}(b_1, 0, \ldots, 0), \ldots, \mathbf{c}_\ell = \mathsf{Enc}_{\mathsf{pk}}(0, \ldots, 0, b_\ell),$$

i.e. $\mathbf{c}^{(i)}$ encrypts a vector which is b_i in index i and 0 everywhere else. The OT-receiver now sends $\mathsf{pk}, \mathbf{c}_1, \ldots, \mathbf{c}_\ell$ to the OT-sender, whose input are messages $(m_{1,0}, m_{1,1}), \ldots, (m_{\ell,0}, m_{\ell,1})$. Using circuit private homomorphic evaluation, the sender computes ciphertexts $\mathbf{c}'_1, \ldots, \mathbf{c}'_\ell$ encrypting $(m_{1,b_1}, 0, \ldots, 0)$, $\ldots, (0, \ldots, 0, m_{\ell,b_\ell})$. Homomorphically computing the sum of the ciphertexts

$\mathbf{c}'_1, \ldots, \mathbf{c}'_\ell$, we obtain a ciphertext $\mathbf{c}'$ encrypting $(m_{1,b_1}, \ldots, m_{\ell,b_\ell})$. Finally, compressing $\mathbf{c}'$ with the compression technique outlined above we obtain a compressed ciphertext $\bar{\mathbf{c}} = (K, c_0, \beta_1, \ldots, \beta_\ell)$ which the OT-sender sends back to the OT-receiver, who can decrypt $(m_{1,b_1}, \ldots, m_{\ell,b_\ell})$.

Note that the size of the sender's message $\bar{\mathbf{c}}$ in this batch OT-protocol is $\mathsf{poly}(\lambda) + \ell$, which means that the *amortized communication cost* per bit-OT approaches 1 bit, and is therefore asymptotically optimal. Even in terms of concrete complexity this seems hard to beat, as the only additional information sent by the sender are the PRF key K and the ciphertext header c_0.

However, in terms of the upload rate, i.e. in terms of the size of the receiver's message, this protocol performs poorly. Specifically, to encrypt ℓ bits $b_1, \ldots, b_\ell$, the receiver needs to send ciphertexts $\mathbf{c}_1, \ldots, \mathbf{c}_\ell$ of total size $\ell^2 \cdot \mathsf{poly}(\lambda)$, which has a worse dependence on ℓ than just repeating the simple protocol from the last paragraph ℓ times.

Clearly, we need a mechanism to compress the receiver's message. Applying the same ElGamal compression technique as for the sender's message quickly runs into problems: Once an ElGamal ciphertext is compressed, the scheme loses its homomorphic capabilities, i.e. we cannot perform any further homomorphic operations on compressed ciphertexts and currently we don't know if it is possible to publicly *decompress* such ciphertexts into "regular" ElGamal ciphertexts.

2.3 Our Approach: Recrypting the Receiver's Message

Instead, our approach will be to encrypt the receiver's message under a different encryption scheme, specifically one which achieves ciphertext rate approaching 1 but at the same time can be decrypted by the homomorphic capabilities of batched ElGamal. Specifically, the decryption procedure of this encryption scheme should be a linear function in the secret key. We can get an encryption scheme which almost fulfills these requirements from the Learning Parity with Noise (LPN) assumption. The LPN assumption states that for a random $m \times n$ matrix $\mathbf{A} \overset{\$}{\leftarrow} \mathbb{Z}_2^{m \times n}$, a random vector $\mathbf{s} \overset{\$}{\leftarrow} \mathbb{Z}_2^n$ and a ρ-Bernoulli distributed[5] $\mathbf{e} \in \mathbb{Z}_2^m$, it holds that

$$(\mathbf{A}, \mathbf{As} + \mathbf{e}) \approx_c (\mathbf{A}, \mathbf{u}),$$

where $\mathbf{u} \overset{\$}{\leftarrow} \mathbb{Z}_2^m$ is chosen uniformly at random. This gives rise to the following simple symmetric-key encryption scheme with *approximate correctness*: Assume that $\mathbf{A}$ is a fixed public parameter, the secret key is a uniformly random $\mathbf{s} \overset{\$}{\leftarrow} \mathbb{Z}_2^n$. To encrypt a message $m \in \mathbb{Z}_2^m$, we compute a ciphertext $\mathbf{d} \leftarrow \mathbf{As} + \mathbf{e} + \mathbf{m}$, where $\mathbf{e} \in \mathbb{Z}_2^m$ is chosen via a ρ-Bernoulli distribution. To decrypt such a ciphertext, we compute $\mathbf{m}' \leftarrow \mathbf{d} - \mathbf{A} \cdot \mathbf{s}$.

Note that this scheme is only approximately correct in the sense that it holds that $\mathbf{m}' = \mathbf{m} + \mathbf{e}$, i.e. in most coordinates $\mathbf{m}'$ is identical to $\mathbf{m}$, but only in few

---

[5] i.e. every component of e_i of $\mathbf{e}$ is independently 0 with probability $1 - \rho$ and 1 with probability ρ.

coordinates $\mathbf{m}'$ and $\mathbf{m}$ differ. Furthermore, one-time security of this encryption scheme follows from the LPN assumption.

The high level strategy to use this symmetric key encryption scheme is now as follows: Assume the matrix $\mathbf{A} \in \mathbb{Z}_2^{m \times n}$ is known to both the sender and the receiver. In the actual protocol this matrix will be chosen by the receiver, and the communication cost of sending $\mathbf{A}$ will be amortized by reusing $\mathbf{A}$ many times.

The OT-receiver chooses a symmetric key $\mathbf{s} \overset{\$}{\leftarrow} \mathbb{Z}_2^n$ uniformly at random and encrypts his vector of choice bits $\mathbf{b} = (b_1, \ldots, b_\ell)$ to $\mathbf{d} = \mathbf{As} + \mathbf{e} + \mathbf{b}$ (where again, $\mathbf{e} \in \mathbb{Z}_2^\ell$ is ρ-Bernoulli distributed). Furthermore, the receiver will encrypt the LPN secret under ElGamal, i.e. he encrypts $\mathbf{s}$ to $\mathbf{c} = \mathsf{Enc}(\mathsf{pk}, \mathbf{s})$. For the moment, assume that $\mathbf{s}$ is encrypted bit-wise with standard ElGamal rather than batched ElGamal. The OT-receiver now sends the ElGamal public key pk and the ciphertexts $\mathbf{c}$ and $\mathbf{d}$ to the OT-sender.

Now, given these values, the sender can homomorphically decrypt the $\mathbf{d}$ into ElGamal, effectively *key-switching* from the ciphertext $\mathbf{d}$ into an ElGamal ciphertext. Concretely: The sender homomorphically evaluates the linear function $f(\mathbf{x}) = \mathbf{d} - \mathbf{Ax}$ on the ElGamal ciphertext $\mathbf{c} = \mathsf{Enc}(\mathsf{pk}, \mathbf{s})$. This produces an ElGamal encryption $\mathbf{c}'$ encrypting $f(\mathbf{s}) = \mathbf{d} - \mathbf{As} = \mathbf{b} + \mathbf{e} = \mathbf{b}'$. In other words, the OT-sender has now obtained an ElGamal encryption of a vector $\mathbf{b}'$ which agrees with $\mathbf{b}$ in most locations.

The high-level idea is now to let the OT-sender use this ciphertext $\mathbf{c}'$ as the encryption of the receiver's choice bits and proceed as in the ElGamal-based OT-protocol above. If we were to naively use $\mathbf{c}'$ in this way, the receiver would obtain the correct output m_{i,b_i} in locations where $\mathbf{b}$ and $\mathbf{b}'$ agree, but would get the wrong output $m_{i,1-b_i}$ in locations where $\mathbf{b}$ and $\mathbf{b}'$ disagree. While there certainly are applications in which a small amount of faulty locations are tolerable, in general this leads to insecure protocols.

There is, however, another issue with this approach. In this paragraph we have implicitly assumed that ElGamal is homomorphic for linear functions modulo 2. However, since the group we implement ElGamal over is of large prime order p, when we evaluate linear functions such as $f(\mathbf{x}) = \mathbf{d} - \mathbf{Ax}$ over a ciphertext encrypting a $\mathbf{s} \in \{0, 1\}^n$, the result of this evaluation is *not* reduced modulo 2, and the resulting ciphertext in fact encrypts $f(\mathbf{s})$ as an integer. This does not cause major problems in terms of correctness, as this integer will still be small (at most of size m), and hence decryption will still be efficient.

However, this does cause major problems in terms of sender-privacy, as we can only guarantee sender privacy for receiver messages that are guaranteed to encrypt a bit $b \in \{0, 1\}$.

For now, we will bypass this problem by relying on a homomorphic encryption scheme which is in fact homomorphic over $\mathbb{Z}_2$ (rather than $\mathbb{Z}_p$), offers function privacy for linear functions modulo 2 and is compatible with ciphertext compression. Such an encryption can in fact be constructed from the Quadratic Residuosity assumption [19].

Another small issue we haven't addressed here is that the compression mechanisms for the sender and the receiver are somewhat orthogonal, in the sense that

the sender's message is compressed by compressing a batched ElGamal ciphertext (which generally does not allow homomorphic evaluation across different
components), whereas the receiver's compression strategy requires the homomorphic evaluation of linear functions with multiple (i.e. vector-valued) inputs.
In the main body (Sect. 7) we will show a tradeoff which allows to reconcile these
requirements, leading to a batch OT protocol with overall rate 1.

We will first discuss how to deal with the issue of errors in the key-switched
ciphertext, and then return to the issue of implementing our approach with
ElGamal instead of QR-based encryption.

2.4 Dealing with LPN Errors

To deal with the LPN errors in the key-switched ciphertext $\mathbf{c}'$, we will pursue the
following high-level strategy: The sender will introduce an additional masking
on the receiver's output, which can only be removed in error-free locations.
This masking effectively erases the receiver's output in locations in which the
receiver's output is corrupted.

To communicate the correct outputs in the locations with errors, the parties
will rely on an additional protocol which is run in parallel. Given that the number
of errors is sufficiently small, the communication cost of this additional protocol
will be insubstantial and not affect the overall asymptotic rate.

We will first address the problem of erasing the receiver's output in corrupted
locations. First observe that the receiver knows the locations with errors (i.e. the
support of the error vector $\mathbf{e}$). Assume that the LPN error vector $\mathbf{e}$ has a fixed
hamming weight $t \approx \rho m$, and note that hardness of fixed-weight LPN follows
routinely from the hardness of Bernoulli LPN[6]. A t-puncturable pseudorandom
function [6,8] is a pseudorandom function [25] which supports punctured keys.
That is, given a PRF key K and t inputs $x_1, \ldots, x_t$, we can efficiently compute
a *punctured key* K' of size $t \cdot \mathrm{poly}(\lambda)$ which allows to evaluate the PRF on all
inputs *except* $x_1, \ldots, x_t$. Furthermore, the key K' does not reveal the function
values at $x_1, \ldots, x_t$, i.e. $\mathsf{PRF}(K, x_1), \ldots, \mathsf{PRF}(K, x_t)$ are pseudorandom given the
punctured key K'.

The approach to erase the receiver's outputs in erroneous locations is now
as follows. The sender chooses a PRF key K and masks both $m_{i,0}$ and $m_{i,1}$
with $\mathsf{PRF}(K, i)$, i.e. instead of using $(m_{i,0}, m_{i,1})$ as OT-inputs, he uses $m'_{i,0} = m_{i,0} \oplus \mathsf{PRF}(K, i)$ and $m'_{i,1} = m_{i,1} \oplus \mathsf{PRF}(K, i)$. Assuming that the sender can
somehow communicate a punctured key K' which is punctured at the locations
$i_1, \ldots, i_t$ of the errors (i.e. $\mathbf{e}_{i_j} = 1$ and $\mathbf{e}$ is 0 everywhere else), the receiver
will be able to remove the mask from error-free locations by computing $m_{i,b_i} = m'_{i,b_i} \oplus \mathsf{PRF}(K', i)$. In the erroneous locations however, $m_{i,1-b_i}$ will be hidden
from the view of the receiver as $\mathsf{PRF}(K, i)$ is pseudorandom even given the
punctured key K'.

How can we communicate the punctured key K' to the receiver with small
communication cost in such a way that the sender does not learn the error-

---

[6] See e.g. [6,18].

locations $i_1, \ldots, i_t$? This could be achieved generically by relying on the punctured PRF construction of [8] and transferring keys using a sublinear private information retrieval (PIR) scheme [17, 19]. However, recently [6] provided a protocol to achieve this task very efficiently via a two round protocol communicating only $t\mathsf{poly}(\lambda)$ bits. In the main body (Sect. 6), we will refer to this primitive as *co-PIR*, since effectively it allows to communicate a large pseudorandom database to a receiver except in a few locations chosen by the receiver.

Finally, to communicate the correct outputs to the receiver in the locations with errors, we will in fact rely on a two-message PIR scheme with polylogarithmic communication. Such schemes are known e.g. from LWE [11] and were recently constructed from a wide variety of assumptions [19], such as DDH and QR. The idea is as follows: For each error location i_j the receiver sends an additional OT message $OT_1(b_{i_j})$ using an off-the-shelf low-rate OT protocol (e.g. the basic ElGamal based protocol sketched above), as well as a PIR message $PIR_1(i_j)$. The sender speculatively completes this OT protocol for each index i (since the index i_j is not known to the sender), collects his OT responses in a database of size ℓ, runs the PIR sender algorithm on this database, and sends the response back to the receiver. The receiver will now be able to recover the correct OT_2 message via PIR, complete the OT and recover $m_{i_j, b_{i_j}}$. We remark that for this protocol to be secure against semi-honest senders, we need a PIR protocol with sender privacy. However, e.g. the protocols provided in [19] readily have this feature.

Carefully putting all these components together, we obtain a batch bit-OT protocol with rate-1, for both the sender and the receiver.

2.5   Emulating Small Subgroups

We now return to the issue that ElGamal does not provide function privacy for linear functions modulo 2. Recall that the issue essentially boils down to the fact that the plaintext space of ElGamal is *natively* $\mathbb{Z}_p$, and when we encode messages in the least significant bits, i.e. encoding a bit b as g^b, then for all practical purposes homomorphic evaluations of linear functions with $\{0, 1\}$ coefficients are over $\mathbb{Z}_2$, i.e. the resulting ciphertext encodes the result of the function evaluation *without* reduction modulo 2.

From an algebraic perspective, this problem is rooted in the fact that since p is prime, $\mathbb{Z}_p$ has no non-trivial subgroup, i.e. it just does not support modular reductions with respect to anything else than p.

To approach this problem, we will take inspiration from the domain of lattice cryptography [35]. There, messages are typically encoded in the high order bits of group elements, i.e. to encode b in $\mathbb{Z}_p$, we would like to encoded it as $b \cdot \frac{p}{2}$. However, since p is odd, first have to round $\frac{p}{2}$ to the nearest integer in order to get a proper $\mathbb{Z}_p$ element, i.e. we encode b via $b \cdot \lceil \frac{p}{2} \rceil$. If we could encode b with respect to $\frac{p}{2} \notin \mathbb{Z}_p$, we would get a subgroup of order 2, i.e. for bits $b, b' \in \{0, 1\}$ it holds that

$$\left(b \cdot \frac{p}{2} + b' \cdot \frac{p}{2} \right) \bmod p = (b + b' \bmod 2) \cdot \frac{p}{2}.$$

However, once we round $\frac{p}{2}$ to the next integer, we get essentially the same problem as before: If we perform group operations on $b\lceil\frac{p}{2}\rceil$ and $b'\lceil\frac{p}{2}\rceil$, then the rounding errors start to accumulate information about b and b' which is cannot be obtained from $b+b'$ mod 2. Specifically

$$b\left\lceil\frac{p}{2}\right\rceil + b'\left\lceil\frac{p}{2}\right\rceil \bmod p = b\left(\frac{p}{2}+\frac{1}{2}\right)+b'\left(\frac{p}{2}+\frac{1}{2}\right) \bmod p$$

$$= (b+b' \bmod 2)\frac{p}{2} + (b+b')\frac{1}{2} \bmod p.$$

Thus, now the least significant bit of $b\lceil\frac{p}{2}\rceil + b'\lceil\frac{p}{2}\rceil$ mod p e.g. leaks if $b=b'=1$, something which cannot be learned from $b+b'$ mod 2.

Consequently, at first glance the idea of encoding a bit b in the "high-order" bits of a $\mathbb{Z}_p$ element seems ineffective. However, the lattice toolkit still has more to offer. In particular, in the context of sampling discrete gaussians from lattices, Peikert [32] considered a technique called *randomized rounding*. The basic idea is, given a a real number $r \in \mathbb{R}$ to not always round to the same value e.g. $\lceil r \rceil$, but to sample a an integer z close to r. In [32], this distribution is a discrete gaussian Z on $\mathbb{Z}$ centered at r, i.e. the expectation of Z is r. Such a discrete gaussian is parametrized by a gaussian parameter σ, which essentially controlls the standard deviation of the discrete gaussian. We denote Z by $\lceil r\rfloor_\sigma$.

Now, given any two $r,r' \in \mathbb{R}$ and $\sigma_1,\sigma_2 > \omega(\sqrt{\log(\lambda)})$ (more generally the *smoothing parameter* of $\mathbb{Z}$), Peikert [32] shows that

$$\lceil r\rfloor_{\sigma_1} + \lceil r'\rfloor_{\sigma_2} \approx_s \lceil r+r'\rfloor_{\sqrt{\sigma_1^2+\sigma_2^2}}.$$

In other words, while $\lceil r\rfloor_{\sigma_1} + \lceil r'\rfloor_{\sigma_2}$ and $\lceil r+r'\rfloor_{\sqrt{\sigma_1^2+\sigma_2^2}}$ are note the same, they are statistically close. This means that anything that can be learned from $\lceil r\rfloor_{\sigma_1} + \lceil r'\rfloor_{\sigma_2}$ could have as well been learned from $\lceil r+r'\rfloor_{\sqrt{\sigma_1^2+\sigma_2^2}}$! While this comes at the expense of an increase "error" term with parameter $\sqrt{\sigma_1^2+\sigma_2^2}$, this *additive error* is very small (of size approx σ) controlling the growth of this error term can be handled by standard techniques.

Returning to our goal of emulating small subgroups in $\mathbb{Z}_p$, our approach follows almost instantly: Instead of encoding a bit $b \in \mathbb{Z}_2$ as $b \cdot \lceil\frac{p}{2}\rceil$, we will encode it as $\lceil b \cdot \frac{p}{2}\rfloor_\sigma$ (for a $\sigma > \omega(\sqrt{\log(\lambda)})$). For $b,b' \in \{0,1\}$ this ensures that

$$\left\lceil b\cdot\frac{p}{2}\right\rfloor_\sigma + \left\lceil b'\cdot\frac{p}{2}\right\rfloor_\sigma \bmod p \approx_s \left\lceil (b+b' \bmod 2)\cdot\frac{p}{2}\right\rfloor_{\sqrt{2}\sigma} \bmod p.$$

Thus, we have ensured that $\lceil b\cdot\frac{p}{2}\rfloor_\sigma + \lceil b'\cdot\frac{p}{2}\rfloor_\sigma$ mod p does not leak more information than $b+b'$ mod 2.

Function-Private Evaluation for ElGamal. We will now briefly discuss how this idea leads to a modulo 2 function private homomorphic evaluation procedure for ElGamal. Say we have two ElGamal ciphertexts $c_1 = (g^{r_1}, h^{r_1} \cdot g^{b_1})$ and $c_2 = (g^{r_2}, h^{r_2} \cdot g^{b_2})$ for a public key $\mathsf{pk} = (g,h)$ and we want to homomorphically evaluate the function $f(x_1, x_2) = a_1 x_1 + a_2 x_2 \mod 2$ (for $a_1, a_2 \in \{0, 1\}$) on this pair of ciphertexts. In the first step, we *randomly encode* the function f as

$$f'(x_1, x_2) = x_1 \cdot \left\lceil a_1 \frac{p}{2} \right\rfloor_\sigma + (1 - x_1) \cdot \lceil 0 \rfloor_\sigma + x_2 \cdot \left\lceil a_2 \frac{p}{2} \right\rfloor_\sigma + (1 - x_2) \cdot \lceil 0 \rfloor_\sigma,$$

noting that this is still a linear function (chosen from a distribution). Homomorphically evaluating f' on the ciphertexts c, c_2 we obtain a ciphertext c' encrypting

$$f'(b_1, b_1) = b_1 \cdot \left\lceil a_1 \frac{p}{2} \right\rfloor_\sigma + (1 - b_1) \cdot \lceil 0 \rfloor_\sigma + b_1 \cdot \left\lceil a_2 \frac{p}{2} \right\rfloor_\sigma + (1 - b_1) \cdot \lceil 0 \rfloor_\sigma$$

$$= \left\lceil b_1 a_1 \frac{p}{2} \right\rfloor_\sigma + \left\lceil b_1 a_2 \frac{p}{2} \right\rfloor_\sigma$$

$$\approx_s \left\lceil (b_1 a_1 + b_1 a_2 \mod 2) \frac{p}{2} \right\rfloor_{\sqrt{2}\sigma}.$$

In other words, this ciphertext could have been simulated knowing only the function result $f(b_1, b_1) = b_1 a_1 + b_1 a_2 \mod 2$, establishing that this homomorphic evaluation procedure is function private.

One aspect to note is that while the messages b_1, b_1 are encoded in c_1, c_2 in the "low-order-bits" via g^{b_1} and g^{b_2}, the function result $f(b_1, b_2)$ encrypted in c' is encoded in the high order bits, i.e. it is encoded as $\approx g^{f(b_1, b_2)\frac{p}{2}}$. This makes it necessary to change the decryption procedure: Let $c' = (c_1', c_2')$ and s be the secret key. To decrypt c' we compute $f = c_2' \cdot (c_1')^{-s} \approx_s g^{\lceil f(s_1, s_2) \cdot \frac{p}{2} \rfloor}$, we test if f is close to $g^0 = 1$ or $g^{\lceil p/2 \rceil}$. This recovers $f(s_1, s_2)$, as the error introduced by the rounding operation is of size at most $\mathsf{poly}(\lambda)$ via standard gaussian tail bounds.

Finally, we remark this this "high-order-bit" encoding is still compatible with ElGamal ciphertext compression, i.e. we can still compress homomorphically evaluated batch ElGamal ciphertexts down asymptotically optimal size, using a slightly different compression mechanism. This mechanism is discussed in Sect. 5. We expect this technique to have additional applications. As one immediate application, it allows to upgrade the key-dependent message secure encryption scheme of Boneh et al. [3] to support arbitrary linear functions modulo 2.

3   Preliminaries

The acronym PPT denotes "probabilistic polynomial time". Throughout this work, λ denotes the security parameter. By $\mathsf{negl}(\lambda)$, we denote a negligible function in λ, that is, a function that vanishes faster than any inverse polynomial in λ. Let $n \in \mathbb{N}$. Then, $[n]$ denotes the set $\{1, \ldots, n\}$. If $\mathcal{A}$ is an algorithm, we denote by $y \leftarrow \mathcal{A}(x)$ the output y after running $\mathcal{A}$ on input x. If S is a (finite) set, we denote by $x \leftarrow_\$ S$ the experiment of sampling uniformly at random an element x from S. If D is a distribution over S, we denote by $x \leftarrow_\$ D$ the element x sampled from S according to D. We denote by $S[i]$ the i-th element of S (where the elements are ordered by ascending order except when explicitly stated otherwise).

For two probability distributions X, Y, we use the notation $X \approx_s Y$ to state that the distributions are statistically indistinguishable.

For two vectors $\mathbf{u}, \mathbf{v} \in \mathbb{F}^n$ over a finite field $\mathbb{F}$, we denote by $\mathbf{u} \odot \mathbf{v}$ their component-wise multiplication. We denote by $\mathsf{Supp}(\mathbf{u})$ the support of $\mathbf{u}$, that is, the set of indices where $\mathbf{u}$ is different from 0.[7] For $S \subseteq [n]$, $\mathbf{u}_S$ denotes the vector $(\mathbf{u}_i)_{i \in S}$. Finally, $\mathbf{u}^T$ denotes the transpose of $\mathbf{u}$ and $\mathsf{hw}(\mathbf{u})$ denotes the hamming weight of $\mathbf{u}$ (that is, the number of coordinates of $\mathbf{u}$ different from 0).

3.1   Lattices and Gaussians

We now review some basic notions of lattices and gaussian distributions.

Let $\mathbf{B} \in \mathbb{R}^{k \times n}$ be a matrix. We denote the lattice generated by $\mathbf{B}$ by $\Lambda = \Lambda(\mathbf{B}) = \{\mathbf{xB} : \mathbf{x} \in \mathbb{Z}^k\}$.[8] The dual lattice Λ^* of a lattice Λ is defined by $\Lambda^* = \{\mathbf{x} \in \mathbb{R}^n : \forall y \in \Lambda, \mathbf{x} \cdot \mathbf{y} \in \mathbb{Z}\}$. It holds that $(\Lambda^*)^* = \Lambda$. The orthogonal lattice $\Lambda_q^\perp$ is defined by $\{\mathbf{y} \in \mathbb{Z}_q^n : \mathbf{Ay}^T = 0 \mod q\}$.

Let $\rho_s(\mathbf{x})$ be probability distribution of the Gaussian distribution over $\mathbb{R}^n$ with parameter s and centered in 0. We define the discrete Gaussian distribution $D_{S,s}$ over S and with parameter s by the probability distribution $\rho_s(\mathbf{x})/\rho(S)$ for all $\mathbf{x} \in S$ (where $\rho_s(S) = \sum_{\mathbf{x} \in S} \rho_s(\mathbf{x})$).

For $\varepsilon > 0$, the smoothing parameter $\eta_\varepsilon(\Lambda)$ of a lattice Λ is the least real $\sigma > 0$ such that $\rho_{1/\sigma}(\Lambda^* \backslash \{0\}) \leq \varepsilon$ [31].

Lemma 1 ([2]). *For all $\alpha \in \mathbb{R}$, $\|\mathbf{x}\| \leq \alpha \sqrt{n}$ for $\mathbf{x} \leftarrow_\$ D_{\mathbb{Z},\alpha}^n$, except with negligible probability in n.*

We will make use of the following convolution property of discrete gaussians.

Lemma 2 ([22], Corollary 4.8). *Let $\Lambda_1, \Lambda_2 \subseteq \mathbb{R}^n$ be lattices, let $\sigma_1, \sigma_2 > 0$ be such that $1/\sqrt{1/\sigma_1^2 + 1/\sigma_2^2} > \eta_\varepsilon(\Lambda_1 \cap \Lambda_2)$ for some $\varepsilon = \mathsf{negl}(\lambda)$. Then it holds for all $\mathbf{a}, \mathbf{b} \in \mathbb{R}^n$ that $D_{\Lambda_1 + \mathbf{a}, \sigma_1} + D_{\Lambda_2 + \mathbf{b}, \sigma_2}$ is statistically close to $D_{\Lambda_1 + \Lambda_2 + \mathbf{a} + \mathbf{b}, \sqrt{\sigma_1^2 + \sigma_2^2}}$.*

We just need the following simple corollary of Lemma 2, which can be obtained by setting $\Lambda_1 = \Lambda_2 = \mathbb{Z}$.

Corollary 1. *Let σ_1, σ_2, $\sigma_3 = \sqrt{\sigma_1^2 + \sigma_2^2}$ be such that $\sigma_1 \sigma_2/\sigma_3 > \eta_\varepsilon(\mathbb{Z})$ for a negligible ε and let $a, b \in \mathbb{Z}$. Then $D_{\mathbb{Z}+a, \sigma_1} + D_{\mathbb{Z}+b, \sigma_2}$ and $D_{\mathbb{Z}+a+b, \sigma_3}$ are statistically close.*

3.2   Distributed GGM-PPRF Correlation

Let $\mathsf{PPRF}_{\mathsf{GGM}} = (\mathsf{KeyGen}, \mathsf{Eval}, \mathsf{Puncture}, \mathsf{EvalPunct})$ be the GGM-PPRF scheme based on [26]. The distributed GGM-PPRF correlation functionality [5] considers two parties: A receiver with input $\alpha \in \{0,1\}^\ell$ and a sender with input $\beta \in \mathbb{F}_{p^r}$ and a GGM-PPRF key K. The functionality outputs a punctured key K_α and a hardwired value $\beta - \mathsf{PPRF.Eval}(K, \alpha)$ to the receiver. We now present the formal definition of the functionality.

---

[7] If there is only one index different from zero, $\mathsf{Supp}(\mathbf{u})$ denotes this index.

[8] The matrix $\mathbf{B}$ is called a basis of $\Lambda(\mathbf{B})$.

Distributed GGM-PPRF Correlation Functionality. The functionality $\mathcal{F}_{\text{PPRF-GGM}}$ is parametrized by integers $\ell, p, r \in \mathbb{N}$. Moreover, let $\text{PPRF}_{\text{GGM}} = (\text{KeyGen}, \text{Eval}, \text{Puncture}, \text{EvalPunct})$ be the GGM PPRF scheme with input space $\{0,1\}^\ell$ and output space $\mathbb{F}_{p^r}$. The functionality works as follows:

- **Receiver phase.** R sends α to $\mathcal{F}_{\text{PPRF-GGM}}$ where $\alpha \in \{0,1\}^\ell$.
- **Sender phase.** S sends (β, K) to $\mathcal{F}_{\text{PPRF-GGM}}$ where $\beta \in \mathbb{F}_{p^r}$ and $K \leftarrow \text{PPRF.KeyGen}(1^\lambda)$. $\mathcal{F}_{\text{PPRF-GGM}}$ sends $K_\alpha \leftarrow \text{PPRF.Puncture}(K, \alpha)$ and $\gamma \leftarrow \beta - \text{PPRF.Eval}(K, \alpha)$ to R.

4 Compression-Friendly Subgroup Emulation via Gaussian Rounding

We will now provide our new subgroup emulation technique. We first define the gaussian rounding functionality.

Definition 1. *Let $\sigma > 0$. For any $x \in \mathbb{R}$, the gaussian rounding $\lceil x \rfloor_\sigma$ is a random variable supported on $\mathbb{Z}$ defined by*

$$\lceil x \rfloor_\sigma = x + D_{\mathbb{Z}-x,\sigma}.$$

In other words, $\lceil x \rfloor_\sigma$ is a discrete gaussian centered on $x \in \mathbb{R}$ but supported on $\mathbb{Z}$.

We will use the following convolution lemma which provides a *simulation property* for gaussian rounding.

Lemma 3. *Let $\epsilon > 0$ be bounded by a sufficiently small constant and let $\sigma_1, \sigma_2 \geq \eta_\epsilon(\mathbb{Z})$. Then it holds for all $x, y \in \mathbb{R}$ that*

$$\lceil x \rfloor_{\sigma_1} + \lceil y \rfloor_{\sigma_2} \approx_s \lceil x + y \rfloor_{\sqrt{\sigma_1^2 + \sigma_2^2}}.$$

It immediately follows from Lemma 3 that it holds for every integer $p \geq 2$ that

$$\lceil x \rfloor_{\sigma_1} + \lceil y \rfloor_{\sigma_2} \mod p \approx_s \lceil x + y \rfloor_{\sqrt{\sigma_1^2 + \sigma_2^2}} \mod p.$$

Please refer to Appendix B of the full version of this paper for the proofs of lemmas in this section.

Lemma 4. *Let $p > q \geq 2$ be integers with $q \leq 2^k$, and let $\sigma > \eta_\epsilon(\mathbb{Z})$ for a negligible ϵ. Let $f : \mathbb{Z}_q^n \to \mathbb{Z}_q$ be given by $f(x_1, \ldots, x_n) = \sum_{i=1}^n a_i x_i + c$ for $a_1, \ldots, a_n, c \in \mathbb{Z}_q$. Define the randomized function $\hat{f} : \{0,1\}^{nk} \to \mathbb{Z}_p^n$ via*

$$\hat{f}(x_{1,1}, \ldots, x_{n,k}) = \sum_{i=1}^n \sum_{j=1}^k \left(x_{i,j} \cdot \left\lceil 2^j \cdot \frac{p}{q} a_i \right\rfloor_\sigma + (1 - x_{i,j}) \lceil 0 \rfloor_\sigma \right) + \left\lceil \frac{p}{q} c \right\rfloor_\sigma.$$

Then it holds for all $x_{1,1}, \ldots, x_{n,k} \in \{0,1\}$ that

$$\hat{f}(x_{1,1}, \ldots, x_{n,k}) \approx_s \left\lceil \frac{p}{q} \cdot f\left(\sum_{j=1}^k x_{1,j} 2^j, \ldots, \sum_{j=1}^k x_{n,j} 2^j \right) \right\rfloor_{\sqrt{2nk+1}\sigma}.$$

5   Rate-1 Circuit-Private Linearly Homomorphic Encryption

In this section we define circuit-private LHE and present constructions based on LWE, DDH or QR[9]. All constructions achieve rate 1.

Definition 2. *A (packed) linearly homomorphic encryption (LHE) scheme* LHE *over a finite group* $\mathbb{G}$ *is composed by a tuple of algorithms* (Keygen, Enc, Eval, Shrink, DecShrink) *such that:*

- KeyGen$(1^\lambda, k)$ *takes as input a security parameter* λ *and* $k \in \mathbb{N}$. *It outputs a pair of public and secret keys* (pk, sk).
- Enc$(\mathsf{pk}, \mathbf{m} = (m_1, \ldots, m_k))$ *takes as input a public key* pk *and a message* $\mathbf{m} = (m_1, \ldots, m_k) \in \mathbb{G}^k$. *It outputs a ciphertext* ct.
- Eval$(\mathsf{pk}, f, (\mathsf{ct}_1, \ldots, \mathsf{ct}_\ell))$ *takes as input a public key* pk, *a linear function* $f : (\mathbb{G}^k)^\ell \to \mathbb{G}^k$ *and* ℓ *ciphertexts* $(\mathsf{ct}_1, \ldots, \mathsf{ct}_\ell)$. *It outputs a new ciphertext* $\tilde{\mathsf{ct}}$.
- Shrink$(\mathsf{pk}, \mathsf{ct})$ *takes as input a public key* pk *and a ciphertext* ct. *It outputs a new shrunken ciphertext* ct′.
- DecShrink$(\mathsf{sk}, \mathsf{ct})$ *takes as input a secret key* sk *and a shrunken ciphertext* ct. *It outputs a message* $\mathbf{m}$.

For simplicity, we define the algorithm Eval&Shrink$(\mathsf{pk}, f, (\mathsf{ct}_1 \ldots, \mathsf{ct}_\ell))$ which outputs a ciphertext $\tilde{\mathsf{ct}}$ and is defined as

$$\mathsf{Eval\&Shrink}(\mathsf{pk}, f, (\mathsf{ct}_1 \ldots, \mathsf{ct}_\ell)) = \mathsf{Shrink}(\mathsf{pk}, \mathsf{Eval}(\mathsf{pk}, f, (\mathsf{ct}_1, \ldots, \mathsf{ct}_\ell)))$$

for any linear function f.

We require the following properties from a (circuit-private) packed LHE: Correctness, semantic security, compactness and circuit-privacy.

Definition 3 (Correctness). *A packed LHE scheme* LHE *is said to be correct if for any* $\ell \in \mathbb{N}$, *any messages* $\mathbf{m}_1, \ldots, \mathbf{m}_\ell$ *and any linear function* $f : (\mathbb{G}^k)^\ell \to \mathbb{G}^k$ *we have that*

$$\Pr\left[\tilde{\mathbf{m}} \leftarrow \mathsf{DecShrink}(\mathsf{sk}, \tilde{\mathsf{ct}}) : \begin{array}{c} (\mathsf{pk}, \mathsf{sk}) \leftarrow \mathsf{KeyGen}(1^\lambda, k) \\ \mathsf{ct}_i \leftarrow \mathsf{Enc}(\mathsf{pk}, \mathbf{m}_i) \text{ for } i \in [\ell] \\ \tilde{\mathsf{ct}} \leftarrow \mathsf{Eval\&Shrink}(\mathsf{pk}, , f, (\mathsf{ct}_1 \ldots, \mathsf{ct}_\ell)) \end{array} \right] = 1$$

where $\tilde{\mathbf{m}} \leftarrow f(\mathbf{m}_1, \ldots, \mathbf{m}_\ell)$.

Definition 4 (Semantic Security). *A packed LHE scheme* LHE *is said to be semantically secure if for all* $\lambda \in \mathbb{N}$, *all* $k = \mathsf{poly}(\lambda)$ *and all adversaries* $\mathcal{A} = (\mathcal{A}_0, \mathcal{A}_1)$ *we have that*

$$\left| \Pr\left[b \leftarrow \mathcal{A}_1(\mathsf{st}, \mathsf{ct}) : \begin{array}{c} (\mathsf{pk}, \mathsf{sk}) \leftarrow \mathsf{KeyGen}(1^\lambda, k) \\ (\mathbf{m}_0, \mathbf{m}_1, \mathsf{st}) \leftarrow \mathcal{A}_0(\mathsf{pk}) \\ b \leftarrow_\$ \{0, 1\} \\ \mathsf{ct} \leftarrow \mathsf{Enc}(\mathsf{pk}, \mathbf{m}_b) \end{array} \right] - \frac{1}{2} \right| \le \mathsf{negl}(\lambda).$$

---

[9] Please refer to Appendix D.1 and D.2 of the full version paper for the construction of LWE and QR.

Definition 5 (Compactness). *We require that a packed LHE scheme* LHE *has the following compactness properties:*

- *For* $(\mathsf{pk}, \mathsf{sk}) \leftarrow \mathsf{KeyGen}(1^\lambda, k)$, *the size of the public key* $|\mathsf{pk}|$ *is bounded by* $k \cdot \mathsf{poly}(n)$.
- *For any linear function* $f : (\mathbb{G}^k)^\ell \to \mathbb{G}^k$ *and any* $(\mathbf{m}_1, \dots, \mathbf{m}_\ell) \in (\mathbb{G}^k)^\ell$ *we have that*
$$\lim_{\lambda \to \infty} \inf \frac{|f(\mathbf{m}_1, \dots, \mathbf{m}_\ell)|}{|\mathsf{Eval\&Shrink}(\mathsf{pk}, , f, (\mathsf{ct}_1 \dots, \mathsf{ct}_\ell))|} \to 1$$

for sufficiently large k, *where* $(\mathsf{pk}, \mathsf{sk}) \leftarrow \mathsf{KeyGen}(1^\lambda, k)$ *and* $\mathsf{ct}_i \leftarrow \mathsf{Enc}(\mathsf{pk}, \mathbf{m}_i)$ *for* $i \in [\ell]$. *In this case, we say that the scheme has rate 1.*

We also need that the packed LHE scheme fulfills circuit privacy (in the semi-honest case).

Definition 6 (Circuit Privacy). *A packed LHE scheme* LHE *is said to be circuit-private if for all messages* $(\mathbf{m}_1, \dots, \mathbf{m}_\ell) \in (\mathbb{G}^k)^\ell$ *and all linear functions* $f : (\mathbb{G}^k)^\ell \to \mathbb{G}^k$, *there exists a simulator* Sim *such that for all adversaries* $\mathcal{A}$ *we have that*

$$\left| \Pr \left[1 \leftarrow \mathcal{A}(\mathsf{pk}, \mathsf{sk}, \tilde{\mathsf{ct}}) : \begin{array}{c} (\mathsf{pk}, \mathsf{sk}) \leftarrow \mathsf{KeyGen}(1^\lambda, k) \\ \mathsf{ct}_i \leftarrow \mathsf{Enc}(\mathsf{pk}, \mathbf{m}_i) \text{ for } i \in [\ell] \\ \tilde{\mathsf{ct}} \leftarrow \mathsf{Eval\&Shrink}(\mathsf{pk}, , f, (\mathsf{ct}_1 \dots, \mathsf{ct}_\ell)) \end{array} \right] - \right.$$
$$\left. \Pr \left[1 \leftarrow \mathcal{A}(\mathsf{pk}, \mathsf{sk}, \tilde{\mathsf{ct}}) : \begin{array}{c} (\mathsf{pk}, \mathsf{sk}) \leftarrow \mathsf{KeyGen}(1^\lambda, k) \\ \tilde{\mathsf{ct}} \leftarrow \mathsf{Sim}(\mathsf{pk}, \tilde{\mathbf{m}}) \end{array} \right] \right| \leq \mathsf{negl}(\lambda)$$

where $\tilde{\mathbf{m}} \leftarrow f(\mathbf{m}_1, \dots, \mathbf{m}_\ell)$.

In other words, since Sim does not use f to compute $\tilde{\mathsf{ct}}$, no information about it is leaked from $\tilde{\mathsf{ct}}$ (apart from what is trivially leaked by f).

Encryption of Matrices. Above, we defined LHE that supports encryption of vectors $\mathbf{m} \in \mathbb{G}^k$. We can easily extend the definition to support encryption of matrices $\mathbf{M} \in \mathbb{G}^{k \times \alpha}$ for any $\alpha = \mathsf{poly}(\lambda)$: Given a public key pk, an encryption $\mathsf{Enc}(\mathsf{pk}, \mathbf{M})$ of $\mathbf{M}$ is defined as

$$\mathsf{Enc}(\mathsf{pk}, \mathbf{M}) = \left(\mathsf{Enc} \left(\mathsf{pk}, \mathbf{m}^{(1)} \right) \dots \mathsf{Enc} \left(\mathsf{pk}, \mathbf{m}^{(\alpha)} \right) \right)$$

where $\mathbf{m}^{(i)}$ is the i-th column of $\mathbf{M}$.

5.1 Construction from DDH

In the following, let $\mathcal{G}$ be a (prime-order) *group generator*, that is, $\mathcal{G}$ is an algorithm that takes as an input a security parameter 1^λ and outputs $(\mathbb{G}, p, g)$, where $\mathbb{G}$ is the description of a multiplicative cyclic group, p is the order of the group which is always a prime number unless differently specified, and g is a generator of the group. In the following we state the decisional version of the Diffie-Hellman (DDH) assumption.

Definition 7 (Decisional Diffie-Hellman Assumption). *Let* $(\mathbb{G}, p, g) \leftarrow_\$ \mathcal{G}$
(1^λ). *We say that the DDH assumption holds (with respect to $\mathcal{G}$) if for any PPT adversary $\mathcal{A}$*

$$\left| \Pr[1 \leftarrow \mathcal{A}((\mathbb{G}, p, g), (g^a, g^b, g^{ab}))] - \Pr[1 \leftarrow \mathcal{A}((\mathbb{G}, p, g), (g^a, g^b, g^c))] \right| \leq \mathsf{negl}(\lambda)$$

where $a, b, c \leftarrow_\$ \mathbb{Z}_p$.

Shrinking Ciphertexts. We first present how we can shrink DDH-based ciphertexts to achieve rate 1. The shrinking mechanism presented below is a modification of the one presented in [9] (which is itself based on previous works [7,19]).

Let $(\mathbb{G}, p, g) \leftarrow_\$ \mathcal{G}(1^\lambda)$ and $k \in \mathbb{Z}$. Consider an El Gamal public key of the form $\mathsf{pk} = (g, (h_1, \ldots, h_k)) = (g, (g^{x_1}, \ldots, g^{x_k})) \in \mathbb{G}^{k+1}$ for $x_1, \ldots, x_k \leftarrow_\$ \mathbb{Z}_p$ (here, $\mathbf{x} = (x_1, \ldots, x_k)$ is the secret key). Consider the following modified El Gamal encryption algorithm where a ciphertext for $\mathbf{m} = (m_1, \ldots, m_k) \in \{0,1\}^k$ is of the form $\mathsf{ct} = (c_1, (c_{2,1}, \ldots, c_{2,k})) \in \mathbb{G}^{k+1}$ where $c_1 = g^r$ and $c_{2,i} = h_i^r g^{\lceil m_i(p/2) \rfloor_\sigma}$.[10] We now show how to compress ciphertexts of this form.

We will need the following ingredients: Let $B, T \in \mathsf{poly}(\lambda)$ and $\mathsf{PRF} = (\mathsf{KeyGen}, \mathsf{Eval})$ be a PRF that maps $g \in \mathbb{G}$ to $\{0,1\}^\tau$ for some $\tau \in \mathbb{Z}$. We also define the function $\mathsf{LEq}_< : \mathbb{G}^2 \to \{0,1\}$ which receives two group elements g_0, g_1 and outputs 1 if $g_0 < g_1$ and 0 otherwise, for some order relation $<$ (e.g. the lexicographic order).

$\mathsf{Shrink}_{\mathsf{DDH}}(\mathsf{pk}, \mathsf{ct})$:
- Parse $\mathsf{pk} = (g, (h_1, \ldots, h_k))$ and $\mathsf{ct} = (c_1, (c_{2,1}, \ldots, c_{2,k}))$. Let $w = g^{\lfloor p/2 \rfloor}$.
- Sample a PRF key $\mathsf{K} \leftarrow_\$ \mathsf{PRF.KeyGen}(1^\lambda)$ such that the following conditions are simultaneously satisfied:
  1. For every $i \in [k]$ and $j \in \{-B, \ldots, B\}$ we have that

     $$\mathsf{PRF.Eval}(\mathsf{K}, c_{2,i} \cdot g^j) \neq 0 \text{ and } \mathsf{PRF.Eval}(\mathsf{K}, c_{2,i} \cdot w \cdot g^j) \neq 0.$$

  2. For all $i \in [k]$ there exists $\ell \in \{B+1, \ldots, T\}$ such that

     $$\mathsf{PRF.Eval}(\mathsf{K}, c_{2,i} \cdot g^\ell) = 0 \text{ and } \mathsf{PRF.Eval}(\mathsf{K}, c_{2,i} \cdot w \cdot g^\ell) = 0.$$

- For every $i \in [k]$, let $\delta_{0,i}, \delta_{1,i} > 0$ be the smallest integer such that

  $$\mathsf{PRF.Eval}(\mathsf{K}, c_{2,i} \cdot g^{\delta_{0,i}}) = 0 \text{ and } \mathsf{PRF.Eval}(\mathsf{K}, c_{2,i} \cdot w \cdot g^{\delta_{1,i}}) = 0.$$

  Let $\alpha_{0,i} = c_{2,i} \cdot g^{\delta_{0,i}}$ and $\alpha_{1,i} = c_{2,i} \cdot w \cdot g^{\delta_{1,i}}$. If $\mathsf{LEq}_<(\alpha_{0,i}, \alpha_{1,i}) = 0$, then set $b_i = 0$. Else, set $b_i = 1$.
- Output $\bar{\mathsf{ct}} = (c_1, \mathsf{K}, (b_1, \ldots, b_k))$.

$\mathsf{DecShrink}_{\mathsf{DDH}}(\mathsf{sk}, \bar{\mathsf{ct}})$:
- Parse $\mathsf{sk} = \mathbf{x} = (x_1, \ldots, x_k)$ and $\bar{\mathsf{ct}} = (c_1, \mathsf{K}, (b_1, \ldots b_k))$. Let $w = g^{\lfloor p/2 \rfloor}$.
- For every $i \in [k]$, compute $\beta_{0,i} = c_1^{x_i}$ and $\beta_{1,i} = c_1^{x_i} \cdot w$.

---

[10] Note that $\lceil \cdot \rfloor_\sigma$ is defined in Sect. 4.

– For every $i \in [k]$, find the smallest integers $\gamma_{0,i}, \gamma_{1,i} > 0$ such that

$$\mathsf{PRF.Eval}(\mathsf{K}, \beta_{0,i} \cdot g^{\gamma_{0,i}}) = 0 \text{ and } \mathsf{PRF.Eval}(\mathsf{K}, \beta_{1,i} \cdot g^{\gamma_{1,i}}) = 0.$$

Let $\bar{\alpha}_{0,i} = \beta_{0,i} \cdot g^{\gamma_{0,i}}$ and $\bar{\alpha}_{1,i} = \beta_{1,i} \cdot g^{\gamma_{1,i}}$. If $\mathsf{LEq}_<(\bar{\alpha}_{0,i}, \bar{\alpha}_{1,i}) = b_i$, set $m_i = 0$. Else, set $m_i = 1$.
– Output $\mathbf{m} = (m_1, \ldots, m_k)$.

Lemma 5 (Correctness). *Let $B = \mathsf{poly}(\lambda)$ be such that $B > \lambda\sigma + 1$. Then the shrinking procedure presented above is correct.*

Please refer to Appendix C.1 of the full version paper for the proof.

Lemma 6 (Runtime). *Let PRF be a PRF, $\tau = \log(8Bk)$ and $T = 2^\tau \lambda \log_e(k) + B(1 + 4k)$. Then, the shrinking algorithm $\mathsf{Shrink}_{\mathsf{DDH}}$ described above terminates in polynomial time, except with negligible probability.*

Please refer to Appendix C.2 of the full version paper for the proof.

Ciphertext Rate. After applying $\mathsf{Shrink}_{\mathsf{DDH}}$ we obtain a ciphertext composed by $\tilde{\mathsf{ct}} = (c_1, \mathsf{K}, (b_1, \ldots, b_k)) \in \mathbb{G} \times \mathcal{K} \times \{0,1\}^k$. Hence,

$$\frac{|\tilde{\mathsf{ct}}|}{|\mathbf{m}|} = \frac{|c_1| + |\mathsf{K}| + |(b_1, \ldots, b_k)|}{k} = \frac{2\lambda + k}{k} = 1 + \frac{2\lambda}{k}$$

which tends to 1 for large enough k.

Function-Private LHE from DDH. We now present our circuit-private LHE over $\mathbb{Z}_2$ based on DDH.

$\mathsf{KeyGen}(1^\lambda, k)$:
 – $(\mathbb{G}, p, g) \leftarrow_\$ \mathcal{G}(1^\lambda)$
 – Sample $x_1, \ldots, x_k \leftarrow_\$ \mathbb{Z}_p$. Compute $h_i = g^{x_i}$.
 – Output $\mathsf{pk} = (\mathbb{G}, p, g, h_1, \ldots, h_k)$ and $\mathsf{sk} = \mathbf{x} = (x_1, \ldots, x_k)$.
$\mathsf{Enc}(\mathsf{pk}, \mathbf{m} = (m_1, \ldots, m_k))$:
 – Parse pk as $(\mathbb{G}, p, g, h_1, \ldots, h_k)$.
 – Sample $r \leftarrow_\$ \mathbb{Z}_p$. Compute $c_1 = g^r$ and $c_{2,i} = h_i^r g^{m_i}$ for $i \in [k]$.
 – Output $\mathsf{ct} = (c_1, (c_{2,1}, \ldots, c_{2,k}))$.
$\mathsf{Eval}(\mathsf{pk}, f, (\mathsf{ct}_1, \ldots, \mathsf{ct}_\ell))$
 – Parse pk as $(\mathbb{G}, p, g, h_1, \ldots, h_k)$, f as $f(\mathbf{x}_1, \ldots, \mathbf{x}_\ell) = \sum_{i=1}^\ell a_i \mathbf{x}_i + \mathbf{b}$ for $\mathbf{a} = (a_1, \ldots, a_\ell) \in \mathbb{Z}_2^\ell$ and $\mathbf{b} \in \mathbb{Z}_2^k$ and ct_i as $(c_{1,i}, \mathbf{c}_{2,i})$ where $\mathbf{c}_{2,i} = (c_{2,1,i}, \ldots, c_{2,k,i})$ for $i \in [\ell]$.
 – Compute $\tilde{\mathsf{ct}} = (\bar{c}_1, (\bar{c}_{2,1}, \ldots, \bar{c}_{2,1}))$ where

$$\bar{c}_1 = \prod_{i=1}^\ell \left(c_{1,i}^{\lfloor a_i \frac{p}{2} \rfloor_\sigma} \cdot (g \cdot c_{1,i}^{-1})^{\lceil 0 \rceil_\sigma} \right) \cdot g^t$$

and

$$\bar{\mathbf{c}}_2 = \bigodot_{i=1}^{\ell} \left(\mathbf{c}_{2,i}^{\lceil a_i \frac{p}{2} \rfloor_\sigma} \odot (g \cdot \mathbf{c}_{2,i}^{-1})^{\lceil 0 \rfloor_\sigma} \right) \odot \left(g^{\lceil b_1 \frac{p}{2} \rfloor_\sigma}, \dots, g^{\lceil b_k \frac{p}{2} \rfloor_\sigma} \right) \odot (h_1^t, \dots, h_k^t).$$

for $t \leftarrow_\$ \mathbb{Z}_p$ and where $\odot$ denotes the component-wise multiplication.
  – Output $\bar{\mathsf{ct}}$.
Shrink(pk, ct): Output $\bar{\mathsf{ct}} \leftarrow \mathsf{Shrink}_{\mathsf{DDH}}(\mathsf{pk}, \mathsf{ct})$.
DecShrink(sk, ct): Output $\mathbf{m} \leftarrow \mathsf{DecShrink}_{\mathsf{DDH}}(\mathsf{sk}, \bar{\mathsf{ct}})$.

Correctness and expected polynomial runtime of the LHE described above is guaranteed by Lemma 5 and Lemma 6 by setting $B > \lambda(\sigma(\sqrt{2\ell} + 1))$. Semantic security of the scheme can be established by a simple reduction to the DDH assumption in a similar way as in many previous works (the reduction is similar to the one that proves that El Gamal is semantically secure). It is also easy to see that the scheme has rate-1 for large enough k.

We now show that the scheme is circuit private. Essentially, circuit privacy can be established by resorting to Lemma 4.

Lemma 7 (Circuit-privacy). *The scheme presented above is circuit private.*

Please refer to Appendix C.3 of the full version paper for the proof.

Larger Plaintext Space. As in the LWE case, in the construction presented above, the plaintext space is $\mathbb{Z}_2^k$. Both the shrinking algorithm and the function-private LHE schemes can be extended to support plaintext space $\mathbb{Z}_q^k$ where $q = \mathsf{poly}(\lambda)$ and $q = 2^\nu$ for some $\nu \in \mathbb{Z}$ (the constrain of q being a power of 2 comes from Lemma 4).

6   Co-private Information Retrieval

In this section, we present a new cryptographic primitive that we call *co-PIR*. In a co-PIR scheme, a receiver (with input a set of indices S) and a sender (with no input) interact such that, at the end, the sender obtains a string $\mathbf{y} \in \mathbb{Z}_q^m$ and receiver obtains $\mathbf{y}_{-S}$ (all positions of y except for the indices in S).

In terms of security, we require that the sender learns nothing about S, whereas the string $\mathbf{y}_S$ looks pseudorandom to the receiver. In terms of efficiency, we require that the total communication of the protocol scales only with $|S|\mathsf{poly}(\lambda)\mathsf{polylog}(m)$ (that is, it scales only poly-logarithmically with m). We present a construction for Co-PIR from the distributed GGM-PPRF correlation (as shown in [5]) in Appendix E.1 of the full version paper; We also present another construction with black-box usage of PPRF and PIR in Appendix E.2 of the full version paper.

6.1   Definition

We start by defining Co-PIR and present its security properties.

Definition 8 (Co-PIR). *A (two-round) Co-PIR scheme* CoPIR *over* $\mathbb{Z}_q$ *is parametrized by an integer* m *where* $m = \mathsf{poly}[\lambda]$, *and is composed by a tuple of algorithms* (Query, Send, Retrieve) *such that*

- Query$(1^\lambda, S)$ *takes as input a set of indices* $S \subseteq [m]$. *It outputs a message* copir_1 *and a private state* st.
- Send(copir_1) *takes as input a first message* copir_1. *It outputs a second message* copir_2 *and a string* $\mathbf{y} \in \mathbb{Z}_q^m$.
- Dec$(\mathsf{copir}_2, \mathsf{st})$ *takes as input a second message* copir_2 *and a state* st. *It outputs a string* $\tilde{\mathbf{y}} \in \mathbb{Z}_q^m$.

Definition 9 (Correctness). *A Co-PIR scheme* CoPIR *is said to be correct if for any* $m = \mathsf{poly}(\lambda)$ *and* $S \subseteq [m]$ *we have that*

$$
\Pr\left[\mathbf{y}_{[m]\setminus S} = \tilde{\mathbf{y}}_{[m]\setminus S} : \begin{array}{l} (\mathsf{copir}_1, \mathsf{st}) \leftarrow \mathsf{Query}(1^\lambda, S) \\ (\mathsf{copir}_2, \mathbf{y}) \leftarrow \mathsf{Send}(\mathsf{copir}_1) \\ \tilde{\mathbf{y}} \leftarrow \mathsf{Retrieve}(\mathsf{copir}_2, \mathsf{st}) \end{array} \right] = 1.
$$

In other words, the strings $\mathbf{y}$ *and* $\tilde{\mathbf{y}}$ *match for every coordinate* $i \in [m]\setminus S$.

In terms of security, we require two properties: receiver security and sender security.

Definition 10 (Receiver security). *A Co-PIR scheme* CoPIR *is said to be receiver secure if for all* $m = \mathsf{poly}(\lambda)$, *any subsets* $S_1, S_2 \subseteq [m]$ *we have that for any adversary* $\mathcal{A}$

$$
\left| \begin{array}{l} \Pr\left[1 \leftarrow \mathcal{A}(k, \mathsf{copir}_1) : (\mathsf{copir}_1, \mathsf{st}) \leftarrow \mathsf{Query}(1^\lambda, S_1) \right] - \\ \Pr\left[1 \leftarrow \mathcal{A}(k, \mathsf{copir}_1) : (\mathsf{copir}_1, \mathsf{st}) \leftarrow \mathsf{Query}(1^\lambda, S_2) \right] \end{array} \right| \leq \mathsf{negl}(\lambda).
$$

Definition 11 (Sender security). *A Co-PIR scheme* CoPIR *is said to be sender secure if for any* $m = \mathsf{poly}(\lambda)$, *any subset* $S \subseteq [m]$ *we have that for all adversaries* $\mathcal{A}$

$$
\left| \begin{array}{l} \Pr\left[1 \leftarrow \mathcal{A}(k, \mathsf{st}, \mathsf{copir}_2, \mathbf{y}_S) : \begin{array}{l} (\mathsf{copir}_1, \mathsf{st}) \leftarrow \mathsf{Query}(1^\lambda, S) \\ (\mathsf{copir}_2, \mathbf{y}) \leftarrow \mathsf{Send}(\mathsf{copir}_1, \mathbf{x}) \end{array} \right] - \\ \Pr\left[1 \leftarrow \mathcal{A}(k, \mathsf{st}, \mathsf{copir}_2, \mathbf{y}_S') : \begin{array}{l} (\mathsf{copir}_1, \mathsf{st}) \leftarrow \mathsf{Query}(1^\lambda, S) \\ (\mathsf{copir}_2, \mathbf{y}) \leftarrow \mathsf{Send}(\mathsf{copir}_1, \mathbf{x}) \\ \mathbf{y}_S' \leftarrow_\$ \mathbb{Z}_q^{|S|} \end{array} \right] \end{array} \right| \leq \mathsf{negl}(\lambda).
$$

Definition 12 (Compactness). *A Co-PIR scheme* CoPIR *is said to be compact if* $|\mathsf{copir}_1|, |\mathsf{copir}_2| = |S| \cdot \mathsf{polylog}(m) \cdot \mathsf{poly}(\lambda$ *for any* $S \subseteq [m]$ *where* $(\mathsf{copir}_1, \mathsf{st}) \leftarrow \mathsf{Query}(1^\lambda, S)$ *and* $(\mathsf{copir}_2, \mathbf{y}) \leftarrow \mathsf{Send}(\mathsf{copir}_1)$. *In other words, the communication complexity depends only poly-logarithmically in* m.

7   Oblivious Transfer with Overall Rate 1

We will now provide our construction of an oblivious transfer protocol with overall rate 1.

Ingredients. We will make use of the following ingredients.

- A packed linearly homomorphic encryption scheme $\mathsf{LHE} = (\mathsf{KeyGen}, \mathsf{Enc}, \mathsf{Eval}, \mathsf{Shrink}, \mathsf{DecShrink})$ with plaintext space $\{0,1\}^\ell$ and a post homomorphism shrinking procedure Shrink which converts ciphertexts into a rate 1 representation.[11]
- The binary $\mathsf{LPN}(n, m, \rho)$ problem with dimension $n = \mathsf{poly}(n)$, $m = n \cdot \ell \cdot \mathsf{poly}(n)$ samples and slightly sub-constant noise-rate $\rho = m^{1-\epsilon}$.
- A 2-round PIR scheme $\mathsf{PIR} = (\mathsf{Query}, \mathsf{Send}, \mathsf{Retrieve})$ with poly-logarithmic communication complexity and sender privacy.
- A 2-round Co-PIR scheme $\mathsf{CoPIR} = (\mathsf{Query}, \mathsf{Send}, \mathsf{Retrieve})$ over $\mathbb{Z}_2$ parametrized by m.

Additional Notation. Furthermore, to declutter notation we define the following embedding functions.

$\mathsf{RowMatrix}(\ell, n, \mathbf{v}_1, \ldots, \mathbf{v}_\ell)$: Takes row-vectors $\mathbf{v}_1, \ldots, \mathbf{v}_\ell \in \{0,1\}^n$ and outputs a matrix

$$\mathbf{V} = \begin{pmatrix} - \mathbf{v}_1 - \\ \vdots \\ - \mathbf{v}_\ell - \end{pmatrix},$$

i.e. for every $i \in [\ell]$ the i-th row of $\mathbf{V}$ is the row-vector $\mathbf{v}_i$.

$\mathsf{SingleRowMatrix}(\ell, n, i, \mathbf{v})$: Takes a row-vector $\mathbf{v} \in \{0,1\}^n$ and outputs a matrix

$$\mathbf{V} = \begin{pmatrix} 0 & \cdots & 0 \\ \vdots & & \vdots \\ 0 & \cdots & 0 \\ - & \mathbf{v} & - \\ 0 & \cdots & 0 \\ \vdots & & \vdots \\ 0 & \cdots & 0 \end{pmatrix},$$

i.e. the i-th row of $\mathbf{V}$ is $\mathbf{v}$, but $\mathbf{V}$ is 0 everywhere else.

$\mathsf{Diag}(n, \mathbf{v})$: Takes a vector $\mathbf{v} = (v_1, \ldots, v_n) \in \{0,1\}^n$ and outputs a matrix

$$\mathbf{D} = \begin{pmatrix} v_1 & & 0 \\ & \ddots & \\ 0 & & v_n \end{pmatrix},$$

---

[11] Recall that we use the notation Eval&Shrink to denote the composition of algorithms Eval and Shrink.

i.e. $\mathbf{D} \in \{0,1\}^{n \times n}$ is a diagonal matrix with the components of $\mathbf{v}$ on its diagonal.

We observe the following:

- For any $\mathbf{v}_1, \ldots, \mathbf{v}_\ell \in \{0,1\}^n$ it holds that

$$\mathsf{RowMatrix}(\ell, n, \mathbf{v}_1, \ldots, \mathbf{v}_\ell) = \sum_{i=1}^{\ell} \mathsf{SingleRowMatrix}(\ell, n, i, \mathbf{v}_i).$$

- For $\mathbf{x}, \mathbf{y} \in \{0,1\}^n$ it holds that

$$\mathbf{x} \cdot \mathsf{Diag}(n, \mathbf{y}) = \mathbf{x} \odot \mathbf{y},$$

where $\odot$ denotes component-wise multiplication.

7.1   The Protocol

The protocol $\mathsf{OT} = (\mathsf{OTR}, \mathsf{OTS}, \mathsf{OTD})$ is given as follows.

$\mathsf{OTR}(\mathbf{b} \in \{0,1\}^{m\ell})$:
- Parse $\mathbf{b} = (\mathbf{b}_1, \ldots, \mathbf{b}_\ell)$, where the $\mathbf{b}_i \in \{0,1\}^m$ are blocks of size m.
- Choose $\mathbf{A} \leftarrow_\$ \{0,1\}^{n \times m}$ uniformly at random and compute a pair of public and secret key $(\mathsf{pk}, \mathsf{sk}) \leftarrow \mathsf{LHE.KeyGen}(1^\lambda, \ell)$.
- For all $i \in [\ell]$, choose $\mathbf{s}_i \leftarrow_\$ \{0,1\}^n$, and $\mathbf{e}_i \leftarrow_\$ \chi_{m,t}$, compute $\mathbf{c}_i \leftarrow \mathbf{s}_i \mathbf{A} + \mathbf{e}_i + \mathbf{b}_i$, and set $\mathbf{S}_i \leftarrow \mathsf{SingleRowMatrix}(\ell, n, i, \mathbf{s}_i)$. Compute a matrix-ciphertext $\mathsf{ct}_i \leftarrow \mathsf{LHE.Enc}(\mathsf{pk}, \mathbf{S}_i)$.
- For all $i \in [\ell]$ set $J_i = \mathsf{Supp}(\mathbf{e}_i)$ to be the support of $\mathbf{e}_i$. Compute $(\mathsf{copir}_{1,i}, \mathsf{st}_i) \leftarrow \mathsf{CoPIR.Query}(J_i)$. Additionally, for $j \in [t]$ compute $(\mathsf{q}_{i,j}, \hat{\mathsf{st}}_{i,j}) = \mathsf{PIR.Query}(J_i[j])$.
- Output $\mathsf{ot}_1 = (\mathsf{pk}, \mathbf{A}, \{\mathsf{ct}_i, \mathbf{c}_i, \mathsf{copir}_{1,i}\}_{i \in [\ell]}, \{\mathsf{q}_{i,j}\}_{i \in [\ell], j \in [t]})$ and $\mathsf{st} = (\mathsf{sk}, \{\mathsf{st}_i, J_i\}_{i \in [\ell]}, \{\hat{\mathsf{st}}_{i,j}\}_{i \in [\ell], j \in [t]})$.

$\mathsf{OTS}((\mathbf{m}_0, \mathbf{m}_1) \in (\{0,1\}^{m\ell})^2, \mathsf{ot}_1)$:
- Parse $\mathbf{m}_0 = (\mathbf{m}_{0,1}, \ldots, \mathbf{m}_{0,\ell})$ and $\mathbf{m}_1 = (\mathbf{m}_{1,1}, \ldots, \mathbf{m}_{1,\ell})$, where each $\mathbf{m}_{b,i} = (m_{b,i,1}, \ldots, m_{b,i,m}) \in \{0,1\}^m$. Parse $\mathsf{ot}_1 = (\mathsf{pk}, \mathbf{A}, \{\mathsf{ct}_i, \mathbf{c}_i, \mathsf{copir}_{1,i}\}_{i \in [\ell]}, \{\mathsf{q}_{i,j}\}_{i \in [\ell], j \in [t]})$.
- For $i \in [\ell]$ $(\mathbf{y}_i, \mathsf{copir}_{2,i}) \leftarrow \mathsf{CoPIR.Send}(\mathsf{copir}_{1,i})$ where $\mathbf{y}_i = (y_{i,1}, \ldots, y_{i,m})$. Set $\mathbf{z}_i = \mathbf{m}_{0,i} + \mathbf{y}_i$.
- Set $\mathbf{Z} = \mathsf{RowMatrix}(\ell, m, \mathbf{z}_1, \ldots, \mathbf{z}_\ell)$.
- For all $i \in [\ell]$ set $\mathbf{C}_i = \mathsf{SingleRowMatrix}(\ell, m, i, \mathbf{c}_i)$ and $\mathbf{D}_i = \mathsf{Diag}(m, \mathbf{m}_{1,i} - \mathbf{m}_{0,i})$.
- Define the $\mathbb{Z}_2$-linear function $f : (\{0,1\}^{\ell \times n})^\ell \to \{0,1\}^{\ell \times m}$ via

$$f(\mathbf{X}_1, \ldots, \mathbf{X}_\ell) = \left(\sum_{i=1}^{\ell} (-\mathbf{X}_i \mathbf{A} + \mathbf{C}_i) \cdot \mathbf{D}_i \right) + \mathbf{Z}.$$

- Compute $\tilde{\mathsf{ct}} \leftarrow \mathsf{LHE.Eval\&Shrink}(\mathsf{pk}, f, \mathsf{ct}_1, \ldots, \mathsf{ct}_\ell)$.

- For $i \in [\ell]$ set $DB_i = (y_{i,1}+(m_{1,i,1}-m_{0,i,1}), \ldots, y_{i,m}+(m_{1,i,m}-m_{0,i,m}))$.
  For all $j \in [t]$ compute $\mathsf{r}_{i,j} \leftarrow \mathsf{PIR.Send}(DB_i, \mathsf{q}_{i,j})$.
- Output $\mathsf{ot}_2 = (\tilde{\mathsf{c}}\mathsf{t}, \{\mathsf{copir}_{2,i}\}_{i\in[\ell]}, \{\mathsf{r}_{i,j}\}_{i\in[\ell],j\in[t]})$.

OTD(ot_2, st):
- Parse $\mathsf{ot}_2 = (\tilde{\mathsf{c}}\mathsf{t}, \{\mathsf{copir}_{2,i}\}_{i\in[\ell]}, \{\mathsf{r}_{i,j}\}_{i\in[\ell],j\in[t]})$ and $\mathsf{st} = (\mathsf{sk}, \{\mathsf{st}_i, J_i\}_{i\in[\ell]},$
  $\{\hat{\mathsf{st}}_{i,j}\}_{i\in[\ell],j\in[t]]})$.
- For all $i \in [\ell]$ compute $\tilde{\mathbf{y}}_i = (\tilde{y}_{i,1}, \ldots, \tilde{y}_{i,m}) \leftarrow \mathsf{CoPIR.Retrieve}(\mathsf{copir}_{2,i}, \mathsf{st}_i)$.
- For $i \in [\ell]$ and $j \in [t]$ compute $\tilde{z}_{i,j} \leftarrow \mathsf{PIR.Retrieve}(\mathsf{r}_{i,j}, \hat{\mathsf{st}}_{i,j})$.
- For $i \in [\ell]$ set $\mathbf{z}_i = (z_{i,1}, \ldots, z_{i,m})$ where

$$z_{i,l} = \begin{cases} \tilde{z}_{i,j} & \text{if } l = J_i[j] \\ \tilde{y}_{i,\ell} & \text{otherwise} \end{cases}.$$

- Set $\mathbf{Z} = \mathsf{RowMatrix}(\ell, m, \mathbf{z}_1, \ldots, \mathbf{z}_\ell)$.
- Compute $\tilde{\mathbf{W}} \leftarrow \mathsf{LHE.DecShrink}(\mathsf{sk}, \tilde{\mathsf{c}}\mathsf{t})$ and $\mathbf{W} = \tilde{\mathbf{W}} - \mathbf{Z}$.
- Let $\mathbf{w}_1, \ldots, \mathbf{w}_\ell$ be the rows of $\mathbf{W}$. Output $\mathbf{w} = (\mathbf{w}_1 \| \ldots \| \mathbf{w}_\ell) \in \{0,1\}^{m\ell}$.

Correctness. We will first show that OT is correct, given that LHE, CoPIR and PIR are correct.

Theorem 1. *Assume that* LHE, CoPIR *and* PIR *are correct. Then the scheme presented above is correct.*

Proof. First note that by linear-homomorphic correctness of LHE it holds that

$$\begin{aligned}
\tilde{\mathbf{W}} &= \mathsf{LHE.DecShrink}(\mathsf{sk}, \mathsf{LHE.Eval\&Shrink}(\mathsf{pk}, f, \mathsf{LHE.Enc}(\mathsf{pk}, \mathbf{S}_1), \ldots, \mathsf{LHE.Enc}(\mathsf{pk}, \mathbf{S}_\ell)) \\
&= f(\mathbf{S}_1, \ldots, \mathbf{S}_\ell) \\
&= \left(\sum_{i=1}^{k}(-\mathbf{S}_i\mathbf{A} + \mathbf{C}_i) \cdot \mathbf{D}_i\right) + \mathbf{Z}
\end{aligned}$$

Let $\tilde{\mathbf{w}}_i$ be the i-th row of $\tilde{\mathbf{W}}$. It holds by definition $\mathbf{S}_i$, $\mathbf{C}_i$ and $\mathbf{Z}_i$ that

$$\begin{aligned}
\tilde{\mathbf{w}}_i &= (-\mathbf{s}_i\mathbf{A} + \mathbf{c}_i)\mathbf{D}_i + \mathbf{z}_i \\
&= (-\mathbf{s}_i\mathbf{A} + \mathbf{s}_i\mathbf{A}_i + \mathbf{e}_i + \mathbf{b}_i)\mathbf{D}_i + \mathbf{m}_{0,i} + \mathbf{y}_i \\
&= \mathbf{b}_i \odot (\mathbf{m}_{1,i} - \mathbf{m}_{0,i}) + \mathbf{m}_{0,i} + \mathbf{e}_i \odot (\mathbf{m}_{1,i} - \mathbf{m}_{0,i}) + \mathbf{y}_i.
\end{aligned}$$

where $\mathbf{y}_i = (y_{i,1}, \ldots, y_{i,m})$ is part of the output of CoPIR.Send.

Let J_i be the support of $\mathbf{e}_i$ and let $\tilde{\mathbf{y}}_i = (\tilde{y}_{i,1}, \ldots, \tilde{y}_{i,m}) \leftarrow$ CoPIR.Retrieve($\mathsf{copir}_{2,i}, \mathsf{st}_i$). By the correctness of the Co-PIR scheme CoPIR we have that $\tilde{y}_{i,j} = y_{i,j}$ for all $j \notin J_i$. On the other hand, by the correctness of the PIR scheme PIR it holds that

$$\tilde{z}_{i,j} = y_{i,j} + (m_{1,i,j} - m_{0,i,j})$$

for all $j \in J_i$. Consequently, we have that

$$z_{i,j} = \begin{cases} y_{i,j} + (m_{1,i,j} - m_{0,i,j}) & \text{if } l = J_i[j] \\ y_{i,j} & \text{otherwise} \end{cases}.$$

In other words, the term $(m_{1,i,j} - m_{0,i,j})$ only appears in the coordinates where $\mathbf{e}_i$ is equal to one. Then, it holds that

$$\mathbf{z}_i = \mathbf{e}_i \odot (\mathbf{m}_{1,i} - \mathbf{m}_{0,i}) + \mathbf{y}_i.$$

We conclude that

$$\mathbf{w} = \tilde{\mathbf{w}}_i - \mathbf{z}_i = \mathbf{b}_i \odot (\mathbf{m}_{1,i} - \mathbf{m}_{0,i}) + \mathbf{m}_{0,i}.$$

Since $\mathbf{w} = (\mathbf{w}_1 \| \dots \| \mathbf{w}_\ell)$ it follows that

$$\mathbf{w} = \mathbf{b} \odot (\mathbf{m}_1 - \mathbf{m}_0) + \mathbf{m}_0,$$

i.e. OT is correct.

Communication Complexity. We will now analyze the communication complexity of OT and show which choice of parameters leads to an overall rate approaching 1.

The bit-size of the message $\mathsf{ot}_1 = \left(\mathsf{pk}, \mathbf{A}, \{\mathsf{ct}_i, \mathbf{c}_i, \mathsf{copir}_{1,i}\}_{i\in[\ell]}, \{\mathsf{q}_{i,j}\}_{i\in[\ell],j\in[t]}\right)$ can be bounded as follows.

- $|\mathsf{pk}| = \ell \cdot \mathsf{poly}(\lambda)$
- $|\mathbf{A}| = n \cdot m$
- $|\{\mathsf{ct}_i\}_{i\in[\ell]}| = \ell^2 \cdot n \cdot \mathsf{poly}(\lambda)$
- $|\{\mathbf{c}_i\}_{i\in[\ell]}| = \ell \cdot m$
- $|\{\mathsf{copir}_{1,i}\}_{i\in[\ell]}| = \ell \cdot t \cdot \mathsf{polylog}(m) \cdot \mathsf{poly}(\lambda)$
- $|\{\mathsf{q}_{i,j}\}_{i\in[\ell],j\in[t]}| = \ell \cdot t \cdot \mathsf{polylog}(m) \cdot \mathsf{poly}(\lambda).$

Consequently, the overall upload-rate ρ_{up} can be bounded by

$$\rho_{\mathsf{up}} = \frac{|\mathsf{pk}| + |\mathbf{A}| + |(\mathsf{ct}_i)_{i\in[\ell]}| + |(\mathbf{c}_i)_{i\in[\ell]}| + |\{\mathsf{copir}_{1,i}\}_{i\in[\ell]}| + |(\mathsf{q}_{i,j})_{i\in[\ell],j\in[t]}|}{\ell m}$$

$$\leq 1 + \frac{\mathsf{poly}(\lambda)}{m} + \frac{n}{\ell} + \frac{\ell \cdot n \cdot \mathsf{poly}(\lambda)}{m} + \frac{t \cdot \mathsf{polylog}(m) \cdot \mathsf{poly}(\lambda)}{m}$$

$$\leq 1 + \frac{n}{\ell} + \frac{\ell \cdot n \cdot \mathsf{poly}(\lambda)}{m} + \frac{t \cdot \mathsf{polylog}(m) \cdot \mathsf{poly}(\lambda)}{m}.$$

We get an overall upload rate of $\rho_{\mathsf{up}} = 1 + O(1/\lambda)$ by choosing $\ell = \lambda \cdot n$ and $m = n^2 \cdot \mathsf{poly}(\lambda)$ for a sufficiently large $\mathsf{poly}(\lambda)$ depending on ϵ (where $t = m^{1-\epsilon}$).

The bit-size of the message $\mathsf{ot}_2 = \left(\tilde{\mathsf{ct}}, \{\mathsf{copir}_{2,i}\}_{i\in[\ell]}, \{\mathsf{r}_{i,j}\}_{i\in[\ell],j\in[t]}\right)$ can be bounded as follows.

- $|\tilde{\mathsf{ct}}| = \ell m (1 + \rho_{\mathsf{LHE}})$, where $1 + \rho_{\mathsf{LHE}}$ is the ciphertext rate of LHE.
- $|\{\mathsf{copir}_{2,i}\}_{i\in[\ell]}| = \ell \cdot t \cdot \mathsf{polylog}(m) \cdot \mathsf{poly}(\lambda)$
- $|\{\mathsf{r}_{i,j}\}_{i\in[\ell],j\in[t]}| = \ell \cdot t \cdot \mathsf{polylog}(m) \cdot \mathsf{poly}(\lambda)$

Thus, the download-rate ρ_{down} can be bounded by

$$\rho_{\mathsf{down}} = \frac{|\tilde{\mathsf{ct}}| + |\{\mathsf{copir}_{2,i}\}_{i\in[\ell]}| + |\{\mathsf{r}_{i,j}\}_{i\in[\ell],j\in[t]}|}{\ell m}$$

$$\leq 1 + \rho_{\mathsf{LHE}} + \frac{\ell \cdot t \cdot \mathsf{polylog}(m) \cdot \mathsf{poly}(\lambda)}{m}.$$

By the above choice of m this comes down to $\rho_{\mathsf{down}} \leq 1 + \rho_{\mathsf{LHE}} + O(1/\lambda)$.

7.2   Security

Receiver Security We now focus on the security of the scheme. We start by proving that the scheme is secure against semi-honest senders.

Theorem 2. *Assume that* LHE *is a semantic secure LHE scheme,* PIR *is a user-private PIR scheme,* CoPIR *is a receiver secure Co-PIR scheme and that the* LPN(n, m, ρ) *assumption holds for* $\rho = m^{1-\varepsilon}$ *for* $\varepsilon > 0$. *Then the scheme presented in Sect. 7.1 is receiver secure against semi-honest adversaries.*

Recall that the receiver's message is composed by LHE ciphertexts, LPN samples, Co-PIR and PIR first messages. In a nutshell, receiver security follows from the fact that the ciphertexts hide the LPN secret, the LPN samples hide the receiver's input **b** and finally the Co-PIR and PIR first messages hide the indices J_i. We prove the above theorem in Appendix G.1 of the full version paper.

Sender Security

Theorem 3. *Assume that* LHE *is a statistically function-private LHE scheme,* PIR *is a sender-private PIR scheme and* CoPIR *is a sender-private Co-PIR scheme. Then the scheme presented in Sect. 7.1 is sender secure.*

In a nutshell, we can use the sender security of PIR and Co-PIR to remove any information about the indices of DB_i that are not in $\mathsf{Supp}(\mathbf{e}_i)$, and finally invoke circuit-privacy of the LHE. We prove sender security in Appendix G.2 of the full version paper.

Hardness assumptions for optimal-rate OT. When we instantiate the LHE with one of the schemes from Sect. 5, the Co-PIR with the construction from Sect. 6 and the PIR with a known black-box construction based on LWE, DDH or QR [19], we obtain the following corollary

Corollary 1. *Assuming the LWE, DDH or QR assumptions together with the* LPN(n, m, ρ), *there is a black-box construction for optimal-rate OT.*

8   Oblivious Matrix-Vector Product and Oblivious Linear Evaluation with Overall Rate 1

In this section we show how we can extend the techniques from the previous section to build protocols for OMV and OLE that achieve optimal rate.

We start by presenting a secure protocol for oblivious matrix-vector product (OMV). In an OMV functionality there is a sender, with input a matrix $\mathbf{M} \in \mathbb{Z}_q^{m \times m}$ and a vector $\mathbf{v} \in \mathbb{Z}_q^m$, and a receiver with input $\mathbf{b} \in \mathbb{Z}_q^m$. In the end, the receiver gets the value $\mathbf{b}\mathbf{M} + \mathbf{v}$ but learns nothing about $\mathbf{M}$ and $\mathbf{v}$ whereas the sender learns nothing about **b**. We start by defining the functionality:

OMV Functionality. The functionality $\mathcal{F}_{\mathsf{OMV}}$ is parametrized by integers $m = \mathsf{poly}(\lambda)$ and q and works as follows:

- **Receiver phase.** R sends $\mathbf{b}$ to $\mathcal{F}_{\mathsf{OMV}}$ where $\mathbf{b} \in \mathbb{Z}_q^m$.
- **Sender phase.** S sends $(\mathbf{M}, \mathbf{v})$ to $\mathcal{F}_{\mathsf{OMV}}$ where $\mathbf{M} \in \mathbb{Z}_q^{m \times m}$ and $\mathbf{v} \in \{0,1\}^m$. $\mathcal{F}_{\mathsf{OMV}}$ sends $\mathbf{bM} + \mathbf{v} \in \mathbb{Z}_q^m$ to R.

We describe the concrete OMV protocol in Appendix H of the full version paper.

8.1   OLE Protocol

An oblivious linear evaluation (OLE) is a protocol between a sender, with input an affine function f, and a receiver, with input a point b. It allows for the receiver to obliviously learn $f(b)$. We now show how we can obtain an OLE using the OMV protocol presented in Appendix H of the full version paper.

We start by defining the functionality:

OLE Functionality. The functionality $\mathcal{F}_{\mathsf{OLE}}$ is parametrized by integers $k = \mathsf{poly}(\lambda)$ and q and works as follows:

- **Receiver phase.** R sends $\mathbf{b}$ to $\mathcal{F}_{\mathsf{OLE}}$ where $\mathbf{b} \in \mathbb{Z}_q^k$.
- **Sender phase.** S sends $(\mathbf{u}_0, \mathbf{u}_1)$ to $\mathcal{F}_{\mathsf{OLE}}$ where $\mathbf{u}_0, \mathbf{u}_1 \in \mathbb{Z}_q^k$. $\mathcal{F}_{\mathsf{OLE}}$ sends $\mathbf{b} \odot \mathbf{u}_0 + \mathbf{u}_1 \in \mathbb{Z}_q^k$ to R.

Protocol for Small Fields. We briefly sketch how we can construct an OLE scheme over $\mathbb{Z}_q$ where $q = \mathsf{poly}(\lambda)$. The protocol follows as a particular case of the protocol of Appendix H. We give a brief overview of the scheme below.

Using the notation of Appendix H, let $\mathbf{b} = (\mathbf{b}_1, \ldots, \mathbf{b}_\ell) \in \mathbb{Z}_q^{m\ell}$ be the receiver's input and let $(\mathbf{u}_0 = (\mathbf{u}_{0,1}, \ldots, \mathbf{u}_{0,\ell}), \mathbf{u}_1 = (\mathbf{u}_{1,1}, \ldots, \mathbf{u}_{1,\ell})) \in (\mathbb{Z}_q^{m\ell})^2$ be the sender's input. To achieve OLE, the sender constructs the matrices $\mathbf{D}_i = \mathsf{Diag}(m, \mathbf{u}_{0,i})$ and sets $\mathbf{v}_i = \mathbf{u}_{1,i}$ for all $i \in [\ell]$. Then they run the OMV protocol where the receiver inputs $\mathbf{b}$ and the sender inputs $\mathbf{D} = (\mathbf{D}_1, \ldots, \mathbf{D}_\ell)$ and $\mathbf{v} = (\mathbf{v}_1, \ldots, \mathbf{v}_\ell)$. It is easy to see that the output of the receiver is $\mathbf{y} = (\mathbf{y}_1, \ldots, \mathbf{y}_\ell)$ where

$$\mathbf{y}_i = \mathbf{b}_i \mathbf{D}_i + \mathbf{v}_i = \mathbf{b}_i \odot \mathbf{u}_{0,i} + \mathbf{u}_{1,i}$$

be the correctness of the OMV protocol.

Moreover, $\mathsf{hw}(\mathbf{D}_i) = 1 \leq m^{1-\zeta}$ for some $\zeta > 0$ such that $\zeta + \epsilon > 1$. Thus the resulting protocol achieves overall rate 1. Finally, in terms of hardness assumptions, the OLE protocol inherits the same security.

Extending OLE to Larger Rings. Following [19], we briefly explain how we can achieve OLE over larger rings (which can potentially have super-polynomial size in λ).

OLE over $\mathbb{Z}_N = \mathbb{Z}_{q_1} \times \cdots \times \mathbb{Z}_{q_\delta}$. Let $N = \prod_{i=1}^{\delta} q_i$ be an integer (which might be superpolynomial in λ) such that for all $i \in [\delta]$ $q_i = \mathsf{poly}(\lambda)$ are different prime numbers. Then, via the Chinese Remainder Theorem, $\mathbb{Z}_N$ is isomorphic to $\mathbb{Z}_{q_1} \times \cdots \times \mathbb{Z}_{q_\delta}$. Thus, performing an OLE over $\mathbb{Z}_N$ boils down to performing δ OLEs over each one of the smaller fields $\mathbb{Z}_{q_i}$. It is easy to see that, if each OLE over $\mathbb{Z}_{q_i}$ has overall rate 1, then the resulting OLE over $\mathbb{Z}_N$ also achieves overall rate 1.

OLE over Extension Fields. We now show how these techniques can be adapted to perform OLE over an extension field $\mathbb{F}_{q^k}$ of order q^k for a prime q. Here, we rely on the fact that multiplication over $\mathbb{F}_{q^k}$ can be expressed as a linear function over the field $\mathbb{Z}_q$. That is, suppose that an element $\mathbf{x} \in \mathbb{F}_{q^k}$ is of the form $\mathbf{x} = x_1 + x_2\alpha + \cdots + x_k\alpha^{k-1}$ where each $x_i \in \mathbb{Z}_q$ and α is a symbol. Then, for elements $\mathbf{a}, \mathbf{x} \in \mathbb{F}_{q^k}$ the product

$$\mathbf{xa} = f_{1,\mathbf{a}}(\mathbf{x}) + f_{2,\mathbf{a}}(\mathbf{x})\alpha + \cdots + f_{k,\mathbf{a}}(\mathbf{x})\alpha^{k-1}$$

where each $f_{i,\mathbf{a}}$ is a $\mathbb{Z}_q$-linear function which depends solely on $\mathbf{a}$.

Given this, we briefly describe how we can perform several OLEs over $\mathbb{F}_{q^k}$ while preserving overall rate 1. The receiver has input $\mathbf{b} = (\mathbf{b}_1, \ldots, \mathbf{b}_t) \in \mathbb{F}_{q^k}^t$ such that $kt = m\ell$ and $k|m$ (using the same notation as in Appendix H). It parses each $\mathbf{b}_i$ as a k-dimensional vectors $\bar{\mathbf{b}}_i \in \mathbb{Z}_q^k$. Then, it organizes all t vectors $\mathbf{b}_i$ in blocks $\mathbf{c}_i \in \mathbb{Z}_q^m$ of size m. It inputs $\mathbf{c} = (\mathbf{c}_1, \ldots, \mathbf{c}_\ell)$ into the OMV protocol.

The sender, with input $\mathbf{u}, \mathbf{v} \in \mathbb{F}_{q^k}$ rearranges $\mathbf{u}, \mathbf{v}$ in the same way as the receiver and obtains $\mathbf{w} = (\mathbf{w}_1, \ldots, \mathbf{w}_\ell), \mathbf{z} = (\mathbf{z}_1, \ldots, \mathbf{z}_\ell)$ respectively. Then, for each $\mathbf{w}_i = (\mathbf{w}_{i,1}, \ldots, \mathbf{w}_{i,m/k})$, it computes the functions $f_{j,\mathbf{w}_{i,r}}$ for each $j \in [k]$, $i \in [\ell]$ and $r \in [m/k]$. Let $\mathbf{f}_{j,\mathbf{w}_{i,r}}$ be the vector composed by the coefficients of $f_{j,\mathbf{w}_{i,r}}$. The sender computes the matrices

$$\bar{\mathbf{D}}_{i,r} = \left(\begin{array}{ccc} | & & | \\ \mathbf{f}_{1,\mathbf{w}_{i,r}} & \cdots & \mathbf{f}_{k,\mathbf{w}_{i,r}} \\ | & & | \end{array} \right)$$

and then sets

$$\mathbf{D}_i = \left(\begin{array}{ccc} \bar{\mathbf{D}}_{i,1} & & \\ & \ddots & \\ & & \bar{\mathbf{D}}_{i,m/k} \end{array} \right).$$

It inputs $\mathbf{D} = (\mathbf{D}_1, \ldots, \mathbf{D}_\ell)$ and $\mathbf{z}$ into the OMV protocol.

It is easy to see that the receiver's output will be $\mathbf{b} \odot \mathbf{u} + \mathbf{v}$ where $\odot$ denotes component-wise multiplication over $\mathbb{F}_{q^k}$. Moreover, $\mathsf{hw}(\mathbf{D}_i) = k$. By choosing k such that $k \leq \mu = m^{1-\varsigma}$ we achieve a protocol with overall rate 1. In particular, we can set the parameters such that $k = \lambda$ and we achieve an OLE over the field $\mathbb{F}_{q^\lambda}$ of exponential size.

Acknowledgment. Zvika Brakerski is supported by the Israel Science Foundation (Grant No. 3426/21), and by the European Union Horizon 2020 Research and Innovation Program via ERC Project REACT (Grant 756482) and via Project PROMETHEUS (Grant 780701).

Pedro Branco thanks the support from DP-PMI and FCT (Portugal) through the grant PD/BD/135181/2017. This work is supported by Security and Quantum Information Group of Instituto de Telecomunicações, by the Fundação para a Ciência e a Tecnologia (FCT) through national funds, by FEDER, COMPETE 2020, and by Regional Operational Program of Lisbon, under UIDB/50008/2020.

Nico Döttling and Sihang Pu were supported by the Helmholtz Association within the project "Trustworthy Federated Data Analytics" (TFDA) (funding number ZT-I-OO1 4).

A   Additional Preliminaries

A.1   UC Security

In terms of security, we work in the standard UC-framework [13]. Let $\mathcal{F}$ be a functionality, π a protocol that implements $\mathcal{F}$ and $\mathcal{E}$ be a environment, an entity that oversees the execution of the protocol in both the real and the ideal worlds. Let $\mathsf{IDEAL}_{\mathcal{F},\mathsf{Sim},\mathcal{E}}$ be a random variable that represents the output of $\mathcal{E}$ after the execution of $\mathcal{F}$ with adversary Sim. Similarly, let $\mathsf{REAL}_{\pi,\mathcal{A},\mathcal{E}}$ be a random variable that represents the output of $\mathcal{E}$ after the execution of π with adversary $\mathcal{A}$.

In this work, we only consider semi-honest adversaries.

Definition 13. *A protocol π implements $\mathcal{F}$ if for every PPT adversary $\mathcal{A}$ there is a PPT simulator Sim such that for all PPT environments $\mathcal{E}$, the distributions $\mathsf{IDEAL}_{\mathcal{F},\mathsf{Sim},\mathcal{E}}$ and $\mathsf{REAL}_{\pi,\mathcal{A},\mathcal{E}}$ are computationally indistinguishable.*

A.2   Learning Parity with Noise

The LPN assumption is closely related to the problem of decoding a random linear code. Informally, it states that it is hard to find a solution for a noisy system of linear equations over $\mathbb{Z}_2$.

Definition 14 (LPN assumption). *Let $n, m, t \in \mathbb{N}$ such that $n \in \mathsf{poly}(\lambda)$ and let $\chi_{m,t}$ be uniform distribution over the set of error vectors of size m and hamming weight t. The Learning Parity with Noise (LPN) assumption $\mathsf{LPN}(n, m, \rho)$ holds if for any PPT adversary $\mathcal{A}$ we have that*

$$\left| \Pr\left[1 \leftarrow \mathcal{A}(\mathbf{A}, \mathbf{sA} + \mathbf{e}) : \begin{array}{c} \mathbf{A} \leftarrow\!\!{}^\$ \{0,1\}^{n \times m} \\ \mathbf{s} \leftarrow\!\!{}^\$ \{0,1\}^n \\ \mathbf{e} \leftarrow\!\!{}^\$ \chi_{m,t} \end{array} \right] - \Pr\left[1 \leftarrow \mathcal{A}(\mathbf{A}, \mathbf{y}) : \begin{array}{c} \mathbf{A} \leftarrow\!\!{}^\$ \{0,1\}^{n \times m} \\ \mathbf{y} \leftarrow\!\!{}^\$ \{0,1\}^m \end{array} \right] \right| \leq \mathsf{negl}(\lambda)$$

where $\rho = m/t$ (ρ is called the noise rate).

In this work, we assume that the noise rate ρ is $m^{1-\varepsilon}$ for any constant $\varepsilon > 0$. The LPN assumption is believed to be hard for that noise rate (see e.g. [5] and references therein).

For other missing preliminaries please refer to the full version paper.

References

1. Alamati, N., Branco, P., Döttling, N., Garg, S., Hajiabadi, M., Pu, S.: Laconic private set intersection and applications. In: Nissim, K., Waters, B. (eds.) TCC 2021. LNCS, vol. 13044, pp. 94–125. Springer, Cham (2021). https://doi.org/10.1007/978-3-030-90456-2_4
2. Banaszczyk, W.: New bounds in some transference theorems in the geometry of numbers. Math. Ann. **296**(4), 625–636 (1993). http://eudml.org/doc/165105
3. Boneh, D., Halevi, S., Hamburg, M., Ostrovsky, R.: Circular-secure encryption from decision Diffie-Hellman. In: Wagner, D. (ed.) CRYPTO 2008. LNCS, vol. 5157, pp. 108–125. Springer, Heidelberg (2008). https://doi.org/10.1007/978-3-540-85174-5_7
4. Bourse, F., Del Pino, R., Minelli, M., Wee, H.: FHE circuit privacy almost for free. In: Robshaw, M., Katz, J. (eds.) CRYPTO 2016, Part II. LNCS, vol. 9815, pp. 62–89. Springer, Heidelberg (2016). https://doi.org/10.1007/978-3-662-53008-5_3
5. Boyle, E., et al.: Efficient two-round OT extension and silent non-interactive secure computation. In: Cavallaro, L., Kinder, J., Wang, X., Katz, J. (eds.) ACM CCS 2019: 26th Conference on Computer and Communications Security, pp. 291–308. ACM Press, 11–15 November 2019
6. Boyle, E., Couteau, G., Gilboa, N., Ishai, Y., Kohl, L., Scholl, P.: Efficient pseudorandom correlation generators: silent OT extension and more. In: Boldyreva, A., Micciancio, D. (eds.) CRYPTO 2019, Part III. LNCS, vol. 11694, pp. 489–518. Springer, Cham (2019). https://doi.org/10.1007/978-3-030-26954-8_16
7. Boyle, E., Gilboa, N., Ishai, Y.: Breaking the circuit size barrier for secure computation under DDH. In: Robshaw, M., Katz, J. (eds.) CRYPTO 2016, Part I. LNCS, vol. 9814, pp. 509–539. Springer, Heidelberg (2016). https://doi.org/10.1007/978-3-662-53018-4_19
8. Boyle, E., Goldwasser, S., Ivan, I.: Functional signatures and pseudorandom functions. In: Krawczyk, H. (ed.) PKC 2014. LNCS, vol. 8383, pp. 501–519. Springer, Heidelberg (2014). https://doi.org/10.1007/978-3-642-54631-0_29
9. Brakerski, Z., Branco, P., Döttling, N., Garg, S., Malavolta, G.: Constant ciphertext-rate non-committing encryption from standard assumptions. In: Pass, R., Pietrzak, K. (eds.) TCC 2020, Part I. LNCS, vol. 12550, pp. 58–87. Springer, Cham (2020). https://doi.org/10.1007/978-3-030-64375-1_3
10. Brakerski, Z., Döttling, N., Garg, S., Malavolta, G.: Leveraging linear decryption: rate-1 fully-homomorphic encryption and time-lock puzzles. In: Hofheinz, D., Rosen, A. (eds.) TCC 2019, Part II. LNCS, vol. 11892, pp. 407–437. Springer, Cham (2019). https://doi.org/10.1007/978-3-030-36033-7_16
11. Brakerski, Z., Vaikuntanathan, V.: Efficient fully homomorphic encryption from (standard) LWE. In: Ostrovsky, R. (ed.) 52nd Annual Symposium on Foundations of Computer Science, pp. 97–106. IEEE Computer Society Press, Palm Springs, 22–25 October 2011
12. Branco, P., Döttling, N., Mateus, P.: Two-round oblivious linear evaluation from learning with errors. Cryptology ePrint Archive, Report 2020/635 (2020). https://eprint.iacr.org/2020/635

13. Canetti, R.: Universally composable security: a new paradigm for cryptographic protocols. In: 42nd Annual Symposium on Foundations of Computer Science, pp. 136–145. IEEE Computer Society Press, Las Vegas, 14–17 October 2001

14. Chase, M., et al.: Reusable non-interactive secure computation. In: Boldyreva, A., Micciancio, D. (eds.) CRYPTO 2019, Part III. LNCS, vol. 11694, pp. 462–488. Springer, Cham (2019). https://doi.org/10.1007/978-3-030-26954-8_15

15. Chase, M., Garg, S., Hajiabadi, M., Li, J., Miao, P.: Amortizing rate-1 OT and applications to PIR and PSI. In: Nissim, K., Waters, B. (eds.) TCC 2021. LNCS, vol. 13044, pp. 126–156. Springer, Cham (2021). https://doi.org/10.1007/978-3-030-90456-2_5

16. Cho, C., Döttling, N., Garg, S., Gupta, D., Miao, P., Polychroniadou, A.: Laconic oblivious transfer and its applications. In: Katz, J., Shacham, H. (eds.) CRYPTO 2017, Part II. LNCS, vol. 10402, pp. 33–65. Springer, Cham (2017). https://doi.org/10.1007/978-3-319-63715-0_2

17. Chor, B., Goldreich, O., Kushilevitz, E., Sudan, M.: Private information retrieval. In: 36th Annual Symposium on Foundations of Computer Science, pp. 41–50. IEEE Computer Society Press, Milwaukee, 23–25, October 1995

18. Döttling, N.: Low noise LPN: KDM secure public key encryption and sample amplification. In: Katz, J. (ed.) PKC 2015. LNCS, vol. 9020, pp. 604–626. Springer, Heidelberg (2015). https://doi.org/10.1007/978-3-662-46447-2_27

19. Döttling, N., Garg, S., Ishai, Y., Malavolta, G., Mour, T., Ostrovsky, R.: Trapdoor hash functions and their applications. In: Boldyreva, A., Micciancio, D. (eds.) CRYPTO 2019, Part III. LNCS, vol. 11694, pp. 3–32. Springer, Cham (2019). https://doi.org/10.1007/978-3-030-26954-8_1

20. Even, S., Goldreich, O., Lempel, A.: A randomized protocol for signing contracts. In: Chaum, D., Rivest, R.L., Sherman, A.T. (eds.) Advances in Cryptology - CRYPTO 1982, pp. 205–210. Plenum Press, New York, Santa Barbara (1982)

21. Garg, S., Hajiabadi, M., Ostrovsky, R.: Efficient range-trapdoor functions and applications: rate-1 OT and more. In: Pass, R., Pietrzak, K. (eds.) TCC 2020, Part I. LNCS, vol. 12550, pp. 88–116. Springer, Cham (2020). https://doi.org/10.1007/978-3-030-64375-1_4

22. Genise, N., Micciancio, D., Peikert, C., Walter, M.: Improved discrete gaussian and subgaussian analysis for lattice cryptography. In: Kiayias, A., Kohlweiss, M., Wallden, P., Zikas, V. (eds.) PKC 2020, Part I. LNCS, vol. 12110, pp. 623–651. Springer, Cham (2020). https://doi.org/10.1007/978-3-030-45374-9_21

23. Gentry, C., Halevi, S.: Compressible FHE with applications to PIR. In: Hofheinz, D., Rosen, A. (eds.) TCC 2019, Part II. LNCS, vol. 11892, pp. 438–464. Springer, Cham (2019). https://doi.org/10.1007/978-3-030-36033-7_17

24. Ghosh, S., Nielsen, J.B., Nilges, T.: Maliciously secure oblivious linear function evaluation with constant overhead. In: Takagi, T., Peyrin, T. (eds.) ASIACRYPT 2017, Part I. LNCS, vol. 10624, pp. 629–659. Springer, Cham (2017). https://doi.org/10.1007/978-3-319-70694-8_22

25. Goldreich, O., Goldwasser, S., Micali, S.: On the cryptographic applications of random functions (extended abstract). In: Blakley, G.R., Chaum, D. (eds.) CRYPTO 1984. LNCS, vol. 196, pp. 276–288. Springer, Heidelberg (1985). https://doi.org/10.1007/3-540-39568-7_22

26. Goldreich, O., Goldwasser, S., Micali, S.: How to construct random functions. J. ACM **33**(4), 792–807 (1986). https://doi.org/10.1145/6490.6503

27. Goldreich, O., Micali, S., Wigderson, A.: How to play any mental game, or a completeness theorem for protocols with honest majority. In: Providing Sound

Foundations for Cryptography: On the Work of Shafi Goldwasser and Silvio Micali, pp. 307–328 (2019)

28. Goyal, R., Vusirikala, S., Waters, B.: New constructions of hinting PRGs, OWFs with encryption, and more. In: Micciancio, D., Ristenpart, T. (eds.) CRYPTO 2020, Part I. LNCS, vol. 12170, pp. 527–558. Springer, Cham (2020). https://doi.org/10.1007/978-3-030-56784-2_18

29. Ishai, Y., Kilian, J., Nissim, K., Petrank, E.: Extending oblivious transfers efficiently. In: Boneh, D. (ed.) CRYPTO 2003. LNCS, vol. 2729, pp. 145–161. Springer, Heidelberg (2003). https://doi.org/10.1007/978-3-540-45146-4_9

30. Ishai, Y., Prabhakaran, M., Sahai, A.: Secure arithmetic computation with no honest majority. In: Reingold, O. (ed.) TCC 2009. LNCS, vol. 5444, pp. 294–314. Springer, Heidelberg (2009). https://doi.org/10.1007/978-3-642-00457-5_18

31. Micciancio, D., Regev, O.: Worst-case to average-case reductions based on Gaussian measures. In: 45th Annual Symposium on Foundations of Computer Science, pp. 372–381. IEEE Computer Society Press, Rome, 17–19 October 2004

32. Peikert, C.: An efficient and parallel gaussian sampler for lattices. In: Rabin, T. (ed.) CRYPTO 2010. LNCS, vol. 6223, pp. 80–97. Springer, Heidelberg (2010). https://doi.org/10.1007/978-3-642-14623-7_5

33. Quach, W., Wee, H., Wichs, D.: Laconic function evaluation and applications. In: Thorup, M. (ed.) 59th Annual Symposium on Foundations of Computer Science, pp. 859–870. IEEE Computer Society Press, Paris, 7–9 October 2018

34. Rabin, M.O.: How to exchange secrets with oblivious transfer. IACR Cryptol. ePrint Arch. 2005(187) (2005)

35. Regev, O.: On lattices, learning with errors, random linear codes, and cryptography. In: Gabow, H.N., Fagin, R. (eds.) 37th Annual ACM Symposium on Theory of Computing, pp. 84–93. ACM Press, Baltimore, 22–24 May 2005

Adaptively Secure Computation for RAM Programs

Laasya Bangalore[1(✉)], Rafail Ostrovsky[2], Oxana Poburinnaya[3], and Muthuramakrishnan Venkitasubramaniam[1]

[1] Georgetown University, Washington, USA
{lb1264,mv783}@georgetown.edu
[2] UCLA, Los Angeles, USA
rafail@cs.ucla.edu
[3] Ligero, Inc., Rochester, USA
oxanapob@bu.edu

Abstract. In this work, we study the communication complexity of secure multiparty computation under minimal assumptions in the presence of an adversary that can adaptively corrupt all parties eventually. Specifically, we are interested in understanding the complexity when modeling the underlying function as a RAM program. Under minimal assumptions, the work of Canetti et al. (STOC 2017) and Benhamouda et al. (TCC 2018) give protocols whose communication complexity grows quadratically in the circuit size when the computation is expressed as a Boolean circuit. In this work, we obtain the first two-round two-party computation protocol, which is secure against adaptive adversaries who can adaptively corrupt all parties where the communication complexity is proportional to the square of the RAM complexity of the function up to polylogarithmic factors assuming the existence of non-committing encryption.

Keywords: Adaptive security · Garbled RAM · Secure computation · Oblivious RAM

1 Introduction

Introduced by Yao [31] and Goldreich, Micali, and Wigderson [21], secure multiparty computation (MPC) allows a set of mutually distrustful agents to collaborate and accomplish a common goal while preserving each agent's privacy to a maximal extent. Secure computation enables anonymous electronic elections, privacy-preserving electronic auctions (or contract biddings), privacy-preserving data mining, fault-tolerant distributed computations, and more.

Typically, an adversary is modeled as a single computational entity that has the capability of hacking, or corrupting, an arbitrary subset of the communicating parties over a network and launching a coordinated attack. The classical and most popular model assumes that the set of corrupted parties are compromised before the target protocol begins. This is referred to as the *static* corruption model. The *adaptive* corruption model, introduced by Canetti et al. [5], considers a stronger

© International Association for Cryptologic Research 2022
O. Dunkelman and S. Dziembowski (Eds.): EUROCRYPT 2022, LNCS 13276, pp. 187–216, 2022.
https://doi.org/10.1007/978-3-031-07085-3_7

adversary that can hijack a host at *any* time during the course of the computation. Arguably, adaptive security provides more meaningful security. In particular, it captures "hacking" attacks where an external attacker breaks into parties' machines in the midst of a protocol execution, and can choose its targets adaptively based on the currently available information. Furthermore, an interesting side-effect of adaptive security is that in many cases it automatically guarantees some form of resilience against leakage from side-channel attacks [3,4].

In this work we focus on *full* adaptive security, namely security against an adversary who can (eventually) corrupt *all participants*. Achieving full adaptive security offers strong protocol compositional features, namely, embedding a full adaptive secure sub-protocol in a larger system enables arguing security of the larger system in a modular way even when all participants in the sub-protocol are corrupted. In the adaptive setting, the case when everybody can be corrupted is usually the most difficult to deal with; this should be contrasted with the static setting, where security in such a case comes for free[1].

Canetti et al. [7] established the feasibility of fully adaptively secure protocol where they designed an $O(d)$-round protocol to securely realize any functionality. In the static setting, constant-round protocols were known [22,26] and the gap in round complexity between what was feasible in the static and fully adaptive regime remained an open problem. When assuming reliable erasures, a constant-round protocol was given by Garg and Sahai [19]. The gap was closed simultaneously in the works of by [6,14,18] where they designed the first constant round protocol. These protocol assumed the trusted generation of a common reference string and relied on the strong assumption of existence of indistinguishability obfuscation. Moreover, these construction required a common reference string proportional to size of the circuit. More recently, Canetti et al. in [9] provided the first constant-round fully adaptively secure protocol from standard (minimal) assumptions. The question of the precise round complexity was finally resolved in the work of [2], where they constructed a two-round fully adaptive protocol. In essence, these works closed the gap in round complexity between static and fully adaptively secure protocols.

In this work, we are interested in understanding the communication complexity of fully adaptive protocols in the constant-round regime under minimal assumptions. The works of [8,14,18] achieve essentially an optimal communication complexity where it is independent of the circuit size. However, as mentioned above, they rely on strong assumptions and the trusted sampling of a common reference string that is as large as the circuit being computed. Moreover, a bound on the size of the circuit to be securely computed was required at the time of the CRS generation. Another vein of works [8,11] show how the complexity can be made proportional to the RAM complexity as opposed to the circuit complexity. The protocol of Cohen, shelat and Wichs [12] improve these works to achieve communication and the CRS size that is only proportional to the *depth* of the circuit.

---

[1] Indeed, in this case the static simulator obtains the inputs of all parties in the protocol and thus can simulate the execution by simply running the protocol.

Under minimal assumptions, we only have the work of Canetti et al. [9] and Benhamouda et al. [2] and their communication complexity grows quadratically in the circuit size when the circuit is expressed as a boolean circuit. The main question that is left open is to understand the communication complexity under minimial assumptions, namely:

What is the communication complexity of constant-round fully adaptive MPC protocols?

In this work, we make progress in answering this question. Specifically, we show how to obtain better complexity that [9] when the circuit is expressed as a RAM computation.

In the static case, RAM-efficient protocols have been obtained in the plain model via *garbled RAM*, a primitive introduced by Lu and Ostrovsky in 2013 [28]. This primitive allows to separately garble the memory, the input, and the RAM program (without converting it into a circuit), such that the size and runtime of the garbled RAM program is only proportional to the runtime of the program, up to polylogarithmic factors. The original paper required a strong circular-security assumption, but in sequence of follow-up works [16,17,20,28] the assumption was improved to a black-box use of any one-way function while maintaining poly-logarithmic overhead in all parameters. Equipped with garbled RAM, several recent works have demonstrated constant round MPC protocols with communication proportional to the RAM complexity in the static setting [15,24].

However, the state of affairs in the adaptive setting leaves us with either a construction proportional to the boolean circuit complexity under minimal assumptions [9] or relying on strong assumptions with a huge CRS [6,8,12,14].

Therefore, the main question that we ask in this paper is this:

Can we construct constant-round secure computation for RAM programs with only poly-logarithmic overhead that withstands (full) adaptive corruptions in the plain model?

In this work, we make a significant step towards answering this question in the affirmtive where we provide a construction whose communication complexity is proportional to the square of the RAM complexity (upto polylogarithmic factors). The question of whether we can reduce the quadratic overhead to linear remains an intriguing one. We remark that even in the case of circuits the best construction we have so far is quadratic in circuit size. To address the malicious case, we additionally design the first RAM-efficient zero-knowledge proof system that is adaptively secure [7,23,27]. Previously such constructions were known only for circuits and required non-constant number of rounds [23].

1.1 Our Results

In this paper, we provide the first construction of a secure two-party computation protocol for RAM programs that withstands adaptive corruption of both parties by an active adversary.

Our first result is an ORAM compiler that is adaptively secure. Informally, we say that an ORAM compiler is adaptively secure if there exists algorithms Sim_1 and Sim_2 such that Sim_1 given memory size and running time as inputs can provide the memory access sequence along with some state information, and Sim_2 given state and the actual input x as inputs can output the randomness for the compiler that leads to the simulated memory access sequence. We have the following theorem:

Theorem 1 (Informal). *There exists an adaptively secure ORAM with* $\mathsf{polylog}(n)$ *worst-case computational overhead and* $\mathsf{polylog}(n)$ *memory overhead, where n is the memory size.*

Next, we construct a functionally equivocal encryption scheme that is RAM-efficient, which we combine with an adaptively-secure ORAM to obtain our main theorem.

Theorem 2 (Informal). *Assume existence of two-round oblivious transfer secure against passive corruption of both parties by an adaptive adversary then there exists:*

- *A minimum interaction (i.e., two-message) two-party general function evaluation protocol for functionalities expressed via a RAM program Π that withstands passive corruption of both parties by an adaptive adversary. The protocol does not use data erasures.*
- *If Π's running time is T, the sum of the input sizes of the parties is n and the size of the memory accessed by Π is M, then our communication complexity is $\widetilde{O}((M+n+T)^2)$. Here $\widetilde{O}(\cdot)$ ignores $\mathsf{poly}(\log T, \log n, \kappa)$ factors where κ is the (computational) security parameter.*

Noting that the required oblivious transfer protocol from the theorem can be constructed based on any non-committing encryption scheme [5], we obtain the first constant-round adaptively secure two-party computation for RAM programs in the plain model based on standard assumptions.

Finally, we design a (RAM-efficient) adaptive zero-knowledge proof in the UC-model whose communication complexity is $\widetilde{O}((M+n+T)^2)$ which we combine with our semi-honest protocol to obtain an adaptively secure 2PC computation that secure against malicious adversaries.[2] Formally, we have:

Theorem 3 (Informal). *Assuming collision resistant hashing and dense cryptosystems, there exists a constant-round* UC-secure *two-party general function evaluation protocol in the common random string model, in face of active corruption of all parties by an adaptive adversary, where communication complexity is $\widetilde{O}((M+n+T)^2)$ and the length of the common random string is independent of the size of the function.*

---

[2] We remark that to obtain our result, it sufficient to obtain a circuit-efficient adaptive zero-knowledge proof.

1.2 Our Techniques

The Challenge of Adaptive Security. When considering adaptive secure computation, the best construction for circuits under minimal assumptions has communication complexity $O(s^2\mathsf{poly}(\kappa))$ for a circuit of s gates. As mentioned before, a long line of research in MPC has focused on measuring the complexity of constructions w.r.t the RAM complexity of the underlying function and designed protocols whose complexity are proportional to the RAM complexity as opposed to the circuit complexity. We recall here that the transforming a RAM program to a circuit is prohibitive where the best constructions that start from a T-time program compile into a circuit of size $O(T^3 \log T)$ [13,29]. Hence, converting a RAM program to a circuit and relying on the construction by [9] would result in a construction of complexity $O(T^6\mathsf{poly}(\log T, \kappa))$. Following analogous works in the static setting, our approach is to design a construction directly for RAM programs.

In a nutshell, our approach extends the equivocal garbling scheme of [9] to garbled RAM. As we describe next, this will not be a simple combination of techniques and we need to overcome a few obstacles. Looking ahead, we will not be able to extend any arbitrary Garbled RAM construction and make it equivocal. This gives rise to three key obstacles.

Obstacle 1: Deterministic vs Randomized Functionality. All Garbled RAM constructions rely on a pre-processing step where the memory sequence is made oblivious, typically by applying an Oblivious RAM (ORAM) compiler. This means that even when the underlying function that we wish to securely evaluate is deterministic, the effective functionality we garble will be randomized. In the adaptive case, randomized functionalities are tricky and they are impossible in the general case [25] at least in the plain model. In the CRS model, we do have constructions [6,8,12,14] based on indistinguishability obfuscation. We resolve this by considering the specific randomization used in the construction and show that it is "equivocable". More precisely, we will need an Oblivious RAM (ORAM) compiler to be adaptively secure. In other words, we need an ORAM scheme where the simulator first provides a sequence of memory accesses before knowing actual program inputs and, later, after learning the inputs, output randomness for the ORAM compiler that maps the actual memory sequence to the simulated one. As our first contribution, we provide the first construction of an ORAM scheme with this adaptive property.

Obstacle 2: Equivocating Memory. Performing memory read and write operations is a challenging component of Garbled RAM constructions as the memory locations to be read are only known during *run* time. In order to incorporate data read from memory into the computation, the labels corresponding to the data need to be provided as input to the garbled step circuits[3]. A common way of doing this is to encrypt the labels under some key and provide a mechanism

---

[3] In a RAM program, a step circuit performs CPU computations at a particular time step.

for determining these keys during the run-time, once the data location to be read is known. Prior works [17,20] incorporate ways to efficiently generate these keys needed to encrypt the labels for the next circuit. In [20], a master key is used to generate keys corresponding to the memory location to be read and then this key is used to encrypt the labels associated with the read bits. In [17], a tree-based structure is used to pick the appropriate key to encrypt the labels associated with the data. At a very high-level, their garbled memory has a tree-structure with the encrypted memory at the leaf nodes. Their construction navigates through the tree towards the data to be read and obtains the appropriate key to encrypt the label (for the next step circuit). A common thread between these techniques is that they obtain efficiency by compressing the keys, either by using a master key to generate other keys or using a tree-structure of keys. But such a compression makes it hard for the simulator to "equivocate" the keys. Consequently, we will not be able to rely on the Garbled RAM constructions of [17,20].

Obstacle 3: RAM-Efficient Equivocal Encryption. A crucial ingredient in [9] is a Functionally Equivocal Encryption (FEE) scheme that allows a private-key encryption scheme to be equivocated with a key size smaller than the message length when the equivocation space can be expressed as the image of a function over a smaller domain. Specifically, [9] provides an FEE scheme for functions expressed as a circuit where the ciphertext size is proportional to the circuit size and the keys are proportional to the input size of the function (rather than message length being encrypted). As Garbled RAM construction employs sequence of circuits that are typically garbled, one approach is to use an FEE scheme to garble these circuits. The issue here is that the function f that defines the message space is a RAM program and relying on the FEE scheme from [9] that is constructed for circuits will be inefficient. The main challenge here is to construct a variant of the equivocal encryption that is efficient for RAM programs. Following the blueprint of [9], we can convert a Garbled RAM construction to an encryption scheme where the key size is small, the main challenge however is to ensure that one can equivocate the randomness consistent with the encryption algorithm. We show how the Garbled RAM scheme of [17] can be converted to a RAM-efficient equivocal scheme.

Obstacle 4: Obtaining Malicious Security. Extending our result to obtain malicious security requires RAM-efficient adaptive zero-knowledge which was previously known only based on indistinguishability obfuscation [9,18]. We obtain malicious security by combining our protocol with an adaptive zero-knowledge proof [7,23,27] using the classic GMW compiler. In order to maintain the communication complexity we need a zero-knowledge proof whose complexity is linear in the circuit size of the NP-relation. The work of [23] provides such a construction, however, it requires a non-constant number of rounds. In fact, the round complexity is proportional to circuit size and will not be sufficient to get our result. We address this by designing a more efficient proof system. In fact, for any NP-relation expressed as a RAM program we design an adaptive zero-knowledge proof with polylogarithmic overhead.

On Database Size. We remark that the database size influences the *online* communication complexity (i.e. the size of the garbled input) of our equivocal garbled RAM. For a database of size M, our equivocal garbled RAM has an *online* communication complexity of $\widetilde{O}((M+n)\cdot n)$. When we consider a scenario $M >> T$, as is typical in RAM applications, our garbling scheme's online complexity will not be efficient (in fact, it is bigger than the size of the computation). On the other hand, if $M << T$ (or even empty) then our garbled RAM scheme will be online efficient. We emphasize here that our main goal is to design a secure two-party computation protocol with a desired communication complexity and the equivocal garbled RAM scheme is only a means to this goal. In other words, even though the stand-alone primitive garbled RAM scheme is not efficient in all regimes, in the context of our 2PC protocol it suffices to consider $M << T$.

Corruption-Adaptive vs. Input-Adaptive Garbling. We note that the term "adaptive" is also used in the literature [1] to denote a very different property which we will call "input-adaptive security", to distinguish it from "corruption-adaptive security". We only focus on achieving "corruption-adaptive security" which we simply refer to as "adaptive security" in this paper. "Corruption-adaptive security" says that the garbling should remain secure even if the adversary prefers to corrupt the evaluator first and sees the communication (i.e. the garbled circuit and garbled input), and later corrupt the garbler and see its internal state (i.e. randomness used to garble the circuit). Whereas the "input-adaptive security" guarantees security against adversaries that can adaptively choose the input to the circuit even after seeing the garbled circuit. In their setting, the input to the circuit may not be fixed when the circuit is being garbled. [1] considers the garbling process to have two phases: the circuit garbling phase followed by the input garbling phase. In particular:

- Input-adaptive garbled circuits remain secure when the input to the computation is chosen adaptively, but lose security properties if randomness of the garbling is revealed to the adversary.
- Corruption-adaptive garbled circuits remain secure when the randomness is revealed to the adversary, but lose security for adaptively chosen inputs.

Outline. For the lack of space, we defer the definitions to the full version; In Sect. 2, we provide an equivocal ORAM compiler. Section 3 contains the description of RAM-efficient Equivocal Encryption. We give our constructions of Equivocal Garbling and adaptive ZK for RAM in Sects. 4 & 5 respectively.

2   Equivocal ORAM

In this section, we prove that the ORAM construction of [10] is adaptively secure. We begin by providing an overview of the ORAM Compiler given by [10]. Consider a client-server setting where a secure client runs a program P that accesses memory D that belongs to an untrusted server. Informally, the ORAM compiler ensures that the server does not learn anything about the client's computation by examining the memory access pattern (*Obliviousness*) while still learning the output of the execution of the RAM program (*Correctness*)[4].

Data Representation. Let the server's memory D, which is of size n, be divided into n/α blocks where the size of each block is α (for some $\alpha > 0$). For any program P with memory of size n, we maintain two main data structures, one at the client's end and the other at the server's end.

The server maintains a complete binary tree of depth $d = \lfloor \log(\frac{n}{\alpha}) \rfloor$. A block is said to be *associated* with a leaf node if the block is stored in one of the nodes on the path from the root to that leaf node. Each node can store at most k tuples of the form (b, l, val), where b denotes the block number, l denotes the leaf node and val denotes the content of block b. If any node has more than k tuples, then we say an overflow has occurred.

The client maintains an array of size n/α, denoted by Pos. This array maps blocks to leaf nodes. More specifically, the ith position of the array i.e. $Pos[i]$, corresponds to the ith block and stores the leaf node *associated* with this block.

Construction. Given a program P with memory D, the ORAM compiler C outputs a program P' with memory D'. Suppose the execution $P^D(x)$ performs m memory access operations. Let the ith operation be represented by $Op(i, addr, val)$ where $addr \in [n]$ denotes the memory address and val denotes the value at memory address $addr$. Also, let $b := addr/n$ be the block that contains the memory cell $addr$ and $r := addr \bmod(n)$ be the relative position of the memory cell within the block b. After the ORAM compilation, the program P' makes $2m$ memory accesses to D', which are denoted by $\{l_1, ..., l_{2m}\}$[5]. The compiler C replaces each memory access $Op(i, addr, val)$ made by P with the following three steps:

1. **Fetch:** If $Pos[b] = \bot$, then set l_{2i} to a randomly sampled leaf node; Otherwise set $l_{2i} := Pos[b]$ i.e. the leaf node associated with block b. Next, traverse the path from the root to the leaf node l_{2i}, reading and writing back the contents of each of the nodes on this path. If any of the nodes contains a tuple of the form (b, l_{2i}, v), then erase this tuple; otherwise set $v = \bot$. Output the value at position r in v.
2. **Update:** Choose a leaf node $l^\star$ uniformly at random and set $Pos[b] := l^\star$. If $val = \bot$ (i.e. it's a write operation), then update val to v. Add the tuple $(b, l^\star, val)$ to the root of the tree. Abort, if an overflow occurs.
3. **Evict:** Choose another leaf node r uniformly at random and set $l_{2i+1} := r$. Traverse each node on the path from the root to leaf node l_{2i+1} such that: every tuple (b', l', v') is pushed down along the path towards l_{2i+1} as long as it is still on the path associated with its leaf node l'. Abort, if an overflow occurs at any of the nodes.

---

[4] We adopt the definition of ORAM from [10].

[5] Note that for simplicity we only specify the leaf nodes accessed by $P'^{D'}(x)$ instead of specifying each node accessed along the path from the root to the leaf.

$\mathsf{Sim}_1(m, n)$

1. Choose $2m$ leaf nodes randomly from $[n/\alpha]$. Let $l_i^{sim} \leftarrow [n/\alpha]$ for each $i \in [1, 2m]$
2. Output $\{l_1^{sim}, ..., l_{2m}^{sim}\}$

Fig. 1. Description of simulator Sim_1, which outputs the memory access pattern of an ORAM

Recursion. In the above construction, the client's memory size is $O(n)$ since it needs to store the position map of size n/α. Instead of storing the position map directly, it can be simulated using the ORAM compiler C. So, any read or write operations to the position map will be performed as described in the construction of C. Now, the client only needs to store a new position of size n/α^2. This reduction in the size of the position map can be done recursively until the size is reduced to just $O(k)$ i.e. constant.

Theorem 4 [10]. *The ORAM compiler C described above is adaptively secure and has worst-case computational complexity of $O(n \cdot \mathsf{polylog}(n))$ and memory complexity of $O(n \cdot \mathsf{polylog}(n))$ where n is the size of the memory.*

Proof. Correctness follows directly from the construction as $P'^{D'}(x)$ has the same output as $P^D(x)$ for any deterministic function P, memory D and input x, whenever overflow does not occur. Using the same argument as [10], it can be shown that overflows occurs with negligible probability.

Obliviousness on the other hand follows trivially from our simulation Sim_1 as it simply chooses two independent random leaf nodes to be traversed for each memory access operation.

Adaptive security can be proved by showing that the adversary can first see the sequence of memory accesses without knowing the input and later gain access to the internal randomness that is consistent with the input (as well as the memory accesses seen earlier). Assume that an overflow does not occur. We first show that the sequence of memory accesses made by the program P' can be generated without knowing the input x. This can be done using the algorithm Sim_1 which chooses a sequence of random memory locations given just the memory size n and the number of memory accesses m (described in Fig. 1). Next, given a fixed sequence of memory locations $\overrightarrow{M}$, memory D and input x, we need to show that there exists randomness that accesses memory locations $\overrightarrow{M}$. That is, we need a way of generating randomness r_{eq} such that the memory accesses made by $P'^{D'}(x)$ exactly correspond to $\overrightarrow{M}$, described by algorithm Sim_2 in Fig. 2. If an overflow occurs, Sim_2 outputs *overflow* instead of outputting the randomness r_{eq}. This does not violate adaptive security as overflow occurs with just negligible probability. The adaptive security hence follows from the existence of algorithms Sim_1 and Sim_2.

$$\mathsf{Sim}_2[\overrightarrow{M}, P](D, x)$$

Parameters. P is the RAM that runs in T steps. Let $\overrightarrow{M}$ parsed as $\{l_1^{sim}, ..., l_{2T}^{sim}\}$ denote the memory accesses made by the program after ORAM compilation[a].

1. If $|\overrightarrow{M}| \neq 2T$, then *abort*. Parse $\overrightarrow{M}$ as $(l_0^{sim}, ..., l_{2T-1}^{sim})$ where $(l_\tau^{sim}, l_{\tau+1}^{sim})$ are the two leaf nodes accessed in the τth time step.
2. Compute the original memory addresses $\overrightarrow{M}_{orig}$ accessed by program P given input x and data D. Parse $\overrightarrow{M}_{orig}$ as $(addr_1, ..., addr_T)$
3. For every memory access operation $\tau \in [T]$, r_τ^{sim} is the randomness used to update the leaf node associated with the fetched block (refer to the *Update* procedure described in ORAM construction). The goal is to compute r_τ^{sim} for each time step τ given $\overrightarrow{M}_{orig}$ and $\overrightarrow{M}$.
4. If there exists a $\tau' > \tau$ such that $addr_{\tau'} = addr_\tau$, then select the smallest such τ' and set $r_\tau^{sim} \leftarrow l_{2\tau'}^{sim}$. Otherwise, set r_τ^{sim} to a randomly chosen leaf node. More specifically, the simulator computes r_τ^{sim} as follows:
   (a) Initialize the set $A := \{(\tau, addr_\tau, l_{2\tau}^{sim})\}_{\tau \in [T]}$.
   (b) Compute the list A' using A such that all the tuples in A are sorted based on $(addr_\tau, \tau)$ i.e. the elements in A are first sorted based on $addr_\tau$ and all the tuples with the same $addr_\tau$ are sorted based on τ. Let $A'[i]$ denote the ith tuple of A.
   (c) Initialize R to empty list of size T. For each $i \in [T]$, the $R[i]$ is computed as follows:
      – Set $(\tau, addr, l) := A'[i]$ and $(\tau', addr', l') := A'[i+1]$.
      – If $addr = addr'$, set $R[i] = (\tau, l')$; otherwise set $R[i] := (\tau, rand)$ where $rand$ is a randomly chosen leaf node.
   (d) Lastly, sort R based on the first element in the tuple i.e. the time step τ. Let the sorted list be $r_{eq} := \{r_1^{sim}, ..., r_T^{sim}\}$
5. Output r_{eq}.

---

[a] We are assuming that the RAM program P accesses at memory every time step; so the number of memory accesses m made by P is equal to T.

Fig. 2. Description of simulator Sim_2, which outputs the randomness used to compute the memory access pattern of a ORAM.

Cost Analysis of Sim_2. The cost of Sim_2 is $O(T \log T)$. This cost arises from the sort operations in steps $4(b)$ and $4(d)$ in Fig. 2, which are used to compute two consecutive memory accesses that access the same memory address.

3   RAM-Efficient Equivocal Encryption

In this section we define and construct *RAM-efficient Equivocal Encryption* (REE) which is similar to Functionally Equivocal Encryption from [9]. As motivated in the introduction, an REE scheme, as opposed to an FEE, provides a more efficient construction of an equivocal garbled RAM. Similar to an FEE, an REE is an equivocal encryption, meaning that the simulator can generate a dummy ciphertext (without knowing the plaintext $m \in \mathcal{M}$) and later equivocate it to some plaintext m', by providing randomness r_{Enc} and the key k consistent with plaintext m' and the dummy (or simulated) ciphertext. There are two main differences between an REE and an FEE. Firstly, FEE equivocates with respect to a function, an REE can equivocate with respect to a RAM program P. Secondly, FEE needs to equivocate based on the input of the function, whereas REE equivocates based on the input as well as the database corresponding to the RAM program. This implies that the key for an FEE comprises of just the garbled input while the key for an REE comprises of the garbled input along with a garbled database.

We begin with the description of the syntax of REE which comprises of the following algorithms (Gen, Enc, Dec, SimTrap, SimEnc, Equiv, Adapt).

- **Key generation.** REE.Gen$(1^\lambda, 1^n; r_{\mathsf{Gen}})$ takes as input security parameter λ, equivocation parameter n, and randomness r_{Gen} of size $\mathsf{poly}(\lambda, n)$. It sets the key $k := r_{\mathsf{Gen}}$ and outputs it.
  Note that the key size only depends on equivocation parameter and security parameter, but not on the plaintext size.
- **Encryption.** REE.Enc$_k$(params, msg; r_{Enc}) takes as input params (which comprises of the description size of the RAM program s and memory size M) and plaintext msg. It outputs an encryption of m with respect to the params using randomness r_{Enc} and key k. Let $c = (\tilde{P}, \tilde{D})$ be the encryption of msg where $\tilde{P}$ and $\tilde{D}$ denote garbled RAM program and garbled memory respectively.
- **Decryption.** REE.Dec$_k(c)$ decrypts ciphertext c using key k and outputs plaintext $m = P^D(x)$.
- **Ciphertext simulation.** Simulating a ciphertext comprises of two algorithms (REE.SimTrap, REE.SimEnc). Algorithm REE.SimTrap takes as input $(1^\lambda, 1^n; r_{\mathsf{td}})$ and outputs the trapdoor td. Algorithm REE.SimEnc on input (params, td; r_{Sim}) outputs a ciphertext $c_{eq} = (\tilde{P}, \tilde{D})$ with respect to params (where params comprises of description of the RAM program P and memory size M).
- **Equivocation.** REE.Equiv(x, td) uses the equivocation trapdoor td to generate a single fake key k_{eq} so that each simulated ciphertext c_{eq} decrypts to $P^D(x)$ under k_{eq}. Note that the c_{eq} was generated with respect to some (P, D) and trapdoor td.
- **Randomness sampling.** REE.Adapt$(P, D, \mathsf{td}, r_{\mathsf{Sim}}, x)$ generates randomness r_{eq}, such that REE.Enc$_{k_{\mathsf{eq}}}$(params, $P^D(x)$; r_{eq}) $= c_{eq}$ where $c_{eq} :=$ REE.SimEnc$(P, D, \mathsf{td}; r_{\mathsf{Sim}})$. In other words, the REE.Adapt algorithm comes up with random coins such that the real garbled RAM program and garbled memory i.e. $(\tilde{P}, \tilde{D})$ look like they are simulated, which makes use of the obliviousness property of Yao's garbling scheme.

Security. The honestly generated encryptions and the simulated encryptions along with the messages, the random coins, and the key, are indistinguishable where the message is the output of the execution of $P^D(x)$, $x \in \{0,1\}^n$ is the input, P is a RAM program from $\{0,1\}^n \rightarrow \{0,1\}^\ell$ and D is the memory accessed by P. More formally, we need to show that for any PPT adversary $\mathcal{A}$ the following two distributions are indistinguishable:

$$D_0^n = \{(P,D,x) \leftarrow \mathcal{A}(1^\lambda, 1^n); \mathsf{td} \leftarrow \mathsf{REE.SimTrap}(1^\lambda, 1^n; r_{\mathsf{td}});$$
$$c_{\mathsf{eq}} := (\tilde{P}_{eq}, \tilde{D}_{eq}) \leftarrow \mathsf{REE.SimEnc}(\mathsf{params}, \mathsf{td}, r_{\mathsf{Sim}});$$
$$k_{\mathsf{eq}} \leftarrow \mathsf{REE.Equiv}(\mathsf{td}, x); r_{\mathsf{eq}} \leftarrow \mathsf{REE.Adapt}(P, D, \mathsf{td}, r_{\mathsf{Sim}}, x) :$$
$$(k_{\mathsf{eq}}, c_{\mathsf{eq}}, r_{\mathsf{eq}})\}$$

$$D_1^n = \{(P,D,x) \leftarrow \mathcal{A}(1^\lambda, 1^n); k \leftarrow \mathsf{REE.Gen}(1^\lambda, 1^n; r_{\mathsf{Gen}});$$
$$c := (\tilde{P}, \tilde{D}) \leftarrow \mathsf{REE.Enc}_k(\mathsf{params}, m; r_{\mathsf{Enc}}) :$$
$$(k, c, r_{\mathsf{Enc}}))\}$$

Overview of [17]. We give an overview of the garbled RAM construction of [17] before presenting the REE. Refer to the full paper for a formal description.

Garbling the Data. Let $m = |D|$ and $d = \log(m/\kappa)$. The garbled data is in the form of a binary tree of keys of depth d. The *plain version* of this tree of keys comprises of data elements (of size κ) at the leaf nodes and random κ-bit values (which are used as PRF keys) at the non-leaf nodes. The *encrypted version* is computed from the *plain version* as follows: each non-root node $r \in \{0,1\}^\kappa$ is encrypted using its parent $s \in \{0,1\}^\kappa$ as the key: $F_s(\text{left/right}, k, r_k)$ (for leaf nodes, data element D_k is encrypted instead of r_k). The protocol $\mathsf{GData}(1^\kappa, D)$ outputs the encrypted version of the tree of keys $\tilde{D}$ and the key corresponding to the root of the tree.

Garbling the Program. Let T be the running time of the program P. We need to garble each of the T CPU steps, which perform a read and write to memory. A CPU step at time step τ is denoted as follows: $C^P_{CPU}(\text{state}, z^{\text{read}}) = (\text{state}', L, z^{\text{write}})$ where L' is the memory location to be read at the next time step i.e. $\tau + 1$, z^{write} is the value to be written into the location L' in the next time step i.e. $\tau + 1$ and z^{read} is the value read from the memory location L, where L is the memory location output by the previous time step $\tau - 1$. Here, a simplifying assumption is that the read and write is made to the same memory location L. For further ease of exposition, the protocol is provided assuming Unprotected Memory Access (UMA).

Without loss of generality, we focus on reading an element from location L and then executing the ith CPU step. Reading an element from the database is done by navigating through the tree of keys all the way to the leaf nodes where the data is located (as described earlier). To traverse from the root to the leaf node of the tree, a sequence of *navigation* circuits C^{nav} are used, one for each level. C^{nav} works as follows: it takes as input two sibling PRF keys and chooses one of them (either the left or right PRF key) based on the location L to be read. Then, C^{nav} uses this chosen key to decrypt and outputs the keys corresponding to its children. These two child PRF keys are used as inputs to the next C^{nav} in the sequence. After navigating through $(d-1)$ level of the tree using C^{nav} circuits, the last level is processed using C^{step} circuit, which does the following:

- Executes CPU computation for the current time step.
- Writes data element z^{write} to location L'.
- Kick starts execution of the next time step by outputting the two PRF keys corresponding to children of the root. This serves as the input to C^{nav} at the start of the next time step.

The outputs of the navigation and step circuits consist of $(write, translate, aux)$ which we explain below.

1. **aux:** comprises of (state, L) where state denotes the state of the computation and L is the memory location to be read. This value is the output of the CPU computation step.
2. **translate:** enables reading of data. The goal is to generate the input label for the next circuit corresponding to the value read from memory. Since the memory location to be read is generated during runtime, *translate* can only be determined during the runtime.
3. **write:** enables writing of data. If the key corresponding to any node needs to be modified/written to a new key, it affects two nodes in the garbled memory: (1) the current node re-encrypts the keys of its children under the new key and (2) the parent of this node is update to store the encryption of the new key.

To overcome the circularity issues of Lu-Ostrovsky's construction, the PRF keys are replaced with fresh ones each time they are used to read. More specifically, the keys are replaced whenever they are used to compute *translate*. The tree structure of the garbled database limits the number of PRF keys that need to be replaced for each CPU step to be polylogarithmic in the memory size. Finally, the protocol GProg($1^\kappa, 1^{\log m}, 1^t, P$) outputs the set of garbled circuits for each CPU step and the set of input keys s^{in}.

Garbling the Input and Evaluation. Let s be the PRF key corresponding to the root of the garbled database. The protocol for input garbling $GInput(1^\kappa, x, s^{in}, s)$ outputs *translate* to enable reading the PRF keys corresponding to the children of root s. Also, it outputs the selection of the labels corresponding to x in s^{in}. The evaluation of each circuit is similar to evaluating any garbled circuit. In addition, we need to obtain the input labels of a circuit from the output labels of the previous circuit in the sequence, which is done using *translate*. This is because the outputs of a circuit are passed as inputs to another circuit.

3.1   Our Construction

We now provide a formal description of the algorithms for our REE. Let $(\mathsf{Gen}^{\mathsf{CPA}}, \mathsf{Enc}^{\mathsf{CPA}}, \mathsf{Dec}^{\mathsf{CPA}})$ be a private-key encryption scheme with the following two properties: (1) has pseudorandom ciphertexts and (2) decrypting a random string with the key outputs a pseudorandom plaintext[6].

Key Generation: REE.Gen on input $(1^\kappa, 1^n; r_{\mathsf{Gen}})$ computes key k as follows:

1. Sample $\overline{\mathsf{lab}}^{inp} = (\overline{\mathsf{lab}}^{aux}, \overline{\mathsf{lab}}^{read})$ where $|aux|$ independent labels $\overline{\mathsf{lab}}^{aux} = (\overline{\mathsf{lab}}_1, \ldots, \overline{\mathsf{lab}}_{|aux|})$ and $|read| = 2\kappa$ independent labels $\overline{\mathsf{lab}}^{read} = (\overline{\mathsf{lab}}_1, \ldots, \overline{\mathsf{lab}}_{2\kappa})$ using $\mathsf{Gen}^{\mathsf{CPA}}(1^\kappa)$.

2. Set $translate^{inp} \leftarrow \mathsf{GenTranslate}(0, 1, 0^d, \overline{\mathsf{lab}}^{read})$ (GenTranslate is described in Fig. 3).

3. Output $k = (translate^{inp}, \overline{\mathsf{lab}}^{aux})$

Encryption: Enc with key $\overline{\mathsf{lab}}^{inp} = (\overline{\mathsf{lab}}^{aux}, \overline{\mathsf{lab}}^{read})$ on input $(P, D, y; r_{\mathsf{Enc}})$, where $|y| = l$, generates ciphertext c as follows:

1. Create a file BookKeeping to keep track of the nodes in the memory that were traversed during the RAM computation.

2. **Generate garbled program $\tilde{P}$:** Let $L^\tau \in [m]$ denote the location of the memory access in time step τ.

   For each *step* $\tau = t - 1$ to 0:

     For each *level* $i = d - 1$ to 0:

      • Sample labels in $\overline{\mathsf{lab}}^{\tau,i} = (\overline{\mathsf{lab}}^{\tau,i,aux}, \overline{\mathsf{lab}}^{\tau,i,read})$ using $\mathsf{Gen}^{\mathsf{CPA}}(1^\kappa)$.

Table 1. Inputs to GSim for different time steps τ and levels i.

τ	i	tag	output
$\{t-1\}$	$\{d-1\}$	final	$write, aux = (y, L^{t-1})$
$\{t-1, \ldots, 0\}$	$\{d-1\}$	step	$write, translate, \overline{\mathsf{lab}}^{\tau+1,0,aux}$
$\{t-1, \ldots, 0\}$	$\{d-2, \ldots, 0\}$	nav	$write, translate, \overline{\mathsf{lab}}^{\tau,i+1,aux}$

     • $write \leftarrow \mathsf{GenWrite}(\tau, i, L^\tau)$

     • $translate \leftarrow \mathsf{GenTranslate}(j, k, L^j, \overline{\mathsf{lab}}^{j,k,read})$ where j and k are chosen as follows: If $i = d - 1$, set $j = \tau + 1$, $k = 0$; otherwise, set $j = \tau$, $k = i + 1$. The descriptions of GenWrite and GenTranslate are given in Fig. 3.

     • If $\tau = 0, i = 0$, then $\tilde{C}^{\tau,i} \leftarrow \mathsf{GSim}(1^\kappa, C^{tag}, \overline{\mathsf{lab}}^{inp}, output)$; otherwise $\tilde{C}^{\tau,i} \leftarrow \mathsf{GSim}(1^\kappa, C^{tag}, \overline{\mathsf{lab}}^{\tau,i}, output)$ where C^{tag} and y are chosen based on τ and i as per Table 1.

3. Set $\tilde{P} := \{C^{\tau,i} \text{ for } \tau \in [t], \ i \in [d]\}$.

---

[6] We note that the PRF-based scheme $(r, F_k(r) \oplus m)$ satisfies both the properties.

Subprotocols for REE.Enc

GenTranslate(τ, i, L, (lab $^{left,\ k}$, lab $^{right,\ k}$))

- Set $r^{left/right,\ k} \leftarrow \{0,1\}^\kappa$ and $rand^{left/right,\ k} \leftarrow \{0,1\}^\kappa$ for all $k \in [\kappa]$. Output

$$translate := \left\{ \begin{matrix} r^{left,\ k} \oplus \mathsf{lab}^{left,\ k} & r^{right,\ k} \oplus \mathsf{lab}^{right,\ k} \\ rand^{left,\ k} & rand^{right,\ k} \end{matrix} \right\}_{k \in [\kappa]}$$

- Let l be the i highest order bits of L. Then add the following entries to the file **BookKeeping** for all $k \in [\kappa]$:
  - $\hat{r}^{i+1,\ 2l,\ k}\{\tau\} = r^{left,\ k}$
  - $\hat{r}^{i+1,\ 2l+1,\ k}\{\tau\} = r^{right,\ k}$

GenWrite(τ, i, L)

- Let l be the i highest order bits of L. Look through **BookKeeping** to find entries $\hat{r}^{i+1,\ 2l,\ k}\{p\}$ and $\hat{r}^{i+1,\ 2l+1,\ k}\{p\}$ such that $p > \tau$ and pick smallest such p if it exists.
- If such a p exists, set $\alpha^{left,\ k} = \hat{r}^{i+1,\ 2l,\ k}\{p\}$ and $\alpha^{right,\ k} = \hat{r}^{i+1,\ 2l+1,\ k}\{p\}$; else set $\alpha^{left,\ k} \leftarrow \{0,1\}^\kappa$ and $\alpha^{right,\ k} \leftarrow \{0,1\}^\kappa$ for all $k \in [\kappa]$.
- Output $(L, (\alpha^{left,\ k}, \alpha^{right,\ k}))$.

Fig. 3. Subprotocols for REE.Enc

4. **Generate garbled memory $\tilde{P}$:** For all $i \in [d+1] - \{0\}$, $j \in [2^i]$, $k \in [\kappa]$, find the smallest entry $\hat{r}^{i,j,k}\{\tau\}$ in BookKeeping such that $\tau > 0$.
   - If such an entry exists, set $\hat{r}^{i,j,k} := \hat{r}^{i,j,k}\{\tau\}$; Else sample a uniformly random $\hat{r}^{i,j,k} \leftarrow \{0,1\}^\kappa$.
   - Set $D^{j,k} := \{\hat{r}^{d,j,k}$ for $j \in [2^d]$, $k \in [\kappa]\}$.
5. Set $\tilde{D} := \{\hat{r}^{i,j,k}$ for all $i \in [d] - \{0\}$, $j \in [2^i]$, $k \in [\kappa]$, $D^{j,k}$ for $j \in [2^d]$, $k \in [\kappa]\}$.
6. Output ciphertext $c = (\tilde{P}, \tilde{D})$.

Decryption. Given ciphertext $c = (\tilde{P}, \tilde{D})$ and key $k = (translate^{inp}, \overline{\mathsf{lab}}^{aux})$, evaluate the simulated garbled RAM program $\tilde{P}$ with the key k using GRAM.Eval$^{\tilde{D}}(\tilde{P}, k)$ and output the result.

Simulating ciphertexts. Let $n = (|aux| + |read|)$. REE.SimTrap$(1^\kappa, 1^n; r_{td})$ samples $2n$ keys using $\widehat{\mathsf{lab}}^{j,0}$ and $\widehat{\mathsf{lab}}^{j,1}$ for $1 \le j \le n$ using Gen$^{CPA}(1^\kappa)$ and outputs td $= (\widehat{\mathsf{lab}}^{aux}, \widehat{\mathsf{lab}}^{read}) = (\widehat{\mathsf{lab}}^{1,0}, \widehat{\mathsf{lab}}^{1,1}, \ldots, \widehat{\mathsf{lab}}^{n,0}, \widehat{\mathsf{lab}}^{n,1})$.
REE.SimEnc on input $(P, td; r_{\mathsf{Sim}})$ computes c_{eq} as follows:

1. Set $(\tilde{P}, root) \leftarrow$ GRAM.Prog$(1^\kappa, 1^{\log m}, 1^t, P, td)$
2. Set $\tilde{D} \leftarrow$ GRAM.Data$(1^\kappa, \mathsf{D})$
3. Finally, output $c_{\mathsf{eq}} = (\tilde{P}, \tilde{D})$.

Equivocation. REE.Equiv on input (x, td) uses the trapdoor $\mathsf{td} = (\widehat{\mathsf{lab}}^{aux}, \widehat{\mathsf{lab}}^{read})$ to compute the key $k_{eq} = \mathsf{GRAM.Inp}(1^\kappa, x, td, root)$.

Randomness sampling. REE.Adapt on input $(P, D, \mathsf{td}, r_{\mathsf{Sim}}, x)$ needs to generate a random string r_{eq} so that $\mathsf{REE.Enc}_{k_{eq}}(\mathsf{params}, P^D(x); r_{\mathsf{eq}}) = c_{\mathsf{eq}} = (\tilde{P}, \tilde{D})$. To generate r_{eq}, it proceeds as follows:

1. Let $\tilde{P} = (\tilde{C}_1, \ldots, \tilde{C}_t)$ and $(\widehat{\mathsf{lab}}^1, \ldots, \widehat{\mathsf{lab}}^t)$ denote the input labels which are determined while generating the RAM program using $\mathsf{GRAM.Prog}$. Also, let $(x_1, \ldots, x_t)$ denote the inputs corresponding to the circuits and are determined while evaluating $P^D(x)$.

2. $r_P = (oSamp(1^\kappa, k_1, x_1), \ldots, oSamp(1^\kappa, k_t, x_t))$

3. $r_D = \{\hat{r}^{i,j} \ \forall i \in [d], j \in [2^i]\}$

4. For each circuit $\tilde{C}^{\tau, i-1}$, let the $translate^{\tau, i-1}$ be:

$$\begin{cases} F_{r^{i-1}, \lfloor j/2 \rfloor}(left, k, 0) \oplus \mathsf{lab}^{left, k, 0} & F_{r^{i-1}, \lfloor j/2 \rfloor}(right, k, 0) \oplus \mathsf{lab}^{right, k, 0} \\ F_{r^{i-1}, \lfloor j/2 \rfloor}(left, k, 1) \oplus \mathsf{lab}^{left, k, 1} & F_{r^{i-1}, \lfloor j/2 \rfloor}(right, k, 1) \oplus \mathsf{lab}^{right, k, 1} \end{cases}_{k \in [\kappa]}$$

The $translate$ given above is used to read the labels for nodes $(r^{i,j,k}, r^{i,j+1,k})$ and is revealed as:

$$r_{translate}^{\tau, i-1} = \begin{cases} r^{left, k} \oplus \mathsf{lab}^{left, k} & r^{right, k} \oplus \mathsf{lab}^{right, k} \\ rand^{left, k} & rand^{right, k} \end{cases}_{k \in [\kappa]}$$

where $r^{left, k} = F_{r^{i-1}, \lfloor j/2 \rfloor}(left, k, r^{i,j,k})$ (corresponds to the active row) and $rand^{left, k} = F_{r^{i-1}, \lfloor j/2 \rfloor}(left, k, 1 \oplus r^{i,j,k}) \oplus \mathsf{lab}^{left, k, 1}$. Similarly, $r^{right, k}$ and $rand^{right, k}$ are defined.

5. For each circuit $C^{\tau, i}$, let the $write$ be:

$$write^{\tau, i} = (F_{r^{i-1}, \lfloor j/2 \rfloor}(left, k, r^{i,j,k}), F_{r^{i-1}, \lfloor j/2 \rfloor}(right, k, r^{i,j+1,k}))$$

be revealed as

$$r_{write}^{\tau, i} = (r^{left, k}, r^{right, k})$$

6. Let $r_{translate} = \{r_{translate}^{\tau, i} \mid \forall \tau \in [t], i \in [d]\}$ and $r_{write} = \{r_{write}^{\tau, i} \mid \forall \tau \in [t], i \in [d]\}$

7. Output $r_{eq} = (r_P, r_D, r_{translate}, r_{write})$.

Theorem 5. *Assuming the encryption scheme is CPA-secure, REE comprising of* $(\mathsf{Gen}, \mathsf{Enc}, \mathsf{Dec}, \mathsf{SimTrap}, \mathsf{SimEnc}, \mathsf{Equiv}, \mathsf{Adapt})$ *is a RAM-efficient Equivocal Encryption scheme with* $\tilde{O}(T + M + n)$ *decryption time complexity and* $\tilde{O}(T + M + n)$ *ciphertext size where T, M and n are the running time, memory size and input size of the RAM program P respectively.*

The proof of this theorem is similar to proof of security of the Garbled RAM from [17] and is given in the full version of our paper.

4   Equivocal Garbled RAM

In this section we discuss how to construct an equivocal garbled RAM by extending [9]'s framework to RAM programs. Roughly speaking, to equivocate RAM programs, we use REE instead of FEE to encrypt the rows of the garbled gates. The garbled RAM construction of [16] primarily involves "communicating" garbled circuits. So the problem of obtaining an equivocal garbled RAM can be reduced to adaptively garbling each of the sub-circuits. In this section, we focus on how to garble the sub-circuits using REE with equivocation. We first define an equivocal garbling scheme for RAM programs and then give an overview of the [16] construction.

Definition 1 (Equivocal garbling scheme for RAM programs). *We say that* GRAM *comprising of* $(Data, Prog, Inp, Eval)$ *is an equivocal garbling scheme for RAM programs, if the following properties hold:*

- **Correctness:** *For any RAM program P, Data D and input to the RAM program x we require the following to hold:*

  $\Pr[r \leftarrow \{0,1\}^{|r|}; K \leftarrow \text{Gen}(1^\lambda); \widetilde{D}, root \leftarrow \text{GRAM.Data}(1^\kappa, D), \widetilde{P} \leftarrow \text{GRAM.Prog}$
  $(1^\kappa, K, P, root; r); \{\widetilde{x}\} \leftarrow \text{GRAM.Inp}(1^\kappa, K, x):$
  $\text{GRAM.Eval}(\widetilde{P}, \widetilde{D}, \widetilde{x}) = P^D(x)] > 1 - \text{negl}(\lambda);$

- **Security:** *There exists a pair of PPT algorithm* $(\text{Sim}_1, \text{Sim}_2)$, *such that any PPT adversary A wins the following game with at most negligible advantage:*
  1. *A gives a RAM program P, memory D and an input x to the challenger;*
  2. *The challenger flips a bit b.*
     If b = 0:
     - *It chooses random garbling key K and randomness r;*
     - *It sets* $(\widetilde{D}, root \leftarrow \text{GRAM.Data}(1^\kappa, D), \widetilde{P} \leftarrow \text{GRAM.Prog}(1^\kappa, K, P, root; r), \{\widetilde{x}\} \leftarrow \text{GRAM.Inp}(1^\kappa, K, x);$
     - *It sends* $\widetilde{P}, \widetilde{D}, \widetilde{x}, K, r$ *to the adversary.*
     If b = 1:
     - *It sets* $y = P^D(x);$
     - *It runs the simulator* $(\widetilde{P}, \widetilde{D}, \widetilde{x}, \text{state}) \leftarrow \text{Sim}_1(P, D, y)$
     - *It runs the simulator* $(K_{eq}, r_{eq}) \leftarrow \text{Sim}_2(\text{state}, x)$
     - *It sends* $\widetilde{P}, \widetilde{D}, \widetilde{x}, K_{eq}, r_{eq}$ *to the adversary.*
  3. *The adversary outputs a bit b'.*
  The adversary wins if b = b'.

Overview of [16]. Garg et al. [16] presented a black box approach to garble RAM programs. Roughly, their construction represents the entire RAM program (including the memory) as a set of circuits which are then garbled. Each circuit *communicate* with the *next* circuit by outputting the input labels corresponding to the *next* circuit. Looking ahead, the observation that all the garbled circuit just output labels corresponding to the input of other garbled circuits in [16] is crucial to the construction of our Equivocal RAM construction.

The mechanism for enabling memory access in [16] is to maintain the garbled data as a *tree* of garbled circuits, known as *memory circuits*, that can *communicate* with the neighboring garbled circuits. This *communication* happens when a garbled circuit outputs the appropriate input labels corresponding to the garbled circuit it intends to communicate with. In order to read/write, the garbled RAM program first passes the control to the root circuit of the garbled database. Depending on the location to be read/written, control is passed through a path of garbled circuits from the root to the leaf node that stores the data that needs to read or written. The leaf garbled circuit, which stores the data, passes control back to the RAM program along with labels corresponding to the data. Over the course of the RAM computation, the control may be passed multiple times to the root garbled circuit, once for each read/write. However, garbled circuits offer no security if they are used more than once i.e., they are evaluated over multiple inputs. So, the root garbled circuit must be refreshed to maintain security. This refreshing of garbled circuits needs to be done with care as it should maintain the property of each of the circuit to communicate with its *neighboring* circuit. This results in the following two main challenges: (i) the *used* garbled circuits must be replaced with fresh ones and (ii) the garbled circuit must *know* the input labels of the circuit it communicates with.

The first issue involves replacing the entire path of garbled circuits from the root to the leaf node with fresh garbled circuits for every memory access. A simple approach of replacing garbled circuits is as follows. If there were T memory accesses overall, then let each node of the garbled tree can have T garbled circuits such that the ith garbled circuit in any node can communicate with the ith garbled circuit at the left and right child nodes. This approach will work but comes at a prohibitively high cost, namely the garbled data size will be $O(TM)$. [16] observed that in this solution most of the garbled circuits are not used, especially at layers closer to the leaf nodes. All the T circuits at the root node are used up because the root is accessed for each of the T steps. But at the next layer there are $2T$ garbled circuit of which only T are used. If we assume memory accesses form a uniform distribution, then each of the left and right children in the first layer would use $T/2$ garbled circuits on average and each node in the second layer would use $T/4$ garbled circuits on average and so on. The reduction in the number of circuits in the subsequent number of layers needs to be done carefully taking into consideration that the number of circuits used can deviate from the expectation. By carefully bounding the number of garbled circuits at each node in every level one can ensure that the probability with which the circuits at these nodes will be over-consumed is negligible while still being efficient. [16] shows that the number of garbled circuits reduces from $O(MT)$ to $O(M)$.

The second issue is to allow a garbled circuits to communicate with "next" garbled circuit within this tree structure of garbled data. In slightly more detail, the garbled data is represented as a tree with each node comprising of a sequence of garbled circuits. A garbled circuit at any node can communicate with (i) its successor i.e. the garbled circuit that is next in sequence at that node, and (ii) its children (more specifically, a window of κ garbled circuits in each of the left and right child nodes). Enabling this communication between garbled circuits is one of the key aspects of the GRAM.Data algorithm. Suppose a garbled circuit C^A needs to communicate with another garbled circuit C^B, then C^A needs to output the input labels for C^B. C^A can either have the input labels of C^B passed as input to it or hard-coded within it. The key aspect of the GRAM.Data is to ensure that the garbled circuits have the appropriate labels to be able to communicate with other circuits. Now we look at the two main types of circuits present in the tree, one corresponding to the internal nodes and the other to the leaf nodes of the tree, which we briefly describe below.

Internal Nodes. Each internal node of the tree is associated with a sequence of circuits, each of which are denoted by C^{node}. These circuits help in navigating control from the root to the leaf node which ultimately enables reading from or writing to memory. Any given circuit can pass control to (1) the next circuit at the same node, (2) one of the circuits located in its left child node or (3) a circuit located in its right child node. The circuits need to know the input labels of the circuits to which control is passed. So, each C^{node} circuit has input labels, corresponding to the three types of circuits mentioned above, hardcoded within it. This elaborate set of connections between the circuits is needed to refresh the circuits as and when they are used up.

Leaf Nodes. The sub-circuits associated with the leaf nodes, say C^{leaf}, enable reading and writing of data into memory. Each leaf node comprises of a sequence of garbled circuits, similar to the internal nodes. The data is stored in these circuits by continually receiving it as input from its predecessor. When the data needs to be read, the C^{leaf} outputs the labels corresponding to data that are later fed into the CPU step circuit. In addition to outputting the input labels for CPU step circuit, it also passes on the data labels as input to the next C^{leaf} sub-circuit in the sequence. To write data into memory, the labels corresponding to the new data are passed as inputs to its successor.

Garbled Program. Garbling a RAM program P essentially involves garbling sub-circuits that carry out CPU computations at every time step. Each of these garbled step circuits outputs the labels for the new CPU state and the memory access information. The new CPU state is fed as input to the next step circuit. The memory access information comprises of labels of (1) the root circuit of the garbled data, (2) the location to read/write and (3) the data to be written. The labels for the root circuit enable passing control from the root to the leaf nodes of the tree of circuits. The leaf nodes store the labels corresponding to the data to be read, which is passed as input to the next step circuit. Thus, the next step circuit receives the labels corresponding to the data as well as the CPU state, which are enough to proceed to the next time step.

Equivocating GRAM. At a high-level, we garble circuits output by the [16] construction using the equivocal garbling scheme of [9] where the underlying encryption scheme is instantiated with an REE (as opposed to an FEE). We provide the details of our construction and a proof sketch below.

4.1 Our Construction

We now present our equivocal garbled RAM construction.

Conventions. Consider a RAM program P with memory D and inputs x with running time T. Let $n = |x|$. We denote the output of the RAM program by $P^D(x)$. We use [16] construction to garble the RAM program and let the garbled versions of these programs be denoted by $\tilde{P}, \tilde{D}, \tilde{x}$. The garbled program and data comprise of three main sub-circuits: C^{step}, C^{node} and C^{leaf}. For the rest of this section, we show how to garble C which could potentially be any of the sub-circuits. Let κ be the security parameter. For any wire w in gate g, let k_w^0, k_w^1 be the λ-bit labels associated with the wires where $\lambda = n\kappa + 1$ and bit_w be the actual bit assigned to w during $P^D(x)$. We consider some gate g with input wires α, β and output wire γ. We also assume without loss of generality that all gates are fan-in two gates.

Garbling Data and Program. GRAM.Data$(1^\kappa, m)$ outputs the garbled data $(\tilde{D}, root)$ and GRAM.Prog $(1^\kappa, 1^{\log m}, P, root)$ outputs $(\tilde{P}, s^{in})$. At a high-level, we follow the garbled RAM construction of [16] to generate $\tilde{P}$ and $\tilde{D}$ with two key technical differences. First, we use an approach similar to equivocal garbling [8] to garble the sub-circuits instead of Yao's Garbling [30]. Secondly, the encryption scheme used to garble the gates is REE instead of FEE used [8] or regular CPA-secure encryption scheme used in Yao's construction.

Recall that the GRAM.Data and GRAM.Prog comprises of garbled circuits communicating with other garbled circuits. So we show how to garble the sub-circuits used in $\tilde{P}$ and $\tilde{D}$. Let C be some sub-circuit with n'-bit input string x_{sub}. We denote by $m = n + \mathsf{gates}(C)$ the total number of wires in C where gates with fan-out more than 1 are counted only once.

We first generate two labels (k_w^0, k_w^1) for every wire w in C using REE.*Gen* and then the garbler generates the following 4 pairs of ciphertexts for each gate g:

$$c_{g,\text{left}}^{00} = \mathsf{REE.Enc}_{k_\alpha^0}(s_{g,\text{left}}^{00}), \quad c_{g,\text{right}}^{00} = \mathsf{REE.Enc}_{k_\beta^0}(s_{g,\text{right}}^{00}),$$

$$c_{g,\text{left}}^{01} = \mathsf{REE.Enc}_{k_\alpha^0}(s_{g,\text{left}}^{01}), \quad c_{g,\text{right}}^{01} = \mathsf{REE.Enc}_{k_\beta^1}(s_{g,\text{right}}^{01}),$$

$$c_{g,\text{left}}^{10} = \mathsf{REE.Enc}_{k_\alpha^1}(s_{g,\text{left}}^{10}), \quad c_{g,\text{right}}^{10} = \mathsf{REE.Enc}_{k_\beta^0}(s_{g,\text{right}}^{10}),$$

$$c_{g,\text{left}}^{11} = \mathsf{REE.Enc}_{k_\alpha^1}(s_{g,\text{left}}^{00}), \quad c_{g,\text{right}}^{11} = \mathsf{REE.Enc}_{k_\beta^1}(s_{g,\text{right}}^{11}),$$

Garbling Inputs. GRAM.Inp$(1^\kappa, x, s^{in}, s)$ outputs $\tilde{x}$ which are the labels corresponding to the input x.

Garbled Evaluation. GRAM.Eval($\tilde{P}, \tilde{D}, \tilde{x}$) evaluated the garbled program and outputs $\tilde{P}^{\tilde{D}}(\tilde{x})$. This function is similar to [16] except that REE.*Dec* is used to decrypt the garbled gates.

Simulation. The simulation has two main parts: (i) simulating the garbled program $\tilde{P}$, garbled data $\tilde{D}$ and garbled inputs $\tilde{x}$ such that $\tilde{P}^{\tilde{D}}(x) = P^D(x)$ and (i) simulating the internal randomness consistent with the revealed inputs.

Simulation of Garbled Program, Garbled Data and Garbled Input. The first step of the simulator is to run $ORAM.Sim_1(T, m)$ and obtain the sequence of memory accesses $\vec{M}$. Similar to the real garbling, it's enough to focus on how to simulate each of the garbled sub-circuits, say C, of $\tilde{P}$ and $\tilde{D}$. For each wire w in C, the simulator chooses $n\kappa$-bit REE keys, random bit Λ_w and an REE trapdoor $\mathsf{td}_w \leftarrow$ REE.SimTrap($1^\kappa, n$). The simulated garbled gate is computed using REE.*Enc* and REE.*SimEnc* as shown in Table 2. Note that each RAM program P_{in} used in REE.SimEnc has $P, C^{\mathsf{type}}, g, k_\gamma, \mathsf{td}_\gamma, \Lambda_\gamma, \vec{M}, \tau, m$ hardcoded within its description, where γ is an output wire of g. The descriptions of the RAM program P_{in} and the database D_{in} used in the REE simulation are given in Fig. 4.

The simulator orders 4 rows of each garbled gate as per $(\Lambda_\alpha, \Lambda_\beta)$ and outputs the 8 ciphertexts. Lastly, the garbled input comprising of the labels $(k_1, \dots, k_n)$ corresponding to the input x (which are the active labels) are output by the simulator.

Simulation of the Internal State of the Garbler. To simulate the internal state of the garbled, we need to present the two main components: (i) the inactive keys $\widehat{k}_w$ for each wire w and (ii) randomness used to generate $\tilde{P}, \tilde{D}$ and $\tilde{x}$ and is consistent with the input. We start by focusing on obtaining the internal sate for the garbled sub-circuits used with the $\tilde{P}$. This approach can be applied to all the sub-circuits in order to obtain the internal state of the garbler.

Table 2. Garbled gate g generated by the simulator.

Row number	Left ciphertext REE	Right ciphertext REE
$(\Lambda_\alpha, \Lambda_\beta)$	$\mathsf{Enc}_{k_\alpha}(s_{g,\mathsf{left}}^{\Lambda_\alpha, \Lambda_\beta})$	$\mathsf{Enc}_{k_\beta}(s_{g,\mathsf{right}}^{\Lambda_\alpha, \Lambda_\beta})$
$(\Lambda_\alpha, 1 \oplus \Lambda_\beta)$	$\mathsf{Enc}_{k_\alpha}(s_{g,\mathsf{left}}^{\Lambda_\alpha, 1 \oplus \Lambda_\beta})$	$\mathsf{SimEnc}(P_{in}^{D_{in}}[\mathsf{prms}, s_{g,\mathsf{left}}^{\Lambda_\alpha, 1 \oplus \Lambda_\beta}])$
$(1 \oplus \Lambda_\alpha, \Lambda_\beta)$	$\mathsf{SimEnc}(P_{in}^{D_{in}}[\mathsf{prms}, s_{g,\mathsf{right}}^{1 \oplus \Lambda_\alpha, \Lambda_\beta}])$	$\mathsf{Enc}_{k_\beta}(s_{g,\mathsf{right}}^{1 \oplus \Lambda_\alpha, \Lambda_\beta})$
$(1 \oplus \Lambda_\alpha, 1 \oplus \Lambda_\beta)$	$\mathsf{SimEnc}(\mathsf{Const}[\mathsf{prms}, s_{g,\mathsf{left}}^{1 \oplus \Lambda_\alpha, 1 \oplus \Lambda_\beta}])$	$\mathsf{SimEnc}(P_{in}^{D_{in}}[\mathsf{prms}, s_{g,\mathsf{left}}^{1 \oplus \Lambda_\alpha, 1 \oplus \Lambda_\beta}])$

Given the input x and data D, the modified input for the program P_{in} is $x||D$. The inactive keys are chosen as $\widehat{k}_w$ for each wire w. It generates these keys by running $\widehat{k}_w \leftarrow$ REE.Equiv($\mathsf{td}_w; \hat{x}$) for each wire w. Now the garbling of P_{in} looks like the real garbling with keys $k_\alpha, \widehat{k}_\alpha, k_\beta, \widehat{k}_\beta$ where k_α, k_β are active for the computation $P_{in}^{D_{in}}(\hat{x})$.

Description of Program $P_{in}[\text{prms}, \text{mask}]$ and Memory D_{in}

Constants: $P, k_\gamma, \text{td}_\gamma, \Lambda_\gamma, \overrightarrow{M}, \tau, m, \text{prms} = \{\tau, C^{\text{type}}, g, b_\alpha \oplus \Lambda_\alpha, b_\beta \oplus \Lambda_\beta\}$
Input: x_{in}
Description of D_{in}. Initialize D_{in} to be an empty database of size $|D|$.
Description of P_{in}. The description of P_{in} follows.

1. Modify the program P to first write the input x into memory D_{in} and then proceed with the logic of P.
2. Run $ORAM.Sim_2[\overrightarrow{M}, P](D, x_{in})$ and write the output r_{eq} onto the random tape of the RAM program.
3. Run the compiler $ORAM.Prog$ with input P and randomness r_{eq}. Let the resulting program be referred to as P'.
4. For every time step $\tau \in T$, the bit assignments $\text{bit}_\alpha, \text{bit}_\beta$ of input wires α, β of gate g are inferred depending on the type of circuit this gate belongs to:

    Cases C^{leaf} and C^{step}: Evaluate the program P' using memory D_{in} with some input to compute the bit assignments corresponding to the inputs of C^{leaf} and C^{step} circuits. Then the bit assignments of the gate g within these circuits can be computed using the inputs.

    Case C^{node}: The bit assignments of all the inputs to C^{node} have already been computed and hence the bits corresponding to gate g can be computed from the inputs without having to evaluate the program P' using memory D_{in} with some input.
5. Generate $\widehat{k}_\gamma \leftarrow \text{REE.Equiv}(\text{td}_\gamma, x)$. If $g(\text{bit}_\alpha, \text{bit}_\beta) = g(b_\alpha \oplus \text{bit}_\alpha, b_\beta \oplus \text{bit}_\beta)$ then output $k_\gamma \oplus \text{mask}$. Else output $\widehat{k}_\gamma \oplus \text{mask}$.

Description of Program $\text{Const}[\text{const}]$

The program is padded to the size of programs P_{in} with memory D_{in} and is the RAM program that outputs the constant const.

Fig. 4. RAM programs and memory used in REE simulation

The second component of the internal state is to present the randomness used in the garbling which is essentially the randomness used to encrypt the ciphertexts in each of the garbled gates. The simulator presents all the randomness used for encryption, a pair of keys per gate as internal state of the garbler and 8 secret shares ciphertexts per garbled gate.

Theorem 6. *Assuming the existence of RAM-efficient equivocal encryption,* GRAM *comprising of $(Data, Prog, Inp, Eval)$ is a Equivocal Garbled RAM scheme with a garbled database size of $\tilde{O}((M + n + T) \cdot M)$, garbled input size of $\tilde{O}((M + n) \cdot n)$, garbled program size and evaluation time of $\tilde{O}((M + n + T) \cdot T)$, where T, M and n are the running time, memory size and input size of the RAM program P respectively.*

Proof Sketch. The correctness of our Equivocal garbled RAM follows from the correctness of the Garbled RAM construction of [16] along with the correctness of the underlying REE. By induction, at each step, the evaluator gets the correct key $k_\gamma^{\text{bit}_\gamma}$ and the correct pointer Λ_γ for the next gate's row.

Description of Hybrids. We define a sequence of hybrids H_0, H_0^{oram}, H_1, ..., H_t, H_{t+1}. The first hybrid H_0 corresponds to the real execution and the hybrid H_{t+1} to simulation. Further, we define m sub-hybrids between each H_i and H_{i+1} where $i \in \{1, ..., t-1\}$: $H_{i,1}^{subcirc}$, ..., $H_{i,m}^{subcirc}$ where $H_{i,m}^{subcirc}$ switches the key $k_{m-i}^{\text{bit}_{m-i}}$ from real to simulated. Here the wires are sorted according to the topological order of the circuit, i.e. that output wires of each gate have larger index than both input wires of that gate (note that our notation $1, ..., n$ for input wires and m for an output wire is consistent with topological order). The descriptions of these hybrids are provided below.

Hybrid H_0^{oram}. In this hybrid we change how the permutation of ciphertexts is generated, without changing the distribution of the hybrid. Instead of generating the memory access sequence by evaluating the program $P^D(x)$, we generate it using the ORAM simulator Sim_1. The garbled $\tilde{P}, \tilde{D}, \tilde{x}$ are generated as follows:

1. Generate the memory access $\overrightarrow{M} \leftarrow ORAM.Sim_1(T, m)$.
2. Compute the randomness $r_{oram} \leftarrow ORAM.Sim_2(\overrightarrow{M})$
3. Compute $P_{oram} \leftarrow ORAM.Prog(P, r_{oram})$ and garbled data $D_{oram} \leftarrow ORAM.Data(D)$
4. Lastly, compute $\tilde{P} \leftarrow \mathsf{GRAM.Prog}(P_{oram})$, $\tilde{D} \leftarrow \mathsf{GRAM.Data}(D_{oram})$ and $\tilde{x} \leftarrow \mathsf{GRAM.Inp}(x)$

The hybrid H_0^{oram} has a distribution similar to he real execution.

Hybrid H_i for $i = 1, ..., t$. Let the sequence of circuits evaluated during the execution of $GRAM.Eval(\tilde{P}, \tilde{D}, \tilde{x})$ be $C_1, ..., C_t$. In hybrid H_i, the first i circuits are simulated and the rest are generated as per the real execution. More specifically, this hybrid is computed as follows: simulate the first i circuits in the reverse order i.e. $C_i, ..., C_1$. This sequence of hybrids are identical to the ones considered in [16]. The main observation from [16] is that in Hybrid H_i, we can replace the real garbling of the ith circuit with a simulated one as the input labels of the ith circuit have been decoupled from the rest of the outputs. We will pursue the same approach with the exception that our real and simulated garbling schemes are according to the equivocal garbling procedure [9] with REE encryption. We consider a sequence of sub-hybrids following [9] between the hybrids H_i and H_{i+1} for $i = 1, ..., t-1$. The indistinguishability follows essentially as in [9], we present the hybrids explicitly rather than defining an equivocal garbling scheme instantiated with the REE.

Sub-Hybrid $H_{i,j}^{subcirc}$ for $j = 1, ..., m$. In this hybrid, the aim is to replace the wires in real garbled circuit C_{i+1} with simulated garbled circuits identical to the hybrids defined in [8] with the difference that REE is used instead of FEE. The real keys k_j corresponding to the jth wire in circuit

C_{i+1} are replaced with simulated keys. The ciphertexts corresponding to the simulated labels $\widehat{K_j}$ are also re simulating the ciphertext generated using these simulated keys. In this hybrid we convert the real labels $k_j^{1 \oplus \mathsf{bit}_j}$ to simulated labels. We essentially replace all the invocations to FEE functions with that of REE function in the hybrids of [8]. The indistinguishability of sub-hybrids $H_{i,j}^{subcirc}$ and $H_{i,j+1}^{subcirc}$ reduces to the security of the underlying REE scheme which has already been shown to be secure.

Hybrid H_{t+1}. In the previous hybrids H_t only the circuits executed during GRAM.Eval($\tilde{P}, \tilde{D}, \tilde{x}$) have been simulated so far. In this hybrid, those garbled circuits that haven't been evaluated will be considered. Note that some of these garbled circuits that weren't evaluated may contain labels to a (proper) subset of the input wires (i.e. partial inputs). These circuits can be topological ordered such that the outputs any circuit only goes as input to the subsequent circuits in the ordering and simulated in the reverse topological ordering.

4.2 Putting It Together

We can essentially use an equivocal garbled RAM scheme in the standard Yao protocol assuming the existence of an adaptively secure oblivious-transfer protocol. The only difference from the standard construction is that we need to rely on the OT-functionality as a communication channel to transmit the garbled circuit and garbled inputs (of the garbler). Another way of achieving this is to additionally assume a non-committing encryption (NCE) scheme and transmitting the data using NCE. We obtain the following theorem.

Theorem 7. *Let f be a two-party functionality expressed via a RAM program π. Assume the existence of a bit-decomposable equivocal garbled RAM scheme and the existence of a 2-round oblivious-transfer protocol secure against passive corruption by an adaptive adversary. Then there exists a 2-round 2-party protocol secure against passive corruption by an adaptive adversary where the communication complexity is $\tilde{O}(T^2 + n)$ where n is the sum of the input size of the two parties to f and T is the upper bound of the running time of π. Here $\tilde{O}(\cdot)$ ignores $\mathsf{poly}(\log T, \log n, \kappa)$ factors where κ is the (computational) security parameter.*

5 Adaptive Zero-Knowledge for RAM

In this section, we describe a simple construction of a UC zero-knowledge proof system for relations expressed as RAM computation. We build it from UC commitments and garbled RAM with a certain property which we call *splitability* We note that our construction also naturally works for circuits. We show that the GRAM construction of [17] is splitable in the full version.

Our proof system is RAM-efficient, meaning that its computation and communication complexity is only proportional to $\tilde{O}(T)$. We then use the standard transformations [7,21] to compile any protocol from active to passive security. In particular, our protocol from Theorem 7 results in an active protocol with computation and communication complexity $\tilde{O}(T^2)$.

Theorem 8 (Adaptive ZK for RAM). *Assume the existence of a UC-secure commitment scheme secure against adaptive adversary, and the existence of static splitable garbled RAM. Then there exists a zero-knowledge proof of knowledge proof system secure against active corruption by an adaptive adversary where the communication complexity is $\widetilde{O}(T^2 + n)$ where n is the sum of the length of the statement and the witness, and T is the upper bound of the running time of the relation R_x. Here $\widetilde{O}(\cdot)$ ignores $\mathsf{poly}(\log T, \log n, \kappa)$ factors where κ is the (computational) security parameter.*

Theorem 9 (Adaptive, active 2PC for RAM). *Let f be a two-party functionality expressed via a RAM program π. Assume the existence of a bit-decomposable equivocal garbled RAM scheme, the existence of a UC-secure 2-round oblivious-transfer protocol secure against active corruption by an adaptive adversary, the existence of adaptive UC-secure commitment scheme, and the existence of static splitable garbled RAM. Then there exists a 2-party protocol secure against active corruption by an adaptive adversary where the communication complexity is $\widetilde{O}(T^2 + n)$ where n is the sum of the input size of the two parties to f and T is the upper bound of the running time of π. Here $\widetilde{O}(\cdot)$ ignores $\mathsf{poly}(\log T, \log n, \kappa)$ factors where κ is the (computational) security parameter.*

5.1 Splitable Garbling

The property of splitability can be defined both for garbled circuits and garbled RAM. For simplicity, we first informally describe it for circuits, but later give a formal definition for RAM programs (since this is what we use in the protocol); the differences are only syntactic.

Let C, x be a circuit and its input. Intuitively, splitability says that the "garbling information" G - i.e. garbled circuit and all labels - can be split into active part G^a and inactive part G^i, with the property that G^a is enough to learn the output $C(x)$. Further, we require that the garbling can be generated in different order: that is, one can either generate the full garbling information G and later, given x, compute G^a; or, one can generate G^a, without knowing x (only $C(x)$), and later complete it to full G, once w is given. We note that we require that the latter method generates the correct distribution of G and G^a (not merely an indistinguishable one). Next, we require verifiability: given G, it should be possible to determine which circuit (or, RAM program) it evaluates. Finally, we require input extractability: given G and G^a corresponding to input x, it should be possible to extract x in polynomial time.

For ease of exposition of our protocol, we also require that $G = G^a \cup G^i$ can be further split into $\{G^a{}_j\}, \{G^i{}_j\}$, such that, when they are shuffled, they jointly don't leak any information about the computation of C on x.

Syntax of Splitable Garbled RAM. For simplicity we assume that the memory D of the computation is empty (but there is still an input x). This will be sufficient for our ZK protocol.

- $G \leftarrow GRAM.Full(P; r_{\mathsf{Gen}})$ computes the full garbling information G;

- $\{G^a, I\} \leftarrow GRAM.Project(G, x)$ computes an active part G^a for computation $P(x)$, and a set of indices I such that G^a is a subset of G corresponding to positions I, i.e. $G^a = G_I$.
- $\{G^a, state, I\} \leftarrow GRAM.Active(P, y)$ computes an active part G^a for program P and its output y, together with positions I.
- $\{G, r_{\mathsf{Gen}}\} \leftarrow GRAM.Complete(G^a, x, state)$ computes the full garbling information G and proper generation randomness r_{Gen}, such that G^a is consistent with x.
- $y \leftarrow GRAM.Eval(G^a)$ computes the output y (supposedly equal to $P(x)$);
- $\{acc, rej\} \leftarrow GRAM.Verify(G, P)$ verifies whether G is a garbled RAM for the program P with empty memory;
- $x \leftarrow GRAM.Extract(G, G^a)$ outputs x such that $P(x) = GRAM.Eval(G^a)$.
- $GRAM.Perm(G)$ outputs a permuted description of G, such that revealing the location of G^a doesn't leak any information beyond $P(x)$.

Now we list the required properties:

- **Correctness:** For all P and x,

$$Pr[y \neq P(x) : r_{\mathsf{Gen}} \leftarrow \{0,1\}^{|r_{\mathsf{Gen}}|}, G \leftarrow GRAM.Full(P; r_{\mathsf{Gen}}),$$

$$G^a \leftarrow GRAM.Project(G, x), y \leftarrow GRAM.Eval(G^a)] \leq negl(\kappa)$$

- **Alternative generation:** For any x, P, and $y = P(x)$, the following distributions are the same:

$$\{(G, G^a, r_{\mathsf{Gen}}, I) : r_{\mathsf{Gen}} \leftarrow \{0,1\}^{|r_{\mathsf{Gen}}|}, G \leftarrow GRAM.Full(P; r_{\mathsf{Gen}}),$$

$$\{G^a, I\} \leftarrow GRAM.Project(G, x)\} \ and$$

$$\{(G, G^a, r_{\mathsf{Gen}}, I) : \{G^a, I, state\} \leftarrow GRAM.Active(P, y),$$

$$\{G, r_{\mathsf{Gen}}\} \leftarrow GRAM.Complete(G^a, x, state)\}.$$

- **Verifiability and Extractability:** For any P, any x, any string G and any substring $G^a = G_I$ (for some set I), if $GRAM.Eval(G^a) = y \neq \perp$, $GRAM.Verify(G, P) = acc$, and $x' \leftarrow GRAM.Extract(G, G^a)$, then $P(x') = y$.
  Naturally, we require that $GRAM.Verify(G, P) = acc$ for honestly generated G.

5.2 Our Adaptive UC ZK Protocol

Our protocol is described on Fig. 5. Completeness follows from correctness of the garbled RAM and correctness of UC commitment. We now explain why proof of knowledge and zero-knowledge properties hold.

The adaptive UC zero-knowledge protocol

Prover's input: statement x and the corresponding relation R_x; witness w.
Verifier's input: statement x and the corresponding relation R_x.
The protocol:

1. The prover chooses random $r_{\mathsf{Gen}} \leftarrow \{0,1\}^{|r_{\mathsf{Gen}}|}$ and computes the splitable garbling of the relation R_x: $G = GRAM.Full(R_x; r_{\mathsf{Gen}})$. Then it computes $G^a, I \leftarrow GRAM.Project(G, w)$ and sets $G^i = G \setminus G^a$.
   The prover sends the verifier N UC commitments, where the committed value in commitment j is $Perm(G)_j$.
2. The verifier sends a random bit b to the prover.
3. If $b = 0$, the prover sends G together with decommitment information for all commitments to the verifier. If $b = 1$, the prover sends G^a together with decommitment information for indices $j \in I$ (which correspond to committed G^a) to the verifier.
4. If $b = 0$, the verifier accepts iff $GRAM.Verify(G, R_x)$ accepts and all decommitments verify. If $b = 1$, the verifier accepts iff $GRAM.Eval(G^a) = 1$ and the decommitments verify.

The simulation:

1. The simulator simulates N executions of the UC commitment.
2. If $b = 0$, the simulator generates $G = GRAM.Full(R_x; r_{\mathsf{Gen}})$, computes $Perm(G)$, and equivocates each commitment j, $j = 1, \ldots, N$, to G_j. It sets G and all the decommitments to be the simulated message of the prover. If $b = 1$, the simulator generates $G^a, I \leftarrow GRAM.Active(R_x, 1)$, equivocates commitments $j \in I$ to $G^a{}_j$ for each j, and sets G^a and the decommitment information to be the simulated message of the prover.
3. Upon corruption of the prover, the simulator learns w such that $R_x(w) = 1$. If $b = 0$, the simulator runs $G^a, I \leftarrow GRAM.Project(G, w)$ and sets $G^i = G \setminus G^a$. If $b = 1$, the simulator runs $\{G, r_{\mathsf{Gen}}\} \leftarrow GRAM.Complete(G^a, w, state)$ It sets $r_{\mathsf{Gen}}, G^a, G, I$, and the simulated coins of the commitment schemes to be the simulated state of the prover.

Fig. 5. The adaptive UC zero-knowledge protocol

Proof Sketch. Intuitively, proof of knowledge (and soundness against unbounded provers) follows from extractability of splitable garbling and binding property of commitments. Let P be a prover which causes an honest verifier to accept with non-negligible probability. Consider an extractor which runs P till the end with verifier message 0, then rewinds P and runs it with verifier message 1. As a result, the extractor obtains G, G^a, and the decommitment information for both values, such that all decommitments verify, $GRAM.Verify(G, R_x) = acc$, and $GRAM.Eval(G^a) = 1$.

The extractor computes $w' = GRAM.Extract(G, G^a)$. By the binding property of commitments, it follows that $G^a = G_I$ for some set I. It then follows from extractability and from the fact that $GRAM.Verify(G, P) = acc$, $GRAM.Eval(G^a) = 1$, $R_x(w') = 1$.

To prove adaptive security, we need to simulate the protocol for an adversary which can adaptively corrupt potentially both parties (simulator described in Fig. 5). Since the verifier is public-coin, it is enough to simulate the case where the adversary first lets the protocol finish and then corrupts the prover. Note that simulatability of this case immediately implies zero-knowledge, since the simulator doesn't have access to the witness when simulating the transcript. We argue that the simulation is computationally indistinguishable from the real execution.

- If $b = 0$, the simulator generates G and G^a honestly. The only difference between simulation and the real execution is that commitments are simulated and later equivocated to G. Indistinguishability follows immediately from the hiding property of commitments.
- If $b = 1$, the simulator uses alternative generation to generate G^a and later complete it to G. Recall that G, G^a, generated in this way, are required to be distributed correctly. Thus, the only difference between simulation and the real execution is that commitments are simulated and later equivocated to G. Indistinguishability follows from the hiding property of commitments.

Acknowledgments. Work of Rafail Ostrovsky was supported by NSF award #2001096, US-Israel BSF grant 2015782, a Google Faculty Award, a JP Morgan Faculty Award, an IBM Faculty Research Award, a Xerox Faculty Research Award, an OKAWA Foundation Research Award, a B. John Garrick Foundation Award, a Teradata Research Award, a Lockheed-Martin Research Award, and the Sunday Group.

References

1. Bellare, M., Hoang, V.T., Rogaway, P.: Adaptively secure garbling with applications to one-time programs and secure outsourcing. In: Wang, X., Sako, K. (eds.) ASIACRYPT 2012. LNCS, vol. 7658, pp. 134–153. Springer, Heidelberg (2012). https://doi.org/10.1007/978-3-642-34961-4_10
2. Benhamouda, F., Lin, H., Polychroniadou, A., Venkitasubramaniam, M.: Two-round adaptively secure multiparty computation from standard assumptions. In: Beimel, A., Dziembowski, S. (eds.) TCC 2018. LNCS, vol. 11239, pp. 175–205. Springer, Cham (2018). https://doi.org/10.1007/978-3-030-03807-6_7
3. Bitansky, N., Canetti, R., Halevi, S.: Leakage-tolerant interactive protocols. In: Cramer, R. (ed.) TCC 2012. LNCS, vol. 7194, pp. 266–284. Springer, Heidelberg (2012). https://doi.org/10.1007/978-3-642-28914-9_15
4. Bitansky, N., Dachman-Soled, D., Lin, H.: Leakage-tolerant computation with input-independent preprocessing. In: Garay, J.A., Gennaro, R. (eds.) CRYPTO 2014, Part II. LNCS, vol. 8617, pp. 146–163. Springer, Heidelberg (2014). https://doi.org/10.1007/978-3-662-44381-1_9
5. Canetti, R., Feige, U., Goldreich, O., Naor, M.: Adaptively secure multi-party computation. In: Proceedings of the Twenty-Eighth Annual ACM Symposium on the Theory of Computing, Philadelphia, Pennsylvania, USA, 22–24 May 1996, pp. 639–648 (1996)

6. Canetti, R., Goldwasser, S., Poburinnaya, O.: Adaptively secure two-party computation from indistinguishability obfuscation. In: Dodis, Y., Nielsen, J.B. (eds.) TCC 2015, Part II. LNCS, vol. 9015, pp. 557–585. Springer, Heidelberg (2015). https://doi.org/10.1007/978-3-662-46497-7_22

7. Canetti, R., Lindell, Y., Ostrovsky, R., Sahai, A.: Universally composable two-party and multi-party secure computation. In: STOC, pp. 494–503 (2002)

8. Canetti, R., Poburinnaya, O., Venkitasubramaniam, M.: Better two-round adaptive multiparty computation. IACR Cryptology ePrint Archive 2016, 614 (2016). http://eprint.iacr.org/2016/614

9. Canetti, R., Poburinnaya, O., Venkitasubramaniam, M.: Equivocating Yao: constant-round adaptively secure multiparty computation in the plain model. In: Proceedings of the 49th Annual ACM SIGACT Symposium on Theory of Computing, STOC 2017, Montreal, QC, Canada, 19–23 June 2017, pp. 497–509 (2017)

10. Chung, K.M., Pass, R.: A simple oram. Technical report, CORNELL UNIV ITHACA NY (2013)

11. Cohen, R., Peikert, C.: On adaptively secure multiparty computation with a short CRS. In: Zikas, V., De Prisco, R. (eds.) SCN 2016. LNCS, vol. 9841, pp. 129–146. Springer, Cham (2016). https://doi.org/10.1007/978-3-319-44618-9_7

12. Cohen, R., Shelat, A., Wichs, D.: Adaptively secure MPC with sublinear communication complexity. In: Boldyreva, A., Micciancio, D. (eds.) CRYPTO 2019, Part II. LNCS, vol. 11693, pp. 30–60. Springer, Cham (2019). https://doi.org/10.1007/978-3-030-26951-7_2

13. Cook, S.A., Reckhow, R.A.: Time bounded random access machines. J. Comput. Syst. Sci. 7(4), 354–375 (1973)

14. Dachman-Soled, D., Katz, J., Rao, V.: Adaptively Secure, Universally Composable, Multiparty Computation in Constant Rounds. In: Dodis, Y., Nielsen, J.B. (eds.) TCC 2015, Part II. LNCS, vol. 9015, pp. 586–613. Springer, Heidelberg (2015). https://doi.org/10.1007/978-3-662-46497-7_23

15. Garg, S., Gupta, D., Miao, P., Pandey, O.: Secure multiparty RAM computation in constant rounds. In: Hirt, M., Smith, A. (eds.) TCC 2016, Part I. LNCS, vol. 9985, pp. 491–520. Springer, Heidelberg (2016). https://doi.org/10.1007/978-3-662-53641-4_19

16. Garg, S., Lu, S., Ostrovsky, R.: Black-box garbled ram. Cryptology ePrint Archive, Report 2015/307 (2015). https://eprint.iacr.org/2015/307

17. Garg, S., Lu, S., Ostrovsky, R., Scafuro, A.: Garbled ram from one-way functions. Cryptology ePrint Archive, Report 2014/941 (2014). https://eprint.iacr.org/2014/941

18. Garg, S., Polychroniadou, A.: Two-round adaptively secure MPC from indistinguishability obfuscation. In: Dodis, Y., Nielsen, J.B. (eds.) TCC 2015, Part II. LNCS, vol. 9015, pp. 614–637. Springer, Heidelberg (2015). https://doi.org/10.1007/978-3-662-46497-7_24

19. Garg, S., Sahai, A.: Adaptively secure multi-party computation with dishonest majority. In: Safavi-Naini, R., Canetti, R. (eds.) CRYPTO 2012. LNCS, vol. 7417, pp. 105–123. Springer, Heidelberg (2012). https://doi.org/10.1007/978-3-642-32009-5_8

20. Gentry, C., Halevi, S., Lu, S., Ostrovsky, R., Raykova, M., Wichs, D.: Garbled RAM revisited. In: Nguyen, P.Q., Oswald, E. (eds.) EUROCRYPT 2014. LNCS, vol. 8441, pp. 405–422. Springer, Heidelberg (2014). https://doi.org/10.1007/978-3-642-55220-5_23

21. Goldreich, O., Micali, S., Wigderson, A.: How to play any mental game or a completeness theorem for protocols with honest majority. In: STOC, pp. 218–229 (1987)

22. Goyal, V.: Constant round non-malleable protocols using one way functions. In: STOC (2011)

23. Hazay, C., Venkitasubramaniam, M.: On the power of secure two-party computation. In: Robshaw, M., Katz, J. (eds.) CRYPTO 2016. LNCS, vol. 9815, pp. 397–429. Springer, Heidelberg (2016). https://doi.org/10.1007/978-3-662-53008-5_14

24. Hazay, C., Yanai, A.: Constant-round maliciously secure two-party computation in the RAM model. In: Hirt, M., Smith, A. (eds.) TCC 2016, Part I. LNCS, vol. 9985, pp. 521–553. Springer, Heidelberg (2016). https://doi.org/10.1007/978-3-662-53641-4_20

25. Ishai, Y., Kumarasubramanian, A., Orlandi, C., Sahai, A.: On invertible sampling and adaptive security. In: Abe, M. (ed.) ASIACRYPT 2010. LNCS, vol. 6477, pp. 466–482. Springer, Heidelberg (2010). https://doi.org/10.1007/978-3-642-17373-8_27

26. Lin, H., Pass, R.: Constant-round non-malleable commitments from any one-way function. In: STOC (2011)

27. Lindell, Y., Zarosim, H.: Adaptive zero-knowledge proofs and adaptively secure oblivious transfer. J. Cryptol. 24(4), 761–799 (2011)

28. Lu, S., Ostrovsky, R.: How to garble RAM programs? In: Johansson, T., Nguyen, P.Q. (eds.) EUROCRYPT 2013. LNCS, vol. 7881, pp. 719–734. Springer, Heidelberg (2013). https://doi.org/10.1007/978-3-642-38348-9_42

29. Pippenger, N., Fischer, M.J.: Relations among complexity measures. J. ACM (JACM) 26(2), 361–381 (1979)

30. Yao, A.C.: Protocols for secure computations (extended abstract). In: FOCS, pp. 160–164 (1982)

31. Yao, A.C.: How to generate and exchange secrets (extended abstract). In: FOCS, pp. 162–167 (1986)

Optimal Broadcast Encryption and CP-ABE from Evasive Lattice Assumptions

Hoeteck Wee[✉]

NTT Research and ENS, Paris, France
wee@di.ens.fr

Abstract. We present a new, simple candidate broadcast encryption scheme for N users with parameter size $\mathsf{poly}(\log N)$. We prove security of our scheme under a non-standard variant of the LWE assumption where the distinguisher additionally receives short Gaussian pre-images while avoiding zeroizing attacks. This yields the first candidate optimal broadcast encryption that is plausibly post-quantum secure, and enjoys a security reduction to a simple assumption. As a secondary contribution, we present a candidate ciphertext-policy attribute-based encryption (CP-ABE) scheme for circuits of a-priori bounded polynomial depth where the parameter size is independent of the circuit size, and prove security under an additional non-standard assumption.

1 Introduction

In this work, we study broadcast encryption [27] as well as attribute-based encryption schemes [10,34,41]. In ciphertext-policy attribute-based encryption (CP-ABE), ciphertexts ct are associated with a predicate f and a message m and keys sk with an attribute x, and decryption returns m when x satisfies f. Broadcast encryption is a special case of CP-ABE where the predicate is specified by a set $S \subseteq [N]$, and decryption returns m when $x \in S$. In both cases, we require security against unbounded collusions, so that an adversary that sees a ciphertext along with secret keys for an arbitrary number of attributes $x_1, x_2, \ldots$ learns nothing about m as long as none of these attributes satisfies f.

Broadcast encryption has been an active area of research since their introduction in the 1990s, where a major goal is to obtain schemes with short parameters, that is, short ciphertexts ct, public keys mpk and secret keys sk. In a celebrated work from 2005, Boneh, Gentry and Waters [13] presented the first broadcast encryption scheme with sublinear-sized parameters from bilinear groups where $|\mathsf{ct}| + |\mathsf{mpk}| + |\mathsf{sk}| = O(N^{1/2})$, [15,22,33], recently improved to $O(N^{1/3})$ [43]. On the other hand, in spite of the tremendous advances in lattice-based cryptography over the past decade, we do not know a LWE-based broadcast encryption scheme achieving $|\mathsf{ct}| = o(N)$.

A more recent line of works focuses on *optimal* broadcast encryption with parameter size $\mathsf{poly}(\log N)$, where the first feasibility results relied on either

© International Association for Cryptologic Research 2022
O. Dunkelman and S. Dziembowski (Eds.): EUROCRYPT 2022, LNCS 13276, pp. 217–241, 2022.
https://doi.org/10.1007/978-3-031-07085-3_8

multi-linear maps [16] or indistinguishability obfuscation [17].[1]. In a recent remarkable break-through, Agrawal and Yamada [7] – along with a follow-up with Wichs [5] – constructed an optimal broadcast encryption scheme from bilinear groups *and* LWE. Independently, Brakerski and Vaikuntathan [20] presented a candidate "lattice-inspired' optimal broadcast encryption scheme that is plausibly post-quantum secure, but they were unable to provide a reduction to LWE or any simple lattice assumption.

Our Contributions. Our main contribution is a new, simple candidate optimal broadcast encryption scheme with poly(log N)-sized parameters. We prove selective security of our scheme assuming *evasive LWE*, a non-standard variant of the LWE assumption where the distinguisher additionally receives short Gaussian pre-images while avoiding zeroizing attacks. This yields the first candidate optimal broadcast encryption that is plausibly post-quantum secure, and enjoys a security reduction to a simple assumption. As a secondary contribution, we present a candidate CP-ABE scheme for circuits of a-priori bounded polynomial depth where the parameter size is independent of the circuit size, and prove security under an additional non-standard assumption. We refer to Fig. 1 for a comparison with prior works, and proceed with a brief overview of our constructions.

2   Technical Overview

Our optimal broadcast encryption scheme follows the Agrawal-Yamada-Wichs, henceforth AYW, blue-print laid out in [5,7] (and partially in [20]): (i) we start with a one-key secure CP-ABE for circuits based on LWE and randomize the secret keys to achieve security against collusions, and (ii) we show that for an appropriate family of circuits, our CP-ABE scheme implies optimal broadcast encryption. The AYW schemes achieve randomization via exponentiation with random scalars in a bilinear group. Security relies on LWE in addition to a hardness assumption about the bilinear group, either the generic group model (GGM) [7], or non-standard knowledge assumption (KOALA) [5,11]. We proceed to sketch two new technical ideas in this work that allows us to eliminate the use of bilinear maps, thereby achieving plausible post-quantum security.

Randomization via Tensors. We randomize secret keys by tensoring with random Gaussian (row) vectors $\mathbf{r} \leftarrow \mathcal{D}_{\mathbb{Z},\chi}^m$, which satisfies the following correctness and security properties:

- Following prior ABE schemes based on LWE [12], given $\mathbf{x} \in \{0,1\}^\ell$, $\mathbf{A} \in \mathbb{Z}_q^{n \times \ell m}$, we can homomorphically evaluate a circuit f on $\mathbf{A} - \mathbf{x} \otimes \mathbf{G}$ to obtain

---

[1] For simplicity of exposition and due to the sheer complexity and impracticality of the ensuing schemes, we ignore obfuscation-based broadcast in the rest of the introduction, deferring a comparison to Sect. 2.3.

Reference	Assumption	Post-Quantum	CP-ABE
AY20 [7]	LWE + bilinear GGM		NC^1, $|ct| = poly(\ell, d, \log s)$
AWY20 [5]	LWE + bilinear KOALA		NC^1, $|ct| = poly(\ell, d, \log s)$
BV22 [20]	×	✓	circuits, $|ct| = poly(\ell, d, \log s)$
Section 5.3	evasive LWE	✓	NC^1, $|ct| = poly(2^d, \log s)$
Section 5.4	evasive LWE + tensor LWE	✓	circuits, $|ct| = poly(d, \log s)$

Fig. 1. Comparison with prior optimal broadcast encryption schemes (sans obfuscation), all of which also yield CP-ABE schemes for either NC^1 or circuits of (a-prior bounded) polynomial depth d. Broadcast encryption for N users correspond to circuits of size $O(N \log N)$ and depth $O(\log \log N)$. CP-ABE decryption time in AY20, AMY20 grows with 2^d, hence the limitation to NC^1 circuits. As in [5], our broadcast encryption schemes achieve selective security, and our CP-ABE schemes achieve very selective security. BV22 only shows LWE-hardness against a subclass of attacks on a specific component of their scheme and does not provide any reduction for their full scheme. Both evasive LWE and bilinear KOALA are non-falsifiable assumptions. Finally, bilinear GGM ⇒ bilinear KOALA.

a quantity of the form $\mathbf{A}_f - f(x)\mathbf{G}$ via right-multiplication by some low-norm matrix $\mathbf{H}_{\mathbf{A},f,\mathbf{x}}$. This property is preserved under tensoring with random Gaussian vectors $\mathbf{r}$: we can homomorphically evaluate f on $(\mathbf{A} - \mathbf{x} \otimes \mathbf{G}) \otimes \mathbf{r}^\top$ to obtain $(\mathbf{A}_f - f(x)\mathbf{G}) \otimes \mathbf{r}^\top$ via right multiplication by $\mathbf{H}_{\mathbf{A},f,\mathbf{x}} \otimes \mathbf{I}$. Note that homomorphic evaluation is not possible if we replace tensor product with vector multiplication (on the right).

- Tensoring "amplifies" a single LWE secret $\mathbf{s}$ into Q independent LWE secrets $\mathbf{s}_1, \ldots, \mathbf{s}_Q$. More formally, under the LWE assumption, we have

$$\left\{ \left(\boxed{\mathbf{s}(\mathbf{I}_n \otimes \mathbf{r}_i^\top) + \mathbf{e}_i}, \mathbf{r}_i^\top \right) \right\}_{i \in [Q]} \approx_c \left\{ \left(\boxed{\mathbf{s}_i}, \mathbf{r}_i^\top \right) \right\}_{i \in [Q]} \tag{1}$$

where $\mathbf{s} \leftarrow \mathbb{Z}_q^{nm}, \mathbf{s}_i \leftarrow \mathbb{Z}_q^n, \mathbf{e}_i \leftarrow \mathcal{D}_{\mathbb{Z},\chi}^n, \mathbf{r}_i \leftarrow \mathcal{D}_{\mathbb{Z},\chi}^m$ [14,21]. In our analysis, Q corresponds to the number of key queries, and having Q independent secrets enables a hybrid argument over the key queries.

An Evasive Lattice Assumption. We describe a simple variant of the *evasive LWE* assumption we put forth in this work. Fix an efficiently samplable distribution $\mathbf{P}$ over $\mathbb{Z}_q^{n \times t}$. The evasive LWE assumption allows us to assert statements of the form

$$(\mathbf{B}, \boxed{\mathbf{sB} + \mathbf{e}}, \mathbf{B}^{-1}(\mathbf{P})) \approx_c (\mathbf{B}, \boxed{\mathbf{c}}, \mathbf{B}^{-1}(\mathbf{P}))$$

where $\mathbf{B} \leftarrow \mathbb{Z}_q^{n \times m}, \mathbf{c} \in \mathbb{Z}_q^{m'}$ are uniformly random, $m = O(n \log q) \leq t$ (so that $\mathbf{P}$ is wider than $\mathbf{B}$). We have two distinguishing strategies in the literature:

- ignore $\mathbf{B}^{-1}(\mathbf{P})$ and distinguish $(\mathbf{B}, \mathbf{sB} + \mathbf{e})$ from $(\mathbf{B}, \mathbf{c})$ – this covers lattice attacks on LWE;

- compute $\mathbf{c}^* = (\mathbf{sB} + \mathbf{e}') \cdot \mathbf{B}^{-1}(\mathbf{P}) \approx \mathbf{sP}$ and distinguish the latter from uniform – this includes zeroizing attacks on multi-linear map and obfuscation candidates [23, 24, 36, 40].

The evasive LWE assumption essentially asserts that these are the only distinguishing attacks. Namely,

$$\text{if} \qquad (\mathbf{B}, \mathbf{P}, \boxed{\mathbf{sB} + \mathbf{e}}, \boxed{\mathbf{sP} + \mathbf{e}''}) \approx_c (\mathbf{B}, \mathbf{P}, \boxed{\mathbf{c}}, \boxed{\mathbf{c}''}),$$

$$\text{then} \qquad (\mathbf{B}, \boxed{\mathbf{sB} + \mathbf{e}}, \mathbf{B}^{-1}(\mathbf{P})) \approx_c (\mathbf{B}, \boxed{\mathbf{c}}, \mathbf{B}^{-1}(\mathbf{P}))$$

where $\mathbf{e}''$ is a fresh noise vector. Note that $\mathbf{sP} + \mathbf{e}'' \approx_c \mathbf{c}''$ implies that the high-order bits of $(\mathbf{sB} + \mathbf{e}') \cdot \mathbf{B}^{-1}(\mathbf{P}) \approx \mathbf{sP}$ are pseudorandom, thereby defeating the second distinguishing strategy.[2] Overall, we note that the statement of evasive LWE is fairly simple and general, and does not refer to tensor products, circuits, or structured distributions like $\mathbf{A} - \mathbf{x} \otimes \mathbf{G}$ or $\mathbf{A}_f$. That is, the assumption encapsulates a principled approach towards (conjectured) computational hardness, rather than one that is tailored to our scheme.

Proof Strategy. Our security proof proceeds in two steps: first, we rely on evasive LWE to reduce security of our scheme to a simpler statement with no short Gaussians, and then we prove this latter statement from LWE, using (1) along the way. For the second step, we need to modify the scheme to perform homomorphic evaluation on $\mathbf{A} - \mathbf{x} \otimes \mathbf{I}$ where $\mathbf{A}$ is a low-norm matrix, and we replaced the gadget matrix $\mathbf{G}$ with the identity matrix $\mathbf{I}$; in the security proof, we will use the fact that if $\mathbf{A} - \mathbf{x} \otimes \mathbf{I}$ is low-norm, then

$$\underline{\mathbf{s}((\mathbf{A} - \mathbf{x} \otimes \mathbf{I}) \otimes \mathbf{r}^\top)} \approx \underline{\mathbf{s}(\mathbf{I} \otimes \mathbf{r}^\top)} \cdot (\mathbf{A} - \mathbf{x} \otimes \mathbf{I})$$

upon which we can invoke (1) to replace $\mathbf{s}(\mathbf{I} \otimes \mathbf{r}^\top)$ on the RHS with random.

Homomorphic evaluation on $\mathbf{A} - \mathbf{x} \otimes \mathbf{I}$ works as before with $\mathbf{G}$, except the noise growth is now doubly (instead of singly) exponential in circuit depth. This yields a CP-ABE scheme with $|\mathsf{ct}| = \mathsf{poly}(2^d, \log s)$ for NC^1 circuits of multiplicative depth d and size s, and we show that this is sufficient for optimal broadcast encryption. In particular, broadcast encryption for N users correspond to circuits of multiplicative depth $O(\log \log N)$ and size $O(N \log N)$. To obtain a CP-ABE for a-prior bounded depth circuits with $|\mathsf{ct}| = \mathsf{poly}(d, \log s)$, we keep $\mathbf{A} - \mathbf{x} \otimes \mathbf{G}$ as before, and instead prove security based a new (falsifiable) "*tensor LWE*" assumption in the second step.

2.1   Our CP-ABE Schemes

We describe our CP-ABE schemes in more detail. The schemes rely on the following strengthening of our earlier statement of evasive LWE: we consider

---

[2] Note that the error distribution $\mathbf{e} \cdot \mathbf{B}^{-1}(\mathbf{P})$ in $\mathbf{c}^*$ is different from the fresh Gaussian error $\mathbf{e}''$. Differences in error distributions can make or break a scheme if $\mathbf{c}^*$ has small norm, but we do not know attacks exploiting these differences when $\mathbf{c}^*$ has large norm, as is the case here.

distributions over pairs of matrices $(\mathbf{A}', \mathbf{P})$ together with auxiliary input aux (instead of just $\mathbf{P}$) and require that

if $(\mathbf{A}', \mathbf{B}, \mathbf{P}, \boxed{\mathbf{sA} + \mathbf{e}'}, \boxed{\mathbf{sB} + \mathbf{e}}, \mathbf{sP} + \mathbf{e}'', \mathsf{aux}) \approx_c (\mathbf{A}', \mathbf{B}, \mathbf{P}, \boxed{\mathbf{c}'}, \boxed{\mathbf{c}}, \boxed{\mathbf{c}''}, \mathsf{aux}),$ (2)

then $(\mathbf{A}', \mathbf{B}, \boxed{\mathbf{sA} + \mathbf{e}'}, \boxed{\mathbf{sB} + \mathbf{e}}, \mathbf{B}^{-1}(\mathbf{P}), \mathsf{aux}) \approx_c (\mathbf{A}', \mathbf{B}, \boxed{\mathbf{c}'}, \boxed{\mathbf{c}}, \mathbf{B}^{-1}(\mathbf{P}), \mathsf{aux})$ (3)

In our applications, the auxiliary input includes the coin tosses used to sample $\mathbf{A}', \mathbf{P}$, which rules out obfuscation-based counter-examples.

A One-Key Secure CP-ABE. We consider CP-ABE for circuits $f : \{0, 1\}^\ell \to \{0, 1\}$ of depth d and size s. Following [7,20], we begin with a one-key secure CP-ABE (where we use curly underlines in place of noise terms):

$$\mathsf{mpk} := \mathbf{B}_1 \leftarrow \mathbb{Z}_q^{n \times m}, \mathbf{A} \leftarrow \mathbb{Z}_q^{n \times \ell m}, \mathbf{u}^\top \leftarrow \mathcal{D}_{\mathbb{Z}, \chi}^m$$
$$\mathsf{ct}_f := \underline{\mathbf{sA}_f \mathbf{u}^\top} + \mu \cdot \mathbf{g}, \underline{\mathbf{sB}_1}, \text{ where } \mathbf{s} \leftarrow \mathbb{Z}_q^n$$
$$\mathsf{sk}_\mathbf{x} := \mathbf{B}_1^{-1}(\mathbf{A} - \mathbf{x} \otimes \mathbf{G})$$

Note that the ciphertext size is independent of ℓ. Decryption for $f(\mathbf{x}) = 0$ uses $(\mathbf{A} - \mathbf{x} \otimes \mathbf{G}) \cdot \mathbf{H}_{\mathbf{A},f,\mathbf{x}} = \mathbf{A}_f - f(\mathbf{x})\mathbf{G}$, which implies $\underline{\mathbf{sB}_1} \cdot \mathbf{B}_1^{-1}(\mathbf{A} - \mathbf{x} \otimes \mathbf{G}) \cdot \mathbf{H}_{\mathbf{A},f,\mathbf{x}} \cdot \mathbf{u}^\top \approx \mathbf{sA}_f \mathbf{u}^\top$.

Next, we show that the scheme is one-key secure assuming LWE and evasive LWE. Intuitively, evasive LWE says that we can replace the terms $\underline{\mathbf{sB}_1}, \mathbf{B}_1^{-1}(\mathbf{A} - \mathbf{x} \otimes \mathbf{G})$ with their product $\underline{\mathbf{s}(\mathbf{A} - \mathbf{x} \otimes \mathbf{G})}$. Then, it suffices to show that μ is hidden given

$$\mathbf{B}_1, \mathbf{A}, \underline{\mathbf{sA}_f \mathbf{u}^\top} + \mu \cdot \mathbf{g}, \underline{\mathbf{s}(\mathbf{A} - \mathbf{x} \otimes \mathbf{G})}$$

Next, we can write $\mathbf{sA}_f \mathbf{u}^\top$ in terms of $\mathbf{s}(\mathbf{A} - \mathbf{x} \otimes \mathbf{G})$ and $f(\mathbf{x}) \cdot \mathbf{sGu}^\top$ using homomorphic computation. Since $f(\mathbf{x}) = 1$, it suffices to show that μ is hidden given

$$\mathbf{B}_1, \mathbf{A}, \underline{\mathbf{sGu}^\top} + \mu \cdot \mathbf{g}, \underline{\mathbf{s}(\mathbf{A} - \mathbf{x} \otimes \mathbf{G})}$$

which follows quite readily from LWE.

Note that this scheme is insecure if the adversary is allowed to make two key queries: given secret keys for 0^ℓ and 1^ℓ, an adversary can compute $\underline{\mathbf{sA}}, \mathbf{s}(\mathbf{A} - 1^\ell \otimes \mathbf{G})$, substract the two to obtain $\mathbf{s}(1^\ell \otimes \mathbf{G})$ and solve for $\mathbf{s}$ and thus μ. To defeat this attack, we randomize the secret keys by tensoring with random Gaussian vectors.

First Modification. We replace $\mathbf{A} - \mathbf{x} \otimes \mathbf{G}$ in sk with $(\mathbf{A} - \mathbf{x} \otimes \mathbf{G}) \otimes \mathbf{r}^\top$ and $\mathbf{sA}_f \mathbf{u}^\top$ in ct with $\mathbf{s}(\mathbf{A}_f \mathbf{u}^\top \otimes \mathbf{I})$, so that

$$\mathsf{ct}_f := \underline{\mathbf{s}(\mathbf{A}_f \mathbf{u}^\top \otimes \mathbf{I})} + \mu \cdot \mathbf{g}, \underline{\mathbf{sB}_1}, \text{ where } \mathbf{s} \leftarrow \mathbb{Z}_q^n$$
$$\mathsf{sk}_\mathbf{x} := \mathbf{B}_1^{-1}((\mathbf{A} - \mathbf{x} \otimes \mathbf{G}) \otimes \mathbf{r}^\top), \mathbf{r}^\top$$

Decryption computes the following quantities:

$$(\underline{\mathbf{s}(\mathbf{A}_f \otimes \mathbf{I})} + \mu \cdot \mathbf{g}) \cdot (\mathbf{I} \otimes \mathbf{r}^\top) \approx \mathbf{s}(\mathbf{A}_f \otimes \mathbf{r}^\top) + \mu \cdot \mathbf{g} \cdot (\mathbf{I} \otimes \mathbf{r}^\top)$$

$$\underline{\mathbf{s}\mathbf{B}_1} \cdot \mathbf{B}_1^{-1}((\mathbf{A} - \mathbf{x} \otimes \mathbf{G}) \otimes \mathbf{r}^\top) \cdot (\mathbf{H}_{\mathbf{A},f,\mathbf{x}} \otimes \mathbf{I}) \approx \mathbf{s}(\mathbf{A}_f \otimes \mathbf{r}^\top)$$

and subtracts the two to recover μ. The attacker from before now learns $\underline{\mathbf{s}(\mathbf{A} \otimes \mathbf{r}_1^\top)}, \underline{\mathbf{s}((\mathbf{A} - 1^\ell \otimes \mathbf{G}) \otimes \mathbf{r}_2^\top}$ and since $\mathbf{r}_1 \neq \mathbf{r}_2$ w.h.p., we can no longer carry out the attack from before.

We do not know an attack on the preceding scheme. However, adapting the security proof for the one-key setting to the many-key setting runs into two difficulties. Upon applying evasive LWE as before, we want to argue that μ is hidden given

$$\mathbf{B}_1, \mathbf{A}, \underline{\mathbf{s}(\mathbf{A}_f \mathbf{u}^\top \otimes \mathbf{I})} + \mu \cdot \mathbf{g}, \left\{ \underline{\mathbf{s}((\mathbf{A} - \mathbf{x}_i \otimes \mathbf{G}) \otimes \mathbf{r}_i^\top)}, \mathbf{r}_i^\top \right\}_{i \in [Q]}$$

- The first difficulty lies in handling $\mathbf{s}(\mathbf{A}_f \mathbf{u}^\top \otimes \mathbf{I})$: using homomorphic computation as before allows us to write $\mathbf{s}(\mathbf{A}_f \mathbf{u}^\top \otimes \mathbf{r}_i^\top)$ in terms of $\mathbf{s}((\mathbf{A} - \mathbf{x}_i \otimes \mathbf{G}) \otimes \mathbf{r}_i^\top)$ and $f(\mathbf{x}_i) \cdot \mathbf{s}(\mathbf{G}\mathbf{u}^\top \otimes \mathbf{r}_i^\top)$. We then need to bridge the gap between $\left\{ \mathbf{s}(\mathbf{A}_f \mathbf{u}^\top \otimes \mathbf{r}_i^\top) \right\}_{i \in [Q]}$ (what we know how to simulate) and $\mathbf{s}(\mathbf{A}_f \mathbf{u}^\top \otimes \mathbf{I})$ (what appears in the ciphertext). The next modification addresses this difficulty while relying only on the LWE assumption.
- This leaves us with arguing pseudorandomness of $\left\{ \underline{\mathbf{s}((\mathbf{A} - \mathbf{x}_i \otimes \mathbf{G}) \otimes \mathbf{r}_i^\top)}, \mathbf{r}_i^\top \right\}_{i \in [Q]}$, for which we present two solutions. The first (and less satisfactory) is to simply assert pseudorandomness via a new assumption, which we refer to as *tensor LWE*. This assumption is qualitatively different from evasive LWE in that there are no Gaussian pre-images. The second solution relies only on the LWE assumption, but incurs a 2^d blow-up, which is nonetheless sufficient for optimal broadcast encryption.

Second Modification. We mask $\mathbf{s}(\mathbf{A}_f \otimes \mathbf{I})$ in the cipertext with a fresh LWE sample $\mathbf{s}_0 \mathbf{A}_0 + \mathbf{e}_0$ and during decryption, compute

$$\mathbf{s}(\mathbf{A}_f \otimes \mathbf{r}^\top) \approx \overbrace{(\mathbf{s}(\mathbf{A}_f \otimes \mathbf{I}_m) + \mathbf{s}_0 \mathbf{A}_0 + \mathbf{e})}^{\text{ct}} \cdot (1 \otimes \overbrace{\mathbf{r}^\top}^{\text{sk}}) - \overbrace{(\mathbf{s}_0 \mathbf{B}_0 + \mathbf{e}_0)}^{\text{ct}} \cdot \overbrace{\mathbf{B}_0^{-1}(\mathbf{A}_0 \mathbf{r}^\top)}^{\text{sk}} \quad (4)$$

where $\mathbf{s}_0 \mathbf{B}_0 + \mathbf{e}_0$ appears in ct_f and $\mathbf{B}_0^{-1}(\mathbf{A}_0 \mathbf{r}^\top)$ in $\mathsf{sk}_\mathbf{x}$. This yields the following CP-ABE scheme for bounded depth circuits:

$$\mathsf{mpk} := \mathbf{A}_0, \mathbf{B}_0 \leftarrow \mathbb{Z}_q^{n \times m}, \mathbf{B}_1 \leftarrow \mathbb{Z}_q^{mn \times m^2}, \mathbf{A} \leftarrow \mathbb{Z}_q^{n \times \ell m}$$

$$\mathsf{ct}_f := \underline{\mathbf{s}_0 \mathbf{B}_0}, \underline{\mathbf{s}(\mathbf{A}_f \otimes \mathbf{I}_m) + \mathbf{s}_0 \mathbf{A}_0} + \mu \cdot \mathbf{g}, \underline{\mathbf{s}\mathbf{B}_1}, \text{ where } \mathbf{s} \leftarrow \mathbb{Z}_q^{mn}, \mathbf{s}_0 \leftarrow \mathbb{Z}_q^n$$

$$\mathsf{sk}_\mathbf{x} := \mathbf{B}_0^{-1}(\mathbf{A}_0 \mathbf{r}^\top), \mathbf{B}_1^{-1}((\mathbf{A} - \mathbf{x} \otimes \mathbf{G}) \otimes \mathbf{r}^\top), \mathbf{r}^\top, \text{ where } \mathbf{r} \leftarrow \mathcal{D}_{\mathbb{Z},\chi}^m$$

Decryption for $f(\mathbf{x}) = 0$ computes (approximately)

$$\mu \cdot \mathbf{g} \cdot (1 \otimes \mathbf{r}^\top) \approx (\mathbf{s}(\mathbf{A}_f \otimes \mathbf{I}_m) + \mathbf{s}_0 \mathbf{A}_0 + \mu \cdot \mathbf{g}) \cdot (1 \otimes \mathbf{r}^\top) - \underline{\mathbf{s}_0 \mathbf{B}_0} \cdot \mathbf{B}_0^{-1}(\mathbf{A}_0 \mathbf{r}^\top)$$
$$+ \underline{\mathbf{s}\mathbf{B}_1} \cdot \mathbf{B}_1^{-1}((\mathbf{A} - \mathbf{x} \otimes \mathbf{G}) \otimes \mathbf{r}^\top) \cdot (\mathbf{H}_{\mathbf{A},f,\mathbf{x}} \otimes \mathbf{I})$$

Again, via the evasive LWE assumption (upon additionally combining $\mathbf{B}_0, \mathbf{B}_1$ into a single matrix $\mathbf{B}$), ABE security reduces to proving pseudorandomness of

$$\mathbf{A}_0, \mathbf{A}, \mathbf{u}^\top, \overbrace{\mathbf{s}(\mathbf{A}_f \mathbf{u}^\top \otimes \mathbf{I}) + \mathbf{s}_0 \mathbf{A}_0}^{\mathbf{c}'}, \left\{ \mathbf{s}((\mathbf{A} - \mathbf{x}_i \otimes \mathbf{G}) \otimes \mathbf{r}_i^\top), \mathbf{s}_0 \mathbf{A}_0 \mathbf{r}_i^\top, \mathbf{r}_i^\top \right\}_{i \in [Q]}$$

Observe that

$$\mathbf{s}_0 \mathbf{A}_0 \mathbf{r}_i^\top \approx \mathbf{c}' \cdot \mathbf{r}_i^\top - \mathbf{s}(\mathbf{A}_f \mathbf{u}^\top \otimes \mathbf{r}_i^\top)$$

We can then use the LWE assumption with secret $\mathbf{s}_0$ to replace $\mathbf{c}'$ with random. This leaves us with proving pseudorandomness of

$$\mathbf{A}_0, \mathbf{A}, \mathbf{u}^\top, \left\{ \mathbf{s}((\mathbf{A} - \mathbf{x}_i \otimes \mathbf{G}) \otimes \mathbf{r}_i^\top), \mathbf{s}(\mathbf{A}_f \mathbf{u}^\top \otimes \mathbf{r}_i^\top), \mathbf{r}_i^\top \right\}_{i \in [Q]}$$

At this point, we can apply homomorphic computation to $\mathbf{s}((\mathbf{A} - \mathbf{x}_i \otimes \mathbf{G}) \otimes \mathbf{r}_i^\top)$ as before in the one-key scheme, upon which we are left with proving pseudo-randomness of

$$\mathbf{A}, \mathbf{u}^\top, \left\{ \mathbf{s}((\mathbf{A} - \mathbf{x}_i \otimes \mathbf{G}) \otimes \mathbf{r}_i^\top), \mathbf{s}(\mathbf{u}^\top \otimes \mathbf{r}_i^\top), \mathbf{r}_i^\top \right\}_{i \in [Q]} \tag{5}$$

The tensor LWE assumption essentially states that the above distribution is pseudorandom.

Third Modification. The third and final modification allows us to handle the second difficulty without introducing the additional tensor LWE assumption but with a 2^d blow-up. The idea is to replace $\mathbf{G}$ in $\mathsf{sk}_\mathbf{x}$ with $\mathbf{I}_m$ and sample $\mathbf{A} \leftarrow \mathcal{D}_{\mathbb{Z},\chi}^{m \times \ell m}$ so that $\mathbf{A} - \mathbf{x} \otimes \mathbf{I}_m$ has low-norm:

$$\mathsf{mpk} := \mathbf{A}_0, \mathbf{B}_0 \leftarrow \mathbb{Z}_q^{n \times m}, \mathbf{B}_1 \leftarrow \mathbb{Z}_q^{m^2 \times O(m^2 \log q)}, \mathbf{A} \leftarrow \mathcal{D}_{\mathbb{Z},\chi}^{m \times \ell m}$$

$$\mathsf{ct}_f := \underline{\mathbf{s}_0 \mathbf{B}_0}, \underline{\mathbf{s}(\mathbf{A}_f \otimes \mathbf{I}_m) + \mathbf{s}_0 \mathbf{A}_0} + \mu \cdot \mathbf{g}, \underline{\mathbf{s} \mathbf{B}_1}, \text{ where } \mathbf{s} \leftarrow \mathbb{Z}_q^{m^2}, \mathbf{s}_0 \leftarrow \mathbb{Z}_q^n$$

$$\mathsf{sk}_\mathbf{x} := \mathbf{B}_0^{-1}(\mathbf{A}_0 \mathbf{r}^\top), \mathbf{B}_1^{-1}((\mathbf{A} - \mathbf{x} \otimes \mathbf{I}) \otimes \mathbf{r}^\top), \mathbf{r}^\top, \text{ where } \mathbf{r} \leftarrow \mathcal{D}_{\mathbb{Z},\chi}^m$$

In the security proof, instead of (5), we need to prove pseudorandomness of

$$\mathbf{A}, \mathbf{u}^\top, \left\{ \mathbf{s}((\mathbf{A} - \mathbf{x}_i \otimes \mathbf{I}_m) \otimes \mathbf{r}_i^\top), \mathbf{s}(\mathbf{u}^\top \otimes \mathbf{r}_i^\top), \mathbf{r}_i^\top \right\}_{i \in [Q]}$$

Both $\mathbf{A} - \mathbf{x}_i \otimes \mathbf{I}_m$ and $\mathbf{u}^\top$ have low-norm, so

$$\mathbf{s}((\mathbf{A} - \mathbf{x}_i \otimes \mathbf{I}_m) \otimes \mathbf{r}_i^\top) \approx \mathbf{s}(\mathbf{I} \otimes \mathbf{r}_i^\top) \cdot (\mathbf{A} - \mathbf{x}_i \otimes \mathbf{I})$$

$$\mathbf{s}(\mathbf{u}^\top \otimes \mathbf{r}_i^\top) \approx \mathbf{s}(\mathbf{I} \otimes \mathbf{r}_i^\top) \cdot \mathbf{u}^\top$$

We may then invoke (1) to replace $\underline{\mathbf{s}(\mathbf{I} \otimes \mathbf{r}_i^\top)}$ with $\mathbf{s}_i \leftarrow \mathbb{Z}_q^m$, upon which it suffices to prove pseudorandomness of

$$\mathbf{A}, \mathbf{u}^\top, \left\{ \mathbf{s}_i(\mathbf{A} - \mathbf{x}_i \otimes \mathbf{I}_m), \mathbf{s}_i \mathbf{u}^\top \right\}_{i \in [Q]}$$

This in turn follows from LWE via a straight-forward hybrid argument over $i \in [Q]$.

2.2   On Evasive Lattice Assumptions

In the past decade, we have witnessed a large number of "lattice-inspired" schemes, on which weaknesses and attacks were subsequently discovered. A partial list includes:

- multi-linear maps and key exchange [28,32] and attacks in [24,25]
- obfuscation for branching programs [29,32,35] and attacks in [23]
- noisy inner product functional encryption [1] with attacks and fixes [4]
- obfuscation from circular security [18,19,31,44] with attacks on [31,44] in [36]

In fact, our evasive LWE assumption shares some structural similarities to the GGH15-based multi-linear maps [32] corresponding to the first two items on the list above. There is however a key conceptual distinction which we briefly alluded to earlier and shall expand on next.

The Zeroizing Regime. All of the afore-mentioned attacks have one thing in common: they pertain to the *zeroizing regime* where an attacker can easily obtain sufficiently many equations in low-norm secret values—low-norm LWE secrets, error vectors, or both—over the integers that information-theoretically determine these secret values.[3] These equations arise naturally from the interaction of the correctness constraints and the security requirements. Such attacks are referred to in the literature as *zeroizing attacks*. Prior zeroizing attacks basically proceed in two steps: (i) collect many of these equations, and (ii) using these equations to recover some secret value and break security. The first step is typically fairly straight-forward; most of the technical and creative work lies in the second step, which varies from computing a linear-algebraic quantity (e.g., kernel [24] or rank [4,23]) of a carefully crafted matrix over the integers/reals, to more sophisticated sum-of-squares attacks [8,39].

Our evasive LWE assumption falls outside of this zeroizing regime in that we do not see any straight-forward way to collect even a single equation of the underlying LWE error vectors over the integers. As explained earlier in the introduction, the straight-forward adaptation of prior attacks would be to compute $\mathbf{c}^* = (\mathbf{sB} + \mathbf{e}_0) \cdot \mathbf{B}^{-1}(\mathbf{P}) \approx \mathbf{sP}$, but the pre-condition for evasive LWE implies that $\mathbf{c}^*$ has large norm and does not yield an equation over the integers. The setting for our assumption is closer to that for prior witness encryption candidates, specifically, the GGH15-based witness encryption candidate in [23], which also fall outside the zeroizing regime. Indeed, there are no known attacks on any witness encryption candidates in the literature, giving us additional confidence in our evasive LWE assumption. For the crypt-analysts who believe that existing witness encryption candidates are broken but haven't found an attack, our evasive LWE assumption provides a much simpler target for crypt-analysis.

---

[3] As a point of comparison, we have examples such as k-LWE [38] and inner product functional encryption [3] based on LWE where it is easy to obtain a few such equations, but the equations do *not* information-theoretically determine the secret values.

Perspective. To the best of our knowledge, our evasive LWE assumption is the first simple lattice assumption that falls outside of the zeroizing regime. We firmly believe that the study of such *evasive* lattice assumptions —hardness, attacks, and constructions— constitutes an important and promising research direction, as well as a rich source of open problems. More broadly, non-standard variants of LWE and evasive lattice assumptions are conceptually similar to q-type assumptions, knowledge assumptions, and generic/algebraic group model assumptions that have played an essential role in our study of group and pairing-based cryptography.[4] This analogy provides additional impetus for the study of evasive lattice assumptions.

Looking Ahead. Looking ahead, we see 4 possible scenarios, starting with the most optimistic:

1. This work ultimately leads to optimal broadcast encryption based on LWE, as has been the case for several lattice-based schemes where the initial candidates were based on non-standard assumptions (outside the zeroizing regime), such as fully homomorphic encryption and its multi-key variant and the Fiat-Shamir heuristic.
2. The evasive LWE assumption surives cryptanalysis: this could enable other advanced encryption primitives. Indeed, in a follow-up work with Vaikuntanathan and Wichs [42], we prove that the GGH15-based witness encryption scheme in [23] is secure under a variant of evasive LWE.
3. The evasive LWE assumption is broken but the broadcast encryption scheme is not. This would require new and valuable crypt-analytic advances beyond the state-of-the-art zeroizing attacks. The current statement of evasive LWE is fairly general, and an attack could guide us towards identify more secure variants of the assumption that would suffice for our broadcast encryption scheme.
4. Both the evasive LWE assumption and the broadcast encryption are broken. Could these new attacks be extended to current GGH15-based witness encryption candidates?

We believe any of these scenarios would advance our current scientific understanding of lattice-based cryptography and assumptions (hardness and/or attacks).

2.3   Additional Related Work

We describe additional related work.

---

[4] Security based on evasive LWE can be viewed as ruling out restricted adversaries that replaces $\mathbf{sB} + \mathbf{e}, \mathbf{B}^{-1}(\mathbf{P})$ with their product $\mathbf{sP} + \mathbf{e}''$ (with fresh noise) and ignoring $\mathbf{B}^{-1}(\mathbf{P})$ thereafter. Viewed this way, evasive LWE can be seen as a partial analogue of the generic/algebraic group model used in group and pairing-based cryptography. Several works studied analogues of the generic group model for multi-linear maps [9,30], but they were in the zeroizing regime.

Relation to GGH15 Multi-linear Maps. Our work draws upon several insights in the study of GGH15 multi-linear maps [21,32]. First, randomization via tensors and the statement in (1) both appeared in [21], but in a different context. Second, the intuition for evasive LWE in terms of an "optimal" distinguishing strategy also underlies earlier GGH15-based schemes, with the crucial distinction that evasive LWE falls outside the zeroizing regime. Our evasive LWE assumption also provides a concise statement of this intuition in a setting that falls outside the zeroizing regime.

Obfuscation-Based Broadcast. We can obtain optimal broadcast encryption schemes by combining the obfuscation-based scheme in [17] with the state-of-the-art obfuscaton schemes/candidates. The ensuing schemes would be extremely complex and impractical, inherited from the current obfuscation schemes/candidates, compounded with the use of non-black-box techniques. Nonetheless, there is value in understanding the ensuing schemes from the perspective of assumptions. In particular, if we rely on the Jain-Lin-Sahai obfuscation scheme [37], we would require both bilinear groups and LWE similar to the AYW schemes, and would not achieve post-quantum security. If we turn to the post-quantum obfuscation candidates, e.g. [4,19,23,31,44], then we would require hardness or assumptions in the zeroizing regime.

CP-ABE from LWE. The state of the art for CP-ABE from LWE is that of Agrawal and Yamada [6] supporting circuits of depth d and size s over $\{0,1\}^\ell$ with $|\mathsf{ct}| = \mathsf{poly}(d,s)$ and key generation running in time $\mathsf{poly}(\ell, d, \log s)$; this improves upon the "trivial" CP-ABE from LWE based on the KP-ABE for circuits from LWE in [12], where key generation runs in time $\mathsf{poly}(d,s)$. Both of these schemes achieve $|\mathsf{sk}| = \mathsf{poly}(d, \log s)$. We note that the recent CP-ABE for NC1 from LWE in [26] achieves $|\mathsf{ct}|, |\mathsf{sk}| = \mathsf{poly}(s)$. In contrast, the CP-ABE schemes described in Fig. 1 achieve $|\mathsf{ct}| = \mathsf{poly}(\ell, d, \log s)$ or $|\mathsf{ct}| = \mathsf{poly}(\ell, 2^d, \log s)$ (i.e., almost independent of circuit size s).

3   Preliminaries

Notations. We use boldface lower case for row vectors (e.g. $\mathbf{v}$) and boldface upper case for matrices (e.g. $\mathbf{V}$). For integral vectors and matrices (i.e., those over $\mathbb{Z}$), we use the notation $|\mathbf{v}|, |\mathbf{V}|$ to denote the maximum absolute value over all the entries. We use $v \leftarrow \mathcal{D}$ to denote a random sample from a distribution $\mathcal{D}$, as well as $v \leftarrow S$ to denote a uniformly random sample from a set S. We use $\approx_s$ and $\approx_c$ as the abbreviation for statistically close and computationally indistinguishable.

Tensor Product. The tensor product (Kronecker product) for matrices $\mathbf{A} = (a_{i,j}) \in \mathbb{Z}^{\ell \times m}$, $\mathbf{B} \in \mathbb{Z}^{n \times p}$ is defined as

$$\mathbf{A} \otimes \mathbf{B} = \begin{bmatrix} a_{1,1}\mathbf{B}, \ldots, a_{1,m}\mathbf{B} \\ \ldots, \ \ldots, \ \ldots \\ a_{\ell,1}\mathbf{B}, \ldots, a_{\ell,m}\mathbf{B} \end{bmatrix} \in \mathbb{Z}^{\ell n \times mp}.$$

The mixed-product property for tensor product says that

$$(\mathbf{A} \otimes \mathbf{B})(\mathbf{C} \otimes \mathbf{D}) = (\mathbf{AC}) \otimes (\mathbf{BD})$$

A useful corollary of the mixed-product property says that for any pair of row vectors $\mathbf{u}, \mathbf{v} \in \mathbb{Z}^n$,

$$\mathbf{u} \otimes \mathbf{v} = (\mathbf{u} \otimes 1)(\mathbf{I}_n \otimes \mathbf{v}) = (1 \otimes \mathbf{v})(\mathbf{u} \otimes \mathbf{I}_n)$$
$$= \mathbf{u}(\mathbf{I}_n \otimes \mathbf{v}) = \mathbf{v}(\mathbf{u} \otimes \mathbf{I}_n)$$

We adopt the convention that matrix multiplication takes precedence over tensor product, so that we can write $\mathbf{A} \otimes \mathbf{BC}$ to mean $\mathbf{A} \otimes (\mathbf{BC})$.

3.1 Lattices Background

We use $\mathcal{D}_{\mathbb{Z},\chi}$ to denote the discrete Gaussian distribution over $\mathbb{Z}$ with standard deviation χ.

Learning with Errors (LWE). Given $n, m, q, \chi \in \mathbb{N}$, the $\mathsf{LWE}_{n,m,q,\chi}$ assumption states that

$$(\mathbf{A}, \mathbf{sA} + \mathbf{e}) \approx_c (\mathbf{A}, \mathbf{c})$$

where

$$\mathbf{A} \leftarrow \mathbb{Z}_q^{n \times m}, \mathbf{s} \leftarrow \mathbb{Z}_q^n, \mathbf{e} \leftarrow \mathcal{D}_{\mathbb{Z}^m,\chi}, \mathbf{c} \leftarrow \mathbb{Z}_q^m$$

Trapdoor and Preimage Sampling. Given any $\mathbf{Z} \in \mathbb{Z}_q^{n \times n'}$, $\sigma > 0$, we use $\mathbf{B}^{-1}(\mathbf{Z}, \sigma)$ to denote the distribution of a matrix $\mathbf{Y}$ sampled from $\mathcal{D}_{\mathbb{Z}^{m \times n'},\sigma}$ conditioned on $\mathbf{BY} = \mathbf{Z} \pmod{q}$. We sometimes suppress σ when the context is clear.

There is a p.p.t. algorithm $\mathsf{TrapGen}(1^n, q)$ that, given the modulus $q \geq 2$ and dimension n, outputs $\mathbf{B} \approx_s U(\mathbb{Z}_q^{n \times 2n \log q})$ with a trapdoor τ. Moreover, there is a p.p.t. algorithm that given $(\mathbf{B}, \tau) \leftarrow \mathsf{TrapGen}(1^n, q)$, $\mathbf{Z} \in \mathbb{Z}_q^{n \times n'}$, and $\sigma \geq 2\sqrt{n \log q}$, outputs a sample from $\mathbf{B}^{-1}(\mathbf{Z}, \sigma)$.

3.2 Attribute-Based Encryption

Syntax. A ciphertext-policy attribute-based encryption (CP-ABE) scheme for some class $\mathcal{F}$ consists of four algorithms:

Setup$(1^\lambda, \mathcal{F}) \rightarrow$ (mpk, msk). The setup algorithm gets as input the security parameter 1^λ and class description $\mathcal{F}$. It outputs the master public key mpk and the master secret key msk.

Enc(mpk, $f, \mu) \rightarrow \mathsf{ct}_f$. The encryption algorithm gets as input mpk, $f \in \mathcal{F}$ and a message $\mu \in \{0, 1\}$. It outputs a ciphertext ct_f.

KeyGen(mpk, msk, $x) \rightarrow \mathsf{sk}_x$. The key generation algorithm gets as input mpk, msk and $x \in \{0, 1\}^\ell$. It outputs a secret key sk_x.

Dec(mpk, $\mathsf{sk}_x, \mathsf{ct}_f) \rightarrow m$. The decryption algorithm gets as input sk_x and ct_f such that $f(x) = 0$ along with mpk. It outputs a message μ.

Correctness. For all inputs x and f with $f(x) = 0$ and all $\mu \in \{0, 1\}$, we require

$$\Pr\left[\mathsf{Dec}(\mathsf{mpk}, \mathsf{sk}_x, \mathsf{ct}_f) = \mu : \begin{array}{l} (\mathsf{mpk}, \mathsf{msk}) \leftarrow \mathsf{Setup}(1^\lambda, \mathcal{F}) \\ \mathsf{sk}_x \leftarrow \mathsf{KeyGen}(\mathsf{mpk}, \mathsf{msk}, x) \\ \mathsf{ct}_f \leftarrow \mathsf{Enc}(\mathsf{mpk}, f, \mu) \end{array} \right] = 1 - \mathrm{negl}(\lambda).$$

Security Definition. For a stateful adversary $\mathcal{A}$, we define the advantage function

$$\mathsf{Adv}^{\mathrm{ABE}}_{\mathcal{A}}(\lambda) := \Pr\left[b = b' : \begin{array}{l} f \leftarrow \mathcal{A}(1^\lambda) \\ (\mathsf{mpk}, \mathsf{msk}) \leftarrow \mathsf{Setup}(1^\lambda, \mathcal{F}) \\ (\mu_0, \mu_1) \leftarrow \mathcal{A}^{\mathsf{KeyGen}(\mathsf{mpk},\mathsf{msk},\cdot)}(\mathsf{mpk}) \\ b \leftarrow \{0, 1\}; \ \mathsf{ct}_f \leftarrow \mathsf{Enc}(\mathsf{mpk}, f, \mu_b) \\ b' \leftarrow \mathcal{A}^{\mathsf{KeyGen}(\mathsf{mpk},\mathsf{msk},\cdot)}(\mathsf{ct}_f) \end{array} \right] - \frac{1}{2}$$

with the restriction that all queries x that $\mathcal{A}$ sent to KeyGen(mpk, msk, $\cdot$) satisfy $f(x) = 0$. An ABE scheme is *selectively secure* if for all PPT adversaries $\mathcal{A}$, the advantage $\mathsf{Adv}^{\mathrm{ABE}}_{\mathcal{A}}(\lambda)$ is a negligible function in λ. Similarly, say that an ABE scheme is *very selectively secure* for the advantage function:

$$\mathsf{Adv}^{\mathrm{ABE}}_{\mathcal{A}}(\lambda) := \Pr\left[b = b' : \begin{array}{l} (f, x_1, \ldots, x_Q) \leftarrow \mathcal{A}(1^\lambda) \\ (\mathsf{mpk}, \mathsf{msk}) \leftarrow \mathsf{Setup}(1^\lambda, \mathcal{F}) \\ \mathsf{sk}_i \leftarrow \mathsf{KeyGen}(\mathsf{mpk}, \mathsf{msk}, x_i), i = 1, \ldots, Q \\ (\mu_0, \mu_1) \leftarrow \mathcal{A}(\mathsf{mpk}, \mathsf{sk}_1, \ldots, \mathsf{sk}_Q) \\ b \leftarrow \{0, 1\}; \ \mathsf{ct}_f \leftarrow \mathsf{Enc}(\mathsf{mpk}, f, \mu_b) \\ b' \leftarrow \mathcal{A}(\mathsf{ct}_f) \end{array} \right] - \frac{1}{2}$$

Broadcast Encryption. Here,

$$\mathcal{X} = \{0, 1\}^N, \mathcal{Y} = [N]$$

where we think of $\{0,1\}^N$ as the power set of $[N]$ (i.e., set of all subsets of $[N]$), and

$$P(S, y) = 1 \iff y \in S$$

As noted in [5,7], very selective security for broadcast encryption implies selective security since an adversary can simply ask for all keys outside S.

4 Evasive LWE

We proceed to provide a formal statement of our evasive LWE assumption, stated informally in Sect. 1.

Evasive LWE. Let Samp be a PPT algorithm that on input 1^λ, outputs

$$\mathbf{A}' \in \mathbb{Z}_q^{n \times m'}, \mathbf{P} \in \mathbb{Z}_q^{n \times t}, \mathsf{aux} \in \{0,1\}^*$$

We define the following advantage functions:

$$\begin{aligned}
\mathsf{Adv}_{\mathcal{A}_0}^{\mathrm{PRE}}(\lambda) := \Pr[\mathcal{A}_0(\boxed{\mathbf{sA}' + \mathbf{e}'}, \boxed{\mathbf{sB} + \mathbf{e}}, \boxed{\mathbf{sP} + \mathbf{e}''}, \mathbf{A}', \mathbf{B}, \mathsf{aux}) = 1] \\
- \Pr[\mathcal{A}_0(\boxed{\mathbf{c}}, \boxed{\mathbf{c}_0}, \boxed{\mathbf{c}'}, \mathbf{A}', \mathbf{B}, \mathsf{aux}) = 1],
\end{aligned} \tag{6}$$

$$\begin{aligned}
\mathsf{Adv}_{\mathcal{A}_1}^{\mathrm{POST}}(\lambda) := \Pr[\mathcal{A}_1(\boxed{\mathbf{sA}' + \mathbf{e}'}, \boxed{\mathbf{sB} + \mathbf{e}}, \mathbf{K}, \mathbf{A}', \mathbf{B}, \mathsf{aux}) = 1] \\
- \Pr[\mathcal{A}_1(\boxed{\mathbf{c}}, \boxed{\mathbf{c}_0}, \mathbf{K}, \mathbf{A}', \mathbf{B}, \mathsf{aux}) = 1]
\end{aligned} \tag{7}$$

where

$$\begin{aligned}
&(\mathbf{A}', \mathbf{P}, \mathsf{aux}) \leftarrow \mathsf{Samp}(1^\lambda) \\
&\mathbf{B} \leftarrow \mathbb{Z}_q^{n \times m}, \mathbf{s} \leftarrow \mathbb{Z}_q^n, \\
&\mathbf{c} \leftarrow \mathbb{Z}_q^{m'}, \mathbf{c}_0 \leftarrow \mathbb{Z}_q^m, \mathbf{c}' \leftarrow \mathbb{Z}_q^t, \\
&\mathbf{e} \leftarrow \mathcal{D}_{\mathbb{Z},\chi}^m, \mathbf{e}' \leftarrow \mathcal{D}_{\mathbb{Z},\chi}^{m'}, \mathbf{e}'' \leftarrow \mathcal{D}_{\mathbb{Z},\chi}^t \\
&\mathbf{K} \leftarrow \mathbf{B}^{-1}(\mathbf{P}) \text{ with standard deviation } O(\sqrt{m \log q})
\end{aligned}$$

We say that the *evasive LWE* assumption holds if for every PPT Samp, $\mathcal{A}_1$, there exists another PPT $\mathcal{A}_0$ and a polynomial $Q(\cdot)$ such that

$$\mathsf{Adv}_{\mathcal{A}_0}^{\mathrm{PRE}}(\lambda) \geq \mathsf{Adv}_{\mathcal{A}_1}^{\mathrm{POST}}(\lambda)/Q(\lambda) - \mathsf{negl}(\lambda)$$

We consider parameter settings for which $\mathsf{LWE}_{n,q,\chi}$ holds.

Remark 1 (restricted samplers). As in [5], we only require that the assumption holds for samplers where aux additionally contains all of the coin tosses used by Samp. This avoids obfuscation-based counter-examples where aux contains an obfuscation of a program related to a trapdoor for matrix $\mathbf{P}$.

Remark 2 (noise magnitudes). For simplicity, we stated the assumption with all the LWE error terms $\mathbf{e}, \mathbf{e}', \mathbf{e}''$ having the same Gaussian parameter χ. It is straight-forward to adapt the assumption and the scheme to a quantitatively weaker variant where the error terms in the post-condition (7) have a larger Gaussian parameter than those in the pre-condition.

Remark 3 (weaker pseudorandomness). For the security of our scheme, it suffices to consider a weaker variant of the assumption where only $\mathbf{s}\mathbf{A}' + \mathbf{e}'$ is required to be pseudorandom in the post-condition.

We refer to Sect. 6 for further discussion on the assumption.

5   Main Constructions

In this section, we present our main constructions:

- a CP-ABE scheme for NC^1 achieving $|\mathsf{ct}| = \mathsf{poly}(2^d, \log s, \lambda)$;
- an "optimal" broadcast encryption scheme for N users with $|\mathsf{mpk}| + |\mathsf{ct}| + |\mathsf{sk}| = \mathsf{poly}(\log N, \lambda)$;
- a CP-ABE scheme for circuits achieving $|\mathsf{ct}| = \mathsf{poly}(d, \log s, \lambda)$;

The first scheme serves as the basis for the second and the third scheme. The first two schemes rely on evasive LWE whereas the third requires an additional "tensor LWE" assumption. We prove very selective security for all three schemes, which implies selective security for broadcast encryption.

5.1   Homomorphic Computation on Matrices

We recall basic homorphic computation on matrices used in prior LWE-based ABE [12].

Lemma 1 (EvalF$_\mathbf{G}$, EvalFX$_\mathbf{G}$). *Fix parameters n, q, ℓ and $m = O(n \log q)$. Given a matrix $\mathbf{A} \in \mathbb{Z}_q^{n \times \ell m}$ and a circuit $f : \{0,1\}^\ell \to \{0,1\}$ of depth d and size s, we can efficiently compute a matrix $\mathbf{A}_f \in \mathbb{Z}_q^{n \times m}$ such that for all $\mathbf{x} \in \{0,1\}^\ell$, there exists a matrix $\mathbf{H}_{\mathbf{A},f,\mathbf{x}} \in \mathbb{Z}^{\ell m \times m}$ with $|\mathbf{H}_{\mathbf{A},f,\mathbf{x}}| = m^{O(d)} \cdot s$ such that*

$$(\mathbf{A} - \mathbf{x} \otimes \mathbf{G}) \cdot \mathbf{H}_{\mathbf{A},f,\mathbf{x}} = \mathbf{A}_f - f(\mathbf{x})\mathbf{G} \tag{8}$$

where $\mathbf{G} \in \mathbb{Z}_q^{n \times m}$ is the gadget matrix. Moreover, $\mathbf{H}_{\mathbf{A},f,\mathbf{x}}$ is efficiently computable given $\mathbf{A}, f, \mathbf{x}$. We use EvalF$_\mathbf{G}(\mathbf{A}, f)$, EvalFX$_\mathbf{G}(\mathbf{A}, f, \mathbf{x})$ to denote the algorithms computing $\mathbf{A}_f, \mathbf{H}_{\mathbf{A},f,\mathbf{x}}$ respectively.

Low-Norm Variant. We also consider a variant where $\mathbf{A}$ has low-norm and we replace $\mathbf{G}$ with $\mathbf{I}$: when deriving $\mathbf{A}_f$, addition gates correspond to matrix addition and multiplication gates correspond to matrix multiplication.[5] The magnitude of the noise squares with each multiplication gate, leading to noise growth that is doubly exponential in d.

Lemma 2 (EvalF, EvalFX). *Fix parameters m, ℓ. Given a matrix $\mathbf{A} \in \mathbb{Z}^{m \times \ell m}$ and a circuit $f : \{0,1\}^\ell \to \{0,1\}$ of depth d and size s, we can efficiently compute a matrix $\mathbf{A}_f \in \mathbb{Z}^{m \times m}$ such that $|\mathbf{A}_f| = (|\mathbf{A}|m)^{O(2^d)} \cdot s$ and for all $\mathbf{x} \in \{0,1\}^\ell$, there exists a matrix $\mathbf{H}_{\mathbf{A},f,\mathbf{x}} \in \mathbb{Z}^{\ell m \times m}$ with $|\mathbf{H}_{\mathbf{A},f,\mathbf{x}}| = (|\mathbf{A}|m)^{O(2^d)} \cdot s$ such that*

$$(\mathbf{A} - \mathbf{x} \otimes \mathbf{I}_m) \cdot \mathbf{H}_{\mathbf{A},f,\mathbf{x}} = \mathbf{A}_f - f(\mathbf{x})\mathbf{I}_m \tag{9}$$

Moreover, $\mathbf{H}_{\mathbf{A},f,\mathbf{x}}$ is efficiently computable given $\mathbf{A}, f, \mathbf{x}$. We use $\mathsf{EvalF}(\mathbf{A}, f)$, $\mathsf{EvalFX}(\mathbf{A}, f, \mathbf{x})$ to denote the algorithms computing $\mathbf{A}_f, \mathbf{H}_{\mathbf{A},f,\mathbf{x}}$ respectively.

5.2 CP-ABE for NC^1 Circuits

We present our CP-ABE scheme for NC^1 circuits.

- $\mathsf{Setup}(1^n, 1^\ell)$: Sample

$$(\mathbf{B}, \tau) \leftarrow \mathsf{TrapGen}(1^{n+m^2}, q), \quad \mathbf{A}_0 \leftarrow \mathbb{Z}_q^{n \times m}, \quad \mathbf{A} \leftarrow \mathcal{D}_{\mathbb{Z}, \chi''}^{m \times \ell m}, \quad \mathbf{u} \leftarrow \mathcal{D}_{\mathbb{Z}, \chi''}^m$$

Output

$$\mathsf{mpk} := (\mathbf{B}, \mathbf{A}_0, \mathbf{A}, \mathbf{u}^\top), \quad \mathsf{msk} := \tau$$

- $\mathsf{Enc}(\mathsf{mpk}, f, \mu \in \{0,1\})$. Compute $\mathbf{A}_f = \mathsf{EvalF}(\mathbf{A}, f)$. Sample

$$\mathbf{s}_0 \leftarrow \mathbb{Z}_q^n, \mathbf{s}_1 \leftarrow \mathbb{Z}_q^{m^2}, \quad \mathbf{e} \leftarrow \mathcal{D}_{\mathbb{Z}, \chi}^m, \mathbf{e}_0 \leftarrow \mathcal{D}_{\mathbb{Z}, \chi}^{O((n+m^2) \log q)},$$

Output

$$\mathsf{ct}_f := \Big(\overbrace{(\mathbf{s}_0 \mid \mathbf{s}_1)\mathbf{B} + \mathbf{e}_0}^{\mathbf{c}_0}, \overbrace{\mathbf{s}_0 \mathbf{A}_0 + \mathbf{s}_1(\mathbf{A}_f \mathbf{u}^\top \otimes \mathbf{I}_m) + \mu \cdot \mathbf{g} + \mathbf{e}}^{\mathbf{c}} \Big)$$

- $\mathsf{KeyGen}(\mathsf{msk}, \mathbf{x})$: Sample

$$\mathbf{r} \leftarrow \mathcal{D}_{\mathbb{Z}, \chi''}^m, \quad \mathbf{K} \leftarrow \mathbf{B}^{-1} \begin{pmatrix} \mathbf{A}_0 \mathbf{r}^\top \\ & \mathbf{A} - \mathbf{x} \otimes \mathbf{I}_m) \otimes \mathbf{r}^\top \end{pmatrix},$$

using τ with standard deviation $O(\sqrt{(n + m^2) \log q})$. Output

$$\mathsf{sk}_\mathbf{x} := (\mathbf{K}, \mathbf{r}^\top)$$

- $\mathsf{Dec}(\mathsf{sk}, \mathbf{x}, \mathsf{ct}, f)$: Compute $\mathbf{H}_{\mathbf{A},f,\mathbf{x}} = \mathsf{EvalFX}(\mathbf{A}, f, \mathbf{x})$. Output

$$\mathsf{round}_{\beta_0} \Big(\mathbf{c} \cdot \mathbf{r}^\top - \mathbf{c}_0 \cdot \mathbf{K} \cdot \begin{pmatrix} 1 \\ \mathbf{K}_1 \cdot \mathbf{H}_{\mathbf{A},f,\mathbf{x}} \mathbf{u}^\top \end{pmatrix} \Big)$$

where $\mathsf{round}_{\beta_0}(x)$ outputs 0 if $|x| < \beta_0$ and 1 otherwise.

---

[5] That is, $x_i + x_j$ corresponds to $\mathbf{A}_i + \mathbf{A}_j$ and $x_i \cdot x_j$ corresponds to $\mathbf{A}_i \cdot \mathbf{A}_j$ instead of $\mathbf{A}_i \cdot \mathbf{G}^{-1}(\mathbf{A}_j)$. More generally, we can represent a circuit f of depth d and size s as a polynomial comprising the sum of s monomials, each of total degree at most 2^d. Then, $\mathbf{A}_f = f(\mathbf{A}_1, \ldots, \mathbf{A}_\ell)$.

	c'	$c'_{1,i}$	$c'_{0,i}$
H_0	$s_0 A_0 + s_1(A_f u^\top \otimes I_m)$	$s_1((A - x_i \otimes I_m) \otimes r_i^\top)$	$s_0 A_0 r_i^\top$
H_1	↓	↓	$c' \cdot r_i^\top - c'_1 \cdot H_{A,f,x_i} u^\top - s_1(u^\top \otimes r_i^\top)$
H_2	$c' \leftarrow \mathbb{Z}_q^m$	↓	↓
H_3	↓	$(s_1(I_m \otimes r_i^\top) + e'_i) \cdot (A - x_i \otimes I_m)$	$c' \cdot r_i^\top - c'_1 \cdot H_{A,f,x_i} u^\top - (s_1(I_m \otimes r_i^\top) + e'_i) \cdot u$
H_4	↓	$s_i (A - x_i \otimes I_m)$	$c' \cdot r_i^\top - c'_1 \cdot H_{A,f,x_i} u^\top - s_i u^\top$
H_5	↓	$c'_{1,i} \leftarrow \mathbb{Z}_q^{\ell m}$	$c'_{0,i} \leftarrow \mathbb{Z}_q$

Fig. 2. Summary of the hybrid sequence, with $H_0 \approx_s H_1 \approx_c H_2 \approx_s H_3 \approx_c H_4 \approx_c H_5$. We suppress the additive noise terms in $c', c'_{1,i}, c'_{0,i}$; ↓ denotes same as previous hybrid; we sample $e'_i \leftarrow \mathcal{D}^m_{\mathbb{Z},\chi''}$ in H_3 and $s_i \leftarrow \mathbb{Z}_q^m$ in H_4.

Parameters. Suppose $|H_{A,f,x}|$ is bounded by β. We set

$$n = \mathsf{poly}(\lambda, \log \beta), \quad m = O(n \log q), \quad \chi'', \chi' = \lambda^{\omega(1)}, \quad \chi = \beta \cdot \lambda^{\omega(1)}, \quad \beta = (\chi'' m)^{O(2^d)} \cdot s$$
$$\beta_0 = \chi^2 \cdot \chi'' \cdot \beta \cdot \mathsf{poly}(m), \quad q = \beta_0 \cdot \lambda^{\omega(1)}$$

In particular, this means

$$|\mathsf{mpk}| = \ell \cdot \mathsf{poly}(2^d, s, \lambda), \quad |\mathsf{ct}| = \mathsf{poly}(2^d, s, \lambda), \quad |\mathsf{sk}| = \ell \cdot \mathsf{poly}(2^d, s, \lambda)$$

Correctness. Fix x, f such that $f(x) = 0$. First, we have

$$c_0 \cdot K \cdot \begin{pmatrix} 1 \\ H_{A,f,x} u^\top \end{pmatrix} \approx (s_0 \mid s_1) B \cdot B^{-1} \begin{pmatrix} A_0 r^\top & \\ & (A - x \otimes I_m) \otimes r^\top \end{pmatrix} \cdot \begin{pmatrix} 1 \\ H_{A,f,x} u^\top \end{pmatrix}$$
$$= s_0 A_0 r^\top + s_1((A - x \otimes I_m) \otimes r^\top) \cdot (H_{A,f,x} u^\top \otimes 1)$$
$$= s_0 A_0 r^\top + s_1((A - x \otimes I_m) \cdot H_{A,f,x} u^\top \otimes I_m) \cdot (1 \otimes r^\top)$$
$$= s_0 A_0 r^\top + s_1(A_f u^\top \otimes I_m) \cdot r^\top$$

where the final equality uses $(A - x \otimes I_m) \cdot H_{A,f,x} = A_f$. This means

$$c \cdot r^\top - c_0 \cdot K \cdot \begin{pmatrix} 1 \\ H_{A,f,x} u^\top \end{pmatrix}$$
$$\approx (s_0 A_0 + s_1(A_f u^\top \otimes I_m) + \mu \cdot g) \cdot r^\top - s_0 A_0 r^\top - s_1(A_f u^\top \otimes I_m) \cdot r^\top$$
$$= \mu \cdot g \cdot r^\top$$

In particular, the error term is bounded by

$$|e \cdot r^\top| + |e_0 \cdot K \cdot \begin{pmatrix} 1 \\ H_{A,f,x} u^\top \end{pmatrix}| \leq \chi^2 \cdot \chi'' \cdot \beta \cdot \mathsf{poly}(m) \leq \beta_0$$

Now, $g \cdot r^\top$ is statistically close to uniform over $\mathbb{Z}_q$, and correctness follows as long as $q \geq \beta_0 \cdot \lambda^{\omega(1)}$.

Security. Suppose the (very selective) ABE adversary $\mathcal{A}$ with randomness $\mathrm{coins}_\mathcal{A}$ queries f and $\mathbf{x}_1, \ldots, \mathbf{x}_Q$ such that $f(\mathbf{x}_1) = \cdots = f(\mathbf{x}_Q) = 1$. We invoke our evasive LWE hardness assumption with the following sampler Samp:

$$\mathsf{aux} = (\overbrace{\mathbf{x}_1, \ldots, \mathbf{x}_Q, f, \mathrm{coins}_\mathcal{A}, \mathbf{r}_1^\top, \ldots, \mathbf{r}_Q^\top, \mathbf{A}_0, \mathbf{A}, \mathbf{u}^\top}^{\mathsf{aux}_0})$$
$$\mathbf{P}_0 = \mathbf{A}_0[\mathbf{r}_1^\top \mid \cdots \mid \mathbf{r}_Q^\top]$$
$$\mathbf{P}_1 = [(\mathbf{A} - \mathbf{x}_1 \otimes \mathbf{I}_m) \otimes \mathbf{r}_1^\top \mid \cdots \mid (\mathbf{A} - \mathbf{x}_Q \otimes \mathbf{I}_m) \otimes \mathbf{r}_Q^\top]$$
$$\mathbf{P} = \begin{pmatrix} \mathbf{P}_0 \\ & \mathbf{P}_1 \end{pmatrix}$$
$$\mathbf{A}' = [\mathbf{A}_0 \mid \mathbf{A}_f \mathbf{u}^\top \otimes \mathbf{I}_m]$$

where $\mathbf{r}_1^\top, \ldots, \mathbf{r}_Q^\top, \mathbf{A}_0, \mathbf{A}, \mathbf{u}^\top$ are sampled as in our CP-ABE scheme. Note that Samp satisfies the restriction in Remark 1. At this point, it suffices to show pseudorandomness of

$$\mathsf{aux}_0, \mathbf{A}_0, \mathbf{A}, \mathbf{u}^\top, \mathbf{B}, \mathbf{s}_0\mathbf{A}_0 + \mathbf{s}_1\mathbf{A}_1 + \mathbf{e}', (\mathbf{s}_0 \mid \mathbf{s}_1)\mathbf{B} + \mathbf{e}_0, \mathbf{s}_0\mathbf{P}_0 + \mathbf{e}_0', \mathbf{s}_1\mathbf{P}_1 + \mathbf{e}_1', \{\mathbf{r}_i^\top\}_{i \in [Q]} \quad (10)$$

where $\mathbf{A}_0, \mathbf{u}^\top, \mathbf{s}_0, \mathbf{s}_1, \mathbf{r}_i^\top$ are also sampled as in the CP-ABE scheme and $\mathbf{e}' \leftarrow \mathcal{D}_{\mathbb{Z},\chi''}^m, \mathbf{e}_{1,i}' \leftarrow \mathcal{D}_{\mathbb{Z},\chi'}^{\ell m}, \mathbf{e}_{0,i}' \leftarrow \mathcal{D}_{\mathbb{Z},\chi}$. Combined with our hardness assumption, the latter would imply:

$$\overbrace{\mathbf{A}_0, \mathbf{A}, \mathbf{u}^\top, \mathbf{B}}^{\mathsf{mpk}}, \overbrace{(\mathbf{s}_0 \mid \mathbf{s}_1)\mathbf{B} + \mathbf{e}_0, \boxed{\mathbf{s}_0\mathbf{A}_0 + \mathbf{s}_1(\mathbf{A}_f\mathbf{u}^\top \otimes \mathbf{I}_m) + \mathbf{e}}}^{\mathsf{ct}} + \mu \cdot \mathbf{g},$$
$$\underbrace{\{\mathbf{B}^{-1}\begin{pmatrix} \mathbf{A}_0\mathbf{r}_i^\top \\ (\mathbf{A} - \mathbf{x}_i \otimes \mathbf{I}_m) \otimes \mathbf{r}_i^\top \end{pmatrix}, \mathbf{r}_i^\top)\}_{i \in [Q]}}_{\mathsf{sk}_i}$$
$$\approx_c \mathbf{A}_0, \mathbf{A}, \mathbf{u}^\top, \mathbf{B}, \mathbf{c}_0, \mathbf{c} + \mu \cdot \mathbf{g},$$
$$\{\mathbf{B}^{-1}\begin{pmatrix} \mathbf{A}_0\mathbf{r}_i^\top \\ (\mathbf{A} - \mathbf{x}_i \otimes \mathbf{I}_m) \otimes \mathbf{r}_i^\top \end{pmatrix}, \mathbf{r}_i^\top)\}_{i \in [Q]}$$

(where the distinguisher additionally gets aux_0) from which ABE security follows readily. Next, we prove pseudorandomness of (10) from LWE via a hybrid sequence summarized in Fig 2:

- H_0: the distribution in (10)

$$\mathsf{aux}_0, \mathbf{A}_0, \mathbf{A}, \mathbf{u}^\top, \mathbf{B}, \overbrace{\mathbf{s}_0\mathbf{A}_0 + \mathbf{s}_1(\mathbf{A}_f\mathbf{u}^\top \otimes \mathbf{I}_m) + \mathbf{e}'}^{\mathbf{c}'},$$
$$\overbrace{(\mathbf{s}_0 \mid \mathbf{s}_1)\mathbf{B} + \mathbf{e}_0}^{\mathbf{c}_0}\{\overbrace{\mathbf{s}_1((\mathbf{A} - \mathbf{x}_i \otimes \mathbf{I}_m) \otimes \mathbf{r}_i^\top) + \mathbf{e}_{1,i}'}^{\mathbf{c}_{1,i}'}, \overbrace{\mathbf{s}_0\mathbf{A}_0\mathbf{r}_i^\top + \mathbf{e}_{0,i}'}^{\mathbf{c}_{0,i}'}, \mathbf{r}_i^\top\}_{i \in [Q]}$$

– H_1: same as H_0, except we compute

$$c'_{0,i} := \boxed{c' \cdot r_i^\top - c'_1 \cdot \mathbf{H}_{\mathbf{A},f,\mathbf{x}_i} \mathbf{u}^\top - s_1(\mathbf{u}^\top \otimes r_i^\top)} + e'_{0,i}.$$

We claim that $H_0 \approx_s H_1$. First, observe that

$$s_0 \mathbf{A}_0 r_i^\top = \overbrace{(s_0 \mathbf{A}_0 + s_1(\mathbf{A}_f \mathbf{u}^\top \otimes \mathbf{I}_m))}^{\approx c'} \cdot r_i^\top - s_1(\mathbf{A}_f \mathbf{u}^\top \otimes r_i^\top)$$

$$= (s_0 \mathbf{A}_0 + s_1(\mathbf{A}_f \mathbf{u}^\top \otimes \mathbf{I}_m)) \cdot r_i^\top - s_1((\mathbf{A} - \mathbf{x}_i \otimes \mathbf{I}_m) \cdot \mathbf{H}_{\mathbf{A},f,\mathbf{x}_i} \mathbf{u}^\top + \mathbf{u}^\top) \otimes r_i^\top)$$

$$= (s_0 \mathbf{A}_0 + s_1(\mathbf{A}_f \mathbf{u}^\top \otimes \mathbf{I}_m)) \cdot r_i^\top - s_1(\overbrace{(\mathbf{A} - \mathbf{x}_i \otimes \mathbf{I}_m) \otimes r_i^\top}^{\approx c'_{1,i}}) \cdot \mathbf{H}_{\mathbf{A},f,\mathbf{x}_i} \mathbf{u}^\top + s_1(\mathbf{u}^\top \otimes r_i^\top)$$

where the first and third equalities uses the mixed-product property, and the second equality uses $(\mathbf{A} - \mathbf{x}_i \otimes \mathbf{I}_m) \cdot \mathbf{H}_{\mathbf{A},f,\mathbf{x}_i} = \mathbf{A}_f - f(\mathbf{x}_i)\mathbf{I}_m$ and $f(\mathbf{x}_i) = 1$. Then, $H_0 \approx_s H_1$ follows from noise flooding using $e'_{0,i}$, namely

$$e'_{0,i} \approx_s e'_{0,i} + e' \cdot r_i^\top - e'_{1,i} \cdot \mathbf{H}_{\mathbf{A},f,\mathbf{x}_i} \mathbf{u}^\top$$

which in turn follows from $\chi \geq \chi' \cdot \beta \cdot \lambda^{\omega(1)}$.

– H_2: same as H_1, except we sample $\boxed{c' \leftarrow \mathbb{Z}_q^m, c_0 \leftarrow \mathbb{Z}_q^{O((n+m^2)\log q)}}$. We have $H_1 \approx_c H_2$, since

$$(\mathbf{A}_0, \mathbf{B}_0, s_0\mathbf{A}_0 + e', s_0\mathbf{B}_0 + e_0,) \approx_c (\mathbf{A}_0, c', c_0), \quad c' \leftarrow \mathbb{Z}_q^m, c_0 \leftarrow \mathbb{Z}_q^{O((n+m^2)\log q)}, \mathbf{B}_0 \leftarrow \mathbb{Z}_q^{n \times O((n+m^2)\log q)}$$

via the LWE assumption. (In the reduction, $\mathbf{B}_0$ corresponds to the top n rows of $\mathbf{B}$.)

– H_3: same as H_2, except we compute

$$s_i := s_1(\mathbf{I}_m \otimes r_i^\top) + e'_i, \quad e'_i \leftarrow \mathcal{D}_{\mathbb{Z},\chi''}^m$$

$$c'_{1,i} := \boxed{s_i(\mathbf{A} - \mathbf{x}_i \otimes \mathbf{I}_m)} + e'_{1,i}$$

$$c'_{0,i} := c' \cdot r_i^\top - c'_1 \cdot \mathbf{H}_{\mathbf{A},f,\mathbf{x}_i} \mathbf{u}^\top - \boxed{s_i}\mathbf{u}^\top + e'_{0,i}$$

We claim that $H_2 \approx_s H_3$. First, observe that

$$\overbrace{s_1((\mathbf{A} - \mathbf{x}_i \otimes \mathbf{I}_m) \otimes r_i^\top)}^{\approx c'_{1,i}} = s_1(\mathbf{I}_m \otimes r_i^\top)((\mathbf{A} - \mathbf{x}_i \otimes \mathbf{I}_m) \otimes 1) = \overbrace{s_1(\mathbf{I}_m \otimes r_i^\top)}^{\approx s_i}(\mathbf{A} - \mathbf{x}_i \otimes \mathbf{I}_m)$$

$$s_1(\mathbf{u}^\top \otimes r_i^\top) = s_1(\mathbf{I}_m \otimes r_i^\top)(\mathbf{u}^\top \otimes 1) = \overbrace{s_1(\mathbf{I}_m \otimes r_i^\top)}^{\approx s_i}\mathbf{u}^\top$$

where the first equality in each line uses the mixed-product property. Then, $H_2 \approx_s H_3$ follows from noise flooding using $e'_{1,i}$ and $e'_{0,i}$, namely

$$e'_{1,i} \approx_s e'_{1,i} + e'_i \cdot (\mathbf{A} - \mathbf{x}_i \otimes \mathbf{I}_m)$$
$$e'_{0,i} \approx_s e'_{0,i} + e'_i \cdot \mathbf{u}^\top$$

which in turn follows from $\chi', \chi'' \geq \lambda^{\omega(1)}$.

– H_4: same as H_3, except we sample $\boxed{\mathbf{s}_i \leftarrow \mathbb{Z}_q^m}$. We have $H_3 \approx_c H_4$, since

$$\left\{ \mathbf{s}_1(\mathbf{I}_m \otimes \mathbf{r}_i^\top), \mathbf{r}_i^\top \right\}_{i \in [Q]} \approx_c \left\{ \mathbf{s}_i, \mathbf{r}_i^\top \right\}_{i \in [Q]}, \quad \mathbf{s}_1 \leftarrow \mathbb{Z}_q^{m^2}, \mathbf{r}_i \leftarrow \mathcal{D}_{\mathbb{Z},\chi}^m, \mathbf{s}_i \leftarrow \mathbb{Z}_q^m$$

via the LWE assumption [14,21]. In particular, if we write $\mathbf{s}_1 = (\mathbf{s}_{1,1}, \ldots, \mathbf{s}_{1,m})$ where $\mathbf{s}_{1,1}, \ldots, \mathbf{s}_{1,m} \in \mathbb{Z}_q^m$, then $\mathbf{s}_1(\mathbf{I}_m \otimes \mathbf{r}_i^\top) = (\mathbf{s}_{1,1}\mathbf{r}_i^\top, \ldots, \mathbf{s}_{1,m}\mathbf{r}_i^\top)$.

– H_5 : same as H_4, except we sample $\boxed{c_{0,i}' \leftarrow \mathbb{Z}_q^{\ell m}, \mathbf{c}_{1,i}' \leftarrow \mathbb{Z}_q^{\ell m}}$. We have $H_4 \approx_c H_5$. This follows from a hybrid argument over $i = 1, \ldots, Q$, where in the i'th step, we switch the distribution of $c_{0,i}', \mathbf{c}_{1,i}'$ to random via:

$$
\begin{aligned}
&(\mathbf{A}, & \mathbf{u}^\top, s_i\mathbf{u}^\top + e_{0,i}', \; s_i(\mathbf{A} - \mathbf{x}_i \otimes \mathbf{I}_m) + \mathbf{e}_{1,i}' \,) \\
\approx_s &(\mathbf{A} + \mathbf{x}_i \otimes \mathbf{I}_m, \mathbf{u}^\top, s_i\mathbf{u}^\top + e_{0,i}', \; s_i\mathbf{A} + \mathbf{e}_{1,i}' &) \\
\approx_c &(\mathbf{A} + \mathbf{x}_i \otimes \mathbf{I}_m, \mathbf{u}^\top, c_{0,i}', & \mathbf{c}_{1,i}' &) \\
\approx_s &(\mathbf{A}, & \mathbf{u}^\top, c_{0,i}', & \mathbf{c}_{1,i}' &)
\end{aligned}
$$

In particular,
- the first and last $\approx_s$ rely on noise flooding with $\mathbf{A} \approx_s \mathbf{A} + \mathbf{x}_i \otimes \mathbf{I}_m$, which in turn follows from $\chi'' \geq \lambda^{\omega(1)}$;
- the $\approx_c$ relies on LWE [14] which tells us

$$(\mathbf{A}, \mathbf{u}^\top, s_i\mathbf{A} + \mathbf{e}_{1,i}', s_i\mathbf{u}^\top + e_{0,i}') \approx_c (\mathbf{A}, \mathbf{u}^\top, \text{random})$$

and where the reduction samples $s_{i+1}, \ldots, s_Q$ and computes $c_{0,i+1}', \ldots, c_{0,Q}', \mathbf{c}_{1,i+1}', \ldots, \mathbf{c}_{1,Q}'$ as in H_5.

5.3   Optimal Broadcast Encryption

To handle broadcast encryption with N users, we identify a user $x \in [N]$ with a bit string $\mathbf{x} \in \{0,1\}^{\lceil \log N \rceil}$. Let $I_\mathbf{y}(\cdot)$ be the point function wrt $\mathbf{y}$, that is,

$$
I_\mathbf{y}(\mathbf{x}) = \begin{cases} 1 & \text{if } \mathbf{x} = \mathbf{y} \\ 0 & \text{otherwise} \end{cases}
$$

We can then associate each set $S \subseteq [N]$ with the circuit $f_S : \{0,1\}^{\lceil \log N \rceil} \to \{0,1\}$ given by

$$
\mathbf{x} \mapsto 1 - \sum_{\mathbf{y} \in S} I_\mathbf{y}(\mathbf{x}) = \begin{cases} 0 & \text{if } \mathbf{x} \in S \\ 1 & \text{if } \mathbf{x} \notin S \end{cases}
$$

It is easy to see that f_S can be computed by a circuit of depth $O(\log \log N)$ and size $O(N \log N)$:[6]

– each $I_\mathbf{y}(\cdot)$ can be computed by a circuit of depth $O(\log \log N)$ and size $O(\log N)$;
– followed by an addition gate with fan-in N.

---

[6] As explained in [12], "To support multiplication and addition of constants, we may assume that we have an extra 0-th input to the circuit that always carries the value 1." That is, we will set $\ell = \lceil \log N \rceil + 1$ in our CP-ABE scheme.

We can then instantiate our CP-ABE scheme with $\beta = \lambda^{\mathsf{poly}(\log N)} \cdot N \log N$ (via the bound in Lemma 2) which yields a broadcast encryption scheme with

$$|\mathsf{mpk}| = \mathsf{poly}(\log N, \lambda), \quad |\mathsf{ct}| = \mathsf{poly}(\log N, \lambda), \quad |\mathsf{sk}| = \mathsf{poly}(\log N, \lambda)$$

5.4   CP-ABE for Polynomial-Depth Circuits

Tensor LWE. We introduce an additional tensor LWE assumption which states that for all $\mathbf{x}_1, \ldots, \mathbf{x}_Q \in \{0,1\}^\ell$, we have

$$\mathbf{A}, \big\{ \mathbf{s}(\mathbf{I}_m \otimes \mathbf{r}_i^\top)(\mathbf{A} - \mathbf{x}_i \otimes \mathbf{G}) + \mathbf{e}_i, \mathbf{r}_i^\top \big\}_{i \in [Q]} \approx_c \mathbf{A}, \big\{ \boxed{\mathbf{c}_i}, \mathbf{r}_i^\top \big\}_{i \in [Q]}$$

where $\mathbf{A} \leftarrow \mathbb{Z}_q^{m \times \ell m}, \mathbf{s} \leftarrow \mathbb{Z}_q^{mn}, \mathbf{e}_i \leftarrow \mathcal{D}_{\mathbb{Z},\chi}^{\ell m}, \mathbf{r}_i^\top \leftarrow \mathcal{D}_{\mathbb{Z},\chi}^m, \mathbf{c}_i \leftarrow \mathbb{Z}_q^{\ell m}$. We consider the same parameter settings as $\mathsf{LWE}_{n,q,\chi}$, with $\ell, Q = \mathsf{poly}(\lambda)$. Our analysis in Sect. 5.2 shows that if we use a low-norm $\mathbf{A}$ and replace $\mathbf{G}$ with $\mathbf{I}$, then LWE implies tensor LWE.

CP-ABE Scheme. We modify our CP-ABE scheme in Sect. 5.2 as follows:

- we sample $\mathbf{A} \leftarrow \mathbb{Z}_q^{n \times \ell m}, (\mathbf{B}_1, \tau_1) \leftarrow \mathsf{TrapGen}(1^{mn}, q), \mathbf{s}_1 \leftarrow \mathbb{Z}_q^{mn}$;
- we replace $\mathbf{I}_m$ in ct, sk with the gadget matrix $\mathbf{G} \in \mathbb{Z}_q^{n \times m}$ and we replace $\mathsf{EvalF}, \mathsf{EvalFX}$ with $\mathsf{EvalF_G}, \mathsf{EvalFX_G}$ respectively;
- we set $\chi'' = \mathsf{poly}(\lambda)$.

That is, we have:

$$\mathsf{ct}_f := \big((\mathbf{s}_0 \mid \mathbf{s}_1)\mathbf{B} + \mathbf{e}_0, \ \mathbf{s}_0\mathbf{A}_0 + \mathbf{s}_1(\mathbf{A}_f\mathbf{u}^\top \otimes \mathbf{G}) + \mu \cdot \mathbf{g} + \mathbf{e} \big)$$

$$\mathsf{sk}_\mathbf{x} := \Big(\mathbf{B}^{-1} \begin{pmatrix} \mathbf{A}_0\mathbf{r}^\top \\ (\mathbf{A} - \mathbf{x} \otimes \mathbf{G}) \otimes \mathbf{r}^\top \end{pmatrix}, \mathbf{r}^\top \Big)$$

As before, we have: $|\mathsf{mpk}| = \ell \cdot \mathsf{poly}(\log \beta, \lambda), |\mathsf{ct}| = \mathsf{poly}(\log \beta, \lambda), |\mathsf{sk}| = \ell \cdot \mathsf{poly}(\log \beta, \lambda)$. Now, for circuits of depth d and size s, we have $|\mathbf{H}_{\mathbf{A},f,\mathbf{x}}| = \lambda^{O(d)} \cdot s$, which yields:

$$|\mathsf{mpk}| = \ell \cdot \mathsf{poly}(d, \log s, \lambda), \quad |\mathsf{ct}| = \mathsf{poly}(d, \log s, \lambda), \quad |\mathsf{sk}| = \ell \cdot \mathsf{poly}(d, \log s, \lambda)$$

Security. The proof of security requires the following modifications:

- H_1:

$$c'_{0,i} := \boxed{\mathbf{c}' \cdot \mathbf{r}_i^\top - \mathbf{c}'_1 \cdot \mathbf{H}_{\mathbf{A},f,\mathbf{x}_i}\mathbf{u}^\top - \mathbf{s}_1(\mathbf{G}\mathbf{u}^\top \otimes \mathbf{r}_i^\top)} + e'_{0,i}.$$

- the proof of $\mathsf{H}_0 \approx_s \mathsf{H}_1$ uses $(\mathbf{A} - \mathbf{x}_i \otimes \mathbf{G}) \cdot \mathbf{H}_{\mathbf{A},f,\mathbf{x}_i} = \mathbf{A}_f - f(\mathbf{x}_i)\mathbf{G}$.
- we omit $\mathsf{H}_3, \mathsf{H}_4$ and directly argue that $\mathsf{H}_2 \approx_c \mathsf{H}_5$. Tensor LWE implies that for all $\mathbf{x}_1, \ldots, \mathbf{x}_Q \in \{0,1\}^\ell$,

$$\mathbf{A}, \mathbf{u}^\top, \big\{ \mathbf{r}_i^\top \big\}_{i \in [Q]}, \big\{ \mathbf{s}_1(\mathbf{I}_m \otimes \mathbf{r}_i^\top)(\mathbf{A} - \mathbf{x}_i \otimes \mathbf{G}) + \mathbf{e}'_{1,i}, \ \mathbf{s}_1(\mathbf{I}_m \otimes \mathbf{r}_i^\top)\mathbf{G}\mathbf{u}^\top + e'_{0,i} \big\}_{i \in [Q]}$$
$$\approx_c \mathbf{A}, \mathbf{u}^\top, \big\{ \mathbf{r}_i^\top \big\}_{i \in [Q]}, \big\{ \mathbf{c}'_{1,i}, \qquad\qquad\qquad\qquad\qquad c'_{0,i} \big\}_{i \in [Q]}$$

Formally, we account for $\mathbf{u}^\top$ by taking tensor LWE with parameter $\ell + 1$ and padding $\mathbf{x}_1, \ldots, \mathbf{x}_\ell$ with a 0.

6   Discussion on Evasive LWE

Recall our informal statement of evasive LWE: for every efficient samplable distributions over $(\mathbf{A}', \mathbf{P}, \mathsf{aux})$,

if $(\mathbf{A}', \mathbf{B}, \mathbf{P}, \boxed{\mathbf{sA} + \mathbf{e}'}, \boxed{\mathbf{sB} + \mathbf{e}}, \mathbf{sP} + \mathbf{e}'', \mathsf{aux}) \approx_c (\mathbf{A}', \mathbf{B}, \mathbf{P}, \boxed{\mathbf{c}'}, \boxed{\mathbf{c}}, \boxed{\mathbf{c}''}, \mathsf{aux}),$

then $(\mathbf{A}', \mathbf{B}, \boxed{\mathbf{sA} + \mathbf{e}'}, \boxed{\mathbf{sB} + \mathbf{e}}, \mathbf{B}^{-1}(\mathbf{P}), \mathsf{aux}) \approx_c (\mathbf{A}', \mathbf{B}, \boxed{\mathbf{c}'}, \boxed{\mathbf{c}}, \mathbf{B}^{-1}(\mathbf{P}), \mathsf{aux})$

We begin with three quick examples:

- if $\mathbf{P}$ is drawn from the uniform distribution over $\mathbb{Z}_q^{n \times t}$, then evasive LWE holds unconditionally, since $\mathbf{B}^{-1}(\mathbf{P})$ is distributed according to a random Gaussian.
- if $\mathbf{P} = \mathbf{0}$, then both the pre and post conditions are false, so evasive LWE is vacuously true.
- if $\mathbf{P} = [\mathbf{U} \mid \mathbf{U}]$ where $\mathbf{U} \leftarrow \mathbb{Z}_q^{n \times t/2}$, then the pre-condition is false, and evasive LWE does not provide any security guarantees.

Algorithmic Attacks. The known algorithmic attacks on the post-condition essentially fall into one of two categories:

- Attacks on LWE ignoring $\mathbf{B}^{-1}(\mathbf{P})$: this is ruled out via the pre-condition;
- Attacks computing $\mathbf{c}^* = (\mathbf{sB} + \mathbf{e}') \cdot \mathbf{B}^{-1}(\mathbf{P}) \approx \mathbf{sP}$: suppose given aux, an attacker can find a low-norm $\mathbf{z}$ such that $\mathbf{P} \cdot \mathbf{z}^\top = \mathbf{0}$; we can then use $\mathbf{z}$ to distinguish $\mathbf{sP} + \mathbf{e}''$ from $\mathbf{c}''$, thereby violating the pre-condition. Zeroizing attacks on multi-linear map and obfuscation candidates fall into this category. The attacks on naive approaches to LWE-based ABE via secret-sharing in [2, Section 6] also falls into this category.

Two Examples. To further our understanding of evasive LWE via cryptanalysis and security reductions, we consider two concrete distributions for $\mathbf{P}$ and where there is no $\mathbf{A}', \mathsf{aux}$:

- Suppose $\mathbf{P}$ is a uniformly random block-diagonal matrix, that is, $\mathbf{P} = \begin{pmatrix} \mathbf{U}_0 & \\ & \mathbf{U}_1 \end{pmatrix}$, where $\mathbf{U}_0, \mathbf{U}_1 \leftarrow \mathbb{Z}_q^{n/2 \times t/2}$. It is easy to see that the pre-condition holds via LWE, and in this case, we can also show that the post-condition holds assuming LWE. Concretely, let $\mathbf{B}_0, \mathbf{B}_1$ denote the top and bottom halves of the matrix $\mathbf{B}$. Then, $\mathbf{B}^{-1}(\mathbf{P}) \approx_s (\mathbf{B}_1^{-1}(\mathbf{0}), \mathbf{B}_0^{-1}(\mathbf{0}))$ via [23], and the post-condition boils down to showing that $(\mathbf{B}, \mathbf{sB} + \mathbf{e}')$ is pseudorandom given trapdoors for $\mathbf{B}_0, \mathbf{B}_1$. As shown in [20, Theorem 5.3], this follows from LWE, where in the reduction, we sample $\mathbf{B}_0 = [\mathbf{A}_0 \mid \mathbf{A}_0\mathbf{R} + \mathbf{G}], \mathbf{B}_1 = [\mathbf{A}_1 \mid \mathbf{A}_1\mathbf{R} - \mathbf{G}]$, where $\mathbf{R}$ is low-norm.
- Suppose $\mathbf{P}$ is drawn from the Gaussian distribution $\mathcal{D}_{\mathbb{Z}, \chi}^{n \times t}$. Then, the pre-condition holds via [14], but we do not know how to prove the post-condition assuming LWE. In this case, $\mathbf{B}^{-1}(\mathbf{P}) \approx_c [\mathbf{B} \mid \mathbf{I}]^{-1}(\mathbf{0})$. The post-condition then boils down to showing that $(\mathbf{B}, \mathbf{sB} + \mathbf{e}')$ is pseudorandom given a low-norm basis for $[\mathbf{B} \mid \mathbf{I}]$.

References

1. Agrawal, S.: Indistinguishability obfuscation without multilinear maps: new methods for bootstrapping and instantiation. In: Ishai, Y., Rijmen, V. (eds.) EUROCRYPT 2019, Part I. LNCS, vol. 11476, pp. 191–225. Springer, Cham (2019). https://doi.org/10.1007/978-3-030-17653-2_7
2. Agrawal, S., Boyen, X., Vaikuntanathan, V., Voulgaris, P., Wee, H.: Functional encryption for threshold functions (or fuzzy IBE) from lattices. In: Fischlin, M., Buchmann, J., Manulis, M. (eds.) PKC 2012. LNCS, vol. 7293, pp. 280–297. Springer, Heidelberg (2012). https://doi.org/10.1007/978-3-642-30057-8_17
3. Agrawal, S., Libert, B., Stehlé, D.: Fully secure functional encryption for inner products, from standard assumptions. In: Robshaw, M., Katz, J. (eds.) CRYPTO 2016, Part III. LNCS, vol. 9816, pp. 333–362. Springer, Heidelberg (2016). https://doi.org/10.1007/978-3-662-53015-3_12
4. Agrawal, S., Pellet-Mary, A.: Indistinguishability obfuscation without maps: attacks and fixes for noisy linear FE. In: Canteaut, A., Ishai, Y. (eds.) EUROCRYPT 2020, Part I. LNCS, vol. 12105, pp. 110–140. Springer, Cham (2020). https://doi.org/10.1007/978-3-030-45721-1_5
5. Agrawal, S., Wichs, D., Yamada, S.: Optimal broadcast encryption from LWE and pairings in the standard model. In: Pass, R., Pietrzak, K. (eds.) TCC 2020, Part I. LNCS, vol. 12550, pp. 149–178. Springer, Cham (2020). https://doi.org/10.1007/978-3-030-64375-1_6
6. Agrawal, S., Yamada, S.: CP-ABE for circuits (and more) in the symmetric key setting. In: Pass, R., Pietrzak, K. (eds.) TCC 2020, Part I. LNCS, vol. 12550, pp. 117–148. Springer, Cham (2020). https://doi.org/10.1007/978-3-030-64375-1_5
7. Agrawal, S., Yamada, S.: Optimal broadcast encryption from pairings and LWE. In: Canteaut, A., Ishai, Y. (eds.) EUROCRYPT 2020, Part I. LNCS, vol. 12105, pp. 13–43. Springer, Cham (2020). https://doi.org/10.1007/978-3-030-45721-1_2
8. Barak, B., Brakerski, Z., Komargodski, I., Kothari, P.K.: Limits on low-degree pseudorandom generators (or: sum-of-squares meets program obfuscation). In: Nielsen, J.B., Rijmen, V. (eds.) EUROCRYPT 2018, Part II. LNCS, vol. 10821, pp. 649–679. Springer, Cham (2018). https://doi.org/10.1007/978-3-319-78375-8_21
9. Bartusek, J., Guan, J., Ma, F., Zhandry, M.: Return of GGH15: provable security against zeroizing attacks. In: Beimel, A., Dziembowski, S. (eds.) TCC 2018, Part II. LNCS, vol. 11240, pp. 544–574. Springer, Cham (2018). https://doi.org/10.1007/978-3-030-03810-6_20
10. Bethencourt, J., Sahai, A., Waters, B.: Ciphertext-policy attribute-based encryption. In: 2007 IEEE Symposium on Security and Privacy, pp. 321–334. IEEE Computer Society Press, May 2007
11. Beullens, W., Wee, H.: Obfuscating simple functionalities from knowledge assumptions. In: Lin, D., Sako, K. (eds.) PKC 2019, Part II. LNCS, vol. 11443, pp. 254–283. Springer, Cham (2019). https://doi.org/10.1007/978-3-030-17259-6_9
12. Boneh, D., et al.: Fully key-homomorphic encryption, arithmetic circuit ABE and compact garbled circuits. In: Nguyen, P.Q., Oswald, E. (eds.) EUROCRYPT 2014. LNCS, vol. 8441, pp. 533–556. Springer, Heidelberg (2014). https://doi.org/10.1007/978-3-642-55220-5_30
13. Boneh, D., Gentry, C., Waters, B.: Collusion resistant broadcast encryption with short ciphertexts and private keys. In: Shoup, V. (ed.) CRYPTO 2005. LNCS, vol. 3621, pp. 258–275. Springer, Heidelberg (2005). https://doi.org/10.1007/11535218_16

14. Boneh, D., Lewi, K., Montgomery, H., Raghunathan, A.: Key homomorphic PRFs and their applications. In: Canetti, R., Garay, J.A. (eds.) CRYPTO 2013, Part I. LNCS, vol. 8042, pp. 410–428. Springer, Heidelberg (2013). https://doi.org/10. 1007/978-3-642-40041-4_23

15. Boneh, D., Waters, B.: A fully collusion resistant broadcast, trace, and revoke system. In: Juels, A., Wright, R.N., De Capitani di Vimercati, S. (eds.) ACM CCS 2006, pp. 211–220. ACM Press, October/November 2006

16. Boneh, D., Waters, B., Zhandry, M.: Low overhead broadcast encryption from multilinear maps. In: Garay, J.A., Gennaro, R. (eds.) CRYPTO 2014, Part I. LNCS, vol. 8616, pp. 206–223. Springer, Heidelberg (2014). https://doi.org/10.1007/978-3-662-44371-2_12

17. Boneh, D., Zhandry, M.: Multiparty key exchange, efficient traitor tracing, and more from indistinguishability obfuscation. In: Garay, J.A., Gennaro, R. (eds.) CRYPTO 2014. LNCS, vol. 8616, pp. 480–499. Springer, Heidelberg (2014). https://doi.org/10.1007/978-3-662-44371-2_27

18. Brakerski, Z., Döttling, N., Garg, S., Malavolta, G.: Candidate iO from homomorphic encryption schemes. In: Canteaut, A., Ishai, Y. (eds.) EUROCRYPT 2020, Part I. LNCS, vol. 12105, pp. 79–109. Springer, Cham (2020). https://doi.org/10. 1007/978-3-030-45721-1_4

19. Brakerski, Z., Döttling, N., Garg, S., Malavolta, G.: Factoring and pairings are not necessary for iO: circular-secure LWE suffices. Cryptology ePrint Archive, Report 2020/1024 (2020)

20. Brakerski, Z., Vaikuntanathan, V.: Lattice-inspired broadcast encryption and succinct ciphertext-policy ABE. In: ITCS, pp. 28:1–28:20 (2022)

21. Canetti, R., Chen, Y.: Constraint-Hiding Constrained PRFs for NC^1 from LWE. In: Coron, J.-S., Nielsen, J.B. (eds.) EUROCRYPT 2017, Part I. LNCS, vol. 10210, pp. 446–476. Springer, Cham (2017). https://doi.org/10.1007/978-3-319-56620-7_16

22. Chen, J., Gay, R., Wee, H.: Improved dual system ABE in prime-order groups via predicate encodings. In: Oswald, E., Fischlin, M. (eds.) EUROCRYPT 2015, Part II. LNCS, vol. 9057, pp. 595–624. Springer, Heidelberg (2015). https://doi.org/10. 1007/978-3-662-46803-6_20

23. Chen, Y., Vaikuntanathan, V., Wee, H.: GGH15 beyond permutation branching programs: proofs, attacks, and candidates. In: Shacham, H., Boldyreva, A. (eds.) CRYPTO 2018, Part II. LNCS, vol. 10992, pp. 577–607. Springer, Cham (2018). https://doi.org/10.1007/978-3-319-96881-0_20

24. Cheon, J.H., Han, K., Lee, C., Ryu, H., Stehlé, D.: Cryptanalysis of the multilinear map over the integers. In: Oswald, E., Fischlin, M. (eds.) EUROCRYPT 2015, Part I. LNCS, vol. 9056, pp. 3–12. Springer, Heidelberg (2015). https://doi.org/10.1007/ 978-3-662-46800-5_1

25. Coron, J.-S., Lee, M.S., Lepoint, T., Tibouchi, M.: Cryptanalysis of GGH15 multilinear maps. In: Robshaw, M., Katz, J. (eds.) CRYPTO 2016. LNCS, vol. 9815, pp. 607–628. Springer, Heidelberg (2016). https://doi.org/10.1007/978-3-662-53008-5_21

26. Datta, P., Komargodski, I., Waters, B.: Decentralized multi-authority ABE for DNFs from LWE. In: Canteaut, A., Standaert, F.-X. (eds.) EUROCRYPT 2021, Part I. LNCS, vol. 12696, pp. 177–209. Springer, Cham (2021). https://doi.org/ 10.1007/978-3-030-77870-5_7

27. Fiat, A., Naor, M.: Broadcast encryption. In: Stinson, D.R. (ed.) CRYPTO 1993. LNCS, vol. 773, pp. 480–491. Springer, Heidelberg (1994). https://doi.org/10.1007/ 3-540-48329-2_40

28. Garg, S., Gentry, C., Halevi, S.: Candidate multilinear maps from ideal lattices. In: Johansson, T., Nguyen, P.Q. (eds.) EUROCRYPT 2013. LNCS, vol. 7881, pp. 1–17. Springer, Heidelberg (2013). https://doi.org/10.1007/978-3-642-38348-9_1

29. Garg, S., Gentry, C., Halevi, S., Raykova, M., Sahai, A., Waters, B.: Candidate indistinguishability obfuscation and functional encryption for all circuits. In: 54th FOCS, pp. 40–49. IEEE Computer Society Press, October 2013

30. Garg, S., Miles, E., Mukherjee, P., Sahai, A., Srinivasan, A., Zhandry, M.: Secure obfuscation in a weak multilinear map model. In: Hirt, M., Smith, A. (eds.) TCC 2016, Part II. LNCS, vol. 9986, pp. 241–268. Springer, Heidelberg (2016). https://doi.org/10.1007/978-3-662-53644-5_10

31. Gay, R., Pass, R.: Indistinguishability obfuscation from circular security. In: STOC (2021)

32. Gentry, C., Gorbunov, S., Halevi, S.: Graph-induced multilinear maps from lattices. In: Dodis, Y., Nielsen, J.B. (eds.) TCC 2015, Part II. LNCS, vol. 9015, pp. 498–527. Springer, Heidelberg (2015). https://doi.org/10.1007/978-3-662-46497-7_20

33. Gentry, C., Waters, B.: Adaptive security in broadcast encryption systems (with short ciphertexts). In: Joux, A. (ed.) EUROCRYPT 2009. LNCS, vol. 5479, pp. 171–188. Springer, Heidelberg (2009). https://doi.org/10.1007/978-3-642-01001-9_10

34. Goyal, V., Pandey, O., Sahai, A., Waters, B.: Attribute-based encryption for fine-grained access control of encrypted data. In: Juels, A., Wright, R.N., De Capitani di Vimercati, S. (eds.) ACM CCS 2006, pp. 89–98. ACM Press, October/November 2006. Available as Cryptology ePrint Archive Report 2006/309

35. Halevi, S., Halevi, T., Shoup, V., Stephens-Davidowitz, N.: Implementing BP-obfuscation using graph-induced encoding. In: Thuraisingham, B.M., Evans, D., Malkin, T., Xu, D. (eds.) ACM CCS 2017, pp. 783–798. ACM Press, October/November 2017

36. Hopkins, S., Jain, A., Lin, H.: Counterexamples to new circular security assumptions underlying iO. In: Malkin, T., Peikert, C. (eds.) CRYPTO 2021, Part II. LNCS, vol. 12826, pp. 673–700. Springer, Cham (2021). https://doi.org/10.1007/978-3-030-84245-1_23

37. Jain, A., Lin, H., Sahai, A.: Indistinguishability obfuscation from well-founded assumptions. Cryptology ePrint Archive, Report 2020/1003 (2020)

38. Ling, S., Phan, D.H., Stehlé, D., Steinfeld, R.: Hardness of k-LWE and applications in traitor tracing. In: Garay, J.A., Gennaro, R. (eds.) CRYPTO 2014, Part I. LNCS, vol. 8616, pp. 315–334. Springer, Heidelberg (2014). https://doi.org/10.1007/978-3-662-44371-2_18

39. Lombardi, A., Vaikuntanathan, V.: Limits on the locality of pseudorandom generators and applications to indistinguishability obfuscation. In: Kalai, Y., Reyzin, L. (eds.) TCC 2017, Part I. LNCS, vol. 10677, pp. 119–137. Springer, Cham (2017). https://doi.org/10.1007/978-3-319-70500-2_5

40. Miles, E., Sahai, A., Zhandry, M.: Annihilation attacks for multilinear maps: cryptanalysis of indistinguishability obfuscation over GGH13. In: Robshaw, M., Katz, J. (eds.) CRYPTO 2016, Part II. LNCS, vol. 9815, pp. 629–658. Springer, Heidelberg (2016). https://doi.org/10.1007/978-3-662-53008-5_22

41. Sahai, A., Waters, B.: Fuzzy identity-based encryption. In: Cramer, R. (ed.) EUROCRYPT 2005. LNCS, vol. 3494, pp. 457–473. Springer, Heidelberg (2005). https://doi.org/10.1007/11426639_27

42. Vaikuntanathan, V., Wee, H., Wichs, D.: Witness encryption and null-iO from evasive LWE. Manuscript (2022)

43. Wee, H.: Broadcast encryption with size $N^{1/3}$ and more from k-lin. In: Malkin, T., Peikert, C. (eds.) CRYPTO 2021, Part IV. LNCS, vol. 12828, pp. 155–178. Springer, Cham (2021). https://doi.org/10.1007/978-3-030-84259-8_6

44. Wee, H., Wichs, D.: Candidate obfuscation via oblivious LWE sampling. In: Canteaut, A., Standaert, F.-X. (eds.) EUROCRYPT 2021, Part III. LNCS, vol. 12698, pp. 127–156. Springer, Cham (2021). https://doi.org/10.1007/978-3-030-77883-5_5

Embedding the UC Model into the IITM Model

Daniel Rausch[1]($\boxtimes$) $\text{\textcircled{iD}}$, Ralf Küsters[1] $\text{\textcircled{iD}}$, and Céline Chevalier[2]

[1] University of Stuttgart, Stuttgart, Germany
{daniel.rausch,ralf.kuesters}@sec.uni-stuttgart.de
[2] CRED, Paris-Panthéon-Assas University, Paris, France
celine.chevalier@ens.fr

Abstract. Universal Composability is a widely used concept for the design and analysis of protocols. Since Canetti's original UC model and the model by Pfitzmann and Waidner several different models for universal composability have been proposed, including, for example, the IITM model, GNUC, CC, but also extensions and restrictions of the UC model, such as JUC, GUC, and SUC. These were motivated by the lack of expressivity of existing models, ease of use, or flaws in previous models. Cryptographers choose between these models based on their needs at hand (e.g., support for joint state and global state) or simply their familiarity with a specific model. While all models follow the same basic idea, there are huge conceptually differences, which raises fundamental and practical questions: (How) do the concepts and results proven in one model relate to those in another model? Do the different models and the security notions formulated therein capture the same classes of attacks? Most importantly, can cryptographers re-use results proven in one model in another model, and if so, how?

In this paper, we initiate a line of research with the aim to address this lack of understanding, consolidate the space of models, and enable cryptographers to re-use results proven in other models. As a start, here we focus on Canetti's prominent UC model and the IITM model proposed by Küsters et al. The latter is an interesting candidate for comparison with the UC model since it has been used to analyze a wide variety of protocols, supports a very general protocol class and provides, among others, seamless treatment of protocols with shared state, including joint and global state. Our main technical contribution is an embedding of the UC model into the IITM model showing that all UC protocols, security and composition results carry over to the IITM model. Hence, protocol designers can profit from the features of the IITM model while being able to use all their results proven in the UC model. We also show that, in general, one cannot embed the full IITM model into the UC model.

1 Introduction

Universal composability is a widely used approach for the modular design and analysis of cryptographic protocols. Protocols are shown to be secure in arbitrary (polynomial-time) contexts, which allows for composing protocols and

O. Dunkelman and S. Dziembowski (Eds.): EUROCRYPT 2022, LNCS 13276, pp. 242–272, 2022.
https://doi.org/10.1007/978-3-031-07085-3_9

re-using security results. Security properties are stated in terms of ideal functionalities/protocols. To prove a real protocol π secure w.r.t. an ideal functionality ϕ one shows that for all network adversaries $\mathcal{A}$ attacking π there is an ideal adversary, called simulator, that interacts with ϕ such that no (polynomial-time) environment $\mathcal{E}$ can distinguish between the real and the ideal world. We write $\pi \leq \phi$ in this case. Composition theorems then immediately imply that one can replace subroutines ϕ used by an arbitrary higher-level protocol ρ with their realization π such that $\rho^{\phi \to \pi} \leq \rho$, where in $\rho^{\phi \to \pi}$ the protocol ρ uses (possibly multiple instances of) π instead of ϕ.

The UC model by Canetti [5,6] and the reactive simulatability model by Pfitzmann and Waidner [20] pioneered this line of research. Since then many different models implementing the same idea of universal composability have been proposed, generally motivated by issues in other existing models such as a lack of expressiveness, overly complicated computational models, and also formal flaws in theorems. To name just a few examples: The JUC [8] and GUC [7] models were proposed as extended variants of the UC model which allow for modeling larger classes of protocols, namely those with joint state (where some state, such as a signature key, is used by multiple protocol sessions) or global state (which is shared with arbitrary other protocols), respectively. The GNUC model [10] was designed as a sound alternative to the UC model, fixing several issues that formally invalidated the UC composition theorem at the time. The IITM model [12,18] offers a simple computational model that supports a very general class of protocols and composition theorems, which, out of the box, support joint state, global state, and arbitrarily shared state, also in combination. The CC model [19] follows a more abstract approach that does not fix a specific computational model, runtime notion, instantiation mechanism, or class of environments.

In the literature, cryptographers often choose the security model based on their needs at hand (for instance support for joint or global state), syntax preferences, or simply their familiarity with a specific model. While all of the above models follow the same basic idea of universal composability, the details are (sometimes drastically) different. It is hence generally unclear how different models and the security results obtained therein relate to each other: Is one model strictly more powerful than another? Can all protocols formalized in one model also be formalized in the other? Are security notions compatible? Do security results carry over from one model to the other? This lack of a deeper understanding of the relationship of models is quite disturbing. For example, we might miss some practical attacks in our security proofs because we, due to a lack of knowledge, chose a model that might actually offer only a weaker security notion than other models. Perhaps worst of all, security results proven in one model currently cannot be used in another model. This drastically limits reusability of security results, contradicting one of the key features of universally composable security and more generally modular analyses.

Our Goal. In this paper, we initiate a line of research with the aim to address this lack of understanding and clarify the relationships between models for universal composability. One of our main goals is to identify, as far as possible, classes of protocols and security results that can be transferred from one model to another. This would enable protocol designers to use a model of their choice, based on their personal preference, the specific needs at hand, as well as the features offered by the model, while still being able to benefit from results shown in another model. This would also provide insights into the concepts employed in one model compared to other models and the strength of the security results obtained within a specific model, potentially justifying that such results are reasonable and cover all practical attacks. Besides consolidating and re-using results, this research can also help consolidating and unifying the space of models themselves. A complete classification of *all* universally composable models is of course out of reach of a single paper. As a first step towards our objective, we here focus on embedding the UC model into the IITM model. We also prove that, in general, the IITM model cannot be embedded into the UC model. To the best of our knowledge our work is the first to study such embeddings, and hence, relate complete models for universal composability. So far, only specific aspects have been considered. For example, in [13] the relationship between security notions employed in various models has been studied, although the study was carried out in one model, and [11,12] discuss runtime notions employed in different models.

On the UC and IITM Models. We choose the UC model [5] since it is currently the most widely used model in the literature on universal composability. The IITM model [12] has also already been used intensively to analyze a wide variety of protocols, including cryptographic protocols (e.g., [14,15]) and also more generally security protocols such as blockchains and distributed ledgers (e.g., [9]). The IITM model is an interesting candidate for a comparison since it supports a very general protocol class and comes with composition theorems which cover joint state and global state out of the box as well as protocols with arbitrary shared state (joint and global state are special cases of shared state) and protocols without pre-established session IDs [15], i.e., parties in one session are not required to share the same SID or fix it upfront (see [4,15,17,18] for overviews of these features). Moreover, all these features can be freely combined since they are all covered within one framework. While recently it has been shown that the UC model directly supports global state [2], combinations of, for example, joint state and global state or features like general shared state and protocols without pre-established SIDs are not yet supported in UC. Hence, an embedding as carried out in this paper enables protocol designers to profit from such features of the IITM model while still being able to access the wide range of existing results shown in the UC model.

For both the UC and IITM model there are recent journal publications; the UC model has been published in the Journal of the ACM [6] and the IITM model in the Journal of Cryptology [18]. These provide a solid basis for a comparison. Such a comparison is far from trivial since the computational frameworks of both models are defined in very different ways, using sometimes drastically different concepts where it is far from obvious how they relate and whether there is a meaningful relationship at all.

Our Contributions. *Conceptual Differences.* After recalling the most important definitions and theorems of the UC and IITM models in Sect. 2, we first
highlight in Sect. 3.1 the major conceptual differences between the two models:
Diff. 1 concerns support for dynamically generated machine code, Diff. 2 to 8
are about message routing and sender/receiver authentication, Diff. 9 concerns
the different polynomial runtime notions employed in the two models, Diff. 10
concerns the classes of environments considered, and Diff. 11 to 14 are about
requirements of the UC security notion and composition theorem that are not
present in the IITM model.

Mapping of Protocols. With that analysis in mind, one main contribution, given
in Sects. 3.2 and 3.5, consists in mapping UC protocols to IITM protocols. This
requires bridging the mentioned differences and to show that the mapping is
faithul, i.e., the original and the mapped protocols have the same behavior (functional, security, complexity) in all contexts they run in (Lemmas 1 and 2). This
then implies that all UC protocols can be expressed as IITM protocols.

Mapping and Preservation of Security Results. We show in Sect. 3.3 that this
mapping also preserves security results. That is, $\pi_{UC} \leq_{UC} \phi_{UC}$ in the UC
model iff $\pi_{IITM} \leq_{IITM} \phi_{IITM}$ for the mapped protocols in the IITM model
(Theorem 4). For the direction from IITM to UC, we require that $\pi_{IITM} \leq_{IITM}$
ϕ_{IITM} can be shown for simulators meeting the UC runtime notion (Theorem 5).
Assuming the existence of time-lock puzzles, we also show that this direction does
not hold in general since the class of IITM simulators is strictly larger than the
class of UC simulators (Lemma 3). This latter result is independent of a specific
protocol mapping, and hence, is a fundamental difference between the models,
which we further discuss in Sect. 3.3.

Mapping and Preservation of Composition Results. Sect. 3.4 discusses composition. One easily observes that Theorem 4 already implies that security results
for composed protocols carry over from UC to IITM by first applying the UC
composition theorem and then mapping the resulting UC protocols to the IITM
model (Corollary 1). But this result does not relate the composition theorems
employed in the models themselves. We therefore show that Corollary 1 can be
obtained directly in the IITM model using the IITM composition theorem and
without relying on the UC theorem (Corollary 2).

 This result also enables composition of mapped UC protocols with arbitrary
other IITM protocols within the IITM model, including those that do not have
a UC counter part and which use features of the IITM model that are out of the
scope of the UC model. We discuss these options in Sect. 3.6.

The Other Direction: Limitations. We discuss in Sect. 4 the other direction of
translating IITM protocols and security results to the UC model. To summarize,
[18] has already shown that the IITM runtime notion permits natural protocols
that cannot be expressed in the UC model. Combined with our results, this shows
that the class of IITM protocols is strictly larger than the class of UC protocols.
Our result from Lemma 3 further shows that also the class of IITM simulators
is strictly larger than the class of UC simulators due to their runtime notions.

So the best one can hope for is a mapping for the class of IITM protocols and simulators that follow the UC runtime notion. We also discuss further obstacles of an embedding of the UC model into the IITM model. We leave it to future work to study this in more details and provide an embedding of (a subset of) the IITM model into the UC model.

Further Insights and Results Obtained Through the Embedding. Firstly, we develop a modeling technique that allows for obtaining a new type of composition as a corollary from existing UC and IITM composition theorems as well as similar models (cf. Sect. 3.4). Secondly, we found several previously unknown technical issues in the UC model that, among others, formally invalidate the UC composition theorem (cf. Sects. 2.1, 3.3, 3.4). We propose fixes for all of these issues which should be compatible with existing UC protocols from the literature.

Altogether, our paper provides deep insights into the UC and IITM models, clarifies the purpose of different concepts employed by the models for achieving similar goals, relates them, also in terms of expressiveness, and uncovers how security results compare to each other. Our main result shows that *all protocols, security, and composability results from the UC model carry over to the IITM model.* As an immediate practical benefit, this opens up entirely new options for protocol designers so far working in the UC model: they can use all their results also in the IITM model, combine their work with protocols in the IITM model and benefit from IITM features including seamless support for joint, global, shared state, and protocols without pre-established session IDs, as well as arbitrary combinations thereof.

2   A Brief Overview of the UC and IITM Models

In this section, we provide brief overviews of the UC and IITM models. We refer the reader to [6,18] for more in-depth information about both models. The presentation here should suffice to follow the rest of the paper.

2.1   The UC Model

The general computational model of the UC model is defined in terms of systems of interactive Turing machines (ITMs or just machines, for short). An interactive Turing machine M in the UC model is a probabilistic Turing machine with three special communication tapes, called *input, subroutine-output* (or simply *output*), and *backdoor tape*. In a run of a system of machines (see also below), *machine instances* are created. Every instance has some machine code that it runs when activated and some identifier. More specifically, each instance has a unique so-called *extended ID* $eid = (c, id)$, consisting of its machine code c and some identity string id that, except for the environment (which has $id = 0$), is of the form $id = (pid, sid)$ for a process/party identifier pid and a session identifier sid. Machine instances have access to two special operations: a *read next message* instruction which moves the head of one of the three mentioned communication tapes to the start of the next received message within a single unit of time and an *external-write* instruction which allows a machine instance to append a message m to one of the (three) communication tapes of another machine instance, and hence, send m to that other instance. On an input tape machine instances receive messages from higher-level protocols or the environment, on subroutine-output tapes they receive messages from subroutines, and on backdoor tapes they receive messages from the network/the adversary.

A system of machines (M, C) consists of the machine code M of the first ITM to be activated and a so-called control function C which can prohibit or alter external-write operations; this is later used to define the security experiment. The first instance to be activated with external input a in a run of this system is a machine instance running code M with ID 0. During a run of such a system, at any time only one machine instance is active and all other machine instances wait for new input via the external write operation. When a machine sends a message m via an external write operation to one of the three communication tapes of another machine, say tape t, there are two main options to specify the recipient: Firstly, by giving an extended ID *eid*. If there does not exist a machine instance with this extended identity yet, then such an instance running the code c specified in its *eid* is first created. Then, m is written to the tape t of the machine instance with extended ID *eid* and that machine becomes active (the sender becomes inactive). This first case is also called *forced-write*. Secondly, by giving a predicate P on extended IDs. In this case, m is written to the tape t of the first existing machine instance (sorted by the order of their first creation) with *eid* such that $P(eid)$ holds true. We will refer to this second case as *non-forced-write*. For both types of external write operations, the sender can either hide or reveal its own extended identity towards the recipient. If an external write operation does not succeed, e.g., when there is no existing machine instance matching the predicate P, then the initial ITM instance $(M, 0)$ is activated again. A run ends when the initial ITM reaches a final halting state. The overall output of such a run is the first bit written on a specific tape of the initial ITM instance.

Two systems of machines (M, C) and (M', C') are called indistinguishable (and we write $(M, C) \equiv (M', C')$) if the difference between the probability that (M, C) outputs 1 and the probability that (M', C') outputs 1 is negligible in the security parameter η and the external input a.[1]

Runtime. Machine instances can receive and send so-called *import* as part of their messages m to/from other machine instances, where import is encoded as a *binary* number contained in a special field of m. A machine M is called *probabilistic polynomial-time* (ppt) iff *(i)* there is a polynomial p such that the overall runtime of (an instance of) M during all points of a run is upper bounded by $p(n_I - n_O)$, where n_I is the sum of all imports received by (that instance of) M and n_O is the sum of all imports sent by (that instance of) M to other machines, and *(ii)* whenever M uses a forced write operation to a machine instance with code M', then M' is also ppt for the same polynomial p.

---

[1] A function $f \colon \mathbb{N} \times \{0, 1\}^* \to \mathbb{R}_{\geq 0}$ is called *negligible* if for all $c, d \in \mathbb{N}$ there exists $\eta_0 \in \mathbb{N}$ such that for all $\eta > \eta_0$ and all $a \in \bigcup_{\eta' \leq \eta^d} \{0, 1\}^{\eta'} \colon f(\eta, a) < \eta^{-c}$.

Furthermore, all machines are parameterized with a security parameter η. All machine instances are required to run only when they hold at least η import, i.e., $n_I - n_O \geq \eta$.

Simulation-Based Security. Security of a protocol π is defined via a security experiment involving an adversary $\mathcal{A}$ and an environment $\mathcal{E}$, where each of these components is modeled via an ITM with code π, $\mathcal{A}$, and $\mathcal{E}$ respectively. More specifically, the experiment is defined via the system $(\mathcal{E}, C_{EXEC}^{\pi,\mathcal{A}})$ where $C_{EXEC}^{\pi,\mathcal{A}}$ is a control function that enforces the following rules of communication:

- The environment $\mathcal{E}$ (with ID 0) can write only to input tapes, only via forced write, and only to IDs of the form (pid, sid) where sid must be the same as in previous write operations (if any exist). This uniquely defined sid is also called *challenge session ID sid_c*. If pid is the special symbol $\diamond$, then the control function changes the code of the recipient to $\mathcal{A}$; otherwise, the code is changed to π. So $\mathcal{E}$ can talk to $\mathcal{A}$ or to π (in session sid_c). Unlike all other machines, the environment is given the additional freedom to freely choose the extended identity that is claimed as a sender of a message.
- The adversary $\mathcal{A}$ (with ID $(\diamond, sid_c)$) may write only to backdoor tapes of other machines and may not use the forced-write mechanism (i.e., he can write only to already existing instances using non-forced-writes).[2]
- All other machine instances (which are part of the protocol stack of π, including subroutines) must always reveal their own sender extended identities. They may write to the backdoor tape of (the unique instance of) $\mathcal{A}$ using non-forced-write without specifying the code of the adversary and without providing import. They may write to input and output tapes of instances other than (the unique instances of) $\mathcal{E}$ and $\mathcal{A}$, subject to the following modification: If the sending instance $(M, (pid, sid))$ has code $M = \pi$, $sid = sid_c$, the recipient tape is the output tape, and the recipient instance does not exist yet, then the message is instead redirected to the output tape of $\mathcal{E}$ with the code M removed from the extended sender identity. The extended identity of the originally intended receiver is also written to the output tape of $\mathcal{E}$.

The initial import for environments is defined to be the length of the external input a, which is at most some polynomial in the security parameter η (as per the definition of negligible functions with external input). Environments are required to be *balanced*, i.e., provide at least as much import to the adversary as they provide in total to all instances of the challenge protocol π, i.e., all instance with extended IDs of the form $(\pi, (pid, sid_c))$, where sid_c is the fixed challenge SID. Given a set of extended identities ξ, an environment is called *ξ-identity-bounded* if it claims only sender extended identities from ξ. The set ξ may be determined

---

[2] The journal version of the UC model [6] formally does not prevent the adversary from revealing its sender extended identity, including its code, to other machines. We found that this option actually causes several severe issues, including a failure of the composition theorem (cf. the full version [21] for details). In what follows, we therefore assume that adversaries must also hide their own sender extended identity. This fixes the issue and is compatible with existing results in the literature.

dynamically via a polytime predicate over the current configuration of the whole system at the time the input it sent to the protocol, which includes (the states of) all existing instances of the environment, adversary, and protocol machines. Given this terminology, the security notion for protocols is defined as follows:

Definition 1. *Let π and ϕ be ppt protocols. Then π realizes ϕ w.r.t. ξ-identity-bounded environments ($\pi \leq_{UC}^{\xi} \phi$) if for all ppt adversaries $\mathcal{A}$ there exists a ppt adversary $\mathcal{S}$ (a simulator or an ideal adversary) such that for all ppt ξ-identity-bounded environments $\mathcal{E}$ it holds true that $(\mathcal{E}, C_{EXEC}^{\pi,\mathcal{A}}) \equiv (\mathcal{E}, C_{EXEC}^{\phi,\mathcal{S}})$.*[3]

Composition Theorem. To state the composition theorem, a bit more terminology is needed. A *session* (with SID *sid*) of a protocol π consists of all instances running code π with SID *sid*. We call these instances *highest-level instances*, i.e., those are exactly the instances that can receive inputs and provide outputs to the environment in the security experiment. The session *sid* of π further includes all instances, i.e., subroutines, that have received an input or output from another instance that is part of the session (except for outputs by highest-level instances, which are intended for the environment/higher-level protocols using the session of π).

A protocol π is called *subroutine respecting* if a protocol session of π interacts with other existing machine instances not belonging to the session only via inputs to and outputs from the highest level instances of the session, even when π is used as a subroutine within a higher-level protocol ρ.[4] The UC model provides a standard implementation of the subroutine respecting property via a subroutine respecting shell code that is added as a wrapper on top of the code of π and its subroutines. A protocol π is called *subroutine exposing* if every session s of the protocol provides an interface to the adversary that the adversary can use to learn whether some extended identity *eid* (specified by the adversary) is part of the session s. The UC model proposes a standard implementation of this mechanism by adding a so-called *directory machine*.

A (higher-level) protocol ρ is called (π, ϕ, ξ)-*compliant* if *(i)* all instances of all sessions of ρ perform write requests to input tapes only via forced-write and ignore outputs from instances that do not reveal their extended identities, *(ii)* there are never two external write requests (made by any instances of any session of ρ) for the same SID but one for code π while the other is for code ϕ, and *(iii)* the extended identities of all instances in all sessions of ρ that pass inputs to an instance with code π or ϕ satisfy the polytime predicate ξ. Given such a (π, ϕ, ξ)-compliant protocol ρ, the protocol $\rho^{\phi \to \pi}$ is defined just as ρ but replaces (input write requests to) subroutine instances of ϕ with (input write

---

[3] The UC model also defines security w.r.t. the *dummy adversary* $\mathcal{A}_{Dum}$, which essentially simply forwards messages between the environment and the protocol, and shows this definition to be equivalent. Also, if ξ always permits all identities, then one simply writes $\leq_{UC}$ instead of $\leq_{UC}^{\xi}$.

[4] The subroutine respecting property ensures that π running within a larger protocol ρ still behaves as in the security experiment, where an environment can interact only with one session of π and only via the highest-level instances of that session.

requests to) subroutine instances of π. In subroutines of ρ this replacement is done as well.[5] Now, the composition theorem is as follows:

Theorem 1 (UC Composition [6]). *Let ρ, π, ϕ be ppt protocols, let ξ be a ppt predicate, such that ρ is (π, ϕ, ξ)-compliant, π and ϕ are both subroutine respecting and subroutine exposing, and $\pi \leq_{UC}^{\xi} \phi$. Then $\rho^{\phi \to \pi} \leq_{UC} \rho$.*

2.2 The IITM Model

The general computational model of the IITM model is defined in terms of systems of (inexhaustible) interactive Turing machines (IITMs or just machines, for short). An interactive Turing machine in the IITM model is a probabilistic Turing machine with an arbitrary number of named bidirectional communication tapes.[6] The names are used for determining pairwise connections between machines in a system of machines.[7] Each machine specifies a CheckAddress and a Compute mode that it can run in, where the former is a ppt algorithm used for addressing individual copies/instances of the same machine and the latter is an algorithm describing the actual computations of instances of the machine (see below).

A *system* $\mathcal{Q}$ of IITMs is a set of IITMs of the form $\mathcal{Q} = \{M_1, \cdots, M_k, \, ! \, M_1', \cdots, \, ! \, M_{k'}'\}$[8] where the M_i and M_j' are machines and each tape name is shared by at most two machines in the system. Two machines are called *connected* if they have tapes with the same name. The operator '!' indicates that in a run of a system an unbounded number of (fresh) instances of a machine may be generated (e.g., to model multiple protocol sessions); for machines without this operator there is at most one instance of this machine in every run of the system. The first instance to be activated with external input a in a run of $\mathcal{Q}$ is an instance of the so-called master IITM; this machine is the only one with a so-called master (input) tape on which it receives external input a given to the system (jumping slightly ahead, the master IITM will be part of the environment). In a run of a system $\mathcal{Q}$, at any time only one machine instance is active and all other instances wait for new input. If, in $\mathcal{Q}$, machines M and M' are connected via a tape, say a tape named n, then an (instance of) M can send a message m to and thus trigger an (instance of) M' by writing m on its tape named n. To determine which instance of M' (if any) gets to process m, the following is done: The message is copied to the tape named n of the first existing instance of M', where instances are sorted by the order of their first creation. (The case that no instance of M' exists yet, is handled below.) That instance then processes m

---

[5] Formally, $\rho^{\phi \to \pi}$ contains an additional so-called UC composition shell code which acts as a wrapper that replaces these write requests.

[6] Formally, the IITM model uses unidirectional tapes. These can be paired to create bidirectional tapes as a special case, as shown in, e.g., [3,4].

[7] Tape names are hidden from and non-accessible to the logic of the machines. Hence, they can be renamed and even reconnected without changing the logic of the machine.

[8] Also written $M_1 \mid \cdots \mid M_k \mid \, ! \, M_1' \mid \cdots \mid \, ! \, M_{k'}'$.

using its CheckAddress algorithm, which either accepts or rejects the input. If the input is accepted, this instance continues processing m using the Compute algorithm. Otherwise, if the input is rejected, then its state is reset to the point before m was written to its tape and the next instance of M' is activated with message m in mode CheckAddress. If none of the existing copies accept and M' is in the scope of a '!', or no copies of M' exist yet, then a new instance of M' is created and runs in mode CheckAddress with input m on tape n. If it accepts, it gets to process m using Compute; otherwise, the fresh instance is deleted again and, as a fallback, an instance of the master IITM of $\mathcal{Q}$ is activated with empty input. The same fallback is also used if an instance (except for instances of the master IITM) stops without sending a message. A run stops if an instance of the master IITM does not produce output or a machine outputs a message on a special tape named decision (just as for the master IITM, only environments have such a special tape). Such a message is considered to be the overall output of the system.

Two systems $\mathcal{Q}$ and $\mathcal{R}$ are called indistinguishable ($\mathcal{Q} \equiv \mathcal{R}$) if the difference between the probability that $\mathcal{Q}$ outputs 1 (on the decision tape) and the probability that $\mathcal{R}$ outputs 1 is negligible in the security parameter η and the external input a (see Footnote 1).

Types of Systems and Their Runtime. We need the following terminology. For a system $\mathcal{Q}$, the tapes of machines in $\mathcal{Q}$ that do not have a matching tape, i.e., there does not exist another machine in $\mathcal{Q}$ with a tape of the same name, are called *external*. External tapes are grouped into *I/O* and *network tapes/interfaces* modeling direct connections to subroutines/higher-level protocols and network communication, respectively. We consider three different types of systems, modeling i) *real* and *ideal protocols/functionalities*, ii) *adversaries* and *simulators*, and iii) *environments*: Protocol systems (protocols) and environmental systems (environments) are systems which have an external I/O and network interface, i.e., they may have I/O and network tapes. Adversarial systems (adversaries) only have an external network interface. Environmental systems may contain a master machine and may produce output on the decision tape.

An environment must be *universally bounded*, i.e., the overall runtime of all instances in a run of an environmental system must be bounded by a single unique polynomial (in the security parameter and length of the external input) even when connected to and running with arbitrary systems. Protocols are required to be *environmentally bounded*, i.e., when combined with an environment, the overall system (which includes all instances of all machines) must run in polynomial time (in the security parameter and length of the external input), except for potentially a negligible set of runs. Note that the polynomial can depend on the environment. Given a protocol, an adversary for that protocol has to satisfy the following condition: the system obtained by combining the adversary and the protocol needs to be environmentally bounded. (Note that, e.g., dummy adversaries belong to this class for all protocols).

Simulation-Based Security. We can now define the security notion of strong simulatability: [9]

Definition 2. *Let $\mathcal{P}$ and $\mathcal{F}$ be protocols with the same I/O interface, the real and the ideal protocol, respectively. Then, $\mathcal{P}$ realizes $\mathcal{F}$ ($\mathcal{P} \leq_{IITM} \mathcal{F}$) if there exists an adversary $\mathcal{S}$ (a simulator or an ideal adversary) such that the systems $\mathcal{P}$ and $\mathcal{S} \mid \mathcal{F}$ have the same external interface and for all environments $\mathcal{E}$, connecting only to the external network and I/O interface of $\mathcal{P}$ (and hence, the external interface of $\mathcal{S} \mid \mathcal{F}$), it holds true that $\mathcal{E} \mid \mathcal{P} \equiv \mathcal{E} \mid \mathcal{S} \mid \mathcal{F}$.*

Composition Theorems. The main IITM composition theorem handles concurrent composition of a fixed number of (potentially different) protocols:

Theorem 2 (IITM Composition [18]). *Let $\mathcal{Q}, \mathcal{P}, \mathcal{F}$ be protocols such that $\mathcal{Q}$ and $\mathcal{P}$ as well as $\mathcal{Q}$ and $\mathcal{F}$ connect only via their external I/O interfaces with each other and $\mathcal{P} \leq_{IITM} \mathcal{F}$. Then, $\mathcal{Q} \mid \mathcal{P} \leq_{IITM} \mathcal{Q} \mid \mathcal{F}$.*

The IITM model also provides another security notion and a composition theorem for unbounded self-composition, which intuitively states the following:

Theorem 3 ((Informal) IITM Unbounded Self Composition). *Let $\mathcal{P}, \mathcal{F}$ be protocols with disjoint sessions. If there exists a simulator $\mathcal{S}$ such that no environment interacting with just a single session of $\mathcal{P}, \mathcal{F}$ can distinguish $\mathcal{P}$ and $\mathcal{S} \mid \mathcal{F}$, then $\mathcal{P} \leq_{IITM} \mathcal{F}$.*

In other words, it is sufficient to analyze the security of a single session of such a protocol to then conclude security of an unbounded number of sessions. This second theorem can be combined with the main composition theorem to obtain a statement similar to Theorem 1 of the UC model since from the assumption of Theorem 3 and if $\mathcal{Q}$ connects only to the external I/O interface of $\mathcal{P}$ (and hence, $\mathcal{F}$), we not only get $\mathcal{P} \leq_{IITM} \mathcal{F}$ but immediately also $\mathcal{Q} \mid \mathcal{P} \leq_{IITM} \mathcal{Q} \mid \mathcal{F}$. Roughly, $\mathcal{Q}$ corresponds to (higher-level machines of) ρ in Theorem 1, and $\mathcal{P}$ and $\mathcal{F}$ to the subroutines π and ϕ, respectively.

3   Embedding the UC Model in the IITM Model

We now show the embedding of the UC model into the IITM model. Formally, we consider arbitrary protocols $\pi_{UC}, \phi_{UC}, \rho_{UC}$ defined in the UC model such that $\pi_{UC} \leq_{UC}^{\xi} \phi_{UC}$ and the UC composition theorem can be applied to ρ_{UC} to obtain $\rho_{UC}^{\phi \to \pi} \leq_{UC} \rho_{UC}$. The overall goal of this section is to show that these protocols, security, and composability results naturally carry over to the IITM model (and then can further be used in the IITM model). We discuss the embedding in the other direction in Sect. 4.

---

[9] The IITM model also supports further security notions, including simulation w.r.t. the dummy adversary $\mathcal{A}_{Dum}$ or w.r.t. arbitrary adversaries $\mathcal{A}$ in the real world. All of these notions have been shown to be equivalent in the IITM model [18].

3.1 Main Conceptual Differences

Let us first list the key conceptual and technical differences of the UC and IITM models in terms of computational models, security definitions, and theorems. We further give pointers to where these difference are bridged.

Support for Dynamically Generated Machine Code (cf. Sect. 3.5)

1. The UC model directly supports dynamically determining the machine code of new machine instances. The IITM model fixes a finite static set of machine codes that can be instantiated during the run of a system.

Message Routing and Sender/Receiver Authentication (cf. Sect. 3.2)

2. Both the UC and IITM models provide an operation for machine instances to send messages to other instances. The UC model allows an instance to send messages to any other instance (subject to a few restrictions imposed by the security experiment). In the IITM model two instances can send messages to each other iff they are instances of two different machines M_1 and M_2 that share a tape with the same name.
3. The UC model distinguishes between two types of messages between protocol machines, namely those that provide input to a subroutine and those that provide output to a higher-level protocol. The IITM model does not have such a distinction but rather uses I/O tapes for both types of messages.
4. The UC model uses IDs of the form (pid, sid) to address messages to different protocol instances with the same machine code. The IITM model instead uses the generic CheckAddress mechanism which can be freely instantiated by protocol designers to capture the desired way of addressing of instances.
5. The UC model authenticates the sender of a message (within a protocol) by revealing its extended ID, consisting of the machine code and the ID of the instance. The IITM model authenticates the sender via the tape a message is received on, but does not guarantee that the receiver learns an ID identifying a specific instance or the code of the sender.
6. The adversary in the UC model cannot spawn any new protocol machine instances; he may only communicate with existing instances. The adversary in the IITM model can spawn new instances.
7. The UC model allows for specifying the receiver of a message via a predicate over the extended IDs of all existing machine instances (non-forced-writes). The CheckAddress algorithm of the IITM model bears some similarity, but runs only over the IDs of instances that share the same machine code.
8. In the UC model, outputs sent from the highest level protocol machines are redirected to the environment under certain conditions, in which case they are also modified by removing the machine code of the sender. Protocols in the IITM model send messages to the environment iff they are written to an external I/O tape, without redirections or modifications.

Polynomial Runtime Notions (cf. Sect. 3.2)

9. The UC and IITM models use different runtime notions, with the former being defined for individual machines that use runtime tokens while the latter is defined for entire systems and does not mandate a specific mechanism for enforcing runtime.

Support for Specific Classes of Environments (cf. Sect. 3.3)

10. The UC security notion supports identity bounded environments that use only sender identities as specified by a polytime predicate ξ. Environments in the IITM model are not required to adhere to any type of predicate.

Additional Requirements of the UC Security Notion and Composition Theorem (cf. Theorem 4 and Corollary 2)

11. The UC model requires environments to be balanced, providing a minimal amount of import to the adversary. Environments in the IITM model are not restricted in a similar way since adversaries in the IITM model do not require import to be able to run.
12. The UC security notion analyzes the security of a single session of a protocol. The IITM model offers two security notions: A single session security notion and a more general multi session security notion.
13. Protocols in the UC model have to be subroutine respecting and subroutine exposing to support composition. The main composition theorem of the IITM model does not have analogous requirements since the underlying security notion considers a more general multi-session setting, where sessions can share state with each other and subroutines can communicate with the environment.
14. Higher-level protocols in the UC model have to be compliant to support composition. Composition in the IITM model instead requires only that higher-level protocols may not connect to the network interface (the UC model enforces the latter at the level of its security notion).

These sometimes drastic technical differences create several challenges that we have to resolve while embedding the UC into the IITM model. For simplicity of presentation, in what follows we at first focus on the case where protocols use only machine codes from an arbitrary static but fixed set of different machine codes, rather than using (ad hoc) dynamically generated code (see Diff. 1); we denote this fixed set by Codes. Note that this is a very natural class of protocols which includes virtually all protocols proposed in the UC literature: generally, the machine codes of honest parties in a protocol are defined and fixed upfront, potentially as a parameter, before the protocol is analyzed. While corrupted parties are typically allowed to choose (almost) arbitrary receiver machine codes for their messages, spawning a new machine with machine code that is not used/recognized by an honest party does not give any additional power to the adversary; the adversary can just internally simulate that machine to obtain the same results. Hence, w.l.o.g. one can assume that corrupted parties in those protocols also communicate only with machines running some code from the set Codes, thereby meeting the above property. Nevertheless, to make our mapping formally complete, we show in Sect. 3.5 how our embedding and all security and composability results can easily be extended to handle also protocols with dynamically generated machine code, i.e., how to bridge Diff. 1.

3.2   Mapping Protocols

Let π_{UC} be a protocol that uses a finite set of machine codes Codes with $n :=$ |Codes|. Note that π_{UC} itself is also one of those codes, in what follows denoted by $c_\pi \in$ Codes to make the distinction between the protocol code c_π and the overall protocol π_{UC} clear.

Normalization. W.l.o.g., let us first bring the protocol π_{UC} and the codes Codes into a normalized form. These purely syntactical changes remove some technical edge cases that would otherwise needlessly complicate the mapping. Recall that, since π_{UC} is subroutine respecting, instances of that protocol can be grouped into disjoint protocol sessions. In each of those sessions, the only instances that can communicate with a higher-level protocol/the environment are instances of the highest-level machine with code c_π *and* with a certain SID sid_c that is specific to that protocol session. We refer to such a protocol session by sid_c. We assume that π_{UC} is such that within each protocol session sid_c there are no instances running code c_π with an SID different from sid_c. Most protocols from the literature naturally meet this property. Other protocols can trivially be modified by, e.g., adding a dummy forwarder on top of π_{UC} that forwards messages between the environment and those instances running code c_π with SID sid_c. This dummy then meets our assumption since the dummy code is now the highest level code and one can easily ensure that it is never called (as a subroutine) with an SID different from sid_c. Note that introducing a dummy does not affect any of the properties of and security results for π_{UC} so is indeed without loss of generality. We also assume that the protocol π_{UC} uses the standard mechanism proposed by the UC model for implementing the "subroutine-respecting" requirement, i.e., all codes in Codes already include the standard subroutine respecting shell code that acts as a wrapper. Among others, this wrapper guarantees that subroutine instances are aware of the SID sid_c of their protocol session since all subroutine instances have SIDs of the form (sid_c, sid'). Again, this is already the case for virtually all protocols from the literature. If a protocol does not use this mechanism, it can be added on top of the protocol since this also does not affect any of the security properties of and results proven for π_{UC} given that π_{UC} is already assumed to be subroutine respecting.

IITMs and Tapes. We model the protocol π_{IITM} in the IITM model via a system containing machines $M_{c_\pi}, M_{c_1}, \ldots, M_{c_{n-1}}$, where Codes $= \{c_\pi, c_1, \ldots, c_{n-1}\}$ and instances of M_c essentially run code $c \in$ Codes; see the left hand-side of Fig. 1 for an illustration of the static structure, i.e., the set of machines and I/O tape connections, of the mapped protocol system π_{IITM}. Just as π_{UC}, π_{IITM} is able

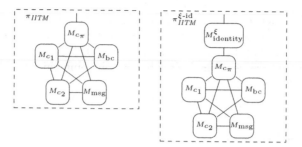

Fig. 1. Left: Static structure of a protocol π_{IITM} using three Codes $= \{c_\pi, c_1, c_2\}$ constructed by our mapping. Right: Static structure of the modified protocol $\pi_{IITM}^{\xi\text{-id}}$ that enforces ξ-identity bounded environments (cf. Sect. 3.3). Lines denote internal connections via I/O tapes and the external I/O tape to the environment. Each Machine also has an external network tape to the adversary (not shown). In a run each machine can be instantiated arbitrarily often, with instances having IDs of the form (pid, sid).

to create an unbounded number of instances of these machines running any of the codes in Codes (see below). Each pair of machines $M_c, M_{c'}$ is connected by a pair (t, t') of uniquely named internal I/O tapes. One of the tapes, say t, is used by (instances of) M_c to provide subroutine inputs to and receive subroutine outputs from $M_{c'}$, while the other tape is used for the reverse direction where $M_{c'}$ provides subroutine inputs to and receives subroutine outputs from M_c.[10] Altogether these connections allow instances of an arbitrary machine to send inputs and outputs to and receive outputs and inputs from any (instance of) *another* machine in the system simply by choosing the appropriate tape. While generally not required by protocols from the literature, if required by π_{UC} we can also extend the protocol π_{IITM} to allow for sending messages between different instances of the *same* machine. This is done by adding a special bouncer machine M_{bc} to the system π_{IITM}. M_{bc} connects to all machines in the system via a pair of I/O tapes each. Each time (a session-specific instance of) this machine receives a message, it returns the same message on the same tape. Hence, a machine M_c can send a message to M_{bc} to effectively send that message to an instance of itself (see below for how we ensure that this message is delivered to the correct receiving instance of M_c). Altogether, these internal I/O tapes bridge Diff. 2 and Diff. 3. In addition to these internal I/O tapes, each machine M_c has one external (unconnected) network tape that can be used to communicate with the network adversary. The machine M_{c_π} also has an unconnected I/O tape which can be used to receive inputs from and send outputs to higher-level protocols/the environment. These external tapes capture permitted communication flows between the protocol, the adversary, and the environment as defined in the security game of the UC model.

---

[10] Typically, the subroutine relation goes only in one direction and in this case just one tape is needed. But in general the relationship is allowed to go both ways, in which case using two tapes allows for distinguishing which relationship is meant.

In addition to the above machines, we also add another machine M_{msg}. Jumping slightly ahead, session specific instances of this machine are responsible for (i) implementing some of the more advanced message transmission and message redirection features of the UC model and (ii) forcing the environment to be balanced, i.e., to provide a minimal amount of import to the adversary. This machine connects via a pair of I/O tapes to all machines M_c, $c \in \mathsf{Codes}$, and offers one external network tape for communication with the adversary. We describe the behavior of M_{msg} along with the description of machines M_c below.

Addressing of Instances. In π_{UC}, an instance of a machine running code c is uniquely addressed by an ID of the form (pid, sid) and learns the ID (pid_s, sid_s) and code c_s of senders who provide input or subroutine output. Furthermore, by our initial normalization of π_{UC}, we have that $sid = (sid_c, sid')$ for internal instances, i.e., instances running code $c \neq c_\pi$, and $sid = sid_c$ for instances running c_π. To capture these unique IDs for instances in π_{IITM}, we use a suitable instantiation of the $\mathsf{CheckAddress}$ mode, cf. Fig. 2. That is, instances of M_c expect incoming inputs/outputs m to be of the form $((pid, sid, c), (pid_s, sid_s, c_s), m')$, where m' is the actual message body.[11] Network messages from the adversary are expected to be of the form $((pid, sid, c), m')$.[12] Furthermore, if $c \neq c_\pi$ (i.e., the current machine instance is an internal subroutine), then it is also required that $sid = (sid', sid'')$ for some sid', sid'', where sid' is interpreted to be the SID sid_c of the protocol session. Messages not conforming to this format are rejected immediately. If the current instance is fresh, i.e., has not previously accepted any messages, then the message is accepted and (in mode $\mathsf{Compute}$) this instance stores (pid, sid) as its own ID. If the instance is not fresh, i.e., has previously accepted a message with receiver ID (pid_0, sid_0), then incoming messages are accepted if and only if they are prefixed by the same ID, i.e., $pid = pid_0$, $sid = sid_0$. Hence, each instance is effectively assigned a unique ID, namely, the first ID (pid_0, sid_0) that it has ever accepted. There will also never be a second instance accepting the same ID since all message for this ID will already be accepted by the first instance with that ID. Given this definition of $\mathsf{CheckAddress}$, an instance (pid_s, sid_s) of machine M_{c_s} can send a message m' to the unique instance (pid, sid) of machine M_c by writing the message $((pid, sid, c), (pid_s, sid_s, c_s), m')$ on one of the two tapes connecting to M_c (this bridges Diff. 4).

---

[11] The only exception are inputs received on the single external I/O tape from the environment, which use the header $((pid, sid), (pid_s, sid_s, c_s), m')$. This directly corresponds to the UC experiment, where environments specify only the receiver ID (pid, sid) but not the receiver code, which is rather determined by the experiment. We also note that, except for outputs returned from the protocol to the environment, it is actually not necessary to include c in the header of any messages on I/O tapes. After all, the receiving machines M_c are already aware of their own code. We chose to nevertheless include c in the header since this matches the format of write commands in the UC model more closely.

[12] Network messages do not contain a sender identity since the sender is always know to be the network adversary.

Mode CheckAddress:

Let m be the message received on some tape.

If this is the highest level machine (i.e., $c = c_\pi$) and m was received on the single external I/O tape from the environment, then try to parse m as $((pid, sid), (pid_s, sid_s, c_s), m')$. Otherwise, if m was received on another I/O tape then try to parse it as $((pid, sid, c), (pid_s, sid_s, c_s), m')$. Try to parse m as $((pid, sid, c), m')$ if it was received on the network tape. Furthermore, if $c \neq c_\pi$, also try to parse sid as (sid', sid'')

If parsing fails, **return reject.** $\begin{cases} id \text{ is a global variable that is } \bot \text{ iff this instance is} \\ \text{fresh. It is set to be the ID of the current instance} \\ \text{in mode Compute upon accepting the first message.} \end{cases}$

if $id = \bot \lor id = (pid, sid)$ **then**

    return accept.

else

    return reject.

end if

Fig. 2. Checkaddress mode of the machine M_c for $c \in$ Codes

All machines M_c are defined in such a way that they never lie about the sender identity of a message, and hence, the receiver always learns the correct identity of the sender (see the Compute mode described below). Specifically, if an instance (pid_s, sid_s) of a machine M_{c_s} sends a message m on some tape, then it will either be of the form $((pid, sid, c), (pid_s, sid_s, c_s), m')$ (if it is sent on an I/O tape) or of the form $((pid_s, sid_s, c_s), m')$ (if it is sent on a network tape connected to the adversary). This bridges Diff. 5 by providing the same level of authentication of the sender instance in π_{IITM} as in π_{UC}.

Runtime Behavior. The Compute mode of a machine M_c is mostly a direct implementation of the protocol logic given by code c (cf. Fig. 3). Upon its first activation in this mode an instance (pid, sid) of M_c stores its own ID (pid, sid) in a global variable id. The machine then checks, also during subsequent activations, if it has already received any inputs/outputs on an I/O tape and stops the activation otherwise. This captures that the network adversary in the UC model is not allowed to spawn new machine instances. That is, even though spawning a new protocol machine instance is technically possible in π_{IITM}, the resulting instance will not do anything until it receives the first input or output from another protocol machine or the environment, which results in a behavior that is equivalent to the one in the UC model (this bridges Diff. 6). Once it receives its first input/output on an I/O tape (and therefore the corresponding instance in π_{UC} is created), the instance registers itself with the instance (ϵ, sid_c) of M_{msg} by sending $((\epsilon, sid_c, c_{M_{msg}}), (pid, sid, c), \texttt{register})$ on an I/O tape connected to M_{msg}. This instance, which is specific to the protocol session sid_c, stores the ID (pid, sid, c) and immediately returns an acknowledgement. Finally, if this is an instance of the highest-level machine M_{c_π} and it receives some import $i > 0$ in a message from the environment, then it sends $((\epsilon, sid_c, c_{M_{msg}}), (pid, sid, c), (\texttt{notifyImport}, i))$ to notify the session specific instance M_{msg} about this amount. M_{msg} stores i and returns an acknowledgement; we describe the purpose of registrations and import notifications later on.

Once all of the above steps are finished (and the instance has not aborted), the instance processes the incoming message m by running the code c. Note that

---

Mode Compute:

Let $m = ((pid, sid, c), (pid_s, sid_s, c_s), m')$ be the message received on some I/O tape t
respectively $m = ((pid, sid, c), m')$ received on the network tape.

if $id = \perp$ then   ⎧ Store the ID of this instance such that the
  $id \leftarrow (pid, sid)$ ⎨ CheckAddress mode can use this information.
end if   ⎩

if this instance has not received any message on an I/O tape yet then
  Stop the current activation of this instance.   {This activates the environment.
end if

if this is the first message received on an I/O tape then
  Send $((\epsilon, sid_c), (pid, sid, c), \mathtt{register})$ on the tape connected to M_{msg}, where sid_c
  can be parsed from sid. Wait for the response and then continue.
end if

if $c = c_\pi$ and m' is a message on the external I/O tape containing import $i > 0$ then
  Send $((\epsilon, sid_c), (pid, sid, c), (\mathtt{notifyImport}, i))$ on the tape connected to M_{msg},
  where sid_c can be parsed from sid. Wait for the response and then continue.
end if

// Main logic //

Run code c using the sender information (pid_s, sid_s, c_s) (or ϵ if the message
is from the network adversary), incoming message m', and the tape type $tt \in$
$\{\mathtt{input}, \mathtt{output}, \mathtt{backdoor}\}$ that m' is written on determined from the tape t.

When c wants to send a message, proceed as described in the paragraph "Sending
messages" on Page 18. In particular, ensure that the resulting message contains the
correct sender identity (pid, sid, c) in the header.

Fig. 3. Compute mode of the machine M_c for $c \in$ Codes

this is indeed possible: M_c can determine whether m is an input, subroutine
output, or a backdoor message depending on the tape m is received on. Inputs
and outputs received from other protocol machines also contain the full extended
identity of the sending instance, including the machine code, so M_c has access to
the same information that instances in π_{UC} have in the UC model upon receiving
a new message.

Sending Messages. During the simulation of code c, whenever the code c
wants to provide input/output m' to an instance (pid', sid') of a machine $M_{c'}$,
M_c chooses the I/O tape t that connects M_c and $M_{c'}$ and which models an
input/output from M_c to $M_{c'}$. Then M_c writes $((pid', sid', c'), (pid, sid, c), m')$
on tape t, where (pid, sid) is the ID of the current instance of M_c. If the code c
wants to send a backdoor message m' to the network adversary, M_c writes the
message $((pid, sid, c), m')$ on its network tape.

We still have to explain how we deal with Diff. 7. That is, code c might choose
to use a non-forced-write command and specify the recipient of a message not by
their extended ID but by a predicate P on extended identities. First, observe that
if a message is sent to a backdoor tape, then it must be for the network adversary by definition of the UC security experiment. Hence, this case is easy to handle in M_c: if the non-forced-write request is to a backdoor tape, then the message is sent as described above to the network adversary. Second, for inputs and
outputs observe that those may not be sent directly to the identities of the envi-

ronment or the adversary. So the predicate may match only identities of (existing) machines within the protocol, i.e., the message will be sent internally. We can easily mimic this in the IITM model via the machine M_{msg}. Recall that, by the above construction, whenever a new machine instance receives the first input or output on an I/O tape in mode Compute, it registers its extended identity (pid, sid, c) at (a session dependent instance of) M_{msg}. The machine M_{msg} offers a "nonForcedWrite" command to the machines M_c that, given message body m', message type $mt \in \{$input, output$\}$, and predicate P, runs the predicate P on the list of existing protocol machine instances to find the first matching one. The message m is then delivered to that instance as described above, but with the I/O tape chosen based on mt and the sender of the message (which is written in the header of the message) set to be the machine instance (pid, sid, c) that called the nonForcedWrite command. If no matching instance is found, then M_{msg} aborts and the environment is activated instead, just as in the UC model.

There is another special case that we have to deal with, namely the highest-level protocol machine M_{c_π} sending a subroutine output (cf. Diff. 8). In the UC model, this output is redirected to the environment (without the code of the sender but instead including the code of the intended receiver) iff the current instance has challenge SID sid_c and the receiver extended identity does not yet exist as an instance of a protocol machine. Observe that by our normalization of π_{UC} all instances of M_{c_π} that are part of protocol session sid_c also have SID sid_c, i.e., the first condition is always met. The second condition can be checked using the information stored in the machine M_{msg}, yielding the following implementation. Whenever an instance (pid_s, sid_s) of M_{c_π} wants to send a subroutine output m' to an extended receiver identity $eid_r = (pid_r, sid_r, c_r)$, M_{c_π} first asks M_{msg} whether eid_r already exists in the system (via a special existsInstance? request). If so, the message is sent by M_{c_π} to the instance (pid_r, sid_r) of machine M_{c_r} as described above. If this instance does not exist yet, then the message $m = ((pid_r, sid_r, c_r), (pid_s, sid_s), m')$ is sent on the single external I/O tape of M_{c_π} that is connected to the environment. Note that, unlike for other messages, the sender machine code c_π is not contained in the header of m in this case. Altogether, this precisely captures the behavior of the UC security experiment and hence bridges Diff. 8.

Import Handling. We still have to explain the purpose of the notifyImport message. Instances of M_{msg} use these notifications to keep track of the list of imports received from the environment in this protocol session. The adversary can send a special totalImport? request to learn the current list of imports. Jumping slightly ahead, this information will be used by the simulator constructed in Sect. 3.3 to bridge Diff. 11: Instead of requiring the environment in the IITM model to be balanced (i.e., it has to provide at least the same amount of import to the simulator as it provides to the protocol), the simulator rather indirectly enforces this property itself. That is, the simulator checks how much import the protocol has received already and, if the protocol has received more than the simulator, adds the missing difference to its own received import. We note that the security notion of the UC model requires runtime bounds to be simulated correctly and hence adversaries/simulators generally must already be aware of the current protocol imports not just for the whole session but even for individual (highest-level) instances in a session. The added `totalImport?` request only makes this property explicit via a fixed mechanism. Nevertheless, we show in the full version [21] that our results can actually also be obtained without adding a `totalImport?` request. This, however, requires a more involved mapping than the one we present here.

Finally, we encode runtime import for the machine codes c in unary instead of binary. This seemingly cosmetic change does not affect the behavior or security results obtained for the protocol π_{UC}. But it allows us to argue that an environment in the IITM model, which may send arbitrary inputs of at most polynomial length to the protocol, can send at most a polynomial amount of import just as an environment in the UC model.

Altogether, we define $\pi_{IITM} := \ !M_{c_\pi} \mid \ !M_{c_1} \mid \ldots \mid \ !M_{c_{n-1}} \mid \ !M_{\mathrm{msg}} \mid \ !M_{\mathrm{bc}}$. Based on the construction and the discussion above, we can easily check that π_{UC} and π_{IITM} behave the same:

Lemma 1. *For all unbounded (including runtime) environments interacting with π_{UC}/π_{IITM} by sending inputs/receiving outputs but also by directly interacting with arbitrary protocol instances over the network, there is a bijective mapping between runs of π_{UC} in the UC model and π_{IITM} in the IITM model such that both protocols behave identically. Both protocols have similar computational complexity.*

Proof. By construction, the only difference between both protocols is the added explicit `totalImport?` request on the network in π_{IITM}. In the UC setting with π_{UC} this request can instead be internally simulated by the environment. □

We show in the next lemma (proven in the full version [21]) that π_{IITM} is a well-defined IITM protocol by showing that it meets the IITM runtime notion for protocols. This bridges Diff. 9 by relating the UC to the IITM runtime notion.

Lemma 2. *The protocol π_{IITM} is environmentally bounded in the IITM model if π_{UC} is ppt in the UC model.*

3.3 UC Security Implies IITM Security

Having defined a mapping of protocols from the UC to the IITM model, we now prove that this mapping preserves security results. That is, if $\pi_{UC} \leq_{UC}^{\xi} \phi_{UC}$, then $\pi_{IITM}^{\xi\text{-id}} \leq_{IITM} \phi_{IITM}^{\xi\text{-id}}$ for protocols mapped as described in Sect. 3.2 plus an additional mechanism to capture ξ-identity bounded environments in the IITM model, which unlike the UC model does not restrict environments. This mechanism does not change the IITM model. We rather show that ξ-identity bounded behavior can be enforced within protocols themselves, thereby bridging Diff. 10.

While designing this mechanism, we found that the definition of ξ-identity bounded environments as used in the UC model actually does not support composition and the proof of the UC composition theorem is flawed. We describe the issue in detail in the full version [21]. In a nutshell, the issue is that the UC model allows for defining the identity set ξ via a predicate over the current configuration of *the whole* system. The configuration of the system and hence potentially the behavior of the predicate is very different in the security experiment, where there are only instances of the environment, adversary, and one session of π_{UC} respectively ϕ_{UC}, compared to the composition theorem, where there are additional instances of a higher-level protocol ρ as well as potentially multiple sessions of π_{UC}/ϕ_{UC}. Hence, even if ρ is ξ-compliant in the setting where instances of ρ and multiple sessions of π_{UC}/ϕ_{UC} exist, this does not imply that an environment internally simulating ρ while running only with π_{UC}/ϕ_{UC} (but with no actual instances of ρ and only a single session of π_{UC}/ϕ_{UC} being present in the system) also is ξ-identity-bounded. Based on this observation, in the full version we show a concrete counterexample for the UC composition theorem.

Therefore, instead of trying to translate the existing identity-bounded mechanism, which does not support composition in the UC model, and hence, would also not support composition when faithfully translated to the IITM model, we propose a fix for the UC model and then transfer that fixed version to the IITM model. Specifically, instead of defining ξ as a predicate over the configuration of the whole system, we define it as a predicate over the (whole history of) inputs sent and outputs received by the environment/ρ to/from one session of the subroutine π/ϕ. This fix, which follows a similar idea as [1], indeed solves the problem: The sequence of messages between ρ and one of its subroutine sessions remains the same (for each respective subroutine session) even if we only simulate ρ within an environment. Hence, such an environment running directly with a single session of the subroutine π/ϕ is indeed ξ-identity-bounded. This fixes this issue of the UC composition theorem and the proof thereof. This fix should also be sufficient for practical purposes; we are not aware of any protocols that have been proven secure for a ξ that falls outside this class. We provide an extended discussion in the full version [21].

We now embed this (fixed) definition of ξ-identity-bounded environments into the IITM model as follows. The obvious option would be to restrict environments in the IITM model in the same way. However, this would require us to change the IITM model and its theorems and proofs. We rather extend the protocols π_{IITM} and ϕ_{IITM} in a generic way to manually enforce the ξ-identity-bounded property for all environments. This is a technique that is commonly used in the IITM model, see for example [14,16]. Formally, we add to each protocol an additional dummy forwarder machine $M_{identity}^{\xi}$ between the environment and the highest-level machine M_{c_π} respectively M_{c_ϕ}, creating new protocols $\pi_{IITM}^{\xi\text{-id}}$ and $\phi_{IITM}^{\xi\text{-id}}$ (cf. right hand-side of Fig. 1). In a run, (a session specific instance of) $M_{identity}^{\xi}$ checks for every input whether ξ is met and, if not, drops the input, thereby activating the environment as a fallback. This achieves the desired goal: On the one hand, environments that are already ξ-identity-bounded are not restricted since for such environments the original protocols π_{IITM}/ϕ_{IITM} and the modified protocols $\pi_{IITM}^{\xi\text{-id}}/\phi_{IITM}^{\xi\text{-id}}$ behave identically. For any other environment $\mathcal{E}$, the combination of $\mathcal{E}$ and $M_{identity}^{\xi}$ constitutes a ξ-identity-bounded environment for the original protocol. Note that the extended protocols are still environmentally bounded as $M_{identity}^{\xi}$ adds only a polynomial number of steps; in particular, ξ can be evaluated in polynomial time by definition. Altogether, this mechanism indeed bridges Diff. 10.

We can now show that $\leq_{UC}$ security implies $\leq_{IITM}$ security for the mapped protocols; we discuss the reverse implication afterwards. In the full version [21], we show that $\leq_{UC}$ implies $\leq_{IITM}$ in general by using a somewhat more involved protocol embedding. Here, using the (simpler) protocol embedding from Sect. 3.2, we formally show this result for a certain though very general class of simulators, in fact, a class of simulators containing virtually all simulators that have ever been considered in the literature so far, as further explained below.

More specifically, first recall that, as stated in the UC model, to prove $\pi \leq_{UC} \phi$ instead of constructing a simulator for every adversary, it suffices to construct a simulator just for the dummy adversary. (From such a simulator, simulators for arbitrary adversaries can be constructed). The dummy adversary as considered in the UC model allows the environment to provide import i via a special message, say $op(i)$, which is different from network messages intended for the protocol. The dummy accepts this import and returns an acknowledgement to the environment without sending a message to the protocol. We therefore consider the class of simulators which also do not require an interaction with the ideal protocol upon receiving import via op from the environment. This is a natural requirement that should be trivially met by simulators for all reasonable protocol definitions, also considering that a protocol in reality cannot rely on the network adversary sending a notification each time the adversary decides to increase its runtime bound. Indeed, we are not aware of any UC protocols from the literature where the simulator has to interact with the ideal protocol upon receiving additional import via op. Simulators are rather defined in a black-box fashion where they implicitly simulate the dummy adversary and only specify their behavior for network messages that are forwarded by the dummy to the real protocol. Since the dummy adversary already handles the input op without sending any network messages to the protocol, all such black-box simulators trivially have the stipulated property. We note again that, as mentioned above, this (though natural) requirement on simulators is not formally necessary.

Theorem 4. *Let* π_{UC}, ϕ_{UC} *be such that* $\pi_{UC} \leq_{UC}^{\xi} \phi_{UC}$. *Then it holds true that* $\pi_{IITM}^{\xi\text{-}id} \leq_{IITM} \phi_{IITM}^{\xi\text{-}id}$.

Proof (sketch). We here show this theorem assuming that the simulator for proving $\pi_{UC} \leq_{UC}^{\xi} \phi_{UC}$ has the properties stipulated above. The proof proceeds in 4 steps (see the full version [21] for details and the general case):

Reduction to UC. We first define an IITM dummy adversary $\mathcal{A}_{Dum,IITM}^{UC\text{-}bounded}$ and an IITM simulator $\mathcal{S}_{IITM}^{UC\text{-}bounded}$ that adhere to the UC runtime notion and enforce the balanced requirement for environments. Specifically, both machines are defined to internally run the UC (real and ideal) adversaries $\mathcal{A}_{Dum,UC}$ and $\mathcal{S}_{UC}$, respectively, but add a wrapper around them. This wrapper handles the added `totalImport?` request on the network itself by forwarding it to M_{msg} and returning the response without involving the internally simulated UC adversary. Also, upon each activation the wrapper first checks whether its protocol has received one or more new imports (via a call to `totalImport?`) such that its total import now exceeds the total import directly provided by the environment to the adversary. If so, the wrapper adds these missing imports to the internally simulated UC adversary via (potentially several calls to) the operation op. Then, and in all other cases, the adversary continues as the internal UC adversary.

Consider an IITM environment $\mathcal{E}_{IITM}^{\text{single},\xi}$ that sends inputs and network messages (via the dummy adversary) only to a single session of the protocol π_{IITM}/ϕ_{IITM}, adheres to the ξ-identity bound, and tries to distinguish the worlds $\mathcal{A}_{Dum,IITM}^{\text{UC-bounded}} \,|\, \pi_{IITM}$ and $\mathcal{S}_{IITM}^{\text{UC-bounded}} \,|\, \phi_{IITM}$. We can reduce this case to the indistinguishability of $\mathcal{A}_{Dum,UC} \,|\, \pi_{UC}$ and $\mathcal{S}_{UC} \,|\, \phi$ in UC by constructing an UC environment $\mathcal{E}_{UC}$ that internally simulates $\mathcal{E}_{IITM}^{\text{single},\xi}$. $\mathcal{E}_{UC}$ further internally simulates responses to `totalImport?` requests. Each time $\mathcal{E}_{IITM}$ wants to provide import as part of an input to the protocol such that the total protocol import exceeds the total import provided to the adversary so far, $\mathcal{E}_{UC}$ first adds the missing difference via a call to op to the adversary and only then sends the input to the protocol. By construction, $\mathcal{E}_{UC}$ is balanced. To see that $\mathcal{E}_{UC}$ has the same distinguishing advantage as $\mathcal{E}_{IITM}^{\text{single},\xi}$, there are only two aspects that we have to argue. Firstly, in the IITM setting a protocol might obtain one or more imports that bring the total above the amount of import of the adversary. Then, as soon as the adversary wrapper becomes active the next time, it calls op for each of these imports, and then the internally simulated adversary processes the message. In the UC world, $\mathcal{E}_{UC}$ first calls op, then provides import to the protocol. This might be repeated several times until, at some point, the adversary processes whatever message $\neq op$ it receives next. So while the same number of calls to op with the same import are used in both UC and IITM setting, formally the state of the protocol might be different when op is executed. Due to the definition of the dummy and assumption on the simulator, op is independent of the state of the protocol, i.e., this formal difference does not actually affect the behavior of the run. (This is the only case where a slight mismatch occurs. All other messages are processed at the same points in the run by construction). Secondly, the UC environment is bounded in its current import, so might not be able to complete the simulation. We can find an external input of suitable length, which determines the initial import, such that this case does not occur.

Environments Without the ξ-Identity Bound. The indistinguishability of $\mathcal{A}_{Dum,IITM}^{\text{UC-bounded}} \,|\, \pi_{IITM}$ and $\mathcal{S}_{IITM}^{\text{UC-bounded}} \,|\, \phi_{IITM}$ for environments $\mathcal{E}_{IITM}^{\text{single},\xi}$ is easily seen to be equivalent to indistinguishability of $\mathcal{A}_{Dum,IITM}^{\text{UC-bounded}} \,|\, \pi_{IITM}^{\xi\text{-id}}$ and $\mathcal{S}_{IITM}^{\text{UC-bounded}} \,|\, \phi_{IITM}^{\xi\text{-id}}$ for arbitrary single session environments $\mathcal{E}_{IITM}^{\text{single}}$.

Indistinguishability for the IITM Dummy. So far, we have only considered the dummy $\mathcal{A}_{Dum,IITM}^{\text{UC-bounded}}$ which adheres to the UC runtime notion and hence might stop whenever he has to forward more bits than he has import. However, we actually have to show $\leq_{IITM}$ for the IITM dummy $\mathcal{A}_{Dum,IITM}$ which never stops and always forwards messages. The idea for constructing a simulator $\mathcal{S}_{IITM}$ for $\mathcal{A}_{Dum,IITM}$ is as follows: Observe that the only difference between $\mathcal{A}_{Dum,IITM}^{\text{UC-bounded}}$ and $\mathcal{A}_{Dum,IITM}$ is that $\mathcal{A}_{Dum,IITM}^{\text{UC-bounded}}$ might stop if it has too little import, which $\mathcal{S}_{IITM}^{\text{UC-bounded}}$ then also simulates. So we define the simulator $\mathcal{S}_{IITM}$ to internally run $\mathcal{S}_{IITM}^{\text{UC-bounded}}$ but, upon each activation, potentially generate additional import via a call to op such that an imaginary $\mathcal{A}_{Dum,IITM}^{\text{UC-bounded}}$, if given the same overall import, would not stop. We show that it is indeed possible to build such a simulator, also while remaining in the polynomial runtime notion of the IITM model (this is because the additional import is polynomial in the runtime of the environment and hence the same argument as in Lemma 2 still applies).

We can then reduce a single session environment $\mathcal{E}_{IITM}^{\text{single}}$ trying to distinguish $\mathcal{A}_{Dum,IITM} \,|\, \pi_{IITM}^{\xi\text{-id}}$ and $\mathcal{S}_{IITM} \,|\, \phi_{IITM}^{\xi\text{-id}}$ to indistinguishability of the worlds $\mathcal{A}_{Dum,IITM}^{\text{UC-bounded}} \,|\, \pi_{IITM}^{\xi\text{-id}}$ and $\mathcal{S}_{IITM}^{\text{UC-bounded}} \,|\, \phi_{IITM}^{\xi\text{-id}}$ by constructing an environment $\mathcal{E}'^{\,\text{single}}_{IITM}$ that internally simulates $\mathcal{E}_{IITM}^{\text{single}}$ plus the additional import generated by the wrapper portion of $\mathcal{S}_{IITM}$.

Indistinguishability of Multiple Sessions. Since the protocols have disjoint sessions and $\mathcal{A}_{Dum,IITM} \,|\, \pi_{IITM}^{\xi\text{-id}}$ and $\mathcal{S}_{IITM} \,|\, \phi_{IITM}^{\xi\text{-id}}$ are indistinguishable for any environment $\mathcal{E}_{IITM}^{\text{single}}$ interacting with just a single session, the second composition theorem of the IITM model (cf. Theorem 3) immediately implies that $\pi_{IITM}^{\xi\text{-id}} \leq_{IITM} \phi_{IITM}^{\xi\text{-id}}$, i.e., there also exists a simulator for arbitrary environments $\mathcal{E}_{IITM}$ interacting with multiple sessions. $\square$

The construction of the simulator $\mathcal{S}_{IITM}^{\text{UC-bounded}}$ in the above proof bridges Diff. 11: Since the IITM model does not require that environments provide a certain minimal amount of import to the adversary (the IITM model does not even require the concept of import), the simulator instead enforces this property itself by manually adding the difference between its own import and the import received by the protocol. The above proof also bridges Diff. 12 by showing that the UC security notion implies the single session IITM security notion. The second composition theorem of the IITM model (cf. Theorem 3) then directly implies security for multiple sessions.

The other implication of Theorem 4 is more involved since the IITM model considers a larger class of adversaries, including simulators, than the UC model. Specifically, the runtime of UC simulators is required to be bounded by a fixed polynomial (in their current import) independently of the environment. An IITM simulator does not need to adhere to any import mechanism. Its polynomial runtime bound is rather taken over η and the length of the external input a and may even depend on the environment. In fact, the following lemma shows that the reverse implication of Theorem 4 does not hold true in general:

Lemma 3. *If time-lock puzzles exist, then there exist protocols π_{UC} and ϕ_{UC} such that for the mapped protocols we have $\pi_{IITM}^{\xi\text{-id}} \leq_{IITM} \phi_{IITM}^{\xi\text{-id}}$ but $\pi_{UC} \leq_{UC} \phi_{UC}$ does not hold true. (These protocols are pretty simple, and hence, the result works for all mappings that preserve the protocols behaviors).*

We recall the definition of time-lock puzzles and formally prove this result in the full version, along with a discussion on the implications for security results. If we consider only the subclass of IITM simulators that corresponds to the class of UC simulators that adhere to the UC runtime notion, such as $S_{IITM}^{UC\text{-bounded}}$ constructed in the proof of Theorem 4, we have the following reverse implication:

Theorem 5. *Let $A_{Dum,IITM}^{UC\text{-bounded}}$ be the IITM dummy adversary that enforces balanced environments and adheres to the UC runtime notion as defined in the proof of Theorem 4. Let $S_{IITM}^{UC\text{-bounded}}$ be an IITM simulator that is of the form as the one described in the proof of Theorem 4.*

If $A_{Dum,IITM}^{UC\text{-bounded}} \mid \pi_{IITM}^{\xi\text{-id}}$ and $S_{IITM}^{UC\text{-bounded}} \mid \phi_{IITM}^{\xi\text{-id}}$ are indistinguishable for all IITM environments interacting with a single session of the protocol, then we have $\pi_{IITM}^{\xi\text{-id}} \leq_{IITM} \phi_{IITM}^{\xi\text{-id}}$ (multi session IITM security) as well as $\pi_{UC} \leq_{UC}^{\xi} \phi_{UC}$.

We provide the proof in the full version [21]. Theorem 5 shows that the implication of Theorem 4 is non-trivial and non-degenerate since our mapping not only preserves security results but also distinguishing attacks. That is, if for all UC simulators there is a ξ-identity bounded UC environment that distinguishes π_{UC} and ϕ_{UC}, then Theorem 5 implies that for all IITM simulators in the UC runtime class there is an IITM environment distinguishing $\pi_{IITM}^{\xi\text{-id}}$ and $\phi_{IITM}^{\xi\text{-id}}$.

3.4 UC Composition Implies IITM Composition

In this section, we investigate in how far composition results carry over from UC to IITM. We first observe the following direct corollary of Theorem 4:

Corollary 1 (Composition from the UC theorem). *Let $\pi_{UC}, \phi_{UC}, \rho_{UC}$ be UC protocols such that $\pi_{UC} \leq_{UC}^{\xi} \phi_{UC}$ and the UC composition theorem can be applied to ρ_{UC} to obtain $\rho_{UC}^{\phi \to \pi} \leq_{UC} \rho_{UC}$. Let ρ_{IITM} and $\rho_{IITM}^{\phi \to \pi}$ be the IITM protocols obtained by applying the mapping from Sect. 3.2 to ρ_{UC} and $\rho_{UC}^{\phi \to \pi}$.[13] Then $\rho_{IITM}^{\phi \to \pi} \leq_{IITM} \rho_{IITM}$.*

While this corollary shows that security results obtained via the UC composition theorem carry over, it does not actually provide insights into how the UC and IITM composition theorems relate. To answer this question, we next show that the same composition statement can be obtained directly from the IITM composition theorem without relying on the UC theorem.

Obtaining Corollary 1 from the IITM Composition Theorem. We start by observing that the IITM theorem requires that higher-level protocols access the subroutine π_{IITM}/ϕ_{IITM} only via its external I/O interface, i.e., the external I/O tapes that the environment had access to in absense of the higher-level protocol. In the special case of our mapped protocols π_{IITM}/ϕ_{IITM}, which offer

---

[13] Note that $\rho_{UC}^{\phi \to \pi}$ also contains some UC composition shell code introduced by the UC composition theorem to replace the code c_ϕ with c_π. $\rho_{IITM}^{\phi \to \pi}$ is thus obtained by mapping the overall machine codes, including the UC composition shell code.

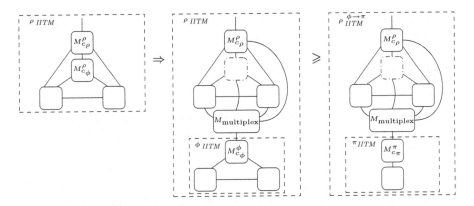

Fig. 4. Overview of the static structures of the protocols in this section. Left: ρ_{IITM} mapped as per Sect. 3.2. Middle: ρ_{IITM} after redirecting all inputs/outputs from $M^{\rho}_{c_{\phi}}$ to ϕ_{IITM}. The machine $M^{\rho}_{c_{\phi}}$ is formally still present but not used in a run. Right: The composed protocol $\rho^{\phi \to \pi}_{IITM}$ after applying the IITM composition theorem, which replaces the protocol (and hence all sessions of) ϕ_{IITM} with the protocol π_{IITM}.

only a single external I/O tape to/from the machine with code c_{π}/c_{ϕ}, this syntactical requirement of the IITM theorem actually corresponds to the "subroutine respecting" requirement for π_{UC}/ϕ_{UC} in the UC theorem.[14] That is, subroutine respecting protocols are required to reject and drop all messages from and never send messages to instances outside of their session of π_{UC}/ϕ_{UC}, except for inputs to and outputs from highest-level instances running code c_{π}/c_{ϕ}. The only difference is that in UC "subroutine respecting" is a semantic requirement imposed on the behavior of machines whereas the IITM requirement enforces the same property on the syntactical level of interfaces by removing any unintended communication channels/tapes. Hence, to be able to apply the IITM composition theorem and conclude $\rho^{\phi \to \pi}_{IITM} \leq_{IITM} \rho_{IITM}$ we have to make some slight syntactical adjustments to ρ_{IITM} such that the semantic "subroutine respecting" property is also reflected by the tape connections.

So let ρ_{IITM} be the protocol mapped according to Sect. 3.3. Then, since ρ_{IITM} uses code $c_{\phi} \in \mathsf{Codes}$ and possibly other codes, ρ_{IITM} looks like depicted in Fig. 4 (left-hand side); we refer to machines of the system ρ_{IITM} by M^{ρ}_i. The middle picture of Fig. 4 illustrates the idea of our syntactical changes to ρ_{IITM}: We extend the protocol ρ_{IITM} by including the full set of machines of ϕ_{IITM}, as obtained by mapping from ϕ_{UC} according to Sect. 3.3. We now change all machines in ρ_{IITM}, i.e., all M^{ρ}_i, to send inputs/receive outputs to/from ϕ_{IITM} instead of $M^{\rho}_{c_{\phi}}$. Since multiple machines need to connect to ϕ_{IITM} but ϕ_{IITM} provides only a single external I/O tape, we introduce a straightforward

---

[14] The IITM composition theorem also supports IITM protocols that offer several external I/O tapes, even to subroutines, which gives the environment and higher-level protocols direct access to those subroutines. Such IITM protocols are more general. They do not and do not have to meet the "subroutine respecting" property.

multiplexer $M_{\mathrm{multiplex}}$ that forwards messages between ϕ_{IITM} and machines M_i^ρ. Since inputs to and outputs from $M_{c_\phi}^\rho$ are the only way for higher-level instances in ρ to interact with instances in any session of the subroutine ϕ (by the subroutine respecting property), this syntactic modification of ρ_{IITM} does not actually change its behavior. It, however, consistently moves all sessions of ϕ to now be instances of the set of machines ϕ_{IITM}. Note that when ϕ_{IITM} calls subroutines (with code in Codes), then ϕ_{IITM} now uses its own subrountine machines, instead of those of ρ_{IITM}. The composed protocol $\rho_{IITM}^{\phi\to\pi}$ is then defined by simply replacing the set of machines ϕ_{IITM} with the set of machines π_{IITM} (right hand-side of Fig. 4). This is as simple as reconnecting the single I/O tape between the multiplexer $M_{\mathrm{multiplex}}$ and ϕ_{IITM} to instead connect to the external I/O tape of π_{IITM}. As a result, in $\rho_{IITM}^{\phi\to\pi}$ all inputs to and outputs from sessions of ϕ_{IITM} are now instead handled by sessions of π_{IITM}, which is just as in $\rho_{UC}^{\phi\to\pi}$. In other words, reconnecting this tape has the same effect as adding the UC composition shell code, which internally changes the code c_ϕ to instead be c_π for such inputs/outputs. So, unlike in Corollary 1, when we use the IITM composition theorem we actually do not need to include this shell code in $\rho_{IITM}^{\phi\to\pi}$. The IITM composition theorem then implies the following:

Corollary 2 (Composition from the IITM theorem). *Let* $\pi_{UC}, \phi_{UC}, \rho_{UC}$ *be UC protocols such that* $\pi_{UC} \leq_{UC}^\xi \phi_{UC}$ *and* ρ_{UC} *meets the requirements of the UC composition theorem. Let* ρ_{IITM} *and* $\rho_{IITM}^{\phi\to\pi}$ *be the IITM protocols from above. Then immediately by the IITM composition theorem,* $\rho_{IITM}^{\phi\to\pi} \leq_{IITM} \rho_{IITM}$.

We provide full details, including the formal definitions of ρ_{IITM}, $\rho_{IITM}^{\phi\to\pi}$ and the proof of Corollary 2 in the full version [21]. In the process of showing this result, we also found and fixed an issue that formally invalidates the UC theorem, namely, additional assumptions on non-forced writes used within ρ are actually necessary. Altogether, the construction shown in Fig. 4 and Corollary 2 illustrate how the additional requirements of the UC theorem from Diff. 13 and Diff. 14 are reflected in the mapped IITM protocols when the IITM theorem is used to obtain the same composition result.

Novel Composition Operation. Recall that the UC theorem applied to a protocol ρ replaces *all* sessions of subroutines running code ϕ with sessions running code π. Similarly, the IITM theorem applied to a protocol ρ replaces *all* sessions of a set of machines ϕ with sessions of a set of machines π. Observe that we can use the above modeling technique not just to move *all* sessions of ϕ to a new set of machines. Under certain conditions, we can rather more generally move a proper subset of the sessions of ϕ to a new set of machines, say ϕ', while moving the other sessions to a different set, say ϕ'', where ϕ' and ϕ'' still run the same code c_ϕ. We then obtain a simple corollary of the UC and IITM composition theorems (also for similar models), where we can replace ϕ' with a realization π' but replace ϕ'' with a different realization π''. In other words, our technique allows for *replacing subsets of sessions*. This can be useful, e.g., if ϕ is an ideal signature functionality, where each session models one key pair. Then we might want to implement certain keys with a signature scheme π' but others with a different signature scheme π'', say, depending on where they are used within a higher-level protocol ρ. We give full details, including requirements on ρ, in [21].

3.5   Capturing Dynamically Generated Machine Code

We now explain how our constructions from the previous sections can be extended to also support an unbounded number of dynamically generated machine codes. This bridges Diff. 1 and thus completes our mapping.

We start by observing that the UC model can be interpreted to be defined on a single universal Turing machine which is instantiated arbitrarily often during a run. Whenever a new instance receives its first input message, which contains the extended identity (pid, sid, c) of that instance, it stores this identity and from then on runs the code c given in its identity. This mechanism, whichs allows the UC model to seamlessly support arbitrary dynamically generated machine codes, can be transferred to an IITM protocol as follows.

Whenever a protocol π_{IITM} requires an unbounded number of different dynamically generated codes, potentially in addition to a finite number of static machine codes Codes as above, then we first map the fixed number of static codes of π_{IITM} as described in Sect. 3.2. We then add a universal Turing machine M_{UT} that all other machines M_{c_i} connect to via pairs of I/O tapes. Each instance of M_{UT} is identified by an ID (pid, sid, c) (instead of (pid, sid) as for machines M_{c_i} with fixed code c_i), where $c \notin$ Codes, and internally runs code c specified by its ID. Whenever an instance of any machine in π_{IITM} wants to send a message to an instance with ID (pid, sid) and code $c \notin$ Codes, i.e., where M_c does not exist in π_{IITM}, then it sends the message to the instance (pid, sid, c) of M_{UT} instead (this is easily done by choosing the appropriate tape; the actual message format, including the headers, does not change). The resulting protocol π_{IITM} behaves just as π_{UC} with dynamically generated codes. Hence, by the same reasoning as for Theorem 4, all realization results carry over for this construction, including results obtained via the UC composition theorem (i.e., Corollary 1). In the full version [21] we argue that also Corollary 2 carries over since the same modeling technique from Sect. 3.4 still applies independently of whether or not there is a universal Turing machine.

This bridges Diff. 1 by showing that the IITM model with its composition theorem also fully supports protocols with an unbounded number of dynamically generated machine codes, including all results available in the UC model.

3.6   Discussion: Beyond UC Protocols

Above, we have considered only IITM protocols that are obtained by mapping some UC protocols. Of course, once we have mapped a UC protocol ϕ_{UC}, including any security and composability results, into the IITM model, we are no longer limited to only considering combinations of ϕ_{IITM} with such mapped protocols. We can rather consider any combination of ϕ_{IITM} with arbitrary other IITM protocols. This includes cases where a higher-level IITM protocol $\mathcal{P}$ is designed based on top of ϕ_{IITM}, which can then, by the IITM composition theorem, be composed with any existing UC realization π_{IITM} of ϕ_{IITM}. One can also consider novel realizations of ϕ_{IITM} via an IITM protocol $\mathcal{P}$.

Such IITM protocols, which are combined with the mapped UC protocols, can then make full use of the features of the IITM model, including seamless support for joint state, global state, arbitrarily shared state, protocols without pre-established SIDs, and arbitrary combinations thereof. For example, a higher-level IITM protocol $\mathcal{P}$ can be defined in such a way that different sessions of $\mathcal{P}$ share the same instance of ϕ_{IITM} and $\mathcal{P}$ could also work without pre-established SIDs etc. We refer the reader to [4,15,17,18] for in-depth overviews, including examples, of IITM protocols with these features which can now be combined with existing UC results. Our mapping thus opens entirely new options for protocol designers so far working in the UC model by allowing them to combine their UC results with these IITM features, including IITM protocols that would require extensions of or are not yet supported by the UC model.

4   Impossibility of Embedding the IITM Model into the UC Model

Having mostly focused on the direction from UC to IITM, we now briefly discuss the other direction. In [18], it has been shown that the IITM runtime notion permits IITM protocols which cannot be expressed in the UC model as they do not meet the UC runtime notion. This includes protocols often encountered in practice, such as protocols that have to deal with ill-formed network messages. Combined with our results, this shows that the class of IITM protocols is strictly larger than the class of UC protocols. Another difference in protocol classes is due to so-called directory machines as required by the UC model for composition. These directory machines provide an oracle to the adversary to test whether a certain extended ID exists and is part of a specific UC protocol session. IITM protocols need not provide such a side channel, i.e., they are able to keep the IDs of internal subroutines secret from the adversary. This is not merely a cosmetic difference. Such an oracle rather changes security properties and might not be simulatable when (the existence of) extended IDs depend on some information that is supposed to remain secret. Finally, in this paper we provide an impossibility result which shows that also the class of IITM adversaries and hence simulators is strictly larger than the class of UC adversaries/simulators (cf. Lemma 3).

So at best one can hope for an embedding of the IITM model into the UC model for a restricted class of IITM protocols that follow the UC runtime notion and provide the same side channel as the directory machine. Realization relations carry over only for simulators that meet the UC runtime notion. Another obstacle to an embedding are IITM protocols that share state between protocol sessions, which includes joint state realizations as a special case. This is because the UC model mandates that UC protocols are subroutine respecting, i.e., have disjoint sessions that do not interact with each other. It might be possible to overcome this mismatch by using an idea briefly mentioned in [4], namely, modeling *all* sessions of an IITM protocol within a *single* session of a UC protocol. We leave exploring the details of this direction for future work.

Acknowledgements. We thank Ran Canetti and Björn Tackmann for helpful discussions on an early draft of this paper.

References

1. Backes, M., Dürmuth, M., Hofheinz, D., Küsters, R.: Conditional reactive simulatability. Int. J. Inf. Secur. (IJIS) **7**(2), 155–169 (2008)
2. Badertscher, C., Canetti, R., Hesse, J., Tackmann, B., Zikas, V.: Universal composition with global subroutines: capturing global setup within plain UC. In: Pass, R., Pietrzak, K. (eds.) TCC 2020, Part III. LNCS, vol. 12552, pp. 1–30. Springer, Cham (2020). https://doi.org/10.1007/978-3-030-64381-2_1
3. Camenisch, J., Enderlein, R.R., Krenn, S., Küsters, R., Rausch, D.: Universal composition with responsive environments. In: Cheon, J.H., Takagi, T. (eds.) ASIACRYPT 2016, Part II. LNCS, vol. 10032, pp. 807–840. Springer, Heidelberg (2016). https://doi.org/10.1007/978-3-662-53890-6_27
4. Camenisch, J., Krenn, S., Küsters, R., Rausch, D.: iUC: flexible universal composability made simple. In: Galbraith, S.D., Moriai, S. (eds.) ASIACRYPT 2019, Part III. LNCS, vol. 11923, pp. 191–221. Springer, Cham (2019). https://doi.org/10.1007/978-3-030-34618-8_7
5. Canetti, R.: Universally composable security: A new paradigm for cryptographic protocols. In: FOCS 2001, pp. 136–145. IEEE Computer Society Press, October 2001
6. Canetti, R.: Universally composable security. J. ACM **67**(5), 28:1–28:94 (2020)
7. Canetti, R., Dodis, Y., Pass, R., Walfish, S.: Universally composable security with global setup. In: Vadhan, S.P. (ed.) TCC 2007. LNCS, vol. 4392, pp. 61–85. Springer, Heidelberg (2007). https://doi.org/10.1007/978-3-540-70936-7_4
8. Canetti, R., Rabin, T.: Universal composition with joint state. In: Boneh, D. (ed.) CRYPTO 2003. LNCS, vol. 2729, pp. 265–281. Springer, Heidelberg (2003). https://doi.org/10.1007/978-3-540-45146-4_16
9. Graf, M., Rausch, D., Ronge, V., Egger, C., Küsters, R., Schröder, D.: A security framework for distributed ledgers. In: ACM CCS 2021, 14–19 November 2021. ACM, Seoul (2021)
10. Hofheinz, D., Shoup, V.: GNUC: a new universal composability framework. J. Cryptol. **28**(3), 423–508 (2015)
11. Hofheinz, D., Unruh, D., Müller-Quade, J.: Polynomial runtime and composability. J. Cryptol. **26**(3), 375–441 (2013)
12. Küsters, R.: Simulation-based security with inexhaustible interactive turing machines. In: Proceedings of the 19th IEEE Computer Security Foundations Workshop (CSFW-19 2006), pp. 309–320. IEEE Computer Society (2006). See [18] for a full and revised version
13. Küsters, R., Datta, A., Mitchell, J.C., Ramanathan, A.: On the relationships between notions of simulation-based security. J. Cryptol. **21**(4), 492–546 (2008)
14. Küsters, R., Rausch, D.: A framework for universally composable Diffie-Hellman key exchange. In: 2017 IEEE Symposium on Security and Privacy, pp. 881–900. IEEE Computer Society Press, May 2017

15. Küsters, R., Tuengerthal, M.: Composition theorems without pre-established session identifiers. In: ACM CCS 2011, pp. 41–50. ACM Press, October 2011
16. Küsters, R., Tuengerthal, M.: Ideal key derivation and encryption in simulation-based security. In: Kiayias, A. (ed.) CT-RSA 2011. LNCS, vol. 6558, pp. 161–179. Springer, Heidelberg (2011). https://doi.org/10.1007/978-3-642-19074-2_12
17. Küsters, R., Tuengerthal, M., Rausch, D.: Joint state theorems for public-key encryption and digital signature functionalities with local computation. J. Cryptol. **33**(4), 1585–1658 (2020)
18. Küsters, R., Tuengerthal, M., Rausch, D.: The IITM model: a simple and expressive model for universal composability. J. Cryptol. **33**(4), 1461–1584 (2020)
19. Maurer, U.: Constructive cryptography - a primer (invited paper). In: Sion, R. (ed.) FC 2010. LNCS, vol. 6052, p. 1. Springer, Heidelberg (2010). https://doi.org/10.1007/978-3-642-14577-3_1
20. Pfitzmann, B., Waidner, M.: Composition and integrity preservation of secure reactive systems. In: ACM CCS 2000, pp. 245–254. ACM Press, November 2000
21. Rausch, D., Küsters, R., Chevalier, C.: Embedding the UC model into the IITM model. Cryptology ePrint Archive, Report 2022/224 (2022). https://eprint.iacr.org/2022/224

Zero-Knowledge Proofs

Zero-Knowledge IOPs with Linear-Time Prover and Polylogarithmic-Time Verifier

Jonathan Bootle[1]($\boxtimes$) , Alessandro Chiesa[2,3]($\boxtimes$), and Siqi Liu[3]

[1] IBM Research, Zurich, Switzerland
jbt@zurich.ibm.com
[2] École polytechnique fédérale de Lausanne, Lausanne, Switzerland
alessandro.chiesa@epfl.ch
[3] University of California, Berkeley, Berkeley, USA
sliu18@berkeley.edu

Abstract. Interactive oracle proofs (IOPs) are a multi-round generalization of probabilistically checkable proofs that play a fundamental role in the construction of efficient cryptographic proofs.

We present an IOP that simultaneously achieves the properties of zero knowledge, linear-time proving, and polylogarithmic-time verification. We construct a zero-knowledge IOP where, for the satisfiability of an N-gate arithmetic circuit over any field of size $\Omega(N)$, the prover uses $O(N)$ field operations and the verifier uses $\mathsf{polylog}(N)$ field operations (with proof length $O(N)$ and query complexity $\mathsf{polylog}(N)$). Polylogarithmic verification is achieved in the holographic setting for every circuit (the verifier has oracle access to a linear-time-computable encoding of the circuit whose satisfiability is being proved).

Our result implies progress on a basic goal in the area of efficient zero knowledge. Via a known transformation, we obtain a zero knowledge argument system where the prover runs in linear time and the verifier runs in polylogarithmic time; the construction is plausibly post-quantum and only makes a black-box use of lightweight cryptography (collision-resistant hash functions).

Keywords: Interactive oracle proofs · Zero knowledge · Succinct arguments

1 Introduction

Zero knowledge proofs enable a prover to convince a verifier that a statement is true without revealing any further information about the statement [28]. The main efficiency measures in a zero knowledge proof are the running time of the prover, the running time of the verifier, and the number of bits exchanged between them. A central goal in the study of zero knowledge proofs is to minimize the complexity of these measures.

Motivated by real-world applications, researchers across multiple communities have invested significant effort, and made much progress, in designing efficient zero knowledge protocols.

© International Association for Cryptologic Research 2022
O. Dunkelman and S. Dziembowski (Eds.): EUROCRYPT 2022, LNCS 13276, pp. 275–304, 2022.
https://doi.org/10.1007/978-3-031-07085-3_10

Several works (e.g., [18,24,31,32,36,52]) focus on prover time. They construct zero-knowledge proofs for circuit satisfiability where the prover's time complexity is linear in circuit size, which is asymptotically optimal.[1] The drawback of these constructions is that communication complexity and verifier time also grow linearly with circuit size, which is undesirable for many applications.

This drawback is inevitable because, even without zero knowledge, interactive proofs for hard languages with sublinear communication are unlikely [25,27]. Nevertheless, if instead of considering proofs we consider *arguments* [15], wherein soundness is required to hold only against efficient adversaries rather than all adversaries, then one can hope to avoid the drawback. For this, rather than studying proofs where zero knowledge holds computationally, one studies arguments where zero knowledge holds statistically.[2]

Succinctness. In a seminal work, Kilian [37] constructed zero knowledge arguments that are *succinct*: communication complexity and verifier time are *polylogarithmic* in computation size. While these are essentially optimal, the prover in Kilian's construction is a polynomial-time algorithm that fails to achieve the asymptotically-optimal linear time achieved via the aforementioned (nonsuccinct) zero knowledge proofs. Improving the prover time in succinct arguments has been a major goal in a subsequent line of work.

Essentially all approaches for constructing succinct arguments follow the same high-level template: first construct a probabilistic proof in some proof model, and then make a black-box use of cryptography to compile the probabilistic proof into an argument system.

A notable exception are zero-knowledge arguments with a linear-time prover and a polylogarithmic-time verifier. This goal is presently achieved as a consequence of the zero-knowledge argument in [13] (see Sect. 1.3), but only via a non-black-box use of cryptography. This is unfortunate, as black-box results are a cryptographic "gold standard" that typically reflect a deeper understanding, and over time lead to more efficient solutions (once each black-box is suitably optimized), when compared to non-black-box results.

Interactive Oracle Proofs. The above status quo is due to inefficiencies in probabilistic proofs. Prior results on zero-knowledge argument systems with a linear-time prover and sublinear-time verifier rely on compiling interactive oracle proofs (IOPs) [8,44] into corresponding succinct arguments via a black-box use of suitable collision-resistant hash functions. The verifier time was sublinear rather than polylogarithmic due to the underlying IOP constructions. In particular, the following basic question has remained open:

Do there exist zero-knowledge IOPs with a linear-time prover and a polylogarithmic-time verifier?

---

[1] Several of these works additionally achieve excellent concrete efficiency, via experiments that demonstrate the ability to prove the satisfiability of circuits with billions of gates.

[2] As soundness is computational then we can hope for zero knowledge to be statistical.

In this paper we give a positive answer to this question for arithmetic computations over a large field, and obtain a corresponding black-box result about zero-knowledge succinct arguments. The question of whether an analogous result can be proved for boolean computations remains an exciting open problem.

IOP	encode circuit cost	prover cost	verifier cost	query complexity	zero-knowledge
[13]	$O(n)$ $\mathbb{F}$-ops	$O(n)$ $\mathbb{F}$-ops	$O(\sqrt{n})$ $\mathbb{F}$-ops	$O(\sqrt{n})$	semi-honest zk
[14]	$O(n)$ $\mathbb{F}$-ops	$O(n)$ $\mathbb{F}$-ops	$O(n^\epsilon)$ $\mathbb{F}$-ops	$O(n^\epsilon)$	not zk
this work	$O(n)$ $\mathbb{F}$-ops	$O(n)$ $\mathbb{F}$-ops	polylog(n) $\mathbb{F}$-ops	$O(\log n)$	semi-honest zk

Fig. 1. Comparison of known IOPs with a linear-time prover, for soundness error $1/2$. The parameters are for an n-gate arithmetic circuit defined over a field $\mathbb{F}$ of size $\Omega(n)$; and ϵ is any positive constant. Sublinear verification is achieved in the holographic setting (the verifier has oracle access to an encoding of the circuit).

1.1 Our Results

Our main result is an interactive oracle proof (IOP) [8,44] that simultaneously achieves zero knowledge, linear-time proving, and polylogarithmic-time verification (so also linear proof length and polylogarithmic query complexity). This implies the first zero-knowledge argument system with linear-time proving and polylogarithmic-time verification (and thus polylogarithmic communication complexity) that makes a black-box use of cryptography. Jumping ahead, our solution uses a lightweight cryptographic primitive (linear-time collision-resistant hash functions) for which there are plausibly post-quantum candidates.

IOP for R1CS. Our IOP is for a standard generalization of arithmetic circuit satisfiability, known as *rank-1 constraint satisfiability* (R1CS), where the "circuit description" is given by coefficient matrices. This NP-complete problem is widely used in the probabilistic proof literature (and beyond) because it efficiently expresses arithmetic circuits[3] and is convenient to use when designing a succinct argument.

Definition 1 (informal). *The R1CS problem asks: given a finite field $\mathbb{F}$, coefficient matrices $A, B, C \in \mathbb{F}^{n \times n}$ each containing at most $m = \Omega(n)$ non-zero entries,[4] and an instance vector $x \in \mathbb{F}^*$, is there a witness vector $w \in \mathbb{F}^*$ such that $z := (x, w) \in \mathbb{F}^n$ and $Az \circ Bz = Cz$? (Here "$\circ$" denotes the entry-wise product.)*

---

[3] Satisfiability of an n-gate arithmetic circuit over the field $\mathbb{F}$ is reducible, *in linear time*, to an R1CS instance also over $\mathbb{F}$ where the coefficient matrices are $n \times n$ and have $m = O(n)$ non-zero entries. (In particular, the coefficient matrices are sparse.).

[4] Note that $m = \Omega(n)$ without loss of generality because if $m < n/3$ then there are variables of z that do not participate in any constraint, which can be dropped. Thus the main size measure for R1CS is the sparsity parameter m.

Merely checking the validity of a witness by directly checking the R1CS condition costs $O(m)$ field operations, so "linear time" for R1CS means computations that cost no more than $O(m)$ field operations.

We construct an IOP for the R1CS problem with the parameters below. Our result significantly improves over prior linear-time IOPs, as summarized in Fig. 1 and further discussed in Sect. 1.2.

Theorem 1 (informal). *There is a public-coin IOP for R1CS over any field $\mathbb{F}$ of size $\Omega(m)$, where:*

- *the prover uses $O(m)$ field operations;*
- *the verifier uses $\mathsf{poly}(|x|, \log m)$ field operations;*
- *round complexity is $O(\log m)$;*
- *proof length is $O(m)$ elements in $\mathbb{F}$;*
- *query complexity is $O(\log m)$;*
- *soundness error is $O(1)$.*

Moreover, the IOP is semi-honest-verifier zero-knowledge.

Succinct Argument for R1CS. The above theorem directly implies a zero-knowledge succinct argument with a linear-time prover and polylogarithmic-time verifier, obtained in a black-box way under standard cryptographic assumptions. The implication involves combining IOPs and linear-time collision resistant hashing [13], as reviewed in Sect. 2.7.

In more detail, the result below relies on any linear-time collision-resistant hash function. Such hash functions are known to exist, e.g., under certain assumptions about finding short codewords in linear codes [1]; moreover, these candidate hash functions are not known to be insecure against quantum adversaries, and so our succinct argument is plausibly post-quantum secure.

Theorem 2 (informal). *Using any linear-time collision-resistant hash function with security parameter λ as a black box, one can obtain an interactive argument for R1CS, over any field of size $\Omega(m)$, where:*

- *time complexity of the prover is bounded by the cost of $O(\lambda + m)$ field operations;*
- *time complexity of the verifier is bounded by the cost of $\mathsf{poly}(\lambda, |x|, \log m)$ field operations;*
- *round complexity is $O(\log m)$;*
- *communication complexity is $\mathsf{poly}(\lambda, \log m)$ field elements;*
- *soundness error is $O(1)$.*

Moreover, the argument is malicious-verifier zero-knowledge with private coins.[5]

---

[5] The private coins come from using the Goldreich–Kahan technique [26]. Achieving public coins is also possible via different relaxations: (i) (ii) we could rely on a reference string (which enables the zero knowledge simulator to access a trapdoor); or (iii) we could relax the goal to honest-verifier zero-knowledge while remaining in the plain model. See [34] for more on these considerations.

On Zero Knowledge. The notion of *semi-honest-verifier* zero-knowledge in Theorem 1 means that the IOP prover leaks no information to an honest IOP verifier for any choice of verifier randomness. This suffices for malicious-verifier zero-knowledge in Theorem 2, as explained in Sect. 2.7. We also present results (see Sect. 2.6) that allow us to prove a variant of Theorem 1 where the IOP satisfies the stronger property of *bounded-query zero-knowledge*, but at the cost of a sublinear verifier time rather than polylogarithmic. Bounded-query zero-knowledge is the hiding notion typically studied for PCPs [38], and often enables reductions in communication complexity when compiling the IOP into a succinct argument. The aforementioned loss in verifier time only comes from the fact that known constructions of "zero knowledge codes" with a linear-time encoder are probabilistic, and the loss could be avoided by derandomizing such families—overcoming this barrier remains an exciting open problem in coding theory.

On Sublinear Verification. The polylogarithmic verifier time in Theorem 1 is achieved in the holographic setting, which means that the verifier is given query access to a linear-length encoding of the coefficient matrices that is computable in linear time. Similarly, polylogarithmic verifier time in Theorem 2 is achieved in the preprocessing setting, which means that the verifier receives as input a short digest of the circuit that can be derived by anyone (in linear time). This follows a general paradigm wherein holographic proofs lead to preprocessing arguments [20,21]. Holography/preprocessing is necessary for sublinear verification in the general case because just reading the R1CS instance takes linear time.[6]

Open Questions. Our IOP works for satisfiability problems over fields of at least linear size, as is the case for all known linear-time IOPs (see Sect. 1.2); obtaining analogous results for all fields, or just the boolean field, is open. Moreover, our IOP achieves constant soundness error, and the question of additionally achieving a sub-constant soundness error (ideally, negligible in a security parameter) is open. Finally, while our focus is asymptotic efficiency, we are optimistic that the ideas in this paper will facilitate further research that may additionally achieve good concrete efficiency. (We point to specific ideas for this in Sect. 2.) Initial progress in this direction has been made in subsequent work discussed in Sect. 1.3.

1.2 Related Work on Probabilistic Proofs

As our main result concerns IOPs, we summarize prior works on probabilistic proofs that study related questions. Further connections to prior work are given in Sect. 2 where we overview our techniques.

First we discuss a line of work on probabilistic proofs with linear proof length, a necessary condition for a linear-time prover (our goal). The first result was [9], which provides a PCP for boolean circuit satisfiability with linear proof length and sublinear query complexity; this is the only known result for PCPs, and constructing PCPs with linear proof length and polylogarithmic query complexity

---

[6] Holography/preprocessing may be avoidable by focusing on R1CS instances with a short description [6] or, more generally, uniform models of computation. Achieving results analogous to ours in such a setting remains an open problem.

remains a major open problem. Subsequently, [4] obtained a 3-round IOP for boolean circuit satisfiability with linear proof length and constant query complexity; and [45] showed how to reduce the multiplicative constant in the proof length to arbitrarily close to 1 at the cost of a slightly larger constant round complexity. None of these works study linear-time proving or sublinear-time verification. Here we omit a discussion of numerous works that achieve IOPs with linear size, but not linear prover time, for many other models of computation.

Next, [13] obtained a zero-knowledge IOP for arithmetic circuit satisfiability with linear-time prover and square-root-time verifier. Then [14] improved the verifier time to any sublinear polynomial, but without zero knowledge. *We improve on this by simultaneously achieving the properties of zero knowledge and polylogarithmic-time verifier.* All of these results require working over a finite field of linear size, and analogous results for boolean circuits are not known. See Fig. 1 for a table comparing these latter works.

Recurring tools across many of these works, as well as this paper, include: the sumcheck protocol for tensor codes [42], proof composition (for PCPs [2] and for IOPs [4]), the linear-time sumcheck [49], and the use of codes without the multiplication property. (The property states that coordinate-wise multiplication of codewords yields codewords in a code whose relative distance is still good.)

The main challenge in designing IOPs with linear-time provers is that one cannot use "useful" codes like the Reed–Solomon code since the encoding time is quasilinear. Instead, prior works resorted to using linear-time encodable codes (e.g., of Spielman [48] or Druk–Ishai [22]) that, unfortunately, do not have the multiplication property, which makes designing IOPs more difficult. (See [41,42] for more on why the multiplication property is useful in constructing probabilistic proofs.)

Our zero-knowledge IOPs with linear-time prover and polylogarithmic-time verifier achieve a central goal in the area of probabilistic proofs, and to construct them we contribute several novel pieces all towards zero knowledge: (i) constructions of linear-time-encodable codes that satisfy a zero-knowledge property; (ii) structural results on the tensor products of codes that satisfy the zero-knowledge property; (iii) a tensor-query zero-knowledge holographic IOP for R1CS with low randomness complexity; (iv) results on zero knowledge preservation under proof composition.

1.3   Related Work on Succinct Arguments

Our main result implies a result on succinct arguments, and below we summarize prior works relevant to that.

A Non-Black-Box Construction. A relaxation of Theorem 2 that makes a non-black-box use of cryptography is a straightforward implication of [13]. In more detail, [13] obtained a zero-knowledge argument system for arithmetic circuit satisfiability over linear-size fields where the prover runs in linear time and the verifier runs in square-root time. The verifier time can be reduced to polylogarithmic, while preserving zero knowledge and a linear-time prover, by using any zero-knowledge succinct argument with subquadratic prover time to prove that the "outer" verifier would have accepted. A similar implication, however from the non-zero-knowledge succinct argument in [14], is described in subsequent work [29,40], and thus we refer the reader to that work for more details on these non-black-box approaches. (We remark that [29,40] additionally contribute ideas and implementations to improve the concrete efficiency of argument systems with a linear-time prover and sublinear-time verifier.)

Black-Box Constructions from Probabilistic Proofs. Essentially all approaches for constructing succinct arguments follow this high-level template: first construct a probabilistic proof in some proof model, and then make a black-box use of cryptography to compile the probabilistic proof into an argument system. The first step alone typically costs more than linear time because it involves (among other things) using the Fast Fourier Transform (FFT) to encode the computation as a polynomial.

Several works [12,16,39,46,47,50,53,54] construct various forms of succinct arguments *without FFTs* by first constructing linear-time probabilistic proofs in certain "algebraic" models and then compiling these into arguments by using homomorphic commitments. However, the cryptography introduces quasilinear work for the prover,[7] usually to perform a linear number of multi-exponentiations over a cryptographically-large group (which translates to a quasilinear number of group operations for the prover);[8] we refer the reader to follow up work [29,40] for a detailed discussion of these quasilinear costs in terms of computation size and the security parameter. In sum, the above line of works has contributed among the best asymptotic prover times for succinct arguments (as well as excellent concrete efficiency), but the cryptography has precluded linear-time provers.

Bootle et al. [13] observe that Kilian's approach to succinct arguments introduces only linear cryptographic costs, when the collision-resistant hash function used for the compilation is suitably instantiated. (We elaborate on this in Sect. 2.7.) Prior work leveraged this observation to construct argument systems with linear-time prover and sublinear-time verifier, given a collision-resistant hash function as a black box.

- [13] achieves an honest-verifier zero knowledge argument system for arithmetic circuit satisfiability with a communication complexity of $O(\sqrt{n})$, where the prover performs $O(n)$ field operations and hash computations while the verifier performs $O(\sqrt{n})$ field operations and hash computations.
- [14] achieves, for every $\epsilon > 0$, an argument system for R1CS with a communication complexity of $O(n^\epsilon)$, where the prover performs $O(n)$ field operations and hash computations while the verifier performs $O(n^\epsilon)$ field operations and hash computations. No zero knowledge property is achieved in this work.

---

[7] The quasilinear costs in some works (due to cryptography [53,54] or an FFT [55]) scale with witness size rather than computation size, and so the prover runs in linear time when the witness is small relative to the computation.

[8] Some of the cited works still refer to such prover time as "linear" or "asymptotically optimal". This is a misnomer.

There are linear-time candidates for the hash function [1], leading to a linear-time prover.

In both cases the technical core is the construction of IOPs with a linear-time prover, but, as discussed in Sect. 1.2, these prior works only achieved sublinear query complexity thereby, after compilation, falling short of the goal of polylogarithmic communication complexity. No prior work thus achieves Theorem 2.

Our main result (Theorem 1) offers improved IOP constructions, and we are then able to improve the state of the art of succinct arguments that make a black-box use of cryptography (Theorem 2).

2   Techniques

We overview our approach towards Theorem 1 in Sect. 2.1 and the construction in Sect. 2.2. We provide additional details behind different aspects of the construction in Sects. 2.3 to 2.6. Finally, in Sect. 2.7 we explain how our result about zero-knowledge succinct arguments (Theorem 2) is a direct implication of our result about zero-knowledge IOPs (Theorem 1).

Throughout, recall that an IOP is a proof model in which a prover and a verifier interact over multiple rounds, and in each round the prover sends a proof message and the verifier replies with a challenge message. The verifier has query access to all received proof messages, in the sense that it can query any of the proof messages at any desired location. The verifier decides to accept or reject depending on its input, its randomness, and answers to its queries. The main information-theoretic efficiency measures in an IOP are proof length (total size of all proof messages) and query complexity (number of read locations across all proof messages), while the main computational efficiency measures are prover time and verifier time.

2.1   Approach Overview

We provide an overview of our approach to Theorem 1.

Review: Proof Composition. Many constructions of PCPs rely on proof composition [2] to achieve the desired goal by combining an "outer" PCP and an "inner" PCP with suitable properties. The composed PCP (roughly) has the prover complexity of the outer PCP, and the verifier complexity of the inner PCP. Informally, the new PCP string consists of the outer PCP string and also, for every choice of randomness of the outer PCP verifier, an inner PCP string attesting that the outer PCP verifier would have accepted the local view of the outer PCP string induced by that choice of randomness. Soundness of the composed PCP requires the outer PCP to be *robust*[9] and the inner PCP to be a *proximity proof*.[10]

---

[9] A proof system is robust if the local view of the verifier is far (e.g. in Hamming distance) from an accepting view with high probability (over the verifier's randomness) whenever the instance is not in the language.

[10] A proximity proof shows that a given input is close to some input in the language.

Proof composition extends to the IOP model [4]: the outer and inner proof systems can be IOPs instead of PCPs, and must satisfy corresponding notions of robustness and proximity; moreover, composition is more efficient because the inner IOP has only to be invoked once rather than for every choice of randomness of the outer IOP verifier (this is because, after running the outer IOP, the verifier can simply send the chosen randomness to the prover and then run the inner IOP on that randomness). Proof composition of IOPs also plays a central role in constructions of IOPs, and we also use it in our construction, as described next.

Our Setting. Using proof composition in our setting involves several considerations.

- *Zero knowledge.* We want the composed IOP to be semi-honest-verifier zero-knowledge, and for this, one can prove that it suffices for the outer IOP to be semi-honest-verifier zero-knowledge, regardless of any zero knowledge properties of the inner IOP. We prove this and other properties about zero knowledge within proof composition in the full version.
- *Prover time.* We want the prover of the composed IOP to run in linear time. The composed prover time is the sum of the outer IOP prover time and the inner IOP prover time. This means that the outer IOP prover must run in time that is linear, e.g., in the R1CS instance. The requirement on the inner IOP prover is less straightforward: the inner IOP prover attests to a computation related to the outer IOP verifier. For example, if the outer IOP verifier runs in cube-root time (relative to the R1CS instance) then we can afford an inner IOP prover that runs in up to cubic time (as the cubic blow up applied to a cube-root time gives linear time overall). In other words, we require the polynomial blow up of the inner IOP prover time to be made up by the savings offered by the outer IOP verifier time.
- *Verifier time.* We want the verifier of the composed IOP to run in polylogarithmic time. The composed verifier time equals the time of the inner IOP verifier when used to test that the outer IOP verifier would have accepted. At minimum, the inner IOP verifier needs to read the description of the outer IOP verifier computation, which consists of its input instance (e.g., the R1CS public input) and its randomness. This implies that the outer IOP verifier can have at most polylogarithmic randomness complexity, and also implies that the compound savings in running time of the outer IOP verifier and inner IOP verifier must lead to a polylogarithmic running time.

The above considerations suggest that one approach that suffices is the following: (i) an inner IOP of proximity for general computations with polylogarithmic verifier time; and (ii) an outer IOP for R1CS that is semi-honest-verifier zero-knowledge, is robust, has a linear prover time, has polylogarithmic randomness complexity, and has a verifier time that is sufficiently small so that we can afford the blowup incurred by the inner IOP prover time. For the inner IOP of proximity we choose the state-of-the-art PCP of proximity for $\mathsf{NTIME}(T)$ due to Mie [43] (discussed later). Our technical contribution is constructing a suitable outer IOP. As the blowup incurred by the inner PCP prover time will be polynomial, we need the outer IOP verifier to run in time that is sufficiently sublinear. We now outline the challenges that arise given prior work.

Challenges. There are two natural paths to explore in order to construct the outer IOP.

1. One path would be to somehow construct the desired outer IOP by starting from the semi-honest-verifier zero-knowledge IOP for arithmetic circuit satisfiability in [13], which works over any field of linear size and has linear prover time and square-root verifier time. This would require addressing some challenges. First, we would need to robustify the IOP, but robustification techniques typically work for verifiers with constant query complexity (possibly over a large alphabet), and so one would have to adapt [13] for this setting. Second, the IOP verifier in [13] would have to be derandomized to achieve polylogarithmic randomness complexity. Third, we cannot afford more than a quadratic blow up in the inner IOP prover time because the verifier in [13] runs in square-root time.
2. An alternative path would be to somehow construct the desired outer IOP by starting from the IOP for R1CS in [14], which over any field of size $O(m)$ has prover time $O(m)$ and verifier time $O(m^\epsilon)$ for any a-priori fixed constant $\epsilon > 0$. This would require somehow additionally achieving zero knowledge (not a goal in [14]), and moreover would still require addressing the robustification and derandomization challenges mentioned above. On the other hand, because we can choose ϵ to be small enough, we can afford an inner proximity proof whose prover runs in any fixed polynomial time (in particular, the PCP of proximity in [43] would suffice).

This Paper. We believe that both paths are plausible. In this paper we use an approach that (roughly) follows the second path, because we can use an off-the-shelf inner proximity proof and we can focus our attention solely on constructing an appropriate outer IOP. Moreover, we believe that building on [14] will contribute new understanding of zero knowledge techniques that are likely to be useful elsewhere, and will lead to a simpler exposition due to the modular nature of that construction.

2.2   Construction Overview

We outline the steps in the construction of an IOP that satisfies Theorem 1. We elaborate on each of these steps in subsequent subsections.

Review: The Tensor-to-Point Approach. The IOP for R1CS in [14] is obtained in two steps: first construct a *tensor IOP* for R1CS with linear prover time and constant query complexity; then apply a compiler that transforms any tensor IOP into a standard IOP. In a tensor IOP, the verifier may make multiple *tensor queries* directly to a proof message Π, each of the form $q = (q_1, \dots, q_t)$ and receiving the corresponding answer $v := \langle \otimes_i q_i, \Pi \rangle$. This differs from a standard IOP, where the verifier makes *point queries*, that is, it queries single locations of proof messages. As mentioned in Sect. 2.1, the resulting (point-query) IOP in [14] has prover time $O(m)$ and verifier time $O(m^\epsilon)$ for any a-priori fixed constant $\epsilon > 0$. (Here m is the maximum number of non-zero entries in an R1CS coefficient matrix.)

Steps in Our Proof. We take an analogous two-step approach as in [14], except that we additionally achieve semi-honest-verifier zero knowledge, while still achieving a prover time of $O(m)$ and reducing the verifier time from $O(m^\epsilon)$ to $\mathsf{poly}(|x|, \log m)$. (Here x is the instance vector of the R1CS instance.)

- *Step 1: tensor IOP for R1CS with zero knowledge.* Given any finite field $\mathbb{F}$, we construct a tensor IOP for R1CS over $\mathbb{F}$ that is semi-honest-verifier zero-knowledge, has soundness error $O(\frac{m}{|\mathbb{F}|})$, has prover time $O(m)$, and has verifier time $O(|x| + \log m)$; moreover, the verifier makes $O(1)$ tensor queries (and also interacts with the prover in a $O(\log m)$-round interactive proof). In Sect. 2.4 we outline the main ideas that we use to additionally achieve zero knowledge compared to the tensor IOP for R1CS in [14].
- *Step 2: from tensor IOPs to standard IOPs while preserving zero knowledge.* Given any finite field $\mathbb{F}$, we construct a compiler that maps a tensor IOP over the field $\mathbb{F}$ into a standard IOP *while preserving the zero knowledge property*; moreover, efficiency measures are preserved up to overheads in the dimension of the tensor and the query complexity of the input tensor IOP. In Sect. 2.3 we outline the main ideas that we use compared to the tensor-query to point-query compiler in [14] (which does not preserve zero knowledge and leads to a large verifier time).

Theorem 1 follows by applying the compiler in the second step to the tensor IOP for R1CS in the first step, as shown diagrammatically in Fig. 2. Below we highlight two aspects of our construction of the compiler.

(a) Proof composition. Differing from the approach overview in Sect. 2.1, the proof composition step actually happens within the tensor-query to point-query compiler rather than as a final step. This choice leads to a compiler that preserves efficiency measures of the tensor IOP up to constants (of independent interest), and moreover invokes the inner proximity proof on a linear computation rather than an arbitrary computation.

(b) Linear codes that are linear-time encodable and zero knowledge. A key ingredient in the construction of our compiler is *tensor codes that simultaneously are linear-time encodable and satisfy a zero-knowledge property* (informally, codewords do not reveal any information about the underlying message when queried in a restricted way). For this, we establish structural properties of zero-knowledge codes and prove that they are preserved under tensor products, which reduces the problem to constructing a linear-time encodable zero-knowledge code to act as the base of the tensor product code. We obtain a suitable base code via an explicit (deterministic) construction of zero-knowledge code based on [48] codes, which protect against a single malicious query. This is enough to prove zero-knowledge against semi-honest verifiers in Theorem 1, which suffices for our main theorem. We also give a probabilistic construction of zero-knowledge codes based on [22] codes which do not reveal information on the underlying message even when the verifier makes queries to a constant fraction of codeword entries. This allows us to prove a variation of Theorem 1 with the stronger property of *bounded-query zero-knowledge*. We review notions of zero knowledge for linear codes in Sect. 2.5, and then describe our results about zero-knowledge codes in Sect. 2.6.

Concrete Efficiency. We do not make any claims regarding the concrete efficiency of our construction. That said, we are optimistic that the ideas introduced in this work can lead to improved constructions with the same asymptotic efficiency but better concrete efficiency. In particular, we believe that further research into zero-knowledge linear-time-encodable codes and further research in specializing the proof composition step to the specific outer statement (a certain linear computation) may significantly improve efficiency. Subsequent work has made progress in this direction [29].

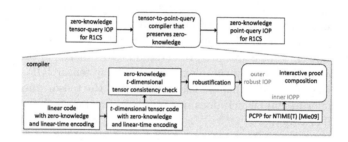

Fig. 2. Diagram of our construction of the IOP for Theorem 1.

2.3   From Tensor-Queries to Point-Queries in Zero-Knowledge

We generically transform any tensor-query IOP into a corresponding point-query IOP, *while preserving zero knowledge*. The transformation is parametrized by a zero-knowledge linear code (a notion explained in more detail in Sect. 2.5) and outputs a point-query IOP that is bounded-query zero knowledge, meaning that malicious queries up to a fixed query bound do not leak any information. In contrast, the tensor-query IOP being transformed is only required to satisfy a weaker notion of zero knowledge, called *semi-honest*-verifier zero knowledge, that we describe further below. Here, "$(\mathbb{F}, k, t)$-tensor IOP" means that each tensor-IOP query $q = (q_1, \ldots, q_t)$ lies in $(\mathbb{F}^k)^t$.

Theorem 3 (informal). *There is an efficient transformation that takes as input a tensor-query IOP and a linear code, and outputs a point-query IOP that has related complexity parameters, as summarized below.*

- Input IOP: *an $(\mathbb{F}, k, t)$-tensor IOP for a relation R with soundness error ϵ, round complexity* rc, *proof length* l, *query complexity* q, *prover arithmetic complexity* tp, *and verifier arithmetic complexity* tv.

- Input code: *a linear code* $\mathcal{C}$ *over* $\mathbb{F}$ *with rate* $\rho = \frac{k}{n}$, *relative distance* $\delta = \frac{d}{n}$, *encoding time* $\Psi(k) \cdot k$, *and description size* $|\mathcal{C}|$. *(The description of a linear code consists of a specification of the circuit used to compute the encoding function, including any random coins used to generate the circuit.)*
- Output IOP: *a point-query IOP with soundness error* $O_{\delta,t}(\epsilon) + O(d^t/|\mathbb{F}|)$, *round complexity* $O_t(\mathsf{rc})$, *proof length* $O_{\rho,t}(\mathsf{q} \cdot \mathsf{l})$, *query complexity* $O_t(\mathsf{q})$, *prover arithmetic complexity* $\mathsf{tp} + O_{\rho,t}(\mathsf{q} \cdot \mathsf{l}) \cdot \Psi(k) + \mathsf{poly}(|\mathcal{C}|, t, \mathsf{q}, k)$, *and verifier arithmetic complexity* $\mathsf{tv} + \mathsf{poly}(|\mathcal{C}|, t, \mathsf{q}, \log k)$.

Moreover, when the tensor-query IOP is semi-honest-verifier zero knowledge the following also holds:

- *if the code* $\mathcal{C}$ *is 1-query zero-knowledge, then the point-query IOP is semi-honest-verifier zero knowledge;*
- *if the code* $\mathcal{C}$ *is b-query zero-knowledge, then the point-query IOP is b-query zero knowledge.*

Finally, the transformation preserves holography up to the multiplicative encoding overhead Ψ *of* $\mathcal{C}$ *and terms that depend on* ρ *and* t: *if the indexer for the input tensor-query IOP runs in time* ti *and produces an index of length* li, *then the indexer for the output point-query IOP runs in time* $\mathsf{ti} + O_{\rho,t}(\mathsf{q} \cdot \mathsf{li}) \cdot \Psi(k)$.

We now explain the main ideas behind our compiler.

Starting Point: An Inefficient Compiler that Breaks Zero Knowledge. Our starting point is the code-based compiler of [14], which takes as input a tensor-query IOP $(\mathbf{P}, \mathbf{V})$ and a linear error-correcting code $\mathcal{C}$ and produces a corresponding point-query IOP $(\hat{\mathbf{P}}, \hat{\mathbf{V}})$. We briefly summarize how the compiler works.

First, the point-query IOP simulates the tensor-query IOP with the modification that: (i) each proof oracle $\Pi \in \mathbb{F}^{k^t}$ is replaced by its encoding $\hat{\Pi} \in \mathbb{F}^{n^t}$ using the tensor product code $\mathcal{C}^{\otimes t}$; (ii) instead of making tensor queries to the proof oracles directly, the new verifier $\hat{\mathbf{V}}$ sends tensor queries $q^{(s)}$ to the prover, who replies with the answers $v^{(s)}$. Second, the new prover $\hat{\mathbf{P}}$ and new verifier $\hat{\mathbf{V}}$ engage in a *consistency test* subprotocol to ensure that the answers $v^{(s)}$ (which may have been computed dishonestly) are consistent with the proofs Π. The consistency test incorporates a *proximity test* to make sure that each proof message $\hat{\Pi}$ is close to a valid encoding of some proof message Π (as a malicious prover may send messages which are far from $\mathcal{C}^{\otimes t}$). As part of the consistency check, the prover sends the verifier "folded" proof messages $c_j^{(s)} = \langle \otimes_{i \leq j} q_i^{(s)}, \Pi \rangle$ encoded under lower-dimensional tensor codes $\mathcal{C}^{\otimes t-j}$. The proximity test works similarly, using random linear combinations of length k sampled by the verifier instead of structured tensor queries. In both cases, the verifier checks linear relations between successive encodings $c_j^{(s)}$ and $c_{j+1}^{(s)}$ by making $O(k)$ point queries.

This compiler preserves prover time up to the encoding overhead $\Psi(k)$ as in our Theorem 3, but has two shortcomings. The compiler does not preserve zero-knowledge, even if the tensor IOP to be compiled is zero knowledge. Moreover, the output IOP has query complexity $\Omega(k)$ and verifier complexity $\Omega(k)$, which does not suffice for Theorem 3 (we can at most afford a polylogarithmic dependence in k). Below we elaborate on how we overcome these shortcomings for zero-knowledge (Sect. 2.3.1) and for efficiency (Sect. 2.3.2).

2.3.1   Preserving Zero-Knowledge

We explain semi-honest verifier zero knowledge (the property of the tensor IOP used to achieve zero knowledge for the output IOP) and then how we preserve zero knowledge in the compiler.

Semi-honest-Verifier Zero Knowledge. Here, "semi-honest" means that there exists a simulator that (perfectly) simulates the honest verifier's view for any fixed choice of the honest verifier's randomness.[11] This requirement is stronger than honest-verifier zero-knowledge, where the simulator must simulate the honest verifier's view for a random choice of its randomness; also, this requirement is weaker than the standard definition of zero-knowledge for IOPs, in which the verifier may deviate from the protocol and make arbitrary queries to the received oracles up to some query bound. Nevertheless, this notion suffices for our compilation procedure, which will produce point-query IOPs with zero-knowledge against semi-honest verifiers or against verifiers making a bounded number of point queries (depending on the zero-knowledge property of the code).

Approach for Zero Knowledge. We need to ensure that, in our compiler, if the tensor-query IOP given as input is semi-honest-verifier zero knowledge then, depending on the zero knowledge property of the code $\mathcal{C}$, the output point-query IOP is either semi-honest verifier zero knowledge or bounded-query zero knowledge. This implication does not hold for the compiler of [14] because, when using a (non-zero-knowledge) linear code $\mathcal{C}$, a point query to any encoded proof message $\hat{\Pi}$ or folded proof message $c_j^{(s)}$ leaks information about Π. We address the information leaked by $\hat{\Pi}$ and $c_j^{(s)}$ in two ways.

We ensure that the folded proof messages $c_j^{(s)}$ do not leak any information by leveraging the fact that the consistency test of [14] is about a linear relation, and thus can be invoked on a random shift of the instance of interest. In more detail, the usual approach to making the messages in such a subprotocol zero-knowledge is to mask the input message as $f = \gamma \Pi + \Xi$, where Ξ is a random message sent by the prover and γ is a random challenge sent by the verifier after that, and then run the consistency test on the *encoding* $c = \gamma \hat{\Pi} + \hat{\Xi}$ [3]. (The claimed tensor-query answers $v^{(s)}$ need to be adjusted accordingly too to account for the contribution of Ξ.) Informally, this enables the simulator to randomly sample c and honestly run the [14] consistency test protocol. Queries on the resulting messages $c_j^{(s)}$ do not reveal any information, since they are derived from c, which is a random tensor codeword. Further, we do not require any zero-knowledge properties from the consistency test.

---

[11] This is related to special honest-verifier zero-knowledge for sigma protocols.

The simulator must still simulate the answers to point queries on $\varXi$ by querying $\hat{\varPi}$ instead. To avoid information leakage from the encoded proofs $\hat{\varPi}$, we use a linear code $\mathcal{C}$ with bounded-query zero-knowledge. This is similar to the notion for IOPs, and means that queries to a codeword up to a fixed query bound do not leak any information. The [14] compiler uses tensor products of codes, and to achieve semi-honest-verifier zero knowledge for the output IOP, it is important that the tensor product code $\mathcal{C}^{\otimes t}$ is 1-query zero-knowledge. Furthermore, to achieve b-query zero knowledge for the output IOP, it is important that the tensor product code $\mathcal{C}^{\otimes t}$ is also zero-knowledge against b queries.[12] This leads to the problem of finding a zero-knowledge code which is encodable in linear time, which we discuss in Sect. 2.6.2, and showing that the zero-knowledge property of codes is preserved under tensor products, which we discuss in Sect. 2.6.1.

2.3.2 Improving Efficiency

Our modifications to the compiler of [14] to preserve zero-knowledge do not affect its efficiency; in particular, if the zero-knowledge code $\mathcal{C}^{\otimes t}$ has a linear-time encoding, then the compiler preserves linear arithmetic complexity of the prover. However, when applied to our $(\mathbb{F}, k, t)$-tensor IOP with $n = \Theta(k^t)$, the improved consistency test has query complexity $O(k)$, prover arithmetic complexity $O(k^t)$, and verifier arithmetic complexity $O(k)$. Though the query complexity and verifier complexity can be improved by increasing t, they remain sublinear in n, which does not suffice for Theorem 3. To prove Theorem 3, we must reduce the query complexity from $\Omega(k)$ to $O(1)$ and the verifier complexity from $\Omega(k)$ to $\mathsf{poly}(\log k)$.

We achieve these goals using interactive proof composition and derandomization techniques. First, we strengthen the improved consistency test through robustification, and then use interactive proof composition for IOPs [4]. This reduces the query complexity so that it is independent of k, and makes the verifier complexity depend only on the randomness complexity of the consistency test verifier. Next, we show that linear prover complexity is preserved. Finally, we explain how to derandomize the consistency test to obtain the desired verifier complexity. (It remains an interesting question whether one can also achieve proof length that approaches witness length, the efficiency goal studied in [45] via related techniques.)

Interactive Proof Composition. Interactive proof composition involves an "outer" IOP that is robust and is for the desired relation, and an "inner" IOP of proximity that is for a relation about the outer IOP's verifier. At a high level, we wish to apply this with the zero-knowledge consistency test from Sect. 2.3.1 as the outer IOP, and the PCP of proximity of [43] as the inner IOP. This requires some care, in part because the consistency check is not robust, and also because our target parameters do not leave much wiggle room. Below, we elaborate on how we robustify the outer protocol, and how we perform proof composition.

---

[12] Note also that query bound b must be at least the number of queries that $\hat{\mathbf{V}}$ makes to the encoded proof $\hat{\varPi}$.

– *Robustification.* Any IOP can be generically robustified by encoding each proof symbol in every round via an appropriate error-correcting code: if the IOP has query complexity q then this transformation yields a robustness parameter $\alpha = O(1/q)$ (over the alphabet of the code).[13] This is a straight-forward generalization of robustifications for IPs (each prover message in each round is encoded) and for PCPs (each proof symbol of the PCP is encoded). This also extends to robustifying IOPPs, in which case each symbol of the witness whose proximity is being proved is also encoded (and this modifies the relation proved by the IOPP slightly).

Superficially, this robustification seems insufficient to prove Theorem 3 because zero-knowledge consistency test from Sect. 2.3.1 has sublinear query complexity $q = O(k) = O(n^{1/t})$, which would lead to a robustness parameter that is sub-constant. However, fortunately, the queries are *bundled*: the verifier always queries entire sets of $O(n^{1/t})$ locations, so the IOPP can be restated as a *constant-query* IOPP over the large alphabet $\mathbb{F}^{O(n^{1/t})}$. To robustify an IOPP over such a large alphabet, we need to use a code with linear-time encoding such as [48] (here zero-knowledge codes are not essential) in order to preserve the linear complexity of the prover. This gives us an IOPP for tensor queries with prover complexity $O(n)$, verifier complexity $O(n^{1/t})$, query complexity $O(n^{1/t})$ over the alphabet $\mathbb{F}$, constant soundness error, and, most importantly, a *constant robustness parameter* α. We are now ready for the next step, proof composition.

– *Composition.* Interactive proof composition [4] applies to any outer IOP that is robust and inner IOP that is a proof of proximity. If the outer IOP is a proof of proximity (as is the case when using the IOPP obtained above) then the composed IOP is also a proof of proximity; similarly, if the inner IOP is robust then the composed IOP is also robust.

We apply proof composition as follows: (i) the outer proof system is the robust zero-knowledge IOPP for tensor queries obtained above; (ii) the inner proof system is the PCP of proximity for $\mathsf{NTIME}(T)$ due to Mie [43] (which achieves any constant soundness error and constant proximity parameter, with proof length $\tilde{O}(T(|\mathbb{x}|))$, query complexity $O(1)$, prover time $\mathsf{poly}(T(|\mathbb{x}|))$, and verifier time $\mathsf{poly}(|\mathbb{x}|, \log T(|\mathbb{x}|))$).

Informally, the new verifier in the composed proof system runs the interactive phase of the IOPP for tensor queries and then, rather than running the query phase of the outer IOPP, runs the PCPP verifier of [43] to check that the witness is close to a tensor encoding of a message that is consistent with all the answers to the tensor queries. This reduces the query complexity from $O(n^{1/t})$ to $O(1)$ queries.

Preserving Prover Complexity. We discuss prover complexity for the composed proof system. The cost of the prover in the composed IOP is $O(n)$

---

[13] An IOP is said to have robustness parameter α if the local view of the verifier is α-close (in relative Hamming distance) to an accepting view with probability bounded by the IOP's soundness error.

field operations to run the prover of the robust IOPP for tensor queries plus $\mathsf{poly}(T(|\mathbb{x}|))$ bit operations to run the PCPP prover in [43]. In our case, the $\mathsf{NTIME}(T)$ relation being checked is the decision predicate for the verifier in the robust IOPP, so that $T = O(n^{1/t})$ (times smaller factors depending on $\log|\mathbb{F}|$ since T refers to bit operations rather than field operations). If we take the tensor power $t \in \mathbb{N}$ to be a sufficiently large constant, then we can ensure that the prover time in the PCPP of [43], which is polynomial in $O(n^{1/t})$, is dominated by $O(n)$ field operations.

Reducing Verifier Complexity. We discuss verifier complexity for the composed proof system. The cost of the verifier in the composed IOP is dominated by $\mathsf{poly}(|\mathbb{x}|, \log T(|\mathbb{x}|))$ bit operations, the time to run the PCPP verifier in [43]. From our discussion of prover complexity for the composed proof system, we know that $T = O(n^{1/t})$ and so $\log T(|\mathbb{x}|) = O(\log n)$. We are thus left to discuss $|\mathbb{x}|$. Here $\mathbb{x}$ is the state used to *describe* (not run) the computation of the decision predicate for the verifier in the robust IOPP. The description consists of: (a) the description of the code $\mathcal{C}$ used for the tensor encoding; (b) the description of the tensor queries whose answers are being checked; and (c) the *verifier randomness* for the robust IOPP.

The second term depends on the tensor queries, but for simplicity here we will ignore it because in our application all the tensor queries can be described via $O(t \log n)$ elements, again a low-order term. The first term depends on the choice of code $\mathcal{C}$, so we keep it as a parameter. As for the last term, the randomness complexity of the robust consistency check is $O(\mathsf{q} \cdot k \cdot t)$, due to the random linear combinations used in the proximity test of [14], whose randomness complexity is unchanged by robustification. In sum, the cost of the verifier in the composed system is $\mathsf{poly}(|\mathcal{C}|, \log n, \mathsf{q} \cdot k \cdot t)$ bit operations. This leads to a sublinear verifier complexity and does not suffice for Theorem 3.

Fortunately, these linear combinations can be derandomized so to reduce their description size to $O(t)$ (a low-order term), as we now explain. The linear combinations are used in the soundness analysis of the [14] proximity test as part of a "distortion statement": if any member of a collection of messages is far (in Hamming distance) from a linear code, then a random linear combination of those messages is also far from the code, except with some small, bounded, failure probability. Ben-Sasson et al. [10] prove distortion statements for linear combinations of the form $\zeta = (\alpha^1, \alpha^2, \alpha^3, \ldots, \alpha^k)$ for a uniformly random $\alpha \in \mathbb{F}$, at the cost of a tolerable increase in failure probability, and thus, in the soundness error of the proximity test. This allows us to dramatically reduce the number of random field elements used in the proximity test from $O(\mathsf{q} \cdot k \cdot t)$ to $O(\mathsf{q} \cdot t)$. After some work, the result is a verifier complexity of $\mathsf{poly}(|\mathcal{C}|, \log n)$ bit operations in the composed system which suffices for Theorem 3.

Remark 1. We use the freedom to choose a large enough t in our robust zero-knowledge IOPP based on [14] to obtain query complexity (and verifier time) that is $O(n^{1/t})$. It is plausible that [13] similarly implies a robust zero-knowledge IOPP with query complexity (and verifier time) $O(n^{1/2})$. We do not know how to leverage such a result because that would require an inner IOPP with sub-quadratic prover time and constant query complexity, and we do not know of such a result. While it is plausible that the prover of [43] prover runs in sub-quadratic time, proving this seems an arduous task.

2.4 Tensor IOP for R1CS with Semi-honest Verifier Zero Knowledge

The input to the compiler in Sect. 2.3 is a tensor IOP for R1CS that is semi-honest-verifier zero knowledge.

Theorem 4 (informal). *For every finite field $\mathbb{F}$ and positive integers $k, t \in \mathbb{N}$, there is a $(\mathbb{F}, k, t)$-tensor holographic IOP for the indexed relation R_{R1CS}, which is semi-honest-verifier zero-knowledge, that supports instances over $\mathbb{F}$ with $m = O(k^t)$, that has the following parameters: (1) soundness error is $O(\frac{m}{|\mathbb{F}|})$; (2) round complexity is $O(\log m)$; (3) proof length is $O(m)$ elements in $\mathbb{F}$; (4) query complexity is $O(1)$; (5) the indexer and prover use $O(m)$ field operations; (6) the verifier uses $O(|x| + \log m)$ field operations.*

Our starting point is the holographic tensor IOP for R1CS in [14], which achieves the same parameters as in the above theorem[14] except that it is not zero knowledge. We use re-randomization techniques to additionally achieve zero knowledge against semi-honest verifiers, while preserving all efficiency parameters. We now elaborate on this: first we review the structure of the tensor IOP in [14], and then explain our ideas for how to additionally achieve zero knowledge.

The Holographic Tensor IOP of BCG. The holographic tensor IOP for R1CS in [14] follows a standard blueprint for constructing protocols for R1CS [7], adapted to the case of tensor queries. The prover first sends oracles containing the full assignment $z = (x, w)$ and its linear combinations $z_A := Az$, $z_B := Bz$, and $z_C := Cz$. The verifier wishes to check that $z_A \circ z_B = z_C$ and that z_A, z_B, z_C are the correct linear combinations of z. To facilitate this, the verifier sends some randomness to the prover, which enables reducing the first condition (a Hadamard product) to a scalar-product condition. The verifier then engages with the prover in scalar-product subprotocols for checking the scalar products, and holographic "lincheck" subprotocols for checking the linear relations (given tensor-query access to suitable linear-time encodings of the matrices A, B, C). The verifier makes a constant number of tensor queries to each of z, z_A, z_B, z_C for concluding the subprotocols and performing other consistency checks (e.g., consistency of z with x).

---

[14] Note that as described in [14], the tensor IOP of [14] achieves verifier complexity $O(|x| + k)$ because some of the verifier's tensor queries are generated from seeds of length $O(k)$. We reduce the verifier complexity by generating the verifier's tensor queries using short seeds.

This protocol is not zero knowledge even for an honest verifier because: (1) the answer to each tensor query to z, z_A, z_B, z_C reveals information about the secret input w (part of the full assignment z); (2) messages sent by the prover during the scalar-product and lincheck protocols reveal further information about z, z_A, z_B, z_C.

Approach for Zero Knowledge. We need to ensure that every prover message and the answer to every tensor query is simulatable. The fact that queries are linear combinations with a tensor structure would make this rather difficult if we had to deal with malicious verifiers.[15] Fortunately, we seek zero knowledge against semi-honest verifiers only, which means that it suffices to consider any valid execution of an honest verifier, and in particular we have the freedom to assume that the verifier's queries have a certain structure. While there are generic techniques for related settings (e.g., a transformation for linear PCPs with degree-2 verifiers in [11]), they do not seem to be useful for our setting (tensor IOPs with linear-time proving). So our approach here will be to modify the protocol in [14] by adapting ideas used in prior works.

We incorporate random values into the protocol in two different ways to address the two types of leakage above. This will enable us to make every prover message and query answer either uniformly random (independent of the witness) or uniquely determined by other prover messages or query answers. The simulator that we construct will then simply sample all the random values and derive the rest from them. We elaborate on this strategy in the paragraphs below.

(1) ZK against verifier queries. The answer to each verifier query is a linear combination (with tensor structure) of elements in the prover's oracle message. Intuitively, if we pad each oracle message with as many random values as the number of queries it receives, and also "force" the linear combination to have non-zero coefficients in the padded region, then all the query answers will be uniformly random and reveal no information. Padding each of z, z_A, z_B, z_C with independent randomness, however, does not preserve completeness because the padded vectors would not satisfy the R1CS condition.

This naive strategy, however, can be fixed as follows. We rely on a small R1CS gadget, whose solutions can be efficiently sampled, for which we can control the amount of independent randomness. Then we augment the original R1CS instance with this gadget.[16] In the first step of the protocol, the prover samples a random solution to the R1CS gadget and appends it to the witness to obtain

---

[15] For example, constructing linear PCPs that are zero knowledge against malicious verifiers remains an open problem. Constructing tensor IOPs that are zero knowledge against malicious verifiers, while formally an easier question, appears similarly hard.

[16] This is distinct from how zero knowledge is achieved for prior IOPs for R1CS based on the Reed–Solomon code [7]. Instead, it is closer in spirit to how semi-honest-verifier zero knowledge was achieved for linear PCPs for circuits or quadratic arithmetic programs in [11,23].

an augmented witness.[17] In the rest of the protocol, the random solution acts as padding as described above, while preserving completeness. The choice of how much to pad depends on how many independent queries each oracle receives.

Though conceptually simple, this approach requires careful design and analysis. Intuitively, this is because the solutions to the R1CS gadget, which act as random padding, satisfy some non-linear relations, and therefore cannot consist entirely of uniformly random field elements. For example, since $z_C = z_A \circ z_B$, if the padding for z_A and z_B was uniformly random, then the padding for z_C would be a sum of products of uniformly random field elements, which would *not* lead to uniformly random answers to queries on z_C. However, introducing uniformly random padding into z_C requires setting some elements of z_A (or z_B) to fixed non-zero elements, which cannot then be used to make queries on z_A uniformly random. In sum, the solutions to the R1CS gadgets must hide not only the results to queries on the vectors z_A, z_B, z_C, but also the dependencies in the solutions themselves.

(2) ZK for the subprotocols. Each lincheck subprotocol checks a linear relation $Uz = z_U$, and as with the point-query compiler, the usual approach to making the messages in such a subprotocol zero-knowledge is to run the subprotocol on the input vector $e = \gamma z + y$, where y is a random vector sent by the prover and γ is a random challenge sent by the verifier after that. (The claimed output vector z_U needs to be adjusted accordingly too.) This enables the simulator to randomly sample e and honestly run the lincheck protocol, which reveals no information, since the honest verifier only queries $e = \gamma z + y$, and never z and y separately. As the lincheck subprotocol is used as a black-box, the holographic properties of our protocol are unaffected by our modifications for zero-knowledge, and are inherited from the lincheck protocol of [14].

The scalar-product subprotocol is a sumcheck protocol on a certain polynomial p. Sumcheck protocols are usually made zero knowledge by following a similar pattern and running the sumcheck protocol on the polynomial $u := \gamma p + q$, where q is a random polynomial [3]. The simulator can randomly sample u and honestly run the sumcheck protocol, while simulating answers to q by querying p instead.

We cannot apply this idea in our setting of linear-time provers without change. In the protocol of [14], the polynomial p is the product of two multilinear polynomials f and g, each with $\log n$ variables (and thus $O(n)$ coefficients). To achieve linear arithmetic complexity for the prover, it is crucial that the prover *does not compute the sumcheck directly on* p, which could have up to $O(n^2)$ coefficients, and works only with f and g following a certain linear-time algorithm [49]. Thus the prover cannot simply sample a random q.

---

[17] We stress that this modification achieves zero knowledge only against semi-honest verifiers, because a malicious verifier could choose to query the padded vectors with a linear combination that leaves out the randomness and thereby learns information about the secret witness. Nevertheless, as discussed in Sect. 2.3, a tensor IOP that is merely semi-honest-verifier zero knowledge suffices for obtaining a point-query IOP with zero knowledge against bounded-query malicious verifiers.

The solution is to re-randomize the multiplicands f and g separately to $\gamma f + r$ and $\gamma g + s$, and run the sumcheck protocol on their product $(\gamma f + r) \cdot (\gamma g + s)$. (If $p = f \cdot g$ sums to α then $(\gamma f + r) \cdot (\gamma g + s)$ sums to $\alpha \gamma^2 + \rho \gamma + \sigma$ for some ρ and σ derived from r and s alone.) The prover can then compute on polynomials with $O(n)$ coefficients, and the simulator can sample each factor of p at random and proceed similarly.

Efficiency. The resulting tensor IOP inherits all efficiency parameters of the non-ZK tensor IOP of [14]: soundness error $O(m/|\mathbb{F}|)$; logarithmic round complexity; linear proof length; constant query complexity; linear-time indexer; linear-time prover; and logarithmic-time verifier.

2.5 Hiding Properties of Linear Codes

Linear codes have been used to achieve hiding properties in many applications, including secret sharing, multi-party computation, and probabilistic proofs. Below we introduce useful notation and then review the properties of linear codes that we use, along with other ingredients, to achieve zero knowledge IOPs. Informally, we consider probabilistic encodings for linear codes with the property that a small number of locations of a codeword reveal no information about the underlying encoded message.

Randomized Linear Codes. Let $\mathcal{C}$ be a linear code over a field $\mathbb{F}$ with message length k and block length n, and let $\mathrm{Enc} \colon \mathbb{F}^k \to \mathbb{F}^n$ be an encoding function for $\mathcal{C}$ (that is, $\mathrm{Enc}(\mathbb{F}^k) = \mathcal{C}$). For a fixed choice of k_m and k_r such that $k_m + k_r = k$, we can derive from Enc the bivariate function $\widetilde{\mathrm{Enc}} \colon \mathbb{F}^{k_m} \times \mathbb{F}^{k_r} \to \mathbb{F}^n$ defined as $\widetilde{\mathrm{Enc}}(m; r) := \mathrm{Enc}(m \| r)$. In turn, this function naturally induces a probabilistic encoding: we define $\widetilde{\mathrm{Enc}}(m)$ to be the random variable $\{\widetilde{\mathrm{Enc}}(m; r)\}_{r \leftarrow \mathbb{F}^{k_r}}$. In other words, we have designated the first k_m inputs of Enc for the message and the remaining k_r inputs for encoding randomness. We shall refer to a code $\mathcal{C}$ specified via a bivariate function $\widetilde{\mathrm{Enc}}$ as a *randomized linear code*.

Bounded-Query Zero Knowledge. A randomized linear code is *b-query zero knowledge* if reading any b locations of a random encoding of a message does not reveal any information about the message. The locations may be chosen arbitrarily and adaptively. In more detail, we denote by $\mathrm{View}(\widetilde{\mathrm{Enc}}(m; r), A)$ the view of an oracle algorithm A that is given query access to the codeword $\widetilde{\mathrm{Enc}}(m; r)$. We say that $\mathcal{C}$ is b-query zero knowledge if there exists a $\mathsf{poly}(n, \log |\mathbb{F}|)$-time simulator algorithm $\mathcal{S}$ such that, for every message $m \in \mathbb{F}^{k_m}$ and b-query algorithm A, the following random variables are identically distributed:

$$\left\{ \mathrm{View}\big(\widetilde{\mathrm{Enc}}(m; r), A\big) \right\}_{r \leftarrow \mathbb{F}^{k_r}} \quad \text{and} \quad \mathcal{S}^A \ .$$

To achieve even 1-query zero knowledge the random encoding cannot be systematic (as otherwise the algorithm A could learn any location of the message by querying the corresponding location in the codeword).

The above notion mirrors the standard notion of bounded-query zero knowledge for several models of probabilistic proofs (PCPs [33,34,38], IPCPs [30], and IOPs [3,5]). Moreover, it is equivalent, in the special case of codes with a polynomial-time encoding, to the message-indistinguishability definition of zero knowledge of [35] (which requires that the encodings of any two messages are equidistributed when restricted to any small-enough subset of coordinates).

Bounded-Query Uniformity. In intermediate steps we also consider a stronger notion of zero knowledge: we say that $\mathcal{C}$ is *b-query uniform* if any b locations of $\{\widetilde{\text{Enc}}(m;r)\}_{r \leftarrow \mathbb{F}^{kr}}$ are uniformly random and independent symbols. This is a strengthening over the prior notion because the simulator for this case is a simple fixed strategy: answer each query with a freshly sampled random symbol. We refer the reader to the full version for more intuition on the difference between the two notions; there we explain how code concatenation, a standard operation on codes, naturally leads to codes that are bounded-query zero knowledge but not bounded-query uniform, and in particular the simulator cannot employ the foregoing simple strategy.

2.6 On Bounded-Query Zero Knowledge

Theorem 1 guarantees zero-knowledge against *semi-honest* verifiers. However, we can achieve *bounded-query* zero-knowledge against a malicious verifier who makes at most $O(m^\epsilon)$ queries, if we relax the verifier time in our construction to $\text{poly}(|x|) + O(m^\epsilon)$ field operations.

The reason behind this is as follows. By Theorem 3, the zero-knowledge property in Theorem 1 relies (among other things) on a family of *explicit* linear-time encodable error-correcting codes which themselves have a zero-knowledge property, whereby a single query to a codeword leaks no information about the encoded message. These codes suffice for semi-honest-verifier zero-knowledge because the honest verifier never learns more than one query of each codeword. By contrast, in the setting of bounded-query zero-knowledge, we require codes with a zero-knowledge property against a sublinear number of queries. The above codes do not satisfy this property. Instead, we show how to obtain suitable codes from a *probabilistic* construction of Druk and Ishai [22], leading to an IOP verifier whose randomness complexity is sublinear.

Obtaining an explicit construction of linear-time encodable zero-knowledge codes remains an interesting open problem, which would allow us to prove Theorem 1 with *both* polylogarithmic verifier complexity and bounded-query zero-knowledge.

2.6.1 Tensor Products of Zero Knowledge Codes

As part of the tensor-query to point-query compiler (see Sect. 2.4), the prover sends to the verifier proof messages $\hat{\Pi}$ consisting of tensor-IOP proof messages Π encoded under a tensor code $\mathcal{C}^{\otimes t}$. The verifier has point-query access to the encoded messages $\hat{\Pi}$. To ensure that these queries do not leak information (up to a certain number of queries), we require the tensor code $\mathcal{C}^{\otimes t}$ to be zero-knowledge. To this end, we prove that the tensor product operation preserves the property of bounded-query zero-knowledge (and bounded-query uniformity). In particular, for $\mathcal{C}^{\otimes t}$ to be zero knowledge it will suffice for $\mathcal{C}$ to be zero knowledge. (We discuss how to obtain a zero-knowledge code that is linear-time encodable after this, in Sect. 2.6.2.)

Theorem 5. *Let $\mathcal{C}$ and $\mathcal{C}'$ be randomized linear codes.*

1. *If $\mathcal{C}$ is b-query zero-knowledge and $\mathcal{C}'$ is b'-query zero-knowledge, then $\mathcal{C} \otimes \mathcal{C}'$ is $\min(b, b')$-query zero-knowledge.*
2. *If $\mathcal{C}$ is b-query uniform and $\mathcal{C}'$ is b'-query uniform, then $\mathcal{C} \otimes \mathcal{C}'$ is $\min(b, b')$-query uniform.*

The formal statement and proof are provided in the full version.

2.6.2 Zero-Knowledge Codes with Linear-Time Encoding

To prove our main theorem, Theorem 1, we require an explicit construction of a randomized linear code, that must be both linear-time encodable and 1-query zero-knowledge. Prior works such as [13, 17] achieve this by applying a 1-out-of-2 secret sharing scheme to every element of the output of an explicit (non zero-knowledge) linear-time encodable code, such as [48]. Given the encoding function Enc for a linear-time encodable code, the new code is defined by $\widetilde{\mathrm{Enc}}(m; r) := (\mathrm{Enc}(m) + r, r)$.

Investigating Bounded-Query Zero-Knowledge. To prove the variation on our main theorem, Theorem 1, with bounded-query zero-knowledge, we require randomized linear codes which are linear-time encodable as above, but with a stronger zero-knowledge property. In this case, the code must be b-query zero-knowledge where b is not only greater than 1, but may even be a constant fraction of the block length.

Prior works achieved these properties separately. For example, it is well-known that the Reed–Solomon code can be made b-query zero-knowledge by using b elements of encoding randomness, but their encoding functions incur costs quasilinear in the message length. On the other hand, the zero-knowledge properties of linear-time encodable codes, such as the explicit family by Spielman [48] or the probabilistic family by Druk and Ishai [22], have not been investigated.

We prove the existence of codes satisfying both requirements, via a probabilistic construction. In the statement below, $H_q \colon [0, 1] \to [0, 1]$ denotes the q-ary entropy function.

Theorem 6. *For every finite field $\mathbb{F}$, every $\epsilon \in (0, 1)$, and every function $\beta \colon \mathbb{N} \to (0, 1)$ bounded away from 1, letting $q := |\mathbb{F}|$, there is a circuit family $\{E_{k_m} \colon \mathbb{F}^{k_m} \times \mathbb{F}^{(H_q(\beta(k_m))+\epsilon) \cdot O(k_m)} \times \mathbb{F}^{O(k_m)} \to \mathbb{F}^{O(k_m)}\}_{k_m \in \mathbb{N}}$ such that: (1) E_{k_m} has size $O(k_m)$; (2) with probability at least $1 - q^{-\Omega_\epsilon(k_m)}$ over $R \in \mathbb{F}^{O(k)}$, the randomized linear code $\mathcal{C}_{k_m}$ whose encoding function is $\widetilde{\mathrm{Enc}}_{k_m}(m; r) := E_{k_m}(m, r, R)$ has constant relative distance and is $O(\beta(k_m) \cdot k_m)$-query uniform.*

The precise statement of the theorem and its proof are provided in the full version.

Below we provide an overview of the proof; and finally discuss related constructions and analyses. Derandomizing Theorem 6, namely the goal of obtaining an explicit family of codes that are both zero knowledge and linear-time encodable, remains an open problem.

Overview of Proof of Theorem 6. We use the same code as in [22], which is a probabilistic construction (which we inherit). Our contribution is to show that their construction additionally satisfies the strong requirement of b-query uniformity, by using ideas from the analysis of [22].

Informally, Druk and Ishai [22] construct a family of distributions $\mathcal{G} = \{\mathcal{G}_k\}_{k \in \mathbb{N}}$ such that, for every $k \in \mathbb{N}$, $\mathcal{G}_k = \{G_R \in \mathbb{F}^{O(k) \times k}\}_{R \in \mathbb{F}^{O(k)}}$ is a distribution over generator matrices such that: (1) matrix-vector multiplication is computable in linear time; (2) for any fixed non-zero vector x, when G_R is sampled at random from the distribution, $G_R x$ is uniformly distributed. This latter property is known as *linear uniform output*, and implies that, with high probability over R, G_R has constant relative distance and dual distance.

We are interested in analyzing what happens if we split the message space of a generator matrix $G \in \mathcal{G}_k$ into two parts, one of length k_m for the actual message and another of length k_r for the encoding randomness, for $k_m + k_r = k$. As in Sect. 2.5, this induces a corresponding split in the generator matrix: $G = \begin{bmatrix} G_m & G_r \end{bmatrix}$. In the full version we show that the probability that this code is b-query uniform is bounded from below by the probability that $(G_r)^\perp$, the dual of G_r, has minimum (absolute) distance at least $b + 1$.

Druk and Ishai [22] show that $G^\perp$ has constant relative distance with high probability. We observe that G_r inherits the linear-uniform output property from G, and then adapt their analysis to $(G_r)^\perp$. We now summarize the main ideas of their analysis when it is applied to our setting of b-query uniformity. Similarly, to the standard probabilistic proof of the Gilbert–Varshamov bound, requiring that $(G_r)^\perp$ has distance at least $b+1$ is equivalent to showing that each non-zero vector $z \in \mathbb{F}^n$ with Hamming weight at most b is not in $(G_r)^\perp$, i.e., $zG_r \neq 0$. The linear-uniform output property of G implies that zG_r is uniformly distributed, over a random choice of G_r; therefore the probability that $z \in \mathbb{F}^n$ is in $(G_r)^\perp$ is at most q^{-k_r}. Taking a union bound over all vectors of weight at most b, of which there are at most $q^{H_q(b/n) \cdot n}$, gives an upper bound on the probability that the distance of $(G_r)^\perp$ is at most b.

We can choose parameters so that $n = O(k_m)$ and $k_r = O(H_q(b/n) \cdot n)$ with suitable constants so that $q^{-k_r} \cdot q^{H_q(b/n) \cdot n} = q^{-\Omega(k_m)}$. In combination with results on the distance of G, this yields Theorem 6.

In sum, we obtain a trade-off between the fraction of the message space allocated to the encoding randomness and the b-query uniformity of the code. For example, if (as we use in this paper) b is linear in n then $H_q(b/n)$ is constant and the encoding randomness is a constant fraction of the input.

Comparison with Related Work. Chen et al. [19] show a result analogous to Theorem 6 for random codes: with high probability over a choice of random code with block length $O(k_m)$, using $H_q(\beta(k_m)) \cdot O(k_m)$ elements of encoding randomness ensures $O(\beta(k_m) \cdot k_m)$-query zero-knowledge. Random codes, however, are not linear-time encodable. Theorem 6 can be viewed as strengthening the result for random codes in [19, Theorem 11] to apply to the linear-time codes of [22] (and to proving the stronger property of bounded-query uniformity). The proofs of both results follow the standard template of the existence proof of codes meeting the Gilbert–Varshamov bound, except that the analyzed code family changes.

Druk and Ishai [22] give a linear-time secret sharing scheme for message vectors of constant length, based on the same code family used to prove Theorem 6. Their construction generalizes to a randomized encoding scheme with b-query zero-knowledge (and most likely b-query uniformity), where b is determined by the distance of the dual code. For this code family, the dual distance is linear in k_m, giving b-query zero-knowledge for $b = \Theta(k_m)$. However, encoding requires solving a system of linear equations whose dimension is the same length as the message, and so fails to be linear-time.

Ishai et al. [35,51] give a generic construction of zero-knowledge codes from any linear code, which works by randomizing a generator matrix for the code, but this does not preserve linear-time encoding.

2.7   Linear-Time Succinct Arguments from Linear-Time IOPs

Known approaches for constructing succinct arguments rely on cryptography to "compile" various forms of probabilistic proofs into argument systems. However, the cryptography used typically introduces super-linear overheads, ruling out a linear-time argument system even when compiling a linear-time probabilistic proof. Bootle et al. [13] observe that Kilian's approach [37] is a notable exception. We review this below because Theorem 1 implies Theorem 2 via this approach; our technical contribution is Theorem 1.

Linear-Time Arguments via Kilian's Approach. The cryptography used in Kilian's approach is collision-resistant hash functions, for which there are linear-time candidates under standard assumptions (e.g., based on the hardness of finding short codewords in linear codes [1]). If we use a linear-time hash function in Kilian's approach to compile a linear-time PCP (over a large-enough alphabet) then we obtain a linear-time argument system.[18] While constructions of linear-time PCPs are not known (and seem far beyond current techniques), the foregoing implication equally holds for IOPs [8,44]. This route was used in

---

[18] In Kilian's approach, the argument prover's cryptographic cost is dominated by the cost to commit to the PCP string via a Merkle tree. In particular, if the PCP has proof length l and the size of a proof symbol is linear in the input size of the hash function, then the running time of the argument prover is within a constant of the running time of the PCP prover.

[13,14] to obtain interactive arguments with linear-time prover and sublinear-time verifier from IOPs with linear-time prover and sublinear-time verifier.

Zero Knowledge. Kilian's approach to additionally achieve zero knowledge makes a non-black-box use of the collision-resistant hash function and the probabilistic proof's verifier.[19] Ishai et al. [34] then proved that if the underlying probabilistic proof satisfies a mild notion of zero knowledge then Kilian's approach can be significantly simplified to yield a zero-knowledge succinct argument where *the collision-resistant hash function and the probabilistic proof are used as black boxes*. This implication, too, preserves linear time of both building blocks to yield a zero-knowledge succinct argument with a linear-time prover.

The notion of zero-knowledge required of the underlying probabilistic proof depends on the desired notion of zero knowledge for the argument system. If the argument system is desired to be honest-verifier zero knowledge (this suffices, e.g., to subsequently apply the Fiat–Shamir heuristic) then the probabilistic proof must be honest-verifier zero knowledge. If instead the argument system is desired to be malicious-verifier zero-knowledge then the probabilistic proof must be *semi*-honest-verifier zero knowledge (the simulator works for any possible fixed execution of the honest verifier). A further strengthening known as bounded-query zero knowledge, the hiding notion typically studied for PCPs [38], enables reductions in communication.

In Sum. The interactive argument in Theorem 2 is constructed via the above approach from the IOP in Theorem 1 (with sublinear verification in the holographic setting mapping to sublinear verification in the preprocessing setting). The semi-honest-verifier zero-knowledge property of the IOP implies the malicious-verifier zero-knowledge property of the interactive argument. The linear prover time and polylogarithmic verifier time of the IOP imply the corresponding running times of the interactive argument, as the given collision-resistant hash function runs in linear time.

References

1. Applebaum, B., Haramaty, N., Ishai, Y., Kushilevitz, E., Vaikuntanathan, V.: Low-complexity cryptographic hash functions. In: Proceedings of the 8th Innovations in Theoretical Computer Science Conference, ITCS 2017, pp. 7:1–7:31 (2017)
2. Arora, S., Safra, S.: Probabilistic checking of proofs: a new characterization of NP. J. ACM **45**(1), 70–122 (1998). Preliminary version in FOCS '92
3. Ben-Sasson, E., Chiesa, A., Forbes, M.A., Gabizon, A., Riabzev, M., Spooner, N.: Zero knowledge protocols from succinct constraint detection. In: Kalai, Y., Reyzin, L. (eds.) TCC 2017. LNCS, vol. 10678, pp. 172–206. Springer, Cham (2017). https://doi.org/10.1007/978-3-319-70503-3_6

---

[19] Modify the Merkle tree to be over hiding commitments to proof symbols (rather than over the proof symbols themselves) and then prove in zero knowledge that opening the queried locations would have made the probabilistic proof verifier accept.

4. Ben-Sasson, E., Chiesa, A., Gabizon, A., Riabzev, M., Spooner, N.: Interactive oracle proofs with constant rate and query complexity. In: Proceedings of the 44th International Colloquium on Automata, Languages and Programming, ICALP 2017, pp. 40:1–40:15 (2017)

5. Ben-Sasson, E., Chiesa, A., Gabizon, A., Virza, M.: Quasi-linear size zero knowledge from linear-algebraic PCPs. In: Kushilevitz, E., Malkin, T. (eds.) TCC 2016. LNCS, vol. 9563, pp. 33–64. Springer, Heidelberg (2016). https://doi.org/10.1007/978-3-662-49099-0_2

6. Ben-Sasson, E., Chiesa, A., Goldberg, L., Gur, T., Riabzev, M., Spooner, N.: Linear-size constant-query IOPs for delegating computation. In: Hofheinz, D., Rosen, A. (eds.) TCC 2019. LNCS, vol. 11892, pp. 494–521. Springer, Cham (2019). https://doi.org/10.1007/978-3-030-36033-7_19

7. Ben-Sasson, E., Chiesa, A., Riabzev, M., Spooner, N., Virza, M., Ward, N.P.: Aurora: transparent succinct arguments for R1CS. In: Ishai, Y., Rijmen, V. (eds.) EUROCRYPT 2019. LNCS, vol. 11476, pp. 103–128. Springer, Cham (2019). https://doi.org/10.1007/978-3-030-17653-2_4

8. Ben-Sasson, E., Chiesa, A., Spooner, N.: Interactive oracle proofs. In: Hirt, M., Smith, A. (eds.) TCC 2016. LNCS, vol. 9986, pp. 31–60. Springer, Heidelberg (2016). https://doi.org/10.1007/978-3-662-53644-5_2

9. Ben-Sasson, E., Kaplan, Y., Kopparty, S., Meir, O., Stichtenoth, H.: Constant rate PCPs for circuit-SAT with sublinear query complexity. In: Proceedings of the 54th Annual IEEE Symposium on Foundations of Computer Science, FOCS 2013, pp. 320–329 (2013)

10. Ben-Sasson, E., Kopparty, S., Saraf, S.: Worst-case to average case reductions for the distance to a code. In: Proceedings of the 33rd ACM Conference on Computer and Communications Security, CCS 2018, pp. 24:1–24:23 (2018)

11. Bitansky, N., Chiesa, A., Ishai, Y., Paneth, O., Ostrovsky, R.: Succinct non-interactive arguments via linear interactive proofs. In: Sahai, A. (ed.) TCC 2013. LNCS, vol. 7785, pp. 315–333. Springer, Heidelberg (2013). https://doi.org/10.1007/978-3-642-36594-2_18

12. Bootle, J., Cerulli, A., Chaidos, P., Groth, J., Petit, C.: Efficient zero-knowledge arguments for arithmetic circuits in the discrete log setting. In: Fischlin, M., Coron, J.-S. (eds.) EUROCRYPT 2016. LNCS, vol. 9666, pp. 327–357. Springer, Heidelberg (2016). https://doi.org/10.1007/978-3-662-49896-5_12

13. Bootle, J., Cerulli, A., Ghadafi, E., Groth, J., Hajiabadi, M., Jakobsen, S.K.: Linear-time zero-knowledge proofs for arithmetic circuit satisfiability. In: Takagi, T., Peyrin, T. (eds.) ASIACRYPT 2017. LNCS, vol. 10626, pp. 336–365. Springer, Cham (2017). https://doi.org/10.1007/978-3-319-70700-6_12

14. Bootle, J., Chiesa, A., Groth, J.: Linear-time arguments with sublinear verification from tensor codes. In: Proceedings of the 18th Theory of Cryptography Conference, TCC 2020, pp. 19–46 (2020)

15. Brassard, G., Chaum, D., Crépeau, C.: Minimum disclosure proofs of knowledge. J. Comput. Syst. Sci. **37**(2), 156–189 (1988)

16. Bünz, B., Bootle, J., Boneh, D., Poelstra, A., Wuille, P., Maxwell, G.: Bulletproofs: short proofs for confidential transactions and more. In: Proceedings of the 39th IEEE Symposium on Security and Privacy, S&P 2018, pp. 315–334 (2018)

17. Cerulli, A.: Efficient zero-knowledge proofs and their applications (2019)

18. Chase, M., et al.: Post-quantum zero-knowledge and signatures from symmetric-key primitives. In: Proceedings of the 24th ACM Conference on Computer and Communications Security, CCS 2017, pp. 1825–1842 (2017)

19. Chen, H., Cramer, R., Goldwasser, S., de Haan, R., Vaikuntanathan, V.: Secure computation from random error correcting codes. In: Naor, M. (ed.) EUROCRYPT 2007. LNCS, vol. 4515, pp. 291–310. Springer, Heidelberg (2007). https://doi.org/10.1007/978-3-540-72540-4_17

20. Chiesa, A., Hu, Y., Maller, M., Mishra, P., Vesely, N., Ward, N.: Marlin: preprocessing zkSNARKs with universal and updatable SRS. In: Canteaut, A., Ishai, Y. (eds.) EUROCRYPT 2020. LNCS, vol. 12105, pp. 738–768. Springer, Cham (2020). https://doi.org/10.1007/978-3-030-45721-1_26

21. Chiesa, A., Ojha, D., Spooner, N.: FRACTAL: post-quantum and transparent recursive proofs from holography. In: Canteaut, A., Ishai, Y. (eds.) EUROCRYPT 2020. LNCS, vol. 12105, pp. 769–793. Springer, Cham (2020). https://doi.org/10.1007/978-3-030-45721-1_27

22. Druk, E., Ishai, Y.: Linear-time encodable codes meeting the Gilbert-Varshamov bound and their cryptographic applications. In: Proceedings of the 5th Innovations in Theoretical Computer Science Conference, ITCS 2014, pp. 169–182 (2014)

23. Gennaro, R., Gentry, C., Parno, B., Raykova, M.: Quadratic span programs and succinct NIZKs without PCPs. In: Johansson, T., Nguyen, P.Q. (eds.) EUROCRYPT 2013. LNCS, vol. 7881, pp. 626–645. Springer, Heidelberg (2013). https://doi.org/10.1007/978-3-642-38348-9_37

24. Giacomelli, I., Madsen, J., Orlandi, C.: ZKBoo: faster zero-knowledge for boolean circuits. In: Proceedings of the 25th USENIX Security Symposium, Security 2016, pp. 1069–1083 (2016)

25. Goldreich, O., Håstad, J.: On the complexity of interactive proofs with bounded communication. Inf. Process. Lett. **67**(4), 205–214 (1998)

26. Goldreich, O., Kahan, A.: How to construct constant-round zero-knowledge proof systems for NP. J. Cryptol. **9**(3), 167–189 (1996). https://doi.org/10.1007/BF00208001

27. Goldreich, O., Vadhan, S., Wigderson, A.: On interactive proofs with a laconic prover. Comput. Complex. **11**(1/2), 1–53 (2002)

28. Goldwasser, S., Micali, S., Rackoff, C.: The knowledge complexity of interactive proof systems. SIAM J. Comput. **18**(1), 186–208 (1989). Preliminary version appeared in STOC '85

29. Golovnev, A., Lee, J., Setty, S., Thaler, J., Wahby, R.: Brakedown: linear-time and post-quantum snarks for r1cs. Cryptology ePrint Archive, Report 2021/1043 (2021)

30. Goyal, V., Ishai, Y., Mahmoody, M., Sahai, A.: Interactive locking, zero-knowledge PCPs, and unconditional cryptography. In: Rabin, T. (ed.) CRYPTO 2010. LNCS, vol. 6223, pp. 173–190. Springer, Heidelberg (2010). https://doi.org/10.1007/978-3-642-14623-7_10

31. Heath, D., Kolesnikov, V.: Stacked garbling for disjunctive zero-knowledge proofs. In: Canteaut, A., Ishai, Y. (eds.) EUROCRYPT 2020. LNCS, vol. 12107, pp. 569–598. Springer, Cham (2020). https://doi.org/10.1007/978-3-030-45727-3_19

32. Ishai, Y., Kushilevitz, E., Ostrovsky, R., Sahai, A.: Zero-knowledge from secure multiparty computation. In: Proceedings of the 39th Annual Symposium on Theory of Computing, STOC 2007, pp. 21–30 (2007)

33. Ishai, Y., Mahmoody, M., Sahai, A.: On efficient zero-knowledge PCPs. In: Cramer, R. (ed.) TCC 2012. LNCS, vol. 7194, pp. 151–168. Springer, Heidelberg (2012). https://doi.org/10.1007/978-3-642-28914-9_9

34. Ishai, Y., Mahmoody, M., Sahai, A., Xiao, D.: On zero-knowledge PCPs: Limitations, simplifications, and applications (2015). http://www.cs.virginia.edu/~mohammad/files/papers/ZKPCPs-Full.pdf

35. Ishai, Y., Sahai, A., Viderman, M., Weiss, M.: Zero knowledge LTCs and their applications. In: Raghavendra, P., Raskhodnikova, S., Jansen, K., Rolim, J.D.P. (eds.) APPROX/RANDOM -2013. LNCS, vol. 8096, pp. 607–622. Springer, Heidelberg (2013). https://doi.org/10.1007/978-3-642-40328-6_42
36. Katz, J., Kolesnikov, V., Wang, X.: Improved non-interactive zero knowledge with applications to post-quantum signatures. In: Proceedings of the 25th ACM Conference on Computer and Communications Security, CCS 2018, pp. 525–537 (2018)
37. Kilian, J.: A note on efficient zero-knowledge proofs and arguments. In: Proceedings of the 24th Annual ACM Symposium on Theory of Computing, STOC 1992, pp. 723–732 (1992)
38. Kilian, J., Petrank, E., Tardos, G.: Probabilistically checkable proofs with zero knowledge. In: Proceedings of the 29th Annual ACM Symposium on Theory of Computing, STOC 1997, pp. 496–505 (1997)
39. Kothapalli, A., Masserova, E., Parno, B.: A direct construction for asymptotically optimal zkSNARKs. Cryptology ePrint Archive, Report 2020/1318 (2020)
40. Lee, J., Setty, S., Thaler, J., Wahby, R.: Linear-time zero-knowledge SNARKs for R1CS. Cryptology ePrint Archive, Report 2021/030 (2021)
41. Meir, O.: Combinatorial PCPs with short proofs. In: Proceedings of the 26th Annual IEEE Conference on Computational Complexity, CCC 2012 (2012)
42. Meir, O.: IP = PSPACE using error-correcting codes. SIAM J. Comput. **42**(1), 380–403 (2013)
43. Mie, T.: Short PCPPs verifiable in polylogarithmic time with o(1) queries. Ann. Math. Artif. Intell. **56**, 313–338 (2009)
44. Reingold, O., Rothblum, R., Rothblum, G.: Constant-round interactive proofs for delegating computation. In: Proceedings of the 48th ACM Symposium on the Theory of Computing, STOC 2016, pp. 49–62 (2016)
45. Ron-Zewi, N., Rothblum, R.: Local proofs approaching the witness length. In: Proceedings of the 61st Annual IEEE Symposium on Foundations of Computer Science, FOCS 2020, pp. 846–857 (2020)
46. Setty, S.: Spartan: efficient and general-purpose zkSNARKs without trusted setup. In: Micciancio, D., Ristenpart, T. (eds.) CRYPTO 2020. LNCS, vol. 12172, pp. 704–737. Springer, Cham (2020). https://doi.org/10.1007/978-3-030-56877-1_25
47. Setty, S., Lee, J.: Quarks: quadruple-efficient transparent zkSNARKs. Cryptology ePrint Archive, Report 2020/1275 (2020)
48. Spielman, D.A.: Linear-time encodable and decodable error-correcting codes. IEEE Trans. Inf. Theory **42**(6), 1723–1731 (1996). Preliminary version appeared in STOC '95
49. Thaler, J.: Time-optimal interactive proofs for circuit evaluation. In: Canetti, R., Garay, J.A. (eds.) CRYPTO 2013. LNCS, vol. 8043, pp. 71–89. Springer, Heidelberg (2013). https://doi.org/10.1007/978-3-642-40084-1_5
50. Wahby, R.S., Tzialla, I., Shelat, A., Thaler, J., Walfish, M.: Doubly-efficient zkSNARKs without trusted setup. In: Proceedings of the 39th IEEE Symposium on Security and Privacy, S&P 2018, pp. 926–943 (2018)
51. Weiss, M.: Secure computation and probabilistic checking (2016)
52. Weng, C., Yang, K., Katz, J., Wang, X.: Wolverine: fast, scalable, and communication-efficient zero-knowledge proofs for boolean and arithmetic circuits. IACR Cryptology ePrint Archive, Report 2020/925 (2020)
53. Xie, T., Zhang, J., Zhang, Y., Papamanthou, C., Song, D.: Libra: succinct zero-knowledge proofs with optimal prover computation. In: Boldyreva, A., Micciancio, D. (eds.) CRYPTO 2019. LNCS, vol. 11694, pp. 733–764. Springer, Cham (2019). https://doi.org/10.1007/978-3-030-26954-8_24

54. Zhang, J., Wang, W., Zhang, Y., Zhang, Y.: Doubly efficient interactive proofs for general arithmetic circuits with linear prover time. Cryptology ePrint Archive, Report 2020/1247 (2020)
55. Zhang, J., Xie, T., Zhang, Y., Song, D.: Transparent polynomial delegation and its applications to zero knowledge proof. In: Proceedings of the 41st IEEE Symposium on Security and Privacy, S&P 2020, pp. 859–876 (2020)

Non-Interactive Zero-Knowledge Proofs with Fine-Grained Security

Yuyu Wang[1]($\boxtimes$)(iD) and Jiaxin Pan[2](iD)

[1] University of Electronic Science and Technology of China, Chengdu, China
wangyuyu@uestc.edu.cn
[2] Department of Mathematical Sciences, NTNU - Norwegian University of Science
and Technology, Trondheim, Norway
jiaxin.pan@ntnu.no

Abstract. We construct the *first* non-interactive zero-knowledge (NIZK) proof systems in the fine-grained setting where adversaries' resources are bounded and honest users have no more resources than an adversary. More concretely, our setting is the NC^1-fine-grained setting, namely, all parties (including adversaries and honest participants) are in NC^1.

Our NIZK systems are for circuit satisfiability (SAT) under the worst-case assumption, $\mathsf{NC}^1 \subsetneq \oplus\mathsf{L}/\mathsf{poly}$. As technical contributions, we propose two approaches to construct NIZKs in the NC^1-fine-grained setting. In stark contrast to the classical Fiat-Shamir transformation, both our approaches start with a simple Σ-protocol and transform it into NIZKs for circuit SAT without random oracles. Additionally, our second approach firstly proposes a *fully homomorphic encryption* (FHE) scheme in the fine-grained setting, which was not known before, as a building block. Compared with the first approach, the resulting NIZK only supports circuits with constant multiplicative depth, while its proof size is independent of the statement circuit size.

Extending our approaches, we obtain two NIZK systems in the uniform reference string model and two non-interactive zaps (namely, non-interactive witness-indistinguishability proof systems in the plain model). While the previous constructions from Ball, Dachman-Soled, and Kulkarni (CRYPTO 2020) require provers to run in polynomial-time, our constructions are the first one with provers in NC^1.

Keywords: Fine-grained cryptography · Non-interactive zero-knowledge proof · Fully homomorphic encryption

Y. Wang—Supported by the National Natural Science Foundation for Young Scientists of China under Grant Number 62002049 and the Fundamental Research Funds for the Central Universities under Grant Number ZYGX2020J017.
J. Pan—Supported by the Research Council of Norway under Project No. 324235.

The original version of this chapter was revised: an erroneous equation in the paper has been corrected. The correction to this chapter is available at
https://doi.org/10.1007/978-3-031-07085-3_31

O. Dunkelman and S. Dziembowski (Eds.): EUROCRYPT 2022, LNCS 13276, pp. 305–335, 2022.
https://doi.org/10.1007/978-3-031-07085-3_11

1 Introduction

Non-interactive zero-knowledge (NIZK) proof systems [11] are a central topic in complexity theory and theoretical cryptography. In the recent years, it also provides numerous novel applications in cryptography. An important line of research is to construct NIZKs based on different assumptions. An earlier work has shown that NIZKs require a trusted setup, such as a common reference string (CRS) [4]. Moreover, Pass and shelat [16] showed that (non-uniform) one-way functions are sufficient for NIZK for AM. Recently, it is possible to construct efficient NIZKs such as Diffie-Hellman-based constructions [12,13]. In this paper, we are interested in NIZKs based on much mild assumptions.

NC^1**-fine-grained cryptography.** Fine-grained cryptography [7] designs cryptographic schemes in a setting where adversaries have only bounded resources and honest users have no more resources than adversaries. In this setting, it is possible to have more efficient schemes and base their security on weaker, or extremely mild assumptions. Although this notion of cryptography was firstly proposed by Degwekar, Vaikuntanathan, and Vasudevan [7], it has long history starting from the Merkle key exchange protocol [15].

In this paper, we consider NC^1-fine-grained cryptography where adversaries are in NC^1. Cryptography in this setting is often based on the worst-case assumption on complexity classes, $\mathsf{NC}^1 \subsetneq \oplus\mathsf{L}/\mathsf{poly}$. Here $\oplus\mathsf{L}/\mathsf{poly}$ is the class of languages with polynomial-size branching programs, and all languages in NC^1 have polynomial-size branching programs of constant width by the Barrington theorem [3]. The $\mathsf{NC}^1 \subsetneq \oplus\mathsf{L}/\mathsf{poly}$ assumption states that there exists at least one language having only polynomial-size branching programs with non-constant width.

We suppose that it is interesting to study NC^1-fine-grained cryptography. First, it is a fundamental question to consider which kind of cryptographic schemes can be constructed in such a setting by assuming $\mathsf{NC}^1 \subsetneq \oplus\mathsf{L}/\mathsf{poly}$. Currently, we know that one-way functions [7], (somewhat homomorphic) public-key encryption [5,7], hash proof systems (HPS) [9], and attribute-based encryption [20] are possible in this setting. We want to explore whether it is possible to push the boundary further. Second, as pointed out in [7], these primitives in NC^1 can be combined with other constructions against polynomial-time adversaries under stronger assumptions. Although the resulting scheme relies on stronger assumptions (e.g., factoring, Diffie-Hellman, and learning with errors) for polynomial-time adversaries, it is secure for NC^1 adversaries as long as $\mathsf{NC}^1 \subsetneq \oplus\mathsf{L}/\mathsf{poly}$.

Current NIZKs in NC^1. We aim at constructing NIZKs in the NC^1-fine-grained setting. To the best of our knowledge, there are three proof systems under the assumption $\mathsf{NC}^1 \subsetneq \oplus\mathsf{L}/\mathsf{poly}$ [2,9,20], but none of them achieves our goal, and, in particular, it is inherently difficult to transform them in achieving our goal.

A fine-grained NIZK proof system has previously been constructed by Ball, Dachman-Soled, and Kulkarni [2] assuming $\mathsf{NC}^1 \subsetneq \oplus\mathsf{L}/\mathsf{poly}$, but in a stronger setting, where the prover is polynomial-time and more powerful than NC^1 circuits and the verifier, simulator, and adversaries are in NC^1. To be a bit more technical, we suppose their requirement on polynomial-time provers is inherent, since their provers need to compute the determinant of some matrix, which cannot be done in NC^1. Another example is the hash proof system (HPS) by Egashira, Wang, and Tanaka [9]. Although in their scheme adversaries and all honest parties are in NC^1, an HPS is a weaker form of NIZK, namely, the designated verifier needs to hold the secret hash key to verify the proof. Recently, Wang, Pan, and Chen [20] proposed a quasi-adaptive NIZK in NC^1 with public verification. However, their scheme can only support languages that can be expressed as linear subspaces, which is rather restricted, and their scheme is in the *weaker* quasi-adaptive model, namely, their CRSs have to be dependent on the language parameter.

1.1 Our Contributions

We construct the *first* NIZK proof systems in the fully NC^1 setting, where adversaries, honest provers, and verifiers are all in NC^1. We note that this is in contrast to schemes in [2] which requires the provers to be polynomial and more powerful than NC^1 circuits. Similar to previous NC^1-fine-grained primitives [5,7,9,20], the security of our scheme is based on the $NC^1 \subsetneq \oplus L/poly$ assumption.

Our approach first constructs a simple Σ-protocol that runs in $AC^0[2]$ which is a subset of NC^1, and then compiles it to NIZKs for circuit satisfiability (SAT) in the CRS model. Our transformation does not require random oracles as in the classical Fiat-Shamir transformation [10], or pairings as in the recent work of Couteau and Hartmann [6].

Our transformation contains several intermediate steps, as described figuratively in Fig. 1. We first transform our Σ-protocol to a NIZK for linear languages, namely, a NIZK for proving whether a vector belongs to

$$L_M = \{t : \exists w \in \{0,1\}^t, \text{ s.t. } t = Mw\},$$

where $M \in \{0,1\}^{n \times t}$. Based on this, we construct an OR-proof system for disjunction.

Fig. 1. Overview of our approaches in constructing NIZK in the CRS model.

Starting from our OR-proof, we have two methods to construct NIZKs for circuit SAT. Our first method uses the additive homomorphic encryption from Degwekar, Vaikuntanathan, and Vasudevan (DVV) [7] (in a non-black-box way) to transform our OR-proof to a NIZK for circuit SAT. Its proof size grows linearly with the size of the statement circuit. The resulting NIZK can prove statements that can be represented as NC^1 circuits, since our provers are NC^1 circuits.

We stress that in the (fully) NC^1-fine-grained setting a statement circuit cannot go beyond NC^1. This is because if the statement circuit is outside NC^1, then even the honest prover in NC^1 cannot decide with the witness if the statement is true or not. However, if we allow the honest prover to run in polynomial-time as in [2], our construction works for any statement circuits with polynomial-size.

Our second method first constructs a fully homomorphic encryption (FHE) scheme in the NC^1 setting, and then uses it to construct a NIZK for circuit SAT. On the one hand, different to our first method, this NIZK's proof size is independent of the statement size. On the other hand, our NIZK from the second method supports statements in $\mathsf{AC}^0_{\mathsf{CM}}[2]$, since our FHE supports homomorphic evaluation of $\mathsf{AC}^0_{\mathsf{CM}}[2]$ circuits. Here $\mathsf{AC}^0_{\mathsf{CM}}[2]$ circuits are $\mathsf{AC}^0[2]$ circuits with constant multiplicative depth, where multiplicative depth can be thought of as the degree of the lowest-degree polynomial in $GF(2)$ evaluating to a circuit [5] (See Definition 4).

Interlude: fine-grained FHE. We highlight that our FHE scheme is of independent interest. To the best of our knowledge, the scheme of Campanelli and Gennaro [5] is the only known somewhat homomorphic encryption (SHE) in the NC^1-fine-grained setting, where SHE is a weaker notion of FHE. Thus, our scheme is the *first* FHE in the NC^1-fine-grained setting. Moreover, our FHE is conceptually simpler and compatible with our OR-proof in constructing NIZK for circuit SAT. In terms of efficiency, our scheme is comparable to the SHE scheme in [5]: our public key has λ^2 bits, while theirs has $O(\lambda^3)$ bits. Also, our scheme uses less parallel running-time, in the sense that it only computes the parity of λ bits in parallel for homomorphic multiplication, while theirs has to compute the parity of λ^2 bits. Here λ is the security parameter.

We leave improving the power of homomorphic computation of our scheme as an open problem. We are also optimistic that all FHE-based applications can be realized in the NC^1-fine-grained setting using our FHE, and we leave a detailed treatment of it as a future work.

Extensions. We extend our NIZKs to construct non-interactive zaps [8] (i.e., non-interactive witness-indistinguishability proof systems in the plain model) by improving the techniques in [12]. The key enabler for this is that all our NIZKs have verifiable correlated key generation which is a property used in [12] and formally defined by us. Roughly speaking, this property states that a perfectly sound CRS (i.e., a binding CRS) is correlated to a perfectly zero-knowledge one (i.e., a hiding CRS), and in some particular case this can even be verified.

All the aforementioned NIZKs are in the CRS model. We further extend them to the uniform random string (URS) model, where a trust setup only samples public coins.

1.2 Technical Details

In this section, we give more details about our techniques with a particular focus on constructing NIZKs for circuit SAT in the CRS model. A figurative overview for this is given in Fig. 1.

Starting point: a Σ-protocol in $\mathsf{AC}^0[2]$. Rather than directly constructing a NIZK under the worst-case assumption $\mathsf{NC}^1 \subsetneq \oplus\mathsf{L/poly}$, we first construct a Σ-protocol with unconditionally special soundness and special honest-verifier zero-knowledge. Our protocol does not require any cryptographic group structure where the discrete logarithm or factoring assumption holds. For the aforementioned linear language $\mathsf{L_M}$, the prover sends the commitment $\mathbf{C} = \mathbf{MR}$, where $\mathbf{R} \xleftarrow{\$} \{0,1\}^{t\times(\lambda-1)}$, to the verifier and receives a challenge $\widetilde{\mathbf{r}} \xleftarrow{\$} \{0,1\}^{\lambda-1}$ back. The response to the challenge is $\mathbf{D} = (\mathbf{R}||\mathbf{w})\mathbf{A}$, where $\mathbf{A} = (\widehat{\mathbf{R}}||\widehat{\mathbf{R}}\widetilde{\mathbf{r}})^{\top}$ and $\widehat{\mathbf{R}} = \begin{pmatrix} \mathbf{0} \\ \mathbf{I}_{\lambda-1} \end{pmatrix} \in \{0,1\}^{\lambda\times(\lambda-1)}$. $\mathbf{I}_{\lambda-1}$ is an identity matrix in $\{0,1\}^{(\lambda-1)\times(\lambda-1)}$. The verifier checks whether $(\mathbf{C}||\mathbf{x})\mathbf{A} = \mathbf{MD}$. In our Σ-protocol, all computations are in $GF(2)$, and all parties can run in $\mathsf{AC}^0[2]$. We refer the reader to Sect. 3 for the detailed proof, which reflects our main technical contribution in this part.

Compiling Σ-protocol to NIZK. Couteau and Hartmann [6] showed how to convert a Σ-protocol into a NIZK for $\mathsf{L}_{(g^\mathbf{M})}$, where $\mathsf{L}_{(g^\mathbf{M})}$ is the language including all group vectors with exponents in the span of $\mathbf{M}$. Their main idea is to put the challenge originally in $\mathbb{Z}_p$ into the group and set it as the common reference string. Verification can be executed by using bilinear map, and finding a valid proof can be reduced to breaking the (extended) kernel matrix Diffie-Hellman assumption. Although this assumption is falsifiable and has analysis in the generic group model and algebraic group model, we want a NIZK based on assumptions weaker than that. Moreover, in the fine-grained cryptographic landscape, we are not aware of the existence of any bilinear map.

Our work exploits the indistinguishability of the following two distributions against NC^1 adversaries used in [2,5,7,9,20]:

$$\underbrace{\{\mathbf{M} \in \{0,1\}^{\lambda\times\lambda} : \mathbf{M}^\top \xleftarrow{\$} \mathsf{ZeroSamp}(\lambda)\}}_{=:D_0} \text{ and } \underbrace{\{\mathbf{M} \in \{0,1\}^{\lambda\times\lambda} : \mathbf{M}^\top \xleftarrow{\$} \mathsf{OneSamp}(\lambda)\}}_{=:D_1}.$$

Here, λ is the security parameter, and the randomized sampling algorithms $\mathsf{ZeroSamp}$ and $\mathsf{OneSamp}$ output matrices with rank $\lambda - 1$ and full rank, respectively. Concrete definitions of these algorithms are given in Sect. 2.2. Note that this indistinguishability holds under the assumption $\mathsf{NC}^1 \subsetneq \oplus\mathsf{L/poly}$ [1,14]. Based on the indistinguishability between D_0 and D_1, we develop a new compiler from a Σ-protocol to a NIZK in NC^1-fine-grained cryptography.

The main idea is to generate $\widehat{\mathbf{R}}$ in our Σ-protocol as $\mathbf{e}_1^\lambda||\widehat{\mathbf{R}} \xleftarrow{\$} \mathsf{LSamp}(\lambda)$ instead of $\begin{pmatrix} \mathbf{0} \\ \mathbf{I}_{\lambda-1} \end{pmatrix}$, where $\mathbf{e}_1^\lambda = (1,0,\cdots,0)^\top$ and LSamp is an intermediate algorithm in $\mathsf{ZeroSamp}$. This makes the distribution of $\mathbf{A} = (\widehat{\mathbf{R}}||\widehat{\mathbf{R}}\widetilde{\mathbf{r}})^\top$ in the Σ-protocol identical to D_0 (see Sect. 2.2 for details). The hiding CRS of the resulting NIZK is $\mathbf{A}$ with $\widetilde{\mathbf{r}}$ being the simulation trapdoor, and a proof consists of $(\mathbf{C}, \mathbf{D})$ (i.e., the first and third round messages of the Σ-protocol). Perfect zero knowledge follows from the honest-verifier zero-knowledge of the aforementioned Σ-protocol. To prove soundness, we switch the distribution of $\mathbf{A}$ from D_0 to D_1, which corresponds to switching a hiding CRS to a binding one. In this case, the kernel of $\mathbf{A}^\top$ becomes empty and there exists no invalid statements passing the verification.

Extension to OR-proof. Let $\mathbf{A}$ be a binding CRS in D_1. From $\mathbf{A}$, we show that a prover can derive a hiding CRS $\mathbf{A}_{1-j}$ with a trapdoor $\tilde{\mathbf{r}}_{1-j}$ and a binding CRS $\mathbf{A}_j$. Moreover, switching the distribution of $\mathbf{A}$ to D_0 leads both $\mathbf{A}_j$ and $\mathbf{A}_{1-j}$ to become hiding CRSs. Based on this crucial step, we develop a fine-grained version of the "OR-proof techniques" [12,17] to achieve the target OR-proof system. Roughly, the prover generates proofs with respect to both $\mathbf{A}_j$ and $\mathbf{A}_{1-j}$. Soundness is guaranteed when one of them is binding, and perfect zero-knowledge is guaranteed when both are hiding.

NIZK for circuit SAT using DVV. We now give an overview on how we construct a NIZK for circuit SAT in NC^1 by using our OR-proof and improving the GOS framework by Groth, Ostrovsky, and Sahai [12].

In the GOS NIZK, for each input/output pair $((w_i, w_j), w_k)$ of a NAND gate, the prover encrypts the bits of wires with an additive homomorphic commitment scheme, and proves that the plaintexts satisfy the relation $w_i + w_j + 2w_k - 2 \in \{0,1\}$.[1] However, since all the computations are performed in $GF(2)$ in NC^1-fine-grained cryptography, $w_i + w_j + 2w_k - 2 \in \{0,1\}$ always holds, and thus proving this relation becomes meaningless.

To address the above problem, we adopt another OR-relation:

$$1 + w_i + w_k = 0 \wedge 1 + w_j = 0 \text{ or } 1 + w_k = 0 \wedge w_j = 0.$$

One can check that each valid input/output pair of a NAND gate should satisfy it.[2] Then we use the DVV encryption scheme by Degwekar, Vaikuntanathan, and Vasudevan [7] to encrypt w_i, w_j, and w_k respectively and prove that the plaintexts satisfy this new relation with our OR-proof. There are two nice properties of the DVV encryption useful in our case: (1) additive homomorphism and (2) a ciphertext of 0 (respectively, 1) is in (respectively, outside) the linear subspace of the public key, which make it compatible with our OR-proof.

NIZK for circuit SAT using FHE. In our NIZK for circuit SAT mentioned above, we generate a ciphertext for each wire of a statement circuit and a proof of compliance for each gate. Thus, the final proof size grows linearly with the circuit size.

Our second construction circumvents this by constructing a fine-grained FHE scheme. In this way, we only have to encrypt the input bits (i.e., witness) and execute the fully homomorphic evaluation of a statement circuit on these ciphertexts to obtain an output ciphertext. Afterwards, we exploit our OR-proof to prove that all the input ciphertexts are valid and the output ciphertext corresponds

---

[1] Recall that any circuit can be converted to one consisting only of NAND gates, and $1 - w_i w_j = 0$ is equivalent to $w_i + w_j + 2w_k - 2 \in \{0,1\}$ in $\mathbb{Z}_p$ for a large number p.

[2] Notice that all the computations are performed in $GF(2)$ and thus addition and subtraction are equivalent.

to 1. The final NIZK proof does not include intermediate ciphertexts generated during the homomorphic evaluation. Thus, the proof size is independent of the circuit size. To verify the final proof, one can just evaluate the ciphertext homomorphically and check the proofs for the input/output ciphertexts. Due to the correctness of the FHE and the soundness of the OR-proof, a valid witness can be extracted from any valid proof with the secret key of the FHE.

Similar to the fine-grained SHE proposed by Campanelli and Gennaro [5], our FHE scheme supports the homomorphic evaluation of circuits in $\mathsf{AC}^0_{\mathsf{CM}}[2]$, which makes the supporting statement of the resulting NIZK somewhat limited. Using the generic technique in [5, Section 3.3], we can extend our FHE to support homomorphic evaluation of circuits in $\mathsf{AC}^0[2]$ with constant number of non-constant fan-in gates. Also, our FHE enjoys short public key size and parallel running-time, and compatibility with our OR-proof.

Extensions to non-interactive zap and NIZK in the URS Model. For the conversion from NIZKs to non-interactive zaps, the bulk of our technical contribution is to prove that all our NIZKs have verifiable correlated key generation. At the core of our proof we show that if $\mathbf{N}_\lambda = \mathbf{A}_0 + \mathbf{A}_1$ for any $(\mathbf{e}_1^\lambda || \overline{\mathbf{A}_0}^\top) \in \mathsf{LSamp}(\lambda)$ and any matrix, where $\mathbf{N}_\lambda$ is some constant matrix (See Sect. 2), either $\mathbf{A}_0$ or $\mathbf{A}_1$ must be a binding CRS with perfect soundness. This allows us to improve the GOS technique to generically convert our NIZKs into non-interactive zaps.

Moreover, we show the existence of an algorithm that can sample matrices with only public coins, while its output distribution is identical to D_0 and D_1 with "half-half" probability. Since the CRSs of our NIZKs consist only of matrices in D_0 and D_1, we can sample CRSs by using this new algorithms for multiple times, and generate proofs for a same statement in parallel. Zero-knowledge follows from that of the underlying NIZK and the indistinguishability between D_0 and D_1. Statistical soundness holds since with high probability, at least one of the CRSs is binding. Since the sampling procedure for CRSs only uses public coins, the resulting NIZK is in the URS model.

2 Preliminaries

Notations. We note that all arithmetic computations are over $GF(2)$ in this work. Namely, all arithmetic computations are performed with a modulus of 2. We write $a \xleftarrow{\$} \mathcal{A}(b)$ (respectively, $a = \mathcal{A}(b)$) to denote the random variable outputted by a probabilistic (respectively, deterministic) algorithm (or circuit) $\mathcal{A}$ on input b. By $x \xleftarrow{\$} \mathcal{S}$ we denote the process of sampling an element x from a set or distribution $\mathcal{S}$ uniformly at random. Let $\mathcal{R}$ be the randomness space of $\mathcal{A}$, $a \xleftarrow{\$} \mathcal{A}(b)$ is equivalent to $a = \mathcal{A}(b; r)$ for $r \xleftarrow{\$} \mathcal{R}$. By $\mathbf{x} \in \{0,1\}^n$ we denote a column vector with size n and by, say, $\mathbf{x} \in \{1\} \times \{0,1\}^{n-1}$ we mean that the first element of $\mathbf{x}$ is 1. By x_i (respectively, x_i) we denote the ith element of a vector $\mathbf{x}$ (respectively, x). By $[n]$ we denote the set $\{1, \cdots, n\}$. By negl we denote an unspecified negligible function.

For a matrix $\mathbf{A} \in \{0,1\}^{n \times t}$ with rank $t' \leq n$, we denote the sets $\{\mathbf{y} \mid \exists \mathbf{x}$ s.t. $\mathbf{y} = \mathbf{A}\mathbf{x}\}$ and $\{\mathbf{x} \mid \mathbf{A}\mathbf{x} = \mathbf{0}\}$ by $\mathrm{Im}(\mathbf{A})$ (i.e., the span of $\mathbf{A}$) and $\mathrm{Ker}(\mathbf{A})$

respectively. By $\mathbf{A}^\perp \in \{0,1\}^{n \times (n-t')}$ we denote a matrix consisting of $n-t'$ linear independent column vectors in the kernel of $\mathbf{A}^\top$. Note that for any $\mathbf{y} \notin \mathrm{Im}(\mathbf{A})$, we have $\mathbf{y}^\top \mathbf{A}^\perp \neq \mathbf{0}$. For a matrix $\mathbf{A} \in \{0,1\}^{\lambda \times \lambda}$, by $\overline{\mathbf{A}}$ (respectively, $\underline{\mathbf{A}}$) we denote the upper $(\lambda - 1) \times \lambda$ matrix (respectively, lower $1 \times \lambda$ vector) of $\mathbf{A}$. Let $b \in \{0,1\}$, by $b\mathbf{A}$ we denote a zero matrix $\mathbf{0} \in \{0,1\}^{n \times t}$ if $b = 0$ or $\mathbf{A}$ if $b = 1$.

By $\mathbf{e}_i^\lambda$ we denote the column vector in $\{0,1\}^\lambda$ with the ith element being 1 and the other elements being 0. By $\mathbf{0}$ we denote a zero vector or matrix. By $\mathbf{I}_n$ we denote an identity matrix in $\{0,1\}^{n \times n}$. By $\mathbf{M}_0^n$, $\mathbf{M}_1^n$, and $\mathbf{N}_n$, we denote the following $n \times n$ matrices: $\mathbf{M}_0^n = \begin{pmatrix} \mathbf{0} & \mathbf{0} \\ \mathbf{I}_{n-1} & \mathbf{0} \end{pmatrix}$, $\mathbf{M}_1^n = \begin{pmatrix} \mathbf{0} & 1 \\ \mathbf{I}_{n-1} & \mathbf{0} \end{pmatrix}$, $\mathbf{N}_n = \begin{pmatrix} \mathbf{0} & \mathbf{0} \\ 1 & \mathbf{0} \end{pmatrix}$.

2.1   Function Families

In this section, we recall the definitions of function family, NC^1 circuits, $\mathsf{AC}^0[2]$ circuits, $\mathsf{AC}_{\mathsf{CM}}^0[2]$ circuits, and $\oplus\mathsf{L}/\mathsf{poly}$ circuits. Note that $\mathsf{AC}^0[2] \subsetneq \mathsf{NC}^1$ [18,19].

Definition 1 (Function family). *A function family is a family of (possibly randomized) functions $\mathcal{F} = \{f_\lambda\}_{\lambda \in \mathbb{N}}$, where for each λ, f_λ has a domain D_λ^f and a range R_λ^f.*

Definition 2 (NC^1). *The class of (non-uniform) NC^1 function families is the set of all function families $\mathcal{F} = \{f_\lambda\}_{\lambda \in \mathbb{N}}$ for which there is a polynomial $p(\cdot)$ and constant c such that for each λ, f_λ can be computed by a (randomized) circuit of size $p(\lambda)$, depth $c \log(\lambda)$, and fan-in 2 using AND, OR, and NOT gates.*

Definition 3 ($\mathsf{AC}^0[2]$). *The class of (non-uniform) $\mathsf{AC}^0[2]$ function families is the set of all function families $\mathcal{F} = \{f_\lambda\}_{\lambda \in \mathbb{N}}$ for which there is a polynomial $p(\cdot)$ and constant c such that for each λ, f_λ can be computed by a (randomized) circuit of size $p(\lambda)$, depth c, and unbounded fan-in using AND, OR, NOT, and PARITY gates.*

One can see that multiplication of a constant number of matrices can be performed in $\mathsf{AC}^0[2]$, since it can be done in constant-depth with PARITY gates.

Next we recall the definitions of multiplicative depth in [5], which can be thought of as the degree of the lowest-degree polynomial in $GF(2)$ evaluating to a circuit.

Definition 4 (Multiplicative depth [5]). *Let C be a circuit, $\mathsf{type}_C(g)$ be the type of a gate g in C, and $\mathsf{parents}_C(g)$ be the list of gates of C whose output is an input to C. The multipicative depth of C is $\mathsf{md}(g_{\mathrm{out}})$, where g_{out} is the output gate and the function md is defined as*

$$\mathsf{md}(g) = \begin{cases} 1 & \text{if } \mathsf{type}_C(g) = \mathsf{input} \\ \max\{\mathsf{md}(g') : g' \in \mathsf{parents}_C(g)\} & \text{if } \mathsf{type}_C(g) = \mathsf{XOR} \\ \sum_{g' \in \mathsf{parents}_C(g)} \mathsf{md}(g') & \text{if } \mathsf{type}_C(g) \in \{\mathsf{AND}, \mathsf{OR}\} \end{cases},$$

where the sum in the last case is over the integers.

Definition 5 ($\mathsf{AC}^0_{\mathsf{CM}}[2]$ [5]). *$\mathsf{AC}^0_{\mathsf{CM}}[2]$ is the class of circuits in $\mathsf{AC}^0[2]$ with constant multiplicative depth (as defined in Definition 4).*

Note that an AND gate of fan-in λ (i.e., the security parameter) cannot be performed in $\mathsf{AC}^0_{\mathsf{CM}}[2]$.

Definition 6 ($\oplus\mathsf{L}/\mathsf{poly}$). *$\oplus\mathsf{L}/\mathsf{poly}$ is the set of all boolean function families $\mathcal{F} = \{f_\lambda\}_{\lambda\in\mathbb{N}}$ for which there is a constant c such that for each λ, there is a non-deterministic Turing machine $\mathcal{M}_\lambda$ such that for each input x with length λ, $\mathcal{M}_\lambda(x)$ uses at most $c\log(\lambda)$ space, and $f_\lambda(x)$ is equal to the parity of the number of accepting paths of $\mathcal{M}_\lambda(x)$.*

2.2 Sampling Procedure

We now recall the definitions of four sampling procedures LSamp, RSamp, ZeroSamp, and OneSamp in Fig. 2. Note that the output of ZeroSamp(n) is always a matrix of rank $n-1$ and the output of OneSamp(n) is always a matrix of full rank [7]. Additionally, in Fig. 3, we define an algorithm $\widetilde{\mathsf{ZeroSamp}}$ which runs in exactly the same way as ZeroSamp except that it additionally outputs a vector

---

LSamp(n):
For all $i, j \in [n]$ and $i < j$:
$\quad r_{i,j} \xleftarrow{\$} \{0,1\}$
Return

$$\begin{pmatrix} 1 & r_{1,2} & \cdots & r_{1,n-1} & r_{1,n} \\ 0 & 1 & r_{2,3} & \cdots & r_{2,n} \\ 0 & 0 & \ddots & & \vdots \\ \vdots & \vdots & \ddots & 1 & r_{n-1,n} \\ 0 & \cdots & 0 & 0 & 1 \end{pmatrix}$$

RSamp(n):
For $i = 1, \cdots, n-1$
$\quad r_i \xleftarrow{\$} \{0,1\}$
Return

$$\begin{pmatrix} 1 & & \cdots & 0 & r_1 \\ 0 & 1 & & & r_2 \\ 0 & 0 & \ddots & & \vdots \\ \vdots & \vdots & & \ddots & 1 & r_{n-1} \\ 0 & \cdots & & 0 & 0 & 1 \end{pmatrix}$$

ZeroSamp(n):
$\mathbf{R}_0 \xleftarrow{\$} \mathsf{LSamp}(n) \in \{0,1\}^{n\times n}$
$\mathbf{R}_1 \xleftarrow{\$} \mathsf{RSamp}(n) \in \{0,1\}^{n\times n}$
Return $\mathbf{R}_0 \mathbf{M}_0^n \mathbf{R}_1 \in \{0,1\}^{n\times n}$

OneSamp(n):
$\mathbf{R}_0 \xleftarrow{\$} \mathsf{LSamp}(n)$
$\mathbf{R}_1 \xleftarrow{\$} \mathsf{RSamp}(n)$
Return $\mathbf{R}_0 \mathbf{M}_1^n \mathbf{R}_1 \in \{0,1\}^{n\times n}$

Fig. 2. Definitions of LSamp, RSamp, ZeroSamp, and OneSamp. $n = n(\lambda)$ is a polynomial in the security parameter λ.

$\widetilde{\mathsf{ZeroSamp}}(n)$:
$\mathbf{R}_0 \xleftarrow{\$} \mathsf{LSamp}(n) \in \{0,1\}^{n\times n}$, $\mathbf{R}_1 = \begin{pmatrix} \mathbf{I}_{\lambda-1} & \widetilde{\mathbf{r}} \\ \mathbf{0} & 1 \end{pmatrix} \xleftarrow{\$} \mathsf{RSamp}(n) \in \{0,1\}^{n\times n}$
Return $(\mathbf{R}_0 \mathbf{M}_0^n \mathbf{R}_1 \in \{0,1\}^{n\times n}, \widetilde{\mathbf{r}})$

Fig. 3. The definition of $\widetilde{\mathsf{ZeroSamp}}$.

$\widetilde{\mathbf{r}} = (r_i)_{i=1}^{n-1}$ consisting of the random bits used in generating $\mathbf{R}_1$. We have $\begin{pmatrix} \widetilde{\mathbf{r}} \\ 1 \end{pmatrix} \in$ $\mathrm{Ker}(\mathbf{R}_0 \mathbf{M}_0^n \mathbf{R}_1)$, since $\mathbf{R}_0 \mathbf{M}_0^n \mathbf{R}_1 \begin{pmatrix} \widetilde{\mathbf{r}} \\ 1 \end{pmatrix} = \mathbf{R}_0 \begin{pmatrix} \mathbf{0} & 0 \\ \mathbf{I}_{\lambda-1} & 0 \end{pmatrix} \begin{pmatrix} \mathbf{I}_{\lambda-1} & \widetilde{\mathbf{r}} \\ 0 & 1 \end{pmatrix} \begin{pmatrix} \widetilde{\mathbf{r}} \\ 1 \end{pmatrix} = \mathbf{0}$. This implies the following lemma.

Lemma 1 (Lemma 3 in [9]). *For all $\lambda \in \mathbb{N}$ and all $\mathbf{M} \in \mathsf{ZeroSamp}(\lambda)$, it holds that $\mathrm{Ker}(\mathbf{M}) = \{\mathbf{0}, \mathbf{k}\}$ where $\mathbf{k}$ is a vector such that $\mathbf{k} \in \{0,1\}^{\lambda-1} \times \{1\}$.*

We now recall an assumption and a lemma on ZeroSamp and OneSamp given in [7].

Definition 7 (Fine-grained matrix linear assumption [7]). *There exists a polynomial $n = n(\lambda)$ in the security parameter λ such that for any family $\mathcal{A} = \{a_\lambda\}_{\lambda \in \mathbb{N}}$ in NC^1 and any $\lambda \in \mathbb{N}$, we have*

$$| \Pr[a_\lambda(\mathbf{M}) = 1 \mid \mathbf{M} \xleftarrow{\$} \mathsf{ZeroSamp}(n)] - $$
$$\Pr[a_\lambda(\mathbf{M}') = 1 \mid \mathbf{M}' \xleftarrow{\$} \mathsf{OneSamp}(n)]| \le \mathsf{negl}(\lambda).$$

Lemma 2 (Lemma 4.3 in [7]). *If $\mathsf{NC}^1 \subsetneq \oplus \mathsf{L}/\mathsf{poly}$, then the fine-grained matrix linear assumption holds.*

Remark. Notice that for any polynomial $n = n(\lambda)$, we have $\{f_n\}_{\lambda \in N} \in \mathsf{NC}^1$ iff $\{f_\lambda\}_{\lambda \in N} \in \mathsf{NC}^1$ since $O(\log(n(\lambda))) = O(\log(\lambda))$. Hence, in the above lemma, we can also set $n(\cdot)$ as an identity function, i.e., $n = \lambda$. For simplicity, in the rest of the paper, we always let $\mathsf{ZeroSamp}(\cdot)$ and $\mathsf{OneSamp}(\cdot)$ take as input λ.

The following lemma indicates a simple relation between the distributions of the outputs of $\mathsf{ZeroSamp}(\lambda)$ and $\mathsf{OneSamp}(\lambda)$.

Lemma 3 (Lemma 7 in [9]). *For all $\lambda \in \mathbb{N}$, the distributions of $\mathbf{M} + \mathbf{N}_\lambda$ and $\mathbf{M}'$ are identical, where $\mathbf{M}^\top \xleftarrow{\$} \mathsf{ZeroSamp}(\lambda)$ and $\mathbf{M}'^\top \xleftarrow{\$} \mathsf{OneSamp}(\lambda)$.*

2.3   Proof Systems

In this section, we give the definitions of Σ-protocol, NIZK, and non-interactive zap. Below, for a language description ρ with the associated language L_ρ and relation R_ρ, by $\mathsf{x} \in \mathsf{L}_\rho$ we mean that there exists w such that $\mathsf{R}_\rho(\mathsf{x}, \mathsf{w}) = 1$.

Σ**-protocol.** The definition of Σ-protocol is as follows.

Definition 8 (Σ-protocol). *A $\mathcal{C}_1$-Σ-protocol for a language distribution $\{\mathcal{D}_\lambda\}_{\lambda \in \mathbb{N}}$ is a function family $\{\mathsf{Prover}_\lambda^1, \mathsf{ChSet}_\lambda, \mathsf{Prover}_\lambda^2, \mathsf{SVer}_\lambda, \mathsf{SExt}_\lambda, \mathsf{SSim}_\lambda\}_{\lambda \in \mathbb{N}} \in \mathcal{C}_1$ with the following properties.*

- $\mathsf{Prover}_\lambda^1(\rho \in \mathcal{D}_\lambda, \mathsf{x}, \mathsf{w})$ *returns a commitment* com *and a state* st.
- ChSet_λ *returns a uniformly random string* ch.
- $\mathsf{Prover}_\lambda^2(\mathsf{ch}, \mathsf{st})$ *returns a response* resp.
- $\mathsf{SVer}_\lambda(\rho, \mathsf{x}, \mathsf{com}, \mathsf{ch}, \mathsf{resp})$ *deterministically returns 1 (accept) or 0 (reject).*
- $\mathsf{SExt}_\lambda(\mathsf{x}, \mathsf{com}, (\mathsf{ch}, \mathsf{resp}), (\mathsf{ch}', \mathsf{resp}'))$ *returns a witness* w.
- $\mathsf{SSim}_\lambda(\rho, \mathsf{x}, \mathsf{ch})$ *returns a commitment* com *and a response* resp.

Completeness *is satisfied if for all* $\lambda \in \mathbb{N}$, *all* $\rho \in \mathcal{D}_\lambda$ *with the associated relation* R_ρ, *all* (x, w) *such that* $\mathsf{R}_\rho(\mathsf{x}, \mathsf{w}) = 1$, *all* $(\mathsf{com}, \mathsf{st}) \in \mathsf{Prover}^1_\lambda(\rho, \mathsf{x}, \mathsf{w})$, *all* $\mathsf{ch} \in \mathsf{ChSet}_\lambda$, *and all* $\mathsf{resp} \in \mathsf{Prover}^2_\lambda(\mathsf{ch}, \mathsf{st})$, *we have* $\mathsf{SVer}_\lambda(\rho, \mathsf{x}, \mathsf{com}, \mathsf{ch}, \mathsf{resp}) = 1$.

Special Soundness *is satisfied if for all* $\lambda \in \mathbb{N}$, *all* $\rho \in \mathcal{D}_\lambda$, *and all* $(\mathsf{x}, \mathsf{com}, (\mathsf{ch}, \mathsf{resp}), (\mathsf{ch}', \mathsf{resp}'))$ *such that* $\mathsf{ch} \neq \mathsf{ch}'$ *satisfying*

$$\mathsf{SVer}_\lambda(\rho, \mathsf{x}, \mathsf{com}, \mathsf{ch}, \mathsf{resp}) = \mathsf{SVer}_\lambda(\rho, \mathsf{x}, \mathsf{com}, \mathsf{ch}', \mathsf{resp}') = 1,$$

we have $\mathsf{R}_\rho(\mathsf{x}, \mathsf{w}) = 1$ *for* $\mathsf{w} = \mathsf{SExt}_\lambda(\mathsf{x}, \mathsf{com}, (\mathsf{ch}, \mathsf{resp}), (\mathsf{ch}', \mathsf{resp}'))$.

Special honest-verifier zero-knowledge *is satisfied if for all* $\lambda \in \mathbb{N}$, *all* $\rho \in \mathcal{D}_\lambda$, *all* (x, w) *such that* $\mathsf{R}_\rho(\mathsf{x}, \mathsf{w}) = 1$, *and all* $\mathsf{ch} \in \mathsf{ChSet}_\lambda$, *the distributions of* $(\mathsf{com}, \mathsf{resp})$ *and* $(\mathsf{com}', \mathsf{resp}')$ *are identical, where* $(\mathsf{com}, \mathsf{st}) \xleftarrow{\$} \mathsf{Prover}^1_\lambda(\rho, \mathsf{x}, \mathsf{w})$, $\mathsf{resp} \xleftarrow{\$} \mathsf{Prover}^2_\lambda(\mathsf{ch}, \mathsf{st})$, *and* $(\mathsf{com}', \mathsf{resp}') \xleftarrow{\$} \mathsf{SSim}_\lambda(\rho, \mathsf{x}, \mathsf{ch})$.

NIZK. We now give the definition of fine-grained NIZK with composable zero-knowledge and statistical/perfect soundness.

Definition 9 (Non-interactive zero-knowledge (NIZK) proof). *A* $\mathcal{C}_1$-*NIZK for a set of language distributions* $\{\mathcal{D}_\lambda\}_{\lambda \in \mathbb{N}}$ *is a function family* $\mathsf{NIZK} = \{\mathsf{Gen}_\lambda, \mathsf{TGen}_\lambda, \mathsf{Prove}_\lambda, \mathsf{Ver}_\lambda, \mathsf{Sim}_\lambda\}_{\lambda \in \mathbb{N}} \in \mathcal{C}_1$ *with the following properties.*

- Gen_λ *returns a binding CRS* crs.
- TGen_λ *returns a hiding CRS* crs *and a simulation trapdoor* td.
- $\mathsf{Prove}_\lambda(\mathsf{crs}, \rho \in \mathcal{D}_\lambda, \mathsf{x}, \mathsf{w})$ *returns a proof* π.
- $\mathsf{Ver}_\lambda(\mathsf{crs}, \rho, \mathsf{x}, \pi)$ *deterministically returns 1 (accept) or 0 (reject).*
- $\mathsf{Sim}_\lambda(\mathsf{crs}, \mathsf{td}, \rho, \mathsf{x})$ *returns a simulated proof* π.

Completeness *is satisfied if for all* $\lambda \in \mathbb{N}$, *all* $\rho \in \mathcal{D}_\lambda$ *with the associated relation* R_ρ, *all* (x, w) *such that* $\mathsf{R}_\rho(\mathsf{x}, \mathsf{w}) = 1$, *all* $\mathsf{crs} \in \mathsf{Gen}_\lambda$, *and all* $\pi \in \mathsf{Prove}_\lambda(\mathsf{crs}, \rho, \mathsf{x}, \mathsf{w})$, *we have* $\mathsf{Ver}_\lambda(\mathsf{crs}, \rho, \mathsf{x}, \pi) = 1$.

$\mathcal{C}_2$-composable zero-knowledge *is satisfied if for any adversary* $\mathcal{A} = \{a_\lambda\}_{\lambda \in \mathbb{N}} \in \mathcal{C}_2$, *we have*

$$\Pr[1 \xleftarrow{\$} a_\lambda(\mathsf{crs}) | \mathsf{crs} \xleftarrow{\$} \mathsf{Gen}_\lambda] - \Pr[1 \xleftarrow{\$} a_\lambda(\mathsf{crs}) | (\mathsf{crs}, \mathsf{td}) \xleftarrow{\$} \mathsf{TGen}_\lambda] \leq \mathsf{negl}(\lambda),$$

and for all $\lambda \in \mathbb{N}$, *all* $\rho \in \mathcal{D}_\lambda$, *and all* (x, w) *such that* $\mathsf{R}_\rho(\mathsf{x}, \mathsf{w}) = 1$, *the following distributions are identical.*

$$\pi \xleftarrow{\$} \mathsf{Prove}_\lambda(\mathsf{crs}, \rho, \mathsf{x}, \mathsf{w}) \; and \; \pi \xleftarrow{\$} \mathsf{Sim}_\lambda(\mathsf{crs}, \mathsf{td}, \rho, \mathsf{x}),$$

where $(\mathsf{crs}, \mathsf{td}) \xleftarrow{\$} \mathsf{TGen}_\lambda$.

Statistical soundness *is satisfied if for all* $\lambda \in \mathbb{N}$ *and all* $\rho \in \mathcal{D}_\lambda$, *we have*

$$\Pr[\exists \mathsf{x} \notin \mathsf{L}_\rho \; and \; \pi, \; s.t. \; \mathsf{Ver}_\lambda(\mathsf{crs}, \rho, \mathsf{x}, \pi) = 1 | \mathsf{crs} \xleftarrow{\$} \mathsf{Gen}_\lambda] \leq \mathsf{negl}(\lambda),$$

where $\mathsf{x} \in \mathsf{L}_\rho$ *iff there exists* w *such that* $\mathsf{R}_\rho(\mathsf{x}, \mathsf{w}) = 1$.

Perfect soundness *is satisfied if the above probability is 0.*

Definition 10 (NIZK in the uniform random string (URS) model.).
A NIZK NIZK $= \{\mathsf{Gen}_\lambda, \mathsf{TGen}_\lambda, \mathsf{Prove}_\lambda, \mathsf{Ver}_\lambda, \mathsf{Sim}_\lambda\}_{\lambda \in \mathbb{N}}$ *is in the* URS *model if* Gen_λ *only samples a public coin* urs $\xleftarrow{\$} \{0,1\}^{p(\lambda)}$ *at random for some polynomial* p *and returns* urs.

Non-interactive Zap. A non-interactive zap is a witness-indistinguishable non-interactive proof system in the plain model, where there is no trusted setup. The definition is as follows.

Definition 11 (Non-interactive zap). *A C_1-non-interactive zap for a set of language distributions* $\{\mathcal{D}_\lambda\}_{\lambda \in \mathbb{N}}$ *is a function family* ZAP $= \{\mathsf{ZProve}_\lambda, \mathsf{ZVer}_\lambda\}_{\lambda \in \mathbb{N}}$ *with the following properties.*

- $\mathsf{ZProve}_\lambda(\rho \in \mathcal{D}_\lambda, \mathsf{x}, \mathsf{w})$ *returns a proof* π.
- $\mathsf{ZVer}_\lambda(\rho, \mathsf{x}, \pi)$ *deterministically returns* 1 *(accept) or* 0 *(reject).*

Completeness is satisfied if for all $\lambda \in \mathbb{N}$, *all* $\rho \in \mathcal{D}_\lambda$, *all* (x, w) *such that* $\mathsf{R}_\rho(\mathsf{x}, \mathsf{w}) = 1$, *and all* $\pi \in \mathsf{ZProve}_\lambda(\rho, \mathsf{x}, \mathsf{w})$, *we have* $\mathsf{ZVer}_\lambda(\rho, \mathsf{x}, \pi) = 1$.

C_2-*witness indistinguishability is satisfied if for all* $\lambda \in \mathbb{N}$, *all* $\rho \in \mathcal{D}_\lambda$ *with the associated relation* R_ρ, *all* $(\mathsf{x}, \mathsf{w}_0, \mathsf{w}_1)$ *such that* $\mathsf{R}_\rho(\mathsf{x}, \mathsf{w}_0) = \mathsf{R}_\rho(\mathsf{x}, \mathsf{w}_1) = 1$, *and any adversary* $\mathcal{A} = \{a_\lambda\}_{\lambda \in \mathbb{N}} \in C_2$, *we have*

$$\Pr[1 \xleftarrow{\$} a_\lambda(\pi) | \pi \xleftarrow{\$} \mathsf{ZProve}_\lambda(\rho, \mathsf{x}, \mathsf{w}_0)] -$$
$$\Pr[1 \xleftarrow{\$} a_\lambda(\pi) | \pi \xleftarrow{\$} \mathsf{ZProve}_\lambda(\rho, \mathsf{x}, \mathsf{w}_1)] \leq \mathsf{negl}(\lambda).$$

Perfect soundness is satisfied if for all $\lambda \in \mathbb{N}$, *all* $\rho \in \mathcal{D}_\lambda$, *all* $\mathsf{x} \notin \mathsf{L}_\rho$, *and all* π, *we have* $\mathsf{ZVer}_\lambda(\rho, \mathsf{x}, \pi) = 0$.

3 $\mathsf{AC}^0[2]$-Σ-Protocol for Linear Languages

Let $\mathcal{D}_\lambda$ be a probability distribution outputting language descriptions $\mathbf{M} \in \{0,1\}^{n \times t}$, where $n(\cdot)$ and $t(\cdot)$ are functions in λ. We define the associated language as $\mathsf{L}_\mathbf{M} = \{\mathbf{t} : \exists \mathbf{w} \in \{0,1\}^t, \text{ s.t. } \mathbf{t} = \mathbf{M}\mathbf{w}\}$. For the associated relation $\mathsf{R}_\mathbf{M}$, we have $\mathsf{R}_\mathbf{M}(\mathbf{x}, \mathbf{w}) = 1$ iff $\mathbf{x} = \mathbf{M}\mathbf{w}$. Let $\widehat{\mathbf{R}} = \begin{pmatrix} \mathbf{0} \\ \mathbf{I}_{\lambda-1} \end{pmatrix}$. We give a Σ-protocol Σ for $\{\mathcal{D}_\lambda\}$ in Fig. 4.

$\underline{\mathsf{Prover}^1_\lambda(\mathbf{M}, \mathbf{x}, \mathbf{w})\text{:}}$ $\mathbf{R} \stackrel{\$}{\leftarrow} \{0,1\}^{t \times (\lambda-1)}$ Return $\mathsf{com} = \mathbf{MR}$ and $\mathsf{st} = (\mathbf{R}, \mathbf{w})$	$\underline{\mathsf{SExt}_\lambda(\mathbf{x}, \mathsf{com}, (\mathsf{ch}, \mathsf{resp}), (\mathsf{ch}', \mathsf{resp}'))\text{:}}$ $\mathbf{r} = \mathsf{ch} - \mathsf{ch}' \in \{0,1\}^{\lambda-1}$ $\mathbf{T} = \mathsf{resp} - \mathsf{resp}' \in \{0,1\}^{t \times \lambda}$ If $\mathbf{r} = \mathbf{0}$, abort Else find the smallest $i \in [\lambda - 1]$ s.t. $r_i = 1$ and return $\mathbf{t}_i$
$\underline{\mathsf{ChSet}_\lambda\text{:}}$ Return $\mathsf{ch} = \widetilde{\mathbf{r}} \stackrel{\$}{\leftarrow} \{0,1\}^{\lambda-1}$	
$\underline{\mathsf{Prover}^2_\lambda(\mathsf{ch}, \mathsf{st})\text{:}}$ $\mathbf{A} = (\widehat{\mathbf{R}} \| \widehat{\mathbf{R}}\widetilde{\mathbf{r}})^\top \in \{0,1\}^{\lambda \times \lambda}$ Return $\mathsf{resp} = (\mathbf{R} \| \mathbf{w})\mathbf{A} \in \{0,1\}^{t \times \lambda}$	$\underline{\mathsf{SSim}_\lambda(\mathbf{M}, \mathbf{x}, \mathsf{ch})\text{:}}$ $\mathbf{R}' \stackrel{\$}{\leftarrow} \{0,1\}^{t \times (\lambda-1)}$ $\mathbf{A} = (\widehat{\mathbf{R}} \| \widehat{\mathbf{R}}\widetilde{\mathbf{r}})^\top \in \{0,1\}^{\lambda \times \lambda}$ $\mathbf{R}' \stackrel{\$}{\leftarrow} \{0,1\}^{t \times (\lambda-1)}$
$\underline{\mathsf{SVer}_\lambda(\mathbf{M}, \mathbf{x}, \mathsf{com} = \mathbf{C}, \mathsf{ch}, \mathsf{resp} = \mathbf{D})\text{:}}$ $\mathbf{A} = (\widehat{\mathbf{R}} \| \widehat{\mathbf{R}}\widetilde{\mathbf{r}})^\top \in \{0,1\}^{\lambda \times \lambda}$ Return 1 iff $(\mathbf{C} \| \mathbf{x})\mathbf{A} = \mathbf{MD}$	$\mathbf{C} = \mathbf{MR}' - \mathbf{x} \cdot \widetilde{\mathbf{r}}^\top$ $\mathbf{D} = (\mathbf{R}' \| \mathbf{0})\mathbf{A}$ Return $\mathsf{com} = \mathbf{C}$ and $\mathsf{resp} = \mathbf{D}$

Fig. 4. Definition of $\Sigma = \{\mathsf{Prover}^1_\lambda, \mathsf{ChSet}_\lambda, \mathsf{Prover}^2_\lambda, \mathsf{SVer}_\lambda, \mathsf{SExt}_\lambda, \mathsf{SSim}_\lambda\}_{\lambda \in \mathbb{N}}$. Note that $\widehat{\mathbf{R}}^\top = (\mathbf{0} \| \mathbf{I}_{\lambda-1})$ where $\mathbf{I}_{\lambda-1}$ is an identity matrix in $\{0,1\}^{(\lambda-1) \times (\lambda-1)}$.

Theorem 1. Σ *is an* $\mathsf{AC}^0[2]$*-Σ-protocol with special soundness and special honest-verifier zero-knowledge.*

Proof. First, we note that $\{\mathsf{Prover}^1_\lambda, \mathsf{ChSet}_\lambda, \mathsf{Prover}^2_\lambda, \mathsf{SVer}_\lambda, \mathsf{SExt}_\lambda, \mathsf{SSim}_\lambda\}_{\lambda \in \mathbb{N}}$ are computable in $\mathsf{AC}^0[2]$, since they only involve operations including multiplication of a constant number of matrices and sampling random bits.

Completeness. Perfect completeness follows from the fact that for $\mathbf{C} = \mathbf{MR}$ and $\mathbf{D} = (\mathbf{R} \| \mathbf{w})\mathbf{A}$, we have $(\mathbf{C} \| \mathbf{x})\mathbf{A} = (\mathbf{MR} \| \mathbf{Mw})\mathbf{A} = \mathbf{M}(\mathbf{R} \| \mathbf{w})\mathbf{A} = \mathbf{MD}$.

Special Soundness. For a statement $\mathbf{x}$, a commitment $(\mathbf{C}, \widehat{\mathbf{R}})$, and two valid challenge/response pairs $((\widetilde{\mathbf{r}}, \mathbf{D}), (\widetilde{\mathbf{r}}', \mathbf{D}'))$ such that $\widetilde{\mathbf{r}} \neq \widetilde{\mathbf{r}}'$, we have

$$(\mathbf{C} \| \mathbf{x}) \begin{pmatrix} \widehat{\mathbf{R}}^\top \\ \widetilde{\mathbf{r}}^\top \widehat{\mathbf{R}}^\top \end{pmatrix} = \mathbf{MD} \quad \text{and} \quad (\mathbf{C} \| \mathbf{x}) \begin{pmatrix} \widehat{\mathbf{R}}^\top \\ \widetilde{\mathbf{r}}'^\top \widehat{\mathbf{R}}^\top \end{pmatrix} = \mathbf{MD}'.$$

Combining the above two equations yields $\mathbf{x}((\widetilde{\mathbf{r}}^\top - \widetilde{\mathbf{r}}'^\top)\widehat{\mathbf{R}}^\top) = \mathbf{M}(\mathbf{D} - \mathbf{D}')$. Since the rank of $\widehat{\mathbf{R}}$ is $\lambda - 1$, we have $\widetilde{\mathbf{r}}^\top \widehat{\mathbf{R}}^\top \neq \widetilde{\mathbf{r}}'^\top \widehat{\mathbf{R}}^\top$ if $\widetilde{\mathbf{r}}^\top \neq \widetilde{\mathbf{r}}'^\top$. Let the ith bit of $(\widetilde{\mathbf{r}}^\top - \widetilde{\mathbf{r}}'^\top)\widehat{\mathbf{R}}^\top$ be 1 and the ith column vector of $\mathbf{D} - \mathbf{D}'$ be $\mathbf{d}_i$, we have $\mathbf{x} = \mathbf{Md}_i$. Therefore, the extractor can successfully extract a witness for $\mathbf{x}$. This completes the proof of special soundness.

Special Honest-Verifier Zero-Knowledge. For $\mathbf{x} = \mathbf{Mw}$, since $\mathbf{MR} = \mathbf{M}(\mathbf{R} + \mathbf{w} \cdot \widetilde{\mathbf{r}}^\top) - \mathbf{x} \cdot \widetilde{\mathbf{r}}^\top$ and

$$(\mathbf{R} \| \mathbf{w}) \begin{pmatrix} \widehat{\mathbf{R}}^\top \\ \widetilde{\mathbf{r}}^\top \widehat{\mathbf{R}}^\top \end{pmatrix} = (\mathbf{R} + \mathbf{w} \cdot \widetilde{\mathbf{r}}^\top)\widehat{\mathbf{R}}^\top = (\mathbf{R} + \mathbf{w} \cdot \widetilde{\mathbf{r}}^\top \| \mathbf{0}) \begin{pmatrix} \widehat{\mathbf{R}}^\top \\ \widetilde{\mathbf{r}}^\top \widehat{\mathbf{R}}^\top \end{pmatrix},$$

and the distribution of $\mathbf{R}+\mathbf{w}\cdot\widetilde{\mathbf{r}}^\top$ is uniform for $\mathbf{R} \xleftarrow{\$} \{0,1\}^{t\times(\lambda-1)}$, the simulator perfect simulates honest proofs, completing the proof of special honest-verifier zero-knowledge.

Putting all the above together, Theorem 1 immediately follows.   □

4 Fine-Grained NIZK for Linear Languages

In this section, we show how to compile the Σ-protocol in Sect. 3 to a fine-grained NIZK for linear languages.

Let $\mathcal{D}_\lambda$ be a probability distribution outputting language descriptions $\mathbf{M}$ of rank $t' < n$ from $\{0,1\}^{n\times t}$, where $n(\cdot)$, $t(\cdot)$, and $t'(\cdot)$ are functions in λ and there exists $\mathbf{M}^\perp \in \{0,1\}^{n\times(n-t')}$ such that $\mathbf{M}^\top\mathbf{M}^\perp = \mathbf{0}$. We define the language as

$$\mathsf{L}_\mathbf{M} = \{\mathbf{x} : \exists\mathbf{w} \in \{0,1\}^t, \text{ s.t. } \mathbf{x} = \mathbf{Mw}\}.$$

For the associated relation $\mathsf{R}_\mathbf{M}$, we have $\mathsf{R}_\mathbf{M}(\mathbf{x},\mathbf{w}) = 1$ iff $\mathbf{x} = \mathbf{Mw}$. We give the construction of NIZK in Fig. 5. Note that each proof of our NIZK consists of a commitment/response pair in our Σ-protocol, and $\mathbf{A}$ used by $\mathsf{Prover}_\lambda^2$ and SVer_λ is generated by using $\mathsf{OneSamp}(\lambda)$ and plays a binding CRS now. A hiding CRS is generated by $\mathsf{ZeroSamp}(\lambda)$, and its trapdoor $\widetilde{\mathbf{r}}$ essentially corresponds to the challenge in the Σ-protocol. Roughly, soundness follows from the fact that when $\mathbf{A}$ is of full rank, the kernel of $\mathbf{A}^\top$ is empty and no invalid proof can pass the verification. Zero-knowledge follows immediately from that of our Σ-protocol when switching $\mathbf{A}$ to a non-full rank matrix.

Gen_λ:	TGen_λ:
$\mathbf{A}^\top \xleftarrow{\$} \mathsf{OneSamp}(\lambda)$	$(\mathbf{A}^\top,\widetilde{\mathbf{r}}) \xleftarrow{\$} \mathsf{ZeroSamp}(\lambda)$
Return $\mathsf{crs} = \mathbf{A} \in \{0,1\}^{\lambda\times\lambda}$	Return $\mathsf{crs} = \mathbf{A} \in \{0,1\}^{\lambda\times\lambda}$ and $\mathsf{td} = \widetilde{\mathbf{r}}$
$\mathsf{Prove}_\lambda(\mathsf{crs}, \mathbf{M} \in \{0,1\}^{n\times t}, \mathbf{x}, \mathbf{w})$:	
$\mathbf{R} \xleftarrow{\$} \{0,1\}^{t\times(\lambda-1)}, \mathbf{C} = \mathbf{MR} \in \{0,1\}^{n\times(\lambda-1)}$	$\mathsf{Sim}_\lambda(\mathsf{crs}, \mathsf{td}, \mathbf{M}, \mathbf{x})$:
$\mathbf{D} = (\mathbf{R}\|\mathbf{w})\mathbf{A} \in \{0,1\}^{t\times\lambda}$	$\mathbf{R}' \xleftarrow{\$} \{0,1\}^{t\times(\lambda-1)}$
Return $\pi = (\mathbf{C},\mathbf{D})$	$\mathbf{C} = \mathbf{MR}' - \mathbf{x}\cdot\widetilde{\mathbf{r}}^\top$
	$\mathbf{D} = (\mathbf{R}'\|\mathbf{0})\mathbf{A}$
$\mathsf{Ver}_\lambda(\mathsf{crs}, \mathbf{M}, \mathbf{x}, \pi)$:	Return $\pi = (\mathbf{C},\mathbf{D})$
Return 1 iff $(\mathbf{C}\|\mathbf{x})\mathbf{A} = \mathbf{MD}$	

Fig. 5. Definition of $\mathsf{LNIZK} = \{\mathsf{Gen}_\lambda, \mathsf{TGen}_\lambda, \mathsf{Prove}_\lambda, \mathsf{Ver}_\lambda, \mathsf{Sim}_\lambda\}_{\lambda\in\mathbb{N}}$ for $\{\mathcal{D}_\lambda\}_{\lambda\in\mathbb{N}}$.

Theorem 2. *If* $\mathsf{NC}^1 \subsetneq \oplus\mathsf{L/poly}$, *then* LNIZK *in Fig. 5 is an* $\mathsf{AC}^0[2]$-*NIZK with perfect soundness and* NC^1-*composable zero-knowledge.*

Proof. First, we note that $\{\mathsf{Gen}_\lambda, \mathsf{TGen}_\lambda, \mathsf{Prove}_\lambda, \mathsf{Ver}_\lambda, \mathsf{Sim}_\lambda\}_{\lambda\in\mathbb{N}}$ are computable in $\mathsf{AC}^0[2]$, since they only involve operations including multiplications of a constant number of matrices and sampling random bits.

Completeness. Completeness follows from the fact that for $\mathbf{x} = \mathbf{Mw}$, $\mathbf{C} = \mathbf{MR}$, and $\mathbf{D} = (\mathbf{R}\|\mathbf{w})\mathbf{A}$, we have $(\mathbf{C}\|\mathbf{x})\mathbf{A} = (\mathbf{MR}\|\mathbf{Mw})\mathbf{A} = \mathbf{M}(\mathbf{R}\|\mathbf{w})\mathbf{A} = \mathbf{MD}$.

NC^1-composable Zero-Knowledge. For any adversary $\mathcal{A} = \{a_\lambda\}_{\lambda \in \mathbb{N}} \in NC^1$, the advantage of a_λ in distinguishing $\mathsf{crs} \xleftarrow{\$} \mathsf{Gen}_\lambda$ from $(\mathsf{crs}, \mathsf{td}) \xleftarrow{\$} \mathsf{TGen}_\lambda$ is the same as its advantage in breaking the fine-grained matrix linear assumption, which is negligible if $NC^1 \subsetneq \oplus L/\mathsf{poly}$, due to Lemma 2.

According to the definition of $\widetilde{\mathsf{ZeroSamp}}$ (see Sect. 2.2), we can give the running procedure of TGen_λ in an explicit way, namely, randomly sampling $\mathbf{R}_0 = (\mathbf{e}_1^\lambda\|\widehat{\mathbf{R}}) \xleftarrow{\$} \mathsf{LSamp}(\lambda)$ and $\mathbf{R}_1 = \begin{pmatrix} \mathbf{I}_{\lambda-1} & \widetilde{\mathbf{r}} \\ \mathbf{0} & 1 \end{pmatrix} \xleftarrow{\$} \mathsf{RSamp}(\lambda)$, and setting $\mathbf{A}^\top = \mathbf{R}_0 \mathbf{M}_0^\lambda \mathbf{R}_1$. In this case, $\mathbf{A}^\top = (\mathbf{e}_1^\lambda\|\widehat{\mathbf{R}}) \begin{pmatrix} \mathbf{0} & \mathbf{0} \\ \mathbf{I}_{\lambda-1} & \mathbf{0} \end{pmatrix} \begin{pmatrix} \mathbf{I}_{\lambda-1} & \widetilde{\mathbf{r}} \\ \mathbf{0} & 1 \end{pmatrix} = (\widehat{\mathbf{R}}\|\widehat{\mathbf{R}}\widetilde{\mathbf{r}})$. Then for $\mathbf{x} = \mathbf{Mw}$, we have $\mathbf{MR} = \mathbf{M}(\mathbf{R} + \mathbf{w} \cdot \widetilde{\mathbf{r}}^\top) - \mathbf{x} \cdot \widetilde{\mathbf{r}}^\top$ and

$$(\mathbf{R}\|\mathbf{w})\mathbf{A} = (\mathbf{R}\|\mathbf{w}) \begin{pmatrix} \widehat{\mathbf{R}}^\top \\ \widetilde{\mathbf{r}}^\top \widehat{\mathbf{R}}^\top \end{pmatrix} = (\mathbf{R} + \mathbf{w} \cdot \widetilde{\mathbf{r}}^\top)\widehat{\mathbf{R}}^\top = (\mathbf{R} + \mathbf{w} \cdot \widetilde{\mathbf{r}}^\top\|\mathbf{0})\mathbf{A}.$$

Moreover, for $\mathbf{R} \xleftarrow{\$} \{0,1\}^{t \times (\lambda-1)}$, the distribution of $\mathbf{R} + \mathbf{w} \cdot \widetilde{\mathbf{r}}^\top$ is uniformly random in $\{0,1\}^{t \times (\lambda-1)}$. Thus, for any statement, the simulator perfect simulates honest proofs, completing the proof of composable zero-knowledge.

Perfect Soundness. For any valid statement/proof pair $(\mathbf{x}, (\mathbf{C}, \mathbf{D}))$ such that $(\mathbf{C}\|\mathbf{x})\mathbf{A} = \mathbf{MD}$ for $\mathbf{M} \in \mathcal{D}_\lambda$, we have $(\mathbf{M}^\perp)^\top(\mathbf{C}\|\mathbf{x})\mathbf{A} = \mathbf{0}$. Since $\mathbf{A}^\top \in$ OneSamp is of full rank, we must have $(\mathbf{M}^\perp)^\top\mathbf{x} = \mathbf{0}$, i.e., $\mathbf{x} \in L_\mathbf{M}$, completing the proof of perfect soundness. Notice that $\mathbf{M}^\perp$ is not necessarily efficiently computable here.

Putting all the above together, Theorem 2 immediately follows. □

Remark. By replacing OneSamp with ZeroSamp in Gen_λ, we immediately achieve a fine-grained NIZK with perfect zero-knowledge and computational soundness. The proof is almost identical to that of Theorem 2 except that we exploit the fine-grained matrix linear assumption in the proof of soundness this time. Similar arguments can also be made for our OR-proof and NIZKs for circuit SAT given in the following sections.

5   Fine-Grained OR-Proof

In this section, we extend LNIZK in Sect. 4 to an OR-proof system.

Let $\mathcal{D}_\lambda^{\mathsf{or}}$ be a probability distribution outputting matrices of rank $t' < n$ from $(\mathbf{M}_0, \mathbf{M}_1) \in \{0,1\}^{n \times t} \times \{0,1\}^{n \times t}$, where $n(\cdot)$, $t(\cdot)$, and $t'(\cdot)$ are functions in λ and there exists $\mathbf{M}_i^\perp \in \{0,1\}^{n \times (n-t')}$ such that $\mathbf{M}_i^\top \mathbf{M}_i^\perp = \mathbf{0}$ for $i \in \{0,1\}$. We define the following language

$$L_{\mathbf{M}_0, \mathbf{M}_1}^{\mathsf{or}} = \{\mathbf{x}_0, \mathbf{x}_1 : \exists \mathbf{w} \in \{0,1\}^t, \text{ s.t. } \mathbf{x}_0 = \mathbf{M}_0\mathbf{w} \vee \mathbf{x}_1 = \mathbf{M}_1\mathbf{w}\}.$$

For the associated relation $\mathsf{R}^{\mathsf{or}}_{\mathbf{M}_0,\mathbf{M}_1}$, we have $\mathsf{R}^{\mathsf{or}}_{\mathbf{M}_0,\mathbf{M}_1}((\mathbf{x}_0,\mathbf{x}_1),\mathbf{w}) = 1$ iff $\mathbf{x}_0 = \mathbf{M}_0\mathbf{w}$ or $\mathbf{x}_1 = \mathbf{M}_1\mathbf{w}$. The OR-proof is given in Fig. 6.

Theorem 3. *If* $\mathsf{NC}^1 \subsetneq \oplus \mathsf{L/poly}$, *then* ORNIZK *in Fig. 6 is an* $\mathsf{AC}^0[2]$*-NIZK with perfect soundness and* NC^1*-composable zero-knowledge.*

Proof. First, we note that $\{\mathsf{ORGen}_\lambda, \mathsf{ORTGen}_\lambda, \mathsf{ORProve}_\lambda, \mathsf{ORVer}_\lambda, \mathsf{ORSim}_\lambda\}_{\lambda \in \mathbb{N}}$ are computable in $\mathsf{AC}^0[2]$, since they only involve operations including multiplications of a constant number of matrices and sampling random bits.

Completeness. Completeness follows from the fact that for $\mathbf{x}_j = \mathbf{M}_j\mathbf{w}$, $\mathbf{C}_j = \mathbf{M}_j\mathbf{R}_j$, and $\mathbf{D}_j = (\mathbf{R}_j\|\mathbf{w})\mathbf{A}_j$, we have

$$(\mathbf{C}_j\|\mathbf{x}_j)\mathbf{A}_j = (\mathbf{M}_j\mathbf{R}_j\|\mathbf{M}_j\mathbf{w})\mathbf{A}_j = \mathbf{M}_j(\mathbf{R}_j\|\mathbf{w})\mathbf{A}_j = \mathbf{M}_j\mathbf{D}_j,$$

and for $\mathbf{A}_{1-j} = \begin{pmatrix} \overline{\mathbf{A}} \\ \widetilde{\mathbf{r}}^\top_{1-j}\overline{\mathbf{A}} \end{pmatrix}$, $\mathbf{C}_{1-j} = \mathbf{M}_{1-j}\mathbf{R}'_{1-j} - \mathbf{x}_{1-j} \cdot \widetilde{\mathbf{r}}^\top_{1-j}$, and $\mathbf{D}_{1-j} = (\mathbf{R}'_{1-j}\|\mathbf{0})\mathbf{A}_{1-j}$, we have

$$(\mathbf{C}_{1-j}\|\mathbf{x}_{1-j})\mathbf{A}_{1-j} = ((\mathbf{M}_{1-j}\mathbf{R}'_{1-j} - \mathbf{x}_{1-j} \cdot \widetilde{\mathbf{r}}^\top_{1-j})\|\mathbf{x}_{1-j}) \begin{pmatrix} \overline{\mathbf{A}} \\ \widetilde{\mathbf{r}}^\top_{1-j}\overline{\mathbf{A}} \end{pmatrix}$$
$$= \mathbf{M}_{1-j}\mathbf{R}'_{1-j}\overline{\mathbf{A}} = \mathbf{M}_{1-j}(\mathbf{R}'_{1-j}\|\mathbf{0})\mathbf{A}_{1-j} = \mathbf{M}_{1-j}\mathbf{D}_{1-j}.$$

ORGen$_\lambda$:
$\mathbf{A}^\top \xleftarrow{\$} \mathsf{OneSamp}(\lambda)$
Return $\mathsf{crs} = \mathbf{A} \in \{0,1\}^{\lambda \times \lambda}$

ORProve$_\lambda(\mathbf{A}, (\mathbf{M}_i, \mathbf{x}_i)_{i=0,1}, \mathbf{w})$:
Let $j \in \{0,1\}$ s.t. $\mathbf{x}_j = \mathbf{M}_j\mathbf{w}$
$\widetilde{\mathbf{r}}_{1-j} \xleftarrow{\$} \{0,1\}^{\lambda-1}$
$\mathbf{A}_{1-j} = \begin{pmatrix} \overline{\mathbf{A}} \\ \widetilde{\mathbf{r}}^\top_{1-j}\overline{\mathbf{A}} \end{pmatrix}$
$\mathbf{A}_j = \begin{pmatrix} \overline{\mathbf{A}} \\ \underline{\mathbf{A}} - \widetilde{\mathbf{r}}^\top_{1-j}\overline{\mathbf{A}} \end{pmatrix}$
$\mathbf{R}_j \xleftarrow{\$} \{0,1\}^{t \times (\lambda-1)}$
$\mathbf{C}_j = \mathbf{M}_j\mathbf{R}_j \in \{0,1\}^{n \times (\lambda-1)}$
$\mathbf{D}_j = (\mathbf{R}_j\|\mathbf{w})\mathbf{A}_j \in \{0,1\}^{t \times \lambda}$
$\mathbf{R}'_{1-j} \xleftarrow{\$} \{0,1\}^{t \times (\lambda-1)}$
$\mathbf{C}_{1-j} = \mathbf{M}_{1-j}\mathbf{R}'_{1-j} - \mathbf{x}_{1-j} \cdot \widetilde{\mathbf{r}}^\top_{1-j}$
$\mathbf{D}_{1-j} = (\mathbf{R}'_{1-j}\|\mathbf{0})\mathbf{A}_{1-j}$
Return $\pi = ((\mathbf{C}_i, \mathbf{D}_i)_{i=0,1}, \underline{\mathbf{A}_0})$

ORTGen$_\lambda$:
$(\mathbf{A}^\top, \widetilde{\mathbf{r}}) \xleftarrow{\$} \widetilde{\mathsf{ZeroSamp}}(\lambda)$
Return $(\mathsf{crs} = \mathbf{A} \in \{0,1\}^{\lambda \times \lambda}, \mathsf{td} = \widetilde{\mathbf{r}})$

ORSim$_\lambda(\mathbf{A}, \widetilde{\mathbf{r}}, (\mathbf{M}_i, \mathbf{x}_i)_{i=0,1})$:
$\widetilde{\mathbf{r}}_0 \xleftarrow{\$} \{0,1\}^{\lambda-1}$, $\widetilde{\mathbf{r}}_1 = \widetilde{\mathbf{r}} - \widetilde{\mathbf{r}}_0$
$\mathbf{A}_0 = \begin{pmatrix} \overline{\mathbf{A}} \\ \widetilde{\mathbf{r}}^\top_0\overline{\mathbf{A}} \end{pmatrix}$, $\mathbf{A}_1 = \begin{pmatrix} \overline{\mathbf{A}} \\ \widetilde{\mathbf{r}}^\top_1\overline{\mathbf{A}} \end{pmatrix}$
For $i = 0, 1$
  $\mathbf{R}'_i \xleftarrow{\$} \{0,1\}^{t \times (\lambda-1)}$
  $\mathbf{C}_i = \mathbf{M}_i\mathbf{R}'_i - \mathbf{x}_i \cdot \widetilde{\mathbf{r}}^\top_i$
  $\mathbf{D}_i = (\mathbf{R}'_i\|\mathbf{0})\mathbf{A}_i$
Return $\pi = ((\mathbf{C}_i, \mathbf{D}_i)_{i=0,1}, \underline{\mathbf{A}_0})$

ORVer$_\lambda(\mathbf{A}, (\mathbf{M}_i, \mathbf{x}_i)_{i=0,1}, \pi)$:
$\mathbf{A}_0 = \begin{pmatrix} \overline{\mathbf{A}} \\ \underline{\mathbf{A}_0} \end{pmatrix}$, $\mathbf{A}_1 = \begin{pmatrix} \overline{\mathbf{A}} \\ \underline{\mathbf{A}} - \underline{\mathbf{A}_0} \end{pmatrix}$
Return 1 iff $(\mathbf{C}_i\|\mathbf{x}_i)\mathbf{A}_i = \mathbf{M}_i\mathbf{D}_i$ for $i = 0, 1$

Fig. 6. Definition of $\mathsf{ORNIZK} = \{\mathsf{ORGen}_\lambda, \mathsf{ORTGen}_\lambda, \mathsf{ORProve}_\lambda, \mathsf{ORVer}_\lambda, \mathsf{ORSim}_\lambda\}_{\lambda \in \mathbb{N}}$ for $\{\mathcal{D}^{\mathsf{or}}_\lambda\}_{\lambda \in \mathbb{N}}$ to $\{\mathcal{D}^{\mathsf{or}}_\lambda\}_{\lambda \in \mathbb{N}}$. Recall that $\overline{\mathbf{A}}$ (respectively, $\underline{\mathbf{A}}$) denotes the upper $(\lambda-1) \times \lambda$ matrix (respectively, lower $1 \times \lambda$ vector) of $\mathbf{A}$.

NC^1-composable Zero-Knowledge. For any adversary $\mathcal{A} = \{a_\lambda\}_{\lambda \in \mathbb{N}} \in \mathsf{NC}^1$, the advantage of a_λ in distinguishing $\mathsf{crs} \xleftarrow{\$} \mathsf{ORGen}_\lambda$ from $(\mathsf{crs}, \mathsf{td}) \xleftarrow{\$} \mathsf{ORTGen}_\lambda$ is negligible if the fine-grained matrix linear assumption holds.

According to the definition of $\widetilde{\mathsf{ZeroSamp}}$ (see Sect. 2.2), we can give the running procedure of ORTGen_λ in an explicit way by randomly sampling $\mathbf{R}_0 = (\mathbf{e}_1^\lambda \| \widehat{\mathbf{R}}) \xleftarrow{\$} \mathsf{LSamp}(\lambda)$ and $\mathbf{R}_1 = \begin{pmatrix} \mathbf{I}_{\lambda-1} & \widetilde{\mathbf{r}} \\ \mathbf{0} & 1 \end{pmatrix} \xleftarrow{\$} \mathsf{RSamp}(\lambda)$ and setting $\mathbf{A}^\top = (\mathbf{e}_1^\lambda \| \widehat{\mathbf{R}}) \begin{pmatrix} \mathbf{0} & \mathbf{0} \\ \mathbf{I}_{\lambda-1} & \mathbf{0} \end{pmatrix} \begin{pmatrix} \mathbf{I}_{\lambda-1} & \widetilde{\mathbf{r}} \\ \mathbf{0} & 1 \end{pmatrix} = (\widehat{\mathbf{R}} \| \widehat{\mathbf{R}}\widetilde{\mathbf{r}})$, where the distribution of $\widetilde{\mathbf{r}}$ is uniform in $\{0,1\}^{\lambda-1}$. Thus we have $\underline{\mathbf{A}} = \widetilde{\mathbf{r}}^\top \overline{\mathbf{A}}$. Therefore, the distributions of $(\mathbf{A}_0, \mathbf{A}_1)$ generated by $\mathsf{ORProve}_\lambda$ and ORSim_λ on input a CRS generated by TGen_λ are identical. Moreover, we have $\mathbf{M}_j\mathbf{R}_j = \mathbf{M}_j(\mathbf{R}_j + \mathbf{w}\cdot\widetilde{\mathbf{r}}^\top) - \mathbf{x}_j\cdot\widetilde{\mathbf{r}}^\top$ and

$$(\mathbf{R}_j\|\mathbf{w})\mathbf{A}_j = (\mathbf{R}_j\|\mathbf{w})\begin{pmatrix} \overline{\mathbf{A}}^\top \\ \widetilde{\mathbf{r}}_j^\top \overline{\mathbf{A}}^\top \end{pmatrix} = (\mathbf{R}_j + \mathbf{w}\cdot\widetilde{\mathbf{r}}_j^\top)\overline{\mathbf{A}}^\top = (\mathbf{R}_j + \mathbf{w}\cdot\widetilde{\mathbf{r}}_j^\top\|\mathbf{0})\mathbf{A}_j$$

for $\mathbf{x}_j = \mathbf{M}_j\mathbf{w}$. Since the distribution of $\mathbf{R}_j + \mathbf{w}\cdot\widetilde{\mathbf{r}}_j^\top$ for $\mathbf{R}_j \xleftarrow{\$} \{0,1\}^{t\times(\lambda-1)}$ is uniform in $\{0,1\}^{t\times(\lambda-1)}$, the simulator perfectly simulate transcripts generated by honest protocol executions, completing the proof of composable zero-knowledge.

Perfect Soundness. For a valid statement/proof pair (x, π) where $\mathsf{x} = (\mathbf{x}_0, \mathbf{x}_1)$ and $\pi = ((\mathbf{C}_i, \mathbf{D}_i)_{i=0,1}, \underline{\mathbf{A}_0})$, we set $\mathbf{A}_0 = \begin{pmatrix} \overline{\mathbf{A}} \\ \underline{\mathbf{A}_0} \end{pmatrix}$ and $\mathbf{A}_1 = \begin{pmatrix} \overline{\mathbf{A}} \\ \underline{\mathbf{A}} - \underline{\mathbf{A}_0} \end{pmatrix}$. Since $\mathbf{A}^\top \in \mathsf{OneSamp}(\lambda)$ is of full rank, at least one of $\mathbf{A}_0$ and $\mathbf{A}_1$ is of full rank.

For $i = 0, 1$ and $(\mathbf{C}_i\|\mathbf{x}_i)\mathbf{A}_i = \mathbf{M}_i\mathbf{D}_i$, we have $(\mathbf{M}_i^\perp)^\top(\mathbf{C}_i\|\mathbf{x}_i)\mathbf{A}_i = \mathbf{0}$. Let $\mathbf{A}_j^\top$ be of full rank for $j = 0$ or $j = 1$. We must have $(\mathbf{M}_j^\perp)^\top\mathbf{x}_j = \mathbf{0}$. This means that $\mathsf{x} \in \mathsf{L}^{\mathsf{or}}_{\mathbf{M}_0, \mathbf{M}_1}$ must hold, completing the proof of perfect soundness. Notice that $\mathbf{M}_j^\perp$ is not necessarily efficiently computable here.

Putting all the above together, Theorem 3 immediately follows.   □

6   Fine-Grained NIZK Proof for Circuit SAT

In this section, we propose a fine-grained NIZK for circuit SAT running in NC^1 and secure against adversaries in NC^1.

Let $\{\mathcal{ND}_\lambda\}_{\lambda \in \mathbb{N}}$ be any family of language distributions such that for all $\rho \in \mathcal{ND}_\lambda$ and all $\mathsf{x} \in \mathsf{L}_\rho$, we have $\{\mathsf{R}_\rho(\mathsf{x}, \cdot)\}_{\lambda \in \mathbb{N}} \in \mathsf{NC}^1$, where L_ρ and R_ρ are the associated language and relation respectively. Without loss of generality, we assume that each $\mathsf{R}_\rho(\mathsf{x}, \cdot)$ only consists of NAND gates, since an NC^1 circuit can be transformed to an NC^1 circuits consisting only of NAND gates, and the transformation can also be performed in NC^1 by changing the gates in parallel. Let $\mathsf{ORNIZK} = \{\mathsf{ORGen}_\lambda, \mathsf{ORTGen}_\lambda, \mathsf{ORProve}_\lambda, \mathsf{ORVer}_\lambda, \mathsf{ORSim}_\lambda\}_{\lambda \in \mathbb{N}}$ be a NIZK for distributions $\{\mathcal{D}^{\mathsf{or}}_\lambda\}_{\lambda \in \mathbb{N}}$ defining the language

$$\mathsf{L}^{\mathsf{or}}_{\mathbf{M}'} = \{\mathbf{x}_0, \mathbf{x}_1 : \exists \mathbf{w} \in \{0,1\}^{2\lambda} \text{ s.t. } \mathbf{x}_0 = \mathbf{M}'\mathbf{w} \vee \mathbf{x}_1 = \mathbf{M}'\mathbf{w}\},$$

$\underline{\text{NCGen}_\lambda:}$
$\text{crs}_\text{or} \xleftarrow{\$} \text{ORGen}_\lambda, \mathbf{M}^\top \xleftarrow{\$} \text{ZeroSamp}(\lambda)$
Return $\text{CRS} = (\text{crs}_\text{or}, \mathbf{M})$

$\underline{\text{NCTGen}_\lambda:}$
$(\text{crs}_\text{or}, \text{td}_\text{or}) \xleftarrow{\$} \text{ORTGen}_\lambda(\lambda), \mathbf{M}^\top \xleftarrow{\$} \text{OneSamp}(\lambda)$
Return $\text{CRS} = (\text{crs}_\text{or}, \mathbf{M})$ and $\text{TD} = \text{td}_\text{or}$

$\underline{\text{NCProve}_\lambda(\text{CRS}, \rho, \mathsf{x}, \mathsf{w}):}$
Extend w to $(\mathsf{w}_1, \cdots, \mathsf{w}_\text{out})$ containing the bits of all wires in the circuit $R_\rho(\mathsf{x}, \cdot)$
Compute $\mathbf{r}_i \xleftarrow{\$} \{0,1\}^\lambda$ and $\text{ct}_i = \mathbf{M}\mathbf{r}_i + \mathbf{e}_\lambda^\lambda \mathsf{w}_i$ for each bit w_i
Set $\mathbf{r}_\text{out} = \mathbf{0}$ and $\text{ct}_\text{out} = \mathbf{e}_\lambda^\lambda$ for the output wire
For each NAND gate with input ciphertexts $\text{ct}_i = \mathbf{M}\mathbf{r}_i + \mathbf{e}_\lambda^\lambda \mathsf{w}_i$ and $\text{ct}_j = \mathbf{M}\mathbf{r}_j + \mathbf{e}_\lambda^\lambda \mathsf{w}_j$
and the output ciphertext $\text{ct}_k = \mathbf{M}\mathbf{r}_k + \mathbf{e}_\lambda^\lambda \mathsf{w}_k$, run

$-\ \mathsf{x}_i = \begin{pmatrix} \mathbf{e}_\lambda^\lambda + \text{ct}_i + \text{ct}_k \\ \mathbf{e}_\lambda^\lambda + \text{ct}_j \end{pmatrix}, \mathbf{r}_i' = \begin{pmatrix} \mathbf{r}_i + \mathbf{r}_k \\ \mathbf{r}_j \end{pmatrix}, \mathsf{x}_j = \begin{pmatrix} \mathbf{e}_\lambda^\lambda + \text{ct}_k \\ \text{ct}_j \end{pmatrix}, \mathbf{r}_j' = \begin{pmatrix} \mathbf{r}_k \\ \mathbf{r}_j \end{pmatrix}$

$-\ \pi_{ij} \xleftarrow{\$} \text{ORProve}_\lambda(\text{crs}_\text{or}, \mathbf{M}', (\mathsf{x}_i, \mathsf{x}_j), \mathbf{r}_b')$ if $\mathsf{x}_b = \mathbf{M}'\mathbf{r}_b'$ for $b \in \{i, j\}$ and abort
   otherwise, where $\mathbf{M}' = \begin{pmatrix} \mathbf{M} & \mathbf{0} \\ \mathbf{0} & \mathbf{M} \end{pmatrix}$

Return Π consisting of all the ciphertexts and proofs

$\underline{\text{NCVer}_\lambda(\text{CRS}, \rho, \mathsf{x}, \Pi):}$
Check that all wires have a corresponding ciphertext and $\text{ct}_\text{out} = \mathbf{e}_\lambda^\lambda$
Check that all NAND gates have a valid NIZK proof of compliance
Return 1 iff all checks pass

$\underline{\text{NCSim}_\lambda(\text{CRS}, \text{TD}, \rho, \mathsf{x}):}$
Compute $\mathbf{r}_i \xleftarrow{\$} \mathbb{Z}_p^\lambda$ and $\text{ct}_i = \mathbf{M}\mathbf{r}_i$ for each wire in the circuit $R_\rho(\mathsf{x}, \cdot)$
For each NAND gate with input ciphertexts ct_i and ct_j and the output ciphertext
ct_k, run

$-\ \mathsf{x}_i = \begin{pmatrix} \mathbf{e}_\lambda^\lambda + \text{ct}_i + \text{ct}_k \\ \mathbf{e}_\lambda^\lambda + \text{ct}_j \end{pmatrix}, \mathsf{x}_j = \begin{pmatrix} \mathbf{e}_\lambda^\lambda + \text{ct}_k \\ \text{ct}_j \end{pmatrix}$

$-\ \pi_{ij} \xleftarrow{\$} \text{ORSim}_\lambda(\text{crs}_\text{or}, \text{td}_\text{or}, \mathbf{M}', (\mathsf{x}_i, \mathsf{x}_j))$ where $\mathbf{M}' = \begin{pmatrix} \mathbf{M} & \mathbf{0} \\ \mathbf{0} & \mathbf{M} \end{pmatrix}$

Return Π consisting of all the ciphertexts and proofs

Fig. 7. Definition of $\text{NCNIZK} = \{\text{NCGen}_\lambda, \text{NCTGen}_\lambda, \text{NCProve}_\lambda, \text{NCVer}_\lambda, \text{NCSim}_\lambda\}_{\lambda \in \mathbb{N}}$ for $\{\mathcal{D}_\lambda\}_{\lambda \in \mathbb{N}}$. Recall that $\mathbf{e}_\lambda^\lambda = (0 \cdots 01)^\top \in \{0,1\}^\lambda$.

where $\mathbf{M}' = \begin{pmatrix} \mathbf{M} & \mathbf{0} \\ \mathbf{0} & \mathbf{M} \end{pmatrix}$ for $\mathbf{M} \in \text{ZeroSamp}(\lambda)$. We give our NIZK for $\{\mathcal{ND}_\lambda\}_{\lambda \in \mathbb{N}}$ in Fig. 7.

Theorem 4. *If $\text{NC}^1 \subsetneq \oplus\text{L}/\text{poly}$ and ORNIZK is an $\text{AC}^0[2]$-NIZK with perfect soundness and NC^1-composable zero-knowledge, then NCNIZK is an NC^1-NIZK with perfect soundness and NC^1-composable zero-knowledge.*

Proof. First, we note that $\{\text{NCGen}_\lambda, \text{NCTGen}_\lambda, \text{NCProve}_\lambda, \text{NCVer}_\lambda, \text{NCSim}_\lambda\}_{\lambda \in \mathbb{N}}$ are computable in NC^1, since they only involve operations including multiplications of a constant number of matrices, sampling random bits, running ORNIZK, and computing $\mathsf{R}_\rho(\mathsf{x}, \mathsf{w}) \in \mathsf{NC}^1$. Notice that after computing the values of all wires, the prover can generate ciphertexts and run ORNIZK for each wire and gate in parallel and the verifier can check the proofs in parallel.

Completeness. Let w_i and w_j be the input bits of a NAND gate, and w_k be the true output. We must have $1 + \mathsf{w}_i + \mathsf{w}_k = 0 \wedge 1 + \mathsf{w}_j = 0$ or $1 + \mathsf{w}_k = 0 \wedge \mathsf{w}_j = 0$. Let $\mathsf{ct}_i = \mathbf{M}\mathbf{r}_i + \mathbf{e}_\lambda^\lambda \mathsf{w}_i$ and $\mathsf{ct}_j = \mathbf{M}\mathbf{r}_j + \mathbf{e}_\lambda^\lambda \mathsf{w}_j$ be the input ciphertexts and $\mathsf{ct}_k = \mathbf{M}\mathbf{r}_k + \mathbf{e}_\lambda^\lambda \mathsf{w}_k$ be the output ciphertext. We have

$$\mathsf{x}_i = \begin{pmatrix} \mathbf{e}_\lambda^\lambda + \mathsf{ct}_i + \mathsf{ct}_k \\ \mathbf{e}_\lambda^\lambda + \mathsf{ct}_j \end{pmatrix} = \mathbf{M}' \begin{pmatrix} \mathbf{r}_i + \mathbf{r}_k \\ \mathbf{r}_j \end{pmatrix} + \begin{pmatrix} \mathbf{e}_\lambda^\lambda(1 + \mathsf{w}_i + \mathsf{w}_k) \\ \mathbf{e}_\lambda^\lambda(1 + \mathsf{w}_j) \end{pmatrix} = \mathbf{M}' \begin{pmatrix} \mathbf{r}_i + \mathbf{r}_k \\ \mathbf{r}_j \end{pmatrix}$$

or

$$\mathsf{x}_j = \begin{pmatrix} \mathbf{e}_\lambda^\lambda + \mathsf{ct}_k \\ \mathsf{ct}_j \end{pmatrix} = \mathbf{M}' \begin{pmatrix} \mathbf{r}_k \\ \mathbf{r}_j \end{pmatrix} + \begin{pmatrix} \mathbf{e}_\lambda^\lambda(1 + \mathsf{w}_k) \\ \mathbf{e}_\lambda^\lambda \mathsf{w}_j \end{pmatrix} = \mathbf{M}' \begin{pmatrix} \mathbf{r}_k \\ \mathbf{r}_j \end{pmatrix}.$$

Therefore, we have $\mathsf{x}_i \in \mathrm{Im}(\mathbf{M}')$ if $\mathsf{w}_j = 1$ and $\mathsf{x}_j \in \mathrm{Im}(\mathbf{M}')$ otherwise. Then the completeness of NCNIZK follows from the completeness of ORNIZK.

NC^1-composable Zero-Knowledge. The indistinguishability of CRSs generated by NCGen_λ and NCTGen_λ follows immediately from Lemma 2 and the composable zero-knowledge of ORNIZK.

Next we define a modified prover $\mathsf{NCProve}'_\lambda$, which is exactly the same as $\mathsf{NCProve}_\lambda$ except that for each NAND gate, π_{ij} is generated as $\pi_{ij} \xleftarrow{\$} \mathsf{ORSim}_\lambda(\mathsf{crs}_{\mathsf{or}}, \mathsf{td}_{\mathsf{or}}, \mathbf{M}', (\mathsf{x}_i, \mathsf{x}_j))$. The following distributions are identical due to the composable zero-knowledge of ORNIZK.

$$\varPi \xleftarrow{\$} \mathsf{NCProve}_\lambda(\mathsf{CRS}, \rho, \mathsf{x}, \mathsf{w}) \text{ and } \varPi \xleftarrow{\$} \mathsf{NCProve}'_\lambda(\mathsf{CRS}, \rho, \mathsf{x}, \mathsf{w}),$$

for $(\mathsf{CRS}, \mathsf{TD}) \xleftarrow{\$} \mathsf{TGen}_\lambda$ and any (x, w) such that $\mathsf{R}_\rho(\mathsf{x}, \mathsf{w}) = 1$.

Moreover, since the distribution of $\mathsf{ct}_i = \mathbf{M}\mathbf{r}_i$ is identical to that of $\mathsf{ct}_i = \mathbf{M}\mathbf{r}_i + \mathbf{e}_\lambda^\lambda \mathsf{w}_i$ for $\mathbf{r}_i \xleftarrow{\$} \{0,1\}^\lambda$ when $\mathbf{M} \in \mathsf{OneSamp}(\lambda)$ is of full rank, the distributions of

$$\varPi \xleftarrow{\$} \mathsf{NCProve}'_\lambda(\mathsf{CRS}, \rho, \mathsf{x}, \mathsf{w}) \text{ and } \varPi \xleftarrow{\$} \mathsf{NCSim}_\lambda(\mathsf{CRS}, \mathsf{TD}, \rho, \mathsf{x}),$$

where $(\mathsf{CRS}, \mathsf{TD}) \xleftarrow{\$} \mathsf{NCTGen}_\lambda$ and $\mathsf{R}_\rho(\mathsf{x}, \mathsf{w}) = 1$, are identical as well, completing the proof of composable zero-knowledge.

Perfect Soundness. Due to the perfect soundness of ORNIZK, for each NAND gate with input ciphertexts $(\mathsf{ct}_i, \mathsf{ct}_j)$ and an output ciphertext ct_k in a valid proof, we have

$$\mathsf{x}_i = \begin{pmatrix} \mathbf{e}_\lambda^\lambda + \mathsf{ct}_i + \mathsf{ct}_k \\ \mathbf{e}_\lambda^\lambda + \mathsf{ct}_j \end{pmatrix} \in \mathrm{Im}(\mathbf{M}') \text{ or } \mathsf{x}_j = \begin{pmatrix} \mathbf{e}_\lambda^\lambda + \mathsf{ct}_k \\ \mathsf{ct}_j \end{pmatrix} \in \mathrm{Im}(\mathbf{M}').$$

Let $\mathbf{k} = (\tilde{\mathbf{r}}^\top, 1)^\top$ be the vector in the kernel of $\mathbf{M}^\top$, which must exist according to Lemma 1. We have

$$\mathbf{k}^\top(\mathbf{e}_\lambda^\lambda + \mathsf{ct}_i + \mathsf{ct}_k) = 1 + \mathbf{k}^\top \mathsf{ct}_i + \mathbf{k}^\top \mathsf{ct}_k = 0 \wedge \mathbf{k}^\top(\mathbf{e}_\lambda^\lambda + \mathsf{ct}_j) = 1 + \mathbf{k}^\top \mathsf{ct}_j = 0$$

or

$$\mathbf{k}^\top(\mathbf{e}_\lambda^\lambda + \mathsf{ct}_k) = 1 + \mathbf{k}^\top\mathsf{ct}_k = 0 \wedge \mathbf{k}^\top\mathsf{ct}_j = 0,$$

i.e., we can extract a true input/output pair $((\mathbf{k}^\top\mathsf{ct}_i, \mathbf{k}^\top\mathsf{ct}_j), \mathbf{k}^\top\mathsf{ct}_k)$ for each NAND gate. For the output wire, we have $\mathbf{k}^\top\mathsf{ct}_{\mathsf{out}} = \mathbf{k}^\top\mathbf{e}_\lambda^\lambda = 1$. As a result, we can extract the bits of all the wires leading to a final output 1, completing the proof of perfect soundness.

Putting all the above together, Theorem 4 immediately follows.   □

Remark. If we relax the restriction on the computational resources of the prover and allow it to run in, say, polynomial-time, our NIZK can also prove statements in NP. The same argument can also be made for our non-interactive zap and NIZK in the URS model (based on this NIZK) given later in Sects. 8.2 and 9. Notice that for the security proof of the non-interactive zap with a polynomial-time prover, we have to ensure that the reduction can simulate proofs in NC^1. This is possible by hard-wiring the extended witness in the reduction beforehand. We refer the reader to the full paper for details.

7   Fine-Grained NIZK for $\mathsf{AC}^0_{\mathsf{CM}}[2]$ with Short Proofs

In this section, we propose another fine-grained NIZK generically constructed from fine-grained NIZKs (instantiated as in Sects. 4 and 5) and a new fine-grained strongly FHE (sFHE) scheme that we give later. Different from the NIZK in Sect. 6, we only consider statement circuits in $\mathsf{AC}^0_{\mathsf{CM}}[2]$ here, while the proof size is independent with the statement circuit size and only dependent on the length of witness. Specifically, while the proof size of the NIZK in Sect. 6 is $l \cdot O(\lambda^2)$, that of the NIZK in this section is $n \cdot O(\lambda^2)$, where l and n are the circuit and witness sizes respectively.

7.1   Definition of Fine-Grained sFHE

For an sFHE scheme, additionally to the properties of a standard FHE, we require that the homomorphic evaluation do not change the form of ciphertexts, and there exist an algorithm $\mathsf{RandEval}_\lambda$ outputting the corresponding randomness of a homomorphically evaluated ciphertext on input the messages and randomness of the originally ciphertexts. Moreover, we define a composable version of indistinguishability against chosen plaintext attacks (CPA), which requires that the adversary cannot distinguish an honest public key with an "invalid" public key, and a ciphertext generated by an invalid public key reveals no information on the message.

Definition 12 (Strongly fully homomorphic encryption (sFHE)). *A $\mathcal{C}_1$-sFHE scheme for $\mathcal{C}_3$ circuits is a function family* $\mathsf{sFHE} = \{\mathsf{FHEGen}_\lambda, \mathsf{FHEGen}'_\lambda, \mathsf{Enc}_\lambda, \mathsf{Dec}_\lambda, \mathsf{Eval}_\lambda, \mathsf{RandEval}_\lambda\}_{\lambda \in \mathbb{N}} \in \mathcal{C}_1$ *with the following properties.*

- FHEGen_λ *returns a public/secret key pair* $(\mathsf{pk}, \mathsf{sk})$.
- FHEGen'_λ *returns a public key* pk.
- $\mathsf{Enc}_\lambda(\mathsf{pk}, \mathsf{m} \in \{0,1\}; \mathsf{r} \in \mathcal{R})$ *returns a ciphertext* ct.
- $\mathsf{Dec}_\lambda(\mathsf{sk}, \mathsf{ct})$ *(deterministically) returns a message* $\mathsf{m} \in \{0,1\}$.
- $\mathsf{Eval}_\lambda(\mathsf{pk}, \mathsf{f} \in \mathcal{C}_3, (\mathsf{ct}_1, \cdots, \mathsf{ct}_n))$ *(deterministically) return a ciphertext* ct. *Without loss of generality, we require that* f *is represented as an arithmetic circuit in* $GF(2)$ *with* XOR *gates of unbounded fan-in and* AND *gates with fan-in* 2.
- $\mathsf{RandEval}_\lambda(\mathsf{pk}, \mathsf{f} \in \mathcal{C}_3, (\mathsf{m}_1, \cdots, \mathsf{m}_n), (\mathsf{r}_1, \cdots, \mathsf{r}_n))$ *(deterministically) return a randomness* $\mathsf{r} \in \mathcal{R}$. *We require that* f *is represented in the same way as above.*

Correctness is satisfied if we have $\mathsf{m} = \mathsf{Dec}_\lambda(\mathsf{sk}, \mathsf{Enc}_\lambda(\mathsf{pk}, \mathsf{m}; \mathsf{r}))$ *for all* $\lambda \in \mathbb{N}$, *all* $\mathsf{m} \in \{0,1\}$, *all* $(\mathsf{pk}, \mathsf{sk}) \in \mathsf{FHEGen}_\lambda$, *and all* $\mathsf{r} \in \mathcal{R}$.

$\mathcal{C}_2$-*composable CPA security is satisfied if for any adversary* $\mathcal{A} = \{a_\lambda\}_{\lambda \in \mathbb{N}} \in \mathcal{C}_2$, *we have*

$$\Pr[1 \xleftarrow{\$} a_\lambda(\mathsf{pk}) | (\mathsf{pk}, \mathsf{sk}) \xleftarrow{\$} \mathsf{FHEGen}_\lambda] - \Pr[1 \xleftarrow{\$} a_\lambda(\mathsf{pk}) | \mathsf{pk} \xleftarrow{\$} \mathsf{FHEGen}'_\lambda] \leq \mathsf{negl}(\lambda),$$

and for all $\lambda \in \mathbb{N}$ *and all* $\mathsf{pk} \in \mathsf{FHEGen}'_\lambda$, *the distributions of* $\mathsf{ct} \xleftarrow{\$} \mathsf{Enc}_\lambda(\mathsf{pk}, 0)$ *and* $\mathsf{ct} \xleftarrow{\$} \mathsf{Enc}_\lambda(\mathsf{pk}, 1)$ *are identical.*

Strong homomorphism is satisfied if for every function family $\{\mathsf{f}_\lambda\}_{\lambda \in \mathbb{N}} \in \mathcal{C}_3$, *all* $\lambda \in \mathbb{N}$, *all* $(\mathsf{pk}, \mathsf{sk}) \in \mathsf{FHEGen}_\lambda$, *all* $\mathsf{m}_1, \cdots, \mathsf{m}_n \in \{0,1\}$, *and all* $\mathsf{r}_1, \cdots, \mathsf{r}_n \in \mathcal{R}$, *we have*

$$\mathsf{Eval}_\lambda(\mathsf{pk}, \mathsf{f}, \mathsf{Enc}_\lambda(\mathsf{pk}, \mathsf{m}_1; \mathsf{r}_1), \cdots, \mathsf{Enc}_\lambda(\mathsf{pk}, \mathsf{m}_n; \mathsf{r}_n))$$
$$= \mathsf{Enc}_\lambda(\mathsf{pk}, \mathsf{f}(\mathsf{m}_1, \cdots, \mathsf{m}_n); \mathsf{RandEval}_\lambda(\mathsf{pk}, \mathsf{f}, (\mathsf{m}_1, \cdots, \mathsf{m}_n), (\mathsf{r}_1, \cdots, \mathsf{r}_n))).$$

One can easily see that composable CPA security implies standard CPA security. Also, strong homomorphism implies standard homomorphism, since a homomorphically evaluated ciphertext can be decrypted to the right value due to correctness.

7.2   Construction of Fine-Grained sFHE

We now give our construction of sFHE $\mathsf{sFHE} = \{\mathsf{FHEGen}_\lambda, \mathsf{FHEGen}'_\lambda, \mathsf{Enc}_\lambda, \mathsf{Dec}_\lambda, \mathsf{Eval}_\lambda, \mathsf{RandEval}_\lambda\}_{\lambda \in \mathbb{N}}$ in Fig. 8. Eval_λ is defined by evaluation algorithms of AND and XOR gates, i.e., $\mathsf{Eval}^{\mathsf{and}}_\lambda$ and $\mathsf{Eval}^{\mathsf{xor}}_\lambda$. Similarly, $\mathsf{RandEval}_\lambda$ is defined by $\mathsf{RandEval}^{\mathsf{and}}_\lambda$ and $\mathsf{RandEval}^{\mathsf{xor}}_\lambda$.

FHEGen$_\lambda$: $(\mathbf{M}^\top, \widetilde{\mathbf{r}}) \xleftarrow{\$} \widetilde{\mathsf{ZeroSamp}}(\lambda)$ Return $(\mathsf{pk}, \mathsf{sk}) = (\mathbf{M}, \widetilde{\mathbf{r}})$	$\mathsf{Eval}_\lambda^{\mathsf{and}}(\mathsf{pk}, (\mathsf{ct}_0, \mathsf{ct}_1))$: Return $\mathsf{ct}_2 = \mathsf{ct}_0\mathsf{ct}_1 \in \{0,1\}^{\lambda \times \lambda}$
FHEGen$'_\lambda$: $\mathbf{M}^\top \xleftarrow{\$} \mathsf{OneSamp}(\lambda)$ Return $\mathsf{pk} = \mathbf{M}$	$\mathsf{Eval}_\lambda^{\mathsf{xor}}(\mathsf{pk}, (\mathsf{ct}_i)_{i=1}^n)$: Return $\mathsf{ct} = \sum_{i=1}^n \mathsf{ct}_i \in \{0,1\}^{\lambda \times \lambda}$
	$\mathsf{RandEval}_\lambda^{\mathsf{and}}(\mathsf{pk}, (\mathsf{m}_0, \mathsf{m}_1), (\mathbf{R}_0, \mathbf{R}_1))$: $\mathsf{ct}_1 = \mathbf{M}\mathbf{R}_1 + \mathsf{m}_1\mathbf{I}_\lambda \in \{0,1\}^{\lambda \times \lambda}$ Return $(\mathbf{R}_0\mathsf{ct}_1 + \mathsf{m}_0\mathbf{R}_1) \in \{0,1\}^{\lambda \times \lambda}$
Enc$_\lambda(\mathsf{pk}, \mathsf{m} \in \{0,1\})$: $\mathbf{R} \xleftarrow{\$} \{0,1\}^{\lambda \times \lambda}$ Return $\mathsf{ct} = \mathbf{M}\mathbf{R} + \mathsf{m}\mathbf{I}_\lambda \in \{0,1\}^{\lambda \times \lambda}$	$\mathsf{RandEval}_\lambda^{\mathsf{xor}}(\mathsf{pk}, (\mathsf{m}_i)_{i=1}^n, (\mathbf{R}_i)_{i=1}^n)$: Return $\sum_{i=1}^n \mathbf{R}_i \in \{0,1\}^{\lambda \times \lambda}$
Dec$_\lambda(\mathsf{sk}, \mathsf{ct})$: Let $\mathbf{c}$ be the λth column vector of ct Return $(\widetilde{\mathbf{r}}^\top\|1)\mathbf{c}$	

Fig. 8. Definition of $\mathsf{sFHE} = \{\mathsf{FHEGen}_\lambda, \mathsf{FHEGen}'_\lambda, \mathsf{Enc}_\lambda, \mathsf{Dec}_\lambda, \mathsf{Eval}_\lambda, \mathsf{RandEval}_\lambda\}_{\lambda \in \mathbb{N}}$ where Eval_λ (respectively, $\mathsf{RandEval}_\lambda$) is defined by $\mathsf{Eval}_\lambda^{\mathsf{and}}$ and $\mathsf{Eval}_\lambda^{\mathsf{xor}}$ (respectively, $\mathsf{RandEval}_\lambda^{\mathsf{and}}$ and $\mathsf{RandEval}_\lambda^{\mathsf{xor}}$). Recall that $\mathbf{I}_\lambda$ is an identity matrix in $\{0,1\}^{\lambda \times \lambda}$.

Theorem 5. *If* $\mathsf{NC}^1 \subsetneq \oplus\mathsf{L}/\mathsf{poly}$, *then* sFHE *is an* $\mathsf{AC}^0[2]$-sFHE *scheme for* $\mathsf{AC}_{\mathsf{CM}}^0[2]$ *circuits that is* NC^1-*composable CPA secure.*

Proof. First, we note that sFHE is computable in $\mathsf{AC}^0[2]$, since the key generation algorithms, the encryption algorithm, and the decryption algorithm only involve operations including multiplications of a constant number of matrices, sampling random bits, and computing parity, and we only consider homomorphic evaluation of circuits in $\mathsf{AC}_{\mathsf{CM}}^0[2]$ (i.e., with constant multiplicative depth), which only involve multiplications of a constant number of matrices as well.

Correctness. Correctness follows from the fact that the λth column vector of a ciphertext for m is in the form of $\mathbf{M}\mathbf{r}_\lambda + \mathbf{e}_\lambda^\lambda\mathsf{m} \in \{0,1\}^\lambda$ (where $\mathbf{e}_\lambda^\lambda = (0, \cdots, 0, 1)^\top$) and we have $(\widetilde{\mathbf{r}}^\top\|1)(\mathbf{M}\mathbf{r}_\lambda + \mathbf{e}_\lambda^\lambda\mathsf{m}) = \mathbf{0} + (\widetilde{\mathbf{r}}^\top\|1)\mathbf{e}_\lambda^\lambda\mathsf{m} = \mathsf{m}$.

Strong Homomorphism. To prove strong homomorphism, we just have to show the correctness of the homomorphic evaluation for XOR and AND gates.

For homomorphic addition, we have

$$\sum_{i=1}^n \mathsf{ct}_i = \mathbf{M}\left(\sum_{i=1}^n \mathbf{R}_i\right) + \left(\sum_{i=1}^n \mathsf{m}_i\right)\mathbf{I}_\lambda.$$

For homomorphic multiplication, we have

$$\mathsf{ct}_0\mathsf{ct}_1 = (\mathbf{M}\mathbf{R}_0 + \mathsf{m}_0\mathbf{I}_\lambda)\mathsf{ct}_1 = \mathbf{M}\mathbf{R}_0\mathsf{ct}_1 + \mathsf{m}_0\mathbf{I}_\lambda(\mathbf{M}\mathbf{R}_1 + \mathsf{m}_1\mathbf{I}_\lambda)$$
$$= \mathbf{M}(\mathbf{R}_0\mathsf{ct}_1 + \mathsf{m}_0\mathbf{R}_1) + \mathsf{m}_0\mathsf{m}_1\mathbf{I}_\lambda.$$

Hence, $\sum_{i=1}^{n} \mathsf{ct}_i$ and $\mathsf{ct}_0\mathsf{ct}_1$ are ciphertexts for $\sum_{i=1}^{n} \mathsf{m}_i$ and $\mathsf{m}_0\mathsf{m}_1$ with randomness $\sum_{i=1}^{n} \mathbf{R}_n$ and $\mathbf{R}_0\mathsf{ct}_1 + \mathsf{m}_0\mathbf{R}_1$ respectively, i.e., strong homomorphism holds.

Composable CPA Security. The security follows immediately from Lemma 2 and the fact that when $\mathbf{M} \in \mathsf{OneSamp}(\lambda)$, $\mathbf{M}$ is of full rank, and thus the distributions of $\mathbf{MR} + \mathbf{I}_\lambda$ and $\mathbf{MR}$ are identical for $\mathbf{R} \xleftarrow{\$} \{0,1\}^{\lambda \times \lambda}$.

Putting all the above together, Theorem 5 immediately follows.   □

We now give some remarks on our scheme.

Remark on $\mathsf{AC}^0_{\mathsf{CM}}[2]$. We follow Campanelli and Gennaro [5] to define $\mathsf{AC}^0_{\mathsf{CM}}[2]$ circuits with constant multiplicative depth. The reason that we only consider this class is that the main overhead for homomorphic evaluation is given by the multiplication gates. Each homomorphic multiplication in our case involves multiplication of two $\lambda \times \lambda$ matrices, which can be performed in an $\mathsf{AC}^0[2]$ circuit with depth 2 (the first layer consists of fan-in 2 multiplication gates and the second layer consists of fan-in λ addition gates). But it requires $\Omega(\log(\lambda))$ depth with fan-in two gates. Hence, a circuit with non-constant multiplicative depth would require an evaluation of $\omega(log(\lambda))$ depth, which cannot be performed in NC^1, while addition of polynomial numbers of matrices and multiplication of a constant depth of matrices can be performed in $\mathsf{AC}^0[2]$.

Remark on Efficiency. In our scheme, the public key size is only λ^2 and the depth of an NC^1 circuit required for homomorphic multiplication is small since it only computes the parity of λ bits (in parallel). In contrast, the somewhat homomorphic encryption in [5] has public keys of length $(L \cdot \lambda^3 + \lambda^2)$, where L is an a-prior fixed upper bound for the multiplicative depth of evaluation circuits, and computes the parity of λ^2 bits in parallel for homomorphic multiplication.

Remark on Proofs for Ciphertexts. We note that our NIZK for linear languages in Sect. 4 and our OR-proof in Sect. 5 support the following two languages respectively including ciphertexts of 1 and all valid ciphertexts.

$$\mathsf{L}^1_{\mathsf{pk}} = \{\mathsf{x} : \exists \mathsf{r} \in \mathcal{R} \text{ s.t. } \mathsf{x} = \mathsf{Enc}_\lambda(\mathsf{pk}, 1; \mathsf{r})\}$$
$$= \{\mathsf{x} : \exists \mathbf{R} \in \{0,1\}^{\lambda \times \lambda}, \mathsf{m} \in \{0,1\} \text{ s.t. } \mathsf{x} + \mathbf{I}_\lambda = \mathbf{MR}\}$$

and

$$\mathsf{L}^{\mathsf{valid}}_{\mathsf{pk}} = \{\mathsf{x} : \exists \mathsf{r} \in \mathcal{R} \text{ s.t. } \mathsf{x} = \mathsf{Enc}_\lambda(\mathsf{pk}, 0; \mathsf{r}) \vee \mathsf{x} = \mathsf{Enc}_\lambda(\mathsf{pk}, 1; \mathsf{r})\}$$
$$= \{\mathsf{x} : \exists \mathbf{R} \in \{0,1\}^{\lambda \times \lambda} \text{ s.t. } \mathsf{x} = \mathbf{MR} \vee \mathsf{x} + \mathbf{I}_\lambda = \mathbf{MR}\}.$$

Here, $\mathsf{pk} = \mathbf{M} \in \{0,1\}^{\lambda \times \lambda}$. The reason is that, say, $\mathsf{x} = \mathbf{MR}$ is equivalent to $\mathsf{x}' = \mathbf{M}'\mathbf{r}'$, where x' and $\mathbf{r}'$ are concatenations of column vectors in x and $\mathbf{R}$ respectively, and $\mathbf{M}' \in \{0,1\}^{\lambda^2 \times \lambda^2}$ is a large matrix with the diagonal being matrices $\mathbf{M}$ and other positions being $\mathbf{0}$.

7.3 Generic Construction of NIZK

Let $\{\mathcal{AD}_\lambda\}_{\lambda \in \mathbb{N}}$ be any family of language distributions such that for all $\rho \in \mathcal{AD}_\lambda$ and all $x \in L_\rho$, we have $\{R_\rho(x, \cdot)\}_{\lambda \in \mathbb{N}} \in \mathsf{AC}^0_{\mathsf{CM}}[2]$, where L_ρ and R_ρ are the associated language and relation respectively.

Let $\mathsf{sFHE} = \{\mathsf{FHEGen}_\lambda, \mathsf{FHEGen}'_\lambda, \mathsf{Enc}_\lambda, \mathsf{Dec}_\lambda, \mathsf{Eval}_\lambda, \mathsf{RandEval}_\lambda\}_{\lambda \in \mathbb{N}}$ be an sFHE scheme with the randomness space $\mathcal{R}$ satisfying NC^1-composable CPA security and $\mathsf{AC}^0_{\mathsf{CM}}[2]$-randomness homomorphism. Let $\mathsf{ORNIZK} = \{\mathsf{ORGen}_\lambda, \mathsf{ORTGen}_\lambda, \mathsf{ORProve}_\lambda, \mathsf{ORVer}_\lambda, \mathsf{ORSim}_\lambda\}_{\lambda \in \mathbb{N}}$ be a NIZK for distributions $\{\mathcal{D}^{\mathsf{or}}_\lambda\}_{\lambda \in \mathbb{N}}$ defining the language $L^{\mathsf{valid}}_\mathbf{M}$ and $\mathsf{LNIZK} = \{\mathsf{Gen}_\lambda, \mathsf{TGen}_\lambda, \mathsf{Prove}_\lambda, \mathsf{Ver}_\lambda, \mathsf{Sim}_\lambda\}_{\lambda \in \mathbb{N}}$ be a NIZK for a distribution $\{\mathcal{D}_\lambda\}_{\lambda \in \mathbb{N}}$ defining $L^1_\mathbf{M}$ (see the remark in Sect. 7.2 for $L^{\mathsf{valid}}_\mathbf{M}$ and $L^1_\mathbf{M}$). We give our NIZK for $\{\mathcal{AD}_\lambda\}_{\lambda \in \mathbb{N}}$ in Fig. 9.

Theorem 6. *If $\mathsf{NC}^1 \subsetneq \oplus\mathsf{L}/\mathsf{poly}$, LNIZK and ORNIZK are $\mathsf{AC}^0[2]$-NIZKs with perfect soundness and NC^1-composable zero-knowledge, and sFHE is an $\mathsf{AC}^0[2]$-sFHE for $\mathsf{AC}^0_{\mathsf{CM}}[2]$ circuits with NC^1-composable CPA security and strong homomorphism, then NCNIZK^* is an $\mathsf{AC}^0[2]$-NIZK with perfect soundness and NC^1-composable zero-knowledge.*

Proof. First, we note that $\{\mathsf{NCGen}_\lambda, \mathsf{NCTGen}_\lambda, \mathsf{NCProve}_\lambda, \mathsf{NCVer}_\lambda, \mathsf{NCSim}_\lambda\}_{\lambda \in \mathbb{N}}$ are computable in $\mathsf{AC}^0[2]$, since they only involve operations including multiplications of a constant number of matrices, sampling random bits, and running $\mathsf{LNIZK}, \mathsf{ORNIZK}$, and homomorphic evaluation for $R_\rho(x, \cdot) \in \mathsf{AC}^0_{\mathsf{CM}}[2]$ is computable in $\mathsf{AC}^0[2]$. Notice that the prover can generate ciphertexts and run ORNIZK for each input wire in parallel, and the verifier can check the proofs in parallel.

Completeness. Due to the strong homomorphism of sFHE, we must have $\mathsf{ct}_{\mathsf{out}} = \mathsf{Enc}_\lambda(\mathsf{pk}, 1; r_{\mathsf{out}}) \in L^1_\mathbf{M}$ when w is a valid witness and $\mathsf{ct}_{\mathsf{out}}$ and r_{out} are honestly generated. Then the completeness of NCNIZK^* follows immediately from the completeness of LNIZK and ORNIZK.

NC^1-composable Zero-Knowledge. The indistinguishability of CRSs generated by NCGen_λ and NCTGen_λ follows immediately from Lemma 2, the composable zero-knowledge of LNIZK and ORNIZK, and the composable CPA security of sFHE.

Next we define a modified prover $\mathsf{NCProve}'_\lambda$, which is exactly the same as $\mathsf{NCProve}_\lambda$ except that for each $i \in [n]$, π^{valid}_i is generated as $\pi^{\mathsf{valid}}_i \xleftarrow{\$} \mathsf{ORSim}_\lambda(\mathsf{crs}_{\mathsf{or}}, \mathsf{td}_{\mathsf{or}}, \mathsf{pk}, \mathsf{ct}_i)$ and π_{out} is generated as $\pi_{\mathsf{out}} \xleftarrow{\$} \mathsf{Sim}_\lambda(\mathsf{crs}, \mathsf{td}, \mathsf{pk}, \mathsf{ct}_{\mathsf{out}})$. Then the following distributions are identical due to the composable zero-knowledge of ORNIZK and LNIZK.

$$\Pi \xleftarrow{\$} \mathsf{NCProve}_\lambda(\mathsf{CRS}, \rho, x, w) \text{ and } \Pi \xleftarrow{\$} \mathsf{NCProve}'_\lambda(\mathsf{CRS}, \rho, x, w),$$

for $(\mathsf{CRS}, \mathsf{TD}) \xleftarrow{\$} \mathsf{NCTGen}_\lambda$ and any (x, w) such that $R_\rho(x, w) = 1$.

Moreover, since the distribution of $\mathsf{ct}_i \leftarrow \mathsf{Enc}_\lambda(\mathsf{pk}, 0)$ is identical to that of $\mathsf{ct}_i \xleftarrow{\$} \mathsf{Enc}_\lambda(\mathsf{pk}, w_i)$ for $\mathsf{pk} \xleftarrow{\$} \mathsf{FHEGen}'_\lambda$, the distributions of

$$\Pi \xleftarrow{\$} \mathsf{NCProve}'_\lambda(\mathsf{CRS}, \rho, x, w) \text{ and } \Pi \xleftarrow{\$} \mathsf{NCSim}_\lambda(\mathsf{CRS}, \mathsf{TD}, \rho, x),$$

NCGen_λ:

$\mathsf{crs_{or}} \overset{\$}{\leftarrow} \mathsf{ORGen}_\lambda$, $\mathsf{crs} \overset{\$}{\leftarrow} \mathsf{Gen}_\lambda$, $(\mathsf{pk}, \mathsf{sk}) \overset{\$}{\leftarrow} \mathsf{FHEGen}_\lambda$

Return $\mathsf{CRS} = (\mathsf{crs_{or}}, \mathsf{crs}, \mathsf{pk})$

NCTGen_λ:

$(\mathsf{crs_{or}}, \mathsf{td_{or}}) \overset{\$}{\leftarrow} \mathsf{ORTGen}_\lambda$, $(\mathsf{crs}, \mathsf{td}) \overset{\$}{\leftarrow} \mathsf{TGen}_\lambda$, $\mathsf{pk} \overset{\$}{\leftarrow} \mathsf{FHEGen}'_\lambda$

Return $\mathsf{CRS} = (\mathsf{crs_{or}}, \mathsf{crs}, \mathsf{pk})$ and $\mathsf{TD} = (\mathsf{td_{or}}, \mathsf{td})$

$\mathsf{NCProve}_\lambda(\mathsf{CRS}, \rho, \mathsf{x}, \mathsf{w} = (\mathsf{w}_i)_{i=1}^n)$:

For $i = 1, \cdots, n$, compute

$\quad r_i \overset{\$}{\leftarrow} \mathcal{R}$, $\mathsf{ct}_i = \mathsf{Enc}_\lambda(\mathsf{pk}, \mathsf{w}_i; r_i)$, and $\pi_i^{\mathsf{valid}} \overset{\$}{\leftarrow} \mathsf{ORProve}_\lambda(\mathsf{crs_{or}}, \mathsf{pk}, \mathsf{ct}_i, r_i)$

Compute $\mathsf{ct_{out}} = \mathsf{Eval}_\lambda(\mathsf{pk}, \mathsf{R}_\rho(\mathsf{x}, \cdot), (\mathsf{ct}_1, \cdots, \mathsf{ct}_n))$

Compute $r_{\mathsf{out}} = \mathsf{RandEval}_\lambda(\mathsf{pk}, \mathsf{R}_\rho(\mathsf{x}, \cdot), (\mathsf{w}_1, \cdots, \mathsf{w}_n), (r_1, \cdots, r_n))$

Compute $\pi_{\mathsf{out}} \overset{\$}{\leftarrow} \mathsf{Prove}_\lambda(\mathsf{crs}, \mathsf{pk}, \mathsf{ct_{out}}, r_{\mathsf{out}})$

Return $\Pi = ((\mathsf{ct}_i)_{i=1}^n, (\pi_i^{\mathsf{valid}})_{i=1}^n, \pi_{\mathsf{out}})$

$\mathsf{NCVer}_\lambda(\mathsf{CRS}, \rho, \mathsf{x}, \Pi)$:

Compute $\mathsf{ct_{out}} = \mathsf{Eval}_\lambda(\mathsf{pk}, \mathsf{R}_\rho(\mathsf{x}, \cdot), (\mathsf{ct}_1, \cdots, \mathsf{ct}_n))$

Check the validity of all NIZK proofs and return 1 iff all checks pass

$\mathsf{NCSim}_\lambda(\mathsf{CRS}, \mathsf{TD}, \rho, \mathsf{x})$:

For $i = 1, \cdots, n$, compute $\mathsf{ct}_i \overset{\$}{\leftarrow} \mathsf{Enc}_\lambda(\mathsf{pk}, 0)$ and $\pi_i^{\mathsf{valid}} \overset{\$}{\leftarrow} \mathsf{ORSim}_\lambda(\mathsf{crs_{or}}, \mathsf{td_{or}}, \mathsf{pk}, \mathsf{ct}_i)$

Compute $\mathsf{ct_{out}} = \mathsf{Eval}_\lambda(\mathsf{pk}, \mathsf{R}_\rho(\mathsf{x}, \cdot), (\mathsf{ct}_1, \cdots, \mathsf{ct}_n))$ and $\pi_{\mathsf{out}} \overset{\$}{\leftarrow} \mathsf{Sim}_\lambda(\mathsf{crs}, \mathsf{td}, \mathsf{pk}, \mathsf{ct_{out}})$

Return $\Pi = ((\mathsf{ct}_i)_{i=1}^n, (\pi_i^{\mathsf{valid}})_{i=1}^n, \pi_{\mathsf{out}})$

Fig. 9. Definition of $\mathsf{NCNIZK}^* = \{\mathsf{NCGen}_\lambda, \mathsf{NCTGen}_\lambda, \mathsf{NCProve}_\lambda, \mathsf{NCVer}_\lambda, \mathsf{NCSim}_\lambda\}_{\lambda \in \mathbb{N}}$ for $\{\mathcal{AD}_\lambda\}_{\lambda \in \mathbb{N}}$.

where $(\mathsf{CRS}, \mathsf{TD}) \overset{\$}{\leftarrow} \mathsf{TGen}_\lambda$ and $\mathsf{R}_\rho(\mathsf{x}, \mathsf{w}) = 1$, are identical as well, completing the proof of composable zero-knowledge.

Perfect Soundness. Let $\Pi = ((\mathsf{ct}_i)_{i=1}^n, (\pi_i^{\mathsf{valid}})_{i=1}^n, \pi_{\mathsf{out}})$ be a valid proof for x. Due to the perfect soundness of ORNIZK and LNIZK, there must exist w_i and r_i such that $\mathsf{ct}_i = \mathsf{Enc}_\lambda(\mathsf{pk}, \mathsf{w}_i; r_i)$ for all i. Then we must have $\mathsf{Dec}_\lambda(\mathsf{sk}, \mathsf{ct_{out}}) = \mathsf{R}_\rho(\mathsf{x}, (\mathsf{w}_i)_{i=1}^n)$ for $\mathsf{ct_{out}} = \mathsf{Eval}_\lambda(\mathsf{pk}, \mathsf{R}_\rho(\mathsf{x}, \cdot), (\mathsf{ct}_1, \cdots, \mathsf{ct}_n))$, due to the homomorphism of sFHE. Moreover, due to the completeness of LNIZK, we have $\mathsf{ct_{out}} \in \mathsf{L}^1$, i.e., $\mathsf{Dec}_\lambda(\mathsf{sk}, \mathsf{ct_{out}}) = 1$. Therefore, we have $\mathsf{R}_\rho(\mathsf{x}, (\mathsf{w}_i)_{i=1}^n) = 1$, completing the proof of perfect soundness.

Putting all the above together, Theorem 4 immediately follows. □

Remark on the CRS. The size of CRS in NCNIZK^* can be further reduced, since we can let LNIZK and ORNIZK share a single matrix $\mathbf{A}$ such that $\mathbf{A}^\top \overset{\$}{\leftarrow} \mathsf{OneSamp}(\lambda)$ as their CRS, and use $\mathbf{A} + \mathbf{N}^\lambda$ as the public-key of the FHE since the distribution of $\mathbf{A} + \mathbf{N}^\lambda$ is identical to $\mathsf{ZeroSamp}(\lambda)$ according to Lemma 3.

8   Fine-Grained Non-Interactive Zap

In this section, we formally define verifiable correlated key generation, and show that all our fine-grained NIZKs have such type of key generation. Then we improve the framework in [12] to transform our NIZKs into zaps in the fine-grained setting.

8.1   Verifiable Correlated Key Generation

Definition 13 (Verifiable correlated key generation). *A C_1-NIZK* NIZK $= \{\mathsf{Gen}_\lambda, \mathsf{TGen}_\lambda, \mathsf{Prove}_\lambda, \mathsf{Ver}_\lambda, \mathsf{Sim}_\lambda\}_{\lambda \in \mathbb{N}}$ *has verifiable correlated key generation if there exists a function family* $\{\mathsf{Convert}_\lambda, \mathsf{Check}_\lambda\}_{\lambda \in \mathbb{N}} \in C_1$ *such that*

1. *the distribution of* $\mathsf{Convert}_\lambda(\mathsf{crs}_0)$ *is identical to that of* crs_1, *where* $\mathsf{crs}_0 \overset{\$}{\leftarrow}$ Gen_λ *and* $(\mathsf{crs}_1, \mathsf{td}_1) \overset{\$}{\leftarrow} \mathsf{TGen}_\lambda$,
2. $\mathsf{Check}_\lambda(\mathsf{crs}_0, \mathsf{Convert}_\lambda(\mathsf{crs}_0)) = 1$ *for all* $\mathsf{crs}_0 \in \mathsf{Gen}_\lambda$, *and*
3. *for any* $\mathsf{crs}_0, \mathsf{crs}_1$ *(not necessarily in the support of* Gen_λ *or* TGen_λ*) such that* $\mathsf{Check}_\lambda(\mathsf{crs}_0, \mathsf{crs}_1) = 1$, *we have* $\mathsf{crs}_0 \in \mathsf{Gen}_\lambda$ *or* $\mathsf{crs}_1 \in \mathsf{Gen}_\lambda$.

Lemma 4. *LNIZK in Sect. 4 (see Fig. 5) and ORNIZK in Sect. 5 (see Fig. 6) have verifiable correlated key generation.*

Proof. For LNIZK and ORNIZK, where a binding (respectively, hiding) CRS consists only of a matrix sampled by $\mathsf{OneSamp}(\lambda)$ (respectively, $\mathsf{ZeroSamp}(\lambda)$), we define $\{\mathsf{Check}_\lambda\}_{\lambda \in \mathbb{N}}$ and $\{\mathsf{Convert}_\lambda\}_{\lambda \in \mathbb{N}}$ as in Fig. 10.

$\mathsf{Convert}_\lambda(\mathbf{A}_0)$:	$\mathsf{Check}_\lambda(\mathbf{A}_0, \mathbf{A}_1)$:
$\mathbf{A}_1 = \mathbf{A}_0 + \mathbf{N}_\lambda$	Return 1 iff $\mathbf{N}_\lambda = \mathbf{A}_0 + \mathbf{A}_1$ and $(\mathbf{e}_1^\lambda \| \overline{\mathbf{A}_0}^\top) \in \mathsf{LSamp}(\lambda)$

Fig. 10. Definitions of $\{\mathsf{Check}_\lambda\}_{\lambda \in \mathbb{N}}$ and $\{\mathsf{Convert}_\lambda\}_{\lambda \in \mathbb{N}}$ for LNIZK and ORNIZK. See Sect. 2 for the definitions of $\mathbf{e}_i^\lambda$, $\mathbf{N}_\lambda$, and LSamp.

First we note that $\{\mathsf{Convert}_\lambda\}_{\lambda \in \mathbb{N}} \in \mathsf{AC}^0[2]$ and $\{\mathsf{Check}_\lambda\}_{\lambda \in \mathbb{N}} \in \mathsf{AC}^0[2]$ since they only involve addition of matrices and it is straightforward that checking whether $(\mathbf{e}_1^\lambda \| \overline{\mathbf{A}_0}^\top) \in \mathsf{LSamp}(\lambda)$ is in $\mathsf{AC}^0[2]$.

For $\mathbf{A}_0^\top \overset{\$}{\leftarrow} \mathsf{OneSamp}(\lambda)$ and $\mathbf{A}_1^\top \overset{\$}{\leftarrow} \mathsf{ZeroSamp}(\lambda)$, the distributions of $\mathbf{A}_0 + \mathbf{N}_\lambda$ and $\mathbf{A}_1$ are identical due to Lemma 3. Thus, the first condition in Definition 13 is satisfied.

We now generate $\mathbf{A}_0^\top$ explicitly by sampling $(\mathbf{e}_1^\lambda \| \widehat{\mathbf{R}}) \overset{\$}{\leftarrow} \mathsf{LSamp}(\lambda)$ and $\begin{pmatrix} \mathbf{I}_{\lambda-1} & \widetilde{\mathbf{r}} \\ \mathbf{0} & 1 \end{pmatrix} \overset{\$}{\leftarrow} \mathsf{RSamp}(\lambda)$ and computing $\mathbf{A}_0^\top = \mathbf{R}_0 \mathbf{M}_1^\lambda \mathbf{R}_1$. In this case,

$$\mathbf{A}_0^\top = (\mathbf{e}_1^\lambda \| \widehat{\mathbf{R}}) \begin{pmatrix} \mathbf{0} & 1 \\ \mathbf{I}_{\lambda-1} & \mathbf{0} \end{pmatrix} \begin{pmatrix} \mathbf{I}_{\lambda-1} & \widetilde{\mathbf{r}} \\ \mathbf{0} & 1 \end{pmatrix} = (\mathbf{e}_1^\lambda \| \widehat{\mathbf{R}}) \begin{pmatrix} \mathbf{0} & 1 \\ \mathbf{I}_{\lambda-1} & \widetilde{\mathbf{r}} \end{pmatrix} = (\widehat{\mathbf{R}} \| \widehat{\mathbf{R}} \widetilde{\mathbf{r}}) + \mathbf{N}_\lambda^\top,$$

i.e., $\overline{\mathbf{A}_0} = \widehat{\mathbf{R}}^\top$. Hence, we must have $(\mathbf{e}_1^\lambda \| \overline{\mathbf{A}_0}^\top) \in \mathsf{LSamp}(\lambda)$ for $\mathbf{A}_0^\top \in \mathsf{OneSamp}(\lambda)$. Moreover, for $\mathbf{A}_1 = \mathbf{A}_0 + \mathbf{N}_\lambda$ we have $\mathbf{N}_\lambda = \mathbf{A}_0 + \mathbf{A}_1$. Hence, the second condition in Definition 13 is satisfied.

According to the above arguments, for $\mathbf{A}_0$ such that $(\mathbf{e}_1^\lambda \| \overline{\mathbf{A}_0}^\top) \in \mathsf{LSamp}(\lambda)$, if $\underline{\mathbf{A}_0}^\top \in \mathsf{Im}(\overline{\mathbf{A}_0}^\top)$, i.e., there exists $\widetilde{\mathbf{r}} \in \{0,1\}^{\lambda-1}$ such that $\underline{\mathbf{A}_0}^\top = \overline{\mathbf{A}_0}^\top \widetilde{\mathbf{r}}$, then $\mathbf{A}_0^\top + \mathbf{N}_\lambda^\top \in \mathsf{OneSamp}(\lambda)$. If $\underline{\mathbf{A}_0}^\top \notin \mathsf{Im}(\overline{\mathbf{A}_0}^\top)$, we must have $(\overline{\mathbf{A}_0}^\top \| \mathbf{e}_1^\lambda) \begin{pmatrix} \widetilde{\mathbf{r}} \\ 1 \end{pmatrix} = \underline{\mathbf{A}_0}^\top$ for some $\widetilde{\mathbf{r}} \in \{0,1\}^{\lambda-1}$, since $(\overline{\mathbf{A}_0}^\top \| \mathbf{e}_1^\lambda)$ is of full rank and $(\overline{\mathbf{A}_0}^\top \| \mathbf{e}_1^\lambda) \begin{pmatrix} \widetilde{\mathbf{r}} \\ 0 \end{pmatrix} \neq \underline{\mathbf{A}_0}^\top$ for any $\widetilde{\mathbf{r}}$. Since $(\overline{\mathbf{A}_0}^\top \| \mathbf{e}_1^\lambda) \begin{pmatrix} \widetilde{\mathbf{r}} \\ 1 \end{pmatrix} = \underline{\mathbf{A}_0}^\top$ (equivalently, $\underline{\mathbf{A}_0} = \widetilde{\mathbf{r}}^\top \overline{\mathbf{A}_0} + \mathbf{e}_1^{\lambda\top}$) implies $\mathbf{A}_0 = \begin{pmatrix} \overline{\mathbf{A}_0} \\ \widetilde{\mathbf{r}}^\top \overline{\mathbf{A}_0} \end{pmatrix} + \mathbf{N}_\lambda$, we have $\mathbf{A}_0^\top \in \mathsf{OneSamp}(\lambda)$. As a result, either $\mathbf{A}_0^\top$ or $\mathbf{A}_1^\top$ must be in the support of $\mathsf{OneSamp}(\lambda)$ when $\mathbf{A}_0 + \mathbf{A}_1 = \mathbf{N}_\lambda$ and $(\mathbf{e}_1^\lambda \| \overline{\mathbf{A}_0}^\top) \in \mathsf{LSamp}(\lambda)$, i.e., the third condition is satisfied.

Putting all the above together, the proof of Lemma 4 immediately follows. □

Lemma 5. *NCNIZK and NCNIZK* in Sects. 6 and 7 (see Figs. 7 and 9) have verifiable correlated key generation if the underlying NIZKs ORNIZK have verifiable correlated key generation.*[3]

Let $\{\mathsf{Check}_\lambda\}_{\lambda \in \mathbb{N}} \in \mathsf{AC}^0[2]$ and $\{\mathsf{Convert}_\lambda\}_{\lambda \in \mathbb{N}} \in \mathsf{AC}^0[2]$ be the checking and converting algorithms for ORNIZK. For NCNIZK and NCNIZK*, we define $\{\mathsf{Check}'_\lambda\}_{\lambda \in \mathbb{N}}$ and $\{\mathsf{Convert}'_\lambda\}_{\lambda \in \mathbb{N}}$ as in Fig. 11.

The proof of Lemma 5 follows immediately from the verifiable correlated key generation of ORNIZK and the proof of Lemma 4. Notice that $\mathbf{M}$ is sampled from $\mathsf{ZeroSamp}(\lambda)$ rather than $\mathsf{OneSamp}(\lambda)$ in the CRS of NCNIZK. However, one can see that this does not make any essential difference and some minor changes on the proof of Lemma 4 is sufficient.

$\mathsf{Convert}'_\lambda(\mathsf{crs}_{\mathsf{or}}, \mathbf{M})$:	$\mathsf{Check}'_\lambda((\mathsf{crs}_{\mathsf{or}}, \mathbf{M}), (\mathsf{crs}'_{\mathsf{or}}, \mathbf{M}'))$:
$\mathsf{crs}'_{\mathsf{or}} = \mathsf{Convert}_\lambda(\mathsf{crs}_{\mathsf{or}})$ $\mathbf{M}' = \mathbf{M} + \mathbf{N}_\lambda$	Return 1 iff $\mathbf{N}_\lambda = \mathbf{M} + \mathbf{M}'$, $(\mathbf{e}_1^\lambda \| \overline{\mathbf{M}}^\top) \in \mathsf{LSamp}(\lambda)$, and $\mathsf{Check}_\lambda(\mathsf{crs}_{\mathsf{or}}, \mathsf{crs}'_{\mathsf{or}}) = 1$

Fig. 11. Definitions of $\{\mathsf{Check}'_\lambda\}_{\lambda \in \mathbb{N}}$ and $\{\mathsf{Convert}'_\lambda\}_{\lambda \in \mathbb{N}}$ for LNIZK and ORNIZK.

8.2 Construction of Fine-Grained Non-Interactive Zap

In this section, we give the transformation from NIZKs with verifiable correlated key generation to non-interactive zaps by using the technique in [12].

---

[3] As remarked in Sect. 7.3, we can make the CRS of NCNIZK* a single matrix in $\mathsf{OneSamp}(\lambda)$.

Let $\{\mathcal{D}_\lambda\}_{\lambda \in \mathbb{N}}$ be any family of language distributions such that for all $\rho \in \mathcal{ND}_\lambda$ and all $\mathsf{x} \in L_\rho$, we can run $\{R_\rho(\mathsf{x}, \cdot)\}_{\lambda \in \mathbb{N}}$ in NC^1, where L_ρ and R_ρ are the associated language and relation of ρ respectively. Let $\mathsf{NIZK} = \{\mathsf{Gen}_\lambda, \mathsf{TGen}_\lambda, \mathsf{Prove}_\lambda, \mathsf{Ver}_\lambda, \mathsf{Sim}_\lambda, \mathsf{Check}_\lambda, \mathsf{Convert}_\lambda\}_{\lambda \in \mathbb{N}}$ be a NIZK with verifiable correlated key generation for $\{\mathcal{D}_\lambda\}_{\lambda \in \mathbb{N}}$. We give a non-interactive zap $\mathsf{ZAP} = \{\mathsf{ZProve}_\lambda, \mathsf{ZVer}_\lambda\}_{\lambda \in \mathbb{N}}$ for $\{\mathcal{D}_\lambda\}_{\lambda \in \mathbb{N}}$ in Fig. 12.

$\mathsf{ZProve}_\lambda(\rho, \mathsf{x}, \mathsf{w})$:	$\mathsf{ZVer}_\lambda(\rho, \mathsf{x}, \pi)$:
$(\mathsf{crs}_0, \mathsf{td}_0) \xleftarrow{\$} \mathsf{TGen}_\lambda,\ \mathsf{crs}_1 = \mathsf{Convert}_\lambda(\mathsf{crs}_0)$	Return 1 iff
$\pi_0 \xleftarrow{\$} \mathsf{Prove}_\lambda(\mathsf{crs}_0, \rho, \mathsf{x}, \mathsf{w})$	$\mathsf{Check}_\lambda(\mathsf{crs}_0, \mathsf{crs}_1) = 1$
$\pi_1 \xleftarrow{\$} \mathsf{Prove}_\lambda(\mathsf{crs}_1, \rho, \mathsf{x}, \mathsf{w})$	$\mathsf{Ver}_\lambda(\mathsf{crs}_0, \rho, \mathsf{x}, \pi_0) = 1$
Return $\pi = (\mathsf{crs}_0, \mathsf{crs}_1, \pi_0, \pi_1)$	$\mathsf{Ver}_\lambda(\mathsf{crs}_1, \rho, \mathsf{x}, \pi_1) = 1$

Fig. 12. Definition of $\mathsf{ZAP} = \{\mathsf{ZProve}_\lambda, \mathsf{ZVer}_\lambda\}_{\lambda \in \mathbb{N}}$ for $\{\mathcal{D}_\lambda\}_{\lambda \in \mathbb{N}}$.

Theorem 7. *If NIZK is an NC^1-NIZK with NC^1-composable zero-knowledge, perfect soundness, and verifiable correlated key generation, then ZAP is an NC^1-non-interactive zap with perfect soundness and NC^1-witness indistinguishability.*

We refer the reader to the full paper for the security proof.

By instantiating the underlying NIZK with our NIZK in Sect. 6, we obtain an NC^1-non-interactive zap with NC^1-witness indistinguishability. Also, by using our NIZK for $\mathsf{AC}^0_{\mathsf{CM}}[2]$ in Sect. 7, we immediately achieve an $\mathsf{AC}^0[2]$-non-interactive zap for $\mathsf{AC}^0_{\mathsf{CM}}[2]$, while the proof is almost identical to that of Theorem 7. Similar argument can also be made for our NIZKs in the URS model in Sect. 9.

9   Fine-Grained NIZK in the URS Model

In this section, we extend our fine-grained NIZKs in the CRS model to ones in the URS model. We first show the existence of a public coin distribution that is identical to the output distributions of $\mathsf{ZeroSamp}(\lambda)$ and $\mathsf{OneSamp}(\lambda)$ with "half-half" probability, and then show how to convert our fine-grained NIZKs into ones in the URS model by exploiting this distribution.

Matrices Represented by Random Coins. Let $\mathbf{r} = (r_{1,2}, \cdots, r_{1,\lambda}, r_{2,3}, \cdots, r_{2,\lambda}, \cdots, r_{\lambda-1,\lambda}) \in \{0,1\}^{\lambda(\lambda-1)/2}$. We define the a function family $\{\mathsf{F}_\lambda\}_{\lambda \in \mathbb{N}}$ such that

$$\mathsf{F}_\lambda(\mathbf{r}) = \begin{pmatrix} r_{1,2} & \cdots & r_{1,\lambda-1} & r_{1,\lambda} \\ 1 & r_{2,3} & \cdots & r_{2,\lambda} \\ 0 & \ddots & & \vdots \\ \vdots & \ddots & 1 & r_{\lambda-1,\lambda} \\ 0 & \cdots & 0 & 1 \end{pmatrix}.$$

One can see that for uniform random $\mathbf{r} \xleftarrow{\$} \{0,1\}^{\lambda(\lambda-1)/2}$, the distribution of $\mathbf{e}_\lambda^\lambda \| \mathsf{F}_\lambda(\mathbf{r})$ is exactly the output distribution of $\mathsf{LSamp}(\lambda)$ in Fig. 2.

Lemma 6. *If* $\mathsf{NC}^1 \subsetneq \oplus\mathsf{L}/\mathsf{poly}$, *for any* $\{a_\lambda\}_{\lambda\in\mathbb{N}} \in \mathsf{NC}^1$, *we have*

$$|\Pr[a_\lambda(\mathsf{F}_\lambda(\mathbf{r})\|\mathbf{s}) = 1|\mathbf{r} \xleftarrow{\$} \{0,1\}^{\lambda(\lambda-1)/2}, \mathbf{s} \xleftarrow{\$} \{0,1\}^\lambda]$$
$$- \Pr[a_\lambda(\mathbf{M})|\mathbf{M} \xleftarrow{\$} \mathsf{ZeroSamp}(\lambda)]| \leq \mathsf{negl}(\lambda).$$

Proof. Let $\widetilde{\mathbf{r}} \xleftarrow{\$} \{0,1\}^{\lambda-1}$, $\mathbf{r} \xleftarrow{\$} \{0,1\}^{\lambda(\lambda-1)/2}$, $\mathbf{s} \xleftarrow{\$} \{0,1\}^\lambda$, and $b \xleftarrow{\$} \{0,1\}$. Since $\mathbf{e}_\lambda^\lambda\|\mathsf{F}_\lambda(\mathbf{r})$ is of full rank, the distribution of $\mathsf{F}_\lambda(\mathbf{r})\widetilde{\mathbf{r}} + \mathbf{e}_1^\lambda \cdot b$, where $\widetilde{\mathbf{r}} \xleftarrow{\$} \{0,1\}^{\lambda-1}$ and $b \xleftarrow{\$} \{0,1\}$, is uniform over $\{0,1\}^\lambda$. Moreover, since the distributions of

$$\mathsf{F}_\lambda(\mathbf{r})\|\mathsf{F}_\lambda(\mathbf{r})\widetilde{\mathbf{r}} = (\mathbf{e}_1^\lambda\|\mathsf{F}_\lambda(\mathbf{r})) \begin{pmatrix} \mathbf{0} & \mathbf{0} \\ \mathbf{I}_{\lambda-1} & \mathbf{0} \end{pmatrix} \begin{pmatrix} \mathbf{I}_{\lambda-1} & \widetilde{\mathbf{r}} \\ \mathbf{0} & 1 \end{pmatrix}$$

and

$$\mathsf{F}_\lambda(\mathbf{r})\|(\mathsf{F}_\lambda(\mathbf{r})\widetilde{\mathbf{r}} + \mathbf{e}_1^\lambda) = (\mathbf{e}_1^\lambda\|\mathsf{F}_\lambda(\mathbf{r})) \begin{pmatrix} \mathbf{0} & 1 \\ \mathbf{I}_{\lambda-1} & \mathbf{0} \end{pmatrix} \begin{pmatrix} \mathbf{I}_{\lambda-1} & \widetilde{\mathbf{r}} \\ \mathbf{0} & 1 \end{pmatrix}$$

are exactly the same as the output distributions of $\mathsf{ZeroSamp}(\lambda)$ and $\mathsf{OneSamp}(\lambda)$ respectively, the distribution of $\mathsf{F}_\lambda(\mathbf{r})\|\mathbf{s}$ is identical to $\mathsf{ZeroSamp}(\lambda)$ and $\mathsf{OneSamp}(\lambda)$ with probability $1/2$ (over the choice of b) respectively. Then Lemma 6 immediately follows from the fine-grained matrix linear assumption (see Lemma 2). □

One can see that the proof of Lemma 6 also implies the following lemma.

Lemma 7. *If* $\mathsf{NC}^1 \subsetneq \oplus\mathsf{L}/\mathsf{poly}$, *for* $\mathbf{r} \in \{0,1\}^{\lambda(\lambda-1)/2}$ *and* $\mathbf{s} \xleftarrow{\$} \{0,1\}^\lambda$, *we have*

$$\Pr[(\mathsf{F}_\lambda(\mathbf{r})\|\mathbf{s}) \in \mathsf{ZeroSamp}(\lambda)] = \Pr[(\mathsf{F}_\lambda(\mathbf{r})\|\mathbf{s}) \in \mathsf{OneSamp}(\lambda)] = 1/2.$$

Moreover, combining Lemmata 6 and 2 immediately yields the following corollary.

Corollary 1. *For any* $\{a_\lambda\}_{\lambda\in\mathbb{N}} \in \mathsf{NC}^1$, *we have*

$$|\Pr[a_\lambda(\mathsf{F}_\lambda(\mathbf{r})\|\mathbf{s}) = 1|\mathbf{r} \xleftarrow{\$} \{0,1\}^{\lambda(\lambda-1)/2}, \mathbf{s} \xleftarrow{\$} \{0,1\}^\lambda]$$
$$- \Pr[a_\lambda(\mathbf{M})|\mathbf{M} \xleftarrow{\$} \mathsf{OneSamp}(\lambda)]| \leq \mathsf{negl}(\lambda).$$

Constructions in the URS Model. Let n be some constant and $\mathsf{NIZK} = \{\mathsf{Gen}_\lambda, \mathsf{TGen}_\lambda, \mathsf{Prove}_\lambda, \mathsf{Ver}_\lambda, \mathsf{Sim}_\lambda\}_{\lambda\in\mathbb{N}}$ be a NIZK with perfect soundness and composable zero-knowledge, where each CRS consists of n matrices outputted by $\mathsf{ZeroSamp}(\lambda)$ or $\mathsf{OneSamp}(\lambda)$. We construct a statistical NIZK URSNIZK in the URS model as follows (Fig. 13).

$$
\begin{array}{|ll|}
\hline
\end{array}
$$

UGen_λ:	UTGen_λ:
For $i = 1, \cdots, \ell$	For $i = 1, \cdots, \ell$
$\quad$ For $j = 1, \cdots, n$	$\quad (\mathsf{crs}_i, \mathsf{td}_i) \overset{\$}{\leftarrow} \mathsf{TGen}_\lambda$
$\qquad \mathbf{r}_{ij} \overset{\$}{\leftarrow} \{0,1\}^{\lambda(\lambda-1)/2}, \ \mathbf{s}_{ij} \overset{\$}{\leftarrow} \{0,1\}^\lambda$	Let $((\mathsf{F}_\lambda(\mathbf{r}_{ij})\|\mathbf{s}_{ij})^\top)_{j=1}^n = \mathsf{crs}_i$
Return $\mathsf{urs} = ((\mathbf{r}_{ij}, \mathbf{s}_{ij})_{j=1}^n)_{i=1}^\ell$	Return $\mathsf{urs} = ((\mathbf{r}_{ij}, \mathbf{s}_{ij})_{j=1}^n)_{i=1}^\ell$
	and $\mathsf{td} = (\mathsf{td}_i)_{i=1}^\ell$
$\mathsf{UProve}_\lambda(\mathsf{urs}, \rho, \mathsf{x}, \mathsf{w})$:	
For $i = 1, \cdots, \ell$	$\mathsf{USim}_\lambda(\mathsf{urs}, \mathsf{td}, \rho, \mathsf{x})$:
$\quad \mathsf{crs}_i = ((\mathsf{F}_\lambda(\mathbf{r}_{ij})\|\mathbf{s}_{ij})^\top)_{j=1}^n$	For $i = 1, \cdots, \ell$
$\quad \pi_i \overset{\$}{\leftarrow} \mathsf{Prove}_\lambda(\mathsf{crs}_i, \rho, \mathsf{x}, \mathsf{w})$	$\quad \mathsf{crs}_i = ((\mathsf{F}_\lambda(\mathbf{r}_{ij})\|\mathbf{s}_{ij})^\top)_{j=1}^n$
Return $\pi = (\pi_i)_{i=1}^\ell$	$\quad \pi_i \overset{\$}{\leftarrow} \mathsf{Sim}_\lambda(\mathsf{crs}_i, \mathsf{td}_i, \rho, \mathsf{x})$
	Return $\pi = (\pi_i)_{i=1}^\ell$
$\mathsf{UVer}_\lambda(\mathsf{urs}, \rho, \mathsf{x}, \pi)$:	
For $i = 1, \cdots, \ell$, $\mathsf{crs}_i = ((\mathsf{F}_\lambda(\mathbf{r}_{ij})\|\mathbf{s}_{ij})^\top)_{j=1}^n$	
Return 1 iff $\mathsf{Ver}_\lambda(\mathsf{crs}_i, \rho, \mathsf{x}, \pi_i) = 1$ for all $i \in [\ell]$	

Fig. 13. Definition of $\mathsf{URSNIZK} = \{\mathsf{UGen}_\lambda, \mathsf{UTGen}_\lambda, \mathsf{UProve}_\lambda, \mathsf{UVer}_\lambda, \mathsf{USim}_\lambda\}_{\lambda \in \mathbb{N}}$ for $\{\mathcal{D}_\lambda\}_{\lambda \in \mathbb{N}}$. ℓ denotes some polynomial in λ and n is some constant.

Theorem 8. *If* $\mathsf{NC}^1 \subsetneq \oplus\mathsf{L}/\mathsf{poly}$ *and* NIZK *is an* NC^1-*NIZK for a set of language distributions* $\{\mathcal{D}_\lambda\}_{\lambda \in \mathbb{N}}$ *with perfect soundness and* NC^1-*composable zero-knowledge, then* $\mathsf{URSNIZK}$ *is an* NC^1-*NIZK for* $\{\mathcal{D}_\lambda\}_{\lambda \in \mathbb{N}}$ *in the URS model with statistical soundness and* NC^1-*composable zero-knowledge.*

The composable zero-knowledge of $\mathsf{URSNIZK}$ follows from that of NIZK and Lemma 6 and Corollary 1. Statistical soundness follows from the fact that among a sufficiently large number of CRSs, at least one of them should be binding with overwhelming probability according to Lemma 7. We refer the reader to the full paper for the formal proof.

References

1. Applebaum, B., Ishai, Y., Kushilevitz, E.: Cryptography in NC^0. In: 45th FOCS, pp. 166–175. IEEE Computer Society Press, October 2004
2. Ball, M., Dachman-Soled, D., Kulkarni, M.: New techniques for zero-knowledge: leveraging inefficient provers to reduce assumptions, interaction, and trust. In: Micciancio, D., Ristenpart, T. (eds.) CRYPTO 2020, Part III. LNCS, vol. 12172, pp. 674–703. Springer, Cham (2020). https://doi.org/10.1007/978-3-030-56877-1_24
3. Barrington, D.A.M.: Bounded-width polynomial-size branching programs recognize exactly those languages in NC^1. In: 18th ACM STOC, pp. 1–5. ACM Press, May 1986
4. Blum, M., Feldman, P., Micali, S.: Non-interactive zero-knowledge and its applications (extended abstract). In: 20th ACM STOC, pp. 103–112. ACM Press, May 1988
5. Campanelli, M., Gennaro, R.: Fine-grained secure computation. In: Beimel, A., Dziembowski, S. (eds.) TCC 2018, Part II. LNCS, vol. 11240, pp. 66–97. Springer, Cham (2018). https://doi.org/10.1007/978-3-030-03810-6_3

6. Couteau, G., Hartmann, D.: Shorter non-interactive zero-knowledge arguments and ZAPs for algebraic languages. In: Micciancio, D., Ristenpart, T. (eds.) CRYPTO 2020, Part III. LNCS, vol. 12172, pp. 768–798. Springer, Cham (2020). https://doi.org/10.1007/978-3-030-56877-1_27
7. Degwekar, A., Vaikuntanathan, V., Vasudevan, P.N.: Fine-grained cryptography. In: Robshaw, M., Katz, J. (eds.) CRYPTO 2016, Part III. LNCS, vol. 9816, pp. 533–562. Springer, Heidelberg (2016). https://doi.org/10.1007/978-3-662-53015-3_19
8. Dwork, C., Naor, M.: Zaps and their applications. In: 41st FOCS, pp. 283–293. IEEE Computer Society Press, November 2000
9. Egashira, S., Wang, Y., Tanaka, K.: Fine-grained cryptography revisited. J. Cryptol. **34**(3), 23 (2021)
10. Fiat, A., Shamir, A.: How to prove yourself: practical solutions to identification and signature problems. In: Odlyzko, A.M. (ed.) CRYPTO 1986. LNCS, vol. 263, pp. 186–194. Springer, Heidelberg (1987). https://doi.org/10.1007/3-540-47721-7_12
11. Goldwasser, S., Micali, S., Rackoff, C.: The knowledge complexity of interactive proof systems. SIAM J. Comput. **18**(1), 186–208 (1989)
12. Groth, J., Ostrovsky, R., Sahai, A.: New techniques for noninteractive zero-knowledge. J. ACM **59**(3), 11:1–11:35 (2012)
13. Groth, J., Sahai, A.: Efficient non-interactive proof systems for bilinear groups. In: Smart, N. (ed.) EUROCRYPT 2008. LNCS, vol. 4965, pp. 415–432. Springer, Heidelberg (2008). https://doi.org/10.1007/978-3-540-78967-3_24
14. Ishai, Y., Kushilevitz, E.: Randomizing polynomials: a new representation with applications to round-efficient secure computation. In: 41st FOCS, pp. 294–304. IEEE Computer Society Press, November 2000
15. Merkle, R.C.: Secure communications over insecure channels. Commun. ACM **21**(4), 294–299 (1978)
16. Pass, Rafael, shelat, abhi: Unconditional characterizations of non-interactive zero-knowledge. In: Shoup, Victor (ed.) CRYPTO 2005. LNCS, vol. 3621, pp. 118–134. Springer, Heidelberg (2005). https://doi.org/10.1007/11535218_8
17. Ràfols, C.: Stretching Groth-Sahai: NIZK proofs of partial satisfiability. In: Dodis, Y., Nielsen, J.B. (eds.) TCC 2015, Part II. LNCS, vol. 9015, pp. 247–276. Springer, Heidelberg (2015). https://doi.org/10.1007/978-3-662-46497-7_10
18. Razborov, A.A.: Lower bounds on the size of bounded depth circuits over a complete basis with logical addition. Math. Notes Acad. Sci. USSR **41**(4), 333–338 (1987)
19. Smolensky, R.: Algebraic methods in the theory of lower bounds for Boolean circuit complexity. In: Aho, A. (ed.) 19th ACM STOC, pp. 77–82. ACM Press, May 1987
20. Wang, Y., Pan, J., Chen, Y.: Fine-grained secure attribute-based encryption. In: Malkin, T., Peikert, C. (eds.) CRYPTO 2021, Part IV. LNCS, vol. 12828, pp. 179–207. Springer, Cham (2021). https://doi.org/10.1007/978-3-030-84259-8_7

On Succinct Non-interactive Arguments in Relativized Worlds

Megan Chen[1]([✉]), Alessandro Chiesa[2]([✉]), and Nicholas Spooner[3]

[1] Boston University, Boston, MA, USA
megchen@bu.edu
[2] EPFL, Lausanne, Switzerland
alessandro.chiesa@epfl.ch
[3] University of Warwick, Coventry, UK
Nicholas.Spooner@warwick.ac.uk

Abstract. Succinct non-interactive arguments of knowledge (SNARKs) are cryptographic proofs with strong efficiency properties. Applications of SNARKs often involve proving computations that include the SNARK verifier, a technique called recursive composition. Unfortunately, SNARKs with desirable features such as a transparent (public-coin) setup are known only in the random oracle model (ROM). In applications this oracle must be heuristically instantiated and used in a non-black-box way.

In this paper we identify a natural oracle model, the low-degree random oracle model, in which there exist transparent SNARKs for all NP computations *relative to this oracle*. Informally, letting $\mathcal{O}$ be a low-degree encoding of a random oracle, and assuming the existence of (standard-model) collision-resistant hash functions, there exist SNARKs relative to $\mathcal{O}$ for all languages in $\mathsf{NP}^{\mathcal{O}}$. Such a SNARK can directly prove a computation about its own verifier.

To analyze this model, we introduce a more general framework, the *linear code random oracle model* (LCROM).

We show how to obtain SNARKs in the LCROM for computations that query the oracle, given an *accumulation scheme* for oracle queries. Then we construct such an accumulation scheme for the special case of a low degree random oracle.

Keywords: Succinct non-interactive arguments · Random oracle model · Accumulation schemes

1 Introduction

Succinct non-interactive arguments (SNARGs) are short cryptographic proofs of NP computations. Many SNARG constructions also have the property of *succinct verification*: a SNARG proof can be verified faster than the original NP witness. This property leads to exciting applications, and one that has received much attention recently, and motivates this paper, is *recursive proof composition*.

Recursive proof composition is a general technique for "bootstrapping" a SNARG of knowledge (SNARK) into an *incremental* proof system for ongoing

© International Association for Cryptologic Research 2022
O. Dunkelman and S. Dziembowski (Eds.): EUROCRYPT 2022, LNCS 13276, pp. 336–366, 2022.
https://doi.org/10.1007/978-3-031-07085-3_12

computations [12]. This technique can be used to build incrementally-verifiable computation (IVC) [38] and proof-carrying data (PCD) [25]. The basic idea is relatively simple: to prove t steps of a computation, prove the NP statement "step t of the computation is correct, and there exists a proof of correctness for the previous $t − 1$ steps". Clearly this is an incremental proof: this statement depends only on a *single* step of the computation and the previous proof.

This technique is "recursive" in that it uses the SNARK to prove a statement *about its own verifier*. The succinct verification property ensures that the statement size can be bounded independently of t. This "non-black-box" use of the SNARK verifier leads to theoretical and practical issues, which we now discuss.

The first *efficient* approach to recursive composition [10] was based on a class of *pairing-based* SNARKs (which includes [13,27,29–31]) that are proven secure under knowledge assumptions or in the generic bilinear group model. This family of constructions yields extremely small proofs and highly efficient verification, but has two significant limitations.

First, all such constructions rely on a *secret setup*: sampling the structured reference string involves secret trapdoor values ("toxic waste") that can be used to attack the scheme. Hence the security of the system depends on these values being discarded—but this is difficult to ensure, even when accounting for the *cryptographic ceremonies* that researchers have designed to mitigate this sampling problem [2,9,16,17]. Second, efficient recursion for these SNARKs relies on *pairing-friendly cycles* of elliptic curves. Only a single construction of such cycles is known, and that cycle's curves have undesirable algebraic properties that weaken their security.

A flurry of recent work has focused on developing new techniques that avoid both of these drawbacks [15,18–20,24,33]. However, all of the proposed schemes share an unfortunate detail: they rely on proving statements about *computations that query random oracles*.

To see how this arises, we consider as an example the construction of [24] (the other schemes work in different ways but the issue is the same in each case). This work presents a SNARK that is secure in the random oracle model, and then applies the recursive composition technique to obtain IVC and PCD. This entails giving a SNARK proof about a verifier that queries the random oracle. It is not known whether there exist SNARKs for such computations in the random oracle model. To avoid this issue, [24] performs a *heuristic step*: they assume that there exists a concrete hash function which yields a secure SNARK when used in place of the random oracle. Under this assumption they obtain a SNARK in the standard model, which can be (provably) recursively composed. All of the cited constructions have similar heuristic steps.

This leads to a natural question: can we retain the benefits of these new constructions without this heuristic step? One approach would be to attempt to design better schemes in the standard or generic group models, but there has been little progress in this direction. In this work we propose a new approach: to build a SNARK in an oracle model which can prove statements *about its own oracle*. Such an oracle model admits a proof of security for recursive composition "within the model", without any heuristic step.

Of course, the resulting system is proven secure only in an idealized model. Nonetheless, we argue that a black-box security proof in an oracle model has several advantages.

- *Flexibility.* The heuristic step in prior constructions requires instantiating the oracle via an efficient circuit. This rules out certain oracle instantiations, such as multi-party protocols or hardware tokens. In contrast, any instantiation of the oracle is possible if the oracle is used as a black box by the construction.
- *Efficiency.* The random oracle is typically instantiated in practice via a concrete "unpredictable" hash function such as SHA-3 or BLAKE. Unfortunately, producing SNARKs about these functions is expensive. This has motivated a line of work on hash functions designed to be more efficient for SNARKs [3–6,28]. These new constructions have received far less scrutiny and cryptanalysis than standard hash functions. Our approach offers a possible alternative: if we can make only black-box use of the oracle, then we do not need to worry about an instantiation's "SNARK-friendliness".
- *Understanding security.* What should be the standard-model analogue of a security property in the ROM? Choosing the correct heuristic assumption is a balancing act between the requirements of the standard model proof and what can be justified by the idealized proof. There are typically *many* details here, and the precise choice of assumption can affect the validity of the result. In the worst case, security flaws might be hidden in the heuristic step! In contrast, security proofs in idealized models provide clear "end-to-end" guarantees. Finally, heuristic assumptions make it difficult to assess the concrete security of a scheme, while security proofs in idealized models often lead to concrete security expressions (the random oracle model is an excellent example of this).

1.1   Our Results

Our main result is to identify a natural oracle model, the low-degree random oracle model, in which there exist SNARKs for all NP computations *relative to the same oracle*. That is, there is a distribution over oracles $\mathcal{O}$ such that, assuming the existence of (standard-model) collision-resistant hash functions, there exist SNARKs relative to $\mathcal{O}$ for all languages in $\mathsf{NP}^{\mathcal{O}}$.

We first introduce a more general model we call the *linear code random oracle model*, and investigate its structural and cryptographic properties. We then describe our construction of SNARKs in the low-degree random oracle model. This construction makes use of an *accumulation scheme* for queries to the oracle, which we consider to be of independent interest. We now discuss these contributions in more detail.

(1) **Linear code random oracles.** We introduce the *linear code random oracle model* (LCROM) and study its structural and security properties. In the LCROM, all parties have oracle access to a codeword $\hat{\rho}$ sampled uniformly at random from a linear code $\mathcal{C} \subseteq (D \to \mathbb{F})$. We require that $\mathcal{C}$ have an associated efficient injective mapping $f \colon \{0,1\}^m \to D$ such that the restriction of $\hat{\rho}$ to

$\mathrm{im}(f)$ is distributed as a uniformly random function $\mathrm{im}(f) \to \mathbb{F}$. This property ensures that we can query the random oracle by querying $\hat{\rho} \circ f$. We show that, while there exist exponential separations between the two models, all linear code random oracles are collision-resistant within $\mathrm{im}(f)$.

A *low-degree random oracle* is a linear code random oracle where $\mathcal{C}$ is a Reed-Muller code: the space of evaluation tables of multivariate polynomials of bounded (individual) degree. The polynomial structure of this code is important in several ways. First, these oracles can be efficiently simulated, which directly implies that standard model computational assumptions continue to hold in this model. Second, it allows for possible concrete instantiations via structured PRFs (see Sect. 2.1). Finally, our accumulation scheme (and hence also our SNARK) relies on polynomial interpolation to perform query reduction.

(2) Transparent SNARKs in the low-degree random oracle model. We show that, if collision-resistant hash functions exist, there exist SNARKs in the low-degree random oracle model (LDROM) that can prove NP computations relative to the same oracle.

Theorem 1. *There exists a transparent SNARK in the LDROM for computations in the LDROM, assuming the existence of collision-resistant hash functions in the standard model.*

The result is obtained by combining a SNARK in the LDROM for NP computations *without* oracles and an *accumulation scheme* for oracle queries in the LDROM. For the former component we use Micali's construction of a SNARK in the random oracle model [35], whose security proof we adapt to the LDROM. The latter component is a new scheme and a key contribution of this work; we discuss this next.

(3) Accumulation scheme for low-degree random oracle queries. An accumulation scheme for an oracle θ is a primitive that allows a verifier, with the help of an untrusted prover, to "store" oracle queries in an *accumulator* that can be efficiently checked later by a *decider*. For non-triviality, we require that the verifier cannot query the oracle, and that the size of the accumulator and the query complexity of the decider be independent of the number of accumulated queries. This is a variation on the notion of accumulation schemes for *predicates* as introduced by [20].

In this work, we build an accumulation scheme for the low-degree random oracle. To do so, we build on a prior interactive query reduction protocol [21,32], which reduces any number of queries to a low-degree polynomial to a single query via interpolation. To obtain an accumulation scheme, we use a variant of the Fiat-Shamir transformation to make (a variant of) the query reduction protocol non-interactive; this introduces an additional oracle query which must also be accumulated. Proving security of the accumulation scheme is the most technically involved part of this paper, and requires developing new tools that we deem of independent interest; see Sect. 2.2 for more details.

1.2   Related Work

Below we summarize prior works related to idealized oracle models and accumulation schemes.

Generic Group Model. Shoup [36] introduced the generic group model (GGM), an model which represents a prime-order group via two oracles: a random injection $L\colon \mathbb{Z}_p \to \{0,1\}^k$ and a mapping from $(L(x), L(y))$ to $L(x+y)$. The generic bilinear group model (GBM), introduced by Boneh and Boyen [14], augments this with an oracle implementing a bilinear map. [39] shows that a generic group or generic bilinear group oracle can be used to construct a random oracle by taking $\rho(x)$ to be the first (say) $k/2$ bits of $L(x)$.[1] A natural question, that we leave open for future work, is whether there exist SNARKs in the GGM/GBM that can prove GGM/GBM computations.

Probabilistic Proofs in Relativized Worlds. Chiesa and Liu [23] give several impossibility results for probabilistic proofs in relativized worlds. They show that there do not exist nontrivial PCPs (or IOPs) for computations relative to a variety of types of oracle, including random oracles, generic group oracles, and, most relevant to us, random low-degree polynomial oracles. It is argued that these separations give evidence that SNARKs relative to these oracles do not exist. We view this work as a counterpoint: the LDROM does not admit efficient PCPs but *does* admit SNARKs (under a cryptographic assumption). This suggests that the relationship between PCPs and SNARKs in relativized worlds is more complex than previously thought.

Algebrization. The notion low-degree random oracles is reminiscent of the algebrization framework [1], introduced to understand the algebraic techniques used to prove non-relativizing results like $\mathsf{PSPACE} \subseteq \mathsf{IP}$. An example of an "algebrizing" inclusion is that for every oracle θ, $\mathsf{PSPACE}^\theta \subseteq \mathsf{IP}^{\hat{\theta}}$, where $\hat{\theta}$ is any low-degree extension of θ. Note that the left side of the containment is relative to the original oracle, whereas the right side is relative to $\hat{\theta}$. This is incomparable to our setting: on the one hand, we want the same low-degree oracle on "both sides"; on the other hand, our results hold only for specific choices of (distributions over) oracles. Nonetheless, some of our techniques for analyzing linear code random oracles are inspired by the study of algebraic query complexity in [1].

2   Techniques

We overview the main ideas behind our results. In Sect. 2.1 we introduce linear code random oracles, as well as the special case of low-degree random oracles. In Sect. 2.2 we describe an accumulation scheme for queries to a low-degree random oracle. Then we discuss technical tools that we use to establish the security of the accumulation scheme: in Sect. 2.3 a forking lemma for algorithms that query any linear code random oracle; and in Sect. 2.4 the hardness of a certain zero-finding game for low-degree random oracles. Finally, in Sect. 2.5 we describe our SNARK construction that relativizes in the random oracle model.

---

[1] This result is sensitive to the way that the generic group is modelled; in particular, it is not known to hold for the [34] formalization of the GGM.

2.1   Linear Code Random Oracles

We informally introduce the model of *linear code random oracles*, in which the oracle is a uniformly random codeword of a linear code. Then, we explain why collision resistance holds for the linear code random oracle. Finally we discuss a notable special case for this paper, low-degree random oracles.

Definition. The (standard) random oracle model considers the setting where every party (honest or malicious) is granted oracle access to the same random function. In this paper we consider the setting where every party is granted oracle access to the same random codeword sampled from a given linear code $\mathcal{C}$.

Recall that a linear code $\mathcal{C}$ is a subspace of the vector space of functions from a domain D to a field $\mathbb{F}$. A *linear code random oracle* is a codeword $\hat{\rho} \colon D \to \mathbb{F}$ chosen uniformly at random from the code $\mathcal{C}$.

For cryptographic applications, it will be helpful to impose an additional requirement on the code $\mathcal{C}$, which we call the "full-rank" condition. Intuitively, the full-rank condition ensures that there is an efficient embedding of the standard random oracle ρ in $\hat{\rho}$. More precisely, we require that $\mathcal{C}$ have an associated efficiently-computable injection $f \colon \{0,1\}^m \to D$ for some $m \in \mathbb{N}$ known as the *arity* of $(\mathcal{C}, f)$. We require that the restriction of $\mathcal{C}$ to the image of f has dimension 2^m (equivalently, $\mathcal{C}$ is systematic on $\mathrm{im}(f)$). This ensures that the function $\hat{\rho} \circ f \colon \{0,1\}^m \to \mathbb{F}$ is uniformly random when $\hat{\rho} \colon D \to \mathbb{F}$ is uniformly random in $\mathcal{C}$. In fact, we can view $\hat{\rho}$ as a (randomized) *systematic encoding* of the random oracle using $\mathcal{C}$.

Definition 1 (informal). *A* **linear code random oracle** $\hat{\rho}$ *is an oracle drawn uniformly at random from a full-rank linear code $\mathcal{C}$. A $\mathcal{C}$-oracle algorithm is an algorithm with oracle access to $c \in \mathcal{C}$. A systematic oracle algorithm is an oracle algorithm making queries in $\{0,1\}^m$.*

A systematic oracle algorithm is a $\mathcal{C}$-oracle algorithm for any full-rank $\mathcal{C}$ via the associated injection. If $\mathcal{C}$ is the space of all functions $\{0,1\}^m \to \mathbb{F}$ (and f is the identity) then we recover the standard random oracle.[2]

Query Complexity. We wish to understand what additional power is granted to the adversary by giving it access to an *encoding* of the random oracle.

A key difference between general linear code random oracles $\hat{\rho}$ and the standard random oracle ρ is that querying $\hat{\rho}$ outside of $\{0,1\}^m$ *can* yield information about evaluations inside $\{0,1\}^m$ that would otherwise be hard to obtain with a small number of queries. To illustrate this, consider the full-rank linear code $\mathcal{C} \subseteq \{0,1\}^m \cup \{\Sigma\} \to \mathbb{F}$ (for a special symbol Σ), consisting of all functions c such that $c(\Sigma) = \sum_{a \in \{0,1\}^m} c(a)$. Clearly, with oracle access to $c \in \mathcal{C}$, one can determine $\sum_{a \in \{0,1\}^m} c(a)$ with a single query. On the other hand, it is not hard to show that no algorithm making fewer than 2^m queries to the *standard* random oracle can compute this quantity.

---

[2] Setting $\mathbb{F}$ to be the field of size 2^λ yields the more familiar definition of a random oracle mapping $\{0,1\}^m \to \{0,1\}^\lambda$; for generality we prefer not to fix the field choice.

Hence in general there is an exponential gap in query complexity between a linear code random oracle model and the standard random oracle model. What about for problems of cryptographic interest? We show that linear code random oracles are collision-resistant; in fact, having access to an encoding of the random oracle using a linear code provides *no advantage* in collision finding.

Lemma 1. *Given oracle access to $\hat{\rho} \leftarrow \mathcal{C}$, a t-query adversary finds $x, y \in \{0, 1\}^m$ such that $\hat{\rho}(x) = \hat{\rho}(y)$ with probability at most $t^2 / |\mathbb{F}|$.*

Note that for this lemma to hold it is crucial that $\mathcal{C}$ be full-rank and that x, y are restricted to $\{0, 1\}^m$. Otherwise finding collisions may be very easy: consider the repetition code $\{(\alpha, \alpha) : \alpha \in \mathbb{F}\}$. We will make use of the collision-resistance property to prove security of our SNARK construction.

Low-Degree Random Oracles. Our protocols rely on a special class of linear code random oracles that we call *low-degree random oracles*, obtained by choosing $\mathcal{C}$ to be the space $\mathbb{F}^{\leq d}[X_1, \ldots, X_m]$ of m-variate polynomials over $\mathbb{F}$ of individual degree at most $d \in \mathbb{N}$, evaluated over the domain $\mathbb{F}^m$. This code is full-rank via the natural bijection between $\{0, 1\}^m$ and $\{0_\mathbb{F}, 1_\mathbb{F}\}^m \subseteq \mathbb{F}^m$, because the latter is an interpolating set for the space of multilinear polynomials.

There is an efficient and perfect stateful simulation of all low-degree random oracles (for polynomial m, d) [8]. This implies that low-degree random oracles do not grant any additional computational power; in particular, it does not impact any "standard model" cryptography. We will use this fact in Sect. 2.2, where our accumulation scheme will require a standard model collision-resistant hash function.

We briefly discuss the possibility of instantiating this model. Given that the low-degree random oracle can be simulated efficiently, it can at least be implemented by a trusted party or hardware token. A candidate cryptographic instantiation is to obfuscate the algebraic pseudorandom functions of Benabbas, Gennaro and Vahlis [11]. They construct a pseudorandom function $F \colon [d]^m \to \mathbb{G}$ (for group $\mathbb{G}$ of prime order p) that additionally allows, given the secret key, the efficient computation of group elements

$$P(x_1, \ldots, x_m) = \sum_{a \in [d]^m} F(a) \cdot x_1^{a_1} \cdots x_m^{a_m}$$

for $x_1, \ldots, x_m \in \mathbb{F}_p$. Note that if F is a random function then P is uniformly random in $\mathbb{F}_p^{\leq d}[X_1, \ldots, X_m]$.[3] Hence if F is pseudorandom, P is indistinguishable from a random polynomial.

Another natural instantiation strategy is to start with some "strong" hash function that we believe suffices to replace the random oracle in existing constructions, then arithmetize it to obtain a polynomial that extends the hash function. Of course, all of the security properties of the original hash function are maintained under this transformation. Unfortunately, directly arithmetizing a hash

---

[3] We view P as a polynomial over $\mathbb{F}_p$ via some isomorphism $\mathbb{G} \to \mathbb{F}_p$ (which need not be efficiently computable).

function yields a polynomial of quite high degree: approximately 2^D, where D is the circuit depth. The latter ranges from 25 to about 3000 for widely-used "strong" hash functions [37]. Since our SNARK construction involves proving a statement of size linear in the degree, this cost becomes prohibitive. While there exist techniques to reduce the degree of an arithmetization, these modify the function significantly so that it no longer behaves like a low-degree random oracle. We leave the question of instantiation via arithmetization to future work.

2.2 Accumulation Scheme for Low-Degree Random Oracles

We describe our construction of an accumulation scheme for accumulating queries to the low-degree random oracle. First we review the notion of an accumulation scheme. Then we describe an interactive protocol based on the query-reduction technique for IPCPs in [21,32], and how this leads, via the Fiat–Shamir transformation, to our accumulation scheme. We conclude by discussing the challenges of proving security, which motivates developing the new tools that we introduce in subsequent sections.

Review: Accumulation Schemes. We review the notion of an accumulation scheme [20], stated for an arbitrary oracle distribution (rather than specifically for the random oracle model) and specialized to the accumulation of oracle queries rather than general predicates.

Definition 1. *An* **accumulation scheme** *for queries to an oracle θ (sampled according to some distribution) is a triple of algorithms (P^θ, V, D^θ), known as the prover, verifier, and decider, that satisfies the following.*

- **Completeness:** *For all accumulators* acc *and query-answer pairs (x, α), if $D^\theta(\mathsf{acc}) = 1$ and $\theta(x) = \alpha$, then for $(\mathsf{acc}', \pi_V) \leftarrow P^\theta(x, \alpha, \mathsf{acc})$ it holds that $V(x, \alpha, \mathsf{acc}, \mathsf{acc}', \pi_V) = 1$ and $D^\theta(\mathsf{acc}') = 1$.*
- **Soundness:** *For efficiently generated accumulators* acc, acc', *query-answer pairs (x, α) and accumulation proofs π_V, if $D^\theta(\mathsf{acc}') = 1$ and $V(x, \alpha, \mathsf{acc}, \mathsf{acc}', \pi_V) = 1$ then $\theta(x) = \alpha$ and $D^\theta(\mathsf{acc}) = 1$ with all but negligible probability.*

The definition extends in a natural way to accumulate n query-answer pairs $[(x_i, \alpha_i)]_{i=1}^n$ and m old accumulators $[\mathsf{acc}_j]_{j=1}^\ell$, as in the formal in Sect. 3.3. For simplicity, below we present our accumulation scheme below for the case of general n and $m = 1$. Note that we do not grant the accumulation verifier V access to the oracle θ—this is a key requirement achieved by our construction and used in our applications.

Review: An Interactive Query Reduction Protocol. [32] describe an interactive query reduction protocol for interactive PCPs (IPCPs), a class of probabilistic proofs; subsequently, [21] adapted and simplified this protocol in their "low-degree" IPCP model. We recast this simplified protocol as an interactive query reduction protocol in the low-degree random oracle model.

Let $\hat{\rho}: \mathbb{F}^m \to \mathbb{F}$ be a polynomial of individual degree at most d (for now, $\hat{\rho}$ need not be random) and let $[q_i]_{i=1}^n = \{(x_1, \alpha_1), \ldots, (x_n, \alpha_n)\}$ be a list of (alleged) query-answer pairs. The prover $\mathcal{P}$ wishes to convince the verifier $\mathcal{V}$ that $\hat{\rho}(x_i) = \alpha_i$ for every $i \in [n]$, in a setting where both parties have oracle access to $\hat{\rho}$. While the verifier $\mathcal{V}$ can straightforwardly check this claim with n queries to $\hat{\rho}$ (and no help from the prover $\mathcal{P}$), the protocol below enables the verifier $\mathcal{V}$ to check this claim with a single query to $\hat{\rho}$ (up to some soundness error). Let $b_1, \ldots, b_n \in \mathbb{F}$ be a list of n distinct field elements, fixed in advance.

1. Both $\mathcal{P}$ and $\mathcal{V}$ compute the unique polynomial g of degree less than n such that $g(b_i) = x_i$ for all $i \in [n]$.
2. The prover $\mathcal{P}$ computes the composed polynomial $f := \hat{\rho} \circ g$, and sends $f: \mathbb{F} \to \mathbb{F}$ to the verifier.
3. The verifier $\mathcal{V}$ chooses a random $\beta \in \mathbb{F}$ and checks that $f(\beta) = \hat{\rho}(g(\beta))$ (by querying $\hat{\rho}$ at $g(\beta)$). Finally, the verifier $\mathcal{V}$ checks that $f(b_i) = \alpha_i$ for every $i \in [n]$.

Observe that $\hat{\rho} \circ g$ is a univariate polynomial of degree less than nmd, and so the communication complexity of this protocol is $O(nmd \cdot \log |\mathbb{F}|)$ bits. If the prover is honest, then $\hat{\rho}(x_i) = \hat{\rho}(g(b_i)) = f(b_i) = \alpha_i$ for every $i \in [n]$. On the other hand, if a cheating prover sends some polynomial $\tilde{f} \neq \hat{\rho} \circ g$, then $\tilde{f}(\beta) \neq \hat{\rho}(g(\beta))$ with probability $1 - \frac{nmd}{|\mathbb{F}|}$ over the choice of $\beta \in \mathbb{F}$, in which case the verifier rejects.

Our Accumulation Scheme. We construct an accumulation scheme for accumulating queries to the low-degree random oracle, based on the above query reduction protocol. At a high level, the accumulation prover and verifier engage in the above query reduction protocol, except that rather than directly checking that $\tilde{f}(\beta) = \hat{\rho}(g(\beta))$, the prover outputs the new accumulator $\mathsf{acc}' := (g(\beta), \tilde{f}(\beta))$ containing the query $g(\beta)$ and claimed answer $\tilde{f}(\beta)$. The decider can check that acc' contains a valid query-answer pair with a single query to the oracle $\hat{\rho}$. Notice that because an accumulator consists of a query-answer pair, we can simply include the old accumulator in the input to the query reduction protocol as an extra pair (x_{n+1}, α_{n+1}).

The challenge now is that an accumulation scheme is a non-interactive protocol while the above query-reduction protocol is interactive. Superficially, achieving non-interactivity appears to be a standard application of the Fiat–Shamir transform [26] because the interactive query-reduction protocol is public-coin. That is, since a low-degree random oracle $\hat{\rho}$ embeds a (standard) random oracle, the accumulation prover can use that random oracle to generate the verifier's random challenge β from the composed polynomial f as $\beta := \hat{\rho}(x_1, \ldots, x_{n+1}, f)$ (the embedding from binary strings into the domain of $\hat{\rho}$ is implicit). Note that we include $x_1, \ldots, x_{n+1}$ as input to $\hat{\rho}$ to achieve adaptive security. However, this setting is quite different from the familiar one for Fiat–Shamir: (i) the original interactive protocol already involves the oracle; (ii) the oracle is a random low-degree oracle rather than a standard random oracle; and (iii) the accumulation verifier cannot query $\hat{\rho}$! We discuss the latter point in more detail next, since resolving it requires modifying the construction; the other two points will be addressed later when we discuss the security proof.

Since the accumulation verifier is not allowed to query the oracle (this is the point of designing an accumulation scheme for oracle queries), it cannot check the query-answer pair $((x_1, \ldots, x_{n+1}, f), \beta)$ for correctness. The natural approach is to store the pair $((x_1, \ldots, x_{n+1}, f), \beta)$ in the accumulator, so that an accumulator contains an additional query-answer pair (x_{n+2}, α_{n+2}). Unfortunately, this results in the length of the Fiat–Shamir query, and hence the accumulator, increasing without bound (it will simply contain all accumulated queries). To address this, we rely on a succinct commitment scheme Commit, and derive the challenge as $\beta := \hat{\rho}(C)$ for $C := \mathsf{Commit}(x_1, \ldots, x_{n+2}, f)$ instead. This ensures that the query to derive the challenge β does not grow in size with each accumulation.

These considerations lead us to design the following accumulation scheme.

- *Accumulation prover:* P receives as input an old accumulator acc and a list of query-answer pairs $[(x_i, \alpha_i)]_{i=1}^n$, and outputs a new accumulator acc' and accumulation proof π_V computed as follows.
  1. *Query-answer list.* The old accumulator acc consists of two query-answer pairs, which we denote by (x_{n+1}, α_{n+1}) and (x_{n+2}, α_{n+2}). Set the query-answer list $Q := [(x_i, \alpha_i)]_{i=1}^{n+2}$.
  2. *Interpolate queries.* Compute the unique polynomial $g \colon \mathbb{F} \to \mathbb{F}^m$ of degree less than $n + 2$ such that $g(b_i) = x_i$ for all $i \in [n + 2]$.
  3. *Compose polynomials.* Compute the polynomial $f := \hat{\rho} \circ g$.
  4. *Commit to polynomials.* Compute the commitment $C := \mathsf{Commit}(x_1, \ldots, x_{n+2}, f)$.
  5. *Fiat–Shamir challenge.* Compute the challenge $\beta := \hat{\rho}(C) \in \mathbb{F}$.
  6. *Output.* Output the new accumulator acc' $:= \{(g(\beta), f(\beta)), (C, \beta)\}$ and accumulation proof $\pi_\mathsf{V} := f$.
- *Accumulation verifier:* V receives as input $([\mathsf{q}_i]_{i=1}^n, \mathsf{acc}, \mathsf{acc}', \pi_\mathsf{V})$, where acc' $= \{(x, \alpha), (C', \beta)\}$, and works as follows. Compute the query-answer list Q as in Step 1 of the prover, the polynomial g as in Step 2 of the prover and the commitment C as in Step 3 of the prover. Then check that $C' = C$, $f(b_i) = \alpha_i$ for all $i \in [n + 2]$, $x = g(\beta)$, and $\alpha = f(\beta)$.
- *Decider:* D checks that the input accumulator acc $= \{(x, \alpha), (C, \beta)\}$ satisfies $\alpha = \hat{\rho}(x)$ and $\beta = \hat{\rho}(C)$.

Intuitively, the accumulation scheme is secure against efficient attackers because the binding property of the commitment scheme ensures that setting the challenge β to $\hat{\rho}(C)$ is as good as $\hat{\rho}(x_1, \ldots, x_{n+2}, f)$, and the latter gives a random challenge based on the prover's first message of the interactive query-reduction protocol.

We remark that the commitment scheme is the *only* part of the construction that uses cryptography outside of the oracle (i.e., is not information theoretic).

Zero-Knowledge. Zero-knowledge for an accumulation scheme means that there exists a simulator that can sample a new accumulator $\mathsf{acc}_i = \{(x, \alpha),$

$(C, \beta)\}$, without access to inputs $[q_i]_{i=1}^n$ or an old accumulator acc_{i-1}. The accumulation scheme described above is *not* zero knowledge, because acc_i includes the value $g(\beta)$, which depends on $[q_i]_{i=1}^n$ and acc_{i-1}. To remedy this, we modify the accumulation scheme so that the prover P additionally accumulates a random query $x_{n+3} \in \mathbb{F}^m$. This ensures that $g(\beta)$ is uniformly random in $\mathbb{F}^m$.[4] We also require Commit to be a hiding commitment, and include the commitment randomness in π_V.

Finally, we note that if zero-knowledge is *not* required, then the commitment scheme used by the prover to obtain C does not need to be hiding; in this case a collision-resistant hash function suffices.

How to Prove Security? Proving the security of the above accumulation scheme is not straightforward, despite the intuition that underlies its design. The main difficulty is that existing tools for establishing security work for standard random oracles rather than low-degree random oracles (e.g., security analyses of the Fiat–Shamir transform). We develop new tools to overcome the above problems. We formulate a *zero-finding game lemma for low-degree random oracles*, which shows that it is computationally hard for an adversary to find $f \not\equiv \hat{\rho} \circ g$ such that $f(z) = (\hat{\rho} \circ g)(z)$ for $z := \hat{\rho}(\mathsf{Commit}(x_1, \ldots, x_{n+2}, f))$. In order to prove this lemma, we additionally prove a *forking lemma for algorithms that query any linear code random oracle*. We discuss these next: first our forking lemma in Sect. 2.3, and then our zero-finding game lemma in Sect. 2.4.

2.3   A Forking Lemma for Linear Code Random Oracles

We review a forking lemma for the standard random oracle, and then describe a new forking lemma for any linear code random oracle.

Review: A Forking Lemma for Random Oracles. In cryptography a forking lemma relates the probability of an adversary winning some game in multiple related executions, as a function of the adversary's winning probability in a single execution. Below we describe a forking lemma (based on [7]) that considers the setting of non-interactive protocols with forks of size 2 via algorithms that run in strict time.[5]

---

[4] Both [32] and [21] also add a random point to the curve. In contrast to our construction, in both cases this point is added by the *verifier* to ensure soundness: the query-reduction protocol is composed with a low-degree test, whose proximity guarantee holds only with respect to a uniform query. In our setting, the oracle is guaranteed to be low degree.

[5] The cryptography literature contains several types of forking lemmas, depending on aspects such as: (i) they apply to interactive protocols (without any oracles) or non-interactive protocols (in the random oracle model); (ii) they have a fork of size 2, or any size; (iii) the forking algorithm runs in strict time or expected time. The specific setting that we study is motivated by the present application, though we expect that the ideas for linear code random oracles that we introduce will extend to other settings as well.

Let p be a predicate that captures the winning condition. Consider an adversary $\mathcal{A}$ that queries the random oracle t times and produces an output (q, o) such that $p(q, o, tr) = 1$ with probability δ, where $tr = \{(q_1, \alpha_1), \ldots, (q_t, \alpha_t)\}$ are the query-answer pairs of $\mathcal{A}$. We think of q as the adversary's "chosen" query, and o as some additional input to the predicate p.

Now suppose that we additionally run $\mathcal{A}$ in a *forked* execution. Let $i := FP(q, tr) \in [t]$ be the location of the query q in its query-answer list tr (abort if q does not appear in tr). Consider the *forking algorithm* Fork that, given access to $\mathcal{A}$ and input (tr, i), works as follows: (i) run $\mathcal{A}$ answering the first $i-1$ queries to the random oracle according to tr; (ii) answer subsequent queries uniformly at random; (iii) output the output (q', o') of $\mathcal{A}$ and the query transcript tr' induced by this execution of $\mathcal{A}$.

The forking lemma below gives a lower bound on the probability that: (1) $p(q, o, tr) = 1$ ($\mathcal{A}$ wins the original game); (2) $p(q', o', tr') = 1$ ($\mathcal{A}$ wins the game in the forked execution); (3) $q = q'$ (the queries output by $\mathcal{A}$ in the two related executions are equal).[6]

Lemma 1. *Suppose that $\mathcal{A}$ is a t-query random oracle algorithm such that*

$$\delta := \Pr_\rho \left[p(q, o, tr) = 1 \mid (q, o; tr) \leftarrow \mathcal{A}^\rho \right] \ .$$

Then

$$\Pr_\rho \left[\begin{array}{c} q = q' \\ \wedge \ p(q, o, tr) = 1 \\ \wedge \ p(q', o', tr') = 1 \end{array} \ \middle| \ \begin{array}{c} (q, o; tr) \leftarrow \mathcal{A}^\rho \\ i \leftarrow FP(q, tr) \\ (q', o', tr') \leftarrow Fork^{\mathcal{A}}(tr, i) \end{array} \right] \geq \delta^2 / t \ .$$

Extending the Forking Lemma to any Linear Code Random Oracle. When extending Lemma 1 to the linear code random oracle setting, a key difficulty is choosing the *fork point i*. The role of the fork point is to ensure that the answer to query q is resampled in the fork, while all prior queries stay the same. For the standard random oracle case, this point is easy to find: it is simply the index of the query q.

Contrastingly, for linear code random oracles, recall from Sect. 2.1 that $\mathcal{A}$ may learn the evaluation of unqueried points due to the structure of the code (e.g., if the code is locally decodable). This makes it unclear at which query $\mathcal{A}$ learns the value of $\hat{\rho}(q)$, or even if a single such query exists at all! We show that the linear structure of the code $\mathcal{C}$ implies that there does exist a query q_i at which $\mathcal{A}$ first learns the value of $\hat{\rho}$ at q (and before that $\mathcal{A}$ knows nothing about it); we define $FP_{\mathcal{C}}(q, tr) := i$.

Can $FP_{\mathcal{C}}$ be efficiently computed? Note that $\mathcal{A}$ may try to obfuscate the fork point by trying to learn $\hat{\rho}(q)$ in some complicated way via the structure of the code. The problem of finding the fork point can be solved via *constraint detection*

---

[6] The bound that appears in [7] is $\geq \frac{\delta^2}{t} - negl(\lambda)$. The negligible term arises from the additional condition that $tr(q) \neq tr'(q)$. Our applications of the forking lemma refer directly to the distribution of $tr'(q)$ and so we do not need this explicit condition.

[8]: the fork point is the first query i at which there is a linear constraint over the set $\{\hat{\rho}(q_1), \ldots, \hat{\rho}(q_i), \hat{\rho}(q)\}$. For low-degree random oracles, we can implement FP_C efficiently using the efficient constraint detection algorithm for Reed–Muller codes of [8]. For many interesting linear codes, efficient constraint detection is an open problem.

To state the forking lemma requires one additional consideration. Strictly speaking, Lemma 1 holds only for adversaries that do not repeat queries (otherwise the adversary can distinguish a fork from the original execution), which is without loss of generality. In the LCROM, this restriction is not enough: the structure of the code might allow an adversary to learn a single query point in a variety of ways. Instead we must restrict our adversary further, so that it does not make any query *whose answer it can already infer*. Any adversary can be converted into a non-redundant adversary via constraint detection; hence we assume non-redundancy for efficient adversaries if C has efficient constraint detection. Due to this complication we prefer to state the non-redundancy condition explicitly in our forking lemma below.

Lemma 2. *Let $\hat{\rho} \leftarrow C$ be a linear code random oracle. Suppose that A is a t-query non-redundant C-oracle algorithm such that*

$$\delta := \Pr_{\hat{\rho}} \left[\mathsf{p}(\mathsf{q}, \mathsf{o}, \mathsf{tr}) = 1 \mid (\mathsf{q}, \mathsf{o}; \mathsf{tr}) \leftarrow A^{\hat{\rho}} \right] .$$

Then

$$\Pr_{\hat{\rho}} \left[\begin{matrix} \mathsf{q} = \mathsf{q}' \in \{0,1\}^m \\ \wedge\ \mathsf{p}(\mathsf{q}, \mathsf{o}, \mathsf{tr}) = 1 \\ \wedge\ \mathsf{p}(\mathsf{q}', \mathsf{o}', \mathsf{tr}') = 1 \end{matrix} \middle| \begin{matrix} (\mathsf{q}, \mathsf{o}; \mathsf{tr}) \leftarrow A^{\hat{\rho}} \\ i \leftarrow \mathsf{FP}_C(\mathsf{tr}, \mathsf{q}) \\ (\mathsf{q}', \mathsf{o}', \mathsf{tr}') \leftarrow \mathsf{Fork}(\mathsf{tr}, i) \end{matrix} \right] \geq \delta^2/t .$$

Note that the Fork algorithm here is *the same* as in Lemma 1, except that we choose the random answers from the alphabet $\mathbb{F}$ of C.

2.4   A Zero-Finding Game for Low-Degree Random Oracles

We review the zero-finding game for *standard* random oracles in [20], and then we describe our variant for *low-degree* random oracles.

Review: A Zero-Finding Game for the Standard Random Oracle. Bünz, Chiesa, Mishra, and Spooner [20] consider a *zero-finding game* where an efficient adversary A with query access to a random oracle ρ is challenged to output a commitment C and a non-zero polynomial $f \in \mathbb{F}^{\leq d}[X_1, \ldots, X_m]$ such that C is a commitment to f and $f(\rho(C)) = 0$. Intuitively, the binding property of the commitment scheme implies that A is unlikely to win the game because the polynomial f is "fixed" before A learns the value of $\rho(C)$, and so the probability that this value is a zero of f is small by the Schwartz–Zippel lemma. Indeed, [20] shows that every efficient adversary A that makes at most t queries to ρ wins with probability at most negligibly more than $\sqrt{(t+1)md/|\mathbb{F}|}$ (note that md is the total degree of f).

Their proof is based on the forking lemma for the standard random oracle (Lemma 1), as we now sketch. We define the forking lemma predicate $p(q, f, tr)$ to be satisfied if and only if: (i) $f \not\equiv 0$; (ii) $f(tr(q)) \neq 0$; and (iii) q is a commitment to f. By increasing the query complexity of $\mathcal{A}$ to $t + 1$ we can ensure that q is in the support of tr. It follows that if $\mathcal{A}$ wins the zero-finding game with probability δ, then it satisfies the premise of Lemma 1, and so the forking experiment succeeds with probability at least $\delta^2/(t + 1)$.

Suppose that the forking experiment succeeds: we obtain (q, f, f', tr, tr') such that f and f' are non-zero polynomials that are both valid openings of the same commitment q, and it holds that $f(tr(q)) \neq 0$ and $f'(tr'(q)) \neq 0$. In the forked execution, $tr'(q)$ is sampled uniformly at random independently of f, and so $\Pr[f(tr'(q)) = 0] \leq md/|\mathbb{F}|$. If $f = f'$ then the probability that $p(q, f', tr')$ is satisfied in this case is at most $md/|\mathbb{F}|$; if instead $f \neq f'$, then we break the commitment scheme, which can occur with at most negligible probability. Hence $\delta^2/(t + 1) \leq md/|\mathbb{F}| + \mathrm{negl}(\lambda)$; rearranging yields the bound.

A Zero-Finding Game for Low-Degree Random Oracles. We require a variant of the zero-finding game to prove security of our accumulation scheme from Sect. 2.2. In more detail, we want to bound the probability that an efficient adversary with query access to a low-degree random oracle $\hat{\rho}$ outputs a commitment C and two polynomials f, g such that: (1) C is a commitment to (f, g); (2) $f \not\equiv \hat{\rho} \circ g$; and (3) the oracle answer $z := \hat{\rho}(C)$ satisfies $f(z) = (\hat{\rho} \circ g)(z)$. For this we prove the following lemma.

Lemma 3 (informal). *Let* Commit *be a binding commitment scheme, and let* $\hat{\rho}$ *be a low-degree random oracle defined over a field* $\mathbb{F}$. *Then for every efficient* t-*query oracle algorithm* $\mathcal{A}$,

$$\Pr_{\hat{\rho}} \left[\begin{array}{c} C = \mathsf{Commit}(f, g; \omega) \\ \wedge\; f(X) \not\equiv \hat{\rho}(g(X)) \\ \wedge\; f(\hat{\rho}(C)) = \hat{\rho}(g(\hat{\rho}(C))) \end{array} \middle| (C, f, g, \omega) \leftarrow \mathcal{A}^{\hat{\rho}} \right] = O \left(\sqrt{t \cdot \frac{m \cdot \deg(\hat{\rho}) \cdot \deg(g)}{|\mathbb{F}|}} \right) + \mathrm{negl}(\lambda) \; .$$

A key difference of our zero-finding game compared to the one in [20] (besides the different oracle models) is in the polynomial equation: the polynomial equation not only involves a random evaluation at a point $\hat{\rho}(C)$ determined by the oracle $\hat{\rho}$ (analogous to $\rho(C)$ before) but it also involves the low-degree oracle $\hat{\rho}$ itself as a polynomial. This causes significant complications to the security proof, as we discuss next.

A natural approach to prove Lemma 3 would be to adapt the proof of the zero-finding game in [20], using our forking lemma for linear code random oracles (Lemma 2) rather than the standard forking lemma. Recall that the non-redundancy requirement is satisfied without loss of generality because low-degree random oracles have efficient constraint detection. To invoke the lemma we must choose a forking predicate $p(C, (f, g, \omega), tr)$ that captures the three conditions on the left. Similarly to before, one condition is "$C = \mathsf{Commit}(f, g; \omega)$". However, translating the other two conditions to be compatible with the forking lemma is much more involved, and requires overcoming several challenges.

Since the predicate p cannot query the oracle $\hat{\rho}$, these conditions must be converted into a statement about the query transcript tr. In the [20] proof, the corresponding condition becomes $f(\mathsf{tr}(C)) = 0$. This is justified in their setting because adversaries that do not query the oracle at C cannot win the game. This is *not* true for low-degree oracles! An adversary can, for example, learn $\hat{\rho}(C)$ by querying points on a curve that passes through C. To handle this issue, we use the structure of the linear code to define a partial function $\tilde{\rho}_{\mathsf{tr}}$ which captures all of the information that the adversary knows about $\hat{\rho}$ given the points it has queried. We show that if $\tilde{\rho}_{\mathsf{tr}}(x) = \bot$, no adversary can determine $\hat{\rho}(x)$ from tr better than guessing.

We summarize the above discussion by describing the forking lemma predicate explicitly. On input query point C, auxiliary input (f, g, ω), and query transcript tr, p accepts if the following three conditions hold:

(1) $C = \mathsf{Commit}(f, g; \omega)$,
(2) $f \not\equiv \tilde{\rho}_{\mathsf{tr}} \circ g$, and
(3) $f(\tilde{\rho}_{\mathsf{tr}}(C)) = \tilde{\rho}_{\mathsf{tr}}(g(\tilde{\rho}_{\mathsf{tr}}(C)))$.

Note that since $\tilde{\rho}_{\mathsf{tr}}$ is a partial function, so is $\tilde{\rho}_{\mathsf{tr}} \circ g$, in general. If $\tilde{\rho}_{\mathsf{tr}} \circ g$ is not total then condition (2) holds immediately, since f is total.

We now continue following the template of [20]. Let $\mathcal{A}$ be an adversary winning the Lemma 3 game with probability δ. Invoking our forking lemma (Lemma 2), we obtain, with probability δ^2/t, $(C, (f, g, \omega), (f', g', \omega'), \mathsf{tr}, \mathsf{tr}')$, where p holds for $(C, (f, g, \omega), \mathsf{tr})$ and $(C, (f', g', \omega'), \mathsf{tr}')$. Similarly to before, by the binding property of Commit we can focus on the case where $(f, g) = (f', g')$. The analogous next step would be to conclude by applying Schwartz–Zippel to the polynomial $f - \tilde{\rho}_{\mathsf{tr}} \circ g$. Here, however, we run into another issue: since this polynomial depends on tr, it may differ between the two forks!

To resolve this, we use a slightly different polynomial. Denote by $\mathsf{tr}|_{i-1}$ the truncation of tr to the first $i-1$ entries, where i is the fork point. By construction, $\mathsf{tr}'|_{i-1} = \mathsf{tr}|_{i-1}$. Hence $\tilde{\rho}_{\mathsf{tr}|_{i-1}} \circ g$ is the same function in both forks. Of course, it may be that $\tilde{\rho}_{\mathsf{tr}|_{i-1}} \circ g$ is not total (even if $\tilde{\rho}_{\mathsf{tr}} \circ g$ is). We show that in this case the adversary is very unlikely to win: in particular, it can be shown that $\tilde{\rho}_{\mathsf{tr}|_{i-1}} \circ g$ is not total only if $\tilde{\rho}_{\mathsf{tr}'|_{i-1}}(g(\alpha)) = \bot$ for all but $m \cdot \deg(\hat{\rho}) \cdot \deg(g)$ choices of $\alpha \in \mathbb{F}$. But then since $\tilde{\rho}_{\mathsf{tr}'}(C)$ is chosen uniformly at random independently of $\mathsf{tr}|_{i-1}$, in this case condition (3) holds with probability at most $m \cdot \deg(\hat{\rho}) \cdot \deg(g)/|\mathbb{F}|$.

In the case that $\tilde{\rho}_{\mathsf{tr}|_{i-1}} \circ g$ is total, we can now apply Schwartz–Zippel to the polynomial $f - \tilde{\rho}_{\mathsf{tr}|_{i-1}} \circ g$, which concludes the proof by rearranging to bound δ as before.

2.5   SNARKs for Oracle Computations

We outline the proof of Theorem 1, which provides a transparent SNARK in the LDROM for computations in the LDROM, assuming the existence of collision-resistant hash functions in the standard model.

The proof is in two steps: first we describe a generic SNARK construction in any oracle model from a SNARK for non-oracle computations and an accumulation scheme for queries to the oracle; then we explain how we instantiate the construction specifically for the low-degree random oracle model.

Step 1: A Generic Construction. Let $\theta \leftarrow \mathcal{O}$ be any oracle (for now not necessarily low-degree). Informally, we can view a computation that has oracle access to θ as made of two parts that share a common (untrusted) witness of query-answer pairs: (i) a computation where oracle answers are read from the witness; and (ii) a computation that checks all query-answer pairs for consistency with the oracle θ. We prove the former using a SNARK $\mathsf{ARG}_{\mathsf{in}} = (\mathcal{P}_{\mathsf{in}}, \mathcal{V}_{\mathsf{in}})$ for non-oracle computations (whose security holds in a model where parties have access to θ), and the latter via an accumulation scheme $\mathsf{AS} = (\mathrm{P}^\theta, \mathrm{V}, \mathrm{D}^\theta)$ for queries to θ. We then combine these two components to obtain a SNARK in the oracle θ model for computations that query θ.

In more detail, our goal is to prove a relation $\mathcal{R}^\theta := \{(\mathbb{x}, \mathbb{w}) : M^\theta(\mathbb{x}, \mathbb{w}) = 1\} \in \mathsf{NP}^\theta$, where M is a polynomial-time oracle Turing machine. To build a SNARK for $\mathcal{R}^\theta$ using our high-level template, we define the following non-oracle relation:

$$\mathcal{R}' := \{((\mathbb{x}, \mathsf{acc}), (\mathbb{w}, \mathsf{tr}, \pi_{\mathrm{V}})) : M'(\mathbb{x}, \mathbb{w}, \mathsf{tr}) = 1 \land \mathrm{V}(\mathsf{tr}, \bot, \mathsf{acc}, \pi_{\mathrm{V}}) = 1\} \in \mathsf{NP} ,$$

where M' works exactly like M except that its oracle queries are answered using tr, V is the accumulation verifier, and $\bot$ denotes an empty accumulator. Intuitively, if $(\mathbb{x}, \mathsf{acc}) \in \mathcal{L}(\mathcal{R}')$ and acc is a valid accumulator, then for tr consistent with θ and some witness $\mathbb{w}$, $M'(\mathbb{x}, \mathbb{w}, \mathsf{tr}) = 1$. This implies that $M^\theta(\mathbb{x}, \mathbb{w}) = 1$, and so $\mathbb{x} \in \mathcal{L}(\mathcal{R})$.

Next, we describe our SNARK construction $\mathsf{ARG}_{\mathsf{out}} = (\mathcal{P}_{\mathsf{out}}^\theta, \mathcal{V}_{\mathsf{out}}^\theta)$ in terms of $\mathcal{R}'$.

1. $\mathcal{P}_{\mathsf{out}}^\theta$ simulates M and records M's oracle transcript tr. Then, $\mathcal{P}_{\mathsf{out}}^\theta$ accumulates the queries in tr using the accumulation prover $\mathsf{acc} \leftarrow \mathrm{P}^\theta(\bot, \mathsf{tr})$. Next, $\mathcal{P}_{\mathsf{out}}^\theta$ runs the SNARK prover $\mathcal{P}_{\mathsf{in}}((\mathbb{x}, \mathsf{acc}), \mathsf{tr})$ to obtain a proof π_{in} that $(\mathbb{x}, \mathsf{acc}) \in \mathcal{R}'$. $\mathcal{P}_{\mathsf{out}}^\theta$ then outputs $\pi_{\mathsf{out}} = (\pi_{\mathsf{in}}, \mathsf{acc})$.
2. $\mathcal{V}_{\mathsf{out}}^\theta$ receives the input $\pi_{\mathsf{out}} = (\pi_{\mathsf{in}}, \mathsf{acc})$, then runs the SNARK verifier $\mathcal{V}_{\mathsf{in}}((\mathbb{x}, \mathsf{acc}), \pi_{\mathsf{in}})$ and the accumulation decider $\mathrm{D}^\theta(\mathsf{acc})$. If both accept, $\mathcal{V}_{\mathsf{out}}^\theta$ accepts.

For (knowledge) soundness, consider a malicious prover $\tilde{\mathcal{P}}$ that outputs an instance $\mathbb{x}$ and a proof $(\pi_{\mathsf{in}}, \mathsf{acc})$ that $\mathcal{V}_{\mathsf{out}}^\theta$ accepts, i.e. $\mathcal{V}_{\mathsf{in}}((\mathbb{x}, \mathsf{acc}), \pi_{\mathsf{in}}) = 1$ and $\mathrm{D}^\theta(\mathsf{acc}) = 1$. By the knowledge guarantee of the SNARK, we can extract a witness $(\mathbb{w}, \mathsf{tr}, \pi_{\mathrm{V}})$. If tr is not consistent with θ, then the soundness of the accumulation scheme implies that $\mathrm{D}^\theta(\mathsf{acc}) = 1$ with at most negligible probability. Hence tr is consistent with θ, which implies that $(\mathbb{x}, \mathbb{w}) \in \mathcal{R}^\theta$ by definition of $\mathcal{R}'$.

For clarity we have omitted parameter generation from the above description. The parameters of $\mathsf{ARG}_{\mathsf{out}}$ are simply the concatenation of the parameters for $\mathsf{ARG}_{\mathsf{in}}$ and AS. If, as in our construction below, both of these have transparent setup, then so does $\mathsf{ARG}_{\mathsf{out}}$.

Step 2: Instantiating the Building Blocks. We explain how to instantiate the above generic construction in the case where θ is a low-degree random oracle.

For the accumulation scheme, we use our construction for low-degree oracle queries from Sect. 2.2. Note that this construction requires a collision-resistant hash function, so our SNARK inherits its public parameters.

Next, we obtain a SNARK for non-oracle computations relative to the low-degree random oracle. It is well known that Micali's SNARG [35], when instantiated with a PCP of knowledge, is a proof of knowledge in the random oracle model via a straightline extractor [38]. Naturally, we can carry this construction over to the low-degree random oracle model. However, it is unclear how to construct a straightline extractor. Instead, we make use of a folklore observation: there is an alternative extractor which uses a forking algorithm. This requires polynomially-many forked transcripts (rather than 2); we observe that our forking lemma in the LCROM (Lemma 2) can easily be extended to support this.

We observe that our technique for proving knowledge is not specific to the low-degree oracle. In fact, our forking lemma (Lemma 2) shows that efficient forking lemmas exist for any linear code random oracle with an efficient constraint detection algorithm. Similarly, all linear code random oracles are collision-resistant. Hence, to build SNARKs for other linear code oracle computations, it suffices to design an accumulation scheme for oracle queries and an efficient constraint detection algorithm for the code.

3 Preliminaries

3.1 Notations

We use $[n]$ to denote the set of integers $\{1, \ldots, n\}$. The notation $\mathbb{F}^{\le d}[X_1, \ldots, X_m]$ refers to the set of m-variate polynomials of individual degree at most d with coefficients in $\mathbb{F}$. In this paper, we write $\deg(\cdot)$ to denote individual degree. For a distribution D, we denote the support of D by $\text{supp}(D)$. For a function f, we denote the image of f with $\text{im}(f)$. We denote by $(X \to Y)$ the set of all functions $\{f \colon X \to Y\}$. We denote by $f \colon X \rightharpoonup Y$ a partial function from X to Y.

Indexed Relations. An *indexed relation* $\mathcal{R}$ is a set of triples (i, x, w) where i is the index, x is the instance, and w is the witness; the corresponding *indexed language* $\mathcal{L}(\mathcal{R}^\theta)$ is the set of pairs (i, x) for which there exists a witness w such that $(i, x, w) \in \mathcal{R}$. For example, the indexed relation of satisfiable Boolean circuits consists of triples where i is the description of a Boolean circuit, x is a partial assignment to its input wires, and w is an assignment to the remaining wires that makes the circuit to output 0.

Security Parameters. For simplicity of notation, we assume that all public parameters have length at least λ, so that algorithms which receive such parameters can run in time $\text{poly}(\lambda)$.

Distributions. For finite set X, we write $x \leftarrow X$ to denote that x is drawn uniformly at random from X.

Oracle Algorithms. For a function $\theta\colon X \to Y$, we write A^θ for an algorithm with oracle access to θ. We say that A is t-query if A makes at most t queries to θ. We say that an oracle algorithm is *systematic* if it only makes queries in $\{0,1\}^m$ for some $m \in \mathbb{N}$.

Random Oracles. Typically, a *random oracle* is a function ρ sampled uniformly at random from $(\{0,1\}^m \to \{0,1\}^n)$ for some $m, n \in \mathbb{N}$. It will be convenient for us to consider a slightly broader definition, where ρ is sampled uniformly at random from $(\{0,1\}^m \to \mathbb{F})$ for some finite field $\mathbb{F}$.

Oracle Relations. For a distribution over oracles $\mathcal{O}$, we write $\mathcal{R}^\mathcal{O}$ to denote the set of indexed relations $\{\mathcal{R}^\theta : \theta \in \mathrm{supp}(\mathcal{O})\}$. We define $\mathcal{R}^\mathcal{O} \in \mathsf{NP}^\mathcal{O}$ if and only if there exists a polynomial-time oracle Turing machine M such that for all $\theta \in \mathrm{supp}(\mathcal{O})$, $\mathcal{R}^\theta = \{(\mathbbm{i}, \mathbbm{x}, \mathbbm{w}) : M^\theta(\mathbbm{i}, \mathbbm{x}, \mathbbm{w}) = 1\}$.

3.2   Non-interactive Arguments in Oracle Models

We follow [22] and define the tuple of algorithms $\mathsf{ARG} = (\mathcal{G}, \mathcal{I}, \mathcal{P}, \mathcal{V})$ to be a (preprocessing) *non-interactive argument* relative to an oracle distribution $\mathcal{O}$ for an indexed oracle relation $\mathcal{R}^\mathcal{O}$ if the algorithms satisfy the following syntax and properties:

1. $\mathcal{G}^\theta(1^\lambda) \to \mathsf{pp}$. On input a security parameter λ (in unary), $\mathcal{G}$ samples public parameters pp for the argument system.
2. $\mathcal{I}^\theta(\mathsf{pp}, \mathbbm{i}) \to (\mathrm{ipk}, \mathrm{ivk})$. On input public parameters pp and an index $\mathbbm{i}$ for the relation $\mathcal{R}$, $\mathcal{I}$ deterministically specializes pp to index-specific proving and verification keys $(\mathrm{ipk}, \mathrm{ivk})$.
3. $\mathcal{P}^\theta(\mathrm{ipk}, \mathbbm{x}, \mathbbm{w}) \to \pi$. On input an index-specific proving key ipk, an instance $\mathbbm{x}$, and a corresponding witness $\mathbbm{w}$, $\mathcal{P}$ computes a proof π that attests to the claim that $(\mathbbm{i}, \mathbbm{x}, \mathbbm{w}) \in \mathcal{R}$.
4. $\mathcal{V}^\theta(\mathrm{ivk}, \mathbbm{x}, \pi) \to b \in \{0,1\}$. On input an index-specific proving key ivk, an instance $\mathbbm{x}$, and a corresponding proof π, $\mathcal{V}$ checks that π is a valid proof.

– **Completeness.** For every adversary $\mathcal{A}$,

$$\Pr\left[\begin{array}{c} (\mathbbm{i}, \mathbbm{x}, \mathbbm{w}) \notin \mathcal{R}^\theta \\ \vee \\ \mathcal{V}^\theta(\mathrm{ivk}, \mathbbm{x}, \pi) = 1 \end{array} \middle| \begin{array}{c} \theta \leftarrow \mathcal{O}(\lambda) \\ \mathsf{pp} \leftarrow \mathcal{G}^\theta(1^\lambda) \\ (\mathbbm{i}, \mathbbm{x}, \mathbbm{w}) \leftarrow \mathcal{A}^\theta(\mathsf{pp}) \\ (\mathrm{ipk}, \mathrm{ivk}) \leftarrow \mathcal{I}^\theta(\mathsf{pp}, \mathbbm{i}) \\ \pi \leftarrow \mathcal{P}^\theta(\mathrm{ipk}, \mathbbm{x}, \mathbbm{w}) \end{array} \right] = 1 \ .$$

– **Soundness.** For every polynomial-size adversary $\tilde{\mathcal{P}}$,

$$\Pr\left[\begin{array}{c} (\mathbbm{i}, \mathbbm{x}) \notin \mathcal{L}(\mathcal{R}^\theta) \\ \wedge \\ \mathcal{V}^\theta(\mathrm{ivk}, \mathbbm{x}, \pi) = 1 \end{array} \middle| \begin{array}{c} \theta \leftarrow \mathcal{O}(\lambda) \\ \mathsf{pp} \leftarrow \mathcal{G}^\theta(1^\lambda) \\ (\mathbbm{i}, \mathbbm{x}, \pi) \leftarrow \tilde{\mathcal{P}}^\theta(\mathsf{pp}) \\ (\mathrm{ipk}, \mathrm{ivk}) \leftarrow \mathcal{I}^\theta(\mathsf{pp}, \mathbbm{i}) \end{array} \right] \leq \mathrm{negl}(\lambda) \ .$$

The above formulation of completeness allows (i, x, w) to depend on the oracle θ and public parameters pp, and the above formulation of soundness allows (i, x) to depend on the oracle θ and public parameters pp.

Knowledge Soundness. We say that ARG has *knowledge soundness* (with respect to auxiliary input distribution $\mathcal{D}$) if there exists an efficient extractor $\mathcal{E}$ such that for every polynomial-size adversary $\tilde{\mathcal{P}}$,

$$\Pr\left[\begin{array}{c|c} \mathcal{V}^\theta(\mathrm{ivk}, x, \pi) = 1 \\ \Downarrow \\ (i, x, w) \in \mathcal{R} \end{array} \middle| \begin{array}{c} \theta \leftarrow \mathcal{O}(\lambda) \\ pp \leftarrow \mathcal{G}^\theta(1^\lambda) \\ \mathrm{ai} \leftarrow \mathcal{D}(pp) \\ (i, x, \pi; r) \leftarrow \tilde{\mathcal{P}}^\theta(pp, \mathrm{ai}) \\ (\mathrm{ipk}, \mathrm{ivk}) \leftarrow \mathcal{I}^\theta(pp, i) \\ w \leftarrow \mathcal{E}^{\tilde{\mathcal{P}}, \theta}(pp, \mathrm{ai}, r) \end{array}\right] \geq 1 - \mathrm{negl}(\lambda) \ .$$

3.3 Accumulation Schemes

We recall the definition of an accumulation scheme from [20]. Let $\Phi\colon \mathcal{O}(*) \times (\{0,1\}^*)^3 \rightarrow \{0,1\}$ be a predicate (for clarity we write $\Phi^\theta(pp_\Phi, i_\Phi, q)$ for $\Phi(\theta, pp_\Phi, i_\Phi, q)$). Let $\mathcal{H}$ be a randomized algorithm with access to θ, which outputs predicate parameters pp_Φ.

An **accumulation scheme for** $(\Phi, \mathcal{H})$ is a tuple of algorithms $\mathsf{AS} = (\mathsf{G}, \mathsf{I}, \mathsf{P}, \mathsf{V}, \mathsf{D})$ all of which (except G) have access to the same oracle θ. These algorithms must satisfy two properties, *completeness* and *soundness*, defined below.

Completeness. For all (unbounded) adversaries $\mathcal{A}$,

$$\Pr\left[\begin{array}{c|c} \forall j \in [\ell], \mathsf{D}^\theta(\mathrm{dk}, \mathrm{acc}_j) = 1 \\ \forall i \in [n], \Phi^\theta(pp_\Phi, i_\Phi, q_i) = 1 \\ \Downarrow \\ \mathsf{V}^\theta(\mathrm{avk}, [q_i]_{i=1}^n, [\mathrm{acc}_j]_{j=1}^\ell, \mathrm{acc}, \pi_\mathsf{V}) = 1 \\ \mathsf{D}^\theta(\mathrm{dk}, \mathrm{acc}) = 1 \end{array} \middle| \begin{array}{c} \theta \leftarrow \mathcal{O}(\lambda) \\ pp \leftarrow \mathsf{G}(1^\lambda) \\ pp_\Phi \leftarrow \mathcal{H}^\theta(1^\lambda) \\ (i_\Phi, [q_i]_{i=1}^n, [\mathrm{acc}_j]_{j=1}^\ell) \leftarrow \mathcal{A}^\theta(pp, pp_\Phi) \\ (\mathrm{apk}, \mathrm{avk}, \mathrm{dk}) \leftarrow \mathsf{I}^\theta(pp, pp_\Phi, i_\Phi) \\ (\mathrm{acc}, \pi_\mathsf{V}) \leftarrow \mathsf{P}^\theta(\mathrm{apk}, [q_i]_{i=1}^n, [\mathrm{acc}_j]_{j=1}^\ell) \end{array}\right] = 1 \ .$$

Note that for $\ell = n = 0$, the precondition on the left-hand side holds vacuously; this is required for the completeness condition to be non-trivial.

Soundness. For every polynomial-size adversary $\mathcal{A}$,

$$\Pr\left[\begin{array}{c|c} \mathsf{V}^\theta(\mathrm{avk}, [q_i]_{i=1}^n, [\mathrm{acc}_j]_{j=1}^\ell, \mathrm{acc}, \pi_\mathsf{V}) = 1 \\ \mathsf{D}^\theta(\mathrm{dk}, \mathrm{acc}) = 1 \\ \Downarrow \\ \forall j \in [\ell], \mathsf{D}^\theta(\mathrm{dk}, \mathrm{acc}_j) = 1 \\ \forall i \in [n], \Phi^\theta(pp_\Phi, i_\Phi, q_i) = 1 \end{array} \middle| \begin{array}{c} \theta \leftarrow \mathcal{O}(\lambda) \\ pp \leftarrow \mathsf{G}^\theta(1^\lambda) \\ pp_\Phi \leftarrow \mathcal{H}^\theta(1^\lambda) \\ \left(\begin{array}{c} i_\Phi \ [q_i]_{i=1}^n \ [\mathrm{acc}_j]_{j=1}^\ell \\ \mathrm{acc} \ \ \pi_\mathsf{V} \end{array}\right) \leftarrow \mathcal{A}^\theta(pp, pp_\Phi) \\ (\mathrm{apk}, \mathrm{avk}, \mathrm{dk}) \leftarrow \mathsf{I}^\theta(pp, pp_\Phi, i_\Phi) \end{array}\right] \geq 1 - \mathrm{negl}(\lambda) \ .$$

Zero Knowledge. There exists a polynomial-time simulator S such that for every polynomial-size "honest" adversary $\mathcal{A}$ (see below) the following distributions are (statistically/computationally) indistinguishable:

$$\left\{ (\theta, \mathsf{pp}, \mathsf{acc}) \;\middle|\; \begin{array}{c} \theta \leftarrow \mathcal{O}(\lambda) \\ \mathsf{pp} \leftarrow \mathrm{G}^{\theta}(1^{\lambda}) \\ \mathsf{pp}_{\Phi} \leftarrow \mathcal{H}^{\theta}(1^{\lambda}) \\ (\mathsf{i}_{\Phi}, [\mathsf{q}_i]_{i=1}^{n}, [\mathsf{acc}_j]_{j=1}^{\ell}) \leftarrow \mathcal{A}^{\theta}(\mathsf{pp}, \mathsf{pp}_{\Phi}) \\ (\mathsf{apk}, \mathsf{avk}, \mathsf{dk}) \leftarrow \mathrm{I}^{\theta}(\mathsf{pp}, \mathsf{pp}_{\Phi}, \mathsf{i}_{\Phi}) \\ \mathsf{acc}, \pi_{\mathrm{V}} \leftarrow \mathrm{P}^{\theta}(\mathsf{apk}, [\mathsf{q}_i]_{i=1}^{n}, [\mathsf{acc}_j]_{j=1}^{\ell}) \end{array} \right\}$$

and

$$\left\{ (\theta, \mathsf{pp}, \mathsf{acc}) \;\middle|\; \begin{array}{c} \theta \leftarrow \mathcal{O}(\lambda) \\ (\mathsf{pp}, \tau) \leftarrow \mathrm{S}^{\theta}(1^{\lambda}) \\ \mathsf{pp}_{\Phi} \leftarrow \mathcal{H}^{\theta}(1^{\lambda}) \\ (\mathsf{i}_{\Phi}, [\mathsf{q}_i]_{i=1}^{n}, [\mathsf{acc}_j]_{j=1}^{\ell}) \leftarrow \mathcal{A}^{\theta}(\mathsf{pp}, \mathsf{pp}_{\Phi}) \\ \mathsf{acc} \leftarrow \mathrm{S}^{\theta}(\mathsf{pp}_{\Phi}, \tau, \mathsf{i}_{\Phi}) \end{array} \right\}.$$

Here $\mathcal{A}$ is *honest* if it outputs, with probability 1, a tuple $(\mathsf{i}_{\Phi}, [\mathsf{q}_i]_{i=1}^{n}, [\mathsf{acc}_j]_{j=1}^{\ell})$ such that $\Phi^{\theta}(\mathsf{pp}_{\Phi}, \mathsf{i}_{\Phi}, \mathsf{q}_i) = 1$ and $\mathrm{D}^{\theta}(\mathsf{dk}, \mathsf{acc}_j) = 1$ for all $i \in [n]$ and $j \in [\ell]$. Note that the simulator S is *not* required to simulate the accumulation verifier proof π_{V}.

3.4 Commitment Schemes

Definition 2. *A* **commitment scheme** *for a family of message universes* $\mathcal{M}_{\mathsf{ck}} = \{0,1\}^{L}$, *commitment universes* $\mathcal{C}_{\mathsf{ck}} = \{0,1\}^{\mathrm{poly}(\lambda, L)}$, *and randomness domains* $\mathcal{R}_{\mathsf{ck}} = \{0,1\}^{\mathrm{poly}(\lambda)}$ *a is a tuple* CM = (CM.Setup, CM.Commit) *with the following syntax.*

- CM.Setup, *on input a security parameter* 1^{λ} *and a message format* L, *outputs a commitment key* ck.
- CM.Commit, *on input a commitment key* ck, *a message* $m \in \mathcal{M}_{\mathsf{ck}}$ *and randomness* $\omega \in \mathcal{R}_{\mathsf{ck}}$, *outputs a commitment* $C \in \mathcal{C}_{\mathsf{ck}}$.

The commitment scheme CM *is* **hiding** *if* ck $\leftarrow$ CM.Setup$(1^{\lambda}, L)$, *then for every efficient adversary* $\mathcal{A}$ *that chooses* $m_0 \neq m_1 \in \mathcal{M}_{\mathsf{ck}}$, *we have that*

$$\{\mathsf{CM.Commit}(\mathsf{ck}, m_0; \omega_0) \mid \omega_0 \leftarrow \mathcal{R}_{\mathsf{ck}}\} \approx \{\mathsf{CM.Commit}(\mathsf{ck}, m_1; \omega_1) \mid \omega_1 \leftarrow \mathcal{R}_{\mathsf{ck}}\}.$$

The commitment scheme CM *is* **binding** *if for every message format* L *such that* $|L| = \mathrm{poly}(\lambda)$ *and for every efficient adversary, the following holds.*

$$\Pr\left[\begin{array}{c} m_0 \neq m_1 \\ \wedge \\ \mathsf{CM.Commit}(\mathsf{ck}, m_0; \omega_0) = \mathsf{CM.Commit}(\mathsf{ck}, m_1; \omega_1) \end{array} \;\middle|\; \begin{array}{c} \mathsf{ck} \leftarrow \mathsf{CM.Setup}(1^{\lambda}, L) \\ ((m_0, \omega_0), (m_1, \omega_1)) \leftarrow \mathcal{A}(\mathsf{ck}) \end{array} \right] \leq \mathrm{negl}(\lambda).$$

Finally, CM *is* **s-compressing** *if for all* ck $\leftarrow$ CM.Setup$(1^{\lambda}, L)$, $\mathcal{C}_{\mathsf{ck}} = \{0,1\}^{s(\lambda)}$.

4 Linear Code Random Oracles

In this section we define our main object of study, *linear code random oracles*. We first recall the definition of a linear code and its dual. For a set D and field $\mathbb{F}$, we write $(D \to \mathbb{F})$ or $\mathbb{F}^D$ for the vector space of functions from D to $\mathbb{F}$.

Definition 3. *Let D be a set, and $\mathbb{F}$ a field. A* **linear code** *$\mathcal{C}$ is a subspace of $\mathbb{F}^D$. The* **dual code** *of $\mathcal{C}$ is the set $\mathcal{C}^{\perp} := \{z \in \mathbb{F}^D : \forall c \in \mathcal{C}, \sum_{x \in D} z(x)c(x) = 0\}$; observe that $\mathcal{C}^{\perp}$ is also a subspace of $\mathbb{F}^D$.*

We are now ready to define a linear code random oracle.

Definition 4 (Linear code random oracle). *Let $\mathcal{C} \subseteq (D \to \mathbb{F})$ be a linear code, and $f \colon \{0,1\}^k \to D$. We say that $(\mathcal{C}, f)$ is* **full-rank** *if $\mathcal{C}|_{\mathrm{im}(f)} = \mathbb{F}^{\mathrm{im}(f)} \simeq \mathbb{F}^{2^k}$ (in particular, f is an injection).*

Let $\mathscr{C} = \{\mathcal{C}_\lambda\}_{\lambda \in \mathbb{N}}$ be a family of linear codes and F an efficient algorithm. We say that $(\mathscr{C}, F)$ is a **linear code random oracle** *of arity m if for each $\lambda \in \mathbb{N}$ if $F(1^\lambda) \colon \{0,1\}^{m(\lambda)} \to D_\lambda$ is a circuit such that $(\mathcal{C}_\lambda, F(1^\lambda))$ is full-rank for all $\lambda \in \mathbb{N}$.*

For the remainder of this work, when it is unambiguous we will typically omit F and write $c(q)$ for $c(F(1^\lambda)(q))$ when $c \in \mathcal{C}_\lambda$ and $q \in \{0,1\}^{m(\lambda)}$. The standard random oracle is the linear code random oracle $(\{(\{0,1\}^{m(\lambda)} \to \mathbb{F}_\lambda)\}_\lambda, I)$ where $I(1^\lambda)(q) = q$ for $q \in \{0,1\}^{m(\lambda)}$. We will often refer to a function sampled uniformly from a linear code random oracle simply as a "linear code random oracle", and we use the symbol $\hat{\rho}$.

An algorithm with oracle access to $c \in \mathcal{C}$, written $\mathcal{A}^c$, can query c at any point in D; we refer to such an algorithm as a $\mathcal{C}$-oracle algorithm. Any systematic oracle algorithm $\mathcal{B}$ can be interpreted as a $\mathcal{C}_\lambda$-oracle algorithm via the efficient injection $F(1^\lambda, \cdot)$; we write $\mathcal{B}^{\hat{\rho}}$, omitting F. The following statement follows immediately from the full-rank condition.

Claim. Let $(\mathscr{C} = \{\mathcal{C}_\lambda \subseteq (D_\lambda \to \mathbb{F}_\lambda)\}_\lambda, F)$ be a linear code random oracle of arity m. For any algorithm $\mathcal{B}$ with access to an oracle $\{0,1\}^{m(\lambda)} \to \mathbb{F}_\lambda$,

$$\Pr_{\rho \leftarrow (\{0,1\}^{m(\lambda)} \to \mathbb{F})} [\mathcal{B}^\rho \to 1] = \Pr_{\hat{\rho} \leftarrow \mathcal{C}_\lambda} [\mathcal{B}^{\hat{\rho}} \to 1] \ .$$

4.1 Query Transcripts and Partial Oracles

We define some notions used in security proofs involving linear code random oracles. A $\mathcal{C}$-query transcript is a list of query-answer pairs consistent with the execution of a $\mathcal{C}$-oracle algorithm. A partial oracle extends a query transcript to include evaluations that are fixed by the structure of the code.

Definition 5. *Let $\mathcal{C} \subseteq (D \to \mathbb{F})$ be a linear code. A $\mathcal{C}$-query transcript is a list $\mathrm{tr} = [(\mathsf{q}_i, \alpha_i)]_{i=1}^t \in (D \times \mathbb{F})^t$ for any $t \in \mathbb{N}$ such that there exists $c \in \mathcal{C}$ with*

$c(q_i) = \alpha_i$ *for all* $i \in [t]$. *A query transcript* tr *induces a partial function* $D \rightharpoonup \mathbb{F}$ *in the natural way, which we also denote by* tr:

$$\mathsf{tr}(q) = \begin{cases} \alpha_i & \textit{if } q = q_i \\ \perp & \textit{if } q \notin \{q_1, \ldots, q_t\}. \end{cases}$$

We then define the **partial oracle** $\tilde{\rho}_{\mathsf{tr}}^{\mathcal{C}} : D \rightharpoonup \mathbb{F}$ *as follows:*

$$\tilde{\rho}_{\mathsf{tr}}^{\mathcal{C}}(q) = \begin{cases} \beta & \textit{if } \forall c \in \mathcal{C}, ((\forall i \in [t], \ c(q_i) = \alpha_i) \Rightarrow c(q) = \beta) \\ \perp & o.w. \end{cases}.$$

When $\mathcal{C}$ *is clear from context we will omit it from the notation.*

4.2 Constraints

In this section we examine properties of the partial oracle arising from the linear structure of $\mathcal{C}$. We first introduce the notion of a *constraint* for elements in the domain of a linear code. The results in this section hold for all linear codes, even those that are not full-rank.

Definition 6. *Let* $\mathcal{C} \subseteq (D \to \mathbb{F})$ *be a linear code. We say that a subset of the domain* $Q \subseteq D$ *is* **constrained** *if there exists a nonzero mapping* $z : Q \to \mathbb{F}$ *such that for all* $c \in \mathcal{C}$, $\sum_{x \in Q} z(x)c(x) = 0$. *Equivalently,* Q *is constrained if there exists* $z \neq 0 \in \mathcal{C}^{\perp}$ *with* $\mathrm{supp}(z) \subseteq Q$. *We refer to* z *as a* **constraint** *on* Q. *We say that* Q *is* **unconstrained** *if it is not constrained.*

We say that $Q \subseteq D$ **determines** $x \in D$ *if either* $x \in Q$ *or there exists a constraint* z *on* $Q \cup \{x\}$ *such that* $z(x) \neq 0$.

The following claim connects constraints and partial oracles.

Claim. Let $\mathcal{C}$ be a linear code, and tr be a $\mathcal{C}$-query transcript. Then for all $x \in D$, $\tilde{\rho}_{\mathsf{tr}}^{\mathcal{C}}(x) \neq \perp$ if and only if $\mathrm{supp}(\mathsf{tr})$ determines x.

In particular, $\tilde{\rho}_{\mathsf{tr}}^{\mathcal{C}}(x) = \beta \in \mathbb{F}$ if and only if $\mathsf{tr}(x) = \beta$, or $\mathsf{tr}(x) = \perp$ and there exists $z \in \mathcal{C}^{\perp}$ such that $\mathrm{supp}(z) \subseteq \mathrm{supp}(\mathsf{tr}) \cup \{x\}$ and $z(x) \neq 0$, and

$$\beta = -z(x)^{-1} \left(\sum_{y \in \mathrm{supp}(\mathsf{tr})} z(y) \mathsf{tr}(y) \right).$$

Next we characterize the distribution of $c(q)$ conditioned on a prior query transcript tr in terms of the value of $\tilde{\rho}_{\mathsf{tr}}^{\mathcal{C}}(q)$.

Claim. Let $\mathcal{C} \subseteq (D \to \mathbb{F})$ be a linear code. For all $q \in D$, $Q \subseteq D$, $c' \in \mathcal{C}$ and $\beta \in \mathbb{F}$,

$$\Pr_{c \leftarrow \mathcal{C}}[c(x) = \beta \mid c|_Q = c'|_Q] = \begin{cases} \frac{1}{|\mathbb{F}|} & \text{if } Q \text{ does not determine } x, \\ 1 & \text{if } Q \text{ determines } x \text{ and } \beta = c'(x), \\ 0 & \text{otherwise.} \end{cases}$$

Equivalently, for all $q \in D$ and all $\mathcal{C}$-query transcripts $\mathsf{tr} = \{(\mathsf{q}_i, \alpha_i)\}_{i=1}^{t}$ and $\beta \in \mathbb{F}$,

$$
\Pr_{c \leftarrow \mathcal{C}}[c(x) = \beta \mid \forall i \in [t],\, c(\mathsf{q}_i) = \alpha_i] = \begin{cases} \frac{1}{|\mathbb{F}|} & \text{if } \tilde{\rho}_{\mathsf{tr}}^{\mathcal{C}}(\mathsf{q}) = \bot, \\ 1 & \text{if } \tilde{\rho}_{\mathsf{tr}}^{\mathcal{C}}(\mathsf{q}) = \beta, \\ 0 & \text{otherwise.} \end{cases}
$$

Proof. The equivalence follows from Sect. 4.2 and the definition of a $\mathcal{C}$-query transcript, so it suffices to prove the second statement. The cases when $\tilde{\rho}_{\mathsf{tr}}(\mathsf{q}) \neq \bot$ are clear, and so we consider the case when $\tilde{\rho}_{\mathsf{tr}}(\mathsf{q}) = \bot$. In this case there exist codewords $c, c' \in \mathcal{C}$ such that $c(\mathsf{q}_i) = c'(\mathsf{q}_i)$ for all i but $c(\mathsf{q}) \neq c'(\mathsf{q})$. It follows by linearity of $\mathcal{C}$ that there exists $c^* = c - c' \in \mathcal{C}$ such that $c^*(\mathsf{q}_i) = 0$ for all i and $c^*(\mathsf{q}) \neq 0$. We can sample from the conditional distribution in the claim by choosing a random $c'' \in \mathcal{C}$ such that $c(\mathsf{q}_i) = \alpha_i$ for all i and a random $\alpha \in \mathbb{F}$ and returning $c'' + \alpha c^*$. The claim follows since $c''(\mathsf{q}) + \alpha c^*(\mathsf{q})$ is uniformly random in $\mathbb{F}$. □

We recall the definition of a constraint detector from [8]. A constraint detector is an algorithm which determines whether a set Q is constrained and, if so, outputs a constraint.

Definition 7 (Constraint detector). *Let $\mathcal{C}$ be a linear code. An algorithm CD is a constraint detector for $\mathcal{C}$ if, given as input a set $Q \subseteq D$,*

- *if Q is constrained, CD outputs a constraint z;*
- *otherwise, CD outputs $\bot$.*

A code family $\{\mathcal{C}_\lambda\}_\lambda$ has efficient constraint detection if there is a polynomial-time algorithm CD such that $\mathsf{CD}(1^\lambda, \cdot)$ is a constraint detector for $\mathcal{C}_\lambda$.

A constraint detector directly yields an implementation of the partial oracle. It also allows us to remove "redundant" queries from any $\mathcal{C}$-oracle algorithm.

Definition 8. *We say that a $\mathcal{C}$-oracle algorithm $\mathcal{A}$ is **non-redundant** if it never makes any query that is determined by its previous queries.*

The following claim, which is straightforward to prove, shows that in many settings we may restrict our attention to non-redundant algorithms without loss of generality.

Claim. Let $\mathcal{A}$ be a t-query $\mathcal{C}$-oracle algorithm. Then there is a non-redundant t-query $\mathcal{C}$-oracle algorithm $\mathcal{A}'$ whose input-output behaviour is identical to $\mathcal{A}$. Moreover, if $\mathcal{C}$ has efficient constraint detection, then if $\mathcal{A}$ is efficient, $\mathcal{A}'$ is also.

4.3 Query Complexity

We study query complexity in the linear code random oracle model. We first give an example showing an exponential gap between linear code random oracles and standard random oracles.

Claim. For every algorithm $\mathcal{A}$ making fewer than 2^m queries,

$$\Pr_{\rho \leftarrow (\{0,1\}^m \to \mathbb{F})} \left[a = \sum_{x \in \{0,1\}^m} \rho(x) \;\middle|\; a \leftarrow \mathcal{A}^\rho \right] = \frac{1}{|\mathbb{F}|}.$$

On the other hand, there exists a linear code random oracle $(\mathscr{C}, F)$ and a 1-query algorithm $\mathcal{B}$ such that for all $\lambda \in \mathbb{N}$,

$$\Pr_{\hat{\rho} \leftarrow \mathscr{C}_\lambda} \left[a = \sum_{x \in \{0,1\}^m} \hat{\rho}(x) \;\middle|\; a \leftarrow \mathcal{B}^{\hat{\rho}} \right] = 1.$$

We now show that linear code random oracles are collision-resistant. To prove this, we will make use of a couple of linear-algebraic tools. First, we show a simple yet important claim about the existence of codewords with some entries fixed to zero.

Claim. Suppose that $(\mathcal{C} \subseteq (D \to \mathbb{F}), f \colon \{0,1\}^m \to D)$ is full-rank. Then for all $q_1, \ldots, q_t \in D$ there exists $c \in \mathcal{C}$ such that

- $c(q_1) = \cdots = c(q_t) = 0$, and
- there exists a set $S \subseteq \{0,1\}^m, |S| \geq 2^m - t$ such that for all $x \in S, c(f(x)) = 1$.

Proof. For $i \in [2^m]$, let $e_i \in \mathbb{F}^{\mathrm{im}(f)}$ be the vector with zeroes everywhere except at $f(\bar{i})$, where $\bar{i}$ is the binary expansion of i. Since $\mathcal{C}$ is full-rank, there is a basis of $\mathcal{C}$ where the first 2^m elements $c_1, \ldots, c_{2^m}$ have $c_i|_{\mathrm{im}(f)} = e_i$ for all i. The claim follows by elementary linear algebra. $\square$

We use this to establish an upper bound on the number of points in $\{0,1\}^m$ determined by a set of size t.

Lemma 2. *Let $\mathcal{C} \subseteq (D \to \mathbb{F})$ be a full-rank linear code of arity m, $Q \subseteq D$. Define $T := \{x \in \{0,1\}^m : Q \text{ determines } x\}$. Then $|T| \leq |Q|$.*

Proof. By Sect. 4.3, there exists $c \in \mathcal{C}$ such that for all $x \in Q$, $c(x) = 0$, and a set $S \subseteq \{0,1\}^m$ of size $2^m - |Q|$ such that for all $x \in S$, $c(x) = 1$. Suppose that $|T| > |Q|$. By the pigeonhole principle, there exists $y \in S \cap T$. By definition of T, there exists $z \colon D \to \mathbb{F}$ with $z(y) \neq 0$ such that $\sum_{x \in Q} z(x)c(x) + z(y)c(y) = 0$, which is a contradiction. $\square$

Lemma 3. *Let $\mathcal{C} \subseteq (D \to \mathbb{F})$ be a full-rank linear code of arity m. For all t-query $\mathcal{C}$-oracle adversaries $\mathcal{A}$,*

$$\Pr_{\hat{\rho} \leftarrow \mathcal{C}} [x, y \in \{0,1\}^m \wedge \hat{\rho}(x) = \hat{\rho}(y) \mid (x, y) \leftarrow \mathcal{A}^{\hat{\rho}}] \leq t^2/|\mathbb{F}|.$$

Proof. Consider running $\mathcal{A}$ and recording its oracle queries in tr. By Lemma 2, the set of points $T = \{x \in \{0,1\}^m : \hat{\rho}_{\mathrm{tr}}(x) \neq \bot\}$ is of size at most t. Moreover for every $x \in T$, $\hat{\rho}(x)$ is sampled uniformly at random. Hence the probability that there exist $x, y \in T$ such that $\hat{\rho}(x) = \hat{\rho}(y)$ is less than $t^2/|\mathbb{F}|$. By Sect. 4.2, if x or y are not in T, then $\Pr[\hat{\rho}(x) = \hat{\rho}(y) \mid \mathrm{tr}] = 1/|\mathbb{F}|$. The lemma follows by a union bound. $\square$

4.4   Low-Degree Random Oracles

We denote by $\mathbb{F}^{\leq d}[X_1, \ldots, X_m]$ the vector space of m-variate polynomials over $\mathbb{F}$ of individual degree at most d.

Definition 9. *Let $\mathscr{F} = \{\mathbb{F}_\lambda\}_{\lambda \in \mathbb{N}}$ be a family of fields, $m, d \colon \mathbb{N} \to \mathbb{N}$. The $(\mathscr{F}, m, d)$-low-degree random oracle is the linear code random oracle $(\{\mathbb{F}_\lambda^{\leq d(\lambda)}[X_1, \ldots, X_{m(\lambda)}]\}_\lambda, F)$, where*

$$F(1^\lambda)(b_1, \ldots, b_{m(\lambda)}) := (i_\lambda(b_1), \ldots, i_\lambda(b_{m(\lambda)}))$$

for the natural injection $i_\lambda \colon \{0,1\} \to \mathbb{F}_\lambda$ mapping 0 to $0_{\mathbb{F}_\lambda}$ and 1 to $1_{\mathbb{F}_\lambda}$.

5   A Forking Lemma for Linear Code Random Oracles

Let $\mathcal{C} \subseteq (D \to \mathbb{F})$ be a full-rank linear code, and let A be a t-query $\mathcal{C}$-oracle algorithm.

For $x \in \{0,1\}^n$, $\boldsymbol{\alpha} \in \mathbb{F}^t$, $\sigma \in \{0,1\}^*$, denote by $(q, o; \mathsf{tr}) \leftarrow A^{\boldsymbol{\alpha}}(x; \sigma)$ the following procedure: Run A on input x and random tape σ. For every $i \in [t]$, answer A's i-th query $q_i \in \{0,1\}^n$ to the oracle with $\alpha_i \in \mathbb{F}$. Parse A's output as (q, o) for $q \in D$. Let $\mathsf{tr} = ((q_1, \alpha_1), \ldots, (q_t, \alpha_t))$ be the transcript of A's queries to the oracle. Denote by $(q, o; \mathsf{tr}, \sigma) \leftarrow A^{\hat{\rho}}(x)$ the same procedure, but where each α_i is adaptively set to $\hat{\rho}(q_i)$, and where σ is the random tape used by A (sampled uniformly).

For a query transcript tr, we define $\mathsf{FP}(\mathsf{tr}, q)$ to be the smallest $i \in [t]$ such that $\{q_1, \ldots, q_i, q\}$ is constrained, or $\perp$ if there is no such i. Note that given an efficient constraint detection algorithm CD, $\mathsf{FP}(\mathsf{tr}, q)$ can be computed in polynomial time. We now describe a general forking algorithm Fork.

$\mathsf{Fork}^A(q, o, \mathsf{tr}, \sigma)$:
1. Let $((q_1, \alpha_1), \ldots, (q_t, \alpha_t)) := \mathsf{tr}$.
2. Set $i := \mathsf{FP}(\mathsf{tr}, q)$. If $i = \perp$, abort and output $\perp$.
3. Otherwise, sample $\alpha_i', \ldots, \alpha_t' \leftarrow \mathbb{F}$, and run $(q', o'; \mathsf{tr}') \leftarrow A^{\mathsf{tr}_{i-1}; \alpha_i', \ldots, \alpha_t'}(\sigma)$.
4. Output $(q', o', \mathsf{tr}', i)$.

Lemma 4 (Forking Lemma).   *For every predicate p and t-query non-redundant $\mathcal{C}$-oracle algorithm A, setting*

$$\delta := \Pr\left[\begin{matrix} \mathsf{FP}(\mathsf{tr}, q) \neq \perp \wedge q \in \{0,1\}^m \\ \wedge\ \mathsf{p}(q, o, \mathsf{tr}) = 1 \end{matrix} \middle| \begin{matrix} \hat{\rho} \leftarrow \mathcal{C}_\lambda \\ (q, o; \mathsf{tr}, \sigma) \leftarrow A^{\hat{\rho}} \end{matrix}\right]$$

we have that

$$\Pr\left[\begin{matrix} \mathsf{FP}(\mathsf{tr}, q) \neq \perp \wedge q \in \{0,1\}^m \\ \wedge\ q = q' \\ \wedge\ \mathsf{p}(q, o, \mathsf{tr}) = 1 \\ \wedge\ \mathsf{p}(q', o', \mathsf{tr}') = 1 \end{matrix} \middle| \begin{matrix} \hat{\rho} \leftarrow \mathcal{C}_\lambda \\ (q, o; \mathsf{tr}, \sigma) \leftarrow A^{\hat{\rho}} \\ (q', o', \mathsf{tr}', i) \leftarrow \mathsf{Fork}^A(q, o, \mathsf{tr}, \sigma) \end{matrix}\right] \geq \delta^2/t .$$

$$(1)$$

Proof. For all $i \in [t], q \in \{0,1\}^m$, we define the set

$$S_{i,q} := \{(\boldsymbol{\alpha}, \sigma) : (q, o; \mathsf{tr}) \leftarrow A^{\boldsymbol{\alpha}}(\mathsf{pp}; \sigma) \wedge \mathsf{FP}(\mathsf{tr}, q) = i \wedge \mathsf{p}(\mathsf{pp}, o, \mathsf{tr}) = 1\} .$$

Next, define

$$\delta_{i,q}(\alpha_1, \ldots, \alpha_{i-1}; \sigma) := \Pr_{\alpha_i', \ldots, \alpha_t' \in \mathbb{F}} [((\alpha_1, \ldots, \alpha_{i-1}, \alpha_i', \ldots, \alpha_t'), \sigma) \in S_{i,q}].$$

Denote by E the event in Eq. 1. Observe that because A is non-redundant, $\Pr[\mathsf{Fork} \mid (\boldsymbol{\alpha}, \sigma) \in S_{i,q}]$ is exactly $\delta_{i,q}(\alpha_1, \ldots, \alpha_{i-1}; \sigma)$.

We now analyze $\Pr[E]$.

$$\Pr[E] = \sum_{i \in [t], q \in \{0,1\}^m} \Pr[E \mid (\boldsymbol{\alpha}, \sigma) \in S_{i,q}] \cdot \Pr[(\boldsymbol{\alpha}, \sigma) \in S_{i,q}]$$

$$= \sum_{i,q} \mathbb{E}_{\boldsymbol{\alpha}, \sigma}[\mathbb{1}_{S_{i,q}}(\boldsymbol{\alpha}, \sigma) \cdot \delta_{i,q}(\alpha_1, \ldots, \alpha_{i-1}; \sigma)]$$

$$= \sum_{i,q} \mathbb{E}_{\alpha_1, \ldots, \alpha_{i-1}, \sigma}[\delta_{i,q}(\alpha_1, \ldots, \alpha_{i-1}; \sigma) \mathbb{E}_{\alpha_i, \ldots, \alpha_t}[\mathbb{1}_{S_{i,q}}(\boldsymbol{\alpha}, \sigma)]]$$

$$= \sum_{i,q} \mathbb{E}_{\alpha_1, \ldots, \alpha_{i-1}, \sigma}[\delta_{i,q}(\alpha_1, \ldots, \alpha_{i-1}; \sigma)^2]$$

where the last equality holds by definition of $\delta_{i,q}$. Let $Q_{i,\alpha,\sigma} := \{q : \delta_{i,q}(\alpha_1, \ldots, \alpha_{i-1}; \sigma) \neq 0\}$. We prove the following claim.

Claim. For all $\boldsymbol{\alpha}, \sigma$, $\sum_i |Q_{i,\alpha,\sigma}| \leq t$.

Proof. For any t-query transcript $\mathsf{tr} = ((q_1, \alpha_1), \ldots, (q_t, \alpha_t))$, let $Q_{i,\mathsf{tr}} := \{q : \mathsf{FP}(\mathsf{tr}, q) = i\}$. By Lemma 2, for all tr it holds that $\sum_i |Q_{i,\mathsf{tr}}| \leq t$. Note that $Q_{i,\mathsf{tr}}$ is a function of $(q_1, \ldots, q_i)$ only.

Now let $(q, o; \mathsf{tr}) := A^{\boldsymbol{\alpha}}(\mathsf{pp}; \sigma)$. For each i, $(q_1, \ldots, q_i)$ is a function of $\alpha_1, \ldots, \alpha_{i-1}, \sigma$ only; hence so is $Q_{i,\mathsf{tr}}$. It follows that $Q_{i,\alpha,\sigma} \subseteq Q_{i,\mathsf{tr}}$ for all i, which proves the claim. □

It follows that

$$\Pr[E] = \mathbb{E}_{\alpha, \sigma}\left[\sum_i \sum_{q \in Q_{i,\alpha,\sigma}} \delta_{i,q}(\alpha_1, \ldots, \alpha_{i-1}; \sigma)^2 \right]$$

$$\geq \frac{1}{t} \cdot \mathbb{E}_{\alpha, \sigma}\left[\left(\sum_i \sum_q \delta_{i,q}(\alpha_1, \ldots, \alpha_{i-1}; \sigma) \right)^2 \right] \geq \frac{\delta^2}{t} ,$$

where the first inequality holds because the number of terms in the sum is at most t, and the second holds by the inequality $\mathbb{E}[X^2] \geq \mathbb{E}[X]^2$. (The outer expectation is taken over $\boldsymbol{\alpha} \in \mathbb{F}^t$ so that all events are over the same probability space.)

6   Oracle Zero-Finding Games

Lemma 5 (Oracle zero-finding game). *Let $\{\mathbb{F}_\lambda\}_\lambda$ be a family of fields. Fix a number of variables $m \in \mathbb{N}$ and a maximum individual degree $d \in \mathbb{N}$. Further, let* CM *be a binding commitment scheme with message format L that is two polynomials $(f \colon \mathbb{F}_\lambda \to \mathbb{F}_\lambda,\ g \colon \mathbb{F}_\lambda \to (\mathbb{F}_\lambda)^m)$. Then for every efficient t-query oracle algorithm $\mathcal{A}$, the following holds.*

$$
\Pr\left[
\begin{array}{c}
f(X) \not\equiv \hat{\rho}(g(X)) \\
\wedge \\
f(z) = \hat{\rho}(g(z))
\end{array}
\;\middle|\;
\begin{array}{c}
\hat{\rho} \leftarrow \mathbb{F}_\lambda^{\leq d}[X_1, \ldots, X_m] \\
\mathsf{ck} \leftarrow \mathsf{CM.Setup}(1^\lambda, L) \\
(f, g, \omega) \leftarrow \mathcal{A}^{\hat{\rho}}(\mathsf{ck}) \\
C \leftarrow \mathsf{CM.Commit}(\mathsf{ck}, f, g, \omega) \\
z \in \mathbb{F}_\lambda \leftarrow \hat{\rho}(C)
\end{array}
\right]
\leq \sqrt{t \cdot \left[\frac{2md \cdot \deg(g) + 1}{|\mathbb{F}_\lambda|}\right]} + \mathsf{negl}(\lambda).
$$

Proof. Let $\mathcal{A}$ be an adversary that wins the above game with probability δ. By Sect. 4.2, we may assume without loss of generality that $\mathcal{A}$ is non-redundant.

We will apply Lemma 4. The forking predicate $\mathsf{p}(\mathsf{pp}, (\mathsf{q}, \alpha), o, \mathsf{tr})$ is the conjunction of the following conditions, where $(f, g) := o$ and $\tilde{\rho}_{\mathsf{tr}}$ is as defined in Sect. 4.1.

- $\mathsf{q} = \mathsf{CM.Commit}(f, g; \omega)$.
- Either $\tilde{\rho}_{\mathsf{tr}} \circ g \colon \mathbb{F} \to \mathbb{F}$ is not total, or $f(X) \not\equiv \tilde{\rho}_{\mathsf{tr}}(g(X))$.
- $f(\alpha) = \tilde{\rho}_{\mathsf{tr}}(g(\alpha))$, where $\alpha := \tilde{\rho}_{\mathsf{tr}}(\mathsf{q})$.

By assumption, from $\mathcal{A}$ we can obtain an adversary satisfying p with probability $> \delta$.

Lemma 4 guarantees that

$$
p := \Pr\left[
\begin{array}{c}
\mathsf{FP}(\mathsf{tr}, q) \neq \bot \wedge q \in \{0,1\}^m \\
\wedge\ q = q' \\
\wedge\ \mathsf{p}(\mathsf{pp}, q, o, \mathsf{tr}) = 1 \\
\wedge\ \mathsf{p}(\mathsf{pp}, q', o', \mathsf{tr}') = 1
\end{array}
\;\middle|\;
\begin{array}{c}
\hat{\rho} \leftarrow \mathcal{C}_\lambda \\
(q, o; \mathsf{tr}, \sigma) \leftarrow \mathcal{A}^{\hat{\rho}}(\mathsf{pp}) \\
(q', o', \mathsf{tr}', i) \leftarrow \mathsf{Fork}^A(q, o, \mathsf{tr}, \sigma)
\end{array}
\right] \geq \delta^2/t \ .
$$

To conclude the proof, we will bound p. Denote by E the event on the left of the above expression.

We first bound the probability that E occurs and $o \neq o'$. By definition of p, if $\mathcal{B}$ succeeds then $\mathsf{CM.Commit}(o) = \mathsf{q} = \mathsf{q}' = \mathsf{CM.Commit}(o')$. However, by the binding property of the commitment scheme CM, the probability $\mathcal{B}$ succeeds and $o \neq o'$ occurs with probability $\leq \mathsf{negl}(\lambda)$. Then the probability that E occurs and $o = o'$ is at least $p - \mathsf{negl}(\lambda)$; call this event E'.

Let $i := \mathsf{FP}(\mathsf{tr}, q)$, and let $\mathsf{tr}|_{i-1}$ denote the truncation of tr to the first $i - 1$ queries. We show that if E' occurs then with high probability, $\mathsf{tr}|_{i-1} \circ g$ is total.

Claim. The probability that E' occurs and $\tilde{\rho}_{\mathsf{tr}|_{i-1}} \circ g$ is not total is at most $(md \cdot \deg(g) + 1)/|\mathbb{F}|$.

Proof. Since for all $c \in \mathcal{C}$, $\deg(c \circ g) \leq d \cdot \deg(g)$, if $\tilde{\rho}_{\mathsf{tr}|_{i-1}} \circ g$ is not total then there are at most $d \cdot \deg(g)$ points $x \in \mathbb{F}$ such that $\tilde{\rho}_{\mathsf{tr}|_{i-1}}(g(x)) \neq \bot$. Then since α' is chosen independently of g and tr, $\Pr[\tilde{\rho}_{\mathsf{tr}|_{i-1}}(g(\alpha')) \neq \bot] \leq md \cdot \deg(g)/|\mathbb{F}|$. Finally, if $\tilde{\rho}_{\mathsf{tr}|_{i-1}}(g(\alpha')) = \bot$, $\Pr[\tilde{\rho}_{\mathsf{tr'}}(g(\alpha')) = f(\alpha')] \leq \frac{1}{|\mathbb{F}|}$, since f and $\mathsf{tr'}$ are independent conditioned on $\mathsf{tr}|_{i-1}$. $\square$

It follows that the probability that E' occurs and $\tilde{\rho}_{\mathsf{tr}|_{i-1}} \circ g$ is total is at least $p - (md \cdot \deg(g) + 1)/|\mathbb{F}| - \mathrm{negl}(\lambda)$. In this case it holds that $\tilde{\rho}_{\mathsf{tr}|_{i-1}} \circ g \not\equiv f$, but $\tilde{\rho}_{\mathsf{tr}|_{i-1}}(g(\alpha')) = f(\alpha')$. Since α' is drawn independently of $\mathsf{tr}|_{i-1}$, g and f, this holds with probability at most $md \cdot \deg(g)/|\mathbb{F}|$.

Rearranging, it follows that

$$p \leq \frac{2md \cdot \deg(g) + 1}{|\mathbb{F}|} + \mathrm{negl}(\lambda) \ ;$$

the statement follows since $p \geq \delta^2/t$. $\square$

7   Accumulation Scheme for Low-Degree Random Oracles

We construct an accumulation scheme $\mathsf{AS} = (\mathsf{G}, \mathsf{I}, \mathsf{P}, \mathsf{V}, \mathsf{D})$ for any low-degree random oracle over a sufficiently large field.

Note that AS is typically defined with respect to a predicate Φ and a randomized algorithm $\mathcal{H}$, which accesses the oracle and outputs predicate parameters pp_Φ. For this construction, $\mathcal{H} = \bot$.

Theorem 1. *Let $\mathcal{C}$ be a $(\mathbb{F}_\lambda, m, d)$-low-degree random oracle.. Let $\mathsf{CM} = (\mathsf{CM.Setup}, \mathsf{CM.Commit})$ be a commitment scheme that is hiding, binding, and has compression to size m. Then, the scheme AS from Construction 1 is an accumulation scheme for $(\Phi, \bot)$, where $\Phi([\mathsf{q}_i]_{i=1}^n) = 1$ if for all $i \in [n]$, the query $\mathsf{q}_i = (x_i, \alpha_i)$ satisfies $\hat{\rho}(x_i) = \alpha_i$.*

We give the construction below. We assume a global ordering of the field $\mathbb{F}_\lambda$, so that $\mathbb{F}_\lambda = \{b_1, \ldots, b_{|\mathbb{F}_\lambda|}\}$.

Construction 1. $\mathsf{AS} = (\mathsf{G}, \mathsf{I}, \mathsf{P}, \mathsf{V}, \mathsf{D})$ is defined as follows:

- Accumulator: The scheme's accumulators are of the form $\mathsf{acc} \in ((\mathbb{F}_\lambda)^n, \mathbb{F}_\lambda)^2$.
- $\mathsf{G}(1^\lambda)$: Output a commitment scheme's commitment key and public parameters $(\mathsf{ck}, \mathsf{pp}_{\mathsf{CM}}) \leftarrow \mathsf{CM.Setup}(L)$, such that the message format L is two polynomials $(f \colon \mathbb{F}_\lambda \to \mathbb{F}_\lambda,\ g \colon \mathbb{F}_\lambda \to (\mathbb{F}_\lambda)^m)$.
- $\mathsf{I}^{\hat{\rho}}(\mathsf{pp} = \mathsf{ck})$: Output $(\mathsf{apk} = \mathsf{ck}, \mathsf{avk} = \mathsf{ck}, \mathsf{dk} = 1^\lambda)$.
- $\mathsf{P}^{\hat{\rho}}(\mathsf{apk} = \mathsf{ck}, [\mathsf{q}_i]_{i=1}^n, [\mathsf{acc}_j]_{j=1}^\ell)$:
    1. Let $Q = [(x_k, \alpha_k)]_{k=1}^{n+2\ell}$ be the concatentation of $[\mathsf{q}_i]_{i=1}^n$ and $[\mathsf{acc}_j]_{j=1}^\ell$.
    2. Sample a random point $x_{n+2\ell+1} \in (\mathbb{F}_\lambda)^\ell$, and set $\alpha_{n+2\ell+1} := \hat{\rho}(x_{n+2\ell+1})$.
    3. Compute the polynomial $g \colon \mathbb{F}_\lambda \to (\mathbb{F}_\lambda)^\ell$ of degree at most $n + 2\ell$ such that for each $k \in [n + 2\ell + 1]$, $g(b_k) = x_k$.

4. Compute the polynomial $f \colon \mathbb{F}_\lambda \to \mathbb{F}_\lambda$ as $f(X) \equiv \hat{\rho}(g(X))$. Note that the degree of f is at most $m \cdot d \cdot (n + 2\ell + 1)$.
5. Sample randomness ω for the commitment scheme, then compute $C := \mathsf{CM.Commit}(\mathsf{ck}, (f, g); \omega) \in \{0, 1\}^m$ and $\beta := \hat{\rho}(C)$.
6. Output the new accumulator $\mathsf{acc} = \{(g(\beta), f(\beta)), (C, \beta)\}$ and proof $\pi_V = (f, \omega, (x_{n+2\ell+1}, \alpha_{n+2\ell+1}))$.

– $\mathsf{V}(\mathsf{avk} = \mathsf{ck}, [\mathsf{q}_i]_{i=1}^n, [\mathsf{acc}_j]_{j=1}^\ell, \mathsf{acc} = \{(x, \alpha), (C, \beta)\}, \pi_V = (f, \omega, (x_{n+2\ell+1}, \alpha_{n+2\ell+1})))$:

1. Compute the list $Q = [(x_k, \alpha_k)]_{k=1}^{n+2\ell}$ and the polynomial g from $[\mathsf{q}_i]_{i=1}^n$ and $[\mathsf{acc}_j]_{j=1}^\ell$ as P does. However, rather than sampling $(x_{n+2\ell+1}, \alpha_{n+2\ell+1})$, use the value received in π_V.
2. Check that $x = g(\beta)$, $\alpha = f(\beta)$ and $C = \mathsf{CM.Commit}(\mathsf{ck}, (f, g); \omega)$.
3. For each $k \in [n + 2\ell + 1]$, check that $f(b_k) = \alpha_k$.
4. Accept if and only if both checks pass.

– $\mathsf{D}^{\hat{\rho}}(\mathsf{dk} = 1^\lambda, \mathsf{acc} = \{(x_1, \alpha_1), (x_2, \alpha_2)\})$: Accept if and only if $\hat{\rho}(x_1) = \alpha_1$ and $\hat{\rho}(x_2) = \alpha_2$.

Remark 1. CM can be replaced by a hash function (sampled from an appropriate hash family) if AS isn't required to be zero knowledge.

Acknowledgments. This research was supported in part by a donation from the Ethereum Foundation, and by DARPA under Agreement No. HR00112020023.

References

1. Aaronson, S., Wigderson, A.: Algebrization: a new barrier in complexity theory. ACM Trans. Comput. Theory **1**(1), 2:1–2:54 (2009)
2. Abdolmaleki, B., Baghery, K., Lipmaa, H., Siim, J., Zając, M.: UC-secure CRS generation for SNARKs. In: Buchmann, J., Nitaj, A., Rachidi, T. (eds.) AFRICACRYPT 2019. LNCS, vol. 11627, pp. 99–117. Springer, Cham (2019). https://doi.org/10.1007/978-3-030-23696-0_6
3. Albrecht, M.R., et al.: Algebraic cryptanalysis of STARK-friendly designs: application to MARVELlous and MiMC. IACR Cryptology ePrint Archive, Report 2019/419 (2019)
4. Albrecht, M.R., et al.: Feistel structures for MPC, and more. IACR Cryptology ePrint Archive, Report 2019/397 (2019)
5. Aly, A., Ashur, T., Ben-Sasson, E., Dhooghe, S., Szepieniec, A.: Design of symmetric-key primitives for advanced cryptographic protocols. IACR Cryptology ePrint Archive, Report 2019/426 (2019)
6. Ashur, T., Dhooghe, S.: MARVELlous: a STARK-friendly family of cryptographic primitives. IACR Cryptology ePrint Archive, Report 2018/1098 (2018)
7. Bellare, M., Neven, G.: Multi-signatures in the plain public-key model and a general forking lemma. In: Proceedings of the 13th ACM Conference on Computer and Communications Security, CCS 2006, pp. 390–399 (2006)
8. Ben-Sasson, E., Chiesa, A., Forbes, M.A., Gabizon, A., Riabzev, M., Spooner, N.: Zero knowledge protocols from succinct constraint detection. In: Kalai, Y., Reyzin, L. (eds.) TCC 2017. LNCS, vol. 10678, pp. 172–206. Springer, Cham (2017). https://doi.org/10.1007/978-3-319-70503-3_6

9. Ben-Sasson, E., Chiesa, A., Green, M., Tromer, E., Virza, M.: Secure sampling of public parameters for succinct zero knowledge proofs. In: Proceedings of the 36th IEEE Symposium on Security and Privacy, S&P 2015, pp. 287–304 (2015)

10. Ben-Sasson, E., Chiesa, A., Tromer, E., Virza, M.: Scalable zero knowledge via cycles of elliptic curves. In: Garay, J.A., Gennaro, R. (eds.) CRYPTO 2014. LNCS, vol. 8617, pp. 276–294. Springer, Heidelberg (2014). https://doi.org/10.1007/978-3-662-44381-1_16

11. Benabbas, S., Gennaro, R., Vahlis, Y.: Verifiable delegation of computation over large datasets. In: Rogaway, P. (ed.) CRYPTO 2011. LNCS, vol. 6841, pp. 111–131. Springer, Heidelberg (2011). https://doi.org/10.1007/978-3-642-22792-9_7

12. Bitansky, N., Canetti, R., Chiesa, A., Tromer, E.: Recursive composition and bootstrapping for SNARKs and proof-carrying data. In: Proceedings of the 45th ACM Symposium on the Theory of Computing, STOC 2013, pp. 111–120 (2013)

13. Bitansky, N., Chiesa, A., Ishai, Y., Paneth, O., Ostrovsky, R.: Succinct non-interactive arguments via linear interactive proofs. In: Sahai, A. (ed.) TCC 2013. LNCS, vol. 7785, pp. 315–333. Springer, Heidelberg (2013). https://doi.org/10.1007/978-3-642-36594-2_18

14. Boneh, D., Boyen, X.: Short signatures without random oracles. In: Cachin, C., Camenisch, J.L. (eds.) EUROCRYPT 2004. LNCS, vol. 3027, pp. 56–73. Springer, Heidelberg (2004). https://doi.org/10.1007/978-3-540-24676-3_4

15. Boneh, D., Drake, J., Fisch, B., Gabizon, A.: Halo infinite: recursive zk-SNARKS from any additive polynomial commitment scheme. ePrint Report 2020/1536 (2020)

16. Bowe, S., Gabizon, A., Green, M.: A multi-party protocol for constructing the public parameters of the Pinocchio zk-SNARK. ePrint Report 2017/602 (2017)

17. Bowe, S., Gabizon, A., Miers, I.: Scalable multi-party computation for zk-SNARK parameters in the random beacon model. ePrint Report 2017/1050 (2017)

18. Bowe, S., Grigg, J., Hopwood, D.: Halo: recursive proof composition without a trusted setup. ePrint Report 2019/1021 (2019)

19. Bünz, B., Chiesa, A., Lin, W., Mishra, P., Spooner, N.: Proof-carrying data without succinct arguments. In: Malkin, T., Peikert, C. (eds.) CRYPTO 2021. LNCS, vol. 12825, pp. 681–710. Springer, Cham (2021). https://doi.org/10.1007/978-3-030-84242-0_24

20. Bünz, B., Chiesa, A., Mishra, P., Spooner, N.: Proof-carrying data from accumulation schemes (2020)

21. Chiesa, A., Forbes, M.A., Gur, T., Spooner, N.: Spatial isolation implies zero knowledge even in a quantum world. In: Proceedings of the 59th Annual IEEE Symposium on Foundations of Computer Science, FOCS 2018, pp. 755–765 (2018)

22. Chiesa, A., Hu, Y., Maller, M., Mishra, P., Vesely, N., Ward, N.: Marlin: preprocessing zkSNARKs with universal and updatable SRS. In: Canteaut, A., Ishai, Y. (eds.) EUROCRYPT 2020. LNCS, vol. 12105, pp. 738–768. Springer, Cham (2020). https://doi.org/10.1007/978-3-030-45721-1_26

23. Chiesa, A., Liu, S.: On the impossibility of probabilistic proofs in relativized worlds. In: Proceedings of the 11th Innovations in Theoretical Computer Science Conference, ITCS 2020, pp. 57:1–57:30 (2020)

24. Chiesa, A., Ojha, D., Spooner, N.: FRACTAL: post-quantum and transparent recursive proofs from holography. In: Canteaut, A., Ishai, Y. (eds.) EUROCRYPT 2020. LNCS, vol. 12105, pp. 769–793. Springer, Cham (2020). https://doi.org/10.1007/978-3-030-45721-1_27

25. Chiesa, A., Tromer, E.: Proof-carrying data and hearsay arguments from signature cards. In: Proceedings of the 1st Symposium on Innovations in Computer Science, ICS 2010, pp. 310–331 (2010)
26. Fiat, A., Shamir, A.: How to prove yourself: practical solutions to identification and signature problems. In: Odlyzko, A.M. (ed.) CRYPTO 1986. LNCS, vol. 263, pp. 186–194. Springer, Heidelberg (1987). https://doi.org/10.1007/3-540-47721-7_12
27. Gennaro, R., Gentry, C., Parno, B., Raykova, M.: Quadratic span programs and succinct NIZKs without PCPs. In: Johansson, T., Nguyen, P.Q. (eds.) EUROCRYPT 2013. LNCS, vol. 7881, pp. 626–645. Springer, Heidelberg (2013). https://doi.org/10.1007/978-3-642-38348-9_37
28. Grassi, L., Khovratovich, D., Rechberger, C., Roy, A., Schofnegger, M.: Poseidon: a new hash function for zero-knowledge proof systems. IACR Cryptology ePrint Archive, Report 2019/458 (2019)
29. Groth, J.: Short pairing-based non-interactive zero-knowledge arguments. In: Abe, M. (ed.) ASIACRYPT 2010. LNCS, vol. 6477, pp. 321–340. Springer, Heidelberg (2010). https://doi.org/10.1007/978-3-642-17373-8_19
30. Groth, J.: On the size of pairing-based non-interactive arguments. In: Fischlin, M., Coron, J.-S. (eds.) EUROCRYPT 2016. LNCS, vol. 9666, pp. 305–326. Springer, Heidelberg (2016). https://doi.org/10.1007/978-3-662-49896-5_11
31. Groth, J., Kohlweiss, M., Maller, M., Meiklejohn, S., Miers, I.: Updatable and universal common reference strings with applications to zk-SNARKs. In: Shacham, H., Boldyreva, A. (eds.) CRYPTO 2018. LNCS, vol. 10993, pp. 698–728. Springer, Cham (2018). https://doi.org/10.1007/978-3-319-96878-0_24
32. Kalai, Y.T., Raz, R.: Interactive PCP. In: Aceto, L., Damgård, I., Goldberg, L.A., Halldórsson, M.M., Ingólfsdóttir, A., Walukiewicz, I. (eds.) ICALP 2008. LNCS, vol. 5126, pp. 536–547. Springer, Heidelberg (2008). https://doi.org/10.1007/978-3-540-70583-3_44
33. Kothapalli, A., Setty, S., Tzialla, I.: Nova: recursive zero-knowledge arguments from folding schemes. ePrint Report 2021/370 (2021)
34. Maurer, U.: Abstract models of computation in cryptography. In: Smart, N.P. (ed.) Cryptography and Coding 2005. LNCS, vol. 3796, pp. 1–12. Springer, Heidelberg (2005). https://doi.org/10.1007/11586821_1
35. Micali, S.: Computationally sound proofs. SIAM J. Comput. **30**(4), 1253–1298 (2000). Preliminary version appeared in FOCS '94
36. Shoup, V.: Lower bounds for discrete logarithms and related problems. In: Fumy, W. (ed.) EUROCRYPT 1997. LNCS, vol. 1233, pp. 256–266. Springer, Heidelberg (1997). https://doi.org/10.1007/3-540-69053-0_18
37. Smart, N.P.: 'Bristol fashion' MPC circuits. https://homes.esat.kuleuven.be/~nsmart/MPC/
38. Valiant, P.: Incrementally verifiable computation or proofs of knowledge imply time/space efficiency. In: Canetti, R. (ed.) TCC 2008. LNCS, vol. 4948, pp. 1–18. Springer, Heidelberg (2008). https://doi.org/10.1007/978-3-540-78524-8_1
39. Zhandry, M., Zhang, C.: The relationship between idealized models under computationally bounded adversaries. Cryptology ePrint Archive, Report 2021/240 (2021)

Families of SNARK-Friendly 2-Chains of Elliptic Curves

Youssef El Housni[1,2,3]([⊠]) [iD] and Aurore Guillevic[4,5]([⊠]) [iD]

[1] ConsenSys, gnark, Paris, France
youssef.elhousni@consensys.net
[2] LIX, CNRS, École Polytechnique, Institut Polytechnique de Paris,
Palaiseau, France
[3] Inria, Saclay, France
[4] Université de Lorraine, CNRS, Inria, LORIA, Nancy, France
aurore.guillevic@inria.fr
[5] Aarhus University, Aarhus, Denmark

Abstract. At CANS'20, El Housni and Guillevic introduced a new 2-chain of pairing-friendly elliptic curves for recursive zero-knowledge Succinct Non-interactive ARguments of Knowledge (zk-SNARKs) made of the former BLS12-377 curve (a Barreto–Lynn–Scott curve over a 377-bit prime field) and the new BW6-761 curve (a Brezing–Weng curve of embedding degree 6 over a 761-bit prime field). First we generalise the curve construction, the pairing formulas ($e\colon \mathbb{G}_1 \times \mathbb{G}_2 \to \mathbb{G}_T$) and the group operations to any BW6 curve defined on top of any BLS12 curve, forming a family of 2-chain pairing-friendly curves.

Second, we investigate other possible 2-chain families made on top of the BLS12 and BLS24 curves. We compare BW6 to Cocks–Pinch curves of higher embedding degrees 8 and 12 (CP8, CP12) at the 128-bit security level. We derive formulas for efficient optimal ate and optimal Tate pairings on our new CP curves. We show that for both BLS12 and BLS24, the BW6 construction always gives the fastest pairing and curve arithmetic compared to Cocks-Pinch curves. Finally, we suggest a short list of curves suitable for Groth16 and KZG-based universal SNARKs and present an optimized implementation of these curves. Based on Groth16 and PlonK (a KZG-based SNARK) implementations in the **gnark** ecosystem, we obtain that the BLS12-377/BW6-761 pair is optimized for the former while the BLS24-315/BW6-672 pair is optimized for the latter.

1 Introduction

A SNARK [7,33,35] is a cryptographic primitive that enables a prover to prove to a verifier the knowledge of a satisfying witness to a non-deterministic (NP) statement by producing a proof π such that the size of π and the cost to verify it are both sub-linear in the size of the witness. If π does not reveal anything about the witness we refer to the cryptographic primitive as a zero-knowledge (zk) SNARK. Today, the most efficient SNARKs require pairing-friendly elliptic curves and trusted setup assumptions as in Groth'16 [25] but in return

© International Association for Cryptologic Research 2022
O. Dunkelman and S. Dziembowski (Eds.): EUROCRYPT 2022, LNCS 13276, pp. 367–396, 2022.
https://doi.org/10.1007/978-3-031-07085-3_13

admit small, constant-size proofs with a constant-time verification. However, the trusted setup is specific to the NP statement to prove. Hence, Groth'16 is not suitable in applications that need to prove many different statements. Fortunately, SNARKs with a universal or transparent setup are an active area of research and recent polynomial-commitment-based constructions allow very efficient constructions. The most efficient universal constructions such as PlonK [21] and Marlin [11] are based on the KZG polynomial commitment [32], which also requires a pairing-friendly elliptic curve.

A pairing-friendly curve E has a bilinear map $e \colon \mathbb{G}_1 \times \mathbb{G}_2 \to \mathbb{G}_T$, where $\mathbb{G}_1, \mathbb{G}_2$ are distinct prime-order r subgroups of E, and $\mathbb{G}_T \subset \mathbb{F}_{q^k}$ of the same order r. On the one hand, one requires two different kind of curves: a curve tailored for Groth'16 should be optimized for operations in $\mathbb{G}_1$, $\mathbb{G}_2$ and for pairings while a curve tailored for KZG-based SNARKs should only focus on $\mathbb{G}_1$ and pairings. On the other hand, both constructions make SNARKs appealing for an incrementally verifiable computation (IVC) [41] in which proofs not only attest to the correct execution of a computation but also, by exploiting succinctness, to the validity of a previous proof. The canonical construction of IVC, or proof-carrying data [8] (PCD) as a generalization, can be achieved via recursive proof composition which was demonstrated to be practical for pairing-based SNARKs in [5]. In such a setting, a prover encodes the statement in the curve's scalar field $\mathbb{F}_r$ (the $\mathbb{G}_i$ are of order r) and a verifier checks the proof π in an extension $\mathbb{F}_{q^k}$ of the curve base field. To allow recursive proof composition, one needs to encode the verification algorithm (which lies in $\mathbb{F}_{q^k}$) as a statement in $\mathbb{F}_r$. However, this is highly impractical as $r \neq q$ and simulating one field's operations in the other incurs a significant overhead. The authors of [5] sidestep this issue by constructing a 2-cycle of pairing-friendly elliptic curves such that the base field of either curve is the scalar field of the other. Unfortunately, only the MNT4/MNT6 [19, Sec. 5] family of pairing-friendly curves is known to satisfy this property and due to their low embedding degrees, secure curves in this family must be constructed over very large (1024-bit) fields, downgrading the performances. To relax this constraint, authors of ZEXE [10] constructed a 2-chain of pairing-friendly elliptic curves such that only the base field of one curve is equal to the scalar field of the other, allowing one-layer recursive proof composition. Namely, the inner curve is a BLS12-377 and the outer curve is a CP6-782. A one-layer recursive proof composition is particularly the building block of two schemes: Decentralized Private Computation (DPC) schemes as introduced in ZEXE [10] and proofs aggregation. This work is directly relevant to these two contructions.

Previous Work. In [15], El Housni and Guillevic introduced a 2-chain of curves made of the previous BLS12-377 and a new BW6-761 curve, a Brezing-Weng curve of embedding degree 6 defined over a 761-bit prime field, which they demonstrated to be orders of magnitude faster than CP6-782.

Contributions. First we are interested in families of 2-chains in which the BW6-761 curve would fall. We present a family of BW6 curves from any BLS12 curve and derive generic formulas, in terms of the BLS12 curve seed u, and integer parameters h_t, h_y. We extend this work to a 2-chain family of BW6 curves from BLS24 curves. We particularly improve the multi-pairing computation on any BW6 curve by deriving a new endomorphism-based optimal Tate pairing (Algorithm 2). To achieve higher levels of security in the target finite field of the outer curves, we compare a larger field characteristic thanks to larger parameters h_t, h_y, to the larger embedding degrees 8 and 12 obtained with Cocks-Pinch curves. Finally, we argue that the BLS12 and BLS24 based families are respectively tailored for Groth'16 and KZG-based SNARKs recursive proof composition, and we present a short list of curves with an optimized implementation along with benchmarks.

Organization of the Paper. Section 2 provides the preliminaries and definitions of SNARK-friendly elliptic curves. In Sect. 3, we argue on the choice of BLS family as the inner curve and present faster group operations. The core of the paper are Sects. 4 and 5. Section 4 exposes the constructions of the outer curves, with optimized pairings and group operations. Finally, Sect. 5 reports on the implementation of the most promising constructions identified in Sect. 4 and compares the performances in relevant practical settings.

2 Preliminaries

We present a short background on pairing-friendly elliptic curves and propose definitions of a SNARK-friendly chain of curves.

2.1 Background on Bilinear Pairings

We briefly recall elementary definitions on pairings and present the computation of two pairings used in practice, the modified Tate and ate pairings. All elliptic curves discussed below are *ordinary* (i.e. non-supersingular).

Let E be an elliptic curve defined over a field $\mathbb{F}_q$, where q is a prime power. Let π_q be the Frobenius endomorphism: $(x, y) \mapsto (x^q, y^q)$. Its minimal polynomial is $X^2 - tX + q$ where t is called the *trace*. Let r be a prime divisor of the curve order $\#E(\mathbb{F}_q) = q + 1 - t$. The r-torsion subgroup of E is denoted $E[r] = \{P \in E(\overline{\mathbb{F}}_q), [r]P = \mathcal{O}\}$ and has two subgroups of order r (eigenspaces of π_q in $E[r]$) that are useful for pairing applications. We define the two groups $\mathbb{G}_1 = E[r] \cap \ker(\pi_q - [1])$ with a generator denoted by G_1, and $\mathbb{G}_2 = E[r] \cap \ker(\pi_q - [q])$ with a generator G_2. The group $\mathbb{G}_2$ is defined over $\mathbb{F}_{q^k}$, where the embedding degree k is the smallest integer $k \in \mathbb{N}^*$ such that $r \mid q^k - 1$.

We recall the Tate and ate pairing definitions, based on the same two steps: evaluating a function $f_{s,Q}$ at a point P, the Miller loop step, and then raising it to the power $(q^k - 1)/r$, the final exponentiation step. The function $f_{s,Q}$ has divisor $div(f_{s,Q}) = s(Q) - ([s]Q) - (s - 1)(\mathcal{O})$ and satisfies, for integers i and j, $f_{i+j,Q} = f_{i,Q}f_{j,Q}\ell_{[i]Q,[j]Q}/v_{[i+j]Q}$, where $\ell_{[i]Q,[j]Q}$ and $v_{[i+j]Q}$ are the two lines needed to compute $[i+j]Q$ from $[i]Q$ and $[j]Q$ (ℓ intersecting the two points and v the vertical). We compute $f_{s,Q}(P)$ with the Miller loop presented in Algorithm 1.

Algorithm 1: MillerLoop(s, P, Q)

   Output: $m = f_{s,Q}(P)$

1 $m \leftarrow 1; S \leftarrow Q$

2 **for** b *from the second most significant bit of s to the least* **do**

3     $\ell \leftarrow \ell_{S,S}(P); S \leftarrow [2]S; v \leftarrow v_{[2]S}(P)$ `// DOUBLING STEP`

4     $m \leftarrow m^2 \cdot \ell/v$

5   **if** $b = 1$ **then**

6         $\ell \leftarrow \ell_{S,Q}(P); S \leftarrow S + Q; v \leftarrow v_{S+Q}(P)$ `// ADDITION STEP`

7         $m \leftarrow m \cdot \ell/v$

8 **return** m

The Tate and ate pairings are defined by

$$\text{Tate}(P, Q) = f_{r,P}(Q)^{(q^k-1)/r}, \qquad \text{ate}(Q, P) = f_{t-1,Q}(P)^{(q^k-1)/r}$$

where $P \in \mathbb{G}_1 \subset E[r](\mathbb{F}_q)$ and $Q \in \mathbb{G}_2 \subset E[r](\mathbb{F}_{q^k})$. The final powering $z \mapsto z^{(q^k-1)/r}$ ensures that the values $\text{Tate}(P, Q)$ and $\text{ate}(Q, P)$ are in the *target group* $\mathbb{G}_T$ of r-th roots of unity in $\mathbb{F}_{q^k}$. It is decomposed into two steps: the easy part $z^{(q^k-1)/\Phi_k(q)}$ with one inversion and some Frobenius powers, and the hard part $z^{\Phi_k(q)/r}$, where Φ_k is the k-th cyclotomic polynomial. In this paper, when abstraction is needed, we denote a pairing as follows: $e\colon \mathbb{G}_1 \times \mathbb{G}_2 \to \mathbb{G}_T$.

It is also important to recall some results with respect to the complex multiplication (CM) discriminant $-D$. When $D = 3$ (resp. $D = 4$), the curve has CM by $\mathbb{Q}(\sqrt{-3})$ (resp. $\mathbb{Q}(\sqrt{-1})$) so that twists of degrees 3 and 6 exist (resp. 4). If moreover the twist degree d divides k, then $\mathbb{G}_2$ is isomorphic to $E'[r](\mathbb{F}_{q^{k/d}})$ for a d-twist E'. Otherwise, in the general case, E admits a single twist (up to isomorphism) and it is of degree 2.

2.2 zk-SNARKs

In this paper, we focus on preprocessing zkSNARKs for NP languages for which we give a basic explanation. Given a public NP program F, public inputs a and b and private input w, such that the program F satisfies the relation $F(a, w) := b$, a zk-SNARK consists in proving this relation succinctly without revealing the private input w. Given a security parameter λ, it consists of the Setup, Prove and Verify algorithms:

$$(\sigma_p, \sigma_v) \leftarrow \text{Setup}(F, \tau, 1^\lambda); \quad \pi \leftarrow \text{Prove}(a, b, w, \sigma_p); \quad 0/1 \leftarrow \text{Verify}(a, b, \pi, \sigma_v)$$

where τ is the setup trapdoor, σ_p the proving key which encodes the program F for the prover, σ_v the verification key that encodes F for the verifier and π the proof.

2.3 SNARK-Friendly Chains

Definition 1. *An m-chain of elliptic curves is a list of distinct curves*

$$E_1/\mathbb{F}_{q_1}, \ldots, E_m/\mathbb{F}_{q_m}$$

where $q_1, \ldots, q_m$ are large primes and

$$q_1 = r_2 \mid \#E_2(\mathbb{F}_{q_2}), \ldots, q_{i-1} = r_i \mid \#E_i(\mathbb{F}_{q_i}), \ldots, q_{m-1} = r_m \mid \#E_m(\mathbb{F}_{q_m}).$$

Definition 2. *An m-chain of SNARK-friendly elliptic curves is an m-chain where each of the $\{E_i/\mathbb{F}_{q_i}\}_{1 \leq i \leq m}$ curves*

- *is pairing-friendly;*
- *has a highly 2-adic subgroup, i.e. $r_i - 1 \equiv 0 \mod 2^L$ for a large $L \geq 1$.*

In particular, a SNARK-friendly 2-chain is a pair of two pairing-friendly elliptic curves $E_1/\mathbb{F}_{q_1}$ and $E_2/\mathbb{F}_{q_2}$ where $q_1 = r_2 \mid \#E_2(\mathbb{F}_{q_2})$ and $r_2 - 1 \equiv r_1 - 1 \equiv 0 \mod 2^L$. We call E_1 the inner curve and E_2 the outer curve.

In this paper, we aim at constructing families of SNARK-friendly 2-chains that are suitable respectively for Groth'16 and KZG-based universal SNARKs.

3   Inner Curves: Barreto–Lynn–Scott (BLS) Curves

We investigate the BLS family as an option for a SNARK-friendly inner curve. We first present our results for a better arithmetic on all BLS curves and then argue on the choice of BLS12 and BLS24 curves for our applications.

3.1   Parameters with a Polynomial Form

BLS curves were introduced in [4]. This is a family of pairing-friendly elliptic curves of embedding degree k multiple of 3 but not multiple of 18. Well-known families are given with $k = 2^i 3^j$ for $i, j \geq 0$: $k = 9, 12, 24, 27, 48$ (Table 1). The curves have j-invariant 0, discriminant $-D = -3$. Each family has polynomial parameters $q(x), r(x), t(x)$ for characteristic, subgroup order of embedding degree k, and trace. The subgroup order is $r(x) = \Phi_k(x)$ the k-th cyclotomic polynomial. The trace has a simple expression $t(x) = x + 1$, so that the ate pairing whose Miller loop computes the function $f_{x,Q}(P)$ is optimal in terms of Vercauteren's paper [42]. The curve order is $q(x) + 1 - t(x)$ and the CM equation is $4q(x) = t(x)^2 + Dy(x)^2$. We state useful lemmas whose proofs are given in [16, Appendix A.1].

Lemma 1. *The cofactor $c(x)$ of BLS curves such that $q(x)+1-t(x) = c(x)r(x)$ has the form*

1. *$(x-1)^2/3 \cdot c_2(x)$ for odd k, where $c_2(x) = (x^{2k/3} + x^{k/3} + 1)/\Phi_k(x) \in \mathbb{Q}[x]$;*
2. *$(x-1)^2/3 \cdot c_2(x)$ for even k, where $c_2(x) = (x^{k/3} - x^{k/6} + 1)/\Phi_k(x) \in \mathbb{Q}[x]$.*

Lemma 2. *For all BLS curves, the polynomial form of the characteristic $q(x)$ is such that $(x-1)/3$ divides $q(x) - 1$.*

Lemma 3. *The parameter $y(x)$ of BLS curves has the form*

$$(x-1)(2x^{k/3}+1)/3 \text{ for odd } k \quad \text{and} \quad (x-1)(2x^{k/6}-1)/3 \text{ for even } k.$$

Lemma 4. *Any BLS curve has endomorphism ring $\mathbb{Z}[\omega]$ where $\omega = (1+\sqrt{-3})/2$.*

Table 1. Parameters of BLS curves for $k = 2^i 3^j$, $i \geq 0$, $j \geq 1$, $18 \nmid k$.

k	$2^i 3^j$, $i, j \geq 1$ $(6, 12, 24, 48, 96, \ldots)$	3^j, $j \geq 1$ $(3, 9, 27, 81, \ldots)$
$t(x)$	$x + 1$	
$y(x)$	$(x-1)(2x^{k/6} - 1)/3$	$(x-1)(2x^{k/3} + 1)/3$
$r(x)$	$x^{k/3} - x^{k/6} + 1$	$x^{2k/3} + x^{k/3} + 1$
$q(x)$	$r(x)(x-1)^2/3 + x$	$r(x)/3(x-1)^2 + x$
$c_2(x)$	1	1
ρ	$1 + 6/k$	$1 + 3/k$

3.2   Faster Co-factor Multiplication

Because $\mathbb{G}_1$ is a proper subgroup of $E(\mathbb{F}_q)$, one multiplies a point $P \in E(\mathbb{F}_q)$ by the cofactor $c(x) = (x-1)^2/3$ to map it to $\mathbb{G}_1$, a.k.a. *cofactor clearing*. Wahby and Boneh noted in [43], that it is sufficient to multiply by $x - 1$ to clear the cofactor of $\mathbb{G}_1$ for the BLS12-381 curve (also in [37, §2]). Here we generalize and prove that it is true for all BLS curves. Let $\mathrm{End}_{\mathbb{F}_q}(E)$ denote the ring of $\mathbb{F}_q$-endomorphisms of E, let $\mathcal{O}$ denote a complex quadratic order of the ring of integers of a complex quadratic number field, and $\mathcal{O}(\Delta)$ denote the complex quadratic order of discriminant Δ.

Theorem 1 ([36, **Proposition 3.7**]). *Let E be an elliptic curve over $\mathbb{F}_q$ and $n \in \mathbb{Z}_{\geq 1}$ with $q \nmid n$. Let π_q denote the Frobenius endomorphism of E and t its trace. Then,*

$$E[n] \subset E(\mathbb{F}_q) \iff \begin{cases} n^2 \mid \#E(\mathbb{F}_q), \\ n \mid q - 1 \text{ and} \\ \pi_q \in \mathbb{Z} \text{ or } \mathcal{O}\left(\frac{t^2 - 4q}{n^2}\right) \subset \mathrm{End}_{\mathbb{F}_q}(E). \end{cases}$$

Proof. Proposition 3.7. in [36].

Corollary 1. *Let $E(\mathbb{F}_{q(x)})$ be a BLS curve of order $c(x)r(x)$ where $r(x)$ is the subgroup prime order and $c(x) = (x-1)^2/3 \cdot c_2(x)$ the cofactor. It is sufficient to multiply by $(x-1)c_2(x)$ to clear the cofactor.*

Proof. Let $n(x) = (x-1)/3$, we show that the full $n(x)$-torsion is in $E(\mathbb{F}_q)$, that is there is no point of order $n^2(x)$ in $E(\mathbb{F}_q)$ but there are $n^2(x)$ points of order $n(x)$. Thus it is sufficient to multiply by $3n(x)$ to clear the $(x-1)^2/3$ cofactor. According to Lemmas 1, 2, 3, and 4, we have $n(x)^2 \mid \#E(\mathbb{F}_q)$, $n(x) \mid q(x) - 1$. Now $(t^2(x) - 4q(x))/n^2(x) = -3y^2(x)/n^2(x) = -3(2x^{k/6} - 1)^2$ for even k, and $-3(2x^{k/3} + 1)^2$ for odd k. Hence $\mathcal{O}\left(\frac{t(x)^2 - 4q(x)}{n^2(x)}\right) \subset \mathrm{End}_{\mathbb{F}_q}(E)$. Thus, Theorem 1 applies and $E[n(x)] \subset E(\mathbb{F}_q)$.

Theorem 1 applied to BLS curves tells us that the curve endomorphism $\phi: E \to E$, $(x, y) \mapsto (\omega x, y)$ with $\omega \in \mathbb{F}_q$ a primitive third root of unity ($\omega^2 +$

$\omega + 1 = 0 \bmod q$) acts as a *distortion map* on $E[n] \simeq \mathbb{Z}/n\mathbb{Z} \oplus \mathbb{Z}/n\mathbb{Z}$. With a Weil pairing e_W, one can embed a discrete logarithm on $E(\mathbb{F}_q)[n]$ into $\mathbb{F}_q^*$, where subexponential DL computation takes place, although the much larger size of q compared to n seems prohibitive. For $G, P \in E[n]$ in the same subgroup of order n, $\log_G(P) = \log_{e_W(G, \phi(G))} e_W(P, \phi(G))$. See [16, Appendix A.2] for more details.

3.3   Subgroup Membership Testing: $\mathbb{G}_T$

Testing membership in $\mathbb{G}_T$ for candidate elements z of $\mathbb{F}_{q^k}$ is done in two steps. First, one checks that z belongs to the *cyclotomic subgroup* of $\mathbb{F}_{q^k}$ (subgroup of order $\Phi_k(q)$), that is $z^{\Phi_k(q)} = 1$. To avoid inversions, one multiplies the positive terms in q^i on one hand, and the negative terms on the other hand, and check for equality: it costs only Frobenius powers. With $k = 6$ and $\Phi_6(q) = q^2 - q + 1$, it means checking that $z^{q^2+1} = z^q$. Second, we propose to use a generalisation of Scott's technique first developed for BN curves, where $r = q + 1 - t$ [39, §8.3]. In the BN case, the computation of z^r is replaced by a Frobenius power z^q and an exponentiation z^{t-1}, and the test $z^q = z^{t-1}$. BLS curves are not of prime order, and we use Proposition 1.

Proposition 1. *Let E be a pairing-friendly curve defined over $\mathbb{F}_q$, of embedding degree k w.r.t. the subgroup order r, and order $\#E(\mathbb{F}_q) = r \cdot c = q + 1 - t$. For $z \in \mathbb{F}_{q^k}^*$, we have this alternative $\mathbb{G}_T$ membership testing:*

$$z^{\Phi_k(q)} = 1 \ \text{and} \ z^q = z^{t-1} \ \text{and} \ \gcd(q + 1 - t, \Phi_k(q)) = r \implies z^r = 1 \ .$$

Proof. If $z^{\Phi_k(q)} = 1$ and $z^{q+1-t} = 1$, then the order of z divides the gcd of the exponents $\gcd(\Phi_k(q), q + 1 - t)$. If this gcd is exactly r, then z is in the subgroup of order r, that is $z^r = 1$.

BLS curves have $c \cdot r = q + 1 - t = q - u$ hence $q \equiv u \bmod r$. As soon as $\gcd(q + 1 - t, \Phi_k(q)) = r$, then the following two tests are enough:

1. test if $z^{\Phi_k(q)} = 1$ with Frobenius maps;
2. test if $z^q = z^u$, using cyclotomic squarings [23] for a faster exponentiation.

Proposition 1 came out of email discussions between cryptographers, and appears in Scott's preprint [37].

Remark 1. For BLS-curves of embedding degree k a power of 3 ($k = 3^j$), the cyclotomic polynomial $\Phi_k(x)$ does not generate primes, actually one has $r(x) = \Phi_k(x)/3$. Moreover a BLS curve has points of order 3, hence $\gcd(q+1-t, \Phi_k(q)) = 3r$ for all $k = 3^j$.

Remark 2. For SNARK-friendly 2-chains, $z^u \in \mathbb{G}_T$ can be implemented efficiently by mixing Granger-Scott's [23] and Karabina's [31] cyclotomic squares. Since $2^L \mid u - 1$, there are $L - 1$ consecutive squarings in the exponentiation. One can use Karabina's method for this series and then switch to Granger-Scott's method for the remaining part. Hence, trading off one inversion in $\mathbb{F}_{q^{k/d}}$ for $2(L-1)$ multiplications in $\mathbb{F}_{q^{k/d}}$. Particularly, for BLS12 and BLS24, this trick yields significant speedups as long as an $\mathbb{F}_q$-inverse costs, respectively, less than $(6L-4)$ and $(18L-16)$ $\mathbb{F}_q$-multiplications, which is the case of curves we are interested in.

3.4   Choosing a Curve Coefficient $b = 1$

Proposition 2. *Half of BLS curves are of the form $Y^2 = X^3 + 1$, these are the curves with odd seed x.*

Proof. Let $E : Y^2 = X^3 + b$ be a BLS curve over $\mathbb{F}_q$ and g neither a square nor a cube in $\mathbb{F}_q$. One choice of $b \in \{1, g, g^2, g^3, g^4, g^5\}$ gives a curve with the correct order (i.e. $r \mid \#E(\mathbb{F}_q)$) [40, §X.5]. For all BLS curves, $x-1 \mid \#E(\mathbb{F}_q)$ (cf Lemma 1, Tables in [16, Appendix A.2]) and $3 \mid x-1$ (which leads to all involved parameters being integers). If, additionally, $2 \mid x-1$ then $2,3 \mid \#E(\mathbb{F}_q)$ and the curve has points of order 2 and 3. A 2-torsion point is $(x_0, 0)$ with x_0 a root of $x^3 + b$, hence $b = (-x_0)^3$ is a cube. The two 3-torsion points are $(0, \pm\sqrt{b})$ hence b is a square. This implies that b is a square and a cube in $\mathbb{F}_q$ and therefore $b = 1$ is the only solution in the set $\{g^i\}_{0 \le i \le 5}$ for half of all BLS curves: those with odd x.

3.5   SNARK-Friendly Inner BLS Curves

This paper focuses on inner SNARK-friendly BLS curves as in Definition 1 at the 128-bit security level and suitable for the Groth'16 and KZG-based universal SNARKs. On the one hand, a Groth'16-tailored curve should optimize $\mathbb{G}_1$ and $\mathbb{G}_2$ operations, and the pairing computation: the proving algorithm involves multi-scalar multiplications (MSM) in $\mathbb{G}_1$ and $\mathbb{G}_2$, and the verification algorithm involves multi-pairings. On the other hand, KZG polynomial commitments only need multi-scalar multiplications in $\mathbb{G}_1$ and multi-pairings.

According to the post[1], an efficient non-conservative choice of a Groth'16-tailored curve at the 128-bit security level is a BLS12 curve of roughly 384 bits. A conservative but efficient alternative is a BLS12 curve of 440 to 448 bits. Then to fulfill SNARK-friendliness, it is sufficient to choose a seed x s.t. $x \equiv 1 \mod 3 \cdot 2^L$ with the desired 2-adicity $L \ge 1$. Consequently, Propositions 1 and 2, and Corollary 1 apply: such an inner BLS12 is always of the form $Y^2 = X^3 + 1$; multiplying by $x-1$ is sufficient to clear the cofactor on $\mathbb{G}_1$, and the efficient $\mathbb{G}_T$ membership testing applies. In fact, for all BLS12 curves, $\gcd(q(x) + 1 - t(x), \Phi_{12}(q(x)))$ is always equal to $r(x)$ and the membership testing boils down to $z^q = (z^q)^q \cdot z$ and $z^q = z^u$ for $z \in \mathbb{G}_T$.

KZG-based SNARKs require a 128-bit secure curve with efficient $\mathbb{G}_1$ operations and fast pairing. For a faster $\mathbb{G}_1$ arithmetic, we consider a BLS24

---

[1] https://members.loria.fr/AGuillevic/pairing-friendly-curves/.

curve of roughly 320 bits, that meets the 128-bit level security [28] and gives the best tradeoff between small $\rho = \log_2 q / \log_2 r$ value ($\rho = 1.25$) and fast pairing. For SNARK-friendliness, cofactor clearing and curve equation ($Y^2 = X^3 + 1$), the same observations as for BLS12 apply. For $\mathbb{G}_T$ membership testing, $\gcd(q(x) + 1 - t(x), \Phi_{24}(q(x)))$ is always equal to $r(x)$ for the BLS24 curves and the test boils down to $z^{q^2} = (z^{q^2})^{q^2} \cdot z$ and $z^q = z^u$ for $z \in \mathbb{G}_T$.

4   Outer Curves: Brezing–Weng, Cocks–Pinch

This section presents the families of 2-chains with a BW6 curve on top of a BLS12 curve (Sect. 4.2), and on top of a BLS24 curve (Sect. 4.3). Cocks-Pinch curves (CP) [19, §4.1] are addressed in Sect. 4.4. For BW6, all parameters and formulas are given as polynomials in the variable x, with integer parameters h_t, h_y that are the lifting cofactors of the Brezing-Weng construction. We use subscripts $q_{\text{bls}}, q_{\text{bw}}, q_{\text{cp}}$ to identify parameters of BLS, BW and CP curves. BW and CP constructions follow the same recipe, but CP deals with integers, while BW deals with polynomials [19, §4.1,§6]. They start from the subgroup order $r_{\text{bw}}(x) = q_{\text{bls}}(x)$, $r_{\text{cp}}(u) = q_{\text{bls}}(u)$, and look for k-th roots of unity $\zeta_k \bmod q_{\text{bls}}$ to set the trace value $t = \zeta_k + 1$. For CP, the existence of ζ_k requires $q_{\text{bls}}(u) \equiv 1 \bmod k$: for $k = 6, 12, 8$ resp., this means $u \equiv 1 \bmod 3$, $1, 10 \bmod 12$, and $1, 10 \bmod 24$ resp. For BW, the number field defined by $q_{\text{bls}}(x)$ only contains $\zeta_k(x)$ for $k \mid 6$, limiting the BW construction to $k = 6$ at most.

4.1   Generic BW6 Curve Parameters

To satisfy Definition 1, a BW curve chained to a BLS curve (of any embedding degree) has a subgroup of prime order $r_{\text{bw}}(x) = q_{\text{bls}}(x)$. To get an embedding degree $k = 6$, a primitive 6-th root of unity ζ_6 modulo $r_{\text{bw}}(x)$ is required, the trace of the curve modulo r_{bw} is then $t_{\text{bw},3} = \zeta_6 + 1 \bmod r_{\text{bw}}$. Alternatively $t_{\text{bw},0} = \overline{\zeta_6} + 1 \bmod r_{\text{bw}}$ with $\zeta_6 = -\overline{\zeta_6} + 1$. With $D = -3$ and $1/\sqrt{-3} = (2\zeta_6 - 1)/3 \bmod r_{\text{bw}}$, then $y_{\text{bw},0} = (t_{\text{bw},0} - 2)/\sqrt{-3} = (\overline{\zeta_6} + 1)/3 = -t_{\text{bw},0}/3$. Or with $1/\sqrt{-3} = -(2\zeta_6 - 1)/3 \bmod r_{\text{bw}}$, one has $y_{\text{bw},3} = (t_{\text{bw},3} - 2)/\sqrt{-3} = (\zeta_6 + 1)/3 = t_{\text{bw},3}/3$. Any BW6 curve will have parameters of the form $t_i = t_{\text{bw},i} \pm h_t r$, $y_i = y_{\text{bw},i} \pm h_y r$, where h_t, h_y are integer lifting cofactors. We label the two cases according to the constant coefficient of the polynomial defining the trace modulo r_{bw}: this is either 0 or 3.

One denotes $q_{\text{bw},0}(x, h_t, h_y) = ((t_{\text{bw},0} + h_t r)^2 + 3(y_{\text{bw},0} + h_y r)^2)/4$. We have

$$q_{\text{bw},0} = t_{\text{bw},0}^2/3 + t_{\text{bw},0} \cdot r_{\text{bw}}(h_t - h_y)/2 + r_{\text{bw}}^2(h_t^2 + 3h_y^2)/4 \,, \tag{1}$$

$$q_{\text{bw},3} = t_{\text{bw},3}^2/3 + t_{\text{bw},3} \cdot r_{\text{bw}}(h_t + h_y)/2 + r_{\text{bw}}^2(h_t^2 + 3h_y^2)/4 \,. \tag{2}$$

The curve cofactor $c_{\text{bw},i}(x, h_t, h_y)$ such that $c_{\text{bw},i} r_{\text{bw}} = q_{\text{bw},i} + 1 - t_{\text{bw},i}$ is

$$c_{\text{bw},0} = (h_t^2 + 3h_y^2)/4r_{\text{bw}} + (h_t - h_y)/2t_{\text{bw},0} + (t_{\text{bw},0}^2/3 - t_{\text{bw},0} + 1)/r_{\text{bw}} - h_t \tag{3}$$

$$c_{\text{bw},3} = (h_t^2 + 3h_y^2)/4r_{\text{bw}} + (h_t + h_y)/2t_{\text{bw},3} + (t_{\text{bw},3}^2/3 - t_{\text{bw},3} + 1)/r_{\text{bw}} - h_t \tag{4}$$

where $(t_{\mathrm{bw},i}^2/3 - t_{\mathrm{bw},i} + 1)/r_{\mathrm{bw}} = \Phi_6(t_{\mathrm{bw},i} - 1)/(3r_{\mathrm{bw}})$ is a polynomial in $\mathbb{Q}[x]$ since by construction r_{bw} divides $\Phi_6(t_{\mathrm{bw},i} - 1)$. Tables 3 and 5 give the explicit values of the polynomials for BLS12 and BLS24 inner curves.

Cofactor of $\mathbb{G}_2$. The group $\mathbb{G}_2$ of order r_{bw} is a subgroup of one of the two sextic twists of E, defined over $\mathbb{F}_q$. Generically, the orders of the two sextic twists are $q + 1 - (t + 3y)/2$ and $q + 1 - (t - 3y)/2$, where y satisfies $t^2 - 4q = -3y^2$. One of the orders is a multiple of r_{bw}, and has cofactor $c'_{\mathrm{bw},i}$. Observe that $(t_{\mathrm{bw},0} - 3y_{\mathrm{bw},0})/2 = t_{\mathrm{bw},0}$ since $y_{\mathrm{bw},0} = -t_{\mathrm{bw},0}/3$. The correct sextic twist has order $q_{\mathrm{bw},0} + 1 - (t_{\mathrm{bw},0} + h_t r_{\mathrm{bw}} - 3(y_{\mathrm{bw},0} + h_y r_{\mathrm{bw}}))/2$, and a calculation gives

$$c'_{\mathrm{bw},0} = c_{\mathrm{bw},0} + (h_t + 3h_y)/2 . \tag{5}$$

For the other trace, $(t_{\mathrm{bw},3} + 3y_{\mathrm{bw},3})/2 = t_{\mathrm{bw},3}$ and the correct sextic twist has order $q_{\mathrm{bw},3} + 1 - (t_{\mathrm{bw},3} + h_t r_{\mathrm{bw}} + 3(y_{\mathrm{bw},3} + h_y r_{\mathrm{bw}}))/2$ a multiple of r_{bw}, and cofactor

$$c'_{\mathrm{bw},3} = c_{\mathrm{bw},3} + (h_t - 3h_y)/2 . \tag{6}$$

Congruences of Cofactors h_t, h_y. One requires $q_{\mathrm{bw},i}$ (Eqs. (1), (2)) to be an integer and a prime. Because $t_{\mathrm{bw},i}$ is always multiple of 3, $t_{\mathrm{bw},i}^2/3$ is an integer. We need $(h_t \pm h_y)/2t_{\mathrm{bw},i} + (h_t^2 + 3h_y^2)/4r_{\mathrm{bw}}$ to be an integer. We now look at $(h_t \pm h_y)$, $(h_t^2 + 3h_y^2)$. We have $t_{\mathrm{bw},0}$ always even, then $(h_t - h_y)t_{\mathrm{bw},0}/2$ is an integer and we require $4 \mid (h_t^2 + 3h_y^2)$. For that we need $h_t - h_y \equiv 0 \bmod 2$ (see Table 2). We have $t_{\mathrm{bw},3}$ always odd. If $(h_t + h_y)$ is odd, then $(h_t + h_y)t_{\mathrm{bw},3}$ is odd but at the same time (see Table 2), $(h_t^2 + 3h_y^2)$ is odd, and the condition is not satisfied. Hence we need $(h_t - h_y)$ to be even, and consequently we have $(h_t^2 + 3h_y^2)/4$ an integer. Finally, for both $t_{\mathrm{bw},0}$ and $t_{\mathrm{bw},3}$, we need $2 \mid (h_t - h_y)$ and consequently we have $4 \mid h_t^2 + 3h_y^2$, to ensure q_{bw} to be an integer. Note also that because $x \equiv 1 \bmod 3$, one has $t_{\mathrm{bw}} = 0 \bmod 3$, and Eqs. (1), (2) give $4q_{\mathrm{bw}} = h_t^2 \bmod 3$. Because q_{bw} needs to be prime, h_t is not multiple of 3, and $3 \nmid (h_t^2 + 3h_y^2)$.

Table 2. Are $2(h_t \pm h_y)$, $h_t^2 + 3h_y^2$ multiple of 4?

h_t	h_y	$h_t \pm h_y$	$h_t^2 + 3h_y^2$	$2(h_t \pm h_y)t_{\mathrm{bw},i} + (h_t^2 + 3h_y^2)r_{\mathrm{bw}} \bmod 4$	
mod 2	mod 2	mod 2	mod 4	$t_{\mathrm{bw},0} = 0 \bmod 2$	$t_{\mathrm{bw},3} = 1 \bmod 2$
0	0	0	0	0	0
0	1	1	3	$3r_{\mathrm{bw}} \neq 0$	$2 + 3r_{\mathrm{bw}} \neq 0$
1	0	1	1	$r_{\mathrm{bw}} \neq 0$	$2 + r_{\mathrm{bw}} \neq 0$
1	1	0	0	0	0

Subgroup Membership Testing: $\mathbb{G}_T$. We apply the technique of Sect. 3.3. BW6 curves over their base field have order $c_{\mathrm{bw},i} \cdot r_{\mathrm{bw}} = q_{\mathrm{bw},i} + 1 - t_{\mathrm{bw},i} - h_t r_{\mathrm{bw}}$, hence

$$q_{\mathrm{bw},i} \equiv t_{\mathrm{bw},i} - 1 \bmod r_{\mathrm{bw}} . \tag{7}$$

As soon as $\gcd(q_{\mathrm{bw},i} + 1 - t_{\mathrm{bw},i}, \Phi_k(q_{\mathrm{bw},i})) = r_{\mathrm{bw}}$, then the following two tests are enough:

1. test if $z^{\Phi_k(q_{bw,i})} = 1$ with Frobenius maps;
2. test if $z^{q_{bw,i}} = z^{t_{bw,i}-1}$ with cyclotomic squarings.

Easy Part of the Final Exponentiation. The final exponentiation raises the Miller loop output f to the power

$$(q^6 - 1)/r = (q^6 - 1)/\Phi_6(q) \cdot \Phi_6(q)/r = (q^3 - 1)(q + 1)(q^2 - q + 1)/r .$$

The easy part $(q^3 - 1)(q + 1)$ costs one conjugation (q^3-Frobenius power), one inversion in $\mathbb{F}_{q^6}$, one q-Frobenius power and two multiplications. We optimise the hard part $(q^2 - q + 1)/r$ in Sect. 4.2, 4.3.

Optimal Pairing Computation. In [15], the authors presented an optimal ate pairing formula that can be generalized as follows: write

$$a_0 + a_1(t_{bw,i} - 1) = 0 \bmod r_{bw} \tag{8}$$

with shortest possible scalars a_0, a_1. On $\mathbb{G}_2$, the Frobenius π_q has eigenvalue $t_{bw,i} - 1$. The optimal ate Miller loop is computed with the formula

$$f_{a_0,Q}(P)f_{a_1,\pi_q(Q)}(P) = f_{a_0,Q}(P)f_{a_1,Q}^q(P) . \tag{9}$$

Moreover, it turned out that $(a_1 - 1) \mid a_2$, and some of the computations were shared. We now introduce another optimisation. We consider Eq. (8) with a new point of view. BW6 curves have an endomorphism $\phi: (x, y) \mapsto (\omega x, -y)$ on $\mathbb{G}_1$ of eigenvalue $\lambda = t_{bw,i} - 1 = q_{bw,i} \bmod r_{bw}$, and characteristic polynomial $\chi^2 - \chi + 1 = 0$. The (bilinear) twisted ate pairing [30, §6] has precisely Miller loop $f_{\lambda,P}(Q)$. However, λ is too large so instead, we consider a multiple of the Tate pairing $f_{hr,P}(Q) = f_{a_0+a_1\lambda,P}(Q)$ for some h (e.g. Eqs. (18), (25)). Instead of decomposing the Miller function $f_{a_0+a_1\lambda,P}(Q)$ into subfunctions $f_{a_0,P}(Q)f_{a_1\lambda,P}(Q)$, we use Lemma 5 (proof in the full version) to get shared squares in $\mathbb{F}_{q^k}$ and shared doubling steps in $\mathbb{G}_1$ (Tate), resp. $\mathbb{G}_2$ (ate), in the same idea as a multi-scalar multiplication. This gives us Algorithm 2. We are in the very particular case of $k/d = 1$, ϕ on $\mathbb{G}_1$ and π_q on $\mathbb{G}_2$ both have eigenvalue $q_{bw,i} \bmod r_{bw}$, and our variant of the twisted ate pairing is competitive with the ate pairing.

Lemma 5. *Let E be a pairing-friendly curve with the usual order-r subgroups $\mathbb{G}_1, \mathbb{G}_2$, two points $P \in \mathbb{G}_i$, $Q \in \mathbb{G}_{1-i}$ of order r, and an endomorphism ϕ of eigenvalue λ over $\mathbb{G}_i$: $\phi(P) = [\lambda]P$, $\lambda = q^e \bmod r$ for some $1 \le e \le k - 1$. The Miller function can be decomposed as follows.*

$$f_{2(u+v\lambda),P}(Q) = f_{u+v\lambda,P}^2(Q)\ell_{(u+v\lambda)P,(u+v\lambda)P}(Q) \tag{10}$$

$$f_{u+1+v\lambda,P}(Q) = f_{u+v\lambda,P}(Q)\ell_{(u+v\lambda)P,P}(Q) \tag{11}$$

$$f_{u+(v+1)\lambda,P}(Q) = f_{u+v\lambda,P}(Q)\ell_{(u+v\lambda)P,\lambda P}(Q) \tag{12}$$

$$f_{u+1+(v+1)\lambda,P}(Q) = f_{u+v\lambda,P}(Q)\ell_{P,\lambda P}(Q)\ell_{(u+v\lambda)P,(1+\lambda)P}(Q) \tag{13}$$

where $\lambda P = \phi(P)$, $(1 + \lambda)P = P + \phi(P)$, and $\ell_{P,\lambda P}(Q)$ can be precomputed.

Algorithm 2: Miller loop for optimal pairing with endomorphism ϕ on $\mathbb{G}_1$ (Tate), resp. $\mathbb{G}_2$ (ate) of eigenvalue λ and degree 2.

Input: $P \in \mathbb{G}_i$, $Q \in \mathbb{G}_{1-i}$, end. ϕ on $\mathbb{G}_i$ of eigenvalue λ, scalars a_0, a_1
   s. t. $a_0 + a_1\lambda = 0 \bmod r$

Output: $f_{a_0+a_1\lambda, P}(Q)$

1   $P_0 \leftarrow P$; $P_1 \leftarrow \phi(P)$
2   **if** $a_0 < 0$ **then** $a_0 \leftarrow -a_0$; $P_0 \leftarrow -P_0$
3   **if** $a_1 < 0$ **then** $a_1 \leftarrow -a_1$; $P_1 \leftarrow -P_1$
4   $P_{1+\lambda} \leftarrow P_0 + P_1$; $\ell_{1,\lambda} \leftarrow \ell_{P_0,P_1}(Q)$
5   $l_0 \leftarrow \text{bits}(a_0)$; $l_1 \leftarrow \text{bits}(a_1)$
6   **if** $\#l_0 = \#l_1$ **then** $S \leftarrow P_{1+\lambda}$; $f \leftarrow \ell_{1,\lambda}$; $n \leftarrow \#l_0$
7   **else if** $\#l_0 < \#l_1$ **then** $S \leftarrow P_1$; $f \leftarrow 1$; $n \leftarrow \#l_1$; pad l_0 with 0 s.t. $\#l_0 = n$
8   **else** $S \leftarrow P_0$; $f \leftarrow 1$; $n \leftarrow \#l_0$; pad l_1 with 0 s.t. $\#l_1 = n$
9   **for** $i = n - 2$ *downto* 0 **do**
10    $f \leftarrow f^2$; $\ell_t \leftarrow \ell_{S,S}(Q)$; $S \leftarrow [2]S$
11   **if** $l_0[i] = 0$ *and* $l_1[i] = 0$ **then** $f \leftarrow f \cdot \ell_t$ // Eq. (10), $m_{\text{full-sparse}}$
12   **else if** $l_0[i] = 1$ *and* $l_1[i] = 1$ **then**   // Eq. (13)
13     $S \leftarrow S + P_{1+\lambda}$; $\ell \leftarrow \ell_{S,P_{1+\lambda}}(Q)$
14     $f \leftarrow (f \cdot \ell_t) \cdot (\ell \cdot \ell_{1,\lambda})$ // $m_k + m_{\text{full-sparse}} + m_{\text{sparse-sparse}}$
15   **else if** $l_0[i] = 1$ **then**   // Eq. (11)
16     $S \leftarrow S + P_0$; $\ell \leftarrow \ell_{S,P_0}(Q)$
17     $f \leftarrow f \cdot (\ell_t \cdot \ell)$ // $m_k + m_{\text{sparse-sparse}}$
18   **else** $(l_1[i] = 1)$ // Eq. (12)
19     $S \leftarrow S + P_1$; $\ell \leftarrow \ell_{S,P_1}(Q)$
20     $f \leftarrow f \cdot (\ell_t \cdot \ell)$ // $m_k + m_{\text{sparse-sparse}}$
21 **return** f

Remark 3. Algorithm 2 shares the squarings in $\mathbb{F}_{q^k}$ and the doubling steps in $\mathbb{G}_1$ (Tate), resp. $\mathbb{G}_2$ (ate). With all parameterized pairing-friendly families, the scalar decomposition gives all but one trivial Miller function, and the ate, or twisted-ate pairing boils down to one Miller loop computation of optimal length, and a few line additions [42]. In our case, while being short, none of the scalars a_0, a_1 is trivial. It is possible to derive a 2-NAF variant of Algorithm 2 (see Table 9). It requires the additional precomputations of $P - \phi(P)$ and $\ell_{P,-\lambda P}(Q)$. From the estimate in Table 9, our Miller loop variant in Algorithm 2 would give up to a 7% speed-up compared to [15, Alg. 5], for BLS24-BW6 curves. Our Algorithm 2 works for Tate and ate pairing. If there is an endomorphism of higher degree on $\mathbb{G}_2$ (or two independent endomorphisms), use Algorithm 4 instead.

4.2 BW6 with BLS-12

Table 3 gives the parameters of the BW6-BLS12 curves in terms of the seed x, and the two lifting cofactors h_t, h_y.

Optimal Ate Pairing Computation. We investigate two pairings on our BW6 curves: optimal ate and optimal Tate. In [15], the authors presented an optimal ate pairing formula, for any BW6 curve with $t_{\text{bw},3}$:

Table 3. Parameters of a BW6 outer curve with a BLS12 inner curve, $x \equiv 1 \bmod 3$.

parameter	value	property
r_{bw}	$q_{\mathrm{bls}} = (x-1)^2/3(x^4 - x^2 + 1) + x$	generates prime
$\bar{\zeta}_6$	$-x^5 + 3x^4 - 3x^3 + x - 1$	
ζ_6	$x^5 - 3x^4 + 3x^3 - x + 2$	
$1/\sqrt{-3}$	$-(2x^5 - 6x^4 + 6x^3 - 2x + 3)/3$	
$t_{\mathrm{bw},0}$	$-x^5 + 3x^4 - 3x^3 + x$	$6 \mid t_{\mathrm{bw},0}$
$t_{\mathrm{bw},3}$	$x^5 - 3x^4 + 3x^3 - x + 3$	$3 \mid t_{\mathrm{bw},3}, 2 \nmid t_{\mathrm{bw},3}$
$y_{\mathrm{bw},0}$	$(x^5 - 3x^4 + 3x^3 - x)/3 = -t_{\mathrm{bw},0}/3$	$2 \mid y_{\mathrm{bw},0}$
$y_{\mathrm{bw},3}$	$(x^5 - 3x^4 + 3x^3 - x + 3)/3 = t_{\mathrm{bw},3}/3$	$2 \nmid y_{\mathrm{bw},3}$
$q_{\mathrm{bw},0}$	$((t_{\mathrm{bw},0} + h_t r_{\mathrm{bw}})^2 + 3(y_{\mathrm{bw},0} + h_y r_{\mathrm{bw}})^2)/4$	generates prime
$q_{\mathrm{bw},3}$	$((t_{\mathrm{bw},3} + h_t r_{\mathrm{bw}})^2 + 3(y_{\mathrm{bw},3} + h_y r_{\mathrm{bw}})^2)/4$	generates prime
$\Phi_6(t_{\mathrm{bw},i} - 1)$	$3r_{\mathrm{bw}}(x^4 - 4x^3 + 7x^2 - 6x + 3)$	
$c_{\mathrm{bw},0}$	$(h_t^2 + 3h_y^2)/4r_{\mathrm{bw}} + (h_t - h_y)/2t_{\mathrm{bw},0} + x^4 - 4x^3 + 7x^2 - 6x + 3 - h_t$	
$c_{\mathrm{bw},3}$	$(h_t^2 + 3h_y^2)/4r_{\mathrm{bw}} + (h_t + h_y)/2t_{\mathrm{bw},3} + x^4 - 4x^3 + 7x^2 - 6x + 3 - h_t$	
$c'_{\mathrm{bw},0}$ ($\mathbb{G}_2$)	$c_{\mathrm{bw},0} + (h_t + 3h_y)/2$	
$c'_{\mathrm{bw},3}$ ($\mathbb{G}_2$)	$c_{\mathrm{bw},3} + (h_t - 3h_y)/2$	

$$m_{\mathrm{opt.\ ate}} = f_{u+1,Q}(P)f^q_{u^3-u^2-u,Q}(P) \quad \text{and} \quad e_{\mathrm{opt.\ ate}} = m_{\mathrm{opt.\ ate}}^{(q^6_{\mathrm{bw}}-1)/r_{\mathrm{bw}}} \tag{14}$$

with optimized computation in [15, Alg. 5]:

$$f_u = f_{u,Q}(P); \ m_{\mathrm{opt.\ ate}} = f_u \cdot (f_u)^q_{u^2-u-1,[u]Q}(P)\ell_{[u]Q,Q}(P), \tag{15}$$

where $[u]Q$ is precomputed together with $f_{u,Q}(P)$. The equivalent formula for a trace $t_{\mathrm{bw},0}$ is

$$f_{u(u^2-u-1),Q}(P)f^q_{u+1,Q}(P) \tag{16}$$

whose optimized version is

$$f_u = f_{u,Q}(P); \ m_{\mathrm{opt.\ ate}} = (f_u \cdot \ell_{[u]Q,Q}(P))^q(f_u)_{u^2-u-1,[u]Q}(P). \tag{17}$$

In the two cases $t_{\mathrm{bw},0}$ and $t_{\mathrm{bw},3}$, the cost in terms of multiplications in the base field are the same.

Optimal Pairing Computation with Algorithm 2. $\mathbb{G}_1$ and $\mathbb{G}_2$ have an endomorphism ϕ_1, ϕ_2 of eigenvalue $\lambda_{\mathrm{bw},i} = t_{\mathrm{bw},i} - 1 \bmod r_{\mathrm{bw}}$. Low degree polynomials (short scalars once evaluated at a seed u) a_0, a_1 s.t. $a_0 + a_1\lambda_{\mathrm{bw},i} = 0 \bmod r_{\mathrm{bw}}$ are

$$(x^3 - x^2 - x) + (x+1)(t_{\mathrm{bw},0} - 1) = -3r_{\mathrm{bw}} \tag{18}$$
$$-x - 1 + (x^3 - x^2 + 1)(t_{\mathrm{bw},0} - 1) = -3(x^2 - 2x + 2)r_{\mathrm{bw}} \tag{19}$$
$$(x+1) + (x^3 - x^2 - x)(t_{\mathrm{bw},3} - 1) = 3(x-1)^2 r_{\mathrm{bw}} \tag{20}$$
$$(x^3 - x^2 + 1) - (x+1)(t_{\mathrm{bw},3} - 1) = -3r_{\mathrm{bw}} \tag{21}$$

The optimal Tate or ate Miller loop with e.g. (19), (21) are:

$$m_{\text{Tate}} = f_{-u-1+(u^3-u^2+1)\lambda_{\text{bw},0},P}(Q), \quad m_{\text{ate}} = f_{-u-1+(u^3-u^2+1)q_{\text{bw},0},Q}(P)$$
$$m_{\text{Tate}} = f_{u^3-u^2+1-(u+1)\lambda_{\text{bw},3},P}(Q), \quad m_{\text{ate}} = f_{u^3-u^2+1-(u+1)q_{\text{bw},3},Q}(P) \ .$$

$\mathbb{G}_1$ **and** $\mathbb{G}_2$ **Membership Testing.** For $\mathbb{G}_1$ membership testing, one uses one of Eqs. (18), (19), resp. (20), (21), with $x = u$. However, these formulas (e.g. $[u^3 - u^2 - u]P + [u + 1]\phi(P)$) will output $\mathcal{O}$ for any point in the subgroup of order $3r_{\text{bw}}$. For $\mathbb{G}_2$ membership testing, the same equations can be re-used: we showed in Sect. 4.1 that the twisted curve E' of $\mathbb{G}_2$ has the same trace as E modulo r_{bw}, either $(t_{\text{bw},0} - 3y_{\text{bw},0})/2 = t_{\text{bw},0}$, or $(t_{\text{bw},3} + 3y_{\text{bw},3})/2 = t_{\text{bw},3}$.

Final Exponentiation. Writing the hard part of the final exponentiation $z^{\Phi_6(q_{\text{bw},i})/r_{\text{bw}}}$ in terms of x, h_t, h_y, Magma runs LLL on multivariate polynomials and provides the result. With $t_{\text{bw},i}$, LLL gives short vectors for the exponent:

$$e_{\text{bw},i} = 3(x + 1)\Phi_k(q_{\text{bw},i})/r_{\text{bw}}(x) \tag{22}$$

and the formulas for $e_{\text{bw},i}$ are

$$e_{\text{bw},0} = 3(c_{\text{bw},0}+h_t)(x^3 - x^2 + 1 - (x + 1)q_{\text{bw},0}) - 9(x^2 - 2x + 2 - q_{\text{bw},0}) \tag{23}$$
$$e_{\text{bw},3} = 3(c_{\text{bw},3}+h_t)(x^3 - x^2 - x + (x + 1)q_{\text{bw},3}) + 9(x^2 - 2x + 1 + q_{\text{bw},3}) \tag{24}$$

We explicit in the full version the link with Hayashida, Hayasaka and Teruya's formulas [29] and show that our formulas are the most efficient.

Cofactor Clearing on $\mathbb{G}_1$ **and** $\mathbb{G}_2$ **with one Endomorphism.** The cofactors are $c_{\text{bw},i}$ for $\mathbb{G}_1$ (Eqs. (3), (4)), resp. $c'_{\text{bw},i}$ for $\mathbb{G}_2$ (Eqs. (5), (6)), Table 3. The curve and its sextic twist for $\mathbb{G}_2$ have an endomorphism defined over $\mathbb{F}_q$, of characteristic polynomial $x^2 + x + 1$ and eigenvalue λ such that $\lambda^2 + \lambda + 1 = 0$ modulo the curve order. There are two formulas, one for each choice of eigenvalue modulo the curve order, and $l_0 + l_1\lambda = 0 \bmod c_{\text{bw},i}$, resp. modulo $c'_{\text{bw},i}$, summarized in Table 4. Formulas with $\bar{\lambda}$ can be found in the full version and the GIT at [17].

Table 4. Cofactor clearing on $\mathbb{G}_i$ with an endomorphism of eigenvalue λ: $\lambda^2 + \lambda + 1 = 0$.

$\mathbb{G}_1$	$c_{\text{bw},0}$	$l_0 = (h_t^2 + 3h_y^2)/4 \cdot (x^3 - x^2 + 1) - h_t(x^2 - 2x + 1) - (h_t - 3h_y)/2$
		$l_1 = (h_t^2 + 3h_y^2)/4 \cdot (x + 1) - (h_t + 3h_y)/2 \cdot (x^2 - 2x + 1) - h_t$
	$c_{\text{bw},3}$	$l_0 = (h_t^2 + 3h_y^2)/4 \cdot (x^3 - x^2 + 1) + h_t + (h_t + 3h_y)/2 \cdot (x - 1)^2$
		$l_1 = (h_t^2 + 3h_y^2)/4 \cdot (x + 1) - (h_t - 3h_y)/2 \cdot (x^2 - 2x + 2) + h_t$
$\mathbb{G}_2$	$c'_{\text{bw},0}$	$l_0 = (h_t^2 + 3h_y^2)/4(x + 1) + (h_t + 3h_y)/2(x^2 - 2x + 2) - h_t$
		$l_1 = (h_t^2 + 3h_y^2)/4(x^3 - x^2 + 1) - (h_t - 3h_y)/2(x^2 - 2x + 1) - h_t$
	$c'_{\text{bw},3}$	$l_0 = -(h_t^2 + 3h_y^2)/4(x + 1) - (h_t - 3h_y)/2(x^2 - 2x + 1) - h_t$
		$l_1 = (h_t^2 + 3h_y^2)/4(x^3 - x^2 - x) + (h_t + 3h_y)/2(x^2 - 2x + 2) - h_t$

Table 5. Parameters of a BW6 outer curve with inner BLS24, $x \equiv 1 \bmod 3$.

r_{bw}	$q_{\text{bls}} = (x-1)^2/3(x^8 - x^4 + 1) + x$	prime
	$(x^{10} - 2x^9 + x^8 - x^6 + 2x^5 - x^4 + x^2 + x + 1)/3$	
$\bar{\zeta_6}$	$-x^9 + 3x^8 - 4x^7 + 4x^6 - 3x^5 + 2x^3 - 2x^2 + x - 1$	
ζ_6	$x^9 - 3x^8 + 4x^7 - 4x^6 + 3x^5 - 2x^3 + 2x^2 - x + 2$	
$1/\sqrt{-3}$	$(2x^9 - 6x^8 + 8x^7 - 8x^6 + 6x^5 - 4x^3 + 4x^2 - 2x + 3)/3$	
$t_{\text{bw},0}$	$-x^9 + 3x^8 - 4x^7 + 4x^6 - 3x^5 + 2x^3 - 2x^2 + x$	$6 \mid t_{\text{bw},0}$
$t_{\text{bw},3}$	$x^9 - 3x^8 + 4x^7 - 4x^6 + 3x^5 - 2x^3 + 2x^2 - x + 3$	$3 \mid t_{\text{bw},3}, 2 \nmid t_{\text{bw},3}$
$y_{\text{bw},0}$	$(x^9 - 3x^8 + 4x^7 - 4x^6 + 3x^5 - 2x^3 + 2x^2 - x)/3$	
$y_{\text{bw},0}$	$-t_{\text{bw},0}/3$	$2 \mid y_{\text{bw},0}$
$y_{\text{bw},3}$	$(x^9 - 3x^8 + 4x^7 - 4x^6 + 3x^5 - 2x^3 + 2x^2 - x + 3)/3$	
$y_{\text{bw},3}$	$t_{\text{bw},3}/3$	$2 \nmid y_{\text{bw},3}$
$q_{\text{bw},0}$	$((t_{\text{bw},0} + h_t r_{\text{bw}})^2 + 3(y_{\text{bw},0} + h_y r_{\text{bw}})^2)/4$	prime
$q_{\text{bw},3}$	$((t_{\text{bw},3} + h_t r_{\text{bw}})^2 + 3(y_{\text{bw},3} + h_y r_{\text{bw}})^2)/4$	prime
$\Phi_6(t_{\text{bw},i}-1)$	$(x^8 - 4x^7 + 8x^6 - 12x^5 + 15x^4 - 14x^3 + 10x^2 - 6x + 3) \cdot 3 \cdot r_{\text{bw}}$	
$c_{\text{bw},0}$	$(h_t^2 + 3h_y^2)/4r_{\text{bw}} + (h_t - h_y)/2t_{\text{bw},0} + \Phi_6(t_{\text{bw},0} - 1)/(3r_{\text{bw}}) - h_t$	
$c_{\text{bw},3}$	$(h_t^2 + 3h_y^2)/4r_{\text{bw}} + (h_t + h_y)/2t_{\text{bw},3} + \Phi_6(t_{\text{bw},3} - 1)/(3r_{\text{bw}}) - h_t$	
$c'_{\text{bw},0}$ ($\mathbb{G}_2$)	$c_{\text{bw},0} + (h_t + 3h_y)/2$	
$c'_{\text{bw},3}$ ($\mathbb{G}_2$)	$c_{\text{bw},3} + (h_t - 3h_y)/2$	

4.3 BW6 with BLS-24

We follow the same process as for BW6-BLS12 and report the parameters in Table 5.

Pairing Computation: Miller Loop. Assuming an endomorphism of eigenvalue $\lambda_{\text{bw},i} = t_{\text{bw},i} - 1$, the formulas are

$$-x - 1 + (x^5 - x^4 + 1)(t_{\text{bw},0} - 1) = -3r_{\text{bw}}((x-1)^2(x^2+1) + 1) \quad (25)$$
$$x^5 - x^4 - x + (x+1)(t_{\text{bw},0} - 1) = -3r_{\text{bw}} \quad (26)$$
$$x + 1 + (x^5 - x^4 - x)(t_{\text{bw},3} - 1) = 3r_{\text{bw}}(x-1)^2(x^2+1) \quad (27)$$
$$x^5 - x^4 + 1 - (x+1)(t_{\text{bw},3} - 1) = -3r_{\text{bw}} \quad (28)$$

and one obtains optimal ate and Tate (a.k.a. twisted ate) pairings from (25), (28)

$$m_{\text{Tate}} = f_{-(u+1)+(u^5-u^4+1)\lambda_{\text{bw},0},P}(Q), \quad m_{\text{Tate}} = f_{u^5-u^4+1-(u+1)\lambda_{\text{bw},3},P}(Q),$$
$$m_{\text{ate}} = f_{-(u+1)+(u^5-u^4+1)q_{\text{bw},0},Q}(P), \quad m_{\text{ate}} = f_{u^5-u^4+1-(u+1)q_{\text{bw},3},Q}(P).$$

Pairing Computation: Final Exponentiation. Like for BLS12-BW6, the hard part can be expressed in terms of $q_{\text{bw},i}, h_t, h_y$. One obtains two cases. Note that according to Table 2, $(h_t^2 + 3_y^2)/4$ and $(h_t - h_y)/2$ are integers. With the parameters of Table 5, the exponent $(q_{\text{bw},i}^2 - q_{\text{bw},i} + 1)/r_{\text{bw}}$ multiplied by $3(x+1)$ has coefficients of low degree in x in basis $q_{\text{bw},i}$. The highest power to compute is u^{15} due to $c_{\text{bw},i}$ of degree 10 in u. The two cases have very similar formulas.

$$(-x^5 + x^4 - 1 + (x+1)q_{\text{bw},0})3(c_{\text{bw},0} + h_t) + 9(x^4 - 2(x^3 - x^2 + x - 1) - q_{\text{bw},0}),$$
$$(x(x^4 - x^3 - 1) + (x+1)q_{\text{bw},3})3(c_{\text{bw},3} + h_t) + 9(x^4 - 2(x^3 - x^2 + x) + 1 + q_{\text{bw},3}).$$

4.4   Two-Chains with Inner BLS and Outer Cocks-Pinch

Section 4.2 showed that a Brezing-Weng outer curve of embedding degree $k = 6$ is optimal with a BLS-12 curve whose prime-order subgroup is about 256 bits long. However BW6 is no longer optimal with BLS24 over a prime field of about 320 bits: we measure the security in the finite field $\mathbb{F}_{q^6}$ whose q is roughly 640 bits long to be about 124 bits in Sect. 5.3. To increase the security in the finite field $\mathbb{F}_{q^k}$, we can increase the size of the prime q thanks to the choice of lifting co-factors h_t, h_y, and obtain a q of 672 bits, or we can increase the embedding degree k, but then the BW construction is no longer available: we move to the Cocks-Pinch construction. To allow twist optimisation, we focus on $k = 8$ with $D = 1$ (quartic twist) and $k = 12$ with $D = 3$ (sextic twist). Our Cocks-Pinch curves are similar to the curves of Guillevic, Masson and Thomé [27]. The lifting cofactor idea appeared before in Fotiadis and Konstantinou paper [18].

With the Cocks-Pinch construction of embedding degree not 6, the optimal ate pairing like for BW6 curves is no longer available because the eigenvalue of the Frobenius endomorphism π_q on a CP curve $E(\mathbb{F}_{q^k})$ does not have a simple polynomial form modulo the subgroup order $r_{\text{cp}} = q_{\text{bls}}$. In other words, there is no k-th root of unity modulo $q_{\text{bls}}(x)$ (as polynomials). However, π_q has an eigenvalue (as a scalar integer) modulo $r_{\text{cp}}(u) \in \mathbb{Z}$, and one can use the LLL algorithm to obtain a decomposition with short scalars a_i, of size $r_{\text{cp}}^{1/4}$: $a_0 + a_1 q_{\text{cp}} + a_2 q_{\text{cp}}^2 + a_3 q_{\text{cp}}^3 = 0 \bmod r_{\text{cp}}$. This 4-fold holds for CP8 and CP12 curves as $\varphi(8) = \varphi(12) = 4$. The optimal ate Miller loop would be

$$f_{a_0,Q}(P)f_{a_1,Q}^q(P)f_{a_2,Q}^{q^2}(P)f_{a_3,Q}^{q^3}(P)\ell_{a_0 Q, a_1 \pi_q(Q)}(P)\ell_{a_2 \pi_{q^2}(Q), a_3 \pi_{q^3}(Q)}$$

But the scalars a_i are not sparse and none of them is trivial, contrary to [42]. Instead, we generalize our Algorithm 2 and obtain Algorithm 4. Algorithm 3 precomputes the data and Algorithm 4 computes the pairing, with the formulas (10)–(13) adapted to the ate pairing with swapped P and Q and $\lambda = q$, and with $C_i = \sum_i c_i q^i$,

$$f_{2C_i,Q}(P) = f_{C_i,Q}^2(P)\ell_{[C_i]Q,[C_i]Q}(P) \tag{29}$$

$$f_{C_i + q^j + q^l + q^m, Q}(P) = f_{C_i,Q}(P)f_{q^j + q^l + q^m, Q}(P)\ell_{[C_i]Q,[q^j + q^l + q^m]Q}(P)$$
$$= f_{C_i,Q}(P)\ell_{[C_i]Q,[q^j + q^l + q^m]Q}(P)\ell_{[q^j + q^l]Q,[q^m]Q}(P)\ell_{[q^j]Q,[q^l]Q}(P) \tag{30}$$

$$f_{C_i + 1 + q + q^2 + q^3, Q}(P) = f_{C_i,Q}(P)f_{1 + q + q^2 + q^3, Q}(P)\ell_{[C_i]Q,[1 + q + q^2 + q^3]Q}(P)$$
$$= f_{C_i,Q}(P)\ell_{[C_i]Q,[1 + q + q^2 + q^3]Q}(P)$$
$$\cdot \ell_{[1+q]Q,[q^2 + q^3]Q}(P)\ell_{Q,[q]Q}(P)\ell_{[q^2]Q,[q^3]Q}(P) \tag{31}$$

The $f_{q^j,Q}(P)$ terms are removed [30]. The points $[q^j]Q$, $[q^j + q^l]Q$, $[q^j + q^l + q^m]Q$, $[1 + q + q^2 + q^3]Q$, lines $\ell_{[q^m]Q,[q^n]Q}(P)$, $\ell_{[q^j + q^l]Q,[q^m]Q}(P)$, $\ell_{[1+q]Q,[q^2 + q^3]Q}(P)$, and their products, are precomputed.

On CP8 curves, $\mathbb{G}_1$ has an endomorphism $\phi: (x,y) \mapsto (-x, \sqrt{-1}y)$ of eigenvalue $\lambda \equiv q^2 \bmod r$, $\lambda^2 \equiv -1 \bmod r$. On CP12 curves, $\mathbb{G}_1$ has the same endomorphism as BW6 curves, of eigenvalue $\lambda \equiv q^2 \bmod r$. The twisted ate pairing on our CP curves has Miller loop $f_{\lambda,P}(Q) = f_{q^2,P}(Q)$, and we derive our optimal Tate pairing like for BW6 curves, with short scalars $a_0 + a_1\lambda \equiv 0 \bmod r$.

Algorithm 3: Precomputations of sums of points and lines

Input: $P \in E(\mathbb{F}_q)[r]$, $Q_0, Q_1, Q_2, Q_3 \in E'(\mathbb{F}_{q^{k/d}})[r]$

Output: array T of length 15, of precomputed points and lines

1   $T \leftarrow$ array of length 15

2   **for** $i = 0$ *to 3* **do**

3      $T[2^i - 1][0] \leftarrow Q_i$; $T[2^i - 1][1] \leftarrow 1$

4   **for** $0 \leq m < n \leq 3$ **do**

5      $i \leftarrow 2^m + 2^n$

6      $T[i - 1][0] \leftarrow T[2^m - 1] + T[2^n - 1]$

7      $T[i - 1][1] \leftarrow \ell_{Q_m, Q_n}(P)$

8   **for** $0 \leq m < n < s \leq 3$ **do**

9      $i \leftarrow 2^m + 2^n + 2^s$

10     $T[i - 1][0] \leftarrow T[2^m + 2^n - 1][0] + T[2^s - 1][0]$

11     $T[i - 1][1] \leftarrow T[2^m + 2^n - 1][1] \cdot \ell_{Q_m + Q_n, Q_s}(P)$

12   $T[15 - 1][0] \leftarrow T[7 - 1][0] + T[8 - 1]$

13   $T[15 - 1][1] \leftarrow T[7 - 1][1] \cdot \ell_{Q_0 + Q_1 + Q_2, Q_3}(P)$

14   **return** T

Algorithm 4: Miller loop for optimal ate pairing, Cocks-Pinch

Input: $P \in \mathbb{G}_1 = E(\mathbb{F}_q)[r]$, $Q \in \mathbb{G}_2 = \ker(\pi_q - [q]) \cap E(\mathbb{F}_{q^k})[r]$, scalars
     a_0, a_1, a_2, a_3 such that $a_0 + a_1 q + a_2 q^2 + a_3 q^3 = 0 \bmod r$

Output: $f_{a_0 + a_1 q + a_2 q^2 + a_3 q^3, Q}(P)$

1   $Q_0 \leftarrow Q$; $Q_1 \leftarrow \pi_q(Q)$; $Q_2 \leftarrow \pi_{q^2}(Q)$; $Q_3 \leftarrow \pi_{q^3}(Q)$

2   **for** $i = 0$ *to 3* **do**

3   **if** $a_i < 0$ **then** $a_i \leftarrow -a_i$; $Q_i \leftarrow -Q_i$

4   $T \leftarrow$ precomputations(Q_0, Q_1, Q_2, Q_3)

5   $l_i \leftarrow bits(a_i)$ for $0 \leq i \leq 3$

6   $i \leftarrow \max_{0 \leq j \leq 3}(\mathrm{len}\, l_j)$

7   $j \leftarrow l_{0,i} + 2l_{1,i} + 4l_{2,i} + 8l_{3,i}$

8   $f \leftarrow T[j - 1][1]$

9   $S \leftarrow T[j - 1][0]$

10   **for** $i = i - 1$ *downto 0* **do**

11     $f \leftarrow f^2$

12     $\ell_t \leftarrow \ell_{S,S}(P)$; $S \leftarrow [2]S$

13     $j \leftarrow l_{0,i} + 2l_{1,i} + 4l_{2,i} + 8l_{3,i}$

14   **if** $j > 0$ **then**

15       $Q_j \leftarrow T[j - 1][0]$; $\ell \leftarrow \ell_{S,Q_j}(P)$; $S \leftarrow S + Q_j$

16       $f \leftarrow f \cdot (\ell_t \cdot \ell)$

17   **if** $T[j - 1][1] \neq 1$ **then** $f \leftarrow f \cdot T[j - 1][1]$

18   **else** $f \leftarrow f \cdot \ell_t$

19   **return** f

4.5   Comparison of BW6, CP8 and CP12 Outer Curve Performances

We reproduce the field arithmetic estimates from [15,27] in Table 6 and the pairing cost estimates in Table 7. Parameters of CP8 and CP12 are in Table 8, BW6 are in Table 12. We justify our choice of seeds and curve parameters in Sec. 5. Ate and Tate pairing estimates of our BW6 and CP curves are in Table 9. We have a speed-up of the optimal ate pairing on BW6 curves compared to [15] with the formula (32) with $v = u^2 - 2u + 1$ for BLS12-BW6 and $v = u^4 - 2(u^3 - u^2 + u) + 1$ for BLS24-BW6 because the 2-NAF Hamming weight of the scalar v is lower.

$$f_{u+1} = f_{u+1,Q}(P), \quad m_{\text{opt. ate}} = (f_{u+1})^q_{v,[u+1]Q}(P)\ell^q_{[(u+1)v]Q,-Q}(P) . \qquad (32)$$

BW6 curves as outer curves of BLS24 have a faster pairing than CP8 and CP12 curves: *a larger characteristic gives better performances than a larger embedding degree.* Assuming a ratio $m_{704}/m_{640} = 1.25$, an ate Miller loop on CP8-632 is 25% slower compared to BW6-672, but the final exp. is 15% faster. A full pairing on CP8 is about 7% slower, and 59% slower on CP12. BLS24-BW6 has a faster pairing than BLS12-BW6, but the 2-adicity of BLS24 curves is much smaller.

Table 6. Cost from [27, Tab. 6] of m_k, s_k and i_k for field extensions $\mathbb{F}_{p^k}$. Inversions in $\mathbb{F}_{p^{ik}}$ come from $i_{2k} = 2m_k + 2s_k + i_k$ and $i_{3k} = 9m_k + 3s_k + i_k$. $\mathbb{F}_{p^{12}}$, resp. $\mathbb{F}_{p^{24}}$ always have a first quadratic, resp. quartic extension, $i_{24} = 2m_{12} + 2s_{12} + i_{12} = 293m + i$ with $i_{12} = 9m_4 + 3s_4 + i_4$, and for $\mathbb{F}_{p^{12}}$, $i_{12} = 2m_6 + 2s_6 + i_6 = 97m + i$ with $i_6 = 9m_2 + 3s_2 + i_2$.

k	1	2	3	4	6	8	12	24
m_k	m	3m	6m	9m	18m	27m	54m	162m
s_k	m	2m	5m	6m	12m	8m	36m	108m
f_k	0	0	2m	2m	4m	6m	10m	22m
s_k^{cyclo}	–	2s	–	4s	6s	12s	18s	54s
$i_k - i_1$	0	2m + 2s	9m + 3s	14m	34m	44m	97m	293m
i_k, with $i_1 = 25m$	25m	29m	37m	39m	59m	69m	119m	318m

Table 7. Miller loop cost in non-affine, Weierstrass model [2,12]. For $6 \mid k$, two sparse-dense multiplications cost $26m_{k/6}$ whereas one sparse-sparse and one multiplication cost $6m_{k/6} + m_k = 24m_{k/6}$. For $4 \mid k$, this is $16m_{k/4}$ compared to $6m_{k/4} + m_k = 15m_{k/4}$.

k	D	curve	DoubleLine and AddLine	ref	SparseM and SparseSparseM
$6 \mid k$	-3	$Y^2 = X^3 + b$ sextic twist	$3m_{k/6} + 6s_{k/6} + (k/3)m$ $11m_{k/6} + 2s_{k/6} + (k/3)m$	[2, §4]	$13m_{k/6}$ $6m_{k/6}$
$4 \mid k$	-1	$Y^2 = X^3 + ax$ quartic twist	$2m_{k/4} + 8s_{k/4} + (k/2)m$ $9m_{k/4} + 5s_{k/4} + (k/2)m$	[12, §4]	$8m_{k/4}$ $6m_{k/4}$

Table 8. CP8 and CP12 outer curve parameters on top of BLS24-315

outer curve	u	(h_t, h_y)	$(t-1)^2+1$ mod r, u	equation	$\mathbb{F}_{q^k}$ (bits)	est. DL in $\mathbb{F}_{q^k}$
BLS24-315-CP8-632	-0xbfcfffff	(6,2)	–	$y^2 = x^3 - x$	5056	140
BLS24-315-CP12-630	-0xbfcfffff	(1,2)	0	$y^2 = x^3 - 1$	7560	166

Table 9. Pairing cost estimates on BLS12-BW6, BLS24-BW6, BLS24-CP8, BLS24-CP12 curves. BLS12-BW6 curves use Eq. (20) with [15, Alg. 5], and $v = u^2 - 2u + 1$. BLS24-BW6 curves use Eq (26), (27) with $v = u^4 - 2(u^3 - u^2 + u) + 1$.

	BLS12-377-BW6-761	BLS12-379-BW6-764
ate $f_{u+1,Q}(f_u)^q_{u^2-u-1,[u]Q}$	7863m$_{768}$	7653m$_{768}$
ate $f_{u+1,Q}(f_{u+1})^q_{v,[u+1]Q}\ell^q_{(u+1)vQ,-Q}$	7555m$_{768}$	7389m$_{768}$
Tate $f_{u+1+(u^3-u^2-u)\lambda,P}$ Algorithm 2	7729m$_{768}$	7540m$_{768}$
Final exp. [15, § 3.3, Tab. 7]	5081m$_{768}$	–
Final exp. Eq. (24)	5195m$_{768}$	5033m$_{768}$
	BLS24-315-BW6-633	BLS24-315-BW6-672
ate $f_{u+1,Q}(f_{u+1})^q_{v,[u+1]Q}\ell^q_{(u+1)vQ,-Q}$	7285m$_{640}$	7285m$_{704}$
Tate $f_{u+1+(u^5-u^4-u)\lambda,P}$ Algorithm 2	6813m$_{640}$	6813m$_{704}$
Final exp.	5027m$_{640}$	5501m$_{704}$
	BLS24-315-CP8-632	BLS24-315-CP12-630
ate $f_{a_0+a_1q+a_2q^2+a_3q^3,Q}$ Algorithm 4	10679m$_{640}$	13805m$_{640}$
Tate $f_{a_0+a_1\lambda,P}$ Algorithm 2	12489m$_{640}$	15780m$_{640}$
Final exp.	5835m$_{640}$	10312m$_{640}$

5   Implementation and Benchmarking

In previous sections, we presented families of SNARK-friendly 2-chains that are suitable for Groth'16 and KZG-based universal SNARKs. These families are composed of BLS12 and BLS24 inner curves and BW6, CP8 and CP12 outer curves. We demonstrated that the pair family BLS12/BW6 is suitable for recursive Groth'16 applications and meets the best security/performance trade-off. Similarly, we showed that BLS24/BW6 is suitable for KZG-based universal SNARKs. We also investigated the family pairs BLS24/CP8 and BLS24/CP12 as more conservative choices and showed that CP8-632 is competitive with BLS24/BW6-672. BW6-633, CP8 and CP12 are defined over a base field of roughly the same bit length, and all have a GLV endomorphism, hence performances on $\mathbb{G}_1$ are expected to be the same. On $\mathbb{G}_2$, BW6 are always faster because they are defined over the same base field as $\mathbb{G}_1$, contrary to CP curves. For the pairing computation, as discussed in Sect. 4.5, CP8 and CP12 are slower than both choices of BW6. Additionally, multi-pairings (as used in SNARKs) scale better on BW6 curves (Algorithm 2) compared to CP8 and CP12. Therefore, we have chosen to focus our benchmarks on BLS12/BW6 and BLS24/BW6 families of curves.

In this section, we first present an open-sourced SageMath library to derive these curves and test our generic formulas. Then, based on additional practical criteria, we recommend a short list of SNARK-friendly 2-chains. Finally, we implement this short-list in the open-sourced gnark ecosystem [9]. We benchmark the relevant curve operations in $\mathbb{G}_1$ and $\mathbb{G}_2$, and the pairings, and compare efficiency of all choices in practical Groth'16 and PlonK settings, which is a popular KZG-based universal SNARK. Both schemes are implemented in gnark and maintained by ConsenSys.

5.1   SageMath Library: Derive the Curves

In this public Git repository [17], we present SageMath scripts to derive all the SNARK-friendly 2-chain families and verify the formulae presented in Sects. 3 and 4, and the pairing cost estimates of Table 9.

5.2   Our Short-List of Curves

For all curves, in addition to SNARK-friendliness and security level λ, we shall consider the following properties:

- A seed u with low Hamming weight $HW(u)$, allowing fast Miller loops in pairings.
- Isogenies of low degree d from a curve with j-invariant different from 0 and 1728, allowing use of the "simplified SWU" method for hashing to the curve [43].
- Small integer α relatively prime to $r - 1$, allowing the use of x^α as an S-box in the algebraic SNARK-hashes (e.g. Poseidon [24]).
- Small non-residues in $\mathbb{F}_q$, for an efficient tower arithmetic.
- "Spare" bits in $\mathbb{F}_q$, for carries, infinity point or compressed point flag.

For outer curves, an additional property is

- Smallest $h_t^2 + 3h_y^2$ with low Hamming weight, allowing fast final exponentiation.

BLS12/BW6. The security of BLS12-384 and BLS12-448 is explained in [28], BLS12-448 being presented as a more conservative choice: it offers about 132 bits of security in $\mathbb{F}_{q^{12}}$ instead of 126 bits. Because a BLS12-448 would imply a much larger BW6-896, we concentrate on the BLS12 curves of 377 to 383 bits of Table 10. Given the above requirements, we short-list BLS12-377 with $u = $ 0x8508c00000000001 and BLS12-379 with $u = $ 0x9b04000000000001. The former was proposed in [10] and used in [15] and the latter is new, of higher 2-adicity. Both have a $HW(u) = 7$, $d = 2$, $\alpha \leq 7$ and tower fields can be constructed as $\mathbb{F}_q \xrightarrow{i^2+5} \mathbb{F}_{q^2} \xrightarrow{v^3-i} \mathbb{F}_{q^6} \xrightarrow{w^2-v} \mathbb{F}_{q^{12}}$.

Now, we construct outer BW6 curves to these inner BLS12 curves. For BLS12-377, we find BW6-761 to be optimal and refer the reader to [15] for a more detailed study. For BLS12-379, we restrict the search to curves up to 768 bits and suggest the corresponding BW6-764 with $h_t = -23$, $h_y = 3$ and equation $Y^2 = X^3 + 1$ (and M-twist $Y^2 = X^3 + 2$). Both BW6-761 and BW6-764 fall in the $t_{bw,3}$ case (Table 3).

BLS24/BW6. A BLS24 curve defined over a 320-bit prime field offers 128 bits of security on the curve thanks to a subgroup of prime order r of 256 bits, and offers around 160 bits in $\mathbb{F}_{q^{24}}$. Accordingly, we find the following SNARK-friendly inner BLS24 curves (Table 11).

Given all the requirements, we choose BLS24-315 ($u = $ -0xbfcfffff) over $\mathbb{F}_q$ of 315 bits and with $\mathbb{F}_r$ of 253 bits. It has 2-adicity 22 and security level almost 128. The tower fields can be constructed as $\mathbb{F}_q \xrightarrow{i^2-13} \mathbb{F}_{q^2} \xrightarrow{v^2-i} \mathbb{F}_{q^4} \xrightarrow{w^2-v} \mathbb{F}_{q^8} \xrightarrow{c^3-w} \mathbb{F}_{q^{24}}$.

Now, we construct outer BW6 curves to BLS24-315. First, we search for less conservative curves over a field of up to 640 bits. We recommend the BW6-633 curve with $h_y = -7, h_y = -1$ and the equation $Y^2 = X^3 + 4$ (and M-twist $Y^2 = X^3 + 8$). For more conservative curves offering 128 bits of security, we search for q_{bw} of exactly 672 bits. We recommend the BW6-672 curve with $h_t = 5111800, h_y = 0$ ($\text{HW}_{2\text{-NAF}}(h_t^2 + 2h_y^2) = 8$) and equation $Y^2 = X^3 - 4$ (D-twist $Y^2 = X^3 - 4/3$). The former falls in the $t_{bw,0}$ and the latter in the $t_{bw,3}$ case.

5.3   Estimated Complexity of a DL Computation in $GF(q^k)$

This section recalls the results from [3,26,28]. A BLS12 curve with r of about 256 bits has q of about 384 bits. In [28, Table 10] the estimated security in $\mathbb{F}_{q^{12}}$ for the BLS12-381 curve is 126 bits. Running the tool from [28], the paper [15] shows that BLS12-377 in $\mathbb{F}_{q^{12}}$ has 125 bits of security, and BW6-761 has 126 bits of security in $\mathbb{F}_{q^6}$. With the same approach and the SageMath tool[2] from [28], our BLS12-379 curve has 125 bits in $\mathbb{F}_{q^{12}}$ and our BLS24-315 curve has 160 bits of security in $\mathbb{F}_{q^{24}}$.

We observe a notable difference between the BW6 outer curves of BLS12 and BLS24 because of the degree of the polynomial $q_{bw}(x)$. This polynomial is the key-ingredient of the Special (Tower) NFS [34]. However when its degree is too high, the general (Tower) NFS performs better, unless a tweak of $q_{bw}(x)$ is possible [26]. This tweak divides by n the degree of $q_{bw}(x)$ while increasing its coefficients by at most u^{n-1}. It works only if either q_{bw} has an automorphism

Table 10. Seeds of SNARK-friendly inner BLS12 curves around 128 bits of security.

u	q (bits)	r (bits)	$\lambda\ E(\mathbb{F}_q)$	$\lambda\ \mathbb{F}_{q^{12}}$	2-adicity L	d	α
0x8508c00000000001	377	253	126	126	47	2	11
-0x7fb80fffffffffff	377	252	126	126	45	2	5
0x9b04000000000001	379	254	127	126	51	2	7
-0xfffbc3ffffffffff	383	256	128	126	43	2	7
-0xfff7c1ffffffffff	383	256	128	126	42	2	7
-0xffc3bfffffffffff	383	256	128	126	47	2	7
0x105a8000000000001	383	257	128	126	52	2	7

---

[2] SageMath code available at https://gitlab.inria.fr/tnfs-alpha/alpha.

Table 11. Seeds of SNARK-friendly inner BLS24 curves around 128 bits of security.

u	q (bits)	r (bits)	$\lambda\, E(\mathbb{F}_q)$	$\lambda\, \mathbb{F}_{q^{24}}$	2-adicity L	d	α
0x60300001	305	245	122	158	22	2	7
-0x950fffff	311	250	125	159	22	2	7
0x9f9c0001	312	251	125	159	20	2	7
-0xbfcfffff	315	253	126	160	22	2	7
-0xc90bffff	315	254	126	160	20	2	13
0xe19c0001	317	255	127	160	20	2	17
-0x10487ffff	319	257	128	161	21	2	11

Table 12. BW6 outer curve parameters, where $y^2 = x^3 + b$.

outer curve	u	(h_t, h_y)	$t \bmod r, u$	b	$\mathbb{F}_{q^k}$ (bits)	est. DL in $\mathbb{F}_{q^k}$
BLS12-377-BW6-761	0x8508c00000000001	(13, 9)	0	−1	4566	126
BLS12-379-BW6-764	0x9b04000000000001	(−25, 3)	0	1	4584	126
BLS24-315-BW6-633	-0xbfcfffff	(−7, −1)	0	4	3798	124
BLS24-315-BW6-672	-0xbfcfffff	(0x4dfff8, 0)	0	−4	4032	128

of degree n, hence the new polynomial has coefficients as small as the initial one, or the seed u is small enough. Here q_{bw} has no automorphism, and u is 32 bits long. We obtain a new $\tilde{q}_{\mathrm{bw}}(x)$ of degree 10 and coefficients of 40 bits. The lowest estimate of DL cost with STNFS is 2^{132} with h of degree 6 for the 633-bit curve. The general TNFS works slightly better: with h of degree 2, and the Conjugation method (Conj), we obtain a DL cost estimate of 2^{124}. This is coherent with MNT-6 curve security estimates, where the same choice of parameters for TNFS apply [27, Fig. 1]. To reach the 2^{128} cost, we increase q_{bw} up to 672 bits. We stress that the tool we use only gives an estimate, and recent progress are being made about TNFS [13]. In case of underestimate of the tool, one can consider a 704-bit BLS24-BW6 curve.

For the Cocks-Pinch construction, the parameters do not have a polynomial form. For the embedding degree 8 we consider the TNFS-Conj algorithm with h of degree 2 according to [27, Fig. 2]. We obtain 140 bits of security in $\mathbb{F}_{q^8}$ for the BLS24-315-CP8-632 curve. For the BLS24-315-CP12-630 curve we measure a DL cost of 166 bits in $\mathbb{F}_{q^{12}}$ with TNFS-Conj and h of degree 3 for the tower.

5.4   Golang Library: Implement the Short-List Curves

In this Git repository [14], we present an optimized implementation, with x86-64 assembly code for the finite fields, of the short-listed curves: BLS12-377, BW6-761, BLS12-379, BW6-764, BLS24-315, BW6-633 and BW6-672 (Table 13). All curve implementations are written in Golang (tested with 1.16 and 1.17 versions) and benefit from $\mathbb{F}_q$ and $\mathbb{F}_r$ x86-64 assembly accelerated arithmetic. Also, they benefit from $D = -3$ endomorphism-based optimizations (GLV and 2-dimensional GLS scalar multiplication, fast subgroup checks and cofactor clearing). For the pairing, we follow optimizations from [1,23,29,38] and Sect. 4.

Table 13. Short-listed curves.

curve, tower fields	equation	twist equation
BLS12-377, $\mathbb{F}_q \xrightarrow{i^2+5} \mathbb{F}_{q^2} \xrightarrow{v^3-i} \mathbb{F}_{q^6} \xrightarrow{w^2-v} \mathbb{F}_{q^{12}}$	$Y^2 = X^3 + 1$	$Y^2 = X^3 + 1/i$
BLS12-379, $\mathbb{F}_q \xrightarrow{i^2+5} \mathbb{F}_{q^2} \xrightarrow{v^3-i} \mathbb{F}_{q^6} \xrightarrow{w^2-v} \mathbb{F}_{q^{12}}$	$Y^2 = X^3 + 1$	$Y^2 = X^3 + 1/(5+i)$
BLS24-315, $\mathbb{F}_q \xrightarrow{i^2-13} \mathbb{F}_{q^2} \xrightarrow{v^2-i} \mathbb{F}_{q^4} \xrightarrow{w^2-v} \mathbb{F}_{q^8} \xrightarrow{c^3-w} \mathbb{F}_{q^{24}}$	$Y^2 = X^3 + 1$	$Y^2 = X^3 + 1/i$
BLS12-377-BW6-761, $\mathbb{F}_q \xrightarrow{i^3+4} \mathbb{F}_{q^3} \xrightarrow{v^2-i} \mathbb{F}_{q^6}$	$Y^2 = X^3 - 1$	$Y^2 = X^3 + 4$
BLS12-379-BW6-764, $\mathbb{F}_q \xrightarrow{i^3-2} \mathbb{F}_{q^3} \xrightarrow{v^2-i} \mathbb{F}_{q^6}$	$Y^2 = X^3 + 1$	$Y^2 = X^3 + 2$
BLS24-315-BW6-633, $\mathbb{F}_q \xrightarrow{i^3-2} \mathbb{F}_{q^3} \xrightarrow{v^2-i} \mathbb{F}_{q^6}$	$Y^2 = X^3 + 4$	$Y^2 = X^3 + 8$
BLS24-315-BW6-672, $\mathbb{F}_q \xrightarrow{i^3-3} \mathbb{F}_{q^3} \xrightarrow{v^2-i} \mathbb{F}_{q^6}$	$Y^2 = X^3 - 4$	$Y^2 = X^3 - 4/3$

5.5 Benchmarking

In this section, we benchmark our Golang implementation for all short-listed curves on two levels. First, independently from the context, we benchmark $\mathbb{G}_1$, $\mathbb{G}_2$ scalar multiplications (with GLV/GLS acceleration [22] and multi-scalar-multiplication (Bucket-list method [6, section 4]). Also, we benchmark the pairing computation (Miller loop, Final exponentiation and total pairing). Then, we benchmark the time to setup, prove and verify Groth'16 and PlonK proofs of circuits with different number of constraints.

The first level benchmarks are run on a AWS z1d.large (3.4 GHz Intel Xeon) and the second level on a an AWS c5a.24xlarge (AMD EPYC 7R32). This allows to handle large proofs and to test different architectures. All with hyperthreading, turbo and frequency scaling disabled. $\mathbb{G}_1$, $\mathbb{G}_2$ **and** $\mathbb{G}_T$ **operations.** $\mathbb{G}_1$ coordinates for all short-listed curves are over $\mathbb{F}_q$ and use $D = -3$ endomorphism to implement GLV. For $\mathbb{G}_2$, BW6 coordinates are over $\mathbb{F}_q$ as well and implements GLV ($D = -3$). For BLS12 and BLS24, the implementation uses 2-dim. GLS [22] over $\mathbb{F}_{q^2}$ and $\mathbb{F}_{q^4}$ respectively. Timings are reported in Tables 14 and 15. For multi-scalar-multiplication, we report timings in Figs. 1 and 2 for different sizes (2^5 to 2^{24} points).

Table 14. $\mathbb{G}_1$ and $\mathbb{G}_2$ scalar multiplication benchmarks.

curve	$\mathbb{G}_1$ scalar mul. (ns)	$\mathbb{G}_2$ scalar mul. (ns)
BLS12-377	77606	261607
BLS12-379	81090	272107
BLS24-315	65825	622044
BLS12-377-BW6-761	377360	377360
BLS12-379-BW6-764	390647	390647
BLS24-315-BW6-633	255600	255600
BLS24-315-BW6-672	300929	300929

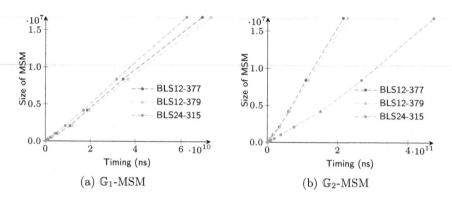

Fig. 1. MSM on $\mathbb{G}_1$ a and $\mathbb{G}_2$ b for short-listed inner curves.

On the one hand, we note that for inner curves BLS24-315 is the fastest on $\mathbb{G}_1$, the slowest on $\mathbb{G}_2$ while still competitive on $\mathbb{G}_T$ (especially for multipairings when the final exponentiation is factored out). Thus, it is suitable for KZG-based SNARKs where only $\mathbb{G}_1$ operations and pairings accounts for the Setup, Prove and Verify algorithms. On the other hand, BLS12-377 presents the best tradeoff on all operations making it suitable for Groth'16 SNARK. For the less conservative choice of outer curve to BLS24-315, namely BW6-633, a pairing computation is almost as fast as on BLS24-315 and MSMs are the fastest on all outer curves given the small field size. For the conservative choice, namely BW6-672, operations on all three groups are reasonably fast and notably faster than on outer curves to BLS12 (BW6-761 and BW6-764).

Groth' 16 and PlonK Schemes. Based on previous paragraph analysis, here, we discard BLS12-379/BW6-764 pair and choose to bench BLS12-377/BW6-761 and BLS24-315/BW6-633/BW6-762 pair of curves in the context of Groth'16

Table 15. Pairing computation benchmarks.

curve	Miller Loop (ns)	Final Exp. (ns)	Pairing (ns)
BLS12-377 opt. ate	377191	422157	799348
BLS12-379 opt. ate	383753	453687	837440
BLS24-315 opt. ate	435958	993500	1429458
BLS12-377-BW6-761 opt. ate (Eq. 14)	1613306	1099533	2712839
BLS12-377-BW6-761 opt. ate (Eq. 32)	1249860	1099533	2349393
BLS12-377-BW6-761 opt. Tate	1249860	1099533	2349393
BLS12-379-BW6-764 opt. ate (Eq. 14)	1548546	1057174	2605720
BLS24-315-BW6-633 opt. ate	918724	727918	1646642
BLS24-315-BW6-633 opt. Tate	809503	727918	1537421
BLS24-315-BW6-672 opt. ate	1073268	977436	2050704
BLS24-315-BW6-672 opt. Tate	973630	977436	1951066

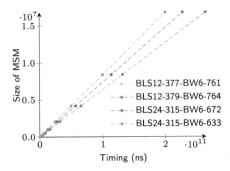

Fig. 2. $\mathbb{G}_1/\mathbb{G}_2$-MSM on short-listed outer curves.

and PlonK SNARKs. We choose a simple circuit (proof of exponentiation: $a^w := b$ (see Sect. 2.2)) to be able to control precisely the number of constraints. We bench the `Setup`, `Prove` and `Verify` algorithms for both Groth16 and PlonK schemes and report timings in Figs. 3, 4, 5, 6 and 7. The benchmark is run, this time, on an AWS c5a.24xlarge (AMD EPYC 7R32) to be able to test large circuits. In Table 16 we recall the cost of SNARK algorithms in terms of preponderant groups operations.

Remark 4. The maximum number of constraints n_{max} a circuit can have is different per SNARK scheme and per curve. For Groth16, $n_{max} = 2^L$ and for PlonK $n_{max} = 2^{L-2}$ where L is the 2-adicity of the chosen curve.

Table 16. Cost of `Setup`, `Prove` and `Verify` algorithms for Groth16 and PlonK. m =number of wires, n =number of multiplications gates, a =number of additions gates and ℓ =number of public inputs. $\mathsf{M}_\mathbb{G}$ =multiplication in $\mathbb{G}$ and P=pairing.

	Setup	Prove	Verify
Groth16	$3n\ \mathsf{M}_{\mathbb{G}_1}, m\ \mathsf{M}_{\mathbb{G}_2}$	$(3n + m - \ell)\ \mathsf{M}_{\mathbb{G}_1}, n\ \mathsf{M}_{\mathbb{G}_2}$	$3\ \mathrm{P}, \ell\ \mathsf{M}_{\mathbb{G}_1}$
PlonK (KZG)	$d_{\geq n+a}\ \mathsf{M}_{\mathbb{G}_1}, 1\ \mathsf{M}_{\mathbb{G}_2}$	$9(n + a)\ \mathsf{M}_{\mathbb{G}_1}$	$2\ \mathrm{P}, 18\ \mathsf{M}_{\mathbb{G}_1}$

It is clear from Figs. 3, 4 and 7 that BLS12-377 is optimized to setup and prove Groth16 proofs while BLS24-315 is suitable to setup and prove PlonK proofs at the cost of acceptably slower verification time. For proof composition, we see from Figs. 5, 6 and 7 that the outer curves to BLS24-315, namely BW6-633 and BW6-672, are faster for all the SNARK algorithms for both Groth16 and PlonK. This confirms the recommendation of BLS24/BW6 pair of curves for KZG-based SNARK. We should also note that for applications where one would like to optimize the cost of generating and proving a proof of several proofs $\{\pi_i\}_{0 \leq i \leq M}$ at the cost of slow generation of π_i (e.g. proof aggregation by light clients of off-chain generated proofs), one could use the BLS24/BW6 pair for Groth16.

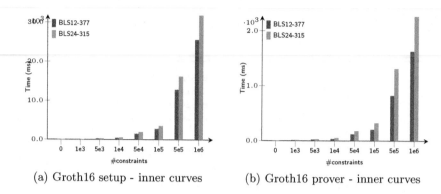

(a) Groth16 setup - inner curves　　　　(b) Groth16 prover - inner curves

Fig. 3. Groth16 Setup (a) and Prove (b) times per number of constraints for inner curves.

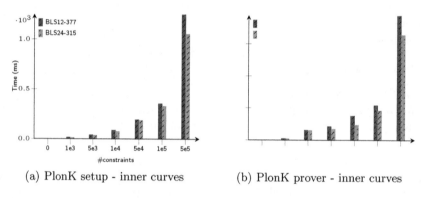

(a) PlonK setup - inner curves　　　　(b) PlonK prover - inner curves

Fig. 4. PlonK Setup (a) and Prove (b) times per number of constraints for inner curves.

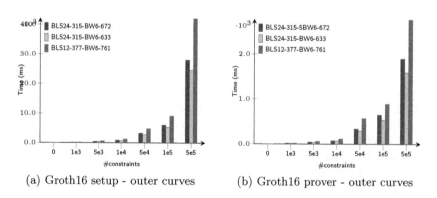

(a) Groth16 setup - outer curves　　　　(b) Groth16 prover - outer curves

Fig. 5. Groth16 Setup (a) and Prove (b) times per number of constraints for outer curves.

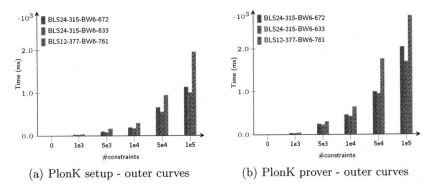

(a) PlonK setup - outer curves   (b) PlonK prover - outer curves

Fig. 6. PlonK `Setup` (a) and `Prove` (b) times per number of constraints for outer curves.

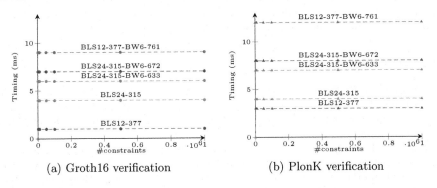

(a) Groth16 verification   (b) PlonK verification

Fig. 7. Groth16 (a) and PlonK (b) `Verify` times on short-listed curves.

6 Conclusion

We generalized the curve construction of [15] and proposed a family in which this curve falls. Precisely, a family of SNARK-friendly 2-chains built on top of BLS12 inner curves. We investigated another family composed of inner BLS24 curves and outer BW6, CP8 and CP12 curves. We first presented our results for a better arithmetic on all BLS curves and then derived generic formulas for group operations and pairings over our outer curves. Then, we analysed and compared the security and performance tradeoffs of all the constructions. In the context of SNARK applications, we short-listed several curves based on practical criteria. Finally, we presented a SageMath library to derive the curves and verify the formulas and an optimized Golang implementation of the short-listed curves along with benchmarks. We concluded that BLS12-377/BW6-761 is optimized in the Groth16 setting while BLS24-315/BW6-672 (or less conservative BW6-633) is optimized in the KZG-based SNARK setting.

As a future work, we would like to investigate optimized pairing algorithms for SNARK circuits (e.g. R1CS). In fact, while pairings are well studied in the classical setting, there isn't much work in the SNARK setting. This would enable faster proof composition with SNARK-friendly 2-chains. Another avenue that is worth noting is combining our work with other techniques that allow proof composition, such as Plookup [20]. This is a protocol for checking whether the values of a committed polynomial are contained in the values of a table but it can be used to emulate non-native field operations in a SNARK circuit. However, this is less efficient than the 2-chains based method and we propose to mix both methods. On a platform where only a target curve is available (e.g. Ethereum blockchain supports BN254 only), one can imagine composing efficiently multiple PlonK proofs with BLS24/BW6 pair of curves and then using the Plookup technique only once to prove the composed BW6-proof over the target curve.

Acknowledgements. We thank Thomas Piellard and Olivier Bégassat for valuable discussions and feedback. We thank Gautam Botrel for helping with the Go implementation. We thank Diego Aranha, Julien Doget and Mike Scott for stimulating discussions on $\mathbb{G}_T$ membership testing and subgroup security in $\mathbb{F}_{q^k}$.

References

1. Aranha, D.F., Barreto, P.S.L.M., Longa, P., Ricardini, J.E.: The realm of the pairings. In: Lange, T., Lauter, K., Lisoněk, P. (eds.) SAC 2013. LNCS, vol. 8282, pp. 3–25. Springer, Heidelberg (2014). https://doi.org/10.1007/978-3-662-43414-7_1

2. Aranha, D.F., Karabina, K., Longa, P., Gebotys, C.H., López, J.: Faster explicit formulas for computing pairings over ordinary curves. In: Paterson, K.G. (ed.) EUROCRYPT 2011. LNCS, vol. 6632, pp. 48–68. Springer, Heidelberg (2011). https://doi.org/10.1007/978-3-642-20465-4_5

3. Barbulescu, R., Duquesne, S.: Updating key size estimations for pairings. J. Cryptol. **32**(4), 1298–1336 (2019). https://doi.org/10.1007/s00145-018-9280-5

4. Barreto, P.S.L.M., Lynn, B., Scott, M.: Constructing elliptic curves with prescribed embedding degrees. In: Cimato, S., Persiano, G., Galdi, C. (eds.) SCN 2002. LNCS, vol. 2576, pp. 257–267. Springer, Heidelberg (2003). https://doi.org/10.1007/3-540-36413-7_19

5. Ben-Sasson, E., Chiesa, A., Tromer, E., Virza, M.: Scalable zero knowledge via cycles of elliptic curves. In: Garay, J.A., Gennaro, R. (eds.) CRYPTO 2014, Part II. LNCS, vol. 8617, pp. 276–294. Springer, Heidelberg (2014). https://doi.org/10.1007/978-3-662-44381-1_16

6. Bernstein, D.J., Doumen, J., Lange, T., Oosterwijk, J.-J.: Faster batch forgery identification. In: Galbraith, S., Nandi, M. (eds.) INDOCRYPT 2012. LNCS, vol. 7668, pp. 454–473. Springer, Heidelberg (2012). https://doi.org/10.1007/978-3-642-34931-7_26

7. Bitansky, N., Canetti, R., Chiesa, A., Tromer, E.: From extractable collision resistance to succinct non-interactive arguments of knowledge, and back again. In: Goldwasser, S. (ed.) ITCS 2012, pp. 326–349. ACM, January 2012. https://doi.org/10.1145/2090236.2090263

8. Bitansky, N., Canetti, R., Chiesa, A., Tromer, E.: Recursive composition and bootstrapping for SNARKS and proof-carrying data. In: Boneh, D., Roughgarden, T., Feigenbaum, J. (eds.) 45th ACM STOC, pp. 111–120. ACM Press, June 2013. https://doi.org/10.1145/2488608.2488623

9. Botrel, G., Piellard, T., Housni, Y.E., Kubjas, I., Tabaie, A.: Consensys/gnark: v0.6.0, January 2022. https://doi.org/10.5281/zenodo.5819105

10. Bowe, S., Chiesa, A., Green, M., Miers, I., Mishra, P., Wu, H.: ZEXE: enabling decentralized private computation. In: 2020 IEEE Symposium on Security and Privacy, pp. 947–964. IEEE Computer Society Press, May 2020. https://doi.org/10.1109/SP40000.2020.00050

11. Chiesa, A., Hu, Y., Maller, M., Mishra, P., Vesely, N., Ward, N.: Marlin: preprocessing zkSNARKs with universal and updatable SRS. In: Canteaut, A., Ishai, Y. (eds.) EUROCRYPT 2020, Part I. LNCS, vol. 12105, pp. 738–768. Springer, Cham (2020). https://doi.org/10.1007/978-3-030-45721-1_26

12. Costello, C., Lange, T., Naehrig, M.: Faster pairing computations on curves with high-degree twists. In: Nguyen, P.Q., Pointcheval, D. (eds.) PKC 2010. LNCS, vol. 6056, pp. 224–242. Springer, Heidelberg (2010). https://doi.org/10.1007/978-3-642-13013-7_14

13. De Micheli, G., Gaudry, P., Pierrot, C.: Lattice enumeration for tower NFS: a 521-bit discrete logarithm computation. In: Tibouchi, M., Wang, H. (eds.) ASIACRYPT 2021, Part I. LNCS, vol. 13090, pp. 67–96. Springer, Cham (2021). https://doi.org/10.1007/978-3-030-92062-3_3

14. El Housni, Y.: A fork of gnark-crypto: Golang library for finite fields, fft, and elliptic curves (2021). https://github.com/yelhousni/gnark-crypto

15. El Housni, Y., Guillevic, A.: Optimized and secure pairing-friendly elliptic curves suitable for one layer proof composition. In: Krenn, S., Shulman, H., Vaudenay, S. (eds.) CANS 2020. LNCS, vol. 12579, pp. 259–279. Springer, Cham (2020). https://doi.org/10.1007/978-3-030-65411-5_13

16. El Housni, Y., Guillevic, A.: Families of SNARK-friendly 2-chains of elliptic curves. ePrint 2021/1359 (2021)

17. El Housni, Y., Guillevic, A.: Families of SNARK-friendly 2-chains of elliptic curves (2021). MIT License. https://gitlab.inria.fr/zk-curves/snark-2-chains

18. Fotiadis, G., Konstantinou, E.: TNFS resistant families of pairing-friendly elliptic curves. Theor. Comput. Sci. **800**, 73–89 (2019). https://doi.org/10.1016/j.tcs.2019.10.017

19. Freeman, D., Scott, M., Teske, E.: A taxonomy of pairing-friendly elliptic curves. J. Cryptol. **23**(2), 224–280 (2010). https://doi.org/10.1007/s00145-009-9048-z

20. Gabizon, A., Williamson, Z.J.: plookup: a simplified polynomial protocol for lookup tables. ePrint 2020/315 (2020)

21. Gabizon, A., Williamson, Z.J., Ciobotaru, O.: PLONK: permutations over lagrange-bases for oecumenical noninteractive arguments of knowledge. ePrint 2019/953 (2019)

22. Galbraith, S.D., Lin, X., Scott, M.: Endomorphisms for faster elliptic curve cryptography on a large class of curves. In: Joux, A. (ed.) EUROCRYPT 2009. LNCS, vol. 5479, pp. 518–535. Springer, Heidelberg (2009). https://doi.org/10.1007/978-3-642-01001-9_30

23. Granger, R., Scott, M.: Faster squaring in the cyclotomic subgroup of sixth degree extensions. In: Nguyen, P.Q., Pointcheval, D. (eds.) PKC 2010. LNCS, vol. 6056, pp. 209–223. Springer, Heidelberg (2010). https://doi.org/10.1007/978-3-642-13013-7_13

24. Grassi, L., Khovratovich, D., Rechberger, C., Roy, A., Schofnegger, M.: Poseidon: a new hash function for zero-knowledge proof systems. In: USENIX Security Symposium (2021)

25. Groth, J.: On the size of pairing-based non-interactive arguments. In: Fischlin, M., Coron, J.-S. (eds.) EUROCRYPT 2016, Part II. LNCS, vol. 9666, pp. 305–326. Springer, Heidelberg (2016). https://doi.org/10.1007/978-3-662-49896-5_11

26. Guillevic, A.: A short-list of pairing-friendly curves resistant to special TNFS at the 128-bit security level. In: Kiayias, A., Kohlweiss, M., Wallden, P., Zikas, V. (eds.) PKC 2020, Part II. LNCS, vol. 12111, pp. 535–564. Springer, Cham (2020). https://doi.org/10.1007/978-3-030-45388-6_19

27. Guillevic, A., Masson, S., Thomé, E.: Cocks-Pinch curves of embedding degrees five to eight and optimal ate pairing computation. Des. Codes Cryptogr. **88**, 1047–1081 (2020). https://doi.org/10.1007/s10623-020-00727-w

28. Guillevic, A., Singh, S.: On the alpha value of polynomials in the tower number field sieve algorithm. Math. Cryptol. **1**(1), 1–39 (2021). https://journals.flvc.org/mathcryptology/article/view/125142

29. Hayashida, D., Hayasaka, K., Teruya, T.: Efficient final exponentiation via cyclotomic structure for pairings over families of elliptic curves. ePrint 2020/875 (2020)

30. Hess, F., Smart, N.P., Vercauteren, F.: The eta pairing revisited. IEEE Trans. Inf. Theory **52**(10), 4595–4602 (2006). https://doi.org/10.1109/TIT.2006.881709

31. Karabina, K.: Squaring in cyclotomic subgroups. Math. Comput. **82**(281), 555–579 (2013). https://doi.org/10.1090/S0025-5718-2012-02625-1

32. Kate, A., Zaverucha, G.M., Goldberg, I.: Constant-size commitments to polynomials and their applications. In: Abe, M. (ed.) ASIACRYPT 2010. LNCS, vol. 6477, pp. 177–194. Springer, Heidelberg (2010). https://doi.org/10.1007/978-3-642-17373-8_11

33. Kilian, J.: A note on efficient zero-knowledge proofs and arguments (extended abstract). In: 24th ACM STOC, pp. 723–732. ACM Press, May 1992. https://doi.org/10.1145/129712.129782

34. Kim, T., Barbulescu, R.: Extended tower number field sieve: a new complexity for the medium prime case. In: Robshaw, M., Katz, J. (eds.) CRYPTO 2016, Part I. LNCS, vol. 9814, pp. 543–571. Springer, Heidelberg (2016). https://doi.org/10.1007/978-3-662-53018-4_20

35. Micali, S.: CS proofs (extended abstracts). In: 35th FOCS, pp. 436–453. IEEE Computer Society Press, November 1994. https://doi.org/10.1109/SFCS.1994.365746

36. Schoof, R.: Nonsingular plane cubic curves over finite fields. J. Comb. Theory Ser. A **46**(2), 183–211 (1987). https://doi.org/10.1016/0097-3165(87)90003-3

37. Scott, M.: A note on group membership tests for $\mathbb{G}_1$, $\mathbb{G}_2$ and $\mathbb{G}_T$ on BLS pairing-friendly curves. ePrint 2021/1130 (2021)

38. Scott, M.: Pairing implementation revisited. ePrint 2019/077 (2019)

39. Scott, M.: Unbalancing pairing-based key exchange protocols. ePrint 2013/688 (2013)

40. Silverman, J.H.: The Arithmetic of Elliptic Curves. Graduate Texts in Mathematics, Springer, Dordrecht (2009). https://doi.org/10.1007/978-0-387-09494-6

41. Valiant, P.: Incrementally verifiable computation or proofs of knowledge imply time/space efficiency. In: Canetti, R. (ed.) TCC 2008. LNCS, vol. 4948, pp. 1–18. Springer, Heidelberg (2008). https://doi.org/10.1007/978-3-540-78524-8_1

42. Vercauteren, F.: Optimal pairings. IEEE Trans. Inf. Theory **56**(1), 455–461 (2010). https://doi.org/10.1109/TIT.2009.2034881

43. Wahby, R.S., Boneh, D.: Fast and simple constant-time hashing to the BLS12-381 elliptic curve. IACR TCHES **2019**(4), 154–179 (2019). https://doi.org/10.13154/tches.v2019.i4.154-179

Fiat–Shamir Bulletproofs are Non-Malleable (in the Algebraic Group Model)

Chaya Ganesh[1], Claudio Orlandi[2], Mahak Pancholi[2(✉)],
Akira Takahashi[2], and Daniel Tschudi[3]

[1] Indian Institute of Science, Bengaluru, India
chaya@iisc.ac.in
[2] Aarhus University, Aarhus, Denmark
{orlandi,mahakp,takahashi}@cs.au.dk
[3] Concordium, Zürich, Switzerland
dt@concordium.com

Abstract. Bulletproofs (Bünz et al. IEEE S&P 2018) are a celebrated ZK proof system that allows for short and efficient proofs, and have been implemented and deployed in several real-world systems.

In practice, they are most often implemented in their *non-interactive* version obtained using the Fiat-Shamir transform, despite the lack of a formal proof of security for this setting.

Prior to this work, there was no evidence that *malleability attacks* were not possible against Fiat-Shamir Bulletproofs. Malleability attacks can lead to very severe vulnerabilities, as they allow an adversary to forge proofs re-using or modifying parts of the proofs provided by the honest parties.

In this paper, we show for the first time that Bulletproofs (or any other similar multi-round proof system satisfying some form of *weak unique response* property) achieve *simulation-extractability* in the *algebraic group model*.

This implies that Fiat-Shamir Bulletproofs are *non-malleable*.

Keywords: Non-interactive zero-knowledge ·
Simulation-extractability · Fiat-Shamir

1 Introduction

Zero-knowledge (ZK) proof systems [24] are one of the most fascinating ideas in modern cryptography, as they allow a prover to persuade a verifier that some statement is true without revealing any other information. In recent years we have observed a new renaissance for ZK proofs, motivated in large part by their applications to advanced Blockchain applications. This has led, among other things, to a standardization effort for ZK proofs.[1]

---

[1] https://zkproof.org.

© International Association for Cryptologic Research 2022
O. Dunkelman and S. Dziembowski (Eds.): EUROCRYPT 2022, LNCS 13276, pp. 397–426, 2022.
https://doi.org/10.1007/978-3-031-07085-3_14

A celebrated modern ZK proof system is Bulletproofs [6]. Bulletproofs offer transparent setup, short proofs and efficient verification (and it is therefore a *zero-knowledge succinct argument of knowledge* or zkSNARK) using only very well established computational assumptions, namely the hardness of discrete logarithms. At the heart of Bulletproofs lies an "inner product" component. This can be used then for general purpose proofs (i.e., where the statement is described as an arithmetic circuit) or for specific purpose proofs (i.e., range proofs, which are the most common use case in practice). Bulletproofs have been implemented in real world systems, especially for confidential transaction systems, like Monero, Mimblewimble, MobileCoin, Interstellar, etc.

Most practical applications of Bulletproofs utilize their non-interactive variant which, since Bulletproofs is a public-coin proof system, can be obtained using the Fiat-Shamir heuristic [17] e.g., the interaction with the verifier (who is only supposed to send uniformly random challenges) is replaced by interacting with a public hash function. Under the assumption that the hash function is a random oracle, one can hope that the prover has no easier time producing proofs for false statements (or for statements for which they do not know a witness) than when interacting with an actual verifier.

While the Fiat-Shamir heuristic has been around for decades, its formal analysis has only been performed much later. It is first in [16] that it was formally proven that the Fiat-Shamir heuristic is indeed sound. However, this proof only applies to classic Σ-protocols [11], which are a special class of ZK protocols with only 3 moves. Therefore this analysis does not cover the case of Bulletproofs, which is a multi-round protocol.

For the case of Bulletproofs, it was first in [22], that it was shown that Fiat-Shamir Bulletproofs are indeed arguments of knowledge e.g., it is not possible for the prover to produce a valid proof without knowing a witness for the statement (a similar result, but with less tight bounds, appeared concurrently also in [8]). However, the results in [22] only consider a malicious prover "in isolation", whereas in most practical applications of Bulletproofs, several provers are producing and exchanging proofs at the same time (e.g., on a Blockchain).

The notion of *non-malleability* in cryptography was introduced in [14], and the notion of non-malleability for zero-knowledge proofs was introduced in [33]. In a nutshell, a malleability attack is one in which the adversary gets to see proofs from honest parties, and then modifies or re-uses parts of the proofs output by the honest parties to forge a proof on some statement for which they do not know a witness. Malleability attacks can have very serious consequences, such as the famous MtGox attack of 2014 [13].

Therefore, it is worrisome that Fiat-Shamir Bulletproofs have been implemented in the wild without any solid evidence that malleability attacks are not possible against them.

Luckily, in this paper we are able to show that Fiat-Shamir Bulletproofs satisfy a strong notion of *simulation-extractability* which in particular implies *non-malleability*. We do so in the *algebraic group model* (AGM) which is a model that only considers restricted classes of adversaries that, in a nutshell, output a group element $z \in \mathbb{G}$ together with its representations $[z]$ w.r.t. all elements they have seen so far. This is a limitation that our result shares with previous results in this area [8,22] that studied concrete knowledge-soundness of Fiat–Shamir Bulletproofs.

1.1 Technical Overview

As already argued, in applications where proof systems are deployed, an adversary who tries to break the system has access to proofs provided by other parties using the same scheme. Thus, any reasonable security notion must require that a ZK proof system be secure against adversaries that potentially see and utilise proofs generated by different parties. *Simulation-soundness* (SIM-SND) and *simulation-extractability* (SIM-EXT) are the notions that guarantee soundness (the prover cannot prove false statements) or the stronger property knowledge-soundness (the prover cannot prove statements without knowing a witness) to hold against adversaries who may see many (simulated) proofs.

Our starting point is the work of [22], that proves that the Fiat-Shamir transform of Bulletproofs (henceforth BP) is knowledge-sound in the AGM and random oracle (RO) model. They do this by first proving that the interactive version of BP satisfies a stronger property of state-restoration witness extended emulation (SR-WEE), where the prover is allowed to rewind the verifier a polynomial number of times (hence the name since the prover can "restore" the state of the verifier). They then turn this into a result for Fiat-Shamir BP by showing that for any adversary who breaks the knowledge-soundness of Fiat-Shamir BP, there exists an adversary for the SR-WEE property of the interactive BP.

The natural question is then, can their proof be easily extend to the case of SIM-EXT (where the result needs to hold even when the simulator has to provide the adversary with simulated proofs on statements of their choice)? To see why this is not straightforward, consider the following natural approach: just answer the proof queries of the adversary by running the honest verifier zero-knowledge simulator of BP, and then program the RO with the challenges returned by the simulator. The RO queries, on the other hand, are simply forwarded to the state-restoration oracle as before. This simple approach works if the underlying protocol satisfies "unique response", which informally means that the adversary cannot generate two distinct accepting transcripts that share a common prefix. (This notion has already been used to prove simulation-extractability of Σ-protocols [16], multi-round public coin interactive protocols [15,30], and Sonic and Plonk [30]). However, BP does not have unique response under their definition: this is simple to see since randomized commitments are sent from the prover during the third round. Therefore, if the forged proof returned by the adversary has a matching prefix as one of the simulated proofs, this forged proof cannot be used to break SR-WEE. [2]

---

[2] In a nutshell, this is because the forged proof may not be an accepting transcript in the SR-WEE game since the shared prefix is a partial transcript that has not been queried to the oracle before. Hence, the oracle has no knowledge of the simulated proofs and therefore any partial transcript that has a matching prefix with a simulated proof.

The next natural attempt might then be to "de-randomize" later rounds of BP e.g., by letting the prover choose and commit all their random coins in the first round, and then prove consistency of all future rounds with these coins. This of course introduces new challenges, since these additional consistency proofs must themselves not use any additional randomness in rounds other than the first one. While these technical challenges could be overcome using the right tools, the final solution would be all but satisfactory. First of all, the new protocol would be less efficient than the original BP. And perhaps more importantly, all real-world implementations of BP would have to decide whether to switch to the new protocol without any evidence that the original BP is insecure.

Instead, we present a new approach here that allows us to prove that Fiat-Shamir BP *as is* satisfies SIM-EXT, which has wide-reaching impact for systems based on BP that are already in use. The diagram in the full version [21] summarizes our modular security analysis towards simulation-extractability of multi-round Fiat–Shamir NIZK. We discuss our new security notions and a chain of implications below.

Unique Response. We introduce two new definitions: state-restoration unique response (SR-UR), and weak unique response (FS-WUR), which are the interactive, and non-interactive definitions for showing unique response of protocols. We show that these two notions are tightly related, i.e., FS-WUR tightly reduces to SR-UR of the interactive protocol (Lemma 1). Both notions require that it should be hard for the adversary, on input a simulated proof, to output a proof which shares a prefix with it. This is opposed to the previous notion of unique response that requires it should be infeasible for the adversary to come up with two different proofs that share a prefix. As an analogy, our notion is akin to second preimage resistance for hash functions, while the previous notion is akin to collision resistance. Clearly, it is easier to show that an existing protocol satisfies the weaker definition. But it is in turn harder to show that the weaker definition is enough to achieve the overall goal. However, note that the weaker variant of the definition is also somewhat closer to the intuitive goal of non-malleability: we do not want the adversary to be able to reuse parts of proofs generated by other parties to forge new proofs.

Simulation-extractability of Multi-round Fiat–Shamir. Once we have FS-EXT (i.e., extractability), FS-WUR, and NIZK for a non-interactive protocol, we are able to show its online simulation-extractability (Lemma 2). Putting together, we prove a general theorem showing that:

Theorem 1 (General Theorem (Informal)). *If a multi-round public-coin interactive protocol satisfies: (1) adaptive state-restoration witness extended emulation (aSR-WEE), (2) perfect HVZK with an algebraic simulator, and (3) state-restoration unique responses (SR-UR), then the non-interactive version of the protocol achieved via the Fiat-Shamir transform, is online simulation-extractable (FS-SIM-EXT) in the algebraic group model and the random oracle model.*

While our framework has been built with Bulletproofs as its main use case, we believe that it is general enough and could be used to show simulation-extractability for other public-coin protocols in the literature.

Non-malleable Bulletproofs. We use our definitional foundation to show that Fiat-Shamir BP is non-malleable and give concrete security bounds for it. The main technical contribution here is to show that BP satisfies our (weaker) definition of unique response, namely SR-UR. For the other assumptions in the theorem, we rely on existing knowledge with some adjustments: BP is already known to satisfy SR-WEE (from [22]), however in our theorem we require a stronger (adaptive) version of the definition, namely aSR-WEE, but it turns out that the proof of SR-WEE in [22] can be used to show the stronger definition as well. Finally, BP is already known to admit a perfect HVZK simulator, which we have to extend to the algebraic setting. Thus, using the general theorem, we get our result. We do this for two versions of BP, namely Bulletproofs for arithmetic circuits (in Sect. 4) and range-proofs Bulletproofs (cf. full version [21]).

1.2   Related Work

Goldwasser and Kalai [23] show that the Fiat-Shamir heuristic is not sound in general, by showing explicit – and somewhat contrived – counterexamples that cannot be proven secure for any hash function. However, there is no evidence that any *natural* construction using the Fiat-Shamir heuristic is insecure.

Faust et al. [16] are the first to analyze SIM-SND and SIM-EXT of Fiat–Shamir NIZK from Σ-protocols. Kohlweiss and Zając [30] extend their result to multi-round protocols with $(n_1, \ldots, n_r)$-special soundness where all-but-one n_i's are equal to 1, which is the case for some modern zkSNARKs (cf. [20,31]), but is not the case for Bulletproofs-style recursive protocols.

Don et al. [15] study multi-round Fiat–Shamir in the quantum random oracle model, but their generic claim (Corollary 15) incurs at least a multiplicative factor $O(q^r)^3$. in the loss in soundness due to Fiat–Shamir, even if the result is downgraded to the classical setting. Hence their result leads to a super-polynomial loss when the number of rounds r depends on the security parameter as in Bulletproofs. They also showed SIM-EXT of multi-round Fiat–Shamir proofs in the QROM assuming the unique response property of the underlying interactive protocols. As we shall see later, Bulletproofs do not meet their definition of unique responses and we are thus motivated to explore alternative paths towards SIM-EXT, but in the classical ROM and the AGM.

There are a limited number of works that analyze the concrete soundness loss incurred by Fiat–Shamir when applied to *non-constant round* protocols. Ben-Sasson et al. [5] show that if the underlying *interactive oracle proof* protocol satisfies *state-restoration soundness* (SR-SND) (a stronger variant of soundness where the prover is allowed to rewind the verifier states) then Fiat–Shamir only introduces $3(q^2 + 1)2^{-\lambda}$ of additive loss both in soundness (SND) and proof

---

[3] Here and below q is the number of queries to the random oracle, r is the number of rounds, and λ is the security parameter.

of knowledge (EXT). Canetti et al. [9,10] propose the closely related notion of *round-by-round soundness* (RBR-SND) which is sufficient to achieve soundness, even without round oracles. Following these works, Holmgren [29] shows SR-SND and RBR-SND are equivalent.

The latest works on this line of research are due to Ghoshal and Tessaro [22] and Bünz et al. [8]. They both provide a detailed analysis of *non-interactive* Bulletproofs in the algebraic group model (AGM) [19] and, in particular, the former shows *state-restoration witness extended emulation* (SR-WEE) of interactive Bulletproofs in the AGM and uses it to argue that EXT of non-interactive Bulletproofs results in $(q + 1)/2^{\mathsf{sLen}(\lambda)}$ in additive loss, where $\mathsf{sLen}(\lambda)$ is the bit length of the shortest challenge. However, none of these works explore SIM-SND or SIM-EXT of non-constant round Fiat–Shamir.

There are also other zkSNARKs that satisfy simulation-extractability such as e.g., [27] and [26,30]. However, these constructions are very different than Bulletproofs since they rely on a structured reference string which comes with a trapdoor, the knowledge of which compromises the soundness. [3] show techniques to make [26] black-box weakly SIM-EXT NIZK using verifiable encryption. A generic framework to turn existing zkSNARKs into SIM-EXT zkSNARKs was presented in [2], but Bulletproofs is not covered by their result since their transform only works for schemes with trusted setup.

2 Preliminaries

Due to space constraints, some standard preliminaries are deferred to the full version [21].

The Algebraic Group Model. The algebraic group model was introduced in [19]. An adversary $\mathcal{A}_{\mathsf{alg}}$ is called *algebraic* if every group element output by $\mathcal{A}_{\mathsf{alg}}$ is accompanied by a representation of that group element in terms of all the group elements that $\mathcal{A}_{\mathsf{alg}}$ has seen so far (input and output). Let $y_1, \ldots, y_k$ be all the group elements previously input and output by $\mathcal{A}_{\mathsf{alg}}$. Then, every group element y output by $\mathcal{A}_{\mathsf{alg}}$, is accompanied by its representation $(x_1, \ldots, x_k)$ such that $y = \prod_{i=1}^{k} y_i^{x_i}$. Following [19], we write $[y]$ to denote a group element enhanced with its representation; $[y] = (y, x_1, \ldots, x_k)$.

Adaptive State-restoration Witness Extended Emulation. Here we define an *adaptive* variant of *state-restoration witness extended emulation* (aSR-WEE) defined in [22]. Intuitively, *state-restoration witness extended emulation* says that having resettable access to the verifier (or "restoring its state", hence the name) should not help a malicious prover in producing a valid proof without knowing a witness for the statement. Formally, the definition consists of two games denoted as $\mathsf{aWEE\text{-}1}_{\Pi}^{\mathcal{P}_{\mathsf{alg}}, \mathcal{D}}$ and $\mathsf{aWEE\text{-}0}_{\Pi, \mathcal{R}}^{\mathcal{E}, \mathcal{P}_{\mathsf{alg}}, \mathcal{D}}$ described in Fig. 1. The former captures the real game, lets the prover $\mathcal{P}_{\mathsf{alg}}$ interact with an oracle $\mathbf{O}_{\mathsf{ext}}^1$, which additionally stores all queried transcripts tr. The latter is finally given to a distinguisher $\mathcal{D}$ which outputs a decision bit. In contrast, the ideal game delegates the role of answering $\mathcal{P}_{\mathsf{alg}}$'s oracle queries to a (stateful) extractor $\mathcal{E}$.

The extractor, at the end of the execution, also outputs a witness candidate w. Due to the adaptive nature of our variant, we also need to redefine the predicate $\mathsf{Acc}()$ so that it accepts a pair $(x^*, \mathcal{T}^*)$ output by the adversary at the end if and only if the pair exists in the execution paths and it gets accepted by the verifier. Formally, $\mathsf{Acc}(\mathsf{tr}, x^*, \mathcal{T}^*)$ now outputs 1 if $(x^*, \mathcal{T}^*) \in \mathsf{tr}$ and $\mathcal{V}(\mathsf{pp}, x^*, \mathcal{T}^*) = 1$, and outputs 0 otherwise. For an interactive proof $\Pi = (\mathsf{Setup}, \mathcal{P}, \mathcal{V})$ and an associated relation $\mathcal{R}$, non-uniform algebraic prover $\mathcal{P}_{\mathsf{alg}}$, a distinguisher $\mathcal{D}$, and an extractor $\mathcal{E}$ we define:

$$\mathbf{Adv}_{\Pi, \mathcal{R}}^{\mathsf{aSR\text{-}WEE}}(\mathcal{E}, \mathcal{P}_{\mathsf{alg}}, \mathcal{D}, \lambda) := \left| \Pr\left[\mathsf{aWEE\text{-}1}_{\Pi}^{\mathcal{P}_{\mathsf{alg}}, \mathcal{D}}(\lambda) \right] - \Pr\left[\mathsf{aWEE\text{-}0}_{\Pi, \mathcal{R}}^{\mathcal{E}, \mathcal{P}_{\mathsf{alg}}, \mathcal{D}}(\lambda) \right] \right|. \quad (1)$$

Definition 1 (aSR-WEE security). *An interactive proof $\Pi = (\mathsf{Setup}, \mathcal{P}, \mathcal{V})$ is online aSR-WEE secure if there exists an efficient $\mathcal{E}$ such that for any (non-uniform algebraic) $\mathcal{P}_{\mathsf{alg}}$ and for any distinguisher $\mathcal{D}$, $\mathbf{Adv}_{\Pi, \mathcal{R}}^{\mathsf{aSR\text{-}WEE}}(\mathcal{E}, \mathcal{P}_{\mathsf{alg}}, \mathcal{D}, \lambda)$ is negligible in λ.*

The main difference with the original definition in [22] is that we allow the adversary to change the statement associated with a transcript in every query, whereas [22] forces the adversary to commit to the fixed statement x in advance. We remark that their results about Bulletproofs still hold under this variant, because nowhere in the proof do they actually exploit the fact that the statement is fixed. Hence, the following is immediate from [22]. We provide more details on this in the full version [21].

Theorem 2 (Adapted from Theorem 6 of [22]). *The protocol* BP *is aSR-WEE secure.*

NIZK and Simulation Oracles. We define zero-knowledge for non-interactive arguments in the explicitly programmable random oracle model where the simulator can program the random oracle. The formalization below can be seen as that of [16] adapted to multi-round protocols. The zero-knowledge simulator $\mathcal{S}_{\mathsf{FS}}$ is defined as a stateful algorithm that operates in two modes. In the first mode, $(c_i, st') \leftarrow \mathcal{S}_{\mathsf{FS}}(1, st, t, i)$ takes care of random oracle calls to H_i on input t. In the second mode, $(\widetilde{\mathcal{T}}, st') \leftarrow \mathcal{S}_{\mathsf{FS}}(2, st, x)$ simulates the actual argument. For convenience we define three "wrapper" oracles. These oracles are stateful and share state.

- $\mathcal{S}_1(t, i)$ to denote the oracle that returns the first output of $\mathcal{S}_{\mathsf{FS}}(1, st, t, i)$;
- $\mathcal{S}_2(x, w)$ that returns the first output of $\mathcal{S}_{\mathsf{FS}}(2, st, x)$ if $(\mathsf{pp}, x, w) \in \mathcal{R}$ and $\bot$ otherwise;
- $\mathcal{S}_2'(x)$ that returns the first output of $\mathcal{S}_{\mathsf{FS}}(2, st, x)$.

Since NIZK is a security property that is only guaranteed for valid statements in the language, the definition below makes use of $\mathcal{S}_2$ as a proof simulation oracle. As we shall see later, *simulation-extractability* on the other hand is defined with respect to an oracle similar to $\mathcal{S}_2'$ following [16].

Definition 2 (Non-interactive Zero Knowledge). *A non-interactive argument* Π_{FS} = (Setup, $\mathcal{P}^H_{FS}$, $\mathcal{V}^H_{FS}$) *for relation* $\mathcal{R}$ *is unbounded* non-interactive zero knowledge *(NIZK) in the random oracle model, if there exist a PPT simulator* $\mathcal{S}_{FS}$ *with wrapper oracles* $\mathcal{S}_1$ *and* $\mathcal{S}_2$ *such that for all PPT distinguisher* $\mathcal{D}$ *there exist a negligible function* $\mu(\lambda)$ *it holds that*

$$| \Pr\left[\mathcal{D}^{H,\mathcal{P}^H_{FS}}(1^\lambda) = 1\right] - \Pr[\mathcal{D}^{\mathcal{S}_1,\mathcal{S}_2}(1^\lambda)]| \leq \mu(\lambda)$$

where both $\mathcal{P}^H_{FS}(\mathsf{pp}, x, w)$ *and* $\mathcal{S}_2$ *return* $\perp$ *if* $(\mathsf{pp}, x, w) \notin \mathcal{R}$.

Given a perfect HVZK simulator $\mathcal{S}$ for Π, we immediately obtain the following *canonical* NIZK simulator $\mathcal{S}_{FS}$ for Π_{FS} by defining responses of each mode as follows.

- To answer query (t, i) with mode 1, $\mathcal{S}_{FS}(1, \mathsf{st}, t, i)$ lazily samples a lookup table $\mathcal{Q}_{1,i}$ kept in state st. It checks whether $\mathcal{Q}_{1,i}[t]$ is already defined. If this is the case, it returns the previously assigned value; otherwise it returns and sets a fresh random value c_i sampled from Ch_i.
- To answer query x with mode 2, $\mathcal{S}_{FS}(2, \mathsf{st}, x)$ calls the perfect HVZK simulator $\mathcal{S}$ of Π to obtain a simulated proof $\pi = (a_1, c_1, \ldots, a_r, c_r, a_{r+1})$. Then, it programs the tables such that $\mathcal{Q}_{1,1}[x, a_1] := c_1, \ldots, \mathcal{Q}_{1,r}[x, a_1, c_1, \ldots, a_r] := c_r$. If any of the table entries has been already defined $\mathcal{S}_{FS}$ aborts, which should happen with negligible probability assuming high min-entropy of a_1.

Online Extractability in the AGM. We introduce the definition of (adaptive) *online extractability* (FS-EXT) in the AGM. Unlike the usual online extraction scenario (e.g., [18,32,34]), where an extractor is only given x^*, $\mathcal{T}^*$ and the random oracle query history as inputs and asked to extract the witness, our definition below requires the extractor to intercept/program the queries/answers to the RO for $\mathcal{P}_{alg}$. We do so because some proofs in [22] (such as Theorem 2 and 3) relating state-restoration witness-extended emulation for Π and argument of knowledge for Π_{FS} do appear to exploit this extra power of the extractor, which to the best of our understanding appears necessary for their proofs to go through.

This modification in turn requires the existence of an extractor $(\mathcal{E}_0, \mathcal{E}_1)$ where $\mathcal{E}_1$ takes care of simulating the RO responses for $\mathcal{P}_{alg}$ and then $\mathcal{E}_0$ produces a valid witness given an adversarial forgery. Our formalization therefore follows variants of extractability in the literature that explicitly introduce a distinguisher to guarantee the validity of simulation conducted by $\mathcal{E}_1$, e.g., [35, Def. 11] for Fiat–Shamir NIZK or [25] for CRS-based NIZK. On the other hand, we do not grant the extractor an oracle access to $\mathcal{P}_{alg}$ to explicitly capture the "online" nature of extraction, i.e., no rewinding step is required.

Note also that the roles of $(\mathcal{E}_0, \mathcal{E}_1)$ and $\mathcal{D}$ below are also analogous to those of the extractor and the distinguisher in aSR-WEE. Thus, our definition allows smooth transition from aSR-WEE to FS-EXT.

Game $\mathsf{aWEE\text{-}1}_{\Pi}^{\mathcal{P}_{\mathsf{alg}},\mathcal{D}}(\lambda)$:

$\mathsf{tr} \leftarrow (\epsilon, \epsilon)$
$\mathsf{pp} \leftarrow \mathsf{Setup}(1^\lambda)$
$([x^*], [\mathcal{T}^*], \mathsf{st}_{\mathcal{P}_{\mathsf{alg}}}) \leftarrow \mathcal{P}_{\mathsf{alg}}^{\mathsf{O}_{\mathsf{ext}}^1}(\mathsf{pp})$
$\tilde{b} \leftarrow \mathcal{D}(\mathsf{st}_{\mathcal{P}_{\mathsf{alg}}}, \mathsf{tr}, x^*, \mathcal{T}^*)$
return $(\tilde{b} = 1)$

Game $\mathsf{aWEE\text{-}0}_{\Pi,\mathcal{R}}^{\mathcal{E},\mathcal{P}_{\mathsf{alg}},\mathcal{D}}(\lambda)$:

$\mathsf{tr} \leftarrow (\epsilon, \epsilon)$
$\mathsf{pp} \leftarrow \mathsf{Setup}(1^\lambda)$
$\mathsf{st}_{\mathcal{E}} \leftarrow \mathsf{pp}$
$([x^*], [\mathcal{T}^*], \mathsf{st}_{\mathcal{P}_{\mathsf{alg}}}) \leftarrow \mathcal{P}_{\mathsf{alg}}^{\mathsf{O}_{\mathsf{ext}}^0}(\mathsf{pp})$
$w \leftarrow \mathcal{E}(\mathsf{st}_{\mathcal{E}}, [x^*], [\mathcal{T}^*])$
$\tilde{b} \leftarrow \mathcal{D}(\mathsf{st}_{\mathcal{P}_{\mathsf{alg}}}, \mathsf{tr}, x^*, \mathcal{T}^*)$
$b \leftarrow (\mathsf{Acc}(\mathsf{tr}, x^*, \mathcal{T}^*) \Rightarrow (\mathsf{pp}, x^*, w) \in \mathcal{R})$
return $(\tilde{b} = 1) \wedge (b = 1)$

Oracle $\mathsf{O}_{\mathsf{ext}}^1([x], [\mathcal{T}], [a_i])$

Parse $\mathcal{T}$ as $\mathcal{T} = (a_1, c_1, \cdots, a_{i-1}, c_{i-1})$
if $(x, \mathcal{T}) \in \mathsf{tr}$ or $(x, \mathcal{T}) = (x, \epsilon)$ **then**
  if $i \leq r$ **then**
    $c_i \overset{\$}{\leftarrow} \mathsf{Ch}_i$
    $\mathsf{tr} \leftarrow \mathsf{tr}\|(x, (\mathcal{T}, a_i, c_i))$
    return c_i
  else if $i = r + 1$ **then**
    $\mathsf{tr} \leftarrow \mathsf{tr}\|(x, (\mathcal{T}, a_i))$
    $d \leftarrow \mathcal{V}(\mathsf{pp}, x, (\mathcal{T}, a_i))$
    return d
return $\perp$

Oracle $\mathsf{O}_{\mathsf{ext}}^0([x], [\mathcal{T}], [a_i])$

Parse $\mathcal{T}$ as $\mathcal{T} = (a_1, c_1, \cdots, a_{i-1}, c_{i-1})$
if $(x, \mathcal{T}) \in \mathsf{tr}$ or $(x, \mathcal{T}) = (x, \epsilon)$ **then**
  if $i \leq r$ **then**
    $(\mathsf{resp}, \mathsf{st}_{\mathcal{E}}) \leftarrow \mathcal{E}(\mathsf{st}_{\mathcal{E}}, [x], [(\mathcal{T}, a_i)])$
    $\mathsf{tr} \leftarrow \mathsf{tr}\|(x, (\mathcal{T}, a_i, \mathsf{resp}))$
    return resp
  else if $i = r + 1$ **then**
    $\mathsf{tr} \leftarrow \mathsf{tr}\|(x, (\mathcal{T}, a_i))$
    $d \leftarrow \mathcal{V}(\mathsf{pp}, x, (\mathcal{T}, a_i))$
    return d
return $\perp$

Fig. 1. Online aSR-WEE Security (adapted from [22], with differences highlighted in orange). (Color figure online)

Game $\mathsf{EXT\text{-}1}_{\Pi_{\mathsf{FS}}}^{\mathsf{H},\mathcal{P}_{\mathsf{alg}},\mathcal{D}}(\lambda)$:

$\mathsf{pp} \leftarrow \mathsf{Setup}(1^\lambda)$
$([x^*], [\mathcal{T}^*], \mathsf{st}_{\mathcal{P}_{\mathsf{alg}}}) \leftarrow \mathcal{P}_{\mathsf{alg}}^{\mathsf{H}}(\mathsf{pp})$
$d \leftarrow \mathcal{V}_{\mathsf{FS}}^{\mathsf{H}}(\mathsf{pp}, x^*, \mathcal{T}^*)$
$\tilde{b} \leftarrow \mathcal{D}(\mathsf{st}_{\mathcal{P}_{\mathsf{alg}}}, x^*, \mathcal{T}^*, \mathcal{Q}_1)$
return $(\tilde{b} = 1)$

Game $\mathsf{EXT\text{-}0}_{\Pi_{\mathsf{FS}},\mathcal{R}}^{\mathcal{E},\mathcal{P}_{\mathsf{alg}},\mathcal{D}}(\lambda)$:

$\mathsf{pp} \leftarrow \mathsf{Setup}(1^\lambda)$
$\mathsf{st}_{\mathcal{E}} \leftarrow \mathsf{pp}$
$([x^*], [\mathcal{T}^*], \mathsf{st}_{\mathcal{P}_{\mathsf{alg}}}) \leftarrow \mathcal{P}_{\mathsf{alg}}^{\mathcal{E}_1}(\mathsf{pp})$
$d \leftarrow \mathcal{V}_{\mathsf{FS}}^{\mathcal{E}_1}(\mathsf{pp}, x^*, \mathcal{T}^*)$
$\tilde{b} \leftarrow \mathcal{D}(\mathsf{st}_{\mathcal{P}_{\mathsf{alg}}}, x^*, \mathcal{T}^*, \mathcal{Q}_1)$
$w \leftarrow \mathcal{E}_0(\mathsf{st}_{\mathcal{E}}, [x^*], [\mathcal{T}^*])$
$b \leftarrow (d = 1 \Rightarrow (\mathsf{pp}, x^*, w) \in \mathcal{R})$
return $(\tilde{b} = 1) \wedge (b = 1)$

Fig. 2. Extractability games. Note that in the EXT-1 experiment, calling the verification algorithm $\mathcal{V}_{\mathsf{FS}}$ has an impact on the RO query set $\mathcal{Q}_1$. In particular, omitting this, there might be trivial distinguishing attacks due to the differences in $\mathcal{Q}_1$ between EXT-1 and EXT-0.

Definition 3 (FS-EXT security). *Let* $\Pi_{\mathsf{FS}} = (\mathsf{Setup}, \mathcal{P}_{\mathsf{FS}}, \mathcal{V}_{\mathsf{FS}})$ *be a NIZK scheme for language* $\mathcal{L}$*. Let* H *be a random oracle.* Π_{FS} *is online extractable (FS-EXT) in the AGM and the ROM if there exists an efficient extractor* $\mathcal{E} = (\mathcal{E}_0, \mathcal{E}_1)$ *such that for every PPT algebraic adversary* $\mathcal{P}_{\mathsf{alg}}$ *and every distinguisher* $\mathcal{D}$*, the following probability is negligible in* λ*:*

$$\mathbf{Adv}_{\Pi_{\mathsf{FS}}, \mathcal{R}}^{\mathsf{FS\text{-}EXT}}(\mathsf{H}, \mathcal{E}, \mathcal{P}_{\mathsf{alg}}, \mathcal{D}, \lambda) := \left| \Pr[\mathsf{EXT\text{-}1}_{\Pi_{\mathsf{FS}}}^{\mathsf{H}, \mathcal{P}_{\mathsf{alg}}, \mathcal{D}}(\lambda)] - \Pr[\mathsf{EXT\text{-}0}_{\Pi_{\mathsf{FS}}, \mathcal{R}}^{\mathcal{E}, \mathcal{P}_{\mathsf{alg}}, \mathcal{D}}(\lambda)] \right|.$$

In Fig. 2, each of $\mathcal{Q}_1 = \{\mathcal{Q}_{1,i}\}_{i \in [1,r]}$ *is a set of query response pairs corresponding to queries to* H *or* $\mathcal{E}_1$ *with random oracle index* i*.*

We recall a relation between aSR-WEE and FS-EXT, because one of our claims (Lemma 2) uses FS-EXT as an assumption. Although Theorem 2 of [22] is for non-adaptive variants of these notions, the proof for the following theorem is almost identical except that we do not ask $\mathcal{P}_{\mathsf{alg}}^*$ to submit the statement x in the beginning, just like in Theorem 2.

Theorem 3. *Let* $\mathcal{R}$ *be a relation. Let* Π *be a* r*-challenge public coin interactive protocol for the relation* $\mathcal{R}$ *where the* i*th challenge is sampled from* Ch_i *for* $i \in [1,r]$*. Let* $\mathcal{E}$ *be an aSR-WEE extractor for* Π*. There exists an FS-EXT extractor* $\mathcal{E}^* = (\mathcal{E}_0^*, \mathcal{E}_1^*)$ *for* Π_{FS} *such that for every non-uniform algebraic prover* $\mathcal{P}_{\mathsf{alg}}^*$ *against* Π_{FS} *that makes* q *random oracle queries, and for every distinguisher* $\mathcal{D}^*$*, there exists a non-uniform algebraic prover* $\mathcal{P}_{\mathsf{alg}}$ *and a distinguisher* $\mathcal{D}$ *such that for all* $\lambda \in \mathbb{N}^+$*,*

$$\mathbf{Adv}_{\Pi_{\mathsf{FS}}, \mathcal{R}}^{\mathsf{FS\text{-}EXT}}(\mathsf{H}, \mathcal{E}^*, \mathcal{P}_{\mathsf{alg}}^*, \mathcal{D}^*, \lambda) \leq \mathbf{Adv}_{\Pi, \mathcal{R}}^{\mathsf{aSR\text{-}WEE}}(\mathcal{E}, \mathcal{P}_{\mathsf{alg}}, \mathcal{D}, \lambda) + (q+1)/|\mathsf{Ch}_{i_0}|$$

where $i_0 \in [1,r]$ *is the round with the smallest challenge set* Ch_{i_0}*. Moreover,* $\mathcal{P}_{\mathsf{alg}}$ *makes at most* q *queries to its oracle and is nearly as efficient as* $\mathcal{P}_{\mathsf{alg}}^*$*. The extractor* $\mathcal{E}^*$ *is nearly as efficient as* $\mathcal{E}$*.*

A proof sketch is found in the full version [21].

3   Simulation-Extractability from State-Restoration Unique Response

Our results make use of the concrete security proof of extractability for Bulletproofs given by [22] in the algebraic group model. Thus, the first step towards proving simulation-extractability for Bulletproofs is to provide a formal definition of simulation-extractability in the algebraic group model, which has not previously appeared in the literature.

3.1   Simulation-Extractability in the AGM

On a high-level, the simulation-extractability (SIM-EXT) property ensures that extractability holds even if the cheating adversary sees simulated proofs. Defining SIM-EXT in the AGM is a non-trivial task: because the algebraic adversary outputs group representation *with respect to all the group elements they have observed so far*, the format of representation gets complex as the adversary receives more simulated proofs, whose representation might not be w.r.t. generators present in pp. To make our analysis simpler, we introduce the notion of *algebraic simulator*.

Definition 4 (Algebraic simulator). *Consider a perfectly HVZK argument of knowledge* (Setup, $\mathcal{P}, \mathcal{V}$) *with a PPT simulator* $\mathcal{S}$. *The simulator* $\mathcal{S}$ *is* algebraic *if on receiving a statement* x *and its group representation* [x] *as input, it outputs a proof* $\widetilde{T}$ *and its group representation* $[\widetilde{T}]$ *with respect to generators in* pp *and generators used for representing* x. *For an algebraic simulator* $\mathcal{S}$, *we denote* $[\widetilde{T}] \leftarrow \mathcal{S}([\text{x}])$.

Definition 5 (Algebraic simulator for NIZK). *Consider a non-interactive argument of knowledge* (Setup, $\mathcal{P}_{\mathsf{FS}}, \mathcal{V}_{\mathsf{FS}}$) *with NIZK simulator* $\mathcal{S}_{\mathsf{FS}}$. *The simulator* $\mathcal{S}_{\mathsf{FS}}$ *is* algebraic *if on receiving a statement* x *and its group representation* [x] *as input, its second mode outputs proofs* $\widetilde{T}$, *their group representations* $[\widetilde{T}]$ *with respect to generators in* pp *and generators used for representing* x. *For an algebraic simulator* $\mathcal{S}_{\mathsf{FS}}$, *we denote* $([\widetilde{T}], st') \leftarrow \mathcal{S}_{\mathsf{FS}}(2, st, [\text{x}])$.

Remark 1. Our use of algebraic is similar in spirit to composability results in the AGM [1] where the environment is required to be algebraic as well, in addition to the adversary; in particular they require the simulator for proving security to be algebraic. Restricting the simulator to be algebraic does not seem to limit the class of protocols that we can analyze, since typical simulators for discrete-log-based protocols are already algebraic. Consider the simulator for the Schnorr protocol: given a statement $x \in \mathbb{G}$ and random challenge ρ the simulator outputs $(g^z x^{-\rho}, \rho, z)$ where z is uniformly sampled from $\mathbb{Z}_q$. In the next section, we show that the simulator for Bulletproofs is also algebraic.

Remark 2. By construction, if we have an algebraic HVZK simulator $\mathcal{S}$ for Π, then the corresponding canonical NIZK simulator $\mathcal{S}_{\mathsf{FS}}$ for Π_{FS} (see the paragraph after Definition 2) fixed by $\mathcal{S}$ is also algebraic, since $\mathcal{S}_{\mathsf{FS}}$ internally invokes $\mathcal{S}$ to obtain a proof.

We now extend the definition of FS-EXT to simulation-extractability, by equipping the cheating algebraic prover with access to proof simulation oracles in addition to the random oracle. Formally, we define simulation-extractability *with respect to a specific NIZK simulator* $\mathcal{S}_{\mathsf{FS}}$ *and the corresponding wrapper oracles* $(\mathcal{S}_1, \mathcal{S}_2')$ *(see Sect. 2)*. That is, $\mathcal{S}_1$ on input (t, i) returns the first output of $\mathcal{S}_{\mathsf{FS}}(1, st, t, i)$ (i.e., corresponding the random oracle H in FS-EXT) and $\mathcal{S}_2'$ on an input statement x returns the first output of $\mathcal{S}_{\mathsf{FS}}(2, st, x)$, respectively.

Following FS-EXT, we define a *simulator-extractor* $\mathcal{E} = (\mathcal{E}_0, \mathcal{E}_1, \mathcal{E}_2)$, where $\mathcal{E}_1$ receives a random oracle query of the form (t, i) (similar to the wrapper oracle $\mathcal{S}_1$) and returns a challenge from Ch_i; $\mathcal{E}_2$ receives a statement query x and returns a simulated proof (similar to the wrapper oracle $\mathcal{S}_2'$); $\mathcal{E}_0$ extracts a witness at the end. The differences with Definition 3 are highlighted in orange.

Game SIM-EXT-$1_{\Pi_{FS}}^{S_1,S_2',\mathcal{P}_{alg},\mathcal{D}}(\lambda)$:	**Game** SIM-EXT-$0_{\Pi_{FS},\mathcal{R}}^{\mathcal{E},\mathcal{P}_{alg},\mathcal{D}}(\lambda)$:
$pp \leftarrow \mathsf{Setup}(1^\lambda)$	$pp \leftarrow \mathsf{Setup}(1^\lambda)$
$([x^*],[\mathcal{T}^*],\mathsf{st}_{\mathcal{P}_{alg}}) \leftarrow \mathcal{P}_{alg}^{S_1,S_2'}(pp)$	$\mathsf{st}_{\mathcal{E}} \leftarrow pp$
$d \leftarrow \mathcal{V}_{FS}^{S_1}(pp,x^*,\mathcal{T}^*)$	$([x^*],[\mathcal{T}^*],\mathsf{st}_{\mathcal{P}_{alg}}) \leftarrow \mathcal{P}_{alg}^{\mathcal{E}_1,\mathcal{E}_2}(pp)$
$\tilde{b} \leftarrow \mathcal{D}(\mathsf{st}_{\mathcal{P}_{alg}},x^*,\mathcal{T}^*,\mathcal{Q}_1,\mathcal{Q}_2)$	$d \leftarrow \mathcal{V}_{FS}^{\mathcal{E}_1}(pp,x^*,\mathcal{T}^*)$
return $(\tilde{b}=1)$	$\tilde{b} \leftarrow \mathcal{D}(\mathsf{st}_{\mathcal{P}_{alg}},x^*,\mathcal{T}^*,\mathcal{Q}_1,\mathcal{Q}_2)$
	$w \leftarrow \mathcal{E}_0(\mathsf{st}_{\mathcal{E}},[x^*],[\mathcal{T}^*])$
	$b \leftarrow \big((d=1 \wedge (x^*,\mathcal{T}^*) \notin \mathcal{Q}_2) \Rightarrow (pp,x^*,w) \in \mathcal{R}\big)$
	return $(\tilde{b}=1) \wedge (b=1)$

Fig. 3. Simulation extractability games. Like in Fig. 2, in the SIM-EXT-1 experiment, calling the verification algorithm $\mathcal{V}_{FS}$ has an impact on the RO query set $\mathcal{Q}_1$.

At a high-level, the security requirement of FS-SIM-EXT is two-fold: (1) $(\mathcal{E}_1,\mathcal{E}_2)$ in the game SIM-EXT-0 correctly simulates the adversary's view in SIM-EXT-1 (indicated by a bit $\tilde{b}$), and (2) the extractor $\mathcal{E}_0$ outputs a valid witness as long as an adversarial forgery $(x^*,\mathcal{T}^*)$ is accepting *and* non-trivial, i.e., not identical to what's obtained by querying a proof simulation oracle (indicated by a bit b).

Definition 6 (FS-SIM-EXT security). *Consider a NIZK scheme* $\Pi_{FS} = (\mathsf{Setup}, \mathcal{P}_{FS}, \mathcal{V}_{FS})$ *for language* $\mathcal{L}$ *with an NIZK simulator* $\mathcal{S}_{FS}$. *Let* $(\mathcal{S}_1,\mathcal{S}_2')$ *be wrapper oracles for* $\mathcal{S}_{FS}$ *as defined in Sect. 2.* Π_{FS} *is* online simulation-extractable *(FS-SIM-EXT) with respect to* $\mathcal{S}_{FS}$ *in the AGM and ROM, if there exists an efficient simulator-extractor* $\mathcal{E} = (\mathcal{E}_0,\mathcal{E}_1,\mathcal{E}_2)$ *such that for every PPT algebraic adversary* $\mathcal{P}_{alg}$ *and every distinguisher* $\mathcal{D}$, *the following probability is negligible in* λ:

$$\mathbf{Adv}_{\Pi_{FS},\mathcal{R}}^{\text{FS-SIM-EXT}}(\mathcal{S}_{FS},\mathcal{E},\mathcal{P}_{alg},\mathcal{D},\lambda)$$
$$:= \left| \Pr[\textit{SIM-EXT-1}_{\Pi_{FS}}^{S_1,S_2',\mathcal{P}_{alg},\mathcal{D}}(\lambda)] - \Pr[\textit{SIM-EXT-0}_{\Pi_{FS},\mathcal{R}}^{\mathcal{E},\mathcal{P}_{alg},\mathcal{D}}(\lambda)] \right|.$$

In Fig. 3, each of $\mathcal{Q}_1 = \{\mathcal{Q}_{1,i}\}_{i \in [1,r]}$ *is a set of query response pairs corresponding to queries to* $\mathcal{S}_1$ *or* $\mathcal{E}_1$ *with random oracle index* i. $\mathcal{Q}_2$ *is a set of statement-transcript pairs* $(x,\widetilde{\mathcal{T}})$, *where* x *is a statement queried to the proof simulation oracle* $\mathcal{S}_2'$ *or* $\mathcal{E}_2$ *by* $\mathcal{P}_{alg}$, *and* $\widetilde{\mathcal{T}}$ *is the corresponding simulated proof, respectively.*

Comparison with Previous SIM-EXT Definitions. Although we borrow the formalization of wrapper oracles $(\mathcal{S}_1,\mathcal{S}_2')$ from [16], our definition of FS-SIM-EXT is different from their "weak" (Definition 6, an extractor requires rewinding access to the adversary) and "full" (Definition 7, an extractor is tasked with extracting a witness by only looking at an adversarial statement-proof pair) SIM-EXT. Indeed, neither of these is suitable in our setting. The former is too weak because we aim for an "online" way of extraction; the latter is too strong since the extractor used for showing reduction from FS-EXT to aSR-WEE (Theorem 3) already needs additional control over RO queries. To the best of our knowledge, there has been no previous work analyzing Fiat–Shamir NIZK under the latter notion even in the AGM.

Another difference with previous FS-SIM-EXT definitions is that ours explicitly handles indistinguishability of two games. This wasn't the case in [16] because their proof of weak SIM-EXT invokes the general forking lemma [4] that implicitly takes care of perfect indistinguishability of two runs. Our definition can essentially be seen as Definition 11 of Unruh [35] extended with a proof simulation oracle, which however was considered "too strong" in that work as its focus is security in the QROM. In contrast, our main focus is analysis in the CROM and online extraction enabled by the AGM (following the previous FS-EXT analysis conducted by [22]). Thus, we believe ours is most suitable for formally analyzing SIM-EXT of Bulletproofs based on the state-of-the-art.

There also exist several SIM-EXT definitions for CRS-NIZK (e.g., [2,3,12,25, 28,33]) but the way they are formulated is naturally different since the plain extractability already varies and simulators for CRS-NIZK behave in a different fashion. Perhaps a variant of Groth [25] is somewhat close to ours: the first part of the extractor handles simulation of CRS (so that it generates a trapdoor without the adversary noticing) and the second part takes care of witness extraction.

Remark 3. In the AGM, the representation submitted by the adversary is w.r.t. the group elements present in pp *and all the simulated proofs they have seen so far.* However, once we assume an algebraic simulator, it is always possible for $\mathcal{E}$ to convert such representation to the one w.r.t. pp and previously queried statements. As we shall see later, this will greatly simplify our security proof in the AGM because it will allow us to reuse the existing extractor analysis (where there is no simulation oracle).

State-restoration Unique Response. Our first definition considers the game $\mathsf{SR\text{-}UR}_{\Pi}^{\mathcal{A}_{\mathsf{alg}},\mathcal{S}}(\lambda)$ in Fig. 4. As the name indicates it has a flavor of aSR-WEE and it is therefore – compared to the the usual UR definition for interactive protocols – both stronger (in the sense that an adversary can rewind the verifier) and weaker (in the sense that an adversary is forced to use the simulated transcript to find a forgery).

Concretely, the prover initially generates an instance x on which it attempts to break the unique response property. Similar to aSR-WEE, we capture the power of the prover to rewind the verifier with an oracle $\mathbf{O}_{\mathsf{ext}}$. Roughly, the oracle allows the prover to build an execution tree, which is extended with each query to it by the prover. The prover succeeds if it comes up with another accepting transcript $\mathcal{T}$ that is part of the execution tree and have a prefix in common with the simulated transcript $\widetilde{\mathcal{T}}$. Let $\mathcal{T} = (a_1, c_1, \ldots, a_r, c_r, a_{r+1})$ denote a transcript. We write $\mathcal{T}|_i$ to denote a partial transcript consisting of the first $2i$ messages of $\mathcal{T}$, i.e., $\mathcal{T}|_i = (a_1, c_1, \ldots, a_i, c_i)$.

Game SR-UR$_\Pi^{\mathcal{A}_{\mathsf{alg}}, \mathcal{S}}(\lambda)$	**Oracle** $\mathsf{O}_{\mathsf{ext}}([\mathcal{T}], [a_i])$

win $\leftarrow$ false
 tr $\leftarrow \epsilon$
 pp $\leftarrow$ Setup(1^λ)
 $([x], \mathsf{st}_{\mathcal{A}}) \leftarrow \mathcal{A}_1(\mathsf{pp})$
 $\widetilde{\mathcal{T}} \leftarrow \mathcal{S}(\mathsf{pp}, x)$
 for $i = 1, \ldots, r$ do
 $\quad$ tr $\leftarrow$ tr $\| (\widetilde{\mathcal{T}}\|_i)$
 end for
 Run $\mathcal{A}_2^{\mathsf{O}_{\mathsf{ext}}}(\widetilde{\mathcal{T}}, \mathsf{st}_{\mathcal{A}})$
 return win
	Parse $\mathcal{T}$ as $\mathcal{T} = (a_1, c_1, \cdots, a_{i-1}, c_{i-1})$
	 if $\mathcal{T} \in$ tr then
	 $\quad$ if $i \le r$ then
	 $\qquad c_i \xleftarrow{\$} \mathsf{Ch}_i$; tr $\leftarrow$ tr$\|(\mathcal{T}, a_i, c_i)$;
	 $\qquad$ return c_i
	 $\quad$ else if $i = r+1$ then
	 $\qquad d_1 \leftarrow \mathcal{V}(\mathsf{pp}, x, (\mathcal{T}, a_i))$
	 $\qquad d_2 \leftarrow \left(\exists j \in [1, r] : \mathcal{T}\|_j = \widetilde{\mathcal{T}}\|_j \wedge a_{j+1} \ne \tilde{a}_{j+1}\right)$
	 $\qquad$ if $d_1 = 1 \wedge d_2 = 1$ then
	 $\qquad\quad$ win $\leftarrow$ true
	 $\qquad$ return d_1
	 return $\bot$

Fig. 4. State-restoration Unique Response.

We also remark that, unlike aSR-WEE, our SR-UR is deliberately made non-adaptive to prove subsequent lemmas with a weaker assumption. Indeed, the reductions we present later will go through even though the resulting simulation-extractability claim has an adaptive flavor.

Definition 7 (SR-UR). *Consider a $(2r + 1)$-round public-coin interactive proof system $\Pi = (\mathsf{Setup}, \mathcal{P}, \mathcal{V})$ that has perfect **HVZK** simulator $\mathcal{S}$. Π is said to have* state-restoration unique response *(SR-UR) with respect to a simulator $\mathcal{S}$, if for all PPT algebraic adversaries $\mathcal{A}_{\mathsf{alg}} = (\mathcal{A}_1, \mathcal{A}_2)$, the advantage* $\mathbf{Adv}_\Pi^{SR\text{-}UR}(\mathcal{A}_{\mathsf{alg}}, \mathcal{S}) := \Pr[SR\text{-}UR_\Pi^{\mathcal{A}_{\mathsf{alg}}, \mathcal{S}}(\lambda)]$ *is* $\mathsf{negl}(\lambda)$.

Weak Unique Response We now present our *weak unique response* definition tailored to non-interactive protocols. While typical unique response properties in the literature are defined for interactive protocols, [30, Definition 7] is in the non-interactive setting. Our definition below is strictly weaker than theirs, as we only need to guarantee the hardness of finding another accepting transcript forked from simulated (honest) one.

Definition 8 (FS-WUR). *Consider a $(2r+1)$-round public-coin interactive proof system $\Pi = (\mathsf{Setup}, \mathcal{P}, \mathcal{V})$ and the resulting **NIZK** $\Pi_{\mathsf{FS}} = (\mathsf{Setup}, \mathcal{P}_{\mathsf{FS}}, \mathcal{V}_{\mathsf{FS}})$ via Fiat-Shamir transform. Let $\mathcal{S}_{\mathsf{FS}}$ be a perfect **NIZK** simulator for Π_{FS} (Definition 2) with wrapper oracles $(\mathcal{S}_1, \mathcal{S}_2')$ as defined in Section 2. Π_{FS} is said to have* weak unique responses *(FS-WUR) with respect to $\mathcal{S}_{\mathsf{FS}}$ if given a transcript $\widetilde{\mathcal{T}} = (\tilde{a}_1, \tilde{c}_1, \ldots, \tilde{a}_r, \tilde{c}_r, \tilde{a}_{r+1})$ simulated by $\mathcal{S}_{\mathsf{FS}}$, it is hard to find another accepting transcript $\mathcal{T} = (a_1, c_1, \ldots, a_r, c_r, a_{r+1})$ that both have a common prefix up to the ith challenge for an instance x. That is, for all PPT algebraic adversaries*

$\mathcal{A}_{alg} = (\mathcal{A}_1, \mathcal{A}_2)$ the advantage $\mathbf{Adv}_{\Pi_{FS}}^{FS\text{-}WUR}(\mathcal{A}_{alg}, \mathcal{S}_{FS})$ defined as the following probability is $\mathsf{negl}(\lambda)$:

$$\Pr\left[\begin{array}{l} \mathcal{V}_{FS}^{\mathcal{S}_1}(\mathsf{pp}, x, \mathcal{T}) = 1 \\ \wedge\ (\exists j \in [1, r] : \mathcal{T}|_j = \widetilde{\mathcal{T}}|_j \\ \wedge\ a_{j+1} \neq \tilde{a}_{j+1}) \end{array} \middle| \begin{array}{l} \mathsf{pp} \leftarrow \mathsf{Setup}(1^\lambda); \\ ([x], \mathsf{st}) \leftarrow \mathcal{A}_1^{\mathcal{S}_1}(\mathsf{pp}); \\ \widetilde{\mathcal{T}} \leftarrow \mathcal{S}_2'(x); \\ [\mathcal{T}] \leftarrow \mathcal{A}_2^{\mathcal{S}_1}(\widetilde{\mathcal{T}}, \mathsf{st}); \end{array}\right].$$

We now show that FS-WUR of Π_{FS} reduces to SR-UR of the interactive proof system Π in the AGM. Informally, the lemma below guarantees that one can construct an adversary breaking unique response in the interactive setting, given an adversary breaking unique response in the non-interactive setting, as long as it makes RO queries for the accepting transcript in right order. As mentioned earlier, the reduction below does not crucially depend on the AGM: if a given protocol meets SR-UR without the AGM the proof holds almost verbatim without the AGM as well. Proof is rather straightforward and thus is deferred to the full version [21].

Lemma 1. *Consider a $(2r + 1)$-round public-coin interactive proof system $\Pi = (\mathsf{Setup}, \mathcal{P}, \mathcal{V})$ and the resulting NIZK $\Pi_{FS} = (\mathsf{Setup}, \mathcal{P}_{FS}, \mathcal{V}_{FS})$ via Fiat-Shamir transform. Let $\mathcal{S}$ be a perfect algebraic HVZK simulator for Π and $\mathcal{S}_{FS}$ be the corresponding canonical NIZK simulator for Π_{FS}. If Π has SR-UR with respect to $\mathcal{S}$, then Π_{FS} has FS-WUR with respect to $\mathcal{S}_{FS}$. That is, for every PPT adversary $\mathcal{A}$ against FS-WUR of Π_{FS} that makes q queries to $\mathcal{S}_1$, there exists a PPT adversary $\mathcal{B}$ against SR-UR of Π such that,*

$$\mathbf{Adv}_{\Pi_{FS}}^{FS\text{-}WUR}(\mathcal{A}, \mathcal{S}_{FS}) \leq \mathbf{Adv}_{\Pi}^{SR\text{-}UR}(\mathcal{B}, \mathcal{S}) + \frac{q+1}{|\mathsf{Ch}_{i_0}|}$$

where $i_0 \in [1, r]$ is the round with the smallest challenge set Ch_{i_0}. Moreover, $\mathcal{B}$ makes at most q queries to its oracle and is nearly as efficient as $\mathcal{A}$.

3.2 From Weak Unique Response to Simulation-extractability

We now prove the simulation-extractability of a non-interactive protocol Π_{FS} assuming it comes with an algebraic NIZK simulator $\mathcal{S}_{FS}$, it is extractable and has weak unique responses with respect to $\mathcal{S}_{FS}$. On a high-level the proof works by constructing another adversary $\mathcal{P}_{alg}$ that forwards the RO queries made by a FS-SIM-EXT adversary $\mathcal{P}_{alg}^*$ to the FS-EXT game, *except for the ones that have prefix in common with any of the simulated transcripts*. This will allow us to invoke the extractor $\mathcal{E}$ that is only guaranteed to work in the FS-EXT setting. On the other hand, thanks to the FS-WUR property we can argue that a cheating prover also has a hard time finding another transcript by reusing any prefix of a simulated transcript.

We stress that, as long as FS-WUR and FS-EXT are satisfied without the AGM the proof below holds almost verbatim without the AGM as well. Interestingly, proof in the AGM requires additional care about representation submitted by $\mathcal{P}_{alg}$: whenever $\mathcal{P}_{alg}$ forwards group elements with representation to external entities (i.e., H, $\mathcal{E}_1$, and $\mathcal{E}_0$), it must always convert representation to the one *only with respect to generators in* pp. This is made possible thanks to an *algebraic* simulator $\mathcal{S}_{FS}$; by probing how $\mathcal{S}_{FS}$ simulates a transcript with respect to the generators in pp, $\mathcal{P}_{alg}$ can translate the group representation submitted by $\mathcal{P}^*_{alg}$ even if it depends on previously simulated transcripts. This is crucial for invoking the extractor from FS-EXT, since a cheating prover against FS-EXT is only allowed to use the generators present in pp. We also remark that the additive security loss due to failure of RO programming by $\mathcal{S}'_2$ is not present in the bound since we use a canonical NIZK simulator as an assumption and such a loss already appears when showing NIZK from HVZK.

Lemma 2. *Consider a NIZK argument system Π_{FS} with an algebraic NIZK simulator $\mathcal{S}_{FS}$. If Π_{FS} is FS-WUR with respect to $\mathcal{S}_{FS}$ and online FS-EXT, then it is online FS-SIM-EXT with respect to $\mathcal{S}_{FS}$.*

Concretely, let $\mathcal{E} = (\mathcal{E}_0, \mathcal{E}_1)$ be an FS-EXT extractor for Π_{FS}. There exists an efficient FS-SIM-EXT simulator-extractor $\mathcal{E}^* = (\mathcal{E}^*_0, \mathcal{E}^*_1, \mathcal{E}^*_2)$ for Π_{FS} such that for every algebraic prover $\mathcal{P}^*_{alg}$ against Π_{FS} that makes q_1 random oracle queries (i.e., queries to $\mathcal{S}_1$ or $\mathcal{E}^*_1$), and q_2 simulation queries (i.e., queries to $\mathcal{S}'_2$ or $\mathcal{E}^*_2$), and for every distinguisher $\mathcal{D}^*$, there exists another algebraic prover $\mathcal{P}_{alg}$, a distinguisher $\mathcal{D}$, and an FS-WUR adversary $\mathcal{A}_{alg}$, such that for all $\lambda \in \mathbb{N}^+$,

$$\mathbf{Adv}^{FS\text{-}SIM\text{-}EXT}_{\Pi_{FS}, \mathcal{R}}(\mathcal{S}_{FS}, \mathcal{E}^*, \mathcal{P}^*_{alg}, \mathcal{D}^*) \leq \mathbf{Adv}^{FS\text{-}EXT}_{\Pi_{FS}, \mathcal{R}}(H, \mathcal{E}, \mathcal{P}_{alg}, \mathcal{D}) + q_2 \cdot \mathbf{Adv}^{FS\text{-}WUR}_{\Pi_{FS}, \mathcal{R}}(\mathcal{A}_{alg}, \mathcal{S}_{FS}).$$

Moreover, $\mathcal{P}_{alg}$ and $\mathcal{A}_{alg}$ make at most q_1 queries to their oracle and is nearly as efficient as $\mathcal{P}^*_{alg}$. The extractor $\mathcal{E}^*$ is nearly as efficient as $\mathcal{E}$.

Proof. Without loss of generality we assume $\mathcal{P}^*_{alg}$ does not repeat the same RO queries. We first construct a cheating prover $\mathcal{P}_{alg}$ against FS-EXT that internally uses the FS-SIM-EXT adversary $\mathcal{P}^*_{alg}$ and simulates its view in FS-SIM-EXT.

We now describe the following simple hybrids.

G_0 This game is identical to SIM-EXT-$1^{\mathcal{S}_1, \mathcal{S}'_2, \mathcal{P}^*_{alg}, \mathcal{D}^*}_{\Pi_{FS}}(\lambda)$. We have

$$\Pr[G_0(\mathcal{P}^*_{alg}, \mathcal{D}^*)] = \Pr[\text{SIM-EXT-}1^{\mathcal{S}_1, \mathcal{S}'_2, \mathcal{P}^*_{alg}, \mathcal{D}^*}_{\Pi_{FS}}(\lambda)].$$

G_1 This game is identical to G_0 except that it aborts if $d = 1$ (i.e., $(x^*, \mathcal{T}^*)$ is accepting) and $(x^*, \mathcal{T}^*) \notin \mathcal{Q}_2$, while there exists some $(x^*, \tilde{\mathcal{T}}) \in \mathcal{Q}_2$ that has prefix in common with $\mathcal{T}^*$ but differs at the response right after that prefix, i.e., for some $j \leq r$ it holds that $\mathcal{T}^*|_j = \tilde{\mathcal{T}}|_j$ and $a^*_{j+1} \neq \tilde{a}_{j+1}$. The abort event implies that there exists an efficient FS-WUR adversary $\mathcal{A}_{alg}$ that internally uses $\mathcal{P}^*_{alg}$. That is,

$$\left| \Pr[G_0(\mathcal{P}^*_{alg}, \mathcal{D}^*)] - \Pr[G_1(\mathcal{P}^*_{alg}, \mathcal{D}^*)] \right| \leq \Pr[G_1(\mathcal{P}^*_{alg}, \mathcal{D}^*) \text{aborts}]$$
$$\leq q_2 \cdot \mathbf{Adv}^{FS\text{-}WUR}_{\Pi_{FS}, \mathcal{R}}(\mathcal{A}_{alg}, \mathcal{S}_{FS}). \tag{2}$$

We defer the reduction deriving (2) to later.

Constructing $\mathcal{P}_{alg}$ and $\mathcal{D}$ for FS-EXT. We now construct a FS-EXT adversary $\mathcal{P}_{alg}$ and a distinguisher $\mathcal{D}$. $\mathcal{P}_{alg}$ plays an FS-EXT game while internally simulating the view of $\mathcal{P}^*_{alg}$ in the game G_1 as follows.

- On receiving pp from $\mathsf{Setup}(1^\lambda)$, $\mathcal{P}_{\mathsf{alg}}$ forwards pp to $\mathcal{P}^*_{\mathsf{alg}}$.
- Whenever $\mathcal{P}^*_{\mathsf{alg}}$ makes a simulation query with input $[x]$, $\mathcal{P}_{\mathsf{alg}}$ internally invokes $\mathcal{S}_{\mathsf{FS}}(2, st, [x])$ to obtain $([\widetilde{T}], st')$ and records a statement-proof pair $(x, \widetilde{T})$ in the set $\mathcal{Q}_2$. $\mathcal{P}_{\mathsf{alg}}$ also separately keeps track of representation of every entry in $\mathcal{Q}_2$. Then it programs the RO tables $\mathcal{Q}_1$ for every challenge in $\widetilde{T}$ as $\mathcal{S}_{\mathsf{FS}}(2, st, [x])$ would do.
- Whenever $\mathcal{P}^*_{\mathsf{alg}}$ (or $\mathcal{V}_{\mathsf{FS}}$ at the end) makes a random oracle query with input $((\mathsf{pp}, [x], [T], [a_i]), i)$, where $T = (a_1, c_1, \ldots, a_{i-1}, c_{i-1})$, $\mathcal{P}_{\mathsf{alg}}$ checks whether there exists some $(x, \widetilde{T}) \in \mathcal{Q}_2$ that has prefix in common with T, i.e., for some $j \leq i - 1$ it holds that $T|_j = \widetilde{T}|_j$. If that is the case, it lazily samples c_i from Ch_i and updates $\mathcal{Q}_{1,i}$ accordingly, as $\mathcal{S}_{\mathsf{FS}}(1, st, (\mathsf{pp}, [x], [T], [a_i]), i)$ would do. Otherwise, it forwards the query $((\mathsf{pp}, x, T, a_i), i)$ to a FS-EXT game with converted group representation, receives $c_i \in \mathsf{Ch}_i$, and updates $\mathcal{Q}_{1,i}$ accordingly.
- When $\mathcal{P}^*_{\mathsf{alg}}$ outputs a forgery $([x^*], [T^*])$, $\mathcal{P}_{\mathsf{alg}}$ first checks whether it causes aborts in the game G_1. If that is the case, $\mathcal{P}_{\mathsf{alg}}$ also aborts because it implies that the challenge values in T^* are not obtained by forwarding the corresponding queries to a FS-EXT game and therefore (x^*, T^*) is not accepting in the FS-EXT game.
- Otherwise, $\mathcal{P}_{\mathsf{alg}}$ outputs $(x^*, T^*, st_{\mathcal{P}_{\mathsf{alg}}})$ to a FS-EXT game with converted group representation, where $st_{\mathcal{P}_{\mathsf{alg}}} = (\mathcal{Q}_1, \mathcal{Q}_2)$.

A FS-EXT distinguisher $\mathcal{D}$ internally invokes $\mathcal{D}^*$ on input $(st_{\mathcal{P}_{\mathsf{alg}}}, x^*, T^*, \mathcal{Q}_1, \mathcal{Q}_2)$ and outputs whatever $\mathcal{D}^*$ returns. By construction, we have

$$\Pr[\mathsf{G}_1(\mathcal{P}^*_{\mathsf{alg}}, \mathcal{D}^*)] = \Pr[\mathsf{EXT\text{-}1}^{\mathsf{H}, \mathcal{P}_{\mathsf{alg}}, \mathcal{D}}_{\Pi_{\mathsf{FS}}}(\lambda)].$$

Constructing $\mathcal{E}^*$ for FS-SIM-EXT. We define a simulator-extractor $\mathcal{E}^* = (\mathcal{E}^*_0, \mathcal{E}^*_1, \mathcal{E}^*_2)$ using a FS-EXT extractor $\mathcal{E} = (\mathcal{E}_0, \mathcal{E}_1)$. $\mathcal{E}^*_1$ answers the random oracle queries made by $\mathcal{P}^*_{\mathsf{alg}}$ as $\mathcal{P}_{\mathsf{alg}}$ would, by using the responses from $\mathcal{E}_1$. $\mathcal{E}^*_2$ answers the simulation queries made by $\mathcal{P}^*_{\mathsf{alg}}$ as $\mathcal{P}_{\mathsf{alg}}$ would, by internally invoking $\mathcal{S}_{\mathsf{FS}}$. $\mathcal{E}^*_0$ outputs whatever $\mathcal{E}_0$ returns on input $(st_{\mathcal{E}}, [x^*], [T^*])$. Note that, if $\mathcal{P}_{\mathsf{alg}}$ does not abort, T^* has no prefix in common with any of the previously simulated transcripts. In that case, thanks to the random oracle simulation conducted by $\mathcal{P}_{\mathsf{alg}}$ as above, for every $i \in [1, r]$, c^*_i has been obtained by querying the random oracle in a FS-EXT game with input $((\mathsf{pp}, x^*, T^*|_{i-1}, a^*_i), i)$. Therefore, (x^*, T^*) gets accepted by $\mathcal{V}^{\mathcal{E}_1}_{\mathsf{FS}}$ whenever it gets accepted by $\mathcal{V}^{\mathcal{E}_1}_{\mathsf{FS}}$, $(x^*, T^*) \notin \mathcal{Q}_2$, and $\mathcal{P}_{\mathsf{alg}}$ does not abort. By construction, $\mathcal{E}^*$ succeeds in extraction if and only if $\mathcal{E}$ does so in the game $\mathsf{EXT\text{-}0}^{\mathcal{E}, \mathcal{P}_{\mathsf{alg}}, \mathcal{D}}_{\Pi_{\mathsf{FS}}, \mathcal{R}}(\lambda)$. Thus we have

$$\Pr[\mathsf{SIM\text{-}EXT\text{-}0}^{\mathcal{E}^*, \mathcal{P}^*_{\mathsf{alg}}, \mathcal{D}^*}_{\Pi_{\mathsf{FS}}, \mathcal{R}}(\lambda)] = \Pr[\mathsf{EXT\text{-}0}^{\mathcal{E}, \mathcal{P}_{\mathsf{alg}}, \mathcal{D}}_{\Pi_{\mathsf{FS}}, \mathcal{R}}(\lambda)].$$

Reduction to FS-WUR. We now bound the probability that the game G_1 aborts. We argue that, if there exists $(\mathcal{P}^*_{\mathsf{alg}}, \mathcal{D}^*)$ that causes $\mathsf{G}_1(\mathcal{P}^*_{\mathsf{alg}}, \mathcal{D}^*)$ to abort (or in other words, that causes $\mathcal{P}_{\mathsf{alg}}$ to abort), one can use $\mathcal{P}_{\mathsf{alg}}^*$ to construct another adversary $\mathcal{A}_{\mathsf{alg}} = (\mathcal{A}_1, \mathcal{A}_2)$ that breaks FS-WUR with respect to $\mathcal{S}_{\mathsf{FS}}$. The reduction goes as follows. The differences with $\mathcal{P}_{\mathsf{alg}}$ are highlighted in orange.

- $\mathcal{A}_1$ first picks a query index $k \in [1, q_2]$ uniformly at random.
- On receiving pp from $\mathsf{Setup}(1^\lambda)$, $\mathcal{A}_1$ forwards pp to $\mathcal{P}_{\mathsf{alg}}^*$.
- Whenever $\mathcal{P}_{\mathsf{alg}}^*$ makes a simulation query with input $[x]$, if this is the kth simulation query then it forwards x to $\mathcal{S}_2'$ in the FS-WUR game with converted group representation. We denote the statement-transcript pair of the kth query by $(x^k, \widetilde{T}^k)$.[4] Otherwise, $\mathcal{A}_1$ internally invokes $\mathcal{S}_{\mathsf{FS}}(2, st, [x])$ to obtain $([\widetilde{T}], st')$. It records a statement-proof pair $(x, \widetilde{T})$ in the set $\mathcal{Q}_2$. $\mathcal{A}$ also separately keeps track of representation of every entry in $\mathcal{Q}_2$. Then it programs the RO tables $\mathcal{Q}_1$ for every challenge in $\widetilde{T}$ as $\mathcal{S}_{\mathsf{FS}}(2, st, [x])$ would do. $\mathcal{A}_2$ also responds to simulation queries in the same way, except that it never forwards a statement to the FS-WUR game.
- Whenever $\mathcal{P}_{\mathsf{alg}}^*$ (or $\mathcal{V}_{\mathsf{FS}}$ at the end) makes a random oracle query with input $((\mathsf{pp}, [x], [T], [a_i]), i)$, where $T = (a_1, c_1, \dots, a_{i-1}, c_{i-1})$, $\mathcal{A}_2$ checks whether $(x^k, \widetilde{T}^k)$ has prefix in common with T, i.e., for some $j \leq i - 1$ it holds that $T|_j = \widetilde{T}^k|_j$. If that is the case, it forwards the query $((\mathsf{pp}, x, T, a_i), i)$ to $\mathcal{S}_1$ in the FS-WUR game with converted group representation, receives $c_i \in \mathsf{Ch}_i$, and updates $\mathcal{Q}_{1,i}$ accordingly. Otherwise, it lazily samples c_i from Ch_i and updates $\mathcal{Q}_{1,i}$ accordingly, as $\mathcal{S}_{\mathsf{FS}}(1, st, (\mathsf{pp}, [x], [T], [a_i]), i)$ would do. $\mathcal{A}_1$ also responds to random oracle queries in the same way, except that it never forwards queries to the FS-WUR game.
- When $\mathcal{P}_{\mathsf{alg}}^*$ outputs a forgery $([x^*], [T^*])$, $\mathcal{A}_{\mathsf{alg}}$ first checks whether it causes aborts in the game G_1. If that is the case, $\mathcal{A}_2$ forwards T^* to the FS-WUR game as a forgery with converted group representation.

The above procedure perfectly simulates $\mathcal{P}_{\mathsf{alg}}^*$'s view in the game G_1. By construction $\mathcal{A}_{\mathsf{alg}}$ breaks FS-WUR with respect to $\mathcal{S}_{\mathsf{FS}}$ if G_1 aborts *and* $(x^* = x^k \wedge T^*$ has some prefix in common with $\widetilde{T}^k)$, because then it is guaranteed that for every $i \in [1, r]$, c_i^* has been obtained by querying the oracles $(\mathcal{S}_1, \mathcal{S}_2')$ in the FS-WUR game. Therefore, T^* does qualify as a valid forgery in the FS-WUR game. Conditioned on the event that G_1 aborts, the probability that $\mathcal{A}_{\mathsf{alg}}$ wins is at least $1/q_2$. Therefore, we have

$$\frac{1}{q_2} \cdot \Pr[\mathsf{G}_1(\mathcal{P}_{\mathsf{alg}}^*, \mathcal{D}^*) \text{aborts}] \leq \mathbf{Adv}_{\Pi_{\mathsf{FS}}, \mathcal{R}}^{\mathsf{FS\text{-}WUR}}(\mathcal{A}_{\mathsf{alg}}, \mathcal{S}_{\mathsf{FS}})$$

which derives (2). Putting together, we obtain

---

[4] We note that $\mathcal{A}_{\mathsf{alg}}$ does not get to know the representation of $\widetilde{T}^k$ unlike other simulated transcripts, as that particular one comes from the FS-WUR game and its representation is not disclosed to the adversary. Therefore, all the subsequent outputs from $\mathcal{P}_{\mathsf{alg}}^*$ are with respect to pp and $\widetilde{T}^k$. This, however, does not prevent us from showing reduction because outputting representation w.r.t. pp and $\widetilde{T}^k$ is indeed allowed in the FS-WUR game.

$$\left| \text{Pr}[\text{SIM-EXT-1}_{\Pi_{FS}}^{\mathcal{S}_1, \mathcal{S}_2', \mathcal{P}_{alg}^*, \mathcal{D}^*}(\lambda)] - \text{Pr}[\text{SIM-EXT-0}_{\Pi_{FS}, \mathcal{R}}^{\mathcal{E}^*, \mathcal{P}_{alg}^*, \mathcal{D}^*}(\lambda)] \right|$$

$$\leq \left| \text{Pr}[\text{EXT-1}_{\Pi_{FS}}^{H, \mathcal{P}_{alg}, \mathcal{D}}(\lambda)] - \text{Pr}[\text{EXT-0}_{\Pi_{FS}, \mathcal{R}}^{\mathcal{E}, \mathcal{P}_{alg}, \mathcal{D}}(\lambda)] \right| + q_2 \cdot \textbf{Adv}_{\Pi_{FS}, \mathcal{R}}^{FS\text{-}WUR}(\mathcal{A}_{alg}, \mathcal{S}_{FS})$$

$$\leq \textbf{Adv}_{\Pi_{FS}, \mathcal{R}}^{FS\text{-}EXT}(H, \mathcal{E}, \mathcal{P}_{alg}, \mathcal{D}) + q_2 \cdot \textbf{Adv}_{\Pi_{FS}, \mathcal{R}}^{FS\text{-}WUR}(\mathcal{A}_{alg}, \mathcal{S}_{FS}).$$

$\square$

3.3 Generic Result on Simulation-Extractability

Theorem 4. *Let $\mathcal{R}$ be a relation. Let Π be a r-challenge public coin interactive protocol for the relation $\mathcal{R}$ where the ith challenge is sampled from Ch_i for $i \in [1, r]$. Suppose Π satisfies: aSR-WEE, perfect HVZK with algebraic simulator $\mathcal{S}$, and SR-UR with respect to $\mathcal{S}$. Let $\mathcal{S}_{FS}$ be the corresponding canonical NIZK simulator for $\mathcal{S}_{FS}$ fixed by $\mathcal{S}$. Then Π_{FS} is FS-SIM-EXT with respect to $\mathcal{S}_{FS}$.*

Concretely, let $\mathcal{E}$ be an aSR-WEE extractor for Π. There exists an efficient FS-SIM-EXT simulator-extractor $\mathcal{E}^*$ for Π_{FS} such that for every non-uniform algebraic prover $\mathcal{P}_{alg}^*$ against Π_{FS} that makes q_1 random oracle queries, and q_2 simulation queries, and for every distinguisher $\mathcal{D}^*$, there exists a non-uniform algebraic prover $\mathcal{P}_{alg}$, an SR-UR adversary $\mathcal{A}_{alg}$, and a distinguisher $\mathcal{D}$ such that for all $\lambda \in \mathbb{N}^+$,

$$\textbf{Adv}_{\Pi_{FS}, \mathcal{R}}^{FS\text{-}SIM\text{-}EXT}(\mathcal{S}_{FS}, \mathcal{E}^*, \mathcal{P}_{alg}^*, \mathcal{D}^*, \lambda)$$

$$\leq \textbf{Adv}_{\Pi, \mathcal{R}}^{aSR\text{-}WEE}(\mathcal{E}, \mathcal{P}_{alg}, \mathcal{D}, \lambda) + q_2 \cdot \textbf{Adv}_{\Pi, \mathcal{R}}^{SR\text{-}UR}(\mathcal{A}_{alg}, \mathcal{S}, \lambda) + \frac{(q_2 + 1)(q_1 + 1)}{|\text{Ch}_{i_0}|}$$

where $i_0 \in [1, r]$ is the round with the smallest challenge set Ch_{i_0}.

Proof. From Theorem 3, aSR-WEE of Π implies FS-EXT security of Π_{FS}. From Lemma 1, SR-UR and HVZK of Π implies FS-WUR security of Π_{FS}. Finally, from Lemma 2, FS-EXT and FS-WUR imply FS-SIM-EXT security of Π_{FS}. Putting together all the concrete bounds, we obtain the result. $\square$

4 Non-Malleability of Bulletproofs – Arithmetic Circuits

The protocol for arithmetic circuit satisfiability as it appears in Bulletproofs (henceforth referred as BP) [7] is formally described in Protocol 1 of the full version [21] and proceeds as follows: In the first round, the prover commits to values on the wire of the circuit (i.e. $\mathbf{a}_L, \mathbf{a}_R$ and $\mathbf{a}_O$), and the blinding vectors ($\mathbf{s}_L, \mathbf{s}_R$). It receives challenges y, z from the verifier. Based on these challenges, the prover defines three polynomials, l, r and t, where $t(X) = \langle l(X), r(X) \rangle$, and commits to the coefficients of the polynomial t in the third round, i.e. commitments $T_1, T_3, T_4, T_5,$ and, T_6[5]. On receiving a challenge x from the verifier, the prover

---

[5] The degree two term is independent of the witness and can be computed by the verifier, therefore there is no T_2 commitment.

evaluates polynomials l, r on this challenge point, computes $\hat{t} = \langle l(x), r(x) \rangle$, and values β_x, μ, and sends $\beta_x, \mu, \hat{t}, \mathbf{l} = l(x)$ and $\mathbf{r} = r(x)$ in the fifth round. The verifier accepts if: the commitments $\{T_i\}_{i=S}$ (for $S = \{1, 3, 4, 5, 6\}$) are to the correct polynomial t and if $\hat{t} = \langle \mathbf{l}, \mathbf{r} \rangle$. To get logarithmic proof size, the prover and verifier define an instance of the inner dot product for checking the condition $\hat{t} = \langle \mathbf{l}, \mathbf{r} \rangle$, instead of sending vectors $\mathbf{l}, \mathbf{r}$ in clear.

The inner product subroutine is presented in the full version [21].

Simulator 1: $\mathcal{S}_{\mathsf{BP}}$

The algebraic simulator $\mathcal{S}_{\mathsf{BP}}$ is given as input:

$$\mathsf{pp} = (n, Q, g, h, u, \mathbf{g}, \mathbf{h}), \ \mathsf{x} = (\mathbf{W}_L, \mathbf{W}_R, \mathbf{W}_O, \mathbf{c})$$

The transcript is simulated as follows where the difference with the original simulator is marked in orange:

1. $x, y, w, z \xleftarrow{\$} \mathbb{Z}_p$
2. $\beta_x, \mu \xleftarrow{\$} \mathbb{Z}_p$
3. $\mathbf{l}, \mathbf{r} \xleftarrow{\$} \mathbb{Z}_p^n$
4. $\hat{t} = \langle \mathbf{l}, \mathbf{r} \rangle$
5. $\rho_I, \rho_O, t_3, t_4, t_5, t_6, \beta_3, \beta_4, \beta_5, \beta_6 \xleftarrow{\$} \mathbb{Z}_p$
6. $A_I = g^{\rho_I}, A_O = u^{\rho_O}$
7. $T_i = g^{t_i} h^{\beta_i}$ for $i \in \{3, 4, 5, 6\}$
8. $\mathbf{h}' = \mathbf{h}^{\mathbf{y}^{-n}}, u' = u^w$
9. $W_L = \mathbf{h}'^{\mathbf{z}_{[1:]}^{Q+1} \cdot \mathbf{W}_L}, \ W_R = \mathbf{g}^{\mathbf{y}^{-n} \circ (\mathbf{z}_{[1:]}^{Q+1} \cdot \mathbf{W}_R)}, \ W_O = \mathbf{h}^{\mathbf{y}^{-n} \circ (\mathbf{z}_{[1:]}^{Q+1} \cdot \mathbf{W}_O)}$
10. $S = \left(A_I^x \cdot A_O^{x^2} \cdot \mathbf{g}^{-1} \cdot (\mathbf{h}')^{-\mathbf{y}^n - \mathbf{r}} \cdot W_L^x \cdot W_R^x \cdot W_O \cdot h^{-\mu} \right)^{-x^{-3}}$
11. $T_1 = \left(h^{-\beta_x} \cdot g^{x^2 \cdot (\delta(y,z) + \langle \mathbf{z}_{[1:]}^{Q+1}, \mathbf{c} \rangle) - \hat{t}} \cdot \prod_{i=3}^{6} T_i^{x^i} \right)^{-x^{-1}}$
12. $\mathcal{T} = (S, A_I, A_O; y, z; \{T_i\}_{i \in S}; x; \hat{t}, \beta_x, \mu; w; \mathbf{l}, \mathbf{r})$
13. Output $[\mathcal{T}]$

4.1 Algebraic Simulation

In Simulator 1 we define an algebraic simulator $\mathcal{S}_{\mathsf{BP}}$ for BP which is going to be used in both the proof of HVZK and SR-UR. The simulator $\mathcal{S}_{\mathsf{BP}}$ essentially works as the simulator from [6], except that, since it needs to explicitly output group representation for each simulated element, it will generate A_I, A_O as well as the T_i's by learning their discrete logarithm in bases g, h, u instead of generically sampling random group elements like in the original proof. This makes no difference for the ZK claim and makes the proof of SR-UR simpler. Note that, since the simulator picks all the challenges at random in the first step, the simulator can easily be changed to satisfy the stronger *special* HVZK. However, by defining the simulator like this we can reuse it in both of the following claims. Note also that while the output of the simulator does not explicitly contain the group representation (t_1, β_1) of T_1 w.r.t base (g, h), it is possible to compute these values from the output of the simulator.

Remark 4. The simulator for the recursive version of Bulletproof e.g., the one that calls InPrd instead of sending $\mathbf{l}, \mathbf{r}$ directly, can easily be constructed from the simulator above by running the InPrd protocol on $\mathbf{l}, \mathbf{r}$. The algebraic simulator also outputs the representation for the elements L_i, R_i generated during this protocol and this representation will be used explicitly in the proof later.

Claim 1. *The protocol* BP *(Protocol 1 of the full version [21]) is perfect HVZK with algebraic simulator* $\mathcal{S}_{\mathsf{BP}}$ *(Simulator 1) .*

Proof. The claim follows directly from the proof of HVZK in [6] by observing that the way $A_I, A_O, T_3, T_4, T_5, T_6$ are generated in our and their simulator produces the exact same distribution (in their case they are sampled as random elements from the group; in ours, we generate them by raising generators to random exponents, and those are not re-used anywhere else).

4.2 State-Restoration Unique Responses

The following claim is crucial for invoking our generic result from Theorem 4. We remind the reader that proving uniqueness of the randomized commitments T_i's is made possible thanks to our relaxed definition: if the adversary was allowed to control both transcripts, it would be trivial to break the (strong) unique response by honestly executing the prover algorithm twice with known witness and by committing to t_i using distinct randomnesses β_i and β_i'. Our proof below on the other hand argues that a cheating prover in SR-UR has a hard time forging T_i once one of the transcripts has been fixed by a simulator. In other words, they cannot reuse parts of simulated proofs without knowing how the simulated messages were generated. This is true even for true statements where the prover might know the witness.

Claim 2. *Protocol* BP *(Protocol 1 of the full version [21]) satisfies state-restoration unique response (SR-UR) with respect to* $\mathcal{S}_{\mathsf{BP}}$ *(Simulator 1) in the AGM, under the assumption that solving the discrete-log relation is hard. That is, for every PPT adversary* $\mathcal{A}_{ur}$ *against SR-UR of BP that makes q queries to* $\mathsf{O}_{\mathsf{ext}}$ *(Fig. 4), there exists a PPT adversary* $\mathcal{A}$ *against DL-REL such that,*

$$\mathbf{Adv}_{\mathsf{BP}}^{\mathsf{SR\text{-}UR}}(\mathcal{A}_{ur}, \mathcal{S}_{\mathsf{BP}}) \le \mathbf{Adv}^{\mathsf{DL\text{-}REL}}(\mathbb{G}_\lambda, \mathcal{A}_\lambda) + \frac{(14n + 8)q}{(p-1)}.$$

Proof. Given an algebraic adversary for SR-UR-game $\mathcal{A}_{ur} = (\mathcal{A}_1, \mathcal{A}_2)$ for protocol BP (Fig. 4), we construct an adversary, $\mathcal{A}$, who breaks the discrete-log relation.

$\mathcal{A}$, upon receiving a discrete-log relation challenge interacts with $\mathcal{A}_{ur}$ as follows: It first runs $\mathcal{A}_1(\mathsf{pp})$ (where pp includes all the generators from the discrete-log relation assumption) to receive an instance $[x]$ and st. $\mathcal{A}$ then invokes the simulator $\mathcal{S}_{\mathsf{BP}}$ on $[x]$ to receive a transcript $\widetilde{\mathcal{T}}$. $\mathcal{A}$ then runs $\mathcal{A}_2$ on $\widetilde{\mathcal{T}}$ and st. Queries to the SR-UR-oracle $\mathbf{O}_{\mathsf{ext}}$ are handled by $\mathcal{A}$ locally as in the SR-UR game, by sampling random challenges and forwarding to $\mathcal{A}_2$. $\mathcal{A}$ locally records the tree of transcripts. Note that when $\mathcal{A}_{ur}$ queries $\mathbf{O}_{\mathsf{ext}}$, it also submits the group representation in terms of all groups elements seen so far. Moreover, the simulator $\mathcal{S}_{\mathsf{BP}}$ is algebraic, and therefore $\mathcal{A}$ can efficiently recover all representation for elements in $\mathcal{T}$ and $\widetilde{\mathcal{T}}$ into an equivalent representation purely in terms of $\mathbf{g}, \mathbf{h}, g, h, u$ which will be used to break the discrete-logarithm assumption.

Since $\mathcal{A}_{ur}$ wins the SR-UR game $[\mathcal{T}]$ is an accepting transcript for statement $[x]$ which is different from $[\widetilde{\mathcal{T}}]$, but has a common prefix. Therefore, at least the first two messages must be equal. In particular, $\mathcal{S}_{\mathsf{BP}}$ outputs transcript of the form

$$\widetilde{\mathcal{T}} = (\tilde{A}_I, \tilde{A}_O, \tilde{S}; \tilde{y}, \tilde{z}; (\tilde{T}_i)_{i \in \mathcal{S}}; \tilde{x}, \tilde{\beta}_x, \tilde{\mu}, \hat{\tilde{t}}, \tilde{w}, \tilde{L}_1, \tilde{R}_1, \tilde{x}_1, \ldots, \tilde{L}_m, \tilde{R}_m, \tilde{x}_m, \tilde{a}, \tilde{b})$$

and $\mathcal{A}_{ur}$ outputs transcripts of the form

$$\mathcal{T} = (\tilde{A}_I, \tilde{A}_O, \tilde{S}; \tilde{y}, \tilde{z}; (T_i)_{i \in \mathcal{S}}; x, \beta_x, \mu, \hat{t}, w, L_1, R_1, x_1, \ldots, L_m, R_m, x_m, a, b)$$

where we denote $m = \log(n)$.

We now proceed with a case by case analysis based on the first message in $\mathcal{T}$ which is different from $\widetilde{\mathcal{T}}$.
If $\tilde{T}_i \neq T_i$ for some $i \in \mathcal{S}$, then the verification equation satisfied by $\mathcal{T}$ is

$$(\mathbf{g}^{(m)})^a (\mathbf{h}^{(m)})^b (u')^{ab}$$
$$= \left(\prod_{i=1}^{m} L_i^{x_i^2} \right) \cdot \left(\prod_{i=1}^{m} R_i^{x_i^{-2}} \right) \cdot h^{-\mu} \cdot \tilde{A}_I^x \cdot \tilde{A}_O^{x^2} \cdot (\tilde{\mathbf{h}}')^{-\tilde{y}^n}$$
$$\cdot \tilde{W}_L^x \cdot \tilde{W}_R^x \cdot \tilde{W}_O \cdot \tilde{S}^{x^3} \cdot (u')^{\hat{t}}.$$

(The values $\tilde{W}_{(\cdot)}$ and $\tilde{\mathbf{h}}'$ are also marked as $\tilde{(\cdot)}$ to remind the reader that they are the same in both $\mathcal{T}$ and $\widetilde{\mathcal{T}}$. Remember that $\mathbf{g}^{(m)}, \mathbf{h}^{(m)}$ are different in the two transcripts and they are generated as part of the InPrd). Dividing it by the verification equation for the simulated transcript, we get

$$(\mathbf{g}^{(m)})^a (\mathbf{h}^{(m)})^b (u')^{ab} \cdot (\tilde{\mathbf{g}}^{(m)})^{-\tilde{a}} (\tilde{\mathbf{h}}^{(m)})^{-\tilde{b}} (\tilde{u}')^{-\tilde{a}\tilde{b}} \qquad (3)$$
$$= \left(\prod_{i=1}^{m} L_i^{x_i^2} \right) \left(\prod_{i=1}^{m} \tilde{L}_i^{-\tilde{x}_i^2} \right) \left(\prod_{i=1}^{m} R_i^{x_i^{-2}} \right) \left(\prod_{i=1}^{m} \tilde{R}_i^{-\tilde{x}_i^{-2}} \right)$$
$$\cdot h^{-(\mu - \tilde{\mu})} \cdot \tilde{A}_I^{x - \tilde{x}} \cdot \tilde{A}_O^{x^2 - \tilde{x}^2} \cdot \tilde{W}_L^{x - \tilde{x}} \cdot \tilde{W}_R^{x - \tilde{x}} \cdot \tilde{S}^{x^3 - \tilde{x}^3} \cdot (u')^{\hat{t}} \cdot (\tilde{u}')^{-\hat{t}}. \qquad (4)$$

We rearrange the exponents w.r.t. the generators $(g, h, \mathbf{g}, \mathbf{h}, u)$. Let us focus on the exponent of g. The only elements with a non-zero component for g are: the simulated $\tilde{A}_I$ and $\tilde{S}$ that have ρ_I and $-\rho_I \tilde{x}^{-2}$ in the exponents of g, respectively; and L_i (resp. R_i) with g-component $l_{i,g}$ (resp. $r_{i,g}$) submitted by the adversary during the oracle queries. Then the exponent of g in (4) is

$$\sum_{i=1}^{m} l_{i,g} x_i^2 + \sum_{i=1}^{m} r_{i,g} x_i^{-2} - \rho_I \tilde{x}^{-2} x^3 + \rho_I x. \tag{5}$$

If (5) is non-zero then we find a non-trivial DL solution since the left-hand side of 4 has g-component 0. Now we argue that (5) vanishes with negligible probability. Since the state-restoration adversary makes queries to $\mathbf{O}_{\text{ext}}$ in order (e.g., it cannot query a transcript whose prefix has not been queried yet), the challenges $x, x_1, \ldots, x_m$ are also assigned in order. Suppose the first m variables are fixed to $x, x_1, \ldots, x_{m-1}$ and regard (5) as a univariate polynomial with indeterminate X_m. Define

$$e_g^{(m)}(X_m) = l_{m,g} X_m^2 + r_{m,g} X_m^{-2} + \sum_{i=1}^{m-1} l_{i,g} x_i^2 + \sum_{i=1}^{m-1} r_{i,g} x_i^{-2} - \rho_I \tilde{x}^{-2} x^3 + \rho_I x.$$

Then, by the Schwartz–Zippel Lemma, if the polynomial $e_g^{(m)}(X_m)$ is non-zero, $e_g^{(m)}(x_m)$ vanishes with probability at most $4/(p-1)$ over the random choice of $x_m \in \mathbb{Z}_p$; if it is a zero-polynomial, it must be that the constant term of $e_g^{(m)}$ is 0. Hence, if the polynomial

$$e_g^{(m-1)}(X_{m-1}) = l_{m-1,g} X_{m-1}^2 + r_{m-1,g} X_{m-1}^{-2} + \sum_{i=1}^{m-2} l_{i,g} x_i^2$$

$$+ \sum_{i=1}^{m-2} r_{i,g} x_i^{-2} - \rho_I \tilde{x}^{-2} x^3 + \rho_I x$$

is non-zero, $e_g^{(m-1)}(x_{m-1})$ vanishes with probability at most $4/(p-1)$ over the random choice of $x_{m-1} \in \mathbb{Z}_p$. Iterating the same argument, we are eventually tasked with showing $e_g^{(0)}(x) = -\rho_I \tilde{x}^{-2} x^3 + \rho_I x = 0$ with negligible probability. This only happens if (1) $\rho_I = 0$, i.e., $e_g^{(0)}(X)$ is a zero-polynomial, or (2) $e_g^{(0)}(x) = 0$ over the random choice of $x \in \mathbb{Z}_p$. The former happens with probability $1/(p-1)$ because ρ_I are uniformly chosen by the simulator; the latter happens with probability at most $3/(p-1)$.

If $\beta_x \neq \tilde{\beta}_x$ or $\hat{t} \neq \tilde{t}$, then we have another transcript

$$\mathcal{T}_{\mathsf{BP}} = (\tilde{A}_I, \tilde{A}_O, \tilde{S}; \tilde{y}, \tilde{z}; (\tilde{T}_i)_{i \in \mathcal{S}}; \tilde{x}, \beta_x, \mu, \hat{t}, w, L_1, R_1, x_1, \ldots, L_m, R_m, x_m, a, b).$$

Since both simulated and adversarial transcripts satisfy the verification equation w.r.t. the same R, we have

$$g^{\hat{t}} h^{\beta_x} = R = g^{\tilde{t}} h^{\tilde{\beta}_x}.$$

which leads to a non-trivial DL relation.

If $\mu \neq \tilde{\mu}$, the analysis is similar to the case where $\tilde{T}_i \neq T_i$. The verification equation satisfied by $\mathcal{T}_{\mathsf{BP}}$ is

$$(\mathbf{g}^{(m)})^a (\mathbf{h}^{(m)})^b (u')^{ab}$$
$$= \left(\prod_{i=1}^{m} L_i^{x_i^2} \right) \cdot \left(\prod_{i=1}^{m} R_i^{x_i^{-2}} \right) \cdot h^{-\mu} \cdot \tilde{A}_I^{\tilde{x}} \cdot \tilde{A}_O^{\tilde{x}^2} \cdot (\tilde{\mathbf{h}}')^{-\check{\mathbf{y}}^n}$$
$$\cdot \tilde{W}_L^{\tilde{x}} \cdot \tilde{W}_R^{\tilde{x}} \cdot \tilde{W}_O \cdot \tilde{S}^{\tilde{x}^3} \cdot (u')^{\hat{t}}.$$

Dividing it by the verification equation for the simulated transcript, we get

$$(\mathbf{g}^{(m)})^a (\mathbf{h}^{(m)})^b (u')^{ab} \cdot (\tilde{\mathbf{g}}^{(m)})^{-\tilde{a}} (\tilde{\mathbf{h}}^{(m)})^{-\tilde{b}} (\tilde{u}')^{-\tilde{a}\tilde{b}}$$
$$= \left(\prod_{i=1}^{m} L_i^{x_i^2} \right) \left(\prod_{i=1}^{m} \tilde{L}_i^{-\tilde{x}_i^2} \right) \left(\prod_{i=1}^{m} R_i^{x_i^{-2}} \right) \left(\prod_{i=1}^{m} \tilde{R}_i^{-\tilde{x}_i^{-2}} \right)$$
$$\cdot h^{-(\mu-\tilde{\mu})} \cdot (u')^{\hat{t}} \cdot (\tilde{u}')^{-\hat{t}}. \tag{6}$$

We rearrange the exponents w.r.t. the generators $(g, h, \mathbf{g}, \mathbf{h}, u)$. Let us focus on the exponent of h. Then the exponent of h in (6) is

$$\sum_{i=1}^{m} l_{i,g} x_i^2 + \sum_{i=1}^{m} r_{i,g} x_i^{-2} - (\mu - \tilde{\mu}) \tag{7}$$

where $l_{i,h}$ (resp. $r_{i,h}$) is the exponent of h available as group representation of L_i (resp. R_i) submitted by the adversary. Using the same argument as before, since the h-component in the left-hand side of 6 is 0, if $\mu \neq \tilde{\mu}$ we obtain non-trivial DL relation except with negligible probability.

If $L_i \neq \tilde{L}_i$ or $R_i \neq \tilde{R}_i$ This part of the proof uses similar techniques as the ones for Lemma 8 in [22], with the main difference that we explicitly show the equalities and constraints that must hold for all exponents of parameters $\mathbf{g}, \mathbf{h}, g, h, u$. For instance, we introduce polynomials $\ell^{\mathbf{g}}$ and $\ell^{\mathbf{h}}$ which are essential for the full analysis, but were absent from proof in [22].

Let the representations output by the adversary for L_i, R_i be

$$L_i = \prod_{j=1}^{n} \left(g_j^{l_{ig_j}} h_j^{l_{ih_j}} \right) g^{l_g} h^{l_h} u^{l_u} \text{ and } R_i = \prod_{j=1}^{n} \left(g_j^{r_{ig_j}} h_j^{r_{ih_j}} \right) g^{r_g} h^{r_h} u^{r_u}$$

and let $P' = \prod_{j=1}^{n} \left(g_j^{p'_{g_j}} h_j^{p'_{h_j}} \right) g^{p'_g} h^{p'_h} u^{p'_u}$ be the representation of P' which is same in both the transcript of the simulator and the one of the adversary. In what follows we prove that the exponents of L_i (resp. R_i) match those of $\tilde{L}_i$ (resp. $\tilde{R}_i$) for $i = 1, \ldots, m$ except with negligible probability and otherwise one can find non-trivial discrete-log relation. Let $\mathrm{bit}(k, i, t)$ be the function that return the bit k_i where $(k_1, \cdots, k_t)$ is the t-bit representation of k.

Since $\mathcal{T}$ is accepting, the outcome of InPrd.V should be 1, and therefore, the following must hold:

$$(\mathbf{g}^{(m)})^a (\mathbf{h}^{(m)})^b (u')^{ab} = \left(\prod_{i=1}^{m} L_i^{x_i^2} \right) P' \left(\prod_{i=1}^{m} R_i^{x_i^{-2}} \right), \tag{8}$$

where $\mathbf{g}^{(m)}, \mathbf{h}^{(m)}$ are parameters for the last round, and a, b are the last round messages. All terms in this equality can be expressed in terms of $\mathbf{g}, \mathbf{h}, g, h, u$ and we can compute the tuple

$$(e_{\mathbf{g}}^{(2)}, e_{\mathbf{h}}^{(2)}, e_g^{(2)}, e_h^{(2)}, e_u^{(2)})$$

such that $\mathbf{g}^{e_{\mathbf{g}}^{(2)}} \mathbf{h}^{e_{\mathbf{h}}^{(2)}} g^{e_g^{(2)}} h^{e_h^{(2)}} u^{e_u^{(2)}} = 1$. We compute $e_{\mathbf{g}}^{(2)}, e_{\mathbf{h}}^{(2)}, e_g^{(2)}, e_h^{(2)}, e_u^{(2)}$ as in Eqs. 9 to 13. Note that if $\mathcal{T}$ is accepting, $(e_{\mathbf{g}}^{(2)}, e_{\mathbf{h}}^{(2)}, e_g^{(2)}, e_h^{(2)}, e_u^{(2)}) = (\mathbf{0}, \mathbf{0}, 0, 0, 0)$, otherwise we get a non-trivial discrete-log relation.

For $k=0$ to $n-1$:

$$e_{g_{k+1}}^{(2)} = 0$$
$$= \left(\sum_{i=1}^{m} (l_{ig_{1+k}} x_i^2 + r_{ig_{1+k}} x_i^{-2}) + p'_{g_{1+k}} \right) - a \cdot \left(\prod_{i=1}^{m} x_i^{(-1)^{1-\text{bit}(k,i,m)}} \right) \tag{9}$$

$$e_{h_{k+1}}^{(2)} = 0$$
$$= \left(\sum_{i=1}^{m} (l_{ih_{1+k}} x_i^2 + r_{ih_{1+k}} x_i^{-2}) + p'_{h_{1+k}} \right) - by^{(-(k))} \cdot \left(\prod_{i=1}^{m} x_i^{(-1)^{\text{bit}(k,i,m)}} \right) \tag{10}$$

$$e_u^{(2)} = 0 = \left(\sum_{i=1}^{m} (l_{iu} x_i^2 + r_{iu} x_i^{-2}) + p'_u \right) - w \cdot ab \tag{11}$$

$$e_g^{(2)} = 0 = \left(\sum_{i=1}^{m} (l_{ig} x_i^2 + r_{ig} x_i^{-2}) + p'_g \right) \tag{12}$$

$$e_h^{(2)} = 0 = \left(\sum_{i=1}^{m} (l_{ih} x_i^2 + r_{ih} x_i^{-2}) + p'_h \right) \tag{13}$$

In order to derive relation between values $l_{ig_j}, r_{ig_j}, l_{ih_j}, r_{ih_j}, u_i$, and the group representation of statement P', we will invoke Schwartz-Zippel lemma in a recursive way. It is convenient to define the following polynomials to invoke the lemma recursively. For all $t \in \{1, \dots, m\}$, for all $j \in \{0, \dots, n-1\}$,

$$f_{t,j}^{\mathbf{g}}(X) = l_{t,g_{1+j}} X^2 + r_{t,g_{1+j}} X^{-2} + p'_{g_{1+j}} + \sum_{i=1}^{k-1} (l_{i,g_{1+j}} x_i^2 + r_{i,g_{1+j}} x_i^{-2}),$$

$$f_{t,j}^{\mathbf{h}}(X) = l_{t,h_{1+j}} X^2 + r_{t,h_{1+j}} X^{-2} + p'_{h_{1+j}} + \sum_{i=1}^{k-1} (l_{i,h_{1+j}} x_i^2 + r_{i,h_{1+j}} x_i^{-2}),$$

and

$$f_t^u(X) = l_{t,u}X^2 + r_{t,u}X^{-2} + p_u' + \sum_{i=1}^{t-1}\left(l_{i,u}x_i^2 + r_{i,u}x_i^{-2}\right).$$

Combining different polynomials, one can eliminate a (and b) from Eq. (9) (and similarly from (10)) and rewrite the resultant equation in terms of polynomial $f_{t,j}^{\mathbf{g}}$ (similarly, $f_{t,j}^{\mathbf{h}}$) to get: For $t \in \{1,\ldots,m\}$, $j \in \{0,\ldots,n/2^t - 1\}$,

$$f_{t,j}^{\mathbf{g}}(x_t) \cdot x_t^2 - f_{t,j+n/2^t}^{\mathbf{g}}(x_t) = 0 \tag{14}$$

and

$$f_{\log(n)}^u(x_{\log(n)}) - w \cdot f_{\log(n),j}^{\mathbf{g}}(x_{\log(n)}) \cdot f_{\log(n),j}^{\mathbf{h}}(x_{\log(n)}) = 0. \tag{15}$$

Since all the challenges are in order, we rewrite (14) as a univariate polynomial in terms of variable X_t:

$$f_{t,j}^{\mathbf{g}}(X_t) \cdot X_t^2 - f_{t,j+n/2^t}^{\mathbf{g}}(X_t) = 0. \tag{16}$$

(16) vanishes with probability at most $6/(p-1)$, and otherwise it is a zero polynomial. Equating each coefficient term to 0, we get

$$r_{t,g_{1+j}} = f_{t-1,j+n/2^t}^{\mathbf{g}}(x_{t-1}),\ l_{t,g_{1+j}} = 0,\ r_{t,g_{j+n/2^t}} = 0, \tag{17}$$

$$l_{t,g_{j+n/2^t}} = p_{g_{1+j}}' + \sum_{i=1}^{t-1}(l_{i,g_{1+j}}x_i^2 + r_{i,g_{1+j}}x_i^{-2}) = \ell_{t-1,j}^{\mathbf{g}}(x_{t-1}) \tag{18}$$

where the last term in (18) can be rewritten as a univariate polynomial:

$$\ell_{t-1,j}^{\mathbf{g}}(X) = l_{t-1,g_{1+j}}X^2 + r_{t-1,g_{1+j}}X^{-2} + p_{g_{1+j}}' + \sum_{i=1}^{t-2}(l_{ig_{1+j}}x_i^2 + r_{ig_{1+j}}x_i^{-2}).$$

Iterating a similar argument for all rounds, for $t = 1$ we get, $r_{1,g_{1+j}} = p_{g_{1+j+n/2}}'$ and $l_{1,g_{j+n/2}} = p_{g_{1+j}}'$. Similarly, arguing for polynomial $f_{k,j}^{\mathbf{h}}$, we get the condition:

$$f_{t-1,j}^{\mathbf{h}}(X_t) \cdot X_t^{-2} - f_{t,j+n/2^t}^{\mathbf{h}}(X_t) = 0. \tag{19}$$

Analogous to polynomial $\ell_{t,j}^{\mathbf{g}}$, we define $\ell_{t,j}^{\mathbf{h}}(X) = l_{t-1,h_{1+j}}X^2 + r_{t-1,h_{1+j}}X^{-2} + p_{h_{1+j}}' + \sum_{i=1}^{t-2}(l_{ih_{1+j}}x_i^2 + r_{ih_{1+j}}x_i^{-2})$. Equalities 16, 19 gives following constraints: For all $t \in \{2,\ldots,m\}$, for all $j \in \{0,\ldots,n/2 - 1\}$:

$$r_{tg_{1+j}} = f_{t-1,j+n/2^t}^{\mathbf{g}}(x_{t-1}),\ l_{tg_{1+j}} = 0,\ r_{t,g_{j+n/2^t}} = 0,$$

$$l_{t,g_{j+n/2^t}} = \ell_{t,j}^{\mathbf{g}}(x_{t-1}),\ r_{th_{1+j}} = 0,\ l_{th_{1+j}} = f_{t-1,j+n/2^t}^{\mathbf{h}}(x_{t-1}) \cdot y^{n/2^t}, \tag{20}$$

$$l_{t,h_{1+j+n/2^t}} = 0,\ r_{t,h_{1+j+n/2^t}} = \ell_{t,j}^{\mathbf{h}}(x_{t-1})$$

For $t = 1$, for all $j \in \{0, \ldots, n/2 - 1\}$:

$$r_{1g_{1+j}} = p'_{g_{1+n/2}},\ l_{1g_{1+j}} = 0,\ r_{1,g_{j+n/2}} = 0,$$

$$l_{1,g_{j+n/2}} = p'_{g_{1+j}},\ r_{1h_{1+j}} = 0, l_{1h_{1+j}} = p'_{h_{1+j+n/2}} \cdot y^{n/2}, \tag{21}$$

$$l_{1,h_{1+j+n/2}} = 0,\ r_{1,h_{1+j+n/2}} = p'_{h_{1+j}} \cdot y^{n/2}$$

Note that the output of polynomials $f^{\mathbf{g}}_{k,j}, f^{\mathbf{h}}_{k,j}, \ell^{\mathbf{g}}_{k,j}, \ell^{\mathbf{h}}_{k,j}$ are deterministic given challenges $(x_1, \ldots, x_k)$. Also note, values $p'_{\mathbf{g}}, \ldots, p'_u$ are fixed as they are equal to the representation output by the simulator. Hence, values for $r_{i,g_{1+j}}, r_{i,h_{1+j}}$, $l_{i,g_{1+j}}$ and $l_{i,h_{1+j}}$ (in Eq. 21) are fixed given previous round challenges.

Now, consider exponents for generators g, h and u. Since Eqs. (11, 12, 13) hold, using Schwartz-Zippel lemma recursively, it can be shown that $l_{i,u}, r_{i,u} = 0, l_{i,g}, r_{i,g}, l_{i,h} = r_{i,h} = 0$.

Note that, for a honest execution of InPrd, the exponents for L_i, R_i are derived using constraints in (21). Thus, L_i, R_i cannot differ from $\tilde{L}_i, \tilde{R}_i$.

Concrete Advantage of the Adversary. This analysis comes directly from the Bad Challenge analysis for ACSPf in [22]. For the case $T_i \neq \tilde{T}_i$, the adversary succeeds in forging if any one of the polynomials $e^{(0)}_g, \ldots, e^{(m)}_g$ vanishes. Using union bound, this happens with probability $4(m + 1)/(p - 1)$. Similarly, for the case $\mu \neq \tilde{\mu}$, we break discrete-log relation except with probability: $4m + 1/(p-1)$. Now, consider the case, $L_i \neq \tilde{L}_i$. The adversary succeeds in forging a proof for a false statement if they were lucky enough to get a challenge x_i such that Eqs. 15, 16 and 19 vanish at x_i. This means, for round $t \in \{1, \ldots, m = \log(n)\}$, if any of the $\sum^{t-1}_{i=1} 2n/2^t$ polynomials of degree at most 4, $2n/2^t$ polynomials of degree at most 6, and one polynomial of degree at most 8, vanish, i.e., adversary succeeding in forging a proof, which turns out to be at most $(14n + 8)/(p - 1)$. Note that the adversary can query $\mathbf{O}_{\mathsf{ext}}$ for SR-UR q times. It is enough to take max of all case-by-case probabilities to get an upper bound for the probability of the adversary succeeding in forging a proof. This is because all the cases are sequential and the adversary succeeds in forging unless we break discrete-log relation for the very first case that the adversary exploits. Thus, adversary succeeds in forging a proof with probability at most $(14n + 8)q/(p - 1)$. $\quad\square$

Combining the results from Theorem 4 and Claim 2, we get the following corollary.

Corollary 1. *Fiat-Shamir transform of* BP *satisfies* **FS-SIM-EXT** *with respect to a canonical simulator* $\mathcal{S}_{\mathsf{FS\text{-}BP}}$ *corresponding to the algebraic simulator* $\mathcal{S}_{\mathsf{BP}}$. *Concretely, there exists an efficient* **FS-SIM-EXT** *extractor* $\mathcal{E}^*$ *for* FS-BP *such that for every non-uniform algebraic prover* $\mathcal{P}^*_{\mathsf{alg}}$ *against* FS-BP *that makes* q_1 *random oracle queries and* q_2 *simulation queries, and for every distinguisher* $\mathcal{D}^*$, *there exists a non-uniform adversary* $\mathcal{A}$ *against* **DL-REL** *with the property that for all* $\lambda \in \mathbb{N}^+$,

$$\mathbf{Adv}^{\textit{FS-SIM-EXT}}_{\textit{FS-BP},\mathcal{R}}(\mathcal{S}_{\textit{FS-BP}},\mathcal{E}^*,\mathcal{P}^*_{\textsf{alg}},\mathcal{D}^*,\lambda) \leq \left(\mathbf{Adv}^{\textit{DL-REL}}(\mathbb{G}_\lambda,\mathcal{A}_\lambda) + \frac{(14n+8)q_1}{(p-1)}\right)$$
$$+q_2 \cdot \left(\mathbf{Adv}^{\textit{DL-REL}}(\mathbb{G}_\lambda,\mathcal{A}_\lambda) + \frac{(14n+8)q_2}{(p-1)}\right) + \frac{(q_2+1)(q_1+1)}{|\textsf{Ch}_{i_0}|}$$

where $i_0 \in [1,r]$ is the round with the smallest challenge set $\textsf{Ch}_{i_0}$.

Acknowledgment. The authors are grateful to Thomas Attema, Matteo Campanelli, Jelle Don, Serge Fehr, Ashrujit Ghoshal, Christian Majenz, Stefano Tessaro, and anonymous reviewers of EUROCRYPT 2022 for helpful comments and insightful discussions. This research was supported by: the Concordium Blockchain Research Center, Aarhus University, Denmark; the Carlsberg Foundation under the Semper Ardens Research Project CF18-112 (BCM); the European Research Council (ERC) under the European Unions's Horizon 2020 research and innovation programme under grant agreement No 803096 (SPEC); Core Research Grant CRG/2020/004488, SERB, Department of Science and Technology.

References

1. Abdalla, M., Barbosa, M., Katz, J., Loss, J., Xu, J.: Algebraic adversaries in the universal composability framework. Cryptology ePrint Archive, Report 2021/1218 (2021). https://ia.cr/2021/1218
2. Abdolmaleki, B., Ramacher, S., Slamanig, D.: Lift-and-shift obtaining simulation extractable subversion and updatable SNARKs generically. In: Ligatti, J., Ou, X., Katz, J., Vigna, G. (eds.) ACM CCS, pp. 1987–2005. ACM Press, New York (2020). https://doi.org/10.1145/3372297.3417228
3. Baghery, K., Kohlweiss, M., Siim, J., Volkhov, M.: Another look at extraction and randomization of groth's zk-snark. Cryptology ePrint Archive, Report 2020/811 (2020). https://ia.cr/2020/811
4. Bellare, M., Neven, G.: Multi-signatures in the plain public-key model and a general forking lemma. In: Juels, A., Wright, R.N., De Capitani di Vimercati, S. (eds.) ACM CCS, pp. 390–399. ACM Press, New York (2006). https://doi.org/10.1145/1180405.1180453
5. Ben-Sasson, E., Chiesa, A., Spooner, N.: Interactive oracle proofs. In: Hirt, M., Smith, A. (eds.) TCC 2016. LNCS, vol. 9986, pp. 31–60. Springer, Heidelberg (2016). https://doi.org/10.1007/978-3-662-53644-5_2
6. Bünz, B., Bootle, J., Boneh, D., Poelstra, A., Wuille, P., Maxwell, G.: Bulletproofs: short proofs for confidential transactions and more. In: 2018 IEEE Symposium on Security and Privacy, pp. 315–334. IEEE Computer Society Press (2018). https://doi.org/10.1109/SP.2018.00020
7. Bünz, B., Bootle, J., Boneh, D., Poelstra, A., Wuille, P., Maxwell, G.: Bulletproofs: short proofs for confidential transactions and more. Cryptology ePrint Archive, Report 2017/1066 (2017). https://eprint.iacr.org/2017/1066
8. Bünz, B., Maller, M., Mishra, P., Tyagi, N., Vesely, P.: Proofs for inner pairing products and applications. Cryptology ePrint Archive, Report 2019/1177 (2019). https://eprint.iacr.org/2019/1177

9. Canetti, R., Chen, Y., Holmgren, J., Lombardi, A., Rothblum, G.N., Rothblum, R.D.: Fiat-Shamir from simpler assumptions. Cryptology ePrint Archive, Report 2018/1004 (2018). https://eprint.iacr.org/2018/1004

10. Canetti, R., et al.: Fiat-Shamir: from practice to theory. In: Charikar, M., Cohen, E. (eds.) 51st ACM STOC, pp. 1082–1090. ACM Press, New York (2019). https://doi.org/10.1145/3313276.3316380

11. Cramer, R., Damgård, I., Schoenmakers, B.: Proofs of partial knowledge and simplified design of witness hiding protocols. In: Desmedt, Y.G. (ed.) CRYPTO 1994. LNCS, vol. 839, pp. 174–187. Springer, Heidelberg (1994). https://doi.org/10.1007/3-540-48658-5_19

12. De Santis, A., Di Crescenzo, G., Ostrovsky, R., Persiano, G., Sahai, A.: Robust noninteractive zero knowledge. In: Kilian, J. (ed.) CRYPTO 2001. LNCS, vol. 2139, pp. 566–598. Springer, Heidelberg (2001). https://doi.org/10.1007/3-540-44647-8_33

13. Decker, C., Wattenhofer, R.: Bitcoin transaction malleability and MtGox. In: Kutyłowski, M., Vaidya, J. (eds.) ESORICS 2014. LNCS, vol. 8713, pp. 313–326. Springer, Cham (2014). https://doi.org/10.1007/978-3-319-11212-1_18

14. Dolev, D., Dwork, C., Naor, M.: Non-malleable cryptography (extended abstract). In: 23rd ACM STOC, pp. 542–552. ACM Press, New York (1991). https://doi.org/10.1145/103418.103474

15. Don, J., Fehr, S., Majenz, C.: The measure-and-reprogram technique 2.0: multiround Fiat-Shamir and more. In: Micciancio, D., Ristenpart, T. (eds.) CRYPTO 2020. LNCS, vol. 12172, pp. 602–631. Springer, Cham (2020). https://doi.org/10.1007/978-3-030-56877-1_21

16. Faust, S., Kohlweiss, M., Marson, G.A., Venturi, D.: On the non-malleability of the Fiat-Shamir transform. In: Galbraith, S., Nandi, M. (eds.) INDOCRYPT 2012. LNCS, vol. 7668, pp. 60–79. Springer, Heidelberg (2012). https://doi.org/10.1007/978-3-642-34931-7_5

17. Fiat, A., Shamir, A.: How To prove yourself: practical solutions to identification and signature problems. In: Odlyzko, A.M. (ed.) CRYPTO 1986. LNCS, vol. 263, pp. 186–194. Springer, Heidelberg (1987). https://doi.org/10.1007/3-540-47721-7_12

18. Fischlin, M.: Communication-efficient non-interactive proofs of knowledge with online extractors. In: Shoup, V. (ed.) CRYPTO 2005. LNCS, vol. 3621, pp. 152–168. Springer, Heidelberg (2005). https://doi.org/10.1007/11535218_10

19. Fuchsbauer, G., Kiltz, E., Loss, J.: The algebraic group model and its applications. In: Shacham, H., Boldyreva, A. (eds.) CRYPTO 2018. LNCS, vol. 10992, pp. 33–62. Springer, Cham (2018). https://doi.org/10.1007/978-3-319-96881-0_2

20. Gabizon, A., Williamson, Z.J., Ciobotaru, O.: PLONK: permutations over lagrange-bases for oecumenical noninteractive arguments of knowledge. Cryptology ePrint Archive, Report 2019/953 (2019). https://eprint.iacr.org/2019/953

21. Ganesh, C., Orlandi, C., Pancholi, M., Takahashi, A., Tschudi, D.: Fiat-shamir bulletproofs are non-malleable (in the algebraic group model). Cryptology ePrint Archive, Report 2021/1393 (2021). https://eprint.iacr.org/2021/1393

22. Ghoshal, A., Tessaro, S.: Tight state-restoration soundness in the algebraic group model. In: Malkin, T., Peikert, C. (eds.) CRYPTO 2021. LNCS, vol. 12827, pp. 64–93. Springer, Cham (2021). https://doi.org/10.1007/978-3-030-84252-9_3

23. Goldwasser, S., Kalai, Y.T.: On the (in)security of the Fiat-Shamir paradigm. In: 44th FOCS, pp. 102–115. IEEE Computer Society Press (2003). https://doi.org/10.1109/SFCS.2003.1238185

24. Goldwasser, S., Micali, S., Rackoff, C.: The knowledge complexity of interactive proof-systems (extended abstract). In: 17th ACM STOC, pp. 291–304. ACM Press (1985). https://doi.org/10.1145/22145.22178

25. Groth, J.: Simulation-sound NIZK proofs for a practical language and constant size group signatures. In: Lai, X., Chen, K. (eds.) ASIACRYPT 2006. LNCS, vol. 4284, pp. 444–459. Springer, Heidelberg (2006). https://doi.org/10.1007/11935230_29

26. Groth, J.: On the size of pairing-based non-interactive arguments. In: Fischlin, M., Coron, J.-S. (eds.) EUROCRYPT 2016. LNCS, vol. 9666, pp. 305–326. Springer, Heidelberg (2016). https://doi.org/10.1007/978-3-662-49896-5_11

27. Groth, J., Maller, M.: Snarky signatures: minimal signatures of knowledge from simulation-extractable SNARKs. In: Katz, J., Shacham, H. (eds.) CRYPTO 2017. LNCS, vol. 10402, pp. 581–612. Springer, Cham (2017). https://doi.org/10.1007/978-3-319-63715-0_20

28. Groth, J., Ostrovsky, R.: Cryptography in the multi-string model. In: Menezes, A. (ed.) CRYPTO 2007. LNCS, vol. 4622, pp. 323–341. Springer, Heidelberg (2007). https://doi.org/10.1007/978-3-540-74143-5_18

29. Holmgren, J.: On round-by-round soundness and state restoration attacks. Cryptology ePrint Archive, Report 2019/1261 (2019). https://eprint.iacr.org/2019/1261

30. Kohlweiss, M., Zając, M.: On simulation-extractability of universal zksnarks. Cryptology ePrint Archive, Report 2021/511 (2021). https://eprint.iacr.org/2021/511

31. Maller, M., Bowe, S., Kohlweiss, M., Meiklejohn, S.: Sonic: zero-knowledge SNARKs from linear-size universal and updatable structured reference strings. In: Cavallaro, L., Kinder, J., Wang, X., Katz, J. (eds.) ACM CCS, pp. 2111–2128. ACM Press, New York (2019). https://doi.org/10.1145/3319535.3339817

32. Pass, R.: On deniability in the common reference string and random oracle model. In: Boneh, D. (ed.) CRYPTO 2003. LNCS, vol. 2729, pp. 316–337. Springer, Heidelberg (2003). https://doi.org/10.1007/978-3-540-45146-4_19

33. Sahai, A.: Non-malleable non-interactive zero knowledge and adaptive chosen-ciphertext security. In: 40th FOCS, pp. 543–553. IEEE Computer Society Press (1999). https://doi.org/10.1109/SFFCS.1999.814628

34. Unruh, D.: Non-interactive zero-knowledge proofs in the quantum random oracle model. In: Oswald, E., Fischlin, M. (eds.) EUROCRYPT 2015. LNCS, vol. 9057, pp. 755–784. Springer, Heidelberg (2015). https://doi.org/10.1007/978-3-662-46803-6_25

35. Unruh, D.: Post-quantum security of Fiat-Shamir. In: Takagi, T., Peyrin, T. (eds.) ASIACRYPT 2017. LNCS, vol. 10624, pp. 65–95. Springer, Cham (2017). https://doi.org/10.1007/978-3-319-70694-8_3

Gemini: Elastic SNARKs for Diverse Environments

Jonathan Bootle[1]([envelope]) [iD], Alessandro Chiesa[2,3], Yuncong Hu[3] [iD],
and Michele Orrú[3]([envelope]) [iD]

[1] IBM Research, Zurich, Switzerland
jbt@zurich.ibm.com
[2] École polytechnique fédérale de Lausanne, Lausanne, Switzerland
alessandro.chiesa@epfl.ch
[3] University of California, Berkeley, Berkeley, USA
{yuncong_hu,michele.orru}@berkeley.edu

Abstract. We introduce a new class of succinct arguments, that we call
elastic. Elastic SNARKs allow the prover to allocate different resources
(such as memory and time) depending on the execution environment
and the statement to prove. The resulting output is independent of the
prover's configuration. To study elastic SNARKs, we extend the streaming paradigm of [Block et al., TCC'20]. We provide a definitional framework for elastic polynomial interactive oracle proofs for R1CS instances
and design a compiler which transforms an elastic PIOP into a preprocessing argument system that supports streaming or random access to
its inputs. Depending on the configuration, the prover will choose different trade-offs for time (either linear, or quasilinear) and memory (either
linear, or logarithmic). We prove the existence of elastic SNARKS by presenting Gemini, a novel FFT-free preprocessing argument. We prove its
security and develop a proof-of-concept implementation in Rust based
on the arkworks framework. We provide benchmarks for large R1CS
instances of tens of billions of gates on a single machine.

Keywords: Succinct non-interactive arguments · Interactive oracle
proofs

1 Introduction

Succinct non-interactive arguments of knowledge (SNARKs) allow for efficient
verification of NP statements. They are an essential component for a number of
protocols, including private transactions [Ben+14b, Zcash], verifiable computation [Ben+14a, Boo+18, Gen+13], and anonymous credentials [Bel+09, GGM14].
Recent years have seen a surge of interest in SNARKs, and after much
dedicated research reducing communication complexity and verifier complexity [Par+13, Boo+16, Tha13], the cost of running the prover algorithm has
emerged as the most relevant bottleneck.

Today, the most important factors are the time and memory required to run
the prover algorithm. For example, in *zk-rollups*[1], some nodes in the network

---

[1] https://ethereum.org/en/developers/docs/scaling/layer-2-rollups/.

© International Association for Cryptologic Research 2022
O. Dunkelman and S. Dziembowski (Eds.): EUROCRYPT 2022, LNCS 13276, pp. 427–457, 2022.
https://doi.org/10.1007/978-3-031-07085-3_15

(called *relayers*) must produce a SNARK proving validity of a large amount of transactions. Here, the instance being proven may contain billions of constraints. Even more resource-intensive is the Filecoin network: daily, Filecoin generates proofs for about 930 B constraints[2]. In both cases, the ability to prove massive statements efficiently is critical, yet many SNARK implementations today can't prove circuits of tens of billions of constraints. This work investigates time- and space-efficient SNARKSs, and the possible compromises that can be made within the same proving algorithm to get the best of both worlds.

Fast Prover. A colossal effort has been put into reducing computational overheads for the prover. A long line of works [Set20, BCG20, Boo+17, Boo+18, Xie+19] focusing on prover efficiency has led to SNARKs whose prover algorithm runs in linear (or *almost-linear*) time with respect to the instance and the witness. Some works [Zha+21, JW17] even rely on specialized hardware to accelerate prover computation. Unfortunately, most linear-time provers [Tha13] exploit dynamic programming techniques and as a consequence also require random access to both instance and witness, and demand space linear in the instance size. When proving large instances, this makes them prohibitively greedy in terms of memory.

Slim Prover. A recent research direction [HR18, Blo+20, Blo+21] investigated, from a theoretical perspective, the possibility of a space-efficient prover. This line of work considers provers that have *streaming access* to the inputs (the statement and the witness), rather than random access to them. It has been shown [Blo+20] that a space-efficient prover needs only logarithmic memory space throughout their entire execution, but requires quasilinear computation time.

Serving Diverse Computing Environments. Each of the above lines of research aims to optimise for a single type of complexity measure. Works which optimise for prover time assume that large amounts of memory are available, which is unlikely to be the case for considerably large instances. On the other hand, for works which focus on optimising for prover space, time efficiency is not a priority, and time overheads may be problematic in practice. In the best case, one could envisage a SNARK which simultaneously runs in linear time and uses only logarithmic memory space by accessing its inputs via streams. Unfortunately, constructing such SNARKs remains a challenging open problem. Complexity-preserving SNARKs [BC12, Bit+13], which aim to preserve both time and space complexity, are a step in the right direction. Sadly, the notion of complexity-preservation in this works allows polylogarithmic blow-ups in time and space, and this looseness makes complexity preserving SNARKs inefficient in practice. In this work, our goal is to meaningfully relax the goal of complexity preservation, in a way that allows us to serve many different computing environments in a concretely-efficient manner.

---

[2] https://research.protocol.ai/sites/snarks/.

1.1 Our Results

(i) Elastic SNARKs. Roughly speaking, we consider SNARKs whose prover admits two different implementations:

- the *time-efficient* prover $\mathcal{P}_t$, which receives as input instance and witness;
- the *space-efficient* prover $\mathcal{P}_s$, which has streaming access to the same inputs.

Provided with this "dual-mode" framework, an elastic prover can choose which implementation to use, and allocate resources depending on the execution environment and the instance size. In addition, the two algorithms are compatible in such a way that during the execution of the protocol the space-efficient prover can stop and transcribe a (compressed) prover state. Then, the prover can switch to the time-efficient implementation, enjoying the benefits of a fast prover.

To achieve the above, we extend the notion of streams of Block et al. [Blo+20]: we study stream composition, and provide a definitional framework for streaming holographic polynomial IOPs for Rank-1 Constraint Systems (R1CSs) instances. We construct a compiler that transforms an elastic PIOP into a preprocessing argument using elastic polynomial commitment schemes.

(ii) An elastic SNARK for R1CS.

We realize the above notion by constructing a novel argument system for R1CS, whose prover admits a time-efficient mode and a space-efficient mode. The two modes are compatible in such a way that it is possible to migrate state from one to the other, and produce the same final proof independently of the prover configuration.

Definition 1. *The R1CS problem asks: given a finite field* $\mathbb{F}$, *coefficient matrices* $A, B, C \in \mathbb{F}^{N \times N}$ *each containing at most* $M = \Omega(N)$ *non-zero entries,[3] and an instance vector* $\mathbf{x}$ *over* $\mathbb{F}$, *is there a witness vector* $\mathbf{w}$ *such that* $\mathbf{z} := (\mathbf{x}, \mathbf{w}) \in \mathbb{F}^N$ *and* $A\mathbf{z} \circ B\mathbf{z} = C\mathbf{z}$?

Above, "○" denotes the entry-wise product. We use standard Landau notation. When referring to time efficiency, the asymptotic number of cryptographic operations (that is, group operations) will be denoted by O_λ, to distinguish them from (less expensive) field operations, that instead we denote with standard big-O notation. Our main contribution is the following theorem:

Theorem 1 (informal). *There exists an elastic SNARK for* $\mathcal{R}_{\text{R1CS}}$ *whose prover admits two implementations:*

- *the* time-efficient *prover runs in* $O_\lambda(M)$ *time and* $O(M)$ *space;*
- *the* space-efficient *prover runs in* $O_\lambda(M \log^2 M)$ *time and* $O(\log M)$ *space,*

where M *is the number of non-zero entries in the R1CS instance. The proof can be verified in* $O_\lambda(|\mathbf{x}| + \log M)$ *time, and has size* $O(\log M)$.

---

[3] Note that $M = \Omega(N)$ without loss of generality because if $M < N/3$ then there are variables of $\mathbf{z}$ that do not participate in any constraint, which can be dropped. Thus the main size measure for R1CS is the sparsity parameter M.

To achieve the above, we study the commitment of Kate et al. [KZG10] from the perspective of an elastic commitment scheme, which involves constructing a streaming interface for commitment and opening algorithms.

Then, we construct an elastic scalar product protocol that runs in linear-time and linear-space, or quasi-linear time and log-space. Our scalar product argument is based on the sumcheck protocol which, thanks to its recursive nature, allows us to easily migrate from a space-efficient instance to a time-efficient one. Using the above elastic scalar product protocol, we build a polynomial IOP [BCS16] for R1CS.

Finally, we give a compiler which uses elastic polynomial commitment schemes and elastic polynomial IOPs to construct elastic cryptographic arguments. This modularity is beneficial not only for protocol design but also reflects the actual implementation. On the one hand, when studying a complex protocol, one can still isolate the cryptographic components from the information-theoretic part to study its complexity and its security. On the other hand, the implementation can benefit from an abstraction layer that reduces the implementation overhead.

Using similar techniques, we provide a preprocessing SNARK with the same complexity.

(iii) Implementation. We implement the construction of Theorem 1 in Rust using the arkworks ecosystem [ark]. Our implementation consists of the main preprocessing argument, and a *non-preprocessing argument* (where the verification procedure is assumed access to the R1CS instance in full). Extending the library with streaming-friendly primitives required a notable engineering effort that we believe could be of independent interest for future space-efficient projects. In Sect. 2.7, we give an overview of the relevant design choices and provide a number of algorithmic optimizations.

(iv) Evaluation. While there are plenty of benchmarks publicly available for time-efficient SNARKs, few works evaluate SNARKs on large circuits. To the best of our knowledge, the largest instance size ever proven in the literature is DIZK [Wu+18], with a maximal instance of size 2^{31}, and using a cluster of 20 machines in 256 executors.

Our benchmarks, described more in-depth in Sect. 2.8 show the following:

- Gemini is able to prove instances of arbitrary size. In particular, using a single machine with around 1 GB of memory budget, we are able to run benchmarks with instances of 2^{32} for the preprocessing argument. If the verifier is allowed to read the entire circuit (that is, a non-preprocessing argument), we were able to carry out proofs for 2^{35} constraints. In contrast, the largest instance ever proven in the literature [Wu+18] is only 2^{31}.

- Gemini is concretely and economically efficient. The preprocessing protocol can prove instances of size 2^{31} within two days and save about 82% (about 400 USD) of expenses when comparing with DIZK on Amazon EC2.

- Gemini provides succinct proofs and verifiers. For instances of size 2^{35}, the proof size is about 27 KB and the verification time is below 30 ms.

1.2 Related Work

There is a long line of work on improving the time complexity of SNARK provers, both asymptotically and concretely; this has culminated in SNARKs with linear-time provers. See [Gol+21] and references therein. However, these optimizations typically come at the expense of space complexity, which is typically linear in the computation size either due to the use of FFTs or dynamic programming algorithms.

Simultaneously optimizing for time and space efficiency was first considered for succinct arguments in [BC12], via the notion of *complexity preservation*. This roughly means that the time and space to prove a computation must be asymptotically close to those for merely running the computation itself. Further constructions of complexity preserving succinct arguments were given in [Bit+13, HR18, Blo+20, Blo+21]. In all of these constructions space efficiency is achieved at the expense of a somewhat higher time complexity, due to the need for either a non-black-box use of cryptography or the need to perform multiple (indeed, logarithmically many) passes on the computation transcript.

Our goal in this work is to study succinct arguments that offer multiple algorithms for the same prover that optimize for different settings, e.g., for time efficiency or space efficiency. Moreover, prior works that study streaming SNARK provers were theoretical, while in this work we additionally study streaming implementations with concrete efficiency.

2 Techniques

In Sect. 2.1, we outline the streaming model. After setting some terminology, we state our main theorem, which is based on elastic polynomial commitment schemes and elastic probabilistic proofs. We describe then the two components separately: first, we describe an elastic polynomial commitment based on KZG in Sect. 2.3, and then we construct a polynomial PIOP for R1CS, which is itself based on a novel elastic scalar-product argument.

2.1 Elasticity and a Streaming Model

The notion of elasticity refers to having multiple realizations of the same algorithm (more precisely, function) for use in different situations. Specifically in this work:

> Elasticity means that we aim for two realizations: a **time-efficient realization** for a setting where time complexity is most important, possibly at the expense of space complexity; and a **space-efficient realization** for a setting where space complexity (i.e., memory consumption) is most important, possibly at the expense of time complexity.

This means that in theorem statements, and in their proofs, we will consider two realizations with different complexities for the same functionality (e.g., the SNARK prover algorithm).

Time-efficient algorithms are a familiar concept. To discuss space-efficiency, however, we must consider *streaming algorithms*, which receive their inputs in *streams* (small pieces at a time) so that we can design algorithms that use less memory than the size of their inputs. Below we describe: (i) a formal model of streams, and (ii) a notion of streaming algorithms, and how their efficiency behaves under composition.

Streams and Streaming Oracles. A *stream* is a tuple consisting of an alphabet Σ, a well-ordered countable set I, and a sequence $K \in \Sigma^I$. Streams can be accessed via special oracles: if K is a sequence, the *streaming oracle* $\mathcal{S}(K)$ of K takes two input commands, start and next; the oracle simply responds to the i-th next command with the i-th element of K; the stream $\mathcal{S}(K)$ can be reset to the first element in the sequence using the start command, in case earlier elements of the stream need to be viewed again. However, the streaming oracle does not allow random access to elements of K. In the full version, we define streaming relations in which the instance and the witness are given as streams.

Streaming Algorithms. A *streaming algorithm* is an algorithm that has access to all of its inputs via streaming oracles and produces a stream as its output, by yielding the next element on upon receiving the next command. The complexity of a streaming algorithm is measured in terms of its time complexity, space complexity, and the number of passes that it makes over each input stream.

Any binary operation over an alphabet can be viewed as a streaming algorithm which takes as input two sequences K and K' over the same alphabet Σ that are indexed by the same set I. In this case, the binary operation acts on successive pairs of elements of K and K', to produce a new stream on the fly. For instance, let $\mathbf{f}, \mathbf{g}$ be two vectors over a prime field $\mathbb{F}$ of order p, and $\mathcal{S}(\mathbf{f})$, $\mathcal{S}(\mathbf{g})$ (respectively) their canonical streams[4]. The stream $\mathcal{S}(\mathbf{f} + \rho\mathbf{g})$ for two vectors $\mathbf{f}, \mathbf{g}$ over a field $\mathbb{F}$ and scalar $\rho \in \mathbb{F}$ can be evaluated as a new stream using $\mathcal{S}(\mathbf{f})$ and $\mathcal{S}(\mathbf{g})$, by responding to each next query in the following way: first query $\mathcal{S}(\mathbf{f})$ to obtain the i-th entry f_i of $\mathbf{f}$, then query $\mathcal{S}(\mathbf{g})$ to obtain g_i, and finally respond with $f_i + \rho g_i$.

Since a streaming algorithm produces a stream as output, multiple streaming algorithms can be *composed* so that the output stream produced by one algorithm acts as the input stream for the next algorithm. The time and space complexity and number of input passes of streaming algorithms behave predictably under composition. If $\mathcal{A}$ is a streaming algorithm with time complexity $t_\mathcal{A}$, space complexity $s_\mathcal{A}$, and $k_\mathcal{A}$ input passes, and $\mathcal{B}$ is a streaming algorithm with time complexity $t_\mathcal{B}$, space complexity $s_\mathcal{B}$, and $k_\mathcal{B}$ input passes, then $\mathcal{A}$ composed with $\mathcal{B}$ has time complexity $t_\mathcal{A} + k_\mathcal{A}t_\mathcal{B}$, space complexity $s_\mathcal{A} + s_\mathcal{B}$, and $k_\mathcal{A}k_\mathcal{B}$ input passes.

2.2   A Modular Construction of Elastic SNARKs

Many succinct arguments are built in two steps. First, construct an information-theoretic probabilistic proof in a model where the verifier has a certain type of

---

[4] The canonical stream of a vector consists of the sequence of its entries, from last to first.

query access to the prover's messages. Second, compile the probabilistic proof into an interactive succinct argument, via a cryptographic commitment scheme that "supports" this query access[5]. Finally, if non-interactivity is desired, apply the Fiat–Shamir transformation [FS86]. This modular approach has enabled researchers to study the efficiency and security of simpler components, which has facilitated much progress in succinct arguments.

We observe that the techniques used in [Chi+20, BFS20] to build a compiler from IOPs to preprocessing arguments *preserve elasticity*: if the ingredients to the approach are elastic then the resulting SNARK is elastic. In more detail, the compiler involves two ingredients.

- *Polynomial IOPs.* A probabilistic proof in which the prover sends polynomial oracles to the verifier, who accesses them via polynomial evaluation queries. This is an interactive oracle proof [BCS16, RRR16] where query access to prover messages is changed from "point queries" to "polynomial evaluation queries".
- *Polynomial commitments.* A cryptographic primitive that enables a sender to commit to a polynomial $\mathbf{f} \in \mathbb{F}[X]$ of bounded degree, and later prove that $\mathbf{f}(z) = v$ for given $v, z \in \mathbb{F}$.

If the polynomial IOP is additionally *holographic* then the resulting succinct argument is a *preprocessing argument*, which means that it is possible, in an offline phase, to perform a public computation that enables sub-linear verification later on. The lemma below summarizes how elasticity is preserved. The formal statement (and its proof) are relative to the formalism for streaming algorithms that we outlined in Sect. 2.1.

Theorem 2 (informal). *Suppose that we are given the following ingredients.*

- *A public-coin polynomial IOP for a relation $\mathcal{R}$ with: (i) time-efficient prover time $t_\mathcal{P}$; (ii) space-efficient prover space $s_\mathcal{P}$ with $k_\mathcal{P}$ passes; (iii) s oracles; (iv) query complexity q (v) verifier complexity $t_\mathcal{V}$*
- *A polynomial commitment scheme PC with (i) time-efficient commit and open time $t_{\mathsf{PC.Com}}$; (ii) space-efficient commit (and open) space $s_{\mathsf{PC.Com}}$ with $k_{\mathsf{PC.Com}}$ passes; and (iii) checking time $t_{\mathsf{PC.Check}}$.*

Then there exists an interactive argument system for the relation $\mathcal{R}$ with (i) time-efficient prover time $t_\mathcal{P} + \mathsf{s} \cdot t_{\mathsf{PC.Com}} + q \cdot t_{\mathsf{PC.Com}}$; (ii) space-efficient prover space $s_\mathcal{P} + \mathsf{s} \cdot s_{\mathsf{PC.Com}}$ with $q \cdot k_{\mathsf{PC.Com}} \cdot k_\mathcal{P}$ passes; and (iii) verifier complexity $t_\mathcal{V} + q \cdot t_{\mathsf{PC.Check}}$. Moreover, the argument system is preprocessing if the given polynomial IOP is holographic (with time and space properties similarly preserved by the transformation).

---

[5] The argument prover and argument verifier emulate the underlying probabilistic proof, with the argument prover sending commitments to proof messages and sending answers to queries together with commitment openings to authenticate those answers.

Roughly speaking, the argument prover commits to each polynomial oracle via the polynomial commitment scheme, and answers polynomial evaluation queries by sending the evaluation along with a proof that it is consistent with the corresponding polynomial commitment. The security and most efficiency measures are studied in [Chi+20, BFS20]. Less obvious is how space complexity is affected.

A streaming implementation of the PIOP prover does not necessarily produce all of its output polynomial streams one by one, and therefore the space complexity of the resulting argument prover is not, e.g., just the sum $s_{\mathcal{P}} + s_{\text{PC.Com}}$ of the PIOP prover space and the PC commitment algorithm space. Indeed, if the PIOP prover's message polynomials all depend on the same input stream, it might be advantageous to produce two polynomials at the same time to avoid making extra passes over the input stream[6]. Furthermore, the commitment algorithm may require several passes over a single input polynomial, so that the argument prover must run the PIOP prover several times in order to completely commit to each polynomial, keeping partially computed commitments to each polynomial in memory. Such considerations lead to the space-efficient argument prover having space complexity $s_{\mathcal{P}} + \mathsf{s} \cdot s_{\text{PC.Com}}$ with $q \cdot k_{\text{PC.Com}} \cdot k_{\mathcal{P}}$ passes. Our PIOP construction actually satisfies the strong property that each polynomial can be produced independently without rerunning the entire prover algorithm, which reduces the space complexity to $s_{\mathcal{P}} + s_{\text{PC.Com}}$.

Remark 1 (types of polynomials). The above discussion is deliberately ambiguous about certain aspects: are the polynomials univariate or multivariate? are the polynomials represented as vectors of coefficients or as vectors of evaluations (or vectors in some other basis)? These details do not matter for Theorem 2 as long as the two components "match up": if the PIOP outputs polynomials represented in a way that is compatible with how the PC scheme expects inputs. Nevertheless, in this paper we focus on the case of univariate polynomials represented as vectors of coefficients, because our construction and implementation are in this setting.

Remark 2 (multilinear vs. univariate). The fact that the approach in [Chi+20, BFS20] preserves space efficiency in the case of multilinear polynomials represented over the boolean hypercube was used in [Blo+20, Blo+21]. Theorem 2 is a straightforward observation about [Chi+20, BFS20] that additionally considers elasticity. In particular, we believe that the constructions in [Blo+20, Blo+21] could be shown to have elastic realizations, by showing that the underlying multilinear PIOP and multilinear PC schemes have elastic realizations. We choose to work with univariate polynomials, instead of multilinear polynomials, because they have seen more success in real world deployments, and thus focus our investigation on the concrete efficiency of elastic SNARKs based on univariate polynomials. We leave the study of concrete efficiency of elastic SNARKs based on multilinear polynomials to future work.

---

[6] For example, if one polynomial consists of all of the even coefficients of another, one can produce streams of the coefficients of both polynomials simultaneously, in half the number of passes required to compute streams of each polynomial one at a time.

Remark 3 (elastic setup and indexer). For any succinct argument, elasticity is a desirable property as the size of the statement to be proven increases. In particular, we are going to focus on elasticity of the prover, which is the current bottleneck for proving large instances.

– *Setup.* We assume the existence of a setup algorithm that samples the public parameters of the system. Despite its complexity can be linear (or more!) in the statement size, we do not discuss setup algorithms in this paper for two reasons: (i) known setup algorithms have straightforward realizations that are simultaneously efficient in time and space (that is, there is less of a tension between optimizing for time or for space as there is for the prover); (ii) public parameters are typically sampled via "cryptographic ceremonies" that realize the setup functionality via secure multi-party protocols [BGM17], and so it is more relevant to discuss the time and space efficiency of these ceremonies.
– *Indexer.* In the case of preprocessing arguments, there is an indexer algorithm that produces the so-called *proving key* and *verification key*. The indexer in our construction and implementation is elastic, but we will not focus on it since all ideas relevant for the indexer can be inferred from the proving algorithm.

2.3 An Elastic Realization of the KZG Polynomial Commitment Scheme

We use a univariate polynomial commitment scheme from [KZG10] to construct our SNARK (see Sect. 2.2). Below we review this scheme and explain how to realize it elastically.

Review: A Polynomial Commitment from [KZG10]. The setup algorithm samples and outputs public parameters for the scheme to support polynomials of degree at most $D \in \mathbb{N}$: the description of a bilinear group $(\mathbb{G}_1, \mathbb{G}_2, \mathbb{G}_T, q, G, H, e)$;[7] the commitment key $\mathsf{ck} := (G, \tau G, \ldots, \tau^D G) \in \mathbb{G}_1^{D+1}$ for a random field element $\tau \in \mathbb{F}_q$; and the receiver key $\mathsf{rk} := (G, H, \tau H) \in \mathbb{G}_1 \times \mathbb{G}_2^2$. The commitment to a polynomial $\mathbf{p} \in \mathbb{F}_q[X]$ of degree at most D is computed as $C := \langle \mathbf{p}, \mathsf{ck} \rangle = \mathbf{p}(\tau)G \in \mathbb{G}_1$. Subsequently, to prove that the committed polynomial $\mathbf{p}$ evaluates to v at $z \in \mathbb{F}_q$, the committer computes the witness polynomial $\mathbf{w}(X) := (\mathbf{p}(X) - \mathbf{p}(z))/(X - z)$, and outputs the evaluation proof $\pi := \langle \mathbf{w}, \mathsf{ck} \rangle = \mathbf{w}(\tau)G \in \mathbb{G}_1$. Finally, to verify the evaluation proof, the receiver checks that $e(C - vG, H) = e(\pi, \tau H - zH)$.

Elastic Realization. An elastic realization of the above scheme requires a time-efficient realization and a space-efficient realization for each relevant algorithm of the scheme. Here we do not discuss the setup algorithm, as it has a natural time-and-space-efficient realization (cf. Remark 3). We do not discuss the verification algorithm either, because it only involves a constant number of scalar

---

[7] Here $|\mathbb{G}_1| = |\mathbb{G}_2| = |\mathbb{G}_T| = q$, G generates $\mathbb{G}_1$, H generates $\mathbb{G}_2$, and $e : \mathbb{G}_1 \times \mathbb{G}_2 \to \mathbb{G}_T$ is a non-degenerate bilinear map.

multiplications and pairings. Our focus is thus on the commitment and opening algorithm.

- *Commitment algorithm.* We are given streams of the commitment key elements $\{\tau^i G\}_{i=0}^d$ and of the coefficients $\{p_i\}_{i=0}^d$ of the polynomial $\mathbf{p}(X) = \sum_{i=0}^d p_i X^i$ to be committed. We compute the commitment $C = \sum_{i=0}^d p_i \tau^i G$ by multiplying each coefficient-key pair $(p_i, \tau^i G)$ together and adding them to a running total. Each scalar-multiplication of $p_i \cdot \tau^i G$ is performed via a double-and-add algorithm in constant space and linear time.

  The above operation is also known as multi-scalar multiplication or multi-exponentiation in the literature, and there exists different algorithms, such as Pippenger's [Pip80], that can greatly improve the concrete efficiency of the multi-scalar multiplication by reducing the number of group operations. Unfortunately, the algorithm requires random access to the vectors of scalars ($\mathbf{p}$) and bases (ck) and, despite Pippenger itself can be transformed into a streaming algorithm (trading off constant memory), the best performance in practice is achieved by setting a constant buffer and computing the result $C = \langle \mathbf{p}, \mathsf{ck} \rangle$ via multiple executions of Pippenger's algorithm. We investigate more non-naïve streaming algorithms in Sect. 2.7.

- *Opening algorithm.* We are given the same streams as above, and an opening location z. By rearranging the expression for the witness polynomial $\mathbf{w}(X) = (\mathbf{p}(X) - \mathbf{p}(z))/(X - z)$, we can stream the coefficients $\{w_i\}_{i=0}^{d-1}$ of $\mathbf{w}(X)$ via Ruffini's rule: $w_i := p_{i+1} + w_{i+1} z$. The evaluation proof $\pi = \sum_{i=0}^{d-1} w_i \tau^i G$ is computed in the same way as the commitment algorithm.

Note that the recurrence relation in the opening algorithm uses w_{j+1} to compute w_j, which means that $\mathbf{w}(X)$ is computed from its highest-order coefficient to its lowest. In turn, this means that the commitment key ck and scalarthe polynomial $\mathbf{p}(X)$ are streamed from highest-degree to lowest-degree coefficient. Setup and commitment algorithms are agnostic to the order elements are being streamed. The above discussion implies the following (informal) lemma.

Lemma 1 (informal). *The polynomial commitment scheme of [KZG10] has an elastic realization.*

2.4   An Elastic Scalar-Product Protocol

A scalar-product protocol enables the prover to convince the verifier that the scalar product of two committed vectors equals a certain target value. In the literature, scalar-product protococols [BCG20] are also known as inner-product arguments or IPAs [Boo+16, DRZ20, Bün+21]. Many constructions of succinct arguments internally rely on scalar-product protocols as their main component for proving NP statements [Boo+16, PLS19, BCG20]. The PIOP for R1CS that we construct in Sects. 2.5 and 2.6 relies on a PIOP for scalar products where the prover has two realizations: (i) one that runs in linear-time and linear-space; and (ii) one that runs in quasilinear-time and logarithmic-space.

Definition 2. *A* **PIOP for scalar products** *is a PIOP where the verifier receives as input* $(\mathbb{F}, N, u)$ *and has (polynomial evaluation) query access to* $\mathbf{f}, \mathbf{g} \in \mathbb{F}^N$, *and checks with the help of the prover that* $\langle \mathbf{f}, \mathbf{g} \rangle = u$.

Theorem 1 (informal). *There is a PIOP for scalar products with proof length* $O(N)$, *query complexity* $O(\log N)$, *verifier time* $O(\log N)$, *and prover that has two realizations:*

– *a time-efficient realization that runs in time* $O(N)$ *and space* $O(N)$;
– *a space-efficient realization that runs in time* $O(N \log N)$ *and space* $O(\log N)$ *in* $O(\log N)$ *passes.*

In the remainder of this section, we outline the scalar-product protocol, deferring to the full version formal security proofs and a more in-depth discussion of the protocol. We also note that our construction uses two slightly different protocols, one for *twisted scalar-products* [BCG20], where $\langle \mathbf{f} \circ \mathbf{y}, \mathbf{g} \rangle = u$ for a vector $\mathbf{y}$ of the form $\mathbf{y} = (1, \rho_0) \otimes (1, \rho_1) \otimes \cdots \otimes (1, \rho_{n-1})$ where $n := \log N$ (we recall that by log we denote the ceil of the logarithm base 2), and one for verifying Hadamard product relations $\mathbf{f} \circ \mathbf{g} = \mathbf{h}$. These only require small modifications to the scalar-product protocol.

We proceed in three steps. First, in Sect. 2.4.1 we describe how to reduce checking a scalar product to checking tensor products of univariate polynomials. Then, we describe a tensor product protocol in Sect. 2.4.2. Finally, in Sect. 2.4.3 we describe how to realize this protocol in an elastic way.

2.4.1 Verifying Scalar Products Using the Sumcheck Protocol

Consider two vectors $\mathbf{f}, \mathbf{g} \in \mathbb{F}^N$ with $\langle \mathbf{f}, \mathbf{g} \rangle = u$ as in Definition 2. The verifier has polynomial evaluation query access to polynomial evaluations of $\mathbf{f}$ and $\mathbf{g}$. That is, the verifier can obtain evaluations of the polynomials $\mathbf{f}(X) = \sum_{i=0}^{N-1} f_i X^i$ and $\mathbf{g}(X) = \sum_{i=0}^{N-1} g_i X^i$ at any point $x \in \mathbb{F}$. Note that the product polynomial $\mathbf{h}(X) := \mathbf{f}(X) \cdot \mathbf{g}(X^{-1})$ has $\langle \mathbf{f}, \mathbf{g} \rangle = \sum_{i=0}^{N-1} f_i g_i$ as the coefficient of X^0, because for every $i, j \in [N]$ the powers of X associated with f_i and g_j multiply together to give X^0 if and only if $i = j$. Therefore, to check the scalar-product $\langle \mathbf{f}, \mathbf{g} \rangle = u$, it suffices to check that the coefficient of X^0 in the product polynomial $\mathbf{h}(X)$ equals u.

However, this check must somehow be performed *without the prover actually computing* $\mathbf{h}(X)$. This is because the fastest algorithm for computing $\mathbf{h}(X)$ requires $O(N \log N)$ time and $O(N)$ space (via FFTs), which is neither time-efficient nor space-efficient. On the other hand, the scalar product $\langle \mathbf{f}, \mathbf{g} \rangle = u$ can be checked (directly) in time $O(N)$ and space $O(1)$, which leaves open the possibility of a scalar-product protocol where the prover does better than computing $\mathbf{h}(X)$ explicitly (and then running some protocol).

This issue is addressed in prior work if the verifier can query the *multilinear* polynomials $\widehat{\mathbf{f}}(\mathbf{X})$ and $\widehat{\mathbf{g}}(\mathbf{X})$ associated to the vectors $\mathbf{f}, \mathbf{g} \in \mathbb{F}^N$: we index the entries of $\mathbf{f}$ using binary vectors, and $f_i = f_{b_0,\ldots,b_{n-1}}$ is the coefficient of $X_0^{b_0} \cdots X_{n-1}^{b_{n-1}}$, where $(b_0, \ldots, b_n)$ is the binary decomposition of i. From previous results [Tha13, Xie+19, BCG20], we have the following lemma.

Lemma 2. *Let $\mathbb{F}$ be a finite field and N be a positive integer. Define $n = \log N$; the sumcheck protocol for*

$$\frac{1}{2^n} \sum_{\omega \in \mathcal{H}^n} (\widehat{\mathbf{f}} \cdot \widehat{\mathbf{g}})(\boldsymbol{\omega}) = u \ . \tag{1}$$

for $\mathcal{H} = \{-1, 1\}$ and two multilinear polynomials $\widehat{\mathbf{f}}(X_0, \ldots, X_{n-1})$ and $\widehat{\mathbf{g}}(X_0, \ldots, X_{n-1})$ has the following properties: soundness error is $O(\log N / |\mathbb{F}|)$ (as a reduction to claims about polynomial evaluations); round complexity is $O(\log N)$; the prover uses $O(\log N)$ field operations; and the verifier uses $O(\log N)$ field operations.

Then, one can use the (multivariate) sumcheck protocol of [Lun+92] to reduce $\langle \mathbf{f}, \mathbf{g} \rangle = u$ to two evaluation queries $\widehat{\mathbf{f}}(\boldsymbol{\rho})$ and $\widehat{\mathbf{g}}(\boldsymbol{\rho})$, where $\boldsymbol{\rho} := (\rho_0, \ldots, \rho_{n-1}) \in \mathbb{F}^n$ are the random verifier challenges used in the sumcheck protocol. Crucially, the prover algorithm in the sumcheck protocol applied to the two product of two multilinear polynomials also has a space-efficient realisation which runs in time $O(N \log N)$ and space $O(\log N)$ [CMT12], which would provide an elastic solution in this multilinear regime.

In our setting the verifier can only query the *univariate* polynomials $\mathbf{f}(X)$ and $\mathbf{g}(X)$ associated with the vectors $\mathbf{f}, \mathbf{g} \in \mathbb{F}^N$. Nevertheless, we follow a similar approach, by running the sumcheck protocol on the *multivariate* polynomials $\widehat{\mathbf{f}}(\mathbf{X})$ and $\widehat{\mathbf{g}}(\mathbf{X})$, producing two claimed evaluations $\widehat{\mathbf{f}}(\boldsymbol{\rho}) = u$ and $\widehat{\mathbf{g}}(\boldsymbol{\rho}) = u'$. We check that these claimed evaluations are consistent with $\mathbf{f}$ and $\mathbf{g}$ using evaluations of the *univariate* polynomials $\mathbf{f}(X)$ and $\mathbf{g}(X)$.

Remark 4 (unstructured fields). While other probabilistic proofs using univariate polynomials, such as the low-degree test in [Ben+18], require the size of the field $\mathbb{F}$ to be *smooth*, so that the field contains high-degree roots of unity or structured linear subspaces. In contrast, using the strategy above, our scalar-product protocol works with univariate polynomials over any sufficiently large field. This allows a much wider range of parameter choices for the [KZG10] polynomial commitment scheme which is likely to lead to better concrete efficiency.

2.4.2   A Tensor-Product Protocol

Consider the claimed evaluation $\widehat{\mathbf{f}}(\boldsymbol{\rho}) = v$. To check that this is correct using univariate polynomial evaluations, note that $\widehat{\mathbf{f}}(\mathbf{X})$ and $\mathbf{f}(X)$ have the same coefficients, and moreover partially evaluating $\widehat{\mathbf{f}}(\mathbf{X})$ by setting X_0 equal to ρ_0, the polynomial $\widehat{\mathbf{f}}(\rho_0, X_1, \ldots, X_{\log N - 1})$ has the same coefficients as the polynomial $\mathbf{f}'(X) := \mathbf{f}_e(X) + \rho_0 \cdot \mathbf{f}_o(X)$. Here, $\mathbf{f}_e(X)$ and $\mathbf{f}_o(X)$ are the unique odd and even parts of $\mathbf{f}(X)$, defined by $\mathbf{f}(X) = \mathbf{f}_e(X^2) + X \mathbf{f}_o(X^2)$.

This suggests a protocol where the prover sends $\mathbf{f}'(X)$ to the verifier. If the verifier can check that $\mathbf{f}'(X)$ was correctly computed from $\mathbf{f}(X)$, then the original problem of consistency between $\mathbf{f}(X)$ and an evaluation of $\widehat{\mathbf{f}}(X_0, \ldots, X_{\log N - 1})$ is reduced to checking consistency between $\mathbf{f}'(X)$ and an evaluation of $\widehat{\mathbf{f}}(\rho_0, X_1, \ldots, X_{\log N - 1})$. Repeating this reduction with every value ρ_j, the prover and verifier eventually arrive at a claim about constant-degree polynomials, which the prover can send to the verifier allowing the verifier to check autonomously.

To check that $\mathbf{f}'(X)$ is consistent with $\mathbf{f}(X)$, the verifier can sample a random challenge point $\beta \in \mathbb{F}^{\times}$ (where $\mathbb{F}^{\times}$ denotes the multiplicative group of $\mathbb{F}$), and make polynomial evaluation queries in order to check the following equations:

$$\mathbf{f}'(\beta^2) = \mathbf{f}_e(\beta) + \rho_0 \cdot \mathbf{f}_o(\beta) = \frac{\mathbf{f}(\beta) + \mathbf{f}(-\beta)}{2} + \rho_0 \cdot \frac{\mathbf{f}(\beta) - \mathbf{f}(-\beta)}{2\beta} . \qquad (2)$$

This is reminiscent of a similar reduction in [Ben+18] used to construct a low-degree test for univariate polynomials. By the Schwartz–Zippel lemma, the check passes with small probability unless $\mathbf{f}'(X)$ was computed correctly.

Noting that $\widehat{\mathbf{f}}(\boldsymbol{\rho}) = \langle \mathbf{f}, \otimes_{j=0}^{n-1}(1, \rho_j) \rangle$, this procedure gives a univariate polynomial IOP for the following relation:

Definition 3. *The* **tensor-product** *relation* $\mathcal{R}_{TC}$ *is the set of tuples*

$$(\mathbb{i}, \mathbb{x}, \mathbb{w}) = (\perp, (\mathbb{F}, N, \rho_0, \ldots, \rho_{n-1}, u), \mathbf{f})$$

where $n = \log N$, $\mathbf{f} \in \mathbb{F}^N$, $u \in \mathbb{F}$, *and* $\langle \mathbf{f}, \otimes_j(1, \rho_j) \rangle = u$.

We give full details of the tensor-product protocol in the full version of this paper. In fact, the tensor check will be useful not only as part of our scalar-product protocol, but also more generally as part of simple checks that take place as part of our R1CS protocols (as described in Sects. 2.5 and 2.6).

2.4.3   Elastic Realization of the Prover Algorithm

Most complexity measures claimed in Theorem 1 follow straightforwardly from the sumcheck protocol described in Lemma 2. What remains is to describe an elastic realization of the prover algorithm for the tensor-product protocol.

The prover's task is to compute the polynomials $\mathbf{f}^{(j)}$ for each round $j \in [n]$. Given $\mathbf{f}^{(j-1)}$, which has degree $O(N/2^j)$, the prover can compute $\mathbf{f}^{(j)}$ in $O(N/2^j)$ operations via Eq. 2. Summing up the prover costs for $j \in [n]$ gives $O(N)$ operations. Therefore, it is easy to see that the tensor-product protocol has a linear-time prover realisation.

Next, we give a space-efficient prover realisation that uses logarithmic space.

Logarithmic Space. We aim for the prover to run in logarithmic space complexity, given streaming access to $\mathbf{f}$ and $\mathbf{g}$. This is more challenging than the time-efficient case, as the prover cannot store $\mathbf{f}^{(j-1)}$ to help it compute $\mathbf{f}^{(j)}$, as this would require linear space complexity (for small j). Instead, the prover computes each $\mathbf{f}^{(j)}$ from scratch using streams of $\mathbf{f}$.

We begin by explaining how the prover can *produce* a stream of $\mathbf{f}^{(j)}$ efficiently, given streaming access to $\mathbf{f}$, in a similar way to streaming evaluations of multivariate polynomials and low-degree extensions in [Blo+21, Blo+20, CMT12]. Our main contribution here is to show that $\mathbf{f}^{(j)}$ can be evaluated in $O(N)$ time and $O(\log N)$ space, saving a logarithmic factor over prior work. Then, we explain how to perform the consistency checks.

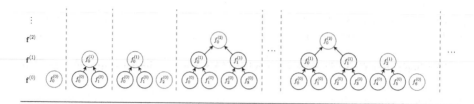

Fig. 1. A streaming algorithm for computing the coefficients of $\mathbf{f}^{(j)}$ from $\mathbf{f}^{(0)} := \mathbf{f}$. Nodes in blue denote the coefficients that are stored in memory at any moment.

- *Streaming* $\mathbf{f}^{(j)}$. Let $\mathbf{f} = \sum_{i=0}^{N-1} f_i X^i$. We can compute $\mathbf{f}' = \sum_{i=0}^{N/2-1}(f_{2i} + \rho f_{2i+1})X^i$ from a stream of coefficients of $\mathbf{f}$ by reading each pair of coefficients f_{2i}, f_{2i+1} from the stream, and produce the next coefficient $f_i' := f_{2i} + \rho f_{2i+1}$ of $\mathbf{f}'$. This process uses a constant amount memory space, storing f_{2i}, and f_{2i+1} and deleting them immediately after computing f_i'. Each coefficient of $\mathbf{f}'$ costs two arithmetic operations to compute.

  The prover can produce the stream $\mathcal{S}(\mathbf{f}^{(j)})$ for $\mathbf{f}^{(j)}$ by applying the same idea recursively as follows. Initialise a stack Stack consisting of pairs $(j, x) \in [\log N] \times \mathbb{F}$, and a list of challenges $\rho_0, \ldots, \rho_j$. To generate $\mathcal{S}(\mathbf{f}^{(j)})$, the prover

  • If the top element in the stack is of the form (j, y) for some $y \in \mathbb{F}$, pop it and return y.

  • If the top two elements in the stack are of the form (k', x') and (k, x) with $k = k'$ (and $k < j$), then pop them and push $(k+1, \ x + \rho_k x')$, where $x + \rho_k x'$ is equal to $f_{k+1}^{(j)}$ (recall that the values are streamed from last to first index);

  • Otherwise, query the stream $\mathcal{S}(\mathbf{f})$ for the next element $x \in \mathbb{F}$ and add $(0, x)$ to the stack.

  The stack Stack must be initialized with some zero-entries if $N \neq 2^n$ (for instance, where N is odd) for correctness, but we avoid discussing this case here for simplicity. A visual representation of this process is displayed in Fig. 1. This procedure produces a stream of $\mathbf{f}^{(j)}$ from a stream of $\mathbf{f}$ in $O(N)$ and using $\log N$ memory space (since the stack Stack holds at most $\log N$ elements at any time).

- *Space-efficient tensor check.* The verifier must perform consistency checks to make sure that each polynomial $\mathbf{f}^{(j)}$ was correctly computed from $\mathbf{f}^{(j-1)}$, and similarly for $\mathbf{g}^{(j)}$. This check requires the computation of $\mathbf{f}^{(0)}, \ldots, \mathbf{f}^{(n-1)}$. We compute them in parallel with a minor modification to the folding algorithm illustrated in Fig. 1. Instead of returning only when the top of the stack has a particular index, we always output the top element in the stack. We thus construct a streaming algorithm $\mathcal{S}(\mathbf{f}^{(0)}, \ldots, \mathbf{f}^{(n-1)})$ that returns elements of the form $(j, x) \in [n] \times \mathbb{F}$ where x is the next coefficient of the polynomial $\mathbf{f}^{(j)}$. With the above stream, it is possible to simulate the streaming oracle $\mathcal{S}(\mathbf{f}^{(j)})$ and the evaluations $\mathbf{f}^{(j)}(\beta^2), \mathbf{f}^{(j)}(+\beta), \mathbf{f}^{(j)}(-\beta)$, for each $j \in [n]$. In particular computing each evaluation requires storing a single $\mathbb{F}$-element; therefore, the total consistency check uses $n = \log N$ memory and N time. This allows to check Eq. 2, substituting $\mathbf{f}' = \mathbf{f}^{(j)}, \mathbf{f} = \mathbf{f}^{(j-1)}$ for $j \in [n]$.

Based on the costs of maintaining the stacks for $\mathbf{f}$ and $\mathbf{g}$, and computing the coefficients of $\mathbf{q}^{(j)}$ incrementally, it follows that each round takes time $O(N)$ and space $O(\log N)$. Therefore, summing over the $O(\log N)$ rounds, the protocol requires time $O(N \log N)$ and space $O(\log N)$.

Remark 5. Based on our tensor product protocol in Sect. 2.4.2, one can construct a linear-time univariate sumcheck protocol with proof length $O(N)$ and query complexity $O(\log N)$, which we believe could be of independent interest for future research. There are other univariate sumcheck protocols in the literature; however, these protocols cannot be used in our setting.

The univariate sumcheck protocol in [Ben+19] is a 1-message PIOP with proof length $O(N)$ and query complexity $O(1)$. That protocol does not seem useful here, because the prover requires $O(N \log N)$ time and $O(N)$ space due to the use of FFTs. In contrast, our protocol achieves elasticity, at the cost of logarithmic round complexity and logarithmic query complexity.

Drake [Dra20] sketches a Hadamard product protocol based on univariate polynomials that does not use FFTs. That protocol, also inspired by the low-degree test in [Ben+18], may conceivably lead to a univariate sumcheck protocol that is elastic. However, no details (or implementations) of the protocol are available.

2.5   Warm-up: An Elastic Non-holographic PIOP for R1CS

We describe an elastic PIOP for R1CS (Definition 1), based on the elastic scalar-product protocol from Sect. 2.4. Due to the large verifier complexity of this protocol, we note that the verifier can also be made elastic using similar techniques to the elastic prover. We will build on this construction later in Sect. 2.6, and construct a *holographic* polynomial IOP with logarithmic verifier complexity.

Theorem 2 (informal). *For every finite field $\mathbb{F}$, there is a PIOP for $\mathcal{R}_{\mathrm{R1CS}}$ over $\mathbb{F}$ with the following parameters:*

- *soundness error $O(N/|\mathbb{F}|)$;*
- *round complexity $O(\log N)$;*
- *proof length $O(N)$ and query complexity $O(\log N)$;*
- *a time-efficient prover that runs in time $O(M)$ and space $O(M)$;*
- *a space-efficient prover that runs in time $O(M \log^2 N)$ and space $O(\log N)$ (with $O(\log N)$ input passes);*
- *a time-efficient verifier that runs in time $O(M)$ and space $O(M)$; and*
- *a space-efficient verifier that runs in time $O(M \log N)$ and space $O(\log N)$.*

Above, N is the matrix size and M the number of non-zero entries in an R1CS instance.

The theorem holds for *any* finite field $\mathbb{F}$, and in particular does not require any smoothness properties for $\mathbb{F}$.

To make the space-efficient realisation of the prover well-defined, we must explain how to stream an R1CS instance. Below we describe a concrete choice of streams that (i) suffices for the theorem; (ii) is realistic (as we elaborate shortly). After that we outline the polynomial IOP for R1CS.

Streaming R1CS. The R1CS problem is captured using the following indexed relation:

Definition 4. *The indexed relation $\mathcal{R}_{\text{R1CS}}$ is the set of all triples:*

$$(\mathbb{i}, \mathbb{x}, \mathbb{w}) = \big((\mathbb{F}, N, M, A, B, C), \mathbb{x}, \mathbb{w}\big)$$

where $\mathbb{F}$ is a finite field, A, B, C are matrices in $\mathbb{F}^{N \times N}$, each having at most M non-zero entries, and $\mathbb{z} := (\mathbb{x}, \mathbb{w})$ is a vector in $\mathbb{F}^N$ such that $A\mathbb{z} \circ B\mathbb{z} = C\mathbb{z}$.

We define streams for each of $\mathbb{i}$, $\mathbb{x}$ and $\mathbb{w}$, with A, B and C in *sparse representation*.

Definition 1. *Let $U \in \mathbb{F}^{N \times N}$ be a matrix with M non-zero entries. The **sparse representation** of U consists of its coordinate-list representation. That is, the stream $\mathcal{S}(U)$ of U is the sequence of elements in the support as tuples (row, column, value), sorted by row index or column index. We denote by $\mathcal{S}_{\text{row}}(U)$ the row-major coordinate list (that is, ordering the entries of the matrix in lexicographic order with row index before column index), and by $\mathcal{S}_{\text{col}}(U)$ the column-major coordinate list.*

In our definition of streams for R1CS, we allow the *computation trace* ($A\mathbb{z}$, $B\mathbb{z}$, $C\mathbb{z}$) of an R1CS instance to be streamed as part of the witness.

Definition 2 (streaming R1CS). *The streams associated with the R1CS instance $((\mathbb{F}, N, M, A, B, C), \mathbb{x}, \mathbb{w})$ are:*

- *the **index streams**: streams $\mathcal{S}(A)$, $\mathcal{S}(B)$, $\mathcal{S}(C)$, the coordinate lists of the R1CS matrices, in row-major and column-major.*
- *the **instance stream**: stream of the instance vector $\mathcal{S}(\mathbb{x})$;*
- *the **witness streams**: stream of the witness $\mathcal{S}(\mathbb{w})$ and the computation trace vectors $\mathcal{S}(A\mathbb{z}), \mathcal{S}(B\mathbb{z}), \mathcal{S}(C\mathbb{z})$.*

The field description $\mathbb{F}$, instance size N, and maximum number M of non-zero entries are explicit inputs.

Including steams for $\mathcal{S}(A\mathbb{z})$, $\mathcal{S}(B\mathbb{z})$, and $\mathcal{S}(C\mathbb{z})$ makes our polynomial IOPs for R1CS space efficient even when matrix multiplication by A, B and C requires a large amount of memory and $A\mathbb{z}$, $B\mathbb{z}$ and $C\mathbb{z}$ cannot be computed element by element on the fly given streaming access to $\mathbb{x}$ and $\mathbb{w}$. On the other hand, for R1CS instances defined by many natural computations, such as a machine computation which repeatedly applies a transition function to a small state, the matrices A, B and C are *banded*; that is, their non-zero entries all lie in a thin, central diagonal band. In this case, it is easy to generate a stream of $\mathcal{S}(A\mathbb{z})$, for example, using streams $\mathcal{S}(\mathbb{x})$, $\mathcal{S}(\mathbb{w})$ and the column-major matrix stream $\mathcal{S}_{\text{col}}(A)$.

The Polynomial IOP Construction. We outline the PIOP construction which proves Theorem 2. The protocol adopts standard ideas from [Ben+19] and an optimization from [Gab20] for concrete efficiency. In the time-efficient realisation of our protocol, the prover takes $\mathbb{i}$, $\mathbb{x}$ and $\mathbb{w}$ as input, and the verifier receives i and x. In the space-efficient realisation, these inputs are provided as streams according to Definition 2.

In the first step of the protocol, the prover sends $\mathbf{z}$ to the verifier. To check that $A\mathbf{z} \circ B\mathbf{z} = C\mathbf{z}$, the verifier replies by sending a random challenge $v \in \mathbb{F}^\times$ to the prover, which the prover expands into a vector $\mathbf{y}_C := (1, v, v^2, \ldots, v^{N-1})$. Then, multiplying $A\mathbf{z} \circ B\mathbf{z} = C\mathbf{z}$ on the left by $\mathbf{y}_C^\mathsf{T}$, the prover and verifier will check that

$$\langle A\mathbf{z} \circ \mathbf{y}_C, \ B\mathbf{z} \rangle = \langle C\mathbf{z}, \mathbf{y}_C \rangle \ . \tag{3}$$

The prover will send the value $u_C := \langle C\mathbf{z}, \mathbf{y}_C \rangle \in \mathbb{F}$ to the verifier. At this point, the prover will convince the verifier that Eq. 3 holds by reducing the two claims $\langle A\mathbf{z} \circ \mathbf{y}_C, \ B\mathbf{z} \rangle = u_C$ and $\langle C\mathbf{z}, \mathbf{y}_C \rangle = u_C$ to *tensor consistency checks* on $\mathbf{z}$, for which we can apply the tensor-product protocol in Sect. 2.4.

As a sub-protocol for the first claim, the prover and verifier run a twisted scalar product protocol, as described in Sect. 2.4. This generates two new claims, one about each of $A\mathbf{z}$ and $B\mathbf{z}$, leaving us with a total of three claims:

$$\begin{aligned} \langle A\mathbf{z}, \mathbf{y}_B \circ \mathbf{y}_C \rangle &= u_A \ , \\ \langle B\mathbf{z}, \mathbf{y}_B \rangle &= u_B \ , \\ \langle C\mathbf{z}, \mathbf{y}_C \rangle &= u_C \ . \end{aligned} \tag{4}$$

Here, $\mathbf{y}_B := \otimes_j (1, \rho_j)$, where $\rho_0, \rho_1, \ldots, \rho_{n-1} \in \mathbb{F}^\times$ are the random challenges sent by the verifier during the sub-protocol. Setting $\mathbf{y}_A := \mathbf{y}_B \circ \mathbf{y}_C$, and moving the matrices A, B and C into the right input argument of the scalar-product relation, we have

$$\begin{aligned} \langle \mathbf{z}, \hat{\mathbf{a}} \rangle &= u_A \ , \\ \langle \mathbf{z}, \hat{\mathbf{b}} \rangle &= u_B \ , \\ \langle \mathbf{z}, \hat{\mathbf{c}} \rangle &= u_C \ , \end{aligned} \tag{5}$$

where $\hat{\mathbf{a}} := \mathbf{y}_A^\mathsf{T} A$, and similarly for $\hat{\mathbf{b}}$ and $\hat{\mathbf{c}}$. Although $\mathbf{y}_B$, $\mathbf{y}_C$, and $\mathbf{y}_A$ all have a tensor structure, $\hat{\mathbf{a}}$, $\hat{\mathbf{b}}$ and $\hat{\mathbf{c}}$ will not generally have the same structure, which means that Eq. 5 cannot be checked directly using the tensor-product protocol. Thus, the verifier sends another random challenge $\eta \in \mathbb{F}^\times$ to the prover. Taking linear combinations of the three claims in Eq. 5 using powers of η yields a single scalar-product claim

$$\langle \mathbf{z}, \ \hat{\mathbf{a}} + \eta \cdot \hat{\mathbf{b}} + \eta^2 \cdot \hat{\mathbf{c}} \rangle = u_A + \eta \cdot u_B + \eta^2 \cdot u_C \ . \tag{6}$$

The prover and verifier run a second twisted scalar-product protocol for Eq. 6. This produces two new claims

$$\langle \mathbf{z}, \mathbf{y} \rangle = u_D \ , \tag{7}$$

$$\langle \hat{\mathbf{a}} + \eta \cdot \hat{\mathbf{b}} + \eta^2 \cdot \hat{\mathbf{c}}, \mathbf{y} \rangle = u_E \ , \tag{8}$$

where again, $\mathbf{y}$ is a vector with the same tensor structure as described in Sect. 2.4, generated using random challenges produced by the verifier.

Finally, the prover and the verifier engage in a tensor-product protocol to check Eq. 7. The verifier can check Eq. 8 directly, since $\hat{\mathbf{a}}$, $\hat{\mathbf{b}}$ and $\hat{\mathbf{c}}$ can be computed directly from the R1CS matrices A, B and C, along with the random challenges used throughout the R1CS protocol.

Time-Efficient Prover. The prover runs in linear time if the prover algorithms for the underlying scalar-product and tensor-product sub-protocols can be realized in linear time. Note that the cost of computing $\hat{a}$, $\hat{b}$ and $\hat{c}$ is linear in the number of non-zero entries in A, B, C. As a result, the verifier also runs in linear time.

Space-Efficient Prover. We start by noting that the streams $\mathcal{S}(A\mathbf{z})$, $\mathcal{S}(B\mathbf{z})$ $\mathcal{S}(C\mathbf{z})$ are provided as input to the prover, and that the stream $\mathcal{S}(\mathbf{z})$ can be produced by chaining the instance stream $\mathcal{S}(\mathbf{x})$ with the witness stream $\mathcal{S}(\mathbf{w})$. In order to run the first twisted scalar-product protocol (cf. Eq. 3), the prover must compute also the stream for the tensor product vector $\mathbf{y}_C = \otimes_j(1, v^{2^j})$. This stream can be generated in linear time: during the i-th iteration, the stream of any vector of the form $\otimes_j(1, v_j)$ must return the product $\prod_{j, b_j \neq 0} v_j$, where $i = (b_0, \ldots, b_{n-1})_2$ in binary. Consider the bit-string representing i: after yielding the i-th element $\prod_{j, b_j \neq 0} v_j$, the next element in the stream has index $(i - 1)$, and it can be either obtained by clearing the last multiplication (that is, multiplying the previous element by v_0^{-1}) or multiplying the previous element by $v_k^{-1} v_{k-1} \cdots v_0$ (when the subtraction has a carry bit propagating k times). The stream, during the initialization phase, stores the incremental products $v_0, v_0 v_1, v_0 v_1 v_2, \ldots, v_0 v_1 \cdots v_{n-1}$ and the "carry elements" $v_0^{-1}, v_1^{-1} v_0, \ldots, v_{n-1}^{-1} v_{n-2} \cdots v_0$ Initialisation of the stream costs $O(\log N)$ field operations and $O(n)$ space; and each new element is produced with a single field multiplication. Using the same idea, it is possible to produce the streams $\mathcal{S}(\mathbf{y}_A)$ and $\mathcal{S}(\mathbf{y}_B)$.

In the second sumcheck (cf. Eq. 6), the stream for $\mathcal{S}(\hat{a}) = \mathcal{S}(\mathbf{y}_A^\mathsf{T} A)$ (respectively, $\mathcal{S}(\hat{b})$ and $\mathcal{S}(\hat{c})$) are not implemented using trivial matrix multiplication from the row-major stream of $\mathcal{S}_{\mathrm{row}}(A)$ (resp. $\mathcal{S}_{\mathrm{row}}(B)$, $\mathcal{S}_{\mathrm{row}}(C)$) with the above tensor product. Instead of using $O(N)$ passes over the stream vector, we compute the i-th element on the fly: using the stream $\mathcal{S}_{\mathrm{row}}(A)$, all elements of i-th row $(i, j, a_{i,j})$ produced by the stream are multiplied by v^i and accumulated in the final result. Overall, producing the next element costs $O(\log N)$ multiplications.

Composing the above streams with the space-efficient realisations of the scalar product and tensor-product sub-protocols described in Sect. 2.4, we obtain a space-efficient prover algorithm which runs in quasilinear time and logarithmic space: overall, the non-holographic protocol can be run in $O(M \log^2 N)$ time and $O(\log N)$ space.

2.6   Elastic Holographic PIOP for R1CS

The verifier complexity in the non-holographic protocol for R1CS described in Sect. 2.5 is linear in the size of the R1CS instance. This is because in order to run a scalar-product protocol to check Eq. 6, the verifier must compute $\hat{a}, \hat{b}, \hat{c}$ via expensive matrix-vector multiplications involving all of the non-zero entries of matrices A, B and C.

In this section, we explain how to construct a *holographic* polynomial IOP protocol for R1CS, in which the verifier's direct access to A, B and C is replaced by query access, as in [Chi+20, COS20]. In this construction, the prover can either run in linear-time and linear-space, or quasilinear-time and log-space, and the verifier runs in log-time and log-space.

Theorem 3 (informal). *There exists an elastic* **holographic** *polynomial IOP for* $\mathcal{R}_{\mathrm{R1CS}}$, *whose prover admits two implementations:*

– *the* **time-efficient** *prover runs in* $O(M)$ *time and* $O(M)$ *space;*
– *the* **space-efficient** *prover runs in* $O(M \log^2 M)$ *time and* $O(\log M)$ *space,*

where N *is the size of the R1CS input, and* M *is the number of non-zero entries in the R1CS instance. The verifier runs in* $O(|\mathbf{x}| + \log M)$ *time and space.*

High-Level Overview. Our holographic protocol follows the same strategy as prior work [BCG20]. Roughly speaking, the core difference between the holographic protocol in this section and the non-holographic protocol in Sect. 2.5 is that the prover and verifier use an alternative strategy to check Eq. 5. Instead of reducing Eq. 5 to Eq. 6, and then verifying Eq. 6 via $\hat{\mathbf{a}}$, $\hat{\mathbf{b}}$ and $\hat{\mathbf{c}}$, the prover sends extra oracle messages to the verifier, corresponding to partial computations of Eq. 5. Then, the prover and the verifier engage in various sub-protocols to check that the partial computations were performed correctly. As in prior works [BCG20], the key sub-protocols are a *look-up* protocol and an *entry-product* protocol (also known as grand product argument [Set20]).

Our main contribution is a space-efficient realisation of these sub-protocols, which leads to a space-efficient holographic R1CS protocol. The main challenge is to show that it is possible to generate the prover's extra messages in a space-efficient manner from a streaming R1CS instance (Definition 2). This places particular restrictions on the design of a space-efficient look-up protocol, which we explain how to deal with in Sect. 2.6.1. We explain how to construct a space-efficient entry-product protocol in Sect. 2.6.2.

Achieving Holography. For a matrix $U \in \{A, B, C\}$, consider the vectors row, col, val $\in \mathbb{F}^M$, such that, for each $i \in [M]$, $\mathsf{val}_i \in \mathbb{F}$ is the $(\mathsf{row}_i, \mathsf{col}_i)$-entry of U, ordered column-major. In the construction of a holographic PIOP, we will assume that the matrices A, B and C have the same support, which means that row $:=$ row$_A =$ row$_B =$ row$_C$ and col $:=$ col$_A =$ col$_B =$ col$_C$. This can easily be achieved by padding val$_A$, val$_B$ and val$_C$ with zeroes as required, and increases the length of row, col and val by at most a factor of 3.

The prover constructs the following vectors and sends them to the verifier as oracle messages:

$$\mathbf{r}_A^* := \mathbf{y}_A|_{\mathsf{row}}\ , \qquad \mathbf{r}_B^* := \mathbf{y}_B|_{\mathsf{row}}\ , \qquad \mathbf{r}_C^* := \mathbf{y}_C|_{\mathsf{row}}\ , \qquad \mathbf{z}^* := \mathbf{z}|_{\mathsf{col}}\ . \qquad (9)$$

In Eq. 9, $\mathbf{r}_A^*$ is the vector whose i-th element is the (row_i)-th element of $\hat{\mathbf{a}}$, and similarly for $\mathbf{r}_B^*$, $\mathbf{r}_C^*$ and $\mathbf{z}^*$. Using Eq. 9, Eq. 4 can be reformulated as:

$$\begin{aligned}
\langle \mathbf{r}_A^* \circ \mathsf{val}_A,\ \mathbf{z}^* \rangle &= u_A\ , \\
\langle \mathbf{r}_B^* \circ \mathsf{val}_B,\ \mathbf{z}^* \rangle &= u_B\ , \\
\langle \mathbf{r}_C^* \circ \mathsf{val}_C,\ \mathbf{z}^* \rangle &= u_C\ .
\end{aligned} \qquad (10)$$

Then, the verifier must check the three claims of Eq. 10, and that $\mathbf{r}_A^*$, $\mathbf{r}_B^*$, $\mathbf{r}_C^*$ and $\mathbf{z}^*$ were correctly computed. The prover and verifier run a twisted scalar-product protocol for the three claims. To check that $\mathbf{r}_A^*$, $\mathbf{r}_B^*$, $\mathbf{r}_C^*$ and $\mathbf{z}^*$ were correctly computed, the prover and verifier run a look-up protocol, which we describe in more detail in Sect. 2.6.1.

Elastic Realization. The twisted scalar-product protocol and look-up protocol are elastic protocols with both time and space-efficient prover realization, and a succinct verifier. Our holographic protocol for R1CS inherits a time-efficient prover and succinct verifier from these sub-protocols. However, to give a space-efficient prover realisation, we must show that the prover can produce streams of $\mathbf{r}_A^*$, $\mathbf{r}_B^*$, $\mathbf{r}_C^*$, using input R1CS streams and the verifier challenges. The R1CS streams $\mathcal{S}_{\mathrm{col}}(A)$, $\mathcal{S}_{\mathrm{col}}(B)$ and $\mathcal{S}_{\mathrm{col}}(C)$ of the matrices A, B and C produce elements of the form $(i, j, e) \in [N] \times [N] \times \mathbb{F}$. Streaming only the first element of the triple produces the stream $\mathcal{S}_{\mathrm{cmrow}}(A) = \mathcal{S}_{\mathrm{cmrow}}(B) = \mathcal{S}_{\mathrm{cmrow}}(C)$ of the vector row (we recall that we assumed the support of A, B, C to be the same, and that row is ordered column-major).

Similarly, the second element of the triple induces a stream $\mathcal{S}_{\mathrm{cmcol}}(A)$ of the vector col, which is also equal to $\mathcal{S}_{\mathrm{cmcol}}(B)$ and $\mathcal{S}_{\mathrm{cmcol}}(C)$, again since the support is the same. Additionally, $\mathcal{S}_{\mathrm{cmcol}}(A)$ is non-increasing: the column indices, in the dense representation of the matrix, are sorted in decreasing order when streamed column-major. As a result, the entries of $\mathbf{z}^*$ can be produced one by one in $O(1)$ space from streams $\mathcal{S}(\mathbf{z})$ and $\mathcal{S}_{\mathrm{col}}(A)$: examine each entry of $\mathcal{S}_{\mathrm{cmcol}}(A)$, advance forwards $\mathbf{z}$ if the column changed, and output that same entry as long as the next element of $\mathcal{S}_{\mathrm{cmcol}}(A)$ stays unchanged.

The streams $\mathcal{S}_{\mathrm{cmval}}(A)$ (respectively, $\mathcal{S}_{\mathrm{cmval}}(B)$ and $\mathcal{S}_{\mathrm{cmval}}(C)$) are defined by projecting onto the third element of the streams $\mathcal{S}_{\mathrm{col}}(A)$ (respectively, $\mathcal{S}_{\mathrm{col}}(B)$ and $\mathcal{S}_{\mathrm{col}}(C)$), and produce the streams for the vectors val_A, val_B, and val_C in column-major order.

For $\mathbf{r}_A^*$, $\mathbf{r}_B^*$ and $\mathbf{r}_C^*$, recall that $\mathbf{y}_B = \otimes_j(1, \rho_j)$, $\mathbf{y}_C = \otimes_j(1, \upsilon^{2^j})$, and $\mathbf{y}_A = \mathbf{y}_B \circ \mathbf{y}_C = \otimes_j(1, \rho_j \upsilon^{2^j})$. Thus, any entry of $\mathbf{r}_B^*$ or $\mathbf{r}_C^*$ (and hence $\mathbf{r}_A^*$) can be computed in $O(\log N)$ operations from $\upsilon \in \mathbb{F}^\times$ and $\rho_0, \ldots, \rho_{n-1} \in \mathbb{F}^\times$.

2.6.1   Lookup Protocol

Lookup protocols enable the prover to convince the verifier that all of the entries in a vector $\mathbf{g}^* \in \mathbb{F}^M$ appear as entries of another vector $\mathbf{g} \in \mathbb{F}^N$ according to the data stored in the *address vector* $\mathsf{addr} \in [N]^M$, i.e.:

$$\{(\mathbf{g}_i^*, \mathsf{addr}_i)\}_{i \in [M]} \subseteq \{(\mathbf{g}_j, j)\}_{j \in [N]} \ .$$

We denote this condition by "$(\mathbf{g}^*, \mathsf{addr}) \subseteq (\mathbf{g}, [N])$". In order to verify that $\mathbf{r}_U^*$ and $\mathbf{z}^*$ were correctly computed, the verifier must check four lookup relations:

$$(\mathbf{r}_A^*, \mathsf{row}) \subseteq (\hat{\mathbf{a}}, [N]) \ , \qquad (\mathbf{r}_B^*, \mathsf{row}) \subseteq (\hat{\mathbf{b}}, [N]) \ ,$$
$$(\mathbf{r}_C^*, \mathsf{row}) \subseteq (\hat{\mathbf{c}}, [N]) \ , \qquad (\mathbf{z}^*, \mathsf{col}) \subseteq (\mathbf{z}, [N]) \ . \tag{11}$$

Note that since $\mathbf{y}_A = \mathbf{y}_B \circ \mathbf{y}_C$, and $\mathbf{r}_A^*$, $\mathbf{r}_B^*$ and $\mathbf{r}_C^*$ come from looking up the entries of $\mathbf{y}_A$, $\mathbf{y}_B$ and $\mathbf{y}_C$ at the indices specified by row. Therefore, instead of checking that $(\mathbf{r}_A^*, \mathsf{row}) \subseteq (\mathbf{y}_A, [N])$, it suffices to check the Hadamard product relation $\mathbf{y}_A = \mathbf{y}_B \circ \mathbf{y}_C$. This can be done using an extension of the twisted scalar product protocol. This leaves four look-up relations to check.

Polynomial Identities for Look-Up Relations. To verify look-up relations, we use the polynomial identity derived by Gabizon and Williams [GW20], and similar strategies to Bootle et al. [BCG20] to construct a polynomial IOP to verify the identity.

We reduce the lookup conditions $(\mathbf{r}_U^*, \mathsf{row}) \subseteq (\mathbf{y}_U, [N])$ and $(\mathbf{z}^*, \mathsf{col}) \subseteq (\mathbf{z}, [N])$ to simpler inclusion conditions such as $\mathbf{f}^* \subseteq \mathbf{f}$, where each entry in the vector $\mathbf{f}^*$ equals some entry in the vector $\mathbf{f}$. To do so, for each matrix $U = A, B, C$, algebraically hash the pairs $(\mathbf{r}_U^*, \mathsf{row})$, $(\mathbf{y}_U, [N])$, $(\mathbf{z}^*, \mathsf{col})$ and $(\mathbf{z}, [N])$ into single vectors by considering a random linear combination of each pair, using a random challenge from the verifier. Let $\mathsf{sort}(\mathbf{g}, \mathbf{f})$ denote the function that sorts the entries of $\mathbf{g} \parallel \mathbf{f}$ according to order of appearance in $\mathbf{f}$.

Lemma 3 ([GW20, Claim 3.1]). *Let $\mathbf{f}^* \in \mathbb{F}^M$ and $\mathbf{f} \in \mathbb{F}^N$. Then $\mathbf{f}^* \subseteq \mathbf{f}$ if and only if there exists $\mathbf{w} \in \mathbb{F}^{M+N}$ such that the equation below in $\mathbb{F}[X, Y]$ is satisfied:*

$$\prod_{j=0}^{M+N-1} \left(Y(1+Z) + w_{j+1} + w_j \cdot Z\right) =$$

$$(1+Z)^M \prod_{j=0}^{M-1} (Y + f_j) \prod_{j=0}^{N-1} \left(Y(1+Z) + f_{j+1} + f_j \cdot Z\right) \quad (12)$$

where indices are taken (respectively) modulo $M + N$, N. If $\mathbf{f}^* \subseteq \mathbf{f}$, then $\mathbf{w} := \mathsf{sort}(\mathbf{f}^*, \mathbf{f})$ satisfies Eq. 12.

The strategy in the look-up protocol is for the prover to compute $\mathbf{w}$ and prove that Eq. 12 is satisfied for every look-up relation that needs to be checked. In the protocol, the prover computes $\mathbf{w}$ and sends it to the verifier. Then, the verifier sends random challenges $v, \zeta \in \mathbb{F}^\times$ to the prover, who computes each of the three product expressions in Eq. 12, evaluated at v and ζ:

$$e_0 = \prod_{i=0}^{M+N-1} \left(v(1+\zeta) + w_{i+1} + w_i \cdot \zeta\right),$$

$$e_1 = \prod_{i=0}^{M-1} (v + f_i^*), \quad (13)$$

$$e_2 = \prod_{i=0}^{N-1} \left(v(1+\zeta) + f_{i+1} + f_i \cdot z\right) .$$

where (again) indices are taken (respectively) modulo $M + N$, N. The prover then sends the three product values e_0, e_1 and e_2 to the verifier. The verifier checks Eq. 12 holds at v and ζ by checking that $e_0 = (1+\zeta)^M e_1 e_2$, and uses three *entry-product* sub-protocols, which we describe in Sect. 2.6.2, to prove that e_0, e_1 and e_2 were correctly computed from $\mathbf{f}^*$, $\mathbf{f}$ and $\mathbf{w}$.

This approach requires polynomial query access to $\mathbf{f}^*_{\circlearrowright}$, the cyclic right-shift of $\mathbf{f}^*$, since the inputs to the entry product protocols depend on $\mathbf{f}^*_{\circlearrowright}$. The look-up protocol of Bootle et al. [BCG20] uses an additional *shift* sub-protocol to check this condition. By contrast, we remove this additional step by considering instead the lookup protocol over vectors with a leading zero coefficient. Now, queries on the right-shift $\mathbf{f}^*_{\circlearrowright}$ can be related to queries on $\mathbf{f}^*$ with a single evaluation query, since the leading coefficient is known in advance. We explain this optimisation further in the full version of this paper.

Elastic Realization. As shown in prior work [BCG20], if the underlying entry product protocols have a linear-time prover realisation and succinct verifier, then the same is true for the look-up protocol. Therefore, we focus on explaining a space-efficient prover realisation of the look-up protocol. Assuming that the entry-product protocol has a suitable space-efficient realisation, it suffices to explain how to simulate streaming access to look-up protocol vectors $\mathbf{f}^*$, $\mathbf{f}$ and $\mathbf{w}$ using previously derived streams.

First we consider $(\mathbf{z}^*, \mathsf{col})$ and $(\mathbf{z}, [N])$. Recall that each pair is algebraically hashed into vectors $\mathbf{f}^*$ and $\mathbf{f}$. It is simple produce the streams $\mathcal{S}(\mathbf{f}^*)$ and $\mathcal{S}(\mathbf{f})$ from the streams $\mathcal{S}(\mathbf{z}^*)$, $\mathcal{S}_{\mathrm{cmcol}}(A)$, $\mathcal{S}(\mathbf{z})$ and $\mathcal{S}([N])$, by applying the same algebraic hash function to pairs of entries on-the-fly. The same applies to input pairs $(\mathbf{r}^*_U, \mathsf{row})$ and $(\mathbf{y}_U, [N])$.

Now, we explain how to generate a stream of $\mathbf{w} = \mathsf{sort}(\mathbf{f}^*, \mathbf{f})$ using little memory space. This is more challenging because storing the entire vectors $\mathbf{f}^*$ and $\mathbf{f}$ and sorting them requires $O(M + N)$ memory. In the case of inputs $(\mathbf{z}^*, \mathsf{col})$ and $(\mathbf{z}, [N])$, as col is a non-decreasing sequence, it turns out that $\mathcal{S}_{\mathrm{cmcol}}(A)$ is already sorted into a suitable order, and it suffices to *merge* the streams of $\mathbf{f}^*$ and $\mathbf{f}$ together to produce a stream for $\mathbf{w}$. The same can't be said for row, which is not necessarily ordered. However, the vector row in non-decreasing form is already available from the inputs: it can be streamed from the dense representation of the matrix in row-major ordering $\mathcal{S}_{\mathrm{row}}(A)$. To apply the same idea to input pairs $\mathbf{r}^*_U$ and row, we build $\mathcal{S}_{\mathrm{rmrow}}(A)$, which is non-decreasing, and use it to produce the stream of the sorted vector for the lookup protocol. We describe our look-up protocol in more detail in the full version.

On Alternative Proof Techniques for Look-Up Relations. Prior work such as [Set20] checks look-up relations using an *offline memory-checking* [Blu+91, Cla+03] abstraction in which the prover shows that $\mathbf{g}^*$ was correctly constructed entry by entry from $\mathbf{g}$ using read and write operations. This leads to an alternative polynomial identity replacing Equation 12, which uses a list of *timestamps* recording when a particular element of $\mathbf{g}^*$ was read from $\mathbf{g}$. In this case though, it is unclear how to generate the timestamps required for by this method without storing linear memory. While in the argument of Gabizon and Williams [GW20] the polynomial relation is independent from the ordering of the matrix $\mathcal{S}(A)$ (row- or column-major), memory-checking arguments require random access to the vector row in order to access the last visited timestamps, which cannot be performed in log-space.

2.6.2 Entry Product Protocol

Let $\mathbf{f} = (f_0, \ldots, f_{N-1}) \in \mathbb{F}^N$ such that $e = f_0 \cdots f_{N-1}$. We describe an entry-product protocol, building on Bootle et al. [BCG20, Sec. 6.4], that reduces an entry product statement $\prod_i f_i = e$ to a single scalar-product relation, using polynomial evaluation query access to $\mathbf{f}$.

Compared with the prior work, our work exploits the structure of univariate polynomials to simplify the scheme and remove the need for *cyclic-shift tests* [BCG20, Sec. 6.3]. We propose additional optimizations in Sect. 2.7 which improve the concrete efficiency of our protocol.

High-Level Overview. Let $\mathbf{f}$ be as above, with $f_{N-1} = 1$.[8] Let $\psi \in \mathbb{F}^\times$ and let $\mathbf{y}' = (1, \psi, \ldots, \psi^{N-1})$. Let $\mathbf{g}$ be the vector of partial products of the entries of $\mathbf{f}$, that is:

$$\mathbf{g} := (\textstyle\prod_{i \geq 0} f_i, \quad \prod_{i \geq 1} f_i, \quad \ldots, \quad f_{N-2}f_{N-1}, \quad f_{N-1}) \tag{14}$$

Then, observe that:

$$
\begin{aligned}
\langle \mathbf{g} \circ \mathbf{y}', \mathbf{f}_\circlearrowright \rangle &= \sum_{i=1}^{N-1} g_i f_{i-1} \psi^i + g_0 f_{N-1} \\
&= \sum_{i=1}^{N-1} g_{i-1} \psi^i + e + g_{N-1}\psi^N - g_{N-1}\psi^N \\
&= \psi \mathbf{g}(\psi) + e - \psi^N
\end{aligned}
\tag{15}
$$

In the entry product protocol, the prover sends the oracle $\mathbf{g}$ to the verifier, and the verifier replies with the random challenge $\psi \in \mathbb{F}^\times$, and makes a polynomial evaluation query $\mathbf{g}(\psi) = v$. Then, both parties engage in a twisted scalar product protocol to verify Eq. 15. Polynomial evaluation queries $\mathbf{f}_\circlearrowright(x)$ for $x \in \mathbb{F}$ made as part of the twisted scalar-product protocol can be computed using evaluation queries $\mathbf{f}(x)$. To do this, note that $\mathbf{f}_\circlearrowright(x) = x\mathbf{f}(x) - x^N + 1$ since $f_{N-1} = 1$; thus the verifier can compute $\mathbf{f}_\circlearrowright(x)$ from $\mathbf{f}(x)$ in $O(\log N)$ operations. The partial products in Eq. 14 are computed starting with f_{N-1} because

Elastic Realization. As with other sub-protocols, the entry-product protocol inherits a linear-time prover realisation and succinct verifier from the underlying twisted scalar-product protocol.

To give a space-efficient realisation, it suffices to show that $\mathbf{g}$ can be generated element-by-element given access to the stream $\mathcal{S}(\mathbf{f})$: the partial products of elements of $\mathbf{f}$ can be produced by streaming each successive element of $\mathcal{S}(\mathbf{f})$ and multiplying it into a running product. Note that the partial products in $\mathbf{g}$ are

---

[8] This restriction is merely didactical. Given any $\mathbf{f} \in \mathbb{F}^N$, representing the coefficients of a degree $N - 1$ polynomial, it is easy to simulate polynomial-evaluation query access to $(\mathbf{f}, 1)$ using the polynomial $\mathbf{f}(X) + X^{N+1}$. For any evaluation query in $x \in \mathbb{F}$, forward evaluation queries to $\mathbf{f}$ and add x^{N+1} before returning. This costs $O(\log N)$ $\mathbb{F}$-ops.

computed from the last entry to the first, starting with f_{N-1}. This is because streams of polynomials move from the highest-order coefficient to the lowest to be compatible with space-efficient commitment algorithms, as explained in Sect. 2.3.

2.7   Implementation and Optimizations

We implemented the elastic argument from Sects. 2.5 and 2.6 by leveraging and extending `arkworks` [ark], a Rust ecosystem for developing and programming with zk-SNARKs. Our implementation, called `ark-gemini`[9], is open-source and freely available under MIT license. The code structure follows the modular design of the protocol, which involves combining an elastic polynomial commitment scheme and an elastic (holographic) PIOP. We deem each of the single components of the protocol (the streaming infrastructure, the commitment scheme, and the sub-protocols for sumcheck, tensor check, entry product, lookup protocol, etc.) to be independent interest for future space-efficient projects. Below, we provide an overview of the streaming infrastructure and the algorithmic optimizations that were adopted in the implementation.

2.7.1   Streaming Infrastructure

We extend the `arkworks` framework with support for streams in order to express our space-efficient protocols. A stream is simply a wrapper over `iter::Iterator`, the Rust interface for dealing iterators. Streams can be restarted and iterated over multiple times. We use Rust's borrow abstractions to produce streams that avoid copying elements whenever possible: a stream either returns a field element, or a reference to a field element. In other words, we have zero-copy interface where data structures do not require to be copied from memory, unless really needed. In practice, input streams could be instantiated with arrays (for instance, a memory-mapped files), or a concurrent stream of data downloaded from the web. Our design supports stream compositions and could be potentially extended to new front-ends.

A recent work by Baum, Malozemoff, Rosen, and Scholl [Bau+21] also studies streaming provers, and provides a space-efficient proving algorithm in Rust. To achieve a space-efficient prover, they rely on Rust's concurrency features (also known as Rust async), which is a more specific interface compatible with our framework based on iterators.

2.7.2   Practical Optimizations

We introduce several algorithmic optimizations that improve the concrete performance of our scheme.

Elastic Provers. One of the benefits of the elastic SNARK is that it allows switching from the space-efficient implementation to the time-efficient one. For example, in the scalar product, if the prover has enough memory, then it can

---

[9] See https://github.com/arkworks-rs/gemini.

transcribe the folded sumcheck claim and proceed with the time-efficient implementation of the prover function. This allows for a more fine-grained control of the memory for the prover, and benefit from the speed-up of the time-efficient prover for the last few rounds of the protocol. Since the prover's messages are the same in both modes, this does not affect the end result. In our implementation, it is possible to enforce a memory budget that, once hit, allows the prover to stop and store the intermediate claim entirely in memory. Once the claim has been stored, it is possible to proceed with the time-efficient implementation.

Batch [KZG10]. Boneh et al. [Bon+20] proposed an optimization of [KZG10] to batch evaluation proofs for a set of evaluation points over different polynomials, exploiting the special structure of univariate polynomials.

We adapt these optimizations to our elastic polynomial commitment scheme, and implement them. In particular, although our tensor product protocol may require the verifier to query different polynomials at a set of different evaluation points, a single constant-size evaluation will have to be sent. This renders the concrete size of the proof significantly better than multi-linear approaches such as [Zha+17, Zha+18], which require a logarithmic-size opening proof.

Offline Memory-Checking. As discussed in Sect. 2.6.1, the offline memory-checking protocol is not compatible with the space-efficient prover, because the computation of timestamps may require random-access over non-zero entries. However, we also observe that given a particular ordering of the non-zero entries, it might be possible to apply the offline memory-checking partially in our polynomial IOP. In the particular implementation of our protocol, the offline memory checking can be used to prove the lookup for $\left(\mathbf{z}_U^\star, \mathsf{col}_U\right) \subseteq \left(\mathbf{z}, [N]\right)$.

We view the offline memory-checking as an optimization because it is concretely more efficient than the plookup protocol. That is because the sender in the plookup protocol must send additional commitments to the verifier; whereas, the commitments in the offline memory-checking can be precomputed by the indexer.

2.8 Evaluation

We run extensive benchmarks over Gemini (both preprocessing and non-preprocessing SNARKs), over an Amazon AWS EC2 c5.9xlarge instance, with 36 cores. We enable multi-threading using `rayon`, a Rust library for parallelism, and use it for efficiently computing multi-scalar multiplications and to run the batched sumcheck in the preprocessing SNARK protocol, where multiple sumcheck instances can be run in parallel. We select BLS12-381 as the pairing-friendly elliptic curve, but we note however that smaller elliptic curves are suitable, due to the remark in Remark 4. Our chosen field $\mathbb{F}$ is the scalar field of BLS12-381.

We perform tests for different instance sizes N, with $M = N$, for the range $N = 2^{18}$ up to 2^{35}. These instance sizes are much larger than what is commonly covered in the literature, and are meant to illustrate the behavior of a proving system over very large instances.

Proving Space. We show that the Gemini prover can support instances with arbitrary sizes. In Fig, 2 it is possible to observe that the memory trace remains constant across large instance sizes, and that is stays consistently below 1 GB of required memory, while the preprocessing SNARK protocol demands slightly more than 1 GB to run. Two main constants influence the overall memory trace of the program:

- the memory budget allocated for multi-scalar multiplication (MSM). Despite the MSM operation can also be implemented in a streaming fashion, either with trivial scalar-multiplication, or by making small changes over Pippenger's algorithm, we noted that, in practice, best performance is achieved by performing Pippenger over buffers of fixed sizes, and then accumulating the partial result. We set the buffer to host 2^{20} field elements.
- the sumcheck round threshold, after which the elastic prover will transcribe the sumcheck instance and proceed with the time-efficient algorithm. We set the threshold to 22. That is, the last 22 rounds of the sumcheck will always be performed with the time-efficient prover.

The memory footprint stays constant because the constants chosen for the multi-scalar multiplication buffer and sumcheck round threshold are much larger than the asymptotic factors of the proving algorithm. The difference in memory is related solely to the batched sumcheck step in the preprocessing SNARK protocol, where multiple instances are being transcribed in memory at the same time once the round threshold hits.

Our benchmarks stop at 2^{35} for the non-preprocessing SNARK and the 2^{32} for the preprocessing one, but the upper limit in our benchmarks is arbitrary: as long as it is possible to generate the input streams for the time prover, then prover will be able to carry out in full the proving algorithm, and keeping the memory footprint very small. Prior works, such as Setty [Set20] and Chiesa et al. [Chi+20] provide public benchmarks for sizes up to 2^{20}. When running benchmarks ourselves to compare our work with previous literature such as Marlin[10], we were unable to proceed over size 2^{24} due to out of memory crashed. Even if we instruct the kernel to allow for memory over-commitment[11], the kernel will refuse to allocate new memory and eventually Rust will panic due to memory allocation failures. Our own prover, when run as a purely time-efficient prover, cannot successfully prove instances of size 2^{25} and 2^{27}.

Proving Time. We present the proving time of elastic provers. The elastic prover will switch to the time-efficient mode if the intermediate state can be loaded within the memory budget. So when the instance size is small, the elastic prover will run purely in the time-efficient mode. As far as runtime is concerned, we make an important initial remark: the most expensive operations in our protocol are given by the cryptographic operations, namely the multi-scalar multiplications. For this reason, in Fig. 2, where we show the running times for for

---

[10] cf. https://github.com/arkworks-rs/marlin.
[11] This is vm.overcommit=2. See https://www.kernel.org/doc/Documentation/vm/overcommit-accounting.

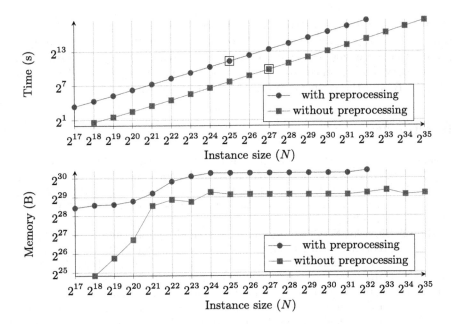

Fig. 2. Runtimes (above) and memory usage (below) for the elastic prover in the *preprocessing* protocol (blue) and the *non-preprocessing* protocol (red), for different R1CS sizes with $N = M$. The black squares indicate the size for which the time-efficient prover triggers an out-of-memory crash.(Color figure online)

different values of N, with $M = N$, it is possible to observe a graph that evolves almost linearly. The squared logarithmic factor does not influence noticeably the overall runtime, as far as we were able to measure within the window of instance sizes of our benchmarks.

We also measure the economic cost of running the Gemini prover. Roughly speaking, the cost per gate of the preprocessing SNARK prover is around than 7.6×10^{-5} seconds per gate. Using the AWS estimator[12] (on-demand hourly cost 1.836 USD), we are able to conclude that, roughly speaking, the cost for the preprocessing SNARK is about 2.30×10^{-5} USD per gate. In particular, the estimated cost for an instance of 2^{31} gates is 89 USD. In contrast, the cost of DIZK [Wu+18] is much higher and around 500 USD for an instance of 2^{31}, because DIZK has to run the computation on 20 more powerful and expensive machines (r3.8xlarge EC2 instances with on-demand hourly cost 2.656 USD) for about 10 h. In the case of non-preprocessing SNARK, the cost is a bit lower and around 40 USD for a circuit of 2^{35}.

---

[12] source: https://calculator.aws.

Verification Time and Proof Size. We measure the proof size and verification time for the preprocessing protocol. Note that the verifier can easily verify the proof for large instances since it does not need to read and load the instance into the memory. For instance size ranging from 2^{12} to 2^{35}, the proof size is about 13–27 KB, and the verification time is about 16–30 ms.

References

[Bau+21] Baum, C., Malozemoff, A.J., Rosen, M.B., Scholl, P.: Mac'n'Cheese: zero-knowledge proofs for Boolean and arithmetic circuits with nested disjunctions. In: Malkin, T., Peikert, C. (eds.) CRYPTO 2021. LNCS, vol. 12828, pp. 92–122. Springer, Cham (2021). https://doi.org/10.1007/978-3-030-84259-8_4

[BC12] Bitansky, N., Chiesa, A.: Succinct arguments from multi-prover interactive proofs and their efficiency benefits. In: Safavi-Naini, R., Canetti, R. (eds.) CRYPTO 2012. LNCS, vol. 7417, pp. 255–272. Springer, Heidelberg (2012). https://doi.org/10.1007/978-3-642-32009-5_16

[BCG20] Bootle, J., Chiesa, A., Groth, J.: Linear-time arguments with sublinear verification from tensor codes. In: Pass, R., Pietrzak, K. (eds.) TCC 2020. LNCS, vol. 12551, pp. 19–46. Springer, Cham (2020). https://doi.org/10.1007/978-3-030-64378-2_2

[BCS16] Ben-Sasson, E., Chiesa, A., Spooner, N.: Interactive oracle proofs. In: Hirt, M., Smith, A. (eds.) TCC 2016. LNCS, vol. 9986, pp. 31–60. Springer, Heidelberg (2016). https://doi.org/10.1007/978-3-662-53644-5_2

[Bel+09] Belenkiy, M., Camenisch, J., Chase, M., Kohlweiss, M., Lysyanskaya, A., Shacham, H.: Randomizable proofs and delegatable anonymous credentials. In: Halevi, S. (ed.) CRYPTO 2009. LNCS, vol. 5677, pp. 108–125. Springer, Heidelberg (2009). https://doi.org/10.1007/978-3-642-03356-8_7

[BFS20] Bünz, B., Fisch, B., Szepieniec, A.: Transparent SNARKs from DARK compilers. In: Canteaut, A., Ishai, Y. (eds.) EUROCRYPT 2020. LNCS, vol. 12105, pp. 677–706. Springer, Cham (2020). https://doi.org/10.1007/978-3-030-45721-1_24

[BGM17] Bowe, S., et al.: Scalable multi-party computation for zk-SNARK parameters in the random beacon model. Cryptology ePrint Archive, Report 2017/1050

[Bit+13] Bitansky, N., et al.: Recursive composition and bootstrapping for SNARKs and proof-carrying data. In: STOC 2013 (2013)

[Blo+20] Block, A.R., Holmgren, J., Rosen, A., Rothblum, R.D., Soni, P.: Public-coin zero-knowledge arguments with (almost) minimal time and space overheads. In: Pass, R., Pietrzak, K. (eds.) TCC 2020. LNCS, vol. 12551, pp. 168–197. Springer, Cham (2020). https://doi.org/10.1007/978-3-030-64378-2_7

[Blo+21] Block, A.R., Holmgren, J., Rosen, A., Rothblum, R.D., Soni, P.: Time- and space-efficient arguments from groups of unknown order. In: Malkin, T., Peikert, C. (eds.) CRYPTO 2021. LNCS, vol. 12828, pp. 123–152. Springer, Cham (2021). https://doi.org/10.1007/978-3-030-84259-8_5

[Blu+91] Blum, M., et al.: Checking the correctness of memories. In: FOCS 1991 (1991)

[Bon+20] Boneh, D., et al.: Efficient polynomial commitment schemes for multiple points and polynomials. Cryptology ePrint Archive, Report 2020/081

[Boo+16] Bootle, J., Cerulli, A., Chaidos, P., Groth, J., Petit, C.: Efficient zero-knowledge arguments for arithmetic circuits in the discrete log setting. In: Fischlin, M., Coron, J.-S. (eds.) EUROCRYPT 2016. LNCS, vol. 9666, pp. 327–357. Springer, Heidelberg (2016). https://doi.org/10.1007/978-3-662-49896-5_12

[Boo+17] Bootle, J., Cerulli, A., Ghadafi, E., Groth, J., Hajiabadi, M., Jakobsen, S.K.: Linear-time zero-knowledge proofs for arithmetic circuit satisfiability. In: Takagi, T., Peyrin, T. (eds.) ASIACRYPT 2017. LNCS, vol. 10626, pp. 336–365. Springer, Cham (2017). https://doi.org/10.1007/978-3-319-70700-6_12

[Boo+18] Bootle, J., Cerulli, A., Groth, J., Jakobsen, S., Maller, M.: Arya: nearly linear-time zero-knowledge proofs for correct program execution. In: Peyrin, T., Galbraith, S. (eds.) ASIACRYPT 2018. LNCS, vol. 11272, pp. 595–626. Springer, Cham (2018). https://doi.org/10.1007/978-3-030-03326-2_20

[Bün+21] Bünz, B., Maller, M., Mishra, P., Tyagi, N., Vesely, P.: Proofs for inner pairing products and applications. In: Tibouchi, M., Wang, H. (eds.) ASIACRYPT 2021. LNCS, vol. 13092, pp. 65–97. Springer, Cham (2021). https://doi.org/10.1007/978-3-030-92078-4_3

[Chi+20] Chiesa, A., Hu, Y., Maller, M., Mishra, P., Vesely, N., Ward, N.: Marlin: preprocessing zkSNARKs with universal and updatable SRS. In: Canteaut, A., Ishai, Y. (eds.) EUROCRYPT 2020. LNCS, vol. 12105, pp. 738–768. Springer, Cham (2020). https://doi.org/10.1007/978-3-030-45721-1_26

[Cla+03] Clarke, D., Devadas, S., van Dijk, M., Gassend, B., Suh, G.E.: Incremental multiset hash functions and their application to memory integrity checking. In: Laih, C.-S. (ed.) ASIACRYPT 2003. LNCS, vol. 2894, pp. 188–207. Springer, Heidelberg (2003). https://doi.org/10.1007/978-3-540-40061-5_12

[CMT12] Cormode, G., et al.: Practical Verified Computation with Streaming Interactive Proofs. In: ITCS 2012 (2012)

[COS20] Chiesa, A., Ojha, D., Spooner, N.: FRACTAL: post-quantum and transparent recursive proofs from holography. In: Canteaut, A., Ishai, Y. (eds.) EUROCRYPT 2020. LNCS, vol. 12105, pp. 769–793. Springer, Cham (2020). https://doi.org/10.1007/978-3-030-45721-1_27

[Dra20] Drake, J.: PLONK without FFTs. https://www.youtube.com/watch?v=ffXgxvlCBvo

[DRZ20] Daza, V., Ràfols, C., Zacharakis, A.: Updateable inner product argument with logarithmic verifier and applications. In: Kiayias, A., Kohlweiss, M., Wallden, P., Zikas, V. (eds.) PKC 2020. LNCS, vol. 12110, pp. 527–557. Springer, Cham (2020). https://doi.org/10.1007/978-3-030-45374-9_18

[FS86] Fiat, A., Shamir, A.: How to prove yourself: practical solutions to identification and signature problems. In: Odlyzko, A.M. (ed.) CRYPTO 1986. LNCS, vol. 263, pp. 186–194. Springer, Heidelberg (1987). https://doi.org/10.1007/3-540-47721-7_12

[Gab20] Gabizon, A.: Lineval Protocol. https://hackmd.io/aWXth2dASPaGVrXiGg1Cmg?view

[Gen+13] Gennaro, R., Gentry, C., Parno, B., Raykova, M.: Quadratic span programs and succinct NIZKs without PCPs. In: Johansson, T., Nguyen, P.Q. (eds.) EUROCRYPT 2013. LNCS, vol. 7881, pp. 626–645. Springer, Heidelberg (2013). https://doi.org/10.1007/978-3-642-38348-9_37

[GGM14] Garman, C., et al.: Decentralized anonymous credentials (2013)

[Gol+21] Golovnev, A., et al.: Brakedown: linear-time and post-quantum SNARKs for R1CS. Cryptology ePrint Archive, Report 2021/1043 (2021)

[GW20] Gabizon, A., et al.: Plookup: a simplified polynomial protocol for lookup tables. Cryptology ePrint Archive, Report 2020/315 (2020)

[HR18] Holmgren, J., et al.: Delegating computations with (almost) minimal time and space overhead. In: FOCS 2018 (2018)

[JW17] Javeed, K., et al.: Low latency flexible FPGA implementation of point multiplication on elliptic curves over GF(p). In: International Journal of Circuit Theory and Applications (2017)

[KZG10] Kate, A., Zaverucha, G.M., Goldberg, I.: Constant-size commitments to polynomials and their applications. In: Abe, M. (ed.) ASIACRYPT 2010. LNCS, vol. 6477, pp. 177–194. Springer, Heidelberg (2010). https://doi. org/10.1007/978-3-642-17373-8_11

[Lun+92] Lund, C., et al.: Algebraic methods for interactive proof systems. J. ACM **39**, 859–868 (1992)

[Par+13] Parno, B., et al.: Pinocchio: nearly practical verifiable computation. In: S&P 2013 (2013)

[Pip80] Pippenger, N.: On the Evaluation of Powers and Monomials (1980)

[PLS19] del Pino, R., Lyubashevsky, V., Seiler, G.: Short discrete log proofs for FHE and ring-LWE ciphertexts. In: Lin, D., Sako, K. (eds.) PKC 2019. LNCS, vol. 11442, pp. 344–373. Springer, Cham (2019). https://doi.org/10.1007/ 978-3-030-17253-4_12

[RRR16] Reingold, O., et al.: Constant-round interactive proofs for delegating computation. In: STOC 2016 (2016)

[Set20] Setty, S.: Spartan: efficient and general-purpose zkSNARKs without trusted setup. In: Micciancio, D., Ristenpart, T. (eds.) CRYPTO 2020. LNCS, vol. 12172, pp. 704–737. Springer, Cham (2020). https://doi.org/10.1007/978- 3-030-56877-1_25

[Tha13] Thaler, J.: Time-optimal interactive proofs for circuit evaluation. In: Canetti, R., Garay, J.A. (eds.) CRYPTO 2013. LNCS, vol. 8043, pp. 71–89. Springer, Heidelberg (2013). https://doi.org/10.1007/978-3-642-40084-1_5

[Wu+18] Wu, H., et al.: DIZK: a distributed zero knowledge proof system. In: USENIX Security 2018 (2018)

[Xie+19] Xie, T., Zhang, J., Zhang, Y., Papamanthou, C., Song, D.: Libra: succinct zero-knowledge proofs with optimal prover computation. In: Boldyreva, A., Micciancio, D. (eds.) CRYPTO 2019. LNCS, vol. 11694, pp. 733–764. Springer, Cham (2019). https://doi.org/10.1007/978-3-030-26954-8_24

[Zcash] Zcash. https://z.cash/

[Zha+17] Zhang, Y., et al.: vSQL: verifying arbitrary SQL queries over dynamic outsourced databases. In: S&P 2017 (2017)

[Zha+18] Zhang, Y., et al.: vRAM: faster verifiable RAM with program-independent preprocessing. In: S&P 2018 (2018)

[Zha+21] Zhang, Y., et al.: PipeZK: accelerating zero-knowledge proof with a pipelined architecture. In: ISCA 2021 (2021)

[Ben+14a] Ben-Sasson, E., et al.: Succinct non-interactive zero knowledge for a von neumann architecture. In: USENIX Security 2014 (2014)

[Ben+14b] Sasson, E.B., et al.: Zerocash: decentralized anonymous payments from bitcoin. In: SP 2014 (2014)

[Ben+18] Ben-Sasson, E., et al.: Fast reed-solomon interactive oracle proofs of proximity. In: ICALP 2018 (2018)

[Ben+19] Ben-Sasson, E., et al.: Aurora: transparent succinct arguments for R1CS. In: EUROCRYPT 2019 (2019)

[ark] arkworks. arkworks: an ecosystem for developing and programming with zkSNARKs.https://github.com/arkworks-rs

Stacking Sigmas: A Framework to Compose Σ-Protocols for Disjunctions

Aarushi Goel[1]([✉]), Matthew Green[1], Mathias Hall-Andersen[2],
and Gabriel Kaptchuk[3]([✉])

[1] Johns Hopkins University, Baltimore, USA
{aarushig,mgreen}@cs.jhu.edu
[2] Aarhus University, Aarhus, Denmark
ma@cs.au.dk
[3] Boston University, Boston, USA
kaptchuk@bu.edu

Abstract. Zero-Knowledge (ZK) Proofs for disjunctive statements have been a focus of a long line of research. Classical results such as Cramer *et al.* [CRYPTO'94] and Abe *et al.* [AC'02] design generic compilers that transform certain classes of ZK proofs into ZK proofs for disjunctive statements. However, communication complexity of the resulting protocols in these results ends up being proportional to the complexity of proving all clauses in the disjunction. More recently, Heath *et al.* [EC'20] exploited special properties of garbled circuits to construct efficient ZK proofs for disjunctions, where the proof size is only proportional to the length of the largest clause in the disjunction. However, these techniques do not appear to generalize beyond garbled circuits.

In this work, we focus on achieving the best of both worlds. We design a *general framework* that compiles a large class of unmodified Σ-protocols, each for an individual statement, into a new Σ-protocol that proves a disjunction of these statements. Our framework can be used both when each clause is proved with the same Σ-protocol and when different Σ-protocols are used for different clauses. The resulting Σ-protocol is concretely efficient and has communication complexity proportional to the communication required by the largest clause, with additive terms that are only logarithmic in the number of clauses.

We show that our compiler can be applied to many well-known Σ-protocols, including classical protocols (*e.g.* Schnorr [JC'91] and Guillou-Quisquater [CRYPTO'88]) and modern MPC-in-the-head protocols such as the recent work of Katz, Kolesnikov and Wang [CCS'18] and the Ligero protocol of Ames *et al.* [CCS'17]. Finally, since all of the protocols in our class can be made non-interactive in the random oracle model using the Fiat-Shamir transform, our result yields the first generic non-interactive zero-knowledge protocol for disjunctions where the communication only depends on the size of the largest clause.

© International Association for Cryptologic Research 2022
O. Dunkelman and S. Dziembowski (Eds.): EUROCRYPT 2022, LNCS 13276, pp. 458–487, 2022.
https://doi.org/10.1007/978-3-031-07085-3_16

1   Introduction

Zero-knowledge proofs and arguments [26] are cryptographic protocols that enable a prover to convince the verifier of the validity of an NP statement without revealing the corresponding witness. These protocols, along with proof of knowledge variants, have now become critical in the construction of larger cryptographic protocols and systems. Since classical results established feasibility of such proofs for all NP languages [24], significant effort has gone into making zero-knowledge proofs more practically efficient *e.g.* [9,10,13,28,31,34,35], resulting in concretely efficient zero-knowledge protocols that are now being used in practice [7,41,42].

Zero-Knowledge for Disjunctive Statements. There is a long history of developing zero-knowledge techniques for *disjunctive statements* [1,17,21]. Disjunctive statements comprise of several *clauses* that are composed together with a logical "OR." These statements also include conditional clauses, *i.e.* clauses that would only be relevant if some condition on the statement is met. The witness for such statements consists of a witness for one of the clauses (also called the *active* clause), along with the index identifying the active clause. Disjunctive statements occur commonly in practice, making them an important target for proof optimizations. For example, disjunctive proofs are often also used to give the prover some degree of privacy, as a verifier cannot determine which clause is being satisfied. Use cases include membership proofs (*e.g.* ring signatures [37]), proving the existence of bugs in a large codebase (as explored in [31]), and proving the correct execution of a processor, which is typically composed of many possible instructions, only one of which is executed at a time [8].

   An exciting line of recent work has emerged that reduces the communication complexity for proving disjunctive statements to the size of the largest clause in the disjunction [31,36]. While succinct proof techniques exist [10,22,27,28], known constructions are plagued by very slow proving times and often require strong assumptions, sometimes including trusted setup. These recent works accept larger proofs in order to get significantly faster proving times and more reasonable assumptions—while still reducing the size of proofs significantly. Intuitively, the authors leverage the observation that a prover only needs to honestly execute the parts of a disjunctive statement that pertain to their witness. Using this observation, these protocols modify existing proof techniques, embedding communication-efficient ways to "cheat" for the inactive clauses of the disjunctive statement. We refer to these techniques as *stacking* techniques, borrowing the term from the work of Heath and Kolesnikov [31].

   Although these protocols achieve impressive results, designing stacking techniques requires significant manual effort. Each existing protocol requires the development of a novel technique that reduces the communication complexity of a specific base protocol. For instance, Heath and Kolesnikov [31] observe that garbled circuit tables can be additively *stacked* (thus the name), allowing the prover in [34] to *un-stack* efficiently, leveraging the topolgy hiding property of garbling. Techniques like these are tailored to optimize the communication complexity of a particular underlying protocol, and do not appear to generalize well to large families of protocols. In contrast, classical results [1, 17] succeed in designing a generic compiler that tranforms a large familily of zero-knowledge proof systems into proofs for disjunction, but fall short of reducing the size of the resulting proof.

In this work, we take a more general approach towards reducing the communication complexity of zero-knowledge protocols for disjunctive statements. Rather than reduce the communication complexity of a specific zero-knowledge protocol, we investigate *generic* stacking techniques for an important family of zero-knowledge protocols—three round public coin proofs of knowledge, popularly known as Σ-protocols. Specifically, we ask the following question:

Can we design a generic compiler that stacks any Σ-protocol without modification?

We take significant steps towards answering this question in the affirmative. While we do not demonstrate a technique for stacking all Σ-protocols, we present a compiler that *stacks* many natural Σ-protocols, including many of practical importance. We focus our attention on Σ-protocols because of their widespread use and because they can be made non-interactive in the random oracle model using the Fiat-Shamir transform [19]. However we expect that the techniques can easily be generalized to public-coin protocols with more rounds.

Benefits of a Generic Stacking Compiler. There are several significant benefits of developing generic stacking compilers, rather than developing bespoke protocols that support stacking. First, automatically compiling multiple Σ-protocols into ones supporting stacking removes the significant manual effort required to modify existing techniques. Moreover, newly developed Σ-protocols can be used to produce stacked proofs immediately, significantly streamlining the deployment process. A second, but perhaps even more practically consequential, benefit of generic compilers is that protocol designers are empowered to tailor their choice of Σ-protocol to their application—without considering if there are known stacking techniques for that particular Σ-protocol. Specifically, the protocol designer can select a proof technique that fits with the natural representation of the relevant statement (*e.g.* Boolean circuit, arithmetic circuit, linear forms or any other algebraic structure). Without a generic stacking compiler, a protocol designer interested in reducing the communication complexity of disjunctive proofs might be forced to apply some expensive NP reduction to encode the statement in a stacking-friendly way. This is particularly relevant because modern Σ-protocols often require that relations are phrased in a very specific manner, *e.g.* Ligero [2] requires arithmetic circuits over a large, finite field, while known stacking techniques [31] focus on Boolean circuits.

A common concern with applying protocol compilers is that they trade generality for efficiency (*e.g.* NP reductions). However, we note that the compiler that we develop in this work is extremely concretely efficient, overcoming this common limitation. For instance, naïvely applying our protocol to the classical Schnorr identification protocol and applying the Fiat-Shamir [19] heurestic yields a ring signature construction with signatures of length $2\lambda \cdot (2 + 2\log(\ell))$ bits, where λ is the security parameter and ℓ is the ring size; this is actually smaller than modern ring signatures from similar assumptions [4,12] without requiring significant optimization.[1]

1.1 Our Contributions

In this work, we give a generic treatment for minimizing the communication complexity of Σ-protocols for disjunctive statements. In particular, we identify some "special properties" of Σ-protocol that make them amenable to "stacking." We refer to protocols that satisfy these properties as *stackable* protocols. Then we present a framework for compiling any stackable Σ-protocols for independent statements into a new, communication-efficient Σ-protocol for the disjunction of those statements. Our framework only requires oracle access to the prover, verifier and simulator algorithms of the underlying Σ-protocols. We present our results in two-steps:

Self-stacking Compiler. First, we present our basic compiler, which we call a "self-stacking" compiler. This compiler composes several instances of the *same* Σ-protocol, corresponding to a particular language into a disjunctive proof. The resulting protocol has communication complexity proportional to the communication complexity of a single instance of the underlying protocol. Specifically, we prove the following theorem:

Informal Theorem 1 (Self-Stacking). *Let Π be a stackable Σ-protocol for an NP language $\mathcal{L}$ that has communication complexity $\mathsf{CC}(\Pi)$. There exists is a Σ-protocol for the language $(x_1 \in \mathcal{L}) \vee \ldots \vee (x_\ell \in \mathcal{L})$, with communication complexity $O(\mathsf{CC}(\Pi) + \lambda \log(\ell))$, where λ is the computational security parameter.*

Cross-Stacking. We then extend the self-stacking compiler to support stacking *different* Σ-protocols for different languages. The communication complexity of the resulting protocol is a function of the largest clause in the disjunction and the similarity between the Σ-protocols being stacked. Let f_{CC} be a function that determines this dependence. For instance, if we compose the same Σ-protocol but corresponding to different languages, then the output of f_{CC} will likely be the same as that of a single instance of that protocol for the language with the largest relation function. However, if we compose Σ-protocols that are very different from each other, then the output of f_{CC} will likely be larger. We prove the following theorem:

Informal Theorem 2 (Cross-Stacking). *For each $i \in [\ell]$, let Π_i be a stackable Σ-protocol for an NP language $\mathcal{L}_i$ There exists is a Σ-protocol for the language $(x_1 \in \mathcal{L}_1) \vee \ldots \vee (x_\ell \in \mathcal{L}_\ell)$, with communication complexity $O(f_{\mathsf{CC}}(\{\Pi_i\}_{i \in [\ell]}) + \lambda \log(\ell))$.*

---

[1] Although concrete efficiency is a central element of our work, applying our compiler to applications is not our focus. The details of this ring signature construction can be found in the full version of the paper.

Examples of Stackable Σ-Protocols. We show many concrete examples of Σ-protocols that are stackable. Specifically, we look at classical protocols like Schnorr [39], Guillio-Quisquater [29] and Blum [11], and modern MPC-in-the-head protocols like KKW [35] and Ligero [2]. Previously it was not known how to prove disjunction over these Σ-protocols with sublinear communication in the number of clauses. When applied to these Σ-protocols, our compiler yields a Σ-protocol which can can made non-interactive in the random oracle model using the Fiat-Shamir heurestic. For example, when instantiated with Ligero our compiler yields a concretely efficient Σ-protocol for disjunction over ℓ different circuits of size $|C|$ each, with communication $O(\sqrt{|C|} + \lambda \log \ell)$. Additionally, we explore how to apply our cross-stacking compiler to stack different stackable Σ-protocols with one another (*e.g.* stacking a KKW proof for one relation with a Ligero proof for another relation).

Partially-Binding Non-interactive Vector Commitments. Central to our compiler is a new variation of commitments called partially-binding non-interactive vector commitment schemes. These schemes allow a committer to commit to a vector of values and equivocate on a subset of the elements in that vector, the positions of which are determined during commitment and are kept hidden. We show how such commitments can be constructed from the discrete log assumption.

Extensions and Implementation Considerations. We finish by discussing extensions of our work and concrete optimizations that improve the efficiency of our compiler when implemented in practice. Specifically, we consider generalizing our work to k-out-of-ℓ proofs of partial knowledge, *i.e.* the threshold analog of disjunctions. We give a version of our compiler that works for these threshold statements. Additionally, we demonstrate the efficiency of our compiler by presenting concrete proof sizes when our compiler is applied to both a disjunction of KKW and Schnorr signatures.

1.2 Related Work

A more in depth overview of these techniques can be found in ??.

Disjunctive Compilers for Zero-Knowledge. The classic work of Cramer *et al.* [17] showed how to compile Σ-protocols into k-of-ℓ disjunctions, but does not provide any communications savings. Abe *et al.* [1] presented an alternative compiler specifically designed for signatures in the random oracle model. More recently, Ciampi *et al.* [15] show how to augment this construction to allow the prover to select instances in the disjunction during the third round. We note that although Ciampi *et al.* make use of a similar commitment scheme, the focus of their work is very different and they do not consider minimizing communication.

Communication Reduction for Disjunctive Zero-Knowledge. In [36], Kolesnikov observed that the topology of a garbled circuit could be decoupled from its tables, resulting in S-universal two party SFE (Secret Function Evaluation). Building on this idea, Heath and Kolesnikov [31] brought the topology-decoupled paradigm to interactive zero-knowledge, based on the works of Jawurek et al. [34] and Frederiksen et al. [20]. This resulted in zero-knowledge with communication complexity proportional to the size of the largest clause in the disjunction, but is inherently interactive. In concurrent work, Baum et al. [5] present Mac'n'Cheese, a constant round zero-knowledge proof system that obtains "free nested disjunctions;" It is not clear how to make these protocols public coin. Heath and Kolesnikov also explored similar ideas to reduce the communication complexity of MPC protocols executed over disjunctions [30,32].

2 Technical Overview

In this section, we give a detailed overview of the techniques that we use to design a generic framework to achieve communication-efficient disjunctions of Σ-protocols without requiring non-trivial[2] changes to the underlying Σ-protocols. Throughout this work, we consider a disjunction of ℓ *clauses*, one (or more) of which are *active*, meaning that the prover holds a witness satisfying the relation encoded into those clauses. For the majority of this technical overview, we focus on the simpler case where the same Σ-protocol is used for each clause. We will then extend our ideas to cover heterogeneous Σ-protocols.

Recall that Σ-protocols are three-round, public-coin zero-knowledge protocols, where the prover sends the first message. In the second round, the verifier sends a random "challenge" message to the prover, that only depends on the random coins of the the verifier. Finally, in the third round, the prover responds with a message based on this challenge. Based on this transcript the verifier then decides whether to accept or reject the proof.

We start by considering the approaches taken by recent works focusing on privacy-preserving protocols for disjunctive statements, *e.g.* [31]. We observe that the "stacking" techniques used in all these works can be broadly classified as taking a *cheat and re-use approach*. In particular, all of these works show how some existing protocols can be modified to allow the parties to "cheat" on the inactive clauses—*i.e.* only executing the active clause honestly—and "re-using" the single honestly-computed transcript to mimic a fake computation of the inactive clauses. Critically, this is done while ensuring that the verifier cannot distinguish the honest execution of the active clause from the fake executions of the inactive clauses.

Our Approach. In this work we extend the *cheat and re-use* approach to design a framework for compiling Σ-protocols into a communication-efficient Σ-protocol for disjunctive statements without requiring modification of the

---

[2] We assume that basic, practice-oriented optimizations have already been applied to the Σ-protocols in question. For instance, we assume that only the minimum amount of information is sent during the third round of protocol. Hereafter, we will ignore these trivial modifications and simply say "without requiring modification." Note that these modifications truly are trivial: the parties only need to repeat existing parts of the transcript in other rounds. We discuss this in the context of MPC-in-the-head protocols in Sect. 5.

underlying protocols. Specifically, we are interested in reducing the number of *third round messages* that a prover must send to the verifier, since the third round message is typically the longest message in the protocol. Intuition extracted from prior work leads us to a natural high-level template for achieving this goal: *Run individual instances of Σ-protocols (one-for each clause in the disjunction) in parallel, such that only one of these instances (the one corresponding to the active clause) is honestly executed, and the remaining instances re-use parts of this honest instance.*

There are two primary challenges we must overcome to turn this rough outline into a concrete protocol: (1) how can the prover cheat on the inactive clauses? and (2) what parts of an honest Σ-protocol transcript can be safely re-used (without revealing the active clause)? We now discuss these challenges, and the techniques we use to overcome them, in more detail.

Challenge 1: How will the Prover Cheat on Inactive Clauses? Since the prover does not have a witness for the inactive clauses, the prover can cheat by creating accepting transcripts for the inactive clauses using the simulator(s) of the underlying Σ-protocols. The traditional method (*e.g.* [17] for disjunctive Schnorr proofs) requires the prover to start the protocol by randomly selecting a challenge for each inactive clause and simulating a transcript with respect to that challenge. In the third round, the prover completes the transcript for each clause and demonstrates that it could only have selected the challenges for all-but-one of the clauses. This approach, however, inherently requires sending many third round messages, which will make it difficult to re-use material across clauses (discussed in more detail below). Similarly, alternative classical approaches for composing Σ-protocols for disjunctives, like that of Abe et al. [1], also require sending a distinct third round message for each clause. As such, we require a new approach for cheating on the inactive clauses.

Our first idea is to defer the selection of first round messages for the inactive clauses until after the verifier sends the challenge (*i.e.* in the third round of the compiled protocol), while requiring that the prover select a first round message honestly for the active clause (*i.e.* in the first round of the compiled protocol). To do this, we introduce a new notion called *non-interactive, partially-binding vector commitments*.[3] These commitments allow the committer to commit to a vector of values and equivocate on a hidden subset of the entries in the vector later on. For instance, a 1-out-of-ℓ binding commitment allows the committer to commit a vector of ℓ values such that that one of the vector positions (chosen when the commitment is computed) is binding, while allowing the committer to modify/equivocate the remaining positions at the time of opening. For a disjunction with ℓ clauses, we can now use this primitive to ensure that the prover computes an honest transcript for at least one of the Σ-protocol instances as follows:

---

[3] A similar notion for interactive commitments was introduced in [15]. Note that this notion of commitments is very different from the similarly named notion of somewhere statistically binding commitments [18].

- **Round 1:** The prover computes an honest first round message for the Σ-protocol corresponding to the active clause. It commits to this message in the binding location of a 1-out-of-ℓ binding commitment, along with $\ell - 1$ garbage values, and sends the commitment to the verifier.
- **Round 2:** The verifier sends a challenge message for the ℓ instances.
- **Round 3:** The prover honestly computes a third round message for the active clause and then simulates first and third round messages for the remaining $\ell - 1$ clauses. It equivocates the commitment with these updated first round messages, and sends an opening of this commitment along with all the ℓ third round messages to the verifier.

While this is sufficient for soundness, we need an additional property from these partially-binding vector commitments to ensure zero-knowledge. In particular, in order to prevent the verifier from learning the index of the active clause, we require these partially-binding commitments to not leak information about the binding vector position. We formalize these properties in terms of a more general t-out-of-ℓ binding vector commitment scheme, which may be of independent interest, and we provide a practical construction based on the discrete log assumption.[4]

Challenge 2: How will the Prover Re-use the Active Transcript? The above approach overcomes the first challenge, but doesn't achieve our goal of reducing the communication complexity of the compiled Σ-protocol. Next, we need to find a way to somehow re-use the honest transcript of the active clause. Our key insight is that for many natural Σ-protocols, it is possible to simulate *with respect to a specific third round message*. That is, it is often easy to simulate an accepting transcript for a given challenge and third round message. This allows the prover to create a transcript for the inactive clauses that share the third round message of the active clause. In order for this compilation approach to work, Σ-protocols must satisfy the following properties (stated here informally):

- *Simulation With Respect To A Specific Third Round Message:* To re-use the active transcript, the prover simulates *with respect to the third round message of the active transcript.* This allows the prover to send a single third round message that can be re-used across all the clauses. More formally, we require that the Σ-protocol have a simulator that can reverse-compute an appropriate first round message to complete the accepting transcript for any given third round message and challenge. While not possible for all Σ-protocols, simulating in this way—i.e., by first selecting a third round message and then "reverse engineering" the appropriate first round message—is actually a common simulation strategy, and therefore possible with most natural Σ-protocols. In order to get communication complexity that only has a logarithmic

---

[4] We also explore a construction that is half the size and leverages random oracles in the full-version of this paper [23].

dependence on the number of clauses, we additionally require this simulator to be deterministic.[5] We formalize this property in Sect. 5.

- *Recyclable Third Round Messages:* To re-use third round messages in this way, the distribution of these third round messages must be the same. Otherwise, simulating the inactive clauses would fail and the verifier could detect the active clause used to produce the third round message. Thus, we require that the distribution of third round messages in the Σ-protocol be the same across all statements of interest. We formalize this property in Sect. 5.

An mentioned before, most natural Σ-protocols satisfy both these properties and we refer to such protocols as *stackable Σ-protocols*. We can compile such Σ-protocols into a communication-efficient Σ-protocol for disjunctions, where the communication only depends on the size of one of the clauses, as follows: Rounds 1 and 2 remain the same as in the protocol sketch above. In the third round, the prover first computes a third round message for the active clause. It then simulates first round messages for the remaining clauses based on the active clause's third round message and the challenge messages. As before, it equivocates the commitment with these updated first round messages.[6] While this allows us to compress the third round messages, we still need to send a vector commitment of the first round messages. In order to get communication complexity that does not depend on the size of all first round messages, the size of this vector commitment should be independent of the size of the values committed. Note that this is easy to achieve using a hash function.

Summary of our Stacking Compiler. Having outlined our main techniques, we now present a detailed description of our compiler for 2 clauses, as depicted in Fig. 1 (similar ideas extend for more than 2 clauses). The right (unshaded) box represents the active clause and the left (shaded) box represents the inactive clause. Each of the following numbered steps refer to a correspondingly numbered arrow in the figure: (1) The prover runs the first round message algorithm of the active clause to produce a first round message a_2. (2) The prover uses the 1-of-2 binding commitment scheme to commit to the vector $\mathbf{v} = (0, a_2)$. (3) The resulting commitment constitutes the compiled first round message a'. (4) The challenge c' is created by the verifier. (5) The prover generates the third round message z for the active clause using the first round message a_2, the challenge c', and the witness w. (6) The prover then uses the simulator for the inactive clause on the challenge c' and the honestly generated third round message z to generate a valid first round message for the inactive clause a_1. (7) The prover equivocates on the contents of the commitment a' – replacing 0 with the simulated first round message a_1. The result is randomness r' that can be used to open commitment

---

[5] We elaborate on the importance of this additional property in the technical sections.

[6] If the simulator computes the first round messages deterministically, then the prover only needs to reveal the randomness used in the commitment in the third round, along with the common third round message to the verifier. Given the third round message, the verifier can compute the first round messages on its own and check if the commitment was valid and that the transcripts verify.

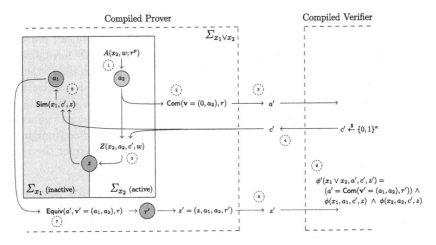

Fig. 1. High level overview of our compiler applied to a Σ-protocol $\Sigma = (A, C, Z, \phi)$ over statements x_1 and x_2. Several details have been omitted or changed to illustrate the core ideas more simply. The red circle contains a value used in the first round, while purple circles contain values used in the third round. We include a_1 and a_2 in the third round message for clarity; in the real protocol, the verifier will be able to deterministically recompute these values on their own. (Color figure online)

a' to the vector $\mathbf{v}' = (a_1, a_2)$. (8) The compiled third round message consists of honestly generated third round message z, the randomness r' of the equivocated commitment, and the two first round messages a_1, a_2.[7] (9) The verifier then verifies the proof by ensuring that each transcript is accepting and that the first round messages constitute a valid opening to the commitment a'.

Complexity Analysis: Communication in the first round only consists of the commitment, which we show can be realized in $O(\ell\lambda)$ bits, where λ is the security parameter. In the last round, the prover sends one third round message of the underlying Σ-protocol that depends on the size of one of the clauses[8] and ℓ first round messages of the underlying Σ-protocol. Thus, naïvely applying our compiler results in a protocol with communication complexity $O(\mathsf{CC}(\Sigma) + \ell \cdot \lambda)$, where $\mathsf{CC}(\Sigma)$ is the communication complexity of the underlying stackable Σ-protocol, when executed for the largest clause. In the technical sections, we show that the resulting protocol is itself "stackable", it can be recursively compiled. This reduces the communication complexity to $O(\mathsf{CC}(\Sigma) + \log(\ell) \cdot \lambda)$.

Stackable Σ-Protocols. While not all Σ-protocols are able to satisfy the first two properties that we require, we show that many natural Σ-protocols

---

[7] In the compiler presented in the main body, a_1 and a_2 are omitted from the third round message and the verifier recomputes them from z and c' directly. We make this simplification in the exposition to avoid introducing more notation.

[8] We can assume w.l.o.g. that all clauses have the same size. This can be done by appropriately padding the smaller clauses.

like Schnorr [38], and Guillio-Quisquater [29] satisfy these properties. We also show that more recent state-of-the-art protocols in MPC-in-the-head paradigm [33] like KKW [35] and Ligero [2] have these properties. We formalize the notion of "$\mathcal{F}$-universally simulatable MPC protocols", which produce stackable Σ-protocols when compiled using MPC-in-the-head [33]. This formalization is highly non-trivial and requires paying careful attention to the distribution of MPC-in-the-head transcripts. Our key observation is that transcripts generated when executing one circuit can often be seamlessly *reinterpreted* as though they were generated for another circuit (usually of similar size). We refer the reader to Sect. 5 for more details on stackable Σ-protocols.

Stacking Different Σ-Protocols. The compiler presented above allows stacking transcripts for a single Σ-protocol, with a single associated NP language, evaluated over different statements e.g., $(x_1 \in \mathcal{L}) \vee \ldots \vee (x_\ell \in \mathcal{L})$. This is quite limiting and does not allow a protocol designer to select the optimal Σ-protocol for each clause in a disjunction. As such, we explore extending our compiler to support stacking *different* Σ-protocols with different associated NP languages, i.e. $(x_1 \in \mathcal{L}_1) \vee (x_2 \in \mathcal{L}_2) \vee \ldots \vee (x_\ell \in \mathcal{L}_\ell)$.

A simple approach would be to rely on NP reductions to define a "meta-language" covering all of $\mathcal{L}_1, \ldots \mathcal{L}_\ell$. Unfortunately, this approach will often result in high concrete overheads. It would be preferable to allow "cross-stacking," or using different Σ-protocols for each clause in the disjunction.[9] The key impediment to applying our self-stacking compiler to different Σ-protocols is that the distribution of third round messages between two different Σ-protocols may be very different. For example, a statement with three clauses may be composed of one Σ-protocol defined over a large, finite field, another operating over a boolean circuit, and a third that is consisting of elements of a discrete logarithm group. Thus, attempting to use the simulator for one Σ-protocol with respect to the third round message of another might result in a domain error; there may be no set of accepting transcripts for the Σ-protocols that share a third round message. As re-using third round messages is the way we reduce communication complexity, this dissimilarity might appear to be insurmountable.

To accommodate these differences, we observe that the extent to which a set of Σ-protocols can be stacked is a function of the similarity of their third round messages. In the self-stacking compiler, these distributions were exactly the same, resulting in a "perfect stacking." With different Σ-protocols, the prover may only be able to re-use a *part* of the third round message when simulating for another Σ-protocol, leading to a "partial stacking." We note, however, that the distributions of common Σ-protocols tend to be quite similar—particularly when seen as an unstructured string of bits. Due to space constraints we include our cross stacking compiler, including case studies on its use, in the full-version of this paper [23].

---

[9] While it might be possible to define a Σ-protocol that uses different techniques for different parts of the relation, this would require the creation of a new, purpose built protocol—something we hope to avoid in this work. Thus, the difference between self-stacking in this work is primarily conceptual, rather than technical.

Paper Organization. The paper is organized as follows: we present required preliminaries Sect. 3 and the interface for partially-binding commitment schemes in Sect. 4. In Sect. 5 we cover the properties of Σ-protocols that our compiler requires and give examples of conforming Σ-protocols. We present our self-stacking compiler in Sect. 6.

3   Preliminaries

3.1   Notation

Throughout this paper we use λ to denote the computational security parameter and κ to denote the statistical security parameter. We denote by $x \xleftarrow{\$} \mathcal{D}$ the sampling of 'x' from the distribution '$\mathcal{D}$'. We use $[n]$ as a short hand for a list containing the first n natrual numbers in order: i.e. $[n] = 1, 2 \ldots, n$. We denote by $x \xleftarrow{\$}_s \mathcal{D}$ the process of sampling 'x' from the distribution '$\mathcal{D}$' using pseudo-random coins derived from a PRG applied to the seed 's', when the expression occurs multiple times we mean that the element is sampled using random coins from disjoint parts of the PRG output. We denote by H a collision-resistant hash function (CRH). We write group operations using multiplicative notation.

3.2 Σ-Protocols

In this section, we recall the definition of a Σ-protocol.

Definition 1 (Σ-Protocol). *Let $\mathcal{R}$ be an NP relation. A Σ-Protocol Π for $\mathcal{R}$ is a 3 move protocol between a prover P and a verifier V consisting of a tuple of PPT algorithms $\Pi = (A, Z, \phi)$ with the following interfaces:*

- *$a \leftarrow A(x, w; r^p)$: On input the statement x, corresponding witness w, such that $\mathcal{R}(x, w) = 1$, and prover randomness r^p, output the first message a that P sends to V in the first round.*
- *$c \xleftarrow{\$} \{0, 1\}^\kappa$: Sample a random challenge c that V sends to P in the second round.*
- *$z \leftarrow Z(x, w, c; r^p)$: On input the statement x, the witness w, the challenge c, and prover randomness r^p, output the message z that P sends to V in the third round.*
- *$b \leftarrow \phi(x, a, c, z)$: On input the statement x, prover's messages a, z and the challenge c, this algorithm run by V, outputs a bit $b \in \{0, 1\}$.*

A Σ-protocol has the following properties:

- ***Completeness:*** *A Σ-Protocol $\Pi = (A, Z, \phi)$ is said to be complete if for any x, w such that $\mathcal{R}(x, w) = 1$, and any prover randomness $r^p \xleftarrow{\$} \{0, 1\}^\lambda$, it holds that,*

$$\Pr\left[\phi(x, a, c, z) = 1 \;\middle|\; a \leftarrow A(x, w; r^p); c \xleftarrow{\$} \{0, 1\}^\kappa; z \leftarrow Z(x, w, c; r^p)\right] = 1$$

- **Special Soundness.** A Σ-Protocol $\Pi = (A, Z, \phi)$ is said to have special soundness if there exists a PPT extractor $\mathcal{E}$, such that given any two transcripts (x, a, c, z) and (x, a, c', z'), where $c \neq c'$ and $\phi(x, a, c, z) = \phi(x, a, c', z') = 1$, it holds that

$$\Pr\left[R(x, w) = 1 \mid w \leftarrow \mathcal{E}(1^\lambda, x, a, c, z, c', z')\right] = 1$$

- **Special Honest Verifier Zero-Knowledge.** A Σ-Protocol $\Pi = (A, Z, \phi)$ is said to be special honest verifier zero-knowledge, if there exists a PPT simulator $\mathcal{S}$, such that for any x, w such that $\mathcal{R}(x, w) = 1$, it holds that

$$\{(a, z) \mid c \xleftarrow{\$} \{0,1\}^\kappa; (a, z) \leftarrow \mathcal{S}(1^\lambda, x, c)\} \approx_c$$
$$\{(a, z) \mid r^p \xleftarrow{\$} \{0,1\}^\lambda; a \leftarrow A(x, w; r^p); c \xleftarrow{\$} \{0,1\}^\kappa; z \leftarrow Z(x, w, c; r^p)\}$$

4   Partially-Binding Vector Commitments

In this section, we introduce *non-interactive partially-binding vector commitments*. These commitments allow a committer to commit to a vector of ℓ elements such that exactly t positions are binding (*i.e.* cannot be opened to another value) and the remaining $\ell - t$ positions can be equivocated. The committer must decide the binding positions of the vector before committing and the binding positions are hidden.

Definition 2 (t-out-of-ℓ Binding Vector Commitment). *A t-out-of-ℓ binding non-interactive vector commitment scheme with message space $\mathcal{M}$, is defined by a tuple of the PPT algorithms (Setup, Gen, EquivCom, Equiv, BindCom) defined as follows:*

- pp $\leftarrow$ Setup(1^λ) *On input the security parameter λ, the setup algorithm outputs public parameters* pp.
- (ck, ek) $\leftarrow$ Gen(pp, B): *Takes public parameters* pp *and a t-subset of indices $B \in \binom{[\ell]}{t}$. Returns a commitment key* ck *and equivocation key* ek.
- (com, aux) $\leftarrow$ EquivCom(pp, ek, $\mathbf{v}$; r): *Takes public parameter* pp, *equivocation key* ek, *ℓ-tuple $\mathbf{v}$ and randomness r. Returns a partially-binding commitment* com *as well as some auxiliary equivocation information* aux.
- $r \leftarrow$ Equiv(pp, ek, $\mathbf{v}$, $\mathbf{v}'$, aux): *Takes public parameters* pp, *equivocation key* ek, *original commitment value $\mathbf{v}$ and updated commitment values $\mathbf{v}'$ with $\forall i \in B : \mathbf{v}_i = \mathbf{v}'_i$, and auxiliary equivocation information* aux. *Returns equivocation randomness r.*
- com $\leftarrow$ BindCom(pp, ck, $\mathbf{v}$; r): *Takes public parameters* pp, *commitment key* ck, *ℓ-tuple $\mathbf{v}$ and randomness r and outputs a commitment* com. *Note that this algorithm does not use the equivocation key* ek. *This algorithm plays a similar role to that of* Open *in a typical commitment scheme.*

The properties satisfied by the above algorithms are as follows:

(Perfect) Hiding: *The commitment key* ck *(perfectly) hides the binding positions B and commitments* com *(perfectly) hide the ℓ committed values in the vector. Formally, for all $\mathbf{v}^{(1)}, \mathbf{v}^{(2)} \in \mathcal{M}^\ell$, $B, B' \in \binom{[\ell]}{t}$, and* pp $\leftarrow$ Setup(1^λ):

$$
\begin{bmatrix}
(\mathsf{ck}, \mathsf{com}) & \begin{array}{l} (\mathsf{ck}, \mathsf{ek}) \leftarrow \mathsf{Gen}(\mathsf{pp}, B); r \xleftarrow{\$} \{0,1\}^\lambda; \\ (\mathsf{com}, \mathsf{aux}) \leftarrow \mathsf{EquivCom}(\mathsf{pp}, \mathsf{ek}, \mathbf{v}; r) \end{array}
\end{bmatrix}
$$
$$
\stackrel{p}{\equiv}
\begin{bmatrix}
(\mathsf{ck}', \mathsf{com}') & \begin{array}{l} (\mathsf{ck}', \mathsf{ek}') \leftarrow \mathsf{Gen}(\mathsf{pp}, B'); r' \xleftarrow{\$} \{0,1\}^\lambda \\ (\mathsf{com}', \mathsf{aux}') \leftarrow \mathsf{EquivCom}(\mathsf{pp}, \mathsf{ek}', \mathbf{v}'; r'); \end{array}
\end{bmatrix}
$$

(Computational) Partial Binding: *It is intractable for an adversary that generates the commitment key* ck *to equivocate on more than $\ell - t$ positions. To formalize this property, we consider the class of adversaries $\mathcal{A}_k$ that produces a single commitment key* ck *and k equivocations to a commitment under that key. We denote the jth opening to the commitment as the vector $\mathbf{v}^{(j)}$ and the ith element of that vector as $v_i^{(j)}$. Formally, for all $k \in \mathrm{poly}(\lambda)$, for all PPT algorithms $\mathcal{A}_k$:*

$$
\Pr \left[\begin{array}{l} \nexists S \subset [\ell], |S| \geq t, \text{ s.t. } i \in S, v_i^{(1)} = \ldots = v_i^{(k)} \wedge \\ \mathsf{BindCom}(\mathsf{pp}, \mathsf{ck}, \mathbf{v}^{(1)}; r_1) = \ldots = \mathsf{BindCom}(\mathsf{pp}, \mathsf{ck}, \mathbf{v}^{(k)}; r_k) \end{array} \middle| \begin{array}{l} \mathsf{pp} \leftarrow \mathsf{Setup}(1^\lambda); \\ (\mathsf{ck}, \mathbf{v}^{(1)}, \ldots, \mathbf{v}^{(k)}, r_1, \ldots, r_k) \leftarrow \mathcal{A}_k(1^\lambda, \mathsf{pp}) \end{array} \right] \leq \mathsf{negl}(\lambda)
$$

Partial Equivocation: *Given a commitment to $\mathbf{v}$ under a commitment key* ck $\leftarrow$ Gen(pp, B), *it is possible to equivocate to any $\mathbf{v}'$ as long as $\forall i \in B : v_i = v_i'$. More formally, for all $B \in \binom{[\ell]}{t}$, and all $\mathbf{v}, \mathbf{v}' \in \mathcal{M}^\ell$ st. $\forall i \in B : v_i = v_i'$ then:*

$$
\Pr \left[\mathsf{BindCom}(\mathsf{pp}, \mathsf{ck}, \mathbf{v}'; r') = \mathsf{com} \middle| \begin{array}{l} \mathsf{pp} \leftarrow \mathsf{Setup}(1^\lambda); r \xleftarrow{\$} \{0,1\}^\lambda; \\ (\mathsf{ck}, \mathsf{ek}) \leftarrow \mathsf{Gen}(\mathsf{pp}, B); \\ (\mathsf{com}, \mathsf{aux}) \leftarrow \mathsf{EquivCom}(\mathsf{pp}, \mathsf{ek}, \mathbf{v}; r); \\ r' \leftarrow \mathsf{Equiv}(\mathsf{ek}, \mathbf{v}, \mathbf{v}', \mathsf{aux}) \end{array} \right] = 1
$$

Throughout this work we will impose the efficiency requirement that the size of the commitment is independent of the size of the elements. We note that this is easy to achieve using a collision resistant hash function, when targeting computational binding.

4.1 Partially-Binding Vector Commitments from Discrete Log

We now present a simple and concretely efficient construction of t-out-of-ℓ partially-binding vector commitments from the discrete log assumption. The idea is to have the committer use a Pedersen commitment for each element in the vector. Recall that a Pedersen commitment to the message $m \in \mathbb{Z}_{|G|}$

$$
\begin{array}{ll}
\text{pp} \leftarrow \mathsf{Setup}(1^\lambda) & (\mathsf{com}, \mathsf{aux}) \leftarrow \mathsf{EquivCom}(\mathsf{pp}, \mathsf{ek}, \mathbf{v}):
\end{array}
$$

$\text{pp} \leftarrow \mathsf{Setup}(1^\lambda)$	$(\mathsf{com}, \mathsf{aux}) \leftarrow \mathsf{EquivCom}(\mathsf{pp}, \mathsf{ek}, \mathbf{v}):$
1: $\mathbb{G} \leftarrow \mathsf{GenGroup}(1^\lambda); g_0, h \xleftarrow{\$} \mathbb{G}$	1: $r \xleftarrow{\$} \mathbb{Z}_{|\mathbb{G}|}^\ell$
2: **return** $(\mathbb{G}, g_0, h)$	2: $\mathsf{com} \leftarrow \mathsf{BindCom}(\mathsf{pp}, \mathsf{ck}, \mathbf{v}, r)$
	3: **return** (com, r)

$(\mathsf{ck}, \mathsf{ek}) \leftarrow \mathsf{Gen}(\mathsf{pp}, B)$

1:    Let $E = [\ell] \setminus B$ (set of equivocal indexes)

2:    **for** $i \in E : y_i \xleftarrow{\$} \mathbb{Z}_{|\mathbb{G}|}, g_i \leftarrow h^{y_i}$ //Generate trapdoors

3:    **for** $j \in [\ell - t] : g_j \leftarrow \prod_{i \in E \cup \{0\}} g_i^{L_{(E \cup \{0\}, i)}(j)}$ //Interpolate first $\ell-t$ elements

4:    $\mathsf{ck} = (g_1, \dots, g_{\ell-t})$

5:    $\mathsf{ek} = (g_1, \dots, g_{\ell-t}, \{y_i\}_{i \in E}, E, B)$

6:    **return** $(\mathsf{ck}, \mathsf{ek})$

$r \leftarrow \mathsf{Equiv}(\mathsf{pp}, \mathsf{ek}, \mathbf{v}, \mathbf{v}', \mathsf{aux}):$

1:    Let $E = [\ell] \setminus B$ (set of equivocal indexes)

2:    Parse $\mathsf{aux} = (r_1, \dots, r_\ell) \in \mathbb{Z}_{|\mathbb{G}|}^\ell$

3:    **for** $j \in [\ell - t, \ell] : g_j \leftarrow \prod_{i \in [\ell-t] \cup \{0\}} g_i^{L_{([\ell-t] \cup \{0\}, i)}(j)}$ //Interpolate other elements

4:    **for** $j \in B : r'_j \leftarrow r_j$

5:    **for** $j \in E : r'_j \leftarrow r_j - y_j \cdot (\mathbf{v}'_j - \mathbf{v}_j)$

6:    **return** r'

$\mathsf{com} \leftarrow \mathsf{BindCom}(\mathsf{pp}, \mathsf{ck}, \mathbf{v}, r):$

1:    **for** $j \in [\ell - t, \ell] : g_j \leftarrow \prod_{i \in [\ell-t] \cup \{0\}} g_i^{L_{([\ell-t] \cup \{0\}, i)}(j)}$ //Interpolate other elements

2:    **for** $j \in [\ell] : \mathsf{com}_j \leftarrow h^{r_j} \cdot g_j^{\mathbf{v}_j}$ //Commit individually

3:    **return** $(\mathsf{com}_1, \dots, \mathsf{com}_\ell)$

Fig. 2. t-of-ℓ binding commitment from discrete log in the CRS model.

with public parameters $g, h \in \mathbb{G}$ is computed as $g^m h^r$ for a random value r. The binding property of Pedersen commitments relies on the committer not knowing the discrete log of g with respect to h. For our partially-binding vector commitment scheme, the commitment key is a set of public parameters for the Pedersen commitments, constructed such a way that the committer knows discrete logs for exactly $\ell - t$ parameters. This is done by having the committer pick $\ell - t$ of the parameters and computing the remaining t parameters by interpolating in the exponent. More formally, let use begin by fixing some notation. Let $\mathbb{Z}_{|\mathbb{G}|}$ be a prime field. In our construction, we implicitly treat indexes $i \in [0, |\mathbb{G}| - 1]$ as field elements, *i.e.* there is an implicit bijective map between

$[0, |\mathbb{G}| - 1]$ and $\mathbb{Z}_{|\mathbb{G}|}$ (e.g. $i \mod |\mathbb{G}| \in \mathbb{Z}/(|\mathbb{G}|)$). Let $\mathcal{X} \subseteq \mathbb{Z}_{|\mathbb{G}|}$ and $j \in \mathcal{X}$, define $L_{(\mathcal{X},j)}(X) := \prod_{m \in \mathcal{X}, m \neq j} \frac{X-m}{j-m} \in \mathbb{Z}_{|\mathbb{G}|}[X]$ i.e. the unique degree $|\mathcal{X}| - 1$ polynomial for which $\forall x \in \mathcal{X} \setminus \{j\} : L_{(\mathcal{X},j)}(x) = 0$ and $L_{(\mathcal{X},j)}(j) = 1$. The formal description of the commitment scheme can be found in Fig. 2. While our construction does require a CRS, we note that the CRS is just two randomly selected group elements[10], which in practice can be generated by hashing a 'nothing-up-by-sleeve' constant to the curve by using a cryptographic hash function.

Theorem 1. *Under the discrete log assumption, for any (t, ℓ) with $t < \ell$: the scheme shown in Fig. 2 is a family of (perfectly hiding, computationally binding) t-of-ℓ partially binding commitment schemes.*

The security reduction is straightforward and tight: for each position i in which the adversary $\mathcal{A}$ manages to equivocate we can extract the discrete log of g_i (as for regular Pedersen commitments), if we extract the discrete log in $\ell - t + 1$ positions, we have sufficient points on the degree $\ell - t$ polynomial to recover $f_{[\ell] \cup \{0\}}(X)$ explicitly and simply evaluate it at 0 to recover the discrete log of g_0 from pp. The full proof can be found in the full-version of this paper [23].

Remark 1. To commit to longer strings a collision resistant hash H : $\{0, 1\}^* \rightarrow \mathbb{Z}_{|\mathbb{G}|}$ is used to compress each coordinate before committing using BindCom/EquivCom as a black-box: by committing to $\mathbf{v}' = (\mathsf{H}(v_1), \ldots, \mathsf{H}(v_\ell))$ instead. Note that the discrete log assumption, used above, also implies the existance of collision resistant hash functions.

5   Stackable Σ-Protocols

In this section, we present the properties of Σ-protocols that our stacking framework requires and show that many Σ-protocols satisfy these properties.

5.1   Well-Behaved Simulators

As outlined in Sect. 2, a critical step of our compilation framework is applying the simulator of the underlying Σ-protocols to the inactive clauses. This raises a technical (mostly definitional) concern: some of inactive clauses may not actually be true, possibly because they were adversarially chosen. At first glance, this might seem like a strange concern. For most interesting NP languages of interest, it should be hard to tell if an instance is in the language, and therefore having false instances in the disjunction should not be a problem. However, the behavior of a simulator is only defined with respect to statements that are in the NP language—that is, true instances. As such, if the disjunction contains false clauses, there is no guarantee that the simulator will produce an accepting transcript. This could cause problems with verification—the verifier will know

---

[10] Like regular Pedersen commitments.

that one of the transcripts is not accepting, but will not know if this is due to a simulation failure or malicious prover. As such, we must carefully consider what simulators will produce when executed on a false instance.

As noted in [25], simulators commonly constructed in proofs of the zero-knowledge property will *usually* output accepting transcripts when executed on these false instances. If the simulator were able to consistently output non-accepting transcripts for false instances, it could be used to decide the NP language in polynomial time. However, it is possible to define a valid simulator that produces an output that is not an accepting transcript with non-negligible probability e.g. (1) the input instance is trivially false (*e.g.* a fully connected graph with 4 nodes is not 3-colorable), or (2) the simulator has a hard-coded set of false instances on which it deviates from its normal behavior. Indeed, a probabilistic simulator may also output a non-accepting transcript in each of these cases only occasionally, possibly depending on the challenge. This behavior will not compromise zero-knowledge, but could result in *correctness or soundness* errors.

We emphasize that this is a corner case: commonly constructed simulators will most likely produce accepting transcripts even on false instances, unless the instance is trivially false or not in the domain of the simulator. Nevertheless, we observe that any Σ-protocol can be generically transformed into one that has a simulator that outputs accepting transcripts for all statements. We refer to such simulators as *well-behaved* simulators. We give a formal definition for well-behaved simulators and present the transformation in the full version [23].

5.2   Properties of Stackable Σ-Protocols

We now formalize the definition of a "stackable" Σ-protocol. As discussed in Sect. 2, a Σ-protocol is stackable (meaning, it can be used by our stacking framework), if it satisfies two main properties: (1) simulation with respect to a specific third round message, and (2) recyclable third round messages.

Cheat Property: "Extended" Honest Verifier Zero-Knowledge. We view "simulation with respect to a specific third round message" as a natural strengthening of the typical special honest verifier zero-knowledge property of Σ-protocols. At a high level, this property requires that it is possible to design a simulator for the Σ-protocol by first sampling a random third round message from the space of admissible third round messages, and then constructing the unique appropriate first round message. We refer to such a simulator as an *extended simulator*. A similar notion is considered by Abe *et al.* [1] in their definition of type-T signature schemes: a type-T signature scheme is essentially the Fiat-Shamir [19] heuristic applied to an EHVZK Σ-protocol.

Definition 3 (EHVZK Σ-Protocol). *Let $\Pi = (A, Z, \phi)$ be a Σ-protocol for the NP relation $\mathcal{R}$, with a well-behaved simulator. We say that Π is "extended honest-verifier zero-knowledge (EHVZK)" if there exists a polynomial time computable <u>deterministic</u> "extended simulator" $\mathcal{S}^{\mathrm{EHVZK}}$ such that for any $(x, w) \in \mathcal{R}$ and $c \in \{0, 1\}^\kappa$, there exists an efficiently samplable distribution $\mathcal{D}_{x,c}^{(z)}$ such that:*

$$\left\{(a,c,z) \mid r^p \xleftarrow{\$} \{0,1\}^\lambda; a \leftarrow A(x,w;r^p); z \leftarrow Z(x,w,c;r^p)\right\}$$

$$\approx \left\{(a,c,z) \mid z \xleftarrow{\$} \mathcal{D}_{x,c}^{(z)}; a \leftarrow \mathcal{S}^{\mathrm{EHVZK}}(1^\lambda, x, c, z)\right\}$$

The natural variants (perfect/statistical/computational) of EHVZK are defined depending on which class of distinguishers for which $\approx$ is defined.

Observation 1 (All Σ-protocols can be made EHVZK.) *In the full version of this paper, we present a transformation that transforms any Σ-protocol into a EHVZK Σ-protocol.*

Re-use Property: Recycle Third Round Messages. The next property that our stacking compilers require is that the distribution of third round messages does not significantly rely on the statement. In more detail, given a fixed challenge, the distribution of possible third round messages for any pair of statements in the language are indistinguishable from each other. We formalize this property by using $\mathcal{D}_c^{(z)}$ to denote a single distribution with respect to a fixed challenge c. We say that a Σ-protocol has recyclable third round messages, if for any statement x in the language the distribution of all possible third round messages corresponding to challenge c is indistinguishable from $\mathcal{D}_c^{(z)}$. We now formally define this property:

Definition 4 (Σ-Protocol with Recyclable Third Messages). *Let $\mathcal{R}$ be an NP relation and $\Pi = (A, Z, \phi)$ be a Σ-protocol for $\mathcal{R}$, with a well-behaved simulator. We say that Π has recyclable third messages if for each $c \in \{0,1\}^\kappa$, there exists an efficiently sampleable distribution $\mathcal{D}_c^{(z)}$, such that for all instance-witness pairs (x, w) st. $\mathcal{R}(x, w) = 1$, it holds that*

$$\mathcal{D}_c^{(z)} \approx \left\{z \mid r^p \xleftarrow{\$} \{0,1\}^\lambda; a \leftarrow A(x,w;r^p); z \leftarrow Z(x,w,c;r^p)\right\}.$$

This property is fundamental to stacking, as it means that the contents of the third round message do not 'leak information' about the statement used to generate the message. This means that the message can be safely re-used to generate transcripts for the non-active clauses and an adversary cannot detect which clause is active.[11] Although this property might seem strange, we will later show that many natural Σ-protocols have this property.

Stackability. With our two-properties formally defined, we are now ready to present the definition of stackable Σ-protocols:

Definition 5 (Stackable Σ-Protocol). *We say that a Σ-protocol $\Sigma = (A, Z, \phi)$ is stackable, if it is EHVZK (see Definition 3) and has recyclable third messages (see Definition 4).*

---

[11] We further elaborate on this in Remark 2.

We now note a useful property of stackable Σ-protocols that follow directly from Definition 5:

Remark 2. Let $\Sigma = (A, Z, \phi)$ be a *stackable* Σ-protocol for the NP relation $\mathcal{R}$, with a well-behaved simulator. Then for each $c \in \{0,1\}^\lambda$ and any instance-witness pair (x, w) with $\mathcal{R}(x, w) = 1$, an honestly computed transcript is computationally indistinguishable from a transcript generated by sampling a random third round message from $\mathcal{D}_c^{(z)}$ and then simulating the remaining transcript using the extended simulator. More formally,

$$\left\{ (a, z) \mid r^p \xleftarrow{\$} \{0,1\}^\lambda; a \leftarrow A(x, w; r^p); z \leftarrow Z(x, w, c; r^p) \right\}$$
$$\approx \left\{ (a, z) \mid z \xleftarrow{\$} \mathcal{D}_c^{(z)}; a \leftarrow \mathcal{S}^{\mathrm{EHVZK}}(1^\lambda, x, c, z) \right\}$$

Looking ahead, these observations will be critical in proving security of our compilers.

5.3   Classical Examples of Stackable Σ-Protocols

In this section, we show some examples of classical Σ-protocols which are stackable. Rather than considering multiple classical Σ-protocols like Schnorr and Guillou-Quisquater separately, we consider the generalization of these protocols as explored in [16]. Once we show that this generalization is stackable, it is simple to see that specific instantiations are also stackable.

Lemma 1 (Σ-protocol for ψ-preimages [16] is stackable). *Let $\mathfrak{G}_1^*$ and $\mathfrak{G}_2^*$ be groups with group operations $*_1, *_2$ respectively (multiplicative notation) and let $\psi : \mathfrak{G}_1^* \to \mathfrak{G}_2^*$ be a one-way group-homomorphism. Recall the simple Σ-protocol (Π_ψ) of Cramer and Damgård [16] for the relation of preimages $\mathcal{R}_\psi(x, w) := x \stackrel{?}{=} \psi(w)$, where $x \in \mathfrak{G}_2^*, w \in \mathfrak{G}_1^*$. The protocol is a generalization of Schnorr [39] and works as follows:*

- *$A(x, w; r^p)$, the prover samples $r \xleftarrow{\$} \mathfrak{G}_1^*$ and sends the image $a = \psi(r) \in \mathfrak{G}_2^*$ to the verifier.*
- *$Z(x, w, c; r^p)$, the prover intreprets c as an integer from a subset $C \subseteq \mathbb{Z}$ and replies with $z = w^c *_1 r$*
- *$\phi(x, a, c, z)$, the verifier checks $\psi(z) = x^c *_2 a$.*

Completeness follows since ψ is a homomorphism: $\psi(z) = \psi(w^c *_1 r) = \psi(w)^c *_2 \psi(r) = x^c *_2 a$. The knowledge soundness error is $1/|C|$ (see [16] for more details). For any homomorphism ψ, Π_ψ is stackable:

Proof. To see that Π_ψ is stackable, define an extended simulator and check for recyclable third messages:

1. *Π_ψ is EHVZK: Let $\mathcal{D}_{x,c}^{(z)} := \{z \mid z \xleftarrow{\$} \mathfrak{G}_1^*\}$, let $\mathcal{S}^{\mathrm{EHVZK}}(1^\lambda, x, c, z) := \psi(z) *_2 x^{-c}$*

2. Π_ψ *has recyclable third messages: Observe that* $\forall x_1, x_2 : \mathcal{D}^{(z)}_{x_1,c} = \mathcal{D}^{(z)}_{x_2,c} = \mathcal{U}(\mathfrak{G}_1^*)^{12}$.

Remark 3. The following variants of Π_ψ (with different choices of $\mathfrak{G}_1^*, \mathfrak{G}_2^*, \psi$) are captured in this generalization (along with other similar Σ-protocols):

(1) Guillou-Quisquater [29] (e-roots in an RSA group) for which $\mathfrak{G}_1^* = \mathfrak{G}_2^* = \mathbb{Z}_n^*$ for a semi-prime $n = pq$, $C = [0, e)$ and $\psi(w) := w^e$ for some prime $e \in \mathbb{N}$.
(2) Schnorr [39] (knowledge of discrete log): for which $\mathfrak{G}_1^* = \mathbb{Z}_{|\mathbb{G}|}^+, \mathfrak{G}_2^* = \mathbb{G}$ where $\mathbb{G}$ is a cyclic group of prime order $|\mathbb{G}|$, $C = [0, |\mathbb{G}|)$ and $\psi(w) := g^w$ for some $g \in \mathbb{G}$.
(3) Chaum-Pedersen [14] (equality of discrete log): for which $\mathfrak{G}_1^* = \mathbb{Z}_{|\mathbb{G}|}^+, \mathfrak{G}_2^* = \mathbb{G} \times \mathbb{G}$ where $\mathbb{G}$ is a cyclic group of prime order $|\mathbb{G}|$, $C = [0, |\mathbb{G}|)$ and $\psi : \mathbb{Z}_{|\mathbb{G}|} \to \mathbb{G} \times \mathbb{G}$, $\psi(w) := (g_1^w, g_2^w)$ for $g_1, g_2 \in \mathbb{G}$.
(4) Attema-Cramer [3] (opening of linear forms): for which $\mathfrak{G}_1^* = \mathbb{Z}_{|\mathbb{G}|}^\ell \times \mathbb{Z}_{|\mathbb{G}|}$, $\mathfrak{G}_2^* = (\mathbb{Z}_{|\mathbb{G}|}, \mathbb{G})$, $C = [0, |\mathbb{G}|)$ and $\psi((\mathbf{x}, \gamma)) := (L(\mathbf{x}), \mathbf{g}^{\mathbf{x}} h^\gamma)$ for some linear form $L(\mathbf{x}) = \langle \mathbf{x}, \mathbf{s} \rangle$, $\mathbf{s} \in \mathbb{Z}_{|\mathbb{G}|}^\ell$

In the full version of this paper, we also show that Blum's classic 3 move protocol [11] for graph Hamiltonicity is stackable.

5.4 Examples of Stackable "MPC-in-the-Head" Σ-Protocols

We now proceed to show that many natural "MPC-in-the-head" style [33] Σ-protocols (with minor modifications) are stackable. MPC-in-the-head (henceforth refereed to as IKOS) is a technique used for designing three-round, public-coin, zero-knowledge proofs using MPC protocols. At a high level, the prover emulates execution of an n-party MPC protocol Π virtually, on the relation function $\mathcal{R}(x, \cdot)$ using the witness w as input of the parties, and commits to the views of each party. An honest verifier then selects a random subset of the views to be opened and verifies that those views are consistent with each other and with an honest execution, where the output of Π is 1.

Achieving EHVZK. Since the first round messages in such protocols only consist of commitments to the views of all virtual partials, a subset of which are opened in the third round, a natural simulation strategy when proving zero-knowledge of such protocols is the following: (1) based on the challenge message, determine the subset of parties whose views will need be opened later, (2) imagining these as the "corrupt" parties, use the simulator of the MPC protocol to simulate their views, and, finally, (3) compute commitments to these simulated views for this subset of the parties and commitments to garbage values for the remaining virtual parties. Clearly, since the first round messages in this simulation strategy are computed after the third round messages, *these protocols are naturally EHVZK.*

---

[12] Uniform distribution over $\mathfrak{G}_1^*$.

Achieving Recyclable Third Messages. To show that these Σ-protocols have recyclable third messages, we observe that in many MPC protocols, an *adversary's view can often be condensed and decoupled from the structure of the functionality/circuit* being evaluated. We elaborate this point with the help of an example protocol—semi-honest BGW [6].

Recall that in the BGW protocol, parties evaluate the circuit in a gate-by-gate fashion on secret shared inputs[13] as follows: (1) for addition gates, the parties locally add their own shares for the incoming wire values to obtain shares of the outgoing wire values. (2) For multiplication gates, the parties first locally multiply their own shares for the incoming wire values and then secret share these multiplied share amongst the other parties. Each party then locally reconstructs these "shares of shares" to obtain shares of the outgoing wire values. (3) Finally, the parties reveal their shares for all the output wires in the circuit to all other parties and reconstruct the output.

By definition, the view of an adversary in any semi-honest MPC protocol is indistinguishable from a view simulated by the simulator with access to the corrupt party's inputs and the protocol output. Therefore, to understand the view of an adversary in this protocol, we recall the simulation strategy used in this protocol:

1. For each multiplication gate in the circuit, the simulator sends random values on behalf of the honest parties to each of the corrupt parties.
2. For the output wires, based on the messages sent to the adversary in the previous step and the circuit that the parties are evaluating, the simulator first computes the messages that the corrupt parties are expected to send to the honest parties. It then uses these messages and the output of protocol to simulate the messages sent by the honest parties to the adversary. Recall that this can be done because these messages correspond to the shares of these parties for the output wire values, and in a threshold secret sharing scheme, the shares of an adversary and the secret, uniquely define the shares of the remaining parties.

Observe that the computation done by the simulator in the first part is independent of the actual circuit or function being computed (it only depends on the number of multiplication gates in the circuit). We refer to the messages computed in (1) and the inputs of the corrupt parties as the *condensed view* of the adversary. Additionally, given these simulated views, the output of the protocol, and the circuit/functionality, the simulated messages of the honest parties in (2) can be computed deterministically. Looking ahead, because the output of relation circuits—the circuits we are interested in simulating—should always be 1 to convince the verifier, this deterministic computation will be straight forward. Since the condensed view is not dependent on the function being computed, it can be used with "any" functionality in the second step to compute the remaining view of the adversary. In other words, given two arithmetic circuits with the

---

[13] These shares are computed using some threshold secret sharing scheme, e.g., Shamir's polynomial based secret sharing [40].

same number of multiplication gates, the condensed views of the adversary in an execution of the BGW protocol for one of the circuits can be re-interpreted as their views in an execution for the other one. We note that circuits can always be "padded" to be the same size, so this property holds more generally.

As a result, for IKOS-style protocols based on such MPC protocols, while some strict structure must be imposed upon third round messages (which are views of a subset of virtual parties) when *verifying* that they have been generated correctly, the third round messages themselves can simply consist of these condensed views (and not correspond to any particular functionality) and hence can be re-used. To make this work, we must make a slight modification to the IKOS compiler. As before, in the first round, the prover will commit to the views (where they are associated with a given function f) of all parties in the first round. However, in the third round, the prover can simply send the condensed views of the opened parties to the verifier. The verifier can deterministically compute the remaining view of these parties w.r.t. the appropriate relation function f and check if they are consistent amongst each other and with the commitments sent in the first round. Since the third round messages in this protocol are not associated with any function, it is now easy to see that they can be the distribution of these messages is independent of the instance.

Building on this intuition, we show that many natural MPC protocols produce stackable Σ-protocols for circuits of the same size when used with the IKOS compiler. Before giving a formal description of the required MPC property, we recall the IKOS compiler in more detail, assuming that the underlying MPC protocol has the following three-functions associated with it: ExecuteMPC emulates execution of the protocol on a given function with virtual parties and outputs the actual views of the parties, CondenseViews takes the views of a subset of the parties as input and outputs their condensed views, and ExpandViews takes the condensed views of a subset of the parties and returns their actual view w.r.t. a particular function.

IKOS Compiler. Let $f = \mathcal{R}(x, \cdot)$. In the first round, the prover runs ExecuteMPC on f and the witness w to obtain views of the parties and commits to each of these views. In the second round, the verifier samples a random subset of parties as its challenge message. Size of this subset is equal to the maximal corruption threshold of the MPC protocol. In the third round, the prover uses CondenseViews to obtain condensed views for this subset of parties and sends them to the verifier along with the randomness used to commit to the original views of these parties in the first round. The verifier runs ExpandViews on f and the condensed views received in the third round to obtain the corresponding original views. It checks if these are consistent with each other and are valid openings to commitments sent in the first round. Depending on the corruption threshold and the security achieved by the underlying MPC protocol, the above steps might be repeated a number of times to reduce the soundness error. Below we restate the main theorem from [33], which also trivially holds for our modified variant.

Theorem 2 (IKOS [33]). *Let $\mathcal{L}$ be an NP language, $\mathcal{R}$ be its associated NP-relation and $\mathcal{F}$ be the function set $\{\mathcal{R}(x, \cdot) : \forall x \in \mathcal{L}\}$. Assuming the existence of non-interactive commitments, the above compiler transforms any MPC protocol for functions in $\mathcal{F}$ into a Σ-protocol for the relation $\mathcal{R}$.*

Next, we formalize the main property of MPC protocols that facilitates in achieving recyclable third messages when compiled with the above IKOS compiler. We characterize this property w.r.t. a function set $\mathcal{F}$, and require the MPC protocol to be such that the condensed views can be expanded for any $f \in \mathcal{F}$. For our purposes, it would suffice, even if the condensed view of the adversary is dependent on the final output of the protocol, as long as it is independent of the functionality. This is because, in our context, the circuit being evaluated will be a relation circuit with the statement hard-coded and should always output 1 in order to convince the verifier.

Definition 6 ($\mathcal{F}$-universally simulatable MPC). *Let Π be an n-party MPC protocol that is capable of securely computing any function $f \in \mathcal{F}$ (where $\mathcal{F} : \mathcal{X}^n \to \mathcal{O}$) against any semi-honest adversary $\mathcal{A}$ who corrupts a set $\mathcal{I} \subset [n]$ of parties, such that $\mathcal{I} \in \mathcal{C}$, where $\mathcal{C}$ is the set of admissible corruption sets. We say that Π is $\mathcal{F}$-universally simulatable if there exists a 3-tuple of PPT functions (ExecuteMPC, ExpandViews, CondenseViews) and a non-uniform PPT simulator $\mathcal{S}^{\text{F-MPC}} : \mathcal{F} \times \mathcal{C} \times \mathcal{O} \to V^*$, defined as follows*

- *$(\{\mathsf{view}_i\}_{i \in [n]}, o) \leftarrow \mathsf{ExecuteMPC}(f, \{x_i\}_{i \in [n]})$: This function takes inputs of the parties $\{x_i\}_{i \in [n]} \in \mathcal{X}^n$ and a function $f \in \mathcal{F}$ as input and returns the views $\{\mathsf{view}_i\}_{i \in [n]}$ of all parties and their output $o \in \mathcal{O}$ in protocol Π.*
- *$\{\mathsf{con.view}_i\}_{i \in \mathcal{I}} \leftarrow \mathsf{CondenseViews}(f, \mathcal{I}, \{\mathsf{view}_i\}_{i \in \mathcal{I}}, o)$: This function takes as input the set of corrupt parties $\mathcal{I} \in \mathcal{C}$, views of the corrupt parties $\{\mathsf{view}_i\}_{i \in \mathcal{I}}$ and the output of the protocol $o \in \mathcal{O}$ and returns their condensed views $\{\mathsf{con.view}_i\}_{i \in \mathcal{I}}$.*
- *$\{\mathsf{view}_i\}_{i \in \mathcal{I}} \leftarrow \mathsf{ExpandViews}(f, \mathcal{I}, \{\mathsf{con.view}_i\}_{i \in \mathcal{I}}, o)$: This function takes as input the functionality $f \in \mathcal{F}$, set of corrupt parties $\mathcal{I} \in \mathcal{C}$, condensed views $\{\mathsf{con.view}_i\}_{i \in \mathcal{I}}$ of the corrupt parties and the output of the protocol $o \in \mathcal{O}$ and returns their views $\{\mathsf{view}_i\}_{i \in \mathcal{I}}$.*
- *$\{\mathsf{con.view}_i\}_{i \in \mathcal{I}} \leftarrow \mathcal{S}^{\text{F-MPC}}(f, \mathcal{I}, \{x_i\}_{i \in \mathcal{I}}, o)$: The simulator takes as input the functionality $f \in \mathcal{F}$, set of corrupt parties $\mathcal{I} \in \mathcal{C}$, inputs of the corrupt parties $\{x_i\}_{i \in \mathcal{I}} \in \mathcal{X}^{|\mathcal{I}|}$ and the output of the protocol $o \in \mathcal{O}$ and returns simulated condensed views $\{\mathsf{con.view}_i\}_{i \in \mathcal{I}}$ of the corrupt parties.*

And these functions satisfy the following properties:

1. ***Condensing-Expanding Views is Deterministic:*** *For all $\{x_i\}_{i \in [n]} \in \mathcal{X}^n$ and $\forall f \in \mathcal{F}$, let $(\{\mathsf{view}_i\}_{i \in [n]}, o) \leftarrow \mathsf{ExecuteMPC}(f, \{x_i\}_{i \in [n]})$. For all $\mathcal{I} \in \mathcal{C}$ it holds that:*

$$\Pr\left[\mathsf{ExpandViews}(f, \mathcal{I}, \mathsf{CondenseViews}(f, \mathcal{I}, \{\mathsf{view}_i\}_{i \in \mathcal{I}}, o), o) = \{\mathsf{view}_i\}_{i \in \mathcal{I}}\right] = 1$$

2. **Indistinguishability of Simulated Views from real execution:** *For all* $\{x_i\}_{i\in[n]} \in \mathcal{X}^n$ *and* $\forall f \in \mathcal{F}$, *let* $(\{\text{view}_i\}_{i\in[n]}, o) \leftarrow \text{ExecuteMPC}(f, \{x_i\}_{i\in[n]})$. *For all* $\mathcal{I} \in \mathcal{C}$ *it holds that:*

$$\text{CondenseViews}(f, \mathcal{I}, \{\text{view}_i\}_{i\in\mathcal{I}}, o) \approx \mathcal{S}^{\text{F-MPC}}(f, \mathcal{I}, \{x_i\}_{i\in\mathcal{I}}, o)$$

3. **Indistinguishability of Simulated Views for all functions:** *For any* $\mathcal{I} \in \mathcal{C}$, *all inputs* $\{x_i\}_{i\in\mathcal{I}} \in \mathcal{X}^{|\mathcal{I}|}$ *of the corrupt parties, and all outputs* $o \in \mathcal{O}$, *there exists a function-independent distribution* $\mathcal{D}_{\{x_i\}_{i\in\mathcal{I}},o}$, *such that* $\forall f \in \mathcal{F}$, *if* $\exists\{x_i\}_{i\in[n]\setminus\mathcal{I}}$ *for which* $f(\{x_i\}_{i\in[n]\setminus\mathcal{I}}, \{x_i\}_{i\in\mathcal{I}}) = o$, *then it holds that:*

$$\mathcal{D}_{\{x_i\}_{i\in\mathcal{I}},o} \approx \mathcal{S}^{\text{F-MPC}}(f, \mathcal{I}, \{x_i\}_{i\in\mathcal{I}}, o)$$

We note that a central notion used in the "stacked-garbling literature" (for communication efficient disjunction for garbled circuit based zero-knowledge proofs) is a special case of $\mathcal{F}$-universally simulatable:

Remark 4 (Topology Decoupled Garbled Circuits and $\mathcal{F}$-universally simulatable MPC.). The notion of topology decoupled garbled circuits introduced by Kolesnikov [36] is a special case of $\mathcal{F}$-universally simulatable MPC: a topology decoupled garbled circuit (E, T) separates the cryptographic material (E, e.g. garbling tables) and topology (T, i.e. wiring) of a garbled circuit and (informally stated) requires that generating E for different topologies introduces indistinguishable distributions. Letting X be the garbled input labels[14] held by the evaluator, in $\mathcal{F}$-universally simulatable terminology (E, X) would constitute the "condensed view", while (E, X, T)[15] would constitute the "expanded views", indistinguishablilty of simulated views for functions with the same number of gates and inputs follows easily from the "topology decoupling"of the garbled circuits and the uniform distribution of the input labels.

In the full version [23], we prove the following theorem, which states that when instantiated with an $\mathcal{F}$-universally simulatable MPC protocol, Theorem 2 yields a stackable Σ-protocol for languages with relation circuits in $\mathcal{F}$.

Theorem 3 ($\mathcal{F}$-universally simulatable implies stackable). *The IKOS compiler (see Theorem 2) yields an stackable Σ-protocol for languages with relation circuit in $\mathcal{F}$ when instantiated with an $\mathcal{F}$-universally simulatable MPC protocol (see Definition 6) with privacy and robustness against a subset of the parties.*

In the full version, we use Theorem 3 to show that two popular IKOS-based Σ-protocols are stackable, namely KKW [35] and Ligero [2].

---

[14] Obtained using an oblivious transfer.

[15] Where T can be computed from f.

Self-Stacking Compiler

Statement: $x = x_1, \ldots, x_n$
Witness: $w = (\alpha, w_\alpha)$

- **First Round:** Prover computes $A'(x, w; r^p) \to a$ as follows:
  - Parse $r^p = (r_\alpha^p \| r)$.
  - Compute $a_\alpha \leftarrow A(x_\alpha, w_\alpha; r_\alpha^p)$.
  - Set $\mathbf{v} = (v_1, \ldots, v_\ell)$, where $v_\alpha = a_\alpha$ and $\forall i \in [\ell] \setminus \alpha, v_i = 0$.
  - Compute $(\mathsf{ck}, \mathsf{ek}) \leftarrow \mathsf{Gen}(\mathsf{pp}, B = \{\alpha\})$.
  - Compute $(\mathsf{com}, \mathsf{aux}) \leftarrow \mathsf{EquivCom}(\mathsf{pp}, \mathsf{ek}, \mathbf{v}; r)$.
  - Send $a = (\mathsf{ck}, \mathsf{com})$ to the verifier.
- **Second Round:** Verifier samples $c \leftarrow \{0,1\}^\lambda$ and sends it to the prover.
- **Third Round:** Prover computes $Z'(x, w, c; r^p) \to z$ as follows:
  - Parse $r^p = (r_\alpha^p \| r)$.
  - Compute $z^* \leftarrow Z(x_\alpha, w_\alpha, c; r_\alpha^p)$.
  - For $i \in [\ell]/\alpha$, compute $a_i \leftarrow \mathcal{S}^{\mathrm{EHVZK}}(x_i, c, z^*)$.
  - Set $\mathbf{v}' = (a_1, \ldots, a_\ell)$
  - Compute $r' \leftarrow \mathsf{Equiv}(\mathsf{pp}, \mathsf{ek}, \mathbf{v}, \mathbf{v}', \mathsf{aux})$ (where aux can be regenerated with r).
  - Send $z = (\mathsf{ck}, z^*, r')$ to the verifier.
- **Verification:** Verifier computes $\phi'(x, a, c, z) \to b$ as follows:
  - Parse $a = (\mathsf{ck}, \mathsf{com})$ and $z = (\mathsf{ck}', z^*, r')$
  - Set $a_i \leftarrow \mathcal{S}^{\mathrm{EHVZK}}(x_i, c, z^*)$
  - Set $\mathbf{v}' = (a_1, \ldots, a_\ell)$
  - Compute and return:

$$b = (\mathsf{ck} \stackrel{?}{=} \mathsf{ck}') \wedge \left(\mathsf{com} \stackrel{?}{=} \mathsf{BindCom}(\mathsf{pp}, \mathsf{ck}, \mathbf{v}'; r')\right) \wedge \left(\bigwedge_{i \in [\ell]} \phi(x_i, a_i, c, z^*)\right)$$

Fig. 3. A compiler for stacking multiple instances of a Σ-protocol.

6 Self-stacking: Disjunctions with the Same Protocol

We now present a self-stacking compiler for Σ-protocols, presented in Fig. 3. By self-stacking, we mean a compiler that takes a *stackable* Σ-protocol Π for a language $\mathcal{L}$ and produces a Σ-protocol for language with disjunctive statements of the form $(x_1 \in \mathcal{L}) \vee (x_2 \in \mathcal{L}) \vee \ldots \vee (x_\ell \in \mathcal{L})$ with communication complexity proportional to the size of a single run of the underlying Σ-protocol (along with an additive factor that is linear in ℓ and λ). The key ingredient in our compiler is the partially-binding vector commitments (See Definition 2), which will allow the prover to efficiently compute verifying transcripts for the inactive clauses.

The compiler generates an accepting transcript (a_α, c, z^*) to the active clause $\alpha \in [\ell]$ using the witness, and then simulates accepting transcripts for each non-active clause, using the extended simulator. Recall that this extended simulator takes in a third round message z and a challenge c and produces a first round message a such that $\phi(x, a, c, z) = 1$. Thus, the prover can *re-use* the third round message z^*, for each simulated transcript, thereby reducing communication to the size of a single third round message. For a more detailed overview, we refer the reader to Sect. 2.

We now present a formal description of the self-stacking compiler, which we prove in the full version of the paper [23].

Theorem 4 (Self-Stacking). *Let $\Pi = (A, Z, \phi)$ be a stackable (See Definition 5) Σ-protocol for the NP relation $\mathcal{R} : \mathcal{X} \times \mathcal{W} \rightarrow \{0, 1\}$ and let* (Setup, Gen, EquivCom, Equiv, BindCom) *be a 1-out-of-ℓ binding vector commitment scheme (See Definition 2). For any pp $\leftarrow$ Setup(1^λ), the compiled protocol $\Pi' = (A', Z', \phi')$ described in Fig. 3 is a <u>stackable</u> Σ-protocol for the relation $\mathcal{R}' : \mathcal{X}^\ell \times ([\ell] \times \mathcal{W}) \rightarrow \{0, 1\}$, where $\mathcal{R}'((x_1, \ldots, x_\ell), (\alpha, w)) := \mathcal{R}(x_\alpha, w)$.*

Communication Complexity. Let $\mathsf{CC}(\Pi)$ be the communication complexity of Π. Then, the communication complexity of the Π' obtained from Theorem 4 is $(\mathsf{CC}(\Pi) + |\mathsf{ck}| + |\mathsf{com}| + |r'|)$, where the sizes of ck, com and r' depends on the choice of partially-binding vector commitment scheme and are independent of $\mathsf{CC}(\Pi)$. With our instantiation of partially binding vector commitments, the size of $|\mathsf{ck}|, |r'|$ will depend linearly on ℓ. However since our resulting protocol Π' is also stackable, the communication complexity can be reduced further to $\mathsf{CC}(\Pi) + 2 \log(\ell)(|\mathsf{ck}| + |\mathsf{com}| + |r'|)$ by recursive application of the compiler as follows: let $\Pi_1 = \Pi$ and for $n > 1$ let Π_{2n} be the outcome of applying the compiler from Theorem 4 with $\ell = 2$ to Π_n. Note that Π_ℓ only applies the stacking compiler $\lceil \log(\ell) \rceil$ times and that $\mathsf{CC}(\Pi_{2n}) = \mathsf{CC}(\Pi_n) + |\mathsf{ck}| + |\mathsf{com}| + |r'|$. Therefore $\mathsf{CC}(\Pi_\ell) = \mathsf{CC}(\Pi) + 2 \log(\ell)(|\mathsf{ck}| + |\mathsf{com}| + |r'|)$.

Computational Complexity. In general, the computation complexity of this protocol is ℓ times that of Π. However, in many protocols, the simulator is much faster than computing an honest transcript. We note that for such protocols, our compiler is expected to also get savings in the computation complexity.

6.1 Extending to Multiple Languages

Many known constructions of Σ-protocols work for more than one language. For instance, most MPC-in-the-head style Σ-protocols (e.g. KKW [35], Ligero [2]) can support all languages with a polynomial sized relation circuit, as long as the underlying MPC protocol works for any polynomial sized function. However, because Σ-protocols are defined w.r.t. a particular NP language/relation, instantiating [35] for two different NP languages $\mathcal{L}_1$ and $\mathcal{L}_2$ will (by definition) result in two distinct Σ-protocols. Therefore, applied naïvely, our compiler could only be used to stack Σ-protocols from [35] for the exact same relation circuit.

We explore two alternatives for overcoming this limitation. First, we note that in many situations it is trivial to generalize our technique to cover "Σ-protocols based on a particular technique," *e.g.* protocols based on [35]. This can be done using a "meta-language" like circuit satisfiability that generalizes across multiple NP languages without introducing a high NP-reduction cost. In the full-version of this paper [23], we explore a conceptually different approach, we call *cross-stacking*. Our cross-stacking compiler applies the self-stacking techniques to different Σ-protocols (both based on a single technique and otherwise) without modifying the Σ-protocols. The major barrier is that the third round message distributions of the Σ-protocols are different, so third round messages may not be recyclable. To overcome this, we define a distribution which captures the "union" of the third round message distributions of each Σ-protocol, and map messages into and out of this distribution. The communication complexity of the resulting protocol is determined by the size of this distribution. We give concrete case studies of cross-stacking various Σ-protocols.

Acknowledgments. We would like to thank the anonymous reviewers of CRYPTO 2021 for their helpful comments on our initial construction of the partially-binding commitments. Additionally, we would like to thank Nicholas Spooner for his helpful comments on the definition of our commitments.

The first and second authors are supported in part by NSF under awards CNS-1653110, and CNS-1801479, and the Office of Naval Research under contract N00014-19-1-2292. The first author is also supported in part by NSF CNS grant 1814919, NSF CAREER award 1942789 and the Johns Hopkins University Catalyst award. The second author is also funded by DARPA under Contract No. HR001120C0084, as well as a Security and Privacy research award from Google. The third author is funded by Concordium Blockhain Research Center, Aarhus University, Denmark. The forth author is supported by the National Science Foundation under Grant #2030859 to the Computing Research Association for the CIFellows Project and is supported by DARPA under Agreements No. HR00112020021 and Agreements No. HR001120C0084. Any opinions, findings and conclusions or recommendations expressed in this material are those of the author(s) and do not necessarily reflect the views of the United States Government or DARPA.

References

1. Abe, M., Ohkubo, M., Suzuki, K.: 1-out-of-n signatures from a variety of keys. In: Zheng, Y. (ed.) ASIACRYPT 2002. LNCS, vol. 2501, pp. 415–432. Springer, Heidelberg (2002). https://doi.org/10.1007/3-540-36178-2_26
2. Ames, S., Hazay, C., Ishai, Y., Venkitasubramaniam, M.: Ligero: lightweight sublinear arguments without a trusted setup. In: Thuraisingham, B.M., Evans, D., Malkin, T., Xu, D. (eds.) ACM CCS 2017, pp. 2087–2104. ACM Press (2017)
3. Attema, T., Cramer, R.: Compressed Σ-protocol theory and practical application to plug & play secure algorithmics. In: Micciancio, D., Ristenpart, T. (eds.) CRYPTO 2020, Part III, LNCS, vol. 12172, pp. 513–543. Springer, Cham (2020). https://doi.org/10.1007/978-3-030-56877-1_18
4. Attema, T., Cramer, R., Fehr, S.: Compressing proofs of k-out-of-n partial knowledge. In: Malkin, T., Peikert, C. (eds.) CRYPTO 2021. LNCS, vol. 12828, pp. 65–91. Springer, Cham (2021). https://doi.org/10.1007/978-3-030-84259-8_3
5. Baum, C., Malozemoff, A.J., Rosen, M.B., Scholl, P.: Mac'n'Cheese: zero-knowledge proofs for Boolean and arithmetic circuits with nested disjunctions. In: Malkin, T., Peikert, C. (eds.) CRYPTO 2021. LNCS, vol. 12828, pp. 92–122. Springer, Cham (2021). https://doi.org/10.1007/978-3-030-84259-8_4

6. Ben-Or, M., Goldwasser, S., Wigderson, A.: Completeness theorems for non-cryptographic fault-tolerant distributed computation (extended abstract). In: 20th ACM STOC, pp. 1–10. ACM Press (1988)

7. Ben-Sasson, E., et al.: Zerocash: decentralized anonymous payments from bitcoin. In: 2014 IEEE Symposium on Security and Privacy, pp. 459–474. IEEE Computer Society Press (2014)

8. Ben-Sasson, E., Chiesa, A., Genkin, D., Tromer, E., Virza, M.: SNARKs for C: verifying program executions succinctly and in zero knowledge. In: Canetti, R., Garay, J.A. (eds.) CRYPTO 2013, Part II, LNCS, vol. 8043, pp. 90–108. Springer, Heidelberg (2013). https://doi.org/10.1007/978-3-642-40084-1_6

9. Ben-Sasson, E., Chiesa, A., Riabzev, M., Spooner, N., Virza, M., Ward, N.P.: Aurora: transparent succinct arguments for R1CS. In: Ishai, Y., Rijmen, V. (eds.) EUROCRYPT 2019, Part I, LNCS, vol. 11476, pp. 103–128. Springer, Cham (2019). https://doi.org/10.1007/978-3-030-17653-2_4

10. Ben-Sasson, E., Chiesa, A., Tromer, E., Virza, M.: Succinct non-interactive zero knowledge for a von Neumann architecture. In: Fu, K., Jung, J. (eds.) USENIX Security 2014, pp. 781–796. USENIX Association (2014)

11. Blum, M.: How to prove a theorem so no one else can claim it. pp. 1444–1451 (1987)

12. Bootle, J., Cerulli, A., Chaidos, P., Ghadafi, E., Groth, J., Petit, C.: Short accountable ring signatures based on DDH. In: Pernul, G., Ryan, P.Y.A., Weippl, E. (eds.) ESORICS 2015, Part I, LNCS, vol. 9326, pp. 243–265. Springer, Cham (2015). https://doi.org/10.1007/978-3-319-24174-6_13

13. Bünz, B., Bootle, J., Boneh, D., Poelstra, A., Wuille, P., Maxwell, G.: Bulletproofs: short proofs for confidential transactions and more. In: 2018 IEEE Symposium on Security and Privacy, pp. 315–334. IEEE Computer Society Press (2018)

14. Chaum, D., Pedersen, T.P.: Transferred cash grows in size. In: Rueppel, R.A. (ed.) EUROCRYPT 1992. LNCS, vol. 658, pp. 390–407. Springer, Heidelberg (1993). https://doi.org/10.1007/3-540-47555-9_32

15. Ciampi, M., Persiano, G., Scafuro, A., Siniscalchi, L., Visconti, I.: Improved OR-composition of sigma-protocols. In: Kushilevitz, E., Malkin, T. (eds.) TCC 2016, Part II, LNCS, vol. 9563, pp. 112–141. Springer, Heidelberg (2016). https://doi.org/10.1007/978-3-662-49099-0_5

16. Cramer, R., Damgård, I.: Zero-knowledge proofs for finite field arithmetic, or: can zero-knowledge be for free? In: Krawczyk, H. (ed.) CRYPTO 1998. LNCS, vol. 1462, pp. 424–441. Springer, Heidelberg (1998). https://doi.org/10.1007/BFb0055745

17. Cramer, R., Damgård, I., Schoenmakers, B.: Proofs of partial knowledge and simplified design of witness hiding protocols. In: Desmedt, Y.G. (ed.) CRYPTO 1994. LNCS, vol. 839, pp. 174–187. Springer, Heidelberg (1994). https://doi.org/10.1007/3-540-48658-5_19

18. Fauzi, P., Lipmaa, H., Pindado, Z., Siim, J.: Somewhere statistically binding commitment schemes with applications. In: Borisov, N., Diaz, C. (eds.) FC 2021. LNCS, vol. 12674, pp. 436–456. Springer, Heidelberg (2021). https://doi.org/10.1007/978-3-662-64322-8_21

19. Fiat, A., Shamir, A.: How to prove yourself: practical solutions to identification and signature problems. In: Odlyzko, A.M. (ed.) CRYPTO 1986. LNCS, vol. 263, pp. 186–194. Springer, Heidelberg (1987). https://doi.org/10.1007/3-540-47721-7_12

20. Frederiksen, T.K., Nielsen, J.B., Orlandi, C.: Privacy-free garbled circuits with applications to efficient zero-knowledge. In: Oswald, E., Fischlin, M. (eds.) EUROCRYPT 2015, Part II, LNCS, vol. 9057, pp. 191–219. Springer, Heidelberg (2015). https://doi.org/10.1007/978-3-662-46803-6_7

21. Garay, J.A., MacKenzie, P., Yang, K.: Strengthening zero-knowledge protocols using signatures. In: Biham, E. (ed.) EUROCRYPT 2003. LNCS, vol. 2656, pp. 177–194. Springer, Heidelberg (2003). https://doi.org/10.1007/3-540-39200-9_11

22. Gennaro, R., Gentry, C., Parno, B., Raykova, M.: Quadratic span programs and succinct NIZKs without PCPs. In: Johansson, T., Nguyen, P.Q. (eds.) EUROCRYPT 2013. LNCS, vol. 7881, pp. 626–645. Springer, Heidelberg (2013). https://doi.org/10.1007/978-3-642-38348-9_37

23. Goel, A., Green, M., Hall-Andersen, M., Kaptchuk, G.: Stacking sigmas: a framework to compose Σ-protocols for disjunctions. Cryptology ePrint Archive, Report 2021/422 (2021). https://eprint.iacr.org/2021/422

24. Goldreich, O., Micali, S., Wigderson, A.: Proofs that yield nothing but their validity and a methodology of cryptographic protocol design (extended abstract). In: 27th FOCS, pp. 174–187. IEEE Computer Society Press (1986)

25. Goldreich, O., Oren, Y.: Definitions and properties of zero-knowledge proof systems. J. Cryptol. $7(1)$, 1–32 (1994). https://doi.org/10.1007/BF00195207

26. Goldwasser, S., Micali, S., Rackoff, C.: The knowledge complexity of interactive proof-systems (extended abstract). In: 17th ACM STOC, pp. 291–304. ACM Press (1985)

27. Groth, J.: Short pairing-based non-interactive zero-knowledge arguments. In: Abe, M. (ed.) ASIACRYPT 2010. LNCS, vol. 6477, pp. 321–340. Springer, Heidelberg (2010). https://doi.org/10.1007/978-3-642-17373-8_19

28. Groth, J.: On the size of pairing-based non-interactive arguments. In: Fischlin, M., Coron, J.-S. (eds.) EUROCRYPT 2016, Part II, LNCS, vol. 9666, pp. 305–326. Springer, Heidelberg (2016). https://doi.org/10.1007/978-3-662-49896-5_11

29. Guillou, L.C., Quisquater, J.-J.: A "paradoxical" indentity-based signature scheme resulting from zero-knowledge. In: Goldwasser, S. (ed.) CRYPTO 1988. LNCS, vol. 403, pp. 216–231. Springer, New York (1990). https://doi.org/10.1007/0-387-34799-2_16

30. Heath, D., Kolesnikov, V.: Stacked garbling - garbled circuit proportional to longest execution path. In: Micciancio, D., Ristenpart, T. (eds.) CRYPTO 2020, Part II, LNCS, vol. 12171, pp. 763–792. Springer, Cham (2020). https://doi.org/10.1007/978-3-030-56880-1_27

31. Heath, D., Kolesnikov, V.: Stacked garbling for disjunctive zero-knowledge proofs. In: Canteaut, A., Ishai, Y. (eds.) EUROCRYPT 2020, Part III, LNCS, vol. 12107, pp. 569–598. Springer, Cham (2020). https://doi.org/10.1007/978-3-030-45727-3_19

32. Heath, D., Kolesnikov, V., Peceny, S.: MOTIF: (almost) free branching in GMW - via vector-scalar multiplication. In: Moriai, S., Wang, H. (eds.) ASIACRYPT 2020, Part III, LNCS, vol. 12493, pp. 3–30. Springer, Cham (2020). https://doi.org/10.1007/978-3-030-64840-4_1

33. Ishai, Y., Kushilevitz, E., Ostrovsky, R., Sahai, A.; Zero-knowledge from secure multiparty computation. In: Johnson, D.S., Feige, U. (eds.) 39th ACM STOC, pp. 21–30. ACM Press (2007)

34. Jawurek, M., Kerschbaum, F., Orlandi, C.: Zero-knowledge using garbled circuits: how to prove non-algebraic statements efficiently. In: Sadeghi, A.-R., Gligor, V.D., Yung, M. (eds.) ACM CCS 2013, pp. 955–966. ACM Press (2013)

35. Katz, J., Kolesnikov, V., Wang, X.: Improved non-interactive zero knowledge with applications to post-quantum signatures. In: Lie, D., Mannan, M., Backes, M., Wang, X. (eds.) ACM CCS 2018, pp. 525–537. ACM Press (2018)

36. Kolesnikov, V.: Free IF: how to omit inactive branches and implement S-universal garbled circuit (almost) for free. In: Peyrin, T., Galbraith, S. (eds.) ASIACRYPT 2018, Part III, LNCS, vol. 11274, pp. 34–58. Springer, Cham (2018). https://doi.org/10.1007/978-3-030-03332-3_2

37. Rivest, R.L., Shamir, A., Tauman, Y.: How to leak a secret. In: Boyd, C. (ed.) ASIACRYPT 2001. LNCS, vol. 2248, pp. 552–565. Springer, Heidelberg (2001). https://doi.org/10.1007/3-540-45682-1_32

38. Schnorr, C.P.: Efficient identification and signatures for smart cards. In: Brassard, G. (ed.) CRYPTO 1989. LNCS, vol. 435, pp. 239–252. Springer, New York (1990). https://doi.org/10.1007/0-387-34805-0_22

39. Schnorr, C.P.: Efficient signature generation by smart cards. J. Cryptol. **4**(3), 161–174 (1991). https://doi.org/10.1007/BF00196725

40. Shamir, A.: How to share a secret. Commun. ACM **22**(11), 612–613 (1979)

41. Swisspost evoting: E-voting system 2019. https://gitlab.com/swisspost-evoting/e-voting-system-2019 (2019)

42. Zaverucha, G.: The picnic signature algorithm. Technical report (2020). https://github.com/microsoft/Picnic/raw/master/spec/spec-v3.0.pdf

One-Shot Fiat-Shamir-Based NIZK Arguments of Composite Residuosity and Logarithmic-Size Ring Signatures in the Standard Model

Benoît Libert[1,2]($\boxtimes$), Khoa Nguyen[3], Thomas Peters[4], and Moti Yung[5]

[1] CNRS, Laboratoire LIP, Lyon, France
[2] ENS de Lyon, Laboratoire LIP (U. Lyon, CNRS, ENSL, Inria, UCBL),
Lyon, France
benoit.libert@ens-lyon.fr
[3] Institute of Cybersecurity and Cryptology, School of Computing and Information
Technology, University of Wollongong, Wollongong, Australia
[4] FNRS and UCLouvain (ICTEAM), Ottignies-Louvain-la-Neuve, Belgium
[5] Google and Columbia University, New York, USA

Abstract. The standard model security of the Fiat-Shamir transform
has been an active research area for many years. In breakthrough results,
Canetti *et al.* (STOC'19) and Peikert-Shiehian (Crypto'19) showed that,
under the Learning-With-Errors (LWE) assumption, it provides soundness by applying correlation-intractable (CI) hash functions to so-called
trapdoor Σ-protocols. In order to be compatible with CI hash functions
based on standard LWE assumptions with polynomial approximation factors, all known such protocols have been obtained via parallel repetitions
of a basic protocol with binary challenges. In this paper, we consider languages related to Paillier's composite residuosity assumption (DCR) for
which we give the first trapdoor Σ-protocols providing soundness in one
shot, via exponentially large challenge spaces. This improvement is analogous to the one enabled by Schnorr over the original Fiat-Shamir protocol in the random oracle model. Using the correlation-intractable hash
function paradigm, we then obtain simulation-sound NIZK arguments
showing that an element of $\mathbb{Z}_{N^2}^*$ is a composite residue, which opens the
door to space-efficient applications in the standard model. As a concrete
example, we build logarithmic-size ring signatures (assuming a common
reference string) with the shortest signature length among schemes based
on standard assumptions in the standard model. We prove security under
the DCR and LWE assumptions, while keeping the signature size comparable with that of random-oracle-based schemes.

Keywords: NIZK arguments · Compactness · Simulation-soundness ·
Composite residuosity · Fiat-Shamir · Ring signatures · Standard
model

K. Nguyen—This work was done while this author was at Nanyang Technological
University, SPMS, Singapore.

O. Dunkelman and S. Dziembowski (Eds.): EUROCRYPT 2022, LNCS 13276, pp. 488–519, 2022.
https://doi.org/10.1007/978-3-031-07085-3_17

1   Introduction

The Fiat-Shamir transform [40] is a famous technique that collapses interactive protocols into non-interactive proof systems by computing the verifier's challenges as hash values of the transcript so far. Since its introduction, it enabled a wide range of applications in the random oracle model (ROM) although it may fail to preserve soundness in general [43]. In the standard model, it was not known to be safely instantiable under standard assumptions until recently. The beautiful work of Canetti et al. [15] and Peikert and Shiehian [66] changed this state-of-affairs by showing the existence of Fiat-Shamir-based non-interactive zero-knowledge (NIZK) proofs for all NP languages under the Learning-With-Errors (LWE) assumption [67]. Their results followed the methodology of *correlation intractable* (CI) hash functions [17], which can sometimes emulate the properties of random oracles in the standard model.

In short, correlation intractability for a relation R requires the infeasibility of finding x such that $(x, H_k(x)) \in R$ given a random hashing key k. This property provides soundness because, with high probability, it prevents a cheating prover's first message from being hashed into a challenge admitting a valid response. Canetti et al. [18] formalized this intuition by observing that it suffices to build CI hash functions for efficiently searchable relations as long as Fiat-Shamir is applied to *trapdoor* Σ-protocols. These are like standard Σ-protocols with two differences. First, they assume a common reference string (CRS). Second, there exists an efficiently computable function BadChallenge that inputs a trapdoor τ_Σ together with a false statement $x \notin \mathcal{L}$ and a first prover message a in order to compute the only challenge Chall such that an accepting transcript (a, Chall, z) exists for some response z. If BadChallenge is efficiently computable, soundness can be achieved using CI hash functions for any efficiently computable relation, which covers the case of the relation R such that $(x, y) \in R$ if and only if $y = \text{BadChallenge}(\tau_\Sigma, x, a)$.

While the results of [15,66] resolve the long-standing problem of realizing NIZK proofs for all NP under standard lattice assumptions, they raise the natural open question of whether LWE-based correlation-intractable hash functions can lead to compact proofs/arguments for specific languages like subgroup membership. In this paper, we consider this problem for Paillier's composite residuosity assumption [64] for which we obtain NIZK arguments that are roughly as short as those obtained from the Fiat-Shamir heuristic in the ROM. In particular, we aim at trapdoor Σ-protocols that ensure soundness in one shot, without going through $\Theta(\lambda)$ parallel repetitions to achieve negligible soundness error.

OUR CONTRIBUTION. We provide space-efficient NIZK arguments showing that an element is a composite residue in the group $\mathbb{Z}_{N^2}^*$, for an RSA modulus $N = pq$. In particular, we can argue that Paillier [64] or Damgård-Jurik [34] ciphertexts decrypt to 0. These arguments extend to handle multiplicative relations between Paillier ciphertexts. We achieve this by showing that several natural Σ-protocols for Paillier-related languages can be extended into trapdoor Σ-protocols with an exponentially large challenge space, which achieve negligible soundness error in a single protocol execution. To our knowledge, we thus obtain the first trapdoor Σ-protocols that guarantee soundness without parallel repetitions.

Our constructions provide multi-theorem statistical NIZK and their soundness can be proved under the Learning-With-Errors (LWE) assumption. In addition, we show how to upgrade them into unbounded simulation-sound NIZK arguments based on the LWE and DCR assumptions. In their single-theorem version, our arguments of composite residuosity are as short as their random-oracle-based counterpart obtained from the Fiat-Shamir heuristic. Their multi-theorem and simulation-sound extensions are only longer by a small constant factor. In particular, we can turn any trapdoor Σ-protocol into an unbounded simulation-sound NIZK argument for the same language while only lengthening the transcript by the size of a Paillier ciphertext and its randomness.

As a main application, we obtain logarithmic-size ring signatures with concretely efficient signature length in the standard model. Recall that ring signatures allow a signer to sign messages while hiding in an *ad hoc* set of users called a *ring*. To this end, the signer only needs to know the public keys of all ring members and its own secret key. So far, the only known logarithmic-size realizations in the standard model under standard assumptions [3,24] incur very large signatures due to the use of witness indistinguishable proofs for NP. In contrast, we obtain fairly short signatures comprised of a small number of Paillier ciphertexts while retaining security under well-studied assumptions. For rings of $R = 2^r$ users, each signature fits within the equivalent of $15r + 7$ RSA moduli, which is only 3 times as large as in a Fiat-Shamir-like construction in the random oracle model under the DCR assumption. The unforgeability of our scheme is proved under the DCR and LWE assumptions while its anonymity holds for unbounded adversaries.

To our knowledge, our NIZK arguments for DCR-related languages give the first examples where, under standard assumptions, Fiat-Shamir-based arguments in the standard model can be almost as short as those in the random oracle model. We believe they can find many other applications than ring signatures. For example, they easily extend to prove multiplicative relations among Paillier ciphertexts, which is a common task in MPC [30] or voting protocols [34]. The trapdoor Σ-protocol of our DCR-based ring signature can also be used in other applications of compact 1-out-of-R proofs [45,46].

TECHNICAL OVERVIEW. Ciampi *et al.* [27] recently showed that any Σ-protocol can be turned into a trapdoor Σ-protocol with small (i.e., binary) challenge space, which requires many repetitions to achieve negligible soundness error. In order to obtain an exponentially large challenge space in one shot, we rely on earlier an observation by Chaidos and Groth [21] who noticed that a certain family of encryption schemes with linearly homomorphic properties over their message *and* randomness spaces admit a trapdoor Σ-protocol for the language $\mathcal{L}^0 = \{x \mid \exists w \in \mathcal{R} : x = \mathcal{E}_{pk}(0; w)\}$ of encryptions of 0. At a high level, if the prover's first message is an encryption $a = \mathcal{E}_{pk}(0; r)$ of 0 and the verifier sends a challenge Chall, the response $z = r + \text{Chall} \cdot w$ satisfies $a \cdot x^{\text{Chall}} = \mathcal{E}_{pk}(0; z)$. If $x \notin \mathcal{L}^0$, the special soundness property ensures that, for any given a, there is at most one Chall such that $a \cdot x^{\text{Chall}} = \mathcal{E}_{pk}(0; z)$ for some $z \in \mathcal{R}$. Moreover, the secret key sk can serve as a trapdoor τ_Σ to compute $\text{BadChallenge}(\tau_\Sigma, x, a)$

for any element a of the ciphertext space. Indeed, if Chall lives a polynomial-size set (say $\{0,1\}^{\log \lambda}$), the bad challenge is efficiently computable by outputting the first Chall $\in \{0,1\}^{\log \lambda}$ for which $\mathcal{D}_{sk}(a \cdot x^{\mathsf{Chall}}) = 0$. The above construction thus decreases the number of parallel repetitions by a factor $O(\log \lambda)$. Using the Okamoto-Uchiyama cryptosystem [63], Chaidos and Groth [21] apply the above technique to identify bad challenges within an exponentially large challenge space. A follow-up work by Lipmaa [58] shows that, although the plaintext space of Paillier's cryptosystem [64] has non-prime order $N = pq$, bad challenges are still computable using the factorization of N as long as the challenge space is contained in $\{0, \ldots, \min(p,q) - 1\}$. We actually identify a gap in [58], which adapts the Chaidos-Groth technique [21] to build designated verifier NIZK proofs that an Elgamal-Paillier ciphertext [13] encrypts 0. The proof of soundness of [58, Theorem 2] implicitly constructs a trapdoor Σ-protocol showing that $(C_0, C_1) = (g^r \bmod N^2, (1+N)^b \cdot h^r \bmod N^2)$ encrypts $b = 0$. We actually show that, for false statements, the extractor may fail to extract the bad challenge when a maliciously generated first prover message is outside the range of the encryption algorithm. Our trapdoor Σ-protocol for DCR proceeds like the extractor of [58, Theorem 2] but avoids this problem as it only relies on the Paillier/Damgård-Jurik encryption scheme, which has the property that all elements of the ciphertext space encrypt something.

In order to obtain a multi-theorem NIZK argument of composite residuosity, we can then apply the construction of [55, Appendix B], which compiles any trapdoor Σ-protocol into a NIZK argument for the same language using a lossy encryption scheme with equivocable lossy mode. As considered [4,72], lossy encryption is a primitive where ciphertexts encrypted under lossy public keys – which are computationally indistinguishable from injective ones – statistically hide the underlying plaintexts. Moreover, the equivocation property (a.k.a. "efficient opening" [4]) makes it possible to trapdoor open any lossy ciphertext exactly as in a trapdoor commitment. It is known [47] that Paillier's cryptosystem [64] provides these properties under the DCR assumption.

However, in the context of the signature-of-knowledge paradigm [23], we need NIZK arguments with unbounded simulation-soundness [35]. Libert et $al.$ [55] showed that any trapdoor Σ-protocol can be turned into an USS argument for the same language using a generalization of the $\mathcal{R}$-lossy encryption primitive introduced by Boyle et $al.$ [9]. In [55], they introduced two distinct equivocation properties and gave a candidate based on the LWE assumption. In order to optimize the signature length, we give an efficient equivocable $\mathcal{R}$-lossy encryption candidate under the DCR assumption. This task is non-trivial since injective keys have to be indistinguishable from lossy keys, even when one of the equivocation trapdoors is given. Yet, our candidate only uses the DCR assumption while [55] used fairly powerful tools (i.e., lattice trapdoors [41]) to equivocate lossy ciphertexts. Although our DCR-based realization satisfies slightly weaker properties than those of [55], we prove it sufficient to obtain simulation-soundness. It thus allows compiling trapdoor Σ-protocols into unbounded simulation-sound NIZK arguments without using lattice trapdoors.

Armed with a DCR-based construction of USS arguments, we then build a simulation-sound NIZK argument that one-out-of-many elements of $\mathbb{Z}_{N^2}^*$ is a composite residue. To this end, we provide a DCR-based variant of the Groth-Kohlweiss (GK) [46] Σ-protocol, which allows proving that one out of R commitments contains 0 with communication cost $O(\log R)$. The reason why DCR is the most promising assumption towards trapdooring [46] is that, in its original version, the GK protocol cannot immediately be turned into a trapdoor Σ-protocol by applying the transformation of Ciampi et al. [27]. The main difficulty is that it only yields $(r + 1)$-special-soundness for $r = O(\log R)$, so that up to r bad challenges may exist for a false statement and a given first prover message. Even if BadChallenge can identify them all for a given protocol iteration, over κ repetitions, we end up with up to r^κ combinations, which are not enumerable in polynomial time for non-constant κ and r.[1] In order to apply the LWE-based CI hash function of [66], we construct a variant of GK with an exponentially large challenge space and where BadChallenge can efficiently enumerate all bad challenges after a single protocol iteration. We achieve this by extending our trapdoor Σ-protocol showing composite residuosity, using a BadChallenge function that computes the roots of a degree-r (instead of a degree-1) polynomial.

Adapting [46] to Paillier-based commitments raises several difficulties if we want to apply it in the context of ring signatures. In our security proofs, we need the Σ-protocol to be statistically honest-verifier zero-knowledge. In the protocol of [46] and our DCR-based variant, this requires that users' public keys be computed as statistically hiding commitments to 0. A first idea is to apply Paillier, where ciphertexts $C = g^m \cdot r^N \bmod N^2$ are perfectly hiding commitments when g is an N-th residue (and extractable commitments when N divides the order of g). Unfortunately, as shown in [57, Section 2.6], using a statistically hiding commitment is not sufficient to ensure statistical anonymity when the adversary can introduce maliciously generated public keys in the ring. In the case of Paillier, when g is an N-th residue, so is any honestly generated commitment. However, in the anonymity game, the adversary can choose a ring containing malformed public keys that are *not* N-th residues in $\mathbb{Z}_{N^2}^*$. This affects the statistical ZK property since the simulator cannot fully randomize commitments by multiplying them with a random commitment to 0. To address this issue, we need a statistically hiding commitment which is "dense" in that commitments to 0 are uniformly distributed over $\mathbb{Z}_{N^2}^*$. In order to obtain trapdoor Σ-protocols, we also need the commitment to be dual-mode as the BadChallenge function should be able to efficiently extract committed messages in the perfectly binding setting. We thus use commitments (suggested in [20] for their online/offline property) of the form $C = (1 + N)^m \cdot h^y \cdot w^N \bmod N^2$, for randomness (y, w), which are perfectly binding if h is an N-th residue and perfectly hiding if N divides the

---

[1] Holmgren et al. [50] recently gave a technique allowing to address the combinatorial explosion of bad challenges induced by parallel repetitions. In the full version of the paper [56], we discuss the applicability of their approach to our setting. Although it allows instantiations under the DDH assumption, these are considerably more expensive that our DCR-based candidate.

order of h. Moreover, the latter configuration provides dense statistically hiding commitments since commitments to 0 are uniformly distributed over $\mathbb{Z}_{N^2}^*$.

A second difficulty arises when we adapt the proof of unforgeability of the Groth-Kohlweiss ring signature, which relies on the extractability property of their Σ-protocol. They apply the forking lemma to extract an opening of a perfectly hiding commitment by replaying the adversary $O(r)$ times. In the standard model, our reduction does not have the degree of freedom of replaying the adversary with a different random oracle. Instead, we proceed with a sequence of hybrid games that exploits the dual-mode property of our DCR-based commitment and moves to a setting where the signer's identity is only computationally hidden. In one game, the commitment is switched to its extractable mode so as to extract the committed bits $\ell_1^\star \ldots \ell_r^\star \in \{0,1\}^r$ of the signer's position $\ell^\star$ in the ring. In the next game, the reduction guesses which honestly generated public key $vk^{(i^\star)}$ will be in the ring position $\ell^\star$ and fails if this guess is incorrect. Finally, we modify the key generation oracle and replace the expected target user's public key $vk^{(i^\star)}$ by a random element of $\mathbb{Z}_{N^2}^*$ in order to force the forgery to prove a false statement. In the last game transition, the problem is that we cannot immediately rely on the DCR assumption to change the distribution of $vk^{(i^\star)}$ while using the factorization of N to extract $\ell_1^\star \ldots \ell_r^\star$. We thus involve two distinct moduli in our DCR-based adaptation of GK. The use of distinct moduli N and $\bar{N}$ requires to adjust our Σ-protocol and force some equality to hold over the integers (and thus modulo both N and $\bar{N}$) between values $a, \ell \in \mathbb{Z}_{\bar{N}}$ that our BadChallenge function extracts from the commitments in the first prover message. We enforce this condition by imposing an unusual range restriction to some component of the response $z = a + \text{Chall} \cdot \ell \in \mathbb{Z}$: Instead of only checking an upper bound for z, the verifier also checks a lower bound to ensure that no implicit modular reduction occurs when homomorphically computing $a + \text{Chall} \cdot \ell$ over commitments sent by a malicious prover.

Using the above ideas, the proof of unforgeability requires reliable erasures. The reason is that the security proof appeals to the NIZK simulator to answer all signing queries. Hence, if the adversary corrupts some user i after a signing query involving $sk^{(i)}$, the challenger has to pretend that the random coins of user i's past signatures have been erased as it cannot efficiently compute randomness that explain the simulated NIZK arguments as real arguments. In a second step, we modify the scheme to get rid of the erasure assumption.

A first idea to avoid erasures is to adapt the proof of unforgeability in such a way that the NIZK simulator is only used to simulate signatures on behalf of the expected target user (whose index $i^\star$ is guessed upfront), while all other users' signatures are faithfully generated. If the guess is correct, user $i^\star$ is never corrupted and the reduction never gets stuck when it comes to explaining the generation of signatures created by adaptively corrupted users. However, this strategy raises a major difficulty since decoding the signer's position $\ell^\star$ in the ring is only possible when the bits $\ell_1^\star \ldots \ell_r^\star \in \{0,1\}^r$ of $\ell^\star$ are committed using extractable commitments $\{L_i^\star\}_{i=1}^r$. At the same time, our security proof requires the guessed index $i^\star$ to be statistically independent of the adversary's view until the forgery stage. In turn, this requires to simulate user i^*'s signatures via *statistical* NIZK arguments. Indeed, computational NIZK proofs would information-theoretically leak the index i^* of the only user for which the NIZK simulator is used in signing queries. Unfortunately, perfectly binding commitments are not compatible with statistical ZK in our setting. To resolve this tension, we need a commitment which is perfectly hiding in all signing queries and extractable in the forgery. Moreover, for anonymity purposes, the perfectly hiding mode should make it possible to perfectly randomize adversarially-chosen commitments when we multiply them with commitments to 0. We instantiate this commitment using a variant (called "dense $\mathcal{R}$-lossy PKE" hereafter) of our DCR-based $\mathcal{R}$-lossy PKE scheme. Like our original $\mathcal{R}$-lossy PKE system, it can be programmed to be statistically hiding in all signing queries and extractable in the forgery, but it features different properties: It does not have to be equivocable, but we need its lossy mode to be dense in $\mathbb{Z}_{N^2}^*$ (a property not met by our equivocable $\mathcal{R}$-lossy PKE) in order to use it in a statistically HVZK Σ-protocol.

RELATED WORK. The negative results (e.g., [17,43]) on the standard-model soundness of Fiat-Shamir did not rule out the existence of secure instantiations when specific protocols are compiled using concrete hash functions. A large body of work [10,14,16,26,29,49,52,59,71] investigated the circumstances under which CI hash functions [17] lead to secure standard model instantiations of the paradigm. Canetti *et al.* [15] showed that correlation intractability for *efficiently searchable* relations suffices to remove interaction from any trapdoor Σ-protocol. This includes their variant of [39] for the language of Hamiltonian graphs, which enables Fiat-Shamir-based proofs for all NP. They also gave candidates assuming the existence of fully homomorphic encryption (FHE) with circular security [18]. Peikert and Shiehian [66] subsequently achieved the same result under the standard LWE assumption [67].

Canetti *et al.* [15,18] gave trapdoor Σ-protocols for the languages of Hamiltonian graphs and quadratic residues in $\mathbb{Z}_N^*$ [42]. Like the generic trapdoor Σ-protocol of [27], they proceed with parallel repetitions of a Σ-protocol with challenge space $\{0,1\}$. CI hash functions were also used to compress protocols with multiple interaction rounds [14,26,52,59] and larger challenges. Lombardi and Vaikuntanathan [59] notably extended the CI paradigm beyond the class of protocols where the BadChallenge function is efficiently computable. In this case, however, evaluating the hash function in polynomial time requires a fairly strong LWE assumption to ensure correlation intractability. Brakerski *et al.* [10] considered a stronger notion of correlation intractability which allows handling relations where the BadChallenge function can only be approximated by a distribution over constant-degree polynomials. They thus obtained Fiat-Shamir-based NIZK arguments from standard assumptions that are not known to imply FHE.

In the following, we consider 3-message protocols where bad challenges are efficiently (and exactly) computable – and thus enable the use of polynomial-time-computable CI hash functions based on standard lattice assumptions – in an exponentially large set after a single protocol run.

Ring signatures were coined by Rivest, Shamir and Tauman [68]. They enable unconditional anonymity and involve no registration phase nor any tracing authority. Whoever has a public key can be appointed as a ring member without being asked for his consent or even being aware of it. The original motivation of ring signatures was to enable the anonymous leakage of secrets, by concealing the identity of a source (e.g., a whistleblower in a political scandal) while simultaneously providing reliability guarantees. Recently, the primitive also found applications in the context of cryptocurrencies [62].

After the work of Rivest, Shamir and Tauman [68], a number of solutions were given under various assumptions [1,2,11,12,46,65,70]. Bender et al. [6] gave stronger definitions and constructions from general assumptions. In the standard model, more efficient schemes were given [8,70] in groups with a bilinear map. Brakerski and Tauman [11] gave the first constructions from lattice assumptions.

In early realizations [8,12,68,70], the size of signatures was linear in the number of ring members. Dodis et al. [36] suggested constant-size ring signatures in the random oracle model. Chase and Lysyanskaya [23] took a similar approach while using simulation-extractable NIZK proofs in the standard model. However, it is not clear how to adapt their approach without using generic NIZK. Assuming a common reference string, constructions with sub-linear-size signatures in the standard model were given in [22,28,44]. Malavolta and Schröder [60] used SNARKs (and thus non-falsifiable assumptions) to obtain constant-size signatures. In the random oracle model, Groth and Kohlweiss [46] obtained an elegant construction with logarithmic-size ring signatures under the discrete logarithm assumption. Lattice-based analogues of [46] were given in [37,38].

The log-size signatures of [46,54,57] are obtained by applying Fiat-Shamir to Σ-protocols that are not immediately compatible with the BadChallenge function paradigm. In their settings, it would require to iterate a basic Σ-protocol (with small challenge space) a super-constant number of times, thus leading to a combinatorial explosion in the total number of bad challenges as each iteration would tolerate more than one bad challenge. Backes et al. [3] and Chatterjee et al. [24] eliminated the need for a CRS while retaining logarithmic signature size. However, they did not provide concrete signature sizes and, due to the use of general NIWI/ZAPs techniques, their constructions would require much longer signatures than ours for any realistic ring cardinality. For instance, even for very small rings, the construction of [24] would incur signatures comprised several hundreds of Megabytes to represent $O(\lambda^3)$ FHE ciphertexts. In stark contrast with earlier solutions, our signatures would still fit within $\approx 1.5\mathrm{Mb}$ (using 3072-bit RSA moduli) for rings as large as the number of atoms in the universe.

While our construction relies on a common reference string, it features (to our knowledge) the first logarithmic-size signatures with concretely efficient signature length *and* security under standard assumptions in the standard model.

2 Background and Definitions

For any $t \geq 2$, we denote by $\mathbb{Z}_t$ the ring of integers with addition and multiplication modulo t. For a finite set S, $U(S)$ stands for the uniform distribution over S. If X and Y are distributions over the same domain, $\Delta(X, Y)$ denotes their statistical distance. For a distribution D, $x \sim D$ means that x is distributed according to D, while $x \hookleftarrow D$ denotes the explicit action of sampling x from D.

2.1 Hardness Assumptions

We first recall the Learning-With-Errors (LWE) assumption.

Definition 2.1 ([67]). *Let $m \geq n \geq 1$, $q \geq 2$ be functions of a security parameter λ and let a distribution χ over $\mathbb{Z}$. The LWE problem consists in distinguishing between the distributions $(\mathbf{A}, \mathbf{As} + \mathbf{e})$ and $U(\mathbb{Z}_q^{m \times n} \times \mathbb{Z}_q^m)$, where $\mathbf{A} \sim U(\mathbb{Z}_q^{m \times n})$, $\mathbf{s} \sim U(\mathbb{Z}_q^n)$ and $\mathbf{e} \sim \chi^m$.*

When χ is the discrete Gaussian distribution $D_{\mathbb{Z}^m, \alpha q}$ with standard deviation αq for some $\alpha \in (0, 1)$, this problem is as hard as worst-case instances of well-studied lattice problems. We now recall the Composite Residuosity assumption.

Definition 2.2 ([34,64]). *Let integers $N = pq$ and $\zeta > 1$ for primes p, q. The ζ-**Decision Composite Residuosity** (ζ-DCR) assumption states that the distributions $\{x = w^{N^\zeta} \bmod N^{\zeta+1} \mid w \leftarrow U(\mathbb{Z}_N^\star)\}$ and $\{x \mid x \leftarrow U(\mathbb{Z}_{N^{\zeta+1}}^\star)\}$ are computationally indistinguishable.*

It is known [34] that the ζ-DCR assumption is equivalent to 1-DCR for any $\zeta > 1$.

2.2 Correlation Intractable Hash Functions

We consider efficiently enumerable [15] relations $R \subseteq \mathcal{X} \times \mathcal{Y}$ where, for each $x \in \mathcal{X}$, there is a polynomial number of elements $y \in \mathcal{Y}$ satisfying $R(x, y) = 1$. Moreover, these are efficiently enumerable.

Definition 2.3. *A relation $R \subseteq \mathcal{X} \times \mathcal{Y}$ is **enumerable** in time T if there exists a function $f_R : \mathcal{X} \to 2^{\mathcal{Y}}$ computable in time T such that, for each $x \in \mathcal{X}$, $f_R(x) = \{y_x \in \mathcal{Y} \mid (x, y_x) \in R\}$. If $\max_{x \in \mathcal{X}} |f_R(x)| \leq 1$, it is called **searchable**.*

Let $\lambda \in \mathbb{N}$ a security parameter. A hash family with input length $n(\lambda)$ and output length λ is a collection $\mathcal{H} = \{h_\lambda : \{0,1\}^{s(\lambda)} \times \{0,1\}^{n(\lambda)} \to \{0,1\}^\lambda\}$ of keyed functions induced by efficient algorithms (Gen, Hash), where $\mathsf{Gen}(1^\lambda)$ outputs a key $k \in \{0,1\}^{s(\lambda)}$ and $\mathsf{Hash}(k, x)$ computes $h_\lambda(k, x) \in \{0,1\}^\lambda$.

Definition 2.4. *For a relation ensemble $\{R_\lambda \subseteq \{0,1\}^{n(\lambda)} \times \{0,1\}^\lambda\}$, a hash function family $\mathcal{H} = \{h_\lambda : \{0,1\}^{s(\lambda)} \times \{0,1\}^{n(\lambda)} \to \{0,1\}^{m(\lambda)}\}$ is R-**correlation intractable** if, for any probabilistic polynomial time (PPT) adversary $\mathcal{A}$, we have $\Pr\left[k \leftarrow \mathsf{Gen}(1^\lambda)), \ x \leftarrow \mathcal{A}(k) : (x, h_\lambda(k, x)) \in R\right] = \mathsf{negl}(\lambda)$.*

Peikert and Shiehian [66] described a CI hash family for any searchable relation defined by functions f of bounded depth. Their construction relies on the standard LWE assumption with polynomial approximation factors. Their proof was given for efficiently searchable relations. However, it also implies correlation intractability for efficiently enumerable relations, as observed in [18,52].

2.3 Admissible Hash Functions

Admissible hash functions were introduced in [7] as a combinatorial tool for partitioning-based security proofs.

Definition 2.5 ([7]). *Let $\ell(\lambda), L(\lambda) \in \mathbb{N}$ be functions of $\lambda \in \mathbb{N}$. Let an efficiently computable function* $\mathsf{AHF} : \{0,1\}^\ell \to \{0,1\}^L$. *For each $K \in \{0,1,\bot\}^L$, let the partitioning function $F_{\mathsf{ADH}}(K, \cdot) : \{0,1\}^\ell \to \{0,1\}$ such that*

$$F_{\mathsf{ADH}}(K, X) := \begin{cases} 0 & \text{if } \forall i \in [L] \quad (\mathsf{AHF}(X)_i = K_i) \ \vee \ (K_i = \bot) \\ 1 & \text{otherwise} \end{cases}$$

We say that AHF *is an* **admissible hash function** *if there exists an efficient algorithm* $\mathsf{AdmSmp}(1^\lambda, Q, \delta)$ *that takes as input $Q \in \mathrm{poly}(\lambda)$ and a non-negligible $\delta(\lambda) \in (0,1]$ and outputs a key $K \in \{0,1,\bot\}^L$ such that, for all $X^{(1)}, \dots, X^{(Q)}, X^\star \in \{0,1\}^\ell$ such that $X^\star \notin \{X^{(1)}, \dots, X^{(Q)}\}$, we have*

$$\Pr_K \left[F_{\mathsf{ADH}}(K, X^{(1)}) = \cdots = F_{\mathsf{ADH}}(K, X^{(Q)}) = 1 \ \wedge \ F_{\mathsf{ADH}}(K, X^\star) = 0 \right] \geq \delta(Q(\lambda)) \ .$$

It is known that admissible hash functions exist for $\ell, L = \Theta(\lambda)$.

Theorem 2.6 ([51, **Theorem 1**]). *Let $(C_\ell)_{\ell \in \mathbb{N}}$ be a family of codes $C_\ell : \{0,1\}^\ell \to \{0,1\}^L$ with minimal distance cL for some constant $c \in (0, 1/2)$. Then, $(C_\ell)_{\ell \in \mathbb{N}}$ is a family of admissible hash functions. Furthermore, $\mathsf{AdmSmp}(1^\lambda, Q, \delta)$ outputs a key $K \in \{0,1,\bot\}^L$ for which $\eta = O(\log \lambda)$ components are not $\bot$ and $\delta(Q(\lambda))$ is a non-negligible function of λ.*

2.4 Trapdoor Σ-protocols

Canetti *et al.* [18] defined a trapdoor variant of the notion of Σ-protocols [31].

Definition 2.7 (**Adapted from** [18]). *Let a language $\mathcal{L}$ associated with an NP relations R. A 3-move interactive proof system $\Pi = (\mathsf{Gen}_{\mathsf{par}}, \mathsf{Gen}_{\mathcal{L}}, \mathsf{P}, \mathsf{V})$ in the common reference string model is a Σ-protocol for $\mathcal{L}$ if it satisfies the following:*

- **3-Move Form:** P *and* V *both input* $\mathsf{crs} = (\mathsf{par}, \mathsf{crs}_{\mathcal{L}})$, *with* $\mathsf{par} \leftarrow \mathsf{Gen}_{\mathsf{par}}(1^\lambda)$ *and* $\mathsf{crs}_{\mathcal{L}} \leftarrow \mathsf{Gen}_{\mathcal{L}}(\mathsf{par}, \mathcal{L})$, *and a statement x. They proceed as follows: (i)* P *inputs* $w \in R(x)$, *computes* $(\mathbf{a}, st) \leftarrow \mathsf{P}(\mathsf{crs}, x, w)$ *and sends* $\mathbf{a}$ *to* V; *(ii)* V *sends back a random challenge* Chall; *(iii)* P *finally sends a response* $\mathbf{z} = \mathsf{P}(\mathsf{crs}, x, w, \mathbf{a}, \mathsf{Chall}, st)$ *to* V; *(iv) On input of* $(\mathbf{a}, \mathsf{Chall}, \mathbf{z})$, V *outputs 1 or 0.*
- **Completeness:** *If* $(x, w) \in R$ *and* P *honestly computes* $(\mathbf{a}, \mathbf{z})$ *for a challenge* Chall, *then* $\mathsf{V}(\mathsf{crs}, x, (\mathbf{a}, \mathsf{Chall}, \mathbf{z}))$ *outputs 1 with probability* $1 - \mathsf{negl}(\lambda)$.
- **Special zero-knowledge:** *There is a PPT simulator* ZKSim *that inputs* crs, $x \in \mathcal{L}$ *and a challenge* $\mathsf{Chall} \in \mathcal{C}$. *It outputs* $(\mathbf{a}, \mathbf{z}) \leftarrow \mathsf{ZKSim}(\mathsf{crs}, x, \mathsf{Chall})$ *such that* $(\mathbf{a}, \mathsf{Chall}, \mathbf{z})$ *is indistinguishable from a real transcript (for* $w \in R(x)$*) with challenge* Chall.
- $(r+1)$-**Special soundness:** *For any CRS* $\mathsf{crs} = (\mathsf{par}, \mathsf{crs}_{\mathcal{L}})$ *obtained as* $\mathsf{par} \leftarrow \mathsf{Gen}_{\mathsf{par}}(1^\lambda)$, $\mathsf{crs}_{\mathcal{L}} \leftarrow \mathsf{Gen}_{\mathcal{L}}(\mathsf{par}, \mathcal{L})$, *any* $x \notin \mathcal{L}$, *and any first message* $\mathbf{a}$ *sent by* P, *the set of challenges* $\mathcal{BADC} = f(\mathsf{crs}, x, \mathbf{a})$ *for which an accepting transcript* $(\mathsf{crs}, x, \mathbf{a}, \mathsf{Chall}, \mathbf{z})$ *exists for some third message* $\mathbf{z}$ *has cardinality* $|\mathcal{BADC}| \leq r$. *The function f is called the "bad challenge function" of Π. That is, if $x \notin \mathcal{L}$ and* $\mathsf{Chall} \notin \mathcal{BADC}$, *the verifier never accepts.*

Canetti *et al.* [18] define *trapdoor Σ-protocols* as Σ-protocols where the bad challenge function is efficiently computable using a trapdoor. They also define instance-dependent trapdoor Σ-protocol where the trapdoor τ_Σ should be generated as a function of some instance $x \notin \mathcal{L}$. Here, we use a definition where x need not be known in advance and the trapdoor does not depend on a specific x. However, the CRS and the trapdoor may depend on the language in our setting. The CRS $\mathsf{crs} = (\mathsf{par}, \mathsf{crs}_\mathcal{L})$ consists of a fixed part par and a language-dependent part $\mathsf{crs}_\mathcal{L}$ which is generated as a function of par and a language description $\mathcal{L}$.

Definition 2.8 (Adapted from [18]**).** *A Σ-protocol $\Pi = (\mathsf{Gen}_{\mathsf{par}}, \mathsf{Gen}_\mathcal{L}, \mathsf{P}, \mathsf{V})$ with bad challenge function f for a trapdoor language $\mathcal{L}$ is a **trapdoor Σ-protocol** if it satisfies the properties of Definition 2.7 and there exist PPT algorithms* (TrapGen, BadChallenge) *with the following properties.*

- $\mathsf{Gen}_{\mathsf{par}}$ *inputs $\lambda \in \mathbb{N}$ and outputs public parameters* $\mathsf{par} \leftarrow \mathsf{Gen}_{\mathsf{par}}(1^\lambda)$.
- $\mathsf{Gen}_\mathcal{L}$ *is a randomized algorithm that, on input of public parameters* par, *outputs the language-dependent part* $\mathsf{crs}_\mathcal{L} \leftarrow \mathsf{Gen}_\mathcal{L}(\mathsf{par}, \mathcal{L})$ *of* $\mathsf{crs} = (\mathsf{par}, \mathsf{crs}_\mathcal{L})$.
- $\mathsf{TrapGen}(\mathsf{par}, \mathcal{L}, \tau_\mathcal{L})$ *inputs public parameters* par *and (optionally) a trapdoor $\tau_\mathcal{L}$ allowing to test membership of $\mathcal{L}$. It outputs* $\mathsf{crs}_\mathcal{L}$ *and a trapdoor τ_Σ.*
- $\mathsf{BadChallenge}(\tau_\Sigma, \mathsf{crs}, x, \mathbf{a})$ *takes in a trapdoor τ_Σ, a CRS $\mathsf{crs} = (\mathsf{par}, \mathsf{crs}_\mathcal{L})$, an instance x, and a first prover message $\mathbf{a}$. It outputs a set $\mathcal{BADC}$.*

In addition, the following properties are required.

- **CRS indistinguishability:** *For any* $\mathsf{par} \leftarrow \mathsf{Gen}_{\mathsf{par}}(1^\lambda)$, *and any trapdoor $\tau_\mathcal{L}$ for the language $\mathcal{L}$, an honestly generated $\mathsf{crs}_\mathcal{L}$ is computationally indistinguishable from a CRS produced by* $\mathsf{TrapGen}(\mathsf{par}, \mathcal{L}, \tau_\mathcal{L})$. *Namely, for any* aux *and any PPT distinguisher $\mathcal{A}$, we have*

$$\mathbf{Adv}^{\text{indist-}\Sigma}_{\mathcal{A}}(\lambda) := |\Pr[\mathsf{crs}_\mathcal{L} \leftarrow \mathsf{Gen}_\mathcal{L}(\mathsf{par}, \mathcal{L}) : \mathcal{A}(\mathsf{par}, \mathsf{crs}_\mathcal{L}) = 1]$$
$$- \Pr[(\mathsf{crs}_\mathcal{L}, \tau_\Sigma) \leftarrow \mathsf{TrapGen}(\mathsf{par}, \mathcal{L}, \tau_\mathcal{L}) : \mathcal{A}(\mathsf{par}, \mathsf{crs}_\mathcal{L}) = 1]| \le \mathsf{negl}(\lambda).$$

- **Correctness:** *There exists a language-specific trapdoor $\tau_\mathcal{L}$ such that, for any instance $x \notin \mathcal{L}$ and all pairs* $(\mathsf{crs}_\mathcal{L}, \tau_\Sigma) \leftarrow \mathsf{TrapGen}(\mathsf{par}, \mathcal{L}, \tau_\mathcal{L})$, *we have* $\mathsf{BadChallenge}(\tau_\Sigma, \mathsf{crs}, x, \mathbf{a}) = f(\mathsf{crs}, x, \mathbf{a})$.

Note that the TrapGen algorithm does not take a specific statement x as input, but only a trapdoor $\tau_\mathcal{L}$ allowing to recognize elements of $\mathcal{L}$.

2.5 $\mathcal{R}$-Lossy Public-Key Encryption with Equivocation

In [55], Libert *et al.* considered a generalization of the notion of $\mathcal{R}$-lossy encryption introduced by Boyle *et al.* [9]. The primitive is a flavor of tag-based encryption [53] where the tag space $\mathcal{T}$ is partitioned into *injective* and *lossy* tags. When ciphertexts are generated for an injective tag, the decryption algorithm recovers the plaintext. On lossy tags, ciphertexts statistically hide the plaintexts. In $\mathcal{R}$-lossy PKE schemes, the tag space is partitioned according to a binary relation $\mathcal{R} \subseteq \mathcal{K} \times \mathcal{T}$. The key generation algorithm inputs an initialization value $K \in \mathcal{K}$

and partitions $\mathcal{T}$ in such a way that injective tags $t \in \mathcal{T}$ are those for which $(K,t) \in \mathcal{R}$ (i.e., all tags t for which $(K,t) \notin \mathcal{R}$ are lossy).

The definition of [55] requires the existence of a lossy key generation algorithm LKeygen that outputs public keys for which all tags t are lossy (in contrast with injective keys where the only lossy tags are those for which $(K,t) \notin \mathcal{R}$). In addition, [55] also asks that a trapdoor allows equivocating lossy ciphertexts (a property called *efficient opening* [4]) using an algorithm called Opener. The application to simulation-soundness [55] involves two opening algorithms Opener and LOpener. The former operates over injective public keys for lossy tags while the latter can equivocate ciphertexts encrypted under lossy keys for any tag.

Definition 2.9. *Let $\mathcal{R} \subseteq \mathcal{K}_\lambda \times \mathcal{T}_\lambda$ be a binary relation. An equivocable $\mathcal{R}$-lossy PKE scheme is a 7-uple of PPT algorithms* (Par-Gen, Keygen, LKeygen, Encrypt, Decrypt, Opener, LOpener) *such that:*

Parameter generation: *Given a security parameter λ, a tag length $L \in \mathsf{poly}(\lambda)$ and a message length $B \in \mathsf{poly}(\lambda)$,* Par-Gen$(1^\lambda, 1^L, 1^B)$ *outputs public parameters Γ that specify a tag space $\mathcal{T}$, a space of initialization values $\mathcal{K}$, a public key space $\mathcal{PK}$, a secret key space $\mathcal{SK}$ and a trapdoor space $\mathcal{TK}$.*

Key generation: *For an initialization value $K \in \mathcal{K}$ and public parameters Γ, algorithm* Keygen(Γ, K) *outputs an injective public key* pk $\in \mathcal{PK}$, *a decryption key* sk $\in \mathcal{SK}$ *and a trapdoor key* tk $\in \mathcal{TK}$. *The public key specifies a ciphertext space* CtSp *and a randomness space R^{LPKE}.*

Lossy Key generation: *Given an initialization value $K \in \mathcal{K}$ and public parameters Γ, the lossy key generation algorithm* LKeygen(Γ, K) *outputs a lossy public key* pk $\in \mathcal{PK}$, *a lossy secret key* sk $\in \mathcal{SK}$ *and a trapdoor key* tk $\in \mathcal{TK}$.

Decryption on injective tags: *For any $\Gamma \leftarrow$ Par-Gen$(1^\lambda, 1^L, 1^B)$, any $K \in \mathcal{K}$, any tag $t \in \mathcal{T}$ such that $(K,t) \in \mathcal{R}$, and any message* Msg $\in$ MsgSp, *we have* $\Pr\big[\exists r \in R^{\mathsf{LPKE}} : \mathsf{Decrypt}(\mathsf{sk}, t, \mathsf{Encrypt}(\mathsf{pk}, t, \mathsf{Msg}; r)) \neq \mathsf{Msg}\big] < \nu(\lambda)$, *for some negligible function $\nu(\lambda)$, where* (pk, sk, tk) $\leftarrow$ Keygen(Γ, K) *and the probability is taken over the randomness of* Keygen.

Indistinguishability: *For any $\Gamma \leftarrow$ Par-Gen$(1^\lambda, 1^L, 1^B)$, the key generation algorithms* LKeygen *and* Keygen *satisfy the following:*

(i) *For any $K \in \mathcal{K}$, the distributions $D_{\mathsf{inj}} = \{(\mathsf{pk}, \mathsf{tk}) \mid (\mathsf{pk}, \mathsf{sk}, \mathsf{tk}) \leftarrow$ Keygen$(\Gamma, K)\}$ and $D_{\mathsf{loss}} = \{(\mathsf{pk}, \mathsf{tk}) \mid (\mathsf{pk}, \mathsf{sk}, \mathsf{tk}) \leftarrow$ LKeygen$(\Gamma, K)\}$ are computationally indistinguishable. For any PPT adversary $\mathcal{A}$, the following advantage function* $\mathbf{Adv}_{\mathcal{A}}^{\mathsf{indist\text{-}LPKE}}(\lambda)$ *is negligible:*

$$\big|\Pr[(\mathsf{pk}, \mathsf{tk}) \hookleftarrow D_{\mathsf{inj}} : \mathcal{A}(\mathsf{pk}, \mathsf{tk}) = 1] - \Pr[(\mathsf{pk}, \mathsf{tk}) \hookleftarrow D_{\mathsf{loss}} : \mathcal{A}(\mathsf{pk}, \mathsf{tk}) = 1]\big|.$$

(ii) *For any initialization values $K, K' \in \mathcal{K}$, the two distributions $\{$pk $\mid$ (pk, sk, tk) $\leftarrow$ LKeygen$(\Gamma, K)\}$ and $\{$pk $\mid$ (pk, sk, tk) $\leftarrow$ LKeygen$(\Gamma, K')\}$ are $2^{-\Omega(\lambda)}$-close in terms of statistical distance.*

Lossiness: *For any $\Gamma \leftarrow$ Par-Gen$(1^\lambda, 1^L, 1^B)$, any initialization value $K \in \mathcal{K}$ and tag $t \in \mathcal{T}$ such that $(K,t) \notin \mathcal{R}$, any* (pk, sk, tk) $\leftarrow$ Keygen(Γ, K), *and any* Msg$_0$, Msg$_1 \in$ MsgSp, *the following distributions are statistically close:*

$\{C \mid C \leftarrow \mathsf{Encrypt}(\mathsf{pk}, t, \mathsf{Msg}_0)\} \approx_s \{C \mid C \leftarrow \mathsf{Encrypt}(\mathsf{pk}, t, \mathsf{Msg}_1)\}$. *For any* $(\mathsf{pk}, \mathsf{sk}, \mathsf{tk}) \leftarrow \mathsf{LKeygen}(\Gamma, K)$, *the above holds for any tag* t.

Equivocation under lossy tags: *For any* $\Gamma \leftarrow \mathsf{Par\text{-}Gen}(1^\lambda, 1^L, 1^B)$, *any* $K \in \mathcal{K}$, *any keys* $(\mathsf{pk}, \mathsf{sk}, \mathsf{tk}) \leftarrow \mathsf{Keygen}(\Gamma, K)$, *let* D_R *the distribution, defined over* R^{LPKE}, *from which the random coins of* $\mathsf{Encrypt}$ *are sampled. For any message* $\mathsf{Msg} \in \mathsf{MsgSp}$ *and ciphertext* C, *let* $D_{\mathsf{pk}, \mathsf{Msg}, C, t}$ *denote the distribution on* R^{LPKE} *with support* $S_{\mathsf{pk}, \mathsf{Msg}, C, t} = \{\bar{r} \in R^{\mathsf{LPKE}} \mid \mathsf{Encrypt}(\mathsf{pk}, t, \mathsf{Msg}, \bar{r}) = C\}$ *and such that, for each* $\bar{r} \in S_{PK, \mathsf{Msg}, C, t}$, *we have*

$$D_{\mathsf{pk}, \mathsf{Msg}, C, t}(\bar{r}) = \Pr_{r' \hookleftarrow D_R}[r' = \bar{r} \mid \mathsf{Encrypt}(\mathsf{pk}, t, \mathsf{Msg}, r') = C] . \tag{1}$$

For any random coins $r \hookleftarrow D_R$, *any tag* $t \in \mathcal{T}_\lambda$ *such that* $(K, t) \notin \mathcal{R}$, *and any messages* $\mathsf{Msg}_0, \mathsf{Msg}_1 \in \mathsf{MsgSp}$, *algorithm* Opener *takes as inputs* $\mathsf{pk}, C = \mathsf{Encrypt}(\mathsf{pk}, t, \mathsf{Msg}_0, r)$, r t, *and* tk. *It outputs a sample* $\bar{r}$ *from a distribution statistically close to* $D_{\mathsf{pk}, \mathsf{Msg}_1, C, t}$.

Equivocation under lossy keys: *For any* $K \in \mathcal{K}$, *any keys* $(\mathsf{pk}, \mathsf{sk}, \mathsf{tk}) \leftarrow \mathsf{LKeygen}(\Gamma, K)$, *any randomness* $r \hookleftarrow D_R$, *any tag* $t \in \mathcal{T}_\lambda$, *and any messages* $\mathsf{Msg}_0, \mathsf{Msg}_1 \in \mathsf{MsgSp}$, *algorithm* $\mathsf{LOpener}$ *inputs* $C = \mathsf{Encrypt}(\mathsf{pk}, t, \mathsf{Msg}_0, r)$, r, t *and* sk. *It outputs* $\bar{r} \in R^{\mathsf{LPKE}}$ *such that* $C = \mathsf{Encrypt}(\mathsf{pk}, t, \mathsf{Msg}_1, \bar{r})$. *We require that, for any tag* $t \in \mathcal{T}_\lambda$ *such that* $(K, t) \notin \mathcal{R}$, *the distribution* $\{\bar{r} \leftarrow \mathsf{LOpener}(\mathsf{pk}, \mathsf{sk}, t, \mathsf{ct}, \mathsf{Msg}_0, \mathsf{Msg}_1, r) \mid r \hookleftarrow D_R\}$ *is statistically close to* $\{\bar{r} \leftarrow \mathsf{Opener}(\mathsf{pk}, \mathsf{tk}, t, \mathsf{ct}, \mathsf{Msg}_0, \mathsf{Msg}_1, r) \mid r \hookleftarrow D_R\}$.

The above definition is slightly weaker than the one of [55] in the property of equivocation under lossy keys. Here, we do not require that the output of $\mathsf{LOpener}$ be statistically close to $D_{\mathsf{pk}, \mathsf{Msg}_1, C, t}$ as defined in (1): We only require that, on lossy keys and lossy tags, Opener and $\mathsf{LOpener}$ sample random coins from statistically close distributions. Our definition turns out to be sufficient for the purpose of simulation-sound arguments (as shown in the full version [56] of the paper) and will allow us to obtain a construction from the DCR assumption.

Definition 2.9 also differs from [55, Definition 2.10] in that the equivocation algorithms ($\mathsf{Opener}, \mathsf{LOpener}$) can use the original random coins $r \in R^{\mathsf{LPKE}}$ of the encryption algorithm. Again, this relaxation will suffice in our setting.

In our ring signature system, we also use a variant of the above $\mathcal{R}$-lossy encryption primitive to instantiate a tag-based commitment scheme.

Definition 2.10. *A dense $\mathcal{R}$-lossy PKE scheme is a tuple* ($\mathsf{Par\text{-}Gen}, \mathsf{Keygen},$ $\mathsf{LKeygen}, \mathsf{Encrypt}, \mathsf{Decrypt}$) *of efficient algorithms that proceed identically to Definition 2.9, except that the lossy mode is dense and the indistinguishability property is relaxed as below. Moreover, no equivocation property is required.*

Weak Indistinguishability: *For any* $\Gamma \leftarrow \mathsf{Par\text{-}Gen}(1^\lambda, 1^L, 1^B)$, *the key generation algorithms* $\mathsf{LKeygen}$ *and* Keygen *satisfy the following:*

(i) *For any* $K \in \mathcal{K}$, $D_{\mathsf{inj}} = \{\mathsf{pk} \mid (\mathsf{pk}, \mathsf{sk}, \mathsf{tk}) \leftarrow \mathsf{Keygen}(\Gamma, K)\}$ *is indistinguishable from* $D_{\mathsf{loss}} = \{\mathsf{pk} \mid (\mathsf{pk}, \mathsf{sk}, \mathsf{tk}) \leftarrow \mathsf{LKeygen}(\Gamma, K)\}$. *For any PPT adversary* $\mathcal{A}$, *the advantage function* $\mathbf{Adv}_{\mathcal{A}}^{\mathsf{weak\text{-}indist\text{-}LPKE}}(\lambda)$, *defined as the* distance $|\Pr[\mathsf{pk} \hookleftarrow D_{\mathsf{inj}} : \mathcal{A}(\mathsf{pk}) = 1] - \Pr[\mathsf{pk} \hookleftarrow D_{\mathsf{loss}} : \mathcal{A}(\mathsf{pk}) = 1]|$, *is negligible as a function of the security parameter.*

(ii) *For any initialization values $K, K' \in \mathcal{K}$, the two distributions $\{\mathsf{pk} \mid (\mathsf{pk}, \mathsf{sk}, \mathsf{tk}) \leftarrow \mathsf{LKeygen}(\Gamma, K)\}$ and $\{\mathsf{pk} \mid (\mathsf{pk}, \mathsf{sk}, \mathsf{tk}) \leftarrow \mathsf{LKeygen}(\Gamma, K')\}$ are $2^{-\Omega(\lambda)}$-close in terms of statistical distance.*

Density of Lossy Mode: *For any $\Gamma \leftarrow \mathsf{Par\text{-}Gen}(1^\lambda, 1^L, 1^B)$, any initialization value $K \in \mathcal{K}$, any $(\mathsf{pk}, \mathsf{sk}, \mathsf{tk}) \leftarrow \mathsf{LKeygen}(\Gamma, K)$ and $\mathsf{Msg} \in \mathsf{MsgSp}$, the distribution of $\{\mathsf{Encrypt}(\mathsf{pk}, \mathsf{Msg}, r) | r \hookleftarrow D_R\}$ is statistically close to $U(\mathsf{CtSp})$.*

2.6   Ring Signatures

A ring signature [68] scheme consists of the following efficient algorithms:

CRSGen(1^λ): Generates a common reference string ρ.

Keygen(ρ): Generates a public key vk and the corresponding secret key sk.

Sign$(\rho, sk, M, \mathsf{R})$: Outputs a signature Σ on the message $M \in \{0,1\}^*$ with respect to the ring $\mathsf{R} = \{vk_0, \ldots, vk_{R-1}\}$ as long as (vk, sk) is a valid key pair produced by $\mathsf{Keygen}(\rho)$ and $vk \in \mathsf{R}$ (otherwise, it outputs $\perp$).

Verify$(\rho, M, \Sigma, \mathsf{R})$: Given a signature Σ on a message M w.r.t. the ring of public keys R, this algorithm outputs 1 if Σ is deemed valid and 0 otherwise.

Correctness requires that users can always sign any message on behalf of a ring they belong to. The standard security requirements for ring signatures are called *unforgeability* and *anonymity*. We use the strong definitions of [6,22], which are recalled in the full version of the paper. In particular, we consider unforgeability with respect to insider corruption and statistical anonymity.

3 $\mathcal{R}$-Lossy Encryption Schemes from **DCR**

Libert *et al.* [55] gave a method that directly compiles any trapdoor Σ-protocol for a trapdoor language into an unbounded simulation-sound NIZK argument for the *same* language. As a building block, their construction uses an LWE-based equivocable $\mathcal{R}$-lossy PKE scheme for the bit-matching relation.

The construction of [55] is recalled in the full version [56] of the paper, where we show that it applies to trapdoor Σ-protocols with $(r+1)$-special-soundness for $r > 1$ as long as we have a CI hash function for efficiently enumerable relations.

Definition 3.1. *Let $\mathcal{K} = \{0, 1, \perp\}^L$ and $\mathcal{T} = \{0,1\}^L$, for some $L \in \mathsf{poly}(\lambda)$. The **bit-matching relation** $\mathcal{R}_{\mathsf{BM}} : \mathcal{K} \times \mathcal{T} \to \{0,1\}$ is defined as $\mathcal{R}_{\mathsf{BM}}(K, t) = 1$ if and only if $K = K_1 \ldots K_L$ and $t = t_1 \ldots t_L$ satisfy $\bigwedge_{i=1}^{L}(K_i = \perp) \vee (K_i = t_i)$.*

In [55], the authors described an $\mathcal{R}_{\mathsf{BM}}$-lossy PKE under the LWE assumption. In order to instantiate their construction with a better efficiency, we now describe a more efficient $\mathcal{R}_{\mathsf{BM}}$-lossy PKE scheme based on the DCR assumption.

3.1 An Equivocable $\mathcal{R}_{BM}$-Lossy PKE Scheme from DCR

Par-Gen$(1^\lambda, 1^L, 1^B)$: Define the spaces $\mathcal{T} = \{0,1\}^L$, $\mathcal{K} = \{0, 1, \bot\}^L$ and the public parameters as $\Gamma = (1^\lambda, 1^B, \mathcal{K}, \mathcal{T})$.

Keygen(Γ, K): Given public parameters Γ and an initialization value $K \in \mathcal{K}$, generate a key pair as follows.

1. Choose an RSA modulus $N = pq$ such that $p, q > 2^{l(\lambda)}$, for some polynomial $l : \mathbb{N} \to \mathbb{N}$ such that $l(\lambda) > L(\lambda)$ for any sufficiently large λ, and an integer $\zeta \in \mathrm{poly}(\lambda)$ such that $N^\zeta > 2^B$.
2. Choose $g \hookleftarrow U(\mathbb{Z}^*_{N^{\zeta+1}})$ and $\alpha_{i,0}, \alpha_{i,1} \hookleftarrow U(\mathbb{Z}^*_N)$ for each $i \in [L]$. Then, for each $i \in [L]$ and $b \in \{0,1\}$, compute $v_{i,b} = g^{\delta_{b,1-K_i}} \cdot \alpha_{i,b}^{N^\zeta} \bmod N^{\zeta+1}$ if $K_i \neq \bot$ and $v_{i,b} = \alpha_{i,b}^{N^\zeta} \bmod N^{\zeta+1}$ if $K_i = \bot$.

Define $R^{\mathsf{LPKE}} = \mathbb{Z}^*_N \times \mathbb{Z}_{N^\zeta}$ and output $\mathsf{sk} = (p, q, K)$ as well as

$$\mathsf{pk} := \Big(N, \zeta, g, \{v_{i,b}\}_{i\in[L], b\in\{0,1\}} \Big), \qquad \mathsf{tk} = \Big(\{\alpha_{i,b}\}_{i\in[L], b\in\{0,1\}}, K \Big).$$

LKeygen(Γ, K): is identical to Keygen except that step 2 generates g by choosing $g_0 \hookleftarrow U(\mathbb{Z}^*_N)$ and computing $g = g_0^{N^\zeta} \bmod N^{\zeta+1}$. The algorithm defines $R^{\mathsf{LPKE}} = \mathbb{Z}^*_N \times \mathbb{Z}_{N^\zeta}$ and outputs the lossy secret key $\mathsf{sk} = (g_0, \mathsf{tk})$ together with $\mathsf{pk} := \Big(N, \zeta, g, \{v_{i,b}\}_{i\in[L], b\in\{0,1\}} \Big)$, $\mathsf{tk} = \Big(\{\alpha_{i,b}\}_{i\in[L], b\in\{0,1\}}, K \Big)$.

Encrypt$(\mathsf{pk}, t, \mathsf{Msg})$: To encrypt $\mathsf{Msg} \in \mathbb{Z}_{N^\zeta}$ for the tag $t = t_1 \ldots t_L \in \{0,1\}^L$, choose $r \hookleftarrow U(\mathbb{Z}^*_N)$, $s \hookleftarrow U(\mathbb{Z}_{N^\zeta})$ and compute

$$\mathsf{ct} = g^{\mathsf{Msg}} \cdot \Big(\prod_{i=1}^{L} v_{i,t_i} \Big)^s \cdot r^{N^\zeta} \bmod N^{\zeta+1} . \tag{2}$$

Decrypt$(\mathsf{sk}, t, \mathsf{ct})$: Given $\mathsf{sk} = (p, q, K)$ and $t = t_1 \ldots t_L \in \{0,1\}^L$, return $\bot$ if $R_{BM}(K, t) = 0$. Otherwise, $\prod_{i=1}^{L} v_{i,t_i} \equiv \Big(\prod_{i=1}^{L} \alpha_{i,t_i} \Big)^{N^\zeta} \pmod{N^{\zeta+1}}$.

1. Compute $\beta_g = \frac{(g^{\lambda(N)} \bmod N^{\zeta+1})-1}{N}$, where $\lambda(N) = \mathrm{lcm}(p-1, q-1)$ and return $\bot$ if $\beta_g = 0$ or $\gcd(\beta_g, N^\zeta) > 1$.
2. Otherwise, compute $\mathsf{Msg} = \frac{(\mathsf{ct}^{\lambda(N)} \bmod N^{\zeta+1})-1}{N} \cdot \beta_g^{-1} \bmod N^\zeta$, where the division is computed over $\mathbb{Z}$, and output $\mathsf{Msg} \in \mathbb{Z}_{N^\zeta}$.

Opener$\big(\mathsf{pk}, \mathsf{tk}, t, \mathsf{ct}, \mathsf{Msg}_0, \mathsf{Msg}_1, (r, s)\big)$: Given $\mathsf{tk} = (\{\alpha_{i,b}\}_{i,b}, K)$, $t \in \{0,1\}^L$, plaintexts $\mathsf{Msg}_0, \mathsf{Msg}_1 \in \mathbb{Z}_{N^s}$ and random coins $(r, s) \in R^{\mathsf{LPKE}}$ such that $\mathsf{ct} = \mathsf{Encrypt}(\mathsf{pk}, t, \mathsf{Msg}_0; (r, s))$, return $\bot$ if $R_{BM}(K, t) = 1$. Otherwise, define

$$v_t \triangleq \prod_{i=1}^{L} v_{i,t_i} \bmod N^{\zeta+1} = g^{d_t} \cdot \Big(\prod_{i=1}^{L} \alpha_{i,t_i} \Big)^{N^\zeta} \bmod N^{\zeta+1}, \tag{3}$$

where $d_t \in \{1, \dots, L\}$ is the number of non-$\bot$ entries of K such that $K_i \neq t_i$. Note that $\gcd(d_t, N^\varsigma) = 1$ since $p, q > L$. Then, compute and output

$$\bar{s} = s + (d_t^{-1} \bmod N^\varsigma) \cdot (\mathsf{Msg}_0 - \mathsf{Msg}_1) \quad \bmod N^\varsigma \qquad (4)$$

$$\bar{r} = r \cdot \prod_{i=1}^{L} \alpha_{i,t_i}^{s-\bar{s}} \cdot g^{(\mathsf{Msg}_0 - \mathsf{Msg}_1 + d_t \cdot (s-\bar{s}))/N^\varsigma} \quad \bmod N,$$

where the division in the exponent above g can be computed over $\mathbb{Z}$ since we have $\mathsf{Msg}_0 + d_t \cdot s \equiv \mathsf{Msg}_1 + d_t \cdot \bar{s} \pmod{N^\varsigma}$. Note that $(\bar{r}, \bar{s})$ satisfy

$$g^{\mathsf{Msg}_1} \cdot v_t^{\bar{s}} \cdot \bar{r}^{N^\varsigma} \equiv g^{\mathsf{Msg}_1} \cdot \left(g^{d_t} \cdot \prod_{i=1}^{L} \alpha_{i,t_i}^{N^\varsigma} \right)^{\bar{s}} \cdot \bar{r}^{N^\varsigma}.$$

$$\equiv g^{\mathsf{Msg}_1} \cdot \left(g^{d_t} \cdot \prod_{i=1}^{L} \alpha_{i,t_i}^{N^\varsigma} \right)^{\bar{s}} \cdot r^{N^\varsigma} \cdot \prod_{i=1}^{L} \alpha_{i,t_i}^{(s-\bar{s}) \cdot N^\varsigma} \cdot g^{(\mathsf{Msg}_0 - \mathsf{Msg}_1 + d_t \cdot (s-\bar{s}))}$$

$$\equiv g^{\mathsf{Msg}_0} \cdot \left(g^{d_t} \cdot \prod_{i=1}^{L} \alpha_{i,t_i}^{N^\varsigma} \right)^{s} \cdot r^{N^\varsigma} \equiv g^{\mathsf{Msg}_0} \cdot v_t^{s} \cdot r^{N^\varsigma} \pmod{N^{\varsigma+1}}$$

$\mathsf{LOpener}(\mathsf{pk}, \mathsf{sk}, t, \mathsf{ct}, \mathsf{Msg}_0, \mathsf{Msg}_1, (r, s))$: Given $\mathsf{sk} = \big(g_0, \mathsf{tk} = (\{\alpha_{i,b}\}_{i,b}, K) \big)$, an arbitrary tag $t \in \{0, 1\}^L$, plaintexts $\mathsf{Msg}_0, \mathsf{Msg}_1 \in \mathbb{Z}_{N^\varsigma}$ and randomness $(r, s) \in R^{\mathsf{LPKE}}$ such that $\mathsf{ct} = \mathsf{Encrypt}(\mathsf{pk}, t, \mathsf{Msg}_0; (r, s))$, let $d_t \in \{0, \dots, L\}$ the number of non-$\bot$ entries such that $K_i \neq t_i$. If $d_t \neq 0$, compute $\bar{s}$ as per (4). Otherwise, choose $\bar{s} \hookleftarrow U(\mathbb{Z}_{N^\varsigma})$. In both cases, output the pair $(\bar{r}, \bar{s})$, where $\bar{r} = r \cdot \prod_{i=1}^{L} \alpha_{i,t_i}^{s-\bar{s}} \cdot g_0^{\mathsf{Msg}_0 - \mathsf{Msg}_1 + d_t \cdot (s-\bar{s})} \bmod N$.

Theorem 3.2. *The above scheme is an equivocable $\mathcal{R}_{\mathsf{BM}}$-lossy PKE scheme under the DCR assumption.* (The proof is given in the full version of the paper.)

By plugging the above system in the construction described in the full version of the paper, we obtain USS arguments from the DCR and LWE assumptions. A difference with [55] is that LWE is only used in the correlation intractable hash function and lattice trapdoors are not needed anywhere. This DCR-based scheme drastically reduces the signature length of our construction. If we were to use the LWE-based $\mathcal{R}$-Lossy PKE scheme from [55], a single ciphertext would already be roughly 20 larger than an entire ring signature, as discussed in the full version of the paper.

3.2 A Dense $\mathcal{R}_{\mathsf{BM}}$-Lossy PKE Scheme from DCR

In order to construct a ring signature without relying on erasures, we will also use a "downgraded" version of the scheme in Sect. 3.1, where we do not need equivocation properties. However, we will rely on the property that its lossy mode induces dense commitments that are uniformly distributed in $\mathbb{Z}^*_{N^{\varsigma+1}}$. The scheme of Sect. 3.1 does not have this density property as its lossy mode induces commitments that live in the subgroup of N^ς-th residues.

Par-Gen$(1^\lambda, 1^L, 1^B)$: Define the spaces $\mathcal{T} = \{0,1\}^L$, $\mathcal{K} = \{0,1,\perp\}^L$ and the public parameters as $\Gamma = (1^\lambda, 1^B, \mathcal{K}, \mathcal{T})$.

Keygen(Γ, K): Given public parameters Γ and an initialization value $K \in \mathcal{K}$, generate a key pair as follows.

1. Choose an RSA modulus $N = pq$ such that $p, q > 2^{l(\lambda)}$, for some polynomial $l : \mathbb{N} \to \mathbb{N}$ such that $l(\lambda) > L(\lambda) - \lambda$ for any sufficiently large λ, and an integer $\zeta \in \mathsf{poly}(\lambda)$ such that $N^\zeta > 2^B$.
2. Choose $\alpha_{i,0}, \alpha_{i,1} \hookleftarrow U(\mathbb{Z}_N^*)$ for each $i \in [L]$. Then, for each $i \in [L]$ and $b \in \{0,1\}$, compute $v_{i,b} = (1+N)^{\delta_{b,1-K_i}} \cdot \alpha_{i,b}^{N^\zeta} \bmod N^{\zeta+1}$ if $K_i \neq \perp$ and $v_{i,b} = \alpha_{i,b}^{N^\zeta} \bmod N^{\zeta+1}$ if $K_i = \perp$.

Define $R^{\mathsf{LPKE}} = \mathbb{Z}_N^* \times \mathbb{Z}_{N^\zeta}$ and output the secret key $\mathsf{sk} = (p, q, K)$ together with $\mathsf{pk} := \left(N, \zeta, \{v_{i,b}\}_{i \in [L], b \in \{0,1\}}\right)$ and $\mathsf{tk} = \perp$.

LKeygen(Γ, K): proceeds identically to Keygen with the difference that step 2 chooses $\{v_{i,b}\}_{i,b}$ at random. For each $i \in [L]$, $b \in \{0,1\}$, the algorithm chooses $v_{i,b} \hookleftarrow U(\mathbb{Z}_{N^{\zeta+1}}^*)$. It defines $R^{\mathsf{LPKE}} = \mathbb{Z}_N^* \times \mathbb{Z}_{N^\zeta}$ and outputs $\mathsf{sk} = \perp$ as well as $\mathsf{pk} := \left(N, \zeta, \{v_{i,b}\}_{i \in [L], b \in \{0,1\}}\right)$, and $\mathsf{tk} = \perp$.

Encrypt$(\mathsf{pk}, t, \mathsf{Msg})$: To encrypt $\mathsf{Msg} \in \mathbb{Z}_{N^\zeta}$ for the tag $t = t_1 \ldots t_L \in \{0,1\}^L$, choose random coins $r \hookleftarrow U(\mathbb{Z}_N^*)$, $s \hookleftarrow U(\mathbb{Z}_{N^\zeta})$ and compute the ciphertext $\mathsf{ct} = (1+N)^{\mathsf{Msg}} \cdot \left(\prod_{i=1}^L v_{i,t_i}\right)^s \cdot r^{N^\zeta} \bmod N^{\zeta+1}$.

Decrypt$(\mathsf{sk}, t, \mathsf{ct})$: Given the secret key $\mathsf{sk} = (p, q, K)$ and the tag $t \in \{0,1\}^L$, return $\perp$ if $R_{\mathsf{BM}}(K, t) = 0$. Otherwise, compute $\mathsf{Msg} = \frac{(\mathsf{ct}^{\lambda(N)} \bmod N^{\zeta+1}) - 1}{N} \bmod N^\zeta$, where the division is computed over $\mathbb{Z}$, and output $\mathsf{Msg} \in \mathbb{Z}_{N^\zeta}$.

Theorem 3.3. *The above system is a dense $\mathcal{R}_{\mathsf{BM}}$-lossy PKE scheme under the DCR assumption. Moreover, the lossy mode is dense in $\mathbb{Z}_{N^{\zeta+1}}^*$.* (The proof is given in the full version of the paper.)

4 Trapdoor Σ-Protocols for DCR-Related Languages

Ciampi *et al.* [27] showed that any Σ-protocol with binary challenges can be turned into a trapdoor Σ-protocol by having the prover encrypt the two possible responses and send them along with its first message. While elegant, this approach requires $\Theta(\lambda)$ repetitions to achieve negligible soundness error. In this section, we give communication-efficient protocols requiring no repetitions.

In the full version of the paper, we show that the standard Σ-protocol that allows proving composite residuosity readily extends into a trapdoor Σ-protocol. By exploiting earlier observations from [46,58], we show that, for a single protocol iteration, the factorization of N allows computing bad challenges within an exponentially large challenge space. In this section, we describe trapdoor Σ-protocols that will serve as building blocks for our ring signature.

4.1 Trapdoor Σ-Protocol Showing that a Paillier Ciphertext/Commitment Contains 0 or 1

We give a trapdoor Σ-protocol allowing to prove that a (lossy) Paillier ciphertext encrypts 0 or 1. This protocol is a DCR-based adaptation of a Σ-protocol proposed in [21,46] for Elgamal-like encryption schemes. The original protocol of [21,46] assumes additively homomorphic properties in the plaintext and randomness spaces. Here, we adapt it to the DCR setting where the randomness space is a multiplicative group. We also describe a BadChallenge function to obtain a trapdoor Σ-protocol with a large challenge space.

The BadChallenge function uses observation from Lipmaa [58] showing that bad challenges are also computable when the message space has composite order $N = pq$ (instead of prime order as in [21]). We actually point out an issue in [58]. Lipmaa aims to identify bad challenges in a Σ-protocol showing that an Elgamal-Paillier ciphertext [13] encrypts 0 or 1. However, in the Elgamal-Paillier scheme, not all elements of $\mathbb{Z}_{N^2}^* \times \mathbb{Z}_{N^2}^*$ are in the range of the encryption algorithm. In the full version of the paper, we show that a cheating prover can send maliciously generated first prover messages for which bad challenges are not efficiently computable although they may exist for false statements.

Here, to avoid this issue, we need a DCR-based dual-mode commitment where the binding mode has the property that any element of $\mathbb{Z}_{N^2}^*$ is in the range of the commitment algorithm. Moreover, even the hiding mode should be dense, meaning that honestly generated commitments to 0 should be uniformly distributed over $\mathbb{Z}_{N^2}^*$. We thus use commitments of the form $C = (1+N)^{\mathsf{Msg}} \cdot h^y \cdot w^N \bmod N^2$, where the distribution of h determines if the commitment is perfectly hiding or perfectly binding. If h is an N-th residue (resp. $h \sim U(\mathbb{Z}_{N^2}^*)$), it is perfectly binding (resp. perfectly hiding). Moreover, the density property of the hiding mode will be crucial to prove the special ZK property of the Σ-protocol.

Let an RSA modulus $N = pq$ and let a random element $h \in \mathbb{Z}_{N^2}^*$. We give a trapdoor Σ-protocol for the following language, which is parametrized by h:

$$\mathcal{L}^{0\text{-}1}(h) = \{ C \in \mathbb{Z}_{N^2}^* \mid \exists b \in \{0,1\} (y,w) \in \mathbb{Z}_N \times \mathbb{Z}_N^* :$$
$$C = (1+N)^b \cdot h^y \cdot w^N \bmod N^2 \}.$$

We include h as a language parameter because we allow the CRS to depend on N, but not on h. We note that, if N divides the order of h, the language $\mathcal{L}^{0\text{-}1}(h)$ is trivial since all elements of $\mathbb{Z}_{N^2}^*$ can be explained as a commitment to a bit. However, the language becomes non-trivial when h is an N-th residue since $C = (1+N)^b h^y w^N \bmod N^2$ is then a perfectly binding commitment to b.

While a trapdoor Σ-protocol for $\mathcal{L}^{0\text{-}1}(h)$ can be obtained from [31], the one below is useful to show that one out of many ciphertexts encrypts 0 [46]. A difference with the Σ-protocols in [21, Figure 2] and [58, Section 3.2] is that, in order to use it in Sect. 4.2, we need the verifier to perform a non-standard interval check for the response over the integers.

$\mathsf{Gen_{par}}(1^\lambda)$: Given the security parameter λ, define $\mathsf{par} = \{\lambda\}$.

Gen$_\mathcal{L}$(par, $\mathcal{L}^{0\text{-}1}$) : Given public parameters par and the description of a language $\mathcal{L}^{0\text{-}1}$, consisting of an RSA modulus $N = pq$ with p and q prime satisfying $p, q > 2^{l(\lambda)}$, for some polynomial $l : \mathbb{N} \to \mathbb{N}$ such that $l(\lambda) > 2\lambda$, define the language-dependent crs$_\mathcal{L} = \{N\}$. The global CRS is crs $= (\{\lambda\}, \text{crs}_\mathcal{L})$.

TrapGen(par, $\mathcal{L}^{0\text{-}1}$, $\tau_\mathcal{L}$) : Given par, a language description $\mathcal{L}^{0\text{-}1}$ that specifies an RSA modulus $N = pq$, and the membership-testing trapdoor $\tau_\mathcal{L} = (p, q)$, output crs $= (\{\lambda\}, \text{crs}_\mathcal{L})$ as in Gen$_\mathcal{L}$ and the trapdoor $\tau_\Sigma = (p, q)$.

P(crs, $\vec{x}, \vec{w}$) $\leftrightarrow$ **V**(crs, $\vec{x}$) : Given crs, a statement $\vec{x} = $ "$C \in \mathcal{L}^{0\text{-}1}(h)$", for some $h \in \mathbb{Z}_{N^2}^*$, P (who has $\vec{w} = (b, y, w)$) and V interact as follows:

1. P chooses $a \leftarrow U(\{2^\lambda, \ldots, 2^{2\lambda} - 1\})$, $d, e \leftarrow U(\mathbb{Z}_N)$, $u, v \leftarrow U(\mathbb{Z}_N^*)$ and sends V the following:

$$A_1 = (1 + N)^a\, h^d\, u^N \bmod N^2, \qquad A_2 = (1 + N)^{-a \cdot b}\, h^e\, v^N \bmod N^2.$$

2. V sends a random challenge Chall $\leftarrow U(\{0, \ldots 2^\lambda - 1\})$.
3. P sends V the response $(z, z_d, z_e, z_u, z_v) \in \mathbb{Z} \times (\mathbb{Z}_N)^2 \times (\mathbb{Z}_N^*)^2$, where

$$
\begin{aligned}
z &= a + \text{Chall} \cdot b, & z_1 &= d + \text{Chall} \cdot y, & z_2 &= e + (z - \text{Chall}) \cdot y, \\
z_d &= z_1 \bmod N, & z_u &= u \cdot w^{\text{Chall}} \cdot h^{\lfloor z_1/N \rfloor} \bmod N, \\
z_e &= z_2 \bmod N, & z_v &= v \cdot w^{z - \text{Chall}} \cdot h^{\lfloor z_2/N \rfloor} \bmod N.
\end{aligned}
$$

4. V returns 1 if and only if $2^\lambda \le z < 2^{2\lambda+1}$ and

$$
\begin{aligned}
A_1 &= C^{-\text{Chall}} \cdot (1 + N)^z \cdot h^{z_d} \cdot z_u^N \bmod N^2, & (5)\\
A_2 &= C^{\text{Chall}-z} \cdot h^{z_e} \cdot z_v^N \bmod N^2.
\end{aligned}
$$

BadChallenge(par, τ_Σ, crs, $\vec{x}, \vec{a}$) : Given a statement $\vec{x} = $ "$C \in \mathcal{L}^{0\text{-}1}(h)$", a trapdoor $\tau_\Sigma = (p, q)$ and $\vec{a} = (A_1, A_2) \in (\mathbb{Z}_{N^2}^*)^2$, return $\perp$ if h is not an N-th residue. Otherwise, decrypt C and (A_1, A_2) to obtain $b = \mathcal{D}_{\tau_\Sigma}(C) \in \mathbb{Z}_N$ and $a_i = \mathcal{D}_{\tau_\Sigma}(A_i) \in \mathbb{Z}_N$ for each $i \in \{1, 2\}$. If $\vec{x}$ is false, we have $b \notin \{0, 1\}$. Consider the following linear system with the unknowns (Chall, z) $\in \mathbb{Z}_N^2$:

$$
\begin{aligned}
z - b \cdot \text{Chall} &\equiv a_1 \pmod{N}, \\
b \cdot (\text{Chall} - z) &\equiv a_2 \pmod{N}.
\end{aligned}
\quad (6)
$$

1. If $b(b - 1) \equiv 0 \pmod{N}$, assume that $b \equiv 0 \pmod{p}$ and $b \equiv 1 \pmod{q}$. Compute $z' = a_1 \bmod p$ and Chall$' = z' - a_1 \bmod q$. Then, return $\perp$ if Chall$' - z' \not\equiv a_2 \pmod{q}$ or $a_2 \not\equiv 0 \pmod{p}$.
2. If $b(b - 1) \not\equiv 0 \pmod{N}$, define $d_b = \gcd(b(b - 1), N)$, so that we have $\gcd(b(b - 1), N/d_b) = 1$. Any solution of (6) also satisfies the system

$$
\begin{aligned}
z - b \cdot \text{Chall} &\equiv a_1 \pmod{N/d_b} \\
b \cdot z - b \cdot \text{Chall} &\equiv -a_2 \pmod{N/d_b},
\end{aligned}
$$

which has a unique solution (Chall$', z'$) $\in (\mathbb{Z}_{N/d_b})^2$.

In both cases, if $2^\lambda \leq z' < 2^{2\lambda+1}$ and $0 \leq \mathsf{Chall}' < 2^\lambda$, return $\mathsf{Chall} = \mathsf{Chall}'$. Otherwise, return $\perp$.

Any honest protocol execution always returns a valid transcript since we have $2^\lambda \leq a + b \cdot \mathsf{Chall} \leq 2^{2\lambda} + 2^\lambda - 2 < 2^{2\lambda+1}$ and

$$
\begin{aligned}
(1+N)^z \cdot h^{z_d} \cdot z_u^N \\
&\equiv (1+N)^{a+\mathsf{Chall}\cdot b} \cdot u^N \cdot w^{N\cdot\mathsf{Chall}} \cdot h^{z_d} \cdot h^{(d+\mathsf{Chall}\cdot y)-(d+\mathsf{Chall}\cdot y \bmod N)} \\
&\equiv (1+N)^{a+\mathsf{Chall}\cdot b} \cdot u^N \cdot w^{N\cdot\mathsf{Chall}} \cdot h^{d+\mathsf{Chall}\cdot y} \\
&\equiv (1+N)^a \cdot u^N \cdot h^d \cdot \left((1+N)^b \cdot w^N \cdot h^y\right)^{\mathsf{Chall}} \equiv A_1 \cdot C^{\mathsf{Chall}} \pmod{N^2}
\end{aligned}
$$

$$
\begin{aligned}
C^{\mathsf{Chall}-z} \cdot h^{z_e} \cdot z_v^N &\equiv \left((1+N)^b \cdot w^N \cdot h^y\right)^{\mathsf{Chall}-z} \cdot v^N \cdot w^{(z-\mathsf{Chall})N} \cdot h^{e+(z-\mathsf{Chall})\cdot y} \\
&\equiv (1+N)^{b(\mathsf{Chall}-z)} \cdot v^N \cdot h^e \equiv (1+N)^{b(-a+(1-b)\cdot\mathsf{Chall})} \cdot v^N \cdot h^e \\
&\equiv (1+N)^{-ab} \cdot v^N \cdot h^e \equiv A_2 \pmod{N^2}
\end{aligned}
$$

The correctness of $\mathsf{BadChallenge}$ follows from the fact that $0 \leq \mathsf{Chall} < 2^\lambda$ (so that $\mathsf{Chall} = \mathsf{Chall} \bmod p = \mathsf{Chall} \bmod q$) and the observation that the verifier never accepts when $z \geq \min(p, q)$. This ensures that a valid response exists for at most one $z \in \mathbb{Z}$ such that $z = z \bmod p = z \bmod q$.

Remark 4.1. When h is a composite residue, the condition $b \in \{0, 1\}$ implies that, over $\mathbb{Z}$, we have either $z = a + b \cdot \mathsf{Chall}$ or $z = a + b \cdot \mathsf{Chall} - N$, where $a = \mathcal{D}_{\tau_\Sigma}(A_1)$ and $b = \mathcal{D}_{\tau_\Sigma}(C)$ (recall that (5) implies $z = a + b \cdot \mathsf{Chall} \bmod N$). The latter case can only occur if $b = 1$ and $N - 2^\lambda \leq a \leq N - 1$. However, this would imply $\mathsf{Chall} - 2^\lambda \leq a + \mathsf{Chall} - N \leq \mathsf{Chall} - 1$, which is not compatible with the lower bound of the verification test $2^\lambda \leq z < 2^{2\lambda+1}$. As a result, the equation $z = a + b \cdot \mathsf{Chall}$ holds over $\mathbb{Z}$, and not only modulo N. While this property is not necessary to ensure the soundness of the above Σ-protocol, it will be crucial for the $\mathsf{BadChallenge}$ function of the trapdoor Σ-protocol in Sect. 4.2.[2] In order to ensure perfect completeness, the prover chooses a in a somewhat unusual interval that does not start with 0. However, we still have statistical completeness and statistical HVZK if a is sampled from $U(\{0, \ldots, 2^{2\lambda} - 1\})$.

4.2 Trapdoor Σ-Protocol Showing that One Out of Many Ciphertexts/Commitments Contains 0

We now present a DCR-based variant of the Σ-protocol of Groth and Kohlweiss [46], which allows proving that one commitment out of $R = 2^r$ contains 0.

INTUITION. The Σ-protocol of [46] relies on a protocol, like the one of Sect. 4.1, showing that a committed b is a bit using a response of the form $z = a + b \cdot \mathsf{Chall}$. To prove that some commitment $C_\ell \in \{C_i\}_{i=0}^{R-1}$ opens to 0 without revealing

---

[2] In contrast, the upper bound for z is crucial here in the first step of $\mathsf{BadChallenge}$.

the index $\ell \in \{0, \ldots, R-1\}$, the bits $\ell_1 \ldots \ell_r \in \{0,1\}^r$ of ℓ are committed and, for each of them, the prover provides evidence that $\ell_j \in \{0,1\}$. The response $z_j = a_j + \ell_j$Chall is seen as a degree-1 polynomial in Chall and used to define polynomials $f_{j,1}[X] = a_j + \ell_j X$ and $f_{f,0}[X] = X - f_j$, which in turn define

$$P_i[X] = \prod_{j=1}^{r} f_{j,i_j}[X] = \delta_{i,\ell} \cdot X^r + \sum_{k=0}^{r-1} p_{i,k} \cdot X^k \qquad \forall i \in \{0, \ldots, R-1\},$$

where $P_i[X]$ has degree r if $i = \ell$ and degree $\leq r-1$ otherwise. In order to prove that one of the $\{P_i[X]\}_{i=0}^{R-1}$ has degree r, Groth and Kohlweiss homomorphically compute $\prod_{i=0}^{R-1} C_i^{P_i(\text{Chall})}$ and multiply it with $\prod_{k=0}^{r-1} C_{d_k}^{-\text{Chall}^k}$, for auxiliary commitments $\{C_{d_k} = \prod_{i=0}^{R-1} C_i^{p_{i,k}}\}_{k=0}^{r-1}$, in order to cancel out the terms of degree 0 to $r-1$ in the exponent. Then, they prove that the product $\prod_{i=0}^{R-1} C_i^{P_i(\text{Chall})} \cdot \prod_{k=0}^{r-1} C_{d_k}^{-\text{Chall}^k}$ is indeed a commitment to 0.

Let $N = pq$ and $\bar{N} = \bar{p}\bar{q}$ denote two RSA moduli. Let also $h \in \mathbb{Z}_{N^2}^*$ and $\bar{h} \in \mathbb{Z}_{\bar{N}^2}^*$. We give a trapdoor Σ-protocol for the language

$$\mathcal{L}_V^{1-R}(h, \bar{h}) := \{((C_0, \ldots, C_{R-1})(L_1, \ldots, L_r)) \in (\mathbb{Z}_{N^2}^*)^R \times (\mathbb{Z}_{\bar{N}^2}^*)^r \mid \qquad (7)$$
$$\exists y \in \mathbb{Z}_N, \ w \in \mathbb{Z}_N^*, \ \exists_{j=1}^r (\ell_j, s_j, t_j) \in \{0,1\} \times \mathbb{Z}_{\bar{N}} \times \mathbb{Z}_{\bar{N}}^* :$$
$$\bigwedge_{j=1}^r L_j = (1 + \bar{N})^{\ell_j} \bar{h}^{s_j} t_j^{\bar{N}} \bmod \bar{N}^2 \ \wedge \ C_\ell = h^y w^N \bmod N^2\}$$

where $R = 2^r$ and $\ell = \sum_{j=1}^r \ell_j \cdot 2^{j-1}$. In (7), $h \in \mathbb{Z}_{N^2}^*$ and $\bar{h} \in \mathbb{Z}_{\bar{N}^2}^*$ are used as language parameters since we allow the CRS to depend on N and $\bar{N}$, but not on h nor $\bar{h}$. The reason is that, in our construction of Sect. 5, we need to generate the CRS before $\bar{h}$ is chosen.

We note that $\mathcal{L}_V^{1-R}(h, \bar{h})$ is a trivial language (i.e., it is $(\mathbb{Z}_{N^2}^*)^R \times (\mathbb{Z}_{\bar{N}^2}^*)^r$) when N and $\bar{N}$ divide the order of h and $\bar{h}$, respectively. However, the security proof of our ring signature will switch to a setting where h and $\bar{h}$ are composite residues, which turns $C_\ell = h^y \cdot w^N \bmod N^2$ into a perfectly binding commitment to 0 (since $C = (1+N)^{\text{Msg}} \cdot h^y \cdot w^N \bmod N^2$ uniquely determines the underlying $\text{Msg} \in \mathbb{Z}_N$) and L_j into a perfectly binding commitment to ℓ_j.

DESCRIPTION. Our Paillier-based adaptation $\Pi_V^{1-R} = (\text{Gen}_{\text{par}}, \text{Gen}_{\mathcal{L}}, \text{P}, \text{V})$ of the Σ-protocol of [46] is described as follows.

$\text{Gen}_{\text{par}}(1^\lambda)$: Given the security parameter λ, define $\text{par} = \{\lambda\}$.

$\text{Gen}_{\mathcal{L}}(\text{par}, \mathcal{L}_V^{1-R})$: Given par and the description of a language $\mathcal{L}_V^{1-R}$, consisting of RSA moduli $N = pq$, $\bar{N} = \bar{p}\bar{q}$ with primes $p, q, \bar{p}, \bar{q}$ satisfying $p, q, \bar{p}, \bar{q} > 2^{l(\lambda)}$, where $l : \mathbb{N} \to \mathbb{N}$ is a polynomial such that $l(\lambda) > 2\lambda$, define the language-dependent $\text{crs}_{\mathcal{L}} = \{N, \bar{N}\}$ and the global CRS $\text{crs} = (\{\lambda\}, \text{crs}_{\mathcal{L}})$.

$\text{TrapGen}(\text{par}, \mathcal{L}_V^{1-R}, \tau_{\mathcal{L}})$: Given par, the description of a language $\mathcal{L}_V^{1-R}$ and a language trapdoor $\tau_{\mathcal{L}}$, it proceeds identically to $\text{Gen}_{\mathcal{L}}$ except that it also outputs the trapdoor $\tau_{\Sigma} = (p, q, \bar{p}, \bar{q})$.

$\mathsf{P}(\mathsf{crs}, \vec{x}, \vec{w}) \leftrightarrow \mathsf{V}(\mathsf{crs}, x)$: P has the witness $\vec{w} = (y, w, \{(\ell_j, s_j, t_j)\}_{j=1}^r)$ to the statement $\vec{x} = ``((C_0, \ldots, C_{R-1}), (L_1, \ldots, L_r)) \in \mathcal{L}_V^{1\text{-}R}(h, \bar{h})"$ and interacts with the verifier V in the following way:

1. For each $j \in [r]$, P chooses $\bar{a}_j \leftarrow U(\{2^\lambda, \ldots, 2^{2\lambda} - 1\})$, $\bar{d}_j, \bar{e}_j, \leftarrow U(\mathbb{Z}_{\bar{N}})$, $\bar{u}_j, \bar{v}_j \leftarrow U(\mathbb{Z}_{\bar{N}}^*)$ and computes

$$\begin{cases} \bar{A}_j = (1 + \bar{N})^{\bar{a}_j} \cdot \bar{h}^{\bar{d}_j} \cdot \bar{u}_j^N \bmod \bar{N}^2, \\ \bar{B}_j = (1 + \bar{N})^{-\bar{a}_j \cdot \ell_j} \cdot \bar{h}^{\bar{e}_j} \cdot \bar{v}_j^N \bmod \bar{N}^2. \end{cases} \tag{8}$$

It then defines degree-1 polynomials $F_{j,1}[X] = \bar{a}_j + \ell_j X \in \mathbb{Z}_N[X]$, $F_{j,0}[X] = X - F_{j,1}[X] \in \mathbb{Z}_N[X]$. For each index $i \in \{0, \ldots, R-1\}$ of binary expansion $i_1 \ldots i_r \in \{0, 1\}^r$, it computes the polynomial

$$P_i[X] = \prod_{j=1}^r F_{j,i_j}[X] = \delta_{i,\ell} \cdot X^r + \sum_{k=0}^{r-1} p_{i,k} \cdot X^k \in \mathbb{Z}_N[X], \tag{9}$$

which has degree $\leq r - 1$ if $i \neq \ell$ and degree r if $i = \ell$. Then, using the coefficients $p_{i,0}, \ldots, p_{i,r-1} \in \mathbb{Z}_N$ of (9), P computes commitments

$$C_{d_k} = \prod_{i=0}^{R-1} C_i^{p_{i,k}} \cdot h^{\mu_k} \cdot \rho_k^N \bmod N^2 \qquad 0 \leq k \leq r - 1, \tag{10}$$

where $\mu_0, \ldots, \mu_{r-1} \leftarrow U(\mathbb{Z}_N)$, $\rho_0, \ldots, \rho_{r-1} \leftarrow U(\mathbb{Z}_N^*)$. Finally, P sends V the message $\vec{a} = \left(\{(\bar{A}_j, \bar{B}_j)\}_{j=1}^r, \{C_{d_k}\}_{k=0}^{r-1}\right)$.

2. V sends a random challenge $\mathsf{Chall} \leftarrow U(\{0, \ldots, 2^\lambda - 1\})$.
3. P sends the response $(z_y, z_w, \{(\bar{z}_j, \bar{z}_{d,j}, \bar{z}_{e,j}, \bar{z}_{u,j}, \bar{z}_{v,j})\}_{j=1}^r)$, where

$$\begin{cases} \bar{z}_{d,j} = \bar{d}_j + \mathsf{Chall} \cdot s_j \bmod \bar{N} \qquad \bar{z}_j = \bar{a}_j + \mathsf{Chall} \cdot \ell_j \\ \bar{z}_{e,j} = \bar{e}_j + (\bar{a}_j + \mathsf{Chall} \cdot (\ell_j - 1)) \cdot s_j \bmod \bar{N} \\ \bar{z}_{u,j} = \bar{u}_j \cdot \bar{t}_j^{\mathsf{Chall}} \cdot \bar{h}^{\lfloor (\bar{d}_j + \mathsf{Chall} \cdot s_j)/\bar{N} \rfloor} \bmod \bar{N} \\ \bar{z}_{v,j} = \bar{v}_j \cdot \bar{t}_j^{\bar{a}_j + \mathsf{Chall} \cdot (\ell_j - 1)} \cdot \bar{h}^{\lfloor (\bar{e}_j + (\bar{a}_j + \mathsf{Chall} \cdot (\ell_j - 1)) \cdot s_j)/\bar{N} \rfloor} \bmod \bar{N} \end{cases} \tag{11}$$

and, letting $P'[X] = y \cdot X^r - \sum_{k=1}^{r-1} \mu_k \cdot X^k \in \mathbb{Z}[X]$,

$$z_y = y \cdot \mathsf{Chall}^r - \sum_{k=0}^{r-1} \mu_k \cdot \mathsf{Chall}^k \bmod N = P'(\mathsf{Chall}) \bmod N,$$

$$z_w = w^{\mathsf{Chall}^r} \prod_{k=0}^{r-1} \rho_k^{-\mathsf{Chall}^k} \prod_{i=0}^{R-1} C_i^{-\lfloor P_i(\mathsf{Chall})/N \rfloor} \cdot h^{\lfloor P'(\mathsf{Chall})/N \rfloor} \bmod N, \tag{12}$$

where $P_i(\mathsf{Chall})$ and $P'(\mathsf{Chall})$ are evaluated over $\mathbb{Z}$ in the exponent.

4. V defines $f_{j,1} = \bar{z}_j$ and $f_{j,0} = \text{Chall} - \bar{z}_j \bmod N$ for each $j \in [r]$. Then, it accepts if and only if $2^\lambda \leq \bar{z}_j < 2^{2\lambda+1}$ for all $j \in [r]$,

$$\forall j \in [r] : \begin{cases} \bar{A}_j = L_j^{-\text{Chall}} \cdot (1 + \bar{N})^{\bar{z}_j} \cdot \bar{h}^{\bar{z}_{d,j}} \cdot \bar{z}_{u,j}^{\bar{N}} \bmod \bar{N}^2 \\ \bar{B}_j = L_j^{\text{Chall}-\bar{z}_j} \cdot \bar{h}^{\bar{z}_{e,j}} \cdot \bar{z}_{v,j}^{\bar{N}} \bmod \bar{N}^2 \end{cases} \tag{13}$$

and, parsing each $i \in \{0, \ldots, R-1\}$ into bits $i_1 \ldots i_r \in \{0,1\}^r$,

$$\prod_{k=0}^{r-1} C_{d_k}^{-\text{Chall}^k} \cdot \prod_{i=0}^{R-1} C_i^{(\prod_{j=1}^r f_{j,i_j} \bmod N)} \equiv h^{z_y} \cdot z_w^N \pmod{N^2}. \tag{14}$$

BadChallenge$(\text{par}, \tau_\Sigma, \text{crs}, \vec{x}, \vec{a})$: On input of a trapdoor $\tau_\Sigma = (p, q, \bar{p}, \bar{q})$, a statement $\vec{x} = $ "$((C_0, \ldots, C_{R-1}), (L_1, \ldots, L_r)) \in \mathcal{L}_V^{1-R}(h, \bar{h})$" and a first prover message $\vec{a} = (\{(\bar{A}_j, \bar{B}_j)\}_{j=1}^r, \{C_{d_k}\}_{k=0}^{r-1})$, return $\perp$ if h is not an N-th residue in $\mathbb{Z}_{N^2}^*$ or $\bar{h}$ is not an $\bar{N}$-th residue in $\mathbb{Z}_{\bar{N}^2}^*$. Otherwise, compute $\ell_j = \mathcal{D}_{\tau_\Sigma}(L_j) \in \mathbb{Z}_{\bar{N}}$ and decrypt $\vec{a}$ so as to obtain $\bar{a}_j = \mathcal{D}_{\tau_\Sigma}(\bar{A}_j) \in \mathbb{Z}_{\bar{N}}$, $\bar{b}_j = \mathcal{D}_{\tau_\Sigma}(\bar{B}_j) \in \mathbb{Z}_{\bar{N}}$, for each $j \in [r]$, and $c_{d_k} = \mathcal{D}_{\tau_\Sigma}(C_{d_k}) \in \mathbb{Z}_N$ for each k. Let also $c_i = \mathcal{D}_{\tau_\Sigma}(C_i) \in \mathbb{Z}_N$ for each $i = 0$ to $R-1$. Since $\vec{x}$ is false, we have either: (i) $\ell_j \notin \{0,1\}$, for some $j \in [r]$; or (ii) $\forall j \in [r] : \ell_j \in \{0,1\}$ but $c_\ell \neq 0 \bmod N$, where $\ell = \sum_{j=1}^r \ell_j \cdot 2^{j-1}$. We consider two cases:

1. If there exists $j \in [r]$ such that $\ell_j \notin \{0,1\}$, then run the $\text{BadChallenge}^{0-1}$ function of Sect. 4.1 on input of elements $(\text{par}, (\bar{p}, \bar{q}), \{\bar{N}\}, L_j, (\bar{A}_j, \bar{B}_j))$ and return whatever it outputs.
2. Otherwise, we have $\ell_j \in \{0,1\}$ for all $j \in [r]$. Define degree-1 polynomials $F_{j,1}[X] = \bar{a}_j + \ell_j X$, $F_{j,0}[X] = X - F_{j,1}[X] \in \mathbb{Z}_N[X]$ and compute $\{P_i[X]\}_{i=0}^{R-1}$ as per (9). For each $i \in \{0, \ldots, R-1\}$, parse the polynomial $P_i[X] \in \mathbb{Z}_N[X]$ as $P_i[X] = \delta_{i,\ell} \cdot X^r + \sum_{k=0}^{r-1} p_{i,k} \cdot X^k$ for some $p_{i,0}, \ldots, p_{i,r-1} \in \mathbb{Z}_N$. Define the polynomial

$$Q[X] \triangleq c_\ell \cdot X^r + \sum_{k=0}^{r-1} \left(\left(\sum_{i=0}^{R-1} c_i \cdot p_{i,k} \right) - c_{d_k} \right) \cdot X^k \in \mathbb{Z}_N[X],$$

which has degree r since $c_\ell \neq 0 \bmod N$. Define $Q_p[X] \triangleq Q[X] \bmod p$ and $Q_q[X] \triangleq Q[X] \bmod q$ over $\mathbb{Z}_p[X]$ and $\mathbb{Z}_q[X]$, respectively. Since at least one of them has degree r, we assume w.l.o.g. that $\deg(Q_p[X]) = r$. Then, compute the roots[3] $\text{Chall}_{p,1}, \ldots, \text{Chall}_{p,r}$ of $Q_p[X]$ over $\mathbb{Z}_p[X]$ in lexicographical order (if it has less than r roots, the non-existing roots are replaced by $\text{Chall}_{p,i} = \perp$). For each $i \in [r]$, do the following:
   a. If $\text{Chall}_{p,i} \notin \{0, \ldots, 2^\lambda - 1\}$, set $\text{Chall}_i = \perp$.
   b. If $\text{Chall}_{p,i} \in \{0, \ldots, 2^\lambda - 1\}$ and $Q_q(\text{Chall}_{p,i}) \equiv 0 \pmod{q}$, then set $\text{Chall}_i = \text{Chall}_{p,i}$. Otherwise, set $\text{Chall}_i = \perp$.

---

[3] This can be efficiently achieved using the Cantor-Zassenhaus algorithm [19], which is a probabilistic algorithm with small failure probability. The CI hash function of [66] is compatible with BadChallenge functions failing with negligible probability.

CORRECTNESS. To see that honestly generated proofs are always accepted by the verifier, we first note that $2^\lambda \leq \bar{a}_j \leq \bar{z}_j = \bar{a}_j + \mathsf{Chall} \cdot \ell_j \leq 2^{2\lambda} + 2^\lambda < 2^{2\lambda+1}$, for all $j \in [r]$, and that the Eqs. (13) are satisfied for the same reasons as in Sect. 4.1. As for Eq. (14), we observe that, if the witnesses $y \in \mathbb{Z}_N$ and $w \in \mathbb{Z}_N^*$ satisfy $C_\ell = h^y \cdot w^N \bmod N^2$, we have

$$h^{z_y} \cdot z_w^N \cdot \prod_{i=0}^{R-1} C_i^{-(\prod_{j=1}^r f_{j,i_j} \bmod N)} \equiv h^{z_y} \cdot z_w^N \cdot \prod_{i=0}^{R-1} C_i^{-P_i(\mathsf{Chall}) \bmod N}$$

$$\equiv h^{z_y} \cdot w^{\mathsf{Chall}^r \cdot N} \cdot \prod_{k=0}^{r-1} \rho_k^{-\mathsf{Chall}^k \cdot N} \cdot \prod_{i=0}^{R-1} C_i^{-P_i(\mathsf{Chall}) + (P_i(\mathsf{Chall}) \bmod N)}$$

$$\cdot h^{P'(\mathsf{Chall}) - z_y} \cdot \prod_{i=0}^{R-1} C_i^{-P_i(\mathsf{Chall}) \bmod N}$$

$$\equiv h^{P'(\mathsf{Chall})} \cdot w^{\mathsf{Chall}^r \cdot N} \cdot \prod_{k=0}^{r-1} \rho_k^{-\mathsf{Chall}^k \cdot N} \cdot \prod_{i=0}^{R-1} C_i^{-P_i(\mathsf{Chall})}$$

$$\equiv h^{\mathsf{Chall}^r \cdot y} \cdot w^{\mathsf{Chall}^r \cdot N} \cdot \prod_{k=0}^{r-1} (h^{-\mathsf{Chall}^k \mu_k} \cdot \rho_k^{-\mathsf{Chall}^k \cdot N})$$

$$\cdot \prod_{i=0}^{R-1} C_i^{-\delta_{i,\ell} \cdot \mathsf{Chall}^r - \sum_{k=0}^{r-1} p_{i,k} \cdot \mathsf{Chall}^k}$$

$$\equiv (h^y \cdot w^N)^{\mathsf{Chall}^r} \cdot \prod_{k=0}^{r-1} (h^{\mu_k} \cdot \rho_k^N)^{-\mathsf{Chall}^k} \cdot C_\ell^{-\mathsf{Chall}^r} \cdot \prod_{i=0}^{R-1} C_i^{-\sum_{k=0}^{r-1} p_{i,k} \cdot \mathsf{Chall}^k}$$

$$\equiv \prod_{k=0}^{r-1} (h^{\mu_k} \cdot \rho_k^N)^{-\mathsf{Chall}^k} \cdot \prod_{k=0}^{r-1} \prod_{i=0}^{R-1} C_i^{-p_{i,k} \cdot \mathsf{Chall}^k} \equiv \prod_{k=0}^{r-1} C_{d_k}^{-\mathsf{Chall}^k} \pmod{N^2}.$$

Lemma 4.2. *The above construction is a trapdoor Σ-protocol for $\mathcal{L}_\vee^{\text{1-R}}$.* (The proof is available in the full version of the paper.)

Following [46] and standard Σ-protocols over the integers, the above Σ-Protocol $\Pi_\vee^{\text{1-R}} = (\mathsf{Gen}_{\mathsf{par}}, \mathsf{Gen}_\mathcal{L}, \mathsf{P}, \mathsf{V})$ is statistically special honest-verifier zero-knowledge. Although the adversary can choose Paillier commitments $\{C_i\}_{i=0}^{R-1}$ of its own (which may be N-th residues or not), we can rely on the fact that h has a component of order N to perfectly randomize commitments $\{C_{d_k}\}_{k=0}^{r-1}$ over the full group $\mathbb{Z}_{N^2}^*$ even if some of the $\{C_i\}_{i=0}^{R-1}$ are maliciously generated.

Lemma 4.3. *For any language $\mathcal{L}_\vee^{\text{1-R}}(h, \bar{h})$ such that N divides the order of $h \in \mathbb{Z}_{N^2}^*$ and $\bar{N}$ divides the order of $\bar{h} \in \mathbb{Z}_{\bar{N}^2}^*$, $\Pi_\vee^{\text{1-R}}(h, \bar{h})$ is statistically special honest-verifier zero-knowledge.* (The proof is given in the full version of the paper.)

5   Logarithmic-Size Ring Signatures in the Standard Model from DCR and LWE

The proof of unforgeability departs from [46] in that we cannot replay the adversary with a different random oracle. Instead, we use Paillier as a dual-mode commitment, which is made extractable at some step to enable the extraction of bits $\ell_1^\star \ldots \ell_r^\star \in \{0,1\}^r$ from the commitments $\{L_j^\star\}_{j=1}^r$ contained in the forgery $\vec{\Sigma}^\star = ((L_1^\star, \ldots, L_r^\star), \vec{\pi}^\star)$. The next step is to have the reduction guess which honestly generated public key $vk^{(i^\star)}$ will belong to the signer identified by decoding the forgery. Then, $vk^{(i^\star)}$ is replaced by a random element of $\mathbb{Z}_{N^2}^\star$ in order to force the adversary to break the simulation-soundness of Π^{uss} by arguing that $vk^{(i^\star)}$ is a commitment to 0, which it is not. The use of two distinct moduli allows us to decode $\ell_1^\star, \ldots, \ell_r^\star \in \{0,1\}^r$ from $\{L_j^\star\}_{j=1}^r$ (which is necessary to check that $\ell^\star = \ell_1^\star \ldots \ell_r^\star$ still identifies the expected verification key $vk^{(i^\star)}$) even when we rely on the DCR assumption to modify the distribution of $vk^{(i^\star)}$.

The security proof of our simplified scheme relies on erasures because the NIZK simulator is used in all signing queries. If the adversary makes a corruption query Corrupt(i) after a signing query involving $sk^{(i)}$, the challenger's loophole is to claim that it erased the signer's randomness in signing queries of the form $(i, \cdot, \cdot)$.

To avoid erasures, we adapt the security proof in such a way that the NIZK simulator only simulates signatures on behalf of the expected target user $i^\star$. All other users' signatures are faithfully generated, thus allowing the challenger to reveal consistent randomness explaining their generation. Since user $i^\star$ is not corrupted with noticeable probability, the challenger never has to explain the generation of a simulated signature. This strategy raises a major difficulty since decoding $\ell_1^\star \ldots \ell_r^\star$ from $\{L_j^\star\}_{j=1}^r$ is only possible when these are extractable commitments. Unfortunately, the NIZK simulator cannot answer signing queries $(i^\star, \cdot, \cdot)$ by computing $\{L_j\}_{j=1}^r$ as perfectly binding commitments as this would not preserve the statistical ZK property of the Σ-protocol of Sect. 4.2. Moreover, relying on computational ZK does not work because we need the guessed index $i^\star$ to be statistically independent of the adversary's view until the forgery stage. If we were to simulate signatures using computational NIZK proofs, they would information-theoretically leak the index $i^\star$ of the only user for which the NIZK simulator is used in signing queries $(i^\star, \cdot, \cdot)$. To resolve this problem, we use a tag-based commitment scheme which is perfectly hiding in all signing queries and extractable in the forgery (with noticeable probability).

We thus commit to the string $\ell \in \{0,1\}^r$ using the dense $\mathcal{R}_{\mathsf{BM}}$-lossy PKE scheme of Sect. 3.2. We use the property that, depending on which tag is used to generate a commitment, it either behaves as perfectly hiding or extractable commitment. In the perfectly hiding mode, we also exploit its density property to ensure the statistical ZK property.

The construction uses the trapdoor Σ-protocol of Sect. 4.2 to prove membership of the parametrized language

$$\mathcal{L}_{\vee}^{1\text{-}R}(h, \bar{h}_{\mathsf{VK}}) := \big\{ \big((C_0, \ldots, C_{R-1})(L_1, \ldots, L_r)\big) \in (\mathbb{Z}_{N^2}^*)^R \times (\mathbb{Z}_{\bar{N}^2}^*)^r \quad | \quad (15)$$
$$\exists y \in \mathbb{Z}_N, \ w \in \mathbb{Z}_N^*, \ s_1, \ldots, s_r \in \mathbb{Z}_{\bar{N}}, \ t_1, \ldots, t_r \in \mathbb{Z}_{\bar{N}}^*,$$
$$(\ell_1, \ldots, \ell_r) \in \{0,1\}^r \ : \ C_\ell = h^y \cdot w^N \bmod N^2$$
$$\wedge \quad L_j = (1 + \bar{N})^{\ell_j} \cdot \bar{h}_{\mathsf{VK}}^{s_j} \cdot t_j^{\bar{N}} \bmod \bar{N}^2 \quad \forall j \in [r] \ \big\},$$

with $R = 2^r$ and $\ell = \sum_{j=1}^r \ell_j \cdot 2^{j-1}$, where $\bar{h}_{\mathsf{VK}}$ changes in each signature.

The construction relies on the following ingredients:

- A trapdoor Σ-protocol $\Pi' = (\mathsf{Gen}'_{\mathsf{par}}, \mathsf{Gen}'_\mathcal{L}, \mathsf{P}', \mathsf{V}')$ for the parametrized language $\mathcal{L}_{\vee}^{1\text{-}R}$ defined in (15).
- A strongly unforgeable one-time signature scheme $\mathsf{OTS} = (\mathcal{G}, \mathcal{S}, \mathcal{V})$ with verification keys of length $\ell_v \in \mathsf{poly}(\lambda)$.
- An admissible hash function $\mathsf{AHF} : \{0,1\}^{\ell_v} \to \{0,1\}^L$, for some $L \in \mathsf{poly}(\lambda)$.
- A dense $\mathcal{R}$-lossy PKE scheme $\mathcal{R}\text{-}\mathsf{LPKE} = (\mathsf{Par\text{-}Gen}, \mathsf{Keygen}, \mathsf{LKeygen}, \mathsf{Encrypt}, \mathsf{Decrypt})$ for $\mathcal{R}_{\mathsf{BM}} : \mathcal{K} \times \mathcal{T} \to \{0,1\}$, where $\mathcal{K} = \{0, 1, \bot\}^L$ and $\mathcal{T} = \{0,1\}^L$.

Our erasure-free ring signature goes as follows.

CRSGen(1^λ) : Given a security parameter λ, conduct the following steps.

1. Generate $\mathsf{par} \leftarrow \mathsf{Gen}_{\mathsf{par}}(1^\lambda)$ for the trapdoor Σ-protocol of Sect. 4.2.
2. Generate an RSA modulus $N = pq$ and choose an element $h \hookleftarrow U(\mathbb{Z}_{N^2}^*)$, which has order divisible by N w.h.p.
3. Choose an admissible hash function $\mathsf{AHF} : \{0,1\}^{\ell_v} \to \{0,1\}^L$. Generate public parameters $\Gamma \hookleftarrow \mathsf{Par\text{-}Gen}(1^\lambda, 1^L, 1^{|N|})$ for the dense $\mathcal{R}_{\mathsf{BM}}$-lossy PKE scheme of Sect. 3.2 with $\zeta = 1$, which is associated with the bit-matching relation $\mathcal{R}_{\mathsf{BM}} : \mathcal{K} \times \mathcal{T} \to \{0,1\}$. Choose a random initialization value $K \hookleftarrow U(\mathcal{K})$ and generate lossy keys $(\mathsf{pk}, \mathsf{sk}, \mathsf{tk}) \leftarrow \mathsf{LKeygen}(\Gamma, K)$. Parse pk as $\mathsf{pk} := (\bar{N}, \{\bar{v}_{i,b}\}_{i \in [L], b \in \{0,1\}})$, for an RSA modulus $\bar{N} = \bar{p}\bar{q}$, where $\bar{v}_{i,b} \sim U(\mathbb{Z}_{\bar{N}^2}^*)$ for each $i \in [L]$, $b \in \{0,1\}$.
4. Generate a pair $(\mathsf{crs}, \tau_{\mathsf{zk}}) \leftarrow \mathsf{Gen}_\mathcal{L}(\mathsf{par}, \mathcal{L}_{\vee}^{1\text{-}R})$ comprised of the CRS crs of an USS argument Π^{uss} (recalled in the full version of the paper) for the language $\mathcal{L}_{\vee}^{1\text{-}R}$ defined in (15) with a simulation trapdoor τ_{zk}. The common reference string crs contains $\mathsf{crs}'_\mathcal{L} = \{N, \bar{N}\}$, which is part of a CRS $\mathsf{crs}' = (\{\lambda\}, \mathsf{crs}'_\mathcal{L})$ for the Σ-protocol of Sect. 4.2.

Output the common reference string $\rho = (\mathsf{crs}, h, \mathsf{AHF}, \mathsf{pk}, \Gamma, \mathsf{OTS})$, where OTS is the specification of a one-time signature scheme.

Keygen(ρ) : Pick $w \hookleftarrow U(\mathbb{Z}_N^*)$, $y \hookleftarrow U(\mathbb{Z}_N)$ and compute $C = h^y \cdot w^N \bmod N^2$. Output (sk, vk), where $sk = (w, y)$ and $vk = C$.

Sign$(\rho, sk, M, \mathsf{R})$: Given a ring $\mathsf{R} = \{vk_0, \ldots, vk_{R-1}\}$ (we assume that $R = 2^r$ for some $r \in \mathbb{N}$), a message M and a secret key $sk = (w, y) \in \mathbb{Z}_N^* \times \mathbb{Z}_N$, let $\ell \in \{0, \ldots, R-1\}$ the index such that $vk_\ell = h^y \cdot w^N \bmod N^2$.

1. Generate a one-time signature key pair $(\mathsf{VK}, \mathsf{SK}) \leftarrow \mathsf{OTS}.\mathcal{G}(1^\lambda)$ and let $\mathsf{VK}' = \mathsf{AHF}(\mathsf{VK}) \in \{0,1\}^L$. Compute $\bar{h}_{\mathsf{VK}} = \prod_{j=1}^{L} \bar{v}_{j,\mathsf{VK}'[j]} \bmod \bar{N}^2$.

2. For each $j \in [r]$, choose $s_j \hookleftarrow U(\mathbb{Z}_{\bar{N}})$, $t_j \hookleftarrow U(\mathbb{Z}_{\bar{N}}^*)$ and compute a commitment $L_j = (1 + \bar{N})^{\ell_j} \cdot \bar{h}_{\mathsf{VK}}^{s_j} \cdot t_j^{\bar{N}} \bmod \bar{N}^2$.

3. Define $\mathsf{lbl} = \mathsf{VK}$ and compute a NIZK argument $\vec{\pi} \leftarrow \mathsf{P}(\mathsf{crs}, \vec{x}, \vec{w}, \mathsf{lbl})$ that $\vec{x} \triangleq ((vk_0, \ldots, vk_{R-1}), (L_1, \ldots, L_r)) \in \mathcal{L}_{\mathsf{V}}^{1\text{-}R}(h, \bar{h}_{\mathsf{VK}})$ by running the prover P with the Σ-protocol of Sect. 4.2 using the witness $\vec{w} = ((\ell_1, \ldots, \ell_r), w, (s_1, \ldots, s_r), (t_1, \ldots, t_r))$.

4. Generate a one-time signature $sig \leftarrow \mathsf{OTS}.\mathcal{S}(\mathsf{SK}, (\vec{x}, M, \mathsf{R}, \vec{\pi})))$.

Output the signature $\vec{\Sigma} = (\mathsf{VK}, (L_1, \ldots, L_r), \vec{\pi}, sig)$.

$\mathsf{Verify}(\rho, M, \vec{\Sigma}, \mathsf{R})$: Given a signature $\vec{\Sigma} = (\mathsf{VK}, (L_1, \ldots, L_r), \vec{\pi}, sig)$, a message M and a ring $\mathsf{R} = \{vk_0, \ldots, vk_{R-1}\}$, return 0 if these do not parse properly. Otherwise, let $\mathsf{lbl} = \mathsf{VK}$ and return 0 if $\mathsf{OTS}.\mathcal{V}(\mathsf{VK}, (\vec{x}, M, \mathsf{R}, \vec{\pi}), sig) = 0$. Otherwise, run $\mathsf{V}(\mathsf{crs}, \vec{x}, \vec{\pi}, \mathsf{lbl})$ which outputs 1 iff $\vec{\pi}$ is a valid argument that $((vk_0, \ldots, vk_{R-1}), (L_1, \ldots, L_r)) \in \mathcal{L}_{\mathsf{V}}^{1\text{-}R}(h, \bar{h}_{\mathsf{VK}})$.

In the full version of the paper, we provide concrete efficiency estimations showing that, in terms of signature length, the above realization competes with its random-oracle-model counterpart. We now state our main security results.

Theorem 5.1. *The above ring signature provides unforgeability if: (i) The one-time signature* OTS *is strongly unforgeable; (ii) The scheme of Sect. 3.2 is a secure dense* $\mathcal{R}_{\mathsf{BM}}$*-lossy PKE scheme; (iii) The* DCR *assumption holds; (iv)* Π^{uss} *is an unbounded simulation-sound NIZK argument for the parametrized language* $\mathcal{L}_{\mathsf{V}}^{1\text{-}R}$. *(The proof is in the full version of the paper.)*

The proof of anonymity follows from the fact that all commitments are perfectly hiding when the CRS ρ is configured as in the real scheme. The proof of Theorem 5.2 is given in the full version of the paper.

Theorem 5.2. *The above construction instantiated with the trapdoor* Σ*-protocol of Sect. 4.2 provides full anonymity under key exposure provided* Π^{uss} *is a statistical NIZK argument for the language* $\mathcal{L}_{\mathsf{V}}^{1\text{-}R}(h, \bar{h}_{\mathsf{VK}})$ *of* (15) *when the order of* h *is a multiple of* N *and the order of* $\bar{h}_{\mathsf{VK}}$ *is a multiple of* $\bar{N}$.

Acknowledgements. This research was partially funded by the French ANR ALAMBIC project (ANR-16-CE39-0006). Khoa Nguyen was supported in part by the Gopalakrishnan - NTU PPF 2018, by A*STAR, Singapore under research grant SERC A19E3b0099, and by Vietnam National University HoChiMinh City (VNU-HCM) under grant number NCM2019-18-01. Thomas Peters is a research associate of the Belgian Fund for Scientific Research (F.R.S.-FNRS).

References

1. Abe, M., Ohkubo, M., Suzuki, K.: 1-out-of-n signatures from a variety of keys. In: Zheng, Y. (ed.) ASIACRYPT 2002. LNCS, vol. 2501, pp. 415–432. Springer, Heidelberg (2002). https://doi.org/10.1007/3-540-36178-2_26

2. Abe, M., Ambrona, M., Bogdanov, A., Ohkubo, M., Rosen, A.: Non-interactive composition of sigma-protocols via share-then-hash. In: Moriai, S., Wang, H. (eds.) ASIACRYPT 2020. LNCS, vol. 12493, pp. 749–773. Springer, Cham (2020). https://doi.org/10.1007/978-3-030-64840-4_25

3. Backes, M., Döttling, N., Hanzlik, L., Kluczniak, K., Schneider, J.: Ring signatures: logarithmic-size, no setup—from standard assumptions. In: Ishai, Y., Rijmen, V. (eds.) EUROCRYPT 2019. LNCS, vol. 11478, pp. 281–311. Springer, Cham (2019). https://doi.org/10.1007/978-3-030-17659-4_10

4. Bellare, M., Hofheinz, D., Yilek, S.: Possibility and impossibility results for encryption and commitment secure under selective opening. In: Joux, A. (ed.) EUROCRYPT 2009. LNCS, vol. 5479, pp. 1–35. Springer, Heidelberg (2009). https://doi.org/10.1007/978-3-642-01001-9_1

5. Bellare, M., Yilek, S.: Encryption schemes secure under selective opening attack. Cryptology ePrint Archive: report 2009/101

6. Bender, A., Katz, J., Morselli, R.: Ring signatures: stronger definitions, and constructions without random oracles. J. Cryptology $22(1)$, 114–138 (2007). https://doi.org/10.1007/s00145-007-9011-9

7. Boneh, D., Boyen, X.: Secure identity based encryption without random oracles. In: Franklin, M. (ed.) CRYPTO 2004. LNCS, vol. 3152, pp. 443–459. Springer, Heidelberg (2004). https://doi.org/10.1007/978-3-540-28628-8_27

8. Boyen, X.: Mesh signatures. In: Naor, M. (ed.) EUROCRYPT 2007. LNCS, vol. 4515, pp. 210–227. Springer, Heidelberg (2007). https://doi.org/10.1007/978-3-540-72540-4_12

9. Boyle, E., Segev, G., Wichs, D.: Fully leakage-resilient signatures. J. Cryptology $26(3)$, 513–558 (2012). https://doi.org/10.1007/s00145-012-9136-3

10. Brakerski, Z., Koppula, V., Mour, T.: NIZK from LPN and trapdoor hash via correlation intractability for approximable relations. In: Micciancio, D., Ristenpart, T. (eds.) CRYPTO 2020. LNCS, vol. 12172, pp. 738–767. Springer, Cham (2020). https://doi.org/10.1007/978-3-030-56877-1_26

11. Brakerski, Z., Tauman-Kalai, Y.: A framework for efficient signatures, ring signatures and identity based encryption in the standard model. Cryptology ePrint Archive: report 2010/086 (2010)

12. Bresson, E., Stern, J., Szydlo, M.: Threshold ring signatures and applications to Ad-hoc groups. In: Yung, M. (ed.) CRYPTO 2002. LNCS, vol. 2442, pp. 465–480. Springer, Heidelberg (2002). https://doi.org/10.1007/3-540-45708-9_30

13. Camenisch, J., Shoup, V.: Practical verifiable encryption and decryption of discrete logarithms. In: Boneh, D. (ed.) CRYPTO 2003. LNCS, vol. 2729, pp. 126–144. Springer, Heidelberg (2003). https://doi.org/10.1007/978-3-540-45146-4_8

14. Canetti, R., Chen, Y., Holmgren, J., Lombardi, A., Rothblum, G., Rothblum, R.: Fiat-Shamir from simpler assumptions. Cryptology ePrint Archive: report 2018/1004

15. Canetti, R., et al.: Fiat-Shamir: from practice to theory. In: Symposium on Theory of Computing (2019)

16. Canetti, R., Chen, Y., Reyzin, L., Rothblum, R.D.: Fiat-Shamir and correlation intractability from strong KDM-secure encryption. In: Nielsen, J.B., Rijmen, V. (eds.) EUROCRYPT 2018. LNCS, vol. 10820, pp. 91–122. Springer, Cham (2018). https://doi.org/10.1007/978-3-319-78381-9_4

17. Canetti, R., Goldreich, O., Halevi, S.: The random oracle methodology, revisted. J. ACM $51(4)$, 557–594 (2004)

18. Canetti, R., Lombardi, A., Wichs, D.: Fiat-Shamir: from practice to theory, part II (NIZK and correlation intractability from circular-secure FHE). Cryptology ePrint Archive: report 2018/1248

19. Cantor, D., Zassenhaus, H.: A new algorithm for factoring polynomials over finite fields. Math. Comput. **36**(154), 587–592 (1981)

20. Catalano, D., Gennaro, R., Howgrave-Graham, N., Nguyen, P. : Paillier's cryptosystem revisited. In: ACM-Conference on Computer and Communications Security (2001)

21. Chaidos, P., Groth, J.: Making sigma-protocols non-interactive without random oracles. In: Katz, J. (ed.) PKC 2015. LNCS, vol. 9020, pp. 650–670. Springer, Heidelberg (2015). https://doi.org/10.1007/978-3-662-46447-2_29

22. Chandran, N., Groth, J., Sahai, A.: Ring signatures of sub-linear size without random oracles. In: Arge, L., Cachin, C., Jurdziński, T., Tarlecki, A. (eds.) ICALP 2007. LNCS, vol. 4596, pp. 423–434. Springer, Heidelberg (2007). https://doi.org/10.1007/978-3-540-73420-8_38

23. Chase, M., Lysyanskaya, A.: On signatures of knowledge. In: Dwork, C. (ed.) CRYPTO 2006. LNCS, vol. 4117, pp. 78–96. Springer, Heidelberg (2006). https://doi.org/10.1007/11818175_5

24. Chatterjee, R., Garg, S., Hajiabadi, M., Khurana, D., Liang, X., Malavolta, G., Pandey, O., Shiehian, S.: Compact ring signatures from learning with errors. In: Malkin, T., Peikert, C. (eds.) CRYPTO 2021. LNCS, vol. 12825, pp. 282–312. Springer, Cham (2021). https://doi.org/10.1007/978-3-030-84242-0_11

25. Chaum, D., Pedersen, T.P.: Wallet databases with observers. In: Brickell, E.F. (ed.) CRYPTO 1992. LNCS, vol. 740, pp. 89–105. Springer, Heidelberg (1993). https://doi.org/10.1007/3-540-48071-4_7

26. Choudhuri, A., Hubacek, P., Kamath, C., Pietrzak, K., Rosen, A., Rothblum, G.: Finding a Nash equilibrium is no easier than breaking Fiat-Shamir. In: Symposium on Theory of Computing (2019)

27. Ciampi, M., Parisella, R., Venturi, D.: On adaptive security of delayed-input sigma protocols and Fiat-Shamir NIZKs. In: Galdi, C., Kolesnikov, V. (eds.) SCN 2020. LNCS, vol. 12238, pp. 670–690. Springer, Cham (2020). https://doi.org/10.1007/978-3-030-57990-6_33

28. Couteau, G., Hartmann, D.: Shorter non-interactive zero-knowledge arguments and zaps for algebraic languages. In: Micciancio, D., Ristenpart, T. (eds.) CRYPTO 2020. LNCS, vol. 12172, pp. 768–798. Springer, Cham (2020). https://doi.org/10.1007/978-3-030-56877-1_27

29. Couteau, G., Katsumata, S., Ursu, B.: Non-interactive zero-knowledge in pairing-free groups from weaker assumptions. In: Canteaut, A., Ishai, Y. (eds.) EUROCRYPT 2020. LNCS, vol. 12107, pp. 442–471. Springer, Cham (2020). https://doi.org/10.1007/978-3-030-45727-3_15

30. Cramer, R., Damgård, I., Nielsen, J.B.: Multiparty computation from threshold homomorphic encryption. In: Pfitzmann, B. (ed.) EUROCRYPT 2001. LNCS, vol. 2045, pp. 280–300. Springer, Heidelberg (2001). https://doi.org/10.1007/3-540-44987-6_18

31. Cramer, R., Damgård, I., Schoenmakers, B.: Proofs of partial knowledge and simplified design of witness hiding protocols. In: Desmedt, Y.G. (ed.) CRYPTO 1994. LNCS, vol. 839, pp. 174–187. Springer, Heidelberg (1994). https://doi.org/10.1007/3-540-48658-5_19

32. Damgård, I.: Efficient concurrent zero-knowledge in the auxiliary string model. In: Preneel, B. (ed.) EUROCRYPT 2000. LNCS, vol. 1807, pp. 418–430. Springer, Heidelberg (2000). https://doi.org/10.1007/3-540-45539-6_30

33. Damgård, I., Fazio, N., Nicolosi, A.: Non-interactive zero-knowledge from homomorphic encryption. In: Halevi, S., Rabin, T. (eds.) TCC 2006. LNCS, vol. 3876, pp. 41–59. Springer, Heidelberg (2006). https://doi.org/10.1007/11681878_3

34. Damgård, I., Jurik, M.: A generalisation, a simplification and some applications of paillier's probabilistic public-key system. In: Kim, K. (ed.) PKC 2001. LNCS, vol. 1992, pp. 119–136. Springer, Heidelberg (2001). https://doi.org/10.1007/3-540-44586-2_9

35. De Santis, A., Di Crescenzo, G., Ostrovsky, R., Persiano, G., Sahai, A.: Robust noninteractive zero knowledge. In: Kilian, J. (ed.) CRYPTO 2001. LNCS, vol. 2139, pp. 566–598. Springer, Heidelberg (2001). https://doi.org/10.1007/3-540-44647-8_33

36. Dodis, Y., Kiayias, A., Nicolosi, A., Shoup, V.: Anonymous identification in *Ad Hoc* groups. In: Cachin, C., Camenisch, J.L. (eds.) EUROCRYPT 2004. LNCS, vol. 3027, pp. 609–626. Springer, Heidelberg (2004). https://doi.org/10.1007/978-3-540-24676-3_36

37. Esgin, M.F., Steinfeld, R., Liu, J.K., Liu, D.: Lattice-based zero-knowledge proofs: new techniques for shorter and faster constructions and applications. In: Boldyreva, A., Micciancio, D. (eds.) CRYPTO 2019. LNCS, vol. 11692, pp. 115–146. Springer, Cham (2019). https://doi.org/10.1007/978-3-030-26948-7_5

38. Esgin, M., Zhao, R., Steinfeld, R., Liu, J., Liu, D.: MatRiCT: efficient, scalable and post-quantum blockchain confidential transactions protocol. In: ACM-Computer and Communications Security (2019)

39. Feige, U., Lapidot, D., Shamir, A.: Multiple non-interactive zero-knowledge under general assumptions. SIAM J. Comput. **29**(1), 1–28 (1999)

40. Fiat, A., Shamir, A.: How to prove yourself: practical solutions to identification and signature problems. In: Odlyzko, A.M. (ed.) CRYPTO 1986. LNCS, vol. 263, pp. 186–194. Springer, Heidelberg (1987). https://doi.org/10.1007/3-540-47721-7_12

41. Gentry, C., Peikert, C., Vaikuntanathan, V.: Trapdoors for hard lattices and new cryptographic constructions. In: Symposium on Theory of computing (2008)

42. Goldwasser, S., Micali, S., Rackoff, C.: The knowledge complexity of interactive proof systems. SIAM J. comput. **18**(1), 186–208 (1989)

43. Goldwasser, S., Tauman Kalai, Y.: On the (in) security of the Fiat-Shamir paradigm. In: Foundations of Computer Science (2003)

44. González, A.: Shorter ring signatures from standard assumptions. In: Lin, D., Sako, K. (eds.) PKC 2019. LNCS, vol. 11442, pp. 99–126. Springer, Cham (2019). https://doi.org/10.1007/978-3-030-17253-4_4

45. Green, M., Ladd, B.-W. , Miers, I.: A Protocol for privately reporting Ad impressions at scale. In: ACM-Computer and Communications Security (2016)

46. Groth, J., Kohlweiss, M.: One-out-of-many proofs: or how to leak a secret and spend a coin. In: Oswald, E., Fischlin, M. (eds.) EUROCRYPT 2015. LNCS, vol. 9057, pp. 253–280. Springer, Heidelberg (2015). https://doi.org/10.1007/978-3-662-46803-6_9

47. Hemenway, B., Libert, B., Ostrovsky, R., Vergnaud, D.: Lossy encryption: constructions from general assumptions and efficient selective opening chosen ciphertext security. In: Lee, D.H., Wang, X. (eds.) ASIACRYPT 2011. LNCS, vol. 7073, pp. 70–88. Springer, Heidelberg (2011). https://doi.org/10.1007/978-3-642-25385-0_4

48. Hofheinz, D., Jager, T., Rupp, A.: Public-key encryption with simulation-based selective-opening security and compact ciphertexts. In: Hirt, M., Smith, A. (eds.) TCC 2016. LNCS, vol. 9986, pp. 146–168. Springer, Heidelberg (2016). https://doi.org/10.1007/978-3-662-53644-5_6

49. Holmgren, J., Lombardi, A.: Cryptographic hashing from strong one-way functions (or: one-way product functions and their applications). In: Foundations of Computer Science (2018)

50. Holmgren, J., Lombardi, A., Rothblum, R.: Fiat-Shamir via list-recoverable codes (or: parallel repetition of GMW is not zero-knowledge). In: Symposium on Theory of Computing (2021)

51. Jager, T.: Verifiable random functions from weaker assumptions. In: Dodis, Y., Nielsen, J.B. (eds.) TCC 2015. LNCS, vol. 9015, pp. 121–143. Springer, Heidelberg (2015). https://doi.org/10.1007/978-3-662-46497-7_5

52. Jawale, R., Tauman-Kalai, Y., Khurana, D., Zhang, R.: SNARGs for bounded depth computations and PPAD hardness from sub-exponential LWE. In: Symposium on Theory of Computing (2021)

53. Kiltz, E.: Chosen-ciphertext security from tag-based encryption. In: Halevi, S., Rabin, T. (eds.) TCC 2006. LNCS, vol. 3876, pp. 581–600. Springer, Heidelberg (2006). https://doi.org/10.1007/11681878_30

54. Libert, B., Ling, S., Nguyen, K., Wang, H.: Zero-knowledge arguments for lattice-based accumulators: logarithmic-size ring signatures and group signatures without trapdoors. In: Fischlin, M., Coron, J.-S. (eds.) EUROCRYPT 2016. LNCS, vol. 9666, pp. 1–31. Springer, Heidelberg (2016). https://doi.org/10.1007/978-3-662-49896-5_1

55. Libert, B., Nguyen, K., Passelègue, A., Titiu, R.: Simulation-sound arguments for LWE and applications to KDM-CCA2 security. In: Moriai, S., Wang, H. (eds.) ASIACRYPT 2020. LNCS, vol. 12491, pp. 128–158. Springer, Cham (2020). https://doi.org/10.1007/978-3-030-64837-4_5

56. Libert, B., Nguyen, K., Peters, T., Yung, M.: One-shot fiat-shamir-based NIZK arguments of composite residuosity and logarithmic-size ring signatures in the standard model. Cryptology ePrint Archive: report 2020/1334

57. Libert, B., Peters, T., Qian, C.: Logarithmic-size ring signatures with tight security from the DDH assumption. In: Lopez, J., Zhou, J., Soriano, M. (eds.) ESORICS 2018. LNCS, vol. 11099, pp. 288–308. Springer, Cham (2018). https://doi.org/10.1007/978-3-319-98989-1_15

58. Lipmaa, H.: Optimally sound sigma protocols under DCRA. In: Kiayias, A. (ed.) FC 2017. LNCS, vol. 10322, pp. 182–203. Springer, Cham (2017). https://doi.org/10.1007/978-3-319-70972-7_10

59. Lombardi, A., Vaikuntanathan, V.: PPAD-hardness and VDFs based on iterated squaring, in the standard model. Crypto (2020)

60. Malavolta, G., Schröder, D.: Efficient ring signatures in the standard model. In: Takagi, T., Peyrin, T. (eds.) ASIACRYPT 2017. LNCS, vol. 10625, pp. 128–157. Springer, Cham (2017). https://doi.org/10.1007/978-3-319-70697-9_5

61. Mohassel, P.: One-time signatures and chameleon hash functions. In: Biryukov, A., Gong, G., Stinson, D.R. (eds.) SAC 2010. LNCS, vol. 6544, pp. 302–319. Springer, Heidelberg (2011). https://doi.org/10.1007/978-3-642-19574-7_21

62. Noether, S.: Ring signature confidential transactions for monero. Cryptology ePrint Archive report 2015/1098 (2015)

63. Okamoto, T., Uchiyama, S.: A new public-key cryptosystem as secure as factoring. In: Nyberg, K. (ed.) EUROCRYPT 1998. LNCS, vol. 1403, pp. 308–318. Springer, Heidelberg (1998). https://doi.org/10.1007/BFb0054135

64. Paillier, P.: Public-key cryptosystems based on composite degree residuosity classes. In: Stern, J. (ed.) EUROCRYPT 1999. LNCS, vol. 1592, pp. 223–238. Springer, Heidelberg (1999). https://doi.org/10.1007/3-540-48910-X_16

65. Park, S., Sealfon, A.: It wasn't me! In: Boldyreva, A., Micciancio, D. (eds.) CRYPTO 2019. LNCS, vol. 11694, pp. 159–190. Springer, Cham (2019). https://doi.org/10.1007/978-3-030-26954-8_6

66. Peikert, C., Shiehian, S.: Noninteractive zero knowledge for NP from (plain) learning with errors. In: Boldyreva, A., Micciancio, D. (eds.) CRYPTO 2019. LNCS, vol. 11692, pp. 89–114. Springer, Cham (2019). https://doi.org/10.1007/978-3-030-26948-7_4

67. Regev. O.: On lattices, learning with errors, random linear codes, and cryptography. STOC (2005)

68. Rivest, R.L., Shamir, A., Tauman, Y.: How to leak a secret. In: Boyd, C. (ed.) ASIACRYPT 2001. LNCS, vol. 2248, pp. 552–565. Springer, Heidelberg (2001). https://doi.org/10.1007/3-540-45682-1_32

69. Sahai, A.: Non-malleable non-interactive zero knowledge and adaptive chosen-ciphertext security. In: Foundations of Computer Science (1999)

70. Shacham, H., Waters, B.: Efficient ring signatures without random oracles. In: Okamoto, T., Wang, X. (eds.) PKC 2007. LNCS, vol. 4450, pp. 166–180. Springer, Heidelberg (2007). https://doi.org/10.1007/978-3-540-71677-8_12

71. Kalai, Y.T., Rothblum, G.N., Rothblum, R.D.: From obfuscation to the security of fiat-shamir for proofs. In: Katz, J., Shacham, H. (eds.) CRYPTO 2017. LNCS, vol. 10402, pp. 224–251. Springer, Cham (2017). https://doi.org/10.1007/978-3-319-63715-0_8

72. Young, A., Yung, M.: Questionable encryption and its applications. In: Dawson, E., Vaudenay, S. (eds.) Mycrypt 2005. LNCS, vol. 3715, pp. 210–221. Springer, Heidelberg (2005). https://doi.org/10.1007/11554868_15

SNARGs for P from Sub-exponential DDH and QR

James Hulett[1,2], Ruta Jawale[1,2], Dakshita Khurana[1,2(✉)],
and Akshayaram Srinivasan[1,2]

[1] University of Illinois, Urbana-Champaign, USA
{jhulett2,jawale2,dakshita}@illinois.edu
[2] Tata Institute of Fundamental Research, Bengaluru, India
akshayaram.srinivasan@tifr.res.in

Abstract. We obtain publicly verifiable Succinct Non-Interactive Arguments (SNARGs) for arbitrary deterministic computations and bounded space non-deterministic computation from standard group-based assumptions, without relying on pairings. In particular, assuming the sub-exponential hardness of both the Decisional Diffie-Hellman (DDH) and Quadratic Residuosity (QR) assumptions, we obtain the following results, where n denotes the length of the instance:

1. A SNARG for any language that can be decided in non-deterministic time T and space S with communication complexity and verifier runtime $(n + S) \cdot T^{o(1)}$.
2. A SNARG for any language that can be decided in deterministic time T with communication complexity and verifier runtime $n \cdot T^{o(1)}$.

1 Introduction

We consider the problem of constructing *succinct, publicly verifiable* arguments to certify the correctness of computation. By succinct, we refer to the setting where the running time of verifier is much smaller than the time required to perform the computation.

The problem of constructing such proof systems has received widespread attention over the last three decades. These are typically called succinct non-interactive arguments (SNARGs), where *argument* refers to any proof system whose soundness holds against polynomial-time provers (under cryptographic assumptions) and the non-interactive setting refers to a single message of communication sent by the prover to the verifier. As in prior work, our work focuses on constructions in the CRS model, where participants have access to a common reference string.

J. Hulett, R. Jawale and D. Khurana—Supported in part by DARPA SIEVE award under contract number HR001120C0024, a gift from Visa Research, and a C3AI DTI award. Any opinions, findings and conclusions or recommendations expressed in this material are those of the author(s) and do not necessarily reflect the views of the United States Government or DARPA.

O. Dunkelman and S. Dziembowski (Eds.): EUROCRYPT 2022, LNCS 13276, pp. 520–549, 2022.
https://doi.org/10.1007/978-3-031-07085-3_18

Until recently, a significant amount of prior work on SNARGs focused on constructions proven secure under non-falsifiable assumptions or shown secure only in idealized models (such as the Random Oracle Model). Indeed, Gentry and Wichs [24] showed that if such an argument system satisfied a strong form of soundness called as adaptive soundness, then such non-falsifiable assumptions are necessary for SNARGs for NP. There has been recent exciting progress on constructing SNARGs for classes that are subsets of NP under falsifiable standard cryptographic assumptions, and in particular the LWE (Learning with Errors assumption), by instantiating the Fiat-Shamir paradigm, discussed next.

The Fiat-Shamir Paradigm. The Fiat-Shamir paradigm is a transformation that converts any public-coin interactive argument $(\mathcal{P}, \mathcal{V})$ for a language L to a non-interactive argument $(\mathcal{P}', \mathcal{V}')$ for L. The CRS consists of randomly chosen hash functions $h_1, \ldots, h_\ell$ from a hash family $\mathcal{H}$, where ℓ is the number of rounds in $(\mathcal{P}, \mathcal{V})$. To compute a non-interactive argument for $x \in L$, the prover $\mathcal{P}'(x)$ generates a transcript corresponding to $(\mathcal{P}, \mathcal{V})(x)$, by emulating $\mathcal{P}(x)$ and replacing each random verifier message by a hash of the transcript so far. The verifier $\mathcal{V}'(x)$ accepts if and only if $\mathcal{V}(x)$ accepts this transcript and all verifier challenges are computed correctly as the output of the hash function on the transcript so far. This paradigm is sound when applied to constant round protocols in the Random Oracle Model (ROM) [6,46]. At the same time there are counterexamples that demonstrate its insecurity in the plain model [4,5,16,25].

The recent work of Canetti *et al.* [15] and subsequent work of Peikert and Shiehian [45] proved the soundness of the Fiat-Shamir paradigm, assuming standard hardness of the Learning With Errors (LWE) problem, when applied to a *specific* zero-knowledge protocol. This gave the first NIZK argument from LWE. This work also obtained a SNARG for all bounded depth computations, assuming the existence of an FHE scheme with optimal circular security – which appears to be an extremely strong assumption. Subsequently, [32] gave an instantiation of the Fiat-Shamir paradigm applied to special classes of succinct proofs, which resulted in SNARGs for bounded depth computations from sub-exponential LWE [32]. Even more recently, Choudhuri et al. [21] gave a construction of SNARGs for the complexity class P from polynomial LWE, using which Kalai et al. [37] gave a construction of SNARGs for bounded-space nondeterministic computation under sub-exponential LWE. The LWE assumption is a structured cryptographic assumption that is known to imply among several other interesting cryptographic primitives, compact (leveled) homomorphic encryption. In fact, all aforementioned constructions of SNARGs implicitly make use of homomorphic encryption.

On the other hand, foundational group-based assumptions such as Decisional Diffie-Hellman and Quadratic Residuosity are not known to imply homomorphic encryption, and yet their (sub-exponential) variants have surprisingly, via the Fiat-Shamir paradigm, been shown to imply non-interactive zero-knowledge [14,31] as well as non-trivial SNARGs for batched NP statements [20]. This motivates the following question:

> *Do there exist SNARGs for* P *(and beyond) from standard group-based assumptions like DDH and QR?*

1.1   Our Results

We address the above question and obtain the following positive results.

- We build a SNARG for the class of all non-deterministic computations requiring time $T(n)$ and space $S(n)$ (denoted by $\mathsf{NTISP}(T(n); S(n))$) where the prover runs in time $\mathsf{poly}(T(n))$ given a witness for the computation and the verifier runs in time $(n + S(n)) \cdot T(n)^{o(1)}$ where n is the instance length.
- Plugging the SNARG above into a compiler from [37], we obtain a SNARG for the class P where the prover runs in time $\mathsf{poly}(T(n))$ and the verifier runs in time $n \cdot T(n)^{o(1)}$.

Our construction for NTISP is obtained in three steps.

1. We develop a new *folding technique* for interactive succinct arguments, where we *recursively* break down a time-T computation into smaller subcomputations, each of time T/k (for an appropriate choice of k) and have the prover send batch proofs of the validity of each subcomputation. This can be viewed as a computational analogue of the RRR interactive proof [47].
2. We instantiate our protocol using batch interactive arguments for NP[1] that are "FS-compatible", which were in particular developed in [20] based on the hardness of QR. Here, FS-compatible refers to the fact that these interactive batch NP arguments can be soundly converted into SNARGs via the Fiat-Shamir paradigm. In addition, we show that our interactive argument for NTISP is FS-compatible as long as the underlying batch NP argument is FS-compatible.
3. We then soundly convert the above succinct interactive argument to a SNARG by making use of correlation-intractable hash functions for low-depth threshold circuits constructed in [31], based on sub-exponential hardness of DDH.

Finally, we note that the works of [2, 28, 41] observed that in addition to interactive proofs, the Fiat-Shamir paradigm can be soundly instantiated for special types of arguments. They observed that this is possible for arguments that have an *unconditionally sound mode*, and where the prover cannot detect whether the argument is unconditionally or computationally sound. These ideas were then extended to the setting of *succinct* arguments in [20, 21]. As a contribution that may be of independent interest, we abstract out a notion of Fiat-Shamir compatibility of argument systems, which captures these broad requirements (including those used in [2, 20, 21, 28, 41]) that interactive *arguments* satisfy in order to soundly instantiate Fiat-Shamir from standard assumptions using known techniques.

---

[1] Batch arguments for NP allow a verifier to verify the correctness of k NP instances with circuit complexity smaller than k times the size of the NP verification circuit.

1.2 Other Prior Work

The works of [7–9,22,23,29,40,42] obtain SNARGs for non-deterministic computations, with security either in the Random Oracle Model [6] or from non-falsifiable "knowledge assumptions." The schemes of [1,10,17–19,39,43] rely on assumptions related to obfuscation, which are both stronger in flavor and less widely studied than the ones used in this work. More recently, [34] constructed a SNARG (for deterministic computations) based on a (new) efficiently falsifiable decisional assumption on groups with bilinear maps. Later, a line of work [15,20,21,32,37] instantiated the Fiat-Shamir paradigm to finally result in SNARGs for P from the learning with errors (LWE) assumption. Very recently, the work of Gonzalez and Zacharias [27] constructed SNARGs from pairing-based assumptions. On the other hand, in this work, we obtain SNARGs from assumptions that hold in pairing-free groups.

Another line of work [3,12,13,33,35,36] built *privately verifiable* schemes for deterministic computations and a sub-class of non-deterministic computations, based on standard assumptions (specifically, the hardness of LWE or ϕ-hiding). These schemes, however, are not publicly verifiable. The CRS is generated together with a secret key which is needed in order to verify the proofs.

In the interactive setting, publicly verifiable schemes exist, even for non-deterministic computations, under standard cryptographic assumptions [11,38,44]. In fact some publicly verifiable interactive proof systems for restricted classes of computations exist even unconditionally, in particular for bounded depth [26] and bounded space computations [47].

2 Technical Overview

We start with a high-level overview of our recursively-built interactive argument. To begin with, we will only focus on languages that can be decided in deterministic time T and space S. The prover will run in time $\mathsf{poly}(T)$, and the size of our proofs will grow (linearly) in S.

2.1 Succinct Interactive Arguments for Bounded Space from Succinct Arguments for Batch NP

In what follows, we describe a form of interactive arguments for bounded space computations that can be soundly compressed via the Fiat-Shamir transform. We discuss why these ideas may seem to necessitate the use of LWE, and then describe how our folding technique helps get around the need for the LWE assumption while achieving $T^{o(1)}$ verification time.

Consider a deterministic computation that takes T steps: the prover and verifier agree on a (deterministic) Turing Machine $\mathcal{M}$, an input $y \in \{0,1\}^n$, and two configurations $u, v \in \{0,1\}^S$ (a configuration includes the machine's internal state, the contents of all memory tapes, and the position of the heads). The prover's claim is that after running the machine $\mathcal{M}$ on input y, starting at configuration u and proceeding for T steps, the resulting configuration is v. This is denoted by

$$(\mathcal{M}, y) : u \xrightarrow{T} v.$$

To prove correctness of this T-step computation, the prover will send $(k-1)$ alleged intermediate configurations

$$(s_1, s_2, \ldots, s_{k-1})$$

and will set $s_0 := u, s_k := v$, where for every $i \in [1, k]$, s_i is the alleged configuration of the machine $\mathcal{M}$ after T/k steps when starting at configuration s_{i-1}.

Now the prover will attempt to prove correctness of all these intermediate configurations: a naïve way to achieve this is to run k executions of the base protocol, one for every $i \in [k]$. But the trick to achieving succinctness will be to prove correctness of all configurations simultaneously in verification time that is significantly smaller than running the base protocol k times, while also not blowing up the prover's complexity by a factor of k. To enable this, the prover and verifier can rely on an appropriate succinct interactive argument for *batch NP* to establish that all responses would have been accepted by the verifier.

In a succinct argument for batch NP, a prover tries to convince a verifier that $(x_1, \ldots, x_k) \in \mathcal{L}^{\otimes k}$, in such a way that the proof size and communication complexity are smaller than the trivial solution where the prover simply sends all witnesses $(w_1, \ldots, w_k)$ to the verifier, and the verifier computes $\bigwedge_{i \in [k]} \mathcal{R}_{\mathcal{L}}(x_i, w_i)$. In particular, [20] recently obtained SNARGs for batching k NP instances (from QR and sub-exponential DDH) where the communication complexity is $\widetilde{O}(|C| + k \log |C|) \cdot \mathsf{poly}(\lambda)$, and verifier runtime is $\widetilde{O}(kn + |C|) \cdot \mathsf{poly}(\lambda)$, where λ is the security parameter, $|C|$ denotes the size of the verification circuit and n denotes the size of each instance. In our setting, $|C| \approx (T/k)$, which means that verification time for the SNARG will be $\widetilde{O}(k + T/k)$. Setting $k = O(\sqrt{T})$, we would obtain communication complexity (and verification runtime) that grows (approx.) with $O(\sqrt{T})$ and this is the best that one can hope for in this case [20]. However, in this work, we would like to achieve an overhead of $T^{o(1)}$.

A Recursive Construction. The argument described above incurred an overhead of T/k because the verification circuit for each subcomputation had size T/k. However, what if we substituted this verification circuit with the (relatively efficient) verifier for a *succinct interactive argument for T/k-time computations?*

Specifically, assume there exists a *public-coin interactive* argument for verifying computations of size T/k. As before, suppose a prover wants to convince a verifier that

$$(\mathcal{M}, y) : u \xrightarrow{T} v.$$

The prover sends $(k-1)$ intermediate configurations, as before, and then prepares the first messages of all k interactive arguments, where the ith interactive argument attests to the correctness of $(\mathcal{M}, y) : s_{i-1} \xrightarrow{T/k} s_i$. Instead of sending these messages in the clear, the prover sends to the verifier a *succinct commitment* to all k first messages. Here, following [20,21,37], one could use a keyed *computationally binding* succinct commitment whose key is placed in the CRS. In fact, looking ahead, we will require a commitment that that is binding to a (hidden) part of the input string [30], and in fact the bound parts of the input should be extractable given a trapdoor. We will call such commitments somewhere-extractable (SE) commitments. In more detail, these commitments have a key generation algorithm $\mathsf{Gen}(1^\lambda, i)$ that on input an index $i \in [k]$ outputs a commitment key ck together with an extraction trapdoor td, and an extraction algorithm that given td and any commitment string c outputs the unique i^{th} committed block (out of a total of k blocks). Moreover, the commitment key hides the index i in a CPA-sense.

Next, the verifier sends a single (public coin) message that serves as a challenge for all k arguments. Subsequently, the prover prepares a third message for all arguments, and commits to these messages, after which the verifier again generates a single (public coin) message that serves as its fourth message for all k arguments. The prover and verifier proceed until all rounds of all k arguments are committed, and then the prover (as before) must prove to the verifier that all committed transcripts would be accepted.

At this point, one solution is for the prover and verifier to engage in a batch NP argument (as before), where the prover must convince the verifier that for every $i \in [k]$, there is an opening to the commitment that would cause the verifier to accept. In what follows, we will rely on the fact that the batch NP SNARG can actually be obtained in two steps: first, build an interactive argument for batch NP, and next compress rounds of interaction via Fiat-Shamir. Indeed, the batch SNARG from [20] that we will use *is obtained* by first building an interactive argument and then compressing it by soundly instantiating the Fiat-Shamir paradigm. From this point on, unless otherwise specified, we will make use of the [20] *interactive* batch NP argument, and later separately use the fact that it can be soundly compressed via Fiat-Shamir based on sub-exponential DDH (a property referred to as FS-compatibility). This modified interactive argument $\langle \mathsf{P}, \mathsf{V} \rangle$ for T-time computations is described in Fig. 1, and it relies on a protocol for T/k-time computations.

Batch NP and the Need for Local Openings. Unfortunately, the protocol described in Fig. 1 is *not succinct*. In particular, each batch NP statement involves verifying an opening of the SE commitment, and therefore the verification complexity of batch NP grows with the complexity of verifying commitment openings. For this to be small, the SE commitment must satisfy an important property: namely, that it is possible to *succinctly decommit* to a part of the committed input in such a way that the size of the opening and complexity of verifying openings depend only on the part being opened, and do not grow with the size of input to the commitment. Unfortunately, such commitments are only known from the learning with errors (LWE) assumption[2]; and therefore we take a different route.

---

[2] In the full version of this paper, we show that one can in fact construct a commitment with somewhat succinct local openings from DDH or QR. However, these are significantly less succinct than their LWE-based counterparts, and using these commitments would lead to marginally worse parameters than one can get with the methods described next.

Emulation Phase.

1. P computes and sends $(k-1)$ intermediate configurations $(s_1, \ldots, s_{k-1})$ to V, where s_i is the configuration of machine $\mathcal{M}$ after T/k steps when starting at configuration s_{i-1}.

2. P prepares the first messages $\{m_1^{(i)}\}_{i \in [k]}$ for k interactive arguments, where the ith interactive argument attests to the correctness of $(\mathcal{M}, x)$: $s_{i-1} \xrightarrow{T/k} s_i$. Next, P computes an SE commitment $c^{(1)}$ to these first messages, and sends the commitment string $c^{(1)}$ to V.

3. V generates a single (public coin) message for (a single copy of) the interactive argument for T/k-sized computation. All k arguments will share the same verifier message.

4. More generally, for every round $j \in [\rho]$ of the underlying interactive argument,
   - P computes the jth round messages for all k interactive arguments where the ith interactive argument attests to the correctness of $(\mathcal{M}, x)$: $s_{i-1} \xrightarrow{T/k} s_i$. Next, P computes an SE commitment $c^{(j)}$ to all these first messages, and sends the commitment string $c^{(j)}$ to V.
   - V generates a single (public coin) message for the underlying interactive argument for T/k-sized computation. All k arguments will share the same verifier message.

Batch NP Phase. P proves to V that there exists an opening of the commitment $c = (c^{(1)}, \ldots, c^{(\rho)})$ where for $i \in [k]$ the ith opened value is an interactive argument such that:

1. The commitment verifier would accept the opening and
2. The verifier for the T/k interactive argument would accept the ith argument.

Fig. 1. Recursively defined interactive argument for bounded space deterministic computation

Coincidentally, in the *interactive arguments* for batch NP due to [20], the first step requires the prover to *commit* to witnesses $(w_1, \ldots, w_k)$ corresponding to each of the k instances $(x_1, \ldots, x_k)$. This is done via an SE commitment in such a way that when the commitment key is binding at index $i \in [k]$, the extraction algorithm outputs the ith committed witness w_i. Moreover, this commitment does not need to have local openings; somewhere extractability suffices[3]. Finally, the [20] protocol is actually an *argument of knowledge for one of the instances*:

---

[3] We remark that [20] also require some additional linear homomorphism properties from the commitment, but these are not necessary for our discussion.

implicit in their proof is the fact that when the SE commitment keys (in the CRS) are binding on index i, no efficient prover can commit to w_i that is a non-witness for x_i and produce an accepting transcript (except with negligible probability).

This gives us a way out: in the Batch NP phase of our protocol, instead of proving that *there exists an opening to the commitment*, we omit sending commitments (since we already committed to all $\frac{T}{k}$ transcripts), and simply prove that for each of the transitions $s_{i-1} \to s_i$, there exists a prover strategy corresponding to verifier coins sent in the emulation phase, that would cause the verifier to accept. That is, the prover demonstrates membership of instances $(\widetilde{x}_1, \ldots, \widetilde{x}_k)$ in the language $\widetilde{\mathcal{L}}$, where for any $i \in [k]$,

$$\widetilde{x}_i = (s_{i-1}, s_i, y, \mathcal{M}, \beta)$$

and $\widetilde{\mathcal{L}}$ is the language of all such $\widetilde{x}$ such that there exist prover messages that when combined with the verifier messages β create an accepting transcript. We note that an honest prover, by the end of the emulation phase in Fig. 1, will already be committed to witnesses for this language.

Thus our final protocol has an emulation phase that is identical to Fig. 1, but the batch NP phase is modified as described in Fig. 2.

It may appear that the language $\widetilde{\mathcal{L}}$ will contain nearly all strings: since the protocol for T/k-sized computations is an *argument*, so there will exist prover messages even for instances not in the language. However, this would only be a problem if we relied on soundness of the batch NP protocol: on the other hand, we are able to use the fact that the [20] protocol is an *argument of knowledge* for the ith statement when the SE commitment key is binding at index i. In particular, this means that if the SE commitment was binding at index i, then it is possible to *efficiently extract* a witness, i.e., an accepting transcript for the ith subcomputation $s_{i-1} \to s_i$.

Now if the prover managed to break soundness of our protocol, this would imply that there exists an index $j \in [k]$ such that the machine $\mathcal{M}$ on input y does not transition from configuration s_{j-1} to s_j. But, if $j = i$, where i is the index where the SE commitment is binding, then one can in fact *extract* an accepting transcript for the jth *incorrect* subcomputation $s_{j-1} \to s_j$. This can therefore be used to build a prover that contradicts soundness of the protocol for T/k-sized computations. Moreover, hiding of the index i ensures that $j = i$ occurs with non-negligible probability.

Finally, we point out that in the base case, i.e., for unit-time computations, the verifier simply checks the statement on its own (this takes one time-step).

The recursive protocol described so far satisfies succinctness for an appropriate choice of k (that we discuss later) but requires multiple rounds, since each round of recursion adds a few rounds of interaction. The goal of this work is to build a *non-interactive* argument, which we achieve by compressing this interactive argument to a SNARG based on correlation-intractable hash functions for low-depth threshold circuits. We discuss this in detail below.

Updated Batch NP Phase
- P and V define instances

$$(\widetilde{x}_1, \ldots \widetilde{x}_k) \text{ where } \widetilde{x}_i = (s_{i-1}, s_i, y, \mathcal{M}, \beta)$$

where β denote all verifier messages from the emulation phase.
- P additionally defines witnesses

$$(\widetilde{w}_1, \ldots \widetilde{w}_k)$$

where for every $i \in [k]$, $\widetilde{w}_i$ contains the prover messages for the ith subcomputation for size $\frac{T}{k}$.
- Finally, define language

$$\widetilde{\mathcal{L}} = \{(s, s', y, \mathcal{M}, \beta) \ : \ \exists \text{ prover messages } \pi \text{ s.t.}$$

$$(\pi, \beta) \text{ is accepting transcript for } (\mathcal{M}, y) : s \xrightarrow{T/k} s'.\}$$

- P and V execute a batch NP argument to prove that for every $i \in [k]$, $\widetilde{x}_i \in \widetilde{\mathcal{L}}$, where they replace the first round of Batch NP (where prover SE-commits to witnesses) with the transcript of the emulation phase.

Fig. 2. Updated batch NP phase for bounded space deterministic computation

2.2 Obtaining a SNARG

We now discuss why this argument can be compressed by relying on the same CI hash functions as used in [20], leading to a sound SNARG.

Fiat-Shamir Compatible Batch NP. To soundly compress their *batch NP* inter-active argument into a SNARG, the work of [20] (building on a line of recent works including [2,14,15,28,31,32,41,45]) relies on a special type of hash function, called a correlation intractable hash function. The prover generates verifier messages for the interactive protocol locally by applying this hash function to its partial transcripts, in effect eliminating the need to interact with a verifier. At a high level, a hash family $\mathcal{H}$ is correlation intractable (CI) for a relation $\mathcal{R}(x, y)$ if it is computationally hard, given a random hash key k, to find any input x such that $(x, \mathcal{H}(k, x)) \in \mathcal{R}$.

Given a CI hash function, the key observation is that if the BAD verifier challenge for the interactive argument, which allows a prover to cheat, can be computed by an *efficient* function, then replacing the verifier message by the output of a CI hash function results in a verifier message that does not allow a prover to cheat, except with negligible probability. But this paradigm is only applicable to protocols where the circuits computing BAD verifier challenges are supported by constructions of CI hash functions exist based on standard assumptions. In particular, CI hash functions from (sub-exponential) DDH are known for functions that are computable by constant (and in fact, $O(\log \log \lambda)$) depth threshold circuits. Recall that the [20] batch NP interactive argument has a first message that contains SE commitments to all witnesses; [20] show that the SE commitment they use (which they construct based on the QR assumption) allows for extraction in constant depth. Moreover, given the witness, all other computations can also be performed by constant depth threshold circuits. Therefore, their interactive arguments can be compressed based on the (sub-exponential) DDH assumption. [20] call this the *strong* FS-compatible property. We will now prove that our interactive arguments for bounded space, also inherit this property.

Fiat-Shamir Compatible Bounded Space Arguments. To begin, we assume that all cryptographic primitives (SE commitments, CI hash functions) satisfy T-security, meaning that no $\mathsf{poly}(T)$-size adversary can break the primitive with advantage better than $\mathsf{negl}(T)$.

Our interactive argument begins with P sending $(k - 1)$ intermediate configurations to V. Observe that it is possible to verify (in time $\leq T$) whether or not a given intermediate configuration is correct[4]. Of course, the verifier should not be verifying intermediate configurations directly (as this will make verification inefficient).

As discussed above, a cheating prover must output at least one pair of consecutive intermediate configurations s_i, s_{i+1} such that $\mathcal{M}$ does not transition from s_i to s_{i+1} in T/k steps. Moreover, by T-index hiding of the SE commitment, if the SE commitment is set to be binding at a random index i', the probability (over the randomness of i') that the prover cheats on the i'^{th} underlying T/k interactive argument must be (negligibly) close to $1/k$. Finally, because the SE commitment is extractable, in this mode, it becomes possible for a reduction to *extract* an accepting transcript of the underlying T/k argument corresponding to a false statement.

Peeling off the recursion just a little, we observe that the (T/k) interactive argument itself begins with the prover sending $(k - 1)$ intermediate configurations, each corresponding to (T/k^2) steps of the Turing Machine $\mathcal{M}$. Again, one pair of consecutive configurations s'_j, s'_{j+1} must be such that $\mathcal{M}$ does not transition from s'_j to s'_{j+1} in (T/k^2) steps. Moreover, by index hiding of the SE commitment used in the (T/k) argument, if the (T/k) commitment is set to be binding at a uniformly random index j', the probability that the prover cheats on the j'^{th} underlying (T/k^2) argument in addition to cheating on the i'^{th} (T/k) argument must be (negligibly) close to $(1/k^2)$. We can recurse $\log_k T$ times all the way to the base case, where the base argument is simply a unit-time computation where the verifier checks the statement on its own. Moreover, letting π denote the unit-time protocol obtained by peeling all layers of the recursion, we

---

[4] This becomes somewhat non-trivial in the non-deterministic setting, which we discuss in an upcoming subsection.

can establish that with probability (close to) $(1/k^{\log_k T}) = 1/T$, π corresponds to a false statement. The rest of our analysis will be conditioned on this event.

Assuming that the base statement π (that the prover is statistically bound to) at the end of the first message is false, we must now understand the distribution of BAD verifier challenges in subsequent messages of the argument system. Note that the very next message will consist of the batch NP phase of the interactive argument for k-size computations, encrypted under $(\log_k T - 1)$ layers of SE commitments. This phase starts with commitments to k witnesses (in this case, the witnesses are empty transcripts), each one proving the correctness of one of the unit-size subcomputations. The false statement from the emulation phase immediately determines which one of the batch statements is incorrect. As long as the SE commitment is binding at this index, the BAD function at this lowest layer of recursion will correspond to the set of verifier challenges in the corresponding batch NP argument that allow the prover to cheat within that argument. This means that the BAD function can be computed by *peeling off* layers of the commitment (i.e. performing $\log_k T$ sequential extractions), and then computing the BAD function for the batch NP argument (which we know is efficiently computable by a constant-depth circuit).

Next, going back up one step, we have the protocol corresponding to k^2-sized computations. It will again be the case that assuming the SE commitment binds at the right index, the BAD function at this layer of recursion will correspond to the set of verifier challenges in the corresponding batch NP argument that allow the prover to cheat within that argument. This means that the BAD function can be computed by peeling off $\log_k T - 1$ layers of the commitment, and then computing the BAD function for the batch NP argument (which we know is efficiently computable by a constant-depth threshold circuit).

More generally, the BAD function of our protocol corresponds to extracting from upto $\log_k T$ layers of commitments, and feeding the result as input to the BAD function circuit of the interactive argument for batch NP.

Communication Complexity and Verifier Runtime. Considering now the efficiency of the verifier, we note that in the emulation phase, the verifier simply has to read prover messages and generate random strings. Thus, for our overview, it suffices to focus on the batch NP phase, as the time taken there will dominate that of the emulation phase. If we were to use a trivial batch NP protocol that simply provided all k witnesses and asked the verifier to check them all, this would mean that the run time of the T verifier would increase by a factor of k over the run time of the T/k verifier. Unrolling the recursion, unfortunately, we would obtain a T-time verifier. Luckily, we are not constrained to use only a trivial batch NP protocol; by being more efficient, we can improve upon the above analysis. Indeed, applying the batch NP described above, we can improve the k multiplicative overhead to a polynomial in λ overhead, where λ is the security parameter of our batch NP scheme.[5]

---

[5] For simplicity of exposition, we are here ignoring some additional additive overhead as well as polylogarithmic multiplicative factors.

By choosing k and λ such that $\lambda << k$, we can ensure that the difference in verifier efficiency over the $\log_k T$ levels between the unit protocol and the T protocol is $\lambda^{c \cdot \log_k T}$ for some constant c, which can be set to $T^{o(1)}$ by a careful choice of parameters. Since the verifier run time is an upper bound on the communication complexity of the protocol (as the verifier needs to at a minimum read all the messages), this gives us the same bound on the size of the proof.

This completes an overview of our SNARGs for deterministic bounded space computation. In what follows, we will discuss how to extend these ideas to the non-deterministic setting.

2.3   SNARGs for Bounded Space Non-deterministic Computation

When the machine $\mathcal{M}$ is non-deterministic it is a-priori no longer clear how to argue or even define "correctness" of intermediate configurations. It may be tempting to consider defining correctness of intermediate configurations with respect to both the instance and the witness. However, the witness used can potentially change every time the prover is queried, and is therefore not well defined. It may also in general be too large to be sent as part of the SNARG.

However, inspired by [3], we observe that if the non-deterministic Turing Machine reads each bit of the witness only once, then it becomes possible to get around this barrier. Similar to [3], we consider the class $\mathsf{NTISP}(T(n), S(n))$ of all languages recognizable by nondeterministic Turing Machines in time $O(T(n))$ and space $O(S(n))$. Recall that a non-deterministic Turing Machine allows each step of the computation to non-deterministically transition to a new state. This, in a sense, corresponds to the setting where each bit of the witness is read at most once (and if the machine wishes to remember previous non-deterministic choices it must explicitly write them down on its worktape). Thus an alternative way to describe this class is as the class of languages $\mathcal{L}$ with a corresponding witness relation $R_{\mathcal{L}}$, recognizable by a layered circuit $C_{n,m}$ parameterized by $n = |x|$ and $m = m(n) = |w|$, that on input a pair (x, w) outputs 1 if and only if $R_{\mathcal{L}}(x, w) = 1$. Each layer of gates in this circuit has input wires that directly read the instance, or directly read the witness, or are the output wires of gates in the previous layer. Moreover, each bit of the witness is read by at most one layer. This circuit has depth $D = O(T(n))$ and width $W = O(S(n))$, where W may be smaller than n and m.

The SNARG Construction. The construction remains largely similar to the one in the deterministic setting. The only (syntactical) difference is that Step 1 in the recursively defined interactive argument from Fig. 1 is modified to send wire assignments $(W_1, \ldots W_{k-1})$ to $(k-1)$ intermediate layers of the circuit, each at a depth interval of D/k from the base layer. Next, for every $i \in [k]$, the prover runs (parallel) interactive arguments proving that there is an assignment to witness wires such that configuration W_i transitions to W_{i+1} in depth D/k.

Analysis. As discussed above, unlike the deterministic setting, it appears difficult define a notion of "correctness" of these intermediate wire assignments. Instead, inspired by [3], we define the notion of an *accepting layer*.

The output layer consists only of the output wire, and thus the only valid assignment for this layer is the symbol 1. For each layer i, we partition the wires that are input to gates in layer i into three sets: intermediate wires, instance wires, and witness wires. Intermediate wires for layer i are all wires connecting gates in layer $(i-1)$ to gates in layer i; instance wires for layer i are all wires that directly read the instance x and are input to gates in layer i; and witness wires for layer i are all wires that directly read the witness and are input to gates in layer i. We define $\mathsf{Acc}^D(x) = 1$. The set $\mathsf{Acc}^{D-1}(x)$ contains all possible assignments to intermediate wires connecting a gate in layer $(D-1)$ to a gate in layer D, such that when the instance wires for layer D are set consistently with x, there exists some assignment to the witness wires for layer D, such that the transition function applied to these wires results in output 1.

For each layer $i < (D-1)$, the set $\mathsf{Acc}^i(x)$ is defined recursively in a similar manner. That is, for $i < (D-1)$, $\mathsf{Acc}^i(x)$ is the set of all possible assignments to intermediate wires connecting gates in layer i to gates in layer $i+1$, such that when the instance wires for layer i are set consistently with x, there exists an assignment to the witness wires for layer $i+1$, such that the transition function applied to these wires outputs intermediate wires connecting layer $i+1$ to layer $(i+2)$ that lie in the set $\mathsf{Acc}^{i+1}(x)$. We note that the lowest i for which this definition is meaningful is $i = 1$, since there are no intermediate wires before the first layer.

By this definition, for $x \notin R_{\mathcal{L}}$, the set $\mathsf{Acc}^1(x)$ is empty. This implies that for any set of claimed intermediate configurations $(W_1, \ldots, W_{k-1})$ sent by P (and for $W_k = 1$), there must exist an $i \in [k-1]$ such that $W_{i+1} \in \mathsf{Acc}^{i+1}(x)$ but $W_i \notin \mathsf{Acc}^i(x)$. This means that there is *no* set of assignments to witness wires that would lead to a correct transition from W_i to W_{i+1}. This means that the prover must be cheating in the ith interactive argument for T/k-time (non-deterministic) computation.

Moreover, as observed in [3], for any width W and depth D non-deterministic computation, it is possible to decide whether a set of wire assignments are in $\mathsf{Acc}^i(x)$, for any $i \in [D]$ in time $\mathsf{poly}(D, 2^W)$. This is done via a straightforward dynamic programming approach. We will set parameters so that the SE commitment is index-hiding against $\mathsf{poly}(T, 2^S)$-size adversaries. This, together with the previous claim implies that if the SE commitment is set to be binding at a random index i', the probability that the prover cheats on the i'^{th} underlying T/k interactive argument must be (negligibly) close to $1/k$. Moreover, because the SE commitment is extractable, in this mode, it becomes possible for a reduction to *extract* an accepting transcript of the underlying T/k argument for a false statement.

At this point, it becomes possible to apply the same recursive argument as in the deterministic setting to argue that with probability (negligibly) close to $1/k^{\log_k T} = 1/T$, the base argument corresponds to a false statement. Conditioned on this event, it becomes possible to analyze the batch NP phase in a manner similar to the analysis in the deterministic setting.

SNARGs *for* P. We rely on the recent work of [37] to compile our SNARGs for non-deterministic bounded-space computations to SNARGs for P.

To this end, we observe that for any language $L \in \mathsf{NTISP}(T, S)$, it holds that $L^{\otimes k} \in \mathsf{NTISP}(kT, S + T)$, where $L^{\otimes k}$ is the language of k instances from L. This implies SNARGs for batch NP with improved parameters than the [20] SNARGs, from sub-exponential DDH and QR. In particular, this implies SNARGs for batching k instances that have a description of size n, and proving that the batched instances are in $L^{\otimes k}$ where $L \in \mathsf{NTISP}(T, S)$, with communication complexity and verifier runtime $k^{o(1)}(n + \mathsf{poly}(T + S))$. By plugging this into a compiler of [37] from Batch SNARGs to SNARGs for P, we obtain SNARGs for T-time deterministic computations with overhead $T^{o(1)}$ from sub-exponential DDH and QR. We point out that the [37] compiler as stated also requires SE commitments that allows for committing to T values with local openings of size $\mathsf{polylog}(T)$. However, we show that for our setting of parameters, it suffices to have a weaker local opening property, where openings are of size $T^{o(1)}$. We build such commitments from any (sub-exponentially index-hiding) SE commitment without local openings, therefore obtaining our final results also from sub-exponential DDH and QR.

FS-compatible Arguments. In the body of our paper, we abstract out some general properties of our interactive arguments, and define a class of FS-compatible interactive arguments that can be soundly compressed using the Fiat-Shamir paradigm based on our technique. We show that any interactive batch NP argument that is an "FS-compatible argument" can also be converted into a proof, (intuitively) as long as its first message essentially contains a succinct commitment to witnesses for all the NP statements. We define FS-compatible interactive arguments to be those that satisfy a variant of round-by-round soundness [15] *w.r.t. a predicate.* This predicate is computed as a function of the first message of the interactive argument[6] and a trapdoor associated with the CRS. Intuitively, we will say that an interactive argument is FS-compatible w.r.t. a predicate ϕ if transcripts that satisfy the predicate, also satisfy round-by-round soundness with sparse and efficiently computable BAD verifier challenges. Moreover, in order to ensure that these arguments can be soundly converted into SNARGs based on CI hash functions, we will require that the predicate be "non-trivial". That is, any adversary that produces accepting transcripts for false statements with non-negligible probability should also produce accepting transcripts *that satisfy the predicate* and correspond to false statements, with non-trivial probability. We show the non-triviality of our predicate using the index hiding property of the underlying SE commitments.

Roadmap. A formalization of the FS-compatible property and a proof that such arguments can be converted to SNARGs can be found in Sect. 4. Next, in Sects. 5 and 6 we formalize our constructions of SNARGs for deterministic and non-deterministic bounded-space computations, respectively. We also combine the latter with recent work [37] to obtain SNARGs for P in Sect. 6.5. Due to shortage

---

[6] More generally, this can be computed as a function of the entire transcript.

of space, we only provide constructions and theorem statements, and defer proofs to the full version of the paper.

3   Preliminaries

In what follows, when we say we assume (T_1, T_2)-hardness of an efficiently falsifiable assumption, we mean that there exists a negligible function $\mu(\cdot)$ such that no $\mathsf{poly}(T_1)$-size adversary can falsify the assumption with probability better than $\mu(T_2)$.

3.1   Correlation Intractable Hash Functions

In this section, we recall the notion of a CI hash family. We start by recalling the notion of a hash function family.

Definition 1. *A hash family $\mathcal{H}$ is associated with algorithms $(\mathcal{H}.\mathsf{Gen}, \mathcal{H}.\mathsf{Hash})$, and a parameter $n = n(\lambda)$, such that:*

- *$\mathcal{H}.\mathsf{Gen}$ is a PPT algorithm that takes as input a security parameter 1^λ and outputs a key k.*
- *$\mathcal{H}.\mathsf{Hash}$ is a polynomial time computable (deterministic) algorithm that takes as input a key $k \in \mathcal{H}.\mathsf{Gen}(1^\lambda)$ and an element $x \in \{0,1\}^{n(\lambda)}$ and outputs an element y.*

We consider hash families $\mathcal{H}$ such that for every $\lambda \in \mathbb{N}$, every key $k \in \mathcal{H}.\mathsf{Gen}(1^\lambda)$ and every $x \in \{0,1\}^{n(\lambda)}$, the output $y = \mathcal{H}.\mathsf{Hash}(k, x)$ is in $\{0,1\}^\lambda$.

Definition 2 (Correlation Intractable). *[15, 16] Fix any $T_1 = T_1(\lambda) \geq \mathsf{poly}(\lambda)$ and $T_2 = T_2(\lambda) \geq \mathsf{poly}(\lambda)$. A hash family $\mathcal{H} = (\mathcal{H}.\mathsf{Gen}, \mathcal{H}.\mathsf{Hash})$ is said to be (T_1, T_2) correlation intractable (CI) for a family $\mathcal{R} = \{\mathcal{R}_\lambda\}_{\lambda \in \mathbb{N}}$ of efficiently enumerable relations if the following two properties hold:*

- *For every $\lambda \in \mathbb{N}$, every $R \in \mathcal{R}_\lambda$, and every $k \in \mathcal{H}.\mathsf{Gen}(1^\lambda)$, the functions R and $\mathcal{H}.\mathsf{Hash}(k, \cdot)$ have the same domain and the same co-domain.*
- *For every $\mathsf{poly}(T_1)$-size $\mathcal{A} = \{\mathcal{A}_\lambda\}_{\lambda \in \mathbb{N}}$ there exists a negligible function μ such that for every $\lambda \in \mathbb{N}$ and every $R \in \mathcal{R}_\lambda$,*

$$\Pr_{\substack{k \leftarrow \mathcal{H}.\mathsf{Gen}(1^\lambda) \\ x \leftarrow \mathcal{A}(k)}} [(x, \mathcal{H}.\mathsf{Hash}(k, x)) \in R] = \mu(T_2(\lambda)).$$

We will use the following theorems from prior work.

Theorem 1. *[31] Fix any $T = T(\lambda) \geq 2^{\lambda^\epsilon}$ for some $0 < \epsilon < 1$. Assuming the (T, T)-hardness of DDH, there exists a constant $c > 0$ such that for any $B = B(\lambda) = \mathsf{poly}(\lambda)$, depth $L \leq O(\log \log \lambda)$ and any family $\mathcal{R} = \{\mathcal{R}_\lambda\}_{\lambda \in \mathbb{N}}$ of relations that are enumerable by threshold circuits of size $B(\lambda)$ and depth L, there exists a (T, T) correlation intractable (CI) hash family $\mathcal{H} = (\mathcal{H}.\mathsf{Gen}, \mathcal{H}.\mathsf{Hash})$ computable in time $(B(\lambda) \cdot \lambda \cdot L)^c$, for $\mathcal{R}$ (Definition 2).*

3.2   Somewhere Extractable (SE) Commitments

Definition 3 (SE Commitments). *A somewhere extractable (SE) commitment consists of PPT algorithms* (Gen, Com, Open, Verify, Extract) *along with an alphabet* $\Sigma = \{0,1\}^{\ell_{\mathsf{blk}}}$ *and a fixed polynomial* $p = p(\cdot)$ *satisfying the following:*

- (ck, ek) ← Gen($1^\lambda, L, \ell_{\mathsf{blk}}, i$): *Takes as input an integer* $L \leq 2^\lambda$, *block length* ℓ_{blk} *and integer* $i \in \{0, \dots, L-1\}$ *and outputs a public commitment key* ck *along with an extraction trapdoor* ek.
- $h \leftarrow$ Com(ck, x): *is a deterministic polynomial time algorithm that takes as input* $x = (x[0], \dots, x[L-1]) \in \Sigma^L$ *and outputs* $h \in \{0,1\}^{\ell_{\mathsf{com}}}$.
- $\pi \leftarrow$ Open(ck, x, i): *Given the commitment key* ck, $x \in \Sigma^L$ *and an index* $i \in \{0, \dots, L-1\}$, *outputs proof* $\pi \in \{0,1\}^{\ell_{\mathsf{open}}}$.
- $b \leftarrow$ Verify(ck, y, i, u, π): *Given a commitment key* ck *and* $y \in \{0,1\}^{\ell_{\mathsf{com}}}$, *an index* $i \in \{0, \dots, L-1\}$, *opened value* $u \in \Sigma$ *and a proof* $\pi \in \{0,1\}^{\ell_{\mathsf{open}}}$, *outputs a decision* $b \in \{0,1\}$.
- $u \leftarrow$ Extract(ek, y): *Given the extraction trapdoor* ek *and a commitment* $y \in \{0,1\}^{\ell_{\mathsf{com}}}$, *outputs an extracted value* $u \in \Sigma$.

We require the following properties:

- **Correctness:** *For any integers* $L \leq 2^\lambda$ *and* $i \in \{0, \dots, L-1\}$, *any* ck ← Gen($1^\lambda, L, i$), $x \in \Sigma^L$, $\pi \leftarrow$ Open(ck, x, j): *we have that* Verify(ck, Com(ck, x), $j, x[j], \pi$) = 1.
- **Index Hiding:** *We consider the following game between an attacker* $\mathcal{A}$ *and a challenger:*
  - *The attacker* $\mathcal{A}(1^{T_1})$ *outputs an integer* L *and two indices* $i_0, i_1 \in \{0, \dots, L-1\}$.
  - *The challenger chooses a bit* $b \leftarrow \{0,1\}$ *and sets* ck ← Gen($1^\lambda, L, i_b$).
  - *The attacker* $\mathcal{A}$ *gets* ck *and outputs a bit* b'.

  We say that an SE commitment satisfies (T_1, T_2) *index-hiding if for every* poly(T_1)-*size attacker* $\mathcal{A}$ *there exists a negligible function* $\mu(\cdot)$ *such that:*

$$\left| \Pr[\mathcal{A} = 1 | b = 0] - \Pr[\mathcal{A} = 1 | b = 1] \right| = \mu(T_2)$$

  in the above game.
- **Somewhere Extractable:** *We say that a commitment is somewhere extractable if there is a negligible function* μ *such that for every* $L(\lambda) \leq 2^\lambda$ *and* $i \in \{0, \dots L-1\}$,

$$\Pr_{(\mathsf{ck},\mathsf{ek}) \leftarrow \mathsf{Gen}(1^\lambda, L, i)} \left[\begin{array}{c} \exists y \in \{0,1\}^{\ell_{\mathsf{com}}}, \quad u \in \Sigma, \quad \pi \in \{0,1\}^{\ell_{\mathsf{open}}} \\ s.t. \ \mathsf{Verify}(\mathsf{ck},y,i,u,\pi)=1 \quad \wedge \quad \mathsf{Extract}(\mathsf{ek},y) \neq u \end{array} \right] = \mu(T_2)$$

Theorem 2 (SE Commitments from QR [20]). *Fix any* $T_1 = T_1(\lambda) \geq$ poly(λ) *and* $T_2 = T_2(\lambda) \geq$ poly(λ). *Assuming* (T_1, T_2) *hardness of QR, there exists an SE commitment satisfying Definition 3 where the extraction algorithm can be implemented by a threshold circuit of constant depth, and which satisfies* (T_1, T_2)-*index hiding. Furthermore, this satisfies the following properties:* $\ell_{\mathsf{com}} = \ell_{\mathsf{blk}}\lambda$, $\ell_{\mathsf{open}} = \ell_{\mathsf{blk}}L$, $|\mathsf{ck}| = \ell_{\mathsf{blk}}L\lambda$, $|\mathsf{ek}| = \ell_{\mathsf{blk}}\lambda$, *the running time of* Gen *and* Verify *is* $\ell_{\mathsf{blk}}L\lambda$ *and the running time of* Extract *is* ℓ_{blk}poly(λ).

4   Fiat-Shamir for Arguments

In this section, we define a class of (multi-round) interactive arguments to which the Fiat-Shamir paradigm can be soundly applied, based on an (appropriate) correlation-intractable hash function. In particular, we will define a few properties that a multi-mode interactive argument should satisfy, in order to be converted to a non-interactive one by applying our technique. We begin with a natural definition of multi-mode interactive arguments:

Definition 4 (N-Mode Protocols). *Let $N(\lambda) \geq \lambda$ be a function. We say that $\Pi = (\mathsf{Setup}, \mathsf{P}, \mathsf{V})$ is an N-mode protocol for a language $\mathcal{L}$ if the following property holds:*

- **Syntax:** Setup *is a randomized algorithm that obtains input a security parameter λ and some $i \in [N(\lambda)]$.* Setup *outputs common reference string* CRS *and auxiliary information* aux *such that* aux *contains i.*

Next, we define a notion of a predicate, that applies to the first prover message, the instance and a trapdoor in the CRS.

Definition 5 (Predicate). *ϕ is a predicate for an N-mode (Definition 4) protocol $\Pi = (\mathsf{Setup}, \mathsf{P}, \mathsf{V})$ if ϕ has the following property:*

- **Syntax:** *For any $i \in [N(\lambda)]$, ϕ takes as input instance x, the first prover message α_1, and some auxiliary information* aux *computed by* $\mathsf{Setup}(1^\lambda, i)$. ϕ *outputs a binary value in $\{0, 1\}$.*

Definition 6 ((T', N)-Non-Trivial Predicate). *Let $\Pi = (\mathsf{Setup}, \mathsf{P}, \mathsf{V})$ be an N-mode (Definition 4) public-coin interactive proof system for a language $\mathcal{L}$. We say that a predicate ϕ for Π (Definition 5) is time-T' non-trivial for Π if the following properties hold:*

- **Syntax:** *For any $\lambda \in \mathbb{Z}^+$, any instance x, any $i \in [N(\lambda)]$, any $(\mathsf{CRS}, \mathsf{aux}) \in$* Support$(\mathsf{Setup}(1^\lambda, i))$, *and any (partial) transcript $\tau = (\alpha_1, \beta_1, \ldots, \alpha_j)$ for some $j \in [\rho(\lambda)]$, we define $\phi(x, \tau, \mathsf{aux}) = \phi(x, \alpha_1, \mathsf{aux})$.*
- **Non-Triviality:** *There exists a polynomial $p(\cdot)$ such that for $\lambda \in \mathbb{Z}^+$, and any* poly(T')-time *adversary $\mathcal{A}$, if there exists a polynomial $q(\cdot)$ such that:*

$$\Pr_{\substack{i \leftarrow [N], \\ (\mathsf{CRS}, \mathsf{aux}) \leftarrow \mathsf{Setup}(1^\lambda, i), \\ (x, \alpha_1) \leftarrow \mathcal{A}(\mathsf{CRS})}} [x \notin \mathcal{L} \wedge x \neq \bot] \geq \frac{1}{q(\lambda)}$$

then

$$\Pr_{\substack{i \leftarrow [N], \\ (\mathsf{CRS}, \mathsf{aux}) \leftarrow \mathsf{Setup}(1^\lambda, i), \\ (x, \alpha_1) \leftarrow \mathcal{A}(\mathsf{CRS})}} [\phi(x, \alpha_1, \mathsf{aux}) = 1 | x \notin \mathcal{L} \wedge x \neq \bot] \geq \frac{1}{p(N(\lambda))}.$$

- **Efficiency:** *ϕ can be evaluated in* poly(T') *time.*

4.1 Round-by-Round Soundness

We now define a notion of round-by-round soundness for interactive arguments w.r.t. a predicate ϕ. The definition below is a generalization of the definition in [15] to the setting of interactive arguments.

Unlike [15], we don't define State on the empty transcript, instead only starting to define it once the first prover message has been sent. The key difference from [15] is that we define the State function on the first prover message to reject when the predicate $\phi(x, \alpha_1, \mathsf{aux}) = 1$, instead of defining it to reject when $x \notin \mathcal{L}$. In particular, if we apply the definition below with the predicate $\phi(x, \alpha_1, \mathsf{aux}) = x \notin \mathcal{L}$ (and modify the syntax of Setup appropriately), we will recover the definition in [15,32].

Definition 7 (b-Round-by-Round Soundness w.r.t. ϕ). *[15] Let $\Pi =$ (Setup, $\mathcal{P}, \mathcal{V}$) be a public-coin N-mode (Definition 4) interactive proof system for a language $\mathcal{L}$. We say that Π is b-round-by-round sound with respect to predicate ϕ (Definition 5), if there exists State such that, denoting the size of every verifier message by λ, for any $i \in [N(\lambda)]$, any (CRS, aux) $\in$ Support(Setup($1^\lambda, i$)), the following properties hold:*

1. ***Syntax:*** *State is a deterministic function that takes as input the CRS, an instance x, a transcript prefix τ, and auxiliary information aux computed by Setup. State outputs either accept or reject.*
   For every x, every non-empty transcript $\tau = (\alpha_1, \beta_1, \ldots, \alpha_j, \beta_j)$, and any next prover message α_{j+1}, we have

$$\mathsf{State}(\mathsf{CRS}, x, \tau, \mathsf{aux}) = \mathsf{State}(\mathsf{CRS}, x, \tau \| \alpha_{j+1}, \mathsf{aux}).$$

2. ***End Functionality:*** *For every x and every first prover message α_1, $\mathsf{State}(\mathsf{CRS}, x, \alpha_1, \mathsf{aux}) = \mathsf{reject}$ iff $\phi(x, \alpha_1, \mathsf{aux}) = 1$. For every complete transcript τ, if $\mathcal{V}(\mathsf{CRS}, x, \tau) = 1$, $\mathsf{State}(\mathsf{CRS}, x, \tau, \mathsf{aux}) = \mathsf{accept}$.*

3. ***Sparsity:*** *For every x and transcript prefix $\tau = (\alpha_1, \beta_1, \ldots, \alpha_{j-1}, \beta_{j-1}, \alpha_j)$, if $\phi(x, \alpha_1, \mathsf{aux}) = 1$ and $\mathsf{State}(\mathsf{CRS}, x, \tau, \mathsf{aux}) = \mathsf{reject}$, it holds that*

$$\Pr_{\beta \leftarrow \{0,1\}^\lambda} [\mathsf{State}(\mathsf{CRS}, x, \tau \| \beta, \mathsf{aux}) = \mathsf{accept}] \leq b(\lambda) \cdot 2^{-\lambda}. \tag{1}$$

4.2 FS-Compatible Arguments

In the following definition, we formalize the requirements from round-by-round sound arguments w.r.t. ϕ that allow them to be compressed by the Fiat-Shamir paradigm via our approach.

Definition 8 (FS-Compatible Multi-mode Argument with Respect to ϕ). *For some $\rho, N : \mathbb{Z}^+ \to \mathbb{Z}^+$, let $\Pi = $ (Setup, P, V) be a ρ-round N-mode (Definition 4) public-coin interactive argument system where Setup is a randomized algorithm that obtains input a security parameter λ and some $i \in [N(\lambda)]$. For any $B, b, d : \mathbb{Z}^+ \to \mathbb{Z}^+$, we say that Π is (B, b, d) FS-compatible with respect to predicate ϕ (Definition 5) if the following properties hold:*

1. **Completeness:** *For any* $\lambda \in \mathbb{Z}^+$, $i \in \{1, 2, \ldots, N(\lambda)\}$, *and* $x \in \mathcal{L}$, *we have*

$$\Pr_{\mathsf{CRS} \leftarrow \mathsf{Setup}(1^\lambda, i)} [\langle \mathsf{P}, \mathsf{V} \rangle (\mathsf{CRS}, x) = \mathsf{accept}] = 1.$$

2. b-**Round-by-round soundness w.r.t.** ϕ**:** Π *is* b-*round-by-round sound with respect to* ϕ *(Definition 7); let* State *be the corresponding state function.*
3. d-**depth** B-**efficient** BAD **w.r.t.** ϕ**:** *For any* $\lambda \in \mathbb{Z}^+$, *any* $i \in [N(\lambda)]$, *any* $(\mathsf{CRS}, \mathsf{aux}) \in \mathsf{Support}(\mathsf{Setup}(1^\lambda, i))$, *there exists a (non-uniform) randomized function* $\mathsf{BAD}_{\mathsf{aux}}$ *that satisfies the following guarantees:*
   - **Syntax:** $\mathsf{BAD}_{\mathsf{aux}}$ *is hardwired with* aux *and takes as input the* CRS, *instance* x, *a partial transcript* $\tau = (\alpha_1, \beta_1, \ldots, \alpha_i)$; *and potentially additional uniform randomness* r.
   - BAD **w.r.t.** ϕ**:** *For every* x *and every* $\tau \triangleq (\alpha_1, \beta_1, \ldots, \alpha_{j-1}, \beta_{j-1}, \alpha_j)$ *s.t.* $\mathsf{State}(\mathsf{CRS}, x, \tau, \mathsf{aux}) = \mathsf{reject}$ *and* $\phi(x, \alpha_1, \mathsf{aux}) = 1$, $\mathsf{BAD}_{\mathsf{aux}}(\mathsf{CRS}, x, \tau)$ *enumerates the set* $\mathcal{B}_{\mathsf{CRS}, \phi, \mathsf{aux}, \tau}$, *where*

   $$\mathcal{B}_{\mathsf{CRS}, \phi, \mathsf{aux}, \tau} := \{\beta : \mathsf{State}(\mathsf{CRS}, x, \tau \| \beta, \mathsf{aux}) = \mathsf{accept}\}.$$

   If $\mathcal{B}_{\mathsf{CRS}, \mathsf{aux}} = \emptyset$, $\mathsf{BAD}_{\mathsf{aux}}(\mathsf{CRS}, x, \tau)$ *outputs* $\perp$. *By Equation* (1), $|\mathcal{B}_{\mathsf{CRS}, \mathsf{aux}}| \leq b(\lambda)$.
   - d-**Depth,** B-**Efficient computation:** $\mathsf{BAD}_{\mathsf{aux}}$ *can be evaluated by a* $d(\lambda)$-*depth (non-uniform) threshold circuit of size* $B = B(\lambda)$.

4.3 From FS-Compatible Arguments to SNARGs

In what follows, we formally state our theorem that arguments satisfying Definition 8 with respect to a non-trivial predicate (Definition 6) can be soundly compressed to obtain a SNARG; the proof of this is deferred to the full version of the paper.

Definition 9 ((T', N)-Sound Non-interactive Arguments). *For any* $T' = T'(\lambda)$ *and* $N = N(\lambda)$, *we say that a* N-*mode protocol (Definition 4)* $\Pi = (\mathsf{Setup}, \mathsf{P}, \mathsf{V})$ *is a non-interactive argument for a language* $\mathcal{L}$ *if the following properties hold:*

- **Completeness:** *For any* $\lambda \in \mathbb{Z}^+$, *any* $i \in [N(\lambda)]$, *and* $x \in \mathcal{L}$, *we have that*

$$\Pr_{\substack{\mathsf{CRS} \leftarrow \mathsf{Setup}(1^\lambda, i) \\ \tau \leftarrow \mathsf{P}(1^\lambda, \mathsf{CRS})}} [\mathsf{V}(\mathsf{CRS}, x, \tau) = \mathsf{accept}] = 1.$$

- N-**Mode Indistinguishability of CRS:** *There exists a negligible function* $\mu(\cdot)$ *such that for any* $i_1, i_2 \in [N(\lambda)]$, *and any* $\mathsf{poly}(T')$-*time adversary* $\mathcal{A}$ *we have that*

$$\left| \Pr_{\mathsf{CRS} \leftarrow \mathsf{Setup}(1^\lambda, i_1)} [\mathcal{A}(\mathsf{CRS}) = 1] - \Pr_{\mathsf{CRS} \leftarrow \mathsf{Setup}(1^\lambda, i_2)} [\mathcal{A}(\mathsf{CRS}) = 1] \right| = \mu(N(\lambda)).$$

- **Adaptive Soundness:** *There exists a negligible function $\mu(\cdot)$ such that for any $\lambda \in \mathbb{Z}^+$, any $i \in [N(\lambda)]$, and any non-uniform $\mathsf{poly}(T')$-time adversary $\mathcal{A}$ we have that*

$$\Pr_{\substack{\mathsf{CRS} \leftarrow \mathsf{Setup}(1^\lambda, i) \\ (x,\tau) \leftarrow \mathcal{A}(1^\lambda, \mathsf{CRS})}} [x \notin \mathcal{L} \ \wedge \ \mathsf{V}(\mathsf{CRS}, x, \tau) = 1] \leq \mu(N(\lambda)).$$

Theorem 3 (FS-Compatible). *Suppose that there exist N, T', B, b, d (all functions of λ) where $N, T' \geq \lambda$. Let $\Pi = (\mathsf{Setup}, \mathsf{P}, \mathsf{V})$ be a $\rho(\lambda)$-round $N(\lambda)$-mode (Definition 4) protocol for a language $\mathcal{L}$ decidable in (deterministic) time $\mathsf{poly}(T')$. Let Π have prover runtime T_P and verifier runtime T_V. Let $\mathcal{H}$ be a hash function. If Π and $\mathcal{H}$ are such that:*

- *Π is (B, b, d)-FS-compatible according to Definition 8 with respect to a (T', N) nontrivial predicate ϕ (Definition 6).*
- *$\mathcal{H}$ is (T', N) CI (Definition 2) for all relations sampleable by d-depth threshold circuits of size B, and is computable in time $p(B)$ for some fixed polynomial $p(\cdot)$.*

Then $\Pi_{\mathsf{FS}}^{\mathcal{H}}$, which is the protocol where every verifier message is computed by the prover by hashing the latest prover message, is a (T', N)-sound non-interactive argument system for $\mathcal{L}$ (Definition 9). $\Pi_{\mathsf{FS}}^{\mathcal{H}}$ has $\rho(\lambda) \cdot p(B(\lambda)) + T_\mathsf{P}$ prover runtime and $\rho(\lambda) \cdot p(B(\lambda)) + T_\mathsf{V}$ verifier runtime.

5   FS-Compatible Arguments for Bounded Space Computations

In this section, we describe and prove FS-compatibility of our interactive arguments for bounded space computation. Before providing a formal theorem, in the following subsection, we define an FS-Compatible Batch NP argument with respect to a batch predicate and SE commitment. We will bootstrap interactive arguments for batch NP satisfying this definition to obtain interactive arguments for bounded space computation.

5.1   FS-Compatible Batch NP Arguments

Let $\Pi_{\mathsf{BNP}} = (\mathsf{Setup}_{\mathsf{BNP}}, \mathsf{P}_{\mathsf{BNP}}, \mathsf{V}_{\mathsf{BNP}})$ be a public-coin argument system for $\mathcal{R}^k$ for some circuit satisfiability relation $\mathcal{R}$ such that $\mathsf{Setup}_{\mathsf{BNP}}(1^\lambda, i)$ runs $(\mathsf{ck}, \mathsf{ek}) \leftarrow \mathcal{C}.\mathsf{Gen}(1^\lambda, k, i)$ for some SE commitment scheme $\mathcal{C}$ and puts ck in CRS and (i, ek) in aux. Then we define a predicate ϕ_{BNP} such that

$$\phi_{\mathsf{BNP}}((x_1, \ldots, x_k), \alpha_1, \mathsf{aux}) = \left((x_i, \mathcal{C}.\mathsf{Extract}(\mathsf{ek}, \alpha_1)) \notin \mathcal{R} \right).$$

Theorem 4 (FS-compatible Batch NP w.r.t. $\mathcal{C}$ [20]). *Assuming the hardness of QR, for any $n = n(\lambda), m = m(\lambda), s = s(\lambda), k = k(\lambda)$, and field $\mathbb{F}$ where $|\mathbb{F}| \leq 2^\lambda$ there exists an FS-compatible Batch NP w.r.t. $\mathcal{C}$ and ϕ_{BNP}, where $\mathcal{C}$ satisfies Definition 3, for $\mathcal{R}_{n,m,s,\mathbb{F}}^k$ where $\mathcal{R}_{n,m,s,\mathbb{F}}$ is any C-SAT relation.*

5.2   Bounded-Space Protocol Construction

For any $T \in \mathbb{N}$, consider a language $\mathcal{L}_T$ that contains the set of all strings $(\mathcal{M}, s_0, s_T, y)$ where $\mathcal{M}$ is the description of a Turing machine, s_0 is the initial state, s_T is the final state and y is an input such that running $\mathcal{M}$ on y with the start state to be s_0 for T time steps results in the final state s_T. We construct an interactive FS-compatible argument for the language $\mathcal{L}_T$.

For any $k, \gamma \geq 1$ where $k^\gamma = T$, for every $\ell \in [\gamma]$, we construct an argument for k^ℓ-time, S-space computations in Fig. 4 in terms of an interactive argument for $k^{\ell-1}$-time, S-space computations.

- Let $\Pi_0 = (\mathsf{Setup}, \mathsf{P}, \mathsf{V})$ denote a trivial protocol (Fig. 3) for unit-time computations where the verifier given a machine $\mathcal{M}$, instance x and states s_0, s_1, outputs 1 if $\mathcal{M}(x, s_0)$ transitions to state s_1 in one time step. $\mathsf{Setup}(1^\lambda)$ outputs $(\bot, \bot)$.
- Let $\Pi_{k^{\ell-1}} = (\mathsf{Setup}, \mathsf{P}, \mathsf{V})$ be a ρ-round public-coin protocol for $(k^{\ell-1})$-time computations with ν-length prover messages whose verifier $\mathsf{V} = (\mathsf{V}_1, \ldots, \mathsf{V}_\rho)$ where $r^{(i)} \leftarrow \mathsf{V}_i(1^\lambda, |x|)$ for $i \in [\rho - 1]$ and $\{0, 1\} \leftarrow \mathsf{V}_\rho(x, \tau)$ for transcript τ.
- Let $\mathcal{C} = (\mathsf{Gen}, \mathsf{Com}, \mathsf{Open}, \mathsf{Verify}, \mathsf{Extract})$ be an SE commitment satisfying Definition 3.
- Let Π_{BNP} be a batch NP protocol for circuit satisfiability that is FS-compatible with respect to the commitment $\mathcal{C}$ (see Sect. 5.1 in the full version of the paper for a formal definition of FS-compatibility for batch NP protocols).

Unit Time Interactive Protocol

P and V obtain an instance $x^{(0)}$, which P wishes to prove is in the language

$$\mathcal{L}^{(0)} \triangleq \left\{ (\mathcal{M}, y, s_0, s_1) \ : \ s_1 \leftarrow \mathcal{M}(y, s_0, 1) \right\}.$$

That is, $\mathcal{M}$ with initial state s_0 reaches state s_1 in one time step on input y.

1. P sends dummy message α to V.
2. V sends dummy message β to P.
3. V computes $s'_1 \leftarrow \mathcal{M}(y, s_0)$. V accepts iff $s'_1 = s_1$.

Fig. 3. Unit time interactive protocol $(\mathsf{Setup}, \mathsf{P}, \mathsf{V})$

Interactive Argument for k^ℓ-Time S-Space Computation

Common Input: The common input for P and V is an instance
$x = (\mathcal{M}, s_0, s_T, y)$ of the language $\mathcal{L}_{k^\ell}$. Setup($1^\lambda, i, k$):

- Parse i as a tuple $(i_1, i_2, \ldots, i_\ell) \in [k]^\ell$.
- Obtain $(\mathsf{ck}, \mathsf{ek}) \leftarrow \mathcal{C}.\mathsf{Gen}(1^\lambda, i_\ell, k)$ and
  $(\mathsf{CRS}', \mathsf{aux}') = \Pi_{k^{\ell-1}}.\mathsf{Setup}(1^\lambda, (i_1, \ldots, i_{\ell-1}), k)$.
- Output $\mathsf{CRS} = (\mathsf{CRS}', \mathsf{ck})$, $\mathsf{aux} = (\mathsf{aux}', \mathsf{ek}, (i_1, \ldots, i_\ell))$.

- **Initial Processing.** P computes $s = (s_0, \ldots, s_k)$ for initial state s_0 and
  $\{s_j \triangleq \mathcal{M}(y, s_0, 1^{T \cdot j/k})\}_{j \in [k]}$. P sends s to V.
- P and V define k instances $(x_1', \ldots, x_k')$ for language $\mathcal{L}_{k^{\ell-1}}$ where $x_j' = (\mathcal{M}, s_{j-1}, s_j, y)$ for $j \in [k]$.

- **Emulation Phase.** For every $r \in [1, \rho]$, let ν denote the maximum
  message size of $\Pi_{k^{\ell-1}}.\mathsf{P}$. P computes k parallel executions of $\Pi_{k^{\ell-1}}.\mathsf{P}$'s
  r^{th} round message, $\Pi_{k^{\ell-1}}.\mathsf{P}_r$:

$$
\pi^{(r)} = \left[\; \pi^{(r)}[1] \;\cdots\; \pi^{(r)}[\nu] \;\right]
$$
$$
\triangleq \begin{bmatrix} - \pi_1^{(r)} \triangleq \Pi_{k^{\ell-1}}.\mathsf{P}_r(\mathsf{CRS}', x_1', \mathcal{L}_{k^{\ell-1}}, \{\beta^{(1)}, \ldots, \beta^{(r-1)}\}) - \\ \cdots \\ - \pi_k^{(r)} \triangleq \Pi_{k^{\ell-1}}.\mathsf{P}_r(\mathsf{CRS}', x_k', \mathcal{L}_{k^{\ell-1}}, \{\beta^{(1)}, \ldots, \beta^{(r-1)}\}) - \end{bmatrix}.
$$

  P sends $C^{(r)} = (C^{(r)}[1], \ldots, C^{(r)}[\nu])$ where $C^{(r)}[j] \triangleq \mathcal{C}.\mathsf{Com}(\mathsf{ck}, \pi^{(r)}[j])$
  for $j \in [\nu]$.
- V sends $\Pi_{k^{\ell-1}}.\mathsf{V}$'s r^{th} round message computed as $\beta^{(r)} \leftarrow \Pi_{k^{\ell-1}}.\mathsf{V}_r(1^\lambda)$.

- **Batch NP Phase.** P and V define the instances $(x_1'', \ldots, x_k'')$ and P
  defines the witnesses $(\omega_1'', \ldots, \omega_k'')$ as follows:
  For $j \in [k]$, $x_j'' = (x_j', \{\beta^{(r)}\}_{r \in [\rho]})$, $\omega_j'' = \{\pi_j^{(r)}\}_{r \in [\rho]}$.
- Define language $\mathcal{L}'' \triangleq$
  $\left\{ (x, \{\beta_r\}_{r \in [\rho]}) : \exists \{\pi_r\}_{r \in [\rho]} \text{ s.t. } \Pi_{k^{\ell-1}}.\mathsf{V}(\mathsf{CRS}', x, \{\pi_r, \beta_r\}_{r \in [\rho]}) = 1 \right\}$.
- P and V execute Π_{BNP} on input ck, instances $(x_1'', \ldots, x_k'')$ and witnesses
  $(\omega_1'', \ldots, \omega_k'')$ where the first round message of P in Π_{BNP} is ignored and
  replaced by $\{C^{(r)}\}_{r \in [\rho]}$ as sent in the emulation phase.
- If $\Pi_{\mathsf{BNP}}.\mathsf{V}$ accepts, then V accepts.

Fig. 4. Bounded space computation protocol Π_{k^ℓ} w.r.t. Π_{BNP} and $\mathcal{C}$

5.3   Non-trivial Predicate for Bounded-Space Protocol

We start with the description of the predicate ϕ for the protocol Π_{k^γ}. Let $\Pi_T = (\mathsf{Setup}, \mathsf{P}, \mathsf{V})$ be the protocol defined by Fig. 4, where $T = k^\gamma$. The predicate ϕ equals ϕ_γ, where ϕ_ℓ is defined recursively for every x, α, aux and $\ell \in [\gamma]$.

- $\phi_0(x, \alpha, \mathsf{aux}) = 1 \iff x \notin \mathcal{L}^{(0)}$.
- $\phi_\ell(x, \alpha, \mathsf{aux})$ for $\ell \in [1, \gamma]$: Parse $\mathsf{aux} = (\mathsf{aux}', ek, (i_1, \ldots, i_\ell))$ and parse $\alpha = ((s_0, \ldots, s_k), C^{(1)})$. Define instances $(x_1', \ldots, x_k')$ as in Fig. 4, where $x_j' = (\mathcal{M}, s_{j-1}, s_j, y)$ for $j \in [k]$.
  Set $\phi_\ell(x, \alpha, \mathsf{aux}) = (x_{i_\ell}' \notin \mathcal{L}_{k^{\ell-1}}) \wedge \phi_{\ell-1}(x_{i_\ell}', C.\mathsf{Extract}(ek, C^{(1)}), \mathsf{aux}')$.

Theorem 5 (Non-trivial predicate). *For every $T = T(\lambda), T' = T'(\lambda)$, assuming the (T', T)-index hiding property of SE commitments, ϕ is a (T', T)-non-trivial predicate for the protocol Π_T.*

5.4   FS-Compatibility for Bounded-Space Protocol

Theorem 6 (FS-Compatibility w.r.t. Predicate ϕ). *Let C be a somewhere extractable commitment (Definition 3) with security parameter λ whose extraction algorithm $\mathsf{Extract}$ has depth d_{Extract} and size B_{Extract}. Suppose that Π_{BNP} is a k-mode $(B_{\mathsf{BNP}}, b_{\mathsf{BNP}}, d_{\mathsf{BNP}})$-FS-compatible batch NP argument with respect to C and ϕ_{BNP} for some $B_{\mathsf{BNP}}, b_{\mathsf{BNP}}, d_{\mathsf{BNP}}, k$ that are all functions of λ.*

Then for any $T = T(\lambda) \geq \lambda$ and $k = k(\lambda)$, Π (Fig. 4) is a T-mode (B, b, d)-FS-compatible argument (Definition 8) with respect to the predicate ϕ, where

$$B = \log_k T \cdot B_{\mathsf{Extract}} + B_{\mathsf{BNP}}, \quad b = b_{\mathsf{BNP}}, \quad d = \log_k T \cdot d_{\mathsf{Extract}} + d_{\mathsf{BNP}}.$$

Furthermore, Π has both communication complexity and verifier complexity $|\Pi_{k^\gamma}.\mathsf{V}| = (kS + |y|) \cdot (\lambda \cdot \log(kS + |y|))^{O(\gamma)}$ and prover complexity $\mathsf{poly}(k^\gamma)$ for a fixed polynomial $\mathsf{poly}(\cdot)$.

Corollary 1. *Assuming the subexponential hardness of QR and subexponential hardness of DDH, there exists a SNARG for any time-T space-S deterministic computation with $\left(T^{\frac{c}{\sqrt{\log\log\log T}}} \cdot (S + n)\right)$ verifier runtime and communication complexity, as well as $\mathsf{poly}(T, S)$ prover runtime, where n denotes the size of the input, and c is a constant > 0.*

6   FS-Compatible Arguments for Non-deterministic Bounded Space

We now describe our interactive arguments for $\mathsf{NTISP}(T(n), S(n))$, which is the class of all languages recognizable by non-deterministic Turing Machines in time $T(n)$ and space $S(n)$. Such a Turing Machine allows each step of the computation to non-deterministically transition to a new state. Thus, in a sense, this corresponds to the setting where each bit of the witness is read at most once[7]. An alternative way to describe this class is as the class of languages L with a corresponding witness relation R_L, recognizable by a deterministic Turing Machines with access to an input tape and a read-only, read-once witness tape, in addition to a work tape where only $O(S(n))$ space is used, and that runs in $O(T(n))$ time.

First, we introduce some notation and provide some background on NTISP computations. The following subsection closely mirrors [3].

6.1   Background

Fix any $L \in \mathsf{NTISP}(T(n), S(n))$. Denote by $\mathcal{R}_L$ its corresponding NP relation, and denote by $M = M_L$ a $T(n)$-time $S(n)$-space (non-deterministic) Turing machine for deciding L. M can alternately be defined as a two-input Turing machine, that takes as input a pair (x, w) and outputs 1 if and only if $(x, w) \in \mathcal{R}_L$.

Corresponding Layered Circuit $C_{n,m}^M$. Any such Turing machine M can be converted into a layered circuit, denoted by $C_{n,m}^M$, which takes as input a pair (x, w), where $n = |x|$ and $|w| = m = m(n)$ (where $m(n)$ is an upper bound on the length of a witness corresponding to a length n instance), and outputs 1 if and only if $M(x, w) = 1$. Moreover, $C_{n,m}^M$ is a layered circuit, with $W = O(S(n))$ denoting the maximum of the number of gates and number of wires in each layer, and depth $D = O(T(n))$, such that an incoming wire to a gate in layer $i + 1$ is either an input wire (i.e. a wire that reads the input), a witness wire (i.e. a wire that is attached to a trivial witness gate with fan-in and fan-out 1 whose output equals its input, and whose input wire reads the witness), or the output wire of a gate in layer i. Moreover, any witness gate has fan-out 1 (this corresponds to read-once access to the witness tape), and any layer of the circuit reads at most one (unique) bit from the witness tape. In addition, there is a deterministic Turing machine M' of space $O(\log T)$ that on input n outputs the (description of the) circuit $C_{n,m}^M$.

6.2   Interactive Arguments for Bounded Space Non-deterministic Computation

For any $\ell \geq 1$, we construct an interactive argument that proves correctness of wire assignments to layered circuits $\mathsf{Ckt}_{n,m}$ where $n = |x|$ and $m = |w|$ that are of the form described above (i.e. corresponding to computations of a Turing Machine M). We will assume that $\mathsf{Ckt}_{n,m}$ has depth $D = k^\ell$ and width W, and describe an interactive argument in terms of an interactive argument for $k^{\ell-1}$-depth, W-width circuits. We will prove in subsequent sections that this protocol is FS-compatible.

---

[7] If a non-deterministic Turing Machine wishes to remember what non-deterministic choices it made, it has to write them down to its work tape.

- Let $\Pi_0 = (\mathsf{Setup}, \mathsf{P}, \mathsf{V})$ denote a trivial protocol for unit-depth circuits where the prover sends a dummy message followed by a dummy verifier message, and the verifier given a circuit $\mathsf{Ckt}_{n,1}$ with a single layer, instance x s.t. $|x| = n$ and states s_0, s_1, outputs 1 iff $s_1 = \mathsf{Ckt}_{n,1}(x, 0, s_0, 1)$ or $s_1 = \mathsf{Ckt}_{n,1}(x, 1, s_0, 1)$. $\mathsf{Setup}(1^\lambda)$ outputs $(\perp, \perp)$.
- Let $\Pi_{k^{\ell-1}} = (\mathsf{Setup}, \mathsf{P}, \mathsf{V})$ be a ρ-round public-coin protocol for $(k^{\ell-1})$-time computations with ℓ-length prover messages whose verifier $\mathsf{V} = (\mathsf{V}_1, \ldots, \mathsf{V}_\rho)$ where $r^{(i)} \leftarrow \mathsf{V}_i(1^\lambda, |x|)$ for $i \in [\rho - 1]$ and $\{0, 1\} \leftarrow \mathsf{V}_\rho(x, \tau)$.
- Let $\mathcal{C} = (\mathsf{Gen}, \mathsf{Com}, \mathsf{Open}, \mathsf{Verify}, \mathsf{Extract})$ be an SE commitment satisfying Definition 3.
- Let Π_{BNP} be a batch NP protocol for circuit satisfiability.

For any $D \in \mathbb{N}$, consider language $\mathcal{L}_D$ defined by the NP relation $\mathcal{R}_{\mathcal{L}_D}$ where $\mathcal{R}_{\mathcal{L}_D}(x, w) = 1$ iff $x = (M', n, s^n, s^D, y)$ where M' outputs a description of a circuit Ckt such that s^n is a set of wire assignments to the intermediate and input wires in the nth layer of the circuit, y and w respectively define assignments to all input and witness wires in the circuit, and s^D is a set of consistent wire assignments to intermediate and input wires of the circuit at layer $D + n$.

Our argument is identical to the one in Fig. 4, except for the following (syntactic) changes to the inputs of both players, and to the initial processing.

Inputs. The common input for P and V is an instance $x = (M', s_0, s_T, y)$ of the language $\mathcal{L}_{k^\ell}$. P also obtains a witness ω, such that $(x, \omega) \in \mathcal{R}_{\mathcal{L}_D}$.

Initial Processing.

- P sends $s = (s_0, \ldots, s_k)$ for $\{s_i \triangleq \mathsf{Ckt}(y, \omega, s_0, iD/k)\}_{i \in [k]}$ to V.
- P and V define instances $(x_1, \ldots, x_k)$ where $\{x_i \triangleq (M', \frac{(i-1)D}{k}, s_{i-1}, s_i, y)\}_{i \in [k]}$ of the language $\mathcal{L}_{k^{\ell-1}}$.
- P partitions ω into witnesses $\omega_1, \ldots, \omega_k$ where for all $i \in [k]$, ω_i is used to generate assignments to witness wires in layers $\frac{(i-1)D}{k}$ through $\frac{iD}{k}$.

6.3   Non-trivial Predicate

Let $\Pi_T = (\mathsf{Setup}, \mathsf{P}, \mathsf{V})$ be the protocol defined by Fig. 4, where $D = k^\gamma$, and with modifications from the previous section. The predicate ϕ equals ϕ_γ, where ϕ_ℓ is defined recursively for every x, α, aux and $\ell \in [\gamma]$.

- $\phi_0(x, \alpha, \mathsf{aux}) = 1 \iff x \notin \mathcal{L}^{(0)}$.
- $\phi_\ell(x, \alpha, \mathsf{aux})$ for $\ell \in [1, \gamma]$: Parse $\mathsf{aux} = (\mathsf{aux}', ek, (i_1, \ldots, i_\ell))$ and parse $\alpha = ((s_0, \ldots, s_k), C^{(1)})$. Define instances $(x'_1, \ldots, x'_k)$ as in Fig. 4, where $x'_j = (\mathcal{M}, s_{j-1}, s_j, y)$ for $j \in [k]$. Finally, set $\phi_\ell(x, \alpha, \mathsf{aux}) = (x'_{i_\ell} \notin \mathcal{L}_{k^{\ell-1}}) \wedge \phi_{\ell-1}(x'_{i_\ell}, \mathcal{C}.\mathsf{Extract}(ek, C^{(1)}), \mathsf{aux}')$.

Theorem 7 (Non-trivial predicate). *Assuming the $(T \cdot 2^S, T)$-index hiding property of SE commitments, ϕ is a $(T \cdot 2^S, T)$-non-trivial predicate for the protocol Π_T where $T = k^\gamma$.*

The proof of this theorem builds on [3] and appears in the full version.

6.4   FS-Compatibility W.r.t. Predicate Φ

Theorem 8 (FS-Compatibility w.r.t. Predicate ϕ). *Let $\mathcal{C}$ be a somewhere extractable commitment (Definition 3) whose extraction circuit has depth d_{Extract} and size B_{Extract}. Let Π_{BNP} be a k-mode ρ-round $(B_{\mathsf{BNP}}, b_{\mathsf{BNP}}, d_{\mathsf{BNP}})$-FS-compatible batch NP with respect to $\mathcal{C}$, for some $B_{\mathsf{BNP}}, b_{\mathsf{BNP}}, d_{\mathsf{BNP}}, k$ (all functions of λ).*

Then for any $T = T(\lambda) \geq \lambda$ and $k = k(\lambda)$, Π defined above is a T-mode (B, b, d)-FS-compatible argument (Definition 8) with respect to the predicate ϕ defined above, where $B = \log_k T \cdot B_{\mathsf{Extract}} + B_{\mathsf{BNP}}$, $b = b_{\mathsf{BNP}}$, $d = \log_k T \cdot d_{\mathsf{Extract}} + d_{\mathsf{BNP}}$.

Furthermore, Π has communication complexity and verifier runtime $|\Pi_{k^\gamma}.\mathsf{V}| = (kS + |y|) \cdot (\lambda \cdot \log(kS + |y|))^{O(\gamma)}$ and prover runtime $\mathsf{poly}(T)$ given the witness, for a fixed polynomial $\mathsf{poly}(\cdot)$.

The proof of this theorem follows identically to that of Theorem 6. In particular, the proofs of completeness, round-by-round soundness, FS-compatibility and efficiency follow identically to that of Theorem 6. We obtain the following corollaries of this theorem.

Corollary 2. *Assuming the $(T \cdot 2^S, T)$-hardness of QR, for any time-T space-S non-deterministic computation, there is a T-mode (B, b, d)-FS-compatible argument (Definition 8) w.r.t. a $(T \cdot 2^S, T)$ non-trivial predicate ϕ, where each verifier message is of size λ (which also denotes the security parameter), and where verifier runtime and communication complexity are bounded by $T^{\frac{c}{\sqrt{\log\log\log T}}} \cdot (S + |y|)$, c is a constant > 0, $|y|$ denotes the size of the input and where $\lambda = T^{\frac{1}{\log\log\log T}}$, where $B = T^{\frac{c}{\sqrt{\log\log\log T}}}, b = \mathsf{poly}(\lambda), d = O(\sqrt{\log\log\log T})$.*

Proof. We set λ such that $\lambda^\gamma = k$, this implies that $T = \lambda^{\gamma^2}$, and $\log T = \gamma^2 \log \lambda$. We also set $\gamma^2 = \log\log\log T$, This implies that $\lambda = T^{\frac{1}{\gamma^2}} = T^{\frac{1}{\log\log\log T}}$, and $\log T < \log^2 \lambda$. Substituting, this implies that there is a constant $c > 0$ such that

$$|\Pi_T.\mathsf{V}| \leq (kS + |y|) \cdot (k^c)$$

which implies that there is a constant $c > 0$ such that

$$|\Pi_T.\mathsf{V}| \leq T^{\frac{c}{\sqrt{\log\log\log T}}} \cdot (S + |y|)$$

Finally, we note that $\lambda = T^{\frac{1}{\log\log\log T}}$, which completes our proof.

The following Corollary follows from Corollary 2, Theorem 3 and Theorem 1, where we set the security parameter $\lambda = \max(S^{1/\epsilon}, T^{\frac{1}{\log\log\log T}})$, where ϵ is the smaller of the subexponential parameters for QR/DDH hardness. Then, $(2^{\lambda^\epsilon}, 2^{\lambda^\epsilon})$-hardness of QR implies the conditions of the corollary above. In addition, $(2^{\lambda^\epsilon}, 2^{\lambda^\epsilon})$-hardness of DDH implies the conditions of Theorem 1.

Corollary 3. *Assuming the subexponential hardness of QR and subexponential hardness of DDH, there exists a SNARG for any time-T space-S nondeterministic computation with verifier runtime and communication complexity $T^{\frac{c}{\sqrt{\log\log\log T}}} \cdot (S + n)$ and prover runtime $\mathsf{poly}(T, S)$ given the witness, where n denotes the size of the input, and c is a constant > 0.*

We also obtain the following corollary about improved SNARGs for Batch NTISP, which follows from the observation that if $L \in \mathsf{NTISP}(T, S)$, then $L^{\otimes k} \in \mathsf{NTISP}(kT, S)$, where $L^{\otimes k}$ is the language containing k instances of L. This is because we can verify the k different instances by verifying each one individually in time T, and reusing the same workspace for every instance.

Corollary 4. *For every $L \in \mathsf{NTISP}(T, S)$ and every $k \geq S$, assuming the subexponential hardness of QR and DDH, there exists a SNARG for $L^{\otimes k}$ where verifier runtime and communication complexity are bounded by $(kT)^{\frac{c}{\sqrt{\log\log\log kT}}} \cdot (S + n)$ and prover runtime is $\mathsf{poly}(k, T, S)$ given the NP witnesses where n denotes the size of the claimed (potentially succinctly described) instance of $L^{\otimes k}$, and $c > 0$ is a constant.*

6.5   SNARGs for P and Beyond

Given the SNARG for batch-NTISP above, we can use methods from [37] to build a SNARG for any language decidable in deterministic time T (and in fact, any language that has a no-signaling PCP, just as in [37]). We instantiate what is essentially their approach with different parameters, specifically, while they obtain $\mathsf{polylog}(T)$ overhead from sub-exponential LWE, we obtain $T^{o(1)}$ overhead from sub-exponential DDH and QR. Thus, we have:

Corollary 5. *Let $\mathcal{L}$ be a language and $T = T(n)$ be a function such that $\mathsf{poly}(n) \leq T(n) \leq \exp(n)$ and $\mathcal{L} \in \mathsf{DTIME}(T)$. Then assuming the subexponential hardness of QR and DDH, there exists a SNARG for $\mathcal{L}$ with prover time $\mathsf{poly}(T)$, verifier time $n \cdot \mathsf{poly}\left(T^{o(1)}\right)$, and communication complexity $n \cdot \mathsf{poly}\left(T^{o(1)}\right)$.*

References

1. Ananth, P., Chen, Y.-C., Chung, K.-M., Lin, H., Lin, W.-K.: Delegating RAM computations with adaptive soundness and privacy. In: Hirt, M., Smith, A. (eds.) TCC 2016. LNCS, vol. 9986, pp. 3–30. Springer, Heidelberg (2016). https://doi.org/10.1007/978-3-662-53644-5_1
2. Badrinarayanan, S., Fernando, R., Jain, A., Khurana, D., Sahai, A.: Statistical ZAP arguments. In: Canteaut, A., Ishai, Y. (eds.) EUROCRYPT 2020. LNCS, vol. 12107, pp. 642–667. Springer, Cham (2020). https://doi.org/10.1007/978-3-030-45727-3_22
3. Badrinarayanan, S., Kalai, Y.T., Khurana, D., Sahai, A., Wichs, D.: Succinct delegation for low-space non-deterministic computation. In: STOC, pp. 709–721 (2018)
4. Barak, B.: How to go beyond the black-box simulation barrier. In: FOCS, pp. 106–115 (2001)

5. Bartusek, J., Bronfman, L., Holmgren, J., Ma, F., Rothblum, R.D.: On the (in)security of Kilian-based SNARGs. In: Hofheinz, D., Rosen, A. (eds.) TCC 2019. LNCS, vol. 11892, pp. 522–551. Springer, Cham (2019). https://doi.org/10.1007/978-3-030-36033-7_20

6. Bellare, M., Rogaway, P.: Random oracles are practical: a paradigm for designing efficient protocols. In: Denning, D.E., Pyle, R., Ganesan, R., Sandhu, R.S., Ashby, V. (eds.) ACM Conference on Computer and Communications Security, pp. 62–73. ACM (1993)

7. Bitansky, N., et al.: The hunting of the SNARK. IACR Cryptol. ePrint Arch. **2014**, 580 (2014). http://eprint.iacr.org/2014/580

8. Bitansky, N., Canetti, R., Chiesa, A., Tromer, E.: Recursive composition and bootstrapping for SNARKS and proof-carrying data. In: STOC, pp. 111–120 (2013)

9. Bitansky, N., Chiesa, A., Ishai, Y., Paneth, O., Ostrovsky, R.: Succinct non-interactive arguments via linear interactive proofs. In: Sahai, A. (ed.) TCC 2013. LNCS, vol. 7785, pp. 315–333. Springer, Heidelberg (2013). https://doi.org/10.1007/978-3-642-36594-2_18, http://dx.doi.org/10.1007/978-3-642-36594-2_18

10. Bitansky, N., Garg, S., Lin, H., Pass, R., Telang, S.: Succinct randomized encodings and their applications. IACR Cryptology ePrint Archive **2015**, 356 (2015)

11. Bitansky, N., Kalai, Y.T., Paneth, O.: Multi-collision resistance: a paradigm for keyless hash functions. In: Diakonikolas, I., Kempe, D., Henzinger, M. (eds.) STOC, pp. 671–684. ACM (2018)

12. Brakerski, Z., Holmgren, J., Kalai, Y.T.: Non-interactive delegation and batch NP verification from standard computational assumptions. In: STOC, pp. 474–482 (2017)

13. Brakerski, Z., Kalai, Y.: Witness indistinguishability for any single-round argument with applications to access control. In: Kiayias, A., Kohlweiss, M., Wallden, P., Zikas, V. (eds.) PKC 2020. LNCS, vol. 12111, pp. 97–123. Springer, Cham (2020). https://doi.org/10.1007/978-3-030-45388-6_4

14. Brakerski, Z., Koppula, V., Mour, T.: NIZK from LPN and trapdoor hash via correlation intractability for approximable relations. In: Micciancio, D., Ristenpart, T. (eds.) CRYPTO 2020. LNCS, vol. 12172, pp. 738–767. Springer, Cham (2020). https://doi.org/10.1007/978-3-030-56877-1_26

15. Canetti, R., et al.: Fiat-Shamir: from practice to theory. In: Charikar, M., Cohen, E. (eds.) STOC, pp. 1082–1090. ACM (2019)

16. Canetti, R., Goldreich, O., Halevi, S.: The random oracle methodology, revisited. J. ACM **51**(4), 557–594 (2004)

17. Canetti, R., Holmgren, J.: Fully succinct garbled RAM. In: ITCS, pp. 169–178. ACM (2016)

18. Canetti, R., Holmgren, J., Jain, A., Vaikuntanathan, V.: Succinct garbling and indistinguishability obfuscation for RAM programs. In: STOC, pp. 429–437. ACM (2015)

19. Chen, Y., Chow, S.S.M., Chung, K., Lai, R.W.F., Lin, W., Zhou, H.: Cryptography for parallel RAM from indistinguishability obfuscation. In: ITCS, pp. 179–190. ACM (2016)

20. Choudhuri, A.R., Jain, A., Jin, Z.: Non-interactive batch arguments for NP from standard assumptions. IACR Cryptol. ePrint Arch. **2021**, 807 (2021). https://eprint.iacr.org/2021/807

21. Choudhuri, A.R., Jain, A., Jin, Z.: Snargs for P from LWE. IACR Cryptol. ePrint Arch, p. 808 (2021). https://eprint.iacr.org/2021/808

22. Damgård, I., Faust, S., Hazay, C.: Secure two-party computation with low communication. In: Theory of Cryptography–9th Theory of Cryptography Conference, TCC 2012, Taormina, Sicily, Italy, 19–21 March 2012. Proceedings, pp. 54–74 (2012). https://doi.org/10.1007/978-3-642-28914-9_4, http://dx.doi.org/10.1007/978-3-642-28914-9_4

23. Gennaro, R., Gentry, C., Parno, B., Raykova, M.: Quadratic span programs and succinct NIZKs without PCPs. In: Johansson, T., Nguyen, P.Q. (eds.) EUROCRYPT 2013. LNCS, vol. 7881, pp. 626–645. Springer, Heidelberg (2013). https://doi.org/10.1007/978-3-642-38348-9_37, http://dx.doi.org/10.1007/978-3-642-38348-9_37

24. Gentry, C., Wichs, D.: Separating succinct non-interactive arguments from all falsifiable assumptions. In: STOC, pp. 99–108 (2011)

25. Goldwasser, S., Kalai, Y.T.: On the (in)security of the fiat-shamir paradigm. In: FOCS, p. 102 (2003)

26. Goldwasser, S., Kalai, Y.T., Rothblum, G.N.: Delegating computation: interactive proofs for muggles. J. ACM **62**(4), 27 (2015)

27. González, A., Zacharakis, A.: Fully-succinct publicly verifiable delegation from constant-size assumptions. In: Nissim, K., Waters, B. (eds.) TCC 2021. LNCS, vol. 13042, pp. 529–557. Springer, Cham (2021). https://doi.org/10.1007/978-3-030-90459-3_18

28. Goyal, V., Jain, A., Jin, Z., Malavolta, G.: Statistical zaps and new oblivious transfer protocols. In: Canteaut, A., Ishai, Y. (eds.) EUROCRYPT 2020. LNCS, vol. 12107, pp. 668–699. Springer, Cham (2020). https://doi.org/10.1007/978-3-030-45727-3_23

29. Groth, J.: Short pairing-based non-interactive zero-knowledge arguments. In: Abe, M. (ed.) ASIACRYPT 2010. LNCS, vol. 6477, pp. 321–340. Springer, Heidelberg (2010). https://doi.org/10.1007/978-3-642-17373-8_19

30. Hubáček, P., Wichs, D.: On the communication complexity of secure function evaluation with long output. In: Roughgarden, T. (ed.) Proceedings of the 2015 Conference on Innovations in Theoretical Computer Science, ITCS 2015, Rehovot, Israel, 11–13 January 2015, pp. 163–172. ACM (2015). https://doi.org/10.1145/2688073.2688105

31. Jain, A., Jin, Z.: Non-interactive zero knowledge from sub-exponential DDH. In: Canteaut, A., Standaert, F.-X. (eds.) EUROCRYPT 2021. LNCS, vol. 12696, pp. 3–32. Springer, Cham (2021). https://doi.org/10.1007/978-3-030-77870-5_1

32. Jawale, R., Kalai, Y.T., Khurana, D., Zhang, R.: SNARGs for bounded depth computations and PPAD hardness from sub-exponential LWE. In: Khuller, S., Williams, V.V. (eds.) STOC 2021: 53rd Annual ACM SIGACT Symposium on Theory of Computing, Virtual Event, Italy, 21–25 June 2021, pp. 708–721. ACM (2021). https://doi.org/10.1145/3406325.3451055

33. Kalai, Y.T., Paneth, O.: Delegating RAM computations. In: Theory of Cryptography - 14th International Conference, TCC 2016-B, Beijing, China, 31 October–3 November 2016, Proceedings, Part II, pp. 91–118 (2016). https://doi.org/10.1007/978-3-662-53644-5_4

34. Kalai, Y.T., Paneth, O., Yang, L.: How to delegate computations publicly. In: Charikar, M., Cohen, E. (eds.) Proceedings of the 51st Annual ACM SIGACT Symposium on Theory of Computing, STOC 2019, Phoenix, AZ, USA, 23–26 June 2019, pp. 1115–1124. ACM (2019). https://doi.org/10.1145/3313276.3316411

35. Kalai, Y.T., Raz, R., Rothblum, R.D.: Delegation for bounded space. In: Symposium on Theory of Computing Conference, STOC 2013, Palo Alto, CA, USA, 1–4 June 2013, pp. 565–574 (2013). https://doi.org/10.1145/2488608.2488679

36. Kalai, Y.T., Raz, R., Rothblum, R.D.: How to delegate computations: the power of no-signaling proofs. In: STOC, pp. 485–494. ACM (2014)

37. Kalai, Y.T., Vaikuntanathan, V., Zhang, R.Y.: Somewhere statistical soundness, post-quantum security, and snargs. Cryptology ePrint Archive, Report 2021/788 (2021). https://ia.cr/2021/788

38. Kilian, J.: A note on efficient zero-knowledge proofs and arguments (extended abstract). In: Proceedings of the 24th Annual ACM Symposium on Theory of Computing, pp. 723–732. ACM (1992)

39. Koppula, V., Lewko, A.B., Waters, B.: Indistinguishability obfuscation for turing machines with unbounded memory. In: STOC, pp. 419–428. ACM (2015)

40. Lipmaa, H.: Progression-free sets and sublinear pairing-based non-interactive zero-knowledge arguments. In: Cramer, R. (ed.) TCC 2012. LNCS, vol. 7194, pp. 169–189. Springer, Heidelberg (2012). https://doi.org/10.1007/978-3-642-28914-9_10

41. Lombardi, A., Vaikuntanathan, V., Wichs, D.: Statistical ZAPR arguments from bilinear maps. In: Canteaut, A., Ishai, Y. (eds.) EUROCRYPT 2020. LNCS, vol. 12107, pp. 620–641. Springer, Cham (2020). https://doi.org/10.1007/978-3-030-45727-3_21

42. Micali, S.: CS proofs (extended abstracts). In: 35th Annual Symposium on Foundations of Computer Science, Santa Fe, New Mexico, USA, 20–22 November 1994, pp. 436–453 (1994). full version in [?]. https://doi.org/10.1109/SFCS.1994.365746, http://dx.doi.org/10.1109/SFCS.1994.365746

43. Paneth, O., Rothblum, G.N.: On zero-testable homomorphic encryption and publicly verifiable non-interactive arguments. In: Kalai, Y., Reyzin, L. (eds.) TCC 2017. LNCS, vol. 10678, pp. 283–315. Springer, Cham (2017). https://doi.org/10.1007/978-3-319-70503-3_9

44. Parno, B., Raykova, M., Vaikuntanathan, V.: How to delegate and verify in public: verifiable computation from attribute-based encryption. In: Cramer, R. (ed.) TCC 2012. LNCS, vol. 7194, pp. 422–439. Springer, Heidelberg (2012). https://doi.org/10.1007/978-3-642-28914-9_24

45. Peikert, C., Shiehian, S.: Noninteractive zero knowledge for NP from (plain) learning with errors. In: Boldyreva, A., Micciancio, D. (eds.) CRYPTO 2019. LNCS, vol. 11692, pp. 89–114. Springer, Cham (2019). https://doi.org/10.1007/978-3-030-26948-7_4

46. Pointcheval, D., Stern, J.: Security proofs for signature schemes. In: Maurer, U. (ed.) EUROCRYPT 1996. LNCS, vol. 1070, pp. 387–398. Springer, Heidelberg (1996). https://doi.org/10.1007/3-540-68339-9_33

47. Reingold, O., Rothblum, G.N., Rothblum, R.D.: Constant-round interactive proofs for delegating computation. In: Proceedings of the 48th Annual ACM SIGACT Symposium on Theory of Computing, STOC 2016, Cambridge, MA, USA, 18–21 June 2016, pp. 49–62 (2016). https://doi.org/10.1145/2897518.2897652, http://doi.acm.org/10.1145/2897518.2897652

Cryptographic Primitives

Optimal Tightness for Chain-Based Unique Signatures

Fuchun Guo$^{(\boxtimes)}$ and Willy Susilo

Institute of Cybersecurity and Cryptology (iC^2),
School of Computing and Information Technology,
University of Wollongong, Wollongong, NSW, Australia
{fuchun,wsusilo}@uow.edu.au

Abstract. Unique signatures are digital signatures with exactly one unique and valid signature for each message. The security reduction for most unique signatures has a natural reduction loss (in the existentially unforgeable against chosen-message attacks, namely EUF-CMA, security model under a non-interactive hardness assumption). In Crypto 2017, Guo *et al.* proposed a particular chain-based unique signature scheme where each unique signature is composed of n BLS signatures computed sequentially like a blockchain. Under the computational Diffie-Hellman assumption, their reduction loss is $n \cdot q_H^{1/n}$ for q_H hash queries and it is logarithmically tight when $n = \log q_H$. However, it is currently unknown whether a better reduction than logarithmical tightness for the chain-based unique signatures exists.

We show that the proposed chain-based unique signature scheme by Guo *et al.* must have the reduction loss $q^{1/n}$ for q signature queries when each unique signature consists of n BLS signatures. We use a meta reduction to prove this lower bound in the EUF-CMA security model under any non-interactive hardness assumption, and the meta-reduction is also applicable in the random oracle model. We also give a security reduction with reduction loss $4 \cdot q^{1/n}$ for the chain-based unique signature scheme (in the EUF-CMA security model under the CDH assumption). This improves significantly on previous reduction loss $n \cdot q_H^{1/n}$ that is logarithmically tight at most. The core of our reduction idea is a *non-uniform* simulation that is specially invented for the chain-based unique signature construction.

Keywords: Unique signatures · Optimal reduction

1 Introduction

A digital signature scheme is a unique signature scheme if there exists a unique and valid signature for each message [5,16,34]. That is, for any message, we cannot find two different signatures that are both valid for that message. Unique signatures prohibit the use of randomness in the signature generation.

It is non-trivial to construct a digital signature scheme that is *tightly secure* in the existentially unforgeable against chosen-message attacks (EUF-CMA)

© International Association for Cryptologic Research 2022
O. Dunkelman and S. Dziembowski (Eds.): EUROCRYPT 2022, LNCS 13276, pp. 553–583, 2022.
https://doi.org/10.1007/978-3-031-07085-3_19

security model under a non-interactive hardness assumption. Intensive research such as [1,3,4,6–10,13,14,17–19,24–28,32,33,36–39,42,43,48,49] have been conducted in this security model or the more advanced multi-user setting model. Most methods must employ randomness in signature generations and are therefore not suitable for unique signatures.

It looks "paradoxical" when proving tight security for a unique signature scheme (in the EUF-CMA model under a non-interactive hardness assumption). Taking the BLS (unique) signature by Boneh *et al.* [11] as an example: upon receiving the public key (g, g^α), the adversary might first query messages to random oracle to know $H(m_1), H(m_2), \cdots, H(m_q)$. For each signature $H(m_i)^\alpha, i \in [1, q]$, it must be either simulatable (the signature is signable by the simulator) or reducible (the signature is unsignable and problem solution can be extracted from the signature) and it cannot be switched. After receiving the public key and all responses to hash queries, the adversary first picks $q - 1$ random messages out of q for their signature queries, and forges the signature on the remaining message. It has been proved in [5,16,34] that the probability of successfully reduction for BLS-like unique signatures is at most $1/q$.

So far, the only known tight security method for unique signature[1] was proposed by Guo *et al.* [27] in Crypto 2017. They constructed a chain-based unique signature scheme (see Subsect. 1.2), where BLS signatures are generated, hashed into messages, and then signed again like a blockchain. Each unique signature has n BLS signatures as block signatures. With this signature structure, they can program the reduction tightly because the simulator will already solve the hard problem before each unique signature is "committed" into simulatable or reducible. In their tight reduction, the adversary must generate and make a special hash query that carries the CDH (Computational Diffie-Hellman) problem solution to the random oracle with probability at least $1/(n \cdot q_H^{1/n})$ if the adversary can successfully forge a signature after making q_H hash queries. This chain-based method was later adopted to construct tightly secure and short unique signatures from RSA signatures by Shacham in [51].

Even though our community has rich methods of tight reduction for digital signatures and other primitives such as the recent results for key exchange [15,25, 31,35], the only tightness method applicable to unique signatures is the chain-based construction[2]. However, it is currently unknown whether there exists a better reduction than [27] for the chain-based unique signatures.

1.1   Our Contributions

In this paper, we analyze the optimal tightness of reductions for the chain-based unique signature scheme in [27] and then propose a reduction with optimal tightness for this scheme.

---

[1] In 2012, Kakvi and Kiltz [37] introduced a conceptual level RSA-FDH scheme with unique signatures and a tight security reduction.

[2] We meant reductions against general adversaries. It is worth noting that BLS-like unique signatures can be proved tight security in the Algebraic Group Model [22] when adversaries are restricted in algebraic operations.

We show that any reduction proof for the chain-based unique signature scheme must have a reduction loss of at least $q^{1/n}$ for q signature queries if each unique signature has n BLS block signatures. This optimal analysis is also applicable in the random oracle model and is proved via meta-reduction under any non-interactive computationally hardness assumption in the EUF-CMA security model. The given optimal analysis indicates that it is necessary to generate a chain-based unique signature having $n = \log(q)$ block signatures in order to obtain tight security. The chain-based unique signature scheme is actually the BLS scheme when $n = 1$ and our corresponding result is in line with the negative results in [5,16,34].

We propose a completely different security reduction for the chain-based BLS scheme in length n with optimal tightness. The core of our reduction idea is a non-uniform programming that perfectly suits the chain-based construction. Our reduction loss is at most $4 \cdot q^{1/n}$ for q signature queries under the CDH assumption in the EUF-CMA security model (using random oracles). This improves significantly on previous $n \cdot q_H^{1/n}$ in [27], because the previous result is logarithmically tight only when $n = \log q_H$ while ours is fully tight when $n = \log q$. Our fully tight reduction does not require to increase the length of signatures (depending on n) because $q \leq q_H$ is always true. In particular, the signatures in our reduction have the same size as in [27] when $q \approx q_H$, and are much shorter than [27] when $q << q_H$ such as $q = 2^{30}$ and $q_H = 2^{100}$.

Our results are also applicable to the Shacham's tightly secure and short RSA unique signatures [51]. Our optimal analysis is general and also applicable to this unique signature scheme. The reduction loss is reduced from logarithmically large to constant, and the computational efficiency is improved because of the decrease of length n when $q << q_H$. The details will be given in the full version.

1.2 Technical Idea

We first review the chain-based BLS scheme proposed in [27] as follows.

KeyGen: Let $(\mathbb{G}, \mathbb{G}_T, p, e, g)$ be a bilinear pairing. The key generation algorithm chooses a random integer $\alpha \in \mathbb{Z}_p$ and a cryptographic hash function $H : \{0,1\}^* \to \mathbb{G}$ that will be viewed as a random oracle in the security proof. It computes $h = g^\alpha$ and chooses an integer n as the scheme parameter. The public key pk is $(\mathbb{G}, \mathbb{G}_T, p, e, g, H, h, n)$, and the secret key sk is α.

Sign: The signing algorithm takes as input a message $m \in \{0,1\}^*$ and the key pair (pk, sk). It computes the signature $\Sigma_m = (\sigma_1, \sigma_2, \cdots, \sigma_n)$ on m as

$$(\sigma_1, \sigma_2, \sigma_3, \cdots, \sigma_n) = \left(H(m|\Sigma_m^0)^\alpha, \ H(m|\Sigma_m^1)^\alpha, \ H(m|\Sigma_m^2)^\alpha, \cdots, H(m|\Sigma_m^{n-1})^\alpha \right),$$

where σ_i for all $i \in [1, n]$ is called block signature, $\Sigma_m^0 = (\ )$, and $\Sigma_m^i = (\sigma_1, \sigma_2, \cdots, \sigma_i)$. The final signature Σ_m on m is Σ_m^n.

> *Note: To be able to distinguish messages and signatures, we must include the symbols " |" and brackets "()" as part of hash inputs. In particular, $m|\Sigma_m^0 = m|(\ )$.*
>
> Verify: The verification algorithm takes as input the public key pk, a message m, and its signature $\Sigma_m = (\sigma_1, \sigma_2, \cdots, \sigma_n)$. It accepts the signature if
>
> $$e\left(\sigma_{i+1}, g\right) = e\left(H(m|\Sigma_m^i), h\right) : \text{ for all } i \in [0, n-1].$$

In the security reduction for the chain-based BLS signature in the random oracle model, a hash query $x = m|\Sigma_m^i$ to H is called type-i query of m . To forge a valid signature on m^*, the adversary must make the type-0 query of m^*, compute $\Sigma_{m^*}^1$, make the type-1 query of m^*, compute $\Sigma_{m^*}^2$ and so on until make the type-$(n-1)$ query of m^*, and compute $\Sigma_{m^*}^n$ as the forged signature.

The chain-based construction enables the simulator to solve the CDH problem with the adversary's hash queries. Given a problem instance (g, g^a, g^b), if $g^\alpha = g^a$ and the type-i query of m is responded with $H(m|\Sigma_m^i) = g^b$, the type-$(i+1)$ query of m generated and made by the adversary contains $\sigma_{i+1} = H(m|\Sigma_m^i)^\alpha = g^{ab}$ that is the solution to the CDH problem. It is worth noting that the hash query used to solve the hard problem does not have to be the query of m^* but can be the query of any message generated by the adversary.

OPTIMAL ANALYSIS OF THE CHAIN-BASED BLS SCHEME. We prove that any security reduction $\mathcal{R}$ for the chain-based BLS scheme in the EUF-CMA security model under any non-interactive computationally hard assumption must be bounded with success probability $1/q^{\frac{1}{n}}$. Otherwise, we construct a meta-reduction $\mathcal{B}$ to break this hardness assumption by following the meta-reduction framework given by Coron in [16], which is described as follows.

- We construct a special hypothetical adversary that can break the chain-based BLS scheme with probability $\epsilon_\mathcal{A}$. When interacting with such a hypothetical adversary, $\mathcal{R}$ would break the hardness assumption with probability $\epsilon_\mathcal{R}$.
- We simulate this hypothetical adversary via rewinding $\mathcal{R}$. When interacting with the simulated adversary, if we can efficiently simulate the hypothetical adversary except with error probability ϵ_E, $\mathcal{R}$ would break the hardness assumption with probability $\epsilon_\mathcal{R} - \epsilon_E$.
- The meta-reduction therefore shows that $\epsilon_\mathcal{R}$ must be not larger than ϵ_E. Otherwise, we can run $\mathcal{R}$ as an oracle to break the hardness assumption.

Based on the Coron's framework, our optimal analysis is to show how a hypothetical adversary will possibly attack and how to simulate this hypothetical adversary successfully except with error probability $\epsilon_E = \epsilon_\mathcal{A}/q^{\frac{1}{n}}$.

The Hypothetical Adversary. A hypothetical adversary might make hash queries and signature queries in the sequence $\mathcal{T}_0(\mathcal{M}_0) \rightarrow \mathcal{S}(\mathcal{M}_0 \setminus \mathcal{M}_1) \rightarrow \mathcal{T}_1(\mathcal{M}_1) \rightarrow \mathcal{S}(\mathcal{M}_1 \setminus \mathcal{M}_2) \rightarrow \cdots \rightarrow \mathcal{S}(\mathcal{M}_{n-1} \setminus \mathcal{M}_n) \rightarrow \mathcal{T}_n(\mathcal{M}_n)$ as long as $\mathcal{R}$ does not fail in responding to queries. The queries are explained as follows.

- $\mathcal{M}_0, \mathcal{M}_1, \cdots, \mathcal{M}_n$ are $n+1$ message sets satisfying that the subset relationship $\mathcal{M}_0 \supset \mathcal{M}_1 \supset \mathcal{M}_1 \supset \mathcal{M}_2 \supset \cdots \supset \mathcal{M}_n$ holds and the set $\mathcal{M}_i$ has $q^{1-\frac{i}{n}}$ messages (we simply treat $q^{\frac{1}{n}}$ as an integer). All messages in the these message sets are randomly chosen by the adversary. In particular, we have $|\mathcal{M}_0| = q$ and $|\mathcal{M}_n| = 1$. We define $\mathcal{M}_i \setminus \mathcal{M}_{i+1}$ to be the set of messages in $\mathcal{M}_i$ but not in $\mathcal{M}_{i+1}$.
- $\mathcal{T}_i(\mathcal{M}_i)$ is the set of type-i queries of all messages in $\mathcal{M}_i$.
- $\mathcal{S}(\mathcal{M}_i \setminus \mathcal{M}_{i+1})$ is the set of signature queries on all messages in $\mathcal{M}_i \setminus \mathcal{M}_{i+1}$.

That is, the (computationally unbounded) adversary first generates type-0 queries of all messages in $\mathcal{M}_0$ and submits all of them to the random oracle. Upon receiving all responses to hash queries, the adversary makes the signature queries on all messages in $\mathcal{M}_0 \setminus \mathcal{M}_1$. If $\mathcal{R}$ aborts, the adversary stops. Otherwise, the adversary generates type-1 queries of all messages in $\mathcal{M}_1$ and repeats the above queries and computations until $\mathcal{T}_n(\mathcal{M}_n)$. Suppose $m^* \in \mathcal{M}_n$. After $\mathcal{T}_n(\mathcal{M}_n)$, the adversary has already generated the type-n query of m^*, namely $m^*|\Sigma_{m^*}^n$. The type-n query implies the signature on m^*. Therefore, at the end of the above query sequence, the adversary can easily return $\Sigma_{m^*} = \Sigma_{m^*}^n$ as the forged signature on a new message m^* whose signature was not queried.

The Simulated Adversary. It is easy to simulate the hash queries $\mathcal{T}_0(\mathcal{M}_0)$ because all hash queries are type-0 queries (namely $m|()$ for $m \in \mathcal{M}_0$) and composed of messages only. The challenge of simulating the hypothetical adversary is to generate and make hash queries $\mathcal{T}_i(\mathcal{M}_i)$ for all $i \in [1, n]$ because the type-i query of m ($m|\Sigma_m^i$) contains block signatures $\Sigma_m^i = (\sigma_1, \sigma_2, \cdots, \sigma_i)$ that cannot be efficiently simulated without knowing the secret key.

We simulate the hypothetical adversary with a rewinding argument. Different from the original meta-reduction in [16], we need to rewind at most n times in order to successfully simulate the hypothetical adversary. The rewinding works as follows from $i = 1$ to $i = n$.

$$
\begin{array}{ccccccc}
& \text{1-st rewind} & & \text{2-nd rewind} & & \text{n-th rewind} & \\
& \nearrow \mathcal{S}(\mathcal{M}_1) & & \nearrow \mathcal{S}(\mathcal{M}_2) & & \nearrow \mathcal{S}(\mathcal{M}_n) & \\
\mathcal{T}_0(\mathcal{M}_0) \to & \mathcal{S}(\mathcal{M}_0 \setminus \mathcal{M}_1) \to \mathcal{T}_1(\mathcal{M}_1) \to & & \mathcal{S}(\mathcal{M}_1 \setminus \mathcal{M}_2) \to \cdots \to & & \mathcal{S}(\mathcal{M}_{n-1} \setminus \mathcal{M}_n) \to \mathcal{T}_n(\mathcal{M}_n)
\end{array}
$$

- Before the i-th time rewind, we first make signature queries $\mathcal{S}(\mathcal{M}_i)$ to $\mathcal{R}$ to obtain signatures $\Sigma_{\mathcal{M}_i} = \{\Sigma_m^n : m \in \mathcal{M}_i\}$.
- Then we rewind $\mathcal{R}$ (the i-th time rewind) to the state it was after the hash queries $\mathcal{T}_{i-1}(\mathcal{M}_{i-1})$. This time, we make signature queries $\mathcal{S}(\mathcal{M}_{i-1} \setminus \mathcal{M}_i)$. We can continue the simulation of making hash queries $\mathcal{T}_i(\mathcal{M}_i) = \{m|\Sigma_m^i : m \in \mathcal{M}_i\}$ with the help of $\Sigma_{\mathcal{M}_i}$ if $\mathcal{R}$ does not abort before the rewind.

The Error Probability. If $\mathcal{R}$ does not abort, the simulated adversary must continue to complete the queries $\mathcal{T}_0(\mathcal{M}_0) \to \mathcal{S}(\mathcal{M}_0 \setminus \mathcal{M}_1) \to \mathcal{T}_1(\mathcal{M}_1) \to \mathcal{S}(\mathcal{M}_1 \setminus \mathcal{M}_2) \to \cdots \to \mathcal{S}(\mathcal{M}_{n-1} \setminus \mathcal{M}_n) \to \mathcal{T}_n(\mathcal{M}_n)$. We note that if $\mathcal{R}$ cannot respond to one of signature queries in this query sequence, the simulation on the hypothetical adversary is still successful because the reduction is aborted by $\mathcal{R}$. We claim that the error happens when there exists an integer $i^\# \in [1, n]$ such that

- $\mathcal{R}$ cannot respond to queries $\mathcal{S}(\mathcal{M}_{i\#})$ before the $i^\#$-th time rewind, but
- $\mathcal{R}$ can respond to queries $\mathcal{S}(\mathcal{M}_{i\#-1} \setminus \mathcal{M}_{i\#})$ after the $i^\#$-th time rewind.

The simulation on the hypothetical adversary fails because the simulated adversary must continue to make the type-$i^\#$ queries $\mathcal{T}_{i\#}(\mathcal{M}_{i\#})$, but the simulated adversary does not have $\Sigma_{\mathcal{M}_{i\#}}$ to simulate these type-$i^\#$ queries.

Let $\mathcal{S}(\mathcal{M}) = 1$ denote that $\mathcal{R}$ can simulate all signature queries on $\mathcal{M}$ and $\mathcal{S}(\mathcal{M}) = 0$ denote the opposite case. When the hypothetical adversary attacks the scheme, no matter what $i \in [1, n]$ is, we have

$$\frac{|\mathcal{M}_i|}{|\mathcal{M}_{i-1}|} = \frac{q^{1-\frac{i}{n}}}{q^{1-\frac{i-1}{n}}} = \frac{1}{q^{\frac{1}{n}}}.$$

Then the error probability will be the same no matter what $i^\# \in [1, n]$ is during the reduction.

Taking $i^\# = 1$ as the example. After the type-0 queries of all messages in $\mathcal{M}_0$ namely $\mathcal{T}_0(\mathcal{M}_0)$, it means that $\mathcal{R}$ cannot compute $H(m|\Sigma_m^0)^\alpha$ for some $m \in \mathcal{M}_0$, while $\mathcal{R}$ can respond to signature queries $\mathcal{S}(\mathcal{M}_0 \setminus \mathcal{M}_1)$ meaning that $m \notin \mathcal{M}_0 \setminus \mathcal{M}_1$. Since the message set $\mathcal{M}_1$ is randomly chosen, we prove that

$$\Pr\left[\mathcal{S}(\mathcal{M}_0 \setminus \mathcal{M}_1) = 1 \middle| \mathcal{S}(\mathcal{M}_0) = 0, \frac{|\mathcal{M}_1|}{|\mathcal{M}_0|} = \frac{1}{q^{\frac{1}{n}}}\right] \leq \frac{1}{q^{\frac{1}{n}}}.$$

The above probability is in line with [5,16,34] when $\mathcal{M}_1$ has one message only. Our case needs to consider multiple messages in $\mathcal{M}_1$.

With the above analysis, we shall prove that the error probability of simulating the hypothetical adversary is at most $\epsilon_\mathcal{A}/q^{\frac{1}{n}}$. This completes the intuitive observation of our optimal analysis.

OPTIMAL TIGHTNESS OF THE CHAIN-BASED BLS SCHEME. The security of the chain-based BLS scheme is based on the CDH hard assumption where it is hard to compute $g^{\hat{a}\hat{b}}$ from $(g, g^{\hat{a}}, g^{\hat{b}})$. In the proof, the simulator sets $\alpha = \hat{a}$ and controls the random oracle. How to respond to each hash query in the random oracle model is the core for obtaining a tight reduction.

Classifications of Hash Queries. All hash queries to the random oracle will be classified into two types called **Normal Query** and **Challenge Query** according to the ways of response by the simulator.

- **Normal Query.** A hash query x is called a normal query if the simulator sets $H(x) = g^z$ in response where $z \in \mathbb{Z}_p$ is randomly chosen by the simulator for the query x. Then $H(x)^\alpha = (g^{\hat{a}})^z$ is computable by the simulator.
- **Challenge Query.** A hash query x is called a challenge query if the simulator sets $H(x) = g^{\hat{b}+z}$ in response, where $z \in \mathbb{Z}_p$ is randomly chosen by the simulator for the query x. Then $H(x)^\alpha = g^{\hat{a}\hat{b}+\hat{a}z}$ and the CDH problem solution $g^{\hat{a}\hat{b}}$ can be extracted from $H(x)^\alpha$ by computing $H(x)^\alpha/(g^{\hat{a}})^z$.

Most importantly, suppose that the type-i query of m, namely $m|\Sigma_m^i$, is set as the challenge query and the adversary makes the type-$(i+1)$ query of m, denoted by $m|\Sigma_m^{i+1}$. We have that $\Sigma_m^{i+1} = (\sigma_1, \sigma_2, \cdots, \sigma_{i+1})$ and the block signature $\sigma_{i+1} = H(m|\Sigma_m^i)^\alpha = g^{\hat{a}\hat{b}+\hat{a}z}$ carries the CDH problem solution.

The Idea in [27]. Let q_H be the number of hash queries. The authors proved that no matter how the adversary adaptively makes hash queries and signature queries in the EUF-CMA security model, there exists an integer $i^* \in [0, n-1]$ such that

- The number of type-i^* queries is not more than $(q_H)^{1-\frac{i^*}{n}}$.
- The number of type-(i^*+1) queries is larger than $(q_H)^{1-\frac{i^*+1}{n}}$.

The integer i^* is dependent on how the adversary adaptively makes hash queries.

In [27], the simulator randomly picks an integer $c^* \in [0, n-1]$ and an integer $l^* \in [1, (q_H)^{1-\frac{c^*}{n}}]$. Then the simulator will set the l^*-th new type-c^* query (of any message m) generated and made by the adversary as the challenge query. When $c^* = i^*$, their proof result guarantees that the adversary will generate and make the type-(c^*+1) query of the same message m with probability

$$\frac{(q_H)^{1-\frac{i^*+1}{n}}}{(q_H)^{1-\frac{i^*}{n}}} = \frac{1}{(q_H)^{\frac{1}{n}}}.$$

Therefore, their reduction loss is $n \cdot (q_H)^{1/n}$ for the chain-based BLS scheme. The features of this logarithmically tight reduction are summarized as follows.

- **Single Challenge.** Only one of q_H hash queries is set as the challenge query. All other hash queries are set as normal queries by the simulator.
- **Uniform Choice.** The simulator will set one type-c^* query as the challenge query, and $c^* \in [0, n-1]$ is uniformly chosen to capture the success probability $\Pr[c^* = i^*] = \frac{1}{n}$ for any adaptive i^* decided by the adversary.
- **Static Setting.** In this reduction, the integers c^* and l^* are chosen by the simulator before the start of hash queries. Which hash query will be set as the challenge query is therefore static.

Our Main Idea. The Single-Uniform-Static approach in [27] (same as in [51]) is based on a natural rule of queries from the adversary. We invent a completely new approach called Multiple-Non-Uniform-Dynamic approach. This approach will allow the simulator to control the simulation such that the probability of success reduction will be increased when the adversary makes more hash queries.

- **Multiple Challenges.** For every message m, the simulator will choose an independent integer $c_m \in [0, n-1]$ and set the type-c_m query of m, denoted by $m|\Sigma_m^{c_m}$, as a challenge query. Then, the type-(c_m+1) query of m carries the problem solution. The integer c_m for m will be chosen when the adversary makes the type-0 query of m. The number of challenge queries is therefore multiple and depends on how many messages are involved in all hash queries.

- **Non-Uniform Choice.** We choose $c_m \in [0, n-1]$ in a non-uniform way. That is, c_m is not uniformly distributed in $[0, n-1]$. In our formal reduction description, we give a general approach of choosing c_m for any scheme parameter n. Here we give a specific choice for $n = \log(q)$ and set

$$\Pr[c_m = i] = \frac{2^i}{2 \cdot 2^n} = \frac{1}{2 \cdot 2^{n-i}}.$$

  That is, for each message m, the challenge query will be set at its type-0 query with probability $1/2^{n+1}$, at its type-1 query with probability $2/2^{n+1}$, and at its type-i query with probability $2^i/2^{n+1}$. It is not hard to achieve this non-uniformity[3].
- **Dynamic Setting.** Generally speaking, the adversary makes type-0 query, type-1 query, and so on until type-k_i query of m_i before signature query on m_i for an adaptive integer $k_i \in [0, n-1]$. If $k_i < c_{m_i}$, it means that no hash query of m_i has yet been set as a challenge query by the simulator. To enable signature simulation, upon receiving the signature query on m_i, the simulator will change $c_{m_i} = \infty$ such that all hash queries of m_i will be set as normal queries and the signature on m_i is computable by the simulator.

This completes the description of our approach. We define that the adversary adaptively chooses $k_i \in [0, n-1]$ and makes type-0 query, type-1 query, and so on until type-k_i query of m_i, denoted by $\mathcal{H}^{k_i}(m_i) = \{m_i|\Sigma_{m_i}^0, m_i|\Sigma_{m_i}^1, \cdots, m_i|\Sigma_{m_i}^{k_i}\}$, before the signature query on m_i, denoted by $\mathcal{S}(m_i)$. We define that the adversary will query the signatures on messages $(m_1, m_2, \cdots, m_q)$ before forging the signature on m^*. According to the setting, we have:

- If $c_{m_i} < k_i$, the simulator can solve the hard problem with type-$(c_{m_i} + 1)$ query of m_i from the adversary according to the truth of $c_{m_i} + 1 \leq k_i$ and the setting of multiple challenges.
- If $c_{m_i} = k_i$, namely the type-k_i query of m_i is set as the challenge query, the simulator has to abort.
- If $c_{m_i} > k_i$, the simulator can simulate the signature according to the dynamic setting.

We cannot directly analyze how the simulator solves the CDH problem because it depends on the adversary's adaptive choice of k_i and the simulator's setting parameter c_{m_i}. What we do instead is to prove **the lower bound of probability of successful reduction.** We are going to prove that

$$\frac{1}{4} \approx \Pr[\mathcal{Q}_{2,0}^*] \leq \Pr[\mathcal{Q}_{2,1}^*] \leq \Pr[\mathcal{Q}_{2,2}^*] \leq \cdots \leq \Pr[\mathcal{Q}_{2,q}^*] \leq \Pr[\mathcal{Q}_{\mathcal{A}}^*],$$

where $\mathcal{Q}^*$ is the query sequence (mixture of hash queries and/or signature queries) made by the adversary $\mathcal{A}$, $\Pr[\mathcal{Q}^*]$ is the success probability of reduction under the query sequence $\mathcal{Q}^*$, $\mathcal{Q}_{\mathcal{A}}^*$ is the real query sequence launched by the adversary during attacks, and all query sequences are defined in Table 1.

---

[3] To implement such a non-uniform choice, we firstly randomly choose an integer $w \in [1, 2^{n+1}]$. Then we find the integer i satisfying $2^i \leq w < 2^{i+1}$ and set $c_m = i$. It is not hard to verify that $\Pr[w \leftarrow_R [1, 2^{n+1}] : 2^i \leq w < 2^{i+1}] = 2^i/2^{n+1} = \Pr[c_m = i]$.

Table 1. The defined query sequences. $\mathcal{H}^{k_1}(m_1) \to \mathcal{S}(m_1)$ means that the adversary will query $\mathcal{H}^{k_1}(m_1)$ first and then query $\mathcal{S}(m_1)$. The differences between two neighbor queries have been highlighted in the same color and $\mathcal{H}^{k_i}(m_i) = \{m_i | \Sigma_{m_i}^0, m_i | \Sigma_{m_i}^1, \cdots, m_i | \Sigma_{m_i}^{k_i}\}$. If the adversary can forge and return the signature $\Sigma_{m^*} = \Sigma_{m^*}^n$ on m^*, it implies that the adversary is able to generate and make hash queries $\mathcal{H}^n(m^*) = \{m^* | \Sigma_{m^*}^0, m^* | \Sigma_{m^*}^1, \cdots, m^* | \Sigma_{m^*}^n\}$.

$\mathcal{Q}_{2,0}^*:$	$\mathcal{H}^0(m_1) \to \mathcal{S}(m_1) \to \mathcal{H}^0(m_2) \to \mathcal{S}(m_2) \to \cdots \to \mathcal{H}^0(m_q) \to \mathcal{S}(m_q) \to \mathcal{H}^n(m^*)$
$\mathcal{Q}_{2,1}^*:$	$\mathcal{H}^{k_1}(m_1) \to \mathcal{S}(m_1) \to \mathcal{H}^0(m_2) \to \mathcal{S}(m_2) \to \cdots \to \mathcal{H}^0(m_q) \to \mathcal{S}(m_q) \to \mathcal{H}^n(m^*)$
$\mathcal{Q}_{2,2}^*:$	$\mathcal{H}^{k_1}(m_1) \to \mathcal{S}(m_1) \to \mathcal{H}^{k_2}(m_2) \to \mathcal{S}(m_2) \to \cdots \to \mathcal{H}^0(m_q) \to \mathcal{S}(m_q) \to \mathcal{H}^n(m^*)$
$\vdots$	
$\mathcal{Q}_{2,q-1}^*:$	$\mathcal{H}^{k_1}(m_1) \to \mathcal{S}(m_1) \to \mathcal{H}^{k_2}(m_2) \to \mathcal{S}(m_2) \to \cdots \to \mathcal{H}^0(m_q) \to \mathcal{S}(m_q) \to \mathcal{H}^n(m^*)$
$\mathcal{Q}_{2,q}^*:$	$\mathcal{H}^{k_1}(m_1) \to \mathcal{S}(m_1) \to \mathcal{H}^{k_2}(m_2) \to \mathcal{S}(m_2) \to \cdots \to \mathcal{H}^{k_q}(m_q) \to \mathcal{S}(m_q) \to \mathcal{H}^n(m^*)$
$\mathcal{Q}_{\mathcal{A}}^*:$	Real query sequence includes $\mathcal{H}^{k_1}(m_1), \mathcal{H}^{k_2}(m_2), \cdots, \mathcal{H}^{k_q}(m_q), \mathcal{H}^n(m^*)$

Now we prove the above inequalities of probabilities step by step.

♠(Step 1) Suppose the adversary can forge a signature without signature queries and the adversary's query sequence is denoted by $\mathcal{Q}_1^* = \mathcal{H}^n(m^*)$. According to the non-uniform parameter $c_{m^*} \in [0, n-1]$ satisfying $\Pr[c_{m^*} = i] = \frac{1}{2 \cdot 2^{n-i}}$ and the adversary will make the type-0 query, the type-1 query and so on until the type-n query of m^*, we immediately have

$$\Pr[\mathcal{Q}_1^*] = \Pr[c_{m^*} \leq n-1] = \sum_{i=0}^{n-1} \Pr[c_{m^*} = i] = \frac{1}{2 \cdot 2^n} + \frac{1}{2 \cdot 2^{n-1}} + \cdots + \frac{1}{2 \cdot 2} = \frac{1}{2} - \frac{1}{2^{n+1}}.$$

♠(Step 2.0) Suppose the adversary's query sequence during attacks is denoted by $\mathcal{Q}_{2,0}^* = \mathcal{H}^0(m_1) \to \mathcal{S}(m_1) \to \mathcal{H}^0(m_2) \to \cdots \to \mathcal{H}^0(m_q) \to \mathcal{S}(m_q) \to \mathcal{H}^n(m^*)$. That is, the adversary only makes the type-0 query of m_i before its signature query for all $i \in [1, q]$.

For each signature query $\mathcal{S}(m_i)$, the simulator aborts if only if the type-0 query of m_i is set as a challenge query and the probability is $\Pr[c_{m_i} = 0] = \frac{1}{2 \cdot 2^n}$. We have $n = \log(q)$. Therefore, the simulator does not abort after q signature queries with probability $(1 - \frac{1}{2^{n+1}})^q = (1 - \frac{1}{2q})^q \geq (1 - \frac{1}{2})^1 = \frac{1}{2}$. Then the simulator will solve the hard problem from $\mathcal{Q}_1^*$ with probability $\Pr[\mathcal{Q}_1^*] \approx \frac{1}{2}$. We therefore approximately obtain $\Pr[\mathcal{Q}_{2,0}^*] \geq \frac{1}{4}$.

♣(Step 2.i) We prove that $\Pr[\mathcal{Q}_{2,i-1}^*] \leq \Pr[\mathcal{Q}_{2,i}^*]$ hold for all $i \in [1, q]$ because of the non-uniform choice c_{m_i} in the programming.

We have the comparison of $\mathcal{Q}_{2,i-1}^*$ and $\mathcal{Q}_{2,i}^*$ as follows.

$$\mathcal{H}^{k_1}(m_1) \to \mathcal{S}(m_1) \to \cdots \to \mathcal{S}(m_{i-1}) \Big\langle \begin{array}{l} \mathcal{H}^0(m_i) \to \mathcal{S}(m_i) \to \mathcal{Q}_{2,[>i]}^* : \mathcal{Q}_{2,i-1}^* \\ \mathcal{H}^{k_i}(m_i) \to \mathcal{S}(m_i) \to \mathcal{Q}_{2,[>i]}^* : \mathcal{Q}_{2,i}^* \end{array}$$

where $\mathcal{Q}_{2,[>i]}^* = \mathcal{H}^0(m_{i+1}) \to \mathcal{S}(m_{i+1}) \to \cdots \to \mathcal{H}^0(m_q) \to \mathcal{S}(m_q) \to \mathcal{H}^n(m^*)$.
Since the two query sequences have the identical sub-sequence before $\mathcal{S}(m_{i-1})$,
we have that the following inequality

$$\Pr[\mathcal{H}^0(m_i) \to \mathcal{S}(m_i) \to \mathcal{Q}_{2,[>i]}^*] \leq \Pr[\mathcal{H}^{k_i}(m_i) \to \mathcal{S}(m_i) \to \mathcal{Q}_{2,[>i]}^*]$$

implies that $\Pr[\mathcal{Q}_{2,i-1}^*] \leq \Pr[\mathcal{Q}_{2,i}^*]$.

Next we prove the correctness of the above inequality. In both query
sequences $\mathcal{H}^0(m_i) \to \mathcal{S}(m_i) \to \mathcal{Q}_{2,[>i]}^*$ and $\mathcal{H}^{k_i}(m_i) \to \mathcal{S}(m_i) \to \mathcal{Q}_{2,[>i]}^*$, the
simulator will either (1) solve hard problem from hash queries of m_i or (2) solve
hard problem from $\mathcal{Q}_{2,[>i]}^*$ when the simulator neither succeeds nor aborts after
$\mathcal{S}(m_i)$. Let $S_i^{(k_i)}$ be the event that the problem solution appears in $\mathcal{H}^{k_i}(m_i)$ of
m_i for integer k_i, and $F_i^{(k_i)}$ be the corresponding event that the simulator fails
in responding to $\mathcal{S}(m_i)$. We have

$$\Pr[\mathcal{H}^0(m_i) \to \mathcal{S}(m_i) \to \mathcal{Q}_{2,[>i]}^*] = \Pr[S_i^{(0)}] + \left(1 - \Pr[S_i^{(0)}] - \Pr[F_i^{(0)}]\right)\Pr[\mathcal{Q}_{2,[>i]}^*]$$

$$\Pr[\mathcal{H}^{k_i}(m_i) \to \mathcal{S}(m_i) \to \mathcal{Q}_{2,[>i]}^*] = \Pr[S_i^{(k_i)}] + \left(1 - \Pr[S_i^{(k_i)}] - \Pr[F_i^{(k_i)}]\right)\Pr[\mathcal{Q}_{2,[>i]}^*]$$

We have the following equations and a positive value X according to the non-
uniform setting $\Pr[c_m = i] = \frac{1}{2 \cdot 2^{n-i}}$.

$$\Pr[S_i^{(k_i)}] - \Pr[S_i^{(0)}] = \Pr[c_{m_i} < k_i] - \Pr[c_{m_i} < 0]$$
$$= \Pr[c_{m_i} = 0] + \Pr[c_{m_i} = 1] + \cdots + \Pr[c_{m_i} = k_i - 1] - 0$$
$$= \frac{1}{2}\left(\frac{1}{2^{n-k_i}} - \frac{1}{2^n}\right) = X,$$
$$\Pr[F_i^{(k_i)}] - \Pr[F_i^{(0)}] = \Pr[c_{m_i} = k_i] - \Pr[c_{m_i} = 0]$$
$$= \frac{1}{2}\left(\frac{1}{2^{n-k_i}} - \frac{1}{2^n}\right) = X.$$

We further have $\Pr[\mathcal{Q}_{2,[>i]}^*] \leq \Pr[\mathcal{Q}_1^*] \leq \frac{1}{2}$ for any $i \in [1, q]$ because signature
queries in $\mathcal{Q}_{2,[>i]}^*$ will decrease the success probability of reduction compared to
no signature query in $\mathcal{Q}_1^*$. We therefore obtain

$$\Pr[\mathcal{H}^{k_i}(m_i) \to \mathcal{S}(m_i) \to \mathcal{Q}_{2,[>i]}^*] - \Pr[\mathcal{H}^0(m_i) \to \mathcal{S}(m_i) \to \mathcal{Q}_{2,[>i]}^*]$$
$$= \Pr[S_i^{(k_i)}] + \left(1 - \Pr[S_i^{(k_i)}] - \Pr[F_i^{(k_i)}]\right)\Pr[\mathcal{Q}_{2,[>i]}^*]$$
$$- \left(\Pr[S_i^{(0)}] + \left(1 - \Pr[S_i^{(0)}] - \Pr[F_i^{(0)}]\right)\Pr[\mathcal{Q}_{2,[>i]}^*]\right)$$
$$= X - 2X \cdot \Pr[\mathcal{Q}_{2,[>i]}^*]$$
$$\geq X - 2X \cdot \frac{1}{2}$$
$$= 0.$$

♣(Step *Final*) We have $\Pr[\mathcal{Q}_{2,q}^*] \leq \Pr[\mathcal{Q}_{\mathcal{A}}^*]$. In comparison with $\mathcal{Q}_{2,q}^*$, the query
sequence $\mathcal{Q}_{\mathcal{A}}^*$ allows the adversary to (1) generate and make hash queries of any

message $m \notin \{m_1, m_2, \cdots, m_q, m^*\}$ without signature query on m, and to (2) make hash queries without following the sequence $\mathcal{Q}^*_{2,q}$, where the adversary could make hash queries of m_i before $\mathcal{S}(m_{i-1})$.

All hash queries will be responded by the simulator without abort. Making hash queries of additional messages without signature queries on them will not increase the failure probability of simulation. In our simulation, a hash query associated with m_i is responded according to the parameter c_{m_i}, which is chosen independently for each message. Whether or not the simulator fails in $\mathcal{S}(m_i)$ depends on (k_i, c_{m_i}) and is not related to when the adversary made hash queries of m_i. We therefore have $\Pr[\mathcal{Q}^*_{2,q}] \leq \Pr[\mathcal{Q}^*_{\mathcal{A}}]$.

This completes the high-level intuition of our reduction with success probability $\frac{1}{4}$ for the chain-based BLS scheme in the EUF-CMA security model under the CDH assumption, no matter what (the polynomial number) q is as long as we have $n = \log q$.

1.3 Impossibility of Reductions

Many excellent research results in the literature have focused on disproving the equivalence between constructed schemes and underlying hardness assumptions.

The impossibility of efficient reduction includes the result [12] that inverting low-exponent RSA may not be equivalent to factoring, the result [47] that breaking ElGamal like discrete-log-based signatures may not be equivalent to discrete log, and the result [41] that breaking some HIBE or ABE system cannot be efficiently reduced to breaking a non-interactive hardness assumption.

The impossibility of reduction better than optimal tightness was first studied by Coron in [16] by introducing the meta-reduction technique. So far, the analysis of optimal tightness has been studied for many primitives including any "simple" reduction for unique signatures or re-randomizable signatures in [5,16,34,44], for specific schemes (like Schnorr-type signatures) in [20,21,23,47,50], for encryption in [5,29], for signatures from identification in [40], for non-interactive key-exchange in [5,15,30], for MACs and PRFs in [45], and the recent result for verifiable random functions in [46].

2 Definitions

Definition 1 (Digital Signatures). *A digital signature scheme consists of the following three algorithms and fulfills correctness.*

KeyGen(1^κ). *The key generation algorithm takes as input a security parameter κ and returns a key pair denoted by (pk, sk).*

Sign(pk, sk, m). *The signing algorithm takes as input (pk, sk) and a message m to be signed. It returns a signature on m denoted by Σ_m.*

Verify(pk, Σ_m, m). *The verification algorithm takes as input pk and a signed message (m, Σ_m). It returns true or false.*

The correctness requires that for any key pair (pk, sk), any message m from message space, and its signature Σ_m, we have $\Pr[\mathsf{Verify}(pk, \Sigma_m, m) = \mathsf{true}] = 1$.

Definition 2 (Unique Signatures [5]). *Let* (KeyGen, Sign, Verify) *be a signature scheme and* $\Sigma(pk, m)$ *be the set of valid signatures on* m *under* pk*, defined as* $\Sigma(pk, m) = \{\Sigma_m : \mathsf{Verify}(pk, \Sigma_m, m) = \mathsf{true}\}$*. We say that* (KeyGen, Sign, Verify) *is a unique signature scheme if* $|\Sigma(pk, m)| = 1$ *for all* pk *and* m*.*

We stress that deterministic signatures (such as [38]) and unique signatures are different. In deterministic signatures, the signature on m generated by the signer is unique. In unique signatures, the signature on m that can pass the verification is unique, which implies that the generated signature must be also unique. That is, a deterministic signature scheme may not be a unique signature scheme, while a unique signature scheme must be a deterministic scheme.

Definition 3 (EUF-CMA Security Model). *The existentially unforgeable against chosen-message attacks (EUF-CMA) security model is defined as follows.*

- **Setup:** *The challenger takes as input security parameter* κ *and generates a key pair* (pk, sk)*. The public key is given to the adversary.*
- **Query:** *The adversary adaptively chooses any message* m *for its signature query. The challenger runs the signing algorithm and sends the output signature* Σ_m *to the adversary.*
- **Forgery:** *The adversary outputs a forged signature* Σ_{m^*} *on message* m^* *and wins the game if* Σ_{m^*} *is valid and no signature query was made on* m^**.*

A digital signature scheme is (t, q, ϵ)*-secure in the EUF-CMA security model if no probabilistic polynomial time adversary can win the game with probability* ϵ *in polynomial time* t *after making at most* q *signature queries, where* ϵ *is a negligible function in* κ*.*

3   Optimal Analysis for the Chain-Based BLS Scheme

We first give a general definition of non-interactive computationally hard assumption that was originally given in [2,5].

Definition 4. *A non-interactive computationally hard assumption, denoted by* (T, V)*, consists of two probabilistic polynomial time algorithms.*

- *Taking as input a security parameter* κ*, the instance generation algorithm* T *outputs a problem instance* ins *and a witness* wit*.*
- *Taking as input* (ins, wit) *and a candidate solution* sol*, the verification algorithm* V *returns* true *or* false*. If* $\mathsf{V}(\mathsf{ins}, \mathsf{wit}, \mathsf{sol}) = \mathsf{true}$*, then we say that* sol *is a valid solution to the problem instance* ins*.*

We say that the assumption (T, V) *is* $(t(\kappa), \epsilon(\kappa))$ *computationally hard if every probabilistic polynomial time algorithm* $\mathcal{B}$ *that stops in* $t(\kappa)$ *polynomial time can only return* sol *to a given instance* ins *with negligible success probability* $\epsilon(\kappa)$*, where the probability is taken over the random coins consumed by* T *and* $\mathcal{B}$*.*

The original definition has been simplified because we focus on computationally hard assumptions instead of general assumptions that include the decisionally hard assumptions.

Our optimal analysis is given below for the chain-based BLS scheme. In comparison with other meta-reductions [5,16,34] in simulating the adversary via rewinding, our meta-reduction proof requires to rewind at most n times in order to simulate the adversary successfully in attacking the chain-based BLS scheme.

Theorem 1. *Let* (T,V) *be a non-interactive computationally hard assumption. Let* $\mathcal{A}$ *be an adversary who can* $(t_{\mathcal{A}}, q, \epsilon_{\mathcal{A}})$-*break the chain-based BLS scheme in the EUF-CMA model. Suppose there exists a reduction* $\mathcal{R}$ *that can* $(t_{\mathcal{A}}, q, \epsilon_{\mathcal{A}}, t_{\mathcal{R}}, \epsilon_{\mathcal{R}})$-*reduce from breaking* (T,V) *assumption to breaking the chain-based BLS scheme by* $\mathcal{A}$. *We can construct an algorithm* $\mathcal{B}$ *that* $(t_{\mathcal{B}}, \epsilon_{\mathcal{B}})$-*breaks* (T,V) *with*

$$t_{\mathcal{B}} \leq O(n \cdot t_{\mathcal{R}}), \quad \epsilon_{\mathcal{B}} \geq \epsilon_{\mathcal{R}} - \frac{\epsilon_{\mathcal{A}}}{q^{\frac{1}{n}}}.$$

Proof. We first describe a potentially hypothetical and inefficient adversary $\mathcal{A}$. Then this adversary will be simulated by us (namely we construct a simulated adversary) in order to run $\mathcal{R}$ to break the hardness assumption.

The Hypothetical Adversary. The hypothetical adversary attacks the chain-based BLS scheme in the corresponding EUF-CMA security model as follows.

Setup: Given an instance ins of (T,V), $\mathcal{R}$ generates a public key pk that is given to the hypothetical adversary.

Query: The adversary flips a biased coin with $\Pr[Coin = 1] = \epsilon_{\mathcal{A}}$ and $\Pr[Coin = 0] = 1 - \epsilon_{\mathcal{A}}$. If $Coin = 0$, abort the attack. Otherwise, the adversary picks q random messages denoted by $\mathcal{M}_0 = \{m_1^*, m_2^*, \cdots, m_q^*\}$, where $q - 1$ of them will be randomly picked for signature queries (satisfies the definition of at most q in the EUF-CMA model) and the last one is used for signature forgery. For simplicity, we assume that the adversary runs an inefficient algorithm that computes the secret key sk from the received public key pk and uses it to generate all involved hash queries.

The adversary computes and makes queries as follows.

- Make type-0 queries of all $m \in \mathcal{M}_0$, denoted by $x = m|\Sigma_m^0 = m|(\ )$.
- Upon receiving all responses to type-0 queries of all messages in $\mathcal{M}_0$, randomly pick $q - q^{1-\frac{1}{n}}$ numbers of messages from $\mathcal{M}_0$ for their signature queries. If $\mathcal{R}$ aborts, the adversary stops. Otherwise, let the remaining messages whose signatures are not queried be in $\mathcal{M}_1$. We have

$$|\mathcal{M}_1| = q - (q - q^{1-\frac{1}{n}}) = q^{1-\frac{1}{n}}.$$

- For $i = 1, 2, 3, \cdots, n - 1$, the adversary makes queries as follows.

- Make type-i queries of all $m \in \mathcal{M}_i$, denoted by $x = m | \Sigma_m^i$.
- Upon receiving all responses to type-i queries of all messages, randomly pick $q^{1-\frac{i}{n}} - q^{1-\frac{i+1}{n}}$ numbers of messages from $\mathcal{M}_i$ for their signature queries. If $\mathcal{R}$ aborts, the adversary stops. Otherwise, let the remaining messages whose signatures are not queried be in $\mathcal{M}_{i+1}$.

$$|\mathcal{M}_{i+1}| = q^{1-\frac{i}{n}} - (q^{1-\frac{i}{n}} - q^{1-\frac{i+1}{n}}) = q^{1-\frac{i+1}{n}}.$$

- Make the type-n query of all $m \in \mathcal{M}_n$, denoted by $x = m | \Sigma_m^n$.

Forgery: We have $|\mathcal{M}_n| = q^0 = 1$. Let the type-$n$ query of message m^* be denoted by $m^* | \Sigma_{m^*}^n$. We have $\Sigma_{m^*}^n = \Sigma_{m^*}$ which is the signature on m^*. Notice that there is no signature query on m^*. The adversary outputs Σ_{m^*} as the forged signature on m^* and $\mathcal{R}$ outputs sol as the solution to ins to break the hardness assumption (T, V).

In summary, the hypothetical adversary makes hash queries and signature queries in the following sequence as long as $\mathcal{R}$ does not abort.

$$\mathcal{T}_0(\mathcal{M}_0) \to \mathcal{S}(\mathcal{M}_0 \setminus \mathcal{M}_1) \to \mathcal{T}_1(\mathcal{M}_1) \to \mathcal{S}(\mathcal{M}_1 \setminus \mathcal{M}_2) \to \cdots \to \mathcal{S}(\mathcal{M}_{n-1} \setminus \mathcal{M}_n) \to \mathcal{T}_n(\mathcal{M}_n).$$

- $\mathcal{T}_i(\mathcal{M}_i)$ is the set of type-i queries of all messages in $\mathcal{M}_i$ defined as

$$\left\{ m | \Sigma_m^i : m \in \mathcal{M}_i, \Sigma_m^i = \left(H(m | \Sigma_m^0)^\alpha, H(m | \Sigma_m^1)^\alpha, \cdots, H(m | \Sigma_m^{i-1})^\alpha \right) \right\}.$$

- $\mathcal{S}(\mathcal{M}_i \setminus \mathcal{M}_{i+1})$ is the set of signature queries on all messages in $\mathcal{M}_i \setminus \mathcal{M}_{i+1}$.
- We have $\mathcal{M}_i \subset \mathcal{M}_{i-1}$ and $|\mathcal{M}_i| = q^{1-\frac{i}{n}}$ for all $i \in [1, n]$.

When interacting with such a hypothetical adversary, $\mathcal{R}$ would break the hardness assumption with probability $\epsilon_\mathcal{R}$ according to the definition.

The Simulated Adversary. Given as input an instance ins of (T, V), $\mathcal{R}$ generates a public key pk and gives it to the simulated adversary. The simulated adversary also tosses a biased coin the same as the hypothetical adversary to continue or abort. When $Coin = 1$, the simulated adversary aims to simulate the hypothetical adversary in making queries as follows unless $\mathcal{R}$ aborts.

$$\mathcal{T}_0(\mathcal{M}_0) \to \mathcal{S}(\mathcal{M}_0 \setminus \mathcal{M}_1) \to \mathcal{T}_1(\mathcal{M}_1) \to \mathcal{S}(\mathcal{M}_1 \setminus \mathcal{M}_2) \to \cdots \to \mathcal{S}(\mathcal{M}_{n-1} \setminus \mathcal{M}_n) \to \mathcal{T}_n(\mathcal{M}_n).$$

It is easy to simulate the adversary in computing hash queries in $\mathcal{T}_0(\mathcal{M}_0)$ because all hash queries are plain messages, namely $m | \Sigma_m^0 = m | ()$, without any block signature (BLS signature). The main difficulty of simulating the adversary is to generate and make all hash queries in $\mathcal{T}_i(\mathcal{M}_i)$ for all $i \in [1, n]$. This is because all these hash queries contain block signatures Σ_m^i that cannot be efficiently computed without knowing the secret key α.

We are going to simulate this hypothetical adversary with a rewinding argument. We will be able to successfully simulate the hypothetical adversary after rewinding $\mathcal{R}$ with the help of signature computed by $\mathcal{R}$ before the rewind. More precisely, for all $i \in [1, n]$, we make signature queries $\mathcal{S}(\mathcal{M}_i)$ to $\mathcal{R}$ and then rewind $\mathcal{R}$ once to simulate hash queries $\mathcal{T}_i(\mathcal{M}_i)$. The details are as follows.

---

1. Let the state after the hash queries $\mathcal{T}_0(\mathcal{M}_0)$ be st_0.
2. At the state st_0, we make signature queries on $\mathcal{M}_1$ to $\mathcal{R}$ as follows.

$$\mathcal{T}_0(\mathcal{M}_0) \overset{st_0}{\to} \mathcal{S}(\mathcal{M}_1).$$

If $\mathcal{R}$ does not abort, we will receive signatures $\Sigma_{\mathcal{M}_1}$ on messages in $\mathcal{M}_1$.
3. We rewind $\mathcal{R}$ to the state st_0. This time, we make signature queries on $\mathcal{M}_0 \backslash \mathcal{M}_1$ to $\mathcal{R}$. That is, $\mathcal{T}_0(\mathcal{M}_0) \overset{st_0}{\to} \mathcal{S}(\mathcal{M}_0 \backslash \mathcal{M}_1)$. If $\mathcal{R}$ aborts, we stop the interaction with $\mathcal{R}$ the same as the hypothetical adversary. Otherwise, $\mathcal{R}$ does not abort and we continue type-1 queries

$$\mathcal{T}_0(\mathcal{M}_0) \overset{st_0}{\to} \mathcal{S}(\mathcal{M}_0 \backslash \mathcal{M}_1) \to \mathcal{T}_1(\mathcal{M}_1),$$

where the hash queries $\mathcal{T}_1(\mathcal{M}_1)$ will be simulated with signatures $\Sigma_{\mathcal{M}_1}$ on $\mathcal{M}_1$ received from $\mathcal{R}$ in the step 2.
4. Let the state after the hash queries $\mathcal{T}_1(\mathcal{M}_1)$ be st_1.

When we are at the state st_1 after the hash queries $\mathcal{T}_1(\mathcal{M}_1)$, we can continue the simulation on $\mathcal{T}_2(\mathcal{M}_2)$ in an analogous way for $\mathcal{T}_1(\mathcal{M}_1)$. In general, when we are at the state st_i after the hash queries $\mathcal{T}_i(\mathcal{M}_i)$ for any $i \in [0, n-1]$ and seeing all responses, we continue the simulation on the adversary as follows.

---

1. Let the state after the hash queries $\mathcal{T}_i(\mathcal{M}_i)$ be st_i.
2. At the state st_i, we make signature queries on $\mathcal{M}_{i+1}$ to $\mathcal{R}$ as follows.

$$\mathcal{T}_0(\mathcal{M}_0) \to \cdots \to \mathcal{T}_i(\mathcal{M}_i) \overset{st_i}{\to} \mathcal{S}(\mathcal{M}_{i+1}).$$

If $\mathcal{R}$ does not abort, we will receive signatures $\Sigma_{\mathcal{M}_{i+1}}$ on $\mathcal{M}_{i+1}$.
3. We rewind $\mathcal{R}$ to the state st_i. This time, we make signature queries on $\mathcal{M}_i \backslash \mathcal{M}_{i+1}$ to $\mathcal{R}$. That is, $\mathcal{T}_0(\mathcal{M}_0) \to \cdots \to \mathcal{T}_i(\mathcal{M}_i) \overset{st_i}{\to} \mathcal{S}(\mathcal{M}_i \backslash \mathcal{M}_{i+1})$. If $\mathcal{R}$ aborts, we stop the interaction with $\mathcal{R}$. Otherwise, $\mathcal{R}$ does not abort and we continue type-$(i+1)$ queries

$$\mathcal{T}_0(\mathcal{M}_0) \to \cdots \to \mathcal{T}_i(\mathcal{M}_i) \overset{st_i}{\to} \mathcal{S}(\mathcal{M}_i \backslash \mathcal{M}_{i+1}) \to \mathcal{T}_{i+1}(\mathcal{M}_{i+1}),$$

where the hash queries $\mathcal{T}_{i+1}(\mathcal{M}_{i+1})$ will be simulated with signatures $\Sigma_{\mathcal{M}_{i+1}}$ on $\mathcal{M}_{i+1}$ received from $\mathcal{R}$ in the step 2.

4. Let the state after the hash queries $\mathcal{T}_{i+1}(\mathcal{M}_{i+1})$ be st_{i+1}.

If $\mathcal{R}$ does not abort in responding to signature queries, after the n-th time rewind, we have successfully simulated the adversary who generated and made queries $\mathcal{T}_0(\mathcal{M}_0) \rightarrow \mathcal{S}(\mathcal{M}_0 \setminus \mathcal{M}_1) \rightarrow \mathcal{T}_1(\mathcal{M}_1) \rightarrow \cdots \rightarrow \mathcal{S}(\mathcal{M}_{n-1} \setminus \mathcal{M}_n) \rightarrow \mathcal{T}_n(\mathcal{M}_n)$. This completes the description of how to simulate the hypothetical adversary.

Next we analyze the correctness of simulating $\mathcal{T}_{i+1}(\mathcal{M}_{i+1})$ in step 3 with $\Sigma_{\mathcal{M}_{i+1}}$ from step 2. At the state st_i, when $\mathcal{R}$ does not abort before the rewind (step 2), we have

$$\Sigma_{\mathcal{M}_{i+1}} = \left\{ \left(H(m|\Sigma_m^0)^\alpha, H(m|\Sigma_m^1)^\alpha, \cdots, H(m|\Sigma_m^{n-1})^\alpha \right) : m \in \mathcal{M}_{i+1} \right\}.$$

When $\mathcal{R}$ does not abort after the rewind (step 3), we need Σ_m^{i+1} to simulate all type-$(i+1)$ queries of $m \in \mathcal{M}_{i+1}$:

$$\mathcal{T}_{i+1}(\mathcal{M}_{i+1}) = \left\{ m \middle| \left(H(m|\Sigma_m^0)^\alpha, H(m|\Sigma_m^1)^\alpha, \cdots, H(m|\Sigma_m^i)^\alpha \right) : m \in \mathcal{M}_{i+1} \right\}.$$

At the state st_i it was after $\mathcal{T}_i(\mathcal{M}_i)$, $\mathcal{R}$ should have responded to all type-i queries of messages in $\mathcal{M}_i$. That is, $\alpha, H(m|\Sigma_m^0), \cdots, H(m|\Sigma_m^i)$ for all $m \in \mathcal{M}_{i+1} \subseteq \mathcal{M}_i$ must be identical before the rewind and after the rewind at the state st_i. Then, the unique block signatures $(H(m|\Sigma_m^0)^\alpha, H(m|\Sigma_m^1)^\alpha, \cdots, H(m|\Sigma_m^i)^\alpha)$ in $\Sigma_{\mathcal{M}_{i+1}}$ and in $\mathcal{T}_{i+1}(\mathcal{M}_{i+1})$ must be identical and therefore we can correctly use $\Sigma_{\mathcal{M}_{i+1}}$ to simulate $\mathcal{T}_{i+1}(\mathcal{M}_{i+1})$.

The Error Probability. We fail in simulating the hypothetical adversary if there exists $i^\# \in [1, n]$ such that we need to continue type-$i^\#$ queries $\mathcal{T}_{i^\#}(\mathcal{M}_{i^\#})$ in step 3 but we did not receive signatures $\Sigma_{\mathcal{M}_{i^\#}}$ in step 2 due to the failure of $\mathcal{R}$.

We define $Stop_i, Bad_i$ for all $i \in [1, n]$ to be events as follows.

$$Bad_i : \mathcal{S}(\mathcal{M}_i) = 0 \wedge \mathcal{S}(\mathcal{M}_{i-1} \setminus \mathcal{M}_i) = 1$$
$$Stop_i : \mathcal{S}(\mathcal{M}_{i-1}) = 0$$

- $\mathcal{S}(\mathcal{M}) = 0$ means that $\mathcal{R}$ cannot respond to signature queries $\mathcal{S}(\mathcal{M})$, while $\mathcal{S}(\mathcal{M}) = 1$ means that $\mathcal{R}$ can respond to signature queries $\mathcal{S}(\mathcal{M})$.
- Bad_i refers to the event that we fail in simulating the adversary after the state st_{i-1} and before the state st_i. More precisely, this event occurs when $\mathcal{R}$ cannot respond to signature queries $\mathcal{S}(\mathcal{M}_i)$ in step 2 denoted by $\mathcal{S}(\mathcal{M}_i) = 0$, but $\mathcal{R}$ can respond to signature queries $\mathcal{S}(\mathcal{M}_{i-1} \setminus \mathcal{M}_i)$ in step 3 denoted by $\mathcal{S}(\mathcal{M}_{i-1} \setminus \mathcal{M}_i) = 1$.
- $Stop_i$ refers to the event that the simulation stops after the state st_{i-1} and before the state st_i. It stops either because $\mathcal{R}$ fails or we fail in simulating the adversary.

Let A_i be the event that the simulation first stops due to the event $Stop_i$.

$$A_i = \overline{Stop_1} \wedge \overline{Stop_2} \wedge \cdots \wedge \overline{Stop_{i-1}} \wedge Stop_i, \text{ where } A_1 = Stop_1.$$

Then we fail in simulating the hypothetical adversary with probability $\Pr[Bad]$:

$$\Pr[Bad] = \sum_{i=1}^{n} \Big(\Pr[Bad_i|A_i] \cdot \Pr[A_i] \Big)$$

We deduct $\Pr[Bad] \leq 1/q^{\frac{1}{n}}$ according to the following two results.

- $\Pr[Bad_i|A_i] \leq \frac{1}{q^{\frac{1}{n}}}$ for all $i \in [1, n]$, which is proved in Lemma 1.
- $\sum_{i=1}^{n} \Pr[A_i] \leq 1$, which is proved as follows. We have the following equation

$$\Pr[\overline{Stop_1} \wedge \overline{Stop_2} \wedge \cdots \wedge \overline{Stop_{i-1}} \wedge \overline{Stop_i}] + \Pr[A_i] = \Pr[\overline{Stop_1} \wedge \overline{Stop_2} \wedge \cdots \wedge \overline{Stop_{i-1}}]$$

for all $i \in [1, n]$ by applying the rule $\Pr[B \wedge \overline{C}] + \Pr[B \wedge C] = \Pr[B]$ for any events B and C. With this equation, we have

$$\Pr[\overline{Stop_1} \wedge \overline{Stop_2} \wedge \cdots \wedge \overline{Stop_n}] + \sum_{i=1}^{n} \Pr[A_i] = \Pr[\overline{Stop_1}] + \Pr[A_1] = 1,$$

which implies $\sum_{i=1}^{n} \Pr[A_i] \leq 1$.

Finally, we fail in simulating the adversary when the events $Coin = 1$ and Bad both occur with probability $\epsilon_\mathcal{A} \cdot \Pr[Bad]$. Otherwise, the bad event does not occur. When interacting with this simulated adversary, according to the meta-reduction framework by Coron in [16], $\mathcal{R}$ would break the hardness assumption for us with probability $\epsilon_\mathcal{R} - \frac{\epsilon_\mathcal{A}}{q^{\frac{1}{n}}}$.

This completes the proof of the theorem. $\qquad\qquad\qquad\qquad\qquad\square$

Lemma 1. $\Pr[Bad_i|A_i] \leq \frac{1}{q^{\frac{1}{n}}}$ for all $i \in [1, n]$.

Proof. The event $A_i = \overline{Stop_1} \wedge \overline{Stop_2} \wedge \cdots \wedge \overline{Stop_{i-1}} \wedge Stop_i$ indicates $\mathcal{S}(\mathcal{M}_{i-1}) = 0$ at the state st_{i-1}. Let $\mathcal{M}_{i-1}^s$ be the largest subset of $\mathcal{M}_{i-1}$ such that $\mathcal{S}(\mathcal{M}_{i-1}^s) = 1$, namely $\mathcal{R}$ can simulate all signatures on messages in $\mathcal{M}_{i-1}^s$. We have

$$|\mathcal{M}_{i-1}^s| \leq |\mathcal{M}_{i-1}| - 1 = q^{1-\frac{i-1}{n}} - 1.$$

By putting all above analysis together, we obtain

$$\begin{aligned}
\Pr[Bad_i|A_i] &= \Pr[\mathcal{S}(\mathcal{M}_i) = 0 \wedge \mathcal{S}(\mathcal{M}_{i-1} \setminus \mathcal{M}_i) = 1 \mid \mathcal{S}(\mathcal{M}_{i-1}) = 0] \\
&\leq \Pr[\mathcal{S}(\mathcal{M}_{i-1} \setminus \mathcal{M}_i) = 1 \mid \mathcal{S}(\mathcal{M}_{i-1}) = 0] \\
&= \Pr[(\mathcal{M}_{i-1} \setminus \mathcal{M}_i) \subseteq \mathcal{M}_{i-1}^s]
\end{aligned}$$

The probability $\Pr[(\mathcal{M}_{i-1} \setminus \mathcal{M}_i) \subseteq \mathcal{M}_{i-1}^s]$ is equivalent to that $|\mathcal{M}_{i-1} \setminus \mathcal{M}_i|$ distinct messages randomly picked from the set $\mathcal{M}_{i-1}$ lie in $\mathcal{M}_{i-1}^s$. By picking messages one by one, the first one lies in $\mathcal{M}_{i-1}^s$ with probability $\frac{|\mathcal{M}_{i-1}^s|}{|\mathcal{M}_{i-1}|}$ and the second one lies in $\mathcal{M}_{i-1}^s$ with probability $\frac{|\mathcal{M}_{i-1}^s|-1}{|\mathcal{M}_{i-1}|-1}$ and so on.

Based on the above analysis, we have

$$
\begin{aligned}
&\Pr[Bad_i | A_i] \\
&\leq \Pr[(\mathcal{M}_{i-1} \setminus \mathcal{M}_i) \subseteq \mathcal{M}_{i-1}^s] \\
&= \frac{|\mathcal{M}_{i-1}^s|}{|\mathcal{M}_{i-1}|} \cdot \frac{|\mathcal{M}_{i-1}^s|-1}{|\mathcal{M}_{i-1}|-1} \cdot \frac{|\mathcal{M}_{i-1}^s|-2}{|\mathcal{M}_{i-1}|-2} \cdots \frac{|\mathcal{M}_{i-1}^s|-|\mathcal{M}_{i-1} \setminus \mathcal{M}_i|+1}{|\mathcal{M}_{i-1}|-|\mathcal{M}_{i-1} \setminus \mathcal{M}_i|+1} \\
&\leq \frac{|\mathcal{M}_{i-1}|-1}{|\mathcal{M}_{i-1}|} \cdot \frac{|\mathcal{M}_{i-1}|-2}{|\mathcal{M}_{i-1}|-1} \cdot \frac{|\mathcal{M}_{i-1}|-3}{|\mathcal{M}_{i-1}|-2} \cdots \frac{|\mathcal{M}_{i-1}|-|\mathcal{M}_{i-1} \setminus \mathcal{M}_i|}{|\mathcal{M}_{i-1}|-|\mathcal{M}_{i-1} \setminus \mathcal{M}_i|+1} \\
&= \frac{|\mathcal{M}_{i-1}|-|\mathcal{M}_{i-1} \setminus \mathcal{M}_i|}{|\mathcal{M}_{i-1}|} \\
&= \frac{q^{1-\frac{i-1}{n}} - \left(q^{1-\frac{i-1}{n}} - q^{1-\frac{i}{n}}\right)}{q^{1-\frac{i-1}{n}}} \\
&= \frac{1}{q^{\frac{1}{n}}}.
\end{aligned}
$$

This completes the proof of the lemma. $\qquad\square$

4   Optimal Tightness for the Chain-Based BLS Scheme

In this section, we formally show how to prove the security of the chain-based BLS scheme with optimal tightness in the EUF-CMA security model under the CDH hardness assumption. In comparison with the high-level intuition proof given in the introduction,

- The formal proof here defines and classifies hash queries including useless or dummy hash queries generated and made by the adversary.
- The formal proof here considers the general parameter setting for any scheme parameter n instead of $n = \log q$. More precisely, the proof will show that given a chain-based BLS scheme instantiated with any integer n, the reduction loss is at most $4 \cdot q^{\frac{1}{n}}$ for q signature queries.

Our security reduction is split into two theorems. In the first theorem, we provide the framework of the reduction without calculating the success probability. We analyze the success probability in the second theorem.

4.1   Framework of Security Reduction

Theorem 2. *Let H be the hash function viewed as the random oracle. Suppose there exists an adversary $\mathcal{A}$ who can (t, q, ϵ)-break the chain-based BLS scheme in the EUF-CMA security model. We can construct a simulator $\mathcal{B}$ that (t', ϵ')-solves the CDH problem, where*

$$
t' = t + O(q_H + q \cdot n), \quad \epsilon' = \Pr[Suc] \cdot \epsilon.
$$

Here q_H is the number of hash queries to the random oracle and $\Pr[Suc]$ is the success probability of solving the CDH problem when the adversary successfully forges a valid signature.

Proof. Suppose there exists an adversary who can (t, q, ϵ)-break the chain-based BLS scheme in the EUF-CMA model. A simulator can be constructed to solve the CDH problem defined over a bilinear pairing $(\mathbb{G}, \mathbb{G}_T, p, e, g)$. Given as input a random instance $(g, g^{\hat{a}}, g^{\hat{b}})$, the simulator aims to compute $g^{\hat{a}\hat{b}}$ and constructs the simulated scheme for the adversary as follows.

Setup: The simulator sets $h = g^{\alpha} = g^{\hat{a}}$ and gives $pk = (\mathbb{G}, \mathbb{G}_T, p, e, g, h, n)$ to the adversary. The hash function H is set as a random oracle controlled by the simulator.

Hash Query: Our reduction uses the adversary's hash queries to the random oracle H to solve the CDH problem. We clarify all hash queries before introducing how to program their responses.

- A hash query x is called type-j query of m if $x = m|\Sigma_m^j$, where $\Sigma_m^j = (\sigma_1, \sigma_2, \cdots, \sigma_j)$ is the first j block (basic) BLS signatures on m and $\sigma_j = H(m|\Sigma_m^{j-1})^{\alpha}$. In particular, the type-0 query of m is $m|(\ )$ composed of m and $\Sigma_m^0 = (\ )$. We define $\mathcal{H}^i(m)$ to be the set of queries of m from type-0 to type-i as $\mathcal{H}^i(m) = \{m|\Sigma_m^0, m|\Sigma_m^1, m|\Sigma_m^2, \cdots, m|\Sigma_m^i\}$. Except hash queries in $\mathcal{H}^n(m)$, other queries of m in our reduction are defined as useless queries because the signature on m is not related to useless queries.
- The simulator uses a hash list to record all hash queries from the adversary $\mathcal{A}$ and their responses. Suppose x is a hash query and y is the response, namely $y = H(x)$. If x is a useless query, the simulator will add the tuple (x, y) into the hash list. Otherwise, $x = m|\Sigma_m^j \in \mathcal{H}^n(m)$ is a type-j query of m, and the simulator will add the tuple $(m, j, \Sigma_m^j, c_m, x, y, z_m^j)$ into the hash list where c_m is a secret related to message m and z_m^j is a secret related to the query x (to be explained later).
- The simulator can easily verify whether a candidate query x lies in $\mathcal{H}^n(m)$. Given a query x, the simulator will judge it as a type-j query of m if x can be parsed as $x = m|(\sigma_1, \cdots, \sigma_j)$ and

$$e\left(\sigma_{i+1}, g\right) = e\left(H(m|\Sigma_m^i), h\right), \text{ for all } i \in [0, j-1].$$

In the above computation, if the type-i query of m for any $i \in [0, j-1]$ was never being queried to the random oracle by the adversary before x, the simulator will firstly respond to the hash query $m|\Sigma_m^i$ before verifying the query x. It guarantees queries in a sequence that if x is the valid type-i query of m, the type-1, type-2, $\cdots$, type-$(i-1)$ queries of m have already been added and responded by the simulator before the type-i query.

- An integer $c_m \in [0, n-1]$ for each message m is chosen independently but non-uniformly satisfying $\Pr[c_m = j] = a_j$. Here $a_0, a_1, \cdots, a_{n-1} > 0$ are values satisfying $0 < a_0 + a_1 + a_2 + \cdots + a_{n-1} \leq \frac{1}{2}$ defined in Theorem 3.

Upon receiving a hash query x from the adversary, the simulator programs the response $y = H(x)$ as follows.

- **Step 1:** If x has already been queried, the simulator responds to this query following the tuple (x, y) or $(m, j, \Sigma_m^j, c_m, x, y, z_m^j)$ in the hash list. Otherwise, the simulator uses the symbols "$|$, ()" to parse the query $x = *|(*)$ for arbitrary strings denoted by $*$. It might be a candidate type-i query or a useless query with structures different from the description in the scheme.
- **Step 2:** Suppose $x \in \mathcal{H}^n(m)$. If message m inside the query $x = m|\Sigma_m^j$ is a new message to the random oracle, the simulator should first choose $c_m \in [0, n-1]$ as stated previously. Otherwise, c_m can be obtained from other tuples about message m in the hash list. The simulator randomly chooses $z_m^j \in \mathbb{Z}_p$ and sets

$$y = H(x) = H(m|\Sigma_m^j) = \begin{cases} g^{z_m^j} & : \quad j \neq c_m \\ g^{\hat{b}+z_m^j} & : \quad j = c_m \end{cases}.$$

The simulator adds $(m, j, \Sigma_m^j, c_m, x, y, z_m^j)$ into the list.
- **Step 3:** Suppose $x \notin \mathcal{H}^n(m)$. The simulator chooses a random $y \in \mathbb{G}$ and adds (x, y) into the hash list.

This completes the description of hash queries and their responses. We classify all hash queries in $\mathcal{H}^n(m)$ into the following three kinds.

- We name the type-c_m query of m as a **challenge query**.
- We name the type-$(c_m + 1)$ query of m as a **solution query**.
- Other queries in $\mathcal{H}^n(m)$ are named as **normal queries**.

That is, if x is a type-c_m query of m, it will be set as a challenge query by the simulator and responded with

$$H(x) = H(m|\Sigma_m^{c_m}) = g^{\hat{b}+z_m^{c_m}}.$$

Then the type-$(c_m + 1)$ query of m, denoted by $m|\Sigma_m^{c_m+1}$, carries the block signatures $\Sigma_m^{c_m+1} = (\sigma_1, \sigma_2, \cdots, \sigma_{c_m+1})$ and σ_{c_m+1} is equal to

$$\sigma_{c_m+1} = H(m|\Sigma_m^{c_m})^\alpha = \left(g^{\hat{b}+z_m^{c_m}}\right)^{\hat{a}} = g^{\hat{a}\hat{b}+\hat{a}z_m^{c_m}}.$$

The CDH problem solution can be extracted from this block signature with the known $z_m^{c_m}$ in the hash list by

$$\frac{\sigma_{c_m+1}}{(g^{\hat{a}})^{z_m^{c_m}}} = \frac{g^{\hat{a}\hat{b}+\hat{a}z_m^{c_m}}}{(g^{\hat{a}})^{z_m^{c_m}}} = g^{\hat{a}\hat{b}}.$$

Therefore, a solution query is a hash query that carries the CDH problem solution. The simulator is able to solve the CDH problem if the adversary generates and makes a solution query to the random oracle. We note that once the simulator extracts the problem solution $g^{\hat{a}\hat{b}}$, it can immediately stops the simulation or can continue the simulation successfully without abort using $g^{\hat{a}\hat{b}}$ until the adversary returns a forged signature.

Signature Query: The adversary adaptively chooses a message m_i for its signature query. Before the signature query on m_i, we assume that the adversary has generated and made the following hash queries to the random oracle

$$\mathcal{H}^{k_i}(m_i) = \{m_i | \Sigma_{m_i}^0, m_i | \Sigma_{m_i}^1, \cdots, m_i | \Sigma_{m_i}^{k_i}\},$$

where $k_i \in [0, n-1]$ is an integer adaptively decided by the adversary and the range is explained as follows. The type-0 query $m_i | \Sigma_{m_i}^0 = m_i |(\ )$ is the plain message. Therefore we simply assume that the adversary makes at least the type-0 query of m_i ($k_i \geq 0$). If the adversary also generates and makes the type-n query of m_i, namely $m_i | \Sigma_{m_i}^n$, the hash query already implies a valid signature on m_i and then there is no need to make its signature query. We therefore also assume that $k_i \leq n-1$.

Recalling that the simulator chose an integer $c_i \in [0, n-1]$ for the message m_i (the symbol c_{m_i} is simplified into c_i for message m_i) in the response to hash queries. The signature simulation falls into the following three cases.

- **Case 1:** $c_i < k_i$. That is, $c_i + 1 \leq k_i$. In this case, the type-c_i query is set as a challenge query and the adversary has already generated and made the type-$(c_i + 1)$ query (the solution query) to the random oracle. The simulator is able to extract the problem solution from this solution query.
- **Case 2:** $c_i = k_i$. The simulator aborts and fails in the signature simulation.
- **Case 3:** $k_i < c_i$. In this case, the adversary has not yet generated and made the type-c_i query of m_i. Then no hash query of m_i is set as the challenge query. Upon receiving the signature query on m_i, the simulator updates c_i with $c_i = \infty$ in all tuples related to message m_i in the hash list. According to the setting of the oracle response, the hash queries

$$x = m_i | \Sigma_{m_i}^j \text{ for all } j = 0, 1, 2, \cdots, n-1$$

will be all normal queries before and after the signature query on message m_i. According to the response to normal queries, we have (the symbol $z_{m_i}^j$ is simplified into z_i^j for message m_i below)

$$H(m_i | \Sigma_{m_i}^j) = g^{z_i^j}, \text{ for all } j = 0, 1, 2, \cdots, n-1.$$

Then all block signatures are equal to

$$\sigma_{j+1} = H(m_i | \Sigma_{m_i}^j)^{\alpha} = \left(g^{z_i^j}\right)^{\hat{a}} = (g^{\hat{a}})^{z_i^j}, \text{ for all } j = 0, 1, 2, \cdots, n-1.$$

Therefore, the simulator is able to compute $\Sigma_{m_i} = (\sigma_1, \sigma_2, \cdots, \sigma_n)$ on m_i for the adversary without knowing the secret key α.

Forgery: The adversary outputs a forged signature on a new message m^* to break the scheme where the signature on m^* was not queried before. Let the forged signature be

$$\Sigma_{m^*} = \left(H(m^*|\Sigma_{m^*}^0)^\alpha, \ H(m^*|\Sigma_{m^*}^1)^\alpha, \cdots, H(m^*|\Sigma_{m^*}^{n-1})^\alpha \right).$$

With the forged signature $\Sigma_{m^*} = \Sigma_{m^*}^n$, one can easily create a type-n query $m^*|\Sigma_{m^*}^n$ of m^*. Therefore, if the adversary can forge a valid signature on m^*, it is equivalent that the adversary must ever generate and make all hash queries in $\mathcal{H}^n(m^*)$ to the random oracle.

This completes the simulation and the reduction. The problem solution will appear in one of the hash queries to the random oracle if a solution query of **any message** is generated and made by the adversary. In the simulation phase, the simulator will continue the simulation until it receives a solution query unless it has to abort.

Our simulated scheme is indistinguishable from the real scheme from the view of the adversary if the simulation is successful. Each hash query x is responded with a random and independent integer z in the computation. All responses therefore are random and independent from the view of the adversary. Further, all simulated signatures are correct by the construction of the random oracle. The simulation therefore is indistinguishable from the real signature scheme.

Each hash query requires $O(1)$ exponentiations and each signature query requires the simulator to generate at most n BLS signatures. Let the success probability of receiving a solution query from the adversary be $\Pr[Suc]$ when the adversary can successfully forge a valid signature on m^*. We obtain the results given in theorem and complete the proof.   □

4.2   Probability Analysis

Theorem 3. *Let the positive values $a_0, a_1, \cdots, a_{n-1}$ in Theorem 2 be a geometric sequence satisfying:*

$$a_j = \frac{d-1}{2d(d^n-1)} \cdot d^j : \ j \in [0, n-1],$$

for the integer d satisfying $d^n = q$. Then $\Pr[Suc]$ in Theorem 2 satisfies

$$\Pr[Suc] \geq \frac{1}{4q^{\frac{1}{n}}},$$

where q is the number of signature queries and n is the scheme parameter.

Proof. We calculate the success probability $\Pr[Suc]$ on the condition that the adversary can successfully forge a valid signature. Namely,

$$\Pr[Suc] = \Pr[\text{The adversary made a solution query}|\mathsf{Verify}(pk, \Sigma_{m^*}, m^*) = \text{true}].$$

Let $m_1, m_2, m_3, \cdots, m_q$ be the order of messages selected for signature queries by the adversary before it forges a valid signature on a new message m^*. We have the following important parameters in Theorem 2.

	m_1	m_2	m_3	$\cdots$	m_q	m^*
The adversary's adaptive choices	k_1	k_2	k_3	$\cdots$	k_q	k^*
The simulator's non-uniform choices	c_1	c_2	c_3	$\cdots$	c_q	c^*

- For each message m_i before its signature query, the adversary will generate and make type-0, type-1, $\cdots$, type-k_i queries of m_i, namely $\mathcal{H}^{k_i}(m_i)$. The integer $k_i \in [0, n-1]$ is adaptively decided by the adversary.
- For the message m^*, a successful forgery $\Sigma_{m^*} = \Sigma_{m^*}^n$ is equivalent to that the adversary will generate and make hash queries $\mathcal{H}^n(m^*)$ to the random oracle. Therefore, we have $k^* = n$.
- For each message m including $(m_1, m_2, \cdots, m_q, m^*)$, the simulator will set its type-c_m query, namely $m|\Sigma_m^{c_m}$, as a challenge query. We have that $c_m \in [0, n-1]$ for each message is chosen independently with

$$\Pr[c_m = j] = a_j = \frac{d-1}{2d(d^n - 1)} \cdot d^j.$$

The reduction is successful if one of the hash queries of any message generated and made by the adversary is a solution query. We note that the solution query does not have to be of message m^*.

Let $\mathcal{Q}_{\mathcal{A}}^*$ be the mixture of hash queries and signature queries made by the adversary in attacking the scheme before returning a forged signature on m^*. In the query sequence $\mathcal{Q}_{\mathcal{A}}^*$, we have that

- The adversary makes queries $\mathcal{H}^{k_i}(m_i) = \{m_i|\Sigma_{m_i}^0, m_i|\Sigma_{m_i}^1, \cdots, m_i|\Sigma_{m_i}^{k_i}\}$ before the signature query on m_i denoted by $\mathcal{S}(m_i)$.
- The adversary makes queries $\mathcal{H}^n(m^*) = \{m^*|\Sigma_{m^*}^0, m^*|\Sigma_{m^*}^1, \cdots, m^*|\Sigma_{m^*}^n\}$ on the message m^*.
- The adversary could generate and make hash queries of any message $m \notin \{m_1, m_2, \cdots, m_q, m^*\}$ without signature query on m.
- The exact sequences of each hash query and each signature query are adaptively decided by the adversary. The adversary could make all hash queries first before signature queries, or will only make hash queries of m_i before signature query on m_i.

The success probability of reduction is rewritten as $\Pr[Suc] = \Pr[\mathcal{Q}_{\mathcal{A}}^*]$, where $\Pr[\mathcal{Q}^*]$ denotes the success probability of reduction against the adversary who makes hash/signature queries according to the sequence $\mathcal{Q}^*$.

It is hard to directly analyze the success probability $\Pr[\mathcal{Q}_{\mathcal{A}}^*]$ because the exact sequence of each hash query and each signature query are unknown by the simulator at the beginning. We solve this difficulty by firstly (1) analyzing the probability $\Pr[\mathcal{Q}_{2,0}^*]$ instead, where $\mathcal{Q}_{2,0}^*$ is a well-format and simplified query sequence whose success probability of reduction is easy in analysis, and then (2) proving that $\Pr[\mathcal{Q}_{\mathcal{A}}^*] \geq \Pr[\mathcal{Q}_{2,0}^*]$.

More precisely, the query sequence $\mathcal{Q}_{2,0}^*$ is defined as $\mathcal{H}^0(m_1) \rightarrow \mathcal{S}(m_1) \rightarrow \mathcal{H}^0(m_2) \rightarrow \mathcal{S}(m_2) \rightarrow \cdots \rightarrow \mathcal{H}^0(m_q) \rightarrow \mathcal{S}(m_q) \rightarrow \mathcal{H}^n(m^*)$, where the adversary only makes type-0 query of m_i after $\mathcal{S}(m_{i-1})$ and before $\mathcal{S}(m_i)$ for all $i \in [1, q]$, and the adversary makes hash queries $\mathcal{H}^n(m^*)$ of m^*.

Next we prove

- $\Pr[\mathcal{Q}_{2,0}^*] \geq \frac{1}{4 \cdot q^{\frac{1}{n}}}$ in Lemma 2.
- $\Pr[\mathcal{Q}_{\mathcal{A}}^*] \geq \Pr[\mathcal{Q}_{2,0}^*]$ in Lemma 3.

This completes the proof of $\Pr[Suc] = \Pr[\mathcal{Q}_{\mathcal{A}}^*] \geq \Pr[\mathcal{Q}_{2,0}^*] \geq \frac{1}{4 q^{1/n}}$. $\qquad\square$

Lemma 2. $\Pr[\mathcal{Q}_{2,0}^*] \geq \frac{1}{4 \cdot q^{\frac{1}{n}}}$.

Proof. The probability $\Pr[\mathcal{Q}_{2,0}^*]$ is calculated in the way that the simulator does not abort in the signature query phase on messages $(m_1, m_2, \cdots, m_q)$ and the solution query appears in one of the hash queries in $\mathcal{H}^n(m^*)$.

The simulator aborts due to the signature query $\mathcal{S}(m_i)$ if and only if the type-0 query of m_i is set as the challenge query. Since the simulator will set the type-c_i query as a challenge query for m_i with probability $\Pr[c_i = 0] = a_0$, the simulator will not abort in the signature query phase with probability

$$
\prod_{i=1}^{q} \left(1 - \Pr[c_i = 0]\right) = \left(1 - a_0\right)^q = \left(1 - \frac{d-1}{2d(d^n - 1)}\right)^q
$$

$$
= \left(1 - \frac{1}{2d(1 + d + d^2 + \cdots + d^{n-1})}\right)^q
$$

$$
\geq \left(1 - \frac{1}{2d^n}\right)^q
$$

$$
= \left(1 - \frac{1}{2q}\right)^q
$$

$$
\geq \left(1 - \frac{1}{2 \cdot 1}\right)^1 = \frac{1}{2}.
$$

For the hash queries of message m^*, the simulator sets the type-c^* query as a challenge query. Since the adversary makes hash queries $\mathcal{H}^n(m^*)$, we have that the solution query appears in $\mathcal{H}^n(m^*)$ as long as $0 \leq c^* \leq n - 1$.

$$
\Pr[c^* \leq n - 1] = a_0 + a_1 + \cdots + a_{n-1}
$$

$$
= \frac{d-1}{2d(d^n - 1)} + \frac{d-1}{2d(d^n - 1)} \cdot d + \cdots + \frac{d-1}{2d(d^n - 1)} \cdot d^{n-1}
$$

$$
= \frac{d-1}{2d(d^n - 1)} \left(1 + d + d^2 + \cdots + d^{n-1}\right)
$$

$$
= \frac{d-1}{2d(d^n - 1)} \cdot \frac{1 - d^n}{1 - d}
$$

$$
= \frac{1}{2d}.
$$

Therefore, we have

$$
\Pr[\mathcal{Q}_{2,0}^*] = \prod_{i=1}^{q} \left(1 - \Pr[c_i = 0]\right) \cdot \Pr[c^* \leq n - 1] \geq \frac{1}{2} \cdot \frac{1}{2d} = \frac{1}{4 q^{\frac{1}{n}}}.
$$

This completes the proof of the lemma.

Lemma 3. $\Pr[\mathcal{Q}_{\mathcal{A}}^*] \geq \Pr[\mathcal{Q}_{2,0}^*]$.

The roadmap of the proof to this lemma is as follows. We define more intermediate query sequences, namely $\mathcal{Q}_{2,1}^*, \mathcal{Q}_{2,2}^*, \mathcal{Q}_{2,3}^*, \cdots, \mathcal{Q}_{2,q}^*$, and prove that

$$\Pr[\mathcal{Q}_{\mathcal{A}}^*] \geq \Pr[\mathcal{Q}_{2,q}^*] \geq \cdots \geq \Pr[\mathcal{Q}_{2,1}^*] \geq \Pr[\mathcal{Q}_{2,0}^*].$$

- Firstly, we define the query sequences $\mathcal{Q}_{2,i}^*$ for all $i \in [1, q]$.
- Secondly, we prove $\Pr[\mathcal{Q}_{2,i}^*] \geq \Pr[\mathcal{Q}_{2,i-1}^*]$ for all $i \in [1, q]$.
- Finally, we prove $\Pr[\mathcal{Q}_{\mathcal{A}}^*] \geq \Pr[\mathcal{Q}_{2,q}^*]$.

Proof. We define the query sequence $\mathcal{Q}_{2,i}^*$ for each $i \in [1, q]$ based on $\mathcal{Q}_{2,0}^*$ and the adaptive integers $(k_1, k_2, \cdots, k_i)$ in $\mathcal{Q}_{\mathcal{A}}^*$. We define $\mathcal{Q}_{2,i}^* = \mathcal{H}^{k_1}(m_1) \to \mathcal{S}(m_1) \to \mathcal{H}^{k_2}(m_2) \to \mathcal{S}(m_2) \to \cdots \to \mathcal{H}^{k_i}(m_i) \to \mathcal{S}(m_i) \to \mathcal{H}^0(m_{i+1}) \to \mathcal{S}(m_{i+1}) \to \cdots \to \mathcal{H}^0(m_q) \to \mathcal{S}(m_q) \to \mathcal{H}^n(m^*)$.

The only difference is the number of hash queries of $(m_1, m_2, \cdots, m_i)$ when compared to $\mathcal{Q}_{2,0}^*$. In $\mathcal{Q}_{2,0}^*$, the hash queries of messages are

$$\mathcal{Q}_{2,0}^*: \quad (m_1, m_2, \cdots, m_q) \Rightarrow \left(\mathcal{H}^0(m_1), \mathcal{H}^0(m_2), \cdots, \mathcal{H}^0(m_q) \right).$$

While in the query sequence $\mathcal{Q}_{2,i}^*$, we define

$$\mathcal{Q}_{2,i}^*: \begin{cases} (m_1, \quad m_2, \quad \cdots, m_i) \Rightarrow \left(\mathcal{H}^{k_1}(m_1), \ \mathcal{H}^{k_2}(m_2), \cdots, \ \mathcal{H}^{k_i}(m_i) \right) \\ (m_{i+1}, m_{i+2}, \cdots, m_q) \Rightarrow \left(\mathcal{H}^0(m_{i+1}), \mathcal{H}^0(m_{i+2}), \cdots, \mathcal{H}^0(m_q) \right) \end{cases}$$

Next, we compare the success probabilities of reduction under the two query sequences $\mathcal{Q}_{2,i-1}^*$ and $\mathcal{Q}_{2,i}^*$. The two query sequences $\mathcal{Q}_{2,i-1}^*$ and $\mathcal{Q}_{2,i}^*$ are compared as follows.

$$\mathcal{H}^{k_1}(m_1) \to \mathcal{S}(m_1) \to \cdots \mathcal{S}(m_{i-1}) \Big\langle \begin{matrix} \mathcal{H}^0(m_i) \to \mathcal{S}(m_i) \to \mathcal{Q}_{2,[>i]}^*: \boxed{\mathcal{Q}_{2,i-1}^*} \\ \\ \mathcal{H}^{k_i}(m_i) \to \mathcal{S}(m_i) \to \mathcal{Q}_{2,[>i]}^*: \boxed{\mathcal{Q}_{2,i}^*} \end{matrix}$$

where $\mathcal{Q}_{2,[>i]}^*$ is a truncated query sequence of $\mathcal{Q}_{2,0}^*$ defined as

$$\mathcal{Q}_{2,[>i]}^* = \mathcal{H}^0(m_{i+1}) \to \mathcal{S}(m_{i+1}) \to \cdots \to \mathcal{H}^0(m_q) \to \mathcal{S}(m_q) \to \mathcal{H}^n(m^*).$$

The two query sequences $\mathcal{Q}_{2,i-1}^*$ and $\mathcal{Q}_{2,i}^*$ have the identical sub-sequence before $\mathcal{S}(m_{i-1})$, and then the reduction will have the identical success probability before $\mathcal{S}(m_{i-1})$ in these two query sequences. The two query sequences have the only difference that the adversary makes hash queries $\mathcal{H}^{k_i}(m_i)$ in $\mathcal{Q}_{2,i}^*$ instead of $\mathcal{H}^0(m_i)$ in $\mathcal{Q}_{2,i-1}^*$. Therefore, we have

$$\Pr[\mathcal{H}^{k_i}(m_i) \to \mathcal{S}(m_i) \to \mathcal{Q}_{2,[>i]}^*] \geq \Pr[\mathcal{H}^0(m_i) \to \mathcal{S}(m_i) \to \mathcal{Q}_{2,[>i]}^*] \quad (1)$$

implies that $\Pr[\mathcal{Q}_{2,i}^*] \geq \Pr[\mathcal{Q}_{2,i-1}^*]$.

Next, we prove the correctness of the inequality (1). In both the two query sub-sequences $\mathcal{H}^0(m_i) \to \mathcal{S}(m_i) \to \mathcal{Q}^*_{2,[>i]}$ and $\mathcal{H}^{k_i}(m_i) \to \mathcal{S}(m_i) \to \mathcal{Q}^*_{2,[>i]}$, the simulator will either (1) obtain a solution query of m_i or (2) obtain a solution query from $\mathcal{Q}^*_{2,[>i]}$ when the simulator neither succeeds nor aborts after $\mathcal{S}(m_i)$. We have

$$\Pr[\mathcal{H}^0(m_i) \to \mathcal{S}(m_i) \to \mathcal{Q}^*_{2,[>i]}] = \Pr[S_i^{(0)}] + \left(1 - \Pr[S_i^{(0)}] - \Pr[F_i^{(0)}]\right) \Pr[\mathcal{Q}^*_{2,[>i]}]$$

$$\Pr[\mathcal{H}^{k_i}(m_i) \to \mathcal{S}(m_i) \to \mathcal{Q}^*_{2,[>i]}] = \Pr[S_i^{(k_i)}] + \left(1 - \Pr[S_i^{(k_i)}] - \Pr[F_i^{(k_i)}]\right) \Pr[\mathcal{Q}^*_{2,[>i]}]$$

where $S_i^{(k_i)}$ is the event that the solution query appears in $\mathcal{H}^{k_i}(m_i)$, and $F_i^{(k_i)}$ is the corresponding event that the simulator fails due to $\mathcal{S}(m_i)$. In particular, we have $\Pr[S_i^{(0)}] = 0$ and $\Pr[F_i^{(0)}] = a_0$.

We have the following results hold according to the setting of a_i.

$$\Pr[S_i^{(k_i)}] - \Pr[S_i^{(0)}] = \left(\Pr[c_i \leq k_i - 1]\right) - 0$$
$$= a_0 + a_1 + \cdots + a_{k_i-1}$$
$$= \frac{d-1}{2d(d^n-1)} + \frac{d-1}{2d(d^n-1)} \cdot d + \cdots + \frac{d-1}{2d(d^n-1)} \cdot d^{k_i-1}$$
$$= \frac{d-1}{2d(d^n-1)}\left(1 + d + d^2 + \cdots + d^{k_i-1}\right)$$
$$= \frac{d-1}{2d(d^n-1)} \cdot \frac{1-d^{k_i}}{1-d}$$
$$= \frac{d^{k_i}-1}{2d(d^n-1)}$$

$$\Pr[F_i^{(k_i)}] - \Pr[F_i^{(0)}] = \left(\Pr[c_i = k_i]\right) - \left(\Pr[c_i = 0]\right)$$
$$= a_{k_i} - a_0$$
$$= \frac{d-1}{2d(d^n-1)} \cdot d^{k_i} - \frac{d-1}{2d(d^n-1)} \cdot d^0$$
$$= \frac{d^{k_i}-1}{2d(d^n-1)} \cdot (d-1)$$

Therefore, we have

$$\Pr[\mathcal{H}^{k_i}(m_i) \to \mathcal{S}(m_i) \to \mathcal{Q}^*_{2,[>i]}] - \Pr[\mathcal{H}^0(m_i) \to \mathcal{S}(m_i) \to \mathcal{Q}^*_{2,[>i]}]$$
$$= \left(\Pr[S_i^{(k_i)}] - \Pr[S_i^{(0)}]\right) + \Pr[\mathcal{Q}^*_{2,[>i]}] \cdot \left(\Pr[S_i^{(0)}] - \Pr[S_i^{(k_i)}] + \Pr[F_i^{(0)}] - \Pr[F_i^{(k_i)}]\right)$$
$$= \frac{d^{k_i}-1}{2d(d^n-1)} + \Pr[\mathcal{Q}^*_{2,[>i]}] \cdot \left(-\frac{d^{k_i}-1}{2d(d^n-1)} - \frac{d^{k_i}-1}{2d(d^n-1)} \cdot (d-1)\right)$$
$$= \frac{d^{k_i}-1}{2d(d^n-1)} - \Pr[\mathcal{Q}^*_{2,[>i]}] \cdot \frac{d^{k_i}-1}{2d(d^n-1)} \cdot d$$
$$= \frac{d^{k_i}-1}{2d(d^n-1)}\left(1 - \Pr[\mathcal{Q}^*_{2,[>i]}] \cdot d\right),$$

which is positive (≥ 0) because we have

- $d \geq 1$ since $d = q^{\frac{1}{n}}$ and $q \geq 1$.
- The inequality $\Pr[\mathcal{Q}^*_{2,[>i]}] \leq \Pr[\mathcal{H}^n(m^*)]$ holds since making type-0 query and then signature query will decrease the success probability of reduction only, such that

$$
\begin{aligned}
\Pr[\mathcal{Q}^*_{2,[>i]}] &= \Pr[\mathcal{H}^0(m_{i+1}) \to \mathcal{S}(m_i) \to \cdots \to \mathcal{H}^0(m_q) \to \mathcal{S}(m_q) \to \mathcal{H}^n(m^*)] \\
&\leq \Pr[\mathcal{H}^n(m^*)] \\
&= \Pr[c^* \leq n-1] \\
&= \frac{1}{2d} \leq \frac{1}{d}
\end{aligned}
$$

Therefore, from the above analysis, we obtain $\Pr[\mathcal{Q}^*_{2,i}] \geq \Pr[\mathcal{Q}^*_{2,i-1}]$.

Finally, we prove $\Pr[\mathcal{Q}^*_{\mathcal{A}}] \geq \Pr[\mathcal{Q}^*_{2,q}]$. In comparison with $\mathcal{Q}^*_{2,q}$, $\mathcal{Q}^*_{\mathcal{A}}$ generates and makes the same hash queries of $(m_1, m_2, \cdots, m_q, m^*)$.

$$
\mathcal{Q}^*_{\mathcal{A}}, \mathcal{Q}^*_{2,q} : \quad (m_1, m_2, \cdots, m_q, m^*) \Rightarrow \left(\mathcal{H}^{k_1}(m_1), \mathcal{H}^{k_2}(m_2), \cdots, \mathcal{H}^{k_q}(m_q), \mathcal{H}^n(m^*) \right).
$$

The only differences are as follows.

- In the real sequence $\mathcal{Q}^*_{\mathcal{A}}$, the adversary could also make hash queries of any message m whose signature was not queried by the adversary.
- In the real sequence $\mathcal{Q}^*_{\mathcal{A}}$, the adversary could make the mixture of hash queries and signature queries without following the well-format sequence. For example, the sub-sequence of $\mathcal{Q}^*_{\mathcal{A}}$ is $\mathcal{H}^{k_1}(m_1) \to \mathcal{H}^{k_2}(m_2) \to \mathcal{S}(m_1)$ instead of $\mathcal{H}^{k_1}(m_1) \to \mathcal{S}(m_1) \to \mathcal{H}^{k_2}(m_2)$ in $\mathcal{Q}^*_q$, where the adversary made hash queries of message m_2 before the signature query on m_1.

Note that any hash query will be responded by the random oracle correctly without abort. Therefore, any query sequence $\mathcal{Q}^*_{\mathcal{A}}$ different from $\mathcal{Q}^*_{2,q}$ would increase the success probability of reduction and then we have $\Pr[\mathcal{Q}^*_{\mathcal{A}}] \geq \Pr[\mathcal{Q}^*_{2,q}]$.

This completes the proof of the lemma. $\qquad\square$

Acknowledgement. We would like to thank Tibor Jager for insightful discussions on the first version of this work in 2020. We would also like to thank the anonymous reviewers from Eurocrypt 2021, Crypto 2021, and Eurocrypt 2022 for their constructive comments.

References

1. Abdalla, M., Fouque, P.-A., Lyubashevsky, V., Tibouchi, M.: Tightly-secure signatures from lossy identification schemes. In: Pointcheval, D., Johansson, T. (eds.) EUROCRYPT 2012. LNCS, vol. 7237, pp. 572–590. Springer, Heidelberg (2012). https://doi.org/10.1007/978-3-642-29011-4_34

2. Abe, M., Groth, J., Ohkubo, M.: Separating short structure-preserving signatures from non-interactive assumptions. In: Lee, D.H., Wang, X. (eds.) ASIACRYPT 2011. LNCS, vol. 7073, pp. 628–646. Springer, Heidelberg (2011). https://doi.org/10.1007/978-3-642-25385-0_34

3. Abe, M., Hofheinz, D., Nishimaki, R., Ohkubo, M., Pan, J.: Compact structure-preserving signatures with almost tight security. In: Katz, J., Shacham, H. (eds.) CRYPTO 2017. LNCS, vol. 10402, pp. 548–580. Springer, Cham (2017). https://doi.org/10.1007/978-3-319-63715-0_19

4. Abe, M., Jutla, C.S., Ohkubo, M., Pan, J., Roy, A., Wang, Y.: Shorter QA-NIZK and SPS with tighter security. In: Galbraith, S.D., Moriai, S. (eds.) ASIACRYPT 2019. LNCS, vol. 11923, pp. 669–699. Springer, Cham (2019). https://doi.org/10.1007/978-3-030-34618-8_23

5. Bader, C., Jager, T., Li, Y., Schäge, S.: On the impossibility of tight cryptographic reductions. In: Fischlin, M., Coron, J.-S. (eds.) EUROCRYPT 2016. LNCS, vol. 9666, pp. 273–304. Springer, Heidelberg (2016). https://doi.org/10.1007/978-3-662-49896-5_10

6. Bellare, M., Poettering, B., Stebila, D.: From identification to signatures, tightly: a framework and generic transforms. In: Cheon, J.H., Takagi, T. (eds.) ASIACRYPT 2016. LNCS, vol. 10032, pp. 435–464. Springer, Heidelberg (2016). https://doi.org/10.1007/978-3-662-53890-6_15

7. Bellare, M., Rogaway, P.: The exact security of digital signatures-how to sign with RSA and Rabin. In: Maurer, U. (ed.) EUROCRYPT 1996. LNCS, vol. 1070, pp. 399–416. Springer, Heidelberg (1996). https://doi.org/10.1007/3-540-68339-9_34

8. Bernstein, D.J.: Proving tight security for Rabin-Williams signatures. In: Smart, N. (ed.) EUROCRYPT 2008. LNCS, vol. 4965, pp. 70–87. Springer, Heidelberg (2008). https://doi.org/10.1007/978-3-540-78967-3_5

9. Blazy, O., Kakvi, S.A., Kiltz, E., Pan, J.: Tightly-secure signatures from chameleon hash functions. In: Katz, J. (ed.) PKC 2015. LNCS, vol. 9020, pp. 256–279. Springer, Heidelberg (2015). https://doi.org/10.1007/978-3-662-46447-2_12

10. Boneh, D., Boyen, X.: Short signatures without random oracles. In: Cachin, C., Camenisch, J.L. (eds.) EUROCRYPT 2004. LNCS, vol. 3027, pp. 56–73. Springer, Heidelberg (2004). https://doi.org/10.1007/978-3-540-24676-3_4

11. Boneh, D., Lynn, B., Shacham, H.: Short signatures from the Weil pairing. In: Boyd, C. (ed.) ASIACRYPT 2001. LNCS, vol. 2248, pp. 514–532. Springer, Heidelberg (2001). https://doi.org/10.1007/3-540-45682-1_30

12. Boneh, D., Venkatesan, R.: Breaking RSA may not be equivalent to factoring. In: Nyberg, K. (ed.) EUROCRYPT 1998. LNCS, vol. 1403, pp. 59–71. Springer, Heidelberg (1998). https://doi.org/10.1007/BFb0054117

13. Boyen, X., Li, Q.: Towards tightly secure lattice short signature and id-based encryption. In: Cheon, J.H., Takagi, T. (eds.) ASIACRYPT 2016. LNCS, vol. 10032, pp. 404–434. Springer, Heidelberg (2016). https://doi.org/10.1007/978-3-662-53890-6_14

14. Chailloux, A., Debris-Alazard, T.: Tight and optimal reductions for signatures based on average trapdoor preimage sampleable functions and applications to code-based signatures. In: Kiayias, A., Kohlweiss, M., Wallden, P., Zikas, V. (eds.) PKC 2020. LNCS, vol. 12111, pp. 453–479. Springer, Cham (2020). https://doi.org/10.1007/978-3-030-45388-6_16

15. Cohn-Gordon, K., Cremers, C., Gjøsteen, K., Jacobsen, H., Jager, T.: Highly efficient key exchange protocols with optimal tightness. In: Boldyreva, A., Micciancio, D. (eds.) CRYPTO 2019. LNCS, vol. 11694, pp. 767–797. Springer, Cham (2019). https://doi.org/10.1007/978-3-030-26954-8_25

16. Coron, J.-S.: Optimal security proofs for PSS and other signature schemes. In: Knudsen, L.R. (ed.) EUROCRYPT 2002. LNCS, vol. 2332, pp. 272–287. Springer, Heidelberg (2002). https://doi.org/10.1007/3-540-46035-7_18

17. Diemert, D., Gellert, K., Jager, T., Lyu, L.: Digital signatures with memory-tight security in the multi-challenge setting. In: Tibouchi, M., Wang, H. (eds.) ASIACRYPT 2021. LNCS, vol. 13093, pp. 403–433. Springer, Cham (2021). https://doi.org/10.1007/978-3-030-92068-5_14

18. Diemert, D., Gellert, K., Jager, T., Lyu, L.: More efficient digital signatures with tight multi-user security. In: Garay, J.A. (ed.) PKC 2021. LNCS, vol. 12711, pp. 1–31. Springer, Cham (2021). https://doi.org/10.1007/978-3-030-75248-4_1

19. El Kaafarani, A., Katsumata, S., Pintore, F.: Lossy CSI-FiSh: efficient signature scheme with tight reduction to decisional CSIDH-512. In: Kiayias, A., Kohlweiss, M., Wallden, P., Zikas, V. (eds.) PKC 2020. LNCS, vol. 12111, pp. 157–186. Springer, Cham (2020). https://doi.org/10.1007/978-3-030-45388-6_6

20. Fischlin, M., Fleischhacker, N.: Limitations of the meta-reduction technique: the case of Schnorr signatures. In: Johansson, T., Nguyen, P.Q. (eds.) EUROCRYPT 2013. LNCS, vol. 7881, pp. 444–460. Springer, Heidelberg (2013). https://doi.org/10.1007/978-3-642-38348-9_27

21. Fleischhacker, N., Jager, T., Schröder, D.: On tight security proofs for Schnorr signatures. In: Sarkar, P., Iwata, T. (eds.) ASIACRYPT 2014. LNCS, vol. 8873, pp. 512–531. Springer, Heidelberg (2014). https://doi.org/10.1007/978-3-662-45611-8_27

22. Fuchsbauer, G., Kiltz, E., Loss, J.: The algebraic group model and its applications. In: Shacham, H., Boldyreva, A. (eds.) CRYPTO 2018. LNCS, vol. 10992, pp. 33–62. Springer, Cham (2018). https://doi.org/10.1007/978-3-319-96881-0_2

23. Garg, S., Bhaskar, R., Lokam, S.V.: Improved bounds on security reductions for discrete log based signatures. In: Wagner, D. (ed.) CRYPTO 2008. LNCS, vol. 5157, pp. 93–107. Springer, Heidelberg (2008). https://doi.org/10.1007/978-3-540-85174-5_6

24. Gay, R., Hofheinz, D., Kohl, L., Pan, J.: More efficient (almost) tightly secure structure-preserving signatures. In: Nielsen, J.B., Rijmen, V. (eds.) EUROCRYPT 2018. LNCS, vol. 10821, pp. 230–258. Springer, Cham (2018). https://doi.org/10.1007/978-3-319-78375-8_8

25. Gjøsteen, K., Jager, T.: Practical and tightly-secure digital signatures and authenticated key exchange. In: Shacham, H., Boldyreva, A. (eds.) CRYPTO 2018. LNCS, vol. 10992, pp. 95–125. Springer, Cham (2018). https://doi.org/10.1007/978-3-319-96881-0_4

26. Goh, E.-J., Jarecki, S.: A signature scheme as secure as the Diffie-Hellman problem. In: Biham, E. (ed.) EUROCRYPT 2003. LNCS, vol. 2656, pp. 401–415. Springer, Heidelberg (2003). https://doi.org/10.1007/3-540-39200-9_25

27. Guo, F., Chen, R., Susilo, W., Lai, J., Yang, G., Mu, Y.: Optimal security reductions for unique signatures: bypassing impossibilities with a counterexample. In: Katz, J., Shacham, H. (eds.) CRYPTO 2017. LNCS, vol. 10402, pp. 517–547. Springer, Cham (2017). https://doi.org/10.1007/978-3-319-63715-0_18

28. Han, S., et al.: Authenticated key exchange and signatures with tight security in the standard model. In: Malkin, T., Peikert, C. (eds.) CRYPTO 2021. LNCS, vol. 12828, pp. 670–700. Springer, Cham (2021). https://doi.org/10.1007/978-3-030-84259-8_23

29. Han, S., Liu, S., Gu, D.: Key encapsulation mechanism with tight enhanced security in the multi-user setting: impossibility result and optimal tightness. In: Tibouchi,

M., Wang, H. (eds.) ASIACRYPT 2021. LNCS, vol. 13091, pp. 483–513. Springer, Cham (2021). https://doi.org/10.1007/978-3-030-92075-3_17

30. Hesse, J., Hofheinz, D., Kohl, L.: On tightly secure non-interactive key exchange. In: Shacham, H., Boldyreva, A. (eds.) CRYPTO 2018. LNCS, vol. 10992, pp. 65–94. Springer, Cham (2018). https://doi.org/10.1007/978-3-319-96881-0_3

31. Hesse, J., Hofheinz, D., Kohl, L., Langrehr, R.: Towards tight adaptive security of non-interactive key exchange. In: Nissim, K., Waters, B. (eds.) TCC 2021. LNCS, vol. 13044, pp. 286–316. Springer, Cham (2021). https://doi.org/10.1007/978-3-030-90456-2_10

32. Hofheinz, D.: Algebraic partitioning: fully compact and (almost) tightly secure cryptography. In: Kushilevitz, E., Malkin, T. (eds.) TCC 2016. LNCS, vol. 9562, pp. 251–281. Springer, Heidelberg (2016). https://doi.org/10.1007/978-3-662-49096-9_11

33. Hofheinz, D., Jager, T.: Tightly secure signatures and public-key encryption. In: Safavi-Naini, R., Canetti, R. (eds.) CRYPTO 2012. LNCS, vol. 7417, pp. 590–607. Springer, Heidelberg (2012). https://doi.org/10.1007/978-3-642-32009-5_35

34. Hofheinz, D., Jager, T., Knapp, E.: Waters signatures with optimal security reduction. In: Fischlin, M., Buchmann, J., Manulis, M. (eds.) PKC 2012. LNCS, vol. 7293, pp. 66–83. Springer, Heidelberg (2012). https://doi.org/10.1007/978-3-642-30057-8_5

35. Jager, T., Kiltz, E., Riepel, D., Schäge, S.: Tightly-secure authenticated key exchange, revisited. In: Canteaut, A., Standaert, F.-X. (eds.) EUROCRYPT 2021. LNCS, vol. 12696, pp. 117–146. Springer, Cham (2021). https://doi.org/10.1007/978-3-030-77870-5_5

36. Jutla, C.S., Ohkubo, M., Roy, A.: Improved (almost) tightly-secure structure-preserving signatures. In: Abdalla, M., Dahab, R. (eds.) PKC 2018. LNCS, vol. 10770, pp. 123–152. Springer, Cham (2018). https://doi.org/10.1007/978-3-319-76581-5_5

37. Kakvi, S.A., Kiltz, E.: Optimal security proofs for full domain hash, revisited. In: Pointcheval, D., Johansson, T. (eds.) EUROCRYPT 2012. LNCS, vol. 7237, pp. 537–553. Springer, Heidelberg (2012). https://doi.org/10.1007/978-3-642-29011-4_32

38. Katz, J., Wang, N.: Efficiency improvements for signature schemes with tight security reductions. In: Jajodia, S., Atluri, V., Jaeger, T. (eds.) ACM CCS 2003, pp. 155–164. ACM (2003)

39. Kiltz, E., Loss, J., Pan, J.: Tightly-secure signatures from five-move identification protocols. In: Takagi, T., Peyrin, T. (eds.) ASIACRYPT 2017. LNCS, vol. 10626, pp. 68–94. Springer, Cham (2017). https://doi.org/10.1007/978-3-319-70700-6_3

40. Kiltz, E., Masny, D., Pan, J.: Optimal security proofs for signatures from identification schemes. In: Robshaw, M., Katz, J. (eds.) CRYPTO 2016. LNCS, vol. 9815, pp. 33–61. Springer, Heidelberg (2016). https://doi.org/10.1007/978-3-662-53008-5_2

41. Lewko, A., Waters, B.: Why proving HIBE systems secure is difficult. In: Nguyen, P.Q., Oswald, E. (eds.) EUROCRYPT 2014. LNCS, vol. 8441, pp. 58–76. Springer, Heidelberg (2014). https://doi.org/10.1007/978-3-642-55220-5_4

42. Libert, B., Joye, M., Yung, M., Peters, T.: Concise multi-challenge CCA-secure encryption and signatures with almost tight security. In: Sarkar, P., Iwata, T. (eds.) ASIACRYPT 2014. LNCS, vol. 8874, pp. 1–21. Springer, Heidelberg (2014). https://doi.org/10.1007/978-3-662-45608-8_1

43. Micali, S., Reyzin, L.: Improving the exact security of digital signature schemes. J. Cryptol. 15(1), 1–18 (2002). https://doi.org/10.1007/s00145-001-0005-8

44. Morgan, A., Pass, R.: On the security loss of unique signatures. In: Beimel, A., Dziembowski, S. (eds.) TCC 2018. LNCS, vol. 11239, pp. 507–536. Springer, Cham (2018). https://doi.org/10.1007/978-3-030-03807-6_19

45. Morgan, A., Pass, R., Shi, E.: On the adaptive security of MACs and PRFs. In: Moriai, S., Wang, H. (eds.) ASIACRYPT 2020. LNCS, vol. 12491, pp. 724–753. Springer, Cham (2020). https://doi.org/10.1007/978-3-030-64837-4_24

46. Niehues, D.: Verifiable random functions with optimal tightness. In: Garay, J.A. (ed.) PKC 2021. LNCS, vol. 12711, pp. 61–91. Springer, Cham (2021). https://doi.org/10.1007/978-3-030-75248-4_3

47. Paillier, P., Vergnaud, D.: Discrete-log-based signatures may not be equivalent to discrete log. In: Roy, B. (ed.) ASIACRYPT 2005. LNCS, vol. 3788, pp. 1–20. Springer, Heidelberg (2005). https://doi.org/10.1007/11593447_1

48. Rotem, L., Segev, G.: Tighter security for Schnorr identification and signatures: a high-moment forking lemma for Σ-protocols. In: Malkin, T., Peikert, C. (eds.) CRYPTO 2021. LNCS, vol. 12825, pp. 222–250. Springer, Cham (2021). https://doi.org/10.1007/978-3-030-84242-0_9

49. Schäge, S.: Tight proofs for signature schemes without random oracles. In: Paterson, K.G. (ed.) EUROCRYPT 2011. LNCS, vol. 6632, pp. 189–206. Springer, Heidelberg (2011). https://doi.org/10.1007/978-3-642-20465-4_12

50. Seurin, Y.: On the exact security of Schnorr-type signatures in the random oracle model. In: Pointcheval, D., Johansson, T. (eds.) EUROCRYPT 2012. LNCS, vol. 7237, pp. 554–571. Springer, Heidelberg (2012). https://doi.org/10.1007/978-3-642-29011-4_33

51. Shacham, H.: Short unique signatures from RSA with a tight security reduction (in the random oracle model). In: Meiklejohn, S., Sako, K. (eds.) FC 2018. LNCS, vol. 10957, pp. 61–79. Springer, Heidelberg (2018). https://doi.org/10.1007/978-3-662-58387-6_4

On Building Fine-Grained One-Way Functions from Strong Average-Case Hardness

Chris Brzuska[1(✉)] and Geoffroy Couteau[2(✉)]

[1] Aalto University, Espoo, Finland
chris.brzuska@aalto.fi
[2] CNRS, IRIF, Université de Paris, Paris, France
geoffroy.couteau@ens.fr

Abstract. Constructing one-way functions from average-case hardness is a long-standing open problem. A positive result would exclude Pessiland (Impagliazzo '95) and establish a highly desirable win-win situation: either (symmetric) cryptography exists unconditionally, or all NP problems can be solved efficiently on the average. Motivated by the lack of progress on this seemingly very hard question, we initiate the investigation of weaker yet meaningful candidate win-win results of the following type: either there are *fine-grained* one-way functions (FGOWF), or nontrivial speedups can be obtained for all NP problems on the average. FGOWFs only require a fixed polynomial gap (as opposed to superpolynomial) between the running time of the function and the running time of an inverter. We obtain three main results:

Construction. We show that if there is an NP language having a very strong form of average-case hardness, which we call *block finding hardness*, then FGOWF exist. We provide heuristic support for this very strong average-case hardness notion by showing that it holds for a random language. Then, we study whether weaker (and more natural) forms of average-case hardness could already suffice to obtain FGOWF, and obtain two negative results:

Separation I. We provide a strong oracle separation for the implication (∃ exponentially average-case hard language $\implies$ ∃ FGOWF).

Separation II. We provide a second strong negative result for an even weaker candidate win-win result. Namely, we rule out a black-box proof for the implication (∃ exponentially average-case hard language *whose hardness amplifies optimally through parallel repetitions* $\implies$ ∃ FGOWF). This separation forms the core technical contribution of our work.

1 Introduction

In his celebrated 1995 position paper [Imp95], Impagliazzo describes his personal view of the study of average-case complexity, an emergent (at the time) and fundamental area of computational complexity initiated in a seminal work of Levin [Lev86], which aims to characterize NP problems which are not only hard for a worst-case choice of inputs, but also for natural distributions over

O. Dunkelman and S. Dziembowski (Eds.): EUROCRYPT 2022, LNCS 13276, pp. 584–613, 2022.
https://doi.org/10.1007/978-3-031-07085-3_20

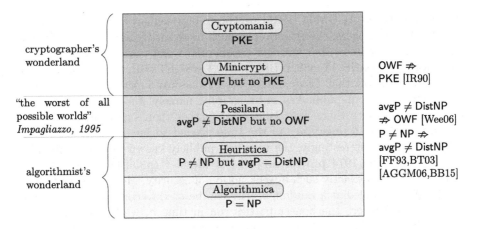

Fig. 1. Impagliazzo's five worlds

the inputs. In Impagliazzo's view, our current understanding of the landscape of complexity theory is best described by considering five possible worlds we might live in, which are now commonly known as the *five worlds of Impagliazzo*, corresponding to the five possible outcomes regarding the existence of worst-case hardness in NP, average-case hardness in NP, one-way function, and public-key cryptography. The corresponding five worlds, Algorithmica, Heuristica, Pessiland, Minicrypt, and Cryptomania, and their relations are summarized on Fig. 1. Algorithmica and Heuristica correspond to the "algorithmist's wonderland", where all NP languages can be decided efficiently on the average. Cryptomania and Minicrypt correspond to the "cryptographer's wonderland",[1] where one-way functions (and therefore, stream ciphers, signatures, pseudorandom functions, etc.) exist. Eventually, Pessiland is what Impagliazzo describes as "the worst of all possible worlds": a world in which many NP problems might be untractable (even on natural instances), yet no one-way function (and thus no cryptography) exists.

One-Way Functions Based on Average-Case Hardness. In this article, we study whether (the existence of) average-case hard NP problems imply (the existence of) one-way functions. Conceptually, a positive answer to this question rules out Pessiland, i.e., it constitutes a win-win result: Either all NP problems can be solved efficiently, on the average, or cryptographic one-way functions exist. Little progress has been made on this question in the past two-and-a-half decades. There is a partial explanation for this lack of success: we know that any construction of one-way functions from average-case hard NP problems must rely on *non-black-box techniques* (Wee [Wee06] attributes this simple observation to Impagliazzo and Rudich). Indeed, similar separations

---

[1] Though we heard that lately, some cryptographers have been found dreaming of an even higher heaven, the mysterious land of Obfustopia.

[IR90, FF93, BT03, AGGM06, BB15] are known between any two of Impagliazzo's worlds. However, there, the situation is much more satisfying: At the bottom of the hierarchy, we know that stronger *exponential* worst-case assumptions imply that avgP $\neq$ DistNP [Yao82, WB86, Sud97, Lev87, STV01]. At the top of the hierarchy, we know that *exponentially secure* one-way functions imply a weak, but useful notion of public-key cryptography, namely *fine-grained* public-key cryptography where there is a polynomial (rather than superpolynomial) gap between the time to encrypt and the time needed to break the cryptosystem [Mer78, BGI08]. Interestingly, the very first publicly-known work on public-key cryptography, the 1974 project proposal of Merkle[2] (published much later in [Mer78]) achieves exactly such a weak notion of security: Merkle shows that an ideal OWF (modeled as a random oracle) can be used to construct a key agreement protocol where the honest parties run in time n, while the best attack requires time n^2. The assumption of an ideal OWF was later relaxed to the existence of exponentially hard OWFs by Biham, Goren and Ishai [BGI08]. Hence, in essence, Merkle establishes a *weak exclusion* of Minicrypt, by showing that strong hardness in Minicrypt already implies some nontrivial form of public-key cryptography, with a quadratic gap between the attacker's runtime and the honest parties' runtime.

1.1   Our Contribution: Inbetween Heuristica and Pessiland

The above result suggests a natural relaxation of Impagliazzo's program: rather than ruling out Pessiland entirely, one could hope to show that sufficiently strong forms of average-case hardness suffice to construct weak forms of cryptography. Such a result would still have a very desirable win-win flavor. For example, if one shows that *exponential* average-case hardness implies *fine-grained* one-way functions, it would show that either *all* NP problems admit nontrivial (subexponential) algorithms on the average, or there must exist *some* form of cryptography, with a polynomial security gap. As the computational power increases, such a gap translates to an increasingly larger runtime gap on concrete instances and thus a larger concrete security margin in realistic situations.

We can also consider starting from even stronger forms of average-case hardness. A very natural target is *non-amortizing* average-case hardness, which states (in essence) that deciding whether k words $(x_1, \cdots, x_k)$ belong to a language $\mathcal{L}$ is k times harder (on average) than deciding membership of a single word. This stronger form of average-case hardness is closely related to the widely studied notion of proofs of work [BRSV18]. Building fine-grained one-way functions from this strong form of average-case hardness would still be a very meaningful win-win: it would show that either we can obtain nontrivial savings on average for all NP problems when amortizing over many instances (which would be an algorithmic breakthrough), or there must exist some weak form of cryptography.

In this work, we initiate the study of these intermediate layers between Heuristica and Pessiland, obtaining both positive and negative results.

---

[2] Ralph Merkle, 1974 project proposal for CS 244 at U.C. Berkeley, http://www.merkle.com/1974/.

Fine-Grained OWFs from Block-Finding Hardness. We mentioned above two natural strengthenings of average-case hardness: exponential average-case hardness, and non-amortizable average-case hardness (deciding whether k words $(x_1, \cdots, x_k)$ belong to $\mathcal{L}$ is k times harder that deciding membership of a single word). Here, we consider even stronger notions: we assume that there is a language where it is already hard to *decide*, given k random words $(x_1, \cdots, x_k)$, whether their language membership satisfies some local structure. As a simple example of such a notion, consider the following (average-case) *block-finding hardness* notion: given k random words $\vec{x} = (x_1, \cdots, x_k)$ and a $t \approx \log k$-bit string s, computed as the t language membership bits of a randomly chosen sequence of t consecutive words in $\vec{x}$, find these consecutive words. The notion states (informally) that finding such a sequence (when it exists, and with probability significantly better than the random guess) cannot be done much faster than by brute-forcing a significant fraction of all the language membership.

To get an intuition of this problem, it is helpful to consider an even simpler formulation: given k random words $(x_1, \cdots, x_k)$ with the promise that t consecutive words are not in the language, find these t consecutive words (with probability significantly better than $1/k$). For a very hard language, it is not clear how to do this without naively brute-forcing the language membership of $\Omega(k/t)$ words. We show that this (very strong) average-case hardness notion already gets us outside of Pessiland: if there is a block-finding hard language, then there exists fine-grained one-way functions (with a quadratic hardness gap).

Heuristically Evaluating the Assumption on Random Languages. Given that this strong form of average-case hardness is new, we provide some heuristic analysis to support the intuition that it plausibly holds for some hard languages. To do so, we introduce a convenient tool for this heuristic analysis, a *random language model* (RLM), analogous to how the random oracle model [BR93] is used to heuristically study the security of constructions when instantiated with a sufficiently strong hash function. The RLM provides oracle access to a truly random NP-language $\mathcal{L}$. In the RLM, each bitstring $x \in \{0,1\}^n$ belongs to $\mathcal{L}$ with probability exactly $1/2$, and the membership witness for a word $x \in \mathcal{L} \cap \{0,1\}^n$ is a uniformly random bitstring from $\{0,1\}^n$.[3] To check membership to the language, the parties have access to an oracle Chk which, on input a pair $(x, w) \in \{0,1\}^n \times \{0,1\}^n$, returns 1 if $x \in \mathcal{L}$ and w is the right corresponding witness, and 0 otherwise. Finding out whether a random bitstring $x \in \{0,1\}^n$ belongs to $\mathcal{L}$ requires 2^{n-1} calls to Chk on the average.[4]

---

[3] Of course, this heuristic is simplified: most real languages can have more than a single witness, and the choice of having $|w| = |x|$ is a somewhat arbitrary way of tuning the hardness to make it exactly 2^n. Still, we believe that there is value in using a simple model to heuristically analyze the plausibility of an assumption – even though, as any heuristic model, it must fail on artificial counter examples.

[4] More precisely, it requires 2^{n-1} calls to Chk on the average to find a witness of language membership if x is indeed in the language. In turn, it requires 2^n calls to confirm that there is indeed no witness if x is not in the language.

The RLM captures idealized hard language where it is not only (exponentially) hard to decide language membership, but also hard to sample an element of the language with probability significantly better than $1/2$ (hence, in particular, it is also hard to generate a word together with the corresponding witness). This captures hard languages where no further structure is assumed beyond the ability to efficiently check a candidate witness; note that the ability to sample instances together with their witness is exactly the additional structure which implies the existence of one-way functions [Imp95], hence the question of building one-way functions from average-case hardness asks precisely about whether this can be done without assuming this additional structure to start with.

In this work, we prove that a random language satisfies block-finding hardness, providing some heuristic support for this strong form of average-case hardness. Hence, we get as a corollary:

Corollary 1 (Informal). *In the Random Language model, there exists a fine-grained one-way function which can be evaluated with n oracle calls, but cannot be inverted with $o(n^2)$ calls to the random language.*

Constructing a FGOWF from Block-Finding Hardness. At a (very) high level, the construction proceeds as follows: suppose that there exists *hard puzzles* where sampling a random puzzle p is easy (it takes time, say, $O(1)$), but finding the unique solution $s = s(p)$ to the puzzle, and verifying that a candidate solution s to the puzzle is correct, are comparatively harder (they take some much larger respective times N_1 and N_2 with $N_1 \approx N_2$). For example, such puzzles can be constructed by sampling $|s|$ words $(x_1, \cdots, x_{|s|})$, and asking for the length-$|s|$ bitstring of the bits indicating for each word x_i whether it belongs to a given hard language $\mathcal{L}$. Then we construct a fine-grained OWF as follows: an input to the function is a list of n puzzles $(p_1, \cdots, p_n)$ for some bound n, and an integer $i \leq n$. The function $F(p_1, \cdots, p_n, i)$ first solves the puzzle p_i, and outputs the solution $s(p_i)$ together with $(p_1, \cdots, p_n)$. Evaluating F takes time $O(n) + N_1$; on the other hand, when $\mathcal{L}$ is an ideally hard language, inverting F requires brute-forcing many of the p_i, which takes time $O(n \cdot N_2)$. Setting $n \approx N_1 \approx N_2$ gives a quadratic hardness gap. We refer to Sect. 3 for a technical overview and the full version of this work [BC20] for a formal proof and analysis of block-finding hardness in the RLM.

Average-Case Hard Languages and Fine-Grained OWF. With the above, we know that a sufficiently strong form of average-case hardness suffices to construct fine-grained one-way functions. The natural next question is whether weaker forms of average-case hardness could possibly suffice. We consider the two natural notions we mentioned previously: exponential average-case hardness, and the stronger *non-amortizing* exponential average-case hardness. For both, our main results are negative and rule out relativizing (black-box) constructions.

For exponential average-case hard languages, we show that *any* construction of fine-grained OWF from an (even exponentially) average-case hard language, even with an arbitrarily small polynomial security gap $N^{1+\varepsilon}$ (for any absolute constant $\varepsilon > 0$), must make a non-black-box use of the language. We prove this by exhibiting an oracle relative to which there exists an exponentially hard language, but no fine-grained one-way functions:

Theorem 2 (Informal). *There is an oracle relative to which there exists an exponentially secure average-case hard language, but any candidate fine-grained OWF f can be inverted with probability $O(1)$ and $\tilde{O}(N)$ calls to the oracle, where N denotes the number of oracle calls to compute f in the forward direction.*

Black-Box Separation Between Non-Amortizable Average-Case Hard Languages and Fine-Grained OWF. We then investigate whether non-amortizability (which states, roughly, that deciding membership of k random instances to $\mathcal{L}$ should take $O(k)$ times longer than deciding membership of a single instance to $\mathcal{L}$) suffices to construct fine-grained OWFs. As we explained, this would still constitute a very interesting win-win result: it would show that either weak forms of cryptography exist unconditionally, or nontrivial speedups can be achieved for *all* NP problems *when amortizing over many random instances*. Below, we sketch another motivation for studying this setting.

Non-Amortizability Helps Circumvent Black-Box Impossibilities. Non-amortizability features have proven to be a key approach to overcoming black-box impossibility results for cryptographic primitives. For example, the Biham-Goren-Ishai construction [BGI08] of fine-grained key agreement from exponential OWFs only provides an inverse-polynomial bound on the probability that an attacker retrieves the shared key when relying on Yao's XOR Lemma. In turn, when relying on a (plausible) version of the XOR Lemma stating that success probability decreases *exponentially fast* in the number of XORed instances, the adversary's success probability can be brought down to negligible. Yet, this "Dream XOR Lemma" cannot be proven under black-box reductions [BGI08]. An even more striking example is given by Simon's celebrated black-box separation between one-way functions and collision-resistant hash functions [Sim98]: Holmgren and Lombardi [HL18] recently showed that a one-way *product* function (i.e., a OWF that amplifies twice, meaning that inverting f on two random images (y_1, y_2) takes twice the time of inverting f on a single random image) suffices to circumvent Simon's impossibility result and build a collision-resistant hash function (in a black-box way).

A Black-Box Separation. Motivated by the above, we investigate the possibility of building fine-grained OWFs from non-amortizable average-case hard languages (i.e., languages whose average-case hardness amplifies through parallel repetitions). Unfortunately, our result turns out to be negative: we prove that there is no black-box construction of an $N^{1+\varepsilon}$-hard OWF (where N is the time it takes to evaluate the function in the forward direction), for an arbitrary constant $\varepsilon > 0$, even from an exponentially average-case hard language whose hardness amplifies at an exponential rate through parallel repetition. Conceptually, our second negative result separates fine-grained one-way functions from a much stronger primitive and can thus be seen as a much stronger result. Note, however, that technically, the two negative results are incomparable since the first one rules out relativizing reductions whereas the latter rules out black-box reductions, see the beginning of Sect. 3 for a discussion.

Theorem 3 (Informal). *There is no black-box construction of an $N^{1+\varepsilon}$-hard OWF f, for an arbitrary constant $\varepsilon > 0$, from exponentially average-case hard languages $\mathcal{L}$ whose hardness amplifies at an exponential rate through parallel repetition.*

In the nomenclature of Reingold, Vadhan and Trevisan [RTV04], we rule out a $\forall\exists$-weakly-reduction, a slightly weaker notion than a relativizing reduction. Namely, the reduction can access the adversary. Our result becomes a full oracle separation if the fine-grained one-way function f would be given black-box access to the adversary $\mathcal{A}$ as well. Reingold, Vadhan and Trevisan point out that in some cases, the adversary $\mathcal{A}$ can be embedded into the oracle O, but doing so did not seem straightforward for our case and is left as an open question. In the CAP nomenclature of Baecher, Brzuska and Fischlin [BBF13], we rule out NNN reductions, since the construction f can depend on the language $\mathcal{L}$, and the reduction $\mathcal{C}$ can depend on both, the adversary and the primitive, i.e., each of these dependencies can be seen as non-black-box, thus NNN.

Why Study Non-amortizability? In the past, non-amortizability proved key to overcome related limitations. For example, if one wants to build fine-grained key exchange with overwhelming security from (exponential) OWFs, a strong non-amortizability property (dubbed *dream XOR lemma*) is known to be necessary [BGI08]. Non-amortizability also allows bridging the gap between OWF and CRHFs [HL18]. Moreover, a very natural and—initially—promising-looking approach towards fine-grained cryptography from weaker-than-usual assumptions inherently goes through (and stops at) non-amortizable languages. Finally, a positive result (non-amortizable languages give FGOWF) would give a really nice win-win (algorithms efficiency vs cryptographic security) result.

Let us elaborate on the approach being natural and looking promising. The goal (FGOWFs from "weaker" assumptions) was set forth in [BRSV17], with a promising path: starting from a worst-case assumption (the exponential time hypothesis (ETH)), one gets structured average-case hardness (through the orthogonal vector problem (OV)); furthermore, this was pushed to *non-amortizable* hardness in follow-up work [BRSV18]. Then, [BRSV17] asked: can we push this OV-based construction further, up to FGOWFs?

One way to read our contributions is the following: our *positive* result can easily be framed as an OV-based construction (*solving a block* becomes finding x such that $F(x) = 1$, where F is an explicit low-degree polynomial). The key technique in [BRSV17, BRSV18] are a worst-case to average-case reduction and an average-case to non-amortizability reductions using the Berlekamp-Welch algorithm, which inherently only works for *search* OV. Block-finding hardness, on the other hand, formalizes what we would *need* to prove to achieve FG-OWF from ETH through this approach. Then, our last separation says: the further the Berlekamp-Welch techniques seems to get us (i.e., to non-amortizing hardness) won't suffice (in a black-box way) to achieve what we need, with *any* candidate construction. In other words, we need new non-black-box techniques that go beyond the Berlekamp-Welch algorithm. Since non-amortizability proved key to overcome related limitations in the past, we actually attempted to *prove* security of our construction from non-amortizing hardness for a long time.

1.2 A Core Abstract Lemma: The Hitting Lemma

At the heart of both our positive result and our black-box separations is an abstract lemma, which we call the *Hitting Lemma*. While the statement of the lemma is very intuitive, its proof is quite technical, and forms one of the core technical contributions of this work. In its abstract form, the Hitting Lemma is a very general probability statement about a simple two-player game between a challenger and an adversary. It shows up naturally on three seemingly unrelated occasions in our work, hence it seems likely that it can have other applications, and we believe it to be of independent interest.

At a high level, the Hitting Lemma provides a strong Chernoff-style bound on the number of witnesses which an adversary can possibly find given oracle access to the relation of a hard language. More precisely, we state the Hitting Lemma in an abstract way, as a game with the following structure:

- First, the game chooses a list of sets V_i. Each set V_i has size bounded by some value 2^n and can be thought of as the set of *candidate witnesses* for a size-n word.
- In each set V_i, the game chooses a uniformly random witness r_i. The sets V_i are allowed to have different sizes, to capture the more general setting where the adversary already obtained preliminary information excluding candidate witnesses.
- Eventually, the adversary interacts with an oracle $\mathsf{Guess}_{r_1 \cdots r_\ell}$ which, on input (i, x), returns 1 if $x = r_i$ and $\perp$ otherwise.

We call a query (i, x) such that $\mathsf{Guess}_{r_1 \cdots r_\ell}(i, x) = 1$ a *hitting query* (or a *hit*). The goal of the adversary is to get as many distinct hits as possible within a bounded number of queries. Intuitively, the most natural strategy to maximize the number of hits is to proceed as follows: first pick the smallest set V_i, and query arbitrary positions one by one, until a hit is obtained. Then, pick the second smallest set V_j and keep proceeding the same way, until all of the r_i are found or the query budget is exhausted.

In essence, the Hitting Lemma states that the above natural strategy is really the best possible strategy, in a strong sense. Namely, denoting m_Q the average number of hits obtained by a Q-query adversary following the above strategy, the Hitting Lemma shows that for *any* possible adversarial strategy, the probability of getting $O(m_Q) + c$ distinct hits using Q queries decreases exponentially with c (for some explicit constant in the $O(\cdot)$). The proof combines a reduction to a simpler probabilistic statement, proven by induction over Q, with a tight concentration bound on the winning probability of the above natural strategy.

Interestingly, the Hitting Lemma extends directly to the non-uniform setting, where the adversary is allowed to receive an arbitrary k-bit advice about the Guess oracle; this properties turns out to be crucial in some of our results. Our bound shows that this advice cannot provide more than k additional hits. More precisely, for any possible adversarial strategy where the adversary receives an arbitrary k-bit advice about the oracle, the probability of getting $O(m_Q) + k + c$ hits decreases exponentially with c. We refer to Sect. 6 for the full statement and analysis of the Hitting Lemma.

Analogy with the ROM. In the Random Oracle Model, a long line of work (see for example [Hel80, Unr07, DGK17, CDGS18] and references therein) has established the hardness of inverting an idealized random function in a non-uniform setting, given a bounded-length advice about the oracle. These results have proven to be important and powerful tools to reason about the Random Oracle Model. At a high level, the hitting lemma provides a comparable tool in the Random Language Model, and captures the hardness of *deciding language membership* for an idealized hard language, even given a non-uniform advice, and even when the adversary tries to amortize over many instances.

1.3   On the Significance of Our Results

We now address some points about how our results should be interpreted, and what they imply.

On Basing FGOWF on the Average-Case Hardness of a Concrete NP-complete Language. Our impossibility results rule out constructions of fine-grained one-way function that would work using black-box access to an *arbitrary* average-case hard language. However, it seems plausible that a construction of FGOWFs from the average-case hardness of an arbitrary language could proceed differently. Typically, such a construction could first reduce the language to a SAT instance (or any other NP-complete problem) using a non-black-box (e.g. Karp) reduction. Then, the construction of FGOWF would build upon the concrete structure of SAT; such a construction would not be ruled out by our results.

Implications of our Negative Results. In this setting, our negative results should be interpreted as saying that if such a construction is possible, then it must crucially rely on specific structural hardness properties of the chosen language, and not solely on natural properties such as its exponential hardness, or its non-amortizability. As it turns out, this has implications to previous attempts of basing cryptography on weaker hardness assumptions. The work of [BRSV17] showed constructions of fine-grained average-case hard languages from the strong exponential-time hypothesis (SETH), using a worst-case to average-case reduction based on the orthogonal vector problem. A major open problem left in their work, which they discuss at length, is whether their construction could be strenghtened to give FGOWFs. In a subsequent work [BRSV18], the authors made a step in the right direction, building *proofs of work* from SETH (building upon their result in [BRSV17]). Their construction precisely exploits that due to the specific structure of the orthogonal vector problem, it is possible to show *non-amortizability* of their fine-grained average-case hard language, which suffices to build proofs of work. Our result shows that this non-amortizability does *not* suffice to build FGOWFs: if there is a construction, it must rely on a different structural hardness property.

In fact, we initially designed the construction of FGOWF from block-finding hardness as a construction based on the average-case hard puzzles of [BRSV18], and dedicated an important effort to trying to reduce its security to the non-amortizable average-case hardness of this puzzle, viewing this approach as the most promising direction to based FGOWFs on a worst-case hardness assumption such as SETH. After failing to prove it secure, we realized that our lack of success might be inherent, and turned this realization into a proof by demonstrating the impossibility of basing a FGOWF on non-amortizing hardness in a blackbox way. We hope and believe that our negative results will therefore guide future attempts of basing FGOWFs on weaker assumptions, even attempts that do not ultimately aim at building them from arbitrary hard languages.

Implications of our Positive Results. Furthermore, our *positive* result hints precisely at the type of hardness which could suffice to build FGOWFs: intuitively, what is needed is that the concrete language satisfies some form of *pattern finding hardness*, where given a list of words $(x_1, \cdots, x_n)$, finding whether there is a sub-vector of words whose membership bits (i.e. the vector of bits indicating for each word whether it is in the language) satisfy a given pattern should require deciding membership of a large fraction of all words. This is formalized as *block-finding hardness* in our work (see Sect. 3.1 and the full version of this work [BC20]). We note that other related forms of hardness – where one must decide whether the membership bits of a vector of words satisfy some locally testable property – can also be shown to imply FGOWFs. We note that actually, a very similar type of structural hardness has been used in [LLW19] to build fine-grained one-way functions from concrete average-case hard problems.

1.4 Related Work

Fine-Grained Cryptography. We already pointed out that Merkle's construction [Mer78] provides the first example of fine-grained cryptography (as well as the first known example of public-key cryptography). It was further studied in [BGI08, BM09], and generalized to the quantum setting in [BS08, BHK+11]. Fine-grained cryptography has only become an explicit subject of study recently. The work of [BRSV17, BRSV18] constructs proofs of work from explicit fine-grained average-case hard languages which can be based on the strong exponential-time hypothesis (SETH), and explicitly poses the problem of building fine-grained one-way functions (while showing some barriers for basing them on SETH via natural approaches). The work of [DVV16] studies a different form of fine-grained cryptography, showing cryptosystems secure against resource-bounded adversaries, such as adversaries in NC_1, under a worst-case hardness assumption. Eventually, the work of [LLW19] is the most closely related to ours: it shows constructions of fine-grained one-way functions and fine-grained encryption schemes from the average-case hardness of concrete problems, such as the Zero-k-Clique problem.

Hardness in Pessiland. While building one-way functions from average-case hardness has remained elusive, some works have investigated other useful forms of hardness which could possibly reside in Pessiland. In particular, in [Wee06], Wee shows that the existence of non-trivial succinct 2-round argument systems for some languages in NP cannot be excluded from Pessiland in a black-box way.

Oracle Techniques. Besides new ideas, our oracle separation relies on several established techniques. We use the *two-oracle* technique of [Sim98,HR04] where one oracle implements the base primitive and the second oracle breaks constructions built from this primitive. As we argue about the *efficiency* of the constructed one-way function, we use similar techniques to Gennaro and Trevisan [GT00] who describe the emulation of a random oracle based on a bounded-length string, implicitly applying a compression argument. We use Borel-Cantelli to extract a single oracle from a distribution of random oracles as the seminal work on black-box separations by Impagliazzo and Rudich [IR89]. In order to make our oracle deterministic, we use the hashing trick of Valiant-Vazirani [VV85] to obtain a unique value out of many pre-image for a one-way function. In particular, we hash *evaluation paths* similar to Bogdanov and Brzuska [BB15] who separate size-verifiable one-way functions from NP-hardness.

On the Relation to Two Recent Works. In a recent work [PV20], Pass and Venkitasubramaniam show that TFNP (the class of total NP search problems) is unconditionally hard in Pessiland. More precisely, they show the following: if there exists average-case hard languages, then either there exists average-case hard TFNP problems, or there exists one-way functions. We note that, since their constructions are black-box, combining their result with our work further implies the following result stating that proving that *total search* average-case hardness suffices to construct fine-grained one-way functions is likely to be hard, since any such black-box proof would unconditionally imply the existence of (full-fledged) one-way functions:

Theorem 4 (this work + [PV20], informal). *If there is a black-box construction of $N^{1+\varepsilon}$-hard one-way function, for an arbitrary constant $\varepsilon > 0$, from average-case TFNP hardness, then one-way functions exist unconditionally.*

In another recent work [PL20], Pass and Liu showed that mild average-case hardness of computing time-bounded Kolmogorov complexity already suffices to establish (in a black-box way) the existence of one-way functions. In particular, we note that, combined with our results, this implies that even exponentially-strong, self-amplifiable average-case hardness in NP does not imply (in a black-box way) mild average-case hardness of time-bounded Kolmogorov complexity.

Theorem 5 (this work + [PL20], informal). *There is no black-box reduction from the mild average-case hardness of computing time-bounded Kolmogorov complexity to the existence of exponentially average-case hard languages whose hardness amplifies at an exponential rate via parallel repetition.*

2 Preliminaries

2.1 Notation, Computational Models and Oracles

For any $n \in \mathbb{N}$, $[n]$ denotes the set $\{1, \cdots, n\}$. Throughout this paper, we represent algorithms as families of boolean circuits (one for each input length), and use circuit size (i.e., the number of wires) as the main measure of efficiency. We model oracle access by allowing circuits to have oracle gates. We measure the size of such an oracle circuit as for a standard circuit, as the number of its wires. Typically, if an oracle takes an n-bit entry as input and outputs an m-bit response, this will be modeled by a fan-in-n fan-out-m oracle gate (hence this gate will contribute $n + m$ to the total circuit size).

As in the standard model for boolean circuits, the wires typically carry bit values. For simplicity and readability, we will generally allow the wires to directly carry other special symbols, such as $\perp$ and err (converting a circuit in this model to a "purely boolean" circuit only introduces some constant blowup which has no impact on our asymptotic results). By default, even when we do not mention it explicitly, we allow all (standard and oracle) gates to receive the symbol err as one of their inputs. If a gate receives err as one of its inputs, it returns the err on all of its output wires. We use pseudo-code as a description language and only argue about the size of the corresponding circuit informally.

2.2 Fine-Grained One-Way Functions

We start by introducing the notion of a fine-grained one-way function (FG-OWF). At a high level, an (ε, δ)-FG-OWF is a function f (modeled as a family $\{f_m\}_m$ of circuits, one for each input size) such that all circuits of size $o(|f|^{1+\delta})$ have probability at most ε to find a preimage of $f(x)$ for a random input x.

Definition 6 (Fine-Grained One-Way Function). *Let $\varepsilon : \mathbb{N} \mapsto \mathbb{R}^+$ be a positive function and $\delta > 0$ be a constant. A function $f : \{0,1\}^* \to \{0,1\}^*$ is an (ε, δ)-fine-grained one-way function if for all circuit families $\mathcal{C} = \{\mathcal{C}_m\}_{m \in \mathbb{N}}$ and all large enough m, if $|\mathcal{C}_m| < |f_m|^{1+\delta}$, then we have*

$$\Pr_{z \leftarrow_{\$} \{0,1\}^m}\left[\mathcal{C}_m(f(z), 1^m) \in f^{-1}(f(z))\right] \leq \varepsilon(m).$$

One can also consider a slightly weaker notion, namely a fine-grained one-way *function distribution* (FG-OWFD), were the hardness of inversion should hold with respect to a randomly sampled function f from a distribution D.

Definition 7 (Fine-Grained One-Way Function Distribution). *Let $\varepsilon : \mathbb{N} \mapsto \mathbb{R}^+$ be a positive function and $\delta > 0$ be a constant. A distribution D over functions $f : \{0,1\}^* \to \{0,1\}^*$ is an (ε, δ)-fine-grained one-way function distribution if for all circuit families $\mathcal{C} = \{\mathcal{C}_m\}_{m \in \mathbb{N}}$ and all large enough m, if $|\mathcal{C}_m| < |f_m|^{1+\delta}$ for all f in the support of D, then it holds that*

$$\Pr_{z \leftarrow \$\{0,1\}^m, f \leftarrow \$ D}\left[\mathcal{C}_m(f, f(z), 1^m) \in f^{-1}(f(z))\right] \leq \varepsilon(m).$$

Any distribution over FG-OWFs induces a FG-OWFD, but the converse need not hold in general.

2.3   Languages

The class NP contains all languages $\mathcal{L}$ of the form $\mathcal{L} = \{x \mid \exists w, (|w| = \mathrm{poly}(|x|)) \wedge (\mathcal{R}(x,w) = 1)\}$, where $\mathcal{R}$ is a *relation* computable by a polysize uniform circuit. This definition naturally extends to the case where an oracle O is available; in this case, we say that the oracle language $\mathcal{L}^O$ is in NP^O if it is of the above form, where $\mathcal{R}$ is computable by a uniform oracle circuit with $|\mathcal{R}| = \mathrm{poly}(|x|)$. When the oracle O is clear from the context, we will sometimes abuse this notation and simply say that the oracle language $\mathcal{L}^O$ is in NP. For a string x, we will denote by $\mathcal{L}(x)$ the bit which is 1 if $x \in \mathcal{L}$, and 0 otherwise. We will also extend this definition to vectors of strings $\vec{x}$ in a natural way.

Average-Case Hard Languages. We now define (exponentially) average-case hard languages (EACHLs). Note that the exponential hardness in the following definition refers to the success probability of the algorithm.

Definition 8 (Exponential Average-Case Hardness). *A language $\mathcal{L}$ is exponentially average-case hard if for any circuit family $\mathcal{C} = \{\mathcal{C}_n\}_{n \in \mathbb{N}}$ and all large enough n,*

$$\Pr_{x \leftarrow \$\{0,1\}^n}\left[\mathcal{C}_n(x) = \mathcal{L}(x)\right] \leq \frac{1}{2} + \frac{|\mathcal{C}_n|}{2^n}.$$

Note that in the most common definition of EACHLs, one does usually not consider an exact bound $|\mathcal{C}_n|$, and instead define a language to be exponentially hard if a polytime algorithm $\mathcal{C}_n$ finds $\mathcal{L}(x)$ with probability at most $1/2 + \mathrm{poly}(n)/2^n$ for a random word $x \in \{0,1\}^n$. However, since we will work in the fine-grained setting, we settle for a stricter definition, with an explicit relation between the running time of $\mathcal{C}_n$ and the probability of finding $\mathcal{L}(x)$. Similarly as for FG-OWFs, we can also define a weaker notion of exponential average-case hard *language distributions* (EACHLD):

Definition 9 (Exponential Average-Case Hard Language Distribution). *A distribution D over languages $\mathcal{L}$ is exponentially average-case hard if for any circuit family $\mathcal{C} = \{C_n\}_{n \in \mathbb{N}}$ and all large enough n,*

$$\Pr_{x \leftarrow \$ \{0,1\}^n, \mathcal{L} \leftarrow \$ D}[C_n(x, \mathcal{L}) = \mathcal{L}(x)] \leq \frac{1}{2} + \frac{|C_n|}{2^n}.$$

Note that any distribution over EACHLs induces an EACHLD, but the converse need not hold in general.

2.4 Pairwise Independent Hash-Functions

Definition 10. *For all $j, i \in \mathbb{N}$, we call a distribution $\mathcal{H}_{j,i}$ over functions $h : \{0,1\}^j \mapsto \{0,1\}^{i+2}$ a distribution of pairwise independent hash-functions, if for all $p, p' \in \{0,1\}^j$ with $p \neq p'$, it holds that*

$$\Pr_{h \leftarrow \$ \mathcal{H}_{j,i+2}}[h(p) = 0^{i+2}] = 2^{-i-2}$$
$$\Pr_{h \leftarrow \$ \mathcal{H}_{j,i+2}}[h(p') = 0^{i+2}] = 2^{-i-2}$$
$$\Pr_{h \leftarrow \$ \mathcal{H}_{j,i+2}}[h(p) = h(p') = 0^{i+2}] = 2^{-2i-4}$$

The following fact is used, e.g., by Valiant and Vazirani in their randomized reduction which solves SAT given a UniqueSAT oracle [VV85].

Claim 1. *For all sets $S \subseteq \{0,1\}^j$ such that $2^i \leq |S| \leq 2^{i+1}$, it holds that*

$$\Pr_{h \leftarrow \$ \mathcal{H}_{j,i+2}}[\exists! p \in S : h(p) = 0^{i+2}] \geq \frac{1}{8}.$$

3 Technical Overview: FGOWFs from Block-Finding Hardness

We first introduce the Random Language Model (RLM), which captures idealized average-case hard languages, in the same way that random oracles capture idealized one-way functions.[5] We will use this model as a heuristic tool to analyze the new form of average-case hardness which we will introduce next. We note that this model has limitations: it is a simplified model, and it is actually not too hard to *directly* build a fine-grained OWF in this model (e.g. one can define the function F which maps x to the list of language memberships of the words $x||1, x \cdots, x||n'$, for an appropriate choice of n'^6). However, such simplified constructions do not correspond to any natural form of average-case hardness that could be formulated on standard NP languages. Rather, our goal is only to use

---

[5] More formally, since we consider an oracle sampled from a distribution over oracles, as for the Random Oracle Model, this captures average-case hard *language distributions*. I.e., the hardness of a language is averaged over the choice of the instance *and* the sampling of the oracle.

[6] We thank an anonymous reviewer for pointing out this construction.

the RLM as a heuristic rule of thumb to evaluate the plausibility of our new average-case hardness notion.

We define a random language $\mathcal{L}$ as follows: for each integer n and each word $x \in \{0,1\}^n$, sample a uniformly random bit $B[x]$. Then the elements of $\mathcal{L}$ are all x with $B[x] = 1$. For notational convenience, we extend this notation to vectors: given a vector $\vec{x}$ of words, $B(\vec{x})$ denotes the vector of the bits $B[x_i]$. For each $x \in \{0,1\}^n$, we also sample a uniformly random *witness* $W[x] \leftarrow\!\!\$ \{0,1\}^n$. To check membership to the language, we introduce an oracle Chk defined as follows: on input a pair (x, w), the oracle checks whether $B[x] = 0$ or $w \neq W[x]$. If one of these conditions hold, it outputs $\bot$; otherwise, it outputs 1 (See Fig. 2). It is relatively easy to see that to check membership of a candidate word x to $\mathcal{L}$ given access to Chk, the best possible strategy is to query (x, w) for all possible values $w \in \{0,1\}^n$, hoping to hit the uniformly random value $W[x]$. Hence, deciding membership of a word x to $\mathcal{L}$ requires on the average 2^{n-1} queries to Chk, which shows that $\mathcal{L}$ is (exponentially) average-case hard.

We now define the notion of block-finding hardness. We will show that (1) block-finding hardness holds for a random language, and (2) if there is a block-finding hard language, then there is an explicit construction of a FG-OWF f such that every adversary running in time $N(n)^{2-\nu}$ for an arbitrarily small constant ν has only a negligible probability of inverting f (in n) – *id est*, there exists a $(\mathsf{negl}(n), 1-\nu)$-FG-OWF, where $\mathsf{negl}(n)$ denotes some negligible function of n.

Distribution $\mathcal{T}$	Chk$[W,B](x,w)$
for $n \in \mathbb{N}$:	**if** $W[x] = w \wedge B[x] = 1$
for $x \in \{0,1\}^n$:	**return** 1
$W[x] \leftarrow\!\!\$ \{0,1\}^n$	**else return** $\bot$
$B[x] \leftarrow\!\!\$ \{0,1\}$	
return (W,B)	

Fig. 2. Distribution $\mathcal{T}$ for sampling a random language $\mathcal{L}^O = \{x \in \{0,1\}^* \mid B[x] = 1\}$ with associated list of witnesses W. The oracle $O = \mathsf{Chk}[W,B]$ allows to check membership of a word $x \in \mathcal{L}^O$ given witness $W[x]$.

3.1 Block-Finding Hardness of $\mathcal{L}$

Informally, we say that a language satisfies *block-finding hardness* if for any adversary $\mathcal{A}$ and any large enough n, the following holds: The adversary $\mathcal{A}$ is given $N \leq 2^n/k$ many length-k vectors $\vec{x}_i$ of distinct words $x_{i,j} \in \{0,1\}^n$ together with the string $s = B[\vec{x}_i]$ (the vector of language membership bits for the words in $\vec{x}_i$) for a uniformly random block index $i \leftarrow\!\!\$ [N]$. If $\mathcal{A}$ finds the block index i with probability significantly better than guessing, it must run in time $\tilde{\Omega}(N \cdot 2^n)$ (in the RLM, this corresponds to making $\tilde{\Omega}(N \cdot 2^n)$ queries to Chk). Intuitively, this means that (up to polylogarithmic factors) the best strategy to find i is to find out the language membership bits of some of the words in each of the blocks, by brute-forcing every possible witness for these words, until one finds membership bits that are consistent with s. Slightly more formally, we show the following:

Lemma 11 (Block-Finding Hardness of $\mathcal{L}$ – Informal Version). *For any adversary $\mathcal{C}$, $n \in \mathbb{N}$, block size k, and number of blocks N (with $k \cdot N \leq 2^n$), and any tuple of blocks $(\vec{x}_i)_{i \leq N} = (x_{i,1}, \cdots, x_{i,k})_{i \leq N}$ such that all the $x_{i,j}$ are distinct:*

$$\Pr_{i \leftarrow \$[N]}[\mathcal{C}_n((\vec{x}_j)_j, B[\vec{x}_i]) = i] \leq \frac{1}{\tilde{O}(N)} \cdot \left(\frac{|\mathcal{C}_n|}{2^n} + 1\right) \cdot 2^{O(k)}.$$

In the RLM, the language $\mathcal{L}$ satisfies block-finding hardness essentially because distinct words have truly independent witnesses and language membership bits. More formally, the above lemma will follow from a strong and generic concentration bound, the *hitting lemma*. We state and formally prove the hitting lemma separately in Sect. 6, Lemma 19, since it turns out that this lemma provides a very convenient and versatile tool to bound the success probability of an adversary which attempts to decide membership of words in an oracle language (the hitting lemma will be needed on three different occasions in this paper). In the context of proving the block-finding hardness of $\mathcal{L}$, we will need a variant of the hitting lemma of the following form:

Lemma 12 (Simplified Hitting Lemma with Advice – Informal Version). *For every integers $n, N, k \in \mathbb{N}$ with $kN \leq 2^n$, vector $\vec{y}$ of kN words, adversary $\mathcal{A}$ getting $\vec{y}$ and $B[\vec{y}_i]$ for a random i (where $\vec{y}_i$ is a vector of k words), and for every integer $c \geq 1$,*

$$\Pr_{(W,B) \leftarrow \mathcal{T}}\left[\#\mathsf{Hit} \geq \frac{O(|\mathcal{A}|)}{2^n} + k + c\right] \leq 2^{-O(c)},$$

where $\#\mathsf{Hit}$ counts the number of witnesses found by $\mathcal{A}$ for distinct words of length n among the entries of $\vec{y}$.

At the same time, conditioned on making less than M hits in different blocks, it is straightforward to show that $\mathcal{A}$ can find i with probability M/N: intuitively, this is because if i belongs to one of the $N - M$ blocks where no hits were made, then the indices of all these blocks are perfectly equiprobable conditioned on the view of $\mathcal{A}$. Applying Bayes rule to combine the above bounds, the probability that $\mathcal{A}$ finds i is upper bounded by the probability that $\mathcal{A}$ finds i conditioned on making less than M hits, plus the probability of making more than M hits. Therefore, for any M, the probability that $\mathcal{A}$ finds i is upper bounded by

$$\frac{M}{N} + 2^{-O(M - |\mathcal{A}|/2^n - k)}.$$

From there, an appropriate choice of M (depending on $|\mathcal{A}|, N$, and n) suffices to conclude that $\mathcal{A}$ finds i with probability at most $\frac{1}{\tilde{O}(N)} \cdot \left(\frac{|\mathcal{C}_n|}{2^n} + 1\right) \cdot 2^{O(k)}$, which concludes the proof.

From Block-Finding Hardness to Fine-Grained One-Way Function. A block-finding hard language immediately leads to a FG-OWF with a quadratic hardness gap: the input to the function is a list of $N = 2^n/k$ blocks $\vec{x}$ of distinct words $\vec{x_i}$ together with an index i. Evaluating the function is done by brute-forcing the languages membership bits of the words in $\vec{x_i}$, which takes at most $k \cdot 2^n$ queries to Chk, and outputting $(\vec{x}, s = B[\vec{x_i}])$. By the block finding hardness of $\mathcal{L}$, inverting the function on a random input, on the other hand, requires $\tilde{O}(N \cdot 2^n) = \tilde{O}(2^{2n}/k)$ queries to Chk to succeed with constant probability when the index i is uniquely defined (i.e., there is a unique index i such that the block $\vec{x_i}$ satisfies $s = B[\vec{x_i}]$). This can be guaranteed to hold except with negligible probability, by choosing $k = \omega(\log n)$. Overall, this leads to a FG-OWF with quadratic hardness gap (up to polylogarithmic factors), with some small but non-negligible inversion probability ε. Parallel amplification can then be used to make the inversion probability negligible, leading to the following corollary:

Corollary 13. *For any $\varepsilon > 0$, there exists a $(\mathsf{negl}(m), 1 - \varepsilon)$-fine-grained one-way function distribution in the Random Language Model.*

4 Overview: No FGOWFs from Average-Case Hardness

Next, we study the possibility of instantiating the above construction using an average-case hard language, instead of a block-finding hard language. At first sight, it is not clear that average-case hardness suffices, since our construction crucially relies on the block-finding hardness of the language, a seemingly much stronger property. Indeed, we show that there exists no construction of essentially any non-trivial FG-OWF making a black-box use of an exponentially average-case hard language. To do so, we exhibit an oracle distribution relative to which there is an exponentially average-case hard language, but no FG-OWF, even with arbitrarily small hardness gap. This proof is the only part of our paper that does not require the hitting lemma.

Language Description. We start by introducing our language. Our oracle defines a somewhat exotic language: for each integer k, we let *all* words $x \in \{0,1\}^n$ such that $k = \lceil \log n \rceil$ have the *same* random witness $w \leftarrow_\$ \{0,1\}^{2^k}$, and we put either all these words simultaneously inside or outside the language, by picking the same random membership bit b_k for all of them. Intuitively, this provides an extreme example of a language which is still hard to decide (since given a word $x \in \{0,1\}^n$, one must still enumerate over $2^{2^{\lceil \log n \rceil}} > 2^n$ candidate witnesses to find out whether $x \in \mathcal{L}$), but whose hardness does not amplify at all (since finding a witness for a single word x gives the witness for all words whose bitlength is close to that of x). This aims at capturing the intuition that any candidate FG-OWF built from an average-case hard language $\mathcal{L}$ must somehow leverage some amplification properties of the hardness of $\mathcal{L}$. Then, the oracle Chk is similar as before: on input (x, w), it returns $\perp$ if $x \notin \mathcal{L}$ or w is not the right witness for x, and 1 otherwise. We will show that any oracle adversary $\mathcal{A}$

requires $O(2^n)$ queries to decide membership of a word $x \in \{0,1\}^n$ to $\mathcal{L}$. The proof is relatively straightforward and relies on the fact that the membership of x to $\mathcal{L}$ remains random conditioned on the view of $\mathcal{A}$ as long as $\mathcal{A}$ did not make any hit, i.e., a query with the right witness for x.

Inexistence of FG-OWF Relative to Chk. Next, we show that for any constant δ, there exists an oracle algorithm $\mathcal{A}$ such that for any candidate FG-OWF f, $\mathcal{A}$ (given access to Chk) of size bounded by $|f|^{1+\delta}$ which inverts f with probability 0.99. The adversary works as follows: for any integer k, it checks whether the function will make "too many" queries of the form (x, w) with x of length n such that $k = \lceil \log n \rceil$ (we call this a k-query), where "too many" is defined as $(2^{2^k})^\varepsilon$ for a value $\varepsilon = (1 + \delta/2)^{-1}$. Intuitively, making more than this number of queries ensures that f will have a noticeable probability of making a hitting query. For all such "heavy queries", $\mathcal{A}$ makes all possible (2^{2^k}) queries to Chk with respect to some fixed word x, until he finds the witness. $\mathcal{A}$ also does the same for all k-queries with $k \leq B(\varepsilon)$ for some bound $B(\varepsilon)$ to be determined later, even when they do not correspond to heavy query (this is to avoid some "border effects" of small queries in the probability calculations). Note that this allows $\mathcal{A}$ to find the witness for *all* words of length n such that $k = \lceil \log n \rceil$, since they all share the same witness. $\mathcal{A}$ defines the following oracle-less function f' that contains all the hardcoded witnesses that $\mathcal{A}$ recovered. Now, on input x, f' runs exactly as f and if f makes a k-query (x, w) for some k, then f' proceeds as follows:

- If k corresponds to a heavy query, then, using (2^{2^k}) queries, $\mathcal{A}$ already computed the witness for all k-queries and thus f' contains the hardcoded witness to correctly answer the query.
- If k does not correspond to a heavy query, f' simulates the answer of the oracle as $\bot$.

We prove that with high probability (at least 0.999), the function f' agrees with f on a random input x; this is because f' disagrees with f only if there is a k-query with $k > 10$ where f makes less than $(2^{2^k})^\varepsilon$ queries, yet hits a witness (for all other types of queries, $\mathcal{A}$ finds the witness by brute-force, hence it can always simulate correctly the answer of the oracle). But this happens only with probability $1 - \sum_{k=B(\varepsilon)+1}^{\infty} (2^{2^k})^\varepsilon \cdot 2^{-2^k}$, which is bounded by 0.999 by picking a sufficiently large bound $B(\varepsilon)$ such that $(1-\varepsilon)2^{B(\varepsilon)} > B(\varepsilon)$. Then, by a straightforward probability calculation, the probability that inverting f' (which $\mathcal{A}$ can easily do locally since f' is oracle-less) corresponds to successfully inverting f on a random input x can be lower-bounded by $0.999^2 > 0.99$, which concludes the proof.

5 Overview: No FG-OWF from Non-Amortizable Hardness

Note that the techniques from our simpler oracle separation crucially exploit that the hardness of the average-case hard language implemented by Chk does not amplify well (in fact, this is the reason why the hitting lemma is not needed in the analysis). We are thus interested in understanding whether we can still provide a black-box impossibility result even when the underlying average-case hard language satisfies *non-amortizable* exponential hardness, or whether non-amortizable average-case hard languages suffice to construct a fine-grained one-way function.

We call a language $\mathcal{L}$ (exponentially) self-amplifiable average-case hard if for any superlogarithmic (computable, total) function $\ell(\cdot)$, for any circuit family $\mathcal{C} = \{\mathcal{C}_n : \{0,1\}^{\ell(n)\cdot n} \mapsto \{0,1\}^n\}_{n \in \mathbb{N}}$ of size at most $2^{O(n)} \cdot \ell(n)$, and for all large enough $n \in \mathbb{N}$,

$$\Pr_{x \leftarrow_{\$} \{0,1\}^{\ell \cdot n}}[\mathcal{C}_n(\vec{x}) = \mathcal{L}(\vec{x})] \leq \mathsf{poly}(n) \cdot 2^{-\left(\ell(n) - \frac{\tilde{O}(|\mathcal{C}_n|)}{2^{O(n)}}\right)}.$$

Informally, this means that to find the language membership bits of $\ell(n)$ challenge words, the best an adversary $\mathcal{C}_n$ can do (up to polylogarithmic factors in $|\mathcal{C}_n|$ and constant factors in n) is to brute-force as many membership bits as it can (roughly, $\tilde{O}(|\mathcal{C}_n|)/2^n$ since brute-forcing a single membership bit requires $O(2^n)$ queries), and guessing the $\ell(n) - \tilde{O}(|\mathcal{C}_n|)/2^n$ missing membership bits at random. Note that self-amplifiable average-case hardness is especially interesting when the circuit $\mathcal{C}_n$ is allowed to run in time larger than 2^n (for small circuits, of size much smaller than 2^n, the standard average-case hardness notion already bounds their probability of guessing correctly a single entry of $\mathcal{L}(\vec{x})$). In this range, the $\mathsf{poly}(n)$ factor in our definition is absorbed in the $\tilde{O}(|\mathcal{C}_n|)$ term in the exponent (note also that adversaries of size larger than $2^{O(n)} \cdot \ell(n)$ can solve the full challenge by brute-force).

Our main result rules out black-box reductions from any exponentially self-amplifiable average-case hard language to fine-grained one-way functions, with arbitrarily small hardness gap. Slightly more formally, we prove the following theorem:

Theorem 14 (Informal). *There exists an oracle O and an oracle language $\mathcal{L}^{\mathsf{O}}$ such that for any fine-grained one-way function f, there exists an (inefficient) adversary $\mathcal{A}$ that inverts f with probability close to 1 such that $\mathcal{L}$ remains exponentially self-amplifiable average-case hard against any candidate reduction $\mathcal{C}$ given oracle access to both O and $\mathcal{A}$.*

We prove Theorem 14 which is phrased in terms of reductions by establishing Theorem 15 which is phrased in terms of oracle worlds.

Theorem 15 (Language Hardness and Good Inversion, Informal). *There exists an oracle O and an oracle Inv such that for all oracle functions f, there exists an inverter $\mathcal{A}$ of size $|\mathcal{A}| = \tilde{O}(|f|)$ which, given oracle access to $(\mathsf{O}, \mathsf{Inv})$ and input (f, y), outputs a preimage of y with respect to f^{O} with probability close to 1. Moreover, there exists an oracle language $\mathcal{L}^{\mathsf{O}}$ which is exponentially self-amplifiable average case hard against any candidate reduction $\mathcal{C}$ given oracle access to $(\mathsf{O}, \mathsf{Inv})$.*

Theorem 15 is slightly different from our main theorem: the inverter $\mathcal{A}$ is now required to be efficient, but gets the help of an additional oracle Inv. Furthermore, the reduction $\mathcal{C}$ is now given oracle access to (O, Inv) instead of $(O, \mathcal{A})$; the implication follows from the fact that the code of $\mathcal{A}$ is linear in its input size, and thus, its code can be hardcoded into the code of $\mathcal{C}$, hence the reduction $\mathcal{C}^{O,\mathcal{A}}$ in our main theorem can be emulated by a reduction $\mathcal{C}_{\mathcal{A}}^{O,Inv}$ in Theorem 15, where $|\mathcal{C}_{\mathcal{A}}| \approx |\mathcal{C}|$. To prove Theorem 15, we rely on a standard method in oracle separations: we first prove a variant of Theorem 15 with respect to a *distribution* over oracles O, Inv (where both the success probability of the inverter and the probability of breaking the self-amplifiable average-case hardness of $\mathcal{L}$ will be over the random choice of O, Inv as well). Then, we apply the Borel-Cantelli lemma to show that with measure 1 over the choice of the oracle, the oracle is "good" and thus, in particular, a single good oracle exists as required by Theorem 15. In summary, to prove Theorem 15 we prove two theorems relative to an explicit distribution $\mathcal{T}$ over oracles O, Inv:

Theorem 16 (Language Hardness, Informal). *For any $\ell : \mathbb{N} \mapsto \mathbb{N}$, circuit family $\mathcal{C} = \{\mathcal{C}_n\}_n$, and for all large enough $n \in \mathbb{N}$,*

$$\Pr_{\vec{x} \leftarrow_\$ \{0,1\}^{\ell \cdot n}, (O, Inv) \leftarrow_\$ \mathcal{T}} \left[\mathcal{C}_n^{O,Inv}(\vec{x}) = \mathcal{L}^O(\vec{x}) \right] \le \mathsf{poly}(n) \cdot 2^{-\left(\ell(n) - \frac{\tilde{O}(|\mathcal{C}_n|)}{2^{O(n)}} \right)}.$$

Theorem 17 (Efficient Inversion, Informal). *Let $f : \{0,1\}^* \to \{0,1\}^*$ be an oracle function. There exists an efficient inverter $\mathcal{A}^{O,Inv}(f, .)$ for f. More precisely, $\mathcal{A}$ is of size $|\mathcal{A}| = \tilde{O}(|f|)$ and for sufficiently large $m \in \mathbb{N}$, it holds that*

$$\Pr_{z \leftarrow_\$ \{0,1\}^m, (O, Inv) \leftarrow_\$ \mathcal{T}} \left[f^O(\mathcal{A}^{O,Inv}(f, f^O(z))) = f^O(z) \right] \approx 1.$$

5.1 Defining the Oracle Distribution $\mathcal{T}$

The distribution $\mathcal{T}$ samples a triple (W, B, H) where:

- B defines a random language $\mathcal{L}$: for every $x \in \{0,1\}^*$, $B[x]$ is set to 0 or 1 with probability $1/2$;
- W defines a set of random *witnesses*: for any $n \in \mathbb{N}$ and $x \in \{0,1\}^n$, $W[x]$ is set to a uniformly random bitstring w_x of length n.
- H contains a pairwise independent hash-function for each triple (i, C, y), where $i \in \mathbb{N}$, C is an encoding of a circuit and y is a bitstring.

A sample (W, B, H) from $\mathcal{T}$ defines a pair of oracles (O, Inv), where the oracle $O = (Chk, Pspace)$ is defined as follows:

- Chk is a membership checking oracle: on input (x, w), it returns $\perp$ if $W[x] \ne w$, and $B[x]$ otherwise. Note that this means that relative to Chk, $\mathcal{L}$ is a random language in NP $\cap$ co-NP, since Chk allows to check both membership and non-membership in $\mathcal{L}$, given the appropriate witness. A *hit* is a query to Chk which does not output $\perp$. To emphasize the dependency of $\mathcal{L}$ on O, we use the notation $\mathcal{L}^O$.

- Pspace is a PSPACE oracle which allows the caller to efficiently perform computations that do not involve calls to the oracles Chk, Inv.

We now turn our attention to the oracle Inv, which is the most involved component: Inv must be defined such that there is an efficient oracle algorithm $\mathcal{A}$ which can, given access to O, Inv, invert any candidate one-way function f^O, yet no algorithm (reduction) can break the self-amplifiable average-case hardness of the language $\mathcal{L}^O$ given access to O, Inv. Hence, the goal of Inv is, given an input (f, y), to help compute preimages z of y with respect to the oracle function f^O, but with carefully chosen safeguards to guarantee that Inv cannot be abused to decide the language $\mathcal{L}^O$. Our solution relies on two crucial safeguards, which we describe below.

First Safeguard: Removing Heavy Paths. The oracle Inv refuses to invert functions f on outputs y if the query-path from the preimage z to y in f^O is "too lucky" with respect to O. To understand this, consider the following folklore construction of a worst-case one-way function f: on input (x, w), it queries $\mathsf{Chk}(x, w)$ and outputs $(x, 1)$ if the check succeeds, and $(x, 0)$ otherwise. Then, querying Inv on input $(f, (x, 1))$ allows the adversary to find the witness w associated to x efficiently, since the function f makes only a single query and thus the inversion query $\mathsf{Inv}(f, (x, 1))$ has small cost for $\mathcal{A}$.

But since f^O is a normal (average-case) one-way function, we can allow the oracle to not invert on a too lucky evaluation path, if we can show that it still inverts sufficiently often. Concretely, on input (f, y), the oracle Inv computes the set S of all *paths* from an input z to $y = f^O(z)$, defined as the sequence of input-output pairs. Then, for all $k \leq |f|$, Inv discards from this set S all *k-heavy paths*, i.e., the paths along which the number of Chk hits on k-bit inputs is much higher[7] than expected, i.e., $N(k)/2^{k-1}$, where $N(k)$ is the number of Chk gates with k-bit inputs in f.

If S is not empty, then Inv samples a uniformly random element from S and returns the set of queries made on the path to the adversary. Since oracles need to be deterministic, we derandomize the sampling via the use of the pairwise independent hash-function stored in the third output H of $\mathcal{T}$ at $H[\log|S|, f, y]$ by the Valiant-Vazirani [VV85] trick that ensures that with probability $\frac{1}{8}$, there is only a unique value in S that hashes to $0^{\log(|S|-1)}$. Note that it suffices to return the *set* of query-answer pairs, as the adversary can use the Pspace oracle to find an input z that leads to y with this set of query-answer pairs produced by f^O. I.e., the Pspace uses the set to emulate the answers to queries made by f and discards a candidate z as soon as it makes a query not in the set.

Let us return to the issue of k-lightness. Firstly, note that we need to check for lightness for all values k, since the oracle Inv accepts functions that make queries to Chk on different k-values, and the Inv-oracle does not "know" the length of the x_i-values for which $\mathcal{C}$ tries to decide membership. Secondly, we now need to clarify that we consider the number of hits as too high above its expected value

---

[7] Determining an appropriate bound on *much higher* is crucial to avoid that deciding $\mathcal{L}^O$ becomes too easy. We return to this issue shortly.

if there are more than $O(N(k))/2^k + \log^2(|f|)$ k-hits on the evaluation path. In this case, if $|f| = O(2^k)$, then on input length k, the adversary could essentially get the same number of hits without Inv queries by using a circuit of slightly bigger size $\tilde{O}(|f|)$ that only makes Chk queries. The point of the additive $\log^2 |f|$ term is to ensure (via a concentration bound) that on a uniformly random input z, the probability that the path on z is light is at least $1 - \frac{1}{\text{superpoly}|f|}$ (while at the same time, the language hardness is maintained).

In turn, when $|f|$ is smaller than, say, $2^{\frac{k}{6}}$, then the additive $\log^2 |f|$ term turns out to allow for too many hits. In this case, the probability of making even a single hit is $2^{-\frac{5(k-1)}{6}}$ and thus exponentially small in k whereas $O(N(k))/2^k + \log^2 |f|$ might potentially allow for many hits. Thus, before performing all steps described in the first saveguard, we first replace f by a shaved function f_s, described below.

Second Safeguard: Shaving High Levels. We *shave* all Chk-gates of $|f|$ that are for *large* input length k, i.e., for all Chk-gates with input length k such that $|f| \leq 2^{\frac{k}{6}}$. To do so, we replace f by a shaved function f_s where the answers of such Chk queries are hardcoded to be $\bot$. The probability (over O and z) that this changes the behaviour of f is equal to the probability of making a hit on one of these high levels and thus $2^{-\frac{5(k-1)}{6}}$ for the smallest k such that $|f| \leq 2^{\frac{k}{6}}$, i.e., $k \geq 6\log(|f|)$. Thus, $2^{-\frac{5(k-1)}{6}} \leq m^{-3}$, where $m = |z|$. Note that later, in the Borel-Cantelli Lemma, we need to sum over these bad events, and thus, it is important that the sum of m^{-3} over all m is a constant.

Putting Everything Together. Finally, with the above two safeguards, our oracle Inv works as follows: on input (f, y), it first shaves f of its higher-level Chk gates, computing $f_s \leftarrow \text{shave}(f)$. Then, it constructs the set S of all paths from some input z to $y = f_s^O(z)$, where a path is defined to be the set of all query pairs to O made during the evaluation of f_s on z. Afterwards, it removes from S all paths which are too heavy, where a path is called heavy if there is a k such that it contains a number $N(k)$ k-Chk queries, out of which more than $O(N(k))/2^k + \log^2|f|$ are hits. Eventually, it returns a path from this set S of light paths using the hashing trick to derandomize the sampling.

As we already outlined, the last output H of T is therefore a set which contains, for every possible triple (i, f, y) where i is an integer, f is an oracle function, and y is a bitstring, a hash function $h = H[i, f, y]$. The guarantee offered by h is that for any set S' of size $2^{i-1} \leq |S'| \leq 2^i$, the probability of the random choice of $h = H[i, f, y]$ that S' contains exactly one entry s such that $h(s) = 0$ is at least $1/8$. Hence, after it computes the set S of light paths, Inv compute the unique integer i such that $2^{i-1} \leq |S| \leq 2^i$, retrieves $h \leftarrow H[i, f, y]$, and output the unique path $p \in S$ such that $h(p) = 0$, or $\bot$ if there is no unique such path. Note that this oracle Inv can fail to return a valid path from an input z to the target output y in f for three reasons: because shaving caused f_s to differ from f on input z (we show that this is uniquely for a random z), because the path from z to y is heavy (again, we show that this is unlikely), and because there is not a unique $p \in S$ such that $h(p) = 0$ (but with probability at least $1/8$, there will be a unique such p). This last source of failure can be later removed by a straightforward parallel amplification, by querying Inv on many pairs (f_k, y) where the f_i are functionally equivalent variants of f (in which case the corresponding $h_k = H[i, f_k, y]$ are independently random by construction). Note that we could have also hardcoded "true" randomness into Inv instead of using the hashing trick. However, as we will see, the hashing trick enables a compression argument since (a) the hash-functions are sampled *independently* from W and B and (b) the sampling can be emulated when only knowing a single element in the set as well as the size of the set S. Details follow in the next section.

5.2   Proving Theorem 16

Fix a function $\ell : \mathbb{N} \mapsto \mathbb{N}$, a circuit family $\mathcal{C}$, and an integer $n \in \mathbb{N}$. We want to bound the probability, over the choice of $\vec{x} \leftarrow_\$ \{0,1\}^{\ell(n) \cdot n}$ and $(\mathsf{O}, \mathsf{Inv}) \leftarrow_\$ \mathcal{T}$, that $\mathcal{C}_n^{\mathsf{O},\mathsf{Inv}}(\vec{x}) = \mathcal{L}^{\mathsf{O}}(\vec{x})$. We proceed in two steps:

- First, we prove an *emulation lemma* which states that there is an explicit algorithm $\mathsf{Emu}^{\mathsf{O}}$ which emulates $\mathcal{C}_n^{\mathsf{O},\mathsf{Inv}}$ without calling the oracle Inv, but using instead some partial information $g(W, B, H)$ about (W, B, H). By emulating, we mean that $\mathsf{Emu}^{\mathsf{O}}(\vec{x}, g(W, B, H)) = \mathcal{C}_n^{\mathsf{O},\mathsf{Inv}}(\vec{x})$, and Emu makes the same number of queries to O as $\mathcal{C}_n$.
- Second, we use the *hitting lemma*, which we already mentioned in Sect. 3 (in the technical overview about the existence of FG-OWFs in the RLM), to bound the number of hits on $\vec{x}$ that Emu can possibly make (where a hit on $\vec{x}$ is a query of the form $(x_i, W[x_i])$ to Chk, from which Emu learns whether $x_i \in \mathcal{L}^{\mathsf{O}}$).

The Emulation Lemma. Concretely, we give an explicit algorithm Emu such that $\mathsf{Emu}^{\mathsf{O}}(L, \vec{x}, \mathcal{C}_n) = \mathcal{C}_n^{\mathsf{O},\mathsf{Inv}}(\vec{x})$ and Emu makes the same queries to O as $\mathcal{C}_n$, where the leakage string L contains the following information:

- The sets H and $(W_{\vec{x}}, B_{\vec{x}})$ of all witnesses and membership bits except for those corresponding to the entries of $\vec{x}$ (intuitively, this corresponds to giving to Emu all information about Inv which is sampled independently of the $W[x_i], B[x_i]$ and does not help with finding $\mathcal{L}^{\mathsf{O}}(\vec{x})$).
- The sets $(W^{\mathsf{Hit}}, B^{\mathsf{Hit}})$ which contains all Chk-hits on $\vec{x}$ in paths obtained by $\mathcal{C}_n$ through queries to Inv.
- The set $W^{\overline{\mathsf{Hit}}}$ which contains all other (non-hitting) Chk-query pairs in paths obtained by $\mathcal{C}_n$ through queries to Inv.
- A list I which for each query (f, y) of $\mathcal{C}_n$ to Inv indicates whether this query returned $\perp$ or not, and if it did not, the value i which was used to select the hash function $h = H[i, f, y]$.

The emulation proceeds by using its information: Emu runs $\mathcal{C}_n$ internally on input $\vec{x}$, forwarding its queries to O. Each time $\mathcal{C}_n$ makes a query (f, y) to Inv, Emu first retrieves from I the information whether Inv outputs $\perp$ or not. If it does not, Emu tries all possible inputs z to f^{O}, but without actually querying O:

for each possible input z, Emu runs $f^O(z)$ by retrieving the answers of O from the sets $(W_{\vec{x}}, B_{\vec{x}}, W^{\mathsf{Hit}}, B^{\mathsf{Hit}}, W^{\overline{\mathsf{Hit}}})$. If $f^O(z)$ makes a query whose answer is not contained in these sets or if $f^O(z)$, Emu discards candidate z.

After trying all inputs to f, Emu has a set S' of candidate inputs z, with a corresponding path. Then, it retrieves the index i from I and selects $h \leftarrow H[i, f, y]$, and sets the output of Inv on (f, y) to be the unique path p associated to some $z \in S'$ such that $h(p) = 0$; by construction, there will be a unique such path. The correctness of the emulation follows by construction and by definition of the sets $(W_{\vec{x}}, B_{\vec{x}}, W^{\mathsf{Hit}}, B^{\mathsf{Hit}}, W^{\overline{\mathsf{Hit}}})$ which Emu gets as input.

This emulation highlights the rationale behind the design of Inv: the use of a hash function h to select the output guarantees that, on top of the sets $(W_{\vec{x}}, B_{\vec{x}}, W^{\mathsf{Hit}}, B^{\mathsf{Hit}}, W^{\overline{\mathsf{Hit}}})$, Emu will only need to receive a *relatively small* amount of additional "leakage", corresponding to the list of all values i for each query to Inv. Now, by definition, i is at most $\log |S|$, where S is a set of paths in f, hence $|S| \leq 2^{|f|}$. Therefore, $i \leq |f|$, hence i can be represented using at most $\log |f|$ bits. By construction, a query (f, y) to Inv can leak information about $\vec{x}$ only if $|f| \geq 2^{n/C}$, because otherwise all n-Chk gates gets removed by shave(f). Hence, our emulator gets a total amount of leakage about $\vec{x}$ bounded by $|\mathcal{C}_n|/2^{O(n)}$. From there, we want to prove that

$$\Pr_{\vec{x} \leftarrow \$\{0,1\}^{\ell \cdot n}, (O, \mathsf{Inv}) \leftarrow \$ \mathcal{T}} \left[\mathcal{C}_n^{O, \mathsf{Inv}}(\vec{x}) = \mathcal{L}^O(\vec{x}) \right] \leq \mathsf{poly}(n) \cdot 2^{-\left(\ell(n) - \frac{\tilde{O}(|\mathcal{C}_n|)}{2^{O(n)}} \right)}.$$

We will do so by proving that

$$\Pr_{\vec{x} \leftarrow \$\{0,1\}^{\ell \cdot n}, (O, \mathsf{Inv}) \leftarrow \$ \mathcal{T}} \left[\mathsf{Emu}^O(L, \vec{x}, \mathcal{C}_n) = \mathcal{L}^O(\vec{x}) \right] \leq \mathsf{poly}(n) \cdot 2^{-\left(\ell(n) - \frac{\tilde{O}(|\mathcal{C}_n|)}{2^{O(n)}} \right)}. \tag{1}$$

Bounding Eq. 1 is the goal of the *hitting lemma*.

Applying the Hitting Lemma. The hitting lemma states that for any circuit $\mathcal{C}_n$, any algorithm $\mathcal{A}$ having only access to the inputs and oracles of $\mathcal{C}_n$'s emulator (i.e., $\mathcal{B}$ has only access to the oracle O and L) cannot possibly make too many hit, even though the emulator gets $|\mathcal{C}_n|/2^{O(n)}$ bits of leakage about the oracle. Let $\mathsf{Hit}_{\mathcal{B}}^O(L, \vec{x}, \mathcal{C}_n)$ be the random variable that counts the number of hits on $\vec{x}$ made by $\mathcal{A}$ on input $(L, \vec{x}, \mathcal{C}_n)$.

Lemma 18 (Hitting Lemma with Advice, Informal). *For every $\ell(\cdot)$, positive integers q, large enough n, challenge $\vec{x}$, L with $|W^{\mathsf{Hit}}| = q$ and list I represented by a string length $|I| = |\mathcal{C}_n|/2^{O(n)}$, adversaries $\mathcal{C}_n, \mathcal{B}$, and for every integer $c \geq 1$,*

$$\Pr_{(W,B,H) \leftarrow \mathcal{T}|_{L_{\tilde{I}}}} \left[\mathsf{Hit}_{\mathcal{B}}^O(L, \vec{x}, \mathcal{C}_n) \geq \frac{O(|\mathcal{C}_n|) + q}{2^n} + c + |I| \right] \leq \frac{1}{2^{\gamma \cdot c}},$$

where $\gamma > 1$, and where the probability is taken over the random sampling of $(W, B, H) \leftarrow \$ \mathcal{T}$, conditioned on L.

We first explain how the hitting lemma implies Eq. 1. First, if Emu^O got a total number of hits t on $\vec{x}$, either through queries to O or through the hits contained in W^{Hit}, then conditioned on all observation seen by Emu, $\ell(n) - t$ bits of $\mathcal{L}^O(\vec{x})$ are truly undetermined. Hence,

$$\Pr_{\vec{x} \leftarrow \$\{0,1\}^{\ell \cdot n},(O,\mathsf{Inv}) \leftarrow \$\mathcal{T}} \left[\mathsf{Emu}^O(L_{\bar{I}}, \vec{x}, \mathcal{C}_n) = \mathcal{L}^O(\vec{x}) \mid \mathsf{Emu} \text{ gets} \leq t \text{ hits on } \vec{x} \right] \leq 2^{-(\ell - t)}.$$

Now, the number of hits seen by Emu is bounded by $\mathsf{Hit}^O_{\mathsf{Emu}}(L_{\bar{I}}, \vec{x}, \mathcal{C}_n) + |W^{\mathsf{Hit}}|$, where $|W^{\mathsf{Hit}}|$ is at most $\mathsf{poly}(n) \cdot \frac{\tilde{O}(|\mathcal{C}_n|)}{2^n}$: this follows from the fact that the number of hits in W^{Hit} is bounded by design by the fact that Inv on input (f, y) only returns light paths, which cannot contain more than $\mathsf{poly}(n) \cdot \frac{\tilde{O}(|f|)}{2^n}$ hits. The result follows by relying on the fact that

$$\Pr_{\vec{x} \leftarrow \$\{0,1\}^{\ell \cdot n},(O,\mathsf{Inv}) \leftarrow \$\mathcal{T}} \left[\mathsf{Emu}^O(L_{\bar{I}}, \vec{x}, \mathcal{C}_n) = \mathcal{L}^O(\vec{x}) \right]$$
$$= \sum_t \Pr[\mathsf{Emu} \text{ gets} \leq t \text{ hits on } \vec{x}] \cdot \Pr\left[\mathsf{Emu}^O(L_{\bar{I}}, \vec{x}, \mathcal{C}_n) = \mathcal{L}^O(\vec{x}) \mid \mathsf{Emu} \text{ gets } t \text{ hits} \right]$$
$$\leq \sum_t 2^{-(\ell - t)} \cdot \Pr[\mathsf{Emu} \text{ gets} \leq t \text{ hits on } \vec{x}].$$

Now, the bound of Eq. 1 will be obtained by plugging the bound on

$$\Pr[\mathsf{Emu} \text{ gets} \leq t \text{ hits on } \vec{x}] \leq \mathsf{Hit}^O_{\mathsf{Emu}}(L, \vec{x}, \mathcal{C}_n) + |W^{\mathsf{Hit}}|,$$

by using the hitting lemma to bound $\mathsf{Hit}^O_{\mathsf{Emu}}(L, \vec{x}, \mathcal{C}_n)$. The proof then follows from the hitting lemma, to which we devote Sect. 6.

5.3   Proving Theorem 17

Let $f : \{0,1\}^* \to \{0,1\}^*$ be an oracle function. We exhibit an efficient inverter $\mathcal{A}^{\mathsf{Inv}}(f, .)$ for f, such that

$$\Pr_{z \leftarrow \$\{0,1\}^m,(O,\mathsf{Inv}) \leftarrow \$\mathcal{T}} \left[f^O(\mathcal{A}^{O,\mathsf{Inv}}(f, f^O(z))) = f^O(z) \right] \approx 1.$$

$\mathcal{A}$ works as follows: to invert a function $f : \{0,1\}^m \mapsto \{0,1\}^*$ given an image y, it queries Inv $\log^3 m$ times on independent inputs (f_k, y), where each f_k are syntactically different but functionally equivalent to f (this guarantees that the failure probabilities introduced by the choice of the hash function h are independent). Then, it takes a path p returned by any successful query to Inv (if any), and returns a uniformly random preimage z consistent with this path (this requires a single query to the PSPACE oracle). The proof that $\mathcal{A}$ is a successful inverter proceeds by a sequence of lemmas. First, we define f_{approx} as $f_s = \mathsf{shave}(f)$, except that it outputs $\bot$ on any input z such that the path in $f_s^O(z)$ is not light.

First Lemma. The first lemma states that

$$\Pr_{O,z \leftarrow \$\{0,1\}^m} \left[f^O_{\mathsf{approx}}(z) = f^O_s(z) \right] \approx 1.$$

This lemma will follow again from the Hitting lemma, which provides a strong concentration bound on the probability that the path of $f_s^O(z)$ is light: by this concentration bound, it follows that the path is light with probability at least $1 - \log|f| \cdot 2^{-O(\log^2|f|)}$ (recall that a path is heavy if, for some k, it contains $N(k)$ k-Chk queries, and more than $O(N(k)) + \log^2|f|$ hits).

Second Lemma. The second lemma states that

$$\Pr_{O, z \leftarrow \$\{0,1\}^m} \left[f_s^O(z) = f^O(z) \right] \approx 1.$$

This lemma follows from the definition of shaving: since only Chk gates with $k \geq 6 \log|f|$ are shaved, the probability that $f_s^O(z) \neq f^O(z)$ is bounded by the sum $\sum_{k \geq 6 \log(|f|)} 2^{-\frac{5k}{6}} \leq 4/m^3$. Combining the above lemmas with an averaging argument, we will show that

$$\Pr_{z \leftarrow \$\{0,1\}^m} \left[f(f_{\mathsf{approx}}^{-1}(f(z), 1^m)) = f(z) \right] \approx 1.$$

When $\mathcal{A}$ makes a single query to Inv, its overall success probability is approximately $1/8$. Since all queries have independent probability of failing due to an unfortunate choice of h, we will show that $\mathcal{A}$ inverts successfully with probability

$$\Pr_{z \leftarrow \$\{0,1\}^m, (O,\mathsf{Inv}) \leftarrow \$\mathcal{T}} \left[f^O(\mathcal{A}^{O,\mathsf{Inv}}(f, f^O(x))) = f^O(x) \right] \approx 1 - \left(\frac{7}{8}\right)^{\log^3 m}.$$

Note that $\mathcal{A}$, on input f, sends $\log^3 m \leq \log^3|f|$ queries to Inv, selects one of the path from the successful queries, and queries it to the PSPACE oracle to select the preimage z it outputs. Therefore, the size of $\mathcal{A}$ is $|\mathcal{A}| = \tilde{O}(|f|)$.

6 The Hitting Lemma

For any $\vec{r} = r_1 \cdots r_\ell$, we define an oracle $\mathsf{Guess}_{\vec{r}}(i, r^*)$ as taking an input r^* and an index i and checking whether $r_i = r^*$. If so, the oracle returns 1. Else, the oracle returns $\bot$. We define $\mathsf{Hit}^{\mathsf{Guess}_{\vec{r}}}(\mathcal{A})$ as the number of distinct queries $\mathcal{A}$ makes which returns something different than $\bot$.

Lemma 19 (Abstract Hitting Lemma). *For every positive integer q, large enough n, $\ell = \ell(n)$, sets $V_1, \cdots, V_\ell$ of size $1 \leq |V_i| \leq 2^n$ such that $q = \ell \cdot 2^n - \sum_{i=1}^{\ell} |V_i|$, for every adversary $\mathcal{A}$, and for every integer $c \geq 1$, $\exists \alpha > 0$, $\exists \gamma > 1$:*

$$\Pr_{\vec{r} \leftarrow \$V_1 \times \cdots \times V_\ell} \left[\mathsf{Hit}^{\mathsf{Guess}_{\vec{r}}}(\mathcal{A}) \geq \frac{16 \cdot \mathsf{qry}_\mathcal{A} + q}{2^n} + c \right] \leq \frac{\alpha}{2^{\gamma c}}.$$

The hitting lemma gives a strong Chernoff-style bound on the number of distinct hits which an arbitrary adversary $\mathcal{A}$ can make using $\mathsf{qry}_\mathcal{A}$ queries. The strength of this bound allows to show that the bound degrades gracefully even if $\mathcal{A}$ is additionally given an arbitrary *advice string* of bounded size about the truth table of the Guess oracle. We discuss applications and variants of the Hitting Lemma in the full version of this work [BC20], and now turn to its proof.

6.1 Proof of the Hitting Lemma – Proof Structure

The goal of $\mathcal{A}$ is to find as many distinct r_i's as possible, where each r_i is sampled randomly from a set V_i of size $|V_i| \leq 2^n$, given access to an oracle which indicates whether a guess is correct or not. Intuitively, $\mathcal{A}$'s best possible strategy is to first choose the smallest set V_{i_1}, query its elements to Guess (in arbitrary order) until it finds r_{i_1}, then move on to the second smallest set V_{i_2}, and so

---

Algorithm $\mathcal{B}_Q$

$\mathsf{qry} \leftarrow 0;\ r_1^*, \cdots, r_\ell^* \leftarrow \perp$
for $i = 1$ **to** ℓ :
  for $j \in [1, v_i]$:
    $\mathsf{qry} \leftarrow \mathsf{qry} + 1$
    if $\mathsf{qry} = Q$ **then return** $(r_1^*, \cdots, r_\ell^*)$
    if $\mathsf{Guess}_{\vec{r}}(i, f_i(j))$ **then** $r_{\sigma(i)}^* \leftarrow f_i(j)$; **break**
return $(r_1^*, \cdots, r_\ell^*)$

Fig. 3. Q-query adversary $\mathcal{B}_Q$

---

on. The proof of the abstract hitting lemma closely follows this intuition: we first show that this strategy is indeed the best possible strategy, then bound it's success probability using a second moment concentration bound. Formally, for any $Q \geq 1$, let $\mathcal{B}_Q$ be a Q-query adversary that implements the following simple strategy: order $V_1, \cdots, V_\ell$ by increasing size, as $V_{\sigma(1)}, \cdots, V_{\sigma(\ell)}$ for some fixed permutation σ such that $|V_{\sigma(1)}| \leq \cdots \leq |V_{\sigma(\ell)}|$. For every $i \leq \ell$, let $v_i \leftarrow |V_{\sigma(i)}|$, and let f_i be an arbitrary bijection between $[v_i]$ and $V_{\sigma(i)}$. The algorithm $\mathcal{B}_Q$ is given on Fig. 3.

The adversary $\mathcal{B}_Q$ sequentially queries the values of the sets V_i ordered by increasing size, following an arbitrary ordering of the values inside each V_i, until it finds r_i (after which it moves to the next smallest larger set) or exhausts its budget of Q queries. To simplify notations, for any vector $\vec{u} \in [v_1] \times \cdots \times [v_\ell]$, we write $\pi(\vec{u}) = f_1^{-1}(u_{\sigma^{-1}(1)}), \cdots, f_\ell^{-1}(u_{\sigma^{-1}(\ell)})$. Observe that for any $t \in \mathbb{N}$,

$$\Pr_{\vec{r} \leftarrow \$ V_1 \times \cdots \times V_\ell}\left[\mathsf{Hit}^{\mathsf{Guess}_{\vec{r}}}(\mathcal{B}_Q) \geq t \right] = \Pr_{\vec{u} \leftarrow \$ [v_1] \times \cdots \times [v_\ell]}\left[\mathsf{Hit}^{\mathsf{Guess}_{\pi(\vec{u})}}(\mathcal{B}_Q) \geq t \right]$$

$$= \Pr_{\vec{u} \leftarrow \$ [v_1] \times \cdots \times [v_\ell]}\left[\sum_{i=1}^{t} u_i \leq Q \right],$$

where the last equality follows from the fact that $\mathcal{B}_Q$ queries the positions one by one in a fixed order, and needs exactly u_i queries to find $r_{\sigma(i)} = f_{\sigma(i)}(u_i)$ for $i = 1$ to t. The proof of the hitting lemma derives directly from two claims. The first claim states that no Q-query adversary can make t distinct hits with probably better than that of $\mathcal{B}_Q$:

Claim 2 ($\mathcal{B}_Q$'s **strategy is the best possible strategy**). *For every integers* $n, Q, \ell = \ell(n)$, *sets* $V_1, .., V_\ell$ *of size* $1 \leq |V_i| \leq 2^n$, *and for any* Q-query *algorithm* $\mathcal{A}$ *and integer* t,

$$\Pr_{\vec{r} \leftarrow \$ V_1 \times \cdots \times V_\ell}\left[\mathsf{Hit}^{\mathsf{Guess}_{\vec{r}}}(\mathcal{A}) \geq t \right] \leq \Pr_{\vec{u} \leftarrow \$ [v_1] \times \cdots \times [v_\ell]}\left[\sum_{i=1}^{t} u_i \leq Q \right].$$

By construction, the average number of hits $\mathbb{E}_{\vec{r}}[\mathsf{Hit}^{\mathsf{Guess}_{\vec{r}}}(\mathcal{B}_Q)]$ made by $\mathcal{B}_Q$ is the largest value m such that $\sum_{i=1}^{m} \frac{v_i+1}{2} \leq Q$. Recall that $q = \ell \cdot 2^n - \sum_{i=1}^{\ell} |V_i| = \ell \cdot 2^n - \sum_{i=1}^{\ell} v_i$ and $v_i \leq 2^n$ for every i, which implies in particular that $\sum_{i=1}^{m} v_i \geq m \cdot 2^n - q$. We thus bound m as a function of $Q, q,$ and 2^n:

$$\sum_{i=1}^{m} \frac{v_i+1}{2} \leq Q \iff m + \sum_{i=1}^{m} v_i \leq 2Q$$

$$\implies m + m \cdot 2^n - q \leq 2Q \iff m \leq \frac{2Q+q}{2^n+1}.$$

The second claim states, in essence, that the probability over $\vec{r}$ that $\mathcal{B}_Q$ does t hits decreases exponentially with the distance of t to the mean m (up to some multiplicative constant).

Claim 3 (Bounding $\mathcal{B}_Q$'s number of hits). *There exists constants $\alpha > 0$ and $\gamma > 1$ such that for every $\ell(\cdot)$, positive integers q, Q, large enough n, integers $v_1, \cdots, v_\ell$ with $1 \leq v_i \leq 2^n$ such that $q = \ell \cdot 2^n - \sum_{i=1}^{\ell} v_i$, and for every integer $c \geq 1$,*

$$\Pr_{\vec{u} \leftarrow_\$ [v_1] \times \cdots \times [v_\ell]} \left[\sum_{i=1}^{t} u_i \leq Q \right] \leq \frac{\alpha}{2^{\gamma c}}, \text{ where } t = \frac{16 \cdot Q + q}{2^n} + c.$$

We prove Claim 2 and Claim 3 in the full version of this work [BC20].

Acknowledgements. We thank Félix Richart for help with the experimental verification of some probability claims, and the anonymous Eurocrypt reviewers for their careful proofreading of the paper. C. Brzuska supported by the academy of Finland. G. Couteau supported by the ANR SCENE.

References

[AGGM06] Akavia, A., Goldreich, O., Goldwasser, S., Moshkovitz, D.: On basing one-way functions on NP-hardness. In: 38th ACM STOC, pp. 701–710. ACM Press, May 2006

[BB15] Bogdanov, A., Brzuska, C.: On basing size-verifiable one-way functions on NP-hardness. In: Dodis, Y., Nielsen, J.B. (eds.) TCC 2015, Part I. LNCS, vol. 9014, pp. 1–6. Springer, Heidelberg (2015). https://doi.org/10.1007/978-3-662-46494-6_1

[BBF13] Baecher, P., Brzuska, C., Fischlin, M.: Notions of black-box reductions, revisited. In: Sako, K., Sarkar, P. (eds.) ASIACRYPT 2013, Part I. LNCS, vol. 8269, pp. 296–315. Springer, Heidelberg (2013). https://doi.org/10.1007/978-3-642-42033-7_16

[BC20] Brzuska, C., Couteau, G.: Towards fine-grained one-way functions from strong average-case hardness. Cryptology ePrint Archive, Report 2020/1326 (2020). https://eprint.iacr.org/2020/1326

[BGI08] Biham, E., Goren, Y.J., Ishai, Y.: Basing weak public-key cryptography on strong one-way functions. In: Canetti, R. (ed.) TCC 2008. LNCS, vol. 4948, pp. 55–72. Springer, Heidelberg (2008). https://doi.org/10.1007/978-3-540-78524-8_4

[BHK+11] Brassard, G., Høyer, P., Kalach, K., Kaplan, M., Laplante, S., Salvail, L.: Merkle puzzles in a quantum world. In: Rogaway, P. (ed.) CRYPTO 2011. LNCS, vol. 6841, pp. 391–410. Springer, Heidelberg (2011). https://doi.org/10.1007/978-3-642-22792-9_22

[BM09]   Barak, B., Mahmoody-Ghidary, M.: Merkle puzzles are optimal—an $O(n^2)$-query attack on any key exchange from a random oracle. In: Halevi, S. (ed.) CRYPTO 2009. LNCS, vol. 5677, pp. 374–390. Springer, Heidelberg (2009). https://doi.org/10.1007/978-3-642-03356-8_22

[BR93]   Bellare, M., Rogaway, P.: Random oracles are practical: a paradigm for designing efficient protocols. In: ACM CCS 1993, pp. 62–73. ACM Press, November 1993

[BRSV17] Ball, M., Rosen, A., Sabin, M., Vasudevan, P.N.: Average-case fine-grained hardness. In: 49th ACM STOC, pp. 483–496. ACM Press, June 2017

[BRSV18] Ball, M., Rosen, A., Sabin, M., Vasudevan, P.N.: Proofs of work from worst-case assumptions. In: Shacham, H., Boldyreva, A. (eds.) CRYPTO 2018, Part I. LNCS, vol. 10991, pp. 789–819. Springer, Cham (2018). https://doi.org/10.1007/978-3-319-96884-1_26

[BS08]   Brassard, G., Salvail, L.: Quantum Merkle puzzles. In: Second International Conference on Quantum, Nano and Micro Technologies (ICQNM 2008), pp. 76–79. IEEE (2008)

[BT03]   Bogdanov, A., Trevisan, L.: On worst-case to average-case reductions for NP problems. In: 44th FOCS, pp. 308–317. IEEE Computer Society Press, October 2003

[CDGS18] Coretti, S., Dodis, Y., Guo, S., Steinberger, J.P.: Random oracles and non-uniformity. In: Nielsen, J.B., Rijmen, V. (eds.) EUROCRYPT 2018, Part I. LNCS, vol. 10820, pp. 227–258. Springer, Cham (2018). https://doi.org/10.1007/978-3-319-78381-9_9

[DGK17] Dodis, Y., Guo, S., Katz, J.: Fixing cracks in the concrete: random oracles with auxiliary input, revisited. In: Coron, J.-S., Nielsen, J.B. (eds.) EUROCRYPT 2017, Part II. LNCS, vol. 10211, pp. 473–495. Springer, Cham (2017). https://doi.org/10.1007/978-3-319-56614-6_16

[DVV16] Degwekar, A., Vaikuntanathan, V., Vasudevan, P.N.: Fine-grained cryptography. In: Robshaw, M., Katz, J. (eds.) CRYPTO 2016, Part III. LNCS, vol. 9816, pp. 533–562. Springer, Heidelberg (2016). https://doi.org/10.1007/978-3-662-53015-3_19

[FF93]   Feigenbaum, J., Fortnow, L.: Random-self-reducibility of complete sets. SIAM J. Comput. **22**(5), 994–1005 (1993)

[GT00]   Gennaro, R., Trevisan, L.: Lower bounds on the efficiency of generic cryptographic constructions. In: 41st FOCS, pp. 305–313. IEEE Computer Society Press, November 2000

[Hel80] Hellman, M.: A cryptanalytic time-memory trade-off. IEEE Trans. Inf. Theory **26**(4), 401–406 (1980)

[HL18]   Holmgren, J., Lombardi, A.: Cryptographic hashing from strong one-way functions (or: one-way product functions and their applications). In: 59th FOCS, pp. 850–858. IEEE Computer Society Press, October 2018

[HR04]   Hsiao, C.-Y., Reyzin, L.: Finding collisions on a public road, or do secure hash functions need secret coins? In: Franklin, M. (ed.) CRYPTO 2004. LNCS, vol. 3152, pp. 92–105. Springer, Heidelberg (2004). https://doi.org/10.1007/978-3-540-28628-8_6

[Imp95] Impagliazzo, R.: A personal view of average-case complexity. In: Proceedings of Structure in Complexity Theory. Tenth Annual IEEE Conference, pp. 134–147. IEEE (1995)

[IR89] Impagliazzo, R., Rudich, S.: Limits on the provable consequences of one-way permutations. In: 21st ACM STOC, pp. 44–61. ACM Press, May 1989

[IR90] Impagliazzo, R., Rudich, S.: Limits on the provable consequences of one-way permutations. In: Goldwasser, S. (ed.) CRYPTO 1988. LNCS, vol. 403, pp. 8–26. Springer, New York (1990). https://doi.org/10.1007/0-387-34799-2_2

[Lev86] Levin, L.A.: Average case complete problems. SIAM J. Comput. **15**(1), 285–286 (1986)

[Lev87] Levin, L.A.: One way functions and pseudorandom generators. Combinatorica **7**(4), 357–363 (1987)

[LLW19] LaVigne, R., Lincoln, A., Williams, V.V.: Public-key cryptography in the fine-grained setting. In: Boldyreva, A., Micciancio, D. (eds.) CRYPTO 2019, Part III. LNCS, vol. 11694, pp. 605–635. Springer, Cham (2019). https://doi.org/10.1007/978-3-030-26954-8_20

[Mer78] Merkle, R.C.: Secure communications over insecure channels. Commun. ACM **21**(4), 294–299 (1978)

[PL20] Pass, R., Liu, Y.: On one-way functions and Kolmogorov complexity. In: FOCS 2020 (2020)

[PV20] Pass, R., Venkitasubramaniam, M.: Is it easier to prove statements that are guaranteed to be true? In: FOCS 2020 (2020)

[RTV04] Reingold, O., Trevisan, L., Vadhan, S.P.: Notions of reducibility between cryptographic primitives. In: Naor, M. (ed.) TCC 2004. LNCS, vol. 2951, pp. 1–20. Springer, Heidelberg (2004). https://doi.org/10.1007/978-3-540-24638-1_1

[Sim98] Simon, D.R.: Finding collisions on a one-way street: can secure hash functions be based on general assumptions? In: Nyberg, K. (ed.) EUROCRYPT 1998. LNCS, vol. 1403, pp. 334–345. Springer, Heidelberg (1998). https://doi.org/10.1007/BFb0054137

[STV01] Sudan, M., Trevisan, L., Vadhan, S.: Pseudorandom generators without the XOR lemma. J. Comput. Syst. Sci. **62**(2), 236–266 (2001)

[Sud97] Sudan, M.: Decoding of Reed Solomon codes beyond the error-correction bound. J. Complex. **13**(1), 180–193 (1997)

[Unr07] Unruh, D.: Random oracles and auxiliary input. In: Menezes, A. (ed.) CRYPTO 2007. LNCS, vol. 4622, pp. 205–223. Springer, Heidelberg (2007). https://doi.org/10.1007/978-3-540-74143-5_12

[VV85] Valiant, L.G., Vazirani, V.V.: NP is as easy as detecting unique solutions. In: 17th ACM STOC, pp. 458–463. ACM Press, May 1985

[WB86] Welch, L.R., Berlekamp, E.R.: Error correction for algebraic block codes (1986). US Patent 4,633,470

[Wee06] Wee, H.: Finding Pessiland. In: Halevi, S., Rabin, T. (eds.) TCC 2006. LNCS, vol. 3876, pp. 429–442. Springer, Heidelberg (2006). https://doi.org/10.1007/11681878_22

[Yao82] Yao, A.C.-C.: Theory and applications of trapdoor functions (extended abstract). In: 23rd FOCS, pp. 80–91. IEEE Computer Society Press, November 1982

On the Multi-user Security of Short Schnorr Signatures with Preprocessing

Jeremiah Blocki[(✉)] and Seunghoon Lee[(✉)]

Purdue University, West Lafayette, IN 47906, USA
{jblocki,lee2856}@purdue.edu

Abstract. The Schnorr signature scheme is an efficient digital signature scheme with short signature lengths, i.e., $4k$-bit signatures for k bits of security. A Schnorr signature σ over a group of size $p \approx 2^{2k}$ consists of a tuple (s, e), where $e \in \{0,1\}^{2k}$ is a hash output and $s \in \mathbb{Z}_p$ must be computed using the secret key. While the hash output e requires $2k$ bits to encode, Schnorr proposed that it might be possible to truncate the hash value without adversely impacting security.

In this paper, we prove that *short* Schnorr signatures of length $3k$ bits provide k bits of multi-user security in the (Shoup's) generic group model and the programmable random oracle model. We further analyze the multi-user security of key-prefixed short Schnorr signatures against preprocessing attacks, showing that it is possible to obtain secure signatures of length $3k + \log S + \log N$ bits. Here, N denotes the number of users and S denotes the size of the hint generated by our preprocessing attacker, e.g., if $S = 2^{k/2}$, then we would obtain secure $3.75k$-bit signatures for groups of up to $N \leq 2^{k/4}$ users.

Our techniques easily generalize to several other Fiat-Shamir-based signature schemes, allowing us to establish analogous results for Chaum-Pedersen signatures and Katz-Wang signatures. As a building block, we also analyze the 1-out-of-N discrete-log problem in the generic group model, with and without preprocessing.

1 Introduction

The Schnorr signature scheme [Sch90] has been widely used due to its simplicity, efficiency and short signature size. In the Schnorr signature scheme, we start with a cyclic group $G = \langle g \rangle$ of prime order p and pick a random secret key $\mathsf{sk} \in \mathbb{Z}_p$. To sign a message m, we pick $r \in \mathbb{Z}_p$ uniformly at random, compute $I = g^r$, $e = \mathsf{H}(I \| m)$, and $s = r + \mathsf{sk} \cdot e \mod p$. Then, the final signature is $\sigma = (s, e)$.

We recall that a signature scheme Π yields k *bits of (multi-user) security* if any attacker running in time at most t can forge a signature with probability at most $\varepsilon_t = t/2^k$ in the (multi-user) signature forgery game, and this should hold for all time bounds $t \leq 2^k$. To achieve k bits of security, we select a hash function H with $2k$-bit outputs, and we select p to be a random $2k$-bit prime so that the length of a signature is $4k$ bits.

In Schnorr's original paper [Sch90], the author proposed the possibility of achieving even shorter Schnorr signatures by selecting a hash function H with

© International Association for Cryptologic Research 2022
O. Dunkelman and S. Dziembowski (Eds.): EUROCRYPT 2022, LNCS 13276, pp. 614–643, 2022.
https://doi.org/10.1007/978-3-031-07085-3_21

k-bit outputs (or truncating to only use the first k bits) so that the final signature $\sigma = (s, e)$ can be encoded with $3k$ bits. We refer to this signature scheme as the *short* Schnorr signature scheme. In this paper, we investigate the following questions:

> *Does the short Schnorr signature scheme achieve k bits of (multi-user) security? If so, is the short Schnorr signature scheme also secure against preprocessing attacks?*

Proving security for the Schnorr signatures has been a challenging task against the interactive attacks. Pointcheval and Stern [PS96] provided a reduction from the discrete-log problem in the random oracle model (ROM) [BR93]. However, their reduction is not tight, i.e., they show that $\mathsf{Adv_{sig}} \leq \mathsf{Adv_{dlog}} \times q_\mathsf{H}$ for any attacker making at most q_H queries to the random oracle. The loss of the factor q_H, which prevents us from concluding that the scheme provides k bits of security, seems to be unavoidable, e.g., see [Seu12,FJS14].

Neven et al. [NSW09] analyzed Schnorr signatures in the generic group model (GGM) [Sho97], showing that the scheme provides k bits of security as long as the hash function satisfies two key properties: random-prefix preimage (rpp) and random-prefix second-preimage (rpsp) security. Interestingly, Neven et al. do not need to assume that H is a random oracle, though a random oracle H would satisfy both rpp and rpsp security. Neven et al. considered the short Schnorr signature scheme, but their upper bounds do not allow us to conclude that the short Schnorr signature scheme provides k bits of security . See the full version [BL19] for further discussion.

An earlier paper of Schnorr and Jakobsson [SJ00] analyzed the security of the short Schnorr signature scheme in the ROM plus the GGM. While they show that the scheme provides k bits of security, they also consider another version of the GGM which is different from the definition proposed by Shoup [Sho97]. The reason is that the version they consider is not expressive enough to capture all known attacks, e.g., any attack that requires the ability to hash group elements including preprocessing attacks of Corrigan-Gibbs and Kogan [CK18] cannot be captured in their GGM. See the full version [BL19] for further discussion.

Galbraith et al. [GMLS02] claimed to have a tight reduction showing that single-user security implies multi-user security of the regular Schnorr signature scheme. However, Bernstein [Ber15] identified an error in the security proof in [GMLS02], proposed a modified "key-prefixed" version of the original Schnorr signature scheme (including the public key as a hash input), and proved that the "key-prefixed" version does provide multi-user security. Derler and Slamanig [DS19] later showed a tight reduction from single-user security to "key-prefixed" multi-user security for a class of key-homomorphic signature schemes including Schnorr signatures. The Internet Engineering Task Force (IETF) adopted the key-prefixed modification of Schnorr signatures to ensure multi-user security [Hao17]. Kiltz et al. [KMP16] later gave a tight security reduction establishing multi-user security of regular Schnorr signatures in the programmable random oracle model plus (another version of) the generic group model without key-prefixing. Our results imply that key-prefixing is not even necessary to establish tight multi-user security of short Schnorr signatures[1]. On the other hand key-prefixing is both necessary and sufficient to establish multi-user security of (short) Schnorr signatures against preprocessing attackers.

1.1 Our Contributions

We show that the *short* Schnorr Signature scheme provides k bits of security against an attacker in *both* the single and multi-user versions of the signature forgery game. Our results assume the programmable ROM and the (Shoup's) GGM. We further analyze the *multi-user* security of key-prefixed short Schnorr signatures against preprocessing attacks. The preprocessing attacker outputs a hint of size S after making as many as 2^{3k} queries to the random oracle and examining the entire generic group oracle. Later on, the online attacker can use the hint to help win the *multi-user* signature forgery game by forging a signature for *any one* of the N users. By tuning the parameters of the key-prefixed short Schnorr signature scheme appropriately, we can obtain $(3k + \log S + \log N)$-bit signatures with k bits of security against a preprocessing attacker.

Single-User Security of Short Schnorr Signatures. As a warm-up, we first consider the single-user security of the *short* Schnorr Signature scheme without preprocessing, showing that short Schnorr signatures provide k bits of security in the (Shoup's) generic group model and the random oracle model.

Theorem 1 (informal). *Any attacker making at most q queries wins the signature forgery game (chosen message attack) against the short Schnorr signature scheme with probability at most $\mathcal{O}\left(q/2^k\right)$ in the generic group model (of order $p \approx 2^{2k}$) plus programmable random oracle model (See Definition 1 and Theorem 4).*

Theorem 1 tells us that the short Schnorr signature obtained by truncating the hash output by half would yield the same k bits of security level with the signature length $3k$, instead of $4k$. A 25% reduction in signature length is particularly significant in contexts where space/bandwidth is limited, e.g., on the blockchain.

Multi-User Security of Short Schnorr Signatures. We show that our proofs can be extended to the multi-user case *even* in the so-called "1-out-of-N" setting, i.e., if the attacker is given N public keys $\mathsf{pk}_1, \ldots, \mathsf{pk}_N$, s/he can forge a signature σ which is valid under any one of these public keys (it does not matter which).

---

[1] The authors of [KMP16] pointed out that their analysis can be adapted to demonstrate multi-user security of short Schnorr signatures (private communication) though the paper itself never discusses short Schnorr signatures. Furthermore, their proof is in a different version of the generic group model which is not suitable for analyzing preprocessing attacks. See discussion in the full version [BL19].

Theorem 2 (informal). *Let N denote the number of distinct users/public keys. Then any attacker making at most q queries wins the multi-user signature forgery game (chosen message attack) against the short Schnorr signature scheme with probability at most $\mathcal{O}\left((q + N)/2^k\right)$ in the generic group model (of order $p \approx 2^{2k}$) plus programmable random oracle model (See Definition 2 and Theorem 6).*

Theorem 2 guarantees that breaking multi-user security of short Schnorr signatures in the 1-out-of-N setting is *not easier* than breaking a single instance, as the winning probability is still in the same order as long as $N \leq q$, which is the typical case. A naïve reduction loses a factor of N, i.e., any attacker winning the multi-user forgery game with probability $\varepsilon_{\mathsf{MU}}$ can be used to win the single-user forgery game with probability $\varepsilon \geq \varepsilon_{\mathsf{MU}}/N$. For example, suppose that $p \approx 2^{224}$ (i.e., $k = 112$), and there are $N = 2^{32}$ instances of short Schnorr signatures, which is more than the half of the entire world population. In the original single-user security game, an attacker wins with probability at most $\varepsilon \leq \mathcal{O}\left(t/2^k\right)$, so an attacker running in time $t = 2^{80}$ would succeed with probability at most $\varepsilon \approx 2^{-32}$. This only allows us to conclude that an attacker succeeds with probability at most $\varepsilon_{\mathsf{MU}} \leq N\varepsilon \approx 1$ in the multi-user security game! Our security proof implies that the attacker will succeed with probability $\varepsilon_{\mathsf{MU}} \approx \varepsilon \approx 2^{-32}$ in the above example. In particular, we don't lose a factor of N in the security reduction.

Security of Key-Prefixed Short Schnorr Signatures Against Preprocessing Attacks. We further show that *key-prefixed short* Schnorr signatures are also secure against preprocessing attacks. Here, we consider a key-prefixed version of Schnorr signatures, because regular Schnorr signatures are trivially vulnerable to preprocessing attacks, e.g., if a preprocessing attacker finds some message m and an integer r such that $e = \mathsf{H}(g^r \| m) = 0$, then $\sigma = (r, 0)$ is *always* a valid signature for *any* public key $\mathsf{pk} = g^{\mathsf{sk}}$ since $g^{r-\mathsf{sk} \cdot 0} = g^r$. We note that several standardized implementations of Schnorr signatures (i.e., BSI [fIS18] or ISO/IEC [fSC18]) slightly deviate from Schnorr's original construction and explicitly disallowing $e = 0$ signatures which defends against our particular preprocessing attack – see the full version [BL19] for further discussion if interested.

We consider a preprocessing attacker who may query the random oracle at up to 2^{3k} points and may also examine the entire generic group oracles before outputting an S-bit hint for the online attacker. We leave it as an interesting open question whether or not the restriction on the number of random oracle queries is necessary. However, from a practical standpoint, we argue that a preprocessing adversary will never be able to make 2^{2k} queries, e.g., if $k \geq 128$, then 2^{2k} operations is already far too expensive for even a nation-state attacker.

Theorem 3 (informal). *Let N denote the number of distinct users/public keys. Then any preprocessing attacker making at most q_{pre} queries and outputs an S-bit hint during the preprocessing phase and making at most q_{on} queries during the online phase wins the multi-user signature forgery game (chosen message attack) against the short Schnorr signature scheme with probability at most*

$\tilde{\mathcal{O}}\left(SN(q_{on} + N)^2/p + q_{on}/2^k + Nq_{pre}q_{on}/p^2\right)$ in the generic group model of order $p > 2^{2k}$ plus programmable random oracle model (see Theorem 8).

Theorem 3 tells us that with suitable parameter setting, key-prefixed short Schnorr signatures also achieve k bits of multi-user security even against preprocessing attacks. In particular, by setting $p \approx 2^{2k}SN$ and maintaining k-bit hash outputs, the short Schnorr signature scheme still maintains k bits of multi-user security against our preprocessing attacker. For example, if $S = 2^{k/2}$ and $N = 2^{k/4}$, then setting $p \approx 2^{2.75k}$ yields signatures of length $k + \log p = 3.75k$. Up to a factor N, the results from Theorem 3 are tight as a preprocessing attacker can succeed with probability at least Sq_{on}^2/p.

Other Fiat-Shamir Signatures. Using similar reductions, we establish similar security bounds for the full-domain hash variant of (key-prefixed) Chaum-Pedersen signatures [CP93] and for Katz-Wang signatures [KW03] with truncated hash outputs. In particular, a preprocessing attacker wins the multi-user signature forgery game with probability at most $\mathcal{O}\left(SNq^2/p + q/2^k\right)$ – see Theorem 10 and Theorem 12 in Sect. 6. Short Katz-Wang signatures [KW03] have the same length as short Schnorr signatures with equivalent security guarantees, while Chaum-Pedersen signatures are a bit longer.

1.2 Our Techniques

The Multi-User Bridge-Finding Game. We introduce an intermediate problem called the 1-*out-of-N bridge-finding game*. Oversimplifying a bit, in a cyclic group $G = \langle g \rangle$, the attacker is given N inputs $g^{x_1}, \ldots, g^{x_N}$, and the goal of the attacker is to produce a non-trivial linear dependence, i.e., $a_1, \ldots, a_N$ and b such that $a_1 x_1 + \ldots + a_N x_N = b$, and $a_i \neq 0$ for at least one $i \leq N$. We then show that in the generic group model, an attacker making at most q generic group queries can succeed with probability at most $\mathcal{O}\left(q^2/p + qN/p\right)$, where $p \approx 2^{2k}$ is the size of the group.

We also show that a preprocessing attacker wins the 1-out-of-N bridge-finding game with probability at most $\mathcal{O}\left(SNq^2 \log p/p\right)$ when given an arbitrary S-bit hint fixed a priori before $x_1, \ldots, x_N$ are chosen. Our proof adapts a compression argument of [CK18] which was used to analyze the security of the regular discrete logarithm problem. In particular, if the probability that our preprocessing attacker wins is $\omega\left(SNq^2 \log p/p\right)$, then we could derive a contradiction by compressing our random injective map τ, mapping group elements to binary strings.

An interesting corollary of these results is that the 1-out-of-N discrete-log problem is hard even for a preprocessing attacker. Intuitively, if a discrete-log attacker can successfully compute x_i for any $i \leq N$, then s/he can also win the 1-out-of-N bridge-finding game.

Restricted Discrete-Log Oracle. In fact, we consider a stronger attacker $\mathcal{A}$ who may query the usual generic group oracle, and is additionally given access to a restricted discrete-log oracle DLog. The oracle DLog will solve the discrete-log problem but only for "fresh" inputs, i.e., given N inputs $g^{x_1}, \ldots, g^{x_N}$, if $h = g^{a_1 x_1 + \cdots + a_N x_N}$ for known values of $a_1, \ldots, a_N$, then this input would not be considered fresh.

We remark that by restricting the discrete-log oracle to fresh queries, we can rule out the trivial attack where the attacker simply queries $\text{DLog}(g^{x_i})$ for any $1 \leq i \leq N$. The restriction also rules out other trivial attacks, where the attacker simply queries $\text{DLog}(g^{x_i + r})$ after computing $g^{x_i + r}$ for some $i \leq N$ and some known value r.

Security Reduction. We then give a reduction showing that any attacker $\mathcal{A}_{\text{sig}}$ that breaks multi-user security of short Schnorr signatures can be used to win the 1-out-of-N bridge-finding game. In the reduction, we interpret the bridge inputs $g^{x_1}, \ldots, g^{x_N}$ as public signing keys, and we simulate the attacker $\mathcal{A}_{\text{sig}}$. The reduction uses the restricted discrete log oracle to ensure that any group element that is submitted as an input to the random oracle has the form $g^{b + a_1 x_1 + \ldots a_N x_N}$ for values $a_1, \ldots, a_N$, and b that are known to the bridge attacker. The reduction also makes use of a programmable random oracle to forge signatures whenever $\mathcal{A}_{\text{sig}}$ queries the signing oracle for a particular user $i \leq N$.

One challenge with carrying out this reduction in the preprocessing setting is that we need to ensure that the hint does not allow the attacker to detect when the random oracle has been programmed. We rely on the observation that the reduction programs the random oracle at random inputs which are unknown to the preprocessing a priori.

A similar reduction allows us to establish multi-user security of other Fiat-Shamir-based signatures such as Chaum-Pedersen signatures [CP93] and Katz-Wang signatures [KW03], with and without preprocessing.

1.3 Related Work

Security Proofs in the Generic Group Model. The generic group model goes back to Nechaev [Nec94] and Shoup [Sho97]. One motivation for analyzing cryptographic protocols in the generic group model is that for certain elliptic curve groups, the best known attacks are all generic [JMV01, FST10, WZ11, BL12, GWZ15]. It is well known that in Shoup's generic group model [Sho97], an attacker requires $\Omega(\sqrt{p})$ queries to solve the discrete-log problem in a group of prime order p and the same lower bound holds for other classical problems like Computational Diffie-Hellman (CDH) and Decisional Diffie-Hellman (DDH). This bound is tight as discrete-log algorithms such as the Baby-Step Giant-Step algorithm by Shanks [Sha71], Pollard's Rho and Kangaroo algorithms [Pol78], and the Pohlig-Hellman algorithm [PH06] can all be described generically in Shoup's model. However, there are some exceptions for other elliptic curves and subgroups of $\mathbb{Z}_p^*$, where the best discrete-log algorithms are not generic and are much more efficient than any generic discrete log algorithms, e.g., see [GHS02, MVO91, Sma99].

Dent [Den02] showed that there are protocols which are provably secure in the generic group model but which are trivially insecure when the generic group is replaced with any (efficiently computable) real one. However, these results were artificially crafted to provide a counterexample. Similar to the random oracle model, experience suggests that protocols with security proofs in the generic group model do not have inherent structural weaknesses, and will be secure as long as we instantiate with a reasonable elliptic curve group. See [KM07, Fis00, JS08] for additional discussion of the strengths/weaknesses of proofs in the generic group model.

Corrigan-Gibbs and Kogan [CK18] analyzed the security of several key cryptographic problems (e.g., discrete-log, computational/decisional Diffie-Hellman, etc.) against preprocessing attacks in the generic group model. We extend their analysis to analyze the multi-user security of key-prefixed short Schnorr signatures against preprocessing attacks. See Sect. 5 for the further details.

Schnorr Signatures and Multi-Signatures. Bellare and Dai [BD20] recently showed that the (single-user) security of Schnorr signatures could be based on the Multi-Base Discrete Logarithm problem which in turn is similar in flavor to the One More Discrete Log Problem [BNPS03]. There has also been an active line of work on adapting the Schnorr signature scheme to design compact multi-signature schemes, e.g., see [BN06, BCJ08, DEF+19, MPSW19]. The goal is for multiple parties to collaborate to generate a single Schnorr signature which is signed using an aggregate public key that can be (publicly) derived from the individually public keys of each signing party. A very recent line of work has reduced the interaction to generate a Schnorr multi-signature to two-rounds without pairings [NRSW20, NRS20, AB20].

Other Short Signatures. Boneh et al. [BLS04] proposed even shorter signatures called BLS signatures, which is as short as $2k$ bits to yield k bits of security in the random oracle model, assuming that the Computational Diffie-Hellman (CDH) problem is hard on certain elliptic curves over a finite field. While BLS signatures yield even shorter signature length than Schnorr signatures, the computation costs for the BLS verification algorithm is several orders of magnitude higher, due to the reliance on bilinear pairings. If we allow for "heavy" cryptographic solutions such as indistinguishability obfuscation [GGH+13] (practically infeasible at the moment), then it becomes possible to achieve k-bit signatures with k bits of security [SW14, RW14, LM17].

2   Preliminaries

Let $\mathbb{N}$ be the set of positive integers, and we define $[N] := \{1, \ldots, N\}$ for $N \in \mathbb{N}$. Throughout the paper, we denote the security parameter by k. We say that $\vec{x} = (x_1, \ldots, x_N) \in \mathbb{Z}_p^N$ is an N-dimensional vector over $\mathbb{Z}_p^N$, and for each $i \in [N]$, we define $\hat{u}_i$ to be the ith N-dimensional unit vector, i.e., the ith element of $\hat{u}_i$ is 1, and all other elements are 0 elsewhere. For simplicity, we let $\log(\cdot)$ be a log with base 2, i.e., $\log x := \log_2 x$. The notation $\leftarrow\!\!\$$ denotes a uniformly random sampling, e.g., we say $x \leftarrow\!\!\$ \mathbb{Z}_p$ when x is sampled uniformly at random from $\mathbb{Z}_p$.

2.1   The Generic Group Model

The generic group model is an idealized cryptographic model proposed by Shoup [Sho97]. Let $G = \langle g \rangle$ be a multiplicative cyclic group of prime order p. In the generic group model, since G is isomorphic to $\mathbb{Z}_p$, we select a random injective map $\tau : \mathbb{Z}_p \to \mathbb{G}$, where $\mathbb{G}$ is the set of bit strings of length ℓ (with $2^\ell \geq p$) and we encode the discrete log of a group element instead of the group element itself.

The key idea in the generic group model is that the map τ does not need to be a group homomorphism, because any adversary against a cryptographic scheme is only available to see a randomly chosen encoding of the discrete log of each group element, not the group element itself. Hence, the generic group model assumes that an adversary has no access to the concrete representation of the group elements. Instead, the adversary is given access to an oracle parametrized by τ, which computes the group operation indirectly in G as well as the encoding of the discrete log of the generator g given as $\mathfrak{g} = \tau(1)$. More precisely, for an input $(\mathfrak{a}, \mathfrak{b}) \in \mathbb{G} \times \mathbb{G}$, the oracles $\mathtt{Mult}(\mathfrak{a}, \mathfrak{b})$, and $\mathtt{Inv}(\mathfrak{a})$ act as following:

$$\mathtt{Mult}(\mathfrak{a}, \mathfrak{b}) = \tau(\tau^{-1}(\mathfrak{a}) + \tau^{-1}(\mathfrak{b})), \text{ and}$$
$$\mathtt{Inv}(\mathfrak{a}) = \tau(-\tau^{-1}(\mathfrak{a})),$$

if $\tau^{-1}(\mathfrak{a}), \tau^{-1}(\mathfrak{b}) \in G$. We remark that the adversary has no access to the map τ itself and does not know what is going on in a group G. Hence, the adversary has no sense that which element in G maps to $\mathtt{Mult}(\mathfrak{a}, \mathfrak{b})$ in $\mathbb{G}$ even if s/he sees the oracle output.

For convenience, we will use the notation $\mathtt{Pow}(\mathfrak{a}, n) = \tau(n\tau^{-1}(\mathfrak{a}))$. Without loss of generality, we do not allow the attacker to directly query $\mathtt{Pow}$ as an oracle, since the attacker can efficiently evaluate this subroutine using the $\mathtt{Mult}$ oracle. In particular, one can evaluate $\mathtt{Pow}(\mathfrak{a}, n)$ using just $\mathcal{O}(\log n)$ calls to $\mathtt{Mult}$ using the standard modular exponentiation algorithm.

2.2   The Schnorr Signature Scheme

The Schnorr signature scheme is a digital signature scheme, which consists of a tuple of probabilistic polynomial-time algorithms $\Pi = (\mathsf{Kg}, \mathsf{Sign}, \mathsf{Vfy})$, where $\mathsf{Kg}(1^k)$ is a key-generation algorithm to generate a secret key $\mathsf{sk} \in \mathbb{Z}_p$ and a public key $\mathsf{pk} = \mathtt{Pow}(\mathfrak{g} = \tau(1), \mathsf{sk}) = \tau(\mathsf{sk})$. The size of the prime number p will be tied to the security parameter k, e.g., $p \approx 2^{2k}$. $\mathsf{Sign}(\mathsf{sk}, m)$ is a signing algorithm which generates a signature σ on a message $m \in \{0,1\}^*$, and $\mathsf{Vfy}(\mathsf{pk}, m, \sigma)$ is a verification algorithm which outputs 1 if the signature is valid, and 0 otherwise.

Throughout the paper, we will consider the notion of the generic group model in the Schnorr signature scheme as described in Fig. 1. We remark that verification works for a correct signature $\sigma = (s, e)$, because $R = \mathtt{Mult}(\tau(s), \mathtt{Pow}(\mathtt{Inv}(\mathsf{pk}), e)) = \tau(s - \mathsf{sk} \cdot e) = \tau(r) = I$ if the signature is valid.

Short Schnorr Signatures. Typically, it is assumed that the random oracle $\mathsf{H}(I\|m)$ outputs a uniformly random element $e \in \mathbb{Z}_p$, where p is a random $2k$-bit prime. Thus, we would need $2k$ bits to encode e. To produce a shorter signature,

$\mathsf{Kg}(1^k)$:	$\mathsf{Sign}(\mathsf{sk}, m)$:	$\mathsf{Vfy}(\mathsf{pk}, m, \sigma)$:
1: $\mathsf{sk} \leftarrow\!\!\$\ \mathbb{Z}_p$	1: $r \leftarrow\!\!\$\ \mathbb{Z}_p$	1: Parse $\sigma = (s, e)$
2: $\mathsf{pk} \leftarrow \mathsf{Pow}(\mathfrak{g}, \mathsf{sk})$	2: $I \leftarrow \mathsf{Pow}(\mathfrak{g}, r)$	2: $R \leftarrow \mathsf{Mult}(\mathsf{Pow}(\mathfrak{g}, s), \mathsf{Pow}(\mathsf{Inv}(\mathsf{pk}), e))$
3: $\mathbf{return}\ (\mathsf{pk}, \mathsf{sk})$	3: $e \leftarrow \mathsf{H}(I\|m)$	3: $\mathbf{if}\ \mathsf{H}(R\|m) = e\ \mathbf{then}$
	4: $s \leftarrow r + \mathsf{sk} \cdot e \mod p$	4: $\quad\mathbf{return}\ 1$
	5: $\mathbf{return}\ \sigma = (s, e)$	5: $\mathbf{else\ return}\ 0$

Fig. 1. The Schnorr signature scheme in the generic group model. Note that instead of the direct group operation in G, we use the encoding by the map τ and the generic group oracle queries.

we can assume that $\mathsf{H}(I\|m)$ outputs a uniformly random integer $e \in \mathbb{Z}_{2^k}$ with just k bits. In practice, the shorter random oracle is *easier* to implement, since we do not need to worry about rounding issues when converting a binary string to $\mathbb{Z}_{2^k}$, i.e., we can simply take the first k bits of our random binary string. The result is a signature $\sigma = (s, e)$, which can be encoded in $3k$ bits – $2k$ bits to encode $s \in \mathbb{Z}_p$ plus k bits to encode e. This natural modification is straightforward and is not new to our paper. The key question we investigate is whether or not short Schnorr signatures can provide k bits of security.

3 Single-User Security of Short Schnorr Signatures

As a warm-up to our main result, we first prove that *short* Schnorr Signatures (of length $3k$) achieve k bits of security. We first describe the standard signature forgery experiment $\mathsf{SigForge}^{\tau}_{\mathcal{A}, \Pi}(k)$ in the generic group model and the random oracle model. Here, an attacker is given the public key $\mathsf{pk} = \tau(\mathsf{sk})$ along with $\mathfrak{g} = \tau(1)$ (the encoding of the group generator 1 of $\mathbb{Z}_p$). The attacker is given oracle access to the signing oracle $\mathsf{Sign}(\cdot)$, as well as the generic group oracles $\mathsf{GO} = (\mathsf{Mult}(\cdot, \cdot), \mathsf{Inv}(\cdot))$, and the random oracle $\mathsf{H}(\cdot)$. The attacker's goal is to eventually output a forgery $(m, \sigma = (s, e))$ for a *fresh* message m that has not previously been submitted to the signing oracle.

Generic Signature Forgery Game. Fixing an encoding map $\tau : \mathbb{Z}_p \to \mathbb{G}$, $\mathfrak{g} = \tau(1)$ and the random oracle H, and an adversary $\mathcal{A}$, consider the following experiment defined for a signature scheme $\Pi = (\mathsf{Kg}, \mathsf{Sign}, \mathsf{Vfy})$:

The Generic Signature Forgery Game $\mathsf{SigForge}^{\tau, \mathsf{H}}_{\mathcal{A}, \Pi}(k)$:

(1) $\mathsf{Kg}(1^k)$ is run to obtain the public and the secret keys $(\mathsf{pk}, \mathsf{sk})$. Here, sk is chosen randomly from the group $\mathbb{Z}_p$ where p is a $2k$-bit prime, and $\mathsf{pk} = \mathsf{Pow}(\mathfrak{g}, \mathsf{sk}) = \tau(\mathsf{sk})$.

(2) Adversary $\mathcal{A}$ is given $(\mathfrak{g} = \tau(1), \mathsf{pk}, p)$ and access to the generic group oracles $\mathsf{GO} = (\mathsf{Mult}(\cdot, \cdot), \mathsf{Inv}(\cdot))$, the random oracle $\mathsf{H}(\cdot)$, and the signing oracle $\mathsf{Sign}(\cdot)$. After multiple access to these oracles, the adversary outputs $(m, \sigma = (s, e))$.

(3) We define $\mathsf{SigForge}_{\mathcal{A},\Pi}^{\tau,\mathsf{H}}(k) = \mathsf{Vfy}(\mathsf{pk}, m, \sigma)$, i.e., the output is 1 when $\mathcal{A}$ succeeds, and 0 otherwise.

Definition 1 formalizes this argument in the sense that an attacker forges a signature if and only if $\mathsf{SigForge}_{\mathcal{A},\Pi}^{\tau,\mathsf{H}}(k) = 1$.

Definition 1. *Consider the generic group model with an encoding map $\tau : \mathbb{Z}_p \to \mathbb{G}$. A signature scheme $\Pi = (\mathsf{Kg}, \mathsf{Sign}, \mathsf{Vfy})$ is said to be $(q_\mathsf{H}, q_\mathsf{G}, q_\mathsf{S}, \varepsilon)$-UF-CMA secure (unforgeable against chosen message attack) if for every adversary $\mathcal{A}$ making at most q_H (resp. q_G, q_S) queries to the random oracle (resp. generic group, signing oracles), the following bound holds:*

$$\Pr\left[\mathsf{SigForge}_{\mathcal{A},\Pi}^{\tau,\mathsf{H}}(k) = 1\right] \leq \varepsilon,$$

where the randomness is taken over the selection of τ, the random coins of $\mathcal{A}$, the random coins of Kg, and the selection of random oracle H.

3.1 Discrete Log Problem with Restricted Discrete Log Oracle

Restricted Discrete-Log Oracle in the Generic Group Model. In the discrete log problem we pick a random $x \in \mathbb{Z}_p$ and the attacker is challenged to recover x given $\mathfrak{g} = \tau(1)$ and $\mathfrak{h} = \mathsf{Pow}(\mathfrak{g}, x)$ after making queries to the generic group oracles Mult and Inv. As we mentioned in Sect. 1.2, we analyze the discrete log problem in a stronger setting where the attacker is additionally given access to a restricted discrete-log oracle DLog. Given the map $\tau : \mathbb{Z}_p \to \mathbb{G}$ and $y \in \mathbb{Z}_p$, $\mathsf{DLog}(\tau(y))$ will output y as long as $\tau(y)$ is a "fresh" group element. More specifically, we say $\tau(y)$ is "fresh" if (1) $\tau(y)$ is not equal to $\mathfrak{h}$, and (2) $\tau(y)$ has not been the output of a previous generic group query.

The requirement that $\tau(y)$ is fresh rules out trivial attacks where the attacker picks $a, b \in \mathbb{Z}_p$, computes $\tau(ax + b) = \mathsf{Mult}(\mathsf{Pow}(\mathfrak{h}, a), \mathsf{Pow}(\mathfrak{g}, b))$ and queries $\mathsf{DLog}(\tau(ax + b))$ and solves for $x = a^{-1}(\mathsf{DLog}(\tau(ax + b)) - b) \mod p$.

The Generic Discrete-Log Game. The formal definition of the discrete log experiment $\mathsf{DLogChal}_{\mathcal{A}}^{\tau}(k)$ is given below:

The Generic Discrete-Log Game $\mathsf{DLogChal}_{\mathcal{A}}^{\tau}(k)$:

(1) The adversary $\mathcal{A}$ is given $(\mathfrak{g} = \tau(1), \tau(x))$ for a random value of $x \in \mathbb{Z}_p$. Here, $\tau : \mathbb{Z}_p \to \mathbb{G}$ is a map from $\mathbb{Z}_p$ to a generic group $\mathbb{G}$ with a $2k$-bit prime p.
(2) $\mathcal{A}$ is allowed to query the usual generic group oracles $(\mathsf{Mult}, \mathsf{Inv})$ and is additionally allowed to query $\mathsf{DLog}(\tau(y))$, but *only* if $\tau(y)$ is "fresh", i.e., $\tau(y)$ is not $\tau(x)$, and $\tau(y)$ has not been the output of a previous random generic group query.
(3) After multiple queries, $\mathcal{A}$ outputs x'.
(4) The output of the game is defined to be $\mathsf{DLogChal}_{\mathcal{A}}^{\tau}(k) = 1$ if $x' = x$, and 0 otherwise.

Lemma 1 upper bounds the probability that an attacker wins the generic discrete-log game $\mathsf{DLogChal}_{\mathcal{A}}^{\tau}(k)$. Intuitively, the proof works by maintaining a list $\mathcal{L}$ of tuples $(\tau(y), a, b)$ such that $y = ax + b$ for every oracle output $\tau(y)$.

Initially, the list $\mathcal{L}$ contains two items $(\tau(x), 1, 0)$ and $(\tau(1), 0, 1)$, and the list is updated after every query to the generic group oracles, e.g., if $(\tau(y_1), a_1, b_1) \in \mathcal{L}$ and $(\tau(y_2), a_2, b_2) \in \mathcal{L}$, then querying $\mathtt{Mult}(\tau(y_1), \tau(y_2))$ will result in the addition of $(\tau(y_1 + y_2), a_1 + a_2, b_1 + b_2)$ into $\mathcal{L}$. If $\mathcal{L}$ already contained a tuple of the form $(\tau(y_1 + y_2), a', b')$ with $a' \neq a_1 + a_2$ or $b' \neq b_1 + b_2$, then we say that the event BRIDGE occurs.

We can use the restricted discrete log oracle to maintain the invariant that every output of our generic group oracles $\mathtt{Mult}$ and $\mathtt{Inv}$ can be added to $\mathcal{L}$. In particular, if we every encounter an input $\mathfrak{y} = \tau(b)$ that does not already appear in $\mathcal{L}$, then $\mathfrak{y}$ is fresh and we can simply query the restricted discrete log oracle to extract $b = \mathtt{DLog}(\mathfrak{y})$, ensuring that the tuple $(\mathfrak{y}, 0, b)$ is added to $\mathcal{L}$ before the generic group query is processed.

The key component of the proof is to upper bound the probability of the event BRIDGE. This is sufficient as any attacker that can recover x will also be able to ensure that $(\tau(x), 0, x)$ is added to $\mathcal{L}$, which would immediately cause the event BRIDGE to occur, since we already have $(\tau(x), 1, 0) \in \mathcal{L}$. We defer the full proof of Lemma 1 to the full version [BL19] for readers who are interested.

Lemma 1. *The probability the attacker making at most q_G generic group oracle queries wins the generic discrete-log game $\mathsf{DLogChal}_{\mathcal{A}}^{\tau}(k)$ (even with access to the restricted DLog oracle) is at most*

$$\Pr\left[\mathsf{DLogChal}_{\mathcal{A}}^{\tau}(k) = 1\right] \leq \frac{6q_G(q_G + 1) + 12}{4p - (3q_G + 2)^2},$$

in the generic group model of prime order p, where the randomness is taken over the selection of τ, the challenge x, as well as any random coins of $\mathcal{A}$.

3.2   Security Reduction

Given Lemma 1, we are now ready to describe our security reduction for short Schnorr signatures of length $3k$. As in our security proof for the discrete-log problem, we will ensure that for every output $\tau(y)$ of a generic group query, we can express $y = ax + b$ for known constants a and b – here x is the secret key that is selected in the security game, i.e., any time $\mathcal{A}_{\mathsf{sig}}$ makes a query involving a fresh element $\tau(y)$, we will simply query $\mathtt{DLog}(\tau(y))$ so that we can add $\tau(y)$ to the list $\mathcal{L}$.

Theorem 4 provides the first rigorous proof of the folklore claim that short ($3k$-bit) Schnorr signatures can provide k bits of security. The formal security proof uses *both* the generic group model and the random oracle model.

Theorem 4. *The* short *Schnorr signature scheme $\Pi_{\mathsf{short}} = (\mathsf{Kg}, \mathsf{Sign}, \mathsf{Vfy})$ of length $3k$ is $(q_H, q_G, q_S, \varepsilon)$-UF-CMA secure with*

$$\varepsilon = \frac{6q_G(q_G + 1) + 12}{4p - (3q_G + 2)^2} + \frac{q_S(q_H + q_S)}{p} + \frac{q_H + q_S}{p - (3q_G + 2)} + \frac{q_H + 1}{2^k} = \mathcal{O}\left(\frac{q}{2^k}\right),$$

in the generic group model of prime order $p \approx 2^{2k}$ and the programmable random oracle model, where q denotes the total number of queries made by an adversary.

Proof Sketch of Theorem 4: Here, we only give the intuition of how the proof works. The full proof of Theorem 4 is similar to that of Theorem 6 and we defer it to the full version [BL19].

We give the proof by reduction, i.e., given an adversary $\mathcal{A}_{\mathsf{sig}}$ attacking short Schnorr signature scheme, we construct an efficient algorithm $\mathcal{A}_{\mathsf{dlog}}$ which solves the discrete-log problem. During the reduction, we simulate the signature signing process without secret key x by programming the random oracle, i.e., to sign a message m we can pick s and e randomly, compute $I = \tau(s - xe)$ by querying adequate generic group oracles[2], and see if the random oracle has been previously queried at $\mathsf{H}(I\|m)$. If not, then we can program the random oracle as $\mathsf{H}(I\|m) := e$ and output the signature (s, e). Otherwise, the reduction simply outputs $\perp$ for failure. Since s and e are selected randomly, we can argue that the probability that we output $\perp$ because $\mathsf{H}(I\|m)$ is already defined is small, i.e., $\approx q_{\mathsf{H}}/p$.

We can use the oracle DLog to maintain the invariant that before processing any random oracle query of the form $\mathsf{H}(\mathfrak{y}\|\cdot)$ that we know a, b such that $\tau(ax + b) = \mathfrak{y}$. In particular, if $\mathfrak{y}$ is a fresh string that has not previously been observed, then we can simply set $a = 0$ and query the restricted discrete log oracle to find b such that $\tau(b) = \mathfrak{y}$. We say that the random oracle query is lucky if $\mathsf{H}(\mathfrak{y}\|m) = -a$, or $\mathsf{H}(\mathfrak{y}\|m) = 0$. Assuming that the event BRIDGE does not occur, it is straightforward to upper bound the probability of a lucky query as $\mathcal{O}(q_{\mathsf{H}}/2^k)$. Similarly, it is straightforward to show that the probability that $\mathcal{A}_{\mathsf{sig}}$ gets lucky and guesses a valid signature (s, e) for a message m without first querying $\mathsf{H}(\tau(s - xe)\|m)$ is $\mathcal{O}(2^{-k})$. Assuming that there are no lucky queries or guesses but the attacker still outputs a successful signature forgery (s, e). In this case we have $I = \tau(s - xe) = \tau(ax + b)$, which allows for us to solve for x using the equation $(a + e)x = (s - b)$. Thus, we can argue that the probability $\mathcal{A}_{\mathsf{dlog}}$ solves the discrete-log challenge correctly is lower bounded by the probability that $\mathcal{A}_{\mathsf{sig}}$ forges a signature minus $\mathcal{O}(q/2^k)$. Finally, by applying Lemma 1 we can upper bound the probability $\mathcal{A}_{\mathsf{sig}}$ wins the generic signature forgery game $\mathsf{SigForge}_{\mathcal{A},\Pi}^{\tau,\mathsf{H}}(k)$ to be $\mathcal{O}(q/2^k)$. $\qquad\square$

4   Multi-user Security of Short Schnorr Signatures

In this section, we prove that short Schnorr signatures also provide k bits of security in the multi-user setting. The reduction uses similar ideas, but requires us to introduce and analyze a game called the *1-out-of-N generic* BRIDGE^N*-finding game*. We first define the *1-out-of-N generic signature forgery game*, where an adversary is given N independent public keys $(\mathsf{pk}_1, \ldots, \mathsf{pk}_N) = (\tau(\mathsf{sk}_1), \ldots, \tau(\mathsf{sk}_N))$ along with oracle access to the signing oracles $\mathsf{Sign}(\mathsf{sk}_1, \cdot), \ldots, \mathsf{Sign}(\mathsf{sk}_N, \cdot)$, the random oracle H, and the generic group oracles. The attacker can succeed if s/he can output a forgery (σ, m)

---

[2] We can compute I without knowledge of x because $\tau(x)$ is given as public key.

which is valid under *any one* public key, e.g., for some public key pk_j we have $\mathsf{Vfy}(\mathsf{pk}_j, m, \sigma) = 1$, while the query m was never submitted to the jth signing oracle $\mathsf{Sign}(\mathsf{sk}_j, \cdot)$. In our reduction, we show that any attacker that wins the 1-out-of-N generic signature forgery game can be used to win the 1-out-of-N generic BRIDGE^N-finding game. We separately upper bound the probability that a generic attacker can win the 1-out-of-N generic BRIDGE^N-finding game.

1-out-of-N Generic Signature Forgery Game. Fixing the injective mapping $\tau : \mathbb{Z}_p \to \mathbb{G}$, a random oracle H, and an adversary $\mathcal{A}$, consider the following experiment defined for a signature scheme $\Pi = (\mathsf{Kg}, \mathsf{Sign}, \mathsf{Vfy})$:

The 1-out-of-N Generic Signature Forgery Game $\mathsf{SigForge}_{\mathcal{A},\Pi}^{\tau,\mathsf{H},N}(k)$:

(1) $\mathsf{Kg}(1^k)$ is run N times to obtain the public and the secret keys $(\mathsf{pk}_i, \mathsf{sk}_i)$ for each $i \in [N]$. Here, for each $i \in [N]$, sk_i is chosen randomly from the group $\mathbb{Z}_p$, where p is a $2k$-bit prime, and $\mathsf{pk}_i = \tau(\mathsf{sk}_i)$.

(2) Adversary $\mathcal{A}$ is given $(\mathfrak{g} = \tau(1), \mathsf{pk}_1, \cdots, \mathsf{pk}_N, p)$, and access to the generic group oracles $\mathsf{GO} = (\mathsf{Mult}(\cdot, \cdot), \mathsf{Inv}(\cdot))$, the random oracle $\mathsf{H}(\cdot)$, and the signing oracles $\mathsf{Sign}(\mathsf{sk}_1, \cdot), \ldots, \mathsf{Sign}(\mathsf{sk}_N, \cdot)$. The experiment ends when the adversary outputs $(m, \sigma = (s, e))$.

(3) $\mathcal{A}$ succeeds to forge a signature if and only if there exists some $j \in [N]$ such that $\mathsf{Vfy}(\mathsf{pk}_j, m, \sigma) = 1$ and the query m was never submitted to the oracle $\mathsf{Sign}(\mathsf{sk}_j, \cdot)$. The output of the experiment is $\mathsf{SigForge}_{\mathcal{A},\Pi}^{\tau,\mathsf{H},N}(k) = 1$ when $\mathcal{A}$ succeeds; otherwise $\mathsf{SigForge}_{\mathcal{A},\Pi}^{\tau,\mathsf{H},N}(k) = 0$.

Definition 2. *Consider the generic group model with an encoding map $\tau : \mathbb{Z}_p \to \mathbb{G}$. A signature scheme $\Pi = (\mathsf{Kg}, \mathsf{Sign}, \mathsf{Vfy})$ is $(N, q_\mathsf{H}, q_\mathsf{G}, q_\mathsf{S}, \varepsilon)$-MU-UF-CMA secure (multi-user unforgeable against chosen message attack) if for every adversary $\mathcal{A}$ making at most q_H (resp. q_G, q_S) queries to the random oracle (resp. generic group, signing oracles), the following bound holds:*

$$\Pr\left[\mathsf{SigForge}_{\mathcal{A},\Pi}^{\tau,\mathsf{H},N}(k) = 1\right] \leq \varepsilon,$$

where the randomness is taken over the selection of τ, the random coins of $\mathcal{A}$, the random coins of Kg, and the selection of random oracle H.

The Discrete-Log Solution List $\mathcal{L}$ in a Multi-User Setting. As before, we will maintain the invariant that for every output $\mathfrak{y}$ of a generic group query that we have recorded a tuple $(\mathfrak{y}, \vec{a}, b)$ in a list $\mathcal{L}$ where $\mathsf{DLog}(\mathfrak{y}) = \vec{a} \cdot \vec{x} + b$ (here, $\vec{a} = (a_1, \ldots, a_N), \vec{x} = (x_1, \ldots, x_N) \in \mathbb{Z}_p^N$). Note that the restricted oracle $\mathsf{DLog}(\cdot)$ will solve $\mathsf{DLog}(\mathfrak{y})$ for any fresh group element $\mathfrak{y}$ such that $\mathfrak{y} \notin \{\tau(1), \tau(x_1), \ldots, \tau(x_N)\}$, and $\mathfrak{y}$ has not been the output of a prior generic group query.

- Initially, $\mathcal{L}$ contains $(\tau(1), \vec{0}, 1)$ and $(\tau(x_i), \hat{u}_i, 0)$ for $1 \leq i \leq N$.
- If the attacker ever submits a fresh group element $\mathfrak{y}$ which was not previously an output of a generic group oracle query, then we can query $b = \mathsf{DLog}(\mathfrak{y})$,

and add $(\mathfrak{y}, \vec{0}, b)$ to our list. Thus, without loss of generality, we can assume that all query inputs to Mult, Inv were first added to $\mathcal{L}$.

- If $(\mathfrak{y}_1, \vec{a}_1, b_1), (\mathfrak{y}_2, \vec{a}_2, b_2) \in \mathcal{L}$, and the attacker queries $\texttt{Mult}(\mathfrak{y}_1, \mathfrak{y}_2)$, then add $(\texttt{Mult}(\mathfrak{y}_1, \mathfrak{y}_2), \vec{a}_1 + \vec{a}_2, b_1 + b_2)$ to $\mathcal{L}$.
- If $(\mathfrak{y}, \vec{a}, b) \in \mathcal{L}$, and $\texttt{Inv}(\mathfrak{y})$ is queried, then add $(\texttt{Inv}(\mathfrak{y}), -\vec{a}, -b)$ to $\mathcal{L}$.

4.1   The Multi-user Bridge-Finding Game

We establish the multi-user security of short Schnorr signatures via reduction from a new game we introduce called the *1-out-of-N generic* BRIDGE^N*-finding game*. As in the 1-out-of-N discrete-log game, the attacker is given $\tau(1)$, as well as $\tau(x_1), \ldots, \tau(x_N)$ for N randomly selected values $\vec{x} = (x_1, \ldots, x_N) \in \mathbb{Z}_p^N$. The key difference between this game and the 1-out-of-N discrete-log game is that the attacker's goal is simply to ensure that the "bridge event" BRIDGE^N occurs, whether or not the attacker is able to solve any of the discrete-log challenges. As in Sect. 3, we will assume that we have access to $\texttt{DLog}(\cdot)$, and we will maintain the invariant that for every output $\tau(y)$ of some generic group query, we have $y = \vec{a} \cdot \vec{x} + b$ for known values $\vec{a} = (a_1, \ldots, a_N) \in \mathbb{Z}_p^N$ and $b \in \mathbb{Z}_p$, i.e., by querying the restricted oracle $\texttt{DLog}(\tau(y))$ whenever we encounter a fresh input.

The 1-out-of-N Generic BRIDGE^N-Finding Game $\mathsf{BridgeChal}_{\mathcal{A}}^{\tau, N}(k, \vec{x})$:

(1) The challenger initializes the list $\mathcal{L} = \{(\tau(1), \vec{0}, 1), (\tau(x_1), \hat{u}_1, 0), \ldots, (\tau(x_N), \hat{u}_N, 0)\}$, and $\vec{x} = (x_1, \cdots, x_N)$.

(2) The adversary $\mathcal{A}$ is given $\mathfrak{g} = \tau(1)$ and $\tau(x_i)$ for each $i \in [N]$.

(3) $\mathcal{A}$ is allowed to query the usual generic group oracles (Mult, Inv).

   (a) If the challenger ever submits any fresh element $\mathfrak{y}$ which does not appear in $\mathcal{L}$ as input to a generic group oracle, then the challenger immediately queries $b_y = \texttt{DLog}(\mathfrak{y})$, and adds the tuple $(\mathfrak{y}, \vec{0}, b_y)$ to the list $\mathcal{L}$.

   (b) Whenever $\mathcal{A}$ submits a query $\mathfrak{y}_1, \mathfrak{y}_2$ to $\texttt{Mult}(\cdot, \cdot)$, we are ensured that there exist tuples $(\mathfrak{y}_1, \vec{a}_1, b_1), (\mathfrak{y}_2, \vec{a}_2, b_2) \in \mathcal{L}$. The challenger adds the tuple $(\texttt{Mult}(\mathfrak{y}_1, \mathfrak{y}_2), \vec{a}_1 + \vec{a}_2, b_1 + b_2)$ to the list $\mathcal{L}$.

   (c) Whenever $\mathcal{A}$ submits a query $\mathfrak{y}$ to $\texttt{Inv}(\cdot)$, we are ensured that some tuple $(\mathfrak{y}, \vec{a}_y, b_y) \in \mathcal{L}$. The challenger adds the tuple $(\texttt{Inv}(\mathfrak{y}), -\vec{a}_y, -b_y)$ to the list $\mathcal{L}$.

(4) If at any point in time we have a collision, i.e., two distinct tuples $(\mathfrak{y}, \vec{a}_1, b_1), (\mathfrak{y}, \vec{a}_2, b_2) \in \mathcal{L}$ with $(\vec{a}_1, b_1) \neq (\vec{a}_2, b_2)$, then the event BRIDGE^N occurs, and the output of the game is 1. If BRIDGE^N never occurs, then the output of the game is 0.

We further define the game $\mathsf{BridgeChal}_{\mathcal{A}}^{\tau, N}(k)$ in which $\vec{x} = (x_1, \ldots, x_N)$ are first sampled uniformly at random, and then we run $\mathsf{BridgeChal}_{\mathcal{A}}^{\tau, N}(k, \vec{x})$. Thus,

$$\Pr_{\mathcal{A}, \tau}[\mathsf{BridgeChal}_{\mathcal{A}}^{\tau, N}(k) = 1] := \Pr_{\mathcal{A}, \tau, \vec{x}}[\mathsf{BridgeChal}_{\mathcal{A}}^{\tau, N}(k, \vec{x}) = 1] .$$

As long as the event BRIDGE^N has not occurred, we can (essentially) view $x_1, \ldots, x_N$ as uniformly random values that are yet to be selected. More precisely, the values $x_1, \ldots, x_N$ are selected subject to a few constraints, e.g., if we know $\mathfrak{f}_1 = \tau(\vec{a}_1 \cdot \vec{x} + b_1) \neq \mathfrak{f}_2 = \tau(\vec{a}_2 \cdot \vec{x} + b_2)$ then we have the constraint that $\vec{a}_1 \cdot \vec{x} + b_1 \neq \vec{a}_2 \cdot \vec{x} + b_2$.

Theorem 5. *For any attackers $\mathcal{A}$ making at most $q_{\mathsf{G}} := q_{\mathsf{G}}(k)$ queries to the generic group oracles,*

$$\Pr\left[\mathsf{BridgeChal}_{\mathcal{A}}^{\tau,N}(k) = 1\right] \leq \frac{q_{\mathsf{G}}N + 3q_{\mathsf{G}}(q_{\mathsf{G}}+1)/2}{p - (N + 3q_{\mathsf{G}} + 1)^2 - N},$$

in the generic group model of prime order p where the randomness is taken over the selection of $x_1, \ldots, x_N, \tau$ as well as any random coins of $\mathcal{A}$.

Proof. Consider the output $\mathfrak{y}_i$ of the ith generic group query. We first analyze the probability that this query results in the event BRIDGE^N conditioning on the event $\overline{\mathsf{BRIDGE}}_{<i}^N$ that the event has not yet occurred, i.e., the event BRIDGE^N has not been occurred until the $(i-1)^{th}$ query. Before we even receive the output $\mathfrak{y}_i$, we already know the values $\vec{a}_i, b_i$ such that the tuple $(\mathfrak{y}_i, \vec{a}_i, b_i)$ will be added to $\mathcal{L}$. If $\mathcal{L}$ does already contain this *exact* tuple, then outputting $\mathfrak{y}_i$ will not produce the event BRIDGE^N. If $\mathcal{L}$ does not already contain this tuple $(\mathfrak{y}_i, \vec{a}_i, b_i)$, then we are interested in the event B_i that some other tuple $(\mathfrak{y}_i, \vec{a}'_i, b'_i)$ has been recorded with $(\vec{a}'_i, b'_i) \neq (\vec{a}_i, b_i)$. Observe that B_i occurs if and only if there exists a tuple of the form $(\cdot, \vec{a}, b)$ with $(\vec{a} - \vec{a}_i) \cdot \vec{x} = b_i - b$ and $(\vec{a}, b) \neq (\vec{a}_i, b_i)$. If we pick $\vec{x}$ randomly, the probability that $(\vec{a} - \vec{a}_i) \cdot \vec{x} = b_i - b$ would be $1/p$. However, we cannot quite view $\vec{x}$ as random due to the restrictions, i.e., because we condition of the event $\overline{\mathsf{BRIDGE}}_{<i}^N$ we know that for any distinct pair $(\mathfrak{y}_i, \vec{a}_i, b_i)$ and $(\mathfrak{y}_j, \vec{a}_j, b_j)$ we know that $\vec{a}_i \cdot \vec{x} + b_i \neq \vec{a}_j \cdot \vec{x} + b_j$.

Consider sampling $\vec{x}$ uniformly at random subject to this restriction. Let $r \leq N$ be an index such that $\vec{a}[r] - \vec{a}_i[r] \neq 0$ and suppose that $x_r = \vec{x}[r]$ is the last value sampled. At this point, we can view x_r as being drawn uniformly at random from a set of at least $p - |\mathcal{L}|^2 - (N - 1)$ remaining values, subject to all of the restrictions. We also observe that $|\mathcal{L}| \leq N + 3q_{\mathsf{G}} + 1$ since each generic group oracle query adds *at most* three new tuples to $\mathcal{L}$—exactly three in the case that we query $\mathsf{Mult}(\mathfrak{y}_1, \mathfrak{y}_2)$ on two fresh elements. Thus, the probability that $(\vec{a} - \vec{a}_i) \cdot \vec{x} = b_i - b$ is at most $\frac{1}{p - (N + 3q_{\mathsf{G}} + 1)^2 - (N-1)}$. Union bounding over all tuples $(\cdot, \vec{a}, b) \in \mathcal{L}$, we have

$$\Pr\left[B_i : \overline{\mathsf{BRIDGE}}_{<i}^N\right] \leq \frac{N + 3i}{p - (N + 3q_{\mathsf{G}} + 1)^2 - N}.$$

To complete the proof, we observe that

$$\Pr\left[\mathsf{BridgeChal}_{\mathcal{A}}^{\mathsf{G0},N}(k) = 1\right] = \sum_{i \leq q_{\mathsf{G}}} \Pr\left[B_i : \overline{\mathsf{BRIDGE}}_{<i}^N\right]$$

$$\leq \sum_{i \leq q_{\mathsf{G}}} \frac{N + 3i}{p - (N + 3q_{\mathsf{G}} + 1)^2 - N} = \frac{q_{\mathsf{G}}N + 3q_{\mathsf{G}}(q_{\mathsf{G}}+1)/2}{p - (N + 3q_{\mathsf{G}} + 1)^2 - N}.$$

$\square$

As an immediate corollary of Theorem 5, we can show that an attacker wins the 1-out-of-N discrete log game with (approximately) the same probability as in the multi-user bridge-finding game. In particular, given any attacker $\mathcal{A}'$ in the 1-out-of-N discrete-log game $\mathsf{1ofNDLog}_{\mathcal{A}}^{\tau,N}(k)$, where the attacker's goal is to output *any* $x \in \{x_1, \ldots, x_N\}$ given input $\tau(1), \tau(x_1), \ldots, \tau(x_N)$, we can construct an attacker $\mathcal{A}$ in the game $\mathsf{BridgeChal}_{\mathcal{A}}^{\tau,N}(k)$. $\mathcal{A}$ simply runs $\mathcal{A}'$ to obtain an output x, and then computes $\tau(x)$ using at most $2 \log p$ queries to the $\mathsf{Mult}(\cdot, \cdot)$ oracle. If $x \in \{x_1, \ldots, x_N\}$, then the bridge event BRIDGE^N must have occurred at some point, since we have $(\tau(x), \vec{0}, x) \in \mathcal{L}$ and $(\tau(x), \hat{u}_i, 0) \in \mathcal{L}$ for some $i \in [N]$.

Corollary 1. *For any attacker $\mathcal{A}$ making at most $q_\mathsf{G} + 2 \log p$ queries,*

$$\Pr\left[\mathsf{1ofNDLog}_{\mathcal{A}}^{\tau,N}(k) = 1\right] \leq \frac{q_\mathsf{G} N + 3 q_\mathsf{G}(q_\mathsf{G} + 1)/2}{p - (N + 3 q_\mathsf{G} + 1)^2 - N},$$

in the generic group model of prime order p, where the randomness is taken over the selection of τ, the challenges $x_1, \ldots, x_N$, and any random coins of $\mathcal{A}$.

4.2   Security Reduction

Theorem 6. *The* short *Schnorr signature scheme* $\Pi_\mathsf{short} = (\mathsf{Kg}, \mathsf{Sign}, \mathsf{Vfy})$ *of length* $3k$ *is* $\left(N, q_\mathsf{H}, q_\mathsf{G}, q_\mathsf{S}, \varepsilon = \mathcal{O}\left(\frac{q+N}{2^k}\right)\right)$*-MU-UF-CMA secure with*

$$\varepsilon = \frac{q_\mathsf{G} N + 3 q_\mathsf{G}(q_\mathsf{G} + 1)/2}{p - (N + 3 q_\mathsf{G} + 1)^2 - N} + \frac{q_\mathsf{S}(q_\mathsf{H} + q_\mathsf{S})}{p} + \frac{q_\mathsf{H} + q_\mathsf{S}}{p - (N + 3 q_\mathsf{G} + 1)} + \frac{q_\mathsf{H} + 1}{2^k},$$

in the generic group model of prime order $p \approx 2^{2k}$ and the programmable random oracle model, where q denotes the total number of queries made by an adversary.

Proof. Given an adversary $\mathcal{A}_\mathsf{sig}$ attacking short Schnorr signature scheme, we construct the following efficient algorithm $\mathcal{A}_\mathsf{bridge}$ which tries to succeed in the 1-out-of-N generic BRIDGE^N-finding game $\mathsf{BridgeChal}_{\mathcal{A}_\mathsf{bridge}}^{\tau,N}(k)$:

Algorithm $\mathcal{A}_\mathsf{bridge}$:
The algorithm is given $p, \mathfrak{g} = \tau(1), \tau(x_i), 1 \leq i \leq N$ as input.

1. Initialize the list $\mathcal{L} = \{(\tau(1), \vec{0}, 1), (\tau(x_i), \hat{u}_i, 0) \text{ for each } i \in [N]\}$, and $\mathsf{H}_\mathsf{resp} = \{\}$, where H_resp stores the random oracle queries.
2. Run $\mathcal{A}_\mathsf{sig}$ with a number of access to the generic oracles $\mathsf{GO} = (\mathsf{Mult}(\cdot, \cdot), \mathsf{Inv}(\cdot)), \mathsf{DLog}_g(\cdot), \mathsf{Sign}_i(\cdot)$ for $1 \leq i \leq N$, and $\mathsf{H}(\cdot)$. The signing oracle without a secret key is described in Fig. 2. Now we consider the following cases:
   (a) Whenever $\mathcal{A}_\mathsf{sig}$ submits a query w to the random oracle H:
      - If there is a pair $(w, R) \in \mathsf{H}_\mathsf{resp}$ for some string R, then return R.
      - Otherwise, select $R \leftarrow^\$ \mathbb{Z}_{2^k}$, and add (w, R) to the set H_resp.

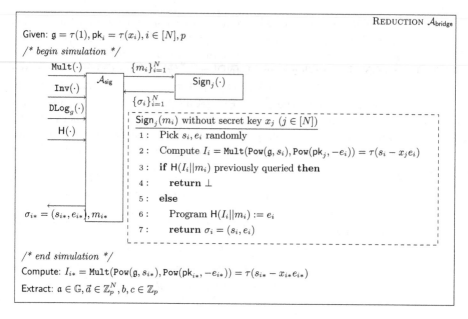

Fig. 2. A reduction to the BridgeChal$_{\mathcal{A}_{\text{bridge}}}^{\tau,N}(k)$ attacker $\mathcal{A}_{\text{bridge}}$ from the short Schnorr signature attacker $\mathcal{A}_{\text{sig}}$.

- If w has the form $w = (\mathfrak{a}\|m_i)$, where the value $\mathfrak{a}$ has not been observed previously (i.e., is not in the list $\mathcal{L}$), then we query $b = \text{DLog}(\mathfrak{a})$, and add $(\mathfrak{a}, \vec{0}, b)$ to $\mathcal{L}$.

(b) Whenever $\mathcal{A}_{\text{sig}}$ submits a query $\mathfrak{a}$ to the generic group oracle $\text{Inv}(\mathfrak{a})$:
  - If $\mathfrak{a}$ is not in $\mathcal{L}$ then we immediately query $b = \text{DLog}(\mathfrak{a})$ and add $(\mathfrak{a}, \vec{0}, b)$ to $\mathcal{L}$.
  - Otherwise, $(\mathfrak{a}, \vec{a}, b) \in \mathcal{L}$. Then we query $\text{Inv}(\mathfrak{a}) = \tau(-\vec{a}\cdot\vec{x}-b)$, output the result and add the result $(\tau(-\vec{a}\cdot\vec{x}-b), -\vec{a}, -b) \in \mathcal{L}$.

(c) Whenever $\mathcal{A}_{\text{sig}}$ submits a query $\mathfrak{a}, \mathfrak{b}$ to the generic group oracle $\text{Mult}(\mathfrak{a}, \mathfrak{b})$:
  - If the element $\mathfrak{a}$ (resp. $\mathfrak{b}$) is not in $\mathcal{L}$, then query $b_0 = \text{DLog}(\mathfrak{a})$ (resp. $b_1 = \text{DLog}(\mathfrak{b})$), and add the element $(\mathfrak{a}, \vec{0}, b_0)$ (resp. $(\mathfrak{b}, \vec{0}, b_1)$) to $\mathcal{L}$.
  - Otherwise, both elements $(\mathfrak{a}, \vec{a}_0, b_0), (\mathfrak{b}, \vec{a}_1, b_1) \in \mathcal{L}$. Then we return $\text{Mult}(\mathfrak{a}, \mathfrak{b}) = \tau((\vec{a}_0 + \vec{a}_1)\cdot\vec{x} + b_0 + b_1)$, and add $(\tau((\vec{a}_0 + \vec{a}_1)\cdot\vec{x} + b_0 + b_1), \vec{a}_0 + \vec{a}_1, b_0 + b_1) \in \mathcal{L}$.

(d) Whenever $\mathcal{A}_{\text{sig}}$ submits a query m_i to the signing oracle $\text{Sign}(x_j, \cdot)$:
  - We use the procedure Sign_j described in Fig. 2 to forge a signature without knowledge of the secret key x_i. Intuitively, the forgery procedure relies on our ability to program the random oracle.

- We remark that a side effect of querying the Sign_j oracle is the addition of the tuples $(\tau(s_i), \vec{0}, s_i)$, $(\tau(x_j e_i), e_i \hat{u}_i, 0)$ and $(\tau(s_i - x_j e_i), -e_i \hat{u}_i, s_i)$ to $\mathcal{L}$, since these values are computed using the generic group oracles $\mathtt{Inv}$ and $\mathtt{Mult}$.

(e) If at any point we find some string $\mathfrak{y}$ such that $(\mathfrak{y}, \vec{a}, b) \in \mathcal{L}$ and $(\mathfrak{y}, \vec{c}, d) \in \mathcal{L}$ for $(\vec{a}, b) \neq (\vec{c}, d)$, then we can immediately have a BRIDGE^N instance $(\tau((\vec{a} - \vec{c}) \cdot \vec{x}), \vec{a} - \vec{c}, 0) \in \mathcal{L}$ and $(\tau(d - b), \vec{0}, d - b) \in \mathcal{L}$ since $\tau((\vec{a} - \vec{c}) \cdot \vec{x}) = \tau(d - b)$.[3] Thus, without loss of generality, we can assume that each string $\mathfrak{y}$ occurs at most once in the list $\mathcal{L}$.

3. After $\mathcal{A}_{\mathsf{sig}}$ outputs $\sigma_{i*} = (s_{i*}, e_{i*})$ and m_{i*}, identify the index $i* \in [N]$ such that $\mathsf{Vfy}(\mathsf{pk}_{i*}, m_{i*}, \sigma_{i*}) = 1$.

4. Compute $\tau(-e_{i*} x_{i*}) = \mathtt{Inv}(\mathtt{Pow}(\tau(x_{i*}), e_{i*}))$ and $\mathfrak{s}_{i*} = \mathtt{Pow}(\mathfrak{g}, s_{i*})$. This will ensure that the elements $(\tau(-e_{i*} x_{i*}), -e_{i*} \hat{u}_{i*}, 0)$ and $(\tau(e_{i*} x_{i*}), e_{i*} \hat{u}_{i*}, 0)$, and $(\mathfrak{s}_{i*}, \vec{0}, s_{i*})$ are all added to $\mathcal{L}$.

5. Compute $I_{i*} = \mathtt{Mult}(\mathfrak{s}_{i*}, \tau(-e_{i*} x_{i*})) = \tau(s_{i*} - x_{i*} e_{i*})$ which ensures that $(I_{i*}, -e_{i*} \hat{u}_{i*}, s_{i*}) \in \mathcal{L}$. Finally, we can check to see if we previously had any tuple of the form $(I_{i*}, \vec{a}, b) \in \mathcal{L}$.

Analysis. We first remark that if the signature is valid then we must have $e_{i*} = \mathsf{H}(I_{i*} \| m_{i*})$ and $\mathsf{DLog}(I_{i*}) = s_{i*} - x_{i*} e_{i*} = \vec{a} \cdot \vec{x} + b$.

We now define failure events $\mathsf{FailtoFind}(I_{i*})$ and $\mathsf{BadQuery}$. $\mathsf{FailtoFind}(I_{i*})$ denotes the event that we find that the signature is valid, but I_{i*} was not previously recorded in our list $\mathcal{L}$ before we computed $\mathtt{Mult}(\mathfrak{s}_{i*}, \tau(-e_{i*} x_{i*}))$ in the last step. Similarly, let $\mathsf{BadQuery}$ denote the event that the signature is valid but for the only prior tuple $(I_{i*}, \vec{a}, b) \in \mathcal{L}$ recorded in $\mathcal{L}$ we have that $\vec{a} = -e_{i*} \hat{u}_{i*}$. If the signature is valid and neither of the events $\mathsf{FailtoFind}(I_{i*})$ and $\mathsf{BadQuery}$ occur, then the bridge event BRIDGE^N must have occurred and we immediately win the game since $(I_{i*}, \vec{a}, b) \in \mathcal{L}$, $(I_{i*}, -e_{i*} \hat{u}_{i*}, s_{i*}) \in \mathcal{L}$ and $\vec{a} \neq -e_{i*} \hat{u}_{i*}$.

We additionally consider then the event $\mathsf{FailtoSign}$ where our reduction outputs $\bot$ in Step 2.(d) due signing oracle failure i.e., because $\mathsf{H}(I_i \| m_i)$ has been queried previously. Intuitively, the attacker will output a valid signature forgery with probability at least $\Pr[\mathsf{SigForge}_{\mathcal{A}_{\mathsf{sig}}, \Pi_{\mathsf{short}}}^{\tau, N}(k) = 1] - \Pr[\mathsf{FailtoSign}]$ after we replace the signing oracle with the procedure Sign_j described in Fig. 2.

Claim 1, Claim 2, and Claim 3 upper bound the probability of our events $\mathsf{FailtoSign}$, $\mathsf{FailtoFind}$ and $\mathsf{BadQuery}$ respectively. We defer the proofs to the full version [BL19].

Claim 1. $\Pr[\mathsf{FailtoSign}] \leq \frac{q_s(q_H + q_s)}{p}$.

Claim 2. $\Pr[\mathsf{FailtoFind}(I_{i*})] \leq \frac{q_H + q_s}{p - |\mathcal{L}|} + \frac{1}{2^k}$.

Claim 3. $\Pr[\mathsf{BadQuery}] \leq \frac{q_H}{2^k}$.

---

[3] Note that $(\vec{a}, b) \neq (\vec{c}, d)$ implies $\vec{a} \neq \vec{c}$ since if $\vec{a} = \vec{c}$ then $\vec{a} \cdot \vec{x} + b = \vec{a} \cdot \vec{x} + d$ implies $b = d$ as $b, d \in \mathbb{Z}_p$.

Since we have $|\mathcal{L}| \leq N + 3q_{\mathsf{G}} + 1$, we can apply Theorem 5 to conclude that

$$\Pr[\mathsf{SigForge}^{\tau, N}_{\mathcal{A}_{\mathsf{sig}}, \Pi_{\mathsf{short}}}(k) = 1]$$

$$\leq \Pr[\mathsf{BridgeChal}^{\tau, N}_{\mathcal{A}_{\mathsf{bridge}}}(k) = 1] + \Pr[\mathsf{FailtoSign}] + \Pr[\mathsf{FailtoFind}(I_{i*})] + \Pr[\mathsf{BadQuery}]$$

$$\leq \frac{q_{\mathsf{G}} N + 3q_{\mathsf{G}}(q_{\mathsf{G}} + 1)/2}{p - (N + 3q_{\mathsf{G}} + 1)^2 - N} + \frac{q_{\mathsf{S}}(q_{\mathsf{H}} + q_{\mathsf{S}})}{p} + \frac{q_{\mathsf{H}} + q_{\mathsf{S}}}{p - (N + 3q_{\mathsf{G}} + 1)} + \frac{q_{\mathsf{H}} + 1}{2^k}$$

$$= \mathcal{O}\left(\frac{q + N}{2^k}\right) .$$

$\square$

5 Multi-user Security of Short Schnorr Signatures with Key-Prefixing Against Preprocessing Attacks

In this section, we analyze the security of short Schnorr signatures against a preprocessing attacker who first outputs an S-bit hint after making (a very large number of) preprocessing queries to the generic group oracles Mult and Inv, as well as the random oracle H. After the public/secret keys are chosen, the signature forgery attacker will try use the hint to help win the signature forgery game. The hint must be fixed *before* the public/secret keys for our signature scheme are selected, otherwise the preprocessing attacker can generate forged signatures and embed them in the hint.

We first observe that Schnorr signatures are trivially broken against a preprocesssing attack, e.g., if the preprocessing attacker finds some message m and an integer r such that $e = \mathsf{H}(\tau(r)\|m) = 0$, then the attacker can simply include the tuple (m, r) as part of the S-bit hint. Observe that the hint is completely independent of the public key pk. In fact, for any public key pk, we have that $\sigma' = (s = r, e = 0)$ is a valid signature for the message m! To see this, note that $R = \tau(s - \mathsf{sk} \cdot 0) = \tau(r) = 0$ and that, by assumption, $\mathsf{H}(R\|m) = \mathsf{H}(\tau(r)\|m) = 0 = e$.

The above attack can easily be addressed with key-prefixing, i.e., to sign a message m, we pick an integer r, compute $e = \mathsf{H}(\mathsf{pk}\|\tau(r)\|m)$, and output the signature $\sigma = (s = r + \mathsf{sk} \cdot e, e)$. Intuitively, since the preprocessing attacker does not know the public key pk in advance, s/he is unlikely to have stored a tuple of the form $(\mathsf{pk}, m, r, \tau(r))$. The key question is whether or not *short Schnorr signatures with key-prefixing* are secure against *any* preprocessing attack. To prove that short Schnorr signatures with key-prefixing are secure against preprocessing attacks, we revisit the 1-out-of-N bridge-finding game in the preprocessing setting.

5.1 Security of BRIDGE^N-Finding Game with Preprocessing

We analyze the BRIDGE^N-finding game in the setting with preprocessing attacks. In particular, an attacker consists of a pair of algorithms $(\mathcal{A}_{\mathsf{pre}}, \mathcal{A}_{\mathsf{on}})$. The basic idea is that we split the attack into two phases, *preprocessing* and *online* phase, so that the attacker has (exponential) time to make preprocessing queries before playing the bridge game. Specifically,

– Algorithm $\mathcal{A}_{\mathsf{pre}}$ runs a preprocessing phase, where it takes as input $\mathfrak{g} = \tau(1)$ and outputs a hint str_τ, which is a binary string after making queries to the generic group oracles $\mathtt{GO} = (\mathtt{Mult}(\cdot,\cdot), \mathtt{Inv}(\cdot))$. Without loss of generality, we can assume that $\mathcal{A}_{\mathsf{pre}}$ is deterministic, and we simply use str_τ to refer to the hint when the random mapping τ is fixed.

– The online attacker $\mathcal{A}_{\mathsf{on}}$ attempts to win the BRIDGE^N-finding game. The online attacker $\mathcal{A}_{\mathsf{on}}$ is given the hint str_τ (which was produced in the preprocessing phase), as well as $(\tau(x_1), \ldots, \tau(x_N))$. However, the challenger picks $(x_1, \ldots, x_N) \in \mathbb{Z}_p^N$ *after* the hint str_τ is fixed. For convenience, we will write $\mathcal{A}_{\mathsf{on},\mathsf{str}_\tau}$ to denote the online attacker with the hint str_τ hardcoded.

We are interested in the setting where the preprocessing algorithm $\mathcal{A}_{\mathsf{pre}}$ can make $q_{\mathsf{G}}^{\mathsf{pre}} \geq 2^{2k}$ queries to the generic group oracles. In other words, the preprocessing algorithm $\mathcal{A}_{\mathsf{pre}}$ can examine the entire input/output table of the mapping τ. However, the length of the hint str_τ given to the online attacker is bounded by S, and the online attacker can make at most $q_{\mathsf{G}}^{\mathsf{on}} < 2^k$ queries to the generic group oracles. Theorem 7 says that the probability of a successful preprocessing attack is at most $\widetilde{\mathcal{O}}(SN(q_{\mathsf{G}}^{\mathsf{on}})^2/p)$.

Theorem 7. *Let $p > 2^{2k}$ be a prime number and $N \in \mathbb{N}$ be a parameter. Let $(\mathcal{A}_{\mathsf{pre}}, \mathcal{A}_{\mathsf{on}})$ be a pair of generic algorithms with an encoding map $\tau : \mathbb{Z}_p \to \mathbb{G}$ such that $\mathcal{A}_{\mathsf{pre}}$ outputs an S-bit hint and $\mathcal{A}_{\mathsf{on}}$ makes at most $q_{\mathsf{G}}^{\mathsf{on}} := q_{\mathsf{G}}^{\mathsf{on}}(k)$ queries to the generic group oracles. Then*

$$\Pr\left[\mathsf{BridgeChal}_{\mathcal{A}_{\mathsf{on},\mathsf{str}_\tau}}^{\tau,N}(k) = 1\right] \leq \widetilde{\mathcal{O}}\left(\frac{SN(q_{\mathsf{G}}^{\mathsf{on}} + N)(q_{\mathsf{G}}^{\mathsf{on}} + 2N)}{p}\right),$$

where the randomness is taken over the selection of τ, the random coins of $\mathcal{A}_{\mathsf{on}}$, and the random coins used by the challenger in the bridge game (the hint $\mathsf{str}_\tau = \mathcal{A}_{\mathsf{pre}}^{\mathtt{GO}}(\mathfrak{g})$ is selected independently of the random coins used by the challenger). In particular, if $q_{\mathsf{G}}^{\mathsf{on}} \geq 10N(1 + 2\log p)$ and $S \geq 10\log(8p)$, then

$$\Pr\left[\mathsf{BridgeChal}_{\mathcal{A}_{\mathsf{on},\mathsf{str}_\tau}}^{\tau,N}(k) = 1\right] \leq \frac{12SN(q_{\mathsf{G}}^{\mathsf{on}})^2 \log p}{p}.$$

Remark 1. The upper bound is essentially tight as a preprocessing attacker can solve a random 1-out-of-N discrete-log challenge with probability $\widetilde{\Omega}((q_{\mathsf{G}}^{\mathsf{on}})^2 S/p)$ which would trivially allow the attacker to win the bridge-finding game. In particular, even when $N = 1$, there is a preprocessing with success probability $\Omega((q_{\mathsf{G}}^{\mathsf{on}})^2 S/p)$, e.g., see [CK18, Section 7.1]. Thus, our upper bound is tight up to a factor of N.   ◁

The proof of Theorem 7 closely follows [CK18, Theorem 2] with a few minor modifications, and the full proof can be found in the full version [BL19]. One small difference is that we need to extend the proofs of [CK18] to handle queries to the inverse oracle $\mathtt{Inv}(\cdot)$, and the restricted discrete log oracle $\mathtt{DLog}$. The proof of Theorem 7 relies on Lemma 2, which is similar to [CK18, Lemma 4]. Intuitively, if the preprocessing attack is too successful, then one can derive a contradiction by compressing the random mapping τ.

Lemma 2. *Let $\mathbb{G}$ be the set of binary strings of length ℓ such that $2^\ell \geq p$ for a prime p. Let $\mathcal{T} = \{\tau_1, \tau_2, \ldots\}$ be a subset of the labeling functions from $\mathbb{Z}_p$ to $\mathbb{G}$. Let $(\mathcal{A}_{\mathsf{pre}}, \mathcal{A}_{\mathsf{on}})$ be a pair of generic algorithms for $\mathbb{Z}_p$ on $\mathbb{G}$ such that for every $\tau \in \mathcal{T}$ and every $\vec{x} = (x_1, \ldots, x_N) \in \mathbb{Z}_p^N$, $\mathcal{A}_{\mathsf{pre}}$ outputs an S-bit advice string, $\mathcal{A}_{\mathsf{on}}$ makes at most q_{on} oracle queries, and $(\mathcal{A}_{\mathsf{pre}}, \mathcal{A}_{\mathsf{on}})$ satisfy $\Pr_{\mathcal{A}_{\mathsf{on}}}\left[\mathsf{BridgeChal}^{\tau, N}_{\mathcal{A}_{\mathsf{on}, \mathsf{str}_\tau}}(k, \vec{x}) = 1\right] \geq \varepsilon$, where $\mathsf{str}_\tau = \mathcal{A}^{\mathsf{G0}}_{\mathsf{pre}}(\tau(1))$. Then, there exists a randomized encoding scheme that compresses elements of $\mathcal{T}$ to bitstrings of length at most*

$$\log \frac{|\mathbb{G}|!}{(|\mathbb{G}| - p)!} + S + 1 - \frac{\varepsilon p}{6 q_{\mathsf{on}}(q_{\mathsf{on}} + N)(N \log p + 1)},$$

and succeeds with probability at least $1/2$.

The full proof of Lemma 2 can be found in the full version [BL19]. Here, we only give the brief idea as follows. To compress τ, our encoding algorithm first runs $\mathcal{A}_{\mathsf{pre}}$ to extract an S-bit hint str_τ. We then execute $\mathcal{A}_{\mathsf{on}}(\mathsf{str}_\tau, \tau(x_1), \ldots, \tau(x_N))$ multiple times with different challenges $x_1, \ldots, x_N$. During each execution we record the responses to the new generic group oracle queries, so that the decoder can also execute $\mathcal{A}_{\mathsf{on}}(\mathsf{str}_\tau, \tau(x_1), \ldots, \tau(x_N))$. Intuitively, whenever the BRIDGE^N event occurs, the decoder can save a few bits by simply recording the index of prior query involved in the collision. This requires just $\log q_{\mathsf{on}}$ bits to encode instead of $\log p$ bits.

5.2 Multi-user Security of Key-Prefixed Short Schnorr Signatures with Preprocessing

Theorem 7 upper bounds the probability that a preprocessing attacker wins the multi-user bridge-finding game. In this setting, we observe that the hint $\mathsf{str} := \mathsf{str}_{\tau, \mathsf{H}}$ that the preprocessing attacker outputs may depend both on the random oracle H as well as the encoding map τ. We show how to adapt our prior reduction to establish the multi-user security of key-prefixed short Schnorr signatures against preprocessing attackers. Recall that in our reduction, we simulated a signature forgery attacker for (non key-prefixed) short Schnorr signatures responding to queries to the signing oracle by programming the random oracle. In the preprocessing setting without key-prefixing, the reduction breaks down immediately. For example, the probability of a lucky random oracle query $\mathsf{H}(\tau(r)\|m) = 0$ is no longer $\approx q_{\mathsf{H}}^{\mathsf{on}}/2^k$, since the preprocessing attacker can simply hardcode the pair (r, m) as part of the hint $\mathsf{str} := \mathsf{str}_{\tau, \mathsf{H}}$. Similarly, the hint $\mathsf{str} := \mathsf{str}_{\tau, \mathsf{H}}$ may be correlated with particular input/output pairs from the random oracle, making it infeasible to program those points.

We address this challenge by considering a model where a preprocessing attacker is *time-bounded*, i.e., the preprocessing attacker can look at the entire generic group oracles but only allowed to query the random oracle at *up to* $q_{\mathsf{H}}^{\mathsf{pre}} = 2^{3k}$ points during the preprocessing phase. We leave it as an interesting theoretical challenge whether or not the bounds can be extended to unbounded preprocessing attacks. However, we would argue that in practice, 2^{3k} greatly overestimates the running time of any preprocessing attacker, e.g., if $k = 112$, then $2^{3k} = 2^{336}$. Intuitively, the signing oracle for key-prefixed short Schnorr signatures involves two random points: a public key $\mathsf{pk} \in \mathbb{G}$ and a random value $r \leftarrow_\$ \mathbb{Z}_p$. The probability that a preprocessing attacker submitted a query of the form $\mathsf{H}(\mathsf{pk}, \tau(r), \cdot)$ is at most $q_\mathsf{H}^{\mathsf{pre}} p^{-2} \leq 2^{-k}$, since the $q_\mathsf{H}^{\mathsf{pre}}$ random oracle queries are fixed before pk and r are sampled.

In our analysis, we consider the bad event that the signing oracle queries the random oracle at a point $\mathsf{H}(\mathsf{pk}_i \| \tau(r_j) \| m)$, which was previously queried by the preprocessing attacker. Note that if this bad event never occurs, then we can view $\mathsf{H}(\mathsf{pk}_i \| \tau(r_j) \| m)$ as a uniformly random string that is uncorrelated with the attacker's state. The probability of this bad event occurring on any single query to the signing oracle is at most $N q_\mathsf{H}^{\mathsf{pre}} / p^2$. In particular, fixing an arbitrary set of $q_\mathsf{H}^{\mathsf{pre}}$ random oracle queries and then sampling $\mathsf{pk}_1, \ldots, \mathsf{pk}_N \in \mathbb{G}$ and $r \in \mathbb{Z}_p$, we can apply union bounds to argue that the probability that the preprocessing attacker previously submitted some query of the form $\mathsf{H}(\mathsf{pk}_i, \tau(r), \cdot)$ for any i is at most $N q_\mathsf{H}^{\mathsf{pre}} / p^2$. Union bounding over the $q_\mathsf{S}^{\mathsf{on}}$ online queries to the signing oracle, the probability of the bad event ever occurring on any query to the signing oracle is at most $N q_\mathsf{H}^{\mathsf{pre}} q_\mathsf{S}^{\mathsf{on}} / p^2$. Assuming that the bad event never occurs, we can safely program the random oracle to simulate queries to the signing oracle when we simulate our signature forgery attacker.

The other challenge that arises in the preprocessing setting is upper bounding the probability of the bad event that the attacker forges a signature without causing the bridge event to occur. Previously, our argument relied on the observation that for "fresh" group elements $r \in \mathbb{Z}_p$, we can effectively view $\tau(r)$ as random bit string that is yet to be fixed. This intuition does not carry over into the preprocessing setting, as the hint str might be correlated with $\tau(r)$. We address these challenges by applying a random oracle compression argument. In particular, if the attacker can generate forged signatures without causing the bridge event to occur, we can use this attacker to predict random oracle outputs, allowing us to derive a contraction by compressing the random oracle.

Theorem 8. *Let $\Pi = (\mathsf{Kg}, \mathsf{Sign}, \mathsf{Vfy})$ be a key-prefixed Schnorr signature scheme and $p > 2^{2k}$ be a prime number. Let $N \in \mathbb{N}$ be a parameter and $(\mathcal{A}_{\mathsf{sig}}^{\mathsf{pre}}, \mathcal{A}_{\mathsf{sig}}^{\mathsf{on}})$ be a pair of generic algorithms with an encoding map $\tau : \mathbb{Z}_p \to \mathbb{G}$ such that $\mathcal{A}_{\mathsf{sig}}^{\mathsf{pre}}$ makes at most $q_\mathsf{H}^{\mathsf{pre}}$ queries to the random oracle $\mathsf{H} : \{0,1\}^* \to \{0,1\}^{k_1}$ and outputs an S-bit hint $\mathsf{str}_{\tau, \mathsf{H}}$, and $\mathcal{A}_{\mathsf{sig}}^{\mathsf{on}}$ makes at most $q_\mathbb{G}^{\mathsf{on}} := q_\mathbb{G}^{\mathsf{on}}(k)$ queries to the generic group oracles and at most $q_\mathsf{H}^{\mathsf{on}}$ queries to the random oracle. Then*
$$\Pr\left[\mathsf{SigForge}_{\mathcal{A}_{\mathsf{sig}, \mathsf{str}_{\tau, \mathsf{H}}}^{\mathsf{on}}, \Pi}^{\tau, N}(k) = 1\right] \leq \varepsilon, \ \text{with}$$

$$\varepsilon = \widetilde{\mathcal{O}}\left(\frac{SN(q_\mathbb{G}^{\mathsf{on}} + N)(q_\mathbb{G}^{\mathsf{on}} + 2N)}{p}\right) + \frac{N q_\mathsf{H}^{\mathsf{pre}} q_\mathsf{S}^{\mathsf{on}}}{p^2} + \frac{q_\mathsf{S}^{\mathsf{on}}(q_\mathsf{S}^{\mathsf{on}} + q_\mathsf{H}^{\mathsf{on}})}{p} + \frac{4(q_\mathsf{H}^{\mathsf{on}} + 1)}{2^{k_1}} + \frac{N^2(S + k_1)}{p},$$

where $q_\mathsf{S}^{\mathsf{on}}$ denotes the number of queries to the signing oracle and the randomness is taken over the selection of τ and the random coins of $\mathcal{A}_{\mathsf{sig}}^{\mathsf{on}}$ (the hint $\mathsf{str}_{\tau, \mathsf{H}} = \mathcal{A}_{\mathsf{sig}}^{\mathsf{pre}, \mathsf{GO}}(\mathfrak{g})$ is selected independently of the random coins used by the challenger).

In particular, if $q_G^{on} \geq 10N(1 + 2\log p)$ and $S \geq 10\log(8p)$, then

$$\varepsilon = \frac{12SN(q_G^{on})^2\log p}{p} + \frac{Nq_H^{pre}q_S^{on}}{p^2} + \frac{q_S^{on}(q_S^{on} + q_H^{on})}{p} + \frac{4(q_H^{on} + 1)}{2^{k_1}} + \frac{N^2(S + k_1)}{p}.$$

Remark 2. The upper bound in Theorem 8 is essentially tight (up to a factor of N), because of the following observations:

- Making the reasonable assumption that $Nq_H^{pre}q_S^{on} < 2^{3k}$ and $q_G^{on} > \sqrt{N}$, the dominating terms in ε are $\widetilde{\mathcal{O}}(SN(q_G^{on})^2/p)$ and/or $\mathcal{O}\left(q_H^{on}/2^{k_1}\right)$.
- A preprocessing attacker can simply solve one of the discrete-log challenges with probability at least $\Omega(S(q_G^{on})^2/p)$ which would recover a secret key and make it trivial to forge a signature.
- Any attacker who makes $q_H^{on} \geq q_S^{on}$ queries to the random oracle can fix an arbitrary message m and pick random numbers $r_1, \ldots, r_{q_H^{on}}$ hoping that $\mathsf{H}(\mathsf{pk}_1 \| \tau(r_j) \| m) = 0$ for some $j \leq q_H^{on}$. In this case, $(r_j, 0)$ is a valid forged signature for m under public key pk_1. Thus, the attacker can succeed with probability $\approx q_H^{on}/2^{k_1}$.   ◁

The full proof of Theorem 8 can be found in the full version [BL19]. The key idea is that we can repeat the essentially same reduction from Sect. 4, i.e., we can build a bridge-finding game attacker ($\mathcal{A}_{bridge}^{pre}, \mathcal{A}_{bridge}^{on}$) *with preprocessing* from the signature forgery attacker ($\mathcal{A}_{sig}^{pre}, \mathcal{A}_{sig}^{on}$) *with preprocessing*, except that when we program a random oracle, we define an additional bad event that we program a random oracle at a point the attacker has already queried the point during the preprocessing phase. We observe that such probability is negligibly small. As long as the failure event does not occur we can program the random oracle and the attacker will not notice the difference.

Instantiating Key-Prefixed Short Schnorr Signatures. We would like to have the success probability in Theorem 8 bounded by $\mathcal{O}(q/2^k)$ for any $q \leq 2^k$, where $q = q_G^{on} + q_H^{on} + q_S^{on}$ is the total number of *online* queries made by a preprocessing attacker. To achieve k bits of multi-user security for key-prefixed short Schnorr signatures with preprocessing, we can fix p such that $p \approx 2^{2k}SN\log p$, and set the length of our hash output to be $k_1 = k$. With these parameters, Theorem 8 tells us that a preprocessing attacker wins the signature forgery game with probability at most $\varepsilon = \mathcal{O}\left((q_H^{on} + q_G^{on})/2^k\right)$. The length of the signatures we obtain will be $k + \log p = 3k + \log N + \log S + \log\log p$.

As a concrete example, if $N \leq 2^{k/4}$ and $S \leq 2^{k/2}$, then we obtain signatures of length $\approx 3.75k + \log 2.75k$. If we want $k \geq 128$ bits of security, then the assumption that $N < 2^{k/4}$ seems quite reasonable, since $2^{32}(\approx 4.3$ billion$)$ is over half of the current global population, and 2^{64} bits exceeds the storage capacity of Facebook's data warehouse[4]. As a second example, if we take $S \leq 2^{80}$ as an upper bound on the storage capacity of any nation state and $N \approx 2^{40}$, then we obtain signatures of length $\approx 3k + 120 + \log(2k + 120)$.

---

[4] See the link: https://engineering.fb.com/2014/04/10/core-data/scaling-the-facebo ok-data-warehouse-to (Retrieved 2/20/2021).

6   Multi-user Security of Other Fiat-Shamir Signatures

In this section, we show that our techniques from Sect. 4 and Sect. 5 apply to other Fiat-Shamir-based signature schemes. We apply our reductions to analyze the multi-user security of the full-domain hash variant of Chaum-Pedersen signatures [CP93], and (short) Katz-Wang signatures [KW03], with and without preprocessing. In practice, the full-domain hash variant of Chaum-Pedersen would be used to ensure that our signature scheme supports the message space $m \in \{0,1\}^*$ instead of requiring that m is a group element. We begin by introducing regular Chaum-Pedersen signatures in the next paragraph before describing the full-domain hash variant (Chaum-Pedersen-FDH) that we analyze.

Security Analysis of Chaum-Pedersen-FDH Signatures. The Chaum-Pedersen signature scheme [CP93] is obtained by applying the Fiat-Shamir transform [FS87] to the Chaum-Pedersen identification scheme and works as follows.

- Given a cyclic group $G = \langle g \rangle$ of prime order p, the key generation algorithm picks $\mathsf{sk} \leftarrow_\$ \mathbb{Z}_p$ and sets $\mathsf{pk} = g^{\mathsf{sk}}$.
- To sign a message $m \in G$ with the secret key sk, we sample $r \leftarrow_\$ \mathbb{Z}_p$ and compute $y = m^{\mathsf{sk}}$, $a = g^r$, $b = m^r$, and $e = \mathsf{H}(m\|y\|a\|b)$. Finally, we output a signature $\sigma = (y, a, b, s)$, where $s := r + \mathsf{sk} \cdot e \mod p$.
- The verification algorithm takes as inputs a signature $\sigma' = (y', a', b', s')$ and computes $e' = \mathsf{H}(m\|y'\|a'\|b')$, $A = g^{s'}$, $B = a' g^{\mathsf{sk} \cdot e'}$, $C = m^{s'}$ and $D = b' y'^{e'}$. Finally, we verify that $(A = B)$ and $(C = D)$ before accepting the signature.

The *full-domain hash variant* of Chaum-Pedersen signature, say *Chaum-Pedersen-FDH signature*, is obtained by hashing a message m into a group element so that we can perform generic group operations when signing the message. That is, in the generic group model, we compute $h = \mathsf{H}'(\mathsf{pk}\|m) := \mathsf{Pow}(\mathfrak{g}, \mathsf{H}(\mathsf{pk}\|m))$ and compute $\mathfrak{y} = \mathsf{Pow}(h, \mathsf{sk})$ and $\mathfrak{b} = \mathsf{Pow}(h, r)$ (which corresponds to $y = h^{\mathsf{sk}}$ and $b = h^r$ when instantiated with a cyclic group $G = \langle g \rangle$) during the signing procedure. Note that key-prefixing is necessary as otherwise an attacker can always forge a signature for a message m, e.g., simply find $m \neq m'$ such that $\mathsf{H}(m) = \mathsf{H}(m')$. The full description for each of these algorithms can be found in the full version [BL19].

Our reduction in Sect. 4 naturally extends to Chaum-Pedersen-FDH signature scheme by using signing oracle in Fig. 3. The signing oracle is able go generate valid signatures *without* the secret key by programming the random oracle. This allows us to prove Theorem 9. We remark that a Chaum-Pedersen-FDH signature with k bits of security has length $8k$—each group element requires $2k$ bits to encode since $p \approx 2^{2k}$. Note that reducing the length of the hash output does not have any effect on Chaum-Pedersen-FDH signature length. Thus, we assume that H is a random oracle with $2k$-bit outputs. The proof of Theorem 9 can be found in the full version [BL19].

Theorem 9. *The Chaum-Pedersen-FDH signature scheme is* $(N, q_\mathsf{H}, q_\mathsf{G}, q_\mathsf{S},$ $\mathcal{O}\left(\frac{q+N}{2^k}\right))$*-MU-UF-CMA secure under the generic group model of prime order*

$p \approx 2^{2k}$ and the programmable random oracle model, where q denotes the total number of queries made by an adversary.

We can also show that the *key-prefixed* Chaum-Pedersen-FDH signature scheme is secure against proprocessing attacks. That is, we apply key-prefixing when computing e, i.e. $e \leftarrow \mathsf{H}(\mathsf{pk}\|h\|\mathfrak{y}\|\mathfrak{a}\|\mathfrak{b})$ during the signing procedure and $e' \leftarrow \mathsf{H}(\mathsf{pk}\|h\|\mathfrak{y}'\|\mathfrak{a}'\|\mathfrak{b}')$ during the verification (see the full version [BL19] for the figure). During the online phase we can request a signature σ for m and output $\sigma' = \sigma$ as our forgery for m'. We defer the full proof of Theorem 10 to the full version [BL19].

Theorem 10. *Let $\Pi = (\mathsf{Kg}, \mathsf{Sign}, \mathsf{Vfy})$ be a key-prefixed Chaum-Pedersen-FDH signature scheme and $p > 2^{2k}$ be a prime number. Let $N \in \mathbb{N}$ be a parameter and $(\mathcal{A}_{\mathsf{sig}}^{\mathsf{pre}}, \mathcal{A}_{\mathsf{sig}}^{\mathsf{on}})$ be a pair of generic algorithms with an encoding map $\tau : \mathbb{Z}_p \to \mathbb{G}$ such that $\mathcal{A}_{\mathsf{sig}}^{\mathsf{pre}}$ makes at most $q_{\mathsf{H}}^{\mathsf{pre}} < 2^{3k}$ queries to the random oracle $\mathsf{H} : \{0,1\}^* \to \{0,1\}^{2k}$ and outputs an S-bit hint $\mathsf{str}_{\tau,\mathsf{H}}$, and $\mathcal{A}_{\mathsf{sig}}^{\mathsf{on}}$ makes at most $q_{\mathsf{G}}^{\mathsf{on}} := q_{\mathsf{G}}^{\mathsf{on}}(k)$ queries to the generic group oracles and at most $q_{\mathsf{H}}^{\mathsf{on}}$ queries to the random oracle. Then $\Pr\left[\mathsf{SigForge}_{\mathcal{A}_{\mathsf{sig}}^{\mathsf{on}}, \mathsf{str}_{\tau,\mathsf{H}}, \Pi}^{\tau, N}(k) = 1\right] \leq \varepsilon$, with*

$$\varepsilon = \widetilde{\mathcal{O}}\left(\frac{SN(q_{\mathsf{G}}^{\mathsf{on}}+N)(q_{\mathsf{G}}^{\mathsf{on}}+2N)}{p}\right) + \frac{Nq_{\mathsf{H}}^{\mathsf{pre}}q_{\mathsf{S}}^{\mathsf{on}}}{p^2} + \frac{q_{\mathsf{S}}^{\mathsf{on}}(q_{\mathsf{G}}^{\mathsf{on}}+q_{\mathsf{H}}^{\mathsf{on}})}{p} + \frac{4(q_{\mathsf{H}}^{\mathsf{on}}+\widetilde{q}_{\mathsf{on}}^2+1)}{2^{2k}} + \frac{3N^2(S+2k)}{2p},$$

where $q_{\mathsf{S}}^{\mathsf{on}}$ denotes the number of queries to the signing oracle, $\widetilde{q}_{\mathsf{on}} = q_{\mathsf{H}}^{\mathsf{on}} + 2q_{\mathsf{S}}^{\mathsf{on}}$, and the randomness is taken over the selection of τ and the random coins of $\mathcal{A}_{\mathsf{sig}}^{\mathsf{on}}$ (the hint $\mathsf{str}_{\tau,\mathsf{H}} = \mathcal{A}_{\mathsf{sig}}^{\mathsf{pre},\mathsf{G0}}(\mathfrak{g})$ is selected independently of the random coins used by the challenger).

Applying Theorem 10, we can fix p such that $p \approx 2^{2k}SN \log p$ to achieve k bits of multi-user security. The final signature size would be $\approx 8k + 4\log S + 4\log N + 4\log(2k + \log SN)$.

Security Analysis of Katz-Wang Signatures. The Katz-Wang signature scheme [KW03] is a double generator version of Schnorr signature scheme. In the generic group model on a cyclic group G of prime order p, we have two generators $p_1, p_2 \in \mathbb{Z}_p$ so that we can associate with g^{p_1} and g^{p_2} to the generators of the group G. Here, the message space for m is arbitrary, i.e., $m \in \{0,1\}^*$.

Given our encoding $\tau : \mathbb{Z}_p \to \mathbb{G}$ and $\mathfrak{g} = \tau(1)$, our key generation algorithm picks $\mathsf{sk} \leftarrow_\$ \mathbb{Z}_p$ and sets $\mathsf{pk} = (p_1, p_2, \mathfrak{h}_1, \mathfrak{h}_2)$, where $\mathfrak{h}_i = \mathsf{Pow}(\tau(p_i), \mathsf{sk})$ for $i = 1, 2$. To sign a message $m \in \{0,1\}^*$ with the secret key sk, we sample $r \leftarrow_\$ \mathbb{Z}_p$, and compute $\mathfrak{a}_i = \mathsf{Pow}(\tau(p_i), r)$ for $i = 1, 2$, $e = \mathsf{H}(\mathsf{pk}\|\mathfrak{a}_1\|\mathfrak{a}_2\|m)$, and $s = r + \mathsf{sk} \cdot e \mod p$. Finally, we output $\sigma = (s, e)$. The verification algorithm takes as inputs a signature $\sigma' = (s', e')$, $\mathsf{pk} = (p_1, p_2, \mathfrak{h}_1, \mathfrak{h}_2)$ and the message m, and compute $\mathfrak{a}_i' = \mathsf{Mult}(\mathsf{Pow}(\tau(p_i), s'), \mathsf{Pow}(\mathsf{Inv}(\mathfrak{h}_i), e'))$ for $i = 1, 2$. Finally, we verify that $e' = \mathsf{H}(\mathsf{pk}\|\mathfrak{a}_1'\|\mathfrak{a}_2'\|m)$ before accepting the signature. The pseudocode for each of these algorithms can be found in the full version [BL19].

We remark that the length of a regular Katz-Wang signature is $4k$ bits when $p \approx 2^{2k}$. Similar to short Schnorr signatures, one can shorten the length of the

Sign$_j(m_i)$ without secret key x_j, $j \in [N]$ (Chaum-Pedersen-FDH)

---

1 : Pick s_i and $e_i \in \mathbb{Z}_p$ randomly
2 : Compute $\mathfrak{s}_i = \text{Pow}(\mathfrak{g}, s_i)$ and $h_{ij} = \text{Pow}(\mathfrak{g}, \text{H}(\text{pk}_j \| m_i))$
3 : Compute $\mathfrak{y}_i = \text{Pow}(\text{pk}_j, \text{H}(\text{pk}_j \| m_i))$
4 : Compute $\mathfrak{a}_i = \text{Mult}(\mathfrak{s}_i, \text{Pow}(\text{Inv}(\text{pk}_j), e_i))$
5 : Compute $\mathfrak{b}_i = \text{Mult}(\text{Pow}(h_{ij}, s_i), \text{Pow}(\text{Inv}(\mathfrak{y}_i), e_i))$
6 : if $\text{H}(h_{ij} \| \mathfrak{y}_i \| \mathfrak{a}_i \| \mathfrak{b}_i) \in$ prior query then
7 :   return $\perp$
8 : else Program $\text{H}(h_{ij} \| \mathfrak{y}_i \| \mathfrak{a}_i \| \mathfrak{b}_i) := e_i$
9 :   return $\sigma_i = (\mathfrak{y}_i, \mathfrak{a}_i, \mathfrak{b}_i, s_i)$

Sign$_j(m_i)$ without secret key x_j, $j \in [N]$ (Katz-Wang)

---

1 : Pick $s_i, e_i \in \mathbb{Z}_p$ randomly
2 : Compute $\mathfrak{a}_{1,i} = \text{Mult}(\text{Pow}(\tau(p_1), s_i), \text{Pow}(\text{Inv}(\text{Pow}(\tau(x_j), p_1)), e_i))$
3 : Compute $\mathfrak{a}_{2,i} = \text{Mult}(\text{Pow}(\tau(p_2), s_i), \text{Pow}(\text{Inv}(\text{Pow}(\tau(x_j), p_2)), e_i))$
4 : if $\text{H}(\text{pk}_j \| \mathfrak{a}_{1,i} \| \mathfrak{a}_{2,i} \| m_i) \in$ prior query then
5 :   return $\perp$
6 : else Program $\text{H}(\text{pk}_j \| \mathfrak{a}_{1,i} \| \mathfrak{a}_{2,i} \| m_i) := e_i$
7 :   return $\sigma_i = (s_i, e_i)$

Fig. 3. The signing oracle without secret key in the Chaum-Pedersen-FDH scheme (top) and the Katz-Wang scheme (bottom). Note that $\text{pk}_j = \tau(x_j)$ is public in both schemes while the signing oracle has no information about x_j. We further remark that in the key-prefixed Chaum-Pedersen-FDH scheme, the only difference is to do a key-prefixing $\text{pk}_j = \tau(x_j)$ to the input of the random oracle (line 6 and 8).

hash output to k bits to obtain $3k$ bit signature. Essentially the same reduction can be used to demonstrate the multi-user security of (short) Katz-Wang signatures, while we use the signing oracle in Fig. 3 without the secret key.

We observe that Katz-Wang signature is already key-prefixed. The security bounds in Theorem 11 and Theorem 12 are equivalent to our bounds for short Schnorr signatures with and without pre-processing. Thus, we obtain $3k$ (resp. $3k + \log N + \log S + \log(2k + \log NS)$)-bit signatures with k bits of security in the multi-user setting without preprocessing (resp. with preprocessing). As before in the preprocessing setting we select our prime number $p \approx 2^{2k} NS \log(2k + \log NS)$ and we fix the length of the hash output to be $k_1 = k$. We defer the full proof of Theorem 11 and Theorem 12 to the full version [BL19].

Theorem 11. *The (short) Katz-Wang signature scheme is $(N, q_H, q_G, q_S,$ $\mathcal{O}\left(\frac{q+N}{2^k}\right))$-MU-UF-CMA secure under the generic group model of prime order $p \approx 2^{2k}$ and the programmable random oracle model, where q denotes the total number of queries made by an adversary.*

Kiltz et al. [KMP16] showed that if the decisional Diffie-Hellman problem is (t, ϵ)-hard then an adversary who tries to forge one out of N (regular) Katz-

Wang signatures running at most time t' can succeed with the probability $\varepsilon' \leq t'(4\varepsilon/t + q_S/p + 1/2^k)$. While their result is similar to Theorem 11, our bounds apply to (short) Katz-Wang signatures, with and without preprocessing.

Theorem 12. *Let $\Pi = (\mathsf{Kg}, \mathsf{Sign}, \mathsf{Vfy})$ be a Katz-Wang signature scheme and $p > 2^{2k}$ be a prime number. Let $N \in \mathbb{N}$ be a parameter and $(\mathcal{A}_{\mathsf{sig}}^{\mathsf{pre}}, \mathcal{A}_{\mathsf{sig}}^{\mathsf{on}})$ be a pair of generic algorithms with an encoding map $\tau : \mathbb{Z}_p \to \mathbb{G}$ such that $\mathcal{A}_{\mathsf{sig}}^{\mathsf{pre}}$ makes at most $q_{\mathsf{H}}^{\mathsf{pre}} < 2^{3k}$ queries to the random oracle at most $q_{\mathsf{H}}^{\mathsf{pre}} < 2^{3k}$ queries to the random oracle $\mathsf{H} : \{0,1\}^* \to \{0,1\}^{k_1}$ and outputs an S-bit hint $\mathsf{str}_{\tau,\mathsf{H}}$, and $\mathcal{A}_{\mathsf{sig}}^{\mathsf{on}}$ makes at most $q_{\mathsf{G}}^{\mathsf{on}} := q_{\mathsf{G}}^{\mathsf{on}}(k)$ queries to the generic group oracles and at most $q_{\mathsf{H}}^{\mathsf{on}}$ queries to the random oracle. Then $\Pr\left[\mathsf{SigForge}_{\mathcal{A}_{\mathsf{sig},\mathsf{str}_{\tau,\mathsf{H}}}^{\mathsf{on}},\Pi}^{\tau,N}(k) = 1\right] \leq \varepsilon$, with*

$$\varepsilon = \tilde{\mathcal{O}}\left(\frac{SN(q_{\mathsf{G}}^{\mathsf{on}}+N)(q_{\mathsf{G}}^{\mathsf{on}}+2N)}{p}\right) + \frac{Nq_{\mathsf{H}}^{\mathsf{pre}}q_{\mathsf{S}}^{\mathsf{on}}}{p^2} + \frac{q_{\mathsf{S}}^{\mathsf{on}}(q_{\mathsf{S}}^{\mathsf{on}}+q_{\mathsf{H}}^{\mathsf{on}})}{p} + \frac{4(q_{\mathsf{H}}^{\mathsf{on}}+1)}{2^{k_1}} + \frac{N^2(S+k_1)}{p},$$

where $q_{\mathsf{S}}^{\mathsf{on}}$ denotes the number of queries to the signing oracle and the randomness is taken over the selection of τ and the random coins of $\mathcal{A}_{\mathsf{sig}}^{\mathsf{on}}$ (the hint $\mathsf{str}_{\tau,\mathsf{H}} = \mathcal{A}_{\mathsf{sig}}^{\mathsf{pre},\mathsf{GO}}(\mathfrak{g})$ is selected independently of the random coins used by the challenger).

Acknowledgements. Jeremiah Blocki was supported in part by the National Science Foundation under NSF CAREER Award CNS-2047272 and NSF Awards CNS-1704587 and CNS-1755708 and CCF-1910659. Seunghoon Lee was supported in part by NSF Award CNS-1755708 and by the Center for Science of Information (NSF CCF-0939370). The opinions in this paper are those of the authors and do not necessarily reflect the position of the National Science Foundation.

References

[AB20] Kilinc Alper, H., Burdges, J.: Two-round trip Schnorr multi-signatures via delinearized witnesses. Cryptology ePrint Archive, Report 2020/1245 (2020). https://eprint.iacr.org/2020/1245

[BCJ08] Bagherzandi, A., Cheon, J.H., Jarecki, S.: Multisignatures secure under the discrete logarithm assumption and a generalized forking lemma. In: Ning, P., Syverson, P.F., Jha, S. (eds.) ACM CCS 2008, pp. 449–458. ACM Press, October 2008

[BD20] Bellare, M., Dai, W.: The multi-base discrete logarithm problem: tight reductions and non-rewinding proofs for Schnorr identification and signatures. In: Bhargavan, K., Oswald, E., Prabhakaran, M. (eds.) INDOCRYPT 2020. LNCS, vol. 12578, pp. 529–552. Springer, Cham (2020). https://doi.org/10.1007/978-3-030-65277-7_24

[Ber15] Bernstein, D.J.: Multi-user Schnorr security, revisited. Cryptology ePrint Archive, Report 2015/996 (2015). http://eprint.iacr.org/2015/996

[BL12] Bernstein, D.J., Lange, T.: Two grumpy giants and a baby. Cryptology ePrint Archive, Report 2012/294 (2012). http://eprint.iacr.org/2012/294

[BL19] bibitem[BL19]ch21cryptoeprint:2019:1105 Blocki, J., Lee, S.: On the multi-user security of short Schnorr signatures with preprocessing. Cryptology ePrint Archive, Report 2019/1105 (2019). https://ia.cr/2019/1105

[BLS04] Boneh, D., Lynn, B., Shacham, H.: Short signatures from the Weil pairing. J. Cryptol. **17**(4), 297–319 (2004). https://doi.org/10.1007/s00145-004-0314-9

[BN06] Bellare, M., Neven, G.: Multi-signatures in the plain public-key model and a general forking lemma. In: Juels, A., Wright, R.N., De Capitani di Vimercati, S. (eds.) ACM CCS 2006, pp. 390–399. ACM Press, October/November 2006

[BNPS03] Bellare, M., Namprempre, C., Pointcheval, D., Semanko, M.: The one-more-RSA-inversion problems and the security of Chaum's blind signature scheme. J. Cryptol. **16**(3), 185–215 (2003). https://doi.org/10.1007/s00145-002-0120-1

[BR93] Bellare, M., Rogaway, P.: Random oracles are practical: a paradigm for designing efficient protocols. In: Denning, D.E., Pyle, R., Ganesan, R., Sandhu, R.S., Ashby, V. (eds.) ACM CCS 1993, pp. 62–73. ACM Press, November 1993

[CK18] Corrigan-Gibbs, H., Kogan, D.: The discrete-logarithm problem with preprocessing. In: Nielsen, J.B., Rijmen, V. (eds.) EUROCRYPT 2018, Part II. LNCS, vol. 10821, pp. 415–447. Springer, Cham (2018). https://doi.org/10.1007/978-3-319-78375-8_14

[CP93] Chaum, D., Pedersen, T.P.: Wallet databases with observers. In: Brickell, E.F. (ed.) CRYPTO 1992. LNCS, vol. 740, pp. 89–105. Springer, Heidelberg (1993). https://doi.org/10.1007/3-540-48071-4_7

[DEF+19] Drijvers, M., et al.: On the security of two-round multi-signatures. In: 2019 IEEE Symposium on Security and Privacy, pp. 1084–1101. IEEE Computer Society Press, May 2019

[Den02] Dent, A.W.: Adapting the weaknesses of the random oracle model to the generic group model. In: Zheng, Y. (ed.) ASIACRYPT 2002. LNCS, vol. 2501, pp. 100–109. Springer, Heidelberg (2002). https://doi.org/10.1007/3-540-36178-2_6

[DS19] Derler, D., Slamanig, D.: Key-homomorphic signatures: definitions and applications to multiparty signatures and non-interactive zero-knowledge. Des. Codes Cryptogr. **87**(6), 1373–1413 (2018). https://doi.org/10.1007/s10623-018-0535-9

[Fis00] Fischlin, M.: A note on security proofs in the generic model. In: Okamoto, T. (ed.) ASIACRYPT 2000. LNCS, vol. 1976, pp. 458–469. Springer, Heidelberg (2000). https://doi.org/10.1007/3-540-44448-3_35

[fIS18] Federal Office for Information Security. Elliptic curve cryptography, version 2.1. Technical Guideline BSI TR-03111, June 2018

[FJS14] Fleischhacker, N., Jager, T., Schröder, D.: On tight security proofs for Schnorr signatures. In: Sarkar, P., Iwata, T. (eds.) ASIACRYPT 2014, Part I. LNCS, vol. 8873, pp. 512–531. Springer, Heidelberg (2014). https://doi.org/10.1007/978-3-662-45611-8_27

[FS87] Fiat, A., Shamir, A.: How to prove yourself: practical solutions to identification and signature problems. In: Odlyzko, A.M. (ed.) CRYPTO 1986. LNCS, vol. 263, pp. 186–194. Springer, Heidelberg (1987). https://doi.org/10.1007/3-540-47721-7_12

[fSC18] International Organization for Standardization and International Electrotechnical Commission. It security techniques - digital signatures with appendix - part 3: Discrete logarithm based mechanisms. ISO/IEC 14888-3, November 2018

[FST10]   Freeman, D., Scott, M., Teske, E.: A taxonomy of pairing-friendly elliptic curves. J. Cryptol. **23**(2), 224–280 (2010). https://doi.org/10.1007/s00145-009-9048-z

[GGH+13] Garg, S., Gentry, C., Halevi, S., Raykova, M., Sahai, A., Waters, B.: Candidate indistinguishability obfuscation and functional encryption for all circuits. In: 54th FOCS, pp. 40–49. IEEE Computer Society Press, October 2013

[GHS02]   Gaudry, P., Hess, F., Smart, N.P.: Constructive and destructive facets of Weil descent on elliptic curves. J. Cryptol. **15**(1), 19–46 (2002). https://doi.org/10.1007/s00145-001-0011-x

[GMLS02] Galbraith, S., Malone-Lee, J., Smart, N.P.: Public key signatures in the multi-user setting. Inf. Process. Lett. **83**(5), 263–266 (2002)

[GWZ15]   Galbraith, S.D., Wang, P., Zhang, F.: Computing elliptic curve discrete logarithms with improved baby-step giant-step algorithm. Cryptology ePrint Archive, Report 2015/605 (2015). http://eprint.iacr.org/2015/605

[Hao17]   Hao, F.: Schnorr Non-interactive Zero-Knowledge Proof. RFC 8235, September 2017

[JMV01]   Johnson, D., Menezes, A., Vanstone, S.: The elliptic curve digital signature algorithm (ECDSA). Int. J. Inf. Secur. **1**(1), 36–63 (2001). https://doi.org/10.1007/s102070100002

[JS08]   Jager, T., Schwenk, J.: On the equivalence of generic group models. In: Baek, J., Bao, F., Chen, K., Lai, X. (eds.) ProvSec 2008. LNCS, vol. 5324, pp. 200–209. Springer, Heidelberg (2008). https://doi.org/10.1007/978-3-540-88733-1_14

[KM07]   Koblitz, N., Menezes, A.: Another look at generic groups (2007)

[KMP16]   Kiltz, E., Masny, D., Pan, J.: Optimal security proofs for signatures from identification schemes. In: Robshaw, M., Katz, J. (eds.) CRYPTO 2016, Part II. LNCS, vol. 9815, pp. 33–61. Springer, Heidelberg (2016). https://doi.org/10.1007/978-3-662-53008-5_2

[KW03]   Katz, J., Wang, N.: Efficiency improvements for signature schemes with tight security reductions. In: Jajodia, S., Atluri, V., Jaeger, T. (eds.) ACM CCS 2003, pp. 155–164. ACM Press, October 2003

[LM17]   Liang, B., Mitrokotsa, A.: Fast and adaptively secure signatures in the random oracle model from indistinguishability obfuscation. Cryptology ePrint Archive, Report 2017/969 (2017). http://eprint.iacr.org/2017/969

[MPSW19] Maxwell, G., Poelstra, A., Seurin, Y., Wuille, P.: Simple Schnorr multi-signatures with applications to bitcoin. Des. Codes Cryptogr. **87**(9), 2139–2164 (2019). https://doi.org/10.1007/s10623-019-00608-x

[MVO91]   Menezes, A., Vanstone, S.A., Okamoto, T.: Reducing elliptic curve logarithms to logarithms in a finite field. In: 23rd ACM STOC, pp. 80–89. ACM Press, May 1991

[Nec94]   Nechaev, V.I.: Complexity of a determinate algorithm for the discrete logarithm. Math. Notes **55**, 165–172 (1994). https://doi.org/10.1007/BF02113297

[NRS20]   Nick, J., Ruffing, T., Seurin, Y.: MuSig2: simple two-round Schnorr multi-signatures. Cryptology ePrint Archive, Report 2020/1261 (2020). https://eprint.iacr.org/2020/1261

[NRSW20] Nick, J., Ruffing, T., Seurin, Y., Wuille, P.: MuSig-DN: Schnorr multi-signatures with verifiably deterministic nonces. Cryptology ePrint Archive, Report 2020/1057 (2020). https://eprint.iacr.org/2020/1057

[NSW09] Neven, G., Smart, N., Warinschi, B.: Hash function requirements for Schnorr signatures. J. Math. Cryptol. **3**, 05 (2009)

[PH06] Pohlig, S., Hellman, M.: An improved algorithm for computing logarithms over $GF(p)$ and its cryptographic significance (corresp.). IEEE Trans. Inf. Theor. **24**(1), 106–110 (2006)

[Pol78] Pollard, J.M.: Monte Carlo methods for index computation mod p. Math. Comput. **32**, 918–924 (1978)

[PS96] Pointcheval, D., Stern, J.: Security proofs for signature schemes. In: Maurer, U. (ed.) EUROCRYPT 1996. LNCS, vol. 1070, pp. 387–398. Springer, Heidelberg (1996). https://doi.org/10.1007/3-540-68339-9_33

[RW14] Ramchen, K., Waters, B.: Fully secure and fast signing from obfuscation. In: Ahn, G.-J., Yung, M., Li, N. (eds.) ACM CCS 2014, pp. 659–673. ACM Press, November 2014

[Sch90] Schnorr, C.-P.: Efficient identification and signatures for smart cards. In: Brassard, G. (ed.) CRYPTO 1989. LNCS, vol. 435, pp. 239–252. Springer, New York (1990). https://doi.org/10.1007/0-387-34805-0_22

[Seu12] Seurin, Y.: On the Exact security of Schnorr-type signatures in the random oracle model. In: Pointcheval, D., Johansson, T. (eds.) EUROCRYPT 2012. LNCS, vol. 7237, pp. 554–571. Springer, Heidelberg (2012). https://doi.org/10.1007/978-3-642-29011-4_33

[Sha71] Shanks, D.: Class number, a theory of factorization, and genera. In: 1969 Number Theory Institute (Proceedings of Symposia in Pure Mathematics, Vol. XX, State University of New York, Stony Brook, N.Y., 1969), pp. 415–440 (1971)

[Sho97] Shoup, V.: Lower bounds for discrete logarithms and related problems. In: Fumy, W. (ed.) EUROCRYPT 1997. LNCS, vol. 1233, pp. 256–266. Springer, Heidelberg (1997). https://doi.org/10.1007/3-540-69053-0_18

[SJ00] Schnorr, C.-P., Jakobsson, M.: Security of signed ElGamal encryption. In: Okamoto, T. (ed.) ASIACRYPT 2000. LNCS, vol. 1976, pp. 73–89. Springer, Heidelberg (2000). https://doi.org/10.1007/3-540-44448-3_7

[Sma99] Smart, N.P.: The discrete logarithm problem on elliptic curves of trace one. J. Cryptol. **12**(3), 193–196 (1999). https://doi.org/10.1007/s001459900052

[SW14] Sahai, A., Waters, B.: How to use indistinguishability obfuscation: deniable encryption, and more. In: Shmoys, D.B. (ed.) 46th ACM STOC, pp. 475–484. ACM Press, May/June 2014

[WZ11] Wang, P., Zhang, F.: Computing elliptic curve discrete logarithms with the negation map. Cryptology ePrint Archive, Report 2011/008 (2011). http://eprint.iacr.org/2011/008

Multi-Designated Receiver Signed Public Key Encryption

Ueli Maurer[1], Christopher Portmann[2], and Guilherme Rito[1]([✉])

[1] Department of Computer Science, ETH Zürich, Zürich, Switzerland
{maurer,gteixeir}@inf.ethz.ch
[2] Concordium, Zürich, Switzerland
cp@concordium.com

Abstract. This paper introduces a new type of public-key encryption scheme, called Multi-Designated Receiver Signed Public Key Encryption (MDRS-PKE), which allows a sender to select a set of designated receivers and both encrypt and sign a message that only these receivers will be able to read and authenticate (*confidentiality* and *authenticity*). An MDRS-PKE scheme provides several additional security properties which allow for a fundamentally new type of communication not considered before. Namely, it satisfies *consistency*—a dishonest sender cannot make different receivers receive different messages—*off-the-record*—a dishonest receiver cannot convince a third party of what message was sent (e.g., by selling their secret key), because dishonest receivers have the ability to forge signatures—and *anonymity*—parties that are not in the set of designated receivers cannot identify who the sender and designated receivers are.

We give a construction of an MDRS-PKE scheme from standard assumptions. At the core of our construction lies yet another new type of public-key encryption scheme, which is of independent interest: Public Key Encryption for Broadcast (PKEBC) which provides all the security guarantees of MDRS-PKE schemes, except authenticity.

We note that MDRS-PKE schemes give strictly more guarantees than Multi-Designated Verifier Signature (MDVS) schemes with privacy of identities. This in particular means that our MDRS-PKE construction yields the first MDVS scheme with privacy of identities from standard assumptions. The only prior construction of such schemes was based on Verifiable Functional Encryption for general circuits (Damgård et al., TCC '20).

1 Introduction

1.1 Public Key Encryption Security Properties

The most common use case for cryptography is sending a message to a single receiver. Here one usually desires to have *confidentiality* (only the desired receiver can read the message) and *authenticity* (the receiver is convinced that the message is from the declared sender). Although one might be interested in signatures

O. Dunkelman and S. Dziembowski (Eds.): EUROCRYPT 2022, LNCS 13276, pp. 644–673, 2022.
https://doi.org/10.1007/978-3-031-07085-3_22

that can be publicly verified (e.g. for a judge to verify a contract), when trying to protect the privacy of personal communication one often wants the opposite: not only is the intended receiver the only one that can verify the signature, but even if this person sells their secret key, no third party will be convinced of the authenticity of the message. This latter property is called *off-the-record* in the Designated Verifier Signature (DVS) literature [12, 16, 19–21, 23, 29–31], and is achieved by designing the scheme so that the receiver's secret key can be used to forge signatures. One may take this a step further and require *anonymity*, i.e. third parties cannot even learn who the sender and receiver are (this is called *privacy of identities* in the (M)DVS literature) [12].[1]

Another setting of interest is where the message is sent to many recipients. Consider, for example, the case of sending an email to multiple receivers. Apart from all the security properties listed above, here one would additionally require *consistency*: all the (intended) receivers will get the same email when decrypting the same ciphertext, even if the sender is dishonest. We note that it is crucial that a receiver can decrypt ciphertexts using only their secret key, i.e. without having to use the public key of the sender and other receivers. It is common in the literature to assume that the receiver knows who the sender and other receivers are so that their public keys can be used for decryption [6, 22]. But in many contexts adding this information in plain to the ciphertext would violate crucial properties, e.g., in broadcast encryption the ciphertext size would not be small any longer and in MDVS schemes anonymity (privacy) would be violated [22].

Many different schemes have been introduced in the literature that satisfy some of the properties listed here, see Sect. 1.5. In this work we propose two new primitives, Public Key Encryption for Broadcast (PKEBC) and Multi-Designated Receiver Signed Public Key Encryption (MDRS-PKE), which we explain in the following two subsections.

1.2   Public Key Encryption for Broadcast

The first type of primitive that we introduce, PKEBC, can be seen as an extension of Broadcast Encryption (BE) [13] which additionally gives consistency guarantees in the case of a dishonest sender.[2] More specifically, we expect PKEBC schemes to provide the following guarantees:

Correctness If a ciphertext c is honestly generated as the encryption of a message m with respect to a vector of receivers, say $\vec{R} := (\text{Bob}, \text{Charlie})$, then we want that if Bob is honest and decrypts c using its secret key, it obtains a pair $((\text{pk}_{\text{Bob}}, \text{pk}_{\text{Charlie}}), m)$, where pk_{Bob} and $\text{pk}_{\text{Charlie}}$ are, respectively, Bob's and Charlie's public keys;

---

[1] With off-the-record, a third party will know that either the alleged sender or the receiver wrote the message, whereas anonymity completely hides who the sender and receiver are. However, anonymity only holds when the receiver is honest whereas off-the-record provides guarantees against a dishonest receiver.

[2] Though BE usually requires the ciphertext size to be sublinear in the number of receivers, which PKEBC does not.

Robustness Let c be the ciphertext from above. We do not want Dave, who is honest but yet not an intended receiver of c, to think c was meant for himself. In other words, we do not want Dave to successfully decrypt c.

Consistency Now consider a dishonest party Alice who wants to confuse Bob and Charlie, both of whom are honest. We do not want Alice to be capable of creating a ciphertext c such that when Bob decrypts c, it obtains some pair $((pk_{Bob}, pk_{Charlie}), m)$, but when Charlie decrypts c it obtains some different pair. Instead, we want that if Bob obtains a pair $((pk_{Bob}, pk_{Charlie}), m)$, then so will Charlie (and vice-versa).

Confidentiality Now, suppose that Alice is honest. If Alice encrypts a message m to Bob and Charlie (who are both honest), we do not want Eve, who is dishonest, to find out what m is.

Anonymity Finally, suppose there are two more honest receivers, say Frank and Grace, to whom Alice could also be sending a message to. If, again, Alice encrypts a message m to both Bob and Charlie, and letting c be the corresponding ciphertext, we do not want Eve to find out that the receivers of ciphertext c are Bob and Charlie; in fact, we do not want Eve to learn anything about the intended receivers of c, other than the number of receivers.

The formal definitions of PKEBC are given in Sect. 3. In Sect. 4 we show how to construct a PKEBC from standard assumptions. Our construction is a generalization of Naor-Yung's scheme [26] that enhances the security guarantees given by the original scheme. In particular, as we will see if the underlying PKE scheme is anonymous, then this anonymity is preserved by the PKEBC construction.

One important difference from other public key schemes for multiple parties is that to decrypt, a receiver only needs to know their own secret key; the decryption of a ciphertext yields not only the underlying plaintext but also the set of receivers for the ciphertext. This then allows the corresponding public keys to be used as needed.[3]

1.3 Multi-Designated Receiver Signed Public Key Encryption

Our main primitive has all of the properties listed in Sect. 1.1. Namely, a MDRS-PKE scheme is expected to provide the following guarantees:

Correctness If a ciphertext c is honestly generated as the encryption of a message m from a sender Alice to a vector of receivers $\vec{R} := (Bob, Charlie)$ then we want that if Bob is honest and decrypts c using its secret key, it obtains a triple $(spk_{Alice}, (rpk_{Bob}, rpk_{Charlie}), m)$, where spk_{Alice} is Alice's public sending key, and rpk_{Bob} and $rpk_{Charlie}$ are, respectively, Bob's and Charlie's receiver public keys;

Consistency Now consider a dishonest party Donald who is a sender and wants to confuse Bob and Charlie, both of whom are honest. We do not want

---

[3] We note that this is only important since we want to achieve anonymity, otherwise once could send the public keys of the other parties together with the ciphertext.

Donald to be able to create a ciphertext c such that when Bob decrypts c, it obtains some triple $(\text{spk}_{\text{Donald}}, (\text{pk}_{\text{Bob}}, \text{pk}_{\text{Charlie}}), m)$, but when Charlie decrypts c it obtains some different triple (or does not even decrypt). Instead, we want that if Bob obtains a triple $(\text{spk}_{\text{Donald}}, (\text{pk}_{\text{Bob}}, \text{pk}_{\text{Charlie}}), m)$, then so will Charlie (and vice-versa).

Unforgeability We do not want that Eve can forge a ciphertext as if it were from an honest sender, say Alice, to a vector of receivers Bob and Charlie.

Confidentiality If an honest sender Alice encrypts a message m to Bob and Charlie (who are both honest), we do not want Eve, who is dishonest, to find out what m is.

Anonymity Suppose there is another honest sender, say Heidi. If Alice encrypts a message m to Bob, and letting c be the corresponding ciphertext, we do not want Eve to find out that Alice is the sender or that Bob is the receiver; Eve should at most learn that someone sent a message to a single receiver.

Off-The-Record Suppose Alice sends a message to Bob, Charlie and Donald. Donald, being dishonest, might be enticed to try convincing Eve that Alice sent some message. However, we do not want Donald to have this capability.

The formal definitions of MDRS-PKE are given in Sect. 5. In Sect. 6 we show how to construct a MDRS-PKE from standard assumptions. As we will see, our construction essentially consists of using the MDVS scheme to sign messages, and then using the PKEBC scheme to encrypt the signed messages, together with their MDVS signatures.

Since an MDRS-PKE scheme is an extension of an MDVS scheme with privacy of identities and confidentiality, any MDRS-PKE scheme yields an MDVS scheme with privacy of identities. Since we give an MDRS-PKE scheme which is secure under standard assumptions, this in particular implies that our construction is the first achieving privacy of identities from standard assumptions. The only previous construction of an MDVS scheme with privacy of identities relied on a Verifiable Functional Encryption scheme for general circuits [12].

1.4   Applications to Secure (Group) Messaging

As we now discuss, one main application of MDRS-PKE schemes is secure messaging, and in particular secure group messaging.

Suppose Alice and Bob are using a secure messaging application to chat with each other. Of course, they expect the messenger to provide basic guarantees such as *Correctness*—if Alice sends a message to Bob, Bob receives this message— *Confidentiality*—no one other than Alice and Bob should learn the contents of the messages—and *Authenticity*—if Alice reads a message m, then Bob must have sent m. Another desirable guarantee they could expect from the messenger is *Anonymity*: suppose that in parallel to Alice and Bob's chat, Charlie and Dave are also chatting; then, if a third party Eve intercepts a ciphertext c from Alice and Bob's chat and Eve cannot *a priori* tell that c came from and/or is addressed to Alice or Bob, then Eve should not gain any additional information about the identity of c's sender and/or receiver from inspecting the contents of ciphertext c itself (in other words, Eve cannot tell if the ciphertext is from Alice and Bob's chat, from Alice and Charlie's chat, from Bob and Charlie's chat, or from Charlie and Dave's chat). Finally, imagine that Bob, who wants to keep the history of his chat with Alice, outsources the storage of the chat's ciphertexts to an external storage service which reliably, but not authentically, stores these ciphertexts. An important additional guarantee Alice expects from the messaging application is *Off-The-Record Deniability (Off-The-Record)* [10,12]: if, somehow, Eve manages to access whatever is stored by Bob's storage service, Eve cannot tell by inspecting the stored ciphertexts, even if Bob chooses to cooperate with Eve[4], if these ciphertexts are authentic ones corresponding to real messages sent by Alice to Bob in their chat, or if they are fake ones generated by Bob (in case Bob is cooperating with Eve) or generated by anyone else (in case Bob is not cooperating with Eve) to incriminate Alice.

A related, yet very different property that secure messaging applications like Signal [11] provide is *Forward Secrecy* [17]. Informally, Forward Secrecy guarantees that even if Eve stores any ciphertexts received by Bob and later *hacks* into Bob's computer to learn his secret key, Eve cannot learn the decryptions (i.e. the plaintexts) of the ciphertexts she previously intercepted. Off-The-Record, on the other hand, does not give any guarantees about hiding the contents of previously exchanged messages. However, it hides from Eve whether Alice really sent a message m to Bob or if Bob faked receiving m. Furthermore, Forward Secrecy assumes Bob is honest: if Bob were dishonest, he could simply store the decryptions of the ciphertexts he receives to later disclose them to Eve. Off-The-Record does not make such assumption: even if Bob is dishonest, Eve cannot tell if it was Alice sending a message m, or if Bob faked receiving m from Alice (in case Bob is dishonest), or anyone else faked Alice sending m to Bob (in case Bob is honest). Finally, as one can deduce, Forward Secrecy is incompatible with parties keeping a history of their chats, whereas this is not the case for Off-The-Record. A different problem is Alice's computer getting *hacked* by Eve. In such scenario it would be desirable to still give the Off-The-Record guarantee to Alice: Eve should not be able to tell if Alice ever sent any message or not. However, current Off-The-Record notions [12], including the one given in this paper, do not capture this.

A natural generalization of two party secure messaging is secure group messaging [2,12]. Suppose Alice, Bob and Charlie now share a group chat. The key difference between Alice, Bob and Charlie sharing a group chat or having multiple two party chats with each other is *Consistency*: even if Charlie is dishonest, he cannot create confusion among Alice and Bob as to whether he sent a message to the group chat or not [12]. In other words, honest group members have a consistent view of the chat. Surprisingly, for the case of MDVS, this guarantee was only recently introduced by Damgård et al. in [12].

To achieve Off-The-Record in the group messaging case, one must consider that any subset of the parties participating in the group chat may be dishon-

---

[4] By Bob collaborating with Eve we mean that Bob shares all his secrets (including secret keys) with Eve.

est [12]. This property, also known as *Any-Subset Off-The-Record Deniability* (or more simply *Off-The-Record*) was first introduced by Damgård et al. in [12]. Returning to Alice, Bob and Charlie's group chat, this property essentially guarantees that regardless of who (among Bob and Charlie) cooperate with Eve in trying to convince her that Alice sent some message, Eve will not be convinced because any of them (or the two together) could have created a fake message to pretend that Alice sent it.

1.5 Related Work

A closely related type of encryption scheme are Broadcast Encryption (BE) schemes [9,13]. However, BE schemes do not give the consistency guarantee that PKEBC give; the main goal of BE schemes is actually making ciphertexts short—ideally the size of ciphertexts would be independent from the number recipients. Conversely, the size of the ciphertexts of the PKEBC scheme construction we give in this paper grows quadratically with the number of recipients. Diament et al. introduce a special type of BE scheme, called Dual-Receiver Encryption schemes, which allow a sender to send messages to two (and only two) receivers. By limiting the number of receivers to two receivers, these schemes allow for efficient constructions with relatively short ciphertexts and public keys from standard assumptions.

As already mentioned, PKEBC schemes allow receivers to decrypt a ciphertext meant for multiple receivers using their secret key only. This problem had been noticed before by Barth et al. in [6], and by Libert et al. in [22]. Barth et al. modify the definition of BE schemes in a way that allows receivers to decrypt ciphertexts without knowing who the other recipients are a priori [6]. Libert et al. strengthens this by guaranteeing that receivers do not learn who the other receivers are, even after decrypting ciphertexts.

Other closely related works are Multi-Designated Verifier Signature (MDVS) schemes [12]. They provide consistency, authenticity, and off-the record and sometimes also anonymity (called privacy). However, to the best of our knowledge, MDVS schemes require the public keys of the sender and other designated receivers to be used to verify signatures, and the existing literature does not discuss how the receiver gets that information, e.g. sending this information in plain would violate privacy. Thus, existing constructions of MDVS with privacy can only be used if the number of combinations of possible sender and receivers is small enough that all combinations can be tried by the verifier.

2 Preliminaries

We now introduce conventions and notation we use throughout the paper. We denote the arity of a vector $\vec{x}$ by $|\vec{x}|$ and its i-th element by x_i. We write $\alpha \in \vec{x}$ to denote $\exists i \in \{1, \ldots, |\vec{x}|\}$ with $\alpha = x_i$. We write $\mathrm{Set}(\vec{x})$ to denote the set induced by vector $\vec{x}$, i.e. $\mathrm{Set}(\vec{x}) := \{x_i \mid x_i \in \vec{x}\}$.

Throughout the paper we frequently use vectors. We use upper case letters to denote vectors of parties, and lower case letters to denote vectors of artifacts such as public keys, messages, sequences of random coins, and so on. Moreover, we use the convention that if $\vec{V}$ is a vector of parties, then $\vec{v}$ denotes $\vec{V}$'s corresponding vector of public keys. For example, for a vector of parties $\vec{V} := (\text{Bob}, \text{Charlie})$, $\vec{v} := (\text{pk}_{\text{Bob}}, \text{pk}_{\text{Charlie}})$ is $\vec{V}$'s corresponding vector of public keys. In particular, V_1 is Bob and v_1 is Bob's public key pk_{Bob}, and V_2 is Charlie and v_2 is Charlie's public key $\text{pk}_{\text{Charlie}}$. More generally, for a vector of parties $\vec{V}$ with corresponding vector of public keys $\vec{v}$, V_i's public key is v_i, for $i \in \{1, \ldots, |\vec{V}|\}$.

3   Public Key Encryption for Broadcast Schemes

We now introduce the first new type of scheme we give in this paper, namely Public Key Encryption for Broadcast (PKEBC). A PKEBC scheme Π with message space $\mathcal{M}$ is a quadruple $\Pi = (S, G, E, D)$ of Probabilistic Polynomial Time Algorithms (PPTs), where:

- S: on input 1^k, generates public parameters pp;
- G: on input pp, generates a receiver key-pair;
- E: on input $(\text{pp}, \vec{v}, m)$, where $\vec{v}$ is a vector of public keys of the intended receivers and m is the message, generates a ciphertext c;
- D: on input $(\text{pp}, \text{sk}, c)$, where sk is the receiver's secret key, D decrypts c using sk, and outputs the decrypted receiver-vector/message pair $(\vec{v}, m)$ (or $\perp$ if the ciphertext did not decrypt correctly).

3.1   The Security of PKEBC Schemes

We now state the definitions of Correctness, Robustness, Consistency, and IND-CCA-2 and IK-CCA-2 security for PKEBC schemes. Before proceeding to the actual definitions, we first introduce some oracles the game systems from Definitions 1, 2 and 3 use. In the following, consider a PKEBC scheme $\Pi = (S, G, E, D)$ with message space $\mathcal{M}$. The oracles below are defined for a game-system with (an implicitly defined) security parameter k:

Public Parameters Oracle: $\mathcal{O}_{PP}$
  1. On the first call, compute and store $\text{pp} \leftarrow S(1^k)$; output pp;
  2. On subsequent calls, output the previously generated pp.
Secret Key Generation Oracle: $\mathcal{O}_{SK}(B_j)$
  1. If $\mathcal{O}_{SK}$ was queried on B_j before, simply look up and return the previously generated key for B_j;
  2. Otherwise, store $(\text{pk}_j, \text{sk}_j) \leftarrow G(\text{pp})$ as B_j's key-pair, and output $(\text{pk}_j, \text{sk}_j)$.
Public Key Generation Oracle: $\mathcal{O}_{PK}(B_j)$
  1. $(\text{pk}_j, \text{sk}_j) \leftarrow \mathcal{O}_{SK}(B_j)$;
  2. Output pk_j.

Encryption Oracle: $\mathcal{O}_E(\vec{V}, m)$
1. $\vec{v} \leftarrow (\mathcal{O}_{PK}(V_1), \ldots, \mathcal{O}_{PK}(V_{|\vec{V}|}))$;
2. Create and output a fresh encryption $c \leftarrow E_{\mathsf{pp},\vec{v}}(m)$.

In addition to the oracles above, the game systems from Definitions 1 and 2 further provide adversaries with access to the following oracles:

Decryption Oracle: $\mathcal{O}_D(B_j, c)$
1. Query $\mathcal{O}_{SK}(B_j)$ to obtain the corresponding secret-key sk_j;
2. Decrypt c using sk_j, $(\vec{v}, m) \leftarrow D_{\mathsf{pp},\mathsf{sk}_j}(c)$, and then output the resulting receivers-message pair $(\vec{v}, m)$, or $\bot$ (if $(\vec{v}, m) = \bot$, i.e. the ciphertext is not valid with respect to B_j's secret key).

Definition 1 (Correctness). *Consider the following game played between between an adversary* **A** *and game system* $\mathbf{G}^{\mathsf{Corr}}$:

- $\mathbf{A}^{\mathcal{O}_{PP}, \mathcal{O}_{PK}, \mathcal{O}_{SK}, \mathcal{O}_E, \mathcal{O}_D}$

A *wins the game if there are two queries* q_E *and* q_D *to* $\mathcal{O}_E$ *and* $\mathcal{O}_D$, *respectively, where* q_E *has input* $(\vec{V}, m)$ *and* q_D *has input* (B_j, c), *satisfying* $B_j \in \vec{V}$, *the input* c *in* q_D *is the output of* q_E, *the output of* q_D *is either* $\bot$ *or* $(\vec{v}', m')$ *with* $(\vec{v}, m) \neq (\vec{v}', m')$, *and* **A** *did not query* $\mathcal{O}_{SK}$ *on input* B_j.

The advantage of **A** *in winning the Correctness game, denoted* $Adv^{\mathsf{Corr}}(\mathbf{A})$, *is the probability that* **A** *wins game* $\mathbf{G}^{\mathsf{Corr}}$ *as described above.*

We say that an adversary **A** $(\varepsilon_{\mathsf{Corr}}, t)$-breaks the (n, d_E, q_E, q_D)-Correctness of a PKEBC scheme Π if **A** runs in time at most t, queries $\mathcal{O}_{PK}$, $\mathcal{O}_E$ and $\mathcal{O}_D$ on at most n different parties[5], makes at most q_E and q_D queries to $\mathcal{O}_E$ and $\mathcal{O}_D$, respectively, with the sum of lengths of the party vectors input to $\mathcal{O}_E$ being at most d_E, and satisfies $Adv^{\mathsf{Corr}}(\mathbf{A}) \geq \varepsilon_{\mathsf{Corr}}$.

The following notion captures the guarantee that if a ciphertext c is an honestly generated ciphertext for a vector of receivers $\vec{R}$ (for some message), then no honest receiver B who is not one of the intended receivers of c can successfully decrypt c (i.e. if $B \notin \vec{R}$ then the decryption of c with B's secret key outputs $\bot$). As one might note, this notion is a variant of the Weak Robustness notion introduced in [1], but adapted to PKEBC schemes.

Definition 2 (Robustness). *Consider the following game played between an adversary* **A** *and game system* $\mathbf{G}^{\mathsf{Rob}}$:

- $\mathbf{A}^{\mathcal{O}_{PP}, \mathcal{O}_{PK}, \mathcal{O}_{SK}, \mathcal{O}_E, \mathcal{O}_D}$

A *wins the game if there are two queries* q_E *and* q_D *to* $\mathcal{O}_E$ *and* $\mathcal{O}_D$, *respectively, where* q_E *has input* $(\vec{V}, m)$ *and* q_D *has input* (B_j, c), *satisfying* $B_j \notin \vec{V}$, *the input* c *in* q_D *is the output of* q_E, *the output of* q_D *is* $(\vec{v}', m')$ *with* $(\vec{v}', m') \neq \bot$, *and* **A** *did not query* $\mathcal{O}_{SK}$ *on input* B_j.

---

[5] Here, querying on most n parties means that the number of different parties in all queries is at most n. In particular, the number of different parties in a query $\mathcal{O}_E((B_1, B_2, B_3), (\ldots))$ is 3, assuming $B_1 \neq B_2 \neq B_3 \neq B_1$; the number of different parties in a query $\mathcal{O}_D(B_j, \cdot)$ is 1.

The advantage of **A** *in winning the Robustness game is the probability that* **A** *wins game* $\mathbf{G}^{\mathsf{Rob}}$ *as described above, and is denoted* $Adv^{\mathsf{Rob}}(\mathbf{A})$.

An adversary **A** $(\varepsilon_{\mathsf{Rob}}, t)$-breaks the Robustness of a PKEBC scheme Π if **A** runs in time at most t and satisfies $Adv^{\mathsf{Rob}}(\mathbf{A}) \geq \varepsilon_{\mathsf{Rob}}$.

Remark 1. Correctness and Robustness are properties only relevant to honest parties. It is common in the literature to either define such security notions without any adversary or to consider a stronger adversary that is unbounded or has access to the honest parties' secret keys. We choose the weaker definitions above for two main reasons: first, it has been proven that analogous Correctness and Robustness notions [1,5] for PKE schemes—also defined with respect to computationally bounded adversaries who are not given access to the secret keys of honest parties—imply (corresponding) composable security notions (see [5] and [18]); second, since the remaining PKEBC security notions (e.g. IND-CCA-2 security) are defined with respect to computationally bounded adversaries that cannot obtain the secret keys of honest parties, there is no advantage in considering strengthened Correctness and Robustness security notions. Nevertheless, as we will see, if the PKE scheme underlying our PKEBC scheme's construction satisfies Correctness against unbounded adversaries, then the PKEBC scheme's construction can be proven to satisfy such stronger Correctness and Robustness security notions.

We now introduce the notion of Consistency. Essentially, this notion captures the guarantee that a dishonest sender cannot create confusion between any pair of honest receivers as to whether they received some message m with respect to a vector of receivers $\vec{R}$ that includes both parties.

Definition 3 (Consistency). *Consider the following game played between an adversary* **A** *and game system* $\mathbf{G}^{\mathsf{Cons}}$:

- $\mathbf{A}^{\mathcal{O}_{PP}, \mathcal{O}_{PK}, \mathcal{O}_{SK}, \mathcal{O}_D}$

A *wins the game if there is a ciphertext* c *such that* $\mathcal{O}_D$ *is queried on inputs* (B_i, c) *and* (B_j, c) *for some* B_i *and* B_j *(possibly with* $B_i = B_j$), *there is no prior query on either* B_i *or* B_j *to* $\mathcal{O}_{SK}$, *query* $\mathcal{O}_D(B_i, c)$ *outputs some* $(\vec{v}, m)$ *satisfying* $(\vec{v}, m) \neq \perp$ *with* $\mathsf{pk}_j \in \vec{v}$ *(where* pk_j *is* B_j's *public key), and query* $\mathcal{O}_D(B_j, c)$ *does not output* $(\vec{v}, m)$.

The advantage of **A** *in winning the Consistency game is denoted* $Adv^{\mathsf{Cons}}(\mathbf{A})$ *and corresponds to the probability that* **A** *wins game* $\mathbf{G}^{\mathsf{Cons}}$ *as described above.*

We say that an adversary **A** $(\varepsilon_{\mathsf{Cons}}, t)$-breaks the (n, q_D)-Consistency of Π if **A** runs in time at most t, queries $\mathcal{O}_{SK}$, $\mathcal{O}_{PK}$ and $\mathcal{O}_D$ on at most n different parties, makes at most q_D queries to $\mathcal{O}_D$ and satisfies $Adv^{\mathsf{Cons}}(\mathbf{A}) \geq \varepsilon_{\mathsf{Cons}}$.

Remark 2. Similarly to Remark 1, Consistency is a security property only relevant to honest receivers, for which reason Definition 3 disallows adversaries from querying for the secret keys of honest receivers. It was proven in [24] that an analogous Consistency notion for MDVS schemes (introduced in [12]) implies composable security. Yet, as we will see, if the PKE scheme underlying our PKEBC scheme's construction satisfies Correctness against unbounded adversaries, then our PKEBC scheme can be proven to satisfy a stronger Consistency notion in which the adversary can query for any party's secret key.

The two following security notions are the multi-receiver variants of IND-CCA-2 security (introduced in [27]) and IK-CCA-2 security (introduced in [7]). The games defined by these notions provide adversaries with access to the oracles $\mathcal{O}_{PP}$ and $\mathcal{O}_{PK}$ defined above as well as to oracles $\mathcal{O}_E$ and $\mathcal{O}_D$. For both notions, $\mathcal{O}_D$ is defined as follows:

Decryption Oracle: $\mathcal{O}_D(B_j, c)$
1. If c was the output of some query to $\mathcal{O}_E$, output test;
2. Otherwise, compute and output $(\vec{v}, m) \leftarrow D_{pp, sk_j}(c)$, where sk_j is B_j's secret key.

The $\mathcal{O}_E$ oracle provided by the IND-CCA-2 games differs from the one provided by the IK-CCA-2 games; for IND-CCA-2, $\mathcal{O}_E$ is as follows:

Encryption Oracle: $\mathcal{O}_E(\vec{V}, m_0, m_1)$
1. For game system $\mathbf{G}_{\mathbf{b}}^{\text{IND-CCA-2}}$, encrypt $m_{\mathbf{b}}$ under $\vec{v}$ (the vector of public keys corresponding to $\vec{V}$); output c.

Adversaries do not have access to $\mathcal{O}_{SK}$ in either notion.

Definition 4 (IND-CCA-2 Security). *Consider the following game played between an adversary* $\mathbf{A}$ *and a game system* $\mathbf{G}_{\mathbf{b}}^{\text{IND-CCA-2}}$, *with* $\mathbf{b} \in \{0, 1\}$:

$$- b' \leftarrow \mathbf{A}^{\mathcal{O}_{PP}, \mathcal{O}_{PK}, \mathcal{O}_E, \mathcal{O}_D}$$

$\mathbf{A}$ *wins the game if* $b' = \mathbf{b}$ *and every query* $\mathcal{O}_E(\vec{V}, m_0, m_1)$ *satisfies* $|m_0| = |m_1|$. *We define the advantage of* $\mathbf{A}$ *in winning the* IND-CCA-2 *game as*

$$Adv^{\text{IND-CCA-2}}(\mathbf{A}) := \left| \Pr[\mathbf{AG}_0^{\text{IND-CCA-2}} = \text{win}] + \Pr[\mathbf{AG}_1^{\text{IND-CCA-2}} = \text{win}] - 1 \right|.$$

For the IK-CCA-2 security notion, $\mathcal{O}_E$ behaves as follows:

Encryption Oracle: $\mathcal{O}_E(\vec{V}_0, \vec{V}_1, m)$
1. For game system $\mathbf{G}_{\mathbf{b}}^{\text{IK-CCA-2}}$, encrypt m under $\vec{v}_{\mathbf{b}}$, the vector of public keys corresponding to $\vec{V}_{\mathbf{b}}$, creating a fresh ciphertext c; output c.

Definition 5 (IK-CCA-2 Security). *Consider the following game played between an adversary* $\mathbf{A}$ *and a game system* $\mathbf{G}_{\mathbf{b}}^{\text{IK-CCA-2}}$, *with* $\mathbf{b} \in \{0, 1\}$:

$$- b' \leftarrow \mathbf{A}^{\mathcal{O}_{PP}, \mathcal{O}_{PK}, \mathcal{O}_E, \mathcal{O}_D}$$

$\mathbf{A}$ *wins the game if* $b' = \mathbf{b}$ *and every query* $\mathcal{O}_E(\vec{V}_0, \vec{V}_1, m)$ *satisfies* $|\vec{V}_0| = |\vec{V}_1|$. *We define the advantage of* $\mathbf{A}$ *in winning the* IK-CCA-2 *security game as*

$$Adv^{\text{IK-CCA-2}}(\mathbf{A}) := \left| \Pr[\mathbf{AG}_0^{\text{IK-CCA-2}} = \text{win}] + \Pr[\mathbf{AG}_1^{\text{IK-CCA-2}} = \text{win}] - 1 \right|.$$

We say that an adversary $\mathbf{A}$ $(\varepsilon_{\text{IND-CCA-2}}, t)$-breaks (resp. $(\varepsilon_{\text{IK-CCA-2}}, t)$-breaks) the (n, d_E, q_E, q_D)-IND-CCA-2 (resp. (n, d_E, q_E, q_D)-IK-CCA-2) security of Π if $\mathbf{A}$ runs in time at most t, queries the oracles it has access to on at most n different parties, makes at most q_E and q_D queries to oracles $\mathcal{O}_E$ and $\mathcal{O}_D$, respectively, with the sum of lengths of all the party vectors input to $\mathcal{O}_E$ being at most d_E, and satisfies $Adv^{\text{IND-CCA-2}}(\mathbf{A}) \geq \varepsilon_{\text{IND-CCA-2}}$ (resp. $Adv^{\text{IK-CCA-2}}(\mathbf{A}) \geq \varepsilon_{\text{IK-CCA-2}}$).

Finally, we say that Π is

$$(\varepsilon_{\text{Corr}}, \varepsilon_{\text{Rob}}, \varepsilon_{\text{Cons}}, \varepsilon_{\text{IND-CCA-2}}, \varepsilon_{\text{IK-CCA-2}}, t, n, d_E, q_E, q_D)\text{-secure},$$

if no adversary $\mathbf{A}$:

- $(\varepsilon_{\text{Corr}}, t)$-breaks the (n, d_E, q_E, q_D)-Correctness of Π;
- $(\varepsilon_{\text{Rob}}, t)$-breaks the Robustness of Π;
- $(\varepsilon_{\text{Cons}}, t)$-breaks the (n, q_D)-Consistency of Π;
- $(\varepsilon_{\text{IND-CCA-2}}, t)$-breaks the (n, d_E, q_E, q_D)-IND-CCA-2 security of Π; or
- $(\varepsilon_{\text{IK-CCA-2}}, t)$-breaks the (n, d_E, q_E, q_D)-IK-CCA-2 security of Π.

4   A PKEBC Scheme from Standard Assumptions

We now present our construction of a PKEBC scheme. The construction is a generalization of Naor-Yung's scheme [26] that enhances the security guarantees given by the original scheme. In particular, if the underlying PKE scheme is anonymous, then this anonymity is preserved by the PKEBC construction. First, while the scheme should preserve the anonymity of the underlying PKE scheme, parties should still be able to obtain the vector of receivers from ciphertexts, using only their own secret key. For this reason, the underlying PKE scheme is used to encrypt not only the messages to be sent, but also the vector of receivers to which each message is being sent to. As one might note, however, to preserve the anonymity of the underlying PKE scheme, the NIZK proof that proves the consistency of the ciphertexts for the various receivers can no longer be a proof for a statement in which the public keys are part of the statement. This introduces an extra complication since for some PKE schemes such as ElGamal, for every ciphertext c and message m, there is a public key pk and a sequence of random coins r such that c is an encryption of m under pk, using r as the sequence of random coins for encrypting m. In particular, this means that the NIZK proof is not actually proving the consistency of the ciphertexts. To solve this issue, we further add a (binding) commitment to the vector of receiver public keys used to encrypt each ciphertext, and then use the NIZK proof to show that each ciphertext is an encryption of this same message under the public keys of the vector to which the commitment is bound. Note, however, that this is still not sufficient: despite now having the guarantee that if the NIZK proof verifies then all ciphertexts are encryptions of the same plaintext with respect a vector of public keys, since a party can still decrypt ciphertexts not meant for itself without realizing it, it could happen that a receiver decrypts the wrong ciphertext, thus getting the wrong vector of receivers-plaintext pair. To avoid this, the commitment additionally commits to the message being sent, and the sequence of random coins used to create the commitment are now encrypted along with the vector of public keys of the parties and the message being sent. This then allows a receiver to recompute the commitment from the vector of parties and message it decrypted. Given the commitment is binding, this implies that if the recomputed commitment matches the one in the ciphertext then decryption worked correctly (as otherwise the recomputed commitment would not match the one in the ciphertext).

We note that our security reductions are tight, and that there are tightly secure instantiations of each of the schemes we use as building blocks for our construction. For instance, ElGamal could be used as the underlying IND-CPA secure encryption scheme, as it is tightly multi-user multi-challenge IND-CPA secure [8].[6] Furthermore, we could use any perfectly correct PKE scheme as the statistically binding commitment scheme needed by our scheme (in particular ElGamal), and the tightly unbounded simulation sound NIZK scheme from [14].

Algorithm 1 gives a construction of a Public Key Encryption for Broadcast scheme $\Pi = (S, G, E, D)$ from a Public Key Encryption scheme $\Pi_{PKE} = (G, E, D)$, a Commitment Scheme $\Pi_{CS} = (G_{CRS}, Commit, Verify)$ and a Non Interactive Zero Knowledge scheme $\Pi_{NIZK} = (G_{CRS}, Prove, Verify, S := (S_{CRS}, S_{Sim}))$. Consider relation R_{Cons} defined as

$$
\begin{aligned}
R_{Cons} := \Big\{ &\big((\mathsf{crs}_{CS}, \mathsf{comm}, \vec{c}), (\rho, \vec{v}, m, \vec{r})\big) \mid \\
&|\vec{c}| = |\vec{v}| \\
&\wedge \mathsf{comm} = \Pi_{CS}.Commit_{\mathsf{crs}}(\vec{v}, m; \rho) \\
&\wedge \big(\forall j \in \{1, \ldots, |\vec{c}|\}, \forall b \in \{0, 1\}, \\
&\quad c_{j,b} = \Pi_{PKE}.E_{v_{j,b}}(\rho, \vec{v}, m; r_{j,b})\big) \Big\}.
\end{aligned}
\tag{4.1}
$$

In Algorithm 1, we consider the language induced by R_{Cons}, which is defined as

$$
\begin{aligned}
L_{Cons} := \Big\{ &\big(\mathsf{crs}_{CS}, \mathsf{comm}, \vec{c}\big) \mid \\
&\exists (\rho, \vec{v}, m, \vec{r}) \\
&\big((\mathsf{crs}_{CS}, \mathsf{comm}, \vec{c}), (\rho, \vec{v}, m, \vec{r})\big) \in R_{Cons} \Big\}.
\end{aligned}
\tag{4.2}
$$

4.1   Security Analysis of PKEBC Construction

We now prove the security of our PKEBC scheme construction. Refer to [25] for a full proof of the following results.

Theorem 1. *If Π_{PKE} is*

$$
\begin{aligned}
&\big(\varepsilon_{PKE\text{-}Corr}, \varepsilon_{PKE\text{-}IND\text{-}CPA}, \varepsilon_{PKE\text{-}IK\text{-}CPA}, \\
&t_{PKE}, n_{PKE}, q_{E\,PKE}, q_{D\,PKE}, \mathsf{Corr}\big)\text{-}secure,
\end{aligned}
\tag{4.3}
$$

---

[6] In the full version of this paper, we show that ElGamal is also tightly multi-user multi-challenge IK-CPA secure under the DDH assumption (see [25]).

Algorithm 1. Construction of a PKEBC scheme $\Pi = (S, G, E, D)$.

$S(1^k)$
  return $(1^k, \Pi_{\text{NIZK}}.G_{CRS}(1^k), \Pi_{\text{CS}}.G_{CRS}(1^k))$

$G(\text{pp} := (1^k, \text{crs}_{\text{NIZK}}, \text{crs}_{\text{CS}}))$
  $(\text{pk}_0, \text{sk}_0) \leftarrow \Pi_{\text{PKE}}.G(1^k)$
  $(\text{pk}_1, \text{sk}_1) \leftarrow \Pi_{\text{PKE}}.G(1^k)$
  return $(\text{pk} := (\text{pk}_0, \text{pk}_1), \text{sk} := ((\text{pk}_0, \text{sk}_0), (\text{pk}_1, \text{sk}_1)))$

$E(\text{pp} := (1^k, \text{crs}_{\text{NIZK}}, \text{crs}_{\text{CS}}), \vec{v} := ((\text{pk}_{1,0}, \text{pk}_{1,1}), \ldots, (\text{pk}_{|\vec{v}|,0}, \text{pk}_{|\vec{v}|,1})), m \in \mathcal{M})$
  $\rho \leftarrow RandomCoins$
  $\text{comm} \leftarrow \Pi_{\text{CS}}.Commit_{\text{crs}_{\text{CS}}}(\vec{v}, m; \rho)$
  for $(\text{pk}_{j,0}', \text{pk}_{j,1}') \in \vec{v}$ do
    $(r_{j,0}, r_{j,1}) \leftarrow (RandomCoins, RandomCoins)$
    $(c_{j,0}, c_{j,1}) \leftarrow (\Pi_{\text{PKE}}.E_{\text{pk}_{j,0}}(\rho, \vec{v}, m; r_{j,0}), \Pi_{\text{PKE}}.E_{\text{pk}_{j,1}}(\rho, \vec{v}, m; r_{j,1}))$
  $\vec{r} := ((r_{1,0}, r_{1,1}), \ldots, (r_{|\vec{v}|,0}, r_{|\vec{v}|,1}))$
  $\vec{c} := ((c_{1,0}, c_{1,1}), \ldots, (c_{|\vec{v}|,0}, c_{|\vec{v}|,1}))$
  $p \leftarrow \Pi_{\text{NIZK}}.Prove_{\text{crs}_{\text{NIZK}}}((\text{crs}_{\text{CS}}, \text{comm}, \vec{c}) \in L_{\text{Cons}}, (\vec{v}, m, \rho, \vec{r}))$
  return $(p, \text{comm}, \vec{c})$

$D(\text{pp} := (1^k, \text{crs}_{\text{NIZK}}, \text{crs}_{\text{CS}}), \text{sk}_j := ((\text{pk}_{j,0}, \text{sk}_{j,0}), (\text{pk}_{j,1}, \text{sk}_{j,1})), c := (p, \text{comm}, \vec{c}))$
  if $\Pi_{\text{NIZK}}.Verify_{\text{crs}_{\text{NIZK}}}((\text{crs}_{\text{CS}}, \text{comm}, \vec{c}) \in L_{\text{Cons}}, p) = \text{valid}$ then
    for $i \in \{1, \ldots, |\vec{c}|\}$ do
      $(\rho, \vec{v} := ((\text{pk}_{1,0}', \text{pk}_{1,1}'), \ldots, (\text{pk}_{|\vec{v}|,0}', \text{pk}_{|\vec{v}|,1}')), m) \leftarrow \Pi_{\text{PKE}}.D_{\text{sk}_{j,0}}'(c_{i,0})$
      if $(\rho, \vec{v}, m) \neq \perp \wedge (\text{pk}_{j,0}, \text{pk}_{j,1}) = (\text{pk}_{i,0}', \text{pk}_{i,1}')$ then
        if $\text{comm} = \Pi_{\text{CS}}.Commit_{\text{crs}_{\text{CS}}}(\vec{v}, m; \rho)$ then
          return $(\vec{v}, m)$
  return $\perp$

Π_{NIZK} is

$$(\varepsilon_{NIZK\text{-Complete}}, \varepsilon_{NIZK\text{-Sound}}, \varepsilon_{NIZK\text{-ZK}}, \varepsilon_{NIZK\text{-SS}},$$
$$t_{NIZK}, q_{P\,NIZK}, q_{V\,NIZK})\text{-secure}, \tag{4.4}$$

and Π_{CS} is

$$(\varepsilon_{CS\text{-Hiding}}, \varepsilon_{CS\text{-Binding}}, t_{CS}, q_{CS}, \text{Binding})\text{-secure}, \tag{4.5}$$

then no adversary $\mathbf{A}$ (ε, t)-breaks Π's

$$(n := n_{PKE}, d_E := q_{E\,PKE}, q_E := q_{P\,NIZK},$$
$$q_D := \min(q_{V\,NIZK}, q_{D\,PKE}))\text{-Correctness},$$

with $\varepsilon > \varepsilon_{CS\text{-Binding}} + \varepsilon_{PKE\text{-Corr}} + \varepsilon_{NIZK\text{-Complete}}$, and $t_{CS}, t_{PKE}, t_{NIZK} \approx t + t_{\text{Corr}}$, where t_{Corr} is the time to run Π's $\mathbf{G}^{\text{Corr}}$ game.

Proof Sketch. Algorithm 1 is composed of a CS, a NIZK and a PKE scheme. The correctness error of this PKEBC protocol is essentially the sum of the errors of these underlying schemes. We prove this by game hoping: we replace each scheme with a perfect version of itself, until the final game has correctness error 0. The advantage in distinguishing between the first and the last game is then the sum of advantages in distinguishing between the underlying schemes and the corresponding perfect versions. □

Remark 3. Theorem 1 states that Π's Correctness holds against computationally bounded adversaries who do not have access to the secret keys of honest parties. However, since we use an underlying PKE with correctness against unbounded adversaries, the proof of Theorem 1 implies something stronger, namely that Π is Correct according to a stronger Correctness notion wherein adversaries are allowed to query for the secret key of any honest receiver.

Theorem 2. *If Π_{CS} is*

$$(\varepsilon_{CS\text{-Hiding}}, \varepsilon_{CS\text{-Binding}}, t_{CS}, q_{CS}, \text{Binding})\text{-secure,} \tag{4.6}$$

then no adversary $\mathbf{A}$ (ε)*-breaks* Π*'s Robustness, with* $\varepsilon > \varepsilon_{CS\text{-Binding}}$.

Proof Sketch. To violate robustness, the same ciphertext must be the encryption of two plaintexts that have different vectors of receivers. But since a commitment to this vector (along with the message) is part of the ciphertext, there must be two vectors of receivers (and messages) that produce the same commitment. And the probability of this happening is bounded by $\varepsilon_{CS\text{-Binding}}$. □

Remark 4. Note that Theorem 2 states that Π's Robustness holds against computationally unbounded adversaries; such adversaries can compute the private key of any party from its public key.

In the following we assume, without loss of generality for any practical purpose, that the NIZK proof verification algorithm is deterministic. For instance, the NIZK scheme given in [14] has deterministic proof verification and is tightly unbounded simulation sound. The reason for this assumptions is that an adversary could potentially come up with a NIZK proof for a valid statement which would only be considered as valid by the NIZK verification algorithm sometimes.

Theorem 3. *If Π_{PKE} is*

$$\begin{gathered}(\varepsilon_{PKE\text{-Corr}}, \varepsilon_{PKE\text{-IND-CPA}}, \varepsilon_{PKE\text{-IK-CPA}}, \\ t_{PKE}, n_{PKE}, q_{E\,PKE}, q_{D\,PKE}, \text{Corr})\text{-secure,}\end{gathered} \tag{4.7}$$

Π_{NIZK} *is*

$$\begin{gathered}(\varepsilon_{NIZK\text{-Complete}}, \varepsilon_{NIZK\text{-Sound}}, \varepsilon_{NIZK\text{-ZK}}, \varepsilon_{NIZK\text{-SS}}, \\ t_{NIZK}, q_{P\,NIZK}, q_{V\,NIZK})\text{-secure,}\end{gathered} \tag{4.8}$$

Π_{CS} *is*

$$(\varepsilon_{CS\text{-Hiding}}, \varepsilon_{CS\text{-Binding}}, t_{CS}, q_{CS}, \text{Binding})\text{-secure,} \tag{4.9}$$

and $\Pi_{NIZK}.V$ is a deterministic algorithm, then no adversary $\mathbf{A}$ (ε, t)*-breaks* Π*'s*

$$(n := n_{PKE}, q_D := q_{V\,NIZK})\text{-Consistency,}$$

with $\varepsilon > \varepsilon_{CS\text{-Binding}} + \varepsilon_{NIZK\text{-Sound}} + \varepsilon_{PKE\text{-Corr}}$ *and with* $t_{PKE}, t_{CS}, t_{NIZK} \approx t + t_{\text{Cons}}$, *where t_{Cons} is the time to run Π's $\mathbf{G}^{\text{Cons}}$ game.*

Proof Sketch. As in the proof of Theorem 1, we proceed by game hoping and replace the CS and NIZK by ideal versions. We then show that if the underlying PKE has perfect correctness, consistency cannot be violated. Hence the final error is that of the CS, the soundness of the NIZK and the correctness of the PKE. □

Remark 5. Theorem 3 states that Π's Consistency holds against computationally bounded adversaries who do not have access to the secret keys of honest parties. However, similarly to Remark 3, its proof implies something stronger, namely that Π is Consistent with respect to a stronger Consistency notion which allows adversaries to query for the secret key of any honest receiver.

Theorem 4. *If Π_{PKE} is*

$$\left(\varepsilon_{PKE\text{-Corr}}, \varepsilon_{PKE\text{-IND-CPA}}, \varepsilon_{PKE\text{-IK-CPA}}, \atop t_{PKE}, n_{PKE}, q_{E\,PKE}, q_{D\,PKE}, \text{Corr}\right)\text{-}secure, \tag{4.10}$$

Π_{NIZK} is

$$\left(\varepsilon_{NIZK\text{-Complete}}, \varepsilon_{NIZK\text{-Sound}}, \varepsilon_{NIZK\text{-ZK}}, \varepsilon_{NIZK\text{-SS}}, \atop t_{NIZK}, q_{P\,NIZK}, q_{V\,NIZK}\right)\text{-}secure, \tag{4.11}$$

and Π_{CS} is

$$\left(\varepsilon_{CS\text{-Hiding}}, \varepsilon_{CS\text{-Binding}}, t_{CS}, q_{CS}, \text{Binding}\right)\text{-}secure, \tag{4.12}$$

then no adversary **A** *(ε, t)-breaks Π's*

$$(n := n_{PKE}, d_E := q_{E\,PKE},$$
$$q_E := \min\left(q_{P\,NIZK}, q_{CS}\right), q_D := q_{V\,NIZK})\text{-IK-CCA-2 } security,$$

with

$$\varepsilon > 4 \cdot \left(\varepsilon_{PKE\text{-IND-CPA}} + \varepsilon_{PKE\text{-Corr}}\right)$$
$$+ 2 \cdot \left(\varepsilon_{NIZK\text{-ZK}} + \varepsilon_{PKE\text{-IK-CPA}} + \varepsilon_{NIZK\text{-SS}}\right)$$
$$+ \varepsilon_{CS\text{-Hiding}},$$
$$t_{PKE}, t_{CS} \approx t + t_{IK\text{-CCA-2}} + q_E \cdot t_{S_{Sim}} + t_{S_{CRS}},$$
$$t_{NIZK} \approx t + t_{IK\text{-CCA-2}},$$

where $t_{IK\text{-CCA-2}}$ is the time to run Π's $\mathbf{G}_b^{IK\text{-CCA-2}}$ game experiment, $t_{S_{Sim}}$ is the runtime of S_{Sim}, and $t_{S_{CRS}}$ is the runtime of S_{CRS}.

Proof Sketch. The definition of IK-CCA-2 security bounds the ability of the adversary to distinguish between two games, one of which generates challenge ciphertexts encrypted for the vector of receivers $\vec{V}_0$ and the other for $\vec{V}_1$. The full proof is a simple generalization of the one from [28] and consists of 16 game hops that bound an adversary's advantage in distinguishing the two game systems. Here we highlight the main ideas in this proof.

The first step in the proof is replacing the NIZK proofs with simulated ones, as this allows creating valid NIZK proofs for false statements. Recall that each PKEBC ciphertext includes, for each receiver, two encryptions of the same plaintext under the two different (and independent) public keys of the receiver. This allows being able to answer the adversary's decryption queries while only knowing one of the two secret keys of the receiver, which is crucial for the reductions to the IND-CPA and IK-CPA security for the underlying PKE scheme. Another key step in the proof is relying on the Simulation Soundness of the underlying NIZK scheme to be able to change the key used for answering decryption queries. Finally, the last main technical idea in the proof is making the sequence of random coins ρ encrypted using the underlying PKE scheme independent of the random coins actually used by the underlying Commitment Scheme when reducing to its Hiding property. □

Theorem 5. *If* Π_{PKE} *is*

$$(\varepsilon_{PKE\text{-Corr}}, \varepsilon_{PKE\text{-IND-CPA}}, \varepsilon_{PKE\text{-IK-CPA}}, \tag{4.13}$$
$$t_{PKE}, n_{PKE}, q_{E\,PKE}, q_{D\,PKE}, \mathsf{Corr})\text{-}secure,$$

Π_{NIZK} *is*

$$(\varepsilon_{NIZK\text{-Complete}}, \varepsilon_{NIZK\text{-Sound}}, \varepsilon_{NIZK\text{-ZK}}, \varepsilon_{NIZK\text{-SS}}, \tag{4.14}$$
$$t_{NIZK}, q_{P\,NIZK}, q_{V\,NIZK})\text{-}secure,$$

and Π_{CS} *is*

$$(\varepsilon_{CS\text{-Hiding}}, \varepsilon_{CS\text{-Binding}}, t_{CS}, q_{CS}, \mathsf{Binding})\text{-}secure, \tag{4.15}$$

then no adversary $\mathbf{A}$ (ε, t)-*breaks* Π's

$$(n := n_{PKE}, d_E := q_{E\,PKE},$$
$$q_E := \min(q_{P\,NIZK}, q_{CS}), q_D := q_{V\,NIZK})\text{-IND-CCA-2 } security,$$

with

$$\varepsilon > 4 \cdot (\varepsilon_{PKE\text{-IND-CPA}} + \varepsilon_{PKE\text{-Corr}})$$
$$+ 2 \cdot (\varepsilon_{NIZK\text{-ZK}} + \varepsilon_{NIZK\text{-SS}})$$
$$+ \varepsilon_{CS\text{-Hiding}}$$
$$t_{PKE} \approx t + t_{\text{IND-CCA-2}} + q_E \cdot t_{S_{Sim}} + t_{S_{CRS}},$$
$$t_{NIZK}, t_{CS} \approx t + t_{\text{IND-CCA-2}},$$

where $t_{\text{IND-CCA-2}}$ *is the time to run* Π's $\mathbf{G}_b^{\text{IND-CCA-2}}$ *game,* $t_{S_{Sim}}$ *is the runtime of* S_{Sim}, *and* $t_{S_{CRS}}$ *is the runtime of* S_{CRS}.

Proof Sketch. The proof of this theorem is a simple adaptation of the proof of Theorem 4, but where one no longer makes game hopping on the IK-CPA security of the PKE scheme Π_{PKE} underlying PKEBC scheme Π's construction. □

5   Multi-Designated Receiver Signed Public Key Encryption Schemes

We now introduce the second new type of scheme we give in this paper: Multi-Designated Receiver Signed Public Key Encryption (MDRS-PKE). An MDRS-PKE scheme $\Pi = (S, G_S, G_V, E, D)$ with message space $\mathcal{M}$ is a five-tuple of PPTs, where:

- S: on input 1^k, generates public parameters pp;
- G_S: on input pp, generates a sender key-pair;
- G_V: on input pp, generates a receiver key-pair;
- E: on input $(\mathsf{pp}, \mathsf{ssk}, \vec{v}, m)$, where ssk is the secret sending key, $\vec{v}$ is a vector of public keys of the intended receivers, and m is the message, generates a ciphertext c;
- D: on input $(\mathsf{pp}, \mathsf{rsk}, c)$, where rsk is the receiver's secret key, D decrypts c using rsk, obtaining a triple sender/receiver-vector/message $(\mathsf{spk}, \vec{v}, m)$ (or $\perp$ if decryption fails) which it then outputs.

5.1   The Security of MDRS-PKE Schemes

Below we state the definitions of Correctness, Consistency, Unforgeability, IND-CCA-2 security, IK-CCA-2 security, and Off-The-Record for MDRS-PKE schemes. Before proceeding to the actual definitions, we first introduce some oracles the game systems for MDRS-PKE use. In the following, consider an MDRS-PKE scheme $\Pi = (S, G_S, G_V, E, D)$ with message space $\mathcal{M}$. The oracles below are defined for a game-system with (an implicitly defined) security parameter k:

Public Parameter Generation Oracle: $\mathcal{O}_{PP}$
    1. On the first call, compute $\mathsf{pp} \leftarrow S(1^k)$; output pp;
    2. On subsequent calls, simply output pp.
Sender Key-Pair Oracle: $\mathcal{O}_{SK}(A_i)$
    1. On the first call on input A_i, compute and store $(\mathsf{spk}_i, \mathsf{ssk}_i) \leftarrow G_S(\mathsf{pp})$; output $(\mathsf{spk}_i, \mathsf{ssk}_i)$;
    2. On subsequent calls, simply output $(\mathsf{spk}_i, \mathsf{ssk}_i)$.
Receiver Key-Pair Oracle: $\mathcal{O}_{RK}(B_j)$
    1. Analogous to the Sender Key-Pair Oracle.
Sender Public-Key Oracle: $\mathcal{O}_{SPK}(A_i)$
    1. $(\mathsf{spk}_i, \mathsf{ssk}_i) \leftarrow \mathcal{O}_{SK}(A_i)$; output spk_i.
Receiver Public-Key Oracle: $\mathcal{O}_{RPK}(B_j)$
    1. Analogous to the Sender Public-Key Oracle.
Encryption Oracle: $\mathcal{O}_E(A_i, \vec{V}, m)$
    1. $(\mathsf{spk}_i, \mathsf{ssk}_i) \leftarrow \mathcal{O}_{SK}(A_i)$;
    2. $\vec{v} \leftarrow (\mathcal{O}_{RPK}(V_1), \ldots, \mathcal{O}_{RPK}(V_{|\vec{V}|}))$;
    3. Output $c \leftarrow E_{\mathsf{pp}}(\mathsf{ssk}_i, \vec{v}, m)$.
Decryption Oracle: $\mathcal{O}_D(B_j, c)$
    1. $(\mathsf{vpk}_j, \mathsf{vsk}_j) \leftarrow \mathcal{O}_{RK}(B_j)$;

2. Output $(\mathrm{spk}, \vec{v} := (\mathrm{rpk}_1, \ldots, \mathrm{rpk}_{|\vec{v}|}), m) \leftarrow D_{\mathrm{pp}}(\mathrm{vsk}_j, c)$.

We now introduce the game-based notions. Let $\Pi = (S, G_S, G_V, E, D)$ be an MDRS-PKE.

Definition 6 (Correctness). *Consider the following game played between an adversary* **A** *and game system* $\mathbf{G}^{\mathsf{Corr}}$:

- $\mathbf{A}^{\mathcal{O}_{PP}, \mathcal{O}_{SPK}, \mathcal{O}_{SK}, \mathcal{O}_{RPK}, \mathcal{O}_{RK}, \mathcal{O}_E, \mathcal{O}_D}$

A *wins the game if there are two queries* q_E *and* q_D *to* $\mathcal{O}_E$ *and* $\mathcal{O}_D$, *respectively, where* q_E *has input* $(A_i, \vec{V}, m)$ *and* q_D *has input* (B_j, c), *satisfying* $B_j \in \vec{V}$, *the input* c *in* q_D *is the output of* q_E, *the output of* q_D *is* $(\mathrm{spk}_i', \vec{v}', m')$ *with* $(\mathrm{spk}_i', \vec{v}', m') = \perp$ *or* $(\mathrm{spk}_i', \vec{v}', m') \neq (\mathrm{spk}_i, \vec{v}, m)$ —*where* spk_i *is* A_i's *public key and* $\vec{v}$ *is the corresponding vector of public keys of the parties of* $\vec{V}$ — *and* **A** *did not query* $\mathcal{O}_{SK}$ *on* A_i *nor* $\mathcal{O}_{RK}$ *on* B_j.

The advantage of **A** *in winning the Correctness game, denoted* $\mathrm{Adv}^{\mathsf{Corr}}(\mathbf{A})$, *is the probability that* **A** *wins game* $\mathbf{G}^{\mathsf{Corr}}$ *as described above.*

As already noted in Remark 1, Correctness is a property only relevant to honest parties. As these parties are not corrupted, their keys do not leak to the adversary. Definition 6 hence disallows adversaries from querying for the secret keys of honest parties. Note that the analogous Correctness notion for MDVS schemes introduced in [24]—which also does not allow adversaries to query for the secret keys of honest parties—is known to imply the composable security of MDVS schemes (see [24]). As noted in Remark 9, the MDRS-PKE construction we give actually satisfies a stronger Correctness notion analogous to the one mentioned in Remark 1, as long as both of the underlying (PKEBC and MDVS) schemes satisfy analogous Correctness notions.

The following notion captures Consistency for MDRS-PKE schemes, and is analogous to the PKEBC Consistency notion.

Definition 7 (Consistency). *Consider the following game played between an adversary* **A** *and game system* $\mathbf{G}^{\mathsf{Cons}}$:

- $\mathbf{A}^{\mathcal{O}_{PP}, \mathcal{O}_{SPK}, \mathcal{O}_{SK}, \mathcal{O}_{RPK}, \mathcal{O}_{RK}, \mathcal{O}_E, \mathcal{O}_D}$

A *wins the game if there is a ciphertext* c *such that* $\mathcal{O}_D$ *is queried on inputs* (B_i, c) *and* (B_j, c) *for some* B_i *and* B_j *(possibly with* $B_i = B_j$), *there is no prior query on either* B_i *or* B_j *to* $\mathcal{O}_{RK}$, *query* $\mathcal{O}_D(B_i, c)$ *outputs some* $(\mathrm{spk}_l, \vec{v}, m)$ *satisfying* $(\mathrm{spk}_l, \vec{v}, m) \neq \perp$, spk_l *is some party* A_l's *public sender key (i.e.* $\mathcal{O}_{SPK}(A_l) = \mathrm{spk}_l$) *and* $\mathrm{rpk}_j \in \vec{v}$ *(where* rpk_j *is* B_j's *public key), and query* $\mathcal{O}_D(B_j, c)$ *does not output the same triple* $(\mathrm{spk}_l, \vec{v}, m)$.

The advantage of **A** *in winning the Consistency game is denoted* $\mathrm{Adv}^{\mathsf{Cons}}(\mathbf{A})$ *and corresponds to the probability that* **A** *wins game* $\mathbf{G}^{\mathsf{Cons}}$ *as described above.*

The following security notion is analogous to the EUF-CMA security notion for Digital Signature Schemes. For the case of a single receiver, it informally states that if a sender A is honest, then no dishonest party can forge a ciphertext that fools an honest receiver into believing A sent it some message that A actually did not send.

Definition 8 (Unforgeability). *Consider the following game played between adversary* **A** *and game system* $\mathbf{G}^{\mathsf{Unforg}}$:

$$- \mathbf{A}^{\mathcal{O}_{PP},\mathcal{O}_{SPK},\mathcal{O}_{SK},\mathcal{O}_{RPK},\mathcal{O}_{RK},\mathcal{O}_E,\mathcal{O}_D}$$

We say that **A** *wins the game if there is a query q to $\mathcal{O}_D$ on an input (B_j, c) that outputs $(\mathrm{spk}_i, \vec{v}, m) \neq \perp$ with spk_i being some party A_i's sender public key (i.e. $\mathcal{O}_{SPK}(A_i) = \mathrm{spk}_i$), there was no query $\mathcal{O}_E(A_i, \vec{V}, m)$ where $\vec{V}$ is the vector of parties with corresponding public keys $\vec{v}$, $\mathcal{O}_{SK}$ was not queried on input A_i, and $\mathcal{O}_{RK}$ was not queried on input B_j.*

The advantage of **A** *in winning the Unforgeability game is the probability that* **A** *wins game $\mathbf{G}^{\mathsf{Unforg}}$ as described above, and is denoted $Adv^{\mathsf{Unforg}}(\mathbf{A})$.*

We say that an adversary **A** (ε, t)-breaks the $(n_S, n_R, d_E, q_E, q_D)$-Correctness, Consistency, or Unforgeability of Π if **A** runs in time at most t, queries $\mathcal{O}_{SPK}$, $\mathcal{O}_{SK}$, $\mathcal{O}_E$ and $\mathcal{O}_D$ on at most n_S different senders, queries $\mathcal{O}_{RPK}$, $\mathcal{O}_{RK}$, $\mathcal{O}_E$ and $\mathcal{O}_D$ on at most n_R different receivers, makes at most q_E and q_D queries to $\mathcal{O}_E$ and $\mathcal{O}_D$, respectively, with the sum of lengths of the party vectors input to $\mathcal{O}_E$ being at most d_E, and **A**'s advantage in winning the (corresponding) security game is at least ε.

The following security notions are the MDRS-PKE variants of Definitions 4 and 5. The games defined by these notions provide adversaries with access to the oracles $\mathcal{O}_{PP}$, $\mathcal{O}_{SPK}$, $\mathcal{O}_{SK}$ and $\mathcal{O}_{RPK}$ defined above as well as to oracles $\mathcal{O}_E$ and $\mathcal{O}_D$. For both notions, $\mathcal{O}_D$ is defined as follows:

Decryption Oracle: $\mathcal{O}_D(B_j, c)$
1. If c was the output of some query to $\mathcal{O}_E$, output test;
2. Otherwise, compute $(\mathrm{spk}_i, \vec{v}, m) \leftarrow D_{\mathrm{pp},\mathrm{sk}_j}(c)$, where sk_j is B_j's secret key; output $(\mathrm{spk}_i, \vec{v}, m)$.

The $\mathcal{O}_E$ oracle provided by the IND-CCA-2 games differs from the one provided by the IK-CCA-2 games; for IND-CCA-2, $\mathcal{O}_E$ is as follows:

Encryption Oracle: $\mathcal{O}_E(A_i, \vec{V}, m_0, m_1)$
1. For game system $\mathbf{G}_b^{\mathsf{IND\text{-}CCA\text{-}2}}$, encrypt m_b under ssk_i (A_i's sender secret key) and $\vec{v}$ ($\vec{V}$'s corresponding vector of receiver public keys); output c.

Definition 9 (IND-CCA-2 Security). *Consider the following game played between an adversary* **A** *and a game system $\mathbf{G}_b^{\mathsf{IND\text{-}CCA\text{-}2}}$, with $\mathbf{b} \in \{0,1\}$:*

$$- b' \leftarrow \mathbf{A}^{\mathcal{O}_{PP},\mathcal{O}_{SPK},\mathcal{O}_{SK},\mathcal{O}_{RPK},\mathcal{O}_E,\mathcal{O}_D}$$

A *wins the game if $b' = \mathbf{b}$ and for every query $\mathcal{O}_E(A_i, \vec{V}, m_0, m_1)$:*

- $|m_0| = |m_1|$; *and*
- *there is no query on A_i to $\mathcal{O}_{SK}$.*

We define the advantage of **A** *in winning the IND-CCA-2 game as*

$$Adv^{\mathsf{IND\text{-}CCA\text{-}2}}(\mathbf{A}) := \left| \Pr[\mathbf{AG}_0^{\mathsf{IND\text{-}CCA\text{-}2}} = \mathtt{win}] + \Pr[\mathbf{AG}_1^{\mathsf{IND\text{-}CCA\text{-}2}} = \mathtt{win}] - 1 \right|.$$

For the IK-CCA-2 security notion, $\mathcal{O}_E$ behaves as follows:

Encryption Oracle: $\mathcal{O}_E((A_{i,0}, \vec{V}_0), (A_{i,1}, \vec{V}_1), m)$
    1. For game system $\mathbf{G}_\mathbf{b}^{\mathsf{IK\text{-}CCA\text{-}2}}$, encrypt m under $\mathsf{ssk}_{i,\mathbf{b}}$ ($A_{i,\mathbf{b}}$'s secret key) and $\vec{v}_\mathbf{b}$ (the vector of public keys corresponding to $\vec{V}_\mathbf{b}$), creating a fresh ciphertext c; output c.

Definition 10 (IK-CCA-2 Security). *Consider the following game played between an adversary* $\mathbf{A}$ *and a game system* $\mathbf{G}_\mathbf{b}^{\mathsf{IK\text{-}CCA\text{-}2}}$, *with* $\mathbf{b} \in \{0,1\}$:

- $b' \leftarrow \mathbf{A}^{\mathcal{O}_{PP}, \mathcal{O}_{SPK}, \mathcal{O}_{SK}, \mathcal{O}_{RPK}, \mathcal{O}_E, \mathcal{O}_D}$

$\mathbf{A}$ *wins the game if* $b' = \mathbf{b}$ *and for every query* $((A_{i,0}, \vec{V}_0), (A_{i,1}, \vec{V}_1), m)$ *to* $\mathcal{O}_E$:

- $|\vec{V}_0| = |\vec{V}_1|$; *and*
- $\mathcal{O}_{SK}$ *is not queried on neither* $A_{i,0}$ *and* $A_{i,1}$.

We define the advantage of $\mathbf{A}$ *in winning the* IK-CCA-2 *security game as*

$$Adv^{\mathsf{IK\text{-}CCA\text{-}2}}(\mathbf{A}) := \left| \Pr[\mathbf{AG}_0^{\mathsf{IK\text{-}CCA\text{-}2}} = \mathtt{win}] + \Pr[\mathbf{AG}_1^{\mathsf{IK\text{-}CCA\text{-}2}} = \mathtt{win}] - 1 \right|.$$

We say that an adversary $\mathbf{A}$ (ε, t)-breaks the (n_R, d_E, q_E, q_D)-IND-CCA-2 security or IK-CCA-2 security of Π if $\mathbf{A}$ runs in time at most t, queries $\mathcal{O}_{RPK}$, $\mathcal{O}_E$ and $\mathcal{O}_D$ on at most n_R different receivers, makes at most q_E and q_D queries to $\mathcal{O}_E$ and $\mathcal{O}_D$, respectively, with the sum of lengths of the party vectors input to $\mathcal{O}_E$ being at most d_E, and has at least ε advantage in winning the corresponding security game.

Remark 6. The IND-CCA-2 and IK-CCA-2 security notions for MDRS-PKE schemes capture, respectively, confidentiality and anonymity. Even though one could define stronger variants of these notions wherein the adversary is allowed to query for the secret key of any sender, we chose these definitions because they are weaker, but yet strong enough to imply composable security (see [3,4,15] for the analogous case of the Outsider Security Model for Signcryption). Nonetheless, our MDRS-PKE construction satisfies the stronger IND-CCA-2 and IK-CCA-2 security notions in which the adversary is allowed to query for the secret key of every sender.

The following notion captures the *Off-The-Record* property of MDRS-PKE schemes, and resembles the (Any-Subset) Off-The-Record security notion introduced in [12] for MDVS schemes. This notion defines two game systems, $\mathbf{G}_0^{\mathsf{OTR\text{-}}Forge}$ and $\mathbf{G}_1^{\mathsf{OTR\text{-}}Forge}$, which are parameterized by an algorithm *Forge*. The game systems also provide adversaries with access to an oracle $\mathcal{O}_E$, whose behavior varies depending on the underlying game system, i.e. depending on $\mathbf{b} \in \{0,1\}$. $\mathcal{O}_E$ behaves as follows:

Encryption Oracle: $\mathcal{O}_E(\mathtt{type} \in \{\mathtt{sign}, \mathtt{forge}\}, A_i, \vec{V}, m, \mathcal{D})$
    For game system $\mathbf{G}_\mathbf{b}^{\mathsf{OTR\text{-}}Forge}$, the oracle behaves as follows:

1. $c_0 \leftarrow E_{pp}(\text{ssk}_i, \vec{v}, m)$;
2. $c_1 \leftarrow Forge_{pp}(\text{spk}_i, \vec{v}, m, \{\text{rsk}_j\}_{B_j \in \mathcal{D}})$;
3. If $\mathbf{b} = 0$, output c_0 if type = sign and c_1 if type = forge;
4. Otherwise, if $\mathbf{b} = 1$, output c_1.

Definition 11. (Off-The-Record). *Let Forge be a PPT algorithm that on input* pp, spk_{i*}, $\vec{v}$, m^* *and* $\{\text{rsk}_j\}_{B_j \in \mathcal{D}*}$, *outputs a forged ciphertext* c'. *For* $\mathbf{b} \in \{0, 1\}$, *consider the following game played between an adversary* $\mathbf{A}$ *and game system* $\mathbf{G}_{\mathbf{b}}^{\text{OTR-}Forge}$:

$-\; b' \leftarrow \mathbf{A}^{\mathcal{O}_{PP}, \mathcal{O}_{SPK}, \mathcal{O}_{SK}, \mathcal{O}_{RPK}, \mathcal{O}_{RK}, \mathcal{O}_E, \mathcal{O}_D}$

$\mathbf{A}$ *wins the game if* $b' = \mathbf{b}$ *and for every query* (type, $A_i, \vec{V}, m, \mathcal{D}$) *to* $\mathcal{O}_E$, *and letting* c *be the output of* $\mathcal{O}_E$, *all of the following hold:*

1. $\mathcal{D} \subseteq Set(\vec{V})$;
2. *for every query* B_j *to* $\mathcal{O}_{VK}$, $B_j \notin Set(\vec{V}) \setminus \mathcal{D}$;
3. *for every query* A_l *to* $\mathcal{O}_{SK}$, $A_l \neq A_i$; *and*
4. *for all queries* $\mathcal{O}_D(A_l, B_j, \vec{V}', m', c')$ *with* $A_l = A_i$ *and* $\vec{V}' = \vec{V}$, $c' \neq c$.

$\mathbf{A}$*'s advantage in winning the Off-The-Record security game with respect to Forge is defined as*

$$Adv^{\text{OTR-}Forge}(\mathbf{A}) := \left| \Pr[\mathbf{A}\mathbf{G}_0^{\text{OTR-}Forge} = \texttt{win}] + \Pr[\mathbf{A}\mathbf{G}_1^{\text{OTR-}Forge} = \texttt{win}] - 1 \right|.$$

We say that an adversary $\mathbf{A}$ $(\varepsilon_{\text{OTR}}, t)$-breaks the $(n_S, n_R, d_E, q_E, q_D)$-Off-The-Record security of Π with respect to algorithm *Forge* if $\mathbf{A}$ runs in time at most t, queries $\mathcal{O}_{SPK}$, $\mathcal{O}_{SK}$, $\mathcal{O}_E$ and $\mathcal{O}_D$ on at most n_S different senders, queries $\mathcal{O}_{RPK}$, $\mathcal{O}_{RK}$, $\mathcal{O}_E$ and $\mathcal{O}_D$ on at most n_R different receivers, makes at most q_E and q_D queries to $\mathcal{O}_E$ and $\mathcal{O}_D$, respectively, with the sum of lengths of the party vectors input to $\mathcal{O}_E$ being at most d_E, and satisfies $Adv^{\text{OTR-}Forge}(\mathbf{A}) \geq \varepsilon_{\text{OTR}}$.

Finally, we say that Π is

$$(\varepsilon_{\text{Corr}}, \varepsilon_{\text{Cons}}, \varepsilon_{\text{Unforg}}, \varepsilon_{\text{IND-CCA-2}}, \varepsilon_{\text{IK-CCA-2}}, \varepsilon_{\text{OTR}},$$
$$t, n_S, n_R, d_E, q_E, q_D, Forge)\text{-secure},$$

if no adversary $\mathbf{A}$:

- $(\varepsilon_{\text{Corr}}, t)$-breaks the $(n_S, n_R, d_E, q_E, q_D)$-Correctness of Π;
- $(\varepsilon_{\text{Cons}}, t)$-breaks the $(n_S, n_R, d_E, q_E, q_D)$-Consistency of Π;
- $(\varepsilon_{\text{Unforg}}, t)$-breaks the $(n_S, n_R, d_E, q_E, q_D)$-Unforgeability of Π;
- $(\varepsilon_{\text{IND-CCA-2}}, t)$-breaks the (n_R, d_E, q_E, q_D)-IND-CCA-2 security of Π;
- $(\varepsilon_{\text{IK-CCA-2}}, t)$-breaks the (n_R, d_E, q_E, q_D)-IK-CCA-2 security of Π; or
- $(\varepsilon_{\text{OTR}}, t)$-breaks the $(n_S, n_R, d_E, q_E, q_D)$-Off-The-Record security of Π with respect to *Forge*.

Remark 7. As one may note, due to the Off-The-Record property of MDRS-PKE schemes (see Definition 11), any receiver B_j can generate a ciphertext that decrypts correctly under B_j's own receiver secret key using only its own secret key and the public keys of the sender and any other receivers. It is thus crucial that, when defining ciphertext Unforgeability (see Definition 8), the adversary is not allowed to query for the secret key of any receiver with respect to which it is trying forge a signature.

It is equally important that the adversary is not allowed to query for the secret keys of honest receivers in the Off-The-Record security notion (Definition 11): as honest receivers do not participate in the ciphertext forgery, due to the Unforgeability of ciphertexts (Definition 8)—which in particular guarantees that if a receiver is honest, then it only decrypts ciphertexts generated by the actual sender, assuming the sender is honest—if an adversary could query for the secret key of an honest receiver B_j, it would be able to distinguish real ciphertexts generated by the sender—which B_j would decrypt successfully using its secret key—from fake ciphertexts generated by dishonest receivers—which, by the Unforgeability of ciphertexts, B_j would not decrypt successfully.

Finally, the adversary can also not be given access to the secret key of any honest receiver B_j in the Consistency game of Definition 7, as otherwise, by the Off-The-Record guarantee (Definition 11), it would be able to use B_j's receiver secret key to forge a ciphertext c that B_j would decrypt successfully (as if it really had been sent by the actual sender), whereas any other honest (designated) receiver's decryption of c would fail.

6   A Multi-Designated Receiver Signed Public Key Encryption Scheme from Standard Assumptions

In this section we give a construction of an MDRS-PKE scheme from a PKEBC scheme and an MDVS scheme (see Algorithm 2). The construction essentially consists of using the MDVS scheme to sign both the messages and the vectors of public PKEBC keys of the receivers, and then using the PKEBC scheme to encrypt the signed message, together with its MDVS signature, the public MDVS signer key of the sender and the vector of public MDVS verifier keys of the receivers.

Remark 8. Even though our MDRS-PKE construction allows parties to locally generate their keys, to achieve the Off-The-Record guarantee it is required that dishonest receivers know their secret keys. This is only so as otherwise one could mount attacks that break the Off-The-Record guarantee. For instance, consider an honest sender Alice that sends a message m to Bob. Bob, who is dishonest wants to convince a non-designated receiver, Eve, that Alice sent m. To do that, Bob could have Eve generating the keys for Bob herself, and give him only the public key (that Bob would claim as being his public key). When Alice sends m, Eve can now learn that Alice sent m as it can use Bob's secret key. Furthermore, since no one other than Eve has Bob's secret key, Eve knows that it cannot be a fake message, implying that it must be Alice's message. Current composable

Algorithm 2. Construction of an MDRS-PKE scheme $\Pi = (S, G_S, G_V, E, D)$ from a PKEBC scheme $\Pi_{\mathrm{PKEBC}} = (G, S, E, D)$, and an MDVS scheme $\Pi_{\mathrm{MDVS}} = (Setup, G_S, G_V, Sign, Vfy)$.

$Setup(1^k)$
> $\mathrm{pp_{MDVS}} \leftarrow \Pi_{\mathrm{MDVS}}.Setup(1^k)$
> $\mathrm{pp_{PKEBC}} \leftarrow \Pi_{\mathrm{PKEBC}}.S(1^k)$
> $\mathrm{pp} := (\mathrm{pp_{MDVS}}, \mathrm{pp_{PKEBC}})$
> **return** pp

$G_S(\mathrm{pp} := (\mathrm{pp_{MDVS}}, \mathrm{pp_{PKEBC}}))$
> $(\mathrm{spk_{MDVS}}, \mathrm{ssk_{MDVS}}) \leftarrow \Pi_{\mathrm{MDVS}}.G_S(\mathrm{pp_{MDVS}})$
> $\mathrm{spk} := \mathrm{spk_{MDVS}}$
> $\mathrm{ssk} := (\mathrm{spk}, \mathrm{ssk_{MDVS}})$
> **return** $(\mathrm{spk}, \mathrm{ssk})$

$G_V(\mathrm{pp} := (\mathrm{pp_{MDVS}}, \mathrm{pp_{PKEBC}}))$
> $(\mathrm{vpk_{MDVS}}, \mathrm{vsk_{MDVS}}) \leftarrow \Pi_{\mathrm{MDVS}}.G_v(\mathrm{pp_{MDVS}})$
> $(\mathrm{pk_{PKEBC}}, \mathrm{sk_{PKEBC}}) \leftarrow \Pi_{\mathrm{PKEBC}}.G(\mathrm{pp_{PKEBC}})$
> $\mathrm{rpk} := (\mathrm{vpk_{MDVS}}, \mathrm{pk_{PKEBC}})$
> $\mathrm{rsk} := (\mathrm{rpk}, (\mathrm{vsk_{MDVS}}, \mathrm{sk_{PKEBC}}))$
> **return** $(\mathrm{rpk}, \mathrm{rsk})$

$E_{\mathrm{pp}}(\mathrm{ssk}_i, \vec{v}, m)$
> **With**
>> $\mathrm{pp} := (\mathrm{pp_{MDVS}}, \mathrm{pp_{PKEBC}})$
>> $\mathrm{ssk}_i := (\mathrm{spk}_i, \mathrm{ssk_{MDVS}}_i)$
>> $\vec{v} := (\mathrm{rpk}_1, \ldots, \mathrm{rpk}_{|\vec{v}|})$
>> **for each** $i \in \{1, \ldots, |\vec{v}|\}$
>>> $\mathrm{rpk}_i := (\mathrm{vpk_{MDVS}}_i, \mathrm{pk_{PKEBC}}_i)$
>
> $\vec{v}_{\mathrm{PKEBC}} \leftarrow (\mathrm{pk_{PKEBC}}_1, \ldots, \mathrm{pk_{PKEBC}}_{|\vec{v}|})$
> $\vec{v}_{\mathrm{MDVS}} \leftarrow (\mathrm{vpk_{MDVS}}_1, \ldots, \mathrm{vpk_{MDVS}}_{|\vec{v}|})$
> $\sigma \leftarrow \Pi_{\mathrm{MDVS}}.Sign_{\mathrm{pp_{MDVS}}}(\mathrm{ssk_{MDVS}}_i, Set(\vec{v}_{\mathrm{MDVS}}), (\vec{v}_{\mathrm{PKEBC}}, m))$
> **return** $\Pi_{\mathrm{PKEBC}}.E_{\mathrm{pp_{PKEBC}}}(\vec{v}_{\mathrm{PKEBC}}, (\mathrm{spk}_i, \vec{v}_{\mathrm{MDVS}}, m, \sigma))$

$D_{\mathrm{pp}}(\mathrm{rsk}_j, c)$
> **With**
>> $\mathrm{pp} := (\mathrm{pp_{MDVS}}, \mathrm{pp_{PKEBC}})$
>> $\mathrm{rsk}_j := (\mathrm{rpk}_j, (\mathrm{vsk_{MDVS}}_j, \mathrm{sk_{PKEBC}}_j))$
>> $\mathrm{rpk}_j := (\mathrm{vpk_{MDVS}}_j, \mathrm{pk_{PKEBC}}_j)$
>
> $(\vec{v}_{\mathrm{PKEBC}}, (\mathrm{spk}_i, \vec{v}_{\mathrm{MDVS}}, m, \sigma)) \leftarrow \Pi_{\mathrm{PKEBC}}.D_{\mathrm{pp_{PKEBC}}}(\mathrm{sk_{PKEBC}}_j, c)$
> **if** $(\vec{v}_{\mathrm{PKEBC}}, (\mathrm{spk}_i, \vec{v}_{\mathrm{MDVS}}, m, \sigma)) = \bot \ \lor \ |\vec{v}_{\mathrm{PKEBC}}| \neq |\vec{v}_{\mathrm{MDVS}}|$ **then**
>> **return** $\bot$
>
> $\vec{v} := ((v_{\mathrm{MDVS}1}, v_{\mathrm{PKEBC}1}), \ldots, (v_{\mathrm{MDVS}|\vec{v}_{\mathrm{PKEBC}}|}, v_{\mathrm{PKEBC}|\vec{v}_{\mathrm{PKEBC}}|}))$
> **if** $\mathrm{rpk}_j \notin \vec{v}$ **then**
>> **return** $\bot$
>
> **if** $\Pi_{\mathrm{MDVS}}.Vfy_{\mathrm{pp_{MDVS}}}(\mathrm{spk}_i, \mathrm{vsk_{MDVS}}_j, Set(\vec{v}_{\mathrm{MDVS}}), (\vec{v}_{\mathrm{PKEBC}}, m), \sigma) \neq \mathtt{valid}$ **then**
>> **return** $\bot$
>
> **return** $(\mathrm{spk}_i, \vec{v}, m)$

---

notions capturing the security of MDVS schemes solve this problem by assuming a trusted third party which generates all key-pairs and gives everyone access to their own key-pair [24][7]. This in particular implies that Bob would have access

---

[7] The composable notions capturing the security of MDVS given in [24] actually assume something even stronger: every dishonest party has access to the secret keys of every other dishonest party.

to its own secret key, and so even if Eve would know Bob's secret key, she would not be able to tell if Alice was the one sending messages or if Bob was faking Alice's messages.

6.1 Security Analysis of the MDRS-PKE Construction

The security of our MDRS-PKE scheme follows from the security of the underlying PKEBC and MDVS schemes. For a full proof of these results, refer to [25].

Theorem 6. *If* Π_{PKEBC} *is*

$$(\varepsilon_{PKEBC\text{-}Corr}, \varepsilon_{PKEBC\text{-}Rob}, \varepsilon_{PKEBC\text{-}Cons}, \varepsilon_{PKEBC\text{-}IND\text{-}CCA\text{-}2}, \varepsilon_{PKEBC\text{-}IK\text{-}CCA\text{-}2},$$
$$t_{PKEBC}, n_{PKEBC}, d_{E\,PKEBC}, q_{E\,PKEBC}, q_{D\,PKEBC})\text{-}secure, \tag{6.1}$$

and Π_{MDVS} *is*

$$(\varepsilon_{MDVS\text{-}Corr}, \varepsilon_{MDVS\text{-}Cons}, \varepsilon_{MDVS\text{-}Unforg}, \varepsilon_{MDVS\text{-}OTR}, \varepsilon_{MDVS\text{-}PI},$$
$$t_{MDVS}, n_{S\,MDVS}, n_{V\,MDVS}, d_{S\,MDVS}, \tag{6.2}$$
$$q_{S\,MDVS}, q_{V\,MDVS}, Forge_{MDVS})\text{-}secure,$$

then no adversary $\mathbf{A}$ (ε, t)*-breaks* Π*'s*

$$(n_S := n_{S\,MDVS},$$
$$n_R := \min(n_{PKEBC}, n_{V\,MDVS}),$$
$$d_E := \min(d_{E\,PKEBC}, d_{S\,MDVS}),$$
$$q_E := \min(q_{E\,PKEBC}, q_{S\,MDVS}),$$
$$q_D := \min(q_{D\,PKEBC}, q_{V\,MDVS}))\text{-}Correctness,$$

with $\varepsilon > \varepsilon_{PKEBC\text{-}Corr} + \varepsilon_{MDVS\text{-}Corr}$, *and* $t_{PKEBC}, t_{MDVS} \approx t + t_{Corr}$, *where* t_{Corr} *is the time to run* Π*'s* $\mathbf{G}^{Corr}$ *game.*

Proof Sketch. To prove this theorem one introduces an intermediate game that assumes the correctness of the Π_{PKEBC} scheme underlying Π's construction. Then, one shows that the advantage of any adversary in winning this intermediate game can only differ from the advantage in winning the original game by at most the advantage that an adversary could have in winning the Correctness game of Π_{PKEBC}. Finally, one shows that the advantage in winning the new game is bound by the advantage in winning the Correctness game of the MDVS scheme Π_{MDVS} underlying Π's construction. $\qquad\square$

Remark 9. Similarly to Remark 3, if Π_{PKEBC}'s correctness holds even when the adversary is allowed to query for the secret key of any receiver, and Π_{MDVS}'s correctness holds even when the adversary is allowed to query for the secret keys of any signer or verifier, then Π's Correctness holds even when the adversary is allowed to query for the secret keys of any sender and receiver.

Theorem 7. *If Π_{PKEBC} is*

$$\left(\varepsilon_{PKEBC\text{-}Corr}, \varepsilon_{PKEBC\text{-}Rob}, \varepsilon_{PKEBC\text{-}Cons}, \varepsilon_{PKEBC\text{-}IND\text{-}CCA\text{-}2}, \varepsilon_{PKEBC\text{-}IK\text{-}CCA\text{-}2},\right.$$
$$\left. t_{PKEBC}, n_{PKEBC}, d_{E\,PKEBC}, q_{E\,PKEBC}, q_{D\,PKEBC}\right)\text{-}secure,$$

$$(6.3)$$

and Π_{MDVS} is

$$\left(\varepsilon_{MDVS\text{-}Corr}, \varepsilon_{MDVS\text{-}Cons}, \varepsilon_{MDVS\text{-}Unforg}, \varepsilon_{MDVS\text{-}OTR}, \varepsilon_{MDVS\text{-}PI},\right.$$
$$t_{MDVS}, n_{S\,MDVS}, n_{V\,MDVS}, d_{S\,MDVS},$$
$$\left. q_{S\,MDVS}, q_{V\,MDVS}, Forge_{MDVS}\right)\text{-}secure,$$

$$(6.4)$$

then no adversary **A** *(ε, t)-breaks Π's*

$$(n_S := n_{S\,MDVS}, n_R := \min\left(n_{PKEBC}, n_{V\,MDVS}\right), d_E := d_{S\,MDVS},$$
$$q_E := q_{S\,MDVS}, q_D := \min\left(q_{D\,PKEBC}, q_{V\,MDVS}\right))\text{-}Consistency,$$

with $\varepsilon > \varepsilon_{PKEBC\text{-}Cons} + \varepsilon_{MDVS\text{-}Cons}$, and $t_{PKEBC}, t_{MDVS} \approx t + t_{\mathsf{Cons}}$, where t_{Cons} is the time to run Π's $\mathbf{G}^{\mathsf{Cons}}$ game.

Proof Sketch. To win the Consistency game, an adversary has to make two queries $\mathcal{O}_D(B_i, c)$ and $\mathcal{O}_D(B_j, c)$ such that $\mathcal{O}_D(B_i, c)$ outputs some $(\mathsf{spk}_l, \vec{v}, m) \neq \perp$—where spk_l is some party A_l's public sender key and B_j's public key is in $\vec{v}$, query $\mathcal{O}_D(B_j, c)$ does not output the same as $\mathcal{O}_D(B_i, c)$, and there is no query to $\mathcal{O}_{RK}$ on B_i or B_j. Note that this is the only possible way to win the Consistency game. With this, one then shows that an adversary winning the Consistency implies that it either broke the consistency of the PKEBC scheme Π_{PKEBC} underlying Π's construction, or that it broke the consistency of the MDVS scheme Π_{MDVS} underlying Π's construction. $\square$

Theorem 8. *If Π_{MDVS} is*

$$\left(\varepsilon_{MDVS\text{-}Corr}, \varepsilon_{MDVS\text{-}Cons}, \varepsilon_{MDVS\text{-}Unforg}, \varepsilon_{MDVS\text{-}OTR}, \varepsilon_{MDVS\text{-}PI},\right.$$
$$t_{MDVS}, n_{S\,MDVS}, n_{V\,MDVS}, d_{S\,MDVS},$$
$$\left. q_{S\,MDVS}, q_{V\,MDVS}, Forge_{MDVS}\right)\text{-}secure,$$

$$(6.5)$$

then no adversary **A** *(ε, t)-breaks Π's*

$$(n_S := n_{S\,MDVS}, n_R := n_{V\,MDVS}, d_E := d_{S\,MDVS},$$
$$q_E := q_{S\,MDVS}, q_D := q_{V\,MDVS})\text{-}Unforgeability,$$

with $\varepsilon > \varepsilon_{MDVS\text{-}Unforg}$, and $t_{MDVS} \approx t + t_{\mathsf{Unforg}}$, where t_{Unforg} is the time to run Π's $\mathbf{G}^{\mathsf{Unforg}}$ game.

Proof Sketch. Any adversary for Π's Unforgeability game can be easily reduced into an adversary for the Unforgeability game of the MDVS scheme Π_{MDVS} underlying Π's construction that has the same advantage in winning Π_{MDVS}'s Unforgeability game. $\square$

Theorem 9. *If Π_{PKEBC} is*

$$(\varepsilon_{PKEBC\text{-Corr}}, \varepsilon_{PKEBC\text{-Rob}}, \varepsilon_{PKEBC\text{-Cons}}, \varepsilon_{PKEBC\text{-IND-CCA-2}}, \varepsilon_{PKEBC\text{-IK-CCA-2}},$$

$$t_{PKEBC}, n_{PKEBC}, d_{E\,PKEBC}, q_{E\,PKEBC}, q_{D\,PKEBC})\text{-}secure,$$

$$(6.6)$$

then no adversary $\mathbf{A}$ (ε, t)-*breaks* Π's

$$(n_R := n_{PKEBC}, d_E := d_{E\,PKEBC},$$

$$q_E := q_{E\,PKEBC}, q_D := q_{D\,PKEBC})\text{-IND-CCA-2} \ security,$$

with $\varepsilon > \varepsilon_{PKEBC\text{-IND-CCA-2}}$, *and* $t_{PKEBC} \approx t + t_{\text{IND-CCA-2}}$, *where* $t_{\text{IND-CCA-2}}$ *is the time to run* Π's $\mathbf{G}^{\text{IND-CCA-2}}$ *games.*

Proof Sketch. Distinguishing Π's (MDRS-PKE) IND-CCA-2 security games can be trivially reduced to distinguishing Π_{PKEBC}'s (PKEBC) IND-CCA-2 security games with the same advantage. $\qquad\square$

Remark 10. Note that Definition 9 and 10 do not allow an adversary to query for the secret keys of any sender A_i that is given as input to a query to $\mathcal{O}_E$. Yet, the proofs of Theorems 9 and 10 actually show something stronger. Namely, that Π is secure according to even the stronger IND-CCA-2 and IK-CCA-2 security notions in which an adversary is allowed to query for the secret key of any sender.

Theorem 10. *If Π_{PKEBC} is*

$$(\varepsilon_{PKEBC\text{-Corr}}, \varepsilon_{PKEBC\text{-Rob}}, \varepsilon_{PKEBC\text{-Cons}}, \varepsilon_{PKEBC\text{-IND-CCA-2}}, \varepsilon_{PKEBC\text{-IK-CCA-2}},$$

$$t_{PKEBC}, n_{PKEBC}, d_{E\,PKEBC}, q_{E\,PKEBC}, q_{D\,PKEBC})\text{-}secure,$$

$$(6.7)$$

then no adversary $\mathbf{A}$ (ε, t)-*breaks* Π's

$$(n_R := n_{PKEBC}, d_E := d_{E\,PKEBC},$$

$$q_E := q_{E\,PKEBC}, q_D := q_{D\,PKEBC})\text{-IK-CCA-2} \ security,$$

with $\varepsilon > \varepsilon_{PKEBC\text{-IND-CCA-2}} + \varepsilon_{PKEBC\text{-IK-CCA-2}}$, *and* $t_{PKEBC} \approx t + t_{\text{IK-CCA-2}}$, *where* $t_{\text{IK-CCA-2}}$ *is the time to run* Π's $\mathbf{G}^{\text{IK-CCA-2}}$ *games.*

Proof Sketch. To prove this theorem we introduce an intermediate game which is just like $\mathbf{G}_0^{\text{IK-CCA-2}}$ except that the $\mathcal{O}_E$ oracle behaves slightly differently: for each query $((A_{i,0}, \vec{V}_0), (A_{i,1}, \vec{V}_1), m)$, $\mathcal{O}_E$ behaves exactly as $\mathbf{G}_0^{\text{IK-CCA-2}}$'s $\mathcal{O}_E$ oracle would behave, except that now it encrypts the PKEBC ciphertext using the vector of public PKEBC keys corresponding to $\vec{V}_1$, rather than using the vector of public keys corresponding to $\vec{V}_0$. An adversary trying to distinguishing $\mathbf{G}_0^{\text{IK-CCA-2}}$ from this intermediate game can be trivially reduced to an adversary distinguishing the two IK-CCA-2 game systems for the underlying Π_{PKEBC} with the same distinguishing advantage; an adversary distinguishing the intermediate game from $\mathbf{G}_1^{\text{IK-CCA-2}}$ can be (again trivially) reduced to an adversary distinguishing the two IND-CCA-2 game systems for the underlying Π_{PKEBC} with the same distinguishing advantage. $\qquad\square$

Algorithm 3. *Forge* algorithm for the construction given in Algorithm 2. In the following, let Π_{MDVS} and Π_{PKEBC} respectively be the MDVS and PKEBC schemes underlying the construction given in Algorithm 2, $Forge_{\text{MDVS}}$ be a signature forging algorithm for Π_{MDVS}, and $\left\{\text{rsk}_{j'}\right\}_{B_{j'} \in \mathcal{D}}$ be the set of secret receiver keys of $\mathcal{D}$, the set of dishonest parties.

$Forge_{\text{pp}}(\text{spk}_i, \vec{v}, m, \left\{\text{rsk}_{j'}\right\}_{B_{j'} \in \mathcal{D}})$

    With

        $\text{pp} := (\text{pp}_{\text{MDVS}}, \text{pp}_{\text{PKEBC}})$

        $\text{spk}_i := \text{spk}_{\text{MDVS}i}$

        for each $\text{rsk}_j \in \left\{\text{rsk}_{j'}\right\}_{B_{j'} \in \mathcal{D}}$

            $\text{rsk}_j := ((\text{vpk}_{\text{MDVS}j}, \text{pk}_{\text{PKEBC}j}), (\text{vsk}_{\text{MDVS}j}, \text{sk}_{\text{PKEBC}j}))$

        $\vec{v} := (\text{rpk}_1, \ldots, \text{rpk}_{|\vec{v}|})$

        for each $i \in \{1, \ldots, |\vec{v}|\}$

            $\text{rpk}_i = (\text{vpk}_{\text{MDVS}i}, \text{pk}_{\text{PKEBC}i})$

    $\vec{v}_{\text{PKEBC}} \leftarrow (\text{pk}_{\text{PKEBC}1}, \ldots, \text{pk}_{\text{PKEBC}|\vec{v}|})$

    $\vec{v}_{\text{MDVS}} \leftarrow (\text{vpk}_{\text{MDVS}1}, \ldots, \text{vpk}_{\text{MDVS}|\vec{v}|})$

    $\sigma_{\text{MDVS}} \leftarrow Forge_{\text{MDVS}_{\text{PP}_{\text{MDVS}}}}(\text{spk}_{\text{MDVS}i}, \text{Set}(\vec{v}_{\text{MDVS}}), (\vec{v}_{\text{PKEBC}}, m), \left\{\text{vsk}_{\text{MDVS}j'}\right\}_{B_{j'} \in \mathcal{D}})$

    return $\Pi_{\text{PKEBC}}.E_{\text{PP}_{\text{PKEBC}}}(\vec{v}_{\text{PKEBC}}, (\text{spk}_{\text{MDVS}i}, \vec{v}_{\text{MDVS}}, m, \sigma_{\text{MDVS}}))$

Theorem 11. *In the following let Forge denote Algorithm 3. If Π_{MDVS} is*

$$(\varepsilon_{MDVS\text{-}Corr}, \varepsilon_{MDVS\text{-}Cons}, \varepsilon_{MDVS\text{-}Unforg}, \varepsilon_{MDVS\text{-}OTR}, \varepsilon_{MDVS\text{-}PI},$$
$$t_{MDVS}, n_{S\,MDVS}, n_{V\,MDVS}, d_{S\,MDVS}, \qquad (6.8)$$
$$q_{S\,MDVS}, q_{V\,MDVS}, Forge_{MDVS})\text{-}secure,$$

then no adversary $\mathbf{A}$ (ε, t)*-breaks* Π*'s*

$$(n_S := n_{S\,MDVS}, n_R := n_{V\,MDVS}, d_E := d_{S\,MDVS},$$
$$q_E := q_{S\,MDVS}, q_D := q_{V\,MDVS}, Forge)\text{-}Off\text{-}The\text{-}Record security,$$

with $\varepsilon > \varepsilon_{MDVS\text{-}OTR}$, *and* $t_{MDVS} \approx t + t_{OTR}$, *where* t_{OTR} *is the time to run* Π*'s* $\mathbf{G}^{OTR}$ *games.*

Proof Sketch. Any adversary for Π's Off-The-Record games can trivially be reduced into an adversary for the Off-The-Record games of the Π_{MDVS} scheme underlying Π's construction that has the same advantage in winning the MDVS Off-The-Record games of Π_{MDVS}. $\qquad\square$

Remark 11. It is easy to see from the proof of Theorem 11 that if Π_{MDVS} satisfies a stronger Off-The-Record notion in which the adversary is allowed to query for the secret key of any sender, then Π would also satisfy the analogous stronger Off-The-Record notion for MDRS-PKE schemes in which the adversary is allowed to query for the secret key of any sender.

Acknowledgments. The authors would like to thank Dennis Hofheinz for helpful discussions and for suggesting Naor-Yung's scheme [26] together with a Simulation Sound NIZK scheme [28] and a Binding Commitment scheme as a starting point to construct the PKEBC scheme. The authors would also like to thank Christian Badertscher, Daniel Jost and Chen-Da Liu-Zhang for helpful discussions.

References

1. Abdalla, M., Bellare, M., Neven, G.: Robust encryption. In: Micciancio, D. (ed.) TCC 2010. LNCS, vol. 5978, pp. 480–497. Springer, Heidelberg (2010). https://doi.org/10.1007/978-3-642-11799-2_28

2. Alwen, J., Coretti, S., Dodis, Y., Tselekounis, Y.: Security analysis and improvements for the IETF MLS standard for group messaging. In: Micciancio, D., Ristenpart, T. (eds.) CRYPTO 2020, Part I. LNCS, vol. 12170, pp. 248–277. Springer, Cham (2020). https://doi.org/10.1007/978-3-030-56784-2_9

3. An, J.H., Dodis, Y., Rabin, T.: On the security of joint signature and encryption. In: Knudsen, L.R. (ed.) EUROCRYPT 2002. LNCS, vol. 2332, pp. 83–107. Springer, Heidelberg (2002). https://doi.org/10.1007/3-540-46035-7_6

4. Badertscher, C., Banfi, F., Maurer, U.: A constructive perspective on signcryption security. In: Catalano, D., De Prisco, R. (eds.) SCN 2018. LNCS, vol. 11035, pp. 102–120. Springer, Cham (2018). https://doi.org/10.1007/978-3-319-98113-0_6

5. Badertscher, C., Maurer, U., Portmann, C., Rito, G.: Revisiting (R)CCA security and replay protection. In: Garay, J.A. (ed.) PKC 2021, Part II. LNCS, vol. 12711, pp. 173–202. Springer, Cham (2021). https://doi.org/10.1007/978-3-030-75248-4_7

6. Barth, A., Boneh, D., Waters, B.: Privacy in encrypted content distribution using private broadcast encryption. In: Di Crescenzo, G., Rubin, A. (eds.) FC 2006. LNCS, vol. 4107, pp. 52–64. Springer, Heidelberg (2006). https://doi.org/10.1007/11889663_4

7. Bellare, M., Boldyreva, A., Desai, A., Pointcheval, D.: Key-privacy in public-key encryption. In: Boyd, C. (ed.) ASIACRYPT 2001. LNCS, vol. 2248, pp. 566–582. Springer, Heidelberg (2001). https://doi.org/10.1007/3-540-45682-1_33

8. Bellare, M., Boldyreva, A., Micali, S.: Public-key encryption in a multi-user setting: security proofs and improvements. In: Preneel, B. (ed.) EUROCRYPT 2000. LNCS, vol. 1807, pp. 259–274. Springer, Heidelberg (2000). https://doi.org/10.1007/3-540-45539-6_18

9. Boneh, D., Gentry, C., Waters, B.: Collusion resistant broadcast encryption with short ciphertexts and private keys. In: Shoup, V. (ed.) CRYPTO 2005. LNCS, vol. 3621, pp. 258–275. Springer, Heidelberg (2005). https://doi.org/10.1007/11535218_16

10. Borisov, N., Goldberg, I., Brewer, E.A.: Off-the-record communication, or, why not to use PGP. In: Atluri, V., Syverson, P.F., di Vimercati, S.D.C. (eds.) WPES 2004, pp. 77–84. ACM (2004). https://doi.org/10.1145/1029179.1029200

11. Cohn-Gordon, K., Cremers, C., Dowling, B., Garratt, L., Stebila, D.: A formal security analysis of the signal messaging protocol. J. Cryptol. **33**(4), 1914–1983 (2020). https://doi.org/10.1007/s00145-020-09360-1

12. Damgård, I., Haagh, H., Mercer, R., Nitulescu, A., Orlandi, C., Yakoubov, S.: Stronger security and constructions of multi-designated verifier signatures. In: Pass, R., Pietrzak, K. (eds.) TCC 2020, Part II. LNCS, vol. 12551, pp. 229–260. Springer, Cham (2020). https://doi.org/10.1007/978-3-030-64378-2_9

13. Fiat, A., Naor, M.: Broadcast encryption. In: Stinson, D.R. (ed.) CRYPTO 1993. LNCS, vol. 773, pp. 480–491. Springer, Heidelberg (1994). https://doi.org/10.1007/3-540-48329-2_40

14. Gay, R., Hofheinz, D., Kiltz, E., Wee, H.: Tightly CCA-secure encryption without pairings. In: Fischlin, M., Coron, J.-S. (eds.) EUROCRYPT 2016, Part I. LNCS, vol. 9665, pp. 1–27. Springer, Heidelberg (2016). https://doi.org/10.1007/978-3-662-49890-3_1

15. Gjøsteen, K., Kråkmo, L.: Universally composable signcryption. In: Lopez, J., Samarati, P., Ferrer, J.L. (eds.) EuroPKI 2007. LNCS, vol. 4582, pp. 346–353. Springer, Heidelberg (2007). https://doi.org/10.1007/978-3-540-73408-6_26

16. Jakobsson, M., Sako, K., Impagliazzo, R.: Designated verifier proofs and their applications. In: Maurer, U. (ed.) EUROCRYPT 1996. LNCS, vol. 1070, pp. 143–154. Springer, Heidelberg (1996). https://doi.org/10.1007/3-540-68339-9_13

17. Jost, D., Maurer, U., Mularczyk, M.: Efficient ratcheting: almost-optimal guarantees for secure messaging. In: Ishai, Y., Rijmen, V. (eds.) EUROCRYPT 2019, Part I. LNCS, vol. 11476, pp. 159–188. Springer, Cham (2019). https://doi.org/10.1007/978-3-030-17653-2_6

18. Kohlweiss, M., Maurer, U., Onete, C., Tackmann, B., Venturi, D.: Anonymity-preserving public-key encryption: a constructive approach. In: De Cristofaro, E., Wright, M. (eds.) PETS 2013. LNCS, vol. 7981, pp. 19–39. Springer, Heidelberg (2013). https://doi.org/10.1007/978-3-642-39077-7_2

19. Laguillaumie, F., Vergnaud, D.: Multi-designated Verifiers Signatures. In: Lopez, J., Qing, S., Okamoto, E. (eds.) ICICS 2004. LNCS, vol. 3269, pp. 495–507. Springer, Heidelberg (2004). https://doi.org/10.1007/978-3-540-30191-2_38

20. Laguillaumie, F., Vergnaud, D.: Designated verifier signatures: anonymity and efficient construction from Any bilinear map. In: Blundo, C., Cimato, S. (eds.) SCN 2004. LNCS, vol. 3352, pp. 105–119. Springer, Heidelberg (2005). https://doi.org/10.1007/978-3-540-30598-9_8

21. Li, Y., Susilo, W., Mu, Y., Pei, D.: Designated verifier signature: definition, framework and new constructions. In: Indulska, J., Ma, J., Yang, L.T., Ungerer, T., Cao, J. (eds.) UIC 2007. LNCS, vol. 4611, pp. 1191–1200. Springer, Heidelberg (2007). https://doi.org/10.1007/978-3-540-73549-6_116

22. Libert, B., Paterson, K.G., Quaglia, E.A.: Anonymous broadcast encryption: adaptive security and efficient constructions in the standard model. In: Fischlin, M., Buchmann, J., Manulis, M. (eds.) PKC 2012. LNCS, vol. 7293, pp. 206–224. Springer, Heidelberg (2012). https://doi.org/10.1007/978-3-642-30057-8_13

23. Lipmaa, H., Wang, G., Bao, F.: Designated verifier signature schemes: attacks, new security notions and a new construction. In: Caires, L., Italiano, G.F., Monteiro, L., Palamidessi, C., Yung, M. (eds.) ICALP 2005. LNCS, vol. 3580, pp. 459–471. Springer, Heidelberg (2005). https://doi.org/10.1007/11523468_38

24. Maurer, U., Portmann, C., Rito, G.: Giving an adversary guarantees (or: how to model designated verifier signatures in a composable framework). In: Tibouchi, M., Wang, H. (eds.) ASIACRYPT 2021. LNCS, vol. 13092, pp. 189–219. Springer, Cham (2021). https://doi.org/10.1007/978-3-030-92078-4_7

25. Maurer, U., Portmann, C., Rito, G.: Multi-designated receiver signed public key encryption. Cryptology ePrint Archive, Report 2022/250 (2022). https://eprint.iacr.org/2022/250

26. Naor, M., Yung, M.: Public-key cryptosystems provably secure against chosen ciphertext attacks. In: 22nd ACM STOC, pp. 427–437. ACM Press, May 1990. https://doi.org/10.1145/100216.100273

27. Rackoff, C., Simon, D.R.: Non-interactive zero-knowledge proof of knowledge and chosen ciphertext attack. In: Feigenbaum, J. (ed.) CRYPTO 1991. LNCS, vol. 576, pp. 433–444. Springer, Heidelberg (1992). https://doi.org/10.1007/3-540-46766-1_35

28. Sahai, A.: Non-malleable non-interactive zero knowledge and adaptive chosen-ciphertext security. In: 40th FOCS, pp. 543–553. IEEE Computer Society Press, October 1999. https://doi.org/10.1109/SFFCS.1999.814628

29. Steinfeld, R., Bull, L., Wang, H., Pieprzyk, J.: Universal designated-verifier signatures. In: Laih, C.-S. (ed.) ASIACRYPT 2003. LNCS, vol. 2894, pp. 523–542. Springer, Heidelberg (2003). https://doi.org/10.1007/978-3-540-40061-5_33

30. Steinfeld, R., Wang, H., Pieprzyk, J.: Efficient extension of standard schnorr/RSA signatures into universal designated-verifier signatures. In: Bao, F., Deng, R., Zhou, J. (eds.) PKC 2004. LNCS, vol. 2947, pp. 86–100. Springer, Heidelberg (2004). https://doi.org/10.1007/978-3-540-24632-9_7

31. Zhang, Y., Au, M.H., Yang, G., Susilo, W.: (Strong) multi-designated verifiers signatures secure against rogue key attack. In: Xu, L., Bertino, E., Mu, Y. (eds.) NSS 2012. LNCS, vol. 7645, pp. 334–347. Springer, Heidelberg (2012). https://doi.org/10.1007/978-3-642-34601-9_25

A Fast and Simple Partially Oblivious PRF, with Applications

Nirvan Tyagi[1]([✉]), Sofía Celi[2]([✉]), Thomas Ristenpart[1], Nick Sullivan[2], Stefano Tessaro[3], and Christopher A. Wood[2]

[1] Cornell Tech, New York, USA
tyagi@cs.cornell.edu
[2] Cloudflare, San Francisco, USA
cherenkov@riseup.net
[3] University of Washington, Seattle, USA

Abstract. We build the first construction of a partially oblivious pseudorandom function (POPRF) that does not rely on bilinear pairings. Our construction can be viewed as combining elements of the 2HashDH OPRF of Jarecki, Kiayias, and Krawczyk with the Dodis-Yampolskiy PRF. We analyze our POPRF's security in the random oracle model via reduction to a new one-more gap strong Diffie-Hellman inversion assumption. The most significant technical challenge is establishing confidence in the new assumption, which requires new proof techniques that enable us to show that its hardness is implied by the q-DL assumption in the algebraic group model.

Our new construction is as fast as the current, standards-track OPRF 2HashDH protocol, yet provides a new degree of flexibility useful in a variety of applications. We show how POPRFs can be used to prevent token hoarding attacks against Privacy Pass, reduce key management complexity in the OPAQUE password authenticated key exchange protocol, and ensure stronger security for password breach alerting services.

Keywords: Verifiable oblivious pseudorandom functions · Diffie-Hellman inversion · Anonymous tokens · Blind signatures

1 Introduction

An oblivious pseudorandom function (OPRF) [23,32] allows a client holding a private input x and a server holding a key sk for a PRF f to engage in a protocol to *obliviously* evaluate f_{sk} on x. The client learns (and optionally verifies) the evaluation $f_{sk}(x)$ while the server learns nothing. *Partially*-oblivious PRFs (POPRF), first introduced by Everspaugh et al. in the context of the Pythia password hardening system [20], extend this functionality to include a public input (or metadata tag) t for the PRF evaluation. A client learns (and, optionally, verifies) $f_{sk}(t, x)$ where t is known by both server and client; the private input x remains hidden.

OPRFs are increasingly becoming a critical cryptographic tool for privacy-preserving protocols. Examples include one-time use anonymous credentials for

© International Association for Cryptologic Research 2022
O. Dunkelman and S. Dziembowski (Eds.): EUROCRYPT 2022, LNCS 13276, pp. 674–705, 2022.
https://doi.org/10.1007/978-3-031-07085-3_23

spam prevention [18], private set intersection (PSI) for checking compromised credentials [36,42], de-identified authenticated logging [26], and password authenticated key exchange [28,30]. In all these applications, we observe that there is a need to "partition" the PRF in a productive manner, i.e., allowing computation of $f_{sk}(t, x)$ using domain separation on some public value t. OPRF blinding protocols do not support this in a secure manner, because the server cannot verify what t is used within a client's oblivious request. Most OPRF applications therefore use a separate key instance for each t, with an associated increase in key management complexity. POPRFs directly provide this functionality. While one can simply use a standard PRF with a master key to derive a key for each t (see, e.g., [29]), there is no known way to make this efficiently verifiable. The only known POPRF supporting efficient verification relies on bilinear pairings [20], which slows performance relative to the best known OPRF and also complicates deployment given the lack of widespread implementation support for pairings.

In this work, we introduce a new POPRF that combines aspects of the 2HashDH OPRF of Jarecki et al. [28], that is the de facto standard used in practice, with the Dodis-Yampolskiy (DY) verifiable random function [19]. Our POPRF is also closely related to a signature scheme suggested by Zhang, Safavi-Naini, and Susilo (ZSS) [46,47]. Our new POPRF, called 3HashSDHI, is essentially as performant as 2HashDH and does not rely on pairings, thereby enabling support for a public input virtually *for free*. While 3HashSDHI's protocol is simple, its analysis is not, requiring a new interactive discrete log (DL) assumption whose security we reduce to q-DL in the algebraic group model [24]. We also provide new formal security notions for POPRFs and (as a special case) OPRFs, which we believe will be of independent interest.

Formal Syntax and Security Notions for POPRFs. We start with the latter contribution. We provide a new formalization for POPRFs, including syntax, semantics, and security definitions. Our formal syntax builds off of [20] and previous OPRF formalizations [28,32]. In terms of security, we propose new property-based security definitions that cover pseudorandomness (in the face of malicious clients) as well as request privacy and verifiability (in the face of malicious servers). Our property-based security games avoid the ideal function based formulations inherited from 2PC and used in prior works on OPRFs; they also avoid the non-standard "one-more" PRF security definition of [20].

Our *pseudorandomness* notion for POPRFs guarantees that the evaluation outputs look random to a malicious client, even when the malicious client has access to a blinded evaluation oracle. It is formalized with a simulation-based indistinguishability game that takes rough inspiration from the UC-style all-in-one OPRF security definition of [28] and prior notions for partially blind signatures [1]. Here an adversary must distinguish between real evaluations of the PRF given access to a blind evaluation oracle, and evaluations of a random function given access to a simulated blind evaluation oracle. The simulator can receive random function evaluations on a limited number of points for any given public input t, where the limit is determined by the number of times the adversary has queried the blind evaluation oracle for that t. This restriction captures that only one random function evaluation is learned for each blind evaluation. Note that our accounting is more granular than the general "ticketing" approaches of blind UC protocols [22, 28, 33], due to the need of tying invocations to particular t values.

Our next notion is *request privacy* which captures that nothing about a client message x should leak to a malicious server during an oblivious evaluation, and, moreover, the server should not be able to associate an output $f_{sk}(t, x)$ to the particular oblivious request transcript used to produce $f_{sk}(t, x)$. The latter is often referred to as a linking attack, and is problematic in various applications of POPRFs. Our request privacy notion comes in two flavors, depending on whether the malicious server behaves passively or actively. The former allows us to analyze the privacy of schemes that do not allow verification that a server legitimately computed the blinded evaluation protocol; the latter requires schemes to allow client-side verification of the server's response.

Finally we formalize a notion of *uniqueness*. It ensures that a malicious server cannot trick clients into accepting inconsistent evaluations, relative to a shareable public key associated to the secret key sk. This is similar to the property of *verifiability*, which, informally, states that servers prove in zero-knowledge that output $f_{sk}(t, x)$ corresponds to the public key associated with sk.

The 3HashSDHI Construction. The main contribution of this work is a new construction of a POPRF, which we call 3HashSDHI. The name refers to its use of three hashes and its reliance on the strong Diffie-Hellman inversion assumption. Its starting point is the 2HashDH construction of Jarecki et al. [28], whose full PRF evaluation we define as $2\mathsf{HashDH}.\mathsf{Ev}(sk, x) = \mathsf{H}_2(x, \mathsf{H}_1(x)^{sk})$. The blinded evaluation protocol has the client send $B = \mathsf{H}_1(x)^r$ for random r, and the server respond with $B' = B^{sk}$. The client can unblind to $(B')^{1/r} = \mathsf{H}_1(x)^{sk}$ in order to complete the evaluation of the function. Here operations are over a prime-order group (written multiplicatively) such as an elliptic curve. Proof of evaluation consists of a simple Chaum-Pedersen proof of discrete log equality [15] proving $\log_g pk = \log_B B'$ where $pk = g^{sk}$ is the server's public key. As mentioned, 2HashDH is already in use in practice [18, 26, 42] and is on track to become a standard [17].

We want a way to extend 2HashDH to allow public tags. To do so, we take inspiration from the Dodis-Yampolskiy PRF, whose evaluation is defined as $\mathsf{DY}.\mathsf{Ev}(sk, t) = g^{1/(sk+t)}$. Put together, the 3HashSDHI scheme gives a PRF evaluated as:

$$\mathsf{3H}.\mathsf{Ev}(sk, t, x) = \mathsf{H}_2\left(t, x, \mathsf{H}_1(x)^{1/(sk+\mathsf{H}_3(t))}\right).$$

It can therefore be interpreted as evaluating the Dodis-Yampolskiy PRF on the public input t over a random generator determined by the private input x, followed by a final hashing step. The basic structure of $\mathsf{H}_1(x)^{1/(sk+\mathsf{H}_3(t))}$ was also described in an attempt to build secure partially blind signatures by ZSS [46]. Their analysis is incorrect, as we discuss further below and in Sect. 4.

To perform a blind evaluation, the client hashes and blinds their private input as $B = \mathsf{H}_1(x)^r$ using a random scalar r and sends B to the server holding sk. The server computes and sends back to the client the strong Diffie-Hellman inversion $B' = B^{1/(sk+\mathsf{H}_3(t))}$ of the blinded element using the secret key and public hash of the public input t. The client can unblind by computing $(B')^{1/r} = \mathsf{H}_1(x)^{1/(sk+\mathsf{H}_3(t))}$ and then complete the evaluation by hashing appropriately. To provide verifiability, the server uses a Chaum-Pedersen zero-knowledge proof (ZKP) of discrete log equality to prove $\log_g pk' = \log_{B'} B$ where $pk' = pk \cdot g^{\mathsf{H}_3(t)}$ which can be easily computed from public values by the client.

Our protocol incurs minimal overhead on top of the OPRF blind evaluation of 2HashDH, requiring only an extra hash computation, group operation, and scalar inversion. It makes use of the same Chaum-Pedersen proof for verifiability, which, as has been observed for 2HashDH, allows for evaluation of a batch of inputs whilst only constructing one Chaum-Pedersen proof [17, 18] (provided the batch is for the same public metadata tag t).

We formally show request privacy against passive adversaries (without ZKP) holds based just on the randomness of the blinding, and that request privacy against malicious adversaries holds additionally assuming the ZKP is sound. The key technical challenge is proving the new POPRF is pseudorandom.

As is seemingly requisite for schemes with blinded evaluation protocols, we prove the pseudorandomness security of our scheme with respect to a one-more gap style assumption [4, 8]. In fact the algebraic structure exposed to adversarial clients by the 3HashSDHI blinded evaluation protocol—raising an arbitrary group element Y to $1/(sk + \mathsf{H}_3(t))$ for adversarial t—requires new proof techniques compared to prior approaches. We start by introducing a new one-more gap strong Diffie-Hellman inversion (OM-Gap-SDHI) assumption, based on the perceived hardness of computing $Y^{1/(x+c)}$ for any base Y and (restricted) scalars c. We show via a relatively straightforward proof that this assumption is sufficient to prove POPRF pseudorandomness for 3HashSDHI, modeling the hash functions as random oracles. Additionally, the verifiable version requires that the ZKP is zero-knowledge.

The main difficulty is analyzing the security of our new computational assumption. In particular, for given distinct constants $c_1, \ldots, c_n$, the assumption considers a setting with an oracle SDH returning $B^{1/(x+c_i)}$ on input (B, i). Given some additional random group elements $Y_1, \ldots, Y_m$, it requires it to be hard to compute ℓ elements $Y_{i_1}^{1/(x+c_i)}, \ldots, Y_{i_\ell}^{1/(x+c_i)}$, for any $i \in [n]$ and for distinct $i_1, \ldots, i_\ell \in [m]$, using fewer than ℓ queries $\mathrm{SDH}(\cdot, i)$. The challenge is that we do *not* restrict the number of queries $\mathrm{SDH}(X, j)$ for $j \neq i$, and this could be for group elements of X that depend on c_i (e.g., X is a prior output of an $\mathrm{SDH}(\cdot, i)$ query). Ultimately, we show in the algebraic group model (AGM) [24] that the assumption reduces to one of the uber assumptions from Bauer, Fuchsbauer, and Loss [3], and therefore, in turn, is implied by the q-DL assumption, where q is a bound on the number of oracle queries. This AGM analysis implies hardness of the new assumption in the generic group model (GGM) [37, 40].

In terms of concrete security, our analysis shows that, roughly speaking, 3HashSDHI is as hard as breaking the q-DL problem. Actually our main AGM proof is loose by a factor that is the maximum number of blind evaluation queries made by an adversary. Whether this AGM analysis can be tightened is an open question, but we observe in the body that a slight alternative to our AGM analysis gives a tight reduction in the GGM. We suggest using this tighter analysis to drive parameter selection: the best known attack against q-DL is due to Cheon [16] and indicates that a 256-bit group suffices for 80-bit security and a 384-bit group for 128-bit security. Importantly this matches the situation for 2HashDH, and so moving to 3HashSDHI does not require changing group parameters to achieve the desired security levels.

Partially-Blind Signatures. Our techniques provide a new approach to building partially-blind signatures [1]. Whereas an OPRF requires access to the private key to verify a given input, a blind signature protocol only requires the public key. This property is useful for a number of applications and deployment settings. For example, in settings where multiple instances of a verifier may check the output of the OPRF, each instance would either (a) require access to the private key or (b) request verification from an entity which holds the private key. The former may be problematic if instances that verify outputs do not mutually trust one another or cannot otherwise share private key material, and the latter may be problematic because it incurs a network performance penalty. Blind signatures avoid both problems by allowing each instance to use the public key for verification.

Blind signatures are used in one-time use anonymous credentials, and are also being proposed as a tool for private click measurement (PCM) in the W3C [45]. One limitation in these use cases is that the protocols do not admit public metadata in the signature computation. PCM, for example, would benefit from binding additional context to signature computations [45].

As previously mentioned, the 3HashSDHI construction is closely related to the ZSS partially blind signature scheme [46], which uses pairings. As we explain in Sect. 4, the original unforgeability proof is however incorrect. We rectify this situation and provide the first formal analysis of the security of ZSS using our new techniques in the full version [43]. To the best of our knowledge, this result provides the most efficient partially-blind signature supporting arbitrary public metadata; previous RSA-based constructions [1,2] require the set of public metadata tags to be incorporated during parameter setup, previous Schnorr-based constructions [2,25] are vulnerable in the concurrent signing setting [7], and other existing constructions are more heavyweight as they are tailored for the anonymous credential setting [10].

Finally, we also show how any unique (partially) blind signature scheme can be used to generically construct a POPRF by hashing the signature using a random oracle. This is apparently a folklore result for OPRFs, and we are unaware of any formal treatment it. We provide one that also covers partial obliviousness/blindness. See the full version [43].

Applications of our POPRF. Equipped with our new POPRF and the underlying design of 3HashSDHI, we return to our motivating applications and show how swapping in a POPRF for the existing OPRF can lead to various benefits for deployments.

One-Time Use Anonymous Credentials. Privacy Pass [12,18] is a protocol in which clients may be issued one-time use tokens that can later be redeemed anonymously to authenticate themselves. It has been proposed for use in the context of content distribution networks and web advertising, requiring users to authenticate with a token, and thereby reducing malicious web requests, protecting against, e.g., denial-of-service attacks and fraudulent advertisement conversions. Tokens are issued to users that prove trustworthiness, e.g., through a CAPTCHA challenge. The protocol is being considered for standardization by both the IETF and the World Wide Web Consortium (W3C), and a prototype deployment is already in production use by Cloudflare, hCaptcha, and others.

An OPRF is the core component of the protocol. Tokens are issued via an OPRF in which users obtain evaluations at random points, storing the point x and evaluation y. Redeeming a token simply involves showing the pair (x, y), which the server can check is valid, but cannot link x back to an issuance due to the oblivious evaluation. The server stores a strikelist of used tokens to prevent double spending. Additionally, all servers perform a global double-spend check to avoid clients from exploiting the possibility of spending tokens more than once against distributed token checking systems. The use of an OPRF leads to a more efficient issuance protocol than alternate approaches for keyed-verification anonymous credentials that support attributes and proofs over attributes [13,14].

An abuse of the protocol that has been observed in its early use is individual users (or groups of users) gathering tokens over a long period of time and redeeming them all at once, e.g., in an attempt to overwhelm a website. We refer to such behavior as a hoarding attack. A conceptually easy way to mitigate the damage of a hoarding attack is to expire old unspent tokens after an amount of time: the way to do this with an OPRF is by rotating the OPRF key. But key rotations are complex, limiting their frequency: establishing trust in a frequently-rotating key is a challenging problem. Trustworthy keys are important in this context, as a server that equivocates on their public key can link token issuances and redemptions, by, for example, using a unique public key for each issuance. As we show, POPRFs address the issue of expiring tokens without the need of rotating keys by using the public metadata input to encode an expiration epoch.

Bucketized PSI for Checking Compromised Credentials. Password breach alerting protocols [36,42] allow a user to query to determine if their username, password pair (u, pw) has appeared in a dataset D of known breaches. If so, the user is vulnerable to credential stuffing attacks and should change their password. Current services for breach alerting rely on an ad hoc 2HashDH-based private-set membership protocol that achieves scalability via bucketization: the user sends a truncated hash $H(u)$ of their username to identify a subset $B \subseteq D$ that have matching truncated username hash. A 2HashDH-based protocol is then performed over B: the client obliviously evaluates 2HashDH.Ev$(sk, u \parallel pw)$ with sk held by server, and also obtains the OPRF outputs for all the values in the bucket B. Bucketization ensures scalability by limiting $|B|$ despite $|D|$ being on the order of billions of username, password pairs.

One issue is that currently deployed protocols provide no cryptographic binding between the bucket identifier $H(u)$ and the blinded OPRF output: a malicious client can query for arbitrary usernames, not just ones that match $H(u)$. Whether this is a significant security problem in practice is not clear, but we note that POPRFs easily rectify it by replacing 2HashDH above with 3HashSDHI and setting $t = H(u)$.

Asymmetric Password-Authenticated Key Exchange. Password authenticated key exchange (PAKE) protocols [6] allow a client and server to establish a shared session key authenticated by a short password. Strong asymmetric PAKE (SaPAKE) protocols [30] additionally ensure that the server stores what amounts to private salted hashes of user passwords. Since these salted hashes are private, an attacker cannot perform offline pre-computation that would lead to instantaneous compromise of user passwords upon the event of a server breach. The OPAQUE [30] SaPAKE protocol uses an OPRF as one of its core components; it is currently being considered for standardization by the IETF [34]. The OPRF suggested for use is 2HashDH.

In OPAQUE the server uses a separate OPRF key for each user. We show how we can instead use our 3HashSDHI POPRF to allow OPAQUE to work with a single master key pk; diversity across users can then be provided using usernames as the public input t to 3HashSDHI. We believe that this will simplify deployments and potentially improve their security, as discussed in the body.

2   Preliminaries

2.1   Algebraic Group Model

In some of our security proofs, we consider security against *algebraic* adversaries which we model using the algebraic group model, following the treatment of [24]. We call an algorithm $\mathcal{A}$ *algebraic* if for all group elements Z that are output (either as final output or as input to oracles), $\mathcal{A}$ additionally provides the representation of Z relative to all previously received group elements. The previous received group elements include both original inputs to the algorithm and outputs received from calls to oracles. More specifically, if $[X]_i$ is the list of group elements $[X_0, \ldots, X_n] \in \mathbb{G}$ that $\mathcal{A}$ has received so far, then, when producing group element Z, $\mathcal{A}$ must also provide a list $[z]_i = [z_0, \ldots, z_n]$ such that $Z = \prod_i X_i^{z_i}$.

2.2   Random Oracle Model

We will prove security using ideal primitives, modeling hash functions as random oracles. Since our schemes will make use of more than one hash function, it will be useful to have a general abstraction for the use of ideal primitives, following the treatment of [27]. An ideal primitive P specifies algorithms $\mathsf{P.Init}$ and $\mathsf{P.Eval}$. The initialization algorithm has syntax $st_{\mathsf{P}} \leftarrow_{\$} \mathsf{P.Init}(1^\lambda)$. The stateful evaluation algorithm has syntax $y \leftarrow_{\$} \mathsf{P.Eval}(x : st_{\mathsf{P}})$. We sometimes use A^{P}

as shorthand for giving algorithm A oracle access to $\mathsf{P.Eval}(\cdot : st_\mathsf{P})$. While, the stateful formulation of the ideal primitive is used to allow for efficient instantiation in our security proofs, e.g., by "lazy sampling", ideal primitives should be *essentially stateless* [27] to prevent contrived behavior. For example, a random oracle can be written to be stateless, but it would inefficient to have to store a huge random table. We can combine access to multiple ideal primitives primitives $\mathsf{P} = \mathsf{P}_1 \times \ldots \times \mathsf{P}_m$ as follows:

$$
\begin{array}{ll}
\underline{\mathsf{P.Init}(1^\lambda)} & \underline{\mathsf{P.Eval}(x : [st_{\mathsf{P},i}]_i^m)} \\
[st_{\mathsf{P},i}]_i^m \leftarrow\!\!\$\; \left[\mathsf{P}_i.\mathsf{Init}(1^\lambda)\right]_i^m & (i, x) \leftarrow x \\
\text{Return } [st_{\mathsf{P},i}]_i^m & y \leftarrow\!\!\$\; \mathsf{P}_i.\mathsf{Eval}(x : st_{\mathsf{P},i}) \\
& \text{Return } y
\end{array}
$$

To concretize the above, we focus on random oracles. We define a random oracle that takes arbitrary input and produces random output from a sampling algorithm Samp. It is captured by the ideal primitive $\mathsf{RO[Samp]} = (\mathsf{RO.Init}, \mathsf{RO.H})$ defined as follows. When the range is clear from context, Samp may be omitted.

$$
\begin{array}{ll}
\underline{\mathsf{RO.Init}(1^\lambda)} & \underline{\mathsf{RO.Eval}(x : T)} \\
T \leftarrow [\cdot] & \text{If } x \notin T \text{ then } T[x] \leftarrow\!\!\$\; \mathsf{Samp}() \\
\text{Return } T & \text{Return } T[x]
\end{array}
$$

When clear from context and in an abuse of notation (since we will use H_i to denote a hash function as well), we will write $\mathsf{P} = \mathsf{H}_1 \times \cdots \times \mathsf{H}_m$ as the ideal primitive that gives access to m random oracles, accessible by querying directly an oracle labeled H_i.

Algebraic Algorithms in the Random Oracle Model. As in [25], to support algebraic algorithms, we will require the structure of the domain and range to be specified for any random oracle RO. We assume an input can be efficiently checked to be a valid member of the domain and perform such checks implicitly returning $\bot$ if they fail. We will require that algebraic algorithms provide representations for any group element input, specified as part of the domain of RO. And similarly, any group element output of RO is included in the list of received group elements for the algebraic adversary.

2.3 Non-interactive Zero Knowledge Proofs

We define a non-interactive proof system NiZK over an efficiently computable relation $\mathcal{R}$ defined over pairs (x, w) where x is called the *statement* and w is called the *witness*. It is made up of the following algorithms. The setup algorithm produces the public parameters for execution, $pp \leftarrow\!\!\$\; \mathsf{NiZK.Setup}(\lambda)$. The proving algorithm takes a witness and statement and produces a proof, $\pi \leftarrow\!\!\$\; \mathsf{NiZK.Prove}_{pp}^\mathsf{P}(w, x)$[1]. The verification algorithm verifies the proof for a statement, $b \leftarrow \mathsf{NiZK.Ver}_{pp}^\mathsf{P}(x, \pi)$. We define the following security properties.

Completeness. A proof system is *complete* if given a true statement, a prover with a witness can convince the verifier. We will make use of a proof system

---

[1] P is an arbitrary ideal primitive.

Game $\text{SOUND}^{\mathcal{A}}_{\text{NiZK},\mathcal{R},\text{P}}(\lambda)$	Game $\text{ZK}^{\mathcal{A},b}_{\text{NiZK},\mathcal{R},\text{S},\text{P}}(\lambda)$	Oracle $\text{PROVE}(x,w)$	Oracle $\text{PRIM}(x)$
$pp \leftarrow\!\!\text{\$}\ \text{NiZK.Setup}(\lambda)$	$pp_1 \leftarrow\!\!\text{\$}\ \text{NiZK.Setup}(\lambda)$	Require $(x,w) \in \mathcal{R}$	$y_1 \leftarrow\!\!\text{\$}\ \text{P.Eval}(x : st_\text{P})$
$st_\text{P} \leftarrow\!\!\text{\$}\ \text{P.Init}(\lambda)$	$st_\text{P} \leftarrow\!\!\text{\$}\ \text{P.Init}(\lambda)$	$\pi_1 \leftarrow\!\!\text{\$}\ \text{NiZK.Prove}^\text{P}(x,w)$	$y_0 \leftarrow\!\!\text{\$}\ \text{S.Eval}(x : st_\text{S})$
$(x,\pi) \leftarrow\!\!\text{\$}\ \mathcal{A}^\text{P}(pp)$	$(st_\text{S}, pp_0) \leftarrow\!\!\text{\$}\ \text{S.Init}(\lambda)$	$\pi_0 \leftarrow\!\!\text{\$}\ \text{S.Prove}(x : st_\text{S})$	Return y_b
Return	$b' \leftarrow\!\!\text{\$}\ \mathcal{A}^{\text{PRIM},\text{PROVE}}(pp_b)$	Return π_b	
$\wedge \begin{pmatrix} \text{NiZK.Ver}^\text{P}(x,\pi) \\ \nexists w \ : \ (x,w) \in \mathcal{R} \end{pmatrix}$	Return b'		

Fig. 1. Soundness (left) and zero knowledge (right) security games for non-interactive zero knowledge proof systems.

with perfect completeness. A proof system has *perfect completeness* if for all $(x,w) \in \mathcal{R}$,

$$\Pr\left[\text{NiZK.Ver}^\text{P}_{pp}(x, \text{NiZK.Prove}^\text{P}_{pp}(w,x)) = 1\right] = 1\ .$$

Knowledge Soundness. A proof system is computationally *knowledge sound* if whenever a prover is able to produce a valid proof for a statement x, it is a true statement, i.e., there exists some witness w such that $(x,w) \in \mathcal{R}$. Knowledge soundness is defined by the security game $\text{SOUND}^{\mathcal{A}}_{\text{NiZK},\mathcal{R},\text{P}}(\lambda)$ (Fig. 1) in which an adversary is tasked with finding a verifying statement and proof where the statement is not in $\mathcal{R}$. The advantage of an adversary is defined as $\text{Adv}^{\text{sound}}_{\text{NiZK},\mathcal{R},\text{P},\mathcal{A}}(\lambda) = \Pr[\text{SOUND}^{\mathcal{A}}_{\text{NiZK},\mathcal{R},\text{P}}(\lambda) = 1]$ with respect to ideal primitive P.

Zero Knowledge. A proof system is computationally *zero-knowledge* if a proof does not leak any information besides the truth of a statement. Zero knowledge is defined by the security game $\text{ZK}^{\mathcal{A},b}_{\text{NiZK},\mathcal{R},\text{S},\text{P}}(\lambda)$ (Fig. 1) in which an adversary is tasked with distinguishing between proofs generated from a valid witness and simulated proofs generated without a witness. The advantage of an adversary is defined as

$$\text{Adv}^{\text{zk}}_{\text{NiZK},\mathcal{R},\text{S},\text{P},\mathcal{A}}(\lambda) = \left|\Pr[\text{ZK}^{\mathcal{A},1}_{\text{NiZK},\mathcal{R},\text{S},\text{P}}(\lambda) = 1] - \Pr[\text{ZK}^{\mathcal{A},0}_{\text{NiZK},\mathcal{R},\text{S},\text{P}}(\lambda) = 1]\right|\ ,$$

with respect to simulator algorithm S and ideal primitive P.

Fiat-Shamir Heuristic for Sigma Protocols. Our protocol requires a non-interactive zero knowledge proof for the relation including two pairs of group elements with equivalent discrete logs:

$$\mathcal{R} = \{(g, U, V, W), (\alpha) \ : \ U = g^\alpha \wedge W = V^\alpha\}\ .$$

This relation falls into a general family of relations of discrete log linear homomorphisms for which there exist so-called "Sigma protocols" [9] to construct interactive proofs of knowledge. These can be made non-interactive using the Fiat-Shamir heuristic in the standard way. We denote $\Sigma_\mathcal{R}[\text{GGen}]$ (shortened to $\Sigma_\mathcal{R}$ for simplicity) as the resulting non-interactive proof system for $\mathcal{R}$ known as the Chaum-Pedersen protocol [15] (shown in Fig. 2); it is perfectly complete, computationally sound, and perfectly zero-knowledge in the random oracle model.

$$\Sigma_{\mathcal{R}}.\mathsf{Prove}^H(\alpha, (g, U, V, W))$$

$r \leftarrow\!\!\$\ \mathbb{Z}_p$

$s_U \leftarrow g^r \ ; \ s_W \leftarrow V^r$

$c \leftarrow H(g \parallel U \parallel V \parallel W \parallel s_U \parallel s_W)$

$z \leftarrow r - c\alpha$

$\pi \leftarrow (z, c)$

Return π

$$\Sigma_{\mathcal{R}}.\mathsf{Ver}^H((g, U, V, W), \pi)$$

$(z, c) \leftarrow \pi$

$s_U \leftarrow g^z U^c \ ; \ s_W \leftarrow V^z W^c$

Return $c = H(g \parallel U \parallel V \parallel W \parallel s_U \parallel s_W)$

$$\mathcal{R} = \{(\alpha), (g, U, V, W) : U = g^\alpha \wedge W = V^\alpha\}$$

Fig. 2. Description of Chaum-Pedersen discrete log equality Sigma protocol [15].

3   Partially Oblivious Pseudorandom Functions

We provide a new formalization for POPRFs, including syntax, semantics, and security. Our formalization builds off that from [20], but we offer new security notions that cover simulation-based security as a PRF (in the presence of a blinded evaluation oracle), client input privacy, and verifiability.

Syntax and Semantics. A partially-oblivious pseudorandom function (POPRF) scheme, Fn, is a tuple of algorithms

$$(\mathsf{Fn.Setup}, \mathsf{Fn.KeyGen}, \mathsf{Fn.Req}, \mathsf{Fn.BlindEv}, \mathsf{Fn.Finalize}, \mathsf{Fn.Ev}).$$

The setup and key generation algorithm generate public parameters pp and a public key, secret key pair (pk, sk), respectively. Oblivious evaluation is carried out as an interactive protocol run between client and server. The protocols we consider in this work make use of only a single round of interaction, so we simplify the syntax of the interactive oblivious evaluation protocol into algorithms $(\mathsf{Fn.Req}, \mathsf{Fn.BlindEv}, \mathsf{Fn.Finalize})$ that work as follows:

(1) First, a client runs the algorithm $\mathsf{Fn.Req}_{pp}^P(pk, t, x)$, which takes input a public key pk, tag (or public input) t, and private input x, and outputs a local state st and a request message req. The message req is sent to a server.

(2) A server runs algorithm $\mathsf{Fn.BlindEv}_{pp}^P(sk, t, req)$, using as input a secret key, a tag t, and the request message. It produces a response message rep that should be sent back to the client.

(3) Finally, the client runs the algorithm $\mathsf{Fn.Finalize}(rep : st)$ and outputs a PRF evaluation or $\bot$ if the response message is rejected, for example, due to the verification check failing.

The unblinded evaluation algorithm $\mathsf{Fn.Ev}$ is deterministic, and takes as input a public key, secret key pair (pk, sk), an input pair (t, x), and outputs a PRF evaluation y. We also define sets $\mathsf{Fn.SK}$, $\mathsf{Fn.PK}$, $\mathsf{Fn.T}$, $\mathsf{Fn.X}$, and $\mathsf{Fn.Out}$ representing the secret key, public key, tag, private input, and output space, respectively. We define the input space $\mathsf{Fn.In} = \mathsf{Fn.T} \times \mathsf{Fn.X}$. We assume efficient algorithms for sampling and membership queries on these sets. When it is clear from context, we drop the prefix Fn and subscript pp from algorithm names.

For correctness, we require that Ev is a function, and that the blinded and unblinded evaluations are consistent. To formalize the latter: we require that for any pp output from Setup, any pk, sk output by KeyGen, and any t, x, it holds that $\Pr[\mathsf{Ev}(sk, t, x) = y] = 1$ where the probability is taken over choice of y via the following process:

$$(st, req) \leftarrow\!\!\!{}_\$ \; \mathsf{Req}^\mathsf{P}(pk, t, x) \; ; \; rep \leftarrow\!\!\!{}_\$ \; \mathsf{BlindEv}^\mathsf{P}(sk, t, req) \; ; \; y \leftarrow\!\!\!{}_\$ \; \mathsf{Finalize}^\mathsf{P}(rep : st) \; .$$

Security. We introduce three new security definitions for POPRFs. We use code-based games mostly following the framework of Bellare and Rogaway [5].

Pseudorandomness. The first definition captures pseudorandomness, i.e., indistinguishability of the POPRF from a random function, even for malicious clients that have access to a blinded evaluation oracle. We borrow some elements from the UC definition for standard OPRFs from [28], but opt for what we believe to be a simpler, standalone formulation. We also extend to handle partial obliviousness, which has some subtleties.

A pseudocode game appears in Fig. 3. The game is parameterized by a security parameter λ, an adversary $\mathcal{A}$, a challenge bit b, a POPRF Fn, a simulator $\mathsf{S} = (\mathsf{S.Init}, \mathsf{S.BlindEv}, \mathsf{S.Eval})$, and an ideal primitive P. The last will be used for random oracles in our main result. A simulator is a triple of algorithms that share state (explicitly denoted by st_S in the game). Algorithm S.Init initializes the simulator state and outputs a public key for the game. Algorithm S.BlindEv simulates blinded evaluation response messages while S.Eval simulates random oracle queries. Importantly, S.BlindEv and S.Eval can obtain Ev outputs, but they can only do so in a circumscribed way: the simulator has oracle access to LIMEV which limits the number of full evaluations it can obtain to be at most the number of queries so far made by the adversary to the BLINDEV. Importantly, this limit is per-metadata value t (indicated via the subscript): the LIMEV query on any particular t is bound by the total number of blinded evaluation queries on that particular t. This follows from similar granular restrictions in the partially blind signatures literature [1].

A weaker version of the game would simply cap the total number of queries to LIMEV by the total number of queries to BLINDEV. This notion is, however, too weak for applications because we would like to ensure that querying, say, three times on public input t_1 cannot somehow help an adversary complete the evaluation for another public input $t_2 \neq t_1$. We note that a recent preprint [41] contained this weaker notion, couched in the context of Privacy Pass. (We discuss this paper further in Sect. 4.)

We let the advantage of a POPRF adversary $\mathcal{A}$ be defined by

$$\mathsf{Adv}^{\mathsf{po\text{-}prf}}_{\mathsf{Fn},\mathsf{S},\mathsf{P},\mathcal{A}}(\lambda) = \left| \Pr\left[\mathrm{POPRF}^{\mathcal{A},1}_{\mathsf{Fn},\mathsf{S},\mathsf{P}}(\lambda) \Rightarrow 1 \right] - \Pr\left[\mathrm{POPRF}^{\mathcal{A},0}_{\mathsf{Fn},\mathsf{S},\mathsf{P}}(\lambda) \Rightarrow 1 \right] \right|$$

where the probability spaces are taken over the random choices made in the games and the events signify that the game outputs the value one.

One could relax our definition in various ways. For example, by setting a parameter $q_{t,\max}$ that upper bounds the total number of BLINDEV queries on

Game POPRF$_{\text{Fn,S,P}}^{\mathcal{A},b}(\lambda)$	Oracle EV(t,x)	Oracle BLINDEV(t, req)
RandFn $\leftarrow\!\!\$ FnGen(Fn.In, Fn.Out)	$y_1 \leftarrow$ Fn.EV$^P(sk, t, x)$	$q_t \leftarrow q_t + 1$
$st_P \leftarrow\!\!\$ P.Init(λ)	$y_0 \leftarrow$ RandFn(t, x)	$rep_1 \leftarrow$ Fn.BlindEv$^P(sk, t, req)$
$pp \leftarrow\!\!\$ Fn.Setup(λ)	Return y_b	$(rep_0, st_S) \leftarrow\!\!\$ S.BlindEv$^{\text{LIMEV}}(t, req : st_S)$
$(sk, pk_1) \leftarrow\!\!\$ Fn.KeyGen$_{pp}^P()$		Return rep_b
$(st_S, pk_0) \leftarrow\!\!\$ S.Init(pp)	Oracle LIMEV(t, x)	
$b' \leftarrow\!\!\$ \mathcal{A}^{\text{EV, BLINDEV, PRIM}}(pp, pk_b)$	$q_{t,s} \leftarrow q_{t,s} + 1$	Oracle PRIM(x)
Return b'	If $q_{t,s} \leq q_t$ then	$y_1 \leftarrow\!\!\$ P.Eval$(x : st_P)$
	$\quad$ Return EV(t,x)	$(y_0, st_S) \leftarrow\!\!\$ S.Eval$^{\text{LIMEV}}(x : st_S)$
	Return $\perp$	Return y_b

Fig. 3. Simulation-based security definition for pseudorandomness against malicious clients, with granular accounting for metadata in queries. The LIMEVAL oracle limits the number of evaluations the simulator can make on a per-metadata tag basis.

tag t over the course of the game and letting the simulator—at any point in the game—obtain $q_{t,\max}$ full evaluations. This would seem to still provide qualitatively the same level of security, but our schemes meet the stronger notion that restricts the simulator over the course of the game. Another relaxation that does not preserve the same level of security would be to allow the simulator more queries than $q_{t,\max}$, for example, $2 \cdot q_{t,\max}$. But this degrades the security guarantee as it means that in q queries to BLINDEV on some t a malicious client can potentially compute up to $2q$ POPRF outputs for that tag t.

Request Privacy and Unlinkability. Our second goal is to capture privacy for clients. This means not only that requests should hide the private input portion x, but also that request/response transcripts and output POPRF values should be unlinkable. We formalize two models for this goal, corresponding to the level of maliciousness by a misbehaving server.

Game POPRIV1 (Fig. 4, left game) captures an indistinguishability experiment in which the adversary can query to obtain full transcripts (including output) resulting from honest blinded evaluation of a POPRF. The transcripts are either returned properly ($b = 0$) or with the request-response pairs swapped relative to the outputs ($b = 1$). Intuitively, if the adversary cannot distinguish between these two worlds, then there is no way to link a POPRF output value to a particular blinded evaluation, despite the adversary knowing the secret POPRF key. This captures also input privacy security: if a request reveals some information about the input x this can be used to win the POPRIV1 game. We sometimes refer to this as request privacy against passive adversaries, because the adversary cannot interfere with the server's proper execution.

The advantage of a POPRIV1 adversary $\mathcal{A}$ in the P-model is defined by

$$\mathsf{Adv}_{\text{Fn,P},\mathcal{A}}^{\text{po-priv1}}(\lambda) = \left| \Pr\left[\text{POPRIV1}_{\text{Fn,P}}^{\mathcal{A},1}(\lambda) \Rightarrow 1 \right] - \Pr\left[\text{POPRIV1}_{\text{Fn,P}}^{\mathcal{A},0}(\lambda) \Rightarrow 1 \right] \right|$$

where the probability spaces are taken over the random choices made in the games and the events signify that the game outputs the value one. We say a Fn scheme is *perfectly private* if $\mathsf{Adv}_{\text{Fn,P},\mathcal{A}}^{\text{po-priv1}}(\lambda) = 0$ for all adversaries $\mathcal{A}$.

Game $\text{POPRIV1}_{\text{Fn,P}}^{\mathcal{A},b}(\lambda)$	Game $\text{POPRIV2}_{\text{Fn,P}}^{\mathcal{A},b}(\lambda)$
$pp \leftarrow\!\!\$\ \text{Fn.Setup}(\lambda)$	$pp \leftarrow\!\!\$\ \text{Fn.Setup}(\lambda)$
$(pk, sk) \leftarrow\!\!\$\ \text{Fn.KeyGen}(pp)$	$st_{\text{P}} \leftarrow\!\!\$\ \text{P.Init}(\lambda)$
$st_{\text{P}} \leftarrow\!\!\$\ \text{P.Init}(\lambda)$	$i \leftarrow 0$
$b' \leftarrow\!\!\$\ \mathcal{A}^{\text{TRANS,P}}(pp, pk, sk)$	$b' \leftarrow\!\!\$\ \mathcal{A}^{\text{REQ,FIN,P}}(pp)$
Return b'	Return b'
Oracle $\text{TRANS}(t, x_0, x_1)$	Oracle $\text{REQ}(pk, t, x_0, x_1)$
$(st_0, req_0) \leftarrow\!\!\$\ \text{Fn.Req}^{\text{P}}(pk, t, x_0)$	$i \leftarrow i + 1$
$(st_1, req_1) \leftarrow\!\!\$\ \text{Fn.Req}^{\text{P}}(pk, t, x_1)$	$(st_{i,0}, req_0) \leftarrow\!\!\$\ \text{Fn.Req}^{\text{P}}(pk, t, x_0)$
$rep_0 \leftarrow\!\!\$\ \text{Fn.BlindEv}^{\text{P}}(sk, t, req_0)$	$(st_{i,1}, req_1) \leftarrow\!\!\$\ \text{Fn.Req}^{\text{P}}(pk, t, x_1)$
$rep_1 \leftarrow\!\!\$\ \text{Fn.BlindEv}^{\text{P}}(sk, t, req_1)$	Return (req_b, req_{1-b})
$y_0 \leftarrow \text{Fn.Finalize}^{\text{P}}(rep_0; st_0)$	Oracle $\text{FIN}(j, rep, rep')$
$y_1 \leftarrow \text{Fn.Finalize}^{\text{P}}(rep_1; st_1)$	If $j > i$ then return $\perp$
$\tau \leftarrow (req_b, rep_b, y_0)$	$y_b \leftarrow \text{Fn.Finalize}^{\text{P}}(st_{j,b}, rep)$
$\tau' \leftarrow (req_{1-b}, rep_{1-b}, y_1)$	$y_{1-b} \leftarrow \text{Fn.Finalize}^{\text{P}}(st_{j,1-b}, rep')$
Return (τ, τ')	If $y_0 = \perp$ or $y_1 = \perp$ then
	$\quad$ Return $\perp$
	Return (y_0, y_1)

Fig. 4. Security definitions for honest-but-curious server unlinkability (**left**) and malicious server unlinkability (**right**).

POPRIV1 security does not capture malicious servers that deviate from the protocol. So, for example, it doesn't rule out attacks in which the server replies with garbage to a blinded evaluation request.

Our next game POPRIV2 allows the adversary to choose the public keys used for request generation and leaves to the adversary how to reply to requests. The game therefore splits transcript generation across two oracles, a request oracle (REQ) and finalize oracle (FIN). The first oracle replies with a randomly ordered pair of request messages based on the challenge bit, and the second oracle can be queried with adversarially chosen response messages. The game requires that neither y_0 nor y_1 is equal to $\perp$—if either is then the finalize oracle returns $\perp$. This prevents the trivial attack of corrupting one reply but not the other.

The advantage of a POPRIV2 adversary $\mathcal{A}$ in the P-model is defined by

$$\text{Adv}_{\text{Fn,P},\mathcal{A}}^{\text{po-priv2}}(\lambda) = \left| \Pr\left[\text{POPRIV2}_{\text{Fn,P}}^{\mathcal{A},1}(\lambda) \Rightarrow 1 \right] - \Pr\left[\text{POPRIV2}_{\text{Fn,P}}^{\mathcal{A},0}(\lambda) \Rightarrow 1 \right] \right|$$

where the probability spaces are taken over the random choices made in the games and the events signify that the game outputs the value one.

POPRIV2 is strictly stronger than POPRIV1. Looking ahead our new POPRF meets POPRIV1 when verification is omitted, and POPRIV2 when verification is required.

Uniqueness. Lastly, we discuss an additional property that is relevant in the verifiable setting when clients want to ensure that servers honestly perform blind evaluations. This means that the output of the blind evaluation protocol should be consistent relative to the public key pair, i.e., consistent with the output of unblinded evaluation using the secret key. Our correctness definition requires this is the case for honest execution of the algorithms. We formalize this correctness property for malicious servers as a uniqueness definition POUNIQ, taking inspiration from definitions used previously for verifiable random functions (c.f., [19]). In short, no malicious server should be able to convince a client into accepting two different outputs for the same (pk, t, x). We show that uniqueness is implied by correctness and POPRIV2. The complete definition for POUNIQ, theorem statement, and proof are deferred to the full version [43].

Relation to Partially Blind Signatures. POPRFs are related to two-move partially blind signatures, which were introduced by Abe and Fujisaki [1]. A partially blind signature is a tuple of algorithms

$$DS = (DS.Setup, DS.KeyGen, DS.Sign, DS.Ver, DS.Req, DS.BlindSign, DS.Finalize)$$

where the first four algorithms define a standard digital signature scheme for message space consisting of pairs (t, m), called the public input (or tag) and private message, respectively. Signatures can also be generated via an interactive protocol which, like we did for POPRFs, we formalize simply as a single round trip protocol initiated by a client running $DS.Req(pk, t, m)$ to generate a request message req and client state st, sending the former to the server which runs $DS.BlindSign(sk, req)$ to generate and send a response rep back to the client, which then computes a signature via $DS.Finalize(st, rep)$. This protocol should achieve blindness, which can be defined similarly to our request privacy definition above for POPRFs.

The main security property targeted is one-more unforgeability, which, roughly speaking, states that an adversarial client can't generate $q + 1$ unique message-signature pairs $(m_1, \sigma_1), \ldots, (m_{q+1}, \sigma_{q+1})$ that all verify under a public key pk and public tag t even when given the ability to query a blind signing oracle with the only restriction being that only q queries can be made for the chosen public tag t. This intuitively enforces that each query to the blind signing oracle only results in one learned signature, and queries for a different public tag do not help in forging a signature for the target tag. We present a complete formal treatment of partially blind signatures in the full version [43].

A partially blind signature is unique if DS.Sign is deterministic and its output on (pk, t, m) matches that of the interactive protocol when initiated on the same triple. A blind signature is just a partially blind signature with t omitted. [28] observed that one can transform unique blind signatures into OPRFs by hashing the signature. A similar transform exists to build a POPRF from a unique partially blind signature. We provide details and proof of this transform in the full version [43] for both cases, with and without public input). (As far as we are aware there has been no formal treatment of this observation.)

Most prior partially blind signature schemes are not unique, e.g., [1,2]. The only unique scheme we are aware of is due to Zhang, Safavi-Naini, and Susilo (ZSS) [46], but it relies on bilinear pairings and so this generic transformation will not achieve our goals for a POPRF. Moreover as mentioned in the introduction, the security analysis in ZSS is wrong. That said, our construction shares much of the underlying structure from the ZSS one. Using our new proof techniques, we furthermore provide the first complete proof of the ZSS partially blind signature scheme (see the full version [43]).

4   The 3HashSDHI POPRF

We now turn to our main result: providing a new POPRF. Our construction combines elements of the 2HashDH construction with a technique used by Dodis and Yampolskiy for their verifiable PRF; it is also related to a partially blind signature scheme suggested by Zhang, Safavi-Naini, and Susilo. We call our construction 3HashSDHI, which we often abbreviate to 3H. The name refers to its use of three hashes and reliance on the strong inverse Diffie-Hellman assumption.

Algorithms. Our protocol relies on a group $\mathbb{G}$ of prime order p and with generator g. As mentioned in the introduction, the 3HashSDHI protocol computes a PRF output as

$$3\mathsf{H}.\mathsf{Ev}(sk, t, x) = \mathsf{H}_2\left(t, x, \mathsf{H}_1(x)^{1/(sk+\mathsf{H}_3(t))}\right)$$

where $\mathsf{H}_1 : \{0,1\}^* \to \mathbb{G}$, $\mathsf{H}_2 : \{0,1\}^* \to \{0,1\}^{\gamma_2}$, and $\mathsf{H}_3 : \{0,1\}^* \to \{0,1\}^{\gamma_3}$ are the titular hash functions. Note that H_1 has range the group $\mathbb{G}$, whereas the second and third hashes output bit strings of length γ_2 and γ_3. By default we set $\gamma_2 = \lambda$ and $\gamma_3 = 2\lambda$. The third hash must be collision resistant for security to hold. Looking ahead to the security analysis, we will model the hash functions as random oracles. The setup, key generation, and full evaluation algorithms are shown in pseudocode below.

$3\mathsf{H}.\mathsf{Setup}(\lambda)$	$3\mathsf{H}.\mathsf{KeyGen}^{\mathsf{H}_1 \times \mathsf{H}_2 \times \mathsf{H}_3}(pp)$	$3\mathsf{H}.\mathsf{Ev}^{\mathsf{H}_1 \times \mathsf{H}_2 \times \mathsf{H}_3}(sk, t, x)$
$(p, g, \mathbb{G}) \leftarrow\!\!{\$}\ \mathsf{GGen}(\lambda)$	$(p, g, \mathbb{G}) \leftarrow pp$	$Y \leftarrow \mathsf{H}_1(x)^{1/(sk+\mathsf{H}_3(t))}$
$pp \leftarrow (p, g, \mathbb{G})$	$sk \leftarrow\!\!{\$}\ \mathbb{Z}_p\ ;\ pk \leftarrow g^{sk}$	$Z \leftarrow \mathsf{H}_2(t, x, Y)$
Return pp	Return (pk, sk)	Return Z

Here, GGen denotes a group parameter generator outputting a triple $(p, g, \mathbb{G})$ consisting of a prime p, (the description of) a group $\mathbb{G}$ of order p, and a generator g of $\mathbb{G}$.

The blind evaluation protocol has a client compute $\mathsf{H}_1(x)$ and mask the resulting group element by raising it to a random scalar r. The client can send the resulting blinded value B to the server, who can then raise B to $1/(sk+\mathsf{H}_3(t))$ and return the result. The client then finalizes by raising the returned value to $1/r$ in order to remove the blinding, followed by the final step of computing the final hash H_2. The blinding ensures request privacy.

We optionally can extend this blinded evaluation protocol to include a proof that the server properly exponentiated B. This is necessary to have the protocol enjoy POPRIV2 security, which is important in some (but not all) applications. At first, it may not be obvious how to prove to the client that the server is returning $B' = B^{1/(sk+\mathsf{H}_3(t))}$ relative to the public key g^{sk}, because the sum appears in the denominator. However, we can use the following trick: the server generates a standard DL proof that $B = (B')^k$ for some k. The client runs

---

$3H.\mathsf{Req}^{\mathsf{H}_1 \times \mathsf{H}_2 \times \mathsf{H}_3 \times \mathsf{H}_4}(pk, t, x)$

$r \leftarrow\!\!\$\ Z_p\ ; \quad B \leftarrow \mathsf{H}_1(x)^r$
Return $((pk, r, t, x), B)$

$\xrightarrow{\quad B, t \quad}$

$3H.\mathsf{BlindEv}^{\mathsf{H}_1 \times \mathsf{H}_2 \times \mathsf{H}_3 \times \mathsf{H}_4}(sk, t, B)$

$k \leftarrow sk + \mathsf{H}_3(t)$
$B' \leftarrow B^{1/k}$
$\pi \leftarrow\!\!\$\ \Sigma_{\mathcal{R}}.\mathsf{Prove}^{\mathsf{H}_4}(k, (g, g^k, B', B))$
Return (B', π)

$3H.\mathsf{Finalize}^{\mathsf{H}_1 \times \mathsf{H}_2 \times \mathsf{H}_3 \times \mathsf{H}_4}(B', \pi; (pk, r, t, x))$

$\xleftarrow{\quad B', \pi \quad}$

$Y \leftarrow (B')^{1/r}$
Require $\Sigma_{\mathcal{R}}.\mathsf{Ver}^{\mathsf{H}_4}((g, g^{\mathsf{H}_3(t)} \cdot pk, B', B), \pi)$
$Z \leftarrow \mathsf{H}_2(t, x, Y)$
Return Z

Fig. 5. Blind evaluation for our 3H POPRF construction. All three algorithms have implicit input the parameters $pp = (p, g, \mathbb{G})$ that describe the group used. The NIZK uses relation $\mathcal{R} = \{(g, U, V, W), (\alpha) : U = g^\alpha \wedge W = V^\alpha\}$.

verification by explicitly reconstructing $g^k = pk \cdot g^{\mathsf{H}_3(t)} = g^{sk + \mathsf{H}_3(t)}$. This means that the verification procedure checks the special structure of the exponent k.

The full protocol, including the NIZK (which uses its own hash H_4), is shown in Fig. 5. Here we show that t is sent from the client to server, though in some applications the server may receive t out-of-band. Execution requires just one round trip. It requires just two group exponentiations on the client side (and, when using the NIZK, those used for its verification). The server uses one exponentiation plus one for the NIZK proof.

Relation to Partially Blind Signatures. 3HashSDHI is closely related to a partially blind signature suggested by Zhang, Safavi-Naini, and Susilo [46]. It uses groups $\mathbb{G}_1, \mathbb{G}_2, \mathbb{G}_T$ each of order p, with generators g_1, g_2, g_T, and that come equipped with an efficient-to-compute pairing $e \colon \mathbb{G}_1 \times \mathbb{G}_2 \to \mathbb{G}_T$ such that for any $\alpha, \beta \in \mathbb{Z}_p$ it holds that $e(g_1^\alpha, g_2^\beta) = g_T^{\alpha\beta}$. Their signature is defined as

$$\mathsf{ZSS1.Ev}(sk, t, x) = \mathsf{H}_{\mathbb{G}_2}(x)^{1/(sk + \mathsf{H}_3(t))}$$

where $\mathsf{H}_{\mathbb{G}_2} \colon \{0, 1\}^* \to \mathbb{G}_2$ hashes onto the group $\mathbb{G}_2$ and H_3 is as defined above for 3HashSDHI. We use ZSS1 to differentiate from our suggested modifications, which we call ZSS2 and discuss in the full version [43]. As can be seen, 3HashS-DHI uses essentially the same structure, combined with a final hash but we dispense with the use of bilinear pairings using instead NIZKs to provide verifiability. We also comment on two aspects of the original security analysis of the partially blind signature scheme in [46]: (1) the analysis of one-more unforgeability is incorrect; and (2) it contains an incorrect claim that so-called "exponential" blinding (see below for discussion in the context of OPRFs) is insecure. More precisely, for (1), the claimed security proof relies on a lemma (stated without a proof) which says that if the scheme is secure, in terms of one-more unforgeability, for any fixed public input, then it is secure as a partially-blind signature – such lemma does not appear to be provable; for (2), the claimed distinguishing test does not work, rather it identifies every pair of signature and signing transcript as a match, regardless of whether they are associated. Our new techniques, in particular a variant of the new gap assumption discussed in the next section, enable a new proof of unforgeability for the ZSS partially blind signature, and we also provide a proof that exponential blinding is secure. See the full version [43] for the details.

Comparison to prior (O)PRFs. Recall that the 2HashDH OPRF is defined by $2\mathsf{HashDH}.\mathsf{Ev}(sk, x) = \mathsf{H}_2(x, \mathsf{H}_1(x)^{sk})$. On the other hand, the DY PRF [19] is evaluated on a message t via $\mathsf{DY}.\mathsf{Ev}(sk, t) = h^{1/(sk+t)}$ for generator h. Thus, our 3HashSDHI can be seen as blending of the two approaches, basically defining, for each x, a separate instance of the DY PRF with generator $h = \mathsf{H}_1(x)$ and input message t. The way we combine them retains the simple blinding mechanism of 2HashDH to allow hiding x. Despite the similarity to the prior constructions, analyzing security requires new techniques (see the next section).

2HashDH is often formulated using an alternative "multiplicative" blinding strategy as opposed to the "exponential" blinding presented here. Multiplicative blinding enables client-side performance improvements of fixed-base exponentiation with precomputation over variable-base exponentiation, but has been shown to have some security drawbacks in the non-verified setting [31]. 3HashSDHI is not compatible with the multiplicative blinding protocol used by 2HashDH, however the full version [43] presents an alternative multiplicative blinding protocol [46] that enjoys the same performance benefits.

Miao et al. construct an oblivious evaluation protocol for the DY PRF [38]. Their approach makes use of the additive-homomorphic Camenisch-Shoup encryption scheme [11] and related proofs of discrete log representation. In contrast, 3HashSDHI uses the more efficient oblivious evaluation approach of 2HashDH and uses the structure of DY to tie in the public metadata, meaning the more expensive DY oblivious evaluation techniques are avoided.

Pythia [20] provided the first POPRF. It uses pairing-friendly groups $\mathbb{G}_1, \mathbb{G}_2, \mathbb{G}_T$ each of order p, with generators g_1, g_2, g_T. Then, the Pythia POPRF is defined by

$$\mathsf{Pythia}.\mathsf{Ev}(sk, t, x) = e(\mathsf{H}_{\mathbb{G}_1}(t), \mathsf{H}_{\mathbb{G}_2}(x))^{sk}$$

where $\mathsf{H}_{\mathbb{G}_2}$ and $\mathsf{H}_{\mathbb{G}_2}$ are hash functions that map to the groups $\mathbb{G}_1, \mathbb{G}_2$. This construction enables blinded evaluation by sending $B \leftarrow \mathsf{H}_{\mathbb{G}_2}(x)^r$, and having the server respond with $e(\mathsf{H}_{\mathbb{G}_1}(t)^{sk}, B)$. It also has some other features that were desirable in the password hardening context for which Pythia was designed, specifically, that one can have compact key rotation tokens of the form $\Delta = sk'/sk$. The token Δ can be shared with a client to help it update previously computed POPRF values for any t, x. Compared to Pythia's POPRF, 3HashSDHI avoids use of pairings. This makes it faster to compute and saves bandwidth.

That said, the 3HashSDHI construction does not support key rotations even if one omits the final H_2 evaluation. To expand, consider using a (non-compact) key rotation in a way analogous to Pythia, i.e., distributing to a client $\Delta_{t_1} = (sk + \mathsf{H}_3(t_1))/(sk' + \mathsf{H}_3(t_1))$ and $\Delta_{t_2} = (sk + \mathsf{H}_3(t_2))/(sk' + \mathsf{H}_3(t_2))$. This would allow rotating (unhashed) POPRF outputs on public inputs t_1 and t_2 from an old key sk to a new key sk'. But this also trivially reveals sk and sk', given that

$H_3(t_1)$ and $H_3(t_2)$ are publicly computable. While in the applications we explore in Sect. 7 we do not need key rotation tokens, the question of finding a POPRF that avoids pairings yet supports key rotations remains open.

Jarecki et al. [29] propose construction of a POPRF F from OPRF F_1 and PRF F_2 as $F.\text{Ev}(sk, t, x) = F_1.\text{Ev}(F_2.\text{Ev}(sk, t), x)$. They go on to propose a construction instantiating F_1 with 2HashDH and F_2 with a symmetric PRF (e.g., HMAC); this construction is highly efficient but does not provide verifiability due to the non-algebraic choice of F_2. 3HashSDHI can be thought of as following this approach composing 2HashDH with the algebraic VRF of Dodis-Yampolskiy [19].

We also compare to the recent attribute-based verifiable OPRF (AB-VOPRF) suggested by Huang et al. of Facebook [26] for use with Privacy Pass. An attribute-based VOPRF is a POPRF that separates out an explicit algorithm for converting a secret key and attribute t (what we call a tag) into a tag-specific public key, secret key pair. As with other VOPRFs, there is a verifiable, blinded evaluation protocol by which a client can obtain an output on some (t, x) pair without revealing x. Any AB-VOPRF gives a POPRF, and vice versa.

Again following the blueprint of [29], Facebook's proposed construction [26] of an AB-VOPRF combines the 2HashDH OPRF with the Naor-Reingold PRF [39]. Evaluation is defined by

$$\text{FB.Ev}(sk, t, x) = H_1(x)^{a_0 \cdot \prod_i a_i^{t[i]}}$$

where $sk = a_0, a_1, \ldots, a_{|t|}$ and $t[i]$ indicates the ith bit of t. To make this verifiable, the scheme must provide a more complex NIZK involving $|t|$ group elements, making it expensive to transmit and verify, particularly in applications where a wide variety of tags t will be used. In comparison 3HashSDHI is as efficient as 2HashDH.

Finally, a concurrent, independent work by Silde and Strand [41] describe what we call the 3HashSDHI protocol and how it could be useful for Privacy Pass and the Facebook de-identified logging application. They formalize a notion of anonymous token security that is more tailored to Privacy Pass style applications (compared to our general POPRF definitions), but this definition contains the aforementioned problem (see Sect. 3) of not performing query accounting on a per public input basis, making it too weak of a security notion for their applications. In addition, the security analysis relative to this notion is incomplete, and so the paper does not yet provide a proof even of this weaker security notion. Nevertheless, their work underscores the benefits of the 3HashSDHI protocol in the applications they explore and our proof techniques (in particular, the new one-more gap SDHI assumption discussed in the next section) should enable improvements to their analysis.

Extension to Private Metadata Bit. Recall a primary application of OPRFs is in the construction of anonymous tokens. We have thus far been concerned with adding support for public metadata, but there are also settings that benefit from being able to associate *private* metadata to tokens that can only be identified by the issuer. To prevent trivial linking attacks by a malicious server, it is necessary that the private metadata space remain small. Kreuter et al. propose a variant of Privacy Pass (based on the 2HashDH OPRF) that supports a single private metadata bit [35]. The high level approach is to simply maintain two keys and prove in zero knowledge that the token is issued under one of the two keys. However, they observe that a deterministic primitive (like a PRF) is insufficient to achieve indistinguishability between private metadata bits. Therefore, the core of their construction is a new anonymous token protocol that can be considered as a randomized variant of 2HashDH. It is likely similar techniques can be applied to construct a randomized version of 3HashSDHI to support public metadata as well as a private metadata bit; we leave the details of such a construction to future work. Silde and Strand propose a construction along these lines, but as mentioned before, the security analysis is incomplete [41].

5   Security Analysis

We show formally that the 3HashSDHI PO-PRF enjoys pseudorandomness and request privacy. The former is the more complex analysis; we start with it.

5.1   Pseudorandomness

The main technical challenge is showing that 3HashSDHI meets our pseudorandomness definition, captured by game POPRF (Fig. 3 in Sect. 3). We start with an overview of our proof strategy, and then state our main result.

Proof Strategy. Our proof of pseudorandomness proceeds in several steps. First, we introduce a new discrete log (DL) type cryptographic hardness assumption: the one-more gap strong Diffie-Hellman inversion problem, denoted (m, n)-OM-GAP-SDHI for parameters m, n that we will explain. The new assumption is a generalization of prior one-more DL assumptions, but extended with two oracles and a more involved one-more winning condition which depends on the number of queries with a specific form to one of the oracles. We show that we can build a POPRF simulator such that, in the ROM, distinguishing between the real ($b = 1$) and ideal worlds ($b = 0$) reduces to breaking an instance of (m, n)-OM-GAP-SDHI where m is the number of H_3 queries made by $\mathcal{A}$ and n is the number of H_1 queries. We note that use of random oracles here allows us to avoid the more complex proof techniques used by Dodis and Yampolskiy [19], and indeed it is unclear what kind of analysis could work for this step without random oracles.

In the second step, we analyze the security of our new assumption, showing that, in the Algebraic Group Model (AGM) [24] it reduces to one of the uber assumptions from Bauer, Fuchsbauer, and Loss (BFL) [3]. In turn, we can use a result from BFL to finally show that our new assumption is implied (again, in the AGM) by the q-DL assumption. This provides good evidence of the difficulty of the problem, and allows us to derive precise concrete security bounds.

The One-More Gap SDHI Assumption. Game (m,n)-OM-GAP-SDHI is shown in Fig. 7. The game generates a group instance and a challenge secret sk. The adversary $\mathcal{A} = (\mathcal{A}_1, \mathcal{A}_2)$ runs in two stages. In the first stage it receives the group description $p, \mathbb{G}$ and outputs a sequence of n scalar values $c_1, \ldots, c_n$. Importantly $\mathcal{A}_1$ does not receive g, forcing it to commit to the c_i values in a way independently of the generator g. We assume that g is randomly chosen; this will be important in our analysis. Then, the second stage $\mathcal{A}_2$ is run on input the generator g, g^{sk}, and a vector of m group elements $g^{y_1}, \ldots, g^{y_n}$. The adversary is given access to two oracles. The SDH oracle returns $B^{1/(sk+c_i)}$ for arbitrary B and one of the previously specified c_i values. The SDDH oracle is a decision oracle that helps the adversary determine whether $Z = Y^{1/(sk+c_i)}$ for arbitrary Y, Z and one of the previously specified c_i values.

The adversary outputs a distinguished index γ indicating a c_γ value, as well as a set of ℓ pairs $(Z_i, \alpha_i) \in \mathbb{G} \times [0..m]$. The adversary wins if $\ell > q_\gamma$ and $Z_i = Y_{\alpha_i}^{1/(sk+c_\gamma)}$ for all $1 \le i \le \ell$. Here q_γ is the number of queries to the SDH with second input set to γ. Without the "one more" restriction of $\ell > q_\gamma$, it is trivial to win. We define the (m,n)-OM-GAP-SDHI-advantage of an adversary $\mathcal{A}$ by

$$\mathsf{Adv}_{\mathsf{GGen},\mathcal{A}}^{(m,n)\text{-om-gap-sdhi}}(\lambda) = \Pr\left[(m,n)\text{-OM-GAP-SDHI}_{\mathsf{GGen}}^{\mathcal{A}}(\lambda) \Rightarrow \mathsf{true} \right] .$$

An adversary $\mathcal{A}$ has query budget $(\vec{q}, q_{\mathsf{SDDH}})$ for $\vec{q} = [\vec{q}_1, \ldots, \vec{q}_n]$ if at the end of the game $\mathcal{A}$ has made at most $\vec{q}_i$ queries to SDH with index i and has made at most q_{SDDH} queries to SDDH. Requiring fixed query budgets is an artifact of existing analysis approaches to Diffie-Hellman inversion-like assumptions; we leave it as an open question whether the per-tag query budget can be handled adaptively.

We note that a weakening of the assumption dispenses with the more granular per-c-value accounting, instead just asking that the adversary can't come up with $\ell > q$ solutions for any mixture of Y_i and c_j values. This variant is much easier to analyze in the AGM, but is not sufficient for our analysis.

Reducing (m,n)-OM-GAP-SDHI to q-DL. In two steps, we show how to reduce this assumption, in the AGM, to the difficulty of q-DL. The latter involves a game q-DL (Fig. 6) that generates a group instance $p, g, \mathbb{G}$ for security parameter λ, and gives an adversary $g, g^x, g^{x^2}, \ldots, g^{x^q}$ for a random scalar x. The adversary must output x. We define the advantage of a q-DL-adversary $\mathcal{A}$ to be $\mathsf{Adv}_{\mathsf{GGen},\mathcal{A}}^{q\text{-dl}}(\lambda) = \Pr\left[q\text{-DL}_{\mathsf{GGen}}^{\mathcal{A}}(\lambda) \Rightarrow \mathsf{true} \right]$.

$$\boxed{\begin{array}{l} \text{Game } q\text{-DL}_{\mathsf{GGen}}^{\mathcal{A}}(\lambda) \\ \hline (p, g, \mathbb{G}) \leftarrow\!\!\$\ \mathsf{GGen}(\lambda) \\ x \leftarrow\!\!\$\ \mathbb{Z}_p \\ x' \leftarrow\!\!\$\ \mathcal{A}\left(p, \mathbb{G}, g, \left[g^{x^i}\right]_{i=1}^q\right) \\ \text{Return } x = x' \end{array}}$$

Fig. 6. The q-type discrete log security game.

As a convenient middle layer, we rely on BFL's "Uber-assumption" [3], formalized via the game m-UBER in Fig. 8. It involves a game where the adversary can obtain $g^{\rho(\vec{x})}$ by querying an arbitrarily chosen m-variate polynomial $\rho(\vec{X})$ to an oracle Ev, for a secret vector $\vec{x} \leftarrow\!\!\$\ \mathbb{Z}_p^m$. The adversary wins if it outputs successfully $g^{\mu(\vec{x})}$ for some polynomial $\mu(\vec{X})$ which is *independent* of the polynomials $\rho_1(\vec{X}), \ldots, \rho_q(\vec{X})$ queried to Ev, i.e., $\mu(\vec{X})$ cannot be expressed as an

$$\begin{array}{ll}
\underline{\text{Game } (m,n)\text{-OM-GAP-SDHI}^{\mathcal{A}}_{\mathsf{GGen}}(\lambda)} & \underline{\text{Oracle SDH}(B,i)} \\
(p,g,\mathbb{G}) \leftarrow\!\!\$\ \mathsf{GGen}(\lambda) & \text{Require } i \notin [1,n] \\
sk \leftarrow\!\!\$\ \mathbb{Z}_p \ ; \ [y_i]_i^m \leftarrow\!\!\$\ [\mathbb{Z}_p]_i^m & q_i \leftarrow q_i + 1 \\
(st_{\mathcal{A}}, [c_i]_i^n) \leftarrow\!\!\$\ \mathcal{A}_1(p,\mathbb{G}) & Z \leftarrow B^{1/(sk+c_i)} \\
\text{Require } \forall_{i\neq j}^n c_i \neq c_j & \text{Return } Z \\
(\gamma, [Z_i, \alpha_i]_i^\ell) \leftarrow\!\!\$\ \mathcal{A}_2^{\text{SDH,SDDH}}\!\left(g, g^{sk}, [g^{y_i}]_i^m : st_{\mathcal{A}}\right) & \\
\text{Require } q_\gamma < \ell \ \wedge\ \forall_{i\neq j}^\ell \alpha_i \neq \alpha_j & \underline{\text{Oracle SDDH}(Y,Z,i)} \\
\text{Return } [Z_i]_i^\ell = \left[g^{y_{\alpha_i}/(sk+c_\gamma)}\right]_i^\ell & \text{Return } Z = Y^{1/(sk+c_i)}
\end{array}$$

Fig. 7. The one-more gap strong Diffie-Hellman inversion security game.

$$\begin{array}{ll}
\underline{\text{Game } m\text{-UBER}^{\mathcal{A}}_{\mathsf{GGen}}(\lambda)} & \underline{\text{Oracle Ev}(\rho(\vec{X}))} \\
(p,g,\mathbb{G}) \leftarrow\!\!\$\ \mathsf{GGen}(\lambda) & Q \leftarrow Q \cup \{\rho(\vec{X})\} \\
Q \leftarrow \{\} & \text{Return } g^{\rho(\vec{x})} \\
\vec{x} = [x_i]_i^m \leftarrow\!\!\$\ [\mathbb{Z}_p]_i^m & \\
(U, \mu(\vec{X})) \leftarrow\!\!\$\ \mathcal{A}^{\text{Ev,Decide}}(p,\mathbb{G},g) & \underline{\text{Oracle Decide}(\rho(\vec{X}), [Y_i]_i^n)} \\
\text{Return } \left(U = g^{\mu(\vec{x})} \wedge Q \perp\!\!\!\perp \{\mu(\vec{X})\}\right) & \vec{y} = [y_i]_i^n \leftarrow [\log_g Y_i]_i^n \\
& \text{Return } \rho(\vec{y}) \equiv_p 0
\end{array}$$

Fig. 8. The interactive, flexible-output, polynomial uber assumption with decision oracle. Here, $\perp\!\!\!\perp$ denotes algebraic independence.

affine combination $\mu(\vec{X}) = \alpha_1 \rho_1(\vec{X}) + \cdots + \alpha_q \rho_q(\vec{X}) + \beta$. The adversary can also query an additional DECIDE oracle with a polynomial $\rho(\vec{X})$, as well as group elements $g^{y_1}, \ldots, g^{y_m}$, and learn whether $g^{\rho(y_1,\ldots,y_m)} = 0$ or not. We denote the corresponding advantage as $\mathsf{Adv}^{m\text{-uber}}_{\mathsf{GGen},\mathcal{A}}(\lambda) = \Pr\left[\, m\text{-UBER}^{\mathcal{A}}_{\mathsf{GGen}}(\lambda) \Rightarrow \mathsf{true} \,\right]$.

We prove the following theorem in the full version [43]. Here and subsequently we use '$\approx$' to denote that runtimes are equal up to small constant factors.

Theorem 1. *For any algebraic adversary $\mathcal{A}_{\text{sdhi}}$ of (m,n)-OM-GAP-SDHI with query budget $(\vec{q} = [q_1, \ldots, q_n], q_{\text{SDDH}})$, and any GGen outputting $(p,g,\mathbb{G})$, where g is a uniformly chosen element of $\mathbb{G}$, we give adversary $\mathcal{A}_{\text{uber}}$ such that*

$$\mathsf{Adv}^{(m,n)\text{-om-gap-sdhi}}_{\mathsf{GGen},\mathcal{A}_{\text{sdhi}}}(\lambda) \leq (q_{\max} + 1) \cdot \mathsf{Adv}^{(m+1)\text{-uber}}_{\mathsf{GGen},\mathcal{A}_{\text{uber}}}(\lambda) + \frac{q}{p},$$

where $q = \sum_i^n q_i$ and $q_{\max} = \max\{q_i\}_i^n$. Also, $\mathcal{A}_{\text{uber}}$ makes at most q queries to its polynomial evaluation oracle with maximum degree $q + 1$, and outputs a polynomial of degree at most q. Further, $T(\mathcal{A}_{\text{sdhi}}) \approx T(\mathcal{A}_{\text{uber}})$.

It is important here to note that the theorem assumes that the query budgets q_i corresponding to different i's are *fixed* a priori, rather than being chosen adaptively.

Combined with a basic reduction from [3], this gives us the following immediate corollary.

Corollary 1. *For any algebraic adversary $\mathcal{A}_{sdhi}$ of (m,n)-OM-GAP-SDHI, with query budget $(\vec{q} = [q_1, \ldots, q_n], q_{SDDH})$, and any GGen outputting $(p, g, \mathbb{G})$, where g is a uniformly chosen element of $\mathbb{G}$, we give adversary $\mathcal{A}_{dl}$ such that*

$$\mathsf{Adv}_{\mathsf{GGen}, \mathcal{A}_{sdhi}}^{(m,n)\text{-om-gap-sdhi}}(\lambda) \leq (q_{max} + 1) \cdot \mathsf{Adv}_{\mathsf{GGen}, \mathcal{A}_{dl}}^{(q+1)\text{-dl}}(\lambda) + \frac{q}{p},$$

where $q = \sum_i^n q_i$ and $q_{max} = \max\{q_i\}_i^n$. Further, $T(\mathcal{A}_{sdhi}) \approx T(\mathcal{A}_{dl})$.

The main difficulty of the proof of Theorem 1 in the full version [43] stems from the one-more requirement $\ell > q_\gamma$ in the winning condition, which is defined in a way that depends on the specific number of queries q_γ to $\mathrm{SDH}(\cdot, \gamma)$. To gain some intuition, it is convenient to think of the game in algebraic terms (and this point of view is also accurate when casting our proof in the AGM).[2] Specifically, let us describe exponents of the elements provided to $\mathcal{A}_2$ as formal polynomials X_0 (standing for the secret key) and $X_1, \ldots, X_m$ (for the values $y_1, \ldots, y_m$). Initially, the adversary has these polynomials available, and now a call to $\mathrm{SDH}(P, i)$ can also be thought of as dividing some polynomial P (or more generally, a rational function) by $(X_0 + c_i)$. The rational function P can be any affine combination of the functions obtained so far, and $\mathrm{SDH}(P, i)$ adds a new rational function to this set of available rational functions. In other words, consecutive queries induce a *transcript* τ consisting of the initial functions $X_0, X_1, \ldots, X_m$, and the functions returned by SDH. The goal of the adversary is to ensure that, for some γ, the span[3] of τ contains $\ell > q_\gamma$ functions of the form

$$\frac{X_{\alpha_1}}{X_0 + c_\gamma}, \quad \ldots, \quad \frac{X_{\alpha_\ell}}{X_0 + c_\gamma}.$$

An adversary cannot achieve this goal naively by querying $\mathrm{SDH}(X_{\alpha_j}, \gamma)$ for $j \in [\ell]$ without violating the query budget. Still, the key difficulty here is that the adversary *could*, after learning (say) $X_1/(X_0 + c_\gamma)$ make a further query that would give $X_1/(X_0 + c_\gamma)(X_0 + c_{\gamma'})$ for some $\gamma' \neq \gamma$. This second query would *not* count towards q_γ, and could potentially be helpful, as it *does* involve c_γ.

The bulk of our proof shows that arbitrary queries to SDH cannot, in fact, help the adversary. We do so via a careful inductive analysis which shows that the transcript τ can be rewritten in an equivalent way, call it τ', without affecting its span. In particular, τ' only involves rational functions whose denominators have form $(X_0 + c_i)^k$ for some i and k, but no products involving multiple c_i's appear in the denominators. We leverage this structure to show that the span of such τ' can include at most q_γ rational functions of the form $\frac{X_i}{X_0 + c_\gamma}$.

Now, given the above algebraic game cannot be won, an adversary winning the game must necessarily produce an output $(\gamma, [Z_i, \alpha_i]_i^\ell)$ where for at least one $i \in [\ell]$, we have that the polynomial $X_{\alpha_i}/(X_0 + c_i)$ is not in the span of the queries

---

[2] We ignore the SDDH oracle in this discussion, and it will be easy to handle in the actual proof via the DECIDE oracle.

[3] By "span" we mean the set of rational functions that can be obtained by taking *affine* combinations of the functions in τ.

to SDH. This lends itself naturally to a reduction to the Uber-assumption, which we describe in full in the proof.

Reducing to (m, n)-OM-GAP-SDHI. We now turn to showing that we can reduce the pseudorandomness security of 3HashSDHI to our new assumption. We focus on the verifiable version of 3HashSDHI; an analysis for the non-verifiable version is easily derived from our analysis here. Our analysis is in the RO model; we model all four hash functions as ROs.

We start by describing the simulator used in the proof. The simulator's goal is to respond to blind evaluation and RO queries so that the resulting transcript of values is indistinguishable from real responses. Importantly, the simulator must do this without making too many calls to the full evaluate oracle for each BLINDEVAL-queried public input t. Intuitively, achieving this security enforces that a malicious client can not exploit the blinded evaluation oracle to do more than help it compute a single POPRF output for the particular requested t.

The simulator works as follows. It chooses its own secret key sk and answers the H_1 and H_3 queries with random group elements and scalars, respectively. To answer a blinded evaluation query, it runs the scheme's blind evaluation algorithm Fn.BlindEv(sk, B), except that it uses the NIZK's simulator to generate the proof π (and to simulate any ideal primitive underlying the NIZK, i.e., H_4). The key challenge is in simulating H_2 queries, that which enables the adversary to "complete" a blinded evaluation. The simulator must arrange that the value it returns in response to H_2 queries is consistent with the random value returned by Ev. To do so, the simulator checks whether a queried point (t, x, Y) is such that $Y = H_1(x)^{1/(sk+H_3(t))}$ and, if so, it queries LIMEV(t, x) and returns the output. Otherwise, it chooses a random point to return. The simulator can perform this check because it chose sk. See the full version [43] for the full details of the simulator.

The simulation can fail should the adversary be able to query it on a point $Y = H_1(x)^{1/(sk+H_3(t))}$ when the simulator cannot make another call to LIMEV for that value t. This can only arise should the adversary query H_2 on more such values t, Y than queries it so far made to BLINDEV on that t. We show that an adversary, that can do so, can also win the (m, n)-OM-GAP-SDHI game where m, n are the total number of queries involving a distinct x value and distinct t value, respectively. (We define this more precisely below.) This step also relies on the collision resistance of H_3, which holds in the ROM.

To formalize this, we state below a theorem using the ideal primitive model in which $P = H_1 \times H_2 \times H_3 \times H_4$ for random oracles over $H_1 : * \rightarrow \mathbb{G}$, $H_2 : * \times * \times \mathbb{G} \rightarrow \{0, 1\}^\lambda$, $H_3 : * \rightarrow \mathbb{Z}_p$, $H_4 : \mathbb{G}^6 \rightarrow \mathbb{Z}_p$ for $(p, \mathbb{G})$ determined by GGen(λ). Here '$*$' denotes the set of arbitrary inputs. We define the query budget for an adversary $\mathcal{A}_{prf}$ in the P model to be a tuple $(m, n, q_E, \vec{q}, q_{H_1}, q_{H_2}, q_{H_3}, q_{H_4})$ where:

- m is the maximum number of distinct x values queried by $\mathcal{A}_{prf}$ to H_1 or H_2;
- n is the maximum number of distinct t values queried by $\mathcal{A}_{prf}$ to BLINDEV, H_2, or H_3;

- $\vec{q} = [\vec{q}_1, \ldots, \vec{q}_n]$ is a vector where each $\vec{q}_i$ is the maximum number of queries by $\mathcal{A}_{\mathrm{prf}}$ to $\mathrm{BLINDEV}(t_i, req)$ for any req and where $t_1, \ldots, t_n$ are the (at most) n values t_i queried in the course of the game in the order of when they are queried. (That is, t_1 is the first t value queried, t_2 is the second, etc.) In words, the adversary is limited to some number n of public inputs t that it can target, and makes a limited number of blinded evaluation queries for each of those inputs t.
- q_{E}, q_{H_1}, q_{H_2}, q_{H_3}, and q_{H_4} are the maximum number of queries made by $\mathcal{A}_{\mathrm{prf}}$ to the EV, H_1, H_2, H_3, and H_4 oracles, respectively.

Note that our query budget requirement $\vec{q}$ does not restrict *which* values t the adversary can use; these can be picked adaptively. But the number of times each t value is queried is restricted by the order in which they are queried. The granular accounting of blinded evaluation queries via $\vec{q}$ will be important when combining the following theorem with Theorem 1.

Theorem 2. *Let $\mathcal{A}_{\mathrm{prf}}$ be a P-model POPRF adversary against* $3\mathsf{H}$ *with query budget* $(m, n, q_{\mathsf{E}}, \vec{q}, q_{\mathsf{H}_1}, q_{\mathsf{H}_2}, q_{\mathsf{H}_3}, q_{\mathsf{H}_4})$. *Then we give a* H_4-*model adversary* $\mathcal{A}_{\mathrm{zk}}$, *an adversary* $\mathcal{A}_{\mathrm{sdhi}}$, *and a simulator* S *such that*

$$\mathsf{Adv}^{\mathrm{po\text{-}prf}}_{3\mathsf{H},\mathsf{S}[\mathsf{S}_{\Sigma}],\mathsf{P},\mathcal{A}_{\mathrm{prf}}}(\lambda) \leq \mathsf{Adv}^{\mathrm{zk}}_{\Sigma_{\mathcal{R}},\mathcal{R},\mathsf{H}_4,\mathsf{S}_{\Sigma},\mathcal{A}_{\mathrm{zk}}}(\lambda) + \mathsf{Adv}^{(m,n)\text{-}\mathrm{om\text{-}gap\text{-}sdhi}}_{\mathsf{GGen},\mathcal{A}_{\mathrm{sdhi}}}(\lambda) + \frac{n^2}{p},$$

Adversary $\mathcal{A}_{\mathrm{zk}}$ *makes* q_{H_4} *queries to its random oracle and* $\mathcal{A}_{\mathrm{sdhi}}$ *has query budget* $(\vec{q}, q_{\mathsf{H}_2})$. *Further,* $T(\mathcal{A}_{\mathrm{prf}}) \approx T(\mathcal{A}_{\mathrm{zk}}) \approx T(\mathcal{A}_{\mathrm{sdhi}})$.

A detailed proof is given in the full version [43]. It proceeds via a sequence of games, starting with the real world $\mathrm{POPRF}^{\mathcal{A}_{\mathrm{po\text{-}prf}},1}_{3\mathsf{H},\mathsf{P},\mathsf{S}}(\lambda)$ and first transitioning to a game that replaces the NIZK π with one generated by the NIZK simulator S_{Σ}. Then we change how Ev queries are handled. Instead of computing the POPRF using sk, we pick a random value and add it to a table R. We also modify the handling of H_2 queries to check if R has been set on a relevant value and, if so, patch up H_2's response so that it maintains consistency. This does not change the distribution of responses to the adversary. Finally, we are in position to perform a reduction to $(q_{\mathsf{H}_1}, q_{\mathsf{H}_3})$-OM-GAP-SDHI: the only difference between this game and the ideal world $\mathrm{POPRF}^{\mathcal{A}_{\mathrm{prf}},0}_{3\mathsf{H},\mathsf{P},\mathsf{S}[\mathsf{S}_{\Sigma}]}(\lambda)$ is when H_2 needs to repair a R value more often than queries to $\mathrm{BLINDEV}$. This reduction step is made relatively simple by our new assumption, which provides the values and oracles necessary to simulate $\mathcal{A}_{\mathrm{prf}}$'s view in a straightforward way.

We can combine the two main theorems with a standard result about the NIZK that we use (restated in Sect. 2) to give the following corollary.

Corollary 2. *Let $\mathcal{A}_{\mathrm{prf}}$ be a P-model POPRF adversary against* $3\mathsf{H}$ *with query budget* $(m, n, q_{\mathsf{E}}, \vec{q}, q_{\mathsf{H}_1}, q_{\mathsf{H}_2}, q_{\mathsf{H}_3}, q_{\mathsf{H}_4})$ *and* GGen *any group parameter generator outputting* $(p, g, \mathbb{G})$, *where p is a prime g is a uniformly chosen element of* $\mathbb{G}$.

Then, we give adversary $\mathcal{A}_{dl}$ and simulator S such that

$$\mathsf{Adv}^{po\text{-}prf}_{3H,S[S_\Sigma],P,\mathcal{A}_{prf}}(\lambda) \leq (q_{max} + 1) \cdot \mathsf{Adv}^{(q+1)\text{-}dl}_{GGen,\mathcal{A}_{dl}}(\lambda)$$
$$+ \frac{q + n^2}{p} + \frac{3q^2 + q(q_{H_4} + 4) + 2}{2^\lambda},$$

where $q = \sum_i^n q_i$, $q_{max} = \max\{q_i\}_i^n$. Further, $T(\mathcal{A}_{prf}) \approx T(\mathcal{A}_{dl})$.

Concrete Security and Parameter Selection. Corollary 2 is interpreted best in the generic-group model (GGM) [37,40], as this yields an absolute bound in terms of $\mathcal{A}_{prf}$'s resources. The advantage of a generic algorithm $\mathcal{A}_{dl}$ running in time T (or more precisely, making T queries to the generic-group oracle) against $(q+1)$-DL in a group of order p is $\mathsf{Adv}^{(q+1)\text{-}dl}_{GGen,\mathcal{A}_{dl}}(\lambda) \leq (T + q + 2)^2(q+1)/(p-1)$ (see, e.g., [3] for a proof). This advantage is multiplied by q_{max} to obtain the dominating term in our final bound. We conjecture however that the bound is somewhat pessimistic, and that the factor q_{max} is an artifact of the proof. In fact, as we discuss below, a different interpretation of our proof flow, which is particularly meaningful in the GGM, avoids this factor altogether. This improved bound omitting q_{max} is also essentially tight, since Cheon's attack [16] extracts[4] the secret key from q BLINDEVAL queries in time $\sqrt{p/q}$, as long as q divides $p - 1$ or $p + 1$.

Cheon's attack can therefore guide parameter selection, as is also done for 2HashDH deployments. For example, a 256-bit group may be sufficient to achieve security for up $T = 2^{80}$, as this would still accommodate up to $q \approx 2^{96}$ blind evaluations without violating our bounds. In contrast, to ensure security up to $T = 2^{128}$, moving to a 384-bit curve appears necessary. The conclusion being that our choice of parameters is consistent with that for 2HashDH, meaning we achieve the same group operation performance while adding public inputs.

We also note that our reduction to the uber assumption requires the generator to be uniformly chosen. We cannot envision any security issues when the generator is instead fixed, and the need for uniformly chosen generators is likely just an artifact of our proof technique.

Tighter GGM Bound. We only sketch the main idea behind the tighter GGM proof, as it is the result of a minor modification of our AGM proof flow. First, note that the $(q_{max} + 1)$ factor in Corollary 2 is inherited from Theorem 1 and is due to our inability to *efficiently* find, within the adversary $\mathcal{A}_{uber}$, a good index $j \in [\ell]$ that leads to a break of the uber-assumption. Therefore, we are left with guessing. However, an alternative is to find such j by computing all ℓ possible polynomials $\mu(\vec{X})$, and outputting the one which is independent from those input to Ev. Unfortunately, this is computationally expensive, and requires time at least $\Omega(q_{max}^2)$. In other words, we could make the proof tight with respect to

---

[4] Define $x = (sk + H_3(t))^{-1}$ for some fixed t. Then, the attacker can just obtain, via consecutive iterative queries, the values $g^x, g^{x^2}, \ldots, g^{x^q}$, and then recover x via Cheon's attack. Finally, $sk = x^{-1} - H_3(t)$.

advantage while losing tightness with respect to time complexity. While in our proof flow in the AGM this needs to be taken into account, in the GGM only the number of group operations matters (i.e., the number of oracle calls), whereas "additional" running time (enumerating polynomials and testing independence) is for free. Thus, if $\mathcal{A}_{\mathrm{prf}}$ makes T queries to its GGM oracles, our proof flow yields (with the proposed modification) an adversary $\mathcal{A}_{\mathrm{dl}}$ with roughly the same number of GGM queries and advantage against $(q+1)$-DL.

5.2   Request Privacy

We now turn to request privacy, which is simpler to analyze. Intuitively, 3HashS-DHI client requests leak no information because the blinding makes them independent of other requests and finalized outputs. The following theorem formalizes this for the case of POPRIV1 for the non-verifiable version of 3HashSDHI.

Theorem 3. *For any* POPRIV1 *adversary* $\mathcal{A}_{\mathrm{po\text{-}priv1}}$ *against* 3H *(without client verification) we have that* $\mathsf{Adv}^{\mathrm{po\text{-}priv1}}_{\mathrm{3H},\mathcal{A}_{\mathrm{po\text{-}priv1}}}(\lambda) = 0$.

Note that the theorem makes no assumptions about the hash functions or group, instead privacy derives directly from the information-theoretic blinding.

Proof. Let G be the same as game $\mathrm{POPRIV1}^{\mathcal{A},b}_{\mathrm{3H},\mathsf{P}}(\lambda)$ except that we replace $(req_d, rep_d) = (\mathsf{H}_1(x_d)^{r_d}, \mathsf{H}_1(x_d)^{r_d \cdot sk})$ with $(req_d, rep_d) = (g^{r_d}, g^{r_d \cdot sk})$ for $d \in \{0,1\}$ and where r_0, r_1 are the random exponents chosen in the two invocations of 3H.Req. Observe that in game G the values returned by REQ are independent of the challenge bit b. Then we have that

$$\Pr\left[\mathrm{POPRIV1}^{\mathcal{A},1}_{\mathrm{3H},\mathsf{P}}(\lambda) \Rightarrow 1 \right] = \Pr\left[\mathrm{G} \Rightarrow 1 \right] = \Pr\left[\mathrm{POPRIV1}^{\mathcal{A},0}_{\mathrm{3H},\mathsf{P}}(\lambda) \Rightarrow 1 \right] .$$

∎

Non-verifiable PO-PRFs, including the non-verifiable version of 3HashSDHI, cannot achieve our stronger notion of malicious request privacy. The attack is straightforward since the adversary can simply replace one of the two responses with garbage, and determine the challenge bit. In detail for the case of 3H, adversary $\mathcal{A}_{\mathrm{po\text{-}priv2}}$ can pick $sk \in \mathbb{G}$ arbitrarily, let $pk = g^{sk}$, and then query $\mathrm{REQ}(pk, t, x_0, x_1)$ for some arbitrary t, x_0, x_1. It obtains back from the oracle req, req', and then parses req as a pair (B, t). It then queries $\mathrm{FIN}(B^{1/(sk+\mathsf{H}_3(t))}, g)$ to get back reply (y_0, y_1). It checks if $y_0 = \mathsf{H}_2(\mathsf{H}_3(x_0)^{1/(sk+\mathsf{H}_3(t))})$ and returns 0 if so. Otherwise it returns one. This adversary wins with probability 1.

The verifiable version of 3HashSDHI achieves our stronger notion of malicious request privacy, due to the ZKP forcing the malicious server to respond honestly to blinded requests (relative to the public key being used). The following theorem formalizes this, where we model the hash used by the ZKP as a random oracle, and all other hashes as standard model.

Theorem 4. *Let $\mathcal{A}_{\text{po-priv2}}$ be a POPRIV2 adversary in the P-model against 3H that makes at most q queries to FIN. We give in the proof below a* SOUND$^{\mathcal{A}}_{\text{NiZK},\mathcal{R},\text{H}_4}$ *adversary $\mathcal{B}_{\text{sound}}$ such that*

$$\text{Adv}^{\text{po-priv2}}_{\text{3H,P},\mathcal{A}_{\text{po-priv2}}}(\lambda) \leq 4q \cdot \text{Adv}^{\text{sound}}_{\text{NiZK},\mathcal{R},\text{H}_4,\mathcal{B}_{\text{sound}}}(\lambda)) \ .$$

Further, $T(\mathcal{B}_{\text{sound}}) \approx T(\mathcal{A}_{\text{po-priv2}})$.

Proof. Consider game POPRIV2$^{\mathcal{A}_{\text{po-priv2}},1}_{\text{3H,P}}(\lambda)$. We consider the event that, in the course of the game, a $\text{FIN}(j,(B'_1,\pi_1),(B'_2,\pi_2))$ query is made such that either

1. $B'_1 \neq B^{1/(sk+\text{H}_3(t_j))}_{j,b}$ but $\Sigma_{\mathcal{R}}.\text{Ver}^{\text{H}_4}((g,g^{\text{H}_3(t_j)} \cdot pk_j, B'_1, B_{j,b}), \pi_1) = 1$; or
2. $B'_2 \neq B^{1/(sk+\text{H}_3(t_j))}_{j,1-b}$ but $\Sigma_{\mathcal{R}}.\text{Ver}^{\text{H}_4}((g,g^{\text{H}_3(t_j)} \cdot pk_j, B'_2, B_{j,1-b}), \pi_2) = 1$.

Here pk_j, t_j are the values queried to the jth call to REQ and we let $sk_j = \text{dlog}_g pk_j$. Recall that here $\mathcal{R} = \{(g,U,V,W),(\alpha) \ : \ U = g^\alpha \wedge W = V^\alpha\}$, and verification is therefore checking, in case (1), that

$$B'_2 = B^{\text{H}_3(t_j)+sk_j}_{j,b} \Leftrightarrow (B'_2)^{1/(sk_j+\text{H}_3(t_j))} = B_{j,b}$$

and a similar equality for case (2). So if this event occurs, this means the adversary has violated the soundness of the ZKP: only a single value $\alpha = sk_j + \text{H}_3(t_j)$ can be the witness for $\mathcal{R}$.

To formally reduce to ZKP soundness, first let game G0 be the same as POPRIV2$^{\mathcal{A}_{\text{po-priv2}}}_{\text{3H,P},b}(\lambda)$ but the bit b is chosen at random from $\{0,1\}$. Let "G0 $\Rightarrow$ b" be the event in game G0 that the game returns the value b. (We use this event notation for subsequent games analogously.) Further we let G0$_{\text{bad}}$ be the same as G0 except that within each FIN it first computes $sk_j = \text{dlog}_g pk_j$ and checks if conditions (1) and (2) hold. If either does not, then it sets a flag bad. Clearly G0$_{\text{bad}}$ is not computationally efficient; our reduction will avoid this computationally inefficient step. Finally we let G1 be the same as game G0 except that all $\text{FIN}(j, rep, rep')$ queries are handled by first replacing rep and rep' with the correct values, i.e., $rep \leftarrow B^{sk_j}_{j,b}$ and $rep' \leftarrow B^{sk_j}_{j,1-b}$ where $sk_j \leftarrow \text{dlog}_g(pk_j)$. Notice that G0$_{\text{bad}}$ and G1 are identical until the first query, if any, that sets the flag bad. We have that

$$\text{Adv}^{\text{po-priv2}}_{\text{3H,P},\mathcal{A}_{\text{po-priv2}}}(\lambda) = 2 \cdot \Pr[\text{G0} \Rightarrow b] - 1 \ .$$

and that

$$\Pr[\text{G0} \Rightarrow b] = \Pr[\text{G0}_{\text{bad}} \Rightarrow b] \leq \Pr[\text{G1} \Rightarrow b] + \Pr[\text{G0}_{\text{bad}} \text{ sets bad}] \ ,$$

where the inequality comes from the fact that G0$_{\text{bad}}$ and G1 are identical-until-bad and application of the fundamental lemma of game playing [5]. We now bound the probability that $\Pr[\text{G0}_{\text{bad}} \text{ sets bad}]$ via reduction to the soundness of the ZKP.

Adversary $\mathcal{B}_{\text{sound}}$ works as follows. First, it randomly chooses a number $q^* \in [1, 2q]$ to serve as its guess for which ZKP π will be forged by the adversary. Here q is the maximum number of FIN queries made by $\mathcal{A}_{\text{po-priv2}}$; each such query includes two proofs. Then $\mathcal{B}_{\text{sound}}$ runs G0, stopping when $\mathcal{A}_{\text{po-priv2}}$ has made $j = \lceil q^*/2 \rceil$ queries to FIN. At this point, $\mathcal{B}_{\text{sound}}$ stops outputting $((g, g^{\mathsf{H_3}(t_j)}pk_j, B'_1, B_{j,b}), \pi_1)$ if q^* is odd and $((g, g^{\mathsf{H_3}(t_j)}pk_j, B'_2, B_{j,1-b}), \pi_2)$ otherwise. Adversary $\mathcal{B}_{\text{sound}}$ avoids computing sk_j; it simply guesses which of the proofs would have caused bad to be set to true, had sk_j been computed and the conditions (1) and (2) been checked. A standard argument yields that

$$\Pr[\, \mathsf{G0}_{\mathsf{bad}} \text{ sets bad} \,] \leq 2q \cdot \mathsf{Adv}^{\text{sound}}_{\mathsf{NiZK}, \mathcal{R}, \mathsf{P}, \mathcal{B}_{\text{sound}}}(\lambda) \,.$$

To finish the proof, we can observe that G1 always correctly computes responses, and a similar argument as we used for POPRIV1 gives that the transcript observed by $\mathcal{A}_{\text{po-priv2}}$ is independent of the challenge bit b, and so $\Pr[\mathsf{G1} \Rightarrow b] = 1/2$. Combining all the above yields the advantage statement in the theorem. ∎

6   Performance Evaluation

We implemented 3HashSDHI to measure the computational cost of the protocol in comparison to related protocols, including the baseline 2HashDH VOPRF from [17], Pythia [20], and the recent attribute-based VOPRF (ABVOPRF) from Facebook [26]. Each protocol was implemented in a minimal fashion, e.g., by omitting domain separating hash function invocations, in order to emphasize the cost of core public key operations. Our implementations use the ristretto255 group [44] where prime-order groups are required, and the bn256 curve for Pythia, where pairing-friendly curves are required. We implemented each protocol in Go using the CIRCL experimental cryptographic library [21] and bn256 package. These benchmarks were evaluated on a machine with a 2.6 GHz 6-Core Intel Core i7 CPU and 32 GB RAM running macOS 10.15.7. We defer the results of our benchmarks to the full version [43].

7   Applications

POPRFs provide a new degree of flexibility that we observe to be useful in a variety of applications. Essentially anywhere an OPRF is used we see opportunity for POPRFs to provide potential benefits in terms of increasing deployment flexibility, reducing key management challenges, and/or improving security. In the full version [43], we discuss further three previously mentioned motivating applications: anonymous one-time-use tokens, password breach alerting, and password-based authenticated key exchange.

Acknowledgments. The authors would like to thank Tjerand Silde, Martin Strand, and Tancrede Lepoint for helpful discussions on early versions of this work. This work was supported in part by NSF grants CNS-1930117 (CAREER), CNS-1926324, CNS-2026774, CNS-2120651, a Sloan Research Fellowship, a JP Morgan Faculty Award, and a Facebook PhD Fellowship.

References

1. Abe, M., Fujisaki, E.: How to date blind signatures. In: Kim, K., Matsumoto, T. (eds.) ASIACRYPT 1996. LNCS, vol. 1163, pp. 244–251. Springer, Heidelberg (1996). https://doi.org/10.1007/BFb0034851

2. Abe, M., Okamoto, T.: Provably secure partially blind signatures. In: Bellare, M. (ed.) CRYPTO 2000. LNCS, vol. 1880, pp. 271–286. Springer, Heidelberg (2000). https://doi.org/10.1007/3-540-44598-6_17

3. Bauer, B., Fuchsbauer, G., Loss, J.: A classification of computational assumptions in the algebraic group model. In: Micciancio, D., Ristenpart, T. (eds.) CRYPTO 2020. LNCS, vol. 12171, pp. 121–151. Springer, Cham (2020). https://doi.org/10.1007/978-3-030-56880-1_5

4. Bellare, M., Namprempre, C., Pointcheval, D., Semanko, M.: The one-more-RSA-inversion problems and the security of Chaum's blind signature scheme. J. Cryptol. **16**(3), 185–215 (2003)

5. Bellare, M., Rogaway, P.: The security of triple encryption and a framework for code-based game-playing proofs. In: Vaudenay, S. (ed.) EUROCRYPT 2006. LNCS, vol. 4004, pp. 409–426. Springer, Heidelberg (2006). https://doi.org/10.1007/11761679_25

6. Bellovin, S., Merritt, M.: Augmented encrypted key exchange: a password based protocol secure against dictionary attacks and password file compromise. In: CCS, pp. 244–250. ACM (1993)

7. Benhamouda, F., Lepoint, T., Loss, J., Orrù, M., Raykova, M.: On the (in)security of ROS. In: Canteaut, A., Standaert, F.-X. (eds.) EUROCRYPT 2021. LNCS, vol. 12696, pp. 33–53. Springer, Cham (2021). https://doi.org/10.1007/978-3-030-77870-5_2

8. Boldyreva, A.: Threshold signatures, multisignatures and blind signatures based on the gap-Diffie-Hellman-group signature scheme. In: Desmedt, Y.G. (ed.) PKC 2003. LNCS, vol. 2567, pp. 31–46. Springer, Heidelberg (2003). https://doi.org/10.1007/3-540-36288-6_3

9. Camenisch, J.: Group signature schemes and payment systems based on the discrete logarithm problem. Ph.D. thesis, ETH Zurich, Zürich, Switzerland (1998)

10. Camenisch, J., Lysyanskaya, A.: Signature schemes and anonymous credentials from bilinear maps. In: Franklin, M. (ed.) CRYPTO 2004. LNCS, vol. 3152, pp. 56–72. Springer, Heidelberg (2004). https://doi.org/10.1007/978-3-540-28628-8_4

11. Camenisch, J., Shoup, V.: Practical verifiable encryption and decryption of discrete logarithms. In: Boneh, D. (ed.) CRYPTO 2003. LNCS, vol. 2729, pp. 126–144. Springer, Heidelberg (2003). https://doi.org/10.1007/978-3-540-45146-4_8

12. Celi, S., Davidson, A., Faz-Hernández, A.: Privacy Pass Protocol Specification. Internet-Draft draft-ietf-privacypass-protocol-00, Internet Engineering Task Force, January 2021. https://datatracker.ietf.org/doc/html/draft-ietf-privacypass-protocol-00. Work in Progress

13. Chase, M., Meiklejohn, S., Zaverucha, G.: Algebraic macs and keyed-verification anonymous credentials. In: CCS, pp. 1205–1216. ACM (2014)

14. Chase, M., Perrin, T., Zaverucha, G.: The signal private group system and anonymous credentials supporting efficient verifiable encryption. In: CCS, pp. 1445–1459. ACM (2020)

15. Chaum, D., Pedersen, T.P.: Wallet databases with observers. In: Brickell, E.F. (ed.) CRYPTO 1992. LNCS, vol. 740, pp. 89–105. Springer, Heidelberg (1993). https://doi.org/10.1007/3-540-48071-4_7

16. Cheon, J.H.: Security analysis of the strong Diffie-Hellman problem. In: Vaudenay, S. (ed.) EUROCRYPT 2006. LNCS, vol. 4004, pp. 1–11. Springer, Heidelberg (2006). https://doi.org/10.1007/11761679_1
17. Davidson, A., Faz-Hernández, A., Sullivan, N., Wood, C.A.: Oblivious Pseudorandom Functions (OPRFs) using Prime-Order Groups. Internet-Draft draft-irtf-cfrg-voprf-05, Internet Engineering Task Force, November 2020. https://datatracker.ietf.org/doc/html/draft-irtf-cfrg-voprf-05. Work in Progress
18. Davidson, A., Goldberg, I., Sullivan, N., Tankersley, G., Valsorda, F.: Privacy pass: bypassing internet challenges anonymously. Proc. Priv. Enhancing Technol. **2018**(3), 164–180 (2018)
19. Dodis, Y., Yampolskiy, A.: A verifiable random function with short proofs and keys. In: Vaudenay, S. (ed.) PKC 2005. LNCS, vol. 3386, pp. 416–431. Springer, Heidelberg (2005). https://doi.org/10.1007/978-3-540-30580-4_28
20. Everspaugh, A., Chatterjee, R., Scott, S., Juels, A., Ristenpart, T.: The pythia PRF service. In: 24th USENIX Security Symposium (USENIX Security 2015), pp. 547–562. USENIX Association (2015). https://www.usenix.org/conference/usenixsecurity15/technical-sessions/presentation/everspaugh
21. Faz-Hernández, A., Kwiatkowski, K.: Introducing CIRCL: An Advanced Cryptographic Library. Cloudflare, June 2019. https://github.com/cloudflare/circl
22. Fischlin, M.: Round-optimal composable blind signatures in the common reference string model. In: Dwork, C. (ed.) CRYPTO 2006. LNCS, vol. 4117, pp. 60–77. Springer, Heidelberg (2006). https://doi.org/10.1007/11818175_4
23. Freedman, M.J., Ishai, Y., Pinkas, B., Reingold, O.: Keyword search and oblivious pseudorandom functions. In: Kilian, J. (ed.) TCC 2005. LNCS, vol. 3378, pp. 303–324. Springer, Heidelberg (2005). https://doi.org/10.1007/978-3-540-30576-7_17
24. Fuchsbauer, G., Kiltz, E., Loss, J.: The algebraic group model and its applications. In: Shacham, H., Boldyreva, A. (eds.) CRYPTO 2018. LNCS, vol. 10992, pp. 33–62. Springer, Cham (2018). https://doi.org/10.1007/978-3-319-96881-0_2
25. Fuchsbauer, G., Plouviez, A., Seurin, Y.: Blind schnorr signatures and signed ElGamal encryption in the algebraic group model. In: Canteaut, A., Ishai, Y. (eds.) EUROCRYPT 2020. LNCS, vol. 12106, pp. 63–95. Springer, Cham (2020). https://doi.org/10.1007/978-3-030-45724-2_3
26. Huang, S., et al.: PrivateStats: De-Identified Authenticated Logging at Scale, January 2021. https://research.fb.com/wp-content/uploads/2021/01/PrivateStats-De-Identified-Authenticated-Logging-at-Scale_final.pdf
27. Jaeger, J., Tyagi, N.: Handling adaptive compromise for practical encryption schemes. In: Micciancio, D., Ristenpart, T. (eds.) CRYPTO 2020. LNCS, vol. 12170, pp. 3–32. Springer, Cham (2020). https://doi.org/10.1007/978-3-030-56784-2_1
28. Jarecki, S., Kiayias, A., Krawczyk, H.: Round-optimal password-protected secret sharing and T-PAKE in the password-only model. In: Sarkar, P., Iwata, T. (eds.) ASIACRYPT 2014. LNCS, vol. 8874, pp. 233–253. Springer, Heidelberg (2014). https://doi.org/10.1007/978-3-662-45608-8_13
29. Jarecki, S., Krawczyk, H., Resch, J.K.: Threshold partially-oblivious PRFs with applications to key management. IACR Cryptology ePrint Archive, p. 733 (2018)
30. Jarecki, S., Krawczyk, H., Xu, J.: OPAQUE: an asymmetric PAKE protocol secure against pre-computation attacks. In: Nielsen, J.B., Rijmen, V. (eds.) EUROCRYPT 2018. LNCS, vol. 10822, pp. 456–486. Springer, Cham (2018). https://doi.org/10.1007/978-3-319-78372-7_15

31. Jarecki, S., Krawczyk, H., Xu, J.: On the (in)security of the Diffie-Hellman oblivious PRF with multiplicative blinding. In: Garay, J.A. (ed.) PKC 2021. LNCS, vol. 12711, pp. 380–409. Springer, Cham (2021). https://doi.org/10.1007/978-3-030-75248-4_14

32. Jarecki, S., Liu, X.: Efficient oblivious pseudorandom function with applications to adaptive OT and secure computation of set intersection. In: Reingold, O. (ed.) TCC 2009. LNCS, vol. 5444, pp. 577–594. Springer, Heidelberg (2009). https://doi.org/10.1007/978-3-642-00457-5_34

33. Kiayias, A., Zhou, H.-S.: Equivocal blind signatures and adaptive UC-security. In: Canetti, R. (ed.) TCC 2008. LNCS, vol. 4948, pp. 340–355. Springer, Heidelberg (2008). https://doi.org/10.1007/978-3-540-78524-8_19

34. Krawczyk, H., Lewi, K., Wood, C.A.: The OPAQUE Asymmetric PAKE Protocol. Internet-Draft draft-irtf-cfrg-opaque-02, Internet Engineering Task Force, February 2021. https://datatracker.ietf.org/doc/html/draft-irtf-cfrg-opaque-02. Work in Progress

35. Kreuter, B., Lepoint, T., Orrù, M., Raykova, M.: Anonymous tokens with private metadata bit. In: Micciancio, D., Ristenpart, T. (eds.) CRYPTO 2020. LNCS, vol. 12170, pp. 308–336. Springer, Cham (2020). https://doi.org/10.1007/978-3-030-56784-2_11

36. Li, L., Pal, B., Ali, J., Sullivan, N., Chatterjee, R., Ristenpart, T.: Protocols for checking compromised credentials. In: CCS, pp. 1387–1403. ACM (2019)

37. Maurer, U.M.: Abstract models of computation in cryptography. In: Smart, N.P. (ed.) Cryptography and Coding 2005. LNCS, vol. 3796, pp. 1–12. Springer, Heidelberg (2005). https://doi.org/10.1007/11586821_1

38. Miao, P., Patel, S., Raykova, M., Seth, K., Yung, M.: Two-sided malicious security for private intersection-sum with cardinality. In: Micciancio, D., Ristenpart, T. (eds.) CRYPTO 2020. LNCS, vol. 12172, pp. 3–33. Springer, Cham (2020). https://doi.org/10.1007/978-3-030-56877-1_1

39. Naor, M., Reingold, O.: Number-theoretic constructions of efficient pseudo-random functions. In: FOCS, pp. 458–467. IEEE Computer Society (1997)

40. Shoup, V.: Lower bounds for discrete logarithms and related problems. In: Fumy, W. (ed.) EUROCRYPT 1997. LNCS, vol. 1233, pp. 256–266. Springer, Heidelberg (1997). https://doi.org/10.1007/3-540-69053-0_18

41. Silde, T., Strand, M.: Anonymous tokens with public metadata and applications to private contact tracing. IACR Cryptol. ePrint Arch. **2021**, 203 (2021)

42. Thomas, K., et al.: Protecting accounts from credential stuffing with password breach alerting. In: USENIX Security Symposium, pp. 1556–1571. USENIX Association (2019)

43. Tyagi, N., Celi, S., Ristenpart, T., Sullivan, N., Tessaro, S., Wood, C.A.: A fast and simple partially oblivious PRF, with applications. IACR Cryptology ePrint Archive, p. 864 (2021)

44. de Valence, H., Grigg, J., Tankersley, G., Valsorda, F., Lovecruft, I., Hamburg, M.: The ristretto255 and decaf448 Groups. Internet-Draft draft-irtf-cfrg-ristretto255-decaf448-00, Internet Engineering Task Force, October 2020. https://datatracker.ietf.org/doc/html/draft-irtf-cfrg-ristretto255-decaf448-00. Work in Progress

45. Wilander, J., Taubeneck, E., Knox, A., Wood, C.: Consider using blinded signatures for fraud prevention - Private Click Measurement (2020). https://github.com/privacycg/private-click-measurement/issues/41

46. Zhang, F., Safavi-Naini, R., Susilo, W.: Efficient verifiably encrypted signature and partially blind signature from bilinear pairings. In: Johansson, T., Maitra, S. (eds.) INDOCRYPT 2003. LNCS, vol. 2904, pp. 191–204. Springer, Heidelberg (2003). https://doi.org/10.1007/978-3-540-24582-7_14

47. Zhang, F., Safavi-Naini, R., Susilo, W.: An efficient signature scheme from bilinear pairings and its applications. In: Bao, F., Deng, R., Zhou, J. (eds.) PKC 2004. LNCS, vol. 2947, pp. 277–290. Springer, Heidelberg (2004). https://doi.org/10.1007/978-3-540-24632-9_20

Hiding in Plain Sight: Memory-Tight Proofs via Randomness Programming

Ashrujit Ghoshal[1]([✉]), Riddhi Ghosal[2], Joseph Jaeger[3], and Stefano Tessaro[1]

[1] Paul G. Allen School of Computer Science & Engineering,
University of Washington, Seattle, USA
{ashrujit,tessaro}@cs.washington.edu
[2] University of California, Los Angeles, USA
riddhi@cs.ucla.edu
[3] Georgia Institute of Technology, Atlanta, GA, USA
josephjaeger@gatech.edu

Abstract. This paper continues the study of *memory-tight reductions* (Auerbach et al., CRYPTO '17). These are reductions that only incur minimal memory costs over those of the original adversary, allowing precise security statements for memory-bounded adversaries (under appropriate assumptions expressed in terms of adversary time and memory usage). Despite its importance, only a few techniques to achieve memory-tightness are known and impossibility results in prior works show that even basic, textbook reductions cannot be made memory-tight.

This paper introduces a new class of memory-tight reductions which leverage random strings in the interaction with the adversary to hide state information, thus shifting the memory costs to the adversary.

We exhibit this technique with several examples. We give memory-tight proofs for digital signatures allowing many forgery attempts when considering randomized message distributions or probabilistic RSA-FDH signatures specifically. We prove security of the authenticated encryption scheme Encrypt-then-PRF with a memory-tight reduction to the underlying encryption scheme. By considering specific schemes or restricted definitions we avoid generic impossibility results of Auerbach et al. (CRYPTO '17) and Ghoshal et al. (CRYPTO '20).

As a further case study, we consider the textbook equivalence of CCA-security for public-key encryption for one or multiple encryption queries. We show two qualitatively different memory-tight versions of this result, depending on the considered notion of CCA security.

Keywords: Provable security · Memory-tightness · Time-memory trade-offs

1 Introduction

The aim of concrete security proofs is to lower bound, as precisely as possible, the resources needed to break a cryptographic scheme of interest, under some plausible assumptions. The traditional resource used in provable security is *time*

© International Association for Cryptologic Research 2022
O. Dunkelman and S. Dziembowski (Eds.): EUROCRYPT 2022, LNCS 13276, pp. 706–735, 2022.
https://doi.org/10.1007/978-3-031-07085-3_24

complexity (as well as related metrics, like data complexity). Recent works [1, 7, 9–12, 15–17, 20–22] have focused on additionally taking the *memory* costs of the adversary into account. This is important, as the amount of available memory can seriously impact the feasibility of an attack.

This paper presents new techniques for *memory-tight reductions*, a notion introduced by Auerbach et al. [1] to relate the assumed time-memory hardness of an underlying computational problem to the security of a scheme. More precisely, the end goal is to prove, via a reduction, that any adversary running in time t and with s bits of memory can achieve at most advantage $\epsilon = \epsilon(t, s)$ in compromising a scheme, by assuming that some underlying computational problem can only be solved with advantage $\delta = \delta(t', s')$ by algorithms running in time t' and with memory s'. A memory-tight reduction guarantees that $s \approx s'$, and usually, we want this to be tight also according to other parameters, i.e., $t \approx t'$ and $\epsilon \approx \delta$.

Memory-tight reductions are of value whenever the underlying problem is (conjectured to) be *memory sensitive*, i.e., the time needed to solve it grows as the amount of memory available to the adversary is reduced. Examples of memory-sensitive problems include classical ones in the public-key setting, such as breaking RSA and factoring, lattice problems and LPN, solving discrete logarithms over finite fields,[1] as well as problems in the secret-key setting, such as finding k-way collisions (for $k > 2$), finding several collisions at once [11], and distinguishing random permutations from random functions [12, 17, 20].

Developing memory-tight reductions is not always easy, and can be (provably) impossible [1, 15, 16, 22]. This makes it fundamental to develop as many techniques as possible to obtain such reductions. In this paper, we identify a class of examples which admit a new kind of memory-tight reductions. Our approach relies on the availability of random strings exchanged between the adversary and the security game, and which the reduction can leverage to encode state which can be recovered from later queries of the adversary, without the need to store this information locally, and thus saving memory. (In particular, the burden of keeping this information remains on the adversary, which needs to reproduce this random string for this state information to be relevant.) We present these techniques abstractly in the next section, with the help of a motivating example, and then move on to an overview of our specific results.

1.1 Our Techniques - An Overview

As a motivating example, consider the standard UFCMA security notion for signatures. It is defined via a game where the attacker, given the verification key vk, obtains signatures for chosen messages $m_1, m_2, \ldots$, after which it outputs a candidate message-signature pair (m^*, σ^*), and wins if m^* was not signed before, and σ^* is valid for m^*. When ignoring memory, this notion is *tightly* equivalent to one (which we refer to as mUFCMA) that allows for an arbitrary number

---

[1] However, the discrete logarithm problem in elliptic-curve groups, or any other group in which the best-known attacks are generic, is not memory sensitive, since optimal memory-less attacks are known.

of "forgery attempts" for pairs (m^*, σ^*), and the adversary wins if one of them succeeds in the above sense. This is convenient: we generally target mUFCMA, but only need to deal with proving the simpler UFCMA notion.

The classical reduction transforms any mUFCMA adversary into a roughly equally efficient UFCMA adversary, which wins with the same probability, by (1) simulating forgery queries using the verification key, and (2) outputting the first forgery query (m^*, σ^*) which validates and such that m^* is fresh. This reduction is however *not* memory-tight, as we need to ensure the freshness of m^*, which requires remembering the previously signed messages. ACFK [1] prove that this is in some sense necessary, by showing that a (restricted) class of reductions cannot be memory-tight via a reduction to streaming lower bounds.

OUR IDEA: EFFICIENT TAGGING. To illustrate our new technique, which we refer to as *efficient tagging*, imagine now that we only use the signature scheme to sign *random* messages $m_1, m_2, \ldots, m_q \leftarrow_{\$} \{0,1\}^\ell$, and consider a corresponding variant of mUFCMA security, which we want to reduce to (plain) UFCMA security. This, intuitively, does not seem to help resolve the above issue, because random messages are hardest to compress.

However, what is important here is that the reduction is responsible for simulating the random messages, and can simulate them in special ways, and *program* them so that they encode state information. For instance, assume that the reduction has access to an *injective* random function $f : [q] \to \{0,1\}^\ell$, with inverse f^{-1}, which can be simulated *succinctly* from a short key as a pseudorandom object. Then, the reduction to UFCMA can set $m_i \leftarrow f(i)$ for the i-th query, and upon simulating a forgery query for (m^*, σ^*), the reduction checks whether $f^{-1}(m^*) \in [q]$ to learn whether m^* is a fresh signing query or not.

Of course, the simulation is not perfect: The original m_i's are not necessarily distinct (this can be handled via the classical "switching lemma"). Also, the reduction could miss a valid forgery if the adversary outputs m_i *before* it is given to the adversary, but this again only occurs with small probability.

INEFFICIENT TAGGING AND NON-TIME-TIGHT REDUCTIONS. In the above example, we can efficiently check that $f^{-1}(m^*) \in [q]$. However, in some cases we may not – again, consider an example where the messages to be signed are sampled as $m_i \leftarrow h(r_i)$, where h is a hard-to-invert function and r_i is random. Then, we could adapt our proof above by setting $m_i \leftarrow h(f(i))$, but now, to detect a prior signing query, we would have to check whether $m^* = h(f(i))$ for some $i \in [q]$, and this can only be done in linear time. The resulting UFCMA adversary runs in time $t' = t + \Theta(q_F \cdot q)$, where t is the running time of the original adversary and q_F is the number of forgery attempts. For example, if $q \approx q_F \approx t$, the reduction is not time tight, and the adversary runs in time $t' = O(t^2)$.

ARE NON-TIME-TIGHT REDUCTIONS USELESS? It turns out that such non-time-tight reductions can still be helpful to infer that breaking a scheme requires memory, although this ultimately depends on the concrete security of the problem targeted by the reduction. Say, for example, a reduction for a given scheme transforms a successful adversary running in time t and using memory s into an adversary running in time t^2 and using memory s breaking discrete logarithms over $\mathbb{F}_p$, for a 4096-bit prime p. It turns out that if we have fewer than 2^{78} bits of memory, no known discrete logarithm algorithm is better than a generic one (i.e. runs in time better than 2^{2048}), which means that our non-time-tight reduction is still sufficient to infer security for any $s < 2^{78}$ as long as $t < 2^{1024}$.

MESSAGE ENCODING. At the highest level, what happens is that the reduction is in control of certain random values which we can exploit to hide state information which can later be uniquely recovered, since triggering a situation where the reduction needs to remember requires the adversary to actually give back to the reduction this value. In the above, this state information is simple, namely whether the query is old or not. But as we will show below, the paradigm can be used to store complex information – we refer to this technique as *message encoding*, and discuss an example below.

A NEW VIEWPOINT: $\mathcal{F}$-ORACLE ADVERSARIES. In our technique described above we needed access to a large random injection, which we argue can be simulated pseudorandomly. Prior works have similarly used PRFs to pseudorandomly simulate random oracles [1,6] with low memory. The fact that one needs to decide how to simulate such objects when stating a memory-tight reduction is rather inconvenient: different instantiations seemingly lead to quantitatively different reductions, although this fact does not appear to be a reflection of any particular reality. In this paper, we propose (and advocate for) what we believe to be the "right" viewpoint: Our reductions are stated in terms of $\mathcal{F}$-oracle adversaries where $\mathcal{F}$ is a set of functions and such an adversary expects oracle access to a random $f \in \mathcal{F}$. Then, a memory-tightness theorem is obtained in one of two ways, by either (1) applying a generic lemma stating that f can be instantiated in low memory using an $\mathcal{F}$-pseudorandom function, or (2) assuming that the use of f does not functionally increase the success chances of the adversary because f is independent of the problem instance being solved (this is provably the case for some information theoretic problems). In particular, (1) is more conservative than (2), but it is very likely that (2) is also a viable approach which leads to cleaner result – indeed, we do not expect any of the considered memory-sensitive problems to become easier given access to an oracle from any natural class $\mathcal{F}$ – e.g., Factoring does not become easier given access to a random injection.

1.2   Our Results

We now move to an overview of our results (summarized in Fig. 1) which exemplify different applications of the tagging and message-encoding techniques.

MULTI-CHALLENGE SECURITY OF DIGITAL SIGNATURES. Our first results consider the security of digital signatures in the face of multiple forgery attempts (i.e., challenge queries), generalizing the examples discussed above. We work with a notion we refer to as UFRMA (unforgeability under randomized message attack). This notion is parameterized by a *message distribution* D and when the attacker makes a signing query for m it receives a signature of $m' = D(m; r)$ for a random r. If m and r can be extracted from m', giving the notion xUFRMA (or mxUFRMA for many forgery attempts), we can generalize our efficient tagging approach above by having the reduction to UFCMA choose $r = f(m, i)$ where each $f(m, \cdot)$ is a random injection. This setting can capture, e.g., the signatures used in key exchange protocols like TLS 1.3 where the server signs a transcript which includes a random 256-bit nonce. A version of our inefficient tagging example works when only m can be extracted from m' (wUFRMA); we pick $r = f(m, i)$ and in verification of a forgery query perform the linear time check of whether $m^* = D(m; f(m, i))$ for some $i \in [q]$. This setting captures places where the message to be signed includes a fresh public key or ciphertext. This includes, for example, the use of signatures for signing certificates, in some key exchange protocols, and in signcryption.

We further prove mUFCMA security for particular schemes. First, we can randomize any digital signature scheme DS (obtaining a scheme we call RDS) by signing $m \parallel r$ for random r chosen by the signing algorithm and including r as part of the signature. An immediate implication of our mxUFCRA result is a tight reduction from the mUFCMA security of RDS to the UFCMA security of the underlying scheme. One particular instantiation of RDS is Probabilistic Full Domain Hash with RSA (RSA-PFDH) which was introduced by Coron [8] to provide a variant of Full Domain Hash [4] with an (advantage-) tighter security proof. Using our efficient tagging technique we obtain a fully tight proof of the *strong* mUFCMA security of RSA-PFDH from the RSA assumption.

In independent and concurrent work, Diemert, Gellert, Jager, and Lyu [10] studied the mUFCMA security of digital signature schemes. They also considered the RDS construction, proving that if DS can be proven strong UFCMA1 secure[2] with a restricted class of "canonical" memory-tight reductions then there is a memory-tight reduction for the strong mUFCMA security of RDS. This complements our result, showing memory-tight strong mUFCMA security of RDS based on a restricted class of schemes while our result proves memory-tight plain mUFCMA security based on any plain UFCMA scheme. They apply their RDS result to establish tight proofs for the strong mUFCMA security of RSA-PFDH (matching our direct proof in Theorem 3). as well as schemes based on lossy identification schemes and pairings.

AUTHENTICATED ENCRYPTION SECURITY. Ghoshal, Jaeger, and Tessaro [15] have recently observed that in the context of authenticated encryption (AE), it is difficult to lift confidentiality of the scheme, in terms of INDR security, to full AE security, when additionally assuming ciphertext integrity, if we want to do so in a memory-tight way. This is well motivated, as several works establish tight time-memory trade-offs for INDR security [9,12,17,20,21], which we would like to lift to their AE security. The difficulty in the proof is that the INDR reduction must simulate a decryption oracle which rejects all ciphertexts *except those forwarded from an encryption query*. Recognizing these forwarded ciphertexts seems to require remembering state.

---

[2] The suffix '1' indicates a variant of UFCMA security in which the adversary can only obtain a single signature per message. The security game always returning the same signature if the adversary repeats signature queries.

Assumption	Scheme	Result	Time	Memory	Advantage	New Technique
1UFCMA	Any	mxUFRMA	✓	✓	✓	Efficient tagging
	RDS	mUFCMA	✓	✓	✓	Efficient tagging
	Any	mwUFRMA	✗	✓	✓	Inefficient tagging
RSA	RSA-PFDH	mSUFCMA	✓	✓	✓	Efficient tagging
(PRF, INDR)	EtP	AE	(✓,✓)	(✗,✓)	(✓,✓)	Efficient tagging
1CCA	Any	mCCA	✗	✓	✗	Inefficient tagging
1$CCA	Any	m$CCA	✓	✓	✗	Message encoding

Fig. 1. Memory-tight reductions we provide. A 1 vs. an m prefix indicates whether one or many challenge queries are allowed. A ✓ vs. an ✗ indicates whether the reduction is tight with respect to that complexity metric. Reductions lacking tightness multiply running time/advantage by $O(q)$ or add $O(q)$ to the memory complexity, where q is the number of queries. An x vs. a w indicates whether the coins underlying the distribution of messages can be extracted from the message. RDS is randomization of any digital signature scheme by padding input messages with randomness. RSA-PFDH is probabilistic full-domain hash with RSA. EtP is the Encrypt-then-PRF AE construction.

Here, we give a different take and show that for specific schemes – in particular, those obtained by adding integrity via a PRF, following the lines of [3,18,19] – a memory-tight reduction *can* be given. Our INDR reduction is applied after arguing that the PRF looks like a random function f and thus forgeries are unlikely to occur. It uses f in a version of our efficient tagging technique to identify whether a ciphertext queried to decryption is fresh.[3]

CHOSEN CIPHERTEXT SECURITY: ONE TO MANY. A classical textbook result for public-key encryption shows that CCA-security against a *single* encryption query (1CCA) implies security against *multiple* queries (mCCA), with a quantitative advantage loss accounting to the number of such queries. ACFK [1] claim, incorrectly, that the associated reduction from 1CCA to mCCA is easy to make memory-tight, but this appears to be an oversight: No such reduction is known, and here we use our techniques to recover a memory-tight version of this result.

Let us consider concretely the "left-or-right" formulation of 1CCA/mCCA-security: The reduction from 1CCA to mCCA, given an adversary $\mathcal{A}$, picks a random $i \leftarrow^\$ [q]$ (where q is the number of encryption queries) and simulates the multi-query challenger to $\mathcal{A}$ by answering its first $i-1$ encryption queries with an encryption of the left message, whereas the last $q-i$ queries are answered by encrypting the right message. Only the answer to the i-th query is answered by the single-query challenger. A problem arises when simulating the decryption queries: Indeed, we need to guarantee that a decryption query for *any* of the challenge ciphertexts $c_1^*, \ldots, c_q^*$ returns an error $\perp$, yet this suggests that we seemingly need to remember the extra challenge ciphertexts c_j^* for $j \neq i$.

---

[3] Ghoshal et al. [15] in fact described three variants of AE with different conventions for how decryption responds to non-fresh queries. By our results, memory-tight reductions to INDR are possible for two of the three variants.

We will resolve this in two ways. First, we give a new memory-tight reduction using the inefficient tagging method, with the same advantage loss as the original textbook reduction. Our reduction is non-time-tight, so may not be suitable for all situations. The main idea here is that we use the *randomness* used to generate the challenge ciphertext as our tag.

To obtain a reduction which is also tight with respect to time, we resort to the observation that changing to a stronger (but still commonly achieved) definition of CCA-security allows for different memory-tight reductions. We give in particular a memory-tight *and* time-tight reduction (with the usual factor q advantage loss) from the notion of 1\$CCA-m security to the notion of m\$CCA-m security. These are variants of CCA security where (1) encryption queries are with respect to a *single* message, and return either the encryption of the message, or a random, independent ciphertext, and (2) decryption queries on a challenge ciphertext c_i^* returns the associated message.

Our reduction uses the full power of our message encoding approach, simulating random ciphertexts in a careful way which allows for recovering the associated challenge plaintext.

A FEW REMARKS. The above results on CCA security show us that the ability to give a memory-tight reduction is strongly coupled with definitional choices. In particular, different equivalent approaches to modeling the decryption oracle in the memory unbounded regime may not be equivalent in the memory-bounded setting. This means in particular that we need to exercise more care in choosing the right definition. We believe, for example, that the approach taken in m\$CCA-m security is the more "natural" one (as it does not require artificially blocking the output of the decryption oracle, by always returning a message), but there may be contexts where other definitional choices are favored.

Another important lesson learnt from our AE result is that impossibility results, such as those in [1, 15, 16, 22], do not preclude positive results in form of memory-tight reductions, either by leveraging the structure of specific schemes, or by considering restricted security notions.

1.3   Paper Outline

Section 2 introduces notation, our computational model, and basic cryptographic background. Section 3 discusses our convention of using $\mathcal{F}$-oracle adversaries. Section 4 gives our memory-tight reduction for digital signature schemes when many forgery attempts are allowed. In particular, the generic results are in Sect. 4.2, while the result specific to RSA-PFDH is in Sect. 4.5. Section 5 proves the security of Encrypt-then-PRF with a memory-tight reduction to the INDR security of the encryption scheme. Section 6 gives our results relating the one- and many-challenge query variants of CCA security. In particular, Sect. 6.1 gives our result for the traditional "left-vs.-right" notion and Sect. 6.2 gives our result for the "indistinguishable from random" variant. The full version of this paper [14] contains omitted proofs.

2 Preliminaries

Let $\mathbb{N} = \{0, 1, \dots\}$ and $[n] = \{1, \dots, n\}$ for $n \in \mathbb{N}$. If $x \in \{0,1\}^*$ is a string, then $|x|$ denotes its length in bits. If S is a set, then $|S|$ denotes its size. We let $x \, \| \, y \, \| \dots$ denote an encoding of the strings $x, y, \dots$ from which the constituent strings can be unambiguously recovered. We identify bitstrings with integers in the standard way.

FUNCTIONS. Let T be a set (called the tweak set) and for each $t \in T$ let D_t and R_t be sets. Then $\mathsf{Fcs}(T, D, R)$ denotes the set of all f such that for each $t \in T$, $f(t, \cdot)$ is a function from D_t to R_t. Similarly, $\mathsf{Inj}(T, D, R)$ denotes the set of all f such that for each $t \in T$, $f(t, \cdot)$ is an injection from D_t to R_t. When D_t or R_t are independent of the choice of t we may omit the subscript.

If $f \in \mathsf{Inj}(T, D, R)$, then its inverse f^{-1} is defined by $f^{-1}(t, f(t, x)) = x$ for all (t, x) and $f^{-1}(t, y) = \perp$ for $y \notin f(t, D_t)$. For such f we let $f^{\pm}$ denote the function defined by $f^{\pm}(+, x) = f(x)$ and $f^{\pm}(-, x) = f^{-1}(x)$. We let $\mathsf{Inj}^{\pm}(T, D, R) = \{f^{\pm} : f \in \mathsf{Inj}(T, D, R)\}$.

2.1 Computational Model

PSEUDOCODE. We regularly use pseudocode inspired by the code-based framework of [5]. We think of algorithms as randomized RAMs when not specified otherwise. If $\mathcal{A}$ is an algorithm, then $y \leftarrow \mathcal{A}^{O_1, \dots}(x_1, \dots; r)$ denotes running $\mathcal{A}$ on inputs $x_1, \dots$ with coins r and access to the oracles $O_1, \dots$ to produce output y. When the coins are implicit we write $\leftarrow\!\!{\scriptstyle\$}$ in place of $\leftarrow$ and omit r.

We let $x \leftarrow\!\!{\scriptstyle\$} \mathcal{D}$ denote sampling x according to the distribution $\mathcal{D}$. If $\mathcal{D}$ is a set, we overload notation and let $\mathcal{D}$ also denote the uniform distribution over elements of $\mathcal{D}$. The domain of $\mathcal{D}$ is denoted by $[\mathcal{D}]$.

Security notions are defined via games; for an example see Fig. 2. The probability that G outputs true is denoted $\Pr[\mathsf{G}]$. In proofs we sometimes define a sequence of "hybrid" games in one figure, using comments of the form "$//\mathsf{H}_{[i,j)}$." A line of code commented thusly is only included in the hybrids H_k for $i \leq k < j$. (We are of course referring only to values of $k \in \mathbb{N}$.) By this convention to identify the differences between H_{k-1} and H_k one looks for comments $\mathsf{H}_{[i,k)}$ (code no longer included in the k-th hybrid) and $\mathsf{H}_{[k,j)}$ (code new to the k-th hybrid).

We let $\perp$ be a special symbol used to indicate rejection. If we do not explicitly include $\perp$ in a set, then $\perp$ is not contained in that set. If $\perp$ is an input to a function or algorithm, then we assume its output is $\perp$. We do not distinguish between $\perp$ and tuples $(\perp, \dots, \perp)$. Algorithms cannot query $\perp$ to their oracles.

COMPLEXITY MEASURES. To measure the complexity of algorithms we follow the conventions of measuring their local complexity, not including the complexity of whatever oracles they interact with. Local complexity was preferred by Auerbach et al. [1] for analyzing memory-limited adversaries so that analysis can be agnostic to minor details of security definitions' implementations. We focus on worst-case runtime $\mathbf{Time}(\mathcal{A})$ and memory complexity $\mathbf{Mem}(\mathcal{A})$ (i.e.

how many bits of state it stores for local computation). These exclude the internal complexity of oracles queried by $\mathcal{A}$, but include the time and memory used to write the query and receive the response. If $\mathcal{A}$ expects access to n oracles then we let $\mathbf{Query}(\mathcal{A}) = (q_1, \ldots, q_n)$ where q_i is an upper bound on the number of queries to its i-th oracle. (Here we index from left to right, so for $\mathcal{A}^{O_1,\ldots,O_n}$ the i-th oracle is O_i.) If S is a scheme, then $\mathbf{Time}(S)$ and $\mathbf{Mem}(S)$ are the sums of the corresponding complexities over all of its algorithms. If G is a game, then we define $\mathbf{Time}(G)$ and $\mathbf{Mem}(G)$ to *exclude* the complexity of any adversaries embedded in the game.

2.2   Cryptographic Background

IDEAL MODELS. Some schemes we look at may be proven secure in ideal models (e.g. the random oracle or ideal cipher models). To capture this we can think of a scheme S as specifying a set of functions S.I. At the beginning of a security game a function h will be sampled from this set. The adversary and all algorithms of S are given oracle access to h.

FUNCTION FAMILIES. A family of functions F specifies, for each $K \in$ F.K, an efficiently computable function $F_K \in$ F.F. We refer to F.F as the function space of F. Pseudorandom (PR) security of F is captured by the game defined in Fig. 2. It measures how F with a random key can be distinguished from a random function in F.F via oracle access. We define $\mathsf{Adv}^{pr}_F(\mathcal{A}) =$ $\Pr[G^{pr}_{F,1}(\mathcal{A})] - \Pr[G^{pr}_{F,0}(\mathcal{A})]$. The standard notions of (tweakable) pseudorandom functions/injections/permutations or strong injections/permutations are captured by appropriate choices of F.F.

Game $G^{pr}_{F,b}(\mathcal{A})$	$\mathrm{Ev}(x)$
$h \leftarrow_\$ F.I$	$y_1 \leftarrow F^h_K(x)$
$K \leftarrow_\$ F.K$	$y_0 \leftarrow f(x)$
$f \leftarrow_\$ F.F$	Return y_b
$b' \leftarrow_\$ \mathcal{A}^{\mathrm{Ev},h}$	
Return $b' = 1$	

Fig. 2. Security game capturing the pseudorandomness of function family F.

SWITCHING LEMMA. We make use of the following standard result which bounds how well a random function and a random injection can be distinguished.

Lemma 1 (Switching Lemma). *Fix T, D, and R. Let $N = \min_{t \in T} |R_t|$. Then for any adversary $\mathcal{A}$ with $q = \mathbf{Query}(\mathcal{A})$ we have that*

$$|\Pr[\mathcal{A}^f \Rightarrow 1] - \Pr[\mathcal{A}^g \Rightarrow 1]| \leq 0 \cdot q^2/N.$$

The probabilities are measured over the coins of $\mathcal{A}$, the uniform choice of f from $\mathsf{Fcs}(T, D, R)$, and the uniform choice of g from $\mathsf{Inj}(T, D, R)$.

Recent papers [11,17,20] have given improved versions of the switching lemma for adversaries with bounded memory complexity, as long as it does not repeat oracle queries. In our application of the switching lemma the adversary's memory complexity is too large for these bounds to provide any improvement.

OTHER PRIMITIVES. We recall relevant syntax and security definitions for digital signatures, nonce-based encryption, and public key encryption schemes in the sections where we consider them (Sects. 4, 5, and 6 respectively).

3 Adversaries with Access to Random Functions

This paper proposes and adopts what we consider to be a better formalism to deal with memory-tight reductions. Namely, all of our reductions will require access to some variety of large random functions which it will query on a small number of inputs (specifically uniformly random functions and invertible random injections). That is, our reduction adversaries can be written in the form shown of the left below, for some set of functions $\mathcal{F}$ and algorithm $\mathcal{A}_2$. (On the right is a pseudorandom version of $\mathcal{A}$ which we will discuss momentarily.)

Adversary $\mathcal{A}^O(in)$	Adversary $\mathcal{A}_{\mathsf{F}}^O(in)$
$f \leftarrow_{\$} \mathcal{F}$	$K \leftarrow_{\$} \mathsf{F.K}$
$out \leftarrow_{\$} \mathcal{A}_2^{O,f}(in)$	$out \leftarrow_{\$} \mathcal{A}_2^{O,\mathsf{F}_K}(in)$
Return out	Return out

We refer to such an $\mathcal{A}$ as an $\mathcal{F}$-oracle adversary. In this section we will generally discuss such adversaries, rather than separately providing the discussion for such adversaries each time we apply them.

The time and memory complexity of any $\mathcal{F}$-oracle adversary must include the complexity of sampling, storing, and evaluating f. This will be significant if $\mathcal{F}$ is large. However, as we will argue, this additional state and time should be assumed to not significantly increase the advantage of $\mathcal{A}$. As such, we will define the *reduced complexity* of $\mathcal{A}$ by

$$\mathbf{Time}^*(\mathcal{A}) = \mathbf{Time}(\mathcal{A}_2) \text{ and } \mathbf{Mem}^*(\mathcal{A}) = \mathbf{Mem}(\mathcal{A}_2).$$

Later we state theorems in terms of reduced complexity.

PSEUDORANDOM REPLACEMENT. The most conservative justification of $\mathcal{F}$-oracle adversaries is to bound how much the oracle can help by replacing it with a pseudorandom version. This was the approach taken by Auerbach et al. [1] when they used pseudorandom functions for purposes such as emulating random oracles and storing the coins required by an adversary with low memory, and has been adopted by follow-up work [7,10,22]. If F is a function family with $\mathsf{F.F} = \mathcal{F}$, then the adversary $\mathcal{A}_{\mathsf{F}}$ we gave above does exactly this. It replaces $\mathcal{A}_2$'s oracle access to f with access to F_K for a random K. The following lemma is straightforward.

Lemma 2. *Let $\mathcal{A}$ be an $\mathcal{F}$-oracle adversary for a game* G. *Then for any function family* F *with* $\mathsf{F.F} = \mathcal{F}$ *we can define a pseudorandomness adversary $\mathcal{A}_i$ such that*

$$\Pr[\mathsf{G}(\mathcal{A})] \leq \Pr[\mathsf{G}(\mathcal{A}_{\mathsf{F}})] + \mathsf{Adv}_{\mathsf{F}}^{\mathsf{pr}}(\mathcal{A}_i), \quad \mathbf{Time}(\mathcal{A}_i) = \mathbf{Time}^*(\mathcal{A}) + \mathbf{Time}(\mathsf{G}(\mathcal{A})),$$

$$\mathbf{Query}(\mathcal{A}_i) = q, \text{ and} \qquad \mathbf{Mem}(\mathcal{A}_i) = \mathbf{Mem}^*(\mathcal{A}) + \mathbf{Mem}(\mathsf{G}(\mathcal{A})).$$

Here q is an upper bound on the number of queries $\mathcal{A}_2$ makes to its second oracle.

Note that the complexity of $\mathcal{A}_\mathsf{F}$ is given by $\mathbf{Time}(\mathcal{A}_\mathsf{F}) = \mathbf{Time}^*(\mathcal{A}) + q \cdot \mathbf{Time}(\mathsf{F})$ and $\mathbf{Mem}(\mathcal{A}_\mathsf{F}) = \mathbf{Mem}^*(\mathcal{A}) + \mathbf{Mem}(\mathsf{F})$. Thus the existence of an appropriate pseudorandom F ensures that the memory and time complexity excluded by $\mathbf{Time}^*$ and $\mathbf{Mem}^*$ cannot significantly aid an adversary. In the use of this technique by Auerbach et al. [1] the reduction $\mathcal{A}_i$ was memory-tight. Note this is not strictly necessary as long as we are willing to assume the existence of F with sufficient security as a function of attackers' time and query complexities without regard to memory complexity.

We could have combined Lemma 2 with any of our coming theorems to obtain bounds in terms of $\mathbf{Time}$ and $\mathbf{Mem}$, rather than their reduced version. However we find the use of reduced complexity cleaner as it simplifies our theorems, allowing us to focus on the conceptual core of the proofs without having to repeat the rote step of replacing random objects with pseudorandom ones.

When combining the lemma with a theorem, game G would correspond to the security game played by the reduction adversary. For our theorems, that game will have low time and memory overhead over that of $\mathcal{A}$, so the application of the lemma would be time- and memory-tight. That said, the tightness of this is less important than the tightness of the other components of the theorem we would apply it to. Note that the definition of $\mathcal{A}_i$ is *independent* of the choice of F. Consequently, we can always choose F with a very high security threshold to counteract any looseness in the lemma. In the full version [14], we summarize the $\mathcal{F}$ used in our theorems and how they could be pseudorandomly instantiated.

ASSUMED INDEPENDENCE. As a second observation why the storage of f may not help $\mathcal{A}$, note that f is completely "independent" of the problem $\mathcal{A}$ is trying to solve (as specified by in and the behavior of O). In various settings it seems likely that such independent state does not help. For example, it would be very surprising (or even a breakthrough) to show a better factoring or lattice algorithm given access to a random function f from a natural set. Indeed, cryptanalytic work often makes use of random oracles without significant comment (from which other types of random functions can be constructed).

INFORMATION THEORETIC SETTINGS. In some information theoretic settings, the "independence" of f from the problem can be made rigorous. Information theoretic results are typically depending only on the query complexity of the attacker or its memory usage, *ignoring code size*. In such settings, we expect bounds of the form $\mathsf{Adv}(\mathcal{A}) \leq \epsilon(\mathbf{Mem}(\mathcal{A}), \mathbf{Query}(\mathcal{A}))$ for some function ϵ. Because this bound *does not* depend on the code size of $\mathcal{A}$, if $\mathcal{A}$ is an $\mathcal{F}$-oracle adversary we should be able to prove $\mathsf{Adv}(\mathcal{A}) \leq \epsilon(\mathbf{Mem}^*(\mathcal{A}), \mathbf{Query}(\mathcal{A}))$ by a coin-fixing argument in which we fix the random choice of function ahead of time and embed it in the description of the adversary. This is, for example, the case for the recent time-memory tradeoffs shown for distinguishing between a random function and a random injection without repeating queries [11,17,20]. A coin-fixing readily shows that these tradeoffs hold when using $\mathbf{Mem}^*(\mathcal{A})$ in place of $\mathbf{Mem}(\mathcal{A}), \mathbf{Query}(\mathcal{A})$.

4   Multi-challenge Security of Digital Signature Schemes

In the context of memory-tightness, the security of digital signature schemes has been considered in several works [1,10,22]. The standard security notion for signatures asks the attacker, given examples, to come up with a forged signature on a fresh message. A straightforward proof shows (in the standard setting where memory efficiency is not a concern) that the security notion is equivalent whether the attacker is allowed one or many forgery attempts. However, Auerbach et al. [1] proved an impossibility result showing that a (certain form of black-box) reduction cannot be time, memory, and advantage tight. The difficulty faced by the reduction is in distinguishing between when the adversary has produced a novel forgery and when it is simply repeating a signature that it was given.

In this section we show a few ways that security against many forgery attempts (i.e., multiple challenges) can be proven to follow from security against a single forgery (i.e., a single challenge) in a memory-tight manner. Our first results consider a variant definition of digital signature security we introduce (called UFRMA) in which the adversary has only partial control over the messages being signed. Using our new techniques, we show that single challenge UFCMA security implies multi-challenge UFRMA security in a memory-tight manner (for some practically relevant distributions over messages). We also consider the security of the RSA full domain hash digital signature scheme. Auerbach et al. [1] gave a memory-, but not advantage-tight proof of the security of the standard version of this scheme in the single challenge setting. By considering a probabilistic variant of the scheme introduced by Coron [8] we are able to provide a memory-, time-, and advantage-tight proof of the many-forgery SUFCMA security of the variant.

4.1   Syntax and Security

DIGITAL SIGNATURE SYNTAX. A digital signature scheme DS specifies a key generation algorithm DS.K, a signing algorithm DS.Sign, and a verification algorithm DS.Ver. The syntaxes of these algorithms are shown in Fig. 3. We capture ideals models by providing DS.Sign and DS.Ver with oracle access to a function h drawn at random from the set DS.I. When relevant we let DS.M denote the set of messages it accepts.

$$\boxed{\begin{array}{l} \underline{\text{DS Syntax}} \\ h \leftarrow\!\!\$\; \text{DS.I} \\ (vk, sk) \leftarrow\!\!\$\; \text{DS.K} \\ \sigma \leftarrow\!\!\$\; \text{DS.Sign}^h(sk, m) \\ d \leftarrow \text{DS.Ver}^h(vk, m, \sigma) \end{array}}$$

Fig. 3. Syntax of digital signature scheme.

The verification and signing keys are respectively denoted by vk and sk. The message to be signed is m, the signature produced is σ, and the decision is $d \in \{\text{true}, \text{false}\}$. Correctness requires $\text{DS.Ver}^h(vk, m, \sigma) = \text{true}$ for all $h \in \text{DS.I}$, all $(vk, sk) \in [\text{DS.K}]$, all $m \in \text{DS.M}$, and all $\sigma \in [\text{DS.Sign}^h(sk, m)]$.

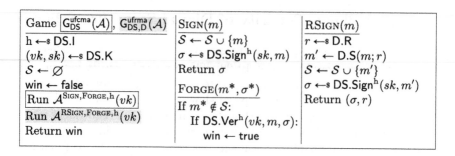

Game $\boxed{\mathsf{G}^{\mathsf{ufcma}}_{\mathsf{DS}}(\mathcal{A})}$, $\mathsf{G}^{\mathsf{ufrma}}_{\mathsf{DS,D}}(\mathcal{A})$	SIGN(m)	RSIGN(m)
$\mathsf{h} \leftarrow_{\$} \mathsf{DS.I}$	$\mathcal{S} \leftarrow \mathcal{S} \cup \{m\}$	$r \leftarrow_{\$} \mathsf{D.R}$
$(vk, sk) \leftarrow_{\$} \mathsf{DS.K}$	$\sigma \leftarrow_{\$} \mathsf{DS.Sign}^{\mathsf{h}}(sk, m)$	$m' \leftarrow \mathsf{D.S}(m; r)$
$\mathcal{S} \leftarrow \varnothing$	Return σ	$\mathcal{S} \leftarrow \mathcal{S} \cup \{m'\}$
win $\leftarrow$ false		$\sigma \leftarrow_{\$} \mathsf{DS.Sign}^{\mathsf{h}}(sk, m')$
$\boxed{\text{Run } \mathcal{A}^{\text{SIGN,FORGE,h}}(vk)}$	FORGE(m^*, σ^*)	Return (σ, r)
Run $\mathcal{A}^{\text{RSIGN,FORGE,h}}(vk)$	If $m^* \notin \mathcal{S}$:	
Return win	If $\mathsf{DS.Ver}^{\mathsf{h}}(vk, m, \sigma)$:	
	win $\leftarrow$ true	

Fig. 4. Security games capturing the unforgeability of a digital signature scheme.

MESSAGE DISTRIBUTION SYNTAX. One of the security notions we consider for digital signature schemes will be parameterized by a message distribution via which the adversary is given incomplete control over the messages which are signed. A message distribution D specifies sampling algorithm D.S which samples an output message m' based on parameters m given as input (written $m' \leftarrow_{\$} \mathsf{D.S}(m)$). The parameters m must be drawn from a set D.M, which we typically leave implicit. When making the randomness of the sampling algorithm explicit we let D.R be the set from which its randomness is drawn and write $m' \leftarrow \mathsf{D.S}(m; r)$. If there exists an extraction algorithm D.X such that $\mathsf{D.X}(\mathsf{D.S}(m; r)) = (m, r)$ for all m, r then we say D is *extractable*. If $\mathsf{D.X}(\mathsf{D.S}(m; r)) = m$ for all m, r then we say D is *weakly extractable*. We assume that $\mathsf{D.X}(m') = \bot$ if $m' \neq \mathsf{D.S}(m; r)$ for all m, r. We define the min-entropy of D as

$$\mathsf{D.H}_{\infty} = -\lg \max_{m} \Pr[r \leftarrow_{\$} \mathsf{D.R} : \mathsf{D.S}(m; r) = m'] .$$

UNFORGEABILITY SECURITY. The unforgeability security notions we consider are defined in Fig. 4. The standard notion of UFCMA (unforgeability under chosen message attack) security is captured by $\mathsf{G}^{\mathsf{ufcma}}$ which includes the boxed but not the highlighted code, giving the adversary access to a regular signing oracle SIGN. The goal of the adversary is to query FORGE with a valid signature σ^* of a message m^* which was not previously included in a signing query (as stored by the set $\mathcal{S}$). We define $\mathsf{Adv}^{\mathsf{ufcma}}_{\mathsf{DS}}(\mathcal{A}) = \Pr[\mathsf{G}^{\mathsf{ufcma}}_{\mathsf{DS}}(\mathcal{A})]$.

Our new security notion UFRMA (unforgeability under randomized message attack) is captured by the game $\mathsf{G}^{\mathsf{ufrma}}$ which is parameterized by a message distribution D. In this game the adversary is instead given access to the randomized signing oracle RSIGN where the message to be signed is chosen by D. Note that the coins used by D are returned to the adversary along with the signature. Otherwise this game matches that of UFCMA security. We define $\mathsf{Adv}^{\mathsf{ufrma}}_{\mathsf{DS,D}}(\mathcal{A}) = \Pr[\mathsf{G}^{\mathsf{ufrma}}_{\mathsf{DS,D}}(\mathcal{A})]$.

We will relate the advantage of attacks making only a single forgery attempt and those making many such attempts. When wanting to make the distinction explicit we prefix the abbreviation of a security notion with an 'm' or '1'. Strong UFCMA security, denoted SUFCMA, is captured by modifying $\mathsf{G}^{\mathsf{ufcma}}$ to store the tuple (σ, m) in $\mathcal{S}$ in SIGN and checking $(m^*, \sigma^*) \notin \mathcal{S}$ in FORGE. We denote this by $\mathsf{G}^{\mathsf{sufcma}}$ and the corresponding advantage by $\mathsf{Adv}^{\mathsf{sufcma}}$. We define SUFRMA, $\mathsf{G}^{\mathsf{sufrma}}$, and $\mathsf{Adv}^{\mathsf{sufrma}}$ analogously. We write xUFRMA when assuming that D is extractable and wUFRMA when assuming it is weakly extractable.

4.2 Multi-challenge Security for Extractable Message Distributions

The first applications we show for our techniques are generic methods of tightly implying security of a digital signature scheme against multiple forgery attempts (i.e., multi-challenge security). Recall that Auerbach et al. [1] gave a lower bound showing that a black-box reduction proving that single UFCMA security implies many UFCMA cannot be made memory-tight and time-tight. We avoid this in two ways; first by considering mUFRMA, rather than mUFCMA, security and then by considering a particular choice of digital signature scheme.

HIGH-LEVEL IDEA. The primary difficulty of a tight proof that 1UFCMA security implies mUFCMA security is that a successful mUFCMA attacker may have made many FORGE queries which verify correctly, one of which is a valid forgery and the rest of which were just forwarded from its SIGN oracle. A 1UFCMA reduction must then somehow be able to identify which of the queries is the true forgery so it can forward this to its own FORGE oracle.

The technical core of the coming proof for mUFRMA is that our reduction adversary will use the random coins of the message distribution D to signal things to its future self. In particular, when $\mathcal{A}_{\mathsf{r}}$ makes a query $\mathrm{RSIGN}(m)$, the reduction will choose coins for D.S via $r \leftarrow f(m, i)$ where i is a counter which is incremented with each query and f is a random tweakable function/injection. The coins then act as a sort of authentication tag for m. On a later $\mathrm{FORGE}(m^*, \sigma^*)$ query, if $m^* = \mathsf{D}.\mathsf{S}(m; r)$ where $r = f(m, i)$ for some $i \in [q_{\mathrm{SIGN}}]$ the reduction can safely assume this message was signed by an earlier RSIGN query.

When D is fully extractable, we can perform the requisite check for FORGE by having f be an injection. We extract m and r from m^* and then compute $i \leftarrow f^{-1}(m, r)$. This is the strategy used in Theorem 1. If we assume only that D is weakly extractable, we can extract m if D has a sufficient amount of entropy, and then individually check if $\mathsf{D}.\mathsf{S}(m; f(m, i))$ holds for each choice of i. This reduction strategy obtains the same advantage at the cost of an extra runtime being needed to iterate over the possible choices of i in FORGE.

EXTRACTABLE MESSAGE DISTRIBUTION. If the message distribution D is extractable, the following theorem captures that 1UFCMA security tightly implies mUFRMA security. The proof makes use of our efficient tagging technique.

Theorem 1 (1UFCMA $\Rightarrow$ mxUFRMA). *Let* DS *be a digital signature scheme and* D *be an extractable message distribution. Let* $\mathcal{A}_{\mathsf{r}}$ *be an adversary with* $(q_{\mathrm{SIGN}}, q_{\mathrm{FORGE}}, q_{\mathsf{h}}) = \mathbf{Query}(\mathcal{A}_{\mathsf{r}})$ *and assume* $q_{\mathsf{Sign}} \leq 0.5|\mathsf{D}.\mathsf{R}|$. *Let* $\mathcal{A}_{\mathsf{u}}$ *be the*

Adversary $\mathcal{A}_u^{\text{Sign,Forge,h}}(vk)$	$\text{SimRSign}(m)$	$\text{SimForge}(m^*, \sigma^*)$
$i \leftarrow 0$	$i \leftarrow i + 1$	$(m, r) \leftarrow \mathsf{D.X}(m^*)$
$f \leftarrow\!\!{}_\$ \, \mathsf{Inj}^{\pm}(\mathsf{DS.M}, [q_{\text{Sign}}], \mathsf{D.R}))$	$r \leftarrow f(m, i)$	If $f^{-1}(m, r) \notin [q_{\text{Sign}}]$:
Run $\mathcal{A}_r^{\text{SimRSign,SimForge,h}}(vk)$	$m' \leftarrow \mathsf{D.S}(m; r)$	If $\mathsf{DS.Ver}^h(vk, m^*, \sigma^*)$:
	$\sigma \leftarrow \text{Sign}(m')$	Query $\text{Forge}(m^*, \sigma^*)$
	Return (σ, r)	Halt execution

Fig. 5. Adversary $\mathcal{A}_u$ used in proof of Theorem 1.

$\mathsf{Inj}^{\pm}(\mathsf{DS.M}, [q_{\text{Sign}}], \mathsf{D.R})$-*oracle adversary shown in Fig. 5. Then,*

$$\mathsf{Adv}_{\mathsf{DS,D}}^{\text{ufrma}}(\mathcal{A}_r) \leq \mathsf{Adv}_{\mathsf{DS}}^{\text{ufcma}}(\mathcal{A}_u) + (0.5 \cdot q_{\text{Sign}}^2 + 2 \cdot q_{\text{Sign}} \cdot q_{\text{Forge}})/|\mathsf{D.R}|$$

$$\mathbf{Query}(\mathcal{A}_u) = (q_{\text{Sign}}, 1, q_h + q_{\text{Forge}} \cdot \mathbf{Query}(\mathsf{DS}))$$

$$\mathbf{Time}^*(\mathcal{A}_u) = \mathbf{Time}(\mathcal{A}_r) + q_{\text{Sign}} \cdot \mathbf{Time}(\mathsf{D}) + q_{\text{Forge}}(\mathbf{Time}(\mathsf{D}) + \mathbf{Time}(\mathsf{DS}))$$

$$\mathbf{Mem}^*(\mathcal{A}_u) = \mathbf{Mem}(\mathcal{A}_r) + \mathbf{Mem}(\mathsf{D}) + \mathbf{Mem}(\mathsf{DS}) + \lg(q_{\text{Sign}}).$$

This is time-tight because $\mathbf{Time}(\mathcal{A}_r) \in \Omega(q_{\text{Sign}} + q_{\text{Forge}})$ must hold and $\mathbf{Time}(\mathsf{D})$ and $\mathbf{Time}(\mathsf{DS})$ will be small. This is memory-tight because $\mathbf{Mem}(\mathsf{D})$, $\mathbf{Mem}(\mathsf{DS})$, and $\lg(q_{\text{Sign}})$ will be small.

The main idea of $\mathcal{A}_u$ is using the output of an invertible random injection f on the message and a counter as coins instead of sampling them uniformly at random when answering RSign queries. Since D is fully extractable, during a Forge query on m^*, we can extract $(m, r) \leftarrow \mathsf{D.X}(m^*)$ and use the fact that f is invertible to compute $f^{-1}(m, r)$ and check if the index is in $[q_{\text{Sign}}]$. This is used to avoid remembering $\mathcal{S}$. If $m^* \in \mathcal{S}$, and $(m, r) \leftarrow \mathsf{D.X}(m^*)$, then there exists $j \in [q_{\text{Sign}}]$ such that $r = f(m, j)$ – so the check passes. We can argue that if $m^* \notin \mathcal{S}$, our check is unlikely to pass. We give the formal proof of this theorem in Sect. 4.3. It applies the switching lemma to argue the use of f cannot be distinguished from honestly sampling r with advantage better than $0.5 \cdot q_{\text{Sign}}^2/|\mathsf{D.R}|$ and shows that the probability of falsely making the check pass is bounded by $2q_{\text{Sign}}q_{\text{Forge}}/|\mathsf{D.R}|$.

We would not be able to use the technique in this proof to prove mxSUFRMA from 1SUFCMA in a memory-tight way. In particular, since the coins r of the message distribution are chosen before σ is known, our trick of using r to signal freshness of a forgery query does not work for a message-signature pair.

4.3   Proof of Theorem 1 (1UFCMA⇒mUFRMA)

Proof. We consider a sequence of hybrids H_0 through H_4 defined in Fig. 6. When examining these hybrids recall our conventions regarding "$//\mathsf{H}_{[i,j]}$" comments described in Sect. 2.1. Of these hybrids we will make the following claims, which establish the upper bound on the advantage of $\mathcal{A}_r$ claimed in the proof.

Games H_h for $0 \leqslant h \leqslant 4$	$\text{RSIGN}(m)$
$h \leftarrow_\$ \text{DS.I}$	$r \leftarrow_\$ \text{D.R} \ //H_{[0,1)}$
$(vk, sk) \leftarrow_\$ \text{DS.K}; \mathcal{S} \leftarrow \varnothing$	$i \leftarrow i + 1 \ //H_{[1,\infty)}$
$\text{win} \leftarrow \text{false}$	$r \leftarrow f(m, i) \ //H_{[1,\infty)}$
$i \leftarrow 0; I[\cdot] \leftarrow \varnothing$	$I[m] \leftarrow I[m] \cup \{i\} \ //H_{[3,4)}$
$f \leftarrow_\$ \text{Fcs}(\text{DS.M}, [q_{\text{SIGN}}], \text{D.R}) \ //H_{[1,2)}$	$m' \leftarrow \text{D.S}(m; r)$
$f \leftarrow_\$ \text{Inj}^{\pm}(\text{DS.M}, [q_{\text{SIGN}}], \text{D.R}) \ //H_{[2,\infty)}$	$\mathcal{S} \leftarrow \mathcal{S} \cup \{m'\} \ //H_{[0,3)}$
Run $\mathcal{A}_r^{\text{RSIGN},\text{FORGE},h}(vk)$	$\sigma \leftarrow_\$ \text{DS.Sign}^h(sk, m')$
Return win	Return (σ, r)
	$\text{FORGE}(m^*, \sigma^*)$
	$(m, r) \leftarrow \text{D.X}(m^*)$
	If $m^* \notin \mathcal{S}: \ //H_{[0,3)}$
	If $f^{-1}(m, r) \notin I[m]: \ //H_{[3,4)}$
	If $f^{-1}(m, r) \notin [q_{\text{SIGN}}]: \ //H_{[4,\infty)}$
	If $\text{DS.Ver}^h(vk, m^*, \sigma^*):$
	win $\leftarrow$ true

Fig. 6. Hybrid games used in proof of Theorem 1.

1. $\Pr[G_{\text{DS,D}}^{\text{ufrma}}(\mathcal{A}_r)] = \Pr[H_0] = \Pr[H_1]$ 4. $\Pr[H_3] \leq \Pr[H_4] + 2q_{\text{SIGN}}q_{\text{FORGE}}/|\text{D.R}|$

2. $\Pr[H_1] \leq \Pr[H_2] + 0.5 \cdot q_{\text{SIGN}}^2/|\text{D.R}|$ 5. $\Pr[H_4] = \text{Adv}_{\text{DS}}^{\text{ufcma}}(\mathcal{A}_u)$

3. $\Pr[H_2] = \Pr[H_3]$

TRANSITION H_0 TO H_1. The hybrid H_0 is simply a copy of the game G^{ufrma}. (We also added code to initialize variables i and $I[\cdot]$ that will be used in later hybrids.) Hence $\Pr[G^{\text{ufrma}}(\mathcal{A}_r)] = \Pr[H_0]$. In hybrid H_1, we replace the random sampling of r for D in RSIGN with the output of a random function f applied to m, using a counter i to provide domain separation between different queries. This method of choosing r is equivalent, so $\Pr[H_0] = \Pr[H_1]$.

TRANSITION H_1 TO H_2. In hybrid H_2 we replace the random function with a random injection. This modifies the behavior of the game only in that values of r are guaranteed not to repeat across different signing queries that used the same message. There are at most q_{SIGN} invocations of f, so the switching lemma (Lemma 1) tells us that $\Pr[H_1] \leq \Pr[H_2] + 0.5 \cdot q_{\text{SIGN}}^2/|\text{D.R}|$.

TRANSITION H_2 TO H_3. In hybrid H_3, we replace the check whether $m^* \notin \mathcal{S}$ in oracle FORGE with a check if $f^{-1}(m, r) \notin I[m]$ where $(m, r) = \text{D.X}(m^*)$. Here $I[\cdot]$ is a new table introduced into the game. In RSIGN, code was added which uses $I[m]$ to store each of the counter values for which $\mathcal{A}_r$ made a signing query for m. Hence $f^{-1}(m, r)$ will be in $I[m]$ iff m^* is in $\mathcal{S}$ and so $\Pr[H_2] = \Pr[H_3]$.

TRANSITION H_3 TO H_4. In the final transition to hybrid H_4 we replace the FORGE check $f^{-1}(m, r) \notin I[m]$ with $f^{-1}(m, r) \notin [q_{\text{SIGN}}]$. This *does* change behavior if $\mathcal{A}_r$ ever makes a successful forgery query for $m^* = \text{D.S}(m; f(m, i))$ without its i-th signing query having used the message m. This would require guessing $f(m, i)$ for some $i \in [q_{\text{SIGN}}] \setminus I[m]$. We can bound the probability of this ever occurring by a union bound over the FORGE queries made by $\mathcal{A}_r$. Consider the set $f(m, [q_{\text{SIGN}}] \setminus I[m]) = \{f(m, i) : i \in [q_{\text{SIGN}}] \setminus I[m]\}$. It has size at most q_{SIGN}. Because f is a random injection it is uniform subset of the set $\text{D.R} \setminus f(m, I[m])$ (which has size at least $|\text{D.R}| - q_{\text{SIGN}}$). Hence the probability of any particular query triggering this different behavior is at most $q_{\text{SIGN}}/(|\text{D.R}| - q_{\text{SIGN}}) \leq 2q_{\text{SIGN}}/|\text{D.R}|$. Applying the union bound gives us $\Pr[\mathsf{H}_3] \leq \Pr[\mathsf{H}_4] + 2q_{\text{SIGN}} \cdot q_{\text{FORGE}}/|\text{D.R}|$.

REDUCTION TO UFCMA. We complete the proof using adversary $\mathcal{A}_u$ from Fig. 5 which simulates hybrid H_4 and succeeds whenever $\mathcal{A}_r$ would. The adversary $\mathcal{A}_u$ samples f at random from $\text{Inj}(\text{DS.M}, [q_{\text{SIGN}}], \text{D.R})$. When run on input vk, it runs $\mathcal{A}_r$ on the same input. It gives $\mathcal{A}_r$ direct access to h. To simulate a query $\text{RSIGN}(m)$, it computes $m' \leftarrow \text{D.S}(m; f(m, i))$, increments i, and queries $\text{SIGN}(m')$, returning the result to $\mathcal{A}_r$. On a query $\text{FORGE}(m^*, \sigma^*)$, it computes $(m, r) \leftarrow \text{D.X}(m^*)$. If $f^{-1}(r) \notin [q_{\text{SIGN}}]$ and $\text{DS.Ver}(vk, m^*, \sigma^*) = \text{true}$ then it queries its own oracle with (m^*, σ^*) and halts. Otherwise it ignores the query.

If adversary $\mathcal{A}_u$ ever makes a FORGE query, it will succeed. It ensured that (m^*, σ^*) is verified correctly and $f^{-1}(r) \notin [q_{\text{SIGN}}]$ ensures that it is has not previously made a SIGN query for m^*. If $\mathcal{A}_r$ would have succeeded in hybrid H_4, its winning query will cause $\mathcal{A}_u$ to make a FORGE query. Hence, we have $\Pr[\mathsf{H}_4] = \text{Adv}_{\text{DS}}^{\text{ufcma}}(\mathcal{A}_u)$.

4.4 Applications and Weakly Extractable Variant

We discuss some applications of Theorem 1. This includes scenarios where extractable message distributions are used and proving security of digital signature schemes when their messages are padded with randomness. Additionally, we give a variant of the theorem when the underlying message distribution is only weakly extractable. The resulting reduction is memory- but not time-tight.

EXAMPLE EXTRACTABLE DISTRIBUTIONS. The simplest extractable distribution does not accept parameters as input and simply outputs its randomness as the message. Security with respect to this is the standard notion of security against random message attacks which was originally introduced by Even, Goldreich, and Micali [13].

Extractable distributions arise naturally when the messages being signed include random values. For example, protocols often include random nonces in messages that are signed. In TLS 1.3, for example, when the server is responding to the Client Hello Message it signs a transcript of the conversation up until that point which includes a 256-bit nonce just chosen by the server. We could think of the security for this setting being captured by an extractable distribution D_{tls} that takes as input message parameter m that specifies all of the transcript other than the nonce and sets the nonce to its randomness $r \in \{0, 1\}^{256}$.

PADDING SCHEMES WITH RANDOMNESS. Using Theorem 1, we can see that augmenting any digital signature scheme by appending auxiliary randomness will give us a memory-tight reduction from the mUFCMA security of the augmented scheme to the 1UFCMA security of the original scheme.

Let DS be a digital signature scheme and R be a set. We define RDS[DS, R] by having RDS[DS, R].Sign(sk, m) do "$r \leftarrow_\$ \mathsf{R}$; Return DS.Sign($sk, m \parallel r) \parallel r$" and having RDS[DS, R].Ver(vk, m, σ') do "$\sigma \parallel r \leftarrow \sigma'$; Return DS.Ver($vk, m \parallel r, \sigma$)." We also define a related message distribution RD[R] by RD[R].R = R and RD[R].S($m; r$) = $m \parallel r$. Clearly it is extractable.

The following reduces the mUFCMA security of RDS to the mUFRMA security of DS. Theorem 1 can in turn be used to reduce this to the 1UFCMA security of DS. It also relates the mSUFCMA security of RDS to the mSUFRMA security of DS. We note this because if DS has unique signatures, then its mSUFRMA and mUFRMA security are identical and hence UFCMA security of DS implies mSUFCMA security of RDS in a memory-tight way.

Theorem 2. *Let* DS *be a digital signature scheme and* R *be a set. Then for any* $\mathcal{A}_u$ *we can construct* $\mathcal{A}_r$ *such that* $\mathsf{Adv}^{\mathsf{ufcma}}_{\mathsf{RDS[DS,R]}}(\mathcal{A}_u) = \mathsf{Adv}^{\mathsf{ufrma}}_{\mathsf{DS,RD[R]}}(\mathcal{A}_r)$. *It additionally holds that* $\mathsf{Adv}^{\mathsf{sufcma}}_{\mathsf{RDS[DS,R]}}(\mathcal{A}_u) = \mathsf{Adv}^{\mathsf{sufrma}}_{\mathsf{DS,RD[R]}}(\mathcal{A}_r)$. *Adversary* $\mathcal{A}_r$ *has essentially the same complexity as* $\mathcal{A}_u$.

Proof (Sketch). The proof of this is straightforward. If $\mathcal{A}_u$ queries SIGN(m), then $\mathcal{A}_r$ queries SIGN(m) and receives (σ, r) and returns $\sigma \parallel r$ to $\mathcal{A}_u$. If $\mathcal{A}_u$ queries FORGE($m^*, \sigma^* \parallel r^*$), then $\mathcal{A}_r$ queries FORGE($m^* \parallel r^*, \sigma^*$). Note that $\mathcal{A}_r$ wins whenever $\mathcal{A}_u$ would. $\square$

In independent and concurrent work, Diemert, Gellert, Jager, and Lyu [10] also considered RDS, proving that if DS can be proven SUFCMA1 secure (in this notion the game records its responses to signature queries and repeats them if the adversary repeats a query) with a restricted class of "canonical" memory-tight reductions, then there is a memory-tight reduction for the mSUFCMA security of RDS. This complements our results as they use a more restrictive assumption to prove mSUFCMA while we use a generic assumption to prove mUFCMA.

In the full version [14], we further show that if D is only *weakly* extractable (but still has high entropy), then we can prove a variant of Theorem 1 with a less efficient reduction. In particular, the running time of the reduction has an additional term of $q_{\mathrm{FORGE}} \cdot q_{\mathrm{SIGN}} \cdot \mathbf{Time}(\mathsf{D.S})$. This difference arises because rather than extracting r and computing $j \leftarrow f^{-1}(m, r)$ in FORGE we instead need to iterate over the possible values of $f(m, j)$ to check for consistency. Thus the proof for this is an instance of our inefficient tagging technique.

4.5 mSUFCMA Security of RSA-PFDH

The RSA-based Probabilistic Full-Domain Hash (RSA-PFDH) scheme, originally introduced by Coron [8], can be viewed as the result of applying the RDS[·] transform to RSA-based Full-Domain Hash [4] (RSA-FDH). Auerbach et al. [1] gave a memory-, but not time-tight reduction from the 1UFCMA security of RSA-FDH to the one-wayness of RSA. Applying Theorems 1 and 2 would give a memory-, but not time-tight reduction for the security of RSA-PFDH.

By a careful combination of our tagging technique with the proof ideas of Coron and of Auerbach et al. we can analyze RSA-PFDH directly. We prove the following result – a time, memory, and advantage tight reduction for the security of RSA-PFDH. The theorem is properly formalized and proven in the full version [14].

Theorem 3 (Informal, mSUFCMA security of RSA-PFDH). *Define* RSA := RDS[RSA-FDH, $\{0,1\}^{\mathsf{rl}}$]. *Let* $\mathcal{A}_{\mathsf{m}}$ *be an adversary with* $(q_{\mathrm{SIGN}}, q_{\mathrm{FORGE}}, q_{\mathsf{h}}) = \mathbf{Query}(\mathcal{A}_{\mathsf{m}})$. *Then we can construct an adversary* $\mathcal{A}_{\mathsf{RSA}}$ *against one-wayness of* rl*-bit RSA such that*

$$\mathsf{Adv}^{\mathsf{sufcma}}_{\mathsf{RSA}}(\mathcal{A}_{\mathsf{m}}) \leq \mathsf{Adv}^{\mathsf{ow-rsa}}(\mathcal{A}_{\mathsf{RSA}}) + (0.5 \cdot q^2_{\mathrm{SIGN}} + 2 \cdot q_{\mathrm{SIGN}} \cdot q_{\mathrm{FORGE}})/2^{\mathsf{rl}}$$

The running time and memory of $\mathcal{A}_{\mathsf{RSA}}$ *is roughly the same as* $\mathcal{A}_{\mathsf{m}}$.

In concurrent work, Diemert, Gellert, Jager, and Lyu [10] also give a time, memory, and advantage tight reduction for RSA-PFDH via a different proof.

5   AE Security of Encrypt-then-PRF

For nonce-based secret-key encryption schemes, we often want Authenticated Encryption (AE) security which simultaneously asks for confidentiality and ciphertext integrity. The common approach to prove AE security of a nonce-based encryption scheme is to give separate reductions to the indistinguishability of its ciphertexts from truly random ones (INDR security) and its ciphertext integrity. Ghoshal et al. [15] proved an impossibility result showing that a (certain form of black-box) reduction from AE security to INDR security and ciphertext integrity cannot be memory-tight. Making the INDR part memory-tight is of particular interest because of results which establish tight time-memory trade-offs for INDR security [9,12,17,20,21].

In this section we look at a particular scheme which we refer to as Encrypt-then-PRF. Given a nonce-based encryption scheme NE that only has INDR security, one generic way to construct a new encryption scheme NE' which also achieves ciphertext integrity is to use a PRF and let the ciphertext of NE' be the concatenation of the ciphertext of NE and a tag which is the evaluation of the PRF on the ciphertext and the nonce.

We show that in the context of Encrypt-then-PRF, for two of the notions of AE security introduced in [15], we can give a memory-tight reduction to the INDR security of the underlying encryption scheme and a non-memory-tight reduction to the security of the PRF. This shows that we can bypass the generic impossibility result of [15] if we consider specific constructions of nonce-based authenticated encryption schemes. In more detail, the impossibility result of [15] rules out lifting the INDR security of a scheme to full AE security in a memory tight way, when additionally assuming ciphertext integrity *for a generic scheme*. Here, we show that for the *specific* case of Encrypt-then-PRF schemes, lifting the INDR security of the encryption scheme to full AE security of Encrypt-then-PRF is possible in a memory-tight way, assuming security of the PRF.

Game $G_{NE,b}^{indr}(\mathcal{A})$	$\mathrm{ENC}_b(n, m)$	$\mathrm{DEC}_b^w(n, c)$
$K \leftarrow_\$ NE.K$	$c_1 \leftarrow NE.E(K, n, m)$	If $M[n, c] \neq \bot$:
$b' \leftarrow \mathcal{A}^{\mathrm{ENC}_b}$	$c_0 \leftarrow_\$ \{0, 1\}^{NE.cl(\|m\|)}$	$\quad$ Return $M[n, c]$ if $w = \mathtt{m}$
Return $b' = 1$	$M[n, c_b] \leftarrow m$	$\quad$ Return $\diamond$ if $w = \diamond$
	Return c_b	$\quad$ Return $\bot$ if $w = \bot$
Game $G_{NE,b}^{ae-w}(\mathcal{A})$		$m_1 \leftarrow NE.D(k, n, c)$
$K \leftarrow_\$ NE.K$		$m_0 \leftarrow \bot$
$b' \leftarrow \mathcal{A}^{\mathrm{ENC}_b, \mathrm{DEC}_b^w}$		Return m_b
Return $b' = 1$		

Fig. 7. Games defining INDR and AE-w security of NE for $w \in \{\mathtt{m}, \diamond, \bot\}$.

5.1 Syntax and Security Definitions

NONCE-BASED ENCRYPTION. A nonce-based (secret-key) encryption scheme NE specifies algorithms NE.K, NE.E, and NE.D. It specifies message space NE.M and nonce space NE.N. The syntax of the algorithms is shown in Fig. 8. The secret key is denoted by K, the message is m, the nonce is n, and the ciphertext is c. The decryption algorithm may return $m = \bot$ to indicate rejection of the ciphertext. Correctness requires for all $K \in [NE.K]$, $n \in NE.N$, and $m \in NE.M$ that $NE.D(K, n, NE.E(K, n, m)) = m$. We assume there is a ciphertext-length function $NE.cl : \mathbb{N} \to \mathbb{N}$ such that for all $K \in [NE.K]$, $n \in NE.N$, and $m \in NE.M$ we have $|c| = NE.cl(|m|)$ where $c \leftarrow NE.E(K, n, m)$. We define $NE.C = \bigcup_{m \in NE.M} \{0, 1\}^{NE.cl(|m|)}$. Typically, a nonce-based encryption scheme also takes associated data as input which is authenticated during encryption. This does not meaningfully affect our proof, so we omit it for simplicity.

ENCRYPT-THEN-PRF. In this section we consider the Encrypt-then-PRF construction of a nonce-based encryption scheme, due to Rogaway [19]. Namprempre et al. [18] gave a more extensive exploration of the many ways to construct an AEAD encryption scheme via generic composition. Given nonce-based encryption scheme NE and function family F, we define EtP[NE, F]

NE Syntax
$K \leftarrow_\$ NE.K$
$c \leftarrow NE.E(K, n, m)$
$m \leftarrow NE.D(K, n, c)$

Fig. 8. Syntax of (nonce-based) secret-key encryption scheme.

by the following algorithms. We refer to the t component of the ciphertext returned by EtP[NE, F].E as the "tag" below. When including associated data, it would be input to F.

EtP[NE, F].K	EtP[NE, F].E(K, n, m)	EtP[NE, F].D(K, n, c)
$K \leftarrow_\$ \text{NE.K}$	$(K, K') \leftarrow K$	$(K, K') \leftarrow K; \ (c', t) \leftarrow c$
$K' \leftarrow_\$ \text{F.K}$	$c' \leftarrow \text{NE.E}(K, n, m)$	If $t = F_{K'}(n, c')$:
Return (K, K')	$t \leftarrow F_{K'}(n, c')$	Return NE.D(K, n, m)
	Return (c', t)	Return $\perp$

Our security result will analyze the authenticated security of EtP assuming NE has ciphertexts indistinguishable from random ciphertexts and F is pseudorandom. Let us recall these security notions.

INDISTINGUISHABILITY FROM RANDOM (INDR) SECURITY. This security notion requires that ciphertexts output by the encryption scheme cannot be distinguished from random strings. Consider the game $G_{NE,b}^{indr}$ defined in Fig. 7. Here an adversary $\mathcal{A}$ is given access to an encryption oracle ENC_b to which it can query a pair (n, m) and receive an honest encryption of message m with nonce n if $b = 1$ or a random string of the appropriate length if $b = 0$. We restrict attention to "valid" adversaries that never repeat the nonce n across different encryption queries. We define $\text{Adv}_{NE}^{indr}(\mathcal{A}) = \Pr[G_{NE,1}^{indr}(\mathcal{A})] - \Pr[G_{NE,0}^{indr}(\mathcal{A})]$.

AUTHENTICATED ENCRYPTION (AE) SECURITY. AE security simultaneously asks for integrity and confidentiality. Consider the games $G_{NE,b}^{ae-w}$ which defines three variants of authenticated encryption security parameterized by $w \in \{\text{m}, \diamond, \perp\}$ shown in Fig. 7. In this game, the adversary is given access to an encryption oracle and a decryption oracle. Its goal is to distinguish between a "real" and "ideal" world. In the real world ($b = 1$) the oracles use NE to encrypt messages and decrypt ciphertexts. In the ideal world ($b = 0$) encryption returns random messages of the appropriate length and decryption returns $\perp$. For simplicity, we will again restrict attention nonce-respecting adversaries which do not repeat nonces across encryption queries. (Note that there is no restriction placed on nonces used for decryption queries.)

The decryption oracle is parameterized by the value $w \in \{\text{m}, \diamond, \perp\}$ corresponding to three different security notions. In all three, we use a table $M[\cdot, \cdot]$ to detect when the adversary forwards encryption queries on to its decryption oracle. When $w = \text{m}$, the decryption oracle returns $M[n, c]$. When $w = \diamond$, it returns a special symbol $\diamond$. When $w = \perp$, it returns the symbol $\perp$ which is also used by the encryption scheme to represent rejection. For $w \in \{\text{m}, \diamond, \perp\}$ we define the advantage of an adversary $\mathcal{A}$ by $\text{Adv}_{NE}^{ae-w}(\mathcal{A}) = \Pr[G_{NE,1}^{ae-w}(\mathcal{A})] - \Pr[G_{NE,0}^{ae-w}(\mathcal{A})]$.

DISCUSSION OF VARIANTS. This choice of considering three variants of the definition follows the same choice made by Ghoshal et al. [15]. First off, we note that *if there are no restrictions on the memory of the adversary, all the three definitions are tightly equivalent.* An adversary can simply remember its past encryption queries and answers, and without loss of generality never make a decryption query on the answer of an encryption query. In the memory restricted setting these definitions *no longer appear to be equivalent.* The only known implication is that $w = \diamond$ security tightly implies $w = \perp$ security. Other implications seem to require remembering all encryption queries to properly simulate the decryption oracle. In Sect. 6 we parameterize public-key encryption CCA definitions similarly. This discussion applies to those definitions as well.

Ghoshal et al. argued that $w = \mathtt{m}$ is the "correct" definition. They argue that chosen ciphertext security is intended to capture the power of an adversary that can observe the behavior of a decrypting party. Both the $w = \bot$ and $w = \diamond$ definitions restrict what the adversary learns about this behavior when honestly generated ciphertexts are forwarded, which does not seem to model anything about real use of encryption. The $w = \mathtt{m}$ definition avoids this unnatural restriction.

We provide some technical context for this philosophical argument. In the full version [14] we give memory-tight proofs for the security of encryption schemes constructed with the KEM/DEM paradigm with $w = \mathtt{m}$ and noting this does not seem possible for the other choices of w. In this section and Sect. 6 we prove the AE/CCA-w security of encryption schemes for differing choices of w. We view this as a general exploration of what results are possible with memory-tight proofs. A proof which works for some w, but not others helps build some understanding of how these notions related.

5.2   Security Result

Now we give a proof of the AE-$\diamond$ security of $\mathsf{EtP}[\mathsf{NE}, \mathsf{F}]$. In particular we provide a memory-tight reduction to the INDR security of NE and a non-memory-tight reduction to the security of F. Such a result is useful if a time-memory tradeoff is known for NE and F is sufficiently secure even against high-memory attackers.

Theorem 4 (Security of EtP). *Let NE be a nonce-based encryption scheme and F be a family of function with $\mathsf{F.F} = \mathsf{Fcs}(\mathsf{NE.N}, \mathsf{NE.C}, \{0, 1\}^\tau)$ for $\tau \in \mathbb{N}$. Let $\mathcal{A}_a$ be an AE-$\diamond$ adversary with $(q_{\mathrm{ENC}}, q_{\mathrm{DEC}}) = \mathbf{Query}(\mathcal{A}_a)$. Define adversaries $\mathcal{A}_\mathsf{p}$ and $\mathcal{A}_r$ as shown in Fig. 9. Then,*

$$\mathsf{Adv}^{\mathsf{ae}\text{-}\diamond}_{\mathsf{EtP}[\mathsf{NE},\mathsf{F}]}(\mathcal{A}_a) \leq \mathsf{Adv}^{\mathsf{pr}}_{\mathsf{F}}(\mathcal{A}_\mathsf{p}) + \mathsf{Adv}^{\mathsf{indr}}_{\mathsf{NE}}(\mathcal{A}_r) + 2q_{\mathrm{DEC}}/2^\tau$$

$$\mathbf{Query}(\mathcal{A}_\mathsf{p}) = q_{\mathrm{ENC}} + q_{\mathrm{DEC}} \qquad \mathbf{Query}(\mathcal{A}_r) = q_{\mathrm{ENC}}$$

$$\mathbf{Time}(\mathcal{A}_\mathsf{p}) = \mathbf{Time}(\mathsf{G}^{\mathsf{ae}\text{-}\diamond}_{\mathsf{EtP}[\mathsf{NE},\mathsf{F}]}(\mathcal{A}_a)) \qquad \mathbf{Time}^*(\mathcal{A}_r) = \mathbf{Time}(\mathcal{A}_a)$$

$$\mathbf{Mem}(\mathcal{A}_\mathsf{p}) = \mathbf{Mem}(\mathsf{G}^{\mathsf{ae}\text{-}\diamond}_{\mathsf{EtP}[\mathsf{NE},\mathsf{F}]}(\mathcal{A}_a)) \qquad \mathbf{Mem}^*(\mathcal{A}_r) = \mathbf{Mem}(\mathcal{A}_a).$$

Adversary $\mathcal{A}_r$ is an $\mathsf{F.F}$-oracle adversary.

The standard (not memory-tight) proof of the security of EtP begins identically to our proof; we start in $\mathsf{G}^{\mathsf{ae}\text{-}\diamond}_{\mathsf{EtP}[\mathsf{NE},\mathsf{F}],1}$ replace the use of F with a truly random function (using $\mathcal{A}_\mathsf{p}$) and then information theoretically argue that the attacker shall be incapable of creating any forgeries. In the standard proof we would transition to a game where the decryption oracle is exactly that of $\mathrm{DEC}^\diamond_0$, i.e. it always returns $\bot$ when $M[n, c] = \bot$. Then we reduce to the security of NE to replace the generated ciphertexts with random. However this standard reduction will not be memory-tight because the attacker must store the table $M[\cdot, \cdot]$ to know whether it should return $\diamond$ or $\bot$ when simulating decryption queries.[4]

---

[4] Note this *would* be memory-tight for AE-$\bot$ security.

Adversary $\mathcal{A}_p^{\mathrm{Ev}}$	SimEnc(n, m)	SimDec(n, c)
$K \leftarrow_{\$} \mathsf{NE.K}$	$c' \leftarrow \mathsf{NE.E}(K, n, m)$	If $M[n, c] \neq \bot$: Return $\diamond$
$b' \leftarrow \mathcal{A}_a^{\mathrm{SimEnc, SimDec}}$	$t \leftarrow \mathrm{Ev}(n, c')$	$(t, c') \leftarrow c$
Return b'	$c \leftarrow (t, c')$	If $t = \mathrm{Ev}(n, c')$:
	$M[n, c] \leftarrow m$	Return $\mathsf{NE.D}(k, n, c')$
	Return c	Return $\bot$

Adversary $\mathcal{A}_r^{\mathrm{Enc}}$	SimEnc(n, m)	SimDec(n, c)
$f \leftarrow_{\$} \mathsf{Fcs}(\mathsf{NE.N}, \mathsf{NE.M}, \{0,1\}^\tau)$	$c' \leftarrow \mathrm{Enc}(n, m)$	$(t, c') \leftarrow c$
$b' \leftarrow \mathcal{A}_a^{\mathrm{SimEnc, SimDec}}$	$t \leftarrow f(n, c')$	If $t = f(n, c')$:
Return b'	$c \leftarrow (t, c')$	Return $\diamond$
	Return c	Return $\bot$

Fig. 9. Adversaries used for proof of Theorem 4.

Instead we first transition to a world where F has been replaced by the random function f and Dec always returns $\diamond$ when given a ciphertext with a correct tag. (Which we can do because either $M[n, c] \neq \bot$ held or the attacker managed to guess a random tag, which is unlikely.) Now we can make our INDR reduction memory-tight. It forwards encryption queries to its encryption oracle and then uses its own function f to create the tag. For decryption queries it checks $f(n, c') = t$, returning $\diamond$ if so and $\bot$ otherwise. Then we can finally conclude by switching to the decryption oracle $\mathrm{Dec}_0^\diamond$ by arguing that noticing this change requires guessing a random tag.

The full proof is given in the full version [14].

It does not seem possible to extend this proof technique to AE-m security because the tag would be too short to embed values of m we need to remember.

6 Chosen Ciphertext Security of Public Key Encryption

Now we apply our techniques to give memory-tight reductions between single- and multi-challenge notions of chosen-ciphertext security. The standard reduction bounds the advantage of an adversary making q_{Enc} encryption queries by q_{Enc} times the advantage of an adversary making 1 query. The reduction requires memory linear in q_{Enc} and so is not memory-tight.[5] In Sect. 6.1, we consider the most common "left-or-right" definition of CCA security and introduce three different variants (mirroring the three notions for AE security in Sect. 5). We give a memory-tight reduction between single- and multi-challenge security for two of

---

[5] Auerbach et al. [1] stated that this reduction is memory-tight for both CPA and CCA security. While the former is correct, the latter depends on the definition of CCA. In personally communication with Auerbach et al. [2], they concurred that their claim was incorrect for their intended definition of CCA security ($w = \diamond$) but pointed out that it does work for an "exclusion" variant, $w = E$, which we discuss in the full version [14].

Game $G_{PKE,b}^{cca-w}(\mathcal{A})$	$ENC_b(m_0, m_1)$	$DEC^w(c)$
$(ek, dk) \leftarrow_\$ PKE.K$	$// \ |m_0| = |m_1|$	If $M[c] \neq \perp$:
$b' \leftarrow \mathcal{A}^{ENC_b, DEC}(ek)$	$c_0 \leftarrow_\$ PKE.E(ek, m_0)$	$\quad$ Return $M[c]$ if $w = \mathtt{m}$
Return $b' = 1$	$c_1 \leftarrow_\$ PKE.E(ek, m_1)$	$\quad$ Return $\diamond$ if $w = \diamond$
	$M[c_b] \leftarrow m_1$	$\quad$ Return $\perp$ if $w = \perp$
	Return c_b	$m \leftarrow PKE.D(dk, c)$
		Return m

Fig. 11. Game defining CCA-w security of PKE for $w \in \{\mathtt{m}, \diamond, \perp\}$.

the three variants ($\diamond$ and $\perp$), but the reduction is not time-tight. In Sect. 6.2, we look at the CCA security variant that requires ciphertexts be indistinguishable from random. We give a memory-tight and time-tight reduction between single- and multi-challenge security for all three variants of this notion.

PUBLIC KEY ENCRYPTION. A public key encryption scheme PKE specifies algorithms PKE.K, PKE.E, and PKE.D. The syntax of these algorithms is shown in Fig. 10. The key generation algorithm PKE.K returns encryption key ek and decryption key dk. The encryption algorithm PKE.E encrypts message m with ek to produce a ciphertext c. We write PKE.E$(ek, m; r)$ when making random coins $r \in$ PKE.R explicit. The decryption algorithm decrypts c with dk to produce m. The decryption algorithm may output $m = \perp$ to indicate rejection.

PKE Syntax
$(ek, dk) \leftarrow_\$ PKE.K$
$c \leftarrow_\$ PKE.E(ek, m)$
$m \leftarrow PKE.D(dk, c)$

Fig. 10. Syntax of a public key encryption scheme PKE.

Correctness requires that PKE.D$(dk, c) = m$ for all $(ek, dk) \in$ [PKE.K], all m, and all $c \in$ [PKE.E(ek, m)]. We define the min-entropy of PKE as

$$PKE.H_\infty = -\lg \max_{m, ek, c} \Pr[r \leftarrow_\$ PKE.R : PKE.E(ek, m; r) = c] .$$

6.1 Left-or-Right CCA Security of PKE

LEFT-OR-RIGHT CCA SECURITY. In this section, we consider the left-or-right definition of CCA-security most commonly used in the literature. For $w \in \{\mathtt{m}, \diamond, \perp\}$ we denote this as CCA-w[6] and the corresponding security game $G_{PKE,b}^{cca-w}$ is defined in Fig. 11. The adversary gets the encryption key ek and has access to an encryption and a decryption oracle. The encryption oracle takes in messages m_0 and m_1 and encrypts m_b where b is the secret bit. The decryption oracle returns the decryption of a ciphertext, unless the ciphertext was previously returned by an encryption query. This is tracked by table M.

---

[6] The discussion in Sect. 5 about the choice to have three variants of the definitions is applicable here as well.

Adversary $\mathcal{A}_1^{\text{Enc},\text{Dec}}(ek)$	$\text{SimEnc}(m_0,m_1)$	$\text{SimDec}(c)$
$k \leftarrow_\$ [q_{\text{Enc}}]$	$i \leftarrow i+1$	If $c = c^*$: Return $\diamond$
$i \leftarrow 0$	For $d \in \{0,1\}$:	$m \leftarrow \text{Dec}(c)$
$D_{(\cdot)} \leftarrow \{0,1\}^{(\cdot)} \times [q_{\text{Enc}}]$	$\quad r_d \leftarrow f(|m_d|,(m_d,i))$	If $m = \bot$: Return $\bot$
$f \leftarrow_\$ \text{Fcs}(\mathbb{N},D,\text{PKE.R})$	$\quad c_d \leftarrow \text{PKE.E}(ek,m_d;r_d)$	For $j \in [i]$ do:
$b' \leftarrow \mathcal{A}_m^{\text{SimEnc},\text{SimDec}}(ek)$	If $i < k$: $c \leftarrow c_1$	$\quad$ If $m \in \{m_0^*,m_1^*\}$ and $j = k$:
Return b'	If $i = k$:	$\quad\quad$ Skip to next j
	$\quad c \leftarrow \text{Enc}(m_0,m_1)$	$\quad r \leftarrow f(|m|,(m,j))$
	$\quad c^* \leftarrow c$	$\quad$ If $\text{PKE.E}(ek,m;r) = c$:
	$\quad (m_0^*,m_1^*) \leftarrow (m_0,m_1)$	$\quad\quad$ Return $\diamond$
	If $i > k$: $c \leftarrow c_0$	Return m
	Return c	

Fig. 12. Adversary $\mathcal{A}_1$ for Theorem 5.

When $w = \text{m}$, the decryption oracle returns $M[c]$ which is m_1 from the earlier encryption query. When $w = \diamond$, it returns $\diamond$. When $w = \bot$, it returns $\bot$ which is also used by the encryption scheme to represent rejection. The advantage of an adversary $\mathcal{A}$ against the CCA-w security of PKE is defined as $\text{Adv}_{\text{PKE}}^{\text{cca-}w}(\mathcal{A}) = \Pr[\mathsf{G}_{\text{PKE},1}^{\text{cca-}w}(\mathcal{A})] - \Pr[\mathsf{G}_{\text{PKE},0}^{\text{cca-}w}(\mathcal{A})]$.

The goal of this section is to relate the advantage of attacks making only a single encryption query and those making many such queries. When wanting to make the distinction explicit we may use the adjectives "many" and "single" or prefix the abbreviation of a security notion with an 'm' or '1'.

1CCA-$\diamond$ IMPLIES mCCA-$\diamond$. The following theorem gives a memory-tight reduction establishing that CCA-$\diamond$ security against adversaries making one encryption query implies security for an arbitrary number of queries. The proof makes use of our inefficient tagging technique. The reduction performs a hybrid over the encryption queries of the original adversary and is thus not advantage-tight.

Theorem 5. (1CCA-$\diamond$ $\Rightarrow$ mCCA-$\diamond$). *Let* PKE *be a public key encryption scheme. Let $\mathcal{A}_m$ be an adversary with $(q_{\text{Enc}}, q_{\text{Dec}}) = \mathbf{Query}(\mathcal{A}_m)$. Define $D_{(\cdot)}$ by $D_n = \{0,1\}^n \times [q_{\text{Enc}}]$. Let $\mathcal{A}_1$ be the $\text{Fcs}(\mathbb{N},D,\text{PKE.R})$-oracle adversary shown in Fig. 12. Then,*

$$\text{Adv}_{\text{PKE}}^{\text{cca-}\diamond}(\mathcal{A}_m) \leq q_{\text{Enc}} \cdot \text{Adv}_{\text{PKE}}^{\text{cca-}\diamond}(\mathcal{A}_1) + 4 \cdot q_{\text{Enc}} \cdot q_{\text{Dec}}/2^{\text{PKE.H}_\infty}$$

$$\mathbf{Query}(\mathcal{A}_1) = (1, q_{\text{Dec}})$$

$$\mathbf{Time}^*(\mathcal{A}_1) = O(\mathbf{Time}(\mathcal{A}_m)) + q_{\text{Enc}}(q_{\text{Dec}}+1)\mathbf{Time}(\text{PKE})$$

$$\mathbf{Mem}^*(\mathcal{A}_1) = O(\mathbf{Mem}(\mathcal{A}_m)) + \mathbf{Mem}(\text{PKE}) + \lg q_{\text{Enc}}.$$

The standard (non-memory-tight) reduction against 1CCA security picks an index $k \in [q_{\text{Enc}}]$ where q_{Enc} is the number of encryption queries made by $\mathcal{A}_m$. It runs $\mathcal{A}_m$, simulating encryption queries as follows. For the first $k-1$ encryption queries, it answers with an encryption of m_1, for the k-th encryption query it forwards the query to its own encryption oracle, and the rest of the queries it

Game $G_{\mathsf{PKE},b}^{\$cca-w}(\mathcal{A})$	$\mathrm{ENC}_b(m)$	$\mathrm{DEC}^w(c)$
$(ek, dk) \leftarrow_\$ \mathsf{PKE.K}$	$c_1 \leftarrow_\$ \mathsf{PKE.E}(ek, m)$	If $M[c] \neq \bot$:
$b' \leftarrow \mathcal{A}^{\mathrm{ENC}_b, \mathrm{DEC}^w}(ek)$	$c_0 \leftarrow_\$ \mathsf{PKE.C}(ek, |m|)$	Return $M[c]$ if $w = \mathbf{m}$
Return $b' = 1$	$M[c_b] \leftarrow m$	Return $\diamond$ if $w = \diamond$
	Return c_b	Return $\bot$ if $w = \bot$
		$m \leftarrow \mathsf{PKE.D}(dk, c)$
		Return m

Fig. 13. Game defining $CCA-w$ security of PKE for $w \in \{\mathbf{m}, \diamond, \bot\}$.

answers with an encryption of m_0. To answer the decryption queries, the reduction returns $\diamond$ if it was ever queried the ciphertext for a previous encryption query. Otherwise, it forwards the query to its own decryption oracle. Finally, the reduction adversary outputs whatever $\mathcal{A}_\mathbf{m}$ outputs. Standard hybrid analysis shows that if the advantage of $\mathcal{A}_\mathbf{m}$ is ϵ, then the advantage of the reduction adversary is $\epsilon/q_{\mathrm{ENC}}$. Simulating decryption queries required remembering all prior encryption queries and hence the reduction is not memory-tight.

We give an adversary $\mathcal{A}_1$ in Fig. 12 that is very similar to the reduction just described, but avoids remembering prior encryption queries. The main idea is that it picks the coins when encrypting m_0 or m_1 locally as the output of a random function f applied to the message and a counter. This allows $\mathcal{A}_1$ to detect whether a ciphertext c queried to the decryption oracle is one it answered to an earlier encryption query as follows: it first asks for the decryption of c from its own decryption oracle and receives m. Then it iterates over all counter values for which encryption queries have been made so far and checks if c was the encryption of m using the output of f on m and the counter as coins. If any of these checks succeed it returns $\diamond$, otherwise it returns m. If c was the answer of an encryption query $\mathcal{A}_1$ detects it successfully. The probability that $\mathcal{A}_1$ returns $\diamond$ for a decryption query when it should not is small. We give the formal proof of Theorem 5 in the full version [14] where we use a sequence of hybrid games to transition from $G_{\mathsf{PKE},b}^{\mathsf{cca}-\diamond}$ to a hybrid game that is simulated by $\mathcal{A}_1$.

Notice that the additional memory overhead for $\mathcal{A}_1$ is just that required to store a counter, run $\mathsf{PKE.E}$, and store (c^*, m_0^*, m_1^*). However, there is an *increase* in runtime by $q_{\mathrm{ENC}} \cdot q_{\mathrm{DEC}} \cdot \mathbf{Time}(\mathsf{PKE})$ because of the iteration over the counters to answer decryption queries. As discussed in the introduction, such reductions may be useful when the best attack for the underlying problem with low memory requires significantly more running time than the best attack with high memory.

The same proof strategy would work essentially unchanged for CCA-$\bot$. For CCA-$\mathbf{m}$, the strategy does not suffice. If the adversary queries the decryption oracle on a ciphertext c which was an answer to a previous query for (m_0, m_1) the oracle needs to return m_1 even if c is an encryption of m_0.

6.2   Indistinguishable from Random CCA Security of PKE

We saw in the previous section that we could have a memory-tight reduction from mCCA-◇ to 1CCA-◇; however, the reduction is not tight with respect to running time. In this section, we show that for a different formalization of CCA security, we can indeed have a memory-tight and time-tight reduction between many- and single-challenge variants.

CIPHERTEXT AND ENCRYPTION KEY SPACE. Before describing the indistinguishable from random formalization of CCA security, we need to make some assumptions on PKE. We define the encryption keyspace by PKE.Ek = $\{ek : (ek, dk) \in$ PKE.K$\}$. We assume for each $ek \in$ PKE.Ek and allowed message length $n \in \mathbb{N}$ there is a set PKE.C(ek, n) such that PKE.E$(ek, m; r) \in$ PKE.C$(ek, |m|)$ always holds. Let PKE.C$^{-1}(ek, c)$ returns n such that $c \in$ PKE.C(ek, n). Correctness implies that PKE.C(ek, n) and PKE.C(ek, n') are disjoint for $n \neq n'$.

INDISTINGUISHABLE FROM RANDOM CIPHERTEXT CCA SECURITY. The security notion we will consider in this section is captured by the game $G^{\$cca\text{-}w}$ shown in Fig. 13. It requires that ciphertexts output by the encryption scheme cannot be distinguished from ciphertexts chosen at random even given access to a decryption oracle. The adversary gets the encryption key ek and has access to an encryption oracle ENC and a decryption oracle DEC. The adversary needs to distinguish the following real and ideal worlds: in the real world, a query to ENC with a message m returns an encryption of m under ek, while in the ideal world, the same query returns a uniformly random element of PKE.C$(ek, |m|)$. The decryption oracle DEC^w acts exactly as the corresponding oracle in $G^{cca\text{-}w}$.[7] The advantage of an adversary $\mathcal{A}$ against the \$CCA-w security of PKE is defined as Adv$^{\$cca\text{-}w}_{\mathsf{PKE}}(\mathcal{A}) = \Pr[G^{\$cca\text{-}w}_{\mathsf{PKE},1}(\mathcal{A})] - \Pr[G^{\$cca\text{-}w}_{\mathsf{PKE},0}(\mathcal{A})]$.

1\$CCA-m IMPLIES m\$CCA-m. The following theorem captures a memory-tight reduction establishing that 1\$CCA-m security implies m\$CCA-m security. The proof makes use of our message encoding technique.

Theorem 6 (1\$CCA-m $\Rightarrow$ m\$CCA-m). *Let* PKE *be a public key encryption scheme. Let τ satisfy* $|\mathsf{PKE.C}(ek, n)| \geq 2^n \cdot 2^\tau$ *for all n, ek. Let $\mathcal{A}_m$ be an adversary with* $(q_{\mathrm{ENC}}, q_{\mathrm{DEC}}, q_h) = \mathbf{Query}(\mathcal{A}_m)$ *and assume* $q_{\mathrm{ENC}} + q_{\mathrm{DEC}} \leq 0.5 \cdot 2^\tau$. *Let $\mathcal{F} = \mathsf{Inj}^{\pm}(T, D, R)$ where T, D, and R are defined by $T = \mathbb{N} \times \mathsf{PKE.Ek}$, $D_{n,ek} = \{0,1\}^n \times [q_{\mathrm{ENC}}]$ and $R_{n,ek} = \mathsf{PKE.C}(ek, n)$. Let $\mathcal{A}_1$ be the $\mathcal{F}$-oracle adversary defined in Fig. 14. Then,*

$$\mathsf{Adv}^{\$cca\text{-}m}_{\mathsf{PKE}}(\mathcal{A}_m) \leq q_{\mathrm{ENC}} \cdot \mathsf{Adv}^{\$cca\text{-}m}_{\mathsf{PKE}}(\mathcal{A}_1) + 8q_{\mathrm{ENC}}q_{\mathrm{DEC}}/2^\tau + 5q^2_{\mathrm{ENC}}/2^\tau$$

$$\mathbf{Query}(\mathcal{A}_1) = (1, q_{\mathrm{DEC}}, q_h)$$

$$\mathbf{Time}^*(\mathcal{A}_1) = O(\mathbf{Time}(\mathcal{A}_m)) + q_{\mathrm{ENC}}\mathbf{Time}(\mathsf{PKE})$$

$$\mathbf{Mem}^*(\mathcal{A}_1) = O(\mathbf{Mem}(\mathcal{A}_m)) + \mathbf{Mem}(\mathsf{PKE}) \lg q_{\mathrm{ENC}}.$$

---

[7] As mentioned, the discussion in Sect. 5 about the three variants definitions is applicable here as well. In the full version [14] we give an example where we can prove CCA security of a KEM/DEM scheme in the memory restricted setting, but only if we use the $w = \mathtt{m}$ definition.

Adversary $\mathcal{A}_1^{\text{ENC,DEC}}(ek)$	$\text{SIMENC}(m)$	$\text{SIMDEC}(c)$
$//\, 0 \leqslant h \leqslant 2$	$i \leftarrow i + 1$	If $c = c^*$: Return m^*
$k \leftarrow^{\$} [q_{\text{ENC}}]$	$c_1 \leftarrow^{\$} \text{PKE.E}(ek, m)$	$n \leftarrow \text{PKE.C}^{-1}(ek, c)$
$i \leftarrow 0$	$c_0 \leftarrow f((|m|, ek), (m, i))$	$(m, j) \leftarrow f^{-1}((n, ek), c)$
$f \leftarrow^{\$} \text{Inj}^{\pm}(T, D, R)$	If $i < k$: $c \leftarrow c_1$	If $m \neq \bot$ and $k \leqslant j \leqslant i$:
$b' \leftarrow \mathcal{A}_m^{\text{SIMENC,SIMDEC}}(ek)$	If $i = k$:	If $(m, j) = (m^*, k)$:
Return b'	$\quad c \leftarrow \text{ENC}(m)$	$\quad$ Skip next line
	$\quad (c^*, m^*) \leftarrow (c, m)$	$\quad$ Return m
	If $i > k$: $c \leftarrow c_0$	$m \leftarrow \text{DEC}(c)$
	Return c	Return m

Fig. 14. Adversary $\mathcal{A}_1$ for Theorem 6.

The standard (non-memory-tight) reduction against 1\$CCA security that runs an m\$CCA adversary $\mathcal{A}_m$ works in a similar manner as the standard reduction from an 1CCA adversary and an mCCA adversary that we described in Sect. 6.1. Again here, simulating decryption queries requires remembering all the answers of the encryption queries, and hence the reduction is not memory-tight.

We give an adversary $\mathcal{A}_1$ in Fig. 14 that is very similar to the standard reduction, but avoids remembering all the answers of the encryption queries. The main idea here is picking the ciphertext c_0 as the output of a random injective function f evaluated on the message and a counter, instead of sampling it uniformly at random. This way of picking the c_0 allows $\mathcal{A}_1$ detect whether a ciphertext c queried to the decryption oracle was the answer to an earlier encryption query as follows: it first checks if the inverse of f on the ciphertext is defined (i.e., not $\bot$), it returns the message part of the inverse. Otherwise it asks for the decryption of the ciphertext to its own decryption oracle and returns the answer. Using our assumption on the size of $\text{PKE.C}(ek, n)$, we can argue that except with small probability, $\mathcal{A}_1$ simulates the decryption oracle correctly. We give the formal proof in the full version [14] where we use a sequence of hybrid games to transition from $G_{\text{PKE},b}^{\text{\$cca-m}}$ to a game that is perfectly simulated by $\mathcal{A}_1$.

The additional memory overhead for $\mathcal{A}_1$ is only a counter. Moreover, there is no increase in the running time of $\mathcal{A}_1$ unlike the adversary in Theorem 5.

EXTENSION TO \$CCA-$\diamond$, \$CCA-$\bot$. We can prove the same result for \$CCA-$\diamond$, \$CCA-$\bot$ but the adversary would not be tight with respect to running time. The adversary in these cases would pick the coins for encrypting m (to compute c_1) like the adversary in Theorem 5. This would require iterating over counters to answer decryption queries and hence lead to looseness with respect to running time. We omit the theorems for these notions because they would not involve any new ideas beyond those presented in Theorems 5 and 6.

Acknowledgements. Ashrujit Ghoshal, Joseph Jaeger, and Stefano Tessaro were partially supported by NSF grants CNS-1930117 (CAREER), CNS-1926324, CNS-2026774, a Sloan Research Fellowship, and a JP Morgan Faculty Award. Joseph Jaeger's work was done while at the University of Washington.

References

1. Auerbach, B., Cash, D., Fersch, M., Kiltz, E.: Memory-tight reductions. In: Katz, J., Shacham, H. (eds.) CRYPTO 2017. LNCS, vol. 10401, pp. 101–132. Springer, Cham (2017). https://doi.org/10.1007/978-3-319-63688-7_4
2. Auerbach, B., Cash, Fersch, M., Kiltz, E.: Personal communication (2021)
3. Bellare, M., Namprempre, C.: Authenticated encryption: relations among notions and analysis of the generic composition paradigm. J. Cryptol. 21(4), 469–491 (2008)
4. Bellare, M., Rogaway, P.: Random oracles are practical: a paradigm for designing efficient protocols. In: Denning, D.E., Pyle, R., Ganesan, R., Sandhu, R.S., Ashby, V. (eds.) ACM CCS, vol. 93, pp. 62–73. ACM Press (1993)
5. Bellare, M., Rogaway, P.: The security of triple encryption and a framework for code-based game-playing proofs. In: Vaudenay, S. (ed.) EUROCRYPT 2006. LNCS, vol. 4004, pp. 409–426. Springer, Heidelberg (2006). https://doi.org/10.1007/11761679_25
6. Bernstein, D.J.: Extending the salsa20 nonce. In: Workshop record of Symmetric Key Encryption Workshop, vol. 2011. Citeseer (2011)
7. Bhattacharyya, R.: Memory-tight reductions for practical key encapsulation mechanisms. In: Kiayias, A., Kohlweiss, M., Wallden, P., Zikas, V. (eds.) PKC 2020. LNCS, vol. 12110, pp. 249–278. Springer, Cham (2020). https://doi.org/10.1007/978-3-030-45374-9_9
8. Coron, J.-S.: Optimal security proofs for PSS and other signature schemes. In: Knudsen, L.R. (ed.) EUROCRYPT 2002. LNCS, vol. 2332, pp. 272–287. Springer, Heidelberg (2002). https://doi.org/10.1007/3-540-46035-7_18
9. Dai, W., Tessaro, S., Zhang, X.: Super-linear time-memory trade-offs for symmetric encryption. In: Pass, R., Pietrzak, K. (eds.) TCC 2020. LNCS, vol. 12552, pp. 335–365. Springer, Cham (2020). https://doi.org/10.1007/978-3-030-64381-2_12
10. Diemert, D., Gellert, K., Jager, T., Lyu, L.: Digital signatures with memory-tight security in the multi-challenge setting. In: Tibouchi, M., Wang, H. (eds.) ASIACRYPT 2021. LNCS, vol. 13093, pp. 403–433. Springer, Cham (2021). https://doi.org/10.1007/978-3-030-92068-5_14
11. Dinur, I.: On the streaming indistinguishability of a random permutation and a random function. In: Canteaut, A., Ishai, Y. (eds.) EUROCRYPT 2020. LNCS, vol. 12106, pp. 433–460. Springer, Cham (2020). https://doi.org/10.1007/978-3-030-45724-2_15
12. Dinur, I.: Tight time-space lower bounds for finding multiple collision pairs and their applications. In: Canteaut, A., Ishai, Y. (eds.) EUROCRYPT 2020. LNCS, vol. 12105, pp. 405–434. Springer, Cham (2020). https://doi.org/10.1007/978-3-030-45721-1_15
13. Even, S., Goldreich, O., Micali, S.: On-line/off-line digital signatures. J. Cryptol. 9(1), 35–67 (1996). https://doi.org/10.1007/BF02254791
14. Ghoshal, A., Ghosal, R., Jaeger, J., Tessaro, S.: Hiding in plain sight: memory-tight proofs via randomness programming. Cryptology ePrint Archive, Report 2021/1409 (2021). https://eprint.iacr.org/2021/1409
15. Ghoshal, A., Jaeger, J., Tessaro, S.: The memory-tightness of authenticated encryption. In: Micciancio, D., Ristenpart, T. (eds.) CRYPTO 2020. LNCS, vol. 12170, pp. 127–156. Springer, Cham (2020). https://doi.org/10.1007/978-3-030-56784-2_5
16. Ghoshal, A., Tessaro, S.: On the memory-tightness of hashed elgamal. In: Canteaut, A., Ishai, Y. (eds.) EUROCRYPT 2020. LNCS, vol. 12106, pp. 33–62. Springer, Cham (2020). https://doi.org/10.1007/978-3-030-45724-2_2

17. Jaeger, J., Tessaro, S.: Tight time-memory trade-offs for symmetric encryption. In: Ishai, Y., Rijmen, V. (eds.) EUROCRYPT 2019. LNCS, vol. 11476, pp. 467–497. Springer, Cham (2019). https://doi.org/10.1007/978-3-030-17653-2_16

18. Namprempre, C., Rogaway, P., Shrimpton, T.: Reconsidering generic composition. In: Nguyen, P.Q., Oswald, E. (eds.) EUROCRYPT 2014. LNCS, vol. 8441, pp. 257–274. Springer, Heidelberg (2014). https://doi.org/10.1007/978-3-642-55220-5_15

19. Rogaway, P.: Nonce-based symmetric encryption. In: Roy, B., Meier, W. (eds.) FSE 2004. LNCS, vol. 3017, pp. 348–358. Springer, Heidelberg (2004). https://doi.org/10.1007/978-3-540-25937-4_22

20. Shahaf, I., Ordentlich, O., Segev, G.: An information-theoretic proof of the streaming switching lemma for symmetric encryption. In: 2020 IEEE International Symposium on Information Theory (ISIT), pp. 858–863 (2020)

21. Tessaro, S., Thiruvengadam, A.: Provable time-memory trade-offs: symmetric cryptography against memory-bounded adversaries. In: Beimel, A., Dziembowski, S. (eds.) TCC 2018. LNCS, vol. 11239, pp. 3–32. Springer, Cham (2018). https://doi.org/10.1007/978-3-030-03807-6_1

22. Wang, Y., Matsuda, T., Hanaoka, G., Tanaka, K.: Memory lower bounds of reductions revisited. In: Nielsen, J.B., Rijmen, V. (eds.) EUROCRYPT 2018. LNCS, vol. 10820, pp. 61–90. Springer, Cham (2018). https://doi.org/10.1007/978-3-319-78381-9_3

Dynamic Collusion Bounded Functional Encryption from Identity-Based Encryption

Rachit Garg[1(✉)], Rishab Goyal[2(✉)], George Lu[1], and Brent Waters[1,3]

[1] UT Austin, Austin, USA
{rachg96,gclu,bwaters}@cs.utexas.edu
[2] MIT, Cambridge, USA
goyal@utexas.edu
[3] NTT Research, Palo Alto, USA

Abstract. Functional Encryption is a powerful notion of encryption in which each decryption key is associated with a function f such that decryption recovers the function evaluation $f(m)$. Informally, security states that a user with access to function keys $\mathsf{sk}_{f_1}, \mathsf{sk}_{f_2}, \ldots$ (and so on) can only learn $f_1(m), f_2(m), \ldots$ (and so on) but nothing more about the message. The system is said to be q-bounded collusion resistant if the security holds as long as an adversary gets access to at most $q = q(\lambda)$ function keys. A major drawback of such *statically* bounded collusion systems is that the collusion bound q must be declared at setup time and is fixed for the entire lifetime of the system.

We initiate the study of *dynamically* bounded collusion resistant functional encryption systems which provide more flexibility in terms of selecting the collusion bound, while reaping the benefits of statically bounded collusion FE systems (such as quantum resistance, simulation security, and general assumptions). Briefly, the virtues of a dynamically bounded scheme can be summarized as:

Fine-grained individualized selection. It lets each encryptor select the collusion bound by weighing the trade-off between performance overhead and the amount of collusion resilience.

Evolving encryption strategies. Since the system is no longer tied to a single collusion bound, thus it allows to dynamically adjust the desired collusion resilience based on any number of evolving factors such as the age of the system, or a number of active users, etc.

R. Goyal—Research supported in part by NSF CNS Award #1718161, an IBM-MIT grant, and by the Defense Advanced Research Projects Agency (DARPA) under Contract No. HR00112020023. Any opinions, findings and conclusions or recommendations expressed in this material are those of the author(s) and do not necessarily reflect the views of the United States Government or DARPA.

B. Waters—Supported by NSF CNS-1908611, CNS-1414082, Packard Foundation Fellowship, and Simons Investigator Award.

O. Dunkelman and S. Dziembowski (Eds.): EUROCRYPT 2022, LNCS 13276, pp. 736–763, 2022.
https://doi.org/10.1007/978-3-031-07085-3_25

Ease and simplicity of updatability. None of the system parameters have to be updated when adjusting the collusion bound. That is, the same key sk_f can be used to decrypt ciphertexts for collusion bound $q = 2$ as well as $q = 2^\lambda$.

We construct such a dynamically bounded functional encryption scheme for the class of all polynomial-size circuits under the general assumption of Identity-Based Encryption.

1   Introduction

Public-key encryption [18] is one of the most fundamental concepts in cryptography. Traditionally, public-key encryption was defined to provide an "all-or-nothing" type functionality and security, where given a decryption key sk, a user can either recover the entire plaintext m from a ciphertext ct or nothing at all. In the recent years, an extremely powerful notion of encryption called Functional Encryption (FE) [11,32] has emerged.

FE provides a fine-grained access control mechanism over encrypted data where a decryption key is now associated with a function f and the decryptor recovers the function evaluation $f(m)$ from the ciphertext. Moreover, a user with access to function keys $sk_{f_1}, \ldots, sk_{f_n}$ can only learn $f_1(m), \ldots, f_n(m)$ but nothing more about the message. This security requirement is commonly captured in a game based indistinguishability definition, where the adversary submits two messages, m_0 and m_1, as a challenge and must be unable to distinguish between encryptions of m_0 and m_1 with non-negligible probability given that $f_i(m_0) = f_i(m_1)$ hold for all keys in adversary's possession.

Over the last several years, FE has been studied extensively. Significant progress has been made towards building various expressive forms of FE under such indistinguishability-based definitions. Starting with initial works [12,29] that built specific forms of predicate encryption over bilinear maps, the search for FE for general circuits under standard cryptographic assumptions culminated in the recent breakthrough work of Jain, Lin, and Sahai [28]. They proposed an FE scheme for general circuits from a combination of PRGs in $\mathbf{NC}^0$, Symmetric eXternal Diffie-Hellman (SXDH), Learning with Errors (LWE), and Learning Parity with Noise (LPN) over large fields assumptions. While this is tremendous progress, an unfortunate limitation of this FE scheme is that it is susceptible to quantum attacks due to the post-quantum insecurity of the SXDH assumption. But even more broadly, pursuing the direction of indistinguishability-based security for FE suffers from the drawback that it is unclear how it captures the intuition that an attacker learns *at most the function evaluation but nothing more*.

For these reasons, FE has also been investigated in the bounded collusion model under simulation-based definitions. In the bounded collusion model, the FE system declares a bound q at the setup time, such that all the system parameters are allowed to grow polynomially with q (in addition to the security parameter λ). Additionally, the security requirement is captured via a simulation-based game, which says that as long as the attacker does not make more than q

key queries, the adversary's view - which includes the ciphertext ct_m and function keys $\mathsf{sk}_{f_1}, \ldots, \mathsf{sk}_{f_q}$ - can be "simulated" given only the function evaluations $f_1(m), \ldots, f_q(m)$ and nothing more about m. Although this more closely captures the intuition behind FE, if the attacker corrupts more than q keys, then no security is provided. Despite its limitations, the bounded collusion model for FE has been very useful in various contexts such as proving negative results in differential privacy [30], applications to tracing [15,26], etc. In some cases, it is the only currently known pathway to certain applications in the post-quantum regime. A notable feature of the bounded collusion model is that under them, FE can be built from the minimal assumption of public-key encryption (and OWFs in case of private-key FE) as studied in a long line of works [1,4,7,15,24,26,31].

The Question. A major drawback of such bounded collusion FE systems is that the setup authority needs to declare the collusion bound q at the very beginning, and the bound q is fixed, once and for all, for the entire lifetime of the system. This puts the authority in a difficult situation, as it requires an incredible amount of foresight at the setup time. In particular, if the authority sets the bound q lower than the eventual number of compromised keys, then the system will be insecure; whereas overestimating the bound q would result in significant performance overhead. Now when the collusion bound is breached, the only option is to do a fresh setup and redistribute the keys which is at best inefficient, and possibly infeasible in certain scenarios. Switching to the state-of-the-art fully collusion resistant FE schemes would suffer from drawbacks discussed above.

With the aforementioned limitations of existing FE systems, we ask the following –

Can we build an FE system for general circuits that reaps the benefits of bounded collusion FE systems – post-quantum security, simulation security, and general assumptions – while at the same time provide more flexibility to the authority in terms of selecting the collusion bound? And, would such an FE system lead to results in the domain of full collusion resistance?

In this work, we study the above question. We answer the first part in affirmative by introducing a new flexible corruption model that we call the "dynamic collusion" model, and building a simulation secure FE system in the dynamic collusion model from the general assumption of Identity-Based Encryption (IBE) [10,16,34] (for which we have quantum-safe instantiations [2,14,22]). Since it is widely believed that the FE for general circuits is significantly more expressive than plain IBE, this seems to answer the latter part negatively. Concurrently[1], the authors of [3] noticed the same gaps and limitations in bounded-collusion FE security, and defined a similar dynamic collusion model. For a more detailed comparison of the concurrent work, refer to Sect. 1.3.

---

[1] Both works, this work and [3], were submitted to Crypto 2021.

Defining Dynamically Bounded Collusion Resistance

In this work, we refer to the traditional notion of bounded collusion resistance for FE as *statically bounded collusion resistance*. Recall that, syntactically, a statically bounded FE is defined exactly as fully collusion resistant FE, that is using four polynomial time algorithms – Setup, KeyGen, Enc, and Dec – except the Setup algorithm now additionally takes the target collusion bound q as an input. As mentioned previously, declaring the collusion bound q upfront lets the setup authority set up the system parameters with enough redundancy, and this typically leads to the running time and sizes of all system parameters (i.e., the keys and ciphertexts) to grow polynomially with q.

In the dynamic collusion model, the Setup algorithm no longer takes the collusion bound as input, but instead the Enc algorithm selects the collusion bound per ciphertext. That is, the setup and key generation algorithms no longer depend on the collusion bound q, but only the encryptor needs to specify the collusion bound.[2] *Basically, this lets the encryptor dynamically decide the size of set of colluding users against which it wants to hide its message.* As a consequence, in the dynamic collusion model, only the size of the ciphertexts potentially grows with the collusion bound q, but the running times of the Setup and KeyGen algorithms (therefore the public and secret keys) are independent of q. The security requirement is again captured via a simulation-based game but where the admissibility constraints on the attacker are lifted such that the number of key queries the attacker is permitted can be adaptively specified at the time of committing the challenge m instead of beginning of the game as in the static model.

Our dynamic collusion model and its comparison with the static model is discussed in detail in Sect. 3. Below we briefly highlight the virtues of the dynamic collusion model.

Fine-grained individualized selection. A dynamically bounded collusion FE scheme allows each user to select the collusion bound by weighing the trade-off between the performance overhead and amount of collusion resilience at encryption time. For example, depending upon the factors such as available computing resources, or the bandwidth on the communication channel, or the sensitivity of data etc., an encryptor might want to increase/decrease the amount of collusion resilience to better fit the computing/communication/privacy constraints.

Evolving encryption strategies. Since the system is no longer statically tied to a single collusion bound at setup time, thus it allows to dynamically adjust the desired collusion resilience based on any number of evolving factors such as the age of the system, or number of active users etc. Thus, the authority does not need to have any foresight about the attackers at setup time in contrast to statically bounded collusion FE systems.

(Of course the ciphertexts in which the collusion bound was exceeded will not be secure, but future attacks can be prevented by adapting to a larger collusion bound.)

---

[2] However, note that it is essential that the master public-secret keys and every function key is resuable for all values of the collusion bound.

Ease and simplicity of updatability. While the above features are already highly desirable, a noteworthy property of these systems is that none of the parameters have to be updated when adjusting the collusion bound. That is, the same function key sk_f can be used to decrypt ciphertexts for collusion bound $q = 2$ as well as $q = 2^\lambda$ without requiring any updates. Also, the storage space for the parameters is bounded by a fixed polynomial in λ.

Next, we provide an overview of our approach and describe the technical ideas. Later on, we discuss some related works and open questions.

1.1   Technical Overview

In this section, we provide a high level overview of our new collusion framework and the corresponding FE construction. The overview is split into five parts which roughly correspond to the proceeding sections of the paper. First, we informally introduce the notion of dynamically bounded collusion resistant FE. Second, we define an efficiency property that we refer to as *weak optimality* for statically bounded collusion FE systems, and show that any weakly optimal FE construction could be generically lifted to a dynamically bounded collusion FE scheme. Next, we build such a weakly optimal FE scheme via the framework of tagged functional encryption scheme, where a tagged FE scheme is same as a regular FE scheme except each ciphertext and secret key is additionally embedded with a tag such that only ciphertexts and keys with the same tag can be combined together. Finally, we build a tagged FE scheme for statically bounded collusions in two steps – first, reduce the problem of constructing tagged FE with static collusions to the simpler setting of at most one key corruption (also referred to as 1-bounded collusion); and second, design a tagged FE system in the simpler setting directly from IBE.

Dynamic vs. Static Bounded Collusion Model

Let us start by recalling the syntax of functional encryption in the static collusion model. An FE scheme in the static collusion model consists of four algorithms with the following semantics:

- Setup takes as input the <u>collusion bound q</u> and samples the master public-secret key pair (mpk, msk).
- KeyGen generates a function key sk_f given function f and master key msk.
- Enc encrypts a message m to a ciphertext ct.
- Dec recovers $f(m)$ from the ciphertext and decryption key.

In the dynamic collusion model, the collusion bound q is not fixed at the system setup, but instead the encryptor chooses the amount of collusion resilience it wants every time a fresh ciphertext is created. This is reflected with the following changes:

- Setup no longer takes the collusion bound q as an input.
- Enc takes <u>the desired collusion bound q as an additional input</u> for sampling the ciphertext.

Note that since the collusion bound q is not specified during setup or key generation at all, thus the efficiency condition for a dynamically bounded collusion FE scheme requires the running time of Setup and KeyGen to be fixed polynomials in λ, whereas in static setting they are allowed to grow polynomially with q.

Static to Dynamic via Weak Optimality

As we mentioned before, our first observation is that a dynamically bounded collusion FE scheme can be constructed from any statically bounded scheme if it satisfies a 'weak optimality' property. Intuitively, the weak optimality property says that the running time of the setup and key generation algorithms grows only poly-logarithmically in the collusion bound q.

Now looking closely at the notion of weakly-optimal statically bounded collusion FE, we observe that the major difference between this and a dynamic system is that the Setup algorithm requires q as an explicit input in the static setting, but not in the dynamic setting. Our idea to get around this is to exploit the efficiency property of the static scheme, where the dynamic collusion FE scheme essentially runs λ independent instances of the static collusion FE scheme in parallel with geometrically increasing collusion bounds. That is, i-th subsystem (running a single instance of the static scheme) is set up with collusion bound $q_i = 2^i$. And, now the master public-secret key pair as well as each function key in the dynamic system contains λ independently sampled keys where the i-th sub-key is sampled using the i-th static FE system. Since the encryption algorithm receives the target collusion bound q as input, thus the encryptor uniquely selects a static FE sub-system under which it encrypts the message. The target collusion bound to subsystem index mapping can simply be defined $i := \lceil \log q \rceil$ (i.e., nearest power of two). Note that setting up the system this way ensures the dynamic system achieves the desired efficiency. This is because the setup and key generation will be efficient (by weak optimality of the static FE scheme), and since $2^i = 2^{\lceil \log q \rceil} < 2q$, thus the running time of encryption and decryption is a polynomial in q.

Since the above transformation is very natural, one would expect the simulation security of the resulting dynamic FE system to also follow directly from the simulation security of the underlying static FE schemes. However, this is not the case. To better understand the technical barrier, let us first consider the most natural simulation strategy described next. The simulator for the dynamic system simply runs the simulator for each of the underlying static systems in parallel, where the ciphertext simulator is only run for the static system corresponding to the adversarially selected challenge target collusion bound q^*. While this seems to compile, there are two subtle issues that need to be carefully handled.

First, the running time of each static FE simulator grows with the underlying collusion bound which grows as large as exponential in λ. For avoiding the problem of inefficient simulation, we additionally require the underlying static FE scheme to have weakly-optimal simulators as well which means that all but the ciphertext simulation phase of the static FE could be performed optimally (i.e., the simulator running time grows only poly-logarithmically in q). However, this is still not enough for proving simulation security. The reason is that typically the simulation security states that the distribution of secret keys and ciphertext are simulatable as long as the adversary does not make more key queries than what is specified by the static collusion bound. That is, if the adversary makes more key queries then no guarantee is provided. Now our dynamic FE simulator must invoke the underlying static FE simulator even for collusion bounds smaller than q^*, thus the standard simulation guarantee is insufficient. To get around this issue, we define a notion called *strong* simulation security for static-bounded-collusion FE schemes under which we require that the real and ideal worlds are also indistinguishable even when the adversary makes more key queries than that specified by the collusion bound as long as the adversary does not make any challenge message queries. More details are provided in Sect. 3.2.

From Tagged FE to Weak Optimality

Our next idea is to embed auxiliary tagging information inside each individual ciphertext and decryption key such that the auxiliary information is useful for achieving weak optimality generically by embedding information about the collusion bound inside the auxiliary information. Formally, in a tagged FE system, the semantics of encryption and key generation are changed as:

- KeyGen, Enc, both also take in a tag string tg as an input.

And, now the decryption algorithm recovers $f(m)$ from the ciphertext and decryption key corresponding to tags tg_1, tg_2 (respectively) iff $tg_1 = tg_2$. Basically, the intuition behind a tagged FE scheme is to efficiently implement many parallel instances of a statically bounded collusion FE scheme such that the master public-secret keys do not grow with number of underlying (untagged) FE instances.

In other words, the idea behind tagged FE is to serve as an extension to regular (untagged) FE in the same way as IBE is to PKE, that is to capture the same master public-secret key compression properties. That is, a tagged FE enables compressing exponentially many parallel instances of untagged FE into a succinct system where all the system parameters are efficient, and the ciphertexts and decryption keys corresponding to each underlying untagged FE system can be efficiently computed given those parameters. In terms of simulation security for tagged FE, the property is a natural extension of statically bounded-collusion security model for FE to the tagged setting, where now the adversary is allowed to query keys and ciphertexts for an unbounded number of tags, and the simulation security must hold for all challenge ciphertexts (queried under separate tags) as long as the number of key queries does not exceed the collusion bound on any tag for which a challenge ciphertext is also requested.

Looking ahead, the benefit of a tagged FE scheme will be that we can distribute the final desired collusion bound over to the auxiliary tag space as well, and not just the collusion bound ingrained in the tagged FE system. And, since tagged FE can encode the tag space more efficiently than the collusion bound, thus this is useful for obtaining the desired weak optimality.

At a high level, to transform any tagged FE scheme into an FE scheme that satisfies the desired weak optimality property, we rely on the linearization trick by Ananth and Vaikuntanathan [7] where they suggested a generic compiler to improve efficiency of a statically bounded-collusion FE scheme from an arbitrary polynomial dependence on the collusion bound, q, to only a linear dependence. Our observation is that if we substitute all the underlying FE scheme in the linearization transformation from [7] with a single tagged FE scheme, then that would result in a statically bounded-collusion FE scheme with weak optimality.

Briefly, collusion bound linearization transformation simply consists of running q many parallel instances of the inefficient (untagged) FE scheme each, but with collusion bound set to be the security parameter λ. While for encrypting the message m, the ciphertext is computed as an encryption of m under each of the underlying FE schemes; the key generator only generated a decryption key for a random instance out of the q inefficient FE systems. By a standard balls and bins concentration argument, it was shown that, with all but negligible probability, the collusion bound of λ was never crossed for any of the underlying FE system as long as only q many total key queries were made. We rely on the same idea for our weak optimality transformation wherein we simply replace the q many paralled untagged FE systems with a single tagged FE system, where now the i-th FE sub-scheme in the [7] transformation is set to be the sub-scheme corresponding to tag value i. The full transformation is provided later in Sect. 5.

Intuitively, we use the linearization trick to absorb the blow-up due to the collusion bound in the tag space of the FE scheme instead. This decouples the desired collusion bound, q, from the resulting FE scheme with the collusion bound fixed inside the underlying tagged FE system thereby allowing us to set the collusion bound for the tagged system to be simply λ. Thus, we can reason from the efficiency of the tagged FE scheme that the resulting scheme only has polylogarithmic dependence in the λ for Setup and KeyGen, making it weakly optimal.

Amplifying Collusion Bound in Tagged FE

The next component in our sequence of transformations is a generic collusion bound amplification procedure for tagged FE, in turn reducing the problem to constructing tagged FE for 1-bounded collusion instead. Our approach follows the general bootstrapping blueprint developed for upgrading collusion bound in untagged FE literature [7,24] which runs a specific multiparty computation protocol in the head.

In such MPC protocols, there are N servers/parties and a single client with an input x with the computation proceeding in two phases – offline and online. In the offline phase, the client encodes its input x into N individual encodings – $\{\hat{x}^1, \ldots, \hat{x}^N\}$ – one for each server. While in the online phase, a function f is encoded into N individual encodings – $\{\hat{f}^1, \ldots, \hat{f}^N\}$ – such that i-th server learns the i-th function encoding, and any subset S of servers of size p can locally decode their individual encodings to obtain partial evaluations, $\hat{y}^i$ for $i \in S$, such that all these p partial evaluations can be publicly combined to compute the function evaluation $f(x)$. And importantly, the security of the MPC protocol assures that, even if at most t servers get corrupted, no information other than actual value $f(x)$ can be adversarially learned given the public partial evaluations. Now for applications to collusion bound amplification in FE, it is important to have MPC protocols in which the client can delegate the computation for multiple functions w.r.t. a single offline phase.

The high level idea is that each ciphertext encodes the message m into various different pieces where each piece corresponds to an individual offline encoding for a particular server, and now the key generator selects a random subset of servers for which it gives the appropriate function encodings for each selected server. In more detail, the bootstrapping procedure works as follows, where 1KeyFE is any 1-bounded collusion untagged FE scheme:

– Setup samples N independent master public-secret key pair $(\mathsf{mpk}_i, \mathsf{msk}_i)$ for the 1KeyFE scheme. These N key pairs are set as the master public-secret key pairs for this scheme respectively.
– Enc encodes the message m using the offline phase to compute encodings $\{\hat{x}^1, \ldots, \hat{x}^N\}$, and encrypts the i-th encoding under the i-th master public key, that is $\mathsf{ct}_i \leftarrow 1\mathsf{KeyFE.Enc}(\mathsf{mpk}_i, \hat{x}^i)$ for $i \in [N]$, and outputs $(\mathsf{ct}_1, \ldots, \mathsf{ct}_N)$ as the full ciphertext.
– KeyGen selects a random subset $S \subseteq [N]$ of size p, and performs the online phase to compute $\{\hat{f}^1, \ldots, \hat{f}^N\}$. Now enable decryption, it creates a FE decryption key for each server $i \in S$ enabling the local circuit computation, that is $\mathsf{sk}_{f,i} \leftarrow 1\mathsf{KeyFE.KeyGen}(\mathsf{msk}_i, \mathsf{Local}(\hat{f}^i, \cdot))$, and sets the final decryption key as these individual decryption keys $\mathsf{sk}_{f,i}$ for $i \in S$.
– Dec first recovers the partial evaluations $\hat{y}^i = \mathsf{Local}(\hat{f}^i, \hat{x}^i)$ for $i \in S$ by running the 1KeyFE decryption, and then combines them to compute $f(m)$.

It turns out that the above compiler amplifies the collusion bound from 1 to q if a simple combinatorial property, regarding the random sets $(S_1, \ldots, S_q)$ sampled for each key, is satisfied. Here $S_j \subseteq [N]$ be the set sampled while answering the j-th key query. Observe that whenever two sets $S_j, S_{j'}$ intersect at an index i, we learn two keys for the underlying 1KeyFE scheme thereby breaking its security, and an adversary can completely learn the underlying encoding $\hat{x}^i$. And, if the security is broken for enough 1KeyFE systems (i.e., $> t$), then our MPC guarantee fails. Thus, to prove security it is sufficient to show that the total number of pairwise intersections is not larger than t. With this combinatorial guarantee, we can rely on the security of 1KeyFE and the MPC protocol to ensure no information other than $f(m)$ is revealed.

Our observation here is that the same blueprint can also be used for tagged FE schemes where for amplifying 1-bounded collusion to q-bounded collusion, we start with a slightly larger tag space for the underlying 1-bounded tagged FE scheme. Basically, to build a q-bounded collusion tagged FE scheme with tag space $\mathcal{T}$, we start with a 1-bounded scheme with tag space $[N] \times \mathcal{T}$, and replace i-th instantiation of the 1KeyFE scheme with 1-bounded tagged FE scheme and the tag is set as (i, tg) where tg is the tag to be embedded (during encryption and key generation, respectively). Now the correctness and security of the resulting compiler closely follows the analysis for untagged FE schemes from [7], with some subtleties in the analysis that arise due to the fact that in tagged FE simulation security we need to be able to jointly simulate multiple ciphertexts (though for distinct tags) at that the same time. More details follow later in Sect. 6.

Adding Tags to 1-Bounded-Collusion FE via IBE

Lastly, to instantiate our above transformations to build a dynamically bounded collusion FE scheme, we need a tagged FE scheme that achieves 1-bounded collusion simulation security. To that end, we look back at the 1-bounded collusion untagged FE construction by Sahai and Seyalioglu [31] which works by combining garbled circuits with plain public-key encryption. In a few words, our idea is to imitate the same ideology for instantiating our tagged FE scheme, but replace the plain public-key encryption scheme with an identity-based encryption scheme to introduce additional space for efficiently embedding tags in the identity space of the IBE scheme.

Recall that in the well-known 1-bounded collusion untagged FE construction, an encryptor garbles the universal circuit U with message m hardwired such that, on an input a description of a circuit C, the hardwired circuit computes $C(m)$. Now the encryptor hides the wire keys for the garbled circuit under the corresponding PKE public keys chosen during setup time, where two PKE key pairs are sampled per bit of the description length of the circuit C. And, the decryption key for a circuit C simply corresponds to half of the PKE secret keys selected on the basis of bit description of C, that $C[i]$-th PKE secret key for each i. Basically, a decryptor first uncovers the wire labels corresponding to circuit C using PKE decryption, and then simply evaluates the garbled circuit to learn the circuit evaluation $C(m)$.

We observe that the same construction can be upgraded to a tagged FE scheme if we simply replace each PKE system in the above transformation with an IBE system[3], where the identity space of the IBE system will be used to encode the "designated tag". Thus, the encryptor simply sets the IBE identity corresponding to which encryption is performed to be the input tag tg, and the decryption key consists of appropriate IBE keys where the identity for each underlying IBE system is the tag tg to be embedded. Clearly, this gives the desired efficiency if the underlying IBE scheme is efficient, and the security follows by a similar argument as to before where a more careful analysis is needed to argue simulation security in presence of multiple tags. While the above transformation is sufficient to prove security in the non-adaptive setting as the original [31] construction, we rely on the delayed/non-committing encryption strategies [13] as in [24,27] to upgrade to adaptive security. Our tagged FE scheme with 1-bounded collusion security is described in Sect. 7.

---

[3] Technically, we compress the keys even further as we replace all the PKE key pairs with a single IBE key pair instead of a sequence of IBE key pairs. However, for the purpose of this overview, we present this simpler version.

1.2 Related Work and Future Directions

Prior Work on Bounded Collusion Resistance. The intial works on bounded collusion resistance for FE were for the specific class of IBE systems. Dodis et al. [19] and Goldwasser, Lewko, and Wilson [23] constructed bounded collusion secure IBE with varying parametere size from regular public-key encryption and special types of linearly key homomorphic public-key encryption, respectively. For more expressive classes of FE, Sahai and Seyalioglu [31] proposed general functional encryption schemes resilient against a single function-key query using garbled circuits [35]. Following [31], GVW [24] build a statically bounded collusion resistant FE scheme for $\mathbf{NC}^1$ circuits from any public-key encryption scheme, and also provided a generic compiler to improve to the class of all polynomial time computable functions by additionally relying on PRFs computable in $\mathbf{NC}^1$. Afterwards, a number of follow-up works [1,4,15,26] improved the concrete efficiency of the statically bounded collusion resistant FE scheme wherein they improved the dependence of the FE scheme parameters on the collusion bound q by relying on more structured algebraic assumptions. Most recently, Ananth and Vaikuntanathan [7] achieved optimally efficient statically secure FE scheme from the minimal assumption of public-key encryption. The optimal efficiency states that the system parameters grow only linearly with the collusion bound q, since any further improvement would lead to a fully collusion resistant FE scheme via the bootstrapping theorems from [5,6,9,21,33].

Comparison with Bundling Functionalities and Encrypt Ahead FE. Goyal, Koppula, and Waters (GKW) [25] proposed the concept of bundling functionalities in FE systems, where bundling functionalities in an FE scheme meant having the property that a single set of public parameters can support the union of all message/function spaces supported by the underlying FE system. They provided a generic transformation that started with IBE (and other implied primitives) and was able to upgrade any FE scheme to its bundled counterpart. One might ask that whether applying the [25] transformation to the family of bounded collusion FE, where the the collusion bound q is treated as part of the functionality index that is bundled, already leads to a dynamically bounded collusion FE system. It turns out this is not the case because such a generic transformation suffers from the limitation that a function key for a given collusion bound is not reusable for other collusion bounds. In particular, this necessitates each user to make additional queries to the authority for obtaining function keys for desired collusion bound, and this only solves the problem of removing the problem of removing the collusion bound dependence for the setup algorithm. Additionally, GKW proposed a novel variant of FE called encrypt ahead FE. One could ask the same question about relationship between encrypt ahead FE and dynamically bounded collusion resistant FE, and the answer is the same as for the case of bundling functionalities which is they are insufficient.

Open Questions. Our work introduces a new interesting avenue for exploring dynamic collusion resilience in FE systems. An interesting research direction is studying similar concepts of dynamic "query" resilience in other cryptographic contexts. For example, one could ask the same question for the concept of CCA-secure encryption where we know that CPA-secure public-key encryption implies (statically-)bounded-query-CCA security for public-key encryption [17]. We believe answering the question of dynamically bounded-query-CCA security might provide more insight in resolving the longstanding open problem of constructing a (general) CCA-secure encryption scheme from a CPA-secure one.

1.3 Concurrent Work

In a concurrent and independent work, Agrawal et al. [3] also define the dynamic collusion model for bounded-collusion functional encryption, with a similar motivation of providing more flexibility in selecting the collusion bound. Their primary construction of dynamic-bounded FE is essentially the same as ours, with the main difference in their presentation. We define abstractions to simplify exposition, while their construction focuses on constructing a ciphertext-policy FE scheme (CPFE) rather than a key-policy FE scheme (KPFE). One can transform any CPFE scheme to a KPFE scheme and vice versa, by using a universal circuit.

Our main results are the same, but [3] extend their results to uniform computation models while relying on specific algebraic assumptions. Finally, they answer the question of the necessity of IBE in building dynamic-bounded collusion FE in the affirmative, which was left as an open problem in an earlier version of this paper.

2 Preliminaries

Notations. Let PPT denote probabilistic polynomial-time. For any integer $q \geq 2$, we let $\mathbb{Z}_q$ denote the ring of integers modulo q. We denote the set of all positive integers upto n as $[n] := \{1, \ldots, n\}$. For any finite set S, $x \leftarrow S$ denotes a uniformly random element x from the set S. Similarly, for any distribution $\mathcal{D}$, $x \leftarrow \mathcal{D}$ denotes an element x drawn from distribution $\mathcal{D}$. The distribution $\mathcal{D}^n$ is used to represent a distribution over vectors of n components, where each component is drawn independently from the distribution $\mathcal{D}$. Two distributions $\mathcal{D}_1$ and $\mathcal{D}_2$, parameterized by security parameter λ, are said to be computationally indistinguishable, represented by $\mathcal{D}_1 \approx_c \mathcal{D}_2$, if for all PPT adversaries $\mathcal{A}$, $|\Pr[\mathcal{A}(x) = 1 : x \leftarrow \mathcal{D}_1] - \Pr[\mathcal{A}(x) = 1 : x \leftarrow \mathcal{D}_2]| \leq \mathsf{negl}(\lambda)$.

2.1 Garbled Circuits

Our definition of garbled circuits [35] is based upon the work of Bellare et al. [8]. Let $\{\mathcal{C}_n\}_n$ be a family of circuits where each circuit in $\mathcal{C}_n$ takes n bit inputs. A garbling scheme GC for circuit family $\{\mathcal{C}_n\}_n$ consists of polynomial-time algorithms Garble and Eval with the following syntax.

- Garble($1^\lambda, C \in \mathcal{C}_n$): The garbling algorithm takes as input the security parameter λ and a circuit $C \in \mathcal{C}_n$. It outputs a garbled circuit $\widetilde{C}$, together with $2n$ wire keys $\{w_{i,b}\}_{i \leq n, b \in \{0,1\}}$.
- Eval($\widetilde{C}, \{w_i\}_{i \leq n}$): The evaluation algorithm takes as input a garbled circuit $\widetilde{C}$ and n wire keys $\{w_i\}_{i \leq n}$ and outputs $y \in \{0,1\}$.

Correctness. A garbling scheme GC for circuit family $\{\mathcal{C}_n\}_n$ is said to be correct if for all λ, n, $x \in \{0,1\}^n$ and $C \in \mathcal{C}_n$, Eval($\widetilde{C}, \{w_{i,x_i}\}_{i \leq n}) = C(x)$, where $(\widetilde{C}, \{w_{i,b}\}_{i \leq n, b \in \{0,1\}}) \leftarrow$ Garble($1^\lambda, C$).

Security. Informally, a garbling scheme is said to be secure if for every circuit C and input x, the garbled circuit $\widetilde{C}$ together with input wires $\{w_{i,x_i}\}_{i \leq n}$ corresponding to some input x reveals only the output of the circuit $C(x)$, and nothing else about the circuit C or input x.

Definition 1. *A garbling scheme* GC $=$ (Garble, Eval) *for a class of circuits* $\mathcal{C} = \{\mathcal{C}_n\}_n$ *is said to be a secure garbling scheme if there exists a polynomial-time simulator* Sim *such that for all* n, $C \in \mathcal{C}_n$ *and* $x \in \{0,1\}^n$, *the following distributions are computationally indistinguishable:*

$$\left\{ \mathsf{Sim}\left(1^\lambda, 1^n, 1^{|C|}, C(x)\right) \right\}_\lambda \approx_c \left\{ \left(\widetilde{C}, \{w_{i,x_i}\}_{i \leq n}\right) : \left(\widetilde{C}, \{w_{i,b}\}_{i \leq n, b \in \{0,1\}}\right) \leftarrow \mathsf{Garble}(1^\lambda, C) \right\}_\lambda.$$

While this definition is not as general as the definition in [8], it suffices for our construction.

2.2   Identity-Based Encryption

An Identity-Based Encryption (IBE) scheme IBE for set of identity spaces $\mathcal{I} = \{\mathcal{I}_n\}_{n \in \mathbb{N}}$ and message spaces $\mathcal{M}$ consists of four polynomial time algorithms (Setup, KeyGen, Enc, Dec) with the following syntax:

Setup($1^\lambda, 1^n$) $\rightarrow$ (mpk, msk). The setup algorithm takes as input the security parameter λ and identity space index n. It outputs the public parameters mpk and the master secret key msk.

KeyGen(msk, id) $\rightarrow$ sk$_\mathsf{id}$. The key generation algorithm takes as input the master secret key msk and an identity id $\in \mathcal{I}_n$. It outputs a secret key sk$_\mathsf{id}$.

Enc(mpk, id, m) $\rightarrow$ ct. The encryption algorithm takes as input the public parameters mpk, a message $m \in \mathcal{M}$, and an identity id $\in \mathcal{I}_n$. It outputs a ciphertext ct.

Dec(sk$_\mathsf{id}$, ct) $\rightarrow m/\bot$. The decryption algorithm takes as input a secret key sk$_\mathsf{id}$ and a ciphertext ct. It outputs either a message $m \in \mathcal{M}$ or a special symbol $\bot$.

Correctness. We say an IBE scheme IBE $=$ (Setup, KeyGen, Enc, Dec) satisfies correctness if for all $\lambda, n \in \mathbb{N}$, (mpk, msk) $\leftarrow$ Setup($1^\lambda, 1^n$), id $\in \mathcal{I}_n$, $m \in \mathcal{M}$, sk$_\mathsf{id}$ $\leftarrow$ KeyGen(msk, id), and ct $\leftarrow$ Enc(mpk, id, m), we have that Dec(sk$_\mathsf{id}$, ct) $= m$.

Definition 2. *We say an IBE scheme* $\mathsf{IBE} = (\mathsf{Setup}, \mathsf{KeyGen}, \mathsf{Enc}, \mathsf{Dec})$ *is secure if for any stateful PPT adversary* $\mathcal{A}$ *there exists a negligible function* $\mathsf{negl}(\cdot)$, *such that for all* $\lambda, n \in \mathbb{N}$, *the probability*

$$\Pr\left[\mathcal{A}_1^{\mathsf{KeyGen}(\mathsf{msk},\cdot)}(\mathsf{st},\mathsf{ct}) = b : \begin{array}{c} (\mathsf{mpk},\mathsf{msk}) \leftarrow \mathsf{Setup}(1^\lambda,1^n); \quad b \leftarrow \{0,1\} \\ (m_0, m_1, \mathsf{id}^*) \leftarrow \mathcal{A}^{\mathsf{KeyGen}(\mathsf{msk},\cdot)}(1^\lambda,1^n,\mathsf{mpk}) \\ \mathsf{ct} \leftarrow \mathsf{Enc}(\mathsf{mpk},\mathsf{id}^*,m_b) \end{array}\right],$$

is $\leq \dfrac{1}{2} + \mathsf{negl}(\lambda)$ *where all identities* id *queried by* $\mathcal{A}$ *satisfy* $\mathsf{id} \neq \mathsf{id}^*$.

3 Functional Encryption: Dynamic Bounded Collusion

In this section, we define the notion of functional encryption (FE) where we start by recalling the regime of (statically) bounded collusion secure FE systems as studied in prior works [24,31]. We follow that by extending the notion to *dynamic* collusion bounded secure FE systems. And, along the way we also introduce a special compactness property for statically bounded collusion secure FE schemes. This will serve as an appropriate intermediate abstraction to build a fully dynamic collusion bounded FE schemes.

Syntax. Let $\mathcal{M} = \{\mathcal{M}_n\}_{n \in \mathbb{N}}$, $\mathcal{R} = \{\mathcal{R}_n\}_{n \in \mathbb{N}}$ be families of sets, and $\mathbb{F} = \{\mathcal{F}_n\}$ a family of functions, where for all $n \in \mathbb{N}$ and $f \in \mathcal{F}_n$, $f : \mathcal{M}_n \to \mathcal{R}_n$. We will also assume that for all $n \in \mathbb{N}$, the set $\mathcal{F}_n$ contains an *empty function* $\epsilon_n : \mathcal{M}_n \to \mathcal{R}_n$. As in [11], the empty function is used to capture information that intentionally leaks from the ciphertext.

A functional encryption scheme FE for a family of function classes $\{\mathcal{F}_n\}_{n \in \mathbb{N}}$ and message spaces $\{\mathcal{M}_n\}_{n \in \mathbb{N}}$ consists of four polynomial-time algorithms (Setup, Enc, KeyGen, Dec) with the following semantics.

$\mathsf{Setup}(1^\lambda, 1^n) \to (\mathsf{mpk}, \mathsf{msk})$. The setup algorithm takes as input the security parameter λ and the functionality index n^4 (in unary), and outputs the master public-secret key pair $(\mathsf{mpk}, \mathsf{msk})$.

$\mathsf{Enc}(\mathsf{mpk}, m \in \mathcal{M}_n) \to \mathsf{ct}$. The encryption algorithm takes as input the master public key mpk and a message $m \in \mathcal{M}_n$ and outputs a ciphertext ct.

$\mathsf{KeyGen}(\mathsf{msk}, f \in \mathcal{F}_n) \to \mathsf{sk}_f$. The key generation algorithm takes as input the master secret key msk and a function $f \in \mathcal{F}_n$ and outputs a function key sk_f.

$\mathsf{Dec}(\mathsf{sk}_f, \mathsf{ct}) \to \mathcal{R}_n$. The decryption algorithm takes as input a ciphertext ct and a secret key sk_f and outputs a value $y \in \mathcal{R}_n$.

---

[4] One coud additionally consider the setup algorithm to take as input a sequence of functionality indices where the function class and message space are characterized by all such indices (e.g., having input length and circuit depth as functionality indices). For ease of notation, we keep a single functionality index in the above definition.

Correctness and Efficiency. A functional encryption scheme FE = (Setup, Enc, KeyGen, Dec) is said to be correct if for all $\lambda, n \in \mathbb{N}$, functions $f \in \mathcal{F}_n$, messages $m \in \mathcal{M}_n$ and (mpk, msk) $\leftarrow$ Setup($1^\lambda, 1^n$), we have that

$$\Pr\left[\mathsf{Dec}(\mathsf{KeyGen}(\mathsf{msk}, f), \mathsf{Enc}(\mathsf{mpk}, m)) = f(m)\right] = 1,$$

where the probability is taken over the coins of key generation and encryption algorithms. And, it is said to be efficient if the running time of the algorithms is a fixed polynomial in the parameters λ and n.

3.1   Bounded Collusion FE: Static and Dynamic

Informally, a functional encryption scheme is said to be secure if an adversary having secret keys for functions $\{f_i\}_{i \leq q}$ and a ciphertext ct for message m learns only $\{f_i(m)\}_{i \leq q}$, $\epsilon(m)$ and nothing else about the underlying message m. Here ϵ is the empty function associated with the message space.

The Static Setting. Now in the "static" bounded collusion setting, the scheme is said to guarantee security so long as q is a polynomial in the security parameter λ and *fixed a-priori at the setup time.* Thus, the syntax of the setup algorithm changes as follows:

Setup($1^\lambda, 1^n, q$) $\rightarrow$ (mpk, msk). The setup algorithm takes as input the security parameter λ and the functionality index n (in unary), and also takes as input the 'collusion bound' q (in binary).[5] It outputs the master public-secret key pair (mpk, msk).

Efficiency. Although the collusion bound q is given in binary to the setup algorithm, the efficiency condition for a statically bounded collusion FE scheme only requires that the running time of the all the algorithms is a fixed polynomial in λ, n and q. That is, the running time of Setup, KeyGen, Enc, and Dec is allowed to polynomially grow with the collusion bound q.

Static Bounded Collusion Security. This is formally captured via the following 'simulation based' security definition as follows. We first provide the adaptive definition, and later provide the non-adaptive definition.

Definition 3 (static-bounded-collusion simulation-security). *A functional encryption scheme* FE = (Setup, Enc, KeyGen, Dec) *is said to be statically-bounded-collusion simulation-secure if there exists a stateful PPT simulator* Sim = (S_0, S_1, S_2, S_3) *such that for every stateful PPT adversary* $\mathcal{A}$, *the following distributions are computationally indistinguishable:*

---

[5] Although most prior works on bounded collusion security consider the collusion bound q to either be a global parameter, or given in unary to the setup algorithm. Here we instead pass it in binary for technical reasons as will become clear in the sequel. See Remark 1 for more details.

$$\left\{ \mathcal{A}^{\mathsf{KeyGen}(\mathsf{msk},\cdot)}(\mathsf{ct}) : \begin{array}{c} (1^n, 1^q) \leftarrow \mathcal{A}(1^\lambda) \\ (\mathsf{mpk}, \mathsf{msk}) \leftarrow \mathsf{Setup}(1^\lambda, 1^n, q) \\ m \leftarrow \mathcal{A}^{\mathsf{KeyGen}(\mathsf{msk},\cdot)}(\mathsf{mpk}) \\ \mathsf{ct} \leftarrow \mathsf{Enc}(\mathsf{mpk}, m) \end{array} \right\}_{\lambda \in \mathbb{N}}$$

$$\approx_c$$

$$\left\{ \mathcal{A}^{\mathsf{S}_3^{U_m(\cdot)}(\mathsf{st}_2,\cdot)}(\mathsf{ct}) : \begin{array}{c} (1^n, 1^q) \leftarrow \mathcal{A}(1^\lambda) \\ (\mathsf{mpk}, \mathsf{st}_0) \leftarrow \mathsf{S}_0(1^\lambda, 1^n, q) \\ m \leftarrow \mathcal{A}^{\mathsf{S}_1(\mathsf{st}_0,\cdot)}(\mathsf{mpk}) \\ (\mathsf{ct}, \mathsf{st}_2) \leftarrow \mathsf{S}_2(\mathsf{st}_1, \Pi^m) \end{array} \right\}_{\lambda \in \mathbb{N}}$$

whenever the following admissibility constraints and properties are satisfied:

- S_1 *and* S_3 *are stateful in that after each invocation, they updates their states* st_1 *and* st_3 *(respectively) which is carried over to its next invocation.*
- Π^m *contains a list of functions* f_i *queried by* $\mathcal{A}$ *in the pre-challenge phase along with the their output on the challenge message* m. *That is, if* f_i *is the i-th function queried by* $\mathcal{A}$ *to oracle* S_1 *and* q_{pre} *be the number of queries* $\mathcal{A}$ *makes before outputting* m, *then* $\Pi^m = ((f_1, f_1(m)), \ldots, (f_{q_{\mathsf{pre}}}, f_{q_{\mathsf{pre}}}(m)))$.[6]
- $\mathcal{A}$ *makes at most* q *queries combined to the key generation oracles in the corresponding games.*
- S_3 *for each queried function* f_i, *in the post-challenge phase, makes a single query to its message oracle* U_m *on the same* f_i *itself.*

Remark 1 (unary vs binary). Note that in the above security games, we require the adversary to specify the collusion bound q in unary at the beginning. This is in contrast to the setup algorithm which gets q in binary as an input. The reason for this distinction is that in the security game for bounded collusion security we do not want to allow the attacker to specify super-polynomial collusion bounds, whereas (as we point out later) allowing the setup algorithm to be run on super-polynomial values of the collusion bound is important for our dynamic collusion bounded FE schemes.

Weak Optimality. Additionally, we also introduce the notion of a "weakly optimal" statically-bounded-collusion secure FE scheme where this system provides better efficiency properties. That is, in a weakly optimal static bounded collusion system, the running time of the setup and key generation algorithms grows only poly-logarithmically in the collusion bound q. Concretely, we define it below.

Definition 4 (weakly optimal statically-bounded-collusion). *A functional encryption scheme* $\mathsf{FE} = (\mathsf{Setup}, \mathsf{Enc}, \mathsf{KeyGen}, \mathsf{Dec})$ *is said to be 'weakly optimal' statically-bounded-collusion FE scheme if the running time of the* Setup *and* KeyGen *algorithm is additionally upper bounded by a fixed polynomial in* λ, n *and* $\log q$.

---

[6] To be more precise, Π^m should also contain the empty function and the evaluation of empty function on challenge message $(\epsilon_n, \epsilon_n(m))$. However, for ease of notation, throughout the paper we assume that to be implicitly added to the list of function-value pairs.

Strengthening the Simulation Guarantee. In this work, we consider a strengthening of the above simulation-secure properties (for the class of weakly optimal static-bounded-collusion FE schemes) which will be be crucial towards building a dynamic-bounded-collusion functional encryption scheme. Note that typically the simulation security states that the distribution of secret keys and ciphertext are simulatable as long as the adversary does not make more key queries than what is specified by the static collusion bound. That is, if the adversary makes more key queries then no guarantee is provided. However, we consider a stronger simulation guarantee below wherein the real world is still simulatable even when the adversary makes more key queries than that specified by the collusion bound as long as the adversary does not make any challenge message queries. That is, either the collusion bound is not crossed, or no challenge ciphertext is queried. In addition to this, we require the running time of the simulator algorithms S_0, S_1 and S_3 (that is, all except the ciphertext simulator S_2) grow only poly-logarithmically in the static collusion bound q. Formally, we define it below.

Definition 5 (strong simulation-security). *A functional encryption scheme* FE = (Setup, Enc, KeyGen, Dec) *is said to be statically-bounded-collusion* strong *simulation-secure if, in the security game defined in Definition 3, the following additional conditions hold:*

1. *the number of key queries made by adversary is allowed to exceed the static collusion bound q as long as the adversary does not submit any challenge message, and*
2. *the running time of the simulator algorithms S_0, S_1 and S_3 is upper bounded by a fixed polynomial in λ, n and $\log q$.*

Lastly, we also define the non-adaptive variant of the simulation security.

Definition 6 (non-adaptive simulation-security). *A functional encryption scheme* FE = (Setup, Enc, KeyGen, Dec) *is said to be statically-bounded-collusion* non-adaptive *(regular/strong) simulation-secure if the adversary is prohibited from making any key queries in the post-challenge phase (that is, after receiving the challenge ciphertext) in its respective security game.*

The Dynamic Setting. Now in the "dynamic" bounded collusion setting, the scheme is no longer tied to a single collusion bound q fixed a-priori at the system setup, but instead the encryptor could choose the amount of collusion resilience it wants. Thus, this changes the syntax of the setup and encryption algorithm when compared to the static setting from above:

Setup($1^\lambda, 1^n$) $\to$ (mpk, msk). The setup algorithm takes as input the security parameter λ and the functionality index n (in unary). It outputs the master public-secret key pair (mpk, msk).
(Note that thus syntactically the setup of a dynamic bounded collusion scheme is same as that of a fully collusion resistant scheme.)

Enc(mpk, $m \in \mathcal{M}_n, 1^q$) → ct. The encryption algorithm takes as input the master public key mpk, a message $m \in \mathcal{M}_n$, and it takes the desired collusion bound q (in unary) as an input. It outputs a ciphertext ct.

Efficiency. Since the collusion bound q is not specified during setup or key generation at all, thus the efficiency condition for a dynamically bounded collusion FE scheme requires the running time of Setup and KeyGen to be fixed polynomials in λ and n. While since the encryptor takes q as input in unary, thus the running time of the Enc algorithm could grow polynomially with collusion bound q. Similarly, the running time of Dec is also allowed to grow polynomially with collusion bound q.

Dynamic Bounded Collusion Security. This is formally captured via a 'simulation based' security definition as in the static setting. The game is similar to that provided in Definition 3, except now the attacker specifies the collusion bound q while making the challenge ciphertext query and the simulator also only receives the collusion bound as input at that point. For completeness, we describe it formally below (both the adaptive and non-adaptive variants).

Definition 7 (dynamic-bounded-collusion simulation-security). *A functional encryption scheme* FE = (Setup, Enc, KeyGen, Dec) *is said to be dynamically-bounded-collusion simulation-secure if there exists a stateful PPT simulator* Sim = (S_0, S_1, S_2, S_3) *such that for every stateful PPT adversary* $\mathcal{A}$, *the following distributions are computationally indistinguishable:*

$$\left\{ \mathcal{A}^{\mathsf{KeyGen(msk,\cdot)}}(\mathsf{ct}) : \begin{array}{c} 1^n \leftarrow \mathcal{A}(1^\lambda) \\ (\mathsf{mpk}, \mathsf{msk}) \leftarrow \mathsf{Setup}(1^\lambda, 1^n) \\ (m, 1^q) \leftarrow \mathcal{A}^{\mathsf{KeyGen(msk,\cdot)}}(\mathsf{mpk}) \\ \mathsf{ct} \leftarrow \mathsf{Enc}(\mathsf{mpk}, m, 1^q) \end{array} \right\}_{\lambda \in \mathbb{N}}$$

$$\approx_c$$

$$\left\{ \mathcal{A}^{S_3^{U_m(\cdot)}(\cdot)}(\mathsf{ct}) : \begin{array}{c} 1^n \leftarrow \mathcal{A}(1^\lambda) \\ \mathsf{mpk} \leftarrow S_0(1^\lambda, 1^n) \\ (m, 1^q) \leftarrow \mathcal{A}^{S_1(\cdot)}(\mathsf{mpk}) \\ \mathsf{ct} \leftarrow S_2(\Pi^m, 1^q) \end{array} \right\}_{\lambda \in \mathbb{N}}$$

whenever the admissibility constraints and properties, as defined in Definition 3, are satisfied.

Definition 8 (non-adaptive simulation-security). *A functional encryption scheme* FE = (Setup, Enc, KeyGen, Dec) *is said to be dynamically-bounded-collusion non-adaptive simulation-secure if, in the security game defined in Definition 7, the adversary is prohibited from making any key queries in the post-challenge phase (that is, after receiving the challenge ciphertext).*

3.2 Upgrading Static to Dynamic Bounded Collusion FE via Weak Optimal Efficiency

In this section, we provide a generic construction of a dynamic-bounded-collusion FE scheme from any static-bounded-collusion FE scheme that satisfies the strong simulation property (Definition 5) and the weak optimality property (Definition 4). Below we provide our construction followed by correctness and security proofs.

Construction. Let Static-FE = (S-FE.Setup, S-FE.Enc, S-FE.KeyGen, S-FE.Dec) be a weakly-optimal static-bounded-collusion FE scheme for a family of function classes $\{\mathcal{F}_n\}_{n\in\mathbb{N}}$ and message spaces $\{\mathcal{M}_n\}_{n\in\mathbb{N}}$. We use Static-FE to build a dynamic-bounded-collusion FE scheme FE = (Setup, Enc, KeyGen, Dec) as follows.

Setup($1^\lambda, 1^n$) → (mpk, msk). The setup algorithm runs the Static-FE setup algorithm λ times with increasing values of the static collusion bound q as follows:

$$\forall i \in [\lambda], \quad (\mathsf{mpk}_i, \mathsf{msk}_i) \leftarrow \text{S-FE.Setup}(1^\lambda, 1^n, q = 2^i).$$

It then sets the master secret and public keys as an λ-tuple of all these keys, i.e. $\mathsf{msk} = (\mathsf{msk}_i)_{i\in[\lambda]}$ and $\mathsf{mpk} = (\mathsf{mpk}_i)_{i\in[\lambda]}$.

KeyGen(msk, f) → sk_f. Let $\mathsf{msk} = (\mathsf{msk}_i)_{i\in[\lambda]}$. The key generation algorithm runs the Static-FE key generation algorithm with all λ keys independently as $\mathsf{sk}_{i,f} \leftarrow$ S-FE.KeyGen(msk_i, f) for $i \in [\lambda]$. It outputs the secret key sk as $\mathsf{sk} = (\mathsf{sk}_{i,f})_{i\in[\lambda]}$.

Enc(mpk, m, 1^Q) → ct. Let $\mathsf{mpk} = (\mathsf{mpk}_i)_{i\in[\lambda]}$. The encryption algorithm simply encrypts the message m under $\lceil \log Q \rceil$-th master public key as ct ← S-FE.Enc($\mathsf{mpk}_{\lceil \log Q \rceil}, m$). (It also includes Q as part of the ciphertext.)

Dec(sk_f, ct) → z. Let $\mathsf{sk}_f = (\mathsf{sk}_{i,f})_{i\in[\lambda]}$. The decryption algorithm runs the Static-FE decryption using the $\lceil \log Q \rceil$-th function key as $z \leftarrow$ S-FE.Dec($\mathsf{sk}_{\lceil \log Q \rceil, f}$, ct).

Correctness, Efficiency, and Security. The correctness of the above scheme follows directly from the correctness of the underlying static-bounded-collusion FE system, while for the desired efficiency consider the following arguments. First, note that by weak optimality of Static-FE we have that the running time of S-FE.Setup and S-FE.KeyGen grows as poly($\lambda, n, \log q$). Since the Setup and S-FE.KeyGen algorithms run S-FE.Setup and S-FE.KeyGen (respectively) λ many times for $\log q \in \{1, \ldots, \lambda\}$, thus we get that running time of Setup and KeyGen is poly(λ, n) as desired. Lastly, the encryption and decryption algorithm run in time at most poly($\lambda, n, 2^{\lceil \log Q \rceil}$) = poly($\lambda, n, Q$) since the $\lceil \log Q \rceil$-th static-bounded-collusion FE system uses $2^{\lceil \log Q \rceil} \leq 2 \cdot Q$ as the static collusion bound. Thus, the resulting FE scheme satisfies the required efficiency properties.
To conclude, we prove the following.

Theorem 1. *If* Static-FE = (S-FE.Setup, S-FE.Enc, S-FE.KeyGen, S-FE.Dec) *is a weakly-optimal static-bounded-collusion simulation-secure FE scheme (as per Definition 5 and 4), then the above scheme* FE = (Setup, Enc, KeyGen, Dec) *is a dynamic-bounded-collusion simulation-secure FE scheme (as per Definition 7).*

The proof follows from a composition of the static-bounded-collusion simulation-security property of Static-FE. Recall that in the static setting, we require the scheme to provide a stronger form of real world vs. ideal world indistinguishability. Where typically the simulation security states that the distribution of secret keys and ciphertext are simulatable as long as the adversary does not make more key queries than what is specified by the static collusion bound. That is, if the adversary makes more key queries then no guarantee is provided. However, in our formalization of simulation security for static-bounded-collusion FE schemes, we require that the real and ideal worlds are also indistinguishable even when the adversary makes more key queries than that specified by the collusion bound as long as the adversary does not make any challenge message queries. That is, either the collusion bound is not crossed, or no challenge ciphertext is queried. Also, the running time of the simulator algorithms S_0, S_1 and S_3 (all except the ciphertext simulator S_2) grow only poly-logarithmically in the collusion bound.

Thus, the simulator for the dynamic-bounded-collusion FE scheme simply runs the S_0 algorithms for all collusion bounds $q = 1, \ldots, 2^\lambda$ to simulate the individual master public keys. It then also runs the S_1 algorithms for simulating the individual function keys for each of these static-bounded-collusion FE systems for answering each adversarial key query. Note that since the running time of S_0 and S_1 is also $\mathsf{poly}(\lambda, n, \log q)$ where $q = 1, \ldots, 2^\lambda$, thus this is efficient.

Now when the adversary makes the challenge query for message m, it also specifies the target collusion bound Q^*. The dynamic-bounded-collusion simulator then runs only the ciphertext simulator algorithm S_2 for the static FE system corresponding to collusion bound $\log q = \lceil \log Q^* \rceil$. Note that the simulator does not run S_2 for the underlying FE schemes with lower (and even higher) collusion bounds. This is important for two reasons: (1) we want to invoke the simulation security of the i-th static FE scheme for $i < \lceil \log Q^* \rceil$ but we can only do this if the ciphertext simulator S_2 is not run for these static FE schemes, (2) the running time of S_2 could grow polynomially with the collusion bound q, thus we should not invoke simulator algorithm S_2 for $i > \lceil \log Q^* \rceil$ as well (since for say $i = \lambda$, the running time would be exponential in λ which would make the dynamic simulator inefficient). Thus, even the ciphertext simulation is efficient and the dynamic simulator is an admissible adversary with respect to static FE challenger, therefore our dynamic FE simulator is both efficient and can rely on simulation security of the underlying static FE schemes. The last phase of simulation (i.e., post-challenge key generation phase) works the same as the second phase simulator (i.e., pre-challenge key generation phase) which is by running S_3 for all collusion bounds.

This completes a high level sketch. A complete proof is provided in our full version [20].

Remark 2 (non-adaptive simulation-security). If the underlying static-bounded-collusion FE scheme only provides security against non-adaptive attackers (as per Definition 6), then the resulting dynamic-bounded-collusion FE scheme is also secure only against non-adaptive attackers (as per Definition 8).

4 Tagged Functional Encryption

In this work, we introduce the concept of tagged functional encryption where the basic difference when compared to regular functional encryption systems is that ciphertexts and secret keys are embedded with a tag value such that only the ciphertexts and keys with the same tags can be combined during decryption.

Formally, a tagged FE scheme in the static collusion model for a set of tag spaces $\mathcal{I} = \{\mathcal{I}_z\}_{z \in \mathbb{N}}$ consists of the same four algorithms with following modification to the syntax:

Setup$(1^\lambda, 1^n, 1^z, 1^q) \to$ (mpk, msk). In addition to the normal inputs taken by a static-bounded FE scheme, the setup also takes in a tag space index z, which fixes a tag space $\mathcal{I}_z$.

Enc(mpk, tg $\in \mathcal{I}_z, m \in \mathcal{M}_n) \to$ ct. The encryption also takes in a tag tg $\in \mathcal{I}_z$ to bind to the ciphertext.

KeyGen(msk, tg $\in \mathcal{I}_z, f \in \mathcal{F}_n) \to$ sk$_{\text{tg},f}$. The key generation also binds the secret keys to a fixed tag tg $\in \mathcal{I}_z$.

Dec(sk$_{\text{tg},f}$, ct) $\to \mathcal{R}_n$. The decryption algorithm has syntax identical to a non-tagged scheme.

Correctness and Efficiency. A tagged FE scheme tgfe is said to be correct if for all $\lambda, n, z, q \in \mathbb{N}$, every function $f \in \mathcal{F}_n$, message $m \in \mathcal{M}_n$, tag tg $\in \mathcal{I}_z$, and (mpk, msk) $\leftarrow$ Setup$(1^\lambda, 1^n, 1^z, 1^q)$, we have that

$$\Pr\left[\mathsf{Dec}(\mathsf{KeyGen}(\mathsf{msk}, \mathsf{tg}, f), \mathsf{Enc}(\mathsf{mpk}, \mathsf{tg}, m)) = f(m)\right] = 1,$$

where the probability is taken over the coins of key generation and encryption algorithms. And, it is said to be efficient if the running time of the algorithms is a fixed polynomial in the parameters λ, n, q and z.

Security. The security definition is modelled in a similar fashion to the ordinary static bounded collusion FE game with the difference that the adversary plays it on multiple tg simultaneously and the simulator must simulate the ciphertexts for every tag. In addition, the adversary is also allowed to make arbitrary many secret key queries for all other tags. The formal definition follows.

Definition 9 (tagged-static-bounded-collusion simulation-security).
For any choice of parameters $\lambda, n, q, z \in \mathbb{N}$, consider the following list of stateful oracles S_0, S_1, S_2 where these oracles simulate the FE setup, key generation, and encryption algorithms respectively, and all three algorithms share and update the same global state of the simulator. Here the attacker interacts with the execution environment $\mathcal{E}$, and the environment makes queries to the simulator oracles. Formally, the simulator oracles and the environment are defined below:

$S_0(1^\lambda, 1^n, 1^z, 1^q)$ *generates the simulated master public key* mpk *of the system, and initializes the global state* st *of the simulator which is used by the next two oracles.*

$S_1(\cdot, \cdot, \cdot)$, *upon a call to generate secret key on a function-tag-value tuple $(f_i, \mathsf{tg}_i, \mu_i)$, where the function value is either $\mu_i = \perp$ (signalling that the adversary has not yet made any encryption query on tag tg_i), or $(m^{\mathsf{tg}_i}, \mathsf{tg}_i)$ has already been queried for encryption (for some message m^{tg_i}), and $\mu_i = f_i(m^{\mathsf{tg}_i})$, the oracle outputs a simulated key $\mathsf{sk}_{f_i, \mathsf{tg}_i}$.*

$S_2(\cdot, \cdot)$, *upon a call to generate ciphertext on a tag-list tuple* $(\mathsf{tg}_i, \Pi^{m^{\mathsf{tg}_i}})$, *where the list* $\Pi^{m^{\mathsf{tg}_i}}$ *is a possibly empty list of the form* $\Pi^{m^{\mathsf{tg}_i}} = ((f_1^{\mathsf{tg}_i}, f_1^{\mathsf{tg}_i}(m^{\mathsf{tg}_i}))$, $\ldots, (f_{q_{\mathsf{pre}}}^{\mathsf{tg}_i}, f_{q_{\mathsf{pre}}}^{\mathsf{tg}_i}(m^{\mathsf{tg}_i})))$ *(that is, contains the list of function-value pairs for which the adversary has already received a secret key for), the oracle outputs a simulated ciphertext* $\mathsf{ct}_{\mathsf{tg}_i}$.

$\mathcal{E}^{S_1, S_2}(\cdot, \cdot)$, *receives two types of queries – secret key query and encryption query. Upon a secret key query on a function-tag pair* (f_i, tg_i), *if* $(m^{\mathsf{tg}_i}, \mathsf{tg}_i)$ *has already been queried for encryption (for some message* m^{tg_i} *) then* $\mathcal{E}$ *queries key oracle* S_1 *on tuple* $(f_i, \mathsf{tg}_i, \mu_i = f_i(m^{\mathsf{tg}_i}))$, *otherwise it adds* (f_i, tg_i) *to the its local state, and queries* S_1 *on tuple* $(f_i, \mathsf{tg}_i, \mu_i = \perp)$. *And, it simply forwards oracle's simulated key* $\mathsf{sk}_{f_i, \mathsf{tg}_i}$ *to the adversary.*

Upon a ciphertext query on a message-tag pair (m_i, tg_i), *if the adversary made an encryption query on the same tag* tg_i *previously, then the query is disallowed (that is, at most one message query per every unique tag is permitted). Otherwise, it computes a (possibly empty) list of function-value pairs of the form* $\Pi^{m_i} = \left((f_1^{\mathsf{tg}_i}, f_1^{\mathsf{tg}_i}(m^{\mathsf{tg}_i})), \ldots, (f_{q_{\mathsf{pre}}}^{\mathsf{tg}_i}, f_{q_{\mathsf{pre}}}^{\mathsf{tg}_i}(m^{\mathsf{tg}_i})) \right)$ *where* $(f_j^{\mathsf{tg}_i}, \mathsf{tg}_i)$ *are stored in* $\mathcal{E}$*'s local state, and removes all such pairs* $(f_j^{\mathsf{tg}_i}, \mathsf{tg}_i)$ *from its local state.* $\mathcal{E}$ *then queries ciphertext oracle* S_2 *on tuple* $(\mathsf{tg}_i, \Pi^{m_i})$, *and simply forwards oracle's simulated ciphertext* $\mathsf{ct}_{\mathsf{tg}_i}$ *to the adversary.*

A tagged functional encryption scheme $\mathsf{FE} = (\mathsf{Setup}, \mathsf{Enc}, \mathsf{KeyGen}, \mathsf{Dec})$ *is said to be tagged-statically-bounded-collusion simulation-secure if there exists a stateful PPT simulator* $\mathsf{Sim} = (S_0, S_1, S_2)$ *such that for every stateful admissible PPT adversary* $\mathcal{A}$, *the following distributions are computationally indistinguishable:*

$$\left\{ \mathcal{A}^{\mathsf{KeyGen}(\mathsf{msk}, \cdot, \cdot), \mathsf{Enc}(\mathsf{mpk}, \cdot, \cdot)}(\mathsf{mpk}) : \begin{array}{c} (1^n, 1^q, 1^z) \leftarrow \mathcal{A}(1^\lambda) \\ (\mathsf{mpk}, \mathsf{msk}) \leftarrow \mathsf{Setup}(1^\lambda, 1^n, 1^z, 1^q) \end{array} \right\}_{\lambda \in \mathbb{N}}$$

$$\approx_c$$

$$\left\{ \mathcal{A}^{\mathcal{E}^{S_1, S_2}(\cdot, \cdot)}(\mathsf{mpk}) : \begin{array}{c} (1^n, 1^q, 1^z) \leftarrow \mathcal{A}(1^\lambda) \\ \mathsf{mpk} \leftarrow S_0(1^\lambda, 1^n, 1^z, 1^q) \end{array} \right\}_{\lambda \in \mathbb{N}}$$

where $\mathcal{A}$ *is an admissible adversary if:*

- $\mathcal{A}$ *makes at most one encryption query per unique tag (that is, if the adversary made an encryption query on some tag* tg_i *previously, then making another encryption query for the same tag is disallowed)*
- $\mathcal{A}$ *makes at most q queries combined to the key generation oracles in the above experiments for all tags* tg_i *such that it also submitted an encryption query for tag* tg_i.

Definition 10 (tagged-static-bounded-collusion non-adaptive simulation-security). *A tagged functional encryption scheme* $\mathsf{FE} = (\mathsf{Setup}, \mathsf{Enc}, \mathsf{KeyGen}, \mathsf{Dec})$ *is said to be tagged-statically-bounded-collusion non-adaptive simulation-secure if, in the security game defined in Definition 9, the adversary is prohibited from making any key queries on any particular tag in the post-challenge phase (that is, if the adversary makes an encryption query w.r.t. tag* tg, *then it must not make any more key queries on the same tag* tg *but can make key queries for other tags*).

5   Tagged to Weakly Optimal Static Collusion FE

In this section we show how to convert the our construction of Q-bounded tagged FE to a weakly optimal statically secure functional encryption scheme with collusion bound Q. The transformation is very similar to the transformation in [7] that achieves linear complexity for any bounded-key FE scheme.

Let Q be the desired collusion bound for the static scheme. The transformation in [7] starts with Q instances of q-bounded statically secure FE, where q is set to some polynomial in the security parameter. The setup parameters are thus linearly bounded in Q. Encryption simply calls the base encrypt algorithm (for the q-bounded collusion scheme) on each instance. Since the base encryption scheme is for collusion bound $q = \mathsf{poly}(\lambda)$, one instance of encrypt takes time polynomial in the security parameter and thus encrypt is linearly bounded in Q. Key generation for a circuit C simply selects one of the instances at random and outputs the key generated by the base scheme on this instance. Correctness holds as the encrytor has encrypted for all possible instances. Security fails only if, after giving out Q secret keys, the load on a particular instance exceeds $q = \mathsf{poly}(\lambda)$ (which happens with only negligible probability via a simple Chernoff argument).

The transformation has the drawback that the setup outputs Q instances and thus all the algorithms depend linearly on Q. Our observation is thar if we start with a tagged FE scheme instead, then we can compress the public and secret parameters using the tag space by setting it proportional to the desired collusion bound Q. Similarly the key generation algorithm takes in a single master public key and master secret key and outputs one instance of the secret key. This helps us satisfy the weakly optimal property. More formal details follow below.

5.1   Construction

Let $\mathsf{tgfe} = (\mathsf{TgFE.Setup}, \mathsf{TgFE.Enc}, \mathsf{TgFE.KeyGen}, \mathsf{TgFE.Dec})$ be a bounded-collusion tagged FE scheme for a family of circuit classes $\{\mathcal{F}_n\}_{n \in \mathbb{N}}$, message spaces $\{\mathcal{M}_n\}_{n \in \mathbb{N}}$, and tag space $\{\mathcal{I}_z = \{0,1\}^z\}_{z \in \mathbb{N}}$. We use TgFE to build $\mathsf{Static\text{-}FE}$ a *weakly-optimal* static-bounded-collusion FE scheme for the same function classes and message spaces.

$\mathsf{Setup}(1^\lambda, 1^n, Q) \to (\mathsf{mpk}, \mathsf{msk})$. The setup algorithm runs the TgFE setup algorithm with the tag space of $\mathcal{I}_z = [2^{\lceil \log Q \rceil}]$ and collusion bound $q = \lambda$ and sets the master public-secret keys as

$$(\mathsf{mpk}, \mathsf{msk}) \leftarrow \mathsf{TgFE.Setup}(1^\lambda, 1^n, 1^z = 1^{\lceil \log Q \rceil}, 1^q = 1^\lambda).$$

Notation. Here and throughout the paper, we represent $\lceil \log Q \rceil$-bit tags as elements over a larger alphabet $[2^{\lceil \log Q \rceil}]$, and when we write $u \leftarrow [Q]$ then that denotes sampling u as a random integer between 1 and Q which can be uniquely encoded as an $\lceil \log Q \rceil$-bit tag.

KeyGen(msk, C) $\rightarrow$ sk$_C$. It samples a tag $u \leftarrow [Q]$, key sk$_{C,u} \leftarrow$ TgFE.KeyGen(msk, u, C), and outputs sk$_C = ($sk$_{C,u}, u)$.

Enc(mpk, $m, 1^Q$) $\rightarrow$ ct. It encrypts the message m for all possible tags, and outputs the ciphertext ct $= ($ct$_1, \ldots,$ct$_Q)$ where each sub-ciphertext is computed as:
$$\forall u \in [Q], \quad \text{ct}_u \leftarrow \text{TgFE.Enc(mpk, } u, m).$$

Dec(sk$_C$, ct) $\rightarrow y$. Let sk$_C = ($sk$_{C,u}, u)$ and ct $= ($ct$_1, \ldots,$ct$_Q)$. The algorithm outputs $y \leftarrow$ TgFE.Dec(sk$_{C,u}$, ct$_u$).

5.2 Correctness, Efficiency, and Security

The correctness of the above scheme follows directly from the correctness of the underlying TgFE scheme. For the efficiency, recall the requirements (Definition 4) which state that the Setup and KeyGen algorithms should be bound by a polynomial in λ, n and $\log Q$. Both Setup and KeyGen run TgFE.Setup and TgFE.KeyGen once respectively. From the efficiency of these algorithms, we know that the running time is poly($\lambda, n, \lceil \log Q \rceil$).

Our full security proof is described in the full version [20].

6 Upgrading Collusion Bound for Tagged FE

Now we show that a bounded-collusion tagged FE scheme where the collusion bound can be any arbitrary polynomial can be generically built from a tagged FE scheme that allows corrupting at most one key per unique tag (i.e., 1-bounded collusion secure) by relying on the client server framework from [7]. The ideas behind this transformation are based on the 1-bounded non-tagged FE to Q-bounded non-tagged FE transformation from [7].

The client server framework is formally defined later in our full version [20] for completeness. Intuitively, in the client server framework, there is a single client and N servers. The computation proceeds in two phases, an offline phase, where the client encrypts an input x of the protocol for N servers where u-th server gets $\hat{x}^u$. This is followed by an online phase which runs in Q sessions for computation on circuits $C_1, \ldots, C_Q$. In each session $j \in [Q]$, client delegates the computation of C_j by computing $\hat{C}_j^u$ for $u \in [\mathsf{N}]$ and sending $\hat{C}_j^u$ to u-th server. Now $S \subseteq [\mathsf{N}]$ where $|S| = \mathsf{p}$ servers come online and for $u \in S$, u-th server computes $\hat{y}_j^u \leftarrow \text{Local}(\hat{C}_j^u, \hat{x}^u)$. Finally the S server send information back to client who computes $y \leftarrow \text{Decode}(\{\hat{y}_j^u\}_{u \in S}, S)$ for each $j \in [Q]$, to compute $C_j(x)$.

The transformation in [7] invokes N (polynomial in Q, λ) many instantiations of the one bounded FE scheme. These N instances act like a separate server in the client server framework. Encryption simply computes the encryption of each one bounded instance on the offline computation on the inputs, i.e. encrypt under $\hat{x}^u$ for $u \in [\mathsf{N}]$ under the one bounded FE algorithm. Key generation computes the online encryption of the circuits, $\hat{C}^u$ for $u \in [\mathsf{N}]$ and picks a random subset S of size p and generates the secret keys on the 1 bounded instance for circuit $\mathsf{Local}(\hat{C}^u, \cdot)$ for $u \in S$. In our transformation, instead of having N independent instances, we instead blowup the tag space for the one tagged FE scheme and perform the key generation and encryption procedures very similarly. The analysis of the correctness and security are very similar to [7], except that in the 1TgFE security game (Definition 9), we allow the adversary to request for multiple challenge ciphertexts (each on a different tag) and thus the security proof is tweaked adequately.

The full construction and proof is described in our full version [20].

7 Building 1-Bounded Collusion Tagged FE from IBE

Here we construct a tagged FE scheme that achieves security in the 1-bounded collusion model and, as we discussed in the previous section, this is sufficient to build a general bounded-collusion tagged FE scheme. Our construction is itself split into two components where first we have a simple construction using garbled circuits and IBE while only achieving non-adaptive security, and later show how to generically upgrade it to full adaptive security by relying on non-committing encryption techiques. We quickly sketch our formal constructions here. Please see the full version of our paper, [20], for the complete proofs.

7.1 Non-Adaptive 1-Bounded Tagged FE from Garbled Circuits and IBE

The non-adaptive construction is a close adaptation of the traditional construction of 1-bounded FE from public key encryption and garbled circuits found in [24,31]. The idea is to simply encrypt all the wire labels of a garbling of a universal circuit using IBE and only give out select IBE secret keys of the wires corresponding to the circuit.

For simplicity, we assume that the functionality class $\mathcal{F}_n$ includes all circuits of size n (the circuit description is n bits long).

$\mathsf{Setup}(1^\lambda, 1^n, 1^z) \to (\mathsf{mpk}, \mathsf{msk})$. Sample an IBE master key pair as (ibe.pk, ibe.msk) $\leftarrow$ IBE.Setup$(1^\lambda, 1^{z+\lceil \log n \rceil + 1})$, and output $\mathsf{mpk} = \mathsf{ibe.pk}, \mathsf{msk} = \mathsf{ibe.msk}$.

Notation. Here and throughout the paper, we use (b, i, tg) to denote the $(z + \lceil \log n \rceil + 1)$-bit identity, where b is a single bit, i encodes $\lceil \log n \rceil$-bits, and tg is encoded in the remaining z bits. Basically, each bit-index-tag tuple is uniquely and efficiently mapped into the identity space.

$\mathsf{Enc}(\mathsf{mpk}, \mathsf{tg}, m \in \mathcal{M}_n) \to \mathsf{ct}$. Let $\mathcal{U}$ be the universal circuit for the family of size n circuits on inputs in $\mathcal{M}_n$ (i.e., $\mathcal{U}(C, m) = C(m)$). Now in the following garble $\mathcal{U}(\cdot, m)$ as $(\hat{\mathcal{U}}, \{w_{i,b}\}_{i \leq n, b \in \{0,1\}}) \leftarrow \mathsf{GC.Garble}(1^\lambda, \mathcal{U})$, and encrypt the labels as

$$\forall i \in n, b \in \{0, 1\}, \quad \mathsf{ct}_{i,b} \leftarrow \mathsf{IBE.Enc}(\mathsf{ibe.pk}, (b, i, \mathsf{tg}), w_{i,b})$$

It finally outputs $\mathsf{ct} = (\hat{\mathcal{U}}, \{\mathsf{ct}_{i,b}\}_{i \leq n, b \in \{0,1\}})$.

KeyGen$(\mathsf{msk}, \mathsf{tg}, C \in \{0,1\}^n) \to \mathsf{sk}_{\mathsf{tg},C}$. Let $C[1], C[2], \ldots C[n]$ denote the bit representation of circuit C. It samples n IBE secret keys as $\mathsf{sk}_i = \mathsf{IBE.KeyGen}(\mathsf{msk}, (C[i], i, \mathsf{tg}))$ for $i \in [n]$, and outputs $\mathsf{sk}_{\mathsf{tg},C} = \{\mathsf{sk}_i\}_{i \in [n]}$.

Dec$(\mathsf{sk}_{\mathsf{tg},C}, \mathsf{ct}) \to y$. It parses the secret key and ciphertext as above. It first decrypts the wire keys as $w_{i,C[i]} \leftarrow \mathsf{IBE.Dec}(\mathsf{sk}_i, \mathsf{ct}_{i,C[i]})$ for $i \in [n]$, and then outputs $y = \mathsf{GC.Eval}(\hat{\mathcal{U}}, \{w_{i,C[i]}\}_{i \in [n]})$.

7.2   Upgrading to Adaptive Security

We can transform any non-adaptive 1-bounded tagged FE scheme to an adaptive one using IBE. This is an analogue of the traditional method of using weak non-committing encryption (which is constructable from plain public key encryption) to make 1-bounded FE adaptive. Here, the encryption has two modes—a 'normal mode', where the scheme functions like a normal public key/IBE scheme, and a non-committing mode, where the encryptor can produce secret keys which equivocate to any value. This enables us to delay simulating the ciphertext of a adaptive key queries until the secret key is requested.

Setup$(1^\lambda, 1^n, 1^z) \to (\mathsf{mpk}, \mathsf{msk})$. The setup algorithm runs the underlying tagged FE and IBE setup algorithms as $(\mathsf{natgfe.pk}, \mathsf{natgfe.msk}) \leftarrow \mathsf{NATgFE.Setup}(1^\lambda, 1^n, 1^z)$, and $(\mathsf{ibe.pk}, \mathsf{ibe.msk}) \leftarrow \mathsf{IBE.Setup}(1^\lambda, 1^{z + \lceil \log n' \rceil + 1})$ where n' denotes the length of natgfe ciphertexts with the above parameters.

It outputs the master keys as $(\mathsf{mpk}, \mathsf{msk}) = ((\mathsf{natgfe.pk}, \mathsf{ibe.pk}), (\mathsf{natgfe.msk}, \mathsf{ibe.msk}))$.

Notation. Here and throughout the paper, we use (b, i, tg) to denote the $(z + \lceil \log n' \rceil + 1)$-bit identity, where b is a single bit, i encodes $\lceil \log n' \rceil$-bits, and tg is encoded in the remaining z bits. Basically, each bit-index-tag tuple is uniquely and efficiently mapped into the identity space.

Enc$(\mathsf{mpk}, \mathsf{tg}, m) \to \mathsf{ct}$. Let $\mathsf{mpk} = (\mathsf{natgfe.pk}, \mathsf{ibe.pk})$. It encrypts m using tagged FE as $\mathsf{ct}' \leftarrow \mathsf{NATgFE.Enc}(\mathsf{natgfe.pk}, \mathsf{tg}, m)$, and it encrypts ct' bit-by-bit under IBE as $c_{b,j} = \mathsf{IBE.Enc}(\mathsf{ibe.pk}, (b, j, \mathsf{tg}), \mathsf{ct}'[j])$ for $b \in \{0,1\}, j \in [n']$. It then outputs $\mathsf{ct} = \{c_{b,j}\}_{b \in \{0,1\}, j \in [n']}$.

KeyGen$(\mathsf{msk}, \mathsf{tg}, C \in \{0,1\}^n) \to \mathsf{sk}_{\mathsf{tg},C}$. Let $\mathsf{msk} = (\mathsf{natgfe.msk}, \mathsf{ibe.msk})$. It samples n' random bits $b_1, b_2, \ldots, b_{n'} \leftarrow \{0,1\}$, and computes secret keys for the underlying systems as:

$$\mathsf{natgfe.sk}_{\mathsf{tg},C} \leftarrow \mathsf{NATgFE.KeyGen}(\mathsf{natgfe.msk}, \mathsf{tg}, C),$$
$$\forall j \in [n'], \quad \mathsf{ibe.sk}_{b_j,j} \leftarrow \mathsf{IBE.KeyGen}(\mathsf{ibe.msk}, (b_j, j, \mathsf{tg})).$$

And it outputs $\mathsf{sk}_{\mathsf{tg},C} = (\mathsf{natgfe.sk}_{\mathsf{tg},C}, \{(b_j, \mathsf{ibe.sk}_{j,b_j})\}_{j \in [n']})$.

Dec$(\mathsf{sk}_{\mathsf{tg},C}, \mathsf{ct}) \to y$. It parses the secret key and ciphertext as above. It first decrypts the IBE ciphertexts as $\mathsf{ct}'[j]$ as $\mathsf{IBE.Dec}(\mathsf{ibe.sk}_{b_j,j}, \mathsf{ct}_{b_j,j})$ for $j \in [n']$, and then computes $y = \mathsf{NATgFE.Dec}(\mathsf{natgfe.sk}_{\mathsf{tg},C}, \mathsf{ct}')$ where $\mathsf{ct}'[i]$ is the i-th bit of ct'.

Acknowledgements. We thank the anonymous reviewers for CRYPTO 2021 for useful feedback regarding our abstractions.

References

1. Agrawal, S.: Stronger security for reusable garbled circuits, general definitions and attacks. In: Katz, J., Shacham, H. (eds.) CRYPTO 2017. LNCS, vol. 10401, pp. 3–35. Springer, Cham (2017). https://doi.org/10.1007/978-3-319-63688-7_1
2. Agrawal, S., Boneh, D., Boyen, X.: Efficient lattice (H)IBE in the standard model. In: Gilbert, H. (ed.) EUROCRYPT 2010. LNCS, vol. 6110, pp. 553–572. Springer, Heidelberg (2010). https://doi.org/10.1007/978-3-642-13190-5_28
3. Agrawal, S., Maitra, M., Vempati, N.S., Yamada, S.: Functional encryption for turing machines with dynamic bounded collusion from LWE. In: Malkin, T., Peikert, C. (eds.) CRYPTO 2021. LNCS, vol. 12828, pp. 239–269. Springer, Cham (2021). https://doi.org/10.1007/978-3-030-84259-8_9
4. Agrawal, S., Rosen, A.: Functional encryption for bounded collusions, revisited. In: Kalai, Y., Reyzin, L. (eds.) TCC 2017. LNCS, vol. 10677, pp. 173–205. Springer, Cham (2017). https://doi.org/10.1007/978-3-319-70500-2_7
5. Ananth, P., Jain, A.: Indistinguishability obfuscation from compact functional encryption. In: Gennaro, R., Robshaw, M. (eds.) CRYPTO 2015. LNCS, vol. 9215, pp. 308–326. Springer, Heidelberg (2015). https://doi.org/10.1007/978-3-662-47989-6_15
6. Ananth, P., Jain, K., Sahai, A.: Indistinguishability obfuscation from functional encryption for simple functions. Cryptology ePrint Archive, Report 2015/730 (2015)
7. Ananth, P., Vaikuntanathan, V.: Optimal bounded-collusion secure functional encryption. In: Hofheinz, D., Rosen, A. (eds.) TCC 2019. LNCS, vol. 11891, pp. 174–198. Springer, Cham (2019). https://doi.org/10.1007/978-3-030-36030-6_8
8. Bellare, M., Hoang, V.T., Rogaway, P.: Foundations of garbled circuits. In: CCS 2012 (2012)
9. Bitansky, N., Vaikuntanathan, V.: Indistinguishability obfuscation from functional encryption. In: FOCS (2015)
10. Boneh, D., Franklin, M.: Identity-based encryption from the weil pairing. In: Kilian, J. (ed.) CRYPTO 2001. LNCS, vol. 2139, pp. 213–229. Springer, Heidelberg (2001). https://doi.org/10.1007/3-540-44647-8_13
11. Boneh, D., Sahai, A., Waters, B.: Functional encryption: definitions and challenges. In: Ishai, Y. (ed.) TCC 2011. LNCS, vol. 6597, pp. 253–273. Springer, Heidelberg (2011). https://doi.org/10.1007/978-3-642-19571-6_16
12. Boneh, D., Waters, B.: Conjunctive, subset, and range queries on encrypted data. In: Vadhan, S.P. (ed.) TCC 2007. LNCS, vol. 4392, pp. 535–554. Springer, Heidelberg (2007). https://doi.org/10.1007/978-3-540-70936-7_29
13. Canetti, R., Feige, U., Goldreich, O., Naor, M.: Adaptively secure multi-party computation. In: Miller, G.L. (ed.) STOC (1996)
14. Cash, D., Hofheinz, D., Kiltz, E., Peikert, C.: Bonsai trees, or how to delegate a lattice basis. J. Cryptol. 25(4), 601–639 (2011). https://doi.org/10.1007/s00145-011-9105-2
15. Chen, Y., Vaikuntanathan, V., Waters, B., Wee, H., Wichs, D.: Traitor-tracing from LWE made simple and attribute-based. In: Beimel, A., Dziembowski, S. (eds.) TCC 2018. LNCS, vol. 11240, pp. 341–369. Springer, Cham (2018). https://doi.org/10.1007/978-3-030-03810-6_13
16. Cocks, C.: An identity based encryption scheme based on quadratic residues. In: Honary, B. (ed.) Cryptography and Coding 2001. LNCS, vol. 2260, pp. 360–363. Springer, Heidelberg (2001). https://doi.org/10.1007/3-540-45325-3_32

17. Cramer, R., et al.: Bounded CCA2-secure encryption. In: Kurosawa, K. (ed.) ASIACRYPT 2007. LNCS, vol. 4833, pp. 502–518. Springer, Heidelberg (2007). https://doi.org/10.1007/978-3-540-76900-2_31

18. Diffie, W., Hellman, M.E.: New directions in cryptography (1976)

19. Dodis, Y., Katz, J., Xu, S., Yung, M.: Key-insulated public key cryptosystems. In: Knudsen, L.R. (ed.) EUROCRYPT 2002. LNCS, vol. 2332, pp. 65–82. Springer, Heidelberg (2002). https://doi.org/10.1007/3-540-46035-7_5

20. Garg, R., Goyal, R., Lu, G., Waters, B.: Dynamic collusion bounded functional encryption from identity-based encryption. Cryptology ePrint Archive (2021)

21. Garg, S., Gentry, C., Halevi, S., Raykova, M., Sahai, A., Waters, B.: Candidate indistinguishability obfuscation and functional encryption for all circuits. In: FOCS (2013)

22. Gentry, S., Peikert, C., Vaikuntanathan, V.: Trapdoors for hard lattices and new cryptographic constructions. In: STOC, pp. 197–206 (2008)

23. Goldwasser, S., Lewko, A., Wilson, D.A.: Bounded-collusion IBE from key homomorphism. In: Cramer, R. (ed.) TCC 2012. LNCS, vol. 7194, pp. 564–581. Springer, Heidelberg (2012). https://doi.org/10.1007/978-3-642-28914-9_32

24. Gorbunov, S., Vaikuntanathan, V., Wee, H.: Functional encryption with bounded collusions via multi-party computation. In: Safavi-Naini, R., Canetti, R. (eds.) CRYPTO 2012. LNCS, vol. 7417, pp. 162–179. Springer, Heidelberg (2012). https://doi.org/10.1007/978-3-642-32009-5_11

25. Goyal, R., Koppula, V., Waters, B.: Semi-adaptive security and bundling functionalities made generic and easy. In: Hirt, M., Smith, A. (eds.) TCC 2016. LNCS, vol. 9986, pp. 361–388. Springer, Heidelberg (2016). https://doi.org/10.1007/978-3-662-53644-5_14

26. Goyal, R., Koppula, V., Waters, B.: Collusion resistant traitor tracing from learning with errors. In: STOC (2018)

27. Goyal, R., Syed, R., Waters, B.: Bounded collusion abe for tms from ibe. Cryptology ePrint Archive, Report 2021/709 (2021)

28. Jain, A., Lin, H., Sahai, A.: Indistinguishability obfuscation from well-founded assumptions. In: STOC (2021)

29. Katz, J., Sahai, A., Waters, B.: Predicate encryption supporting disjunctions, polynomial equations, and inner products. In: Smart, N. (ed.) EUROCRYPT 2008. LNCS, vol. 4965, pp. 146–162. Springer, Heidelberg (2008). https://doi.org/10.1007/978-3-540-78967-3_9

30. Kowalczyk, L., Malkin, T., Ullman, J., Wichs, D.: Hardness of non-interactive differential privacy from one-way functions. In: Shacham, H., Boldyreva, A. (eds.) CRYPTO 2018. LNCS, vol. 10991, pp. 437–466. Springer, Cham (2018). https://doi.org/10.1007/978-3-319-96884-1_15

31. Sahai, A., Seyalioglu, H.: Worry-free encryption: functional encryption with public keys. In: CCS (2010)

32. Sahai, A., Waters, B.: Fuzzy identity-based encryption. In: Cramer, R. (ed.) EUROCRYPT 2005. LNCS, vol. 3494, pp. 457–473. Springer, Heidelberg (2005). https://doi.org/10.1007/11426639_27

33. Sahai, A., Waters, B.: How to use indistinguishability obfuscation: deniable encryption, and more. In: STOC, pp. 475–484 (2014)

34. Shamir, A.: Identity-based cryptosystems and signature schemes. In: Blakley, G.R., Chaum, D. (eds.) CRYPTO 1984. LNCS, vol. 196, pp. 47–53. Springer, Heidelberg (1985). https://doi.org/10.1007/3-540-39568-7_5

35. Yao, A.: How to generate and exchange secrets. In: FOCS, pp. 162–167 (1986)

Property-Preserving Hash Functions for Hamming Distance from Standard Assumptions

Nils Fleischhacker[1]([⊠]) [iD], Kasper Green Larsen[2] [iD], and Mark Simkin[3] [iD]

[1] Ruhr University Bochum, Bochum, Germany
mail@nilsfleischhacker.de
[2] Aarhus University, Aarhus, Denmark
larsen@cs.au.dk
[3] Ethereum Foundation, Aarhus, Denmark
mark.simkin@ethereum.org

Abstract. Property-preserving hash functions allow for compressing long inputs x_0 and x_1 into short hashes $h(x_0)$ and $h(x_1)$ in a manner that allows for computing a predicate $P(x_0, x_1)$ given only the two hash values without having access to the original data. Such hash functions are said to be adversarially robust if an adversary that gets to pick x_0 and x_1 after the hash function has been sampled, cannot find inputs for which the predicate evaluated on the hash values outputs the incorrect result.

In this work we construct robust property-preserving hash functions for the hamming-distance predicate which distinguishes inputs with a hamming distance at least some threshold t from those with distance less than t. The security of the construction is based on standard lattice hardness assumptions.

Our construction has several advantages over the best known previous construction by Fleischhacker and Simkin (Eurocrypt 2021). Our construction relies on a single well-studied hardness assumption from lattice cryptography whereas the previous work relied on a newly introduced family of computational hardness assumptions. In terms of computational effort, our construction only requires a small number of modular additions per input bit, whereas the work of Fleischhacker and Simkin required several exponentiations per bit as well as the interpolation and evaluation of high-degree polynomials over large fields. An additional benefit of our construction is that the description of the hash function can be compressed to λ bits assuming a random oracle. Previous work has descriptions of length $\mathcal{O}(\ell\lambda)$ bits for input bit-length ℓ.

We prove a lower bound on the output size of any property-preserving hash function for the hamming distance predicate. The bound shows that the size of our hash value is not far from optimal.

N. Fleischhacker—Funded by the Deutsche Forschungsgemeinschaft (DFG, German Research Foundation) under Germany's Excellence Strategy - EXC 2092 CASA - 390781972.

K. Green Larsen—Supported by Independent Research Fund Denmark (DFF) Sapere Aude Research Leader Grant No. 9064-00068B.

O. Dunkelman and S. Dziembowski (Eds.): EUROCRYPT 2022, LNCS 13276, pp. 764–781, 2022.
https://doi.org/10.1007/978-3-031-07085-3_26

1   Introduction

Efficient algorithms that compress large amounts of data into small digests that preserve certain properties of the original input data are ubiquitous in computer science and hardly need an introduction. Sketching algorithms [5], approximate membership data structures [8], locality-sensitive hash functions [15], streaming algorithms [20], and compressed sensing [11] are only a few among many examples.

Commonly, these algorithms are studied in benign settings where no adversarial parties are present. More concretely, these randomized algorithms usually state their (probabilistic) correctness guarantees by quantifying over all inputs and arguing that with high probability over the chosen random coins, the algorithm will behave as it should. Importantly, the inputs to the algorithm are considered to be *independent* of the random coins used.

In real world scenarios, however, the assumption of a benign environment may not be justified and an adversary may be incentivized to manipulate a given algorithm into outputting incorrect results by providing malicious inputs. Adversaries that choose their inputs adaptively *after* the random coins of the algorithm have been sampled, were previously studied in the context of sketching and streaming algorithms [6,7,9,10,12,14,19,21]. These works show that algorithms which work well in benign environments are not guaranteed to work well in the presence of adaptive malicious inputs and several algorithms with security guarantees against malicious inputs were proposed.

The focus of this work are adversarially robust property-preserving hash (PPH) functions recently introduced by Boyle, LaVigne, and Vaikuntanathan [9], which allow for compressing long inputs x_0 and x_1 into short hashes $h(x_0)$ and $h(x_1)$ in a manner that allows for evaluating a predicate $P(x_0, x_1)$ given only the two hash values without having access to the original data. A bit more concretely, a PPH function for a predicate $P : X \times X \to \{0, 1\}$ is composed of a deterministic compression function $h : X \to Y$ and an evaluation algorithm $\mathsf{Eval} : Y \times Y \to \{0, 1\}$. Such a pair of functions is said to be adversarially robust if no computationally bounded adversary $\mathcal{A}$, who is given a random (h, Eval) from an appropriate family, can find inputs x_0 and x_1, such that $P(x_0, x_1) \neq \mathsf{Eval}(h(x_0), h(x_1))$.

BLV constructed PPH functions that compress inputs by a constant factor for the gap hamming predicate, which distinguishes inputs with very small hamming distance from those with a large distance[1]. For inputs that have neither a very small or very large distance, their construction provided no guarantees.

Subsequently Fleischhacker and Simkin [12] constructed PPH functions for the exact hamming distance predicate, which distinguishes inputs with distance at least t from those with distance less than t. Their construction compresses arbitrarily long inputs into hash values of size $\mathcal{O}(t\lambda)$, where λ is the computational security parameter. Unfortunately, their construction is based on a new

---

[1] We do not care about the exact size of their gap, since we will focus on a strictly stronger predicate in this work.

family of computational assumptions, which is introduced in their work, meaning that the security of their result is not well understood. From a computational efficiency point of view, their construction is rather expensive. It requires $\mathcal{O}(\ell)$ exponentiations for hashing a single ℓ-bit long input and evaluating the predicate on the hashes requires interpolating and evaluating high-degree polynomials over large fields.

1.1   Our Contribution

In this work we present a new approach for constructing PPH functions for the exact hamming distance predicate, which improves upon the result of Fleischhacker and Simkin in several ways.

The security of our construction relies on a well-studied hardness assumption from the domain of lattice-based cryptography. Both hashing an input and evaluating a predicate on hash values only involves fast operations, such as modular additions, xor, and evaluating a few t-wise independent hash functions. The size of our hash values is $\tilde{\mathcal{O}}(\lambda^2 t)$ bits. We present a lower bound of $\Omega(t \log(\ell/t))$ on the size of the hash value of any PPH function for the exact hamming distance predicate, showing that our result is not far from optimal.

Our hash functions can be described by a uniformly random bit string of sufficient length. This means that, assuming a random oracle, these descriptions can compressed into λ bits by replacing it with a short seed. This compression is not applicable to the work of Fleischhacker and Simkin, since their hash function descriptions are $\Theta(\ell\lambda)$-long bit strings with a secret structure that is only known to the sampling algorithm.

1.2   Technical Overview

Let x_0 and x_1 be two ℓ-bit strings, which we would like to compress using a hash function h in a manner that allows us to use $h(x_0)$ and $h(x_1)$ to check whether $d(x_0, x_1) < t$, where d is the hamming distance and t is some threshold. We start with a simple observation from the work of Fleischhacker and Simkin [12]. We can encode bit strings $x = x_1 x_2 \ldots x_\ell$ into sets $X = \{2i - x_i \mid i = 1, \ldots, \ell\}$ and for $x_0, x_1 \in \{0,1\}^\ell$ we have that $d(x_0, x_1) < t$, if and only if $|X_0 \triangle X_1| < 2t$. Thus, from now on we can focus on hashing sets and constructing a property-preserving hash function for the symmetric set difference, which turns out to be an easier task.

Conceptually, our construction is inspired by Invertible Bloom Lookup Tables (IBLTs), which were introduced by Goodrich and Mitzenmacher [13]. This data structure allows one to encode a set into an $\tilde{\mathcal{O}}(t)$ sketch with the following properties: Two sketches can be subtracted from each other, resulting in a new sketch that corresponds to an encoding of the symmetric set difference of the original sets. If a sketch contains at most $\mathcal{O}(t)$ many set elements, then it can be decoded with high probability, meaning that the elements within it can be fully recovered.

Given this data structure, one could attempt the following construction of a PPH function for the symmetric set difference predicate. Given an input set, encode it as an IBLT. To evaluate the symmetric set difference predicate on two hash values, subtract the two given IBLTs and attempt to decode the resulting data structure. If decoding succeeds, then count the number of decoded elements and check, whether it's more or less than $2t$. If decoding fails, then conclude that the symmetric set difference is too large. The main issue with this construction is that IBLTs do not provide any correctness guarantees for inputs that are chosen adversarially. Thus, the main contribution of this work is to construct a robust set encoding similar to IBLTs that remains secure in the presence of an adversary.

Our robust set encoding is comprised of "random" functions $r_i : \{0,1\}^* \to \{1,\ldots,2t\}$ for $i = 1,\ldots,k$ and a "special" collision-resistant hash function A. To encode a set X, we generate an initially empty $k \times 2t$ matrix H. Each element $x \in X$ is then inserted by adding $A(x)$ in each row i to column $r_i(x)$ in H, i.e., $H[i,r_i(x)] = H[i,r_i(x)] + A(x)$ for $i = 1,\ldots,k$. To subtract two encodings, we simply subtract the two matrices entry-wise. To decode a matrix back into a set, we repeatedly look for entries in H that contain a single hash value $A(x)$, i.e., for cells i,j with $|H[i,j]| = A(x)$ for some x, and peel them away. That is, whenever we find such an entry, we find x corresponding to $A(x)$ and then remove x from all positions, where it was originally inserted in H. Then we repeat the process until the matrix H is empty or until the process gets stuck, because no cell contains a single set element by itself.

To prove security of our construction, we will show two things. First, we will show that no adversary can find a pair of sets that have a small symmetric set difference, where the peeling process will get stuck. Actually, we will show something stronger, namely that such pairs do not exist with overwhelming probability over the random choices of $r_1,\ldots,r_k$. Secondly, we will need to show that no (computationally bounded) adversary can find inputs, which decode incorrectly. In particular, we will have to argue that the peeling process never decodes an element that was not actually encoded, i.e., that the sum of several hash values in some cell $H[i,j]$ never looks like $A(x)$ for some single set element x. To argue that such a bad sum of hash values does not exist, one would need to pick the output length of A too big in the sense that our resulting PPH function would not be compressing. Instead, we will show that for an appropriate choice of A these sums may exist, but finding them is hard and can be reduced to the computational hardness of solving the Short Integer Solution Problem [4], a well-studied assumption from lattice-based cryptography.

2   Preliminaries

This section introduces notation, some basic definitions and lemmas that we will use throughout this work. We denote by $\lambda \in \mathbb{N}$ the security parameter and by $\mathsf{poly}(\lambda)$ any function that is bounded by a polynomial in λ. A function f in λ is negligible, if for every $c \in \mathbb{N}$, there exists some $N \in \mathbb{N}$, such that for all

$\lambda > N$ it holds that $f(\lambda) < 1/\lambda^c$. We denote by $\mathsf{negl}(\lambda)$ any negligible function. An algorithm is PPT if it is modeled by a probabilistic Turing machine with a running time bounded by $\mathsf{poly}(\lambda)$.

We write e_i to denote the i-th canonical unit vector, i.e. the vector of zeroes with a one in position i, and assume that the dimension of the vector is known from the context. For a row vector v, we write v^T to denote its transpose. Let $n \in \mathbb{N}$, we denote by $[n]$ the set $\{1, \ldots, n\}$. Let X, Y be sets, we denote by $|X|$ the size of X and by $X \triangle Y$ the symmetric set difference of X and Y, i.e., $X \triangle Y = (X \cup Y) \setminus (X \cap Y) = (X \setminus Y) \cup (Y \setminus X)$. We write $x \leftarrow X$ to denote the process of sampling an element of X uniformly at random. For $x, y \in \{0,1\}^n$, we write $w(x)$ to denote the Hamming weight of x and we write $d(x,y)$ to denote the Hamming distance between x and y, i.e., $d(x,y) = w(x \oplus y)$. We write x_i to denote the i-th bit of x.

2.1 Property-Preserving Hash Functions

The following definition of property-preserving hash functions is taken almost verbatim from [9]. In this work, we consider the strongest of several different security notions that were proposed in [9].

Definition 1 (Property-Preserving Hash). *For a $\lambda \in \mathbb{N}$ an η-compressing property-preserving hash function family $\mathcal{H}_\lambda = \{h : X \to Y\}$ for a two-input predicate requires the following three efficiently computable algorithms:*

$\mathsf{Sample}(1^\lambda) \to h$ *is an efficient randomized algorithm that samples an efficiently computable random hash function from $\mathcal{H}$ with security parameter λ.*

$\mathsf{Hash}(h, x) \to y$ *is an efficient deterministic algorithm that evaluates the hash function h on x.*

$\mathsf{Eval}(h, y_0, y_1) \to \{0,1\}$: *is an efficient deterministic algorithm that on input h, and $y_0, y_1 \in Y$ outputs a single bit.*

We require that $\mathcal{H}$ must be compressing, meaning that $\log |Y| \leq \eta \log |X|$ for $0 < \eta < 1$.

For notational convenience we write $h(x)$ for $\mathsf{Hash}(h, x)$.

Definition 2 (Direct-Access Robustness). *A family of PPH functions $\mathcal{H} = \{h : X \to Y\}$ for a two-input predicate $P : X \times X \to \{0,1\}$ is a family of direct-access robust PPH functions if, for any PPT adversary $\mathcal{A}$ it holds that,*

$$\Pr\left[\begin{array}{l} h \leftarrow \mathsf{Sample}(1^\lambda); \\ (x_0, x_1) \leftarrow \mathcal{A}(h) \end{array} : \mathsf{Eval}(h, h(x_0), h(x_1)) \neq P(x_0, x_1)\right] \leq \mathsf{negl}(\lambda),$$

where the probability is taken over the internal random coins of Sample and $\mathcal{A}$.

Two-Input Predicates. We define the following two-input predicates, which will be the main focus of this work.

Definition 3 (Hamming Predicate). *For $x, y \in \{0,1\}^n$ and $t > 0$, the two-input predicate is defined as*

$$\mathsf{HAM}^t(x,y) = \begin{cases} 1 & \text{if } d(x,y) \geq t \\ 0 & \text{Otherwise} \end{cases}$$

2.2   Lattices

In the following we recall some lattice hardness assumptions and the relationships between them. We start by revisiting one of the most well-studied computational problems.

Definition 4 (Shortest Independent Vector Problem). *For an approximation factor of $\gamma := \gamma(n) \geq 1$, the (n, γ)-SIVP is defined as follows: Given a lattice $\mathcal{L} \subset \mathbb{R}^n$, output n linearly independent lattice vectors, which have all euclidean length at most $\gamma \cdot \lambda_n(\mathcal{L})$, where $\lambda_n(\mathcal{L})$ is the minimum possible.*

Starting with the celebrated work of Lenstra, Lenstra, and Lovász [16], a long line of research works [1–3] has been dedicated to finding fast algorithms for solving the exact and approximate shortest independent vector problem. All existing algorithms for finding any $\mathsf{poly}(n)$-approximation run in time $2^{\Omega(n)}$ and it is believed that one can not do better asymptotically as is captured in the following assumption.

Assumption 5. *For large enough n, there exists no $2^{o(n)}$-time algorithm for solving the (n, γ)-SIVP with $\gamma = \mathsf{poly}(n)$.*

A different computationally hard problem that has been studied extensively is the short integer solution problem.

Definition 6 (Short Integer Solution Problem). *For parameters n, m, q, $\beta_2, \beta_\infty \in \mathbb{N}$, the $(n, m, q, \beta_2, \beta_\infty)$-SIS problem is defined as follows: Given a uniformly random matrix $A \in \mathbb{Z}_q^{n \times m}$, find $s \in \mathbb{Z}^m$ with $\|s\|_2 \leq \beta_2$ and $\|s\|_\infty \leq \beta_\infty$, such that $As^\mathsf{T} = 0$.*

It was shown by Micciancio and Peikert that the difficulty of solving the SIS problem fast on average is related to the difficulty of solving the SIVP in the worst-case.

Theorem 1 (Worst-Case to Average-Case Reduction for SIS [17]). *Let n, $m := m(n)$, and $\beta_2 \geq \beta_\infty \geq 1$ be integers. Let $q \geq \beta_2 \cdot n^\delta$ for some constant $\delta > 0$. Solving the $(n, m, q, \beta_2, \beta_\infty)$-SIS problem on average with non-negligible probability in n is at least as hard as solving the (n, γ)-SIVP in the worst-case to within $\gamma = \max(1, \beta_2 \cdot \beta_\infty / q) \cdot \tilde{\mathcal{O}}(\beta_2 \sqrt{n})$.*

Combining the above result with Assumption 5, we get the following corollary.

Corollary 2. *Let $n \in \Theta(\lambda)$ and $m = \mathsf{poly}(\lambda)$ be integers, let $\beta_\infty = 2$, and let $\beta_2 = \sqrt{m + \nu}$ for some constant ν. Let $q > \beta_2 \cdot n^\delta$ for some constant $\delta > 0$. If Assumption 5 holds, then for large enough λ, there exists no PPT adversary that solves the $(n, m, q, \beta_2, \beta_\infty)$-SIS problem with non-negligible (in λ) probability.*

3 Robust Set Encodings

In this section, we define our notion of robust set encodings. The encoding transforms a possibly large set into a smaller sketch. Given two sketches of sets with a small enough symmetric set difference, one should be able to decode the symmetric set difference. The security of our encodings guarantees that no computationally bounded adversary can find a pair of sets where decoding either returns the incorrect result or fails even though the symmetric set difference between the encoded sets is small.

Definition 7 (Robust Set Encodings). *A robust set encoding for a universe U is comprised of the following algorithms:*

$\mathsf{Sample}(1^\lambda, t) \to f$ *is an efficient randomized algorithm that takes the security parameter λ and threshold t as input and returns an efficiently computable set encoding function f sampled from the family $\mathcal{E}$.*

$\mathsf{Encode}(f, X) \to y$ *is an efficient deterministic algorithm that takes set encoding function f and set $X \subset U$ as input and returns encoding y.*

$\mathsf{Decode}(f, y_0, y_1) \to X'/\bot$ *is an efficient deterministic algorithm that takes set encoding function f and two set encodings y_0, y_1 as input and returns set X' or $\bot$.*

We denote by $\mathsf{Len}_{\mathcal{E}} : \mathbb{N} \times \mathbb{N} \to \mathbb{N}$ the function that describes the length of the encoding for a given security parameter λ and threshold t. For any two sets X_0, X_1 we use $X' \leftarrow \mathsf{Diff}(f, X_0, X_1)$ as a shorthand notation for

$$X' \leftarrow \mathsf{Decode}(f, \mathsf{Encode}(f, X_0), \mathsf{Encode}(f, X_1)).$$

We say a set encoding is robust, if for any PPT adversary $\mathcal{A}$ and any threshold $t \in \mathbb{N}$ it holds that,

$$\Pr\left[\begin{array}{l} f \leftarrow \mathsf{Sample}(1^\lambda, t); \\ (X_0, X_1) \leftarrow \mathcal{A}(f, t); \\ X' \leftarrow \mathsf{Diff}(f, X_0, X_1) \end{array} : \begin{array}{l} X' \notin \{X_0 \bigtriangleup X_1, \bot\} \\ \vee\ (|X_0 \bigtriangleup X_1| < t \wedge X' = \bot) \end{array}\right] \leq \mathsf{negl}(\lambda),$$

where the probability is taken over the random coins of the adversary $\mathcal{A}$ and Sample.

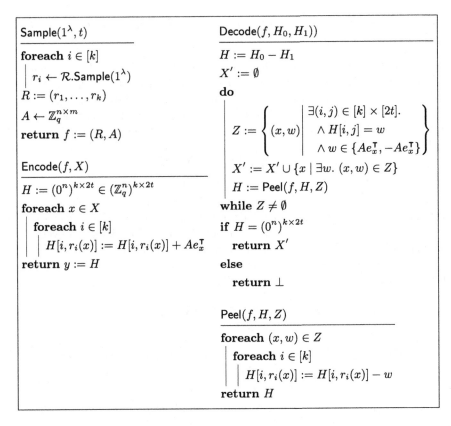

Fig. 1. Construction of a robust set encoding for universe $[m]$.

3.1 Instantiation

In this section we construct a set encoding for universe $[m]$ with $m = \mathsf{poly}(\lambda)$ by modifying Invertible Bloom Lookup Tables [13] to achieve security against adaptive malicious inputs. Since we are only encoding polynomially large sets and can leverage the cryptographic hardness of the SIS problem, we can get away with only maintaining a matrix of hash values in our sketch and we do not require the additional counter or value fields that were present in the original construction of Goodrich and Mitzenmacher. Refer to Fig. 1 for a full description of the construction. Before we prove that the construction is a robust set encoding we will first prove a few of its properties that will be useful in the following.

The following lemma effectively states that given the difference of two encodings there will always be a least one element that can be peeled if the symmetric set difference is small enough.

Lemma 3. *Let $\mathcal{R}$ be a family of t-wise independent hash functions $r : [m] \to [2t]$ and let $k \geq 2 \log_{3/e} m$. With probability at least $1 - 2^{-\Omega(k)}$, it simultaneously holds for all sets $T \subseteq [m]$ with $0 < |T| \leq t$ that there is at least one $x \in T$ and one* *index $i \in [k]$ such that $r_i(x) \neq r_i(y)$ for all $y \in T \setminus \{x\}$. Here the probability is taken over the random choice of the r_i's.*

Proof. Let E denote the event that there is a set T with $0 < |T| \leq t$ such that for all $x \in T$ and all $i \in [k]$, there is a $y \in T \setminus \{x\}$ with $r_i(x) = r_i(y)$. We show that $\Pr[E]$ is small. The proof follows from a union bound over all $T \subseteq [m]$ with $2 \leq |T| \leq t$. So fix one such T. Let E_T denote the event that there is no $i \in [k]$ and $x \in T$ such that $r_i(x) \neq r_i(y)$ for all $y \in T \setminus \{x\}$. Then by a union bound, we have

$$\Pr[E] \leq \Pr\left[\bigcup_{T \subseteq [m]} E_T\right] \leq \sum_{T \subseteq [m]} \Pr[E_T].$$

To bound $\Pr[E_T]$, notice that conditioned on E_T, the number of distinct hash values $|\{r_i(x) \mid x \in T\}|$ for the ith hash function is at most $|T|/2$, as every hash value is *hit* by either 0 or at least 2 elements from T. Now define an event $E_{T,S}$ for every k-tuple $S = (S_1, \ldots, S_k)$ where S_i is a subset of $|T|/2$ values in $[k]$. The event $E_{T,S}$ occurs if $r_i(x) \in S_i$ for every $x \in T$ and every $i \in [k]$. If E_T happens then at least one event $E_{T,S}$ happens. Thus

$$\Pr[E_T] \leq \Pr\left[\bigcup_S E_{T,S}\right] \leq \sum_S \Pr[E_{T,S}].$$

To bound $\Pr[E_{T,S}]$, notice that by t-wise independence, the values $r_i(x)$ are independent and fall in S_i with probability exactly $|T|/(2 \cdot 2t)$. Since this must happen for every i and every $x \in T$, we get that $\Pr[E_{T,S}] \leq (|T|/(4t))^{|T|k}$ and $\Pr[E_T] \leq \binom{2t}{|T|/2}^k (|T|/(4t))^{|T|k}$. A union bound over all T gives us $\Pr[E] \leq \sum_{j=2}^t \binom{m}{j}\binom{2t}{j/2}^k (j/(4t))^{jk}$. Using the bound $\binom{n}{k} \leq (en/k)^k$ for all $0 \leq k \leq n$ and the bound $\binom{m}{j} \leq m^j$, we finally conclude:

$$\Pr[E] \leq \sum_{j=2}^t \binom{m}{j}\left(\frac{2t}{j/2}\right)^k (j/(4t))^{jk}$$

$$\leq \sum_{j=2}^t m^j (4et/j)^{jk/2}(j/(4t))^{jk}$$

$$= \sum_{j=2}^t m^j (e/3)^{jk/2}(3j/(4t))^{jk/2}$$

For $k \geq 2\log_{3/e} m$ we have $(e/3)^{k/2} \leq 1/m$. The above is thus bounded by

$$\Pr[E] \leq \sum_{j=2}^t (3j/(4t))^{jk/2}$$

$$\leq \sum_{j=2}^t (3/4)^{jk/2}$$

For any $k \geq 2$, the terms in this sum go down by a factor at least $4/3$ and thus is bounded by $2^{-\Omega(k)}$. □

In the next lemma we show that correctly peeling one layer of elements during decoding leads to a state that is equivalent to never having inserted those elements in the first place.

Lemma 4. *For any security parameter λ, any threshold t, any encoding function $f \leftarrow \mathsf{Sample}(1^\lambda, t)$, any pair of subsets $X_0, X_1 \subseteq [m]$ and any set*

$$Z \subseteq \{(x, Ae_x^\mathsf{T}) \mid x \in X_0 \setminus X_1\} \cup \{(x, -Ae_x^\mathsf{T}) \mid x \in X_1 \setminus X_0\}$$

and $X := \{x \mid \exists w. (x, w) \in Z\}$ it holds that

$$\mathsf{Peel}(\mathsf{Encode}(f, X_0) - \mathsf{Encode}(f, X_1), Z) = \mathsf{Encode}(f, X_0 \setminus X) - \mathsf{Encode}(f, X_1 \setminus X).$$

Proof. Let $H_b := \mathsf{Encode}(f, X_b)$, $H_b' := \mathsf{Encode}(f, X_b' \setminus X)$ and $H := \mathsf{Peel}(f, H_0 - H_1, Z)$ For any $(i, j) \in [k] \times [2t]$, let $S_{i,j} = \{x \in [m] \mid r_i(x) = j\}$. Then for each $(i, j) \in [k] \times [2t]$ we have

$$H[i,j] = H_0[i,j] - H_1[i,j] - \sum_{x \in X \cap S_{i,j}} Z(x) \tag{1}$$

$$= \sum_{x \in X_0 \cap S_{i,j}} Ae_x^\mathsf{T} - \sum_{x \in X_1 \cap S_{i,j}} Ae_x^\mathsf{T} - \sum_{x \in X \cap S_{i,j}} Z(x) \tag{2}$$

$$= \sum_{x \in X_0 \cap S_{i,j}} Ae_x^\mathsf{T} - \sum_{x \in X_1 \cap S_{i,j}} Ae_x^\mathsf{T} - \sum_{x \in X \cap X_0 \cap S_{i,j}} Z(x) - \sum_{x \in X \cap X_1 \cap S_{i,j}} Z(x) \tag{3}$$

$$= \sum_{x \in X_0 \cap S_{i,j}} Ae_x^\mathsf{T} - \sum_{x \in X_1 \cap S_{i,j}} Ae_x^\mathsf{T} - \sum_{x \in X \cap X_0 \cap S_{i,j}} Ae_x^\mathsf{T} + \sum_{x \in X \cap X_1 \cap S_{i,j}} Ae_x^\mathsf{T} \tag{4}$$

$$= \sum_{x \in (X_0 \setminus X) \cap S_{i,j}} Ae_x^\mathsf{T} - \sum_{x \in (X_1 \setminus X) \cap S_{i,j}} Ae_x^\mathsf{T} \tag{5}$$

$$= H_0'[i,j] - H_1'[i,j], \tag{6}$$

where we denote by $Z(x)$ the unique value w such that $(x, w) \in Z$. Equations 1 and 2 follow from the definitions of Peel and Encode respectively. Equations 3 and 5 follow from the fact that X is a subset of the symmetric set difference of X_0 and X_1. Equation 4 follows from the fact that $w = (-1)^b Ae_x^\mathsf{T}$ iff $x \in X_b$. Finally, Eq. 6 follows again from the definition of Encode. □

The following lemma essentially states that during the decoding process we will never peel an element that is not in the symmetric set difference *and* all elements will be peeled correctly, i.e., the decoding algorithm correctly identifies whether an element is from X_0 or from X_1.

Lemma 5. *For an encoding function $f \leftarrow \mathsf{Sample}(1^\lambda, t)$ and two sets X_0, X_1, let $Z_1, Z_2, \ldots$ denote the sequence of sets peeled during the execution of*

$$\mathsf{Decode}(f, \mathsf{Encode}(f, X_0), \mathsf{Encode}(f, X_1)).$$

Let further $X_b^c = X_b \setminus \{y \mid \exists w. (y, w) \in Z_1 \cup \cdots \cup Z_{c-1}\}$. If the $(n, m, q, \sqrt{m+3}, 2)$-SIS problem is hard, then for any PPT algorithm $\mathcal{A}$, it holds that

$$\Pr\left[\begin{array}{l} f := \mathsf{Sample}(1^\lambda, t); \\ (X_0, X_1) \leftarrow \mathcal{A}(f) \end{array} \exists c. Z_c \not\subseteq \begin{array}{l} \{(x, Ae_x^\mathsf{T}) \mid x \in X_0^c \setminus X_1^c\} \\ \cup \{(x, -Ae_x^\mathsf{T}) \mid x \in X_1^c \setminus X_0^c\} \end{array}\right] \leq \mathsf{negl}(\lambda).$$

Proof. Let $\mathcal{A}$ be an arbitrary PPT algorithm with

$$\Pr\left[\begin{array}{l} f := \mathsf{Sample}(1^\lambda, t); \\ (X_0, X_1) \leftarrow \mathcal{A}(f) \end{array} \exists c. Z_c \not\subseteq \begin{array}{l} \{(x, Ae_x^\mathsf{T}) \mid x \in X_0^c \setminus X_1^c\} \\ \cup \{(x, -Ae_x^\mathsf{T}) \mid x \in X_1^c \setminus X_0^c\} \end{array}\right] = \epsilon(\lambda).$$

We construct an algorithm $\mathcal{B}$ that solves $(n, m, q, \sqrt{m+3}, 2)$-SIS as follows. $\mathcal{B}$ receives as input a random matrix $A \in \mathbb{Z}_q^{n \times m}$, samples $r_i \leftarrow \mathcal{R}$ for $i \in [k]$ and invokes $\mathcal{A}$ on $f = (A, (r_1, \ldots, r_k))$. Once $\mathcal{A}$ outputs X_0, X_1, $\mathcal{B}$ runs $H_0 := \mathsf{Encode}(f, X_0)$ and $H_1 := \mathsf{Encode}(f, X_1)$ and then starts to execute $\mathsf{Decode}(f, H_0, H_1)$. Let Z_c denote the set Z in the c-th iteration of the main loop of Decode. In each iteration, if

$$Z_c \not\subseteq \{(x, Ae_x^\mathsf{T}) \mid x \in X_0^c \setminus X_1^c\} \cup \{(x, -Ae_x^\mathsf{T}) \mid x \in X_1^c \setminus X_0^c\},$$

then $\mathcal{B}$ stops the decoding process and proceeds as follows.

Let $S_{i,j} = \{x \in [m] \mid r_i(x) = j\}$. By definition of Z, there must exists at least one element $(x, w) \in Z_c$, such that

$$H[i, j] = (-1)^b Ae_x^\mathsf{T} \quad \text{and} \quad x \notin X_b^c \setminus X_{1-b}^c \tag{7}$$

for some cell (i, j) and some bit b. $\mathcal{B}$ identifies one such cell by exhaustive search and outputs the vector

$$s := \sum_{y \in X_0^c \cap S_{i,j}} e_y - \sum_{y \in X_1^c \cap S_{i,j}} e_y - (-1)^b e_x.$$

If the decoding procedure terminates without such a Z_c occurring, $\mathcal{B}$ outputs $\perp$.

To analyze the success probability of $\mathcal{B}$, consider that by Lemma 4 and since Z_c is the *first* set in which an element as specified above exists, we have that $H = \mathsf{Encode}(f, X_0') - \mathsf{Encode}(f, X_1')$, i.e.

$$(-1)^b Ae_x^\mathsf{T} = H[i, j] = \sum_{y \in X_0^c \cap S_{i,j}} Ae_y^\mathsf{T} - \sum_{y \in X_1^c \cap S_{i,j}} Ae_y^\mathsf{T}$$

Thus, whenever $\mathcal{B}$ outputs a vector s, it holds that $As^\mathsf{T} = 0$. Furthermore, this vector consists of the sum of at most m unique canonical unit vectors and one additional canonical unit vector. This implies that $\|s\|_2 \leq \sqrt{m+3}$ and $\|s\|_\infty \leq 2$. It remains to argue that s is non-zero. The vector s is zero, iff

$$\sum_{y \in X_0^c \cap S_{i,j}} e_y - \sum_{y \in X_1^c \cap S_{i,j}} e_y = (-1)^b e_x.$$

Observe that, since we are summing up canonical unit vectors, this can hold only if $x \in X_b^c \setminus X_{1-b}^c$. However, by Eq. 7 this does not occur, therefore s is non-zero.

We can conclude that $\mathcal{B}$ solves $(n, m, q, \sqrt{m+3}, 2)$-SIS, with probability $\epsilon(\lambda)$. Since $(n, m, q, \sqrt{m+3}, 2)$-SIS is assumed to be hard, $\epsilon(\lambda)$ must be negligible. $\square$

The following lemma states that with overwhelming probability the decoding process will output either $\perp$ or a subset of the symmetric set difference, even for maliciously chosen sets X_0, X_1.

Lemma 6. *If the $(n, m, q, \sqrt{m+3}, 2)$-SIS problem is hard, then for any PPT adversary $\mathcal{A}$ it holds that*

$$\Pr \left[\begin{array}{l} f := \mathsf{Sample}(1^\lambda, t); \\ (X_0, X_1) \leftarrow \mathcal{A}(f); \quad : \quad X' \neq \perp \wedge X' \not\subseteq X_0 \triangle X_1 \\ X' := \mathsf{Diff}(f, X_0, X_1) \end{array} \right] \leq \mathsf{negl}(\lambda)$$

Proof. Let $Z_1, Z_2, \ldots$ denote the sequence of sets peeled during the execution of

$$\mathsf{Decode}(f, \mathsf{Encode}(f, X_0), \mathsf{Encode}(f, X_0)).$$

If an algorithm outputs X_0, X_1, such that $X' \not\subseteq X_0 \triangle X_1$, there must exist an $x \in X'$ such that

$$x' \notin X_0 \triangle X_1 = (X_0 \setminus X_1) \cup (X_1 \setminus X_0).$$

Since $X' := \{x \mid \exists w. (x, w) \in Z_1 \cup \ldots\}$, this can only happen with negligible probability by Lemma 5. $\square$

The following lemma states that with overwhelming probability the decoding process will never output a *strict* subset of the symmetric set difference, even for maliciously chosen sets X_0, X_1.

Lemma 7. *If the $(n, m, q, \sqrt{m+3}, 2)$-SIS problem is hard, then for any PPT adversary $\mathcal{A}$ it holds that*

$$\Pr \left[\begin{array}{l} f := \mathsf{Sample}(1^\lambda, t); \\ (X_0, X_1) \leftarrow \mathcal{A}(f); \quad : \quad X' \subsetneq X_0 \triangle X_1 \\ X' := \mathsf{Diff}(f, X_0, X_1) \end{array} \right] \leq \mathsf{negl}(\lambda)$$

Proof. Let $\mathcal{A}$ be a PPT an adversary for the above experiment. We construct an adversary $\mathcal{B}$ against $(n, m, q, \sqrt{m+3}, 2)$-SIS as follows. $\mathcal{B}$ is given matrix A, samples $r_i \leftarrow \mathcal{R}$ for $i \in [k]$ and invokes $\mathcal{A}$ on $f = (A, (r_1, \ldots, r_k))$. Adversary $\mathcal{A}$ returns X_0 and X_1 and $\mathcal{B}$ computes $X' := \mathsf{Diff}(f, X_0, X_1)$. If $X' \subsetneq X_0 \triangle X_1$, then $\mathcal{B}$ computes $X'_b = X_b \setminus X'$ for $b \in \{0, 1\}$ and finds an index i, j such that there exists an $x \in X'_0 \triangle X'_1$ with $r_i(x) = j$. $\mathcal{B}$ returns

$$s := \sum_{y \in X'_0 \cap S_{i,j}} e_y - \sum_{y \in X'_1 \cap S_{i,j}} e_y.$$

Since every canonical unit vector appears at most once in the sum above, it follows that $\|s\|_2 \leq \sqrt{m}$ and $\|s\|_\infty = 1$. Further, since, by construction, there exists at least one $y \in (X_0' \cap S_{i,j}) \triangle (X_1' \cap S_{i,j})$ it follows that $s \neq 0$.

To analyze the probability that $As^\mathsf{T} = 0$ we consider the following. Let H' be the value of the matrix H when the decoding procedure terminates. By Lemma 5 and Lemma 4 it holds with overwhelming probability that $H' = H_0' - H_1' = \mathsf{Encode}(f, X_0') - \mathsf{Encode}(f, X_1')$. However, since the decoding terminates successfully, it must also hold that $H' = (0^n)^{k \times 2t}$. It follows that for all i, j, we have $H_0'[i, j] - H_1'[i, j] = 0$ and therefore $As = 0$ with overwhelming probability. Since $(n, m, q, \sqrt{m+3}, 2)$-SIS is assumed to be hard the lemma follows.   □

By combining Lemma 6 and Lemma 7 we obtain the following corollary stating that with overwhelming probability the decoding process will output *either* the correct symmetric set difference *or* the error symbol $\perp$.

Corollary 8. *If the $(n, m, q, \sqrt{m+3}, 2)$-SIS problem is hard, then for any PPT adversary $\mathcal{A}$ it holds that*

$$\Pr\left[\begin{array}{l} f := \mathsf{Sample}(1^\lambda, t); \\ (X_0, X_1) \leftarrow \mathcal{A}(f); \;\; : \;\; X' \notin \{X_0 \triangle X_1, \perp\} \\ X' := \mathsf{Diff}(f, X_0, X_1) \end{array}\right] \leq \mathsf{negl}(\lambda)$$

The following lemma states that with overwhelming probability the decoding process will not output $\perp$ if the symmetric set difference is small.

Lemma 9. *If the $(n, m, q, \sqrt{m+3}, 2)$-SIS problem is hard, then for any PPT adversary $\mathcal{A}$ it holds that*

$$\Pr\left[\begin{array}{l} f \leftarrow \mathsf{Sample}(1^\lambda, t); \\ (X_0, X_1) \leftarrow \mathcal{A}(f, t); \;\; : \;\; |X_0 \triangle X_1| < t \wedge X' = \perp \\ X' \leftarrow \mathsf{Diff}(f, X_0, X_1) \end{array}\right] \leq \mathsf{negl}(\lambda)$$

Proof. Let $\mathcal{A}$ be an arbitrary PPT algorithm. By Lemma 5 and Lemma 4 it holds that in each iteration c we have $H = H_{c,0} - H_{c,1}$, where $H_{c,b} = \mathsf{Encode}(f, X_{c,0}, X_{c,1})$ and $X_{c,b} = X_b \setminus \{x \mid \exists w. (x, w) \in Z_1 \cup \cdots \cup Z_{c-1}\}$. Since it must hold that $|X_0 \triangle X_1| < t$ it in particular holds that $|X_{c,0} \triangle X_{c,1}| < t$ in each iteration. By Lemma 3, in each iteration where $X_{c,1} \triangle X_{c,2} \neq \emptyset$ it holds that $Z_c \neq \emptyset$ with overwhelming probability. Therefore, the decoding process terminates after at most t steps, with $X' = X_0 \triangle X_1$. Since each peeling step was correct with overwhelming probability it must hold that $H = (0^n)^{k \times 2t}$.   □

Given the above lemmas, we can now easily prove the following theorem.

Theorem 10. *Let $\mathcal{R}$ be a family of t-wise independent hash functions $r : [m] \to [2t]$ and let $k \geq \max\{\lambda, 2 \log_{3/e} m\}$. Then the construction in Fig. 1 is a robust set encoding for universe $[m]$ if the $(n = n(\lambda), m, q, \sqrt{m+3}, 2)$-SIS problem is hard.*

Sample(1^λ)	Hash(h, x)	Eval(h, y_0, y_1)
$f \leftarrow \mathcal{E}.\mathsf{Sample}(1^\lambda, 2t)$	$X := \{2i - x_i \mid i \in [\ell]\}$	$X' := \mathcal{E}.\mathsf{Decode}(h, y_0, y_1)$
return $h := f$	$y := \mathcal{E}.\mathsf{Encode}(h, X)$	if $X' = \bot$ or $\lvert X' \rvert \geq 2t$
	return y	return 1
		else
		return 0

Fig. 2. A family of direct-access robust PPHs for the predicate HAM^t over the domain $\{0,1\}^\ell$ for any $\ell \in \mathbb{N}$.

Proof. Let $\mathcal{A}$ be an arbitrary PPT algorithm, using Corollary 8, Lemma 9 and a simple union bound we can conclude that

$$\Pr \begin{bmatrix} f \leftarrow \mathsf{Sample}(1^\lambda, t); \\ (X_0, X_1) \leftarrow \mathcal{A}(f, t); \\ X' \leftarrow \mathsf{Diff}(f, X_0, X_1) \end{bmatrix} : \begin{array}{c} X' \notin \{X_0 \triangle X_1, \bot\} \\ \vee \, (\lvert X_0 \triangle X_1 \rvert < t \wedge X' = \bot) \end{array} \end{bmatrix}$$

$$\leq \Pr \begin{bmatrix} f \leftarrow \mathsf{Sample}(1^\lambda, t); \\ (X_0, X_1) \leftarrow \mathcal{A}(f, t); \\ X' \leftarrow \mathsf{Diff}(f, X_0, X_1) \end{bmatrix} : X' \notin \{X_0 \triangle X_1, \bot\} \end{bmatrix}$$

$$+ \Pr \begin{bmatrix} f \leftarrow \mathsf{Sample}(1^\lambda, t); \\ (X_0, X_1) \leftarrow \mathcal{A}(f, t); \\ X' \leftarrow \mathsf{Diff}(f, X_0, X_1) \end{bmatrix} : \lvert X_0 \triangle X_1 \rvert < t \wedge X' = \bot \end{bmatrix}$$

$$\leq \mathsf{negl}(\lambda).$$

Remark 1. Instantiated as specified, the construction has keys that consist of k many t-wise independent hash functions and a matrix $A \in \mathbb{Z}_q^{m \times n}$, leading to a key length of $kt \cdot \log m + mn \cdot \log q$. Note that the entire key can be represented by a public uniformly random $kt \cdot \log m + mn \cdot \log q$ bit string. Assuming the existence of a random oracle, this string can be replaced by a short λ bit seed.

4 Construction

In this section we construct property-preserving hash functions for the exact hamming distance predicate based on robust set encodings.

4.1 PPH for the Hamming Distance Predicate

Theorem 11. *Let $\ell = \mathsf{poly}(\lambda)$ and $t \leq \ell$. Let $\mathcal{E}$ be a robust set encoding for universe $[2\ell]$ with encoding length $\mathsf{Len}_\mathcal{E}$. Then, the construction in Fig. 2 is a $\mathsf{Len}_\mathcal{E}(\lambda, 2t)/\ell$-compressing direct-access robust property-preserving hash function family for the two-input predicate HAM^t and domain $\{0,1\}^\ell$.*

Proof. Let $\mathcal{A}$ be an arbitrary PPT adversary against the direct-access robustness of $\mathcal{H}$. We construct an adversary $\mathcal{B}$ against the robustness of $\mathcal{E}$ as follows. Upon input e, $\mathcal{B}$ invokes $\mathcal{A}$ on input $h := f$. When $\mathcal{A}$ outputs x_0, x_1, $\mathcal{B}$ outputs $X_0 := \{2i - x_{0,i} \mid i \in [\ell]\}$ and $X_1 := \{2i - x_{1,i} \mid i \in [\ell]\}$. We note that it holds that

$$
\Pr\left[\begin{array}{l} h \leftarrow \mathsf{Sample}(1^\lambda); \\ (x_0, x_1) \leftarrow \mathcal{A}(h) \end{array} : \mathsf{Eval}(h, h(x_0), h(x_1)) \neq \mathsf{HAM}^t(x_0, x_1)\right] \tag{8}
$$

$$
= \Pr\left[\begin{array}{l} f \leftarrow \mathcal{E}.\mathsf{Sample}(1^\lambda, 2t); \\ (X_0, X_1) \leftarrow \mathcal{B}(f); \\ y_0 := \mathcal{E}.\mathsf{Encode}(f, X_0); \\ y_1 := \mathcal{E}.\mathsf{Encode}(f, X_1) \end{array} : \mathsf{Eval}(f, y_0, y_1) \neq \mathsf{HAM}^t(x_0, x_1)\right] \tag{9}
$$

$$
= \Pr\left[\begin{array}{l} f \leftarrow \mathcal{E}.\mathsf{Sample}(1^\lambda, 2t); \\ (X_0, X_1) \leftarrow \mathcal{B}(f); \\ X' := \mathsf{Diff}(f, X_0, X_1) \end{array} : \begin{array}{l} (d(x_0, x_1) \geq t \wedge X' \neq \bot \wedge |X'| < 2t) \\ \vee (d(x_0, x_1) < t \wedge (X' = \bot \vee |X'| \geq 2t)) \end{array}\right] \tag{10}
$$

$$
= \Pr\left[\begin{array}{l} f \leftarrow \mathcal{E}.\mathsf{Sample}(1^\lambda, 2t); \\ (X_0, X_1) \leftarrow \mathcal{B}(f); \\ X' := \mathsf{Diff}(f, X_0, X_1) \end{array} : \begin{array}{l} (|X_0 \triangle X_1| \geq 2t \wedge X' \neq \bot \wedge |X'| < 2t) \\ \vee (|X_0 \triangle X_1| < 2t \wedge (X' = \bot \vee |X'| \geq 2t)) \end{array}\right] \tag{11}
$$

$$
= \Pr\left[\begin{array}{l} f \leftarrow \mathcal{E}.\mathsf{Sample}(1^\lambda, 2t); \\ (X_0, X_1) \leftarrow \mathcal{B}(f); \\ X' := \mathsf{Diff}(f, X_0, X_1) \end{array} : \begin{array}{l} (|X_0 \triangle X_1| \geq 2t \wedge X' \neq \bot \wedge |X'| < 2t) \\ \vee (|X_0 \triangle X_1| < 2t \wedge X' \neq \bot \wedge |X'| \geq 2t) \\ \vee (|X_0 \triangle X_1| < 2t \wedge X' = \bot) \end{array}\right] \tag{12}
$$

$$
= \Pr\left[\begin{array}{l} f \leftarrow \mathcal{E}.\mathsf{Sample}(1^\lambda, 2t); \\ (X_0, X_1) \leftarrow \mathcal{B}(f); \\ X' := \mathsf{Diff}(f, X_0, X_1) \end{array} : \begin{array}{l} (X' \neq \bot \wedge |X_0 \triangle X_1| \neq |X'|) \\ \vee (|X_0 \triangle X_1| < 2t \wedge X' = \bot) \end{array}\right] \tag{13}
$$

$$
\leq \Pr\left[\begin{array}{l} f \leftarrow \mathcal{E}.\mathsf{Sample}(1^\lambda, 2t); \\ (X_0, X_1) \leftarrow \mathcal{B}(f); \\ X' := \mathsf{Diff}(f, X_0, X_1) \end{array} : \begin{array}{l} X' \notin \{X_0 \triangle X_1, \bot\} \\ \vee (|X_0 \triangle X_1| < 2t \wedge X' = \bot) \end{array}\right]. \tag{14}
$$

Here Eq. 9 follows from the definition of Sample and Hash and Eq. 10 follows from the definition of Eval as well as the exact hamming distance predicate. Equation 11 follows from the definition of the sets X_0, X_1: for each position i where the $x_{0,i} = x_{1,i}$, the sets share an element, whereas for every position where $x_{0,i} \neq x_{1,i}$, one of them contains the element $2i$ and the other $2i - 1$, thus $d(x_0, x_1) = t \iff |X_0 \triangle X_1| = 2t$. Equations 12 and 13 follow by first splitting the bottom clause and then rewriting the top two clauses.

Finally, since $\mathcal{E}$ is a robust set encoding it holds by assumption that the probability in Eq. 14 is negligible and the theorem thus follows.

Corollary 12. *Instantiating the construction from Fig. 2 using the robust set encoding from Sect. 3 with $k = n = \lambda$ and $q = \sqrt{\lambda(2\ell + 3)}$ leads to a $\frac{2tkn \log q}{\ell} = \frac{t\lambda^2 \log(\lambda(2\ell+3))}{\ell}$ compressing PPH for exact hamming distance.*

5   Lower Bound

In this section, we show a lower bound on the output length of a PPH for exact Hamming distance. We prove the lower bound by reduction from indexing. In the indexing problem, there are two parameters k and m. The first player Alice is given a string $x = (x_1, \ldots, x_m) \in [k]^m$, while the second player Bob is given an integer $i \in [m]$. Alice sends a single message to Bob and Bob should output x_i. The following lower bound holds:

Lemma 13 ([18]). *In any one-way protocol for indexing in the joint random source model with success probability at least $1 - \delta$ over a uniform random string x and uniform random index i, Alice must send a message of size $\Omega((1-\delta)m \log k - m)$ in expectation.*

Here the joint random source model means that Alice and Bob have shared randomness that is drawn independently of their inputs. Note that we have strengthened the lemma a bit over the original result, to allow the failure probability to be "on average" over a uniform random index. The proof of the above lemma is very short using modern techniques:

Proof. Let $X = (X_1, \ldots, X_m)$ be a uniform random string over $[k]^m$ and let I be a uniform random index in $[m]$. Let R be a random variable giving the shared randomness between Alice and Bob (independent of their inputs) drawn from some universe $\mathcal{R}$ of finite bit strings. Let $\pi : [k]^m \times \mathcal{R} \to \{0,1\}^*$ give Alice's message in a protocol and let $\tau : \{0,1\}^* \times [m] \times \mathcal{R} \to [k]$ be Bob's decoding. That is, $\pi(X, R)$ is Alice's message and $\tau(\pi(X, R), I, R)$ is Bob's output. Assume $\Pr_{X,I,R}[\tau(\pi(X, R), I, R) = X_I] \geq 1 - \delta$. For every $i \in [m]$, let $\delta_i = \Pr_{X,R}[\tau(\pi(X, R), i, R) \neq X_i]$. Then $\sum_{i=1}^{m} \delta_i/m \leq \delta$. Thus given Alice's message $\pi(X, R)$, Bob may reconstruct X_i except with probability δ_i by computing $\tau(\pi(X, R), i, R)$. By Fano's inequality, this implies that $H(X_i \mid \pi(X, R), R) \leq H_b(\delta_i) + \delta_i \log k \leq 1 + \delta_i \log k$ (here $H_b(\cdot)$ denotes binary entropy). Therefore, we have $H(X \mid \pi(X, R), R) \leq \sum_{i=1}^{m} 1 + \delta_i \log k \leq m + \delta m \log k$. But $H(X \mid R) = m \log k$. Thus $H(\pi(X, R)) \geq H(\pi(X, R) \mid R) \geq I(X; \pi(X, R) \mid R) = H(X \mid R) - H(X \mid R, \pi(X, R)) \geq (1-\delta)m \log k - m$. Since the entropy of a bit string is no more than its expected length, the lower bound follows.

Using the above lemma, we prove the following lower bound:

Theorem 14. *Any PPH for the exact Hamming distance predicate on ℓ-bit strings with threshold t and success probability at least $1 - \delta$ (This means that the direct access robustness error is at most δ.), must have an output length of $\Omega((1 - \delta)(t - 1) \log(\ell/t) - t)$ bits.*

Proof. Assume that there exists a PPH-family $\mathcal{H}$ for the predicate HAM^t and input length ℓ with $t \leq \ell$ and direct robustness error at most δ. Let s denote the output length of $\mathcal{H}$. We then use $\mathcal{H}$ to solve indexing with parameters $k = \lfloor \ell/t \rfloor$ and $m = t - 1$. When Alice receives a string $x \in [k]^m$, she constructs a binary string y consisting of m chunks of k bits. If $mk < \ell$, she pads this string with 0's. Each chunk in y has a single 1 in position x_i and 0's elsewhere. She then computes the hash value $h(y)$, where h is sampled from $\mathcal{H}$ using joint randomness, and sends it to Bob, costing s bits.

From his index $i \in [m]$, Bob constructs k bit strings $z_1, \ldots, z_k$ of length ℓ, such that z_j has a 1 in the position corresponding to the j'th position of the i'th chunk of y, and 0 everywhere else. He then computes the hash values $h(z_1), \ldots, h(z_k)$ (using the joint randomness to sample h) and runs $\mathsf{Eval}(h, h(y), h(z_j))$. Bob outputs as his guess for x_i, an index j, such that $\mathsf{Eval}(h, h(y), h(z_j)) = 0$. Notice that the Hamming distance between z_j and y is $m + 1 \geq t$ if $j \neq x_i$ and it is $m - 1 < t$ otherwise. Thus if all k evaluations are correct, Bob succeeds in reporting x_i. The probability that all evaluations are correct is at least $1 - \delta$, since otherwise an adversary could break the direct access robustness of $\mathcal{H}$ with probability greater than δ by sampling x and i uniformly at random, simulating the above protocol, checking for which z_j the evaluation is correct and outputting y, z_j. Thus, Bob is correct with probability at least $1 - \delta$. By Lemma 13, we conclude $s = \Omega((1 - \delta)(t - 1) \log(\ell/t) - t)$.

Remark 2. We note that for $\delta = \mathsf{negl}(\lambda)$, $t > 2$, and $\ell > 4t$ the lower bound from Theorem 14 simplifies to $\Omega(t \log(\ell/t))$.

References

1. Aggarwal, D., Dadush, D., Regev, O., Stephens-Davidowitz, N.: Solving the shortest vector problem in 2^n time using discrete Gaussian sampling: extended abstract. In: Servedio, R.A., Rubinfeld, R. (eds.) 47th Annual ACM Symposium on Theory of Computing, pp. 733–742. ACM Press, Portland, OR, USA (2015). https://doi.org/10.1145/2746539.2746606
2. Aggarwal, D., Li, J., Nguyen, P.Q., Stephens-Davidowitz, N.: Slide reduction, revisited—Filling the gaps in SVP approximation. In: Micciancio, D., Ristenpart, T. (eds.) CRYPTO 2020. LNCS, vol. 12171, pp. 274–295. Springer, Cham (2020). https://doi.org/10.1007/978-3-030-56880-1_10
3. Aggarwal, D., Stephens-Davidowitz, N.: Just take the average! An embarrassingly simple 2^n-time algorithm for SVP (and CVP). In: Seidel, R. (ed.) 1st Symposium on Simplicity in Algorithms (SOSA 2018). OpenAccess Series in Informatics (OASIcs), vol. 61, pp. 12:1–12:19. Schloss Dagstuhl-Leibniz-Zentrum fuer Informatik, Dagstuhl, Germany (2018). https://doi.org/10.4230/OASIcs.SOSA.2018.12
4. Ajtai, M.: Generating hard instances of lattice problems (extended abstract). In: 28th Annual ACM Symposium on Theory of Computing, pp. 99–108. ACM Press, Philadelphia, PA, USA (1996). https://doi.org/10.1145/237814.237838
5. Alon, N., Matias, Y., Szegedy, M.: The space complexity of approximating the frequency moments. In: 28th Annual ACM Symposium on Theory of Computing, pp. 20–29. ACM Press, Philadelphia, PA, USA (1996). https://doi.org/10.1145/237814.237823

6. Ben-Eliezer, O., Jayaram, R., Woodruff, D.P., Yogev, E.: A framework for adversarially robust streaming algorithms. In: Proceedings of the 39th ACM SIGMOD-SIGACT-SIGAI Symposium on Principles of Database Systems, pp. 63–80 (2020)
7. Ben-Eliezer, O., Yogev, E.: The adversarial robustness of sampling. In: Proceedings of the 39th ACM SIGMOD-SIGACT-SIGAI Symposium on Principles of Database Systems, pp. 49–62 (2020)
8. Bloom, B.H.: Space/time trade-offs in hash coding with allowable errors. Commun. ACM **13**(7), 422–426 (1970)
9. Boyle, E., LaVigne, R., Vaikuntanathan, V.: Adversarially robust property-preserving hash functions. In: Blum, A. (ed.) ITCS 2019: 10th Innovations in Theoretical Computer Science Conference, vol. 124, pp. 16:1–16:20. LIPIcs, San Diego, CA, USA (2019). https://doi.org/10.4230/LIPIcs.ITCS.2019.16
10. Clayton, D., Patton, C., Shrimpton, T.: Probabilistic data structures in adversarial environments. In: Cavallaro, L., Kinder, J., Wang, X., Katz, J. (eds.) ACM CCS 2019: 26th Conference on Computer and Communications Security, pp. 1317–1334. ACM Press (2019). https://doi.org/10.1145/3319535.3354235
11. Donoho, D.L.: Compressed sensing. IEEE Trans. Inf. Theory **52**(4), 1289–1306 (2006)
12. Fleischhacker, N., Simkin, M.: Robust property-preserving hash functions for hamming distance and more. In: Canteaut, A., Standaert, F.-X. (eds.) EUROCRYPT 2021. LNCS, vol. 12698, pp. 311–337. Springer, Cham (2021). https://doi.org/10.1007/978-3-030-77883-5_11
13. Goodrich, M.T., Mitzenmacher, M.: Invertible bloom lookup tables. In: 2011 49th Annual Allerton Conference on Communication, Control, and Computing (Allerton), pp. 792–799. IEEE (2011)
14. Hardt, M., Woodruff, D.P.: How robust are linear sketches to adaptive inputs? In: Boneh, D., Roughgarden, T., Feigenbaum, J. (eds.) 45th Annual ACM Symposium on Theory of Computing, pp. 121–130. ACM Press, Palo Alto, CA, USA (2013). https://doi.org/10.1145/2488608.2488624
15. Indyk, P., Motwani, R.: Approximate nearest neighbors: towards removing the curse of dimensionality. In: 30th Annual ACM Symposium on Theory of Computing, pp. 604–613. ACM Press, Dallas, TX, USA (1998). https://doi.org/10.1145/276698.276876
16. Lenstra, A.K., Lenstra, H.W., Lovász, L.: Factoring polynomials with rational coefficients. Math. Ann. **261**, 515–534 (1982)
17. Micciancio, D., Peikert, C.: Hardness of SIS and LWE with small parameters. In: Canetti, R., Garay, J.A. (eds.) CRYPTO 2013. LNCS, vol. 8042, pp. 21–39. Springer, Heidelberg (2013). https://doi.org/10.1007/978-3-642-40041-4_2
18. Miltersen, P.B., Nisan, N., Safra, S., Wigderson, A.: On data structures and asymmetric communication complexity. J. Comput. Syst. Sci. **57**(1), 37–49 (1998)
19. Mironov, I., Naor, M., Segev, G.: Sketching in adversarial environments. In: Ladner, R.E., Dwork, C. (eds.) 40th Annual ACM Symposium on Theory of Computing, pp. 651–660. ACM Press, Victoria, BC, Canada (2008). https://doi.org/10.1145/1374376.1374471
20. Muthukrishnan, S.: Data streams: algorithms and applications. In: 14th Annual ACM-SIAM Symposium on Discrete Algorithms, p. 413. ACM-SIAM, Baltimore, MD, USA (2003)
21. Naor, M., Yogev, E.: Bloom filters in adversarial environments. In: Gennaro, R., Robshaw, M. (eds.) CRYPTO 2015. LNCS, vol. 9216, pp. 565–584. Springer, Heidelberg (2015). https://doi.org/10.1007/978-3-662-48000-7_28

Short Pairing-Free Blind Signatures with Exponential Security

Stefano Tessaro and Chenzhi Zhu[✉]

Paul G. Allen School of Computer Science & Engineering,
University of Washington, Seattle, USA
{tessaro,zhucz20}@cs.washington.edu

Abstract. This paper proposes the first practical pairing-free three-move blind signature schemes that (1) are concurrently secure, (2) produce short signatures (i.e., *three* or *four* group elements/scalars), and (3) are provably secure either in the generic group model (GGM) or the algebraic group model (AGM) under the (plain or one-more) discrete logarithm assumption (beyond additionally assuming random oracles). We also propose a partially blind version of one of our schemes.

Our schemes do not rely on the hardness of the ROS problem (which can be broken in polynomial time) or of the mROS problem (which admits sub-exponential attacks). The only prior work with these properties is Abe's signature scheme (EUROCRYPT '02), which was recently proved to be secure in the AGM by Kastner et al. (PKC '22), but which also produces signatures twice as long as those from our scheme.

The core of our proofs of security is a new problem, called *weighted fractional* ROS (WFROS), for which we prove (unconditional) exponential lower bounds.

1 Introduction

Blind signatures [1] allow a *user* to interact with a *signer* to produce a valid signature that cannot be linked back by the signer to the interaction that produced it. Blind signatures are used in several applications, such as e-cash systems [1,2], anonymous credentials (e.g., [3]), privacy-preserving ad-click measurement [4], and various forms of anonymous tokens [5,6]. They are also covered by an RFC draft [7].

This paper develops the first practical pairing-free three-move blind signature schemes that (1) are concurrently secure, (2) produce short signatures (i.e., *three* or *four* group elements/scalars), and (3) are provably secure either in the *generic group model* (GGM) [8,9] or in the *algebraic group model* (AGM) [10] under the discrete logarithm (DL) or the one-more discrete logarithm (OMDL) assumption (in addition to assuming *random oracles* [11]). Our DL-based scheme also admits a *partially blind* version [12], roughly following a paradigm by Abe and Okamoto [13], that targets applications where signatures need to depend on some public input (e.g., an issuing date) known to the signer. An overview of our schemes is given in Table 1.

© International Association for Cryptologic Research 2022
O. Dunkelman and S. Dziembowski (Eds.): EUROCRYPT 2022, LNCS 13276, pp. 782–811, 2022.
https://doi.org/10.1007/978-3-031-07085-3_27

Unlike blind Schnorr [14], Okamoto-Schnorr [15], and other generic constructions based on identification schemes [16], we do not rely on the hardness of the ROS problem, for which a polynomial-time attack has recently been presented [17]. Also, unlike Clause Blind Schnorr (CBS) signatures [18], we do not rely on the assumed hardness of the mROS problem, which is subject to (mildly) sub-exponential attacks and we can thus support smaller group sizes.[1] In fact, our schemes all admit tight bounds, and this suggests that they can achieve $(\lambda/2)$-bit of security on λ-bit elliptic curves, supporting an instantiation with 256-bit curves. Our security proofs rely on a reduction to a new variant of the ROS problem, called *weighted fractional* ROS (WFROS), for which we prove an exponential, unconditional lower bound. Therefore, another benefit over CBS, beyond concrete parameters, is that we do not need to rely on an additional assumption.

Perhaps as a testament of the unsatisfactory status of pairing-free schemes, the *only* other scheme known to achieve exponential, concurrent, security is Abe's scheme [19]. Although its original (standard-model) proof was found to be flawed, proofs were then given both in the GGM [20] and the AGM [21], along with a proof for the restricted setting of sequential security [22]. Still, it produces longer signatures and public keys, and is overall less efficient. Also, it only offers computational blindness (under DDH), whereas our scheme provides perfect blindness.

DISCRETE-LOGARITHM BASED BLIND SIGNATURES. We stress that our focus here is making pairing-free schemes as practical and as secure as possible. Indeed, very simple pairing-based blind signature schemes in the ROM can be obtained from BLS signatures [23,24]. Blind BLS offers a different trade-off: signatures are short (i.e., one group element) and signing requires only *two* moves, but signature verification requires a more expensive (and more complex) pairing evaluation. Indeed, the current blind signature RFC draft [7] favors RSA over BLS, also due to lesser availability of pairings implementations. In particular, several envisioned applications of blind signatures are inherently browser-based, and the available cryptographic libraries (e.g., NSS for Firefox and BoringSSL for Chrome) do not yet offer pairing-friendly curve implementations.

In contrast, (non-blind) Schnorr signatures [25,26] (such as EdDSA [27]) are short, can rely on standard libraries, and outperform RSA. Though their blind evaluation requires three rounds, this may be less concerning in applications where verification cost is the dominating factor and the signing application can easily keep state. Indeed, [7] identifies CBS as the only plausible alternative to RSA, and our schemes improve upon CBS by avoiding the mROS assumption. Once the group order is adjusted to resist sub-exponential attacks, we achieve comparable signature size, more efficient signing, and accommodate for partial

---

[1] The best known attack against mROS [18] runs in time $2^{\ell+\log(\ell+1)+\lambda/(1+\log(\ell+1))}$, where λ is the security parameter and ℓ corresponds to the number of concurrent sessions. The worst ℓ gives a $2^{O(\lambda/\log\lambda)}$ attack, and in practice, this suggests a choice of $\lambda = 512$ to achieve 128-bit security for all ℓ's.

Table 1. Overview of our results. The four schemes proposed in this paper compared to pairing-free schemes that admit GGM/AGM security proofs in the literature. All schemes are three-move and secure assuming the ROM; All schemes except BS$_1$ admit AGM security proofs; further $p = |\mathbb{G}|$. As in plain Schnorr signatures, most schemes allow replacing one element in $\mathbb{Z}_p$ with a group element in the signature. The ROS assumption can be broken in polynomial time unless the scheme is restricted to tolerate only a very small number of sessions. Also, the mROS assumption admits sub-exponential attacks, which require the choice of a larger order p over all schemes (roughly 512-bit for 128-bit security [18]).

Scheme	PK size	Sig. size	Assumption	Communication
BS$_1$ (Sect. 4)	1 G	3 $\mathbb{Z}_p$	GGM	2 G + 3 $\mathbb{Z}_p$
BS$_2$ (full version)	1 G	4 $\mathbb{Z}_p$	OMDL	2 G + 4 $\mathbb{Z}_p$
BS$_3$ (Sect. 5.1)	2 G	4 $\mathbb{Z}_p$	DL	2 G + 4 $\mathbb{Z}_p$
PBS (Sect. 6)	1 G	4 $\mathbb{Z}_p$	DL	2 G + 4 $\mathbb{Z}_p$
Blind Schnorr [18]	1 G	2 $\mathbb{Z}_p$	OMDL + ROS	1 G + 2 $\mathbb{Z}_p$
Clause Blind Schnorr [18]	1 G	2 $\mathbb{Z}_p$	OMDL + mROS	2 G + 4 $\mathbb{Z}_p$
Abe [19,21]	3 G	2 G + 6 $\mathbb{Z}_p$	DL	λ bits + 3 G + 6 $\mathbb{Z}_p$

blindness. (No partially blind version of CBS is known to the best of our knowledge.)

Finally, note that it is easier to prove security of pairing-free schemes under sequential access to the signer. For example, Kastner et al. [21] prove that plain blind Schnorr signatures are secure in this case, in the AGM, assuming the hardness of OMDL. Also, Baldimtsi and Lysyanskaya [22] (implicitly) prove sequential security of Abe's scheme. However, many applications, like PCM, easily enable concurrent attacks.

ON IDEAL MODELS. The use of the AGM or the GGM, along with the ROM, still appears necessary for the most practical pairing-free schemes with concurrent security. As of now, solutions solely assuming the ROM can only handle bounded concurrency [16] or, alternatively, their communication and computation costs grow with the number of signing sessions [28–30].

A number of other schemes [31–37] partially or completely avoid ideal models, some of which are fairly practical. However, they do not yet appear suitable for at-scale deployment.

1.1 A Scheme in the GGM

Our simplest scheme only admits a proof in the generic-group model (GGM) but best illustrates our ideas, in particular, how we bypass ROS-style attacks. It is slightly less efficient than Schnorr signatures, i.e., a signature that consists of *three* scalars mod p (or alternatively, two scalars and a group element). Nonetheless, it has a very similar flavor (in particular, signature verification can be built on top of a suitable implementation of Schnorr signatures in a black-box way).

PREFACE: BLIND SCHNORR SIGNATURES AND ROS. Recall that we seek an interactive scheme (1) that is one-more unforgeable (i.e., no adversary should be able to generate $\ell + 1$ signatures by interacting only ℓ times with the signer), and (2) for which interaction can be blinded. It is helpful to illustrate the main technical barrier behind proving (1) for *interactive* Schnorr signatures. Recall that the verification key is $X = g^x$ for a generator g of a cyclic group $\mathbb{G}$ of prime order p, and a signing key x. The signer starts the session by sending $A = g^a$, for a random $a \in \mathbb{Z}_p$. Then, the user sends a challenge $c = H(A, m)$ for a hash function H and a message m to be signed. Finally, the signer responds with $s = a + c \cdot x$, and the signature is $\sigma = (c, s)$.

Let us now consider an adversary that obtains ℓ initial messages $A_1, \ldots, A_\ell$ from the signer, where $A_i = g^{a_i}$. By solving the so-called *ROS problem* [16,18,38], the attacker can find $\ell+1$ vectors $\boldsymbol{\alpha}_1, \ldots, \boldsymbol{\alpha}_{\ell+1} \in \mathbb{Z}_p^\ell$ and a vector $(c_1, \ldots, c_\ell) \in \mathbb{Z}_p^\ell$ such that

$$\sum_{j=1}^{\ell} \alpha_i^{(j)} \cdot c_j = c_i^* \tag{1}$$

for all $i \in [\ell + 1]$, where $c_i^* = H(\prod_{j=1}^{\ell} A_j^{\alpha_i^{(j)}}, m_i^*)$, for some message $m_i^* \in \{0,1\}^*$. (Here, $\alpha_i^{(j)}$ is the j-th component of $\boldsymbol{\alpha}_i$.) Then, the attacker can obtain $s_j = a_j + c_j x$ from the signer for all $j \in [\ell]$ by completing the ℓ signing sessions. It is now easy to verify that (c_i^*, s_i^*) is a valid signature for m_i^* for all $i \in [\ell+1]$, where $s_i^* = \sum_{j=1}^{\ell} \alpha_i^{(j)} \cdot s_j$. Benhamouda et al. [17] recently gave a simple polynomial-time algorithm to solve the ROS problem for the case $\ell > \log(p)$, which thus breaks one-more unforgeability.[2]

Fuchsbauer et al. [18] propose a different interactive signing process for Schnorr signatures that is one-more unforgeable (in the AGM + ROM) assuming that a variant of the ROS problem, called mROS, is hard. The mROS problem, however, admits sub-exponential attacks, and as it gives approximately only 70 bits of security from an implementation on a 256-bit curve, it effectively forces the use of 512-bit curves.[3]

OUR FIRST SCHEME. We take a different path which completely avoids the ROS and mROS problems to obtain our first scheme, BS_1. Again, we present a non-blind version – the scheme can be made blind via fairly standard tricks, as we explain in the body of the paper below. Again, the public key is $X = g^x$ for a secret key x. Then, the signer and the user engage in the following protocol to sign $m \in \{0,1\}^*$:

1. The signer sends $A = g^a$ and $Y = X^y$ for random $a, y \in \mathbb{Z}_p$.
2. The user responds with $c = H(A, Y, m)$

---

[2] Many envisioned implementations allow for $\ell > \log(p)$. Still, is worth noting that the scheme retains some security for $\ell < \log(p)$ even in the standard model [16].

[3] mROS depends on a parameter ℓ, with a similar role as in ROS – sub-exponential attacks require $\ell < \log(p)$, but a one-more unforgeability attack for a small ℓ implies one for any $\ell' > \ell$ simply by generating $(\ell' - \ell)$ additional valid signatures.

3. The signer returns a pair (s, y), where $s = a + cxy$.
4. The user accepts the signature $\sigma = (c, s, y)$ iff $g^s = A \cdot Y^c$ and $Y = X^y$.

Verification simply checks that $H(g^s X^{-yc}, X^y, M) = c$. In particular, note that (c, s) is a valid Schnorr signature with respect to the public-key X^y – this can be leveraged to implement the verification algorithm on top of an existing implementation of basic Schnorr signatures that also hash the public key (EdDSA does exactly this).[4] Further, as in Schnorr signatures, we could replace c with A in σ, and our results would be unaffected.

SECURITY INTUITION. To gather initial insights about the security of BS_1, it is instructive to *attempt* an ROS-style attack. The attacker opens ℓ sessions and obtains pairs $(A_1, Y_1), \ldots, (A_\ell, Y_\ell)$, where $A_i = g^{a_i}$ and $Y_i = X^{y_i} = g^{xy_i}$ for all $i \in [\ell]$. One natural extension of the ROS attack is to find $\ell + 1$ vectors $\boldsymbol{\alpha}_i \in \mathbb{Z}_p^\ell$ along with messages $m_1^*, m_2^*, \ldots \in \{0, 1\}^*$ such that

$$c_i^* = H \left(\prod_{j=1}^{\ell} A_j^{\alpha_i^{(j)}}, \prod_{j=1}^{\ell} Y_j^{\alpha_i^{(j)}}, m_i^* \right)$$

for all $i \in [\ell + 1]$ and then find $(c_1, \ldots, c_\ell) \in \mathbb{Z}_p^\ell$ such that

$$\sum_{j=1}^{\ell} \alpha_i^{(j)} \cdot y_j \cdot c_j = c_i^* \cdot \sum_{j=1}^{\ell} \alpha_i^{(j)} \cdot y_j , \tag{2}$$

for all $i \in [\ell + 1]$. Indeed, if this succeeded, the adversary could complete the ℓ sessions to learn (s_j, y_j) by inputting c_j, where y_j is random and $s_j = a_j + c_j \cdot x \cdot y_j$. One could generate $\ell + 1$ signatures (c_i^*, s_i^*, y_i^*) for $i \in [\ell + 1]$ by setting $s_i^* = \sum_{j=1}^{\ell} \alpha_i^{(j)} s_j$ and $y_i^* = \sum_{j=1}^{\ell} \alpha_i^{(j)} \cdot y_j$. These would be valid because

$$g^{s_i^*} = g^{\sum_{j=1}^{\ell} \alpha_i^{(j)}(a_j + c_j x y_j)}$$

$$= \prod_{j=1}^{\ell} A_j^{\alpha_i^{(j)}} \cdot X^{\sum_{j=1}^{\ell} \alpha_i^{(j)} c_j y_j} \overset{(2)}{=} \prod_{j=1}^{\ell} A_j^{\alpha_i^{(j)}} \cdot \left(\prod_{j=1}^{\ell} Y_j^{\alpha_i^{(j)}} \right)^{c_i^*} .$$

However, finding $(c_1, \ldots, c_\ell)$ that satisfy (2) for $\ell + 1$ i's simultaneously is *much harder* than ROS. An initial intuition here is that X^y *completely hides* y to the point where y is revealed later in the session, where it appears like a random and fresh weight in the sum, *independent of c_i*. This intuition is however not correct, as an attacker can use the group element X^y and can try to gain information about y, but our proof will show (among other things) that in the GGM no useful information is obtained about y, and y is (close to) uniform when it is later revealed.

---

[4] Note that this only superficially resembles key-blinding for Schnorr signatures [39]. Here, the "blinding" y is actually public and part of the signature.

THE WFROS PROBLEM. The above attack paradigm is in fact generalized in terms of a new ROS-like problem that we call WFROS (this stands for *Weighted Fractional ROS*), for which we prove an unconditional lower bound. WFROS considers a game with two oracles that can be invoked adaptively in an interleaved way:

- The first oracle, H, accepts as input a pair of vectors $\boldsymbol{\alpha}, \boldsymbol{\beta} \in \mathbb{Z}_p^{2\ell+1}$, which are then associated with a random $\delta \in \mathbb{Z}_p^*$.
- The second oracle, S, allows to bind, for some $i \in [\ell]$, chosen input $c_i \in \mathbb{Z}_p$ with a random *weight* $y_i \in \mathbb{Z}_p^*$. During the course of the game, this latter oracle must be called *exactly* once for each $i \in [\ell]$.

The adversary finally commits to a subset of $\ell + 1$ prior H queries and wins if for each query in the subset, which has defined a pair of vector $\boldsymbol{\alpha}, \boldsymbol{\beta}$ and returned δ, we have $A/B = \delta$, where

$$A = \alpha^{(0)} + \sum_{i \in [\ell]} y_i(\alpha^{(2i-1)} + c_i \cdot \alpha^{(2i)}), \quad B = \beta^{(0)} + \sum_{i \in [\ell]} y_i(\beta^{(2i-1)} + c_i \cdot \beta^{(2i)}).$$

Here, $v^{(i)}$ denotes the i-th component of vector $\boldsymbol{v}$. Our main result (Theorem 1) says that no adversary making Q_H queries to H can win this game with probability better than $(Q_H^2 + 2\ell Q_H)/(p-1)$, or, in other words, $Q_H \geqslant \min\{\sqrt{p}, p/\ell\}$ is needed to win with constant probability. Note that $\ell \ll \sqrt{p}$ is generally true, as for our usage, ℓ is bounded by the number of signing sessions.

Our GGM proof for BS_1 transforms any generic attacker into one breaking the WFROS problem. This transformation is actually not immediate because a one-more unforgeability attacker can learn functions of the secret key x when obtaining the second message from the signer. A similar challenge occurs in proving hardness of the OMDL problem in the GGM, which was recently resolved by Bauer et al. [40], and we rely on their techniques.

1.2 AGM Security and Partial Blindness

The Algebraic Group Model (AGM) [10] can be seen as a weaker idealization than the GGM. In particular, AGM proofs deal with actual groups (as opposed to representing group elements with random labels) and proceed via *reductions* that apply only to "algebraic adversaries", which provide representation of the group elements they output to the reduction. AGM has become a very popular model for validating security of a number of practical group-based protocols.

The main barrier to proving one-more unforgeability of BS_1 in the AGM is that the representation of X^y could leak some information about y that would not be available in the GGM, and thus we would not be able to apply our argument showing that y is still (close to) random looking when it is later revealed – our reduction in the GGM security proof crucially relies on this. To overcome this issue, for the two schemes BS_2 and BS_3, we replace X^y with a *hiding* commitment to y. In particular, we propose two different ways of achieving this:

Scheme BS$_2$. Here, X^y is replaced by $g^t X^y$. Later, the signer responds to challenge c with (s, y, t), where $s = a + c \cdot y \cdot x$. A signature is $\sigma = (c, s, y, t)$.

Scheme BS$_3$. Here, $g^t X^y$ is replaced by $g^t Z^y$, where Z is an extra random group element included in the verification key.

We consider BS$_2$ mostly for pedagogical reasons. Indeed, we can prove security of BS$_3$ in the AGM based *solely* on the discrete logarithm problem (DL). In contrast, BS$_2$ relies on the hardness of the (stronger) *one-more* DL problem (OMDL) [41], which asks for the hardness of breaking $\ell + 1$ DL instances given access to an oracle that can solve at most ℓ (adaptively chosen) DL instances. While we know that OMDL is generally not easier than DL [40], a prudent instantiation may prefer relying on the (non-interactive) DL problem. While BS$_3$ requires a longer key, one could mitigate this by obtaining Z as the output of a hash function (assumed to be a random oracle) evaluated on some public input.

The proof of security for both schemes consists of showing that any adversary breaking one-more unforgeability can be transformed into one breaking either OMDL or DL (depending on the scheme) *or* into one breaking the WFROS problem. For the latter, however, we can resort to our unconditional hardness lower bound (Theorem 1).

ADDING PARTIAL BLINDNESS. Finally, we note that it is not too hard to add partial blindness to BS$_3$, which is another reason to consider this scheme. In particular, to obtain the resulting PBS scheme, we can adopt a framework by Abe and Okamoto [13]. The main idea is simply to use a hash function (modeled as a random oracle) to generate the extra group element Z in a way that is dependent on a public input upon which the signature depends. We target in particular a stronger notion of one-more unforgeability, which shows that if the protocol is run ℓ times for a public input, then no $\ell+1$ signatures can be generated for that public input regardless of how many signatures have been generated for *different* public inputs. We defer more details to Sect. 6.

Outline of the Paper

Section 2 will introduce some basic preliminaries. Section 3 will then introduce the WFROS problem, and prove a lower bound for it. We will then discuss our GGM-based scheme in Sect. 4, whereas variants secure in the AGM are presented in Sect. 5. Finally, we give a partially blind instantiation of our AGM scheme in Sect. 6.

2   Preliminaries

NOTATION. For positive integer n, we write $[n]$ for $\{1, \ldots, n\}$. We use λ to denote the security parameter. We use $\mathbb{G}$ to denote an (asymptotic) family of cyclic groups $\mathbb{G} := \{\mathbb{G}_\lambda\}_{\lambda>0}$, where $|\mathbb{G}_\lambda| > 2^\lambda$. We use $g(\mathbb{G}_\lambda)$ to denote the generator of $\mathbb{G}_\lambda$, and we will work over prime-order groups. We tacitly assume standard group operations can be performed in time polynomial in λ in $\mathbb{G}_\lambda$ and adopt multiplicative notation. We will often compute over the finite field $\mathbb{Z}_p$ (for a prime p) – we usually do not write modular reduction explicitly when it is clear from the context. We write $\mathbb{Z}_p^* = \mathbb{Z}_p \setminus \{0\}$. We often need to consider vectors $\boldsymbol{\alpha} \in \mathbb{Z}_p^\ell$ and usually refer to the i-th component of $\boldsymbol{\alpha}$ as $\alpha^{(i)} \in \mathbb{Z}_p$.

BLIND SIGNATURES. This paper focuses on *three-move* blind signature schemes, and our notation is similar to that of prior works (e.g., [16,18]). Formally, a (three-move) *blind signature scheme* BS is a tuple of efficient (randomized) algorithms

$$\text{BS} = (\text{BS.Setup}, \text{BS.KG}, \text{BS.S}_1, \text{BS.S}_2, \text{BS.U}_1, \text{BS.U}_2, \text{BS.Ver}) ,$$

with the following behavior:

- The *parameter generation* algorithm $\text{BS.Setup}(1^\lambda)$ outputs a string of parameters *par*, whereas the *key generation* algorithm $\text{BS.KG}(par)$ outputs a keypair (sk, pk), where sk is the *secret* (or *signing*) key and pk is the *public* (or *verification*) key.
- The interaction between the user and the signer to sign a message $m \in \{0,1\}^*$ with key-pair (pk, sk) is defined by the following experiment:

$$(\text{st}^s, \text{msg}_1) \leftarrow \text{BS.S}_1(sk) , \quad (\text{st}^u, \text{chl}) \leftarrow \text{BS.U}_1(pk, \text{msg}_1, m) ,$$
$$\text{msg}_2 \leftarrow \text{BS.S}_2(\text{st}^s, \text{chl}) , \quad \sigma \leftarrow \text{BS.U}_2(\text{st}^u, \text{msg}_2) . \tag{3}$$

Here, σ is either the resulting *signature* or an *error message* $\bot$.
- The (deterministic) *verification algorithm* outputs a bit $\text{BS.Ver}(pk, \sigma, m)$.

We say that BS is (perfectly) *correct* if for every message $m \in \{0,1\}^*$, with probability one over the sampling of parameters and the key pair (pk, sk), the experiment in (3) returns σ such that $\text{BS.Ver}(pk, \sigma, m) = 1$. All of our schemes are going to be perfectly correct.

ONE-MORE UNFORGEABILITY. The standard notion of security for blind signatures is *one-more unforgeability* (OMUF). OMUF ensures that no adversary playing the role of a user interacting with the signer ℓ times, in an arbitrarily concurrent fashion, can issue $\ell + 1$ signatures (or more, of course). The $\text{OMUF}_{\text{BS}}^{\mathcal{A}}$ game for a blind signature scheme BS is defined in Fig. 1. The corresponding advantage of $\mathcal{A}$ is defined as $\text{Adv}_{\text{BS}}^{\text{omuf}}(\mathcal{A}, \lambda) := \Pr[\text{OMUF}_{\text{BS}}^{\mathcal{A}}(\lambda) = 1]$. All of our analyses will further assume one or more random oracles, which are modeled as an additional oracle to which the adversary $\mathcal{A}$ is given access.

BLINDNESS. We also consider the standard notion of blindness against a malicious server that can, in particular, attempt to publish a malformed public key. The corresponding game $\text{Blind}_{\text{BS}}^{\mathcal{A}}$ is defined in Fig. 2, and for any adversary $\mathcal{A}$, we define its advantage as $\text{Adv}_{\text{BS}}^{\text{blind}}(\mathcal{A}, \lambda) := \left| \Pr[\text{Blind}_{\text{BS}}^{\mathcal{A}}(\lambda) = 1] - \frac{1}{2} \right|$. We say the scheme is perfectly blind if and only if $\text{Adv}_{\text{BS}}^{\text{blind}}(\mathcal{A}, \lambda) = 0$ for any $\mathcal{A}$ and all λ.

Game $\mathrm{OMUF}_{\mathsf{BS}}^{\mathcal{A}}(\lambda)$:	Oracle S_1 :
$par \leftarrow \mathsf{BS.Setup}(1^\lambda)$	$sid \leftarrow sid + 1$
$(sk, pk) \leftarrow \mathsf{BS.KG}(par)$	$(\mathsf{st}_{sid}^s, \mathsf{msg}_1) \leftarrow \mathsf{BS.S}_1(sk)$
$sid \leftarrow 0 \; ; \; \ell \leftarrow 0 \; ; \; \mathcal{I}_{\mathrm{fin}} \leftarrow \varnothing$	Return (sid, msg_1)
$\{(m_k^*, \sigma_k^*)\}_{k \in [\ell+1]} \leftarrow^{\$} \mathcal{A}^{\mathsf{S}_1, \mathsf{S}_2}(pk)$	
If $\exists \; k_1 \neq k_2$ such that $(m_{k_1}^*, \sigma_{k_1}^*) = (m_{k_2}^*, \sigma_{k_2}^*)$	Oracle $\mathsf{S}_2(i, c_i)$:
then return 0	If $i \notin [sid] \backslash \mathcal{I}_{\mathrm{fin}}$ then return $\bot$
If $\exists \; k \in [\ell+1]$ such that $\mathsf{BS.Ver}(pk, \sigma_k^*, m_k^*) = 0$	$\mathsf{msg}_2 \leftarrow \mathsf{BS.S}_2(\mathsf{st}_i^s, c_i)$
then return 0	$\mathcal{I}_{\mathrm{fin}} \leftarrow \mathcal{I}_{\mathrm{fin}} \cup \{i\}$
Return 1	$\ell \leftarrow \ell + 1$
	Return msg_2

Fig. 1. The OMUF security game for a blind signature scheme BS.

Game $\mathrm{Blind}_{\mathsf{BS}}^{\mathcal{A}}(\lambda)$:	Oracle $\mathsf{U}_1(i, \mathsf{msg}_1^{(i)})$:
$par \leftarrow \mathsf{BS.Setup}(1^\lambda)$	If $i \notin \{0, 1\}$ or $sess_i \neq \mathtt{init}$ then return $\bot$
$b \leftarrow^{\$} \{0, 1\} \; ; \; b_0 \leftarrow b \; ; \; b_1 \leftarrow 1 - b$	$sess_i \leftarrow \mathtt{open}$
$b' \leftarrow^{\$} \mathcal{A}^{\mathrm{INIT}, \mathsf{U}_1, \mathsf{U}_2}(par)$	$(\mathsf{st}_i^u, \mathsf{chl}^{(i)}) \leftarrow \mathsf{BS.U}_1(pk, \mathsf{msg}_1^{(i)}, m_{b_i})$
If $b' = b$ then return 1	Return $\mathsf{chl}^{(i)}$
Return 0	
	Oracle $\mathsf{U}_2(i, \mathsf{msg}_2^{(i)})$:
Oracle $\mathrm{INIT}(\tilde{pk}, \tilde{m}_0, \tilde{m}_1)$:	If $i \notin \{0, 1\}$ or $sess_i \neq \mathtt{open}$ then return $\bot$
$sess_0 \leftarrow \mathtt{init}$	$sess_i \leftarrow \mathtt{closed}$
$sess_1 \leftarrow \mathtt{init}$	$\sigma_{b_i} \leftarrow \mathsf{BS.U}_2(\mathsf{st}_i^u, \mathsf{msg}_2^{(i)})$
$pk \leftarrow \tilde{pk}$	If $sess_0 = sess_1 = \mathtt{closed}$ then
$m_0 \leftarrow \tilde{m}_0 \; ; \; m_1 \leftarrow \tilde{m}_1$	If $\sigma_0 = \bot$ or $\sigma_1 = \bot$ then return $(\bot, \bot)$
	Return (σ_0, σ_1)
	Return $(i, \mathtt{closed})$

Fig. 2. The Blind security game for a blind signature scheme BS.

GAME-PLAYING PROOFS. Several of our proofs adopt a lightweight variant of the standard "Game-Playing Framework" by Bellare and Rogaway [42].

3 The Weighted Fractional ROS Problem

This section introduces and analyzes an unconditionally hard problem underlying all of our proofs, which we call the *Weighted Fractional ROS* problem (WFROS). It is a variant of the original ROS problem [16,18,38], which, in turn, stands for <u>R</u>andom inhomogeneities in a <u>O</u>verdetermined <u>S</u>olvable system *of linear equations*. While ROS can be solved in polynomial time [17] and its mROS variant can be solved in sub-exponential time [18], we are going to prove an *exponential* lower bound for WFROS.

THE WFROS PROBLEM. The problem is defined via the game $\mathrm{WFROS}_{\ell,p}^{\mathcal{A}}$, described in Fig. 3, which involves an adversary $\mathcal{A}$ and depends on two integer parameters ℓ and p, where p is a prime. The adversary here interacts with

Game WFROS$_{\ell,p}^{\mathcal{A}}$:	Oracle H$(\boldsymbol{\alpha},\boldsymbol{\beta})$:
hid $\leftarrow 0$; $\mathcal{I}_{\text{fin}} \leftarrow \varnothing$	hid $\leftarrow$ hid $+1$
$\mathcal{J} \leftarrow \mathcal{A}^{\text{H},\text{S}}(p)$	$\boldsymbol{\alpha}_{\text{hid}} \leftarrow \boldsymbol{\alpha}$; $\boldsymbol{\beta}_{\text{hid}} \leftarrow \boldsymbol{\beta}$
If $\mathcal{J} \not\subseteq [\text{hid}]$ or $|\mathcal{J}| \leqslant \ell$ or $\mathcal{I}_{\text{fin}} \neq [\ell]$ then	$\delta_{\text{hid}} \leftarrow\!\!{\$}\ \mathbb{Z}_p^*$
$\quad$ Return 0	Return δ_{hid}, hid
For each $j \in \mathcal{J}$,	
$\quad A_j \leftarrow \alpha_j^{(0)} + \sum_{i \in [\ell]} y_i(\alpha_j^{(2i-1)} + c_i \cdot \alpha_j^{(2i)})$	Oracle S(i, c_i) :
$\quad B_j \leftarrow \beta_j^{(0)} + \sum_{i \in [\ell]} y_i(\beta_j^{(2i-1)} + c_i \cdot \beta_j^{(2i)})$	If $i \notin [\ell] \backslash \mathcal{I}_{\text{fin}}$ then return $\bot$
If $\forall j \in \mathcal{J} : (A_j = \delta_j B_j \ \wedge\ B_j \neq 0)$ then	$y_i \leftarrow\!\!{\$}\ \mathbb{Z}_p^*$
$\quad$ Return 1	$\mathcal{I}_{\text{fin}} \leftarrow \mathcal{I}_{\text{fin}} \cup \{i\}$
Return 0	Return y_i

Fig. 3. The WFROS problem. Here, $\boldsymbol{\alpha},\boldsymbol{\beta} \in \mathbb{Z}_p^{2\ell+1}$, which is indexed as $\boldsymbol{\alpha} = (\alpha^{(0)},\ldots,\alpha^{(2\ell)})$ and $\boldsymbol{\beta} = (\beta^{(0)},\ldots,\beta^{(2\ell)})$.

two oracles, H and S. The first oracle allows the adversary to link a vector pair $\boldsymbol{\alpha},\boldsymbol{\beta} \in \mathbb{Z}_p^{2\ell+1}$ with a random inhomogeneous part $\delta \in \mathbb{Z}_p^*$ – each such query defines implicitly an equation $A/B = \delta$ in the unknowns $C_1,\ldots,C_\ell$ and $Y_1,\ldots,Y_\ell$. A call to S(i,c_i) lets us set the value of C_i to c_i and set Y_i to a random value y_i. The second oracle S$(i,\cdot)$ must be called once for every $i \in [\ell]$. It is noteworthy to stress that the c_i's can be chosen arbitrarily, whereas the corresponding y_i's are random and independent.

In the end, the adversary wins the game if a subset of $\ell+1$ equations defined by the H queries is satisfied by the assignment defined by querying S. In particular, we define $\mathsf{Adv}_{\ell,p}^{\text{wfros}}(\mathcal{A}) = \Pr\left[\text{WFROS}_{\ell,p}^{\mathcal{A}} = 1\right]$. Note that it would be possible to carry out some of the following security proofs using restricted versions of the WFROS game, but the above formulation lets us handle all schemes via a single notion.

A LOWER BOUND FOR WFROS. The following theorem, our main result on WFROS, shows that any adversary winning WFROS with constant probability requires $Q_H = \Omega(\min\{\sqrt{p}, p/\ell\})$ queries. (Also, note that all applications of interest assume $\ell \ll \sqrt{p}$.)

Theorem 1 (Lower bound for WFROS). *For any $\ell > 0$, any prime number p, and any adversary $\mathcal{A}$ playing the WFROS$^{\ell,p}$ game that makes at most Q_H queries to H, we have*

$$\mathsf{Adv}_{\ell,p}^{\text{wfros}}(\mathcal{A}) \leqslant \frac{Q_H(2\ell + Q_H)}{p-1} .$$

The proof is given in the next section. To gain some very high-level intuition, we observe that a key contributor to the hardness of WFROS are values y_i, which are defined *after* the c_i's are fixed and hence randomize the A_j and B_j's. Therefore, to satisfy $A_j = \delta_j \cdot B_j$, the adversary is restricted in the way it plays. For example, to satisfy an equation defined by an H query $(\boldsymbol{\alpha}_j,\boldsymbol{\beta}_j)$, the adversary can pick c_i's such that $(\alpha_j^{(2i-1)} + c_i \alpha_j^{(2i)}) = \delta_j \cdot (\beta_j^{(2i-1)} + c_i \beta_j^{(2i)})$ for all $i \in [\ell]$. Then, the equation $A_j = \delta_j B_j$ is satisfied no matter what the y_i's are. Our proof shows that the adversary *has* to pick c_i's this way – and in fact, it has to follow even more restrictions. Finally, we show that under these restrictions, no set of $\ell + 1$ equations can be satisfied simultaneously.

3.1   Proof of Theorem 1

Let $\mathcal{A}$ be an adversary for the WFROS game that makes at most Q_H queries to H. Without loss of generality, we assume that $\mathcal{A}$ makes exactly one query (i, c_i) to S for each $i \in [\ell]$ and that $\mathcal{A}$ always outputs $\mathcal{J} \subseteq [Q_H]$.

In the $\text{WFROS}_{\ell,p}^{\mathcal{A}}$ game, for each $j \in [Q_H]$, denote the event W_j as

$$\alpha_j^{(0)} + \sum_{i\in[\ell]} y_i(\alpha_j^{(2i-1)} + c_i \cdot \alpha_j^{(2i)}) = \delta_j \left(\beta_j^{(0)} + \sum_{i\in[\ell]} y_i(\beta_j^{(2i-1)} + c_i \cdot \beta_j^{(2i)})\right) \quad (\text{W1})$$

$$\wedge \ \beta_j^{(0)} + \sum_{i\in[\ell]} y_i(\beta_j^{(2i-1)} + c_i \cdot \beta_j^{(2i)}) \neq 0 . \quad (\text{W2})$$

In other words, W_j is the event that the equation defined by the j-th H query is satisfied. Then, $\mathcal{A}$ wins if and only if $|\mathcal{J}| > \ell$ and W_j occur for each $j \in \mathcal{J}$. Denote $W := (|\mathcal{J}| > \ell) \wedge \left(\bigwedge_{j\in\mathcal{J}} W_j\right)$ and we have $\text{Adv}_{\ell,p}^{\text{wfros}}(\mathcal{A}) = \Pr[W]$.

To bound $\Pr[W]$, we need notation to refer to some values (formally, random variables) defined in the execution of the $\text{WFROS}_{\ell,p}^{\mathcal{A}}$ game. First, denote as $\mathcal{I}_{\text{fin}}^{(j)}$ the contents of the set $\mathcal{I}_{\text{fin}}$ when the adversary makes the j-th query to H, and let (α_j, β_j) be the input of this query to H, which is answered with δ_j. Also, let $\mathcal{I}_{\text{unk}}^{(j)} := [\ell] \setminus \mathcal{I}_{\text{fin}}^{(j)}$, i.e., the set of indices $i \in [\ell]$ for which $\mathcal{A}$ has not yet made any query $(i, \cdot)$ to S when the j-th query to H is made. Further, $c_1, \ldots, c_\ell$ and $y_1, \ldots, y_\ell$ are the values defined by querying S.

Now, for each $j \in [Q_H]$, we define the following events:

Event $E_j^{(1)}$. First, let $E_{1,j}^{(1)}$ be the event that $\beta_j^{(0)} + \sum_{i\in\mathcal{I}_{\text{fin}}^{(j)}} y_i \left(\beta_j^{(2i-1)} + c_i \cdot \beta_j^{(2i)}\right)$ $\neq 0$. For each $i \in \mathcal{I}_{\text{unk}}^{(j)}$, also let $E_{2,(j,i)}^{(1)}$ be the event that $\alpha_j^{(2i-1)} + c_i \cdot \alpha_j^{(2i)} \neq$ $\delta_j \left(\beta_j^{(2i-1)} + c_i \cdot \beta_j^{(2i)}\right)$. Finally, let $E_j^{(1)} := E_{1,j}^{(1)} \vee \left(\bigvee_{i\in\mathcal{I}_{\text{unk}}^{(j)}} E_{2,(j,i)}^{(1)}\right)$.

Event $E_j^{(2)}$. We denote the event $E_j^{(2)}$ as the event where

$$\forall \ i \in \mathcal{I}_{\text{unk}}^{(j)} : \alpha_j^{(2i)} \cdot \beta_j^{(2i-1)} = \alpha_j^{(2i-1)} \cdot \beta_j^{(2i)} . \quad (4)$$

Note that events $E_j^{(1)}$ and $E_j^{(2)}$ are, by themselves, not necessarily unlikely – the adversary can certainly provoke them. However, we intend to show that this has implications on the ability to satisfy the j-th equation. In particular, we prove the following two lemmas in Sects. 3.2 and 3.3 below, respectively.

Lemma 1. $\Pr[W_j \wedge E_j^{(1)}] \leq \frac{\ell+1}{p-1}$.

Lemma 2. $\Pr[W_j \wedge (\neg E_j^{(1)}) \wedge E_j^{(2)}] \leq \frac{\ell}{p-1}$.

Now, if we denote $E^{(1)} := \bigvee_{j\in[Q_{\mathrm{H}}]}(W_j \wedge E_j^{(1)})$ and $E^{(2)} := \bigvee_{j\in[Q_{\mathrm{H}}]}(W_j \wedge (\neg E_j^{(1)}) \wedge E_j^{(2)})$, the union bound yields $\Pr[E^{(1)}] \leq \frac{Q_{\mathrm{H}}(\ell+1)}{p-1}$ and $\Pr[E^{(2)}] \leq \frac{Q_{\mathrm{H}}\cdot\ell}{p-1}$. Our final lemma (proved in Sect. 3.4) is then the following:

Lemma 3. $\Pr[W \wedge (\neg E^{(1)}) \wedge (\neg E^{(2)})] \leq \frac{Q_{\mathrm{H}}(Q_{\mathrm{H}}-1)}{p-1}$.

The three lemmas can be combined to obtain

$$\Pr[W] \leq \Pr[E^{(1)}] + \Pr[E^{(2)}] + \Pr[W \wedge (\neg E^{(1)}) \wedge (\neg E^{(2)})] \leq \frac{Q_{\mathrm{H}}(2\ell + Q_{\mathrm{H}})}{p-1} .$$

which concludes the proof. In the next three sections, we prove the three perceding lemmas.

3.2 Proof of Lemma 1

Throughout this proof, let us fix $j \in [Q_{\mathrm{H}}]$. We first define a sequence of random variables $(D_0, D_1, \ldots, D_n, X_1, \ldots, X_n)$, where $n = \ell + 1$, such that $E_j^{(1)}$ implies one of $D_0, \ldots, D_n$ is not equal to 0 and $D_0 + \sum_{k\in[n]} D_k X_k = 0$. Further, we also ensure that X_k is uniformly distributed over $\mathbb{Z}_p^*$ independent of $(D_0, D_1, \ldots, D_k, X_1, \ldots, X_{k-1})$ for each $k \in [n]$ and use this to bound $\Pr[E_j^{(1)}]$. More concretely:

- Let $D_0 := \alpha_j^{(0)} + \sum_{i\in\mathcal{I}_{\mathrm{fin}}^{(j)}} y_i\left(\alpha_j^{(2i-1)} + c_i \cdot \alpha_j^{(2i-1)}\right)$, $X_1 := -\delta_j$, $D_1 := \beta_j^{(0)} + \sum_{i\in\mathcal{I}_{\mathrm{fin}}^{(j)}} y_i\left(\beta_j^{(2i-1)} + c_i \cdot \beta_j^{(2i)}\right)$, and note that $E_{1,j}^{(1)}$ is equivalent to $D_1 \neq 0$.
- Further, for $1 \leq k \leq |\mathcal{I}_{\mathrm{unk}}^{(j)}|$, denote $i_k \in \mathcal{I}_{\mathrm{unk}}^{(j)}$ as the index such that (i_k, c_{i_k}) is the k-th query made to S among the indexes in $\mathcal{I}_{\mathrm{unk}}^{(j)}$ and let $X_{k+1} = y_{i_k}$, $D_{k+1} := \alpha_j^{(2i_k-1)} + c_{i_k} \cdot \alpha_j^{(2i_k)} - \delta_j\left(\beta_j^{(2i_k-1)} + c_{i_k} \cdot \beta_j^{(2i_k)}\right)$, we have $E_{2,(j,i_k)}^{(1)}$ occurs is equivalent to $D_{k+1} \neq 0$.
- For $|\mathcal{I}_{\mathrm{unk}}^{(j)}| + 1 < k \leq n$, let $D_k = 0$ and X_k be a random variable uniformly distributed in $\mathbb{Z}_p^*$ independent of $(D_0, D_1, \ldots, D_k, X_1, \ldots, X_{k-1})$.[5]

Note that $D_0 + \sum_{k=1}^n D_k X_k = \alpha_j^{(0)} + \sum_{i\in[\ell]} y_i \cdot \left(\alpha_j^{(2i-1)} + c_i \cdot \alpha_j^{(2i)}\right) - \delta_j \cdot \left(\beta_j^{(0)} + \sum_{i\in[\ell]} y_i \left(\beta_j^{(2i-1)} + c_i \cdot \beta_j^{(2i)}\right)\right)$. Therefore, by (W1), we know W_j occurs implies $D_0 + \sum_{i=1}^n D_i X_i = 0$. Thus, the event $W_j \wedge E_j^{(1)}$ implies, in addition, that one of $D_0, \ldots, D_n$ is not equal to 0. Then, the upper bound $\Pr[W_j \wedge E_j^{(1)}] \leq \frac{\ell+1}{p-1}$

---

[5] For $|\mathcal{I}_{\mathrm{unk}}^{(j)}| + 1 < k \leq n$, D_k, X_k act as placeholders so that we can apply Lemma 4 for an a priori fixed value n instead of a random variable $|\mathcal{I}_{\mathrm{unk}}^{(j)}| + 1$.

follows by combining the following lemma[6] and claim. The proofs of the lemma and claim are presented in the full version of this paper.

Claim 1. *For each $k \in [n]$, X_k is uniformly distributed over $\mathbb{Z}_p^*$ independent of $(D_0, \ldots, D_k, X_1, \ldots, X_{k-1})$.*

Lemma 4. *Let p be prime. Let $D_0, D_1, \ldots, D_n, X_1, \ldots, X_n \in \mathbb{Z}_p$ be random variables such that for all $k \in [n]$, X_k is uniform over $U_k \subseteq \mathbb{Z}_p$ and independent of $(D_0, \ldots, D_k, X_1, \ldots, X_{k-1})$. Then,*

$$\Pr\left[\exists\, i \in \{0, \ldots, n\} \ : \ D_i \neq 0 \ \wedge \ D_0 + \sum_{j=1}^{n} D_j X_j = 0\right] \leq \sum_{i=1}^{n} \frac{1}{|U_i|}.$$

3.3   Proof of Lemma 2

It is easier to introduce a new event F_j and show that $W_j \ \wedge \ (\neg E_j^{(1)})$ implies F_j. We will then bound $\Pr[F_j \ \wedge \ E_j^{(2)}]$. In particular, define the event F_j as

$$\forall\, i \in \mathcal{I}_{\text{unk}}^{(j)} \ : \ \alpha_j^{(2i-1)} + c_i \cdot \alpha_j^{(2i)} - \delta_j \left(\beta_j^{(2i-1)} + c_i \cdot \beta_j^{(2i)}\right) = 0 \tag{F1}$$

$$\wedge \sum_{i \in \mathcal{I}_{\text{unk}}^{(j)}} y_i \left(\beta_j^{(2i-1)} + c_i \cdot \beta_j^{(2i)}\right) \neq 0, \tag{F2}$$

and we have the following lemma.

Lemma 5. *If $W_j \ \wedge \ (\neg E_j^{(1)})$ occurs, then the event F_j occurs.*

We also denote

$$\mathcal{D}_j := \left\{ \frac{\alpha_j^{(2i)}}{\beta_j^{(2i)}} \ \Big|\ i \in \mathcal{I}_{\text{unk}}^{(j)}, \beta_j^{(2i)} \neq 0 \right\} \cup \left\{ \frac{\alpha_j^{(2i-1)}}{\beta_j^{(2i-1)}} \ \Big|\ i \in \mathcal{I}_{\text{unk}}^{(j)}, \beta_j^{(2i)} = 0, \beta_j^{(2i-1)} \neq 0 \right\}.$$

We have $|\mathcal{D}_j| \leq |\{i \in \mathcal{I}_{\text{unk}}^{(j)} \mid \beta_j^{(2i)} \neq 0\} \cup \{i \in \mathcal{I}_{\text{unk}}^{(j)} \mid \beta_j^{(2i)} = 0\}| = |\mathcal{I}_{\text{unk}}^{(j)}|$.

Claim 2. *The event $F_j \ \wedge \ E_j^{(2)}$ implies $\delta_j \in \mathcal{D}_j$.*

The proofs of the above claim and lemma are presented in the full version of this paper. Note that δ_j is generated uniformly at random, independently of $\mathcal{D}_j$, since the latter is defined by the j-th H query. Therefore, Lemma 5 and Claim 2 yield $\Pr[W_j \ \wedge \ (\neg E_j^{(1)}) \ \wedge \ E_j^{(2)}] \leq \Pr[F_j \ \wedge \ E_j^{(2)}] \leq \Pr[\delta_j \in \mathcal{D}_j] \leq \frac{|\mathcal{I}_{\text{unk}}^{(j)}|}{p-1} \leq \frac{\ell}{p-1}$.

---

[6] Note that Lemma 4 cannot be directly derived from the Schwartz-Zippel lemma by viewing $D_0 + \sum_{j=1}^{n} D_j X_j = 0$ as a polynomial of $X_1, \ldots, X_n$, since we cover for example the case where $D_0, D_1, \ldots, D_n$ are adaptively chosen, i.e., each D_i can depend on $X_1 \ldots, X_{i-1}$.

3.4 Proof of Lemma 3

To conclude the analysis, we introduce yet another event, $E^{(3)}$. We will show below that $W \land (\neg E^{(1)}) \land (\neg E^{(2)})$ implies $E^{(3)}$, and thus it is enough to upper bound the probability of $E^{(3)}$ occurring. Concretely, $E^{(3)}$ is defined as follows (the definition of the following events $F_{j'}$ is given in Sect. 3.3).

Event $E^{(3)}$. For each $j_1, j_2 \in [Q_H]$ and $j_1 < j_2$, denote the event $E^{(3)}_{(j_1,j_2)}$ as

$$\exists\, i \in \mathcal{I}^{(j_1)}_{\mathrm{unk}} \cap \mathcal{I}^{(j_2)}_{\mathrm{unk}} : \alpha^{(2i)}_{j_1} \cdot \beta^{(2i-1)}_{j_1} \neq \alpha^{(2i-1)}_{j_1} \cdot \beta^{(2i)}_{j_1} \land \alpha^{(2i)}_{j_2} \cdot \beta^{(2i-1)}_{j_2} \neq \alpha^{(2i-1)}_{j_2} \cdot \beta^{(2i)}_{j_2}.$$

Denote $E'^{(3)}_{(j_1,j_2)} := E^{(3)}_{(j_1,j_2)} \land F_{j_1} \land F_{j_2}$ and $E^{(3)} := \bigvee_{j_1,j_2 \in [Q_H], j_1 < j_2} E'^{(3)}_{(j_1,j_2)}$.

To see why the above implication is true, assume that W indeed occurs, but both $E^{(1)}$ and $E^{(2)}$ do not occur. We now fix some $j \in \mathcal{J}$. We know W_j occurs, but both $E^{(1)}_j$ and $E^{(2)}_j$ do not occur. In particular, by the definition of $E^{(2)}_j$, we know there exists $i \in \mathcal{I}^{(j)}_{\mathrm{unk}}$ such that $\alpha^{(2i)}_j \cdot \beta^{(2i-1)}_j \neq \alpha^{(2i-1)}_j \cdot \beta^{(2i)}_j$.

Let $i^{(j)}_{\min}$ be the smallest index in $\mathcal{I}^{(j)}_{\mathrm{unk}}$ such that $\alpha^{(2i^{(j)}_{\min})}_j \cdot \beta^{(2i^{(j)}_{\min}-1)}_j \neq \alpha^{(2i^{(j)}_{\min}-1)}_j \cdot \beta^{(2i^{(j)}_{\min})}_j$. Since W occurs, we know $|\mathcal{J}| > \ell$. Then, since $i^{(j)}_{\min} \in \mathcal{I}^{(j)}_{\mathrm{unk}} \subseteq [\ell]$ for each $j \in \mathcal{J}$ and $|\mathcal{J}| > \ell$, by the pigeonhole principle, we know there exists $j_1, j_2 \in \mathcal{J}$ such that $j_1 < j_2$ and $i^{(j_1)}_{\min} = i^{(j_2)}_{\min}$, which implies $E^{(3)}_{(j_1,j_2)}$ occurs. Also, since we know both $W_{j_1} \land (\neg E^{(1)}_{j_1})$ and $W_{j_2} \land (\neg E^{(1)}_{j_2})$ occur, by Lemma 5, we have F_{j_1} and F_{j_2} both occur. Therefore, we know $E'^{(3)}_{(j_1,j_2)} = E^{(3)}_{(j_1,j_2)} \land F_{j_1} \land F_{j_2}$ occurs, which implies $E^{(3)}$ occurs.

Therefore, we have $\Pr\left[W \land (\neg E^{(1)}) \land (\neg E^{(2)})\right] \leqslant \Pr[E^{(3)}]$. We now just need to bound $\Pr[E'^{(3)}_{(j_1,j_2)}]$ for any $j_1 < j_2$.

To gain insight, suppose $E'^{(3)}_{(j_1,j_2)}$ occurs. We can show that there exists $i \in \mathcal{I}^{(j_1)}_{\mathrm{unk}} \cap \mathcal{I}^{(j_2)}_{\mathrm{unk}}$ such that $\alpha^{(2i)}_{j_1} - \delta_{j_1}\beta^{(2i)}_{j_1} \neq 0$ and $\alpha^{(2i)}_{j_2} - \delta_{j_2}\beta^{(2i)}_{j_2} \neq 0$. Then, since F_{j_1} and F_{j_2} occur, by (F1), it holds that $\dfrac{\alpha^{(2i-1)}_{j_1} - \delta_{j_1} \cdot \beta^{(2i-1)}_{j_1}}{\alpha^{(2i)}_{j_1} - \delta_{j_1} \cdot \beta^{(2i)}_{j_1}} = c_i = \dfrac{\alpha^{(2i-1)}_{j_2} - \delta_{j_2} \cdot \beta^{(2i-1)}_{j_2}}{\alpha^{(2i)}_{j_2} - \delta_{j_2} \cdot \beta^{(2i)}_{j_2}}$. However, this can occur with only small probability since δ_{j_1} and δ_{j_2} are sampled independently. The following claim makes this formal. The proof is presented in the full version of this paper.

Claim 3. *For any $j_1, j_2 \in [Q_H]$ such that $j_1 < j_2$, suppose $E'^{(3)}_{(j_1,j_2)}$ occurs. Let i_{dif} be the smallest index in $\mathcal{I}^{(j_1)}_{\mathrm{unk}} \cap \mathcal{I}^{(j_2)}_{\mathrm{unk}}$ such that $\alpha^{(2i_{\mathrm{dif}})}_{j_1} \cdot \beta^{(2i_{\mathrm{dif}}-1)}_{j_1} \neq \alpha^{(2i_{\mathrm{dif}}-1)}_{j_1} \cdot \beta^{(2i_{\mathrm{dif}})}_{j_1}$ and $\alpha^{(2i_{\mathrm{dif}})}_{j_2} \cdot \beta^{(2i_{\mathrm{dif}}-1)}_{j_2} \neq \alpha^{(2i_{\mathrm{dif}}-1)}_{j_2} \cdot \beta^{(2i_{\mathrm{dif}})}_{j_2}$. Then, we have $\alpha^{(2i_{\mathrm{dif}})}_{j_1} - \delta_{j_1}\beta^{(2i_{\mathrm{dif}})}_{j_1} \neq 0$. Moreover, let $T = \dfrac{\alpha^{(2i_{\mathrm{dif}}-1)}_{j_1} - \delta_{j_1} \cdot \beta^{(2i_{\mathrm{dif}}-1)}_{j_1}}{\alpha^{(2i_{\mathrm{dif}})}_{j_1} - \delta_{j_1} \cdot \beta^{(2i_{\mathrm{dif}})}_{j_1}}$, and we have $\beta^{(2i_{\mathrm{dif}}-1)}_{j_2} - T \cdot \beta^{(2i_{\mathrm{dif}})}_{j_2} \neq 0$ and $\delta_{j_2} = \dfrac{\alpha^{(2i_{\mathrm{dif}}-1)}_{j_2} - T \cdot \alpha^{(2i_{\mathrm{dif}})}_{j_2}}{\beta^{(2i_{\mathrm{dif}}-1)}_{j_2} - T \cdot \beta^{(2i_{\mathrm{dif}})}_{j_2}}$.*

Algorithm $BS_1.Setup(1^\lambda)$:	Algorithm $BS_1.U_1(pk, msg_1, m)$:
$p \leftarrow |\mathbb{G}_\lambda|$	$X \leftarrow pk$; $(A, Y) \leftarrow msg_1$
Let g be the generator of $\mathbb{G}_\lambda$	$r_1, r_2 \leftarrow_\$ \mathbb{Z}_p$; $\gamma \leftarrow_\$ \mathbb{Z}_p^*$
Select $H : \{0,1\}^* \to \mathbb{Z}_p$	$Y' \leftarrow Y^\gamma$; $A' \leftarrow g^{r_1} \cdot A^\gamma \cdot Y'^{r_2}$
Return $par \leftarrow (p, g, H)$	$c' \leftarrow H(A' \| Y' \| m)$
	$c \leftarrow c' + r_2$
Algorithm $BS_1.KG(par)$:	$st^u \leftarrow (c, c', r_1, \gamma, X, Y, A)$
$(p, g, H) \leftarrow par$	Return (st^u, c)
$x \leftarrow_\$ \mathbb{Z}_p^*$; $X \leftarrow g^x$	
$sk \leftarrow x$; $pk \leftarrow X$	Algorithm $BS_1.U_2(st^u, msg_2)$:
Return (sk, pk)	$(c, c', r_1, \gamma, X, Y, A) \leftarrow st^u$
	$(s, y) \leftarrow msg_2$
Algorithm $BS_1.S_1(sk)$:	If $y = 0$ or $Y \neq X^y$ or $g^s \neq A \cdot Y^c$
$x \leftarrow sk$; $X \leftarrow g^x$	then return $\perp$
$a \leftarrow_\$ \mathbb{Z}_p$; $y \leftarrow_\$ \mathbb{Z}_p^*$	$s' \leftarrow \gamma \cdot s + r_1$; $y' \leftarrow \gamma \cdot y$
$A \leftarrow g^a$; $Y \leftarrow X^y$	Return $\sigma \leftarrow (c', s', y')$
$st^s \leftarrow (a, y, x)$; $msg_1 \leftarrow (A, Y)$	
Return (st^s, msg_1)	Algorithm $BS_1.Ver(pk, \sigma, m)$:
	$(c, s, y) \leftarrow \sigma$
Algorithm $BS_1.S_2(st^s, c)$:	If $y = 0$ then return 0
$(a, y, x) \leftarrow st^s$	$Y \leftarrow X^y$; $A \leftarrow g^s \cdot Y^{-c}$
$s \leftarrow a + c \cdot y \cdot x$	If $c \neq H(A \| Y \| m)$ then return 0
Return $msg_2 \leftarrow (s, y)$	Return 1

Fig. 4. The blind signature scheme $BS_1 = BS_1[\mathbb{G}]$.

Let T and i_{dif} be the values defined in the above claim. Consider the step when δ_{j_2} is generated. We know the j_2-th query to H has been made, and thus α_{j_2} and β_{j_2} are determined. Also, since $j_1 < j_2$, the j_1-th query to H has returned, and thus α_{j_1}, α_{j_2}, and δ_{j_1} are determined. Therefore, we know i_{dif} and T are also determined. Thus, we know δ_{j_2} is picked uniformly at random from $\mathbb{Z}_p^*$ independent of i_{dif}, α_{j_1}, α_{j_2}, β_{j_1}, β_{j_2}, δ_{j_1}, and T. Then, by the above claim,

$$\Pr[E'^{(3)}_{(j_1, j_2)}] \leqslant \Pr \left[\begin{array}{c} \alpha_{j_1}^{(2i_{dif})} - \delta_{j_1}\beta_{j_1}^{(2i_{dif})} \neq 0 \\ \wedge \ \beta_{j_2}^{(2i_{dif}-1)} - T \cdot \beta_{j_2}^{(2i_{dif})} \neq 0 \end{array} \wedge \ \delta_{j_2} = \frac{\alpha_{j_2}^{(2i_{dif}-1)} - T \cdot \alpha_{j_2}^{(2i_{dif})}}{\beta_{j_2}^{(2i_{dif}-1)} - T \cdot \beta_{j_2}^{(2i_{dif})}} \right]$$

$$\leqslant \Pr \left[\delta_{j_2} = \frac{\alpha_{j_2}^{(2i_{dif}-1)} - T \cdot \alpha_{j_2}^{(2i_{dif})}}{\beta_{j_2}^{(2i_{dif}-1)} - T \cdot \beta_{j_2}^{(2i_{dif})}} \ \middle| \ \begin{array}{c} \alpha_{j_1}^{(2i_{dif})} - \delta_{j_1}\beta_{j_1}^{(2i_{dif})} \neq 0 \\ \wedge \ \beta_{j_2}^{(2i_{dif}-1)} - T \cdot \beta_{j_2}^{(2i_{dif})} \neq 0 \end{array} \right]$$

$$\leqslant \frac{1}{p-1} .$$

4   Efficient Blind Signatures in the GGM

This section introduces our first scheme, BS_1, which relies on a prime-order cyclic group and a hash function H. We describe this scheme formally in Fig. 4. Roughly, it extends (blind) Schnorr Signatures by sending an additional group element $Y = X^y$ in the first round. Then, the signer's final response to challenge c reveals y along with $s = a + cxy$. We also note that we could consider a variant of the scheme where the signature consists of $\sigma = (A', s', y')$, where A' replaces c'.

SECURITY ANALYSIS. First off, we observe that the protocol is blind. We give a complete proof of the following theorem in the full version of this paper.

Theorem 2. *Let $\mathbb{G}$ be an (asymptotic) family of prime-order cyclic groups. Then, the blind signature scheme $\mathsf{BS}_1[\mathbb{G}]$ is perfectly blind.*

Our main result shows OMUF security of BS_1 in the *generic-group model* (GGM) following Shoup's original formalization [8], which encodes every group element with a random label. To this end, we present in Fig. 5 a game describing a GGM-version of OMUF security for BS_1, adapting the one from Sect. 2. We also define a corresponding advantage $\mathsf{Adv}^{\mathrm{omuf\text{-}ggm}}_{\mathsf{BS}_1[\mathbb{G}]}(\mathcal{A}, \lambda)$ to measure the probability that $\mathcal{A}$ wins the game. Note that to keep notation homogenous, it is convenient to allow the game to depend on $\mathbb{G}$, although the game itself only makes use of the order of the group. The game also models the hash function H as a random oracle, to which the adversary is given oracle access.

The following theorem states our main result in the form of a reduction to WFROS and is proved in Sect. 4.1.

Theorem 3 (OMUF Security of BS_1). *Let $\mathbb{G}$ be an (asymptotic) family of prime-order cyclic groups. For any adversary $\mathcal{A}$ for the $\mathrm{OMUF\text{-}GGM}^{\mathsf{BS}_1[\mathbb{G}]}(\lambda)$ game making at most Q_Π queries to Π, Q_{S_1} queries to S_1, and Q_H queries to the random oracle H, there exists an adversary $\mathcal{B}$ for the $\mathrm{WFROS}_{Q_{\mathsf{S}_1},p}$ problem, where $p = |\mathbb{G}_\lambda|$, making at most $Q_\mathrm{H} + Q_{\mathsf{S}_1} + 1$ queries to the random oracle H such that $\mathsf{Adv}^{\mathrm{omuf\text{-}ggm}}_{\mathsf{BS}_1[\mathbb{G}]}(\mathcal{A}, \lambda) \leqslant \mathsf{Adv}^{\mathrm{wfros}}_{Q_{\mathsf{S}_1},p}(\mathcal{B}) + \frac{Q_\Phi(Q_\Phi + 2Q_\mathrm{H} + 2Q_{\mathsf{S}_1} + 2)}{p - (1 + Q_{\mathsf{S}_1} + Q_\Phi^2)}$, where Q_Φ is the maximum number of queries to Φ during the game $\mathrm{OMUF\text{-}GGM}$, and we have $Q_\Phi = Q_\Pi + 4Q_{\mathsf{S}_1} + 4$.*

By Theorem 1, we have the following corollary.

Corollary 1. *Let $\mathbb{G}$ be an (asymptotic) family of prime-order cyclic groups. For any adversary $\mathcal{A}$ playing game $\mathrm{OMUF\text{-}GGM}^{\mathsf{BS}_1[\mathbb{G}]}(\lambda)$ making at most Q_Π queries to Π, Q_{S_1} queries to S_1, and Q_H queries to the random oracle H, we have $\mathsf{Adv}^{\mathrm{omuf\text{-}ggm}}_{\mathsf{BS}_1[\mathbb{G}]}(\mathcal{A}, \lambda) \leqslant \frac{2Q_\Phi(Q_\Phi + 2Q_\mathrm{H} + 2Q_{\mathsf{S}_1} + 2)}{p - (1 + Q_{\mathsf{S}_1} + Q_\Phi^2)}$, where $Q_\Phi = Q_\Pi + 4Q_{\mathsf{S}_1} + 4$.*

We note in particular that the concrete security of BS_1 in the GGM is comparable to that of the discrete logarithm problem, in that $Q_\Phi = \Omega(\min\{\sqrt{p}, p/Q_\mathrm{H}, p/Q_{\mathsf{S}_1}\})$ is necessary to break security with constant probability.

Game OMUF-GGM$_{\mathsf{BS}_1[\mathbb{G}]}^{\mathcal{A}}(\lambda)$:

$p \leftarrow |\mathbb{G}_\lambda|$; $x \leftarrow_\$ \mathbb{Z}_p^*$
$\mathsf{sid} \leftarrow 0$; $\ell \leftarrow 0$; $\mathcal{I}_{\mathsf{fin}} \leftarrow \varnothing$; $\mathsf{Cur} \leftarrow \varnothing$
$\varXi \leftarrow ()$; $T \leftarrow ()$
$\{(m_k, \sigma_k)\}_{k \in [\ell+1]} \leftarrow_\$ \mathcal{A}^{\varPi, \mathsf{S}_1, \mathsf{S}_2, \mathsf{H}}(p, \varPhi(1), \varPhi(x))$
If $\exists\, k_1 \neq k_2$ such that $(m_{k_1}, \sigma_{k_1}) = (m_{k_2}, \sigma_{k_2})$ then
    Return 0
If $\exists\, k \in [\ell+1]$ such that $y_k^* = 0$
    or $c_k \neq \mathsf{H}(\varPhi(s_k - c_k \cdot y_k \cdot x) \,\|\, \varPhi(y_k \cdot x) \,\|\, m_i)$
where $(c_k, s_k, y_k) = \sigma_k$ then return 0
Return 1

Oracle $\varPhi(v)$:

If $v \in \mathsf{Cur}$ then return $\varXi(v)$
$\varXi(v) \leftarrow_\$ \{0,1\}^{\log(p)} \setminus \varXi(\mathsf{Cur})$
$\mathsf{Cur} \leftarrow \mathsf{Cur} \cap \{v\}$
Return $\varXi(v)$

Oracle $\varPi(\xi, \xi', b)$:

If $\exists v, v' \in \mathsf{Cur}$ such that $\xi = \varXi(v)$ and $\xi' = \varXi(v')$ then
    Return $\varPhi(v + (-1)^b v')$
Else return $\bot$

Oracle S_1 :

$\mathsf{sid} \leftarrow \mathsf{sid} + 1$
$a_{\mathsf{sid}} \leftarrow_\$ \mathbb{Z}_p$; $y_{\mathsf{sid}} \leftarrow_\$ \mathbb{Z}_p^*$
$\mathsf{st}_{\mathsf{sid}}^s \leftarrow (a_{\mathsf{sid}}, y_{\mathsf{sid}})$
$\mathsf{msg}_1 \leftarrow (\varPhi(a_{\mathsf{sid}}), \varPhi(x y_{\mathsf{sid}}))$
Return $(\mathsf{sid}, \mathsf{msg}_1)$

Oracle $\mathsf{S}_2(i, c_i)$:

If $i \notin [\mathsf{sid}] \setminus \mathcal{I}_{\mathsf{fin}}$ then
    Return $\bot$
$(a_i, y_i) \leftarrow \mathsf{st}_i^s$
$s_i \leftarrow a_i + c_i \cdot y_i \cdot x$
$\mathsf{msg}_2 \leftarrow (s_i, y_i)$
$\mathcal{I}_{\mathsf{fin}} \leftarrow \mathcal{I}_{\mathsf{fin}} \cup \{i\}$
$\ell \leftarrow \ell + 1$
Return msg_2

Oracle $\mathsf{H}(\mathsf{str})$:

If $T(\mathsf{str}) = \bot$ then
    $T(\mathsf{str}) \leftarrow_\$ \mathbb{Z}_p$
Return $T(\mathsf{str})$

Fig. 5. The OMUF security game in GGM for the blind signature scheme $\mathsf{BS}_1[\mathbb{G}]$.

4.1   Proof of Theorem 3

Let us fix an adversary $\mathcal{A}$ that makes (without loss of generality) exactly $Q_\varPi$ queries to $\varPi$, Q_{S_1} queries to S_1, and Q_{H} queries to the random oracle H. Without loss of generality, assume it also makes exactly one query (i, c_i) to S_2 for each $i \in [Q_{\mathsf{S}_1}]$. Then, after $\mathcal{A}$ returns, we know $\ell = Q_{\mathsf{S}_1}$ and $\mathcal{I}_{\mathsf{fin}} = [Q_{\mathsf{S}_1}]$. Also, it is clear that the overall number of queries to $\varPhi$ in OMUF-GGM$_{\mathsf{BS}_1}^{\mathcal{A}}$ is at most $Q_\varPhi := Q_\varPi + 4Q_{\mathsf{S}_1} + 4$.

We prove the theorem by going through a series of games, from Game$_0$ to Game$_4$, where Game$_0$ is the OMUF-GGM$_{\mathsf{BS}_1}^{\mathcal{A}}$ game and Game$_4$ is an intermediate game that enables an easier reduction to WFROS. Here, however, we first introduce Game$_4$ and Lemma 6 and then discuss the reduction to WFROS, which is the core of the proof. We leave the definition of the intermediate games between Game$_0$ to Game$_4$ to the proof of Lemma 6. The game-hopping argument is non-trivial, but it follows the same blueprint as in [40].

DEFINITION OF Game$_4$. The pseudocode description of Game$_4$ is given in Fig. 6. The main difference from OMUF-GGM$_{\mathsf{BS}_1}^{\mathcal{A}}$ is that the encoding oracle $\varPhi$ takes as input a polynomial instead of an integer in $\mathbb{Z}_p$. (Note that the adversary cannot query $\varPhi$ directly, and thus this difference is not directly surfaced.) This essentially captures the algebraic core of our proof.

Also, for a valid query (i, c_i) to S_2, the output values (s_i, y_i) are directly sampled uniformly from $\mathbb{Z}_p \times \mathbb{Z}_p^*$. Furthermore, when this happens, two polyno-

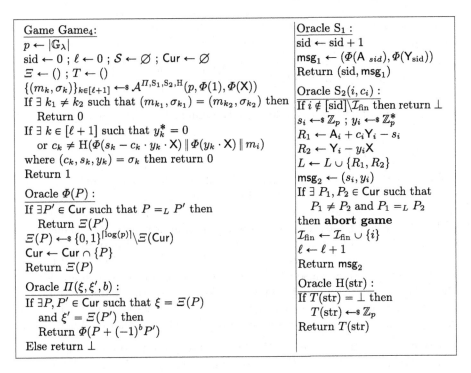

Fig. 6. The definition of Game₄. The symbols P and P' denote polynomials over variables $\mathsf{X}, \{\mathsf{A}_i, \mathsf{Y}_i\}_{i\in[\text{sid}]}$. Also, a new equality notation, "$=_L$", is used. We say $P_1 =_L P_2$ if and only if $P_1 - P_2$ can be represented as a linear combination of polynomials in L.

mials, $R_1 = \mathsf{A}_i + c_i \cdot \mathsf{Y}_i - s_i$ and $R_2 = \mathsf{Y}_i - y_i \cdot \mathsf{X}$, are recorded in the set L. Then, in the encoding oracle Φ, two polynomials, P_1 and P_2, are considered to differ if and only if $P_1 \neq_L P_2$, where $P_1 =_L P_2$ means that $P_1 - P_2$ can be generated as a linear combination of polynomials in L. Still, $P_1 \neq_L P_2$ could occur when queries P_1 and P_2 are made to Φ, but they becomes equal (in the sense of "$=_L$") after L is updated. The game aborts when this happens.

Overall, we have the following lemma. The proof is presented in the full version of this paper.

Lemma 6. $\mathsf{Adv}_{\mathsf{BS}_1[\mathbb{G}]}^{\text{omuf-ggm}}(\mathcal{A}, \lambda) \leqslant \Pr[\mathsf{Game}_4^{\mathcal{A}} = 1] + \frac{Q_\Phi^2}{p - (1 + Q_{\mathsf{S}_1} + Q_\Phi^2)}.$

REDUCTION TO WFROS. The core of the proof is to relate the probability of the adversary $\mathcal{A}$ winning Game₄ with the advantage of an adversary $\mathcal{B}$ winning the WFROS problem, as stated in the following lemma. The proof is given in Sect. 4.2.

Lemma 7. *For every λ, there exists an adversary $\mathcal{B}$ for the* WFROS$_{Q_{S_1},p}$ *problem, where $p = |\mathbb{G}_\lambda|$, making at most $Q_H + Q_{S_1} + 1$ queries to H such that*

$$\Pr[\text{Game}_4^{\mathcal{A}} = 1] \leq \text{Adv}_{Q_{S_1},p}^{\text{wfros}}(\mathcal{B}) + \frac{(2Q_\Phi + 1)(Q_H + Q_{S_1} + 1)}{p - Q_\Phi}. \tag{5}$$

The statement of Theorem 3 follows by combining Lemmas 6 and 7.

4.2   Proof of Lemma 7

We construct $\mathcal{B}$ that interacts with $\mathcal{A}$ by simulating the oracles from Game$_4$ using the two oracles S and H in WFROS. In particular, we extract suitable vectors $\boldsymbol{\alpha}$ and $\boldsymbol{\beta}$ to query to H in WFROS, i.e., each RO query str is decomposed as str $= \xi^A \| \xi^Y \| m$, where ξ^A and ξ^Y are encodings of group elements. If both encodings are valid, there must exist P^A, P^Y such that $\Xi(P^A) = \xi^A$ and $\Xi(P^Y) = \xi^Y$; then, $\mathcal{B}$ defines two vectors $\boldsymbol{\alpha}$ and $\boldsymbol{\beta}$ to make a corresponding query to H in WFROS. The oracle S is also used to simulate the signer's second stage. Finally, when $\mathcal{A}$ outputs $Q_{S_1} + 1$ different valid message-signature pairs in Game$_4$, $\mathcal{B}$ tries to map each valid message-signature pair to a query to H in WFROS. We show that this strategy succeeds with probability close to that of $\mathcal{A}$ succeeding.

THE ADVERSARY $\mathcal{B}$. Specifically, $\mathcal{B}$ initializes the variables sid, Cur, $\mathcal{I}_{\text{fin}}$, Ξ, and T as in Game$_4$. In addition, $\mathcal{B}$ initializes an empty table Hid, used later in the simulation of $\hat{H}$.

Then, $\mathcal{B}$ runs $\mathcal{A}$ on input $(p, \hat{\Phi}(1), \hat{\Phi}(X))$ and with access to the oracles $\hat{\Pi}$, $\hat{S}_1$, $\hat{S}_2$, and $\hat{H}$. These oracles, along with $\hat{\Phi}$, operate as follows:

Oracles $\hat{\Phi}, \hat{\Pi}$: Same as in Game$_4$. In particular, L is updated by calls to $\hat{S}_2$.
Oracle $\hat{S}_1$: Same as in Game$_4$.
Oracle $\hat{S}_2$: Same as Game$_4$ except that instead of sampling y_i randomly, if $i \in [\text{sid}] \setminus \mathcal{I}_{\text{fin}}$, $\mathcal{B}$ makes a query (i, c_i) to S and uses its output as the value y_i.
Oracle $\hat{H}$: After receiving a query str, if $T(\text{str}) \neq \perp$, the value $T(\text{str})$ is returned. Otherwise, str is decomposed as str $= \xi^A \| \xi^Y \| m$ such that the length of ξ^A and ξ^Y is $\lceil \log(p) \rceil$.
  – If there exist $P^A, P^Y \in$ Cur such that $\Xi(P^A) = \xi^A$ and $\Xi(P^Y) = \xi^Y$, denote the coefficients of P^A, P^Y as

$$P^A = \hat{\alpha}^g + \hat{\alpha}^X X + \sum_{i \in [\text{sid}]} \hat{\alpha}^{A_i} A_i + \sum_{i \in [\text{sid}]} \hat{\alpha}^{Y_i} Y_i, \tag{6}$$

$$P^Y = \hat{\beta}^g + \hat{\beta}^X X + \sum_{i \in [\text{sid}]} \hat{\beta}^{A_i} A_i + \sum_{i \in [\text{sid}]} \hat{\beta}^{Y_i} Y_i. \tag{7}$$

Then, $\mathcal{B}$ issues the query $(\boldsymbol{\alpha}, \boldsymbol{\beta})$ to H, where $\boldsymbol{\alpha}, \boldsymbol{\beta} \in \mathbb{Z}_p^{2Q_{S_1}+1}$ are such that

$$
\alpha^{(i')} = \begin{cases}
\hat{\alpha}^X, & i' = 0 \\
\hat{\alpha}^{Y_i}, & i' = 2i - 1, \ i \in [\mathsf{sid}] \\
-\hat{\alpha}^{A_i}, & i' = 2i, \ i \in [\mathsf{sid}] \\
0, & o.w.
\end{cases},
$$

$$
\beta^{(i')} = \begin{cases}
-\hat{\beta}^X, & i' = 0 \\
-\hat{\beta}^{Y_i}, & i' = 2i - 1, \ i \in [\mathsf{sid}] \\
\hat{\beta}^{A_i}, & i' = 2i, \ i \in [\mathsf{sid}] \\
0, & o.w.
\end{cases}.
\tag{8}
$$

After receiving the output $(\delta_{\mathsf{hid}}, \mathsf{hid})$, $\mathcal{B}$ sets $T(\mathsf{str}) \leftarrow \delta_{\mathsf{hid}}$ and $\mathsf{Hid}(\mathsf{str}) \leftarrow \mathsf{hid}$.

- Otherwise, if $\xi^A \notin T(\mathsf{Cur})$ or $\xi^Y \notin T(\mathsf{Cur})$ (or if the decomposition of str is not possible), $\mathcal{B}$ samples $T(\mathsf{str})$ uniformly from $\mathbb{Z}_p$ and sets $\mathsf{Hid}(\mathsf{str}) = \bot$.

Finally, $\mathcal{B}$ returns $T(\mathsf{str})$.

After $\mathcal{A}$ outputs $\{(m_k^*, \sigma_k^*)\}_{k \in [Q_{S_1}+1]}$, $\mathcal{B}$ aborts if the signatures are not valid, i.e., one of the following conditions is not satisfied:

$$
\forall \ k_1, k_2 \in [Q_{S_1} + 1] \text{ and } k_1 \neq k_2 \ : \ (m_{k_1}^*, \sigma_{k_1}^*) \neq (m_{k_2}^*, \sigma_{k_2}^*),
\tag{9}
$$

$$
\forall \ k \in [Q_{S_1} + 1] \ : \ y_k^* \neq 0 \ \wedge \ c_k^* = \hat{\mathsf{H}}(\mathsf{str}_k^*),
\tag{10}
$$

where $(c_k^*, s_k^*, y_k^*) = \sigma_k^*$ and $\mathsf{str}_k^* = \hat{\Phi}(s_k^* - c_k^* \cdot y_k^* \cdot X) \,\|\, \hat{\Phi}(y_k^* \cdot X) \,\|\, m_k^*$. (Here, $\hat{\mathsf{H}}$ and $\hat{\Phi}$ are the oracles described previously.) Further, $\mathcal{B}$ aborts if the following condition does not hold:

$$
\forall \ k \in [Q_{S_1} + 1] \ : \ \mathsf{Hid}(\mathsf{str}_k^*) \neq \bot.
\tag{11}
$$

Otherwise, $\mathcal{B}$ outputs $\mathcal{J} := \{\mathsf{Hid}(\mathsf{str}_k^*)\}_{k \in [Q_{S_1}+1]}$.

ANALYSIS OF $\mathcal{B}$. Note that $\mathcal{B}$ queries to H at most once when it receives a query to $\hat{\mathsf{H}}$ and makes $Q_{S_1} + 1$ more queries to $\hat{\mathsf{H}}$ when checking the validity of the output. Therefore, $\mathcal{B}$ makes at most $Q_{\mathsf{H}} + Q_{S_1} + 1$ queries to H. Also, it is clear that $\mathcal{B}$ simulates oracles S_1, S_2 in Game$_4$ perfectly. For the simulation of $\hat{\mathsf{H}}$, the only difference is that the distribution of δ_{hid} outputting from H in WFROS is uniformly over $\mathbb{Z}_p^*$, where in Game$_4$ it is always uniformly from $\mathbb{Z}_p$. However, the statistical distance between the two distributions is $1/p$. Since $\mathcal{B}$ makes at most $Q_{\mathsf{H}} + Q_{S_1} + 1$ queries to H, the statistical difference between the view of $\mathcal{A}$ in Game$_4$ and that in the one simulated by $\mathcal{B}$ is bounded by $(Q_{\mathsf{H}} + Q_{S_1} + 1)/p$.

Denote the event E_1 such that when $\mathcal{B}$ checks the output from $\mathcal{A}$, both (9) and (10) hold. As these are exactly the winning conditions of Game$_4$, which is simulated statistically closed to perfect, we have $\Pr[E_1] + \frac{Q_{\mathsf{H}} + Q_{S_1} + 1}{p} \geqslant \Pr[\mathsf{Game}_4^{\mathcal{A}} =$

1]. Also, let E_2 be the event for which the condition (11) holds immediately afterward. If E_2 does not happen, but E_1 does, then we know $\mathcal{A}$ outputs a valid message-signature pair (m_k^*, σ_k^*) such that $\mathrm{Hid}(\mathrm{str}_k^*) = \perp$, which is unlikely to happen. The following formalizes this.

Claim 4. $\Pr[E_1 \wedge (\neg E_2)] \leqslant \frac{2Q_\Phi(Q_\mathrm{H} + Q_{\mathrm{S}_1} + 1)}{p - Q_\Phi}$.

Then, we can conclude the proof with the following claim.

Claim 5. *If both E_1 and E_2 happen, then $\mathcal{B}$ outputs a valid WFROS solution $\mathcal{J}$, which in turn implies that $\Pr[E_1 \wedge E_2] \leqslant \mathrm{Adv}_{Q_{\mathrm{S}_1}, p}^{\mathrm{wfros}}(\mathcal{B})$.*

The proofs of the above two claim are presented in the full version of this paper.

5   Efficient Blind Signatures in the AGM

We now present schemes that are secure in the *algebraic group model* (AGM) [10]. This model considers security for *algebraic adversaries* - these are adversaries that, when used within a reduction, provide a representation of any group element they output in terms of all prior group elements input to the adversary. (We dispense with a more formal definition since the use of the AGM is self-evident in our proofs.)

5.1   A Protocol Secure Under the DL Assumption

In this section, we introduce a scheme, which we refer to as BS_3, that relies on the hardness of the (plain) discrete logarithm (DL) problem, which is formalized in Fig. 8. In contrast to BS_1, our new scheme (described in Fig. 7) requires an extra group element Z in the public key, and the commitment X^y in is replaced by $g^t Z^y$. (This will necessary result in an additional scalar in the signature.) However, one could generate Z as an output of a hash function (assuming the hash function is a random oracle, which we assume anyways), although, interestingly, our proof for BS_3 will show that blindness holds even when Z is chosen maliciously by the signer (who may consequently also know its discrete logarithm). We also present a slightly simpler alternative protocol, called BS_2, in the full version of this paper, that avoids the need of such an extra group element, at the cost of relying on the hardness of a stronger assumption, the *one-more discrete logarithm* (OMDL) problem. (Needless to say, a scheme based on DL only is seen as more desirable than a scheme based on the OMDL assumption [43].)

The additional group element Z will in fact allow us to develop a *partially blind* version of BS_3, which we refer to as PBS, which we discuss in Sect. 6 below. We note that in fact *all* results about BS_3 can be obtained as a corollary of our analysis of PBS, because a blind signature scheme is of course a special case of a partially blind one. However, we are opting for a separate presentation, as the main ideas behind the reduction are much simpler to understand in (plain) BS_3, and the proof of PBS adds some extra complexity (in particular, in order to obtain a tighter bound), which obfuscates the main ideas.

Algorithm $\mathsf{BS_3.Setup}(1^\lambda)$:	Algorithm $\mathsf{BS_3.U_1}(pk, \mathsf{msg}_1, m)$:
$p \leftarrow |\mathbb{G}_\lambda|$; $g \leftarrow g(\mathbb{G}_\lambda)$	$X \leftarrow pk$; $(A, C) \leftarrow \mathsf{msg}_1$
Select $\mathsf{H} : \{0,1\}^* \to \mathbb{Z}_p^*$	$r_1, r_2 \leftarrow_\$ \mathbb{Z}_p$; $\gamma_1, \gamma_2 \leftarrow_\$ \mathbb{Z}_p^*$
Return $par \leftarrow (p, \mathbb{G}_\lambda, g, \mathsf{H})$	$A' \leftarrow g^{r_1} \cdot A^{\gamma_1/\gamma_2}$; $C' \leftarrow C^{\gamma_1} g^{r_2}$
	$c' \leftarrow \mathsf{H}(A' \| C' \| m)$
Algorithm $\mathsf{BS_3.KG}(par)$:	$c \leftarrow c' \cdot \gamma_2$
$(p, \mathbb{G}_\lambda, g, \mathsf{H}) \leftarrow par$	$\mathsf{st}^u \leftarrow (c, c', r_1, r_2, \gamma_1, \gamma_2, X, Z, A, C)$
$x \leftarrow_\$ \mathbb{Z}_p$; $X \leftarrow g^x$; $Z \leftarrow_\$ \mathbb{G}_\lambda$	Return (st^u, c)
$sk \leftarrow x$; $pk \leftarrow (X, Z)$	
Return (sk, pk)	Algorithm $\mathsf{BS_3.U_2}(\mathsf{st}^u, \mathsf{msg}_2)$:
	$(c, c', r_1, r_2, \gamma_1, \gamma_2, X, Z, A, C) \leftarrow \mathsf{st}^u$
Algorithm $\mathsf{BS_3.S_1}(sk)$:	$(s, y, t) \leftarrow \mathsf{msg}_2$
$x \leftarrow sk$; $X \leftarrow g^x$	If $y = 0$ or $C \neq g^t Z^y$ or $g^s \neq A \cdot X^{c \cdot y}$
$a, t \leftarrow_\$ \mathbb{Z}_p$; $y \leftarrow_\$ \mathbb{Z}_p^*$	then return $\perp$
$A \leftarrow g^a$; $C \leftarrow g^t Z^y$	$s' \leftarrow (\gamma_1/\gamma_2) \cdot s + r_1$
$\mathsf{st}^s \leftarrow (a, y, t, x)$; $\mathsf{msg}_1 \leftarrow (A, C)$	$y' \leftarrow \gamma_1 \cdot y$; $t' \leftarrow \gamma_1 \cdot t + r_2$
Return $(\mathsf{st}^s, \mathsf{msg}_1)$	Return $\sigma \leftarrow (c', s', y', t')$
Algorithm $\mathsf{BS_3.S_2}(\mathsf{st}^s, c)$:	Algorithm $\mathsf{BS_3.Ver}(pk, \sigma, m)$:
If $c = 0$ then return $\perp$	$(c, s, y, t) \leftarrow \sigma$
$(a, y, t, x) \leftarrow \mathsf{st}^s$	If $y = 0$ then return 0
$s \leftarrow a + c \cdot y \cdot x$	$C \leftarrow g^t Z^y$; $A \leftarrow g^s \cdot X^{-c \cdot y}$
Return $\mathsf{msg}_2 \leftarrow (s, y, t)$	If $c \neq \mathsf{H}(A \| C \| m)$ then return 0
	Return 1

Fig. 7. The blind signature scheme $\mathsf{BS_3} = \mathsf{BS_3}[\mathbb{G}]$.

SECURITY ANALYSIS. The following theorem establishes the blindness of $\mathsf{BS_3}$. (Its proof is presented in the full version of this paper.)

Theorem 4. *Let $\mathbb{G}$ be an (asymptotic) family of prime-order cyclic groups. Then, the blind signature scheme $\mathsf{BS_3}[\mathbb{G}]$ is perfectly blind.*

The core of the analysis is once again a proof that the scheme is one-more unforgeable in the AGM, i.e., we only prove security against algebraic adversaries. In particular, we model the selected hash function as a random oracle H, to which the adversary is given explicit access.

Theorem 5. *Let $\mathbb{G}$ be an (asymptotic) family of prime-order cyclic groups. For any algebraic adversary $\mathcal{A}_{alg}$ for the game $\mathsf{OMUF}^{\mathsf{BS_3}[\mathbb{G}]}(\lambda)$ making at most Q_{S_1} queries to S_1 and Q_H queries to the random oracle H, there exists an adversary $\mathcal{B}_{dlog}$ for the DLog problem running in a similar running time as $\mathcal{A}_{alg}$ such that*
$$\mathsf{Adv}_{\mathsf{BS_3}[\mathbb{G}]}^{omuf}(\mathcal{A}_{alg}, \lambda) \leqslant 2\mathsf{Adv}_\mathbb{G}^{dlog}(\mathcal{B}_{dlog}, \lambda) + \frac{(Q_\mathsf{H} + Q_{\mathsf{S}_1} + 1)(Q_\mathsf{H} + 3Q_{\mathsf{S}_1} + 1)}{p - 1}.$$

Proof (of Theorem 5). Let us fix an adversary $\mathcal{A}_{alg}$ that makes at most Q_{S_1} queries to S_1 and Q_H queries to the random oracle H. Without loss of generality, assume $\mathcal{A}_{alg}$ makes exactly Q_{S_1} queries to S_1 and exactly one query (i, c_i) to S_2 for each $i \in [Q_{\mathsf{S}_1}]$. Then, after $\mathcal{A}_{alg}$ returns, we know $\ell = Q_{\mathsf{S}_1}$ and $\mathcal{I}_{fin} = [Q_{\mathsf{S}_1}]$.

$$\boxed{\begin{array}{l}
\text{Game DLog}_{\mathbb{G}}^{\mathcal{A}}(\lambda): \\
\hline
p \leftarrow |\mathbb{G}_\lambda| \; ; \; g \leftarrow g(\mathbb{G}_\lambda) \; ; \; X \leftarrow_\$ \mathbb{G}_\lambda \\
y \leftarrow \mathcal{A}(p, g, \mathbb{G}_\lambda, X) \\
\text{If } g^y = X \text{ then return } 1 \\
\text{Return } 0
\end{array}}$$

Fig. 8. The DLog game.

$$\boxed{\begin{array}{l|l}
\begin{array}{l}
\text{Game OMUF}_{\mathsf{BS}_3[\mathbb{G}]}^{\mathcal{A}_{\text{alg}}}(\lambda): \\
\hline
p \leftarrow |\mathbb{G}_\lambda| \; ; \; g \leftarrow g(\mathbb{G}_\lambda) \; ; \; x \leftarrow_\$ \mathbb{Z}_p \; ; \; X \leftarrow g^x \; ; \; Z \leftarrow \mathbb{G}_\lambda \\
\text{sid} \leftarrow 0 \; ; \; \ell \leftarrow 0 \; ; \; \mathcal{I}_{\text{fin}} \leftarrow \varnothing \; ; \; T \leftarrow () \; ; \; \text{hid} \leftarrow 0 \; ; \; \text{Hid} \leftarrow () \\
\{(m_k^*, \sigma_k^*)\}_{k \in [\ell+1]} \leftarrow_\$ \mathcal{A}_{\text{alg}}^{\mathsf{S}_1, \mathsf{S}_2, \mathsf{H}}(p, g, \mathbb{G}_\lambda, X, Z) \\
\text{If } \exists\, k_1 \neq k_2 \text{ such that } (m_{k_1}^*, \sigma_{k_1}^*) = (m_{k_2}^*, \sigma_{k_2}^*) \text{ then} \\
\quad \text{Return } 0 \\
\text{If } \exists\, k \in [\ell+1] \text{ such that } y_k^* = 0 \\
\quad \text{or } c_k^* \neq \mathsf{H}(g^{s_k^*} X^{-c_k^* \cdot y_k^*} \,\|\, g^{t_k^*} Z^{y_k^*} \,\|\, m_k^*) \\
\text{where } (c_k^*, s_k^*, y_k^*, t_k^*) = \sigma_k^* \text{ then return } 0 \\
\text{Return } 1 \\[4pt]
\text{Oracle } \mathsf{H}(A \,\|\, C \,\|\, m): \\
\hline
\text{If } T(A \,\|\, C \,\|\, m) = \bot \text{ then} \\
\quad T(A \,\|\, C \,\|\, m) \leftarrow_\$ \mathbb{Z}_p \\
\quad \text{hid} \leftarrow \text{hid} + 1 \; ; \; \text{Hid}(A \,\|\, C \,\|\, m) \leftarrow \text{hid} \\
\quad /\!/ \; A = g^{\hat{\alpha}g} X^{\hat{\alpha}X} Z^{\hat{\alpha}Z} \prod_{i \in [\text{sid}]} A_i^{\hat{\alpha}A_i} C_i^{\hat{\alpha}C_i} \\
\quad /\!/ \; C = g^{\hat{\beta}g} X^{\hat{\beta}X} Z^{\hat{\beta}Z} \prod_{i \in [\text{sid}]} A_i^{\hat{\beta}A_i} C_i^{\hat{\beta}C_i} \\
\quad \delta_{\text{hid}} \leftarrow T(A \,\|\, C \,\|\, m) \; ; \; \hat{\alpha}_{\text{hid}} \leftarrow \hat{\alpha} \; ; \; \hat{\beta}_{\text{hid}} \leftarrow \hat{\beta} \\
\text{Return } T(A \,\|\, C \,\|\, m)
\end{array}
&
\begin{array}{l}
\text{Oracle } \mathsf{S}_1: \\
\hline
\text{sid} \leftarrow \text{sid} + 1 \\
a_{\text{sid}}, t_{\text{sid}} \leftarrow_\$ \mathbb{Z}_p \\
y_{\text{sid}} \leftarrow_\$ \mathbb{Z}_p^* \\
\text{st}_{\text{sid}}^s \leftarrow (a_{\text{sid}}, y_{\text{sid}}, t_{\text{sid}}) \\
A_{\text{sid}} \leftarrow g^{a_{\text{sid}}} \\
C_{\text{sid}} \leftarrow g^{t_{\text{sid}}} Z^{y_{\text{sid}}} \\
\text{msg}_1 \leftarrow (A_{\text{sid}}, C_{\text{sid}}) \\
\text{Return } (\text{sid}, \text{msg}_1) \\[4pt]
\text{Oracle } \mathsf{S}_2(i, c_i): \\
\hline
\text{If } i \notin [\text{sid}] \setminus \mathcal{I}_{\text{fin}} \\
\quad \text{or } c_i = 0 \text{ then} \\
\quad \text{Return } \bot \\
(a_i, y_i, t_i) \leftarrow \text{st}_i^s \\
s_i \leftarrow a_i + c_i \cdot y_i \cdot x \\
\text{msg}_2 \leftarrow (s_i, y_i, t_i) \\
\mathcal{I}_{\text{fin}} \leftarrow \mathcal{I}_{\text{fin}} \cup \{i\} \\
\ell \leftarrow \ell + 1 \\
\text{Return } \text{msg}_2
\end{array}
\end{array}}$$

Fig. 9. The OMUF security game for the blind signature scheme $\mathsf{BS}_3[\mathbb{G}]$.

The $\text{OMUF}_{\mathsf{BS}_3[\mathbb{G}]}^{\mathcal{A}_{\text{alg}}}$ game is formally defined in Fig. 9. In addition to the original OMUF game (defined in Fig. 1), for each query $(A \,\|\, C \,\|\, m)$ to H, its corresponding hid is recorded in $\text{Hid}(A \,\|\, Y \,\|\, m)$, and the output of the query is recorded as δ_{hid}. Also, since $\mathcal{A}_{\text{alg}}$ is algebraic, it also provides the representations of A and C, and the corresponding coefficient $\hat{\alpha}$ and $\hat{\beta}$ are recorded as $\hat{\alpha}_{\text{hid}}$ and $\hat{\beta}_{\text{hid}}$.

Denote the event WIN as $\mathcal{A}_{\text{alg}}$ wins the $\text{OMUF}_{\mathsf{BS}_3[\mathbb{G}]}^{\mathcal{A}_{\text{alg}}}$ game, i.e., all output message-signature pairs $\{m_k^*, \sigma_k^*\}_{k \in [Q_{\mathsf{S}_1}+1]}$ are distinct and valid. Furthermore, let us denote $\text{str}_k^* := g^{s_k^*} X^{-c_k^* \cdot y_k^*} \,\|\, g^{t_k^*} Z^{y_k^*} \,\|\, m_k^*$. We let E be the event in the $\text{OMUF}_{\mathsf{BS}_3[\mathbb{G}]}^{\mathcal{A}_{\text{alg}}}$ game for which, after the validity of the output is checked, for each $k \in [Q_{\mathsf{S}_1}+1]$ and $j = \text{Hid}(\text{str}_k^*)$,[7] the following conditions hold:

---

[7] Here, $\text{Hid}(\text{str}_k^*)$ must be defined since a query str_k^* is made to H when checking the validity of the output (m_k^*, σ_k^*).

$$\hat{\alpha}_j^{\mathsf{X}} - \sum_{i \in [Q_{\mathsf{S}_1}]} y_i \cdot c_i \cdot \hat{\alpha}_j^{\mathsf{A}_i} = -\delta_j \cdot y_k^* \,, \tag{12}$$

$$\hat{\beta}_j^{\mathsf{Z}} + \sum_{i \in [Q_{\mathsf{S}_1}]} y_i \cdot \hat{\beta}_j^{\mathsf{C}_i} = y_k^* \,. \tag{13}$$

Since $\mathsf{Adv}_{\mathsf{BS}_3[\mathbb{G}]}^{\mathrm{omuf}}(\mathcal{A}_{\mathrm{alg}}, \lambda) = \Pr[\mathsf{WIN}] = \Pr[\mathsf{WIN} \wedge E] + \Pr[\mathsf{WIN} \wedge (\neg E)]$, the theorem follows by combining the following two lemmas with Theorem 1.

Lemma 8. *There exists an adversary $\mathcal{B}_{\mathrm{wfros}}$ for the $\mathrm{WFROS}_{Q_{\mathsf{S}_1}, p}$ problem making at most $Q_{\mathsf{H}} + Q_{\mathsf{S}_1} + 1$ queries to the random oracle $\hat{\mathsf{H}}$ such that $\mathsf{Adv}_{Q_{\mathsf{S}_1}, p}^{\mathrm{wfros}}(\mathcal{B}_{\mathrm{wfros}}) \geqslant \Pr[\mathsf{WIN} \wedge E]$.*

Lemma 9. *There exists an adversary $\mathcal{B}_{\mathrm{dlog}}$ for the DLog problem running in a similar running time as $\mathcal{A}_{\mathrm{alg}}$ such that $\mathsf{Adv}_{\mathbb{G}}^{\mathrm{dlog}}(\mathcal{B}_{\mathrm{dlog}}, \lambda) \geqslant \frac{1}{2} \Pr[\mathsf{WIN} \wedge (\neg E)]$.*

$\square$

The proof of Lemma 8 is presented in the full version of this paper, which is similar to the proof of Lemma 7.

5.2 Proof of Lemma 9

Proof. We first partition the event $\mathsf{WIN} \wedge (\neg E)$ into two cases. Denote F_1 as the event in the $\mathrm{OMUF}_{\mathsf{BS}_3[\mathbb{G}]}^{\mathcal{A}_{\mathrm{alg}}}$ game that there exists $k \in [Q_{\mathsf{S}_1} + 1]$ such that (12) does not hold, and denote F_2 as the event that there exists $k \in [Q_{\mathsf{S}_1} + 1]$ such that (13) does not hold. Then, if E does not occur, we know either F_1 or F_2 occurs. Therefore, we have $\mathsf{WIN} \wedge (\neg E) = (\mathsf{WIN} \wedge F_1) \vee (\mathsf{WIN} \wedge F_2)$. We then prove the following two claims.

Claim 6. *There exists $\mathcal{B}_{\mathrm{dlog}}^{(0)}$ for the DLog problem running in a similar running time as $\mathcal{A}_{\mathrm{alg}}$ such that $\Pr[\mathsf{WIN} \wedge F_1] \leqslant \mathsf{Adv}_{\mathbb{G}}^{\mathrm{dlog}}(\mathcal{B}_{\mathrm{dlog}}^{(0)}, \lambda)$.*

Claim 7. *There exists $\mathcal{B}_{\mathrm{dlog}}^{(1)}$ for the DLog problem running in a similar running time as $\mathcal{A}_{\mathrm{alg}}$ such that $\Pr[\mathsf{WIN} \wedge F_2] \leqslant \mathsf{Adv}_{\mathbb{G}}^{\mathrm{dlog}}(\mathcal{B}_{\mathrm{dlog}}^{(1)}, \lambda)$.*

From the above two claims, we can conclude the lemma by construct the adversary $\mathcal{B}_{\mathrm{dlog}}$ that runs either $\mathcal{B}_{\mathrm{dlog}}^{(0)}$ or $\mathcal{B}_{\mathrm{dlog}}^{(1)}$ with $1/2$ probability. $\square$

Proof (of Claim 6). We first give a detailed description of $\mathcal{B}_{\mathrm{dlog}}^{(0)}$ playing the $\mathrm{DLog}_{\mathbb{G}}$ game.

THE ADVERSARY $\mathcal{B}_{\mathrm{dlog}}^{(0)}$. Initially, $\mathcal{B}_{\mathrm{dlog}}^{(0)}$ initializes sid, $\mathcal{I}_{\mathrm{fin}}$, ℓ, T, hid, and Hid as described in the $\mathrm{OMUF}_{\mathsf{BS}_3[\mathbb{G}]}^{\mathcal{A}_{\mathrm{alg}}}$ game. After $\mathcal{B}_{\mathrm{dlog}}^{(0)}$ receives $(p, g, \mathbb{G}_\lambda, W)$ from the $\mathrm{DLog}_{\mathbb{G}}$ game, $\mathcal{B}_{\mathrm{dlog}}^{(0)}$ samples z uniformly from $\mathbb{Z}_p$ and sets $X \leftarrow W$, $Z \leftarrow g^z$. Then, $\mathcal{B}_{\mathrm{dlog}}^{(0)}$ runs $\mathcal{A}_{\mathrm{alg}}$ on input $(p, g, \mathbb{G}_\lambda, X)$ and with access to the oracles $\hat{\mathsf{S}}_1$, $\hat{\mathsf{S}}_2$, and $\hat{\mathsf{H}}$. These oracles operate as follows:

Oracle $\hat{\mathsf{S}}_1$: $\mathcal{B}_{\mathrm{dlog}}^{(0)}$ samples $s_{\mathrm{sid}}, t'_{\mathrm{sid}}$ uniformly from $\mathbb{Z}_p$ and y'_{sid} uniformly from $\mathbb{Z}_p^*$ and sets $A_{\mathrm{sid}} = g^{s_{\mathrm{sid}}} X^{-y'_{\mathrm{sid}}}$ and $C_{\mathrm{sid}} = g^{t'_{\mathrm{sid}}}$. Then, $\mathcal{B}_{\mathrm{dlog}}^{(0)}$ returns $(\mathrm{sid}, A_{\mathrm{sid}}, C_{\mathrm{sid}})$.

Oracle $\hat{\mathsf{S}}_2$: Same as in the $\mathrm{OMUF}_{\mathsf{BS}_3[\mathbb{G}]}^{\mathcal{A}_{\mathrm{alg}}}$ game if $i \notin [\mathrm{sid}] \setminus \mathcal{I}_{\mathrm{fin}}$ or $c_i = 0$. Otherwise, after receiving a query (i, c_i) to $\hat{\mathsf{S}}_2$ from $\mathcal{A}_{\mathrm{alg}}$, $\mathcal{B}_{\mathrm{dlog}}^{(0)}$ sets $y_i \leftarrow y'_i/c_i$ and $t_i \leftarrow t'_i - y_i \cdot z$. Then, $\mathcal{B}_{\mathrm{dlog}}^{(0)}$ returns (s_i, y_i, t_i) to $\mathcal{A}_{\mathrm{alg}}$.

Oracle $\hat{\mathsf{H}}$: Same as in the $\mathrm{OMUF}_{\mathsf{BS}_3[\mathbb{G}]}^{\mathcal{A}_{\mathrm{alg}}}$ game.

After receiving the output $\{(m_k^*, \sigma_k^*)\}_{k \in [Q_{S_1} + 1]}$, $\mathcal{B}_{\mathrm{dlog}}^{(0)}$ aborts if the event WIN $\wedge$ F_1 does not occur.

It is clear that $\mathcal{B}_{\mathrm{dlog}}^{(0)}$ simulates the $\mathrm{OMUF}_{\mathsf{BS}_3[\mathbb{G}]}^{\mathcal{A}_{\mathrm{alg}}}$ game perfectly. Therefore, it is left to show that if the event WIN $\wedge$ F_1 occurs within the simulation, $\mathcal{B}_{\mathrm{dlog}}^{(0)}$ can compute the discrete log of X, which equals to W.

Suppose WIN $\wedge$ F_1 occurs. There exists $k \in [Q_{S_1} + 1]$ and $j = \mathrm{Hid}(\mathrm{str}_k^*)$ such that (12) does not hold. Since $\mathrm{Hid}(\mathrm{str}_k^*) = j$ and $\delta_j = c_k^*$, we have

$$g^{s_k^*} X^{-\delta_j \cdot y_k^*} = g^{s_k^*} X^{-c_k^* \cdot y_k^*} = g^{\hat{\alpha}_j^g} X^{\hat{\alpha}_j^X} Z^{\hat{\alpha}_j^Z} \prod_{i \in [\mathrm{sid}]} A_i^{\hat{\alpha}_j^{A_i}} C_i^{\hat{\alpha}_j^{C_i}}. \tag{14}$$

Similar to the preceding case, since $\mathcal{B}_{\mathrm{dlog}}^{(0)}$ knows the discrete log of Z as z and (12) does not hold, by substituting $A_i = g^{s_i} X^{-c_i \cdot y_i}$, $C_i = g^{t_i} Z^{y_i}$, and $Z = g^z$ into (14), $\mathcal{B}_{\mathrm{dlog}}^{(0)}$ can compute the discrete log of X as

$$x := \frac{s_k^* - \hat{\alpha}_j^g - \hat{\alpha}_j^Z \cdot z - \sum_{i \in [Q_{S_1}]} (\hat{\alpha}_j^{A_i} \cdot s_i + \hat{\alpha}_j^{C_i} \cdot (t_i + y_i \cdot z))}{\hat{\alpha}_j^X - \sum_{i \in [Q_{S_1}]} y_i \cdot c_i \cdot \hat{\alpha}_j^{A_i} + \delta_j \cdot y_k^*}.$$

$\square$

The proof of Claim 7 is presented in the full version of this paper, which is analogous to the proof of Claim 6.

6   Partially Blind Signatures

This section presents our partially blind signature scheme, PBS, which is detailed in Fig. 10. The scheme builds on top of the BS_3 scheme by replacing the extra generator Z contained in the public key with the output of a hash function F (also modeled as a random oracle in the OMUF proof) applied to the public input info. We do not formally redefine the syntax of partially blind signatures, but we note that it simply extends that of blind signatures by adding the extra input info $\in \{0, 1\}^*$ to the signer, the user, and the verification algorithm.

BLINDNESS. We first study the blindness of PBS. The $\mathrm{PBlind}_{\mathsf{PBS}}^{\mathcal{A}}$ game is defined in Fig. 11. The only difference between PBlind and Blind is that initially, the

Algorithm PBS.Setup(1^λ) :	Algorithm PBS.U$_1$($pk, \mathsf{msg}_1, \mathsf{info}, m$) :
$p \leftarrow |\mathbb{G}_\lambda|$; $g \leftarrow g(\mathbb{G}_\lambda)$	$X \leftarrow pk$; $(A, C) \leftarrow \mathsf{msg}_1$; $Z \leftarrow \mathrm{F}(\mathsf{info})$

Algorithm PBS.Setup(1^λ) :

$p \leftarrow |\mathbb{G}_\lambda|$; $g \leftarrow g(\mathbb{G}_\lambda)$
Select $\mathrm{H} : \{0,1\}^* \to \mathbb{Z}_p^*$
Select $\mathrm{F} : \{0,1\}^* \to \mathbb{G}_\lambda$
Return $par \leftarrow (p, \mathbb{G}_\lambda, g, \mathrm{H}, \mathrm{F})$

Algorithm PBS.KG(par) :

$(p, \mathbb{G}_\lambda, g, \mathrm{H}, \mathrm{F}) \leftarrow par$
$x \leftarrow_\$ \mathbb{Z}_p$; $X \leftarrow g^x$
$sk \leftarrow x$; $pk \leftarrow X$
Return (sk, pk)

Algorithm PBS.S$_1$(sk, info) :

$x \leftarrow sk$; $X \leftarrow g^x$; $Z \leftarrow \mathrm{F}(\mathsf{info})$
$a, t \leftarrow_\$ \mathbb{Z}_p$; $y \leftarrow_\$ \mathbb{Z}_p^*$
$A \leftarrow g^a$; $C \leftarrow g^t Z^y$
$\mathsf{st}^s \leftarrow (a, y, t, x)$; $\mathsf{msg}_1 \leftarrow (A, C)$
Return $(\mathsf{st}^s, \mathsf{msg}_1)$

Algorithm PBS.S$_2$(st^s, c) :

If $c = 0$ then return $\bot$
$(a, y, t, x) \leftarrow \mathsf{st}^s$
$s \leftarrow a + c \cdot y \cdot x$
Return $\mathsf{msg}_2 \leftarrow (s, y, t)$

Algorithm PBS.U$_1$($pk, \mathsf{msg}_1, \mathsf{info}, m$) :

$X \leftarrow pk$; $(A, C) \leftarrow \mathsf{msg}_1$; $Z \leftarrow \mathrm{F}(\mathsf{info})$
$r_1, r_2 \leftarrow_\$ \mathbb{Z}_p$; $\gamma_1, \gamma_2 \leftarrow_\$ \mathbb{Z}_p^*$
$A' \leftarrow g^{r_1} \cdot A^{\gamma_1/\gamma_2}$; $C' \leftarrow C^{\gamma_1} g^{r_2}$
$c' \leftarrow \mathrm{H}(\mathsf{info} \,\|\, A' \,\|\, C' \,\|\, m)$
$c \leftarrow c' \cdot \gamma_2$
$\mathsf{st}^u \leftarrow (c, c', r_1, r_2, \gamma_1, \gamma_2, X, Z, A, C)$
Return (st^u, c)

Algorithm PBS.U$_2$($\mathsf{st}^u, \mathsf{msg}_2$) :

$(c, c', r_1, r_2, \gamma_1, \gamma_2, X, Z, A, C) \leftarrow \mathsf{st}^u$
$(s, y, t) \leftarrow \mathsf{msg}_2$
If $y = 0$ or $C \neq g^t Z^y$ or $g^s \neq A \cdot X^{c \cdot y}$
  then return $\bot$
$s' \leftarrow (\gamma_1/\gamma_2) \cdot s + r_1$
$y' \leftarrow \gamma_1 \cdot y$; $t' \leftarrow \gamma_1 \cdot t + r_2$
Return $\sigma \leftarrow (c', s', y', t')$

Algorithm PBS.Ver($pk, \mathsf{info}, \sigma, m$) :

$X \leftarrow pk$; $Z \leftarrow \mathrm{F}(\mathsf{info})$; $(c, s, y, t) \leftarrow \sigma$
If $y = 0$ then return 0
$C \leftarrow g^t Z^y$; $A \leftarrow g^s \cdot X^{-c \cdot y}$
If $c \neq \mathrm{H}(\mathsf{info} \,\|\, A \,\|\, C \,\|\, m)$ then return 0
Return 1

Fig. 10. The partially blind signature scheme PBS = PBS[$\mathbb{G}$].

adversary $\mathcal{A}$ also picks a public information info and interacts with PBS.U$_1$ and PBS.U$_2$ for signing (info, m_0) and (info, m_1). Denote the advantage of the adversary $\mathcal{A}$ as $\mathsf{Adv}_{\mathsf{PBS}}^{\mathrm{pblind}}(\mathcal{A}, \lambda) := \left| \Pr[\mathrm{PBlind}_{\mathsf{PBS}}^{\mathcal{A}}(\lambda) = 1] - \frac{1}{2} \right|$. We say a partially blind signature scheme PBS is perfectly blind if and only if $\mathsf{Adv}_{\mathsf{PBS}}^{\mathrm{pblind}}(\mathcal{A}) = 0$ for any $\mathcal{A}$.

Theorem 6. *Let $\mathbb{G}$ be an (asymptotic) family of prime-order cyclic groups. The partially blind signature scheme PBS[$\mathbb{G}$] is perfectly blind.*

Since the algorithm PBS.U$_1$ and PBS.U$_2$ are almost the same as BS$_3$.U$_1$ and BS$_3$.U$_2$, we can use a proof similar to the one for BS$_3$ (Sect. 5.1) to show PBS[$\mathbb{G}$] is perfectly blind. The only difference is that in BS$_3$, Z is given in the public key, while in PBS[$\mathbb{G}$], Z is given by $\mathrm{F}(\mathsf{info})$.

OMUF SECURITY. We next study the OMUF security of PBS. Note that the definition must also be adjusted: The main difference is that the adversary wins as long as it can produce $\ell + 1$ valid message-signature pairs for some info for which it has run only ℓ signing sessions, regardless of how many signing sessions are run with $\mathsf{info}' \neq \mathsf{info}$ (i.e., their number could be higher than ℓ). We present the corresponding game for the specific case of the scheme PBS and prove the following theorem in the full version of this paper.

Game $\mathrm{PBlind}_{\mathsf{PBS}}^{\mathcal{A}}(\lambda)$:	Oracle $U_1(i, \mathsf{msg}_1^{(i)})$:
$par \leftarrow \mathsf{BS.Setup}(1^\lambda)$	If $i \notin \{0,1\}$ or $\mathsf{sess}_i \neq \mathtt{init}$ then return $\perp$
$b \leftarrow_{\$} \{0,1\}$; $b_0 \leftarrow b$; $b_1 \leftarrow 1 - b$	$\mathsf{sess}_i \leftarrow \mathtt{open}$
$b' \leftarrow_{\$} \mathcal{A}^{\mathrm{INIT}, U_1, U_2}(par)$	$(\mathsf{st}_i^u, \mathsf{chl}^{(i)}) \leftarrow \mathsf{PBS.U}_1(pk, \mathsf{msg}_1^{(i)}, \mathsf{info}, m_{b_i})$
If $b' = b$ then return 1	Return $\mathsf{chl}^{(i)}$
Return 0	
	Oracle $U_2(i, \mathsf{msg}_2^{(i)})$:
Oracle $\mathrm{INIT}(\tilde{pk}, \tilde{\mathsf{info}}, \tilde{m}_0, \tilde{m}_1)$:	If $i \notin \{0,1\}$ or $\mathsf{sess}_i \neq \mathtt{open}$ then return $\perp$
$\mathsf{sess}_0 \leftarrow \mathtt{init}$	$\mathsf{sess}_i \leftarrow \mathtt{closed}$
$\mathsf{sess}_1 \leftarrow \mathtt{init}$	$\sigma_{b_i} \leftarrow \mathsf{PBS.U}_2(\mathsf{st}_i^u, \mathsf{msg}_2^{(i)})$
$pk \leftarrow \tilde{pk}$	If $\mathsf{sess}_0 = \mathsf{sess}_1 = \mathtt{closed}$ then
$\mathsf{info} \leftarrow \tilde{\mathsf{info}}$	If $\sigma_0 = \perp$ or $\sigma_1 = \perp$ then return $(\perp, \perp)$
$m_0 \leftarrow \tilde{m}_0$; $m_1 \leftarrow \tilde{m}_1$	Return (σ_0, σ_1)
	Return $(i, \mathtt{closed})$

Fig. 11. The PBlind security game for a partially blind signature scheme PBS.

Theorem 7. *Let $\mathbb{G}$ be an (asymptotic) family of prime-order cyclic groups. Let $\mathcal{A}_{\mathrm{alg}}$ be an algebraic adversary for the game $\mathrm{OMUF}^{\mathsf{PBS}[\mathbb{G}]}(\lambda)$ such that for each public information info, makes at most Q_{S_1} queries to S_1 and Q_H queries to the random oracle H that start with info. Also, let the total number of distinct public information info's queried by $\mathcal{A}_{\mathrm{alg}}$ to S_1 be bounded by Q_{info}. Then, there exists an adversary $\mathcal{B}_{\mathrm{dlog}}$ for the DLog problem running in similar running time as $\mathcal{A}_{\mathrm{alg}}$ such that $\mathsf{Adv}_{\mathsf{PBS}[\mathbb{G}]}^{\mathrm{omuf}}(\mathcal{A}_{\mathrm{alg}}, \lambda) \leqslant 2\mathsf{Adv}_{\mathbb{G}}^{\mathrm{dlog}}(\mathcal{B}_{\mathrm{dlog}}, \lambda) + \frac{Q_{\mathsf{info}}(Q_H + 3Q_{S_1} + 1)^2 + 2}{p - 1}$.*

The proof is very similar to that for BS_3 except we need to additionally perform a hybrid argument over queries to F, guessing which info will be the one leading to a one-more forgery. However, we need to work harder here to ensure the discrete logarithm advantage does not scale with Q_{info}.

We also note that we have no argument supporting the fact that the information-theoretic term in Theorem 7 is tight and the inclusion of info in H is necessary. However, a tighter analysis appears to require studying a more general version of WFROS. We leave this to future work.

Acknowledgments. The authors wish to thank Christopher A. Wood for extensive discussions. Both authors were partially supported by NSF grants CNS-1930117 (CAREER), CNS-1926324, CNS-2026774, a Sloan Research Fellowship, and a JP Morgan Faculty Award.

References

1. Chaum, D.: Verification by anonymous monitors. In: Gersho, A. (ed.) CRYPTO 1981, volume ECE Report 82–04, pp. 138–139. U.C. Santa Barbara, Department of Electrical and Computer Engineering (1981)
2. Chaum, D., Fiat, A., Naor, M.: Untraceable electronic cash. In: Goldwasser, S. (ed.) CRYPTO 1988. LNCS, vol. 403, pp. 319–327. Springer, New York (1990). https://doi.org/10.1007/0-387-34799-2_25

3. Camenisch, J., Lysyanskaya, A.: Signature schemes and anonymous credentials from bilinear maps. In: Franklin, M. (ed.) CRYPTO 2004. LNCS, vol. 3152, pp. 56–72. Springer, Heidelberg (2004). https://doi.org/10.1007/978-3-540-28628-8_4

4. PCM: Click fraud prevention and attribution sent to advertiser. https://webkit.org/blog/11940/pcm-click-fraud-prevention-and-attribution-sent-to-advertiser/, Accessed 30 Sept 2021

5. Hendrickson, S., Iyengar, J., Pauly, T., Valdez, S., Wood, C.A.: Private Access Tokens. Internet-Draft draft-private-access-tokens-01, Internet Engineering Task Force (2021). Work in Progress

6. Trust tokens. https://developer.chrome.com/docs/privacy-sandbox/trust-tokens/, Accessed 11 Jan 2022

7. Denis, F., Jacobs, F., Wood, C.A.: RSA Blind Signatures. Internet-Draft draft-irtf-cfrg-rsa-blind-signatures-02, Internet Engineering Task Force (2021). Work in Progress

8. Shoup, V.: Lower bounds for discrete logarithms and related problems. In: Fumy, W. (ed.) EUROCRYPT 1997. LNCS, vol. 1233, pp. 256–266. Springer, Heidelberg (1997). https://doi.org/10.1007/3-540-69053-0_18

9. Maurer, U.: Abstract models of computation in cryptography. In: Smart, N.P. (ed.) Cryptography and Coding 2005. LNCS, vol. 3796, pp. 1–12. Springer, Heidelberg (2005). https://doi.org/10.1007/11586821_1

10. Fuchsbauer, G., Kiltz, E., Loss, J.: The algebraic group model and its applications. In: Shacham, H., Boldyreva, A. (eds.) CRYPTO 2018. LNCS, vol. 10992, pp. 33–62. Springer, Cham (2018). https://doi.org/10.1007/978-3-319-96881-0_2

11. Bellare, M., Rogaway, P.: Random oracles are practical: a paradigm for designing efficient protocols. In: Denning, D.E., Pyle, R., Ganesan, R., Sandhu, R.S., Ashby, V. (eds.) ACM CCS 93, pp. 62–73. ACM Press (1993)

12. Abe, M., Fujisaki, E.: How to date blind signatures. In: Kim, K., Matsumoto, T. (eds.) ASIACRYPT 1996. LNCS, vol. 1163, pp. 244–251. Springer, Heidelberg (1996). https://doi.org/10.1007/BFb0034851

13. Abe, M., Okamoto, T.: Provably secure partially blind signatures. In: Bellare, M. (ed.) CRYPTO 2000. LNCS, vol. 1880, pp. 271–286. Springer, Heidelberg (2000). https://doi.org/10.1007/3-540-44598-6_17

14. Chaum, D., Pedersen, T.P.: Wallet databases with observers. In: Brickell, E.F. (ed.) CRYPTO 1992. LNCS, vol. 740, pp. 89–105. Springer, Heidelberg (1993). https://doi.org/10.1007/3-540-48071-4_7

15. Pointcheval, D., Stern, J.: Security arguments for digital signatures and blind signatures. J. Cryptol. 13(3), 361–396 (2000)

16. Hauck, E., Kiltz, E., Loss, J.: A modular treatment of blind signatures from identification schemes. In: Ishai, Y., Rijmen, V. (eds.) EUROCRYPT 2019. LNCS, vol. 11478, pp. 345–375. Springer, Cham (2019). https://doi.org/10.1007/978-3-030-17659-4_12

17. Benhamouda, F., Lepoint, T., Loss, J., Orrù, M., Raykova, M.: On the (in)security of ros. In: Canteaut, A., Standaert, F.-X. (eds.) EUROCRYPT 2021. LNCS, vol. 12696, pp. 33–53. Springer, Cham (2021). https://doi.org/10.1007/978-3-030-77870-5_2

18. Fuchsbauer, G., Plouviez, A., Seurin, Y.: Blind schnorr signatures and signed elgamal encryption in the algebraic group model. In: Canteaut, A., Ishai, Y. (eds.) EUROCRYPT 2020. LNCS, vol. 12106, pp. 63–95. Springer, Cham (2020). https://doi.org/10.1007/978-3-030-45724-2_3

19. Abe, M.: A secure three-move blind signature scheme for polynomially many signatures. In: Pfitzmann, B. (ed.) EUROCRYPT 2001. LNCS, vol. 2045, pp. 136–151. Springer, Heidelberg (2001). https://doi.org/10.1007/3-540-44987-6_9

20. Ohkubo, M., Abe, M.: Security of some three-move blind signature schemes reconsidered. In: The 2003 Symposium on Cryptography and Information Security (2003)

21. Kastner, J., Loss, J., Rosenberg, M., Xu, J.: On pairing-free blind signature schemes in the algebraic group model. In: PKC 2022 (2022). to appear

22. Baldimtsi, F., Lysyanskaya, A.: Anonymous credentials light. In: Sadeghi, A.R., Gligor,V.D., Yung, M. (eds.) ACM CCS 2013, pp. 1087–1098. ACM Press (2013)

23. Boneh, D., Lynn, B., Shacham, H.: Short signatures from the weil pairing. In: Boyd, C. (ed.) ASIACRYPT 2001. LNCS, vol. 2248, pp. 514–532. Springer, Heidelberg (2001). https://doi.org/10.1007/3-540-45682-1_30

24. Boldyreva, A.: Threshold signatures, multisignatures and blind signatures based on the gap-diffie-hellman-group signature scheme. In: Desmedt, Y.G. (ed.) PKC 2003. LNCS, vol. 2567, pp. 31–46. Springer, Heidelberg (2003). https://doi.org/10.1007/3-540-36288-6_3

25. Schnorr, C.P.: Efficient identification and signatures for smart cards. In: Brassard, G. (ed.) CRYPTO 1989. LNCS, vol. 435, pp. 239–252. Springer, New York (1990). https://doi.org/10.1007/0-387-34805-0_22

26. Schnorr, C.P.: Efficient signature generation by smart cards. J. Cryptol. 4(3), 161–174 (1991). https://doi.org/10.1007/BF00196725

27. Bernstein, D.J., Duif, N., Lange, T., Schwabe, P., Yang, B.-Y.: High-speed high-security signatures. J. Cryptogr. Eng. 2(2), 77–89 (2012)

28. Katz, J., Loss, J., Rosenberg, M.: Boosting the security of blind signature schemes. In: Tibouchi, M., Wang, H. (eds.) ASIACRYPT 2021. LNCS, vol. 13093, pp. 468–492. Springer, Cham (2021). https://doi.org/10.1007/978-3-030-92068-5_16

29. Chairattana-Apirom, R., Lysyanskaya, A.: Compact cut-and-choose: boosting the security of blind signature schemes, compactly. Cryptology ePrint Archive, Report 2022/003 (2022). https://ia.cr/2022/003

30. Wagner, B., Hanzlik, L., Loss, J.: Pi-cut-choo! parallel instance cut and choose for practical blind signatures. Cryptology ePrint Archive, Report 2022/007 (2022). https://ia.cr/2022/007

31. Garg, S., Rao, V., Sahai, A., Schröder, D., Unruh, D.: Round optimal blind signatures. In: Rogaway, P. (ed.) CRYPTO 2011. LNCS, vol. 6841, pp. 630–648. Springer, Heidelberg (2011). https://doi.org/10.1007/978-3-642-22792-9_36

32. Blazy, O., Fuchsbauer, G., Pointcheval, D., Vergnaud, D.: Short blind signatures. J. Comput. Secur. 21(5), 627–661 (2013)

33. Garg, S., Gupta, D.: Efficient round optimal blind signatures. In: Nguyen, P.Q., Oswald, E. (eds.) EUROCRYPT 2014. LNCS, vol. 8441, pp. 477–495. Springer, Heidelberg (2014). https://doi.org/10.1007/978-3-642-55220-5_27

34. Fuchsbauer, G., Hanser, C., Slamanig, D.: Practical round-optimal blind signatures in the standard model. In: Gennaro, R., Robshaw, M. (eds.) CRYPTO 2015. LNCS, vol. 9216, pp. 233–253. Springer, Heidelberg (2015). https://doi.org/10.1007/978-3-662-48000-7_12

35. Fuchsbauer, G., Hanser, C., Kamath, C., Slamanig, D.: Practical round-optimal blind signatures in the standard model from weaker assumptions. In: Zikas, V., De Prisco, R. (eds.) SCN 2016. LNCS, vol. 9841, pp. 391–408. Springer, Cham (2016). https://doi.org/10.1007/978-3-319-44618-9_21

36. Ghadafi, E.: Efficient round-optimal blind signatures in the standard model. In: Kiayias, A. (ed.) FC 2017. LNCS, vol. 10322, pp. 455–473. Springer, Cham (2017). https://doi.org/10.1007/978-3-319-70972-7_26

37. Katsumata, S., Nishimaki, R., Yamada, S., Yamakawa, T.: Round-optimal blind signatures in the plain model from classical and quantum standard assumptions. In: Canteaut, A., Standaert, F.-X. (eds.) EUROCRYPT 2021. LNCS, vol. 12696, pp. 404–434. Springer, Cham (2021). https://doi.org/10.1007/978-3-030-77870-5_15

38. Schnorr, C.P.: Security of blind discrete log signatures against interactive attacks. In: Qing, S., Okamoto, T., Zhou, J. (eds.) ICICS 2001. LNCS, vol. 2229, pp. 1–12. Springer, Heidelberg (2001). https://doi.org/10.1007/3-540-45600-7_1

39. Hopper, N.: Proving security of tor's hidden service identity blinding protocol (2013). https://www-users.cse.umn.edu/~hoppernj/basic-proof.pdf

40. Bauer, B., Fuchsbauer, G., Plouviez, A.: The one-more discrete logarithm assumption in the generic group model. Cryptology ePrint Archive, Report 2021/866 (2021). https://ia.cr/2021/866

41. Bellare, M., Namprempre, C., Pointcheval, D., Semanko, M.: The one-more-RSA-inversion problems and the security of Chaum's blind signature scheme. J. Cryptol. 16(3), 185–215 (2003)

42. Bellare, M., Rogaway, P.: The security of triple encryption and a framework for code-based game-playing proofs. In: Vaudenay, S. (ed.) EUROCRYPT 2006. LNCS, vol. 4004, pp. 409–426. Springer, Heidelberg (2006). https://doi.org/10.1007/11761679_25

43. Koblitz, N., Menezes, A.: Another look at non-standard discrete log and diffie-hellman problems. J. Math. Cryptol. 2(4), 311–326 (2008)

Real-World Systems

CoCoA: Concurrent Continuous Group Key Agreement

Joël Alwen[1], Benedikt Auerbach[2], Miguel Cueto Noval[2], Karen Klein[3],
Guillermo Pascual-Perez[2]([✉]), Krzysztof Pietrzak[2], and Michael Walter[4]

[1] AWS Wickr, New York, USA
alwenjo@amazon.com
[2] ISTA, Klosterneuburg, Austria
{bauerbac,mcuetono,gpascual,pietrzak}@ist.ac.at
[3] ETH Zurich, Zürich, Switzerland
karen.klein@inf.ethz.ch
[4] Zama, Paris, France
michael.walter@zama.ai

Abstract. Messaging platforms like Signal are widely deployed and provide strong security in an asynchronous setting. It is a challenging problem to construct a protocol with similar security guarantees that can *efficiently* scale to large groups. A major bottleneck are the frequent key rotations users need to perform to achieve post compromise forward security.

In current proposals – most notably in TreeKEM (which is part of the IETF's Messaging Layer Security (MLS) protocol draft) – for users in a group of size n to rotate their keys, they must each craft a message of size $\log(n)$ to be broadcast to the group using an (untrusted) delivery server.

In larger groups, having users sequentially rotate their keys requires too much bandwidth (or takes too long), so variants allowing any $T \leq n$ users to simultaneously rotate their keys in just 2 communication rounds have been suggested (e.g. "Propose and Commit" by MLS). Unfortunately, 2-round concurrent updates are either damaging or expensive (or both); i.e. they either result in future operations being more costly (e.g. via "blanking" or "tainting") or are costly themselves requiring $\Omega(T)$ communication for each user [Bienstock et al., TCC'20].

M. Walter—Benedikt Auerbach and Krzysztof Pietrzak have received funding from the European Research Council (ERC) under the European Union's Horizon 2020 research and innovation programme (682815 - TOCNet); Karen Klein was supported in part by ERC CoG grant 724307 and conducted part of this work at IST Austria, funded by the ERC under the European Union's Horizon 2020 research and innovation programme (682815 - TOCNeT); Guillermo Pascual-Perez was funded by the European Union's Horizon 2020 research and innovation programme under the Marie Skłodowska-Curie Grant Agreement No.665385; Michael Walter conducted part of this work at IST Austria, funded by the ERC under the European Union's Horizon 2020 research and innovation programme (682815 - TOCNeT).

© International Association for Cryptologic Research 2022
O. Dunkelman and S. Dziembowski (Eds.): EUROCRYPT 2022, LNCS 13276, pp. 815–844, 2022.
https://doi.org/10.1007/978-3-031-07085-3_28

In this paper we propose CoCoA; a new scheme that allows for T concurrent updates that are neither damaging nor costly. That is, they add no cost to future operations yet they only require $\Omega(\log^2(n))$ communication per user. To circumvent the [Bienstock et al.] lower bound, CoCoA increases the number of rounds needed to complete all updates from 2 up to (at most) $\log(n)$; though typically fewer rounds are needed.

The key insight of our protocol is the following: in the (non-concurrent version of) TreeKEM, a delivery server which gets T concurrent update requests will approve one and reject the remaining $T - 1$. In contrast, our server attempts to apply all of them. If more than one user requests to rotate the same key during a round, the server arbitrarily picks a winner. Surprisingly, we prove that regardless of how the server chooses the winners, all previously compromised users will recover after at most $\log(n)$ such update rounds.

To keep the communication complexity low, CoCoA is a server-aided CGKA. That is, the delivery server no longer blindly forwards packets, but instead actively computes individualized packets tailored to each user. As the server is untrusted, this change requires us to develop new mechanisms ensuring robustness of the protocol.

1   Introduction

End-to-end (E2E) secure cryptographic protocols are rapidly becoming ubiquitous tools in the daily life of billions of people. The most prominent examples are secure messaging protocols (such as those based on the Double Ratchet) and E2E encrypted VoIP conference calling protocols. The demands of practical E2E security are non-trivial; all the more so when the goal is to allow *groups* to communicate in a single session. Almost all current (aka. "1st generation") E2E protocols for groups are built on top of some underlying black-box 1-on-1 E2E secure protocol [28]. However, this approach seems to unavoidably result in the complexity of (at least some critical) operations scaling linearly in the group size n.[1] This has resulted in practical limits in the groups sizes for deployed E2E protocols (to date, often in 10s or low 100s and never more than 1000).

Motivated by this, Cohn-Gordon et al. [16] initiated the study of E2E protocols whose complexity scales *logarithmically* in n. Starting with this work, research in the area has focused on a fundamental class of primitives called *Continuous Group Key Agreement* (CGKA).[2] Intuitively, CGKA is to, say, E2E secure messaging what Key Agreement is to Public Key Encryption. That is, CGKA protocols capture many of the challenges involved in building practical higher-level E2E secure applications (like messaging) while still providing enough functionality to make building such applications comparatively easy using known techniques [4]. Thus they present a very useful subject for research in the area.

---

[1] In fact, this holds true even for the few 1st generation E2E protocols designed from the ground up with groups in mind [22].

[2] Also referred to as *Group Ratcheting* [11] or *Continuous Group Key Distribution* [13].

In a bit more detail, a CGKA protocol allows an evolving set of group members to continuously agree on a fresh symmetric key. Every time a new party joins, or an existing one leaves or refreshes (a.k.a. "updates") their cryptographic state, a new epoch begins in the session. Each epoch E is equipped with its own group key k_E which can be derived by all parties that are members of the group during E. CGKA protocol sessions are expected to last for very long periods of time (e.g. years). Thus, they must provide a property sometimes referred to as *post compromise forward security* (PCFS) [5]. That means that the group key of a target epoch should look random to an adversary despite having compromised any number of group members in both earlier and later epochs as long as the compromised parties either left the group or performed an update between their compromise and the target epoch.[3] In the spirit of distributed E2E security (and unlike, say, Broadcast Encryption or Dynamic Group Key Agreement) CGKA protocols must achieve this without the help of trusted group managers or other specially designated trusted parties.

With a few exceptions discussed below, most CGKA protocols today [3,5, 7,9,16,25] were designed with an asynchronous communication setting in mind (likely motivated by the application of secure asynchronous messaging). That is, parties may remain offline for extended periods of time, not ever actually being online at the same time as each other. Once they do come online, though, they should be able to immediately "catch up" and even initiate a new epoch (e.g. by unilaterally adding a new member to the group). To facilitate this, protocols are designed to communicate via an untrusted network which buffers protocol packets for parties until they come online again.

The Problem of Coordination. One property the first generation of CGKA protocols [3,9,16,25] share is that they require *all* protocol packets to be processed in exactly the same order by every group member. However, ensuring this level of coordination can present real challenges in a variety of settings; especially for large groups (e.g. with 50,000 members as is targeted by the IETF's upcoming E2E secure messaging standard MLS [8]). In particular, it might lead to the problem sometimes called "starvation" where a client's packets are constantly rejected by the group (e.g. when the client is on a slow network connection and so can never distribute its own packets fast enough).

There do not seem to be any practical solutions to convincingly provide this level of coordination without significant drawbacks. Implementing the buffering mechanism via a single server does not automatically address the issue of

---

[3] We note that PCFS is strictly stronger than providing the two more commonly discussed properties of Forward Security (FS) and Post Compromise Security (PCS). Indeed, a successful attack on an epoch E may require compromises *both* before *and* after E. Such an attack is neither an FS attack nor a PCS attack. Moreover, literature usually speaks informally of FS and PCS as separate notions asking that they both hold. Yet the notions do not necessarily compose. For example, the MLS messaging standard has both strong FS and PCS properties but significantly worse PCFS [3]. Fortunately, all *formal* security definitions for CGKA we are aware of do in fact capture (some variation of) PCFS instead of treating FS and PCS separately.

starvation of clients with a slow connection. Nor is a round-robin "speaking slot" approach a satisfactory solution (even assuming universal time), as it would severely impact responsiveness; especially for larger groups. It's also not just responsiveness that suffers from a reduction of the rate at which parties can send new packets to the group. The quality of the security of a session (e.g. the speed with which privacy is recovered after a group member's local state is leaked) is also tightly dependent on the rate at which participants can send out packets. After all, if a compromised party has not even been able to send anything new to the group since a compromise, they have no way to update the leaked cryptographic material to something the adversary cannot simply derive itself.

Concurrency at a High Price. To mitigate this problem the MLS messaging protocol introduced a new syntax referred to as the "propose-and-commit" (P&C) paradigm. Since then it was adopted by most second generation CGKA protocols [5,7] as it allows for some degree of concurrency. In particular, group members (and even designated external parties) may concurrently propose changes to the group state e.g. "Alice proposes adding Bob", "Charlie proposes updating his keys", etc. At any point a group member can collect such proposal into a commit message which is broadcast to the group and actually affects all changes in the referenced proposals. Note, however, that the commit messages still must be processed in a globally unique order. Moreover, in each of these protocols there is a high price being paid for large amounts of concurrency. Namely, the greater the number of proposals in a single commit message, the less efficient (e.g. greater packet size) certain future commits will be. In fact, efficiency can degenerate to the point where (starting from an arbitrary group state) a commit to $\Theta(n)$ proposals can produce a state where the next commit packet is forced to have size $\Omega(n)$; a far cry from the desired $O(\log(n))$.

Lower-Bounds on Communication Complexity. Bienstock et al. [11] showed that there are limits to what we could hope for in terms of reducing communication complexity. Specifically, they show that T group members updating concurrently incurs a communication cost per user in the following round that is linear in T in any "reasonable" protocol.[4] In fact, if all n parties wish to update concurrently within 2 rounds then this has complexity at least $\Omega(n^2)$.

1.1   Our Contributions

In this paper (full version in [2]) we propose a new CGKA protocol called CoCoA (for *COncurrent COntinuous group key Agreement*) which is designed specifically to allow for efficient concurrent group operations. In contrast to past CGKA

---

[4] For the lower bound, [11] considered a symbolic model of execution, which only applies to protocols constructed by using "practical" primitives combined in a "standard" way. For definitions of what "practical" and "standard" mean in this context we refer to [11], but we remark, that our protocol and the TreeKEM variants considered in this work fall into this category.

protocols, update operations may require more than 2 rounds (in the worst case $\log(n)$ rounds). However, even when all n users update their keys concurrently in $\log(n)$ rounds, the total communication complexity of any user is only roughly $(\log(n))^2$ (constant size) ciphertexts. This circumvents [11] as their lower-bound only holds for updates that complete in at most 2 rounds. So, for the price of more interaction CoCoA can *greatly* decrease the actual bandwidth consumed.

To emphasize this even more, consider the cost of transitioning from a fully blanked tree to a fully unblanked one. We believe this to be a particularly interesting case as it captures the transition from any freshly created group into a bandwidth-optimal one. The faster/cheaper this transition can be completed, the faster an execution can begin optimal complexity behaviour. TreeKEM [9], the CGKA scheme used in the MLS messaging protocol, needs $n/2$ rounds with receiver complexity, i.e. number of ciphertexts downloaded per user, $\Omega(n \log(n))$. The protocol in [11], in turn, would be able to unblank the whole tree in 2 rounds with linear sender and recipient communication per user. In contrast, in CoCoA the tree could be unblanked in 1 round with linear sender cost, but only logarithmic recipient cost. For big groups this difference is very significant.

With such low communication, a user cannot learn all the $2n-1$ fresh public-keys in the distributed group state (usually called "ratchet-tree" or "key-tree"). Fortunately, for CoCoA, users only need to know the $\log(n)$ secret keys and another $2\log(n)$ public keys. So in our protocol, users will not have a complete view of the public state as in previous protocols, but only know the partial state that is relevant to them. As a consequence, the server no longer acts as a relay but instead computes packets tailored to the individual receiving user. This comes with a new challenge that we address in this work: ensuring consistency across all users is not as straightforward anymore. This is crucial for security, since users disagreeing e.g. on the set of group members can lead to severe attacks.

Once we take into account operations like adding and removing group members, efficiency might degrade (though not to anything worse than past protocols). Nevertheless, in a typical execution we can expect to see far more updates than adds/removes. In particular, the more updates parties perform the faster the protocol heals from past compromises so it is generally in users' interest to perform updates as regularly as they can. By (greatly) reducing the cost of updates compared to past CGKA protocols, we allow groups to have quantitatively better security for the same amount of communication complexity spent.

In terms of security, we prove CoCoA secure in an "partially active setting". A bit more precisely, the adaptive adversary can (repeatedly) leak parties local states including any random coins they use and query users to generate protocol messages. As the sever is untrusted, the adversary is allowed to send arbitrary (potentially malformed) server messages and deviate from the server specification. However, as users sign their protocol messages and the adversary does not get access to signing keys, it is not able to generate such messages by itself. While the latter is a strong assumption, it is common for such protocols. We discuss this in more detail in Sect. 5. Note that [25] uses the term partially active to refer to security against weaker adversaries that have control of the delivery server, but are not allowed to send arbitrary messages.

Signature Keys. One caveat to the above discussion are signature keys. Apart from the aforementioned public and secret keys, each group member must know the signature verification key of each other group member (as these are used to authenticate packets, amongst other things). In principle, this means that just distributing n new signature key pairs (as part of n parties updating) already imposes $\Omega(n)$ communication complexity for each group member (regardless of how many rounds are used or even of concurrency).

However, in practice, there are several mitigating aspects to this problem. As was observed already during the design of MLS, in some real-world deployments of CGKAs fresh signature keys may be much harder to come by than simply locally generating new ephemeral key material. That is because each new signature key is typically bound to some external identity (like an account name) via some generic "authenticator" and this binding may be an expensive and slow process. E.g. a certificate that must be obtained manually from a CA. For this reason CoCoA (like MLS) explicitly permits *lite updates*; that is, updates which refresh all secret key material of the sender *except* for their signature keys. While lite updates are clearly not ideal from a security perspective, they do allow for frequently refreshing the remaining key material without being bogged down by the cost of certifying fresh signature keys. Moreover, CoCoA (like MLS) derives authenticity of packets not just from signatures but also by requiring senders to, effectively, prove knowledge of the previous epoch's group key. Thus, leaking a group members' signing keys does not automatically confer the ability to forge on their behalf. Indeed, if the victims all perform a lite update, a fresh epoch is initiated with a secure group key.

1.2 Related Work

The study of CGKA based protocols was initiated by the ART protocol [16], based on which the first version of MLS [8] was built shortly before transitioning to TreeKEM [9]. TreeKEM has since been the subject of several security analysis including [3,4,10,13,17]. More generally, the study of CGKAs has, roughly speaking, focused on several topics: stronger security definitions, more efficient constructions, better support for concurrency and new security properties.

Several works have studied CGKA's supporting varying degrees of concurrent operations. Weidner's Causal TreeKEM [26] explores the idea of updates *re-randomizing* key material instead of overwriting it (though it lacks forward secrecy and a complete security proof). Recently, [30] proposed a decentralized CGKA protocol; albeit with linear communication complexity. Finally, a paper by Bienstock *et al.* [11] studies the trade-off between PCS, concurrency and communication complexity, showing a lower bound for the latter and proposing a close to optimal protocol in their synchronous model for a fixed group in a weak security model.

A similar security model to the one in our paper can be found in [25]. That work was the first to require security against an *adaptive* adversary. The security model of [3] is weak but incomparable to our model. Their adversaries must deliver all packets in the same order to all parties (though not at the same time or even at all) and they do not learn the coins of corrupt parties. On the other hand, the adversary may modify and even inject new packets; albeit only if honest parties would reject the resulting adversarial packet. A different approach to security notions was initiated in [4] where the *history graph* technique was introduced to describe the semantics of any given CGKA executions. They also provided the first black-box construction of secure group messaging from CGKA (and other primitives). [5] presented the first ideal/real CGKA security notion. Their notion captures security against powerful adaptive and fully active adversaries that can corrupt parties at will and even *set* their random coins. Finally, building on that work, [7] extend their adversaries to also account for how corrupt insiders might interact with a (very weak) PKI. The formal notion was later adapted in [6,21] to capture essentially the same intuition but for the server-aided CGKA setting. A third approach to defining adaptive and active security is taken in [10] who use an "event driven" language to define adaptive security a CGKA. The notion of server-aided CGKA was first formalized in [6]. However, the earlier work of [18] and the concurrent work of [21] both include (implicit) server-aided CGKAs as well.

The work of [24] initiated the study of post-quantum primitives for CGKA by building primitives designed for use in TreeKEM (and similar CGKAs). However, it turned out that their security notion was lacking (e.g. it seems to not allow for adaptive security of the resulting CGKA) so in a follow up paper [21] a new (more secure) PQ primitive is proposed along with a novel server-aided CGKA (proven secure in the classic model) designed to reduce receiver communication cost. Cremers *et al.* compared the PCS properties in the multi-group setting of MLS to the Signal group protocol [17]. In [1] more efficient CGKA constructions in the multi-group setting are given. In [5] zero-knowledge proofs are used to improve the robustness of CGKA protocols. The approach was made a bit more practical in [18] by, amongst other things, introducing tailor-made ZK proofs. Very recently, [20] initiated the study of membership privacy for CGKAs.

A closely related family of protocols to CGKA are the older Group Key Exchange (GKE) protocols which allow a fixed group of users to derive a common key. These can be traced to early publications like [14,23]. In contrast to CGKA, GKE protocols do not target PCS and are designed for the synchronous setting. Initial GKE results were followed by a long list of works exploring additional features; notably, supporting changes to group membership mid-session (aka. Dynamic GKE) [12,19]. Another notion very related to CGKA are Logical Key Hierarchies [15,29,31], introduced as a solution to very related primitive of Multicast Encryption [27]. They allow a changing group of users to maintain a common key with the help of a trusted group manager.

2   Preliminaries

2.1   Continuous Group-key Agreement

To begin with, we define the notion of continuous group-key agreement (CGKA). Parties participating in the execution of a CGKA protocol will maintain a local state γ, allowing them to keep track of a common ratchet tree, to derive a shared secret. Parties will be able to add and remove users to the execution, and to rotate the keys along sections of the tree, thus achieving FS and PCS. Our definition is similar to that of [25], with the main difference that operations do not need to be confirmed individually by the server. Instead, the stateful server works in rounds, collects operations into batches and sends them out at the end of each round (note that setting the batch size equal to 1 would just return the definition from [25]). Accordingly, a party issuing an operation will no longer be able to pre-compute its new state should the operation be confirmed.

Definition 1 (Asynchronous Continuous Group-key Agreement]). *An asynchronous continuous group-key agreement (CGKA) scheme is an 8-tuple of algorithms* CGKA = (CGKA.Gen, CGKA.Init, CGKA.Add, CGKA.Rem, CGKA.Upd, CGKA.Dlv, CGKA.Proc, CGKA.Key) *with the following syntax and semantics:*

KEY GENERATION: *Fresh InitKey pairs* $((\mathsf{pk}, \mathsf{sk}), (\mathsf{ssk}, \mathsf{svk})) \leftarrow$ CGKA.Gen(1^λ) *consist of a pair of public key encryption keys and a pair of digital signing keys. They are generated by users prior to joining a group, where* λ *denotes the security parameter. Public keys are used to invite parties to join a group.*

INITIALIZE A GROUP: *Let* $\mathsf{G} = (\mathsf{ID}_1, \dots, \mathsf{ID}_n)$. *For* $i \in [2, n]$ *let* pk_i *be an InitKey PK of party* ID_i. *Party* ID_1 *creates a new group with membership* G *by running:*

$$(\gamma, [W_2, \dots, W_n]) \leftarrow \mathsf{CGKA.Init}\,(\mathsf{G}, [\mathsf{pk}_1, \dots, \mathsf{pk}_n], [\mathsf{svk}_1, \dots, \mathsf{svk}_n], \mathsf{sk}_1)$$

and sending welcome *message* W_i *for party* ID_i *to the server. Finally,* ID_1 *stores its* local state γ *for later use.*

ADDING A MEMBER: *A group member with local state* γ *can add party* ID *to the group by running* $(\gamma, W, T) \leftarrow$ CGKA.Add$(\gamma, \mathsf{ID}, \mathsf{pk}, \mathsf{svk})$ *and sending* welcome *message* W *for party* ID *and the* add *message* T *for all group members (including* ID*) to the server.*

REMOVING A MEMBER: *A group member with local state* γ *can remove group member* ID *by running* $(\gamma, T) \leftarrow$ CGKA.Rem(γ, ID) *and sending the* remove *message* T *for all group members (*ID*) to the server.*

UPDATE: *A group member with local state* γ *can perform an update by running* $(\gamma, T) \leftarrow$ CGKA.Upd(γ) *and sending the* update *message* T *to the server.*

COLLECT AND DELIVER: *The delivery server, upon receiving a set of CGKA protocol messages* $T = (T_1, \dots, T_k)$ *(including welcome messages) generated by a set of parties, sends out a round message* $(\gamma_{\mathrm{ser}}, (\mathfrak{M}_1, \dots, \mathfrak{M}_n)) =$ CGKA.Dlv$(\gamma_{\mathrm{ser}}, T)$, *where* $\mathfrak{M}_i$ *is the message for user* i *and* γ_{ser} *is the server's internal state. Each* $\mathfrak{M}_i$ *contains a counter* c_i *indicating whether* $\mathfrak{M}_i$ *includes an update message generated by user* i, *and which one of the potentially several they might have generated.*

PROCESS: *Upon receiving an incoming CGKA message $\mathfrak{M}_i$, a party immediately processes it by running $\gamma \leftarrow \mathsf{CGKA.Proc}(\gamma, \mathfrak{M}_i)$.*

GET GROUP KEY: *At any point a party can extract the current group key K from its local state γ by running $K \leftarrow \mathsf{CGKA.Key}(\gamma)$.*

2.2 Ratchet Trees

Our protocol builds on TreeKEM, and thus uses the same underlying structure of a *ratchet tree* for deriving shared secrets among the group members. A ratchet tree is a directed binary tree $\mathfrak{T} = (V_{\mathfrak{T}}, E_{\mathfrak{T}})$, with edges pointing towards the root node v_{root}[5] and each user in the group associated to a leaf. We will use the notation $\mathfrak{T}^i = (V_{\mathfrak{T}}^i, E_{\mathfrak{T}}^i)$ to refer to the ratchet tree associated to round i.

Tree Structure. Given a node v, we will denote its child by $\mathsf{child}(v)$, its left and right parents respectively as $\mathsf{lparent}(v), \mathsf{rparent}(v)$, and will write $\mathsf{parents}(v) = (\mathsf{lparent}(v), \mathsf{rparent}(v))$. Given a leaf node, we denote its path to the root as $\mathsf{path}(v) = (v_0 = v, v_1, \ldots, v_k = v_{root})$, where $v_i = \mathsf{child}(v_{i-1})$. Similarly, we denote its co-path as $\mathsf{co\text{-}path}(v) = (v_1', \ldots, v_k')$, where v_i' is the parent of v_i not in $\mathsf{path}(v)$. We will often just refer to such a (co-)path as v's (co-)path. For a user ID we will denote its associated leaf node by $\mathsf{leaf}(\mathsf{ID})$, and accordingly sometimes refer to $\mathsf{leaf}(\mathsf{ID})$'s (co-)path as just ID's (co-)path or $(\mathsf{co\text{-}path}(\mathsf{ID}))$ $\mathsf{path}(\mathsf{ID})$. Given two leaves l, l', let $\mathsf{Int}(l, l')$ be their least common descendant, i.e. the first node where their paths intersect. For a node $v \in \mathfrak{T}$, we set $v.\mathsf{isLeaf} := \mathsf{true}$ if v is a leaf of $\mathfrak{T}$, and $v.\mathsf{isLeaf} := \mathsf{false}$ otherwise.

Node States. Each node v has an associated node state $\gamma(v)$. Sometimes during the protocol execution, nodes can be marked as *blank*, meaning that their state is empty. Blank nodes become *unblanked* if their state is repopulated at a later point in time.

The non-blank node state contains: a PKE key-pair $(\gamma(v).\mathsf{sk}, \gamma(v).\mathsf{pk})$, sometimes written as $(\mathsf{sk}_v, \mathsf{pk}_v)$ for simplicity; a vector of public keys PK^{pr} called the *predecessor keys* which correspond to the public keys of the nodes in the resolution of v (defined below) in the round right before the current key pk_v was first introduced, see Sect. 3.4; a pair of hash values h_v called the parent hash of v; an identifier corresponding to the party ID_v generating the node's key pair; a signature σ_v under the private signing key of ID_v; a transcript hash value, $\mathcal{H}_{trans}$, committing to the state of ID_v at the time of sampling that node's key pair (defined below in Sect. 3.3); a confirmation tag value $\mathsf{confTag}$ (defined below in Sect. 3.4); an optional pair of hash values $o_v = (o_{v,1}, o_{v,2})$ corresponding to partial openings of a Merkle commitment sent by the server and encoding the state of the parent nodes of v; and a set of of so called *unmerged leaves* $\gamma(v).\mathsf{Unmerged}$, or simply $\mathsf{Unmerged}(v)$, corresponding to the leaves (and their

---

[5] The non standard direction of the edges here captures that knowledge of (the secret key associated to) the source node implies knowledge of (the secret key associated to) the sink node. Note that nodes therefore have one child and two parents.

associated public keys) of the subtree rooted at v whose users have no knowledge of sk_v (this will be the case, temporarily, for newly added users). In a slight abuse of notation, given a set of nodes S, we define its set of unmerged nodes to be $\mathsf{Unmerged}(S) = \cup_{v \in S}\mathsf{Unmerged}(v)$. Finally, the state of leaves l additionally contains a signing and verification key-pair $(\mathsf{ssk}_l, \mathsf{svk}_l)$ corresponding to the user ID_l associated to that leaf. For an internal node v, we will write ssk_v to refer to the secret signing key of party ID_v.

The *secret part* of $\gamma(v)$ consists of sk_v, and ssk_v in case v is a leaf. In turn, the *public part*, $^P\gamma(v)$, of $\gamma(v)$ consists of $\gamma(v)$ minus the secret part. While the public part of nodes' states can be accessed by all users, users should only have partial knowledge of the secret parts. Indeed, the protocol ensures that the secret part of $\gamma(v)$ is known only by users whose leaf is in the sub-tree rooted at v; this is known as the *tree invariant*.

Looking ahead, parties might end up (through a misbehaving delivery server) having different views on the state of a given node, and so we will refer to the view of party ID_i of v at round n as $\gamma_i^n(v)$.

Resolution and Effective Parents. The set of blank and non-blank nodes in a ratchet tree gives rise to the *resolution* of a node v. Intuitively, it is the minimal set S of non-blank nodes such that for each ancestor v' of v the set S contains at least one node on the path from v' to v. Formally, it is defined as follows.

Definition 2. *Let $\mathfrak{T}$ be a tree with vertex set $V_\mathfrak{T}$. The resolution $\mathsf{Res}(v) \subset V_\mathfrak{T}$ of $v \in V_\mathfrak{T}$ is defined as follows:*

- *If v is not blank, then $\mathsf{Res}(v) = \{v\}$.*
- *If v is a blank leaf, then $\mathsf{Res}(v) = \emptyset$.*
- *Otherwise, $\mathsf{Res}(v) = \cup_{v' \in \mathsf{parents}(v)}\mathsf{Res}(v')$*

In a slight abuse of notation, given a set of nodes V, we define the resolution of V to be $\mathsf{Res}(V) = \bigcup_{v \in V}\mathsf{Res}(v)$.

Re-keying. Users will often need to sample new keys along their leaves' paths. This is done following the MLS specification, through the hierarchical derivation captured in the algorithm $\mathsf{Re\text{-}key}(v)$ (Algorithm 1). Given a leaf v, it outputs a list of seeds and key-pairs for nodes along v's path. We use Δ_{root} or the expression *root seed* to refer to the seed associated to v_{root}. The algorithm will use two independent hash functions H_1 and H_2. These can be easily defined by taking a hash function H, fixing two different tags x_1 and x_2 and defining $\mathsf{H}_i(\cdot) = \mathsf{H}(\cdot, x_i)$.

3 The CoCoA Protocol

We start with a high level description of the CoCoA protocol in Sect. 3.1, but refer the reader to the full version [2] for a more in detail introductory discussion. Section 3.2 covers users' states and the key schedule, Sect. 3.3 robustness and the round hash, Sect. 3.4 the parent hash mechanism (again, more complete in [2]), and Sect. 3.5 formally defines the protocol procedures.

Algorithm 1: Re-key computes new seeds and keys along a path.

Input: A leaf node v in a tree $\mathfrak{T}$ of depth d.

Output: A vector of hierarchically derived seeds, and another vector of corresponding keys for all nodes in v's path to the root.

1 $\Delta_1 \xleftarrow{\$} \mathfrak{S}(\lambda)$ // λ security parameter; $\mathfrak{S}(\lambda)$ seed space

2 $(\mathsf{sk}_1, \mathsf{pk}_1) \leftarrow \mathsf{PKE.Gen}(\mathsf{H}_2(\Delta_1))$

3 **for** $i \leftarrow 2$ **to** d **do**

4       $\Delta_i = \mathsf{H}_1(\Delta_{i-1})$

5       $(\mathsf{sk}_i, \mathsf{pk}_i) \leftarrow \mathsf{PKE.Gen}(\mathsf{H}_2(\Delta_i))$

6 $\Delta \leftarrow (\Delta_1, \ldots, \Delta_d)$

7 $\mathsf{K} \leftarrow ((\mathsf{sk}_1, \mathsf{pk}_1), \ldots, (\mathsf{sk}_d, \mathsf{pk}_d))$

8 **return** (Δ, K)

3.1 Overview

Concurrent Updates in CGKA. To recover from compromise, CGKA protocols allow users to refresh the secret key material known to them. Broadly, a user does this by re-sampling all keys they know (those on the user's path in the case of a ratchet tree), encoding them in an update message, and sending this to the server, which broadcasts it to the other group members. However, it is unclear how to handle concurrent update attempts by several users.

As a first approach, it seems natural to simply reject all but one update. Using a fixed rule to determine whose update to implement, however, might lead to starvation, with users blocked from updating and thus not recovering from compromise (compare Fig. 1, column (a)). Even if parties that did not update for the longest time are prioritized, it may take a linear number of update attempts to fully recover security of the ratchet tree (compare Fig. 1, column (b)).

To amend this issue the MLS protocol introduced the "propose and commit" paradigm. Roughly, update proposals refresh a user's leaf key and signal the intent to perform an update. A commit then allows a user to implement several concurrent update proposals. While this allows the ratchet tree to fully recover within two rounds, this comes at the cost of destroying the binary structure of the tree, as, in order to preserve the tree invariant, nodes not on the path of the committing party are blanked. In the worst case, this can lead to future updates having a size linear in the number of parties (compare Fig. 1, column (c)).

The approach we take with the CoCoA protocol is to implement all updates simultaneously, albeit some of them only partially. Intuitively, while the ratchet tree might not fully recover immediately, every updating party still makes progress towards recovery; and after logarithmically many updates of every compromised user, security is restored (compare Fig. 1, column (d)).

Updates in the CoCoA Protocol. The main idea in the CoCoA protocol is, given several concurrent update messages, to apply all of them simultaneously, while resolving conflicts by means of an ordering of the operations. As a consequence, some updates might only be applied partially. More precisely, the

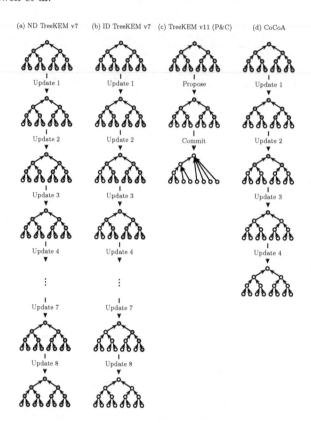

Fig. 1. Comparison of number of rounds required to recover from corruption for different TreeKEM variants, ND stands for "Naïve Delivery", ID for "Ideal Delivery". Red nodes indicate key material known to the adversary. In each round all parties (try to) update. In columns (a) and (d) update requests are prioritized from left to right. In column (b) update requests are prioritized from left to right among all parties that did not update yet. In column (c) all parties propose an update, then the leftmost party commits. (Color figure online)

protocol parameters contain an ordering $\prec$. This could be, e.g. the lexicographic ordering, however, the particular choice does not affect our security results. Then, given a set of update messages $\{U_1, \ldots, U_k\}$, if a node in the ratchet tree would be affected by several U_i, the one that is minimal with respect to $\prec$ takes precedence and replaces its key pair. Consider the example of Fig. 2, in which the users A, C, G in a group of size 8 concurrently update, with C's update taking precedence over the other two. Note that since the updates are concurrent, new keys get encrypted to keys of the previous round. Assume, e.g., that C and G were compromised. Then, after the updates, all compromised keys are replaced. However, only the first three keys in C's and G's update paths are secure, while the new Δ_{root} was encrypted to an old, compromised key and hence is known to

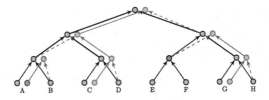

Fig. 2. Example; concurrent updates in the CoCoA protocol. The former state of the ratchet tree (black) is changed by concurrent updates of A (blue), C (green), and G (red). The ordering is $U_C \prec U_A \prec U_G$. In the updates solid edges correspond to seeds obtained by hashing, dashed edges to encryptions. (Color figure online)

Table 1. User's local state γ.

$\gamma.\text{ID}$	An identifier for the party
$\gamma.G$	The set of current members of the group
$\gamma.\text{ssk}$	The party's signing key
$\gamma(v)$	Node state for every $v \in \mathcal{P}(\gamma.\text{ID})$, only public part for $v \in \text{Res}(\text{co-path}(\gamma.\text{ID}))$
$\gamma.\mathcal{H}_{trans}$	Current value of the transcript hash
$\gamma.\text{appSecret}$	Current round's application secret
$\gamma.\text{confKey}$	Current round's confirmation key
$\gamma.\text{initSec}$	Current round's initialization secret
γ'	Pending state encoding operations not yet confirmed

the adversary. So, while the ratchet tree did not fully recover, it made progress towards it. In Sect. 5 we discuss the security of CoCoA in more detail.

3.2 Users' States and the Key Schedule

Each user keeps track solely of the state of nodes on either their path or the resolution of their co-path; we define $\mathcal{P}(\text{ID}) = \text{path}(\text{ID}) \cup \text{Res}(\text{co-path}(\text{ID}))$ to be the set comprising exactly those nodes. More in detail, each user stores a local state γ, described in Table 1, which gets updated after every round message. We will write γ^n to refer to a state corresponding to round n.

Key Schedule. CoCoA's *key schedule* for round n is defined via hash function H_5 as follows:

$$\gamma.\text{epochSecret}(n) = \mathsf{H}_5(\gamma.\text{initSec}(n-1) \,||\, \Delta_{root}(n) \,||\, \mathcal{H}_{trans}(n))$$
$$\gamma.\text{appSecret}(n) = \mathsf{H}_5(\gamma.\text{epochSecret}(n) \,||\, \text{'appsecret'})$$
$$\gamma.\text{confKey}(n) = \mathsf{H}_5(\gamma.\text{epochSecret}(n) \,||\, \text{'confirm'})$$
$$\gamma.\text{initSec}(n) = \mathsf{H}_5(\gamma.\text{epochSecret}(n) \,||\, \text{'init'})$$

The epoch secret $\gamma.\text{epochSecret}(n)$ is used to derive all other keys from it; the application secret $\gamma.\text{appSecret}(n)$ serves as the group key in epoch n and is to be used in higher level protocols, e.g. secure group messaging; the confirmation key $\gamma.\mathsf{confKey}(n)$ will be used to authenticate next epoch's protocol messages through a MAC termed the confirmation tag;[6] and the initialization secret $\gamma.\mathsf{initSec}(n)$ seeds next round's key schedule, tying it to the current one. Finally, the transcript hash $\mathcal{H}_{trans}(n)$ encodes the transcript of the execution up until round n - it is defined in the following section.

3.3   Robustness, Round Hash, and Transcript Hash

In this section we discuss CoCoA's robustness. We show that two parties accepting messages containing the same round hash value, will transition into consistent states. We start by defining the concept of a round hash and consistent states.

In the following we assume a fixed rule, that can be locally computed by the users on input a ratchet tree $\mathfrak{T}$ and a set of operations that determines a total ordering of said operations. This ordering ensures all users will compute the same round hash and also, when applied to adds A_i, determines the free leaf that the user added by A_i is assigned to.

Definition 3. *Let H_3 be a hash function, and n a round with associated protocol messages $T = (U, R, A) = ((U_1, \ldots, U_k), (R_1, \ldots, R_l), (A_1, \ldots, A_m))$, where the U_i correspond to Update messages; and the R_i and A_i correspond to the packets, as sent by their issuers, of any remove and add operation, respectively; and let each vector U, R, A be ordered with respect to the ordering $\prec$. Let $\mathfrak{T}^n$ be the ratchet tree resulting from applying the operations in T with respect to $\prec$ to $\mathfrak{T}^{n-1}$, and $^P\gamma(v)$ the public state of v in $\mathfrak{T}^n$ (note that $^P\gamma(v) = \mathtt{blank}$ if the node is to be blanked as a result of some removal in R). We define the map ℓ taking nodes in $\mathfrak{T}^n$ to labels as follows:*

$$\ell(v) = \begin{cases} \mathsf{H}_3(^P\gamma(v)), & \textit{if } v \textit{ is a leaf.} \\ \mathsf{H}_3(\ell(\mathsf{lparent}(v)), \ell(\mathsf{rparent}(v)), ^P\gamma(v)), & \textit{if } v \textit{ is an internal node.} \end{cases}$$

The round hash $\mathcal{H}_{round}(n)$ of n is defined to be $\mathcal{H}_{round}(n) = \mathsf{H}_3(\ell(v_{root}), R, A)$.

In short, the round hash is essentially a Merkle commitment to the ratchet tree's public keys and the round's dynamic operations. The benefit of this approach is that every user can verify that the round hash sent by the server faithfully encodes the operations affecting their local state, by just receiving at most a logarithmic number of values irrespective of the number of updates (note that a user will necessarily need to hear about all dynamic operations). In particular, a user ID receiving the appropriate group operations should have access to the inputs corresponding to dynamic operations, and to the new keys of nodes in $\mathcal{P}(\mathsf{ID})$. The server does this by sending the user $\mathcal{H}_{round}(n)$, as well as the output

---

[6] This MAC, also present in TreeKEM, is there to mitigate active attacks. The latter are not reflected in our security model, but we chose to keep it, as it is the main security mechanism in response to a leaking of signature keys.

of openRH, which, on input a user ID, returns a vector of hash values, corresponding to the labels of nodes not in $\mathcal{P}(\mathsf{ID})$, but that are parents of a node in $\mathcal{P}(\mathsf{ID})$. Given these values, the user is able to verify the received round message by running verifyRH, which recomputes $\mathcal{H}_{round}(n)$ with respect to their updated ratchet tree and compares it to the round hash provided by the server. For a formal description of both algorithms we refer to the full version of this work [2].

The transcript hash is defined as $\mathcal{H}_{trans}(0) = 0$, and, for subsequent rounds, given a verified round hash:

$$\mathcal{H}_{trans}(n) = \mathsf{H}_3(\mathcal{H}_{trans}(n-1) \| \mathcal{H}_{round}(n)) \ .$$

With this we can define what it means for parties to have consistent states, which informally requires them to have consistent views of the tree (i.e. agree on the states of nodes on the intersection of their states), and agree on the group key, group members, and group history, i.e. on the transcript hash.

Definition 4. *Let* ID *and* ID^* *be two group members with states* γ *and* γ^*. *They have consistent states if* $^P\gamma(v) = {}^P\gamma^*(v)$ *for all* $v \in \mathcal{P}(\mathsf{ID}) \cap \mathcal{P}(\mathsf{ID}^*)$, $\gamma.\mathsf{appSecret} = \gamma^*.\mathsf{appSecret}$, *and* $(\gamma.G, \gamma.\mathcal{H}_{trans}) = (\gamma^*.G, \gamma^*.\mathcal{H}_{trans})$.

Note that we only define consistency of states for users who have joined the group. More in detail, we say that a user ID has (in their view) joined the group if there exists a query $\mathsf{CGKA.Proc}(\mathsf{ID}, \cdot)$ in the execution, where ID accepts the corresponding round message, i.e. where the state for ID changes (is initialized) as a result of said query.

3.4 Parent Hash

Ratchet trees in TreeKEM contain so-called *parent hashes*, which were introduced to the standard in TreeKEM v9, and analyzed and improved by Alwen *et al.* [7]. These ensure, on the one hand, that for every node $v \in \mathfrak{T}$, whoever sampled sk_v had knowledge of the secret signing key for some leaf l of the subtree rooted at v; and on the other, that at the moment this secret was generated it was not communicated to any user whose leaf is not in this subtree. This protects against active attacks where a user is added to a malformed group where the tree invariant is violated, potentially causing him to communicate to a set of users different to the one he believes to be communicating to.

To adapt parent hash to CoCoA we have to overcome the two issues that (a), since parties update concurrently, parent hash values can be defined with respect to keys on the copath that were overwritten by a concurrent update, and (b), since the resolution of a user's copath and in turn the corresponding public keys that are known to the user may change from round to round, the user needs to be able to verify the authenticity of such keys without having access to the state of leaves below it. We address the first issue by having users store the public keys of one previous round: each node state $\gamma(v)$ now contains an associated list of predecessor keys, $\mathsf{PK}^{\mathsf{pr}}$, containing the public keys corresponding to nodes in the resolution of v in the epoch when the current key was sampled, and excluding those that where unmerged at $\mathsf{child}(v)$;[7] i.e. if the Update sampling pk_v unblanked v, the predecessor keys will be a list, else it will just contain the previous public key. The second issue we solve by not only signing the parent hash value of users' leaves but by introducing a signature at every node in their update path (that which is sent with the packet containing the new public key when it is first announced). Last, to ensure consistency between users' views, we add two further values to the parent hash and node state: a commitment to the subtree under the node's sibling and a commitment to the whole ratchet tree. We now define more formally the slightly modified parent-hash algorithm, compatible with our construction, with respect to signature scheme Sig.

As in TreeKEM, parent hash values of a node are updated whenever the key corresponding to the node is updated. More in detail, let ID compute an Update U containing new keys for nodes along their path (see full definition in Sect. 3.5), which get stored in pending state γ'. Parent hashing algorithm PHash.Sig on input (ID, γ') first fetches ID's update path $\mathsf{path}(v_{\mathsf{ID}}) = (v_0 = v_{\mathsf{ID}}, v_1, \ldots, v_k = v_{root})$. For $i \in \{0, \ldots, k-1\}$ let v_i' denote the parent of v_{i+1} that is not part of $\mathsf{path}(v_{\mathsf{ID}})$, and let $\mathcal{R} = \mathsf{Res}(v_i') \setminus \mathsf{Unmerged}(v_{i+1})$. Then, we define $h_{1,k} = h_{2,k} = 0$, and using hash function H_4, compute:

$$h_{1,i} \leftarrow \ell(v_i') \qquad\qquad\qquad\qquad\qquad\qquad \text{for } i \in (k-1, \ldots, 0)$$
$$h_{2,i} \leftarrow \mathsf{H}_4(\mathsf{pk}_{v_{i+1}}, \mathsf{PK}^{\mathrm{pr}}_{v_{i+1}}, h_{2,i+1}, \{\mathsf{pk}_v\}_{v \in \mathcal{R}}) \qquad \text{for } i \in (k-1, \ldots, 0)$$
$$\sigma_i \leftarrow \mathsf{Sig.Sig}\,(\gamma(\mathsf{ID}).\mathsf{ssk}, m) \qquad\qquad\qquad\qquad \text{for } i \in (0, \ldots, k)$$

where $\ell(v)$ is the label of v as in Definition 3 above, $\mathsf{PK}^{\mathrm{pr}}_v \leftarrow 0$ if v did not have a key before U, $h_i = (h_{1,i}, h_{2,i})$, and $m = (\mathsf{pk}_{v_i}, \mathsf{PK}^{\mathrm{pr}}_{v_i}, (h_{1,i}, h_{2,i}), \mathcal{H}_{trans}, \mathsf{confTag})$

Algorithm PHash.Sig then adds the values $(H, \Sigma) = (h_0, \ldots, h_k, \sigma_0, \ldots, \sigma_k)$ to U, substitutes the parent hash values h_i and signatures σ_i in γ' by the newly computed ones, and returns U.

Verification. A user receiving a tree T from the server can verify its authenticity by running the algorithm $\mathsf{PHash.Ver}(T)$. This will be run by users in two different scenarios: on the one hand, when joining the group, they will verify the whole ratchet tree (in this case $T = \mathfrak{T}$); on the other, when processing a round message containing one or more Removes, they will verify the received keys for nodes in the new resolution of their co-path (in this case T is the union of $\mathcal{P}(\mathsf{ID}_i)$ for all removed ID_i). The algorithm runs as follows:

The algorithm first checks that all non-blank nodes in the tree have a complete public state, and that for any internal node v, the associated identifier ID_v is associated to one of the leaves of the sub-tree rooted at v.[8] If any of these checks does not pass, the algorithm aborts. Next, it checks that $h_{2,v_{root}}$, and then, verifies the following conditions hold:

---

[7] The exclusion of these unmerged leaves responds to the fact that these could correspond to parties added *after* the state for $\mathsf{child}(v)$ was last updated.

[8] A user who is already part of the group will have knowledge of the leaf index of each group member, and can check this without necessarily having a full view of the tree.

1. For any non-blank non-leaf node v in T the following equalities hold with either p and p' being the left and right parents of v or, if not, with p' being the left parent of v and p the right parent, setting $p \leftarrow \mathsf{lparent}(p)$ if p is blank, until p is either non-blank or an empty leaf, in which case $0 \leftarrow \mathsf{PHash.Ver}(T)$.[9]

   (a) $h_{2,p} = \mathsf{H}_4(\mathsf{pk}_v, \mathrm{PK}_v^{\mathrm{pr}}, h_{2,v}, \{\mathsf{pk}_w\}_{w \in R})$ and $h_{1,p} = \ell(p')$ or
   (b) $h_{2,p} = \mathsf{H}_4(\mathsf{pk}_v, \mathrm{PK}_v^{\mathrm{pr}}, h_{2,v}, \mathrm{PK}_{p'}^{\mathrm{pr}})$ and $\mathcal{H}_{trans,p} = \mathcal{H}_{trans,p'}$.

   where $R = \mathsf{Res}(p') \setminus \mathsf{Unmerged}(v)$.
2. $\mathsf{Sig.Ver}_{\mathsf{svk}_w}((\mathsf{pk}_w, \mathrm{PK}_w^{\mathrm{pr}}, h_w, \mathcal{H}_{trans,w}, \mathsf{confTag}_w), \sigma_w) = 1$ for all $w \in T$.

3.5   The Protocol: CoCoA and Partial Updates

In the description below, we use γ for the state of the party issuing the appropriate operation. The ordering used to resolve conflicts caused by concurrent updates is denoted by $\prec$.

Initialization. To initialize a group with parties $G = \{\mathsf{ID}_1, \ldots, \mathsf{ID}_n\}$, ID_1 creates a ratchet tree as follows. First, ID_1 retrieves the public initialization keys $(\mathbf{pk}, \mathbf{svk}) = (\{\mathsf{pk}_{\mathsf{ID}_1}, \ldots, \mathsf{pk}_{\mathsf{ID}_n}\}, \{\mathsf{svk}_{\mathsf{ID}_1}, \ldots, \mathsf{svk}_{\mathsf{ID}_n}\})$ of all group members (including themselves), redefines $G \leftarrow (G, \mathbf{pk}, \mathbf{svk})$ to include these, and initializes a left-balanced binary tree with n leaves, assigning each pair of keys in $(\mathbf{pk}, \mathbf{svk})$ to a leaf. Let v be ID_1's leaf. They then sample new secrets for v's path $(\Delta, K) \leftarrow \mathsf{Re\text{-}key}(v)$, store the new keypairs $(\mathsf{sk}_j, \mathsf{pk}_j)$ in the corresponding nodes on the created tree and compute and store in γ' the parent hashes and signatures for the nodes in $\mathsf{path}(v)$: $(H, \Sigma) \leftarrow \mathsf{PHash.Sig}(\mathsf{ID}_1, \gamma')$, where recall that each $\sigma_j \in \Sigma$ is a signature of $(\mathsf{pk}_j, 0, h_j, \mathcal{H}_{trans}, 0)$ for some $v_j \in \mathsf{path}(v)$ with $h_j \in H$ its corresponding new parent hash pair (here $\mathrm{PK}_v^{\mathrm{pr}}$ and $\mathsf{confTag}$ are set to 0 initially). For every $v_j \in \mathsf{path}(v) \setminus v$, let w_j be the parent of v_j not in $\mathsf{path}(v)$. Then, for each $y_{j,l} \in \mathsf{Res}(w_j)$, ID_1 computes $e_{j,l} = \mathsf{PKE.Enc}(\mathsf{pk}_{y_{j,l}}, \Delta_j)$, together with the signature $\sigma_{j,l}^s = \mathsf{Sig.Sig}_{\mathsf{ssk}_i}(e_{j,l})$. Next, they send out the initialization message $I = ('init', \mathsf{ID}_1, G, \mathbf{pk}, P, S)$; where P is the vector with entries $p_j = (\mathsf{pk}_j, h_j, \mathcal{H}_{trans}, \sigma_j)$, one per node in $\mathsf{path}(\mathsf{ID}_1)$; and S is the vector with entries $s_{j,l} = (e_{j,l}, \sigma_{j,l}^s)$, containing all the necessary encryptions and values to be authenticated, for each $v_j \in \mathsf{path}(v)$. Finally, ID_1 erases the seeds Δ_i, and sets all internal nodes outside their path in their local tree copy to be blank.

Update. To issue an update, user ID_i with state γ and at leaf v, first computes new secrets along their path $(\Delta, K) \leftarrow \mathsf{Re\text{-}key}(v)$, stores the new keys in γ' and computes and stores the parent hashes and signatures for the nodes in $\mathsf{path}(v)$: $(H, \Sigma) \leftarrow \mathsf{PHash.Sig}(\mathsf{ID}_i, \gamma')$. Second, they set $\mathsf{confTag} = \mathsf{MAC.Tag}(\gamma.\mathsf{confKey}, \gamma.\mathcal{H}_{trans})$. For every $v_j \in \mathsf{path}(v) \setminus v$, let w_j be the parent of v_j not in $\mathsf{path}(v)$ and let $L_j = \mathsf{Res}(w_j) \cup \mathsf{Unmerged}(\mathsf{Res}(w_j))$ be the set of nodes that are either in the

---

[9] The recursion in the second case is needed to account for the possible blank nodes introduced between p and v as a result of adding to new leaves to accomodate new parties, so that p and p' correspond to the parents of v at the time the state of v was created.

resolution of w_j or are leaves that are unmerged at some node in said resolution. Then, for each $y_{j,l} \in L_j$, ID_i computes $e_{j,l} = \mathsf{PKE.Enc}(\mathsf{pk}_{y_{j,l}}, \Delta_j)$, together with the signature $\sigma_{j,l}^s = \mathsf{Sig.Sig}_{\mathsf{ssk}_i}(e_{j,l}, \mathsf{confTag})$. Next, they send out the update message $U = (\mathsf{ID}_i, P, S, c_i)$; where P is a vector of entries $p_j = (\mathsf{pk}_j, h_j, \mathcal{H}_{trans}, \mathsf{confTag}, \sigma_j,)$ containing the new public states and necessary authentication values for each $v_j \in \mathsf{path}(v)$;[10] S is the vector with entries $s_{j,l} = (e_{j,l}, \mathsf{confTag}, \sigma_{j,l}^s)$, containing all the necessary encryptions and values to be authenticated, for each $v_j \in \mathsf{path}(v)$; and a counter c_i, the number of updates (including this one) sent by ID_i since they last processed a round message. Last, they erase the seeds Δ.

Remove. To remove party ID_j, ID_i sends out a $remove(\mathsf{ID}_j)$ plaintext request together with $\mathsf{confTag} = \mathsf{MAC.Tag}(\gamma.\mathsf{confKey}, \gamma.\mathcal{H}_{trans})$, and a signature σ under their signing key of the remove message and the confirmation tag. This will have the effect of blanking the nodes in ID_j's path. Following a removal, an Update operation must be issued immediately so that a new group key is created.

Add. Additions of parties work in two rounds. To add party ID_j, ID_i first sends a plaintext add request $add(\mathsf{ID}_j, \mathsf{pk}, \mathsf{svk})$ containing ID_j's public init key pair $(\mathsf{pk}, \mathsf{svk})$, $\mathsf{confTag} = \mathsf{MAC.Tag}(\gamma.\mathsf{confKey}, \gamma.\mathcal{H}_{trans})$ and a signature under ID_i's signing key of the add request and the confirmation tag. This will allow all group members to learn the identity of the new party and therefore to encrypt future protocol messages to them. In the following round, ID_i[11] must send ID_j a signed welcome message $\mathcal{W} = (\mathcal{H}_{round}, \gamma.\mathcal{H}_{trans}, \gamma.G, \gamma.\mathsf{confKey}, \gamma.\mathsf{initSec})$, encrypted under pk, allowing them to initialize their state and key schedule, as well as checking the correctness of the tree sent by the server. Moreover, some user must send an Update during that round, thus creating a new application secret.

Collect and Deliver. Whenever the server receives an initialization message I, it just forwards it to all the new group members, initializing its local state γ_{ser} with the members of the new group and the public information of the ratchet tree included in I. For all other messages, it does as follows: given concurrent group messages $T = (U, R, A, W) = (U_a, R_b, A_c, W_d : a \in [p], b \in [q], c \in [r], d \in [s])$ sent during a round, corresponding to Updates, Removes, Adds, and Welcome messages, respectively, the delivery server will first check if any two or more updates come from the same user, deleting all of them except for the one received last. The server first updates its local copy of the public state of $\mathfrak{T}$, stored in γ_{ser}, by updating the public keys of nodes refreshed by any U_a, blanking any nodes affected by any R_b, and adding a public key and identifier to any leaf newly populated as a result of an A_c; here if two or more operations affect a given node, the operation that is minimal with respect to $\prec$ will be the one

---

[10] note that, as in an initialization message, the signature included in each of the p_j does not exactly cover the rest of the elements of p_j, but also includes the predecesor key $\mathrm{PK}^{\mathrm{pr}}$ at that node. This is not a problem for verification, as this is set to 0 for new groups, and in any other cases, parties will have access to the key at that node before they processed said update.

[11] an alternative specification could allow any group member online to do this instead.

determining the state of the node. A few considerations must be observed here, which we discuss further below: first, all Removes must precede any Updates, so that a node is blanked whenever a leaf under it is removed, irrespective of which Updates take place; second, conflicting Removes take effect simultaneously, blanking nodes in both paths; third, new users are added on the left-most free leaves in the tree according to some fixed rule that the receiving parties can reproduce locally. Once the server's view $\mathfrak{T}$ is updated, it computes the labels for it, defining $\mathfrak{T}_\ell$, and the round hash $\mathcal{H}_{round}$, as prescribed in Definition 3; and computes opening vectors $O_i \leftarrow \mathsf{openRH}(\mathsf{ID}_i, \mathfrak{T}_\ell)$ for all group members $\mathsf{ID}_i \in G$ (note that these will be computed with respect to the set $\mathcal{P}(\mathsf{ID}_i)$ resulting from (un)blanking nodes as implied by T). Then, it crafts round messages $\mathfrak{M}_i$ for each user, containing the following information: first, the vectors R and A or Removes and Adds; second the vector O_i and the round hash $\mathcal{H}_{round}$; third, the public states $\gamma(v) = (\mathsf{pk}_v, \mathrm{PK}_v^{\mathrm{pr}}, h_v, \mathsf{ID}_v, \sigma_v, \mathcal{H}_{trans,v}, \mathsf{confTag}_v, o_v, \mathsf{Unmerged}(v))$ at the beginning of the round of the nodes $v \in \mathcal{N}_i = (\cup_{j \in R_{id}} \mathcal{P}(\mathsf{ID}_j)) \setminus \mathcal{P}(\mathsf{ID}_i)$ where R_{id} is the set of indices of parties removed by R, i.e., the new nodes on the resolution of ID_i's and the extra states needed to verify the validity of the received keys[12]; and fourth, for each node $v \in \mathcal{P}(\mathsf{ID}_i)$ (after the (un)blanking implied by T) whose keys get rotated as a result of some (winning w.r.t. $\prec$) update $U_a = (\mathsf{ID}, P, S)$, the server adds $u_v = (\mathsf{ID}, p_j)$ to $\mathfrak{M}_i$, where $p_j \in P$ is the public state of corresponding to v; if, besides, $v \in \mathsf{path}(\mathsf{ID}_i)$ and is the lowest node in $\mathsf{path}(\mathsf{ID}_i)$ updated by U_a, the server also includes the tuple $s_{j,l} \in S$ into u_v, corresponding to the encryption of v's seed to the node in $\mathsf{path}(\mathsf{ID}_i)$ which is in the resolution of the co-path of U_a's author. Last, the server also includes a counter c_i, equal to that of ID_i's update included in $\mathfrak{M}_i$ if there is one, and 0 otherwise. Finally, for each newly-added ID_i, the round message $\mathfrak{M}_i$ additionally contains the corresponding $\mathcal{W}$, as well as a copy of the public state of $\mathfrak{T}$.

Process. Upon receipt of a round message $\mathfrak{M}$ containing associated Updates $U = (U_1, \ldots, U_p)$, Removes $R = (R_1, \ldots, R_q)$, Adds $A = (A_1, \ldots, A_r)$, openings vector O, public states for nodes in $\mathcal{N}$, round hash $\mathcal{H}_{round}$, and counter c, user ID processes it as follows. First, if $c \neq 0$, they check if, from the time they last processed a round message, they issued an update with counter c, aborting if not. Next, they check that $\mathsf{MAC.Ver}(\gamma.\mathsf{confKey}, \mathsf{confTag}) = 1$ for every update, remove and add; that for the all update packets U_a the transcript hash value included with the new public values for a node is the same as $\gamma.\mathcal{H}_{trans}$; and that the associated signature verifies under the public key of the sender (using the current node key in place of $\mathrm{PK}^{\mathrm{pr}}$ to verify signatures of updates); and similarly

---

[12] note that the leaves of the sub-tree of $\mathfrak{T}$ with vertex set $\mathcal{N}_i$ correspond to the new nodes in the resolution of ID that were not part of their state.

abort if any of these verifications does not pass.[13] If these checks pass, they copy their local state γ corresponding to the current round to γ', incorporating into it any node states previously stored there as part of the generation of said update with counter c (this update is empty if $c = 0$). Then, they update the public state of nodes needed to verify the round hash, as prescribed by the received operations: first, for every $v \in \mathcal{P}(\mathsf{ID})$, they blank v if it is in the path affected by some R_i and update $\mathcal{P}(\mathsf{ID})$ to include its new resolution as follows: they check that the set of nodes $\mathcal{N}$ consists of the nodes outside $\mathcal{P}(\mathsf{ID})$ that are in the paths and resolutions of co-paths of removed users. If more than one user is removed, it could be that $\mathcal{N}$ consists of several disconnected subtrees of $\mathfrak{T}$. For each such subtree T, ID checks that its leaves are all non-blank; that all the leaves (w.r.t to $\mathfrak{T}$) of removed parties as described in R are included in it; and, finally, that $\mathsf{PHash.Ver}(\gamma, T) = 1$. Moreover, for each blanked node w (as a result of $\mathfrak{M}$), they will use the received openings for the leaves of T, together with the received states, to reconstruct the Merkle hash openings o_v associated to v and check that the stored values match these. If all the checks pass, ID incorporates in γ' the public states of the nodes in $\mathcal{N}$ that belong to the new nodes in $\mathcal{P}(\mathsf{ID})$, together with the received openings for each such node, and aborts otherwise. Next, if any v in the new $\mathcal{P}(\mathsf{ID})$ set is affected by an update U_a, they overwrite its public key, parent hash value, signature, identifier, transcript hash value, and confirmation tag to the one set by U_a, and update the unmerged leaves and predecessor keys appropriate; and else, if corresponding to a newly populated leaf, determine the corresponding added party from (U, R, A) and add the new public key and identifier ID^* to the leaf. If several nodes in their state are affected by updates, they also check that for every such node in their path, the update setting a new state for it is the same setting a state for one of its parents. Once the updating of the public state of $\mathfrak{T}$ is done, they run $\mathsf{verifyRH}(\gamma', \mathfrak{M})$, aborting if the output is 0. Once those verifications are passed, for all nodes affected by some U_i, they decrypt the appropriate seed, derive the new key-pairs from it as in algorithm $\mathsf{Re\text{-}key}$, check that the received public key matches the derived one, aborting if not, and otherwise, overwrite the public and secret keys with them; set $\mathsf{Unmerged}(v) \leftarrow \emptyset$, and then $\mathsf{Unmerged}(v) \leftarrow \mathsf{Unmerged}(v) \cup l_i$ for each leaf l_i that is an ancestor of v corresponding to an added party. After that, they update $\gamma.G$ to account for membership changes as per R and A. Finally, they compute the key schedule for the current round, set $\gamma \leftarrow \gamma'$, deleting both the old key schedule and the old key material from node states, and delete $\gamma' \leftarrow \emptyset$.

If the user is not yet part of the group, $\mathfrak{M}$ will also contain a welcome message $\mathcal{W} = (\mathcal{H}_{round}, \mathcal{H}_{trans}, G, \texttt{confKey}, \texttt{initSec})$ together with a copy of the public

---

[13] Observe that this could allow an active adversary to continuously send inconsistent messages, preventing users from updating. Since this falls outside of our model, we do not consider it here for simplicity, but note that it could be prevented by having users process all operations that do verify and compute an updated round hash, hashing together the received value and the operations that failed verification, inputting this into the transcript hash instead. This would ensure that parties agree on the transcript hash if and only if they processed exactly the same operations.

Table 2. Comparison of the communication complexity of different CGKA protocols. For a detailed discussion of the table see Sect. 4. The values x depicted in the last 5 columns are to be understood as $\mathcal{O}(x)$. We assume that the ratchet-tree based protocols start with a fully unblanked tree. †: In the uncoordinated case, the protocol's recipient communication is n^2 (case (a)) and $t^2(1+\log(n/t))$ (case (b)), respectively. Regarding the subsequent update cost, while the protocol formally has a worst case subsequent update cost of $\log(n)$, it is only secure in a weak security model. Modifying it to obtain PCS guarantees similar to the other protocols, e.g. by tainting [25], would lead to future worst-case update cost of n (case (a)) and $t(1+\log(n/t))$ (case (b)), respectively.

Protocol type	Rounds to heal t corruptions	Cumulative sender communication		Per-user recipient communication	Subsequent per-user update cost	
		No coordination	Coordination		Worst	Average
(a) Corrupted parties unknown						
Original TreeKEM & variants [3,8,25,26]	n	$n^2\log(n)$	$n\log(n)$	$n\log(n)$	$\log(n)$	$\log(n)$
Propose-commit TreeKEM [8]	2	n^2	n	n	n	n
Bienstock et al. [11]	2	n^2	n	$n^\dagger$	$\log(n)^\dagger$	$\log(n)^\dagger$
Bidirectional channels [30]	2	n^2	n^2	n	n	n
This work	$\lceil\log(n)\rceil+1$	$n\log^2(n)$	$n\log^2(n)$	$\log^2(n)$	$\log(n)$	$\log(n)$
(b) Corrupted parties known						
Original TreeKEM & variants [3,8,25,26]	t	$t^2\log(n)$	$t\log(n)$	$t\log(n)$	$\log(n)$	$\log(n)$
Propose-commit TreeKEM [8]	2	$t^2(1+\log(n/t))$	$t(1+\log(n/t))$	$t(1+\log(n/t))$	$t(1+\log(n/t))$	$\frac{t^2+(n-t)\log(n)}{n}$
Bienstock et al. [11]	2	$t^2(1+\log(n/t))$	$t(1+\log(n/t))$	$t(1+\log(n/t))^\dagger$	$\log(n)^\dagger$	$\log(n)$
Bidirectional channels [30]	2	tn	tn	t	n	n
This work	$\lceil\log(n)\rceil+1$	$t\log^2(n)$	$t\log^2(n)$	$\log(n)\cdot\min(t,\log(n))$	$\log(n)$	$\log(n)$

state of the ratchet tree $\mathfrak{T}$, allowing the user to initialize their state prior to executing the instructions above. The newly added user ID_i will first check that G matches the leaf identifiers in $\mathfrak{T}$, compute the round hash from $\mathfrak{T}$, R and A as in Definition 3, and check that it matches the received value $\mathcal{H}_{round}$ (and skip this step when later processing the rest of the round message). If any of these checks fails, the user immediately aborts. Next, they will initialize their state γ by setting $\gamma.\mathsf{ID} \leftarrow \mathsf{ID}_i$, $\gamma.\mathcal{H}_{trans} \leftarrow \mathcal{H}_{trans}$, $\gamma.G \leftarrow G$, $\gamma.\mathsf{confKey} \leftarrow \mathsf{confKey}$, and $\gamma.\mathsf{initSec} \leftarrow \mathsf{initSec}$. Finally, they set the state $\gamma(l)$ of the leaf l to contain the init key with which they were added - note that they will not have at this point knowledge of the secret keys of any other node, but they will obtain some as soon as they process any U_a. When doing so, note that for the verification of the signature they will need to make use of the keys in $\mathfrak{T}$. Last, to process an initialization message $I = ('init', \tilde{\mathsf{ID}}, G, P, S)$, ID verifies the parent hash for the node public states in P, using $\mathsf{PK}_v^{\mathrm{pr}} = 0$ for all nodes $v \in \mathsf{path}_{\tilde{\mathsf{ID}}}$, derives the keys for $\tilde{\mathsf{ID}}$'s path from S, and creates a ratchet tree with users in G as leaves and the obtained keys. Last, they initialize the key schedule, with initial value 0 for $\gamma.\mathsf{initSec}$ and $\mathcal{H}_{trans}$, storing all in the newly created state γ.

Get Group Key. A user with local state γ fetches $K = \gamma.\mathsf{appSecret}$.

4 Efficiency

In this section we discuss the communication complexity of our protocol and compare it with other CGKA schemes. We focus on the cost incurred by several users updating concurrently to recover from compromise, as this is the main setting we aim to tackle with this work. An overview is given in Table 2.

Considered Setting. Not only does the sequence of operations preceding concurrent update operations (in the case of ratchet-tree based CGKA schemes) have a crucial impact on the resulting communication cost, but also, whether the participating parties know which of the other parties have been compromised and when they are planning to update. Among the different settings one could compare, we restrict our view to the following, quite natural in our opinion.

We consider a group of n users, t of which have been compromised. For ratchet-tree-based protocols we assume that the tree is fully unblanked/untainted, as this should typically be the case, with Updates being the most common operation. Our analysis differentiates between the settings (a) where it is only known that the group has been compromised, but not who the particular t corrupted users are, and (b) where the set of compromised users is known to everyone. Note that the former essentially forces every member of the group to update, while in the latter scenario only the t compromised users have to act.

The first value we are interested in is the number of rounds of (potentially) concurrent updates, after which the group key is guaranteed to be secure again. The second is the cumulative sender complexity (measured over all rounds), which essentially corresponds to the number of public keys and ciphertexts sent to the server. Here, we again distinguish between two settings. Namely, whether the parties act coordinated or not. In the latter case the participating parties are not aware of whether other parties are concurrently preparing updates/commits, which, depending on the scheme, potentially leads to the server having to reject packages. In the former case, on the other hand, they have this knowledge. In practice, this could be implemented by introducing an additional mechanism, that requires parties to wait for a confirmation by the server before preparing and sending update packages. We further track the per-user recipient communication complexity, again measured as a total over all rounds required to recover from compromise. The final considered value is the sender communication cost of a single, non-concurrent, update/commit in a subsequent round. Here, we state both the cost of the worst-case party as well as the average cost.

In Table 2 we mark schemes that perform substantially better or worse in one of the categories in green and red, respectively.

The Communication Complexity of CoCoA. We first discuss the number of rounds required to recover from compromise of t users. As we will show in Sect. 5, it is sufficient for the group to recover that all corrupted users concurrently update in $\lceil \log(n) \rceil + 1$ rounds.

Regarding the sender communication complexity, the size of update packages sent by a user ID to update in the CoCoA protocol is proportional to the size of the resolution of ID's co-path, which will be of order $\log(n)$ for a fully unblanked tree[14]. However, this value could be up to linear in a tree with many blanks, as is the case in TreeKEM and its variants, where blanks (or taints in the case of TTKEM) degrade communication efficiency. In CoCoA concurrent updates are merged and thus none are ever rejected by the server. Hence, in the considered scenario CoCoA in both the coordinated and uncoordinated setting has the same sender communication complexity of order $n \log(n)^2$ (corresponding to n users sending an update of size $\log(n)$ in $\lceil \log(n) \rceil + 1$ many rounds) and $t \log(n)^2$ (corresponding to t users sending an update of size $\log(n)$ in $\lceil \log(n) \rceil + 1$ many rounds), for cases (a) and (b) respectively.

With regards to the recipient communication complexity, user ID in our protocol needs to only receive at most a single ciphertext per update (zero if said update does not rotate the keys of any node in their state), and never more than $\mathsf{path}(\mathsf{ID}) = \lceil \log(n) \rceil$ in total. They will also receive at most $|\mathcal{P}(\mathsf{ID})|$ public keys per round.[15] Thus in case (a) ID would incur a download cost of order $\log(n)$ per round, and $\mathcal{O}(\log(n)^2)$ across the $\lceil \log(n) \rceil + 1$ rounds. In case (b) only t parties are updating per round, implying that the per round recipient cost is of order $\min(t, \log(n))$ and the cost over all $\lceil \log(n) \rceil + 1$ rounds is of order $\log(n) \cdot \min(t, \log(n))$. Finally, as in CoCoA concurrent updates do not affect the ratchet tree structure and in particular do not require blanks, the cost of subsequent updates remains of order $\log(n)$.

The Communication Complexity of Other CGKA Schemes. In Table 2 we contrast CoCoA to other CGKA schemes. For a more detailed breakdown of theses values we refer to the full version of this work [2]. The first class of considered schemes are ratchet-tree based schemes that do not rely on the P&C framework, as TreeKEM v7 and earlier versions [8], rTreeKEM [3], TTKEM [25], and Causal TreeKEM [26][16]. Further, with TreeKEM v8 [8] and later versions and the protocol by Bienstock et al. [11] we consider ratchet-tree based protocols following the P&C paradigm. Finally, we give values for the protocol by Weidner et al. [30] based on bidirectional channels. We point out that this work targets a different network model and has thus a different focus than ours.

Summary and Comparison. CoCoA diverges across two different axes from what could be considered a common paradigm until now. On the one hand, users are no longer required to keep track of the full state of the ratchet tree, reducing the recipient communication cost and the storage costs for users, and making this cost differ substantially from the total amount of upload communication. Indeed, this is a big change, as this distinction is not really present in previous

---

[14] an additional ciphertext would need to be sent for each unmerged leaf across ID's path, but this will not account for much in typical protocol executions.

[15] Note that the size of $\mathcal{P}(\mathsf{ID})$ grows at most by 1 per every blank node.

[16] Causal TreeKEM proposes an interesting idea of re-randomizing node secrets through a concrete homomorphic operation, instead of re-sampling them. Thus it actually allows for concurrent updates. However, the presented security statement still requires updates of every compromised party in *different* rounds, thus leading to communication complexity as presented in the table.

works, where the majority of uploaded packets are downloaded by everyone. On the other hand, we consider a more flexible PCS guarantee that only requires users to heal after $\lceil \log(n) \rceil + 1$ rounds. This is in contrast to previous works requiring PCS to hold after a constant number of rounds or only after n rounds. The effect of allowing concurrent updates to be merged is that, on one hand, the protocol is agnostic to coordination, i.e., no additional mechanism is needed that ensures that users do not send update/commit packages that will be rejected by the server, and, on the other hand, it allows the protocol to handle concurrent update operations without introducing blanks in the ratchet tree.

The trade-off with TreeKEM versions that precede the P&C paradigm is clear: we are paying a $\log(n)$ factor in sender communication in exchange for faster PCS that is independent from the number of compromised users. The comparison with P&C TreeKEM is not as straightforward, as the t compromised users can heal in only 2 rounds. The main advantage CoCoA over has this scheme is that it does not introduce blanks in the ratchet tree when handling concurrent operations, which leads to an improved update cost in subsequent rounds. However, this comes at the cost of slower healing and a factor of $\log^2(n)$ (or roughly $\log(n)$ in case (b)) in sender communication cost. We point out that the P&C framework of TreeKEM allows for more flexibility, e.g. by performing the required updates in several batches over multiple rounds. The exact trade-off achieved by such an intermediate approach is hard to quantify, but, again, due to blanking the cost of future updates will suffer. Finally, CoCoA has the advantage, over all versions of TreeKEM, of reduced recipient communication complexity and that users can prepare updates without the need of extra communication with the server to prevent rejection of said updates.

As a final remark, CoCoA seems to have a slightly worse efficiency than TreeKEM based protocols predating the P&C paradigm, since it requires slightly larger sender communication overall. However, as we show in Sect. 5, this is only the case if fast PCS is required for many users. In fact, a round with a single update will immediately grant PCS to its sender, just as in TreeKEM. Thus, CoCoA can be seen as an extension of pre-P&C TreeKEM, which incorporates the possibility of trading bandwidth for faster collective healing.

5   Security

Given a set of parties whose state has leaked, TreeKEM and related variants achieve PCS exactly after all of them perform an update. This is still true in our protocol *as long as the updates are applied sequentially*. In the case of concurrent updates, on the other hand, we show that every corrupted party sending logarithmically many updates is sufficient.

5.1   Security Model and Safe Predicate

To analyze the security of CoCoA, we essentially use the security model from [25], which allows the adversary to act partially actively and fully adaptively: in this model, the adversary can adaptively decide which users perform which operations, and can actively control the delivery server; however it can not issue messages on behalf of the users. In [25] this is enforced by assuming authenticated channels. Since in CoCoA the signing of protocol messages is more involved, parent hash plays an important role also for security against partially active adversaries, and the server no longer just relays messages, we make the use of signatures explicit in this work. As we restrict our analysis to partially active adversaries, the adversary does not get access to signing keys via corruptions. While this might look artificial, it has importance in practice as discussed in the introduction, and we still obtain meaningful results in the vein of [25]. Nevertheless, we consider the analysis of CoCoA's security against fully active adversaries an important question for future work.

Except for explicit signatures, the differences in the setting of *concurrent* CGKA to the one of [25] are that 1) users process concurrent messages, 2) no messages are ever rejected by the server, and 3) the server is allowed to send arbitrary (potentially malformed) messages. Regarding 2), it is however possible that messages get lost and even that a user does not process an update they generated. Whether a user ID_i's update message (and which one) is contained in a round message $\mathfrak{M}_i$, is represented by a counter c_i. Finally, regarding 3), while our security notion is strictly stronger than the one from [25] (where the server could only forward existing messages), the security of protocols such as TreeKEM and TTKEM can trivially be upgraded to our notion: This is true since round messages in these protocols only consist of *signed* messages and the adversary does not learn any party's signing key. In our protocols, in contrast, the server is assumed to perform some computation on users' messages, hence it makes sense to consider a stronger model where this computation is not trusted.

Definition 5 (Asynchronous CGKA Security). *The security for CGKA is modeled using a game between a challenger* C *and an adversary* A. *At the beginning of the game, the adversary queries* **create-group**(G) *and the challenger initializes the group* G *with identities* $(\mathsf{ID}_1, \ldots, \mathsf{ID}_\ell)$. *The adversary* A *can then make a sequence of queries, enumerated below, in any arbitrary order. On a high level,* **add-user** *and* **remove-user** *allow the adversary to control the structure of the group, whereas* **process** *allows it to control the scheduling of the messages. The query* **update** *simulates the refreshing of a local state. Finally,* **start-corrupt** *and* **end-corrupt** *enable the adversary to corrupt the users for a time period. The entire state and random coins of a corrupted user are leaked to the adversary during this period, except for the user's signing key.*

1. **add-user**(ID, ID′): *a user* ID *requests to add another user* ID′ *to the group.*
2. **remove-user**(ID, ID′): *a user* ID *requests to remove another user* ID′ *from the group.*
3. **update**(ID): *the user* ID *requests to refresh its current local state* γ.
4. **process**(𝔐, ID): *for some message* 𝔐 *and party* ID, *this action sends* 𝔐 *to* ID *which immediately processes it.*
5. **start-corrupt**(ID): *from now on the entire internal state and randomness of* ID *except for the signing key* $\mathsf{ssk}_{\mathsf{ID}}$ *is leaked to the adversary.*

6. **end-corrupt**(ID): *ends the leakage of user* ID*'s internal state and randomness to the adversary.*

7. **challenge**(q^*): *A picks a query q^* corresponding to anaction* a* = **update**(ID) *or the initialization (if $q^* = 0$). Let K_0 denote the group key that is sampled during this operation and K_1 be a fresh random key. The challenger tosses a coin b and – if the safe predicate below is satisfied – the key K_b is given to the adversary (if the predicate is not satisfied the adversary gets nothing).*

At the end of the game, the adversary outputs a bit b' and wins if $b' = b$. We call a CGKA scheme (Q, ϵ, t)-CGKA-secure if for any adversary A making at most Q queries of the form **add-user**$(\cdot, \cdot)$, **remove-user**$(\cdot, \cdot)$, or **update**$(\cdot)$ and running in time t it holds

$$\mathsf{Adv}_{\mathsf{CGKA}}(A) := |\Pr[1 \leftarrow A|b = 0] - \Pr[1 \leftarrow A|b = 1]| < \epsilon.$$

In contrast to the security definition of [25], process queries do not point to specific queries here. Thus, in order to define our safe predicate, we first need to define what we mean by saying that a party processed another party's update.

Definition 6. *Let* ID *and* ID* *be two (not necessarily different) users and* $(\gamma_q, T) \leftarrow$ CGKA.Upd(γ_{q-1}) *an update with associated counter c, generated by* ID *in query q. Let* $\mathcal{R}(\mathsf{ID}, \gamma_q)$ *be the set of round messages* $\mathfrak{M}$ *that*

(a) are efficiently computable from the public transcript and private states of all parties,
(b) have counter c for party ID*, and*
(c) will be accepted by ID *in state* γ_q*, i.e.,* CGKA.Proc$(\gamma_q, \mathfrak{M})$ *outputs a new state γ_{q+1} such that* CGKA.Key$(\gamma_{q+1}) \neq$ CGKA.Key(γ_q)*.*

Then we say that ID* processes the update T (or equivalently q) at time $q^* > q$ if ID* processes some round message $\mathfrak{M}^*$ at time q^* resulting in state γ_{q^*}, and CGKA.Key$(\gamma_{q^*}) \in \{$CGKA.Key(CGKA.Proc$(\gamma_q, \mathfrak{M})) \mid \mathfrak{M} \in \mathcal{R}(\mathsf{ID}, \gamma_q)\}$.

As a special case we say that ID* processes the single update T (or equivalently q), if in item (c) additionally the only changes to $\mathcal{P}(\mathsf{ID})$ resulting from updates are due to T.

With this notion in place, we will now define the safe predicate similar to the one in [25]. In particular, it rules out all trivial winning strategies, while preserving simplicity by ignoring protocol-specific details such as the relative position of users within the tree.

Definition 7 (Critical window, safe user). *Let* ID *and* ID* *be two (not necessarily different) users and $q^* \in [Q]_0$ be some* **update**$(\cdot)$ *or* **create-group**$(\cdot)$ *query. Let $q^- < q^*$ be maximal such that one of the following holds:*

- *There exist $L := \lceil \log(n) \rceil + 1$ update queries* $\mathsf{a}^i_{\mathsf{ID}} :=$ **update**(ID) *($i \in [L]$) that were generated for* ID *and processed by* ID* *within the time interval $[q^-, q^*]$. If* ID* *does not process L such queries then we set $q^- = 1$, the first query. We denote the last such update query as q^L.*

– *There exists an update query* $a_{ID}^- := \textbf{update}(ID)$ *that was generated by* ID *and processed by* ID^* *as a single update within the time interval* $[q^-, q^*]$*. In this case, we set* $q^L := q^-$.

Furthermore, let $q^+ > q^L$ *be the first query that invalidates* ID*'s current key (in the view of* ID^**), i.e., in query* q^+*,* ID *processes a (partial) update* $a_{ID}^+ := \textbf{update}(ID) \notin \{a_{ID}^i\}_{i \in [L]}$*. If* ID *does not process any such query then we set* $q^+ = Q$*, the last query.*

We say that the window $[q^-, q^+]$ is critical *for* ID *at time* q^* *in the view of* ID^**. Moreover, if the user* ID *is* not corrupted *at any time point in the critical window, we say that* ID *is* safe *at time* q^* *in the view of* ID^**.*

Similar to [25], we define a group key as *safe* if all the users that ID^* considers to be in the group are individually safe, i.e., not corrupted in their critical windows, in the view of ID^*.

Definition 8 (Safe predicate). *Let* K^* *be a group key generated in an action* $a^* \in \{\textbf{update}(ID^*), \textbf{create-group}(ID^*, \cdot)\}$ *at time point* $q^* \in [Q]_0$ *and let* G^* *be the set of users which would end up in the group if query* q^* *was processed, as viewed by the generating user* ID^**. Then the key* K^* *is considered* safe *if for all users* $ID \in G^*$ *(including* ID^**) we have that* ID *is safe at time* q^* *in the view of* ID^* *(as per Definition 7).*

Note that the second case in Definition 7 exactly captures the case where only *single* updates are accepted in each round. Thus, the security of CoCoA is strictly stronger than sequential variants of TreeKEM. Further, the bound of $\lceil \log(n) \rceil + 1$ updates as required in Definition 7 is indeed tight, as we show with an example given in the full version of this work [2].

5.2 Security of CoCoA

Regarding the security of CoCoA we obtain the following.

Theorem 1. *If the encryption scheme used in CoCoA is* (ϵ_{Enc}, t)*-IND-CPA-secure, the signature scheme is* $(\epsilon_{Sig}, t, (n + 2\log(n))Q)$*-UF-CMA-secure, and the used hash functions are modeled as random oracles, then CoCoA is* $(Q, \mathcal{O}(\epsilon_{Enc} \cdot (nQ)^2 + \epsilon_{Sig} \cdot n), t)$*-CGKA-secure.*

Due to space limitations we only give a high level overview on the proof, and refer to the full version of this work [2] for the formal proof. To prove security of CoCoA, we follow the approach of [25] and consider the graph structure that is generated throughout the security experiment. A node i in the so-called *CGKA graph* is associated with seeds Δ_i and $s_i := H_2(\Delta_i)$, and a key-pair $(pk_i, sk_i) := \text{Gen}(s_i)$. The edges of the graph, on the other hand, are induced by dependencies via the hash function H_1 or (public-key) encryptions. To be more precise, an edge (i, j) corresponds to either:

(a) a ciphertext of the form $\mathsf{Enc}_{\mathsf{pk}_i}(\Delta_j)$; or
(b) an application of H_1 of the form $\Delta_j = \mathsf{H}_1(\Delta_i)$ used in hierarchical derivation.

Naturally, the structure of the CGKA graph depends on the **update, add-user** or **remove-user** queries made by the adversary, and is therefore generated adaptively. To argue security of a challenge group key, we consider the subgraph of the CGKA graph that consists of all ancestors of the node associated to the challenge group key – the so-called *challenge graph*. By functionality of the CGKA protocol, the challenge group key can be derived from any secret key/seed associated to a node in the challenge graph. To argue security, none of the secret keys in the challenge graph must be leaked to the adversary by corruption. We prove that this is indeed the case for CoCoA if the safe predicate is satisfied. Our proof follows the ideas from [25], but involves a new combinatorial argument to establish the upper bound of $\lceil \log(n) \rceil + 1$ updates for healing the state of every user. Further, the fact that in CoCoA users only keep track of a part of the ratchet tree substantially complicates the proof of this statement.

In more detail, the proof for the protocol in [25] relies on the property that every key in the challenge graph must stem from an update that the party ID^*, who generated the challenge key, processed. This can easily be ensured for protocols keeping track of the full ratchet tree, by forcing parties, who do not agree for every point in time in the protocol execution on every key associated to a node in the ratchet tree, into inconsistent states, thus making future communication between them impossible. Note that this implies the desired property. In this case, if a user ID, while generating an update, encrypts the seed of a key pk to some pk', and later ID^* encrypts to pk, then ID^* must have had pk' in their state at some point in time, and, in particular, processed the update establishing it.

Unfortunately, while in an execution where the server behaves honestly, this property would also be true with respect to the relatively simple definition of processing an update of Definition 6, it is no longer true if we allow an untrusted server. Since in CoCoA the server might send malformed round messages, this property turns out to not hold anymore. We overcome this issue by giving a more involved definition (which is equivalent to Definition 6 in the honest server setting) of *weakly processing* an update and then essentially show, in the ROM, that every key in a user's state must stem from a weakly processed update. Further, we show that users that do not agree on the same history of weakly processed updates transition to inconsistent states. For this we have to show, for example, that all keys introduced into a user's state after a change to the resolution of their copath must have been weakly processed in an earlier round (even in the case that at this point in time this update did not affect the user's limited view of the ratchet tree). To prove these properties we rely on the consistency mechanisms of transcript hash and parent hash.

With these statements in place we are finally able to show that no key in the challenge graph is leaked to the adversary, where we use the observation that this property holding with respect to processing an update as defined in Definition 6 is implied by it holding with respect to the relaxed definition.

Acknowledgements. We thank Marta Mularczyk and Yiannis Tselekounis for their very helpful feedback on an earlier draft of this paper.

References

1. Alwen, J., et al.: Grafting key trees: efficient key management for overlapping groups. In: Nissim, K., Waters, B. (eds.) TCC 2021. LNCS, vol. 13044, pp. 222–253. Springer, Cham (2021). https://doi.org/10.1007/978-3-030-90456-2_8

2. Alwen, J., et al.: Cocoa: Concurrent continuous group key agreement (2022). Cryptology ePrint Archive, Report 2022/251, https://eprint.iacr.org/2022/251

3. Alwen, J., Coretti, S., Dodis, Y., Tselekounis, Y.: Security analysis and improvements for the IETF MLS standard for group messaging. In: Micciancio, D., Ristenpart, T. (eds.) CRYPTO 2020. LNCS, vol. 12170, pp. 248–277. Springer, Cham (2020). https://doi.org/10.1007/978-3-030-56784-2_9

4. Alwen, J., Coretti, S., Dodis, Y., Tselekounis, Y.: Modular design of secure group messaging protocols and the security of MLS. In: Vigna, G., Shi, E. (eds.) ACM CCS 2021, pp. 1463–1483. ACM Press (2021)

5. Alwen, J., Coretti, S., Jost, D., Mularczyk, M.: Continuous group key agreement with active security. In: Pass, R., Pietrzak, K. (eds.) TCC 2020. LNCS, vol. 12551, pp. 261–290. Springer, Cham (2020). https://doi.org/10.1007/978-3-030-64378-2_10

6. Alwen, J., Hartmann, D., Kiltz, E., Mularczyk, M.: Server-aided continuous group key agreement. Cryptology ePrint Archive, Report 2021/1456, 2021. https://eprint.iacr.org/2021/1456

7. Alwen, J., Jost, D., Mularczyk, M.: On the insider security of MLS. Cryptology ePrint Archive, Report 2020/1327 (2020). https://eprint.iacr.org/2020/1327

8. Barnes, R., Beurdouche, B., Millican, J., Omara, E., Cohn-Gordon, K., Robert, R.: The Messaging Layer Security (MLS) Protocol. Internet-Draft draft-ietf-mls-protocol-11, Internet Engineering Task Force (2020). Work in Progress

9. Bhargavan, K., Barnes, R., Rescorla, E.: TreeKEM: asynchronous decentralized key management for large dynamic groups (2018). https://mailarchive.ietf.org/arch/attach/mls/pdf1XUH6o.pdf

10. Bhargavan, K., Beurdouche, B., Naldurg, P.: Formal Models and Verified Protocols for Group Messaging: Attacks and Proofs for IETF MLS. Research report, Inria Paris (2019)

11. Bienstock, A., Dodis, Y., Rösler, P.: On the price of concurrency in group ratcheting protocols. In: Pass, R., Pietrzak, K. (eds.) TCC 2020. LNCS, vol. 12551, pp. 198–228. Springer, Cham (2020). https://doi.org/10.1007/978-3-030-64378-2_8

12. Bresson, E., Chevassut, O., Pointcheval, D.: Dynamic group diffie-hellman key exchange under standard assumptions. In: Knudsen, L.R. (ed.) EUROCRYPT 2002. LNCS, vol. 2332, pp. 321–336. Springer, Heidelberg (2002). https://doi.org/10.1007/3-540-46035-7_21

13. Brzuska, C., Cornelissen, E., Kohbrok, K.: Cryptographic security of the mls rfc, draft 11. Cryptology ePrint Archive, Report 2021/137 (2021). https://eprint.iacr.org/2021/137

14. Burmester, M., Desmedt, Y.: A secure and efficient conference key distribution system. In: De Santis, A. (ed.) EUROCRYPT 1994. LNCS, vol. 950, pp. 275–286. Springer, Heidelberg (1995). https://doi.org/10.1007/BFb0053443

15. Canetti, R., Garay, J.A., Itkis, G., Micciancio, D., Naor, M., Pinkas, B.: Multicast security: a taxonomy and some efficient constructions. In: IEEE INFOCOM 1999, New York, NY, USA, 21–25 March 1999, pp. 708–716 (1999)
16. Cohn-Gordon, K., Cremers, C., Garratt, L., Millican, J., Milner, K.: On ends-to-ends encryption: asynchronous group messaging with strong security guarantees. In: Lie, D., Mannan, M., Backes, M., Wang, X. (eds.) ACM CCS 2018, pp. 1802–1819. ACM Press (2018)
17. Cremers, C., Hale, B., Kohbrok, K.: The complexities of healing in secure group messaging: Why cross-group effects matter. In: Bailey, M., Greenstadt, R. (eds.) USENIX Security 2021, pp. 1847–1864. USENIX Association (2021)
18. Devigne, J., Duguey, C., Fouque, P.-A.: MLS group messaging: how zero-knowledge can secure updates. In: Bertino, E., Shulman, H., Waidner, M. (eds.) ESORICS 2021. LNCS, vol. 12973, pp. 587–607. Springer, Cham (2021). https://doi.org/10.1007/978-3-030-88428-4_29
19. Dutta, R., Barua, R.: Dynamic group key agreement in tree-based setting. In: Boyd, C., González Nieto, J.M. (eds.) ACISP 2005. LNCS, vol. 3574, pp. 101–112. Springer, Heidelberg (2005). https://doi.org/10.1007/11506157_9
20. Emura, K., Kajita, K., Nojima, R., Ogawa, K., Ohtake, G.: Membership privacy for asynchronous group messaging. Cryptology ePrint Archive, Report 2022/046 (2022). https://eprint.iacr.org/2022/046
21. Hashimoto, K., Katsumata, S., Postlethwaite, E., Prest, T., Westerbaan, B.: A concrete treatment of efficient continuous group key agreement via multi-recipient PKEs. In: Vigna, G., Shi, E. (eds.) ACM CCS 2021, pp. 1441–1462. ACM Press (2021)
22. Howell, C., Leavy, T., Alwen, J.: Wickr messaging protocol: technical paper (2019). https://1c9n2u3hx1x732fbvk1ype2x-wpengine.netdna-ssl.com/wp-content/uploads/2019/12/WhitePaper_WickrMessagingProtocol.pdf
23. Ingemarsson, I., Tang, D., Wong, C.: A conference key distribution system. IEEE Trans. Inf. Theory **28**(5), 714–720 (1982)
24. Hashimoto, K., Katsumata, S., Postlethwaite, E., Prest, T., Westerbaan, B.: A concrete treatment of efficient continuous group key agreement via multi-recipient PKEs. In: Vigna, G., Shi, E. (eds.) ACM CCS 2021, pp. 1441–1462. ACM Press (2021)
25. Klein, K., et al.: Keep the dirt: tainted TreeKEM, adaptively and actively secure continuous group key agreement. In: 2021 IEEE Symposium on Security and Privacy, pp. 268–284. IEEE Computer Society Press (2021)
26. Weidner, M.A.: Group Messaging for Secure Asynchronous Collaboration. Master's thesis, University of Cambridge (2019)
27. Panjwani, S.: Tackling adaptive corruptions in multicast encryption protocols. In: Vadhan, S.P. (ed.) TCC 2007. LNCS, vol. 4392, pp. 21–40. Springer, Heidelberg (2007). https://doi.org/10.1007/978-3-540-70936-7_2
28. Perrin, T., Marlinspike, M.: The Double Ratchet Algorithm (2016). https://signal.org/docs/specifications/doubleratchet/
29. Wallner, D.M., Harder, E.J., Agee, R.C.: Key management for multicast: Issues and architectures. Internet Draft (1998). http://www.ietf.org/ID.html
30. Weidner, M., Kleppmann, M., Hugenroth, D., Beresford, A.R.: Key agreement for decentralized secure group messaging with strong security guarantees. In: Vigna, G., Shi, E. (eds.) ACM CCS 2021, pp. 2024–2045. ACM Press (2021)
31. Wong, C.K., Gouda, M.G., Lam, S.S.: Secure group communications using key graphs. In: Proceedings of ACM SIGCOMM, Vancouver, BC, Canada, 31 August–4 September 1998, pp. 68–79 (1998)

Efficient Schemes for Committing Authenticated Encryption

Mihir Bellare[1] and Viet Tung Hoang[2(✉)]

[1] Department of Computer Science and Engineering,
University of California San Diego, La Jolla, USA
`mihir@eng.ucsd.edu`
[2] Department of Computer Science, Florida State University, Tallahassee, USA
`tvhoang@cs.fsu.edu`
`https://cseweb.ucsd.edu/~mihir/, https://cs.fsu.edu/~tvhoang/`

Abstract. This paper provides efficient authenticated-encryption (AE) schemes in which a ciphertext is a commitment to the key. These are extended, at minimal additional cost, to schemes where the ciphertext is a commitment to all encryption inputs, meaning key, nonce, associated data and message. Our primary schemes are modifications of GCM (for basic, unique-nonce AE security) and AES-GCM-SIV (for misuse-resistant AE security) and add both forms of commitment without any increase in ciphertext size. We also give more generic, but somewhat more costly, solutions.

1 Introduction

Symmetric encryption is the canonical primitive of cryptography, with which the field is often identified in the popular mind. Over time, the primitive has evolved. Failures of privacy-only schemes lead to the understanding that the goal should be *authenticated* encryption [10,32]. The underlying syntax, meanwhile, has gone from randomized or counter-based [7] to nonce-based [39,40].

Recent attacks and applications [3,4,25,27,34] motivate another evolution. Namely, a ciphertext should be a commitment to the key, and beyond that, possibly even to other or all the inputs to the encryption process.

In this paper we contribute definitions and new schemes for such committing authenticated encryption. Our schemes combine efficiency, security and practicality attributes that may make them attractive for inclusion in cryptographic software libraries or for standardization.

BACKGROUND. In a nonce-based symmetric encryption scheme SE, encryption takes key K, nonce N, associated data A and message M to deterministically return a ciphertext $C \leftarrow \mathsf{SE.Enc}(K, N, A, M)$, with decryption recovering via $M \leftarrow \mathsf{SE.Dec}(K, N, A, C)$ [39,40]. AE security asks for both privacy and authenticity of the message. In its most basic form, called UNAE (Unique-Nonce AE security) this is under the assumption that nonces are unique, meaning never reused across encryptions [39,40]. MRAE (Misuse-resistant AE security) is stronger,

© International Association for Cryptologic Research 2022
O. Dunkelman and S. Dziembowski (Eds.): EUROCRYPT 2022, LNCS 13276, pp. 845–875, 2022.
https://doi.org/10.1007/978-3-031-07085-3_29

asking in addition for best-possible security under any reuse of an encryption nonce [41].

A central scheme is GCM [36]. It is a government standard [23] and is used in TLS [42]. Other standardized and widely-used schemes are XSalsa20/Poly1305 and ChaCha20/Poly1305 [15–17]. All these are UNAE-secure. AES-GCM-SIV [28, 43] is a leading MRAE scheme poised for standardization.

For both UNAE and MRAE, proofs are the norm, but the bar is now high: not only multi-user (mu) security [13]—reflecting that deployment settings like TLS have millions of users—but with bounds that are good, meaning almost the same as for the single-user setting. Dedicated analyses show that GCM has such UNAE security [13, 29, 35], and likewise for the MRAE security of AES-GCM-SIV [20]. Henceforth when we refer to UNAE or MRAE, it means in the mu setting

COMMITTING SECURITY. We formalize, in a systematic way, different notions of what it means for a ciphertext $C \leftarrow$ SE.Enc(K, N, A, M) to be a commitment. For the purposes of this Introduction, we can confine attention to two notions, CMT-1 and CMT-4. The primary, CMT-1 notion asks that the commitment be to the key K. In the game formalizing this, the adversary returns a pair $((K_1, N_1, A_1, M_1), (K_2, N_2, A_2, M_2))$ satisfying $K_1 \neq K_2$, and is successful if SE.Enc$(K_1, N_1, A_1, M_1) =$ SE.Enc(K_2, N_2, A_2, M_2). Extending this, CMT-4 asks that the commitment be, not just to the key, but to K, N, A, M, meaning to *all* the inputs to SE.Enc. The game changes only in the requirement $K_1 \neq K_2$ being replaced by $(K_1, N_1, A_1, M_1) \neq (K_2, N_2, A_2, M_2)$. As a mnemonic, think of the integer ℓ in the notation CMT-ℓ as the number of inputs of SE.Enc to which we commit.

Clearly CMT-4 $\rightarrow$ CMT-1, meaning any scheme that is CMT-4-secure is also CMT-1-secure, and it is easy to see that the implication is strict. (There exist CMT-1-secure schemes that are not CMT-4-secure.)

In Sect. 3, we also consider CMT-3, simpler than, but equivalent to, CMT-4; we give alternative, decryption-based formulations of all these definitions but show the two equivalent for schemes that, like all the ones we consider, satisfy the syntactic requirement of tidiness [38]; and finally we extend the notions from 2-way committing security to s-way committing security for a parameter $s \geq 2$ which will enter results.

Simple counterexamples show that neither UNAE nor MRAE security imply even CMT-1-security. And the gap is real: attacks from [4, 27, 34] show that GCM, XSalsa20/Poly1305, ChaCha20/Poly1305 and OCB [40] are all CMT-1-insecure.

PRIOR NOTIONS. The notion of key-committing (KC) security, asking that a ciphertext is a commitment to the key, starts with Abdalla, Bellare and Neven (ABN) [3], who called it robustness and studied it for PKE and IBE. Their definitions were strengthened by Farshim, Libert, Paterson and Quaglia [24]. Now calling it key-robustness, Farshi, Orlandi and Rosie (FOR) [25] bring it to randomized symmetric encryption. Albertini, Duong, Gueron, Kölbl, Luykx and Schmieg (ADGKLS) [4] and Len, Grubbs and Ristenpart (LGR) [34] consider it for nonce-based symmetric encryption, giving definitions slightly weaker than CMT-1.

Grubbs, Lu and Ristenpart (GLR) [27] consider committing to the header and message. CMT-4 is stronger in that it asks for the commitment to be not just to these but also to the key and nonce. However, we do not consider or require what GLR [27] call compact commitment.

WHY COMMIT TO THE KEY? The canonical method for password-based encryption (PKCS#5 [31]) uses a symmetric encryption scheme SE, such as GCM, as a tool. In a surprising new attack, LGR [34] show that absence of key-committing (KC) security in SE leads to a break of the overlying password-based encryption scheme. This attack is circumvented if SE is CMT-1-secure.

Broadly, we have seen protocols failing due to absence of key-committing security in an underlying encryption scheme and then fixed by its being added. ABN [3] illustrate this when the protocol is PEKS [19]; they also note that when encryption strives to be anonymous, key-committing security is necessary for unambiguous decryption. FOR [25] illustrate the issue for an encryption-using Oblivious Transfer protocol and note that encryption not being key-committing has lead to attacks on Private Set Intersection protocols [33]. ADGKLS [4] describe in detail three real-world security failures—the domains are key rotation, envelope encryption and subscribe-with-Google—arising from lack of key-committing security.

WHY COMMIT TO EVERYTHING? CMT-4 is a simple, optimally-strong goal: we commit to everything. This means all 4 of the inputs to the encryption algorithm: key, nonce, associated data and message. Some motivation comes from applications; for example, GLR [27] show that committing to header and message is needed for an AE scheme to provide message franking, a capability in messaging systems that allows a receiver to report the receipt of abusive content. But the larger benefit is to increase ease of use and decrease risk of error or misuse. An application designer is spared the burden of trying to understand to exactly which encryption inputs the application needs a commitment; with CMT-4, she is covered.

PATH TO SCHEMES. Our starting points are existing AE schemes. Given one such, call it SE, we will modify it to a CMT-1 scheme SE-1 and then further into a CMT-4 scheme SE-4. These modifications must of course retain AE security: for XX $\in$ {UN, MR}, if SE is XXAE-secure then so are SE-1, SE-4. The ciphertext overhead (length of ciphertext in new scheme minus that in old) is kept as small as possible, and is zero for our primary schemes. Computational overhead will always be independent of the length of the message.

Proofs of AE security for our schemes are in the multi-user setting, with bounds as good as those for the starting schemes. This requires significant analytical effort.

Modern encryption standards are purely blockcipher based, meaning do not use a cryptographic hash function like SHA256; this allows them to most effectively exploit the AES-NI instructions for speed, and also lowers their real-estate in hardware. We aim, as much as possible, to retain this. For CMT-1, we succeed, reaching this without cryptographic hash functions. The extension to CMT-4

Scheme	AE security	Committing security	Ciphertext overhead	Starts from
CAU-C1	UNAE	CMT-1	0	GCM
HtE[CAU-C1, ·]	UNAE	CMT-4	0	GCM
CAU-SIV-C1	MRAE	CMT-1	0	AES-GCM-SIV
HtE[CAU-SIV-C1, ·]	MRAE	CMT-4	0	AES-GCM-SIV
UtC[SE, ·]	UNAE	CMT-1	1 block	any UNAE SE
HtE[UtC[SE, ·], ·]	UNAE	CMT-4	1 block	any UNAE SE
RtC[SE, ·, ·]	MRAE	CMT-1	1 block	any MRAE SE
HtE[RtC[SE, ·, ·], ·]	MRAE	CMT-4	1 block	any MRAE SE

Fig. 1. Summary of attributes of our schemes. Ciphertext overhead is length of ciphertext in our scheme minus that in the scheme from which it starts. Computational overhead is always independent of message length. A "·" as an argument to a transform refers to some suitable auxiliary primitive discussed in the text.

however requires a function H that we would instantiate via a cryptographic hash function.

The step from CMT-1 to CMT-4 is done via a general, zero ciphertext-overhead transform, called HtE, that we discuss next. Figure 1 summarizes the attributes of the different new schemes that we give and will discuss below.

FROM CMT-1 TO CMT-4 VIA HtE. We give a generic way to turn a CMT-1 scheme into into a CMT-4 one. (That is, once you can commit to the key, it is easy to commit to everything.) The transform incurs no ciphertext overhead and preserves both UNAE and MRAE security. The computational overhead involves processing only the nonce and associated data, and is independent of message length.

We now give some detail. Given a symmetric encryption scheme SE-1, and a function H, our HtE (Hash then Encrypt) transform defines the scheme SE-4 ← HtE[SE-1, H] in which SE-4.Enc(K, N, A, M) lets $L \leftarrow H(K, (N, A))$ and returns SE-1.Enc(L, N, ε, M). Here outputs of H have the same length as keys of SE-1. There is no ciphertext overhead: ciphertexts in SE-4 have the same length as in SE-1. The computational overhead, namely the computation of H, is independent of message length. Theorem 1 shows that SE-4 is CMT-4 assuming SE-1 is CMT-1 and H is collision resistant. Theorem 2 shows that if H is a PRF then (1) If SE-1 is UNAE then so is SE-4, and (2) If SE-1 is MRAE then so is SE-4. All these results are with good bounds.

We stress that we avoid assuming H is a random oracle; we instead make the standard-model assumption that it is a collision-resistant PRF. Section 3 discusses instantiations of H based on HMAC [5], SHA256 or SHA3.

CAU SCHEMES. GCM [36] is a UNAE scheme that, due to its standardization [23] and use in TLS [42], is already widely implemented. Attacks [4,27,34] however show that it is not CMT-1-secure. Making only a tiny modification to GCM, we obtain a new scheme, that we CAU-C1, that is UNAE and CMT-1 secure. Theorem 3 establishes CMT-1 security of CAU-C1, and Theorem 4 establishes UNAE security with good mu bounds.

CAU-C1 changes only how the last block GCM block is encrypted so that the tag is a Davies-Meyer hash. (See Fig. 9.) The locality and minimality of the change means that it should be easy to modify existing GCM code to obtain CAU-C1 code, making CAU-C1 attractive for implementation. With regard to performance, CAU-C1 incurs essentially no overhead; in particular, the ciphertext size remains the same as in GCM.

We can obtain a UNAE and CMT-4-secure scheme, that we call CAU-C4, by applying our above-discussed HtE transform to CAU-C1 and a suitable collision-resistant PRF H. Ciphertext overhead continues to be zero: CAU-C4 ciphertexts have the same size as CAU-C1, and thus GCM, ones.

With the above, we have obtained CMT-1 and CMT-4 UNAE schemes that offer minimal overhead, good quantitative security and ease of implementation. We now turn to MRAE, doing the same. Here our starting point is AES-GCM-SIV [28,43], a leading MRAE scheme poised for standardization. We give CAU-SIV-C1, a tiny modification of AES-GCM-SIV that is MRAE and CMT-1-secure. Theorem 5 establishes CMT-1 security of CAU-SIV-C1, and Theorem 6 establishes MRAE security with good mu bounds. Again, applying HtE to CAU-SIV-C1 yields a MRAE and CMT-4 scheme CAU-SIV-C4 that continues to be a small modification of AES-GCM-SIV. There is no growth in ciphertext size.

GENERIC TRANSFORMS. With the four schemes discussed above, we have obtained CMT-1 and CMT-4 security for both UNAE and MRAE schemes, with zero ciphertext overhead and almost zero computational overhead. These schemes however are intrusive, making small modifications to GCM or AES-GCM-SIV. We now give ways to add committing security via generic transforms that invoke the given scheme only in a blackbox way. The price we will pay is some ciphertext overhead.

We give a generic transform UtC that takes any UNAE scheme SE and returns a scheme $\overline{\text{SE}} \leftarrow \text{UtC}[\text{SE}, \text{F}]$ that is UNAE and CMT-1-secure. Here F is a committing PRF, a primitive we introduce that generalizes the notion of a key-robust PRF from FOR [25]. We build a cheap committing PRF, that we call CX, from (only) a blockcipher. Proposition 5 proves its security with good bounds. Theorem 7 establishes CMT-1 security of $\overline{\text{SE}}$, and also shows that $\overline{\text{SE}}$ inherits the mu UNAE security of SE without degradation in the bound. Ciphertexts in $\overline{\text{SE}}$ are one block longer than those in SE. Applying HtE to $\overline{\text{SE}}$ and a suitable collision-resistant PRF H, we obtain a UNAE CMT-4 scheme, leaving ciphertext overhead at one block.

UtC however does not preserve MRAE security. We give a second generic transform, RtC, that takes any MRAE scheme SE and returns a scheme $\overline{\text{SE}} \leftarrow \text{RtC}[\text{SE}, \text{F}, \text{H}]$ that is MRAE and CMT-1-secure. Here F as before is a committing PRF that we set to CX, and H is a collision-resistant PRF that we instantiate via the Davies-Meyer method. Theorem 8 establishes CMT-1 security of $\overline{\text{SE}}$, and also shows that $\overline{\text{SE}}$ inherits the mu MRAE security of SE without degradation in the bound. Ciphertexts in $\overline{\mathsf{SE}}$ are one block longer than those in SE. Again, applying HtE to $\overline{\mathsf{SE}}$ yields a MRAE CMT-4 scheme, leaving ciphertext overhead at one block.

EXTENSIONS AND REMARKS. For an integer parameter $s \geq 2$, we can extend CMT-1 to a notion CMT_s-1 of multi-input committing security. Here the adversary returns an s-tuple $((K_1, N_1, A_1, M_1), \ldots (K_s, N_s, A_s, M_s))$ in which $K_1, \ldots, K_s$ are all distinct, and is successful if $\mathsf{SE.Enc}(K_1, N_1, A_1, M_1), \ldots, \mathsf{SE.Enc}(K_s, N_s, A_s, M_s)$ are all the same. CMT-4 is likewise extended to CMT_s-4. Clearly CMT-n implies CMT_s-n ($n \in \{1, 4\}$). Our results however consider CMT_s-n (not just CMT-n) and prove bounds on its being violated that degrade quickly with s. This allows us to give better guarantees for security against partitioning oracle attacks [34]. Namely, we can show that, with use of one of our CMT-1 schemes, the probability that an attacker can speed up the attack by a factor s decreases quickly as a function of s.

RELATED WORK. We start by noting a few "firsts." (1) Prior nonce-based committing schemes were only for UNAE. We are giving the first ones for MRAE. (2) We give the first schemes that commit to all encryption inputs, meaning achieve CMT-4. (3) We give the first schemes (our four CAU schemes) that have zero ciphertext overhead (4) We give analyses of multi-input committing security with bounds that degrade quickly in the number s of inputs.

FOR [25] take a broad, systematic approach, giving general methods to build key-committing primitives. Their key-committing encryption schemes however are randomized rather than nonce-based. Also, they don't show multi-user security with good bounds.

Many of the schemes of GLR [27] are randomized. Their leading nonce-based scheme, Committing Encrypt-and-PRF (CEP), has a block of ciphertext overhead, unlike our CAU schemes. CEP also seems to fare somewhat more poorly than our schemes with regard to performance and extent of software change. They don't show good multi-user security.

The DGRW scheme [22] is randomized, not nonce-based. It uses a compression function that is assumed collision resistant and RKA-PRF-secure [9]. Instantiating the latter via Davies-Meyers yields a blockcipher-based scheme, but speed with AES-NI is reduced because the blockcipher key changes with each message block. They incur ciphertext overhead, and don't show good multi-user security.

It should be noted that GLR [27] and DGRW [22] are targeting and achieving properties beyond key-commiting security, as needed for message franking. In particular, their schemes, unlike ours, produce a *compact* commitment to the message.

ADGKLS [4] consider nonce-based schemes and give a generic way to add key-committing security to a UNAE scheme. Their transform uses a pair of collision-resistant PRFs. UtC generalizes this, using instead our (new) committing PRF abstraction; instantiation with CX yields efficiency improvements over ADGKLS. They also give a padding-based key-committing extension of GCM, but, unlike our CAU-C1, it increases ciphertext size.

LGR [34] say "our results suggest that future work should design, standardize, and add to libraries, AE schemes designed to be key-committing." Our schemes are intended as a response.

2 Preliminaries

NOTATION AND TERMINOLOGY. Let ε denote the empty string. For a string x we write $|x|$ to refer to its bit length, and $x[i:j]$ is the bits i through j (inclusive) of x, for $1 \le i \le j \le |x|$. By $\mathsf{Func}(\mathsf{Dom}, \mathsf{Rng})$ we denote the set of all functions $f : \mathsf{Dom} \to \mathsf{Rng}$ and by $\mathsf{Perm}(\mathsf{Dom})$ the set of all permutations $\pi : \mathsf{Dom} \to \mathsf{Dom}$. We use $\bot$ as a special symbol to denote rejection, and it is assumed to be outside $\{0,1\}^*$. In the context that we use a blockcipher $E : \{0,1\}^k \times \{0,1\}^n \to \{0,1\}^n$, the *block length* of a string x, denoted as $|x|_n$, is $\max\{1, \lceil |x|/n \rceil\}$. If X is a finite set, we let $x \leftarrow_\$ X$ denote picking an element of X uniformly at random and assigning it to x.

SYMMETRIC ENCRYPTION. A (nonce-based) symmetric encryption (SE) scheme SE specifies deterministic algorithms $\mathsf{SE.Enc} : \mathcal{K} \times \mathcal{N} \times \{0,1\}^* \times \{0,1\}^* \to \{0,1\}^*$ and $\mathsf{SE.Dec} : \mathcal{K} \times \mathcal{N} \times \{0,1\}^* \times \{0,1\}^* \to \{0,1\}^* \cup \{\bot\}$. Here $\mathcal{K}, \mathcal{N}$ are the associated key and nonce spaces. The encryption algorithm takes as input a key $K \in \mathcal{K}$, a nonce $N \in \mathcal{N}$, associated data $A \in \{0,1\}^*$ and a message $M \in \mathcal{M}$, and returns a ciphertext $C \leftarrow \mathsf{SE.Enc}(K, N, A, M)$. The decryption algorithm takes as input K, N, A, C and returns either a message $M \in \{0,1\}^*$ or the special symbol $\bot$ indicating invalidity or rejection. The correctness requirement says that decryption reverses encryption, namely if $C \leftarrow \mathsf{SE.Enc}(K, N, A, M)$ then $\mathsf{SE.Dec}(K, N, A, C)$ returns M. We assume that there is a ciphertext-length function $\mathsf{SE.len} : \mathbb{N} \to \mathbb{N}$ such that the length of $\mathsf{SE.Enc}(K, N, A, M)$ is exactly $\mathsf{SE.len}(|M|)$ bits for all K, N, A, M.

We say that SE is *tidy* [38] if $M \leftarrow \mathsf{SE.Dec}(K, N, A, C)$ implies that $\mathsf{SE.Enc}(K, N, A, M)$ returns C. Combining correctness and tidiness means that functions $\mathsf{SE.Enc}(K, N, A, \cdot)$ and $\mathsf{SE.Dec}(K, N, A, \cdot)$ are the inverse of each other. The schemes we consider will be tidy.

AE SECURITY. Let SE be a symmetric encryption scheme with key space $\mathcal{K}$ and nonce space $\mathcal{N}$. We now define its security as an authenticated encryption (AE) scheme in the multi-user setting, following the formalization of [13]. The first, basic requirement, called unique-nonce AE (UNAE), asks for security assuming encryption never repeats a nonce for any given user. The second, advanced requirement, called misuse-resistant AE (MRAE) drops this condition. Consider games $\mathbf{G}_{\mathsf{SE}}^{\mathrm{real}}(\mathcal{A})$ and $\mathbf{G}_{\mathsf{SE}}^{\mathrm{rand}}(\mathcal{A})$ in Fig. 2. We define the mrae advantage of an adversary $\mathcal{A}$ as

$$\mathbf{Adv}_{\mathsf{SE}}^{\mathrm{mrae}}(A) = \Pr[\mathbf{G}_{\mathsf{SE}}^{\mathrm{real}}(\mathcal{A})] - \Pr[\mathbf{G}_{\mathsf{SE}}^{\mathrm{rand}}(\mathcal{A})] \ .$$

To avoid trivial wins, we forbid the adversary from repeating a query to either its ENC or its VF oracles. Moreover, if the adversary previously received $C \leftarrow \mathrm{ENC}(i, N, A, M)$ then later it is not allowed to query $\mathrm{VF}(i, N, A, C)$. We can

Game $\mathbf{G}_{\mathsf{SE}}^{\mathrm{real}}(\mathcal{A})$	Game $\mathbf{G}_{\mathsf{SE}}^{\mathrm{rand}}(\mathcal{A})$
$b' \leftarrow_{\$} \mathcal{A}^{\mathrm{NEW, ENC, VF}}$; return b'	$b' \leftarrow_{\$} \mathcal{A}^{\mathrm{NEW, ENC, VF}}$; return b'
$\underline{\mathrm{NEW}()}$	$\underline{\mathrm{NEW}()}$
$v \leftarrow v + 1;\ K_v \leftarrow_{\$} \mathcal{K}$	$v \leftarrow v + 1$
$\underline{\mathrm{ENC}(i, N, A, M)}$	$\underline{\mathrm{ENC}(i, N, A, M)}$
If $i \notin \{1, \ldots, v\}$ return $\perp$	If $i \notin \{1, \ldots, v\}$ return $\perp$
$C \leftarrow \mathsf{SE.Enc}(K_i, N, A, M)$	$C \leftarrow_{\$} \{0,1\}^{\mathsf{SE.len}(|M|)}$
Return C	Return C
$\underline{\mathrm{VF}(i, N, A, C)}$	$\underline{\mathrm{VF}(i, N, A, C)}$
If $i \notin \{1, \ldots, v\}$ return $\perp$	If $i \notin \{1, \ldots, v\}$ return $\perp$
$V \leftarrow \mathsf{SE.Dec}(K_i, N, A, C)$; return $(V \neq \perp)$	return false

Fig. 2. Games defining misuse-resistance security of a SE scheme SE.

now recover UNAE security by restricting attention to *unique-nonce* adversaries, these being ones that never repeat an (i, N) pair across their ENC queries. (That is, a nonce is never reused for a given user.) We stress that there is no such restriction on decryption queries. If $\mathcal{A}$ is a unique-nonce adversary, then we write its advantage as $\mathbf{Adv}_{\mathsf{SE}}^{\mathrm{unae}}(\mathcal{A})$ for clarity.

MULTI-COLLISION RESISTANCE. Let $H : \mathsf{Dom} \to \mathsf{Rng}$ be a function. Let $s \geq 2$ be an integer. An s-way collision for H is a tuple $(X_1, \ldots, X_s)$ of distinct points in Dom such that $H(X_1) = \cdots = H(X_s)$. For an adversary $\mathcal{A}$, define its advantage in breaking the s-way multi-collision resistance of H as

$$\mathbf{Adv}_{H,s}^{\mathrm{coll}}(\mathcal{A}) = \Pr[(X_1, \ldots, X_s)\ \text{is an } s\text{-way collision for } H]$$

where the probability is over $(X_1, \ldots, X_s) \leftarrow_{\$} \mathcal{A}$. When $s = 2$ we recover the classical notion of collision resistance.

AXU HASHING. Let $G : \{0,1\}^n \times \{0,1\}^* \times \{0,1\}^* \to \{0,1\}^n$ be a keyed hash function. We say that G is c-*almost xor universal* if for all $(M, A) \neq (M', A')$ and all $\Delta \in \{0,1\}^n$,

$$\Pr_{K \leftarrow_{\$} \{0,1\}^n}[G_K(M, A) \oplus G_K(M', A') = \Delta] \leq \frac{c \cdot \max\{|M|_n + |A|_n, |M'|_n + |A'|_n\}}{2^n}.$$

PRFs AND PRPs. For a function $\mathsf{F} : \{0,1\}^k \times \mathsf{Dom} \to \mathsf{Rng}$ and an adversary $\mathcal{A}$, we define the advantage of $\mathcal{A}$ in breaking the (multi-user) PRF security of F [6] as

$$\mathbf{Adv}_{\mathsf{F}}^{\mathrm{prf}}(\mathcal{A}) = 2\Pr[\mathbf{G}_{\mathsf{F}}^{\mathrm{prf}}(\mathcal{A})] - 1 \ ,$$

where game $\mathbf{G}_{\mathsf{F}}^{\mathrm{prf}}(\mathcal{A})$ is shown in Fig. 3. For a blockcipher $E : \{0,1\}^k \times \{0,1\}^n \to \{0,1\}^n$ and an adversary $\mathcal{A}$, we define the advantage of $\mathcal{A}$ in breaking the multi-user PRP security of E as

$$\mathbf{Adv}_E^{\mathrm{prp}}(\mathcal{A}) = 2\Pr[\mathbf{G}_E^{\mathrm{prp}}(\mathcal{A})] - 1 \ ,$$

Game $\mathbf{G}_{\mathsf{F}}^{\mathrm{prf}}(\mathcal{A})$	NEW()	EVAL(i, M)
$v \leftarrow 0; \ b \leftarrow \!\! \$ \{0,1\}$	$v \leftarrow v + 1$	If $i \notin \{1, \ldots, v\}$ return $\perp$
$b' \leftarrow \!\! \$ \ \mathcal{A}^{\mathrm{NEW},\mathrm{EVAL}}$	$K_v \leftarrow \!\! \$ \{0,1\}^k$	$C_1 \leftarrow \mathsf{F}(K_i, M); \ C_0 \leftarrow f_i(M)$
return $(b' = b)$	$f_v \leftarrow \!\! \$ \ \mathsf{Func}(\mathsf{Dom}, \mathsf{Rng})$	return C_b

Game $\mathbf{G}_{E}^{\mathrm{prp}}(\mathcal{A})$	NEW()	EVAL(i, M)
$v \leftarrow 0; \ b \leftarrow \!\! \$ \{0,1\}$	$v \leftarrow v + 1$	If $i \notin \{1, \ldots, v\}$ return $\perp$
$b' \leftarrow \mathcal{A}^{\mathrm{NEW},\mathrm{EVAL}}$	$K_v \leftarrow \!\! \$ \{0,1\}^k$	$C_1 \leftarrow E(K_i, M); \ C_0 \leftarrow \pi_i(M)$
return $(b' = b)$	$\pi_v \leftarrow \!\! \$ \ \mathsf{Perm}(\{0,1\}^n)$	return C_b

Fig. 3. Games defining PRF security of F and PRP security of E.

where game $\mathbf{Adv}_{\mathsf{F}}^{\mathrm{prp}}(\mathcal{A})$ is defined in Fig. 3. Mouha and Luykx [37] show that if we model E as an ideal cipher then for any adversary making q evaluation queries and p ideal-cipher queries, $\mathbf{Adv}_{E}^{\mathrm{prp}}(\mathcal{A}) \leq (q^2 + 2pq)/2^{k+1}$.

3 Committing AE Framework

Let SE be a symmetric encryption scheme with key space $\mathcal{K}$ and nonce space $\mathcal{N}$. We define a hierarchy of levels of committing security CMTD-1 $\leftarrow$ CMTD-3 $\leftrightarrow$ CMTD-4, where the "D" indicates these are decryption-based. For each $\ell \in \{1, 3, 4\}$ we also recast CMTD-ℓ as an encryption-based notion CMT-ℓ that is simpler but equivalent if SE is tidy. We give relations between the notions, and then extend all this to s-way committing security for $s \geq 2$.

Think of ℓ here as indicating that we commit to the first ℓ inputs of the encryption algorithm. Since popular schemes, and the ones in this paper in particular, are tidy, the CMT-ℓ notions become our focus moving forward. The Introduction had discussed only CMT-1 and CMT-4; here we introduce the $\ell = 3$ notions as simpler than, but equivalent to, the $\ell = 4$ ones, something our results will exploit.

This section concludes with a simple transform, called EtH, that promotes $\ell = 1$ security to $\ell = 4$ security with minimal overhead.

WHAT IS COMMITTED? In asking that a ciphertext $C \leftarrow \mathsf{SE.Enc}(K, N, A, M)$ be a committal, the question is, to what? We consider this in a fine-grained way. We define a function WiC_ℓ (What is Committed) that on input (K, N, A, M) returns the part of the input to which we want the ciphertext to be a commitment. It is defined as shown in the table in Fig. 4. Thus, when $\ell = 1$, we are asking that we commit to the key; this corresponds to robustness [3], also called key-robustness [25] or key-committing [4] security. When $\ell = 3$, we commit to the key, nonce and associated data. Finally $\ell = 4$ means we commit, additionally, to the message, and thus to all the inputs of $\mathsf{SE.Enc}$.

Game $\mathbf{G}_{\mathsf{SE}}^{\text{cmtd-}\ell}(\mathcal{A})$

$\big(C, (K_1, N_1, A_1, M_1), (K_2, N_2, A_2, M_2)\big) \leftarrow_{\$} \mathcal{A}$
Require: $\mathsf{WiC}_\ell(K_1, N_1, A_1, M_1) \neq \mathsf{WiC}_\ell(K_2, N_2, A_2, M_2)$
Return $((M_1 = \mathsf{SE.Dec}(K_1, N_1, A_1, C)$ and $M_2 = \mathsf{SE.Dec}(K_2, N_2, A_2, C))$

Game $\mathbf{G}_{\mathsf{SE}}^{\text{cmt-}\ell}(\mathcal{A})$

$\big((K_1, N_1, A_1, M_1), (K_2, N_2, A_2, M_2)\big) \leftarrow_{\$} \mathcal{A}$
Require: $\mathsf{WiC}_\ell(K_1, N_1, A_1, M_1) \neq \mathsf{WiC}_\ell(K_2, N_2, A_2, M_2)$
Return $(\mathsf{SE.Enc}(K_1, N_1, A_1, M_1) = \mathsf{SE.Enc}(K_2, N_2, A_2, M_2))$

ℓ	1	3	4
$\mathsf{WiC}_\ell(K, N, A, M)$	K	(K, N, A)	(K, N, A, M)

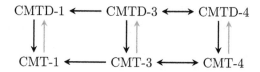

Fig. 4. Games defining committing security of a symmetric encryption scheme SE. Below them are the associated what-is-committed functions WiC_ℓ, and then the relations between the notions. The gray arrows hold for tidy SE.

THE D-NOTIONS. Let $\ell \in \{1, 3, 4\}$ be an integer representing the level of committing security. Consider game $\mathbf{G}_{\mathsf{SE}}^{\text{cmtd-}\ell}(\mathcal{A})$ in Fig. 4, and define the advantage of adversary $\mathcal{A}$ as $\mathbf{Adv}_{\mathsf{SE}}^{\text{cmtd-}\ell}(\mathcal{A}) = \Pr[\mathbf{G}_{\mathsf{SE}}^{\text{cmtd-}\ell}(\mathcal{A})]$. In the game, the adversary provides a ciphertext C together with a pair of tuples (K_1, N_1, A_1, M_1) and (K_2, N_2, A_2, M_2). (No entry of a tuple is allowed to be $\perp$.) The adversary wins if both decryptions of C equal the respective adversary-provided messages. The game requires that the outputs of the WiC_ℓ function on the adversary-provided tuples be different, precluding a trivial win. The only difference between the different levels indicated by ℓ is in the value of $\mathsf{WiC}_\ell(K, N, M, A)$ as given in the table. We denote the resulting notions by CMTD-ℓ for $\ell \in \{1, 3, 4\}$.

Our CMTD-1 notion is stronger than the key-committing notion in prior work [4], since we allow the adversary to specify *different* nonces N_1 and N_2. In contrast, the key-committing notion requires the two nonces to be the same.

On the other hand, achieving CMTD-4 security requires processing the associated data under a collision-resistant hash function. To see why, note that in settings where messages are the empty string, a ciphertext is a *compact* commitment of the associated data.

THE E-NOTIONS. Let $\ell \in \{1, 3, 4\}$ be an integer representing the level of committing security. Consider game $\mathbf{G}_{\mathsf{SE}}^{\text{cmt-}\ell}(\mathcal{A})$ in Fig. 4, and define the advantage of adversary $\mathcal{A}$ as $\mathbf{Adv}_{\mathsf{SE}}^{\text{cmt-}\ell}(\mathcal{A}) = \Pr[\mathbf{G}_{\mathsf{SE}}^{\text{cmt-}\ell}(\mathcal{A})]$. In the game, the adversary

$$\boxed{\begin{array}{l}
\text{Game } \mathbf{G}_{\mathsf{SE},s}^{\mathrm{cmtd}\text{-}\ell}(\mathcal{A}) \\
\hline
(C,(K_1,N_1,A_1,M_1),\ldots,(K_s,N_s,A_s,M_s)) \leftarrow\!\!\$\ \mathcal{A} \\
\text{Require: } \mathsf{WiC}_\ell(K_1,N_1,A_1,M_1),\ldots,\mathsf{WiC}_\ell(K_s,N_s,A_s,M_s) \text{ are all distinct} \\
\text{Return } (\forall i : M_i = \mathsf{SE.Dec}(K_i,N_i,A_i,C_i))
\end{array}}$$

$$\boxed{\begin{array}{l}
\text{Game } \mathbf{G}_{\mathsf{SE},s}^{\mathrm{cmt}\text{-}\ell}(\mathcal{A}) \\
\hline
((K_1,N_1,A_1,M_1),\ldots,(K_s,N_s,A_s,M_s)) \leftarrow\!\!\$\ \mathcal{A} \\
\text{Require: } \mathsf{WiC}_\ell(K_1,N_1,A_1,M_1),\ldots,\mathsf{WiC}_\ell(K_s,N_s,A_s,M_s) \text{ are all distinct} \\
\text{Return } (\mathsf{SE.Enc}(K_1,N_1,A_1,M_1) = \cdots = \mathsf{SE.Enc}(K_s,N_s,A_s,M_s))
\end{array}}$$

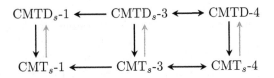

Fig. 5. Games defining s-way committing security of a symmetric encryption scheme SE for $s \geq 2$. Below them are the relations between the notions. The gray arrows hold for tidy SE.

provides a pair of tuples (K_1, N_1, A_1, M_1) and (K_2, N_2, A_2, M_2). (No entry of a tuple is allowed to be $\perp$.) The functions WiC_ℓ are unchanged. The game returns true (the adversary wins) if the encryptions of the two tuples are the same. We denote the resulting notions by CMT-ℓ for $\ell \in \{1, 3, 4\}$.

RELATIONS. The bottom of Fig. 4 shows the relations between the notions of committing security. An arrow A $\rightarrow$ B, read as A implies B, means that any scheme SE that is A-secure is also B-secure. A gray arrow means the implication holds when SE is tidy. The relations in the picture are justified in [8].

MULTI-INPUT COMMITTING SECURITY. The notions above considered an adversary successful if it opened a ciphertext in two different ways (D) or provided two encryption inputs with the same output (E). We now generalize from "two" to an integer parameter $s \geq 2$, the prior notions being the special case $s = 2$. The games, in Fig. 5, are parameterized, as before, with symmetric encryption scheme SE, but now also with s. Again there are "D" and "E" variants. The functions WiC_ℓ remain as in Fig. 4. The advantages of an adversary $\mathcal{A}$ are defined as $\mathbf{Adv}_{\mathsf{SE},s}^{\mathrm{cmtx}\text{-}\ell}(\mathcal{A}) = \Pr[\mathbf{G}_{\mathsf{SE},s}^{\mathrm{cmtx}\text{-}\ell}(\mathcal{A})]$ for $\mathrm{x} \in \{\mathrm{d}, \varepsilon\}$ and $\ell \in \{1, 3, 4\}$. We denote the resulting notions by CMTX$_s$-ℓ for $\mathrm{X} \in \{\mathrm{D}, \varepsilon\}$ and $\ell \in \{1, 3, 4\}$. Their relations remain as before and for completeness are also illustrated in Fig. 5.

WHY GENERALIZE? It is easy to see that CMTX-ℓ implies CMTX$_s$-ℓ for all $s \geq 2$ and $\mathrm{X} \in \{\mathrm{D}, \varepsilon\}$, meaning if a scheme SE is CMTX-ℓ-secure then it is also CMTX$_s$-ℓ for all $s \geq 2$. So why consider $s > 2$? The reason is that we can give schemes for which the bound on adversary advantage gets better as s gets larger, indeed even decaying exponentially with s. Indeed, one can break CMT-1-security of the scheme CAU-C1 in Sect. 5 in about 2^{64} operations. However, for

$\overline{\mathsf{SE}}.\mathsf{Enc}(K, N, A, M)$	$\overline{\mathsf{SE}}.\mathsf{Dec}(K, N, A, C^* \| T')$
$L \leftarrow H(K, (N, A))$	$L \leftarrow H(K, (N, A))$
$C \leftarrow \mathsf{SE}.\mathsf{Enc}(L, N, \varepsilon, M)$	$M \leftarrow \mathsf{SE}.\mathsf{Dec}(L, N, \varepsilon, C)$
Return C	Return M

Fig. 6. The scheme $\overline{\mathsf{SE}} = \mathsf{HtE}[\mathsf{SE}, H]$ defined via the Hash-then-Encrypt transform applied to a symmetric encryption scheme SE and a function H.

any adversary $\mathcal{A}$ that spends at most 2^{80} operations, the chance that it can break CMT_3-1 security of CAU-C1 is at most 2^{-62}. This allows us to offer a much stronger guarantee for situations like the Partitioning Oracle attack [34]. Recall that here, breaking CMT_s-1 security speeds up the time to find the underlying password used for key derivation by a factor of s. Thus our results say that despite investing 2^{80} operations, $\mathcal{A}$ can at best speed up its password search by a factor of two.

DISCUSSION. Practical schemes tend to be tidy, and all the ones we consider are, so, moving forward, we make tidiness an implicit assumption and focus on the E notions. Our primary focus is (s-way) CMT-1 because this is already non-trivial, what was targeted in many previous works, and enough for many applications. Below we give a generic way to promote CMT-1 security to CMT-4 security.

FROM CMT-1 TO CMT-4. We give a way to turn CMT-1 security into CMT-4 security, for both unique-nonce and misuse-resistance security. (That is, if you can commit to the key, it is easy to commit to everything.) It takes the form of a transform we call HtE (Hash then Encrypt). The ingredients are a base symmetric encryption scheme SE with key space $\{0,1\}^k$, and a function $H : \{0,1\}^k \times \{0,1\}^* \rightarrow \{0,1\}^k$. The encryption and decryption algorithms of the scheme $\overline{\mathsf{SE}} = \mathsf{HtE}[\mathsf{SE}, H]$ are shown in Fig. 6. The key-space and nonce-space remain that of SE.

With regard to performance, HtE preserves ciphertext length, meaning we are promoting CMT-1 to CMT-4 without increase in ciphertext size. The computational overhead, which is the computation of $H(K, (N, A))$, is optimal, since achieving CMT-4 requires processing the associated data with a collision-resistant hash function. In practice, associated data is often short (for example, IP headers are at most 60B), and thus HtE typically incurs just a constant computational overhead over the base scheme SE.

With regard to security, intuitively, if H is collision-resistant then the sub-key L is a commitment to the master key K, the nonce N and the associated data A. As a result, if the ciphertext is a commitment to the subkey L then it is also a commitment to (K, N, A). Hence the CMT-1 security of SE implies the CMT-3 security of $\overline{\mathsf{SE}}$, and thus, as per the relations in Fig. 4, also its CMT-4 security. Furthermore we will show that HtE preserves both unique-nonce and misuse-resistance security assuming H is a PRF.

We note that we do not assume H is a random oracle, instead making the standard-model assumption that it is a collision-resistant PRF. We now give formal results confirming the intuition above. The following shows that HtE indeed promotes CMT-1 security to CMT-4 security. The proof is in [8].

Theorem 1. *Let* SE *be an SE scheme with key length* k, *and let* $H : \{0,1\}^k \times \{0,1\}^* \to \{0,1\}^k$ *be a hash function. Let* $\overline{\text{SE}} = \text{HtE}[\text{SE}, H]$. *Fix an integer* $s \geq 2$ *and let* $t = \lceil \sqrt{s} \rceil$. *Then given an adversary* $\mathcal{A}$, *we can construct adversaries* $\mathcal{B}_0$ *and* $\mathcal{B}_1$ *such that*

$$\mathbf{Adv}_{\overline{\text{SE}},s}^{\text{cmt-4}}(\mathcal{A}) \leq \max\{\mathbf{Adv}_{H,t}^{\text{coll}}(\mathcal{B}_0), \mathbf{Adv}_{\text{SE},t}^{\text{cmt-1}}(\mathcal{B}_1)\} \ .$$

Each $\mathcal{B}_i$ *runs* $\mathcal{A}$ *and then runs* H *on* s *pairs (nonce, associated data) of* $\mathcal{A}$.

The next result shows that HtE preserves both unique-nonce and misuse-resistance security, provided that H is a good PRF. The proof is in [8].

Theorem 2. *Let* SE *be an SE scheme with key length* k, *and let* $H : \{0,1\}^k \times \{0,1\}^* \to \{0,1\}^k$ *be a hash function. Let* $\overline{\text{SE}} = \text{HtE}[\text{SE}, H]$. *Then given an adversary* $\mathcal{A}$ *that makes at most* q *queries of totally* σ_a *bits for (nonce, AD) pairs and at most* B *queries per (user, nonce, AD) triples, we can construct adversaries* $\mathcal{B}$ *and* $\mathcal{D}$ *such that*

$$\mathbf{Adv}_{\overline{\text{SE}}}^{\text{mrae}}(\mathcal{A}) \leq \mathbf{Adv}_H^{\text{prf}}(\mathcal{B}) + \mathbf{Adv}_{\text{SE}}^{\text{mrae}}(\mathcal{D}) \ .$$

If $\mathcal{A}$ *is unique-nonce then so is* $\mathcal{D}$, *and we can rewrite the bound as*

$$\mathbf{Adv}_{\overline{\text{SE}}}^{\text{unae}}(\mathcal{A}) \leq \mathbf{Adv}_H^{\text{prf}}(\mathcal{B}) + \mathbf{Adv}_{\text{SE}}^{\text{unae}}(\mathcal{D}) \ .$$

Adversary $\mathcal{B}$ *makes at most* q *queries on at most* σ_a *bits. Its running time is about that of* $\mathcal{A}$ *plus the time to encrypt/decrypt* $\mathcal{A}$'s *queries. Adversary* $\mathcal{D}$ *makes* q *queries of the total length as* $\mathcal{A}$, *but it makes only* B *queries per user. Its running time is about that of* $\mathcal{A}$ *plus* $O(\sigma_a \log(B))$.

We now discuss the choice of H. If nonce length is fixed, one can instantiate $H(K, (N, A))$ via HMAC-SHA256$(K\|N\|A)[1 : k]$ or SHA3$(K\|N\|A)[1 : k]$. We stress that if one considers using SHA256$(K\|N\|A)[1 : k]$, one must beware of the extension attack, to avoid which one should only use this if $k = 128$ [21].

4   Some Building Blocks

We give building blocks, technical results and information that we will use later. Some of the results are interesting in their own right, and may have applications beyond the context of committing AE.

MULTI-USER PRP/PRF SWITCHING. Lemma 1 below generalizes the classical PRP/PRF Switching Lemma [12] to the multi-user setting; see [8] for a proof. If one uses a hybrid argument on the standard single-user PRP/PRF Switching Lemma, one will obtain a weak bound $uB^2/2^n$, where u is the number of users. If there are $\Theta(q)$ users and some user makes $\Theta(q)$ queries then this bound is in the order of $q^3/2^n$, whereas our bound is just $q^2/2^n$ in this case.

Alternatively, if one parameterizes on q only, as in [35], one will end up with another weak bound $q^2/2^n$. In the setting where each user makes approximately B queries, this bound is even weaker than the trivial bound $uB^2/2^n$. Lemma 1 instead uses a different parameterization to obtain a sharp bound $qB/2^n$. The idea of using both B and q as parameters in multi-user analysis is first introduced in [20].

Lemma 1 (Multi-user PRP/PRF Switching Lemma). *Let $E : \{0,1\}^k \times \{0,1\}^n \to \{0,1\}^n$ be a blockcipher. For any adversary $\mathcal{A}$, if it makes at most q evaluation queries in total, with at most B queries per user, then*

$$\mathbf{Adv}_E^{\mathrm{prf}}(\mathcal{A}) \leq \mathbf{Adv}_E^{\mathrm{prp}}(\mathcal{A}) + \frac{Bq}{2^n} \ .$$

SIMPLIFYING UNAE/MRAE PROOFS. In UNAE/MRAE proofs, an adversary can adaptively interleave encryption and verification queries. Proofs will be simpler if the adversary is *orderly*, meaning that (i) its verification queries are made at the very end, and (ii) each verification query does not depend on the answers of prior verification queries, but may still depend on the answers of prior encryption queries. Proposition 1 shows that one can consider only orderly adversaries in UNAE/MRAE notions with just a small loss in the advantage; see [8] for a proof. The idea of restricting to orderly adversaries has been used in prior works [11,20]. They show that one can factor an UNAE/MRAE adversary $\mathcal{A}$ into two adversaries $\mathcal{B}_0$ and $\mathcal{B}_1$ attacking privacy and authenticity respectively, where $\mathcal{B}_1$ is orderly. Here we instead transform $\mathcal{A}$ to another orderly UNAE/MRAE adversary $\mathcal{B}$.

Proposition 1. *Let SE be a symmetric encryption scheme such that its ciphertext is at least τ-bit longer than the corresponding plaintext. For any adversary $\mathcal{A}$ that makes q_v verification queries, we can construct another orderly adversary $\mathcal{B}$ of about the same running time such that*

$$\mathbf{Adv}_{\mathsf{SE}}^{\mathrm{mrae}}(\mathcal{A}) \leq \mathbf{Adv}_{\mathsf{SE}}^{\mathrm{mrae}}(\mathcal{B}) + \frac{2q_v}{2^\tau} \ .$$

Adversary $\mathcal{B}$ has the same query statistics as $\mathcal{A}$. Moreover, if $\mathcal{A}$ is unique-nonce then so its $\mathcal{B}$, and thus in that case we can rewrite the bound as

$$\mathbf{Adv}_{\mathsf{SE}}^{\mathrm{unae}}(\mathcal{A}) \leq \mathbf{Adv}_{\mathsf{SE}}^{\mathrm{unae}}(\mathcal{B}) + \frac{2q_v}{2^\tau} \ .$$

For both notions, if every ciphertext of SE is exactly τ-bit longer than its plaintext then the term $2q_v/2^\tau$ can be improved to $q_v/2^\tau$.

COMMITTING AE VIA COLLISION-RESISTANT HASH. Intuitively, from the definition of committing AE, to achieve this goal, one needs to include the image of the key under some (multi)collision-resistant hash function in the ciphertext.

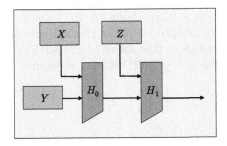

Fig. 7. Illustration of the cascade of the two hash functions H_0 and H_1.

This connection has been recognized and explored in prior works. For example, (i) the OPAQUE protocol [30] recommends the use of the Encrypt-then-HMAC construction, (ii) Albertini et al. [4] suggest using a hash-based key-derivation function to add key-committing security into legacy AE schemes; and (iii) Dodis et al. [22] propose a hash-based AE design for Facebook's message franking. The definition was recalled in Sect. 2. We now give some new fundamental results.

THE TRUNCATED DAVIES-MEYER CONSTRUCTION. A common way to build a collision-resistant compression function from a blockcipher is the Davies-Meyer construction. Our paper makes extensive use of this construction to have a cheap commitment of the key for obtaining committing security. It appears in both the AE schemes of Sects. 5 and 6. While the collision resistance of the Davies-Meyer construction is well-known [18], its multi-collision resistance has not been studied before. Moreover, in our use of Davies-Meyer, we usually have to truncate the output, and even ordinary collision resistance of truncated Davies-Meyer has not been investigated.

In particular, let $E : \{0,1\}^k \times \{0,1\}^n \to \{0,1\}^n$ be a blockcipher. Let $m \le n$ be an integer, and define $\mathsf{DM}[E, m] : \{0,1\}^k \times \{0,1\}^n \to \{0,1\}^m$ via

$$\mathsf{DM}[E, m](X, Y) = \big(E_X(Y) \oplus Y\big)[1 : m] \ .$$

We write $\mathsf{DM}[E]$ for the special case $m = n$ (meaning there is no truncation). Proposition 2 below analyzes the multi-collision resistance of $\mathsf{DM}[E, m]$; see [8] for a proof. The result is in the ideal-cipher model, that is, the adversary is given oracle access to both E and its inverse, and the number of ideal-cipher queries refers to the total queries to these two oracles.

Proposition 2. *Let* $E : \{0,1\}^k \times \{0,1\}^n \to \{0,1\}^n$ *be a blockcipher that we will model as an ideal cipher. Let* $s \ge 2$ *and* $m \le n$ *be integers. For an adversary* $\mathcal{A}$ *that makes at most* $p \le 2^{n-1} - s$ *ideal-cipher queries,*

$$\mathbf{Adv}^{\mathrm{coll}}_{\mathsf{DM}[E,m],s}(\mathcal{A}) \le 2^{1-m} + \binom{p}{s} \cdot 2^{(1-m)(s-1)} \ .$$

For the case $s = 2$ and $m = n$, our bound is $2^{1-n} + p(p-1)/2^n$, which slightly improves the classical bound $p(p+1)/2^n$ of Black, Rogaway, and Shrimpton [18]. For a general s, in [8], we show that for an ideal hash function on range $\{0,1\}^m$, there is an attack on the s-way multi-collision resistance of advantage

$$\frac{1}{4} \cdot \binom{p}{s} \cdot 2^{-m(s-1)} .$$

Thus the Truncated Davies-Meyer construction achieves essentially the best possible multi-collision resistance that we can hope for the output length m.

THE ITERATIVE TRUNCATED-PERMUTATION CONSTRUCTION. Let $E : \{0,1\}^k \times \{0,1\}^n \to \{0,1\}^n$ be a blockcipher. Let $r < n$ be a positive integer, and let $m \leq 2n$ be a positive even integer. Let $\mathsf{pad} : \{0,1\}^r \times \{1,2\} \to \{0,1\}^n$ be a one-to-one mapping. Define $\mathsf{ITP}[E, r, m] : \{0,1\}^k \times \{0,1\}^r \to \{0,1\}^{2m}$ via

$$\mathsf{ITP}[E, r, m](K, X) = E_K(\mathsf{pad}(X, 1))[1 : m/2] \| E_K(\mathsf{pad}(X, 2))[1 : m/2] .$$

The ITP construction is used in the key-derivation function of AES-GCM-SIV, where $r = 96$ and $m = n = 128$, and $\mathsf{pad}(X, i)$ is the concatenation of X and an $(n - r)$-bit encoding of i. For proving the committing security of the variants of AES-GCM-SIV in Sect. 6, we need to show that in using ITP to derive subkeys, one is also committing the master key and the nonce to one of the subkeys. Proposition 3 below analyzes the multi-collision resistance of ITP; see [8] for a proof. The analysis is difficult because ITP was *not* designed for collision resistance. This result is in the ideal-cipher model, meaning that the adversary is given oracle access to both E and E^{-1}, and the number of ideal-cipher queries refers to the total queries to both oracles. Note that for $r \leq 3n/4$ and $m = n$ (which holds for the situation of AES-GCM-SIV), ITP has birthday-bound security or better.

Proposition 3. *Let m, r, n be positive integers such that $r < n$, and $m \leq 2n$ is even. Let $E : \{0,1\}^k \times \{0,1\}^n \to \{0,1\}^n$ be a blockcipher that we will model as an ideal cipher. Let $s \geq 2$ be an integer. For an adversary $\mathcal{A}$ that makes at most $p \leq 2^{n-3} - s$ ideal-cipher queries,*

$$\mathbf{Adv}^{\mathrm{coll}}_{\mathsf{ITP}[E,r,m],s}(\mathcal{A}) \leq 2^{1-m} + \frac{4p^s}{s! \cdot 2^{(m-2)(s-1)}} + \frac{2^{m/2+1} \cdot p^s}{s! \cdot 2^{(m/2+n-r-2)s}} .$$

Compared to the lower bound $\binom{p}{s} \cdot 2^{-m(s-1)}$, the ITP construction has some security degradation due to the last term in the bound of Proposition 3. In [8], we give an attack that matches this term, implying that the bound of Proposition 3 is tight.

MULTI-COLLISION RESISTANCE ON A CASCADE. Let $c \geq 2$ be an integer. For each $i \in \{0, \ldots, c - 1\}$, let $H_i : \mathcal{L}_i \times \mathcal{R}_i \to \mathsf{Rng}_i$ be a hash function such that $\mathsf{Rng}_i \subseteq \mathcal{R}_{i+1}$. Define the *cascade* $H_0 \circ H_1$ of H_0 and H_1 as the hash function H such that $H(X, Y, Z) = H_1(Z, H_0(X, Y))$; see Fig. 7 for an illustration. The cascade $H_0 \circ \cdots \circ H_i$ of $H_0, \ldots, H_i$ is defined recursively as $(H_0 \circ \cdots \circ H_{i-1}) \circ$

H_i. Cascading appears in AE schemes of Sect. 6 where one first commits the master key into a subkey, and then includes a commitment of the subkey into the ciphertext. The following result shows how to bound the multi-collision resistance of $H_0 \circ \cdots \circ H_{c-1}$; see [8] for a proof.

Proposition 4. *Let H be the cascade of hash functions $H_0, H_1, \ldots, H_{c-1}$ as above. Let $s \geq 2$ be an integer, and let $t = \lceil \sqrt[c]{s} \rceil$. Then for any adversary $\mathcal{A}$, we can construct adversaries $\mathcal{B}_0, \ldots, \mathcal{B}_{c-1}$ such that*

$$\mathbf{Adv}_{H,s}^{\mathrm{coll}}(\mathcal{A}) \leq \max \left\{ \mathbf{Adv}_{H_0,t}^{\mathrm{coll}}(\mathcal{B}_0), \ldots, \mathbf{Adv}_{H_{c-1},t}^{\mathrm{coll}}(\mathcal{B}_{c-1}) \right\} .$$

Each adversary $\mathcal{B}_i$ runs $\mathcal{A}$, and then runs the cascade of $H_0, \ldots, H_{\min\{c-2,i\}}$ on the s inputs of $\mathcal{A}$.

5   A Committing Variant of GCM

In this section, we describe a close variant CAU-SIV-C1 of AES-GCM-SIV that achieves both CMT-1 and unique-nonce security with the same speed and bandwidth costs as GCM. In this entire section, let $E : \{0,1\}^k \times \{0,1\}^n \to \{0,1\}^n$ be a blockcipher. Following Bellare and Tackmann [14], we consider a generalization CAU of GCM. This scheme loosely follows the encrypt-then-MAC paradigm, where the encryption scheme is the CTR mode, and the MAC is the Carter-Wegman construction via an almost-xor-universal (AXU) hash function. (The name CAU is a mnemonic for the use of the CTR mode and an AXU hash function.) In GCM, the function G is instantiated by a 1.5-AXU hash GHASH.

THE SCHEME CAU. We now describe the scheme CAU. Let $G : \{0,1\}^n \times \{0,1\}^* \times \{0,1\}^* \to \{0,1\}^n$ be an AXU hash function. Let $\mathcal{N} = \{0,1\}^r$ be the nonce space, where $r < n$ is an integer. In GCM, $n = 128$ and $r = 96$. For a string $N \in \mathcal{N}$, we write $\mathsf{pad}(N)$ to refer to $N \| 0^{n-r-1} \| 1$. Let $\tau \leq n$ be the tag length. The scheme $\mathsf{CAU}[E, G, \tau]$ is specified in Fig. 8; it only accepts messages of at most $2^{n-r} - 2$ blocks. See also Fig. 9 for an illustration.

SPECIFICATION OF CAU-C1. The code of $\mathsf{CAU-C1}[E, G, \tau]$ is shown in Fig. 8. Like CAU, it only accepts messages of at most $2^{n-r} - 2$ blocks. Compared to CAU, the change occurs in how we derive the tag, as illustrated in Fig. 9. In particular, in CAU, one obtains the tag by using the Carter-Wegman paradigm, applying a one-time pad $E_K(\mathsf{pad}(N))$ to the output R of the AXU hash. In contrast, in CAU-C1, we use a different Carter-Wegman flavor, enciphering $V \leftarrow R \oplus \mathsf{pad}(N)$. However, to ensure committing security, instead of using $T \leftarrow E_K(V)[1 : \tau]$, we employ the Truncated Davies-Meyer method, outputting $T \leftarrow \mathsf{DM}[E, \tau](K, V)$.

   We note that if one instead computes $T \leftarrow \mathsf{DM}[E, \tau](K, R)$ then the resulting scheme will not have unique-nonce security. In particular, once we obtain a valid ciphertext C under nonce N and associated data A, the pair (A, C) remains valid for any nonce N', and thus breaking authenticity is trivial. Xor'ing $\mathsf{pad}(N)$ to R ensures that the tag T depends on all of N, A, C.

$\underline{\mathsf{Enc}(K, N, A, M)}$

// $0 \le |M_m| < n$ and $|M_i| = n$ otherwise
$Y \leftarrow \mathsf{pad}(N)$; $M_1 \cdots M_m \leftarrow M$
// Encrypt with CTR mode and IV $Y + 1$
For $i \leftarrow 1$ to $m - 1$ do $C_i \leftarrow M_i \oplus E_K(Y + i)$
$C_m \leftarrow M_m \oplus E_K(Y + m)[1 : |M_m|]$; $C \leftarrow C_1 \cdots C_m$
// Use Carter-Wegman on G
$L \leftarrow E_K(0^n)$; $R \leftarrow G_L(A, C)$; $\boxed{T \leftarrow \mathsf{Tag}(K, Y, R)}$
Return $C \| T$

$\underline{\mathsf{Dec}(K, N, A, C \| T)}$

// $0 \le |C_m| < n$ and $|C_i| = n$ otherwise
$Y \leftarrow \mathsf{pad}(N)$; $C_1 \cdots C_m \leftarrow C$
// Decrypt with CTR mode and IV $Y + 1$
For $i \leftarrow 1$ to $m - 1$ do $M_i \leftarrow C_i \oplus E_K(Y + i)$
$M_m \leftarrow C_m \oplus E_K(Y + m)[1 : |C_m|]$; $M \leftarrow M_1 \cdots M_m$
// Use Carter-Wegman on G
$L \leftarrow E_K(0^n)$; $R \leftarrow G_L(A, C)$; $\boxed{T' \leftarrow \mathsf{Tag}(K, Y, R)}$
If $T' \ne T$ then return $\perp$ else return M

$\underline{\mathsf{Tag}(K, Y, R)}$ // CAU	$\underline{\mathsf{Tag}(K, Y, R)}$ // CAU-C1
$S \leftarrow E_K(Y) \oplus R$	$V \leftarrow Y \oplus R$; $S \leftarrow E_K(V) \oplus V$
Return $S[1 : \tau]$	Return $S[1 : \tau]$

Fig. 8. The common blueprint for encryption (top) and decryption (middle) of $\mathsf{CAU}[E, G, \tau]$ and $\mathsf{CAU\text{-}C1}[E, G, \tau]$. The two schemes only differ on how they implement the internal procedure Tag, as shown in the bottom panels.

Farshim, Orlandi, and Roşie [25] also point out that in Encrypt-and-MAC, if the encryption scheme and the PRF can use the same key, and the PRF is committing, then the composition has key-committing security. Their result is however for probabilistic AE, so it does not imply the key-committing security of CAU-C1.

DISCUSSION. Our CAU-C1 scheme has several merits. (1) The change to CAU is small, making it easy to modify existing CAU code to get CAU-C1 code. (2) The speed of CAU-C1 is about the same as CAU for moderate and large messages. Moreover, the absence of any ciphertext overhead over CAU means there is no additional bandwidth cost. In contrast, prior proposed solutions [4,22,25,27,30] have to sacrifice either speed or bandwidth. (3) As we will show later, for short tag length, CAU-C1 has much better UNAE security than CAU.

It however does have some limitations. (1) Since it requires modifying CAU's code, one may not be able to use CAU-C1 in some legacy systems. (2) In the encryption algorithm of CAU-C1, the blockcipher call for the tag must be computed strictly after all other blockcipher calls are completed. In contrast, in CAU, all blockcipher calls can be done in parallel. This slowdown can be significant for tiny messages.

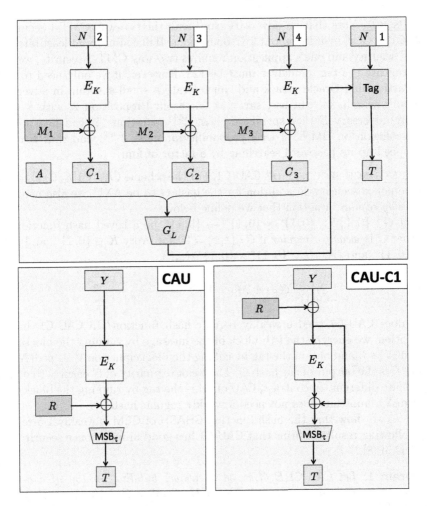

Fig. 9. A pictorial comparison of the encryption schemes of CAU and CAU-C1. The two scheme have the same blueprint on the top panel. They however have different implementations for the internal procedure Tag, illustrated in the bottom panels. Here the trapezoid MSB_τ outputs the τ-bit prefix of the input.

CMT-1 SECURITY OF CAU-C1. The following Theorem 3 analyzes CMT-1 security of CAU-C1; the proof is in [8]. The result is in the standard model, although it relies on the multi-collision of the truncated Davies-Meyer that is justified in the ideal-cipher model via Proposition 2.

Theorem 3. *Let* CAU-C1$[E, G, \tau]$ *be as above. Let* $s \geq 2$ *be an integer. Then for any adversary* $\mathcal{A}$, *we can construct an adversary* $\mathcal{B}$ *such that*

$$\mathbf{Adv}^{\mathrm{cmt\text{-}1}}_{\mathsf{CAU\text{-}C1}[E,G,\tau],s}(\mathcal{A}) \leq \mathbf{Adv}^{\mathrm{coll}}_{\mathsf{DM}[E,\tau],s}(\mathcal{B}) \ .$$

Adversary $\mathcal{B}$ *runs* $\mathcal{A}$ *and makes* s *other calls on* E.

DISCUSSION. Note that an adversary can break the two-way CMT-1 security of CAU-C1[E, G, τ] by using about $2^{\tau/2}$ operations. If one aims for at least birthday-bound security and one's application requires two-way CMT-1 security, we must not truncate the tag, namely τ must be 128. However, if we only need to resist the Partitioning-Oracle attack and can tolerate a small speedup in adversarial password search, we can use, say $\tau = 96$. From Proposition 2, with $\tau = 96$, for any adversary $\mathcal{B}$ that spends at most 2^{64} operations, it can find a 5-way multi-collision on DM[E, τ] with probability at most 2^{-60}, and thus $\mathcal{B}$ can at best speed up its password searching by a factor of four.

UNIQUE-NONCE SECURITY OF CAU-C1. For the scheme CAU-C1[E, G, τ] to have unique-nonce security, in addition for the hash G to be AXU, we also need it to be *weakly regular*, a notion that we define below.

Let $G : \{0,1\}^n \times \{0,1\}^* \times \{0,1\}^* \to \{0,1\}^n$ be a keyed hash function. We say that G is *weakly c-regular* if $G_K(\varepsilon, \varepsilon) = 0^n$ for every $K \in \{0,1\}^n$, and for all $Y \in \{0,1\}^n$ and $(A, M) \in \{0,1\}^* \times \{0,1\}^* \backslash (\varepsilon, \varepsilon)$,

$$\Pr_{K \leftarrow\$ \{0,1\}^n}[G_K(A, M) = Y] \le \frac{c \cdot (|M|_n + |A|_n)}{2^n} .$$

Why does CAU-C1 need a weakly regular hash function? In CAU-C1, in each encryption, we encrypt the i-th block of the message by running the blockcipher on pad(N)+i, and obtain the tag by calling the blockcipher on $V \leftarrow$ pad(N)$\oplus R$, where R is the output of the hash G. The weak regularity of G ensures that these inputs are different. In contrast, CAU obtains the tag by running the blockcipher on pad(N), and thus does not need a weakly regular hash.

In [8] we show that the hash function GHASH of GCM is weakly 1.5-regular. The following result confirms that CAU-C1 has good unique-nonce security. The proof is in [8].

Theorem 4. *Let* CAU-C1[E, G, τ] *be as above, building on top of a c-AXU, weakly c-regular hash function G and a blockcipher $E : \{0,1\}^k \times \{0,1\}^n \to \{0,1\}^n$. Then for an adversary $\mathcal{A}$ that makes at most q queries of σ blocks and q_v verification queries in total, with at most B blocks per user, we can construct another $\mathcal{B}$ of at most $\sigma + q$ queries such that*

$$\mathbf{Adv}^{\mathrm{unae}}_{\mathrm{CAU\text{-}C1}[E,G,\tau]}(\mathcal{A}) \le \mathbf{Adv}^{\mathrm{prf}}_E(\mathcal{B}) + \frac{(4c+2)B\sigma + (2c+2)Bq}{2^n} + \frac{2q_v}{2^\tau} .$$

The running time of $\mathcal{B}$ is about that of $\mathcal{A}$ plus the time to use G on $\mathcal{A}$'s messages and associated data.

ON SHORT TAGS. When the tag length τ is short, CAU-C1 has much better unique-nonce security than CAU. In particular, Ferguson [26] gives a (single-user) attack of q_v decryption queries, each of ℓ blocks, to break the security of CAU with advantage $q_v \ell / 2^\tau$. In contrast, CAU-C1 enjoys a smaller term $q_v / 2^\tau$.

CAU-C4 FOR CMT-4-SECURITY. Applying the HtE transform of Sect. 3, with a suitable choice of H, to CAU-C1, yields a CMT-4 and UNAE scheme that we call

CAU-C4. There is no increase in ciphertext size. The computational overhead, running H on the key, nonce and associated data, is independent of the message length.

6   A Committing Variant of AES-GCM-SIV

In this section, we describe a close variant CAU-SIV-C1 of AES-GCM-SIV that achieves both CMT-1 and misuse-resistance security with the same speed and bandwidth costs as AES-GCM-SIV. In this entire section, let n be an even integer, and let $E : \{0,1\}^k \times \{0,1\}^n \to \{0,1\}^n$ be a blockcipher, with $k \in \{n, 2n\}$. We will consider a generalization CAU-SIV of AES-GCM-SIV that we describe below. The name CAU-SIV is a mnemonic for the use of (i) the classic SIV paradigm [41] in achieving misuse-resistance security, (ii) (a variant of) the CTR mode and (iii) an AXU hash function.

THE PRF GMAC$^+$. Like CAU, the scheme CAU-SIV is based on a c-AXU hash. As shown in [20], the hash function POLYVAL of AES-GCM-SIV is 1.5-AXU. In CAU-SIV, the AXU hash function is used to build a PRF that Bose, Hoang, and Tessaro [20] call GMAC$^+$. We begin with the description of this PRF.

For strings X and Y such that $|X| < |Y| = n$, let $X \boxplus Y$ denote the string obtained by setting the first bit of $(0^{n-|X|}\|X) \oplus Y$ to 0. Let $r < n$ be an integer, and let $\mathcal{N} = \{0,1\}^r$. Define GMAC$^+[E, G] : \{0,1\}^{k+n} \times \mathcal{N} \times \{0,1\}^* \times \{0,1\}^* \to \{0,1\}^n$ via

$$\mathsf{GMAC}^+[E, G](K_{\mathsf{in}} \| K_{\mathsf{out}}, N, A, M) = E(K_{\mathsf{out}}, X) \ ,$$

where $X \leftarrow N \boxplus G(K_{\mathsf{in}}, M, A)$. See Fig. 11 for an illustration of GMAC$^+$.

THE KEY-DERIVATION FUNCTION KD1. In each encryption, CAU-SIV derives subkeys by applying a key-derivation function (which we call KD1) on the given nonce. Specifically, KD1 is exactly the ITP hash function in Sect. 4 with padding $\mathsf{pad}(N, i) = N\|[i]_{n-r}$, where $[i]_{n-r}$ denote an $(n-r)$-bit encoding of an integer i. The code of KD1 is given in the second-top panel of Fig. 10 for completeness.

CTR MODE. CAU-SIV is based on the following variant of the CTR mode. Let $r < n$ be an integer. (For AES-GCM-SIV, $r = 96$ and $n = 128$.) Let add be an operation on $\{0,1\}^n \times \{0, 1, \ldots, 2^{n-r} - 1\}$ such that

$$\mathsf{add}(X, i) = 1\|X[2 : r]\|(X[r+1 : n] + i \bmod 2^{n-r}) \ .$$

The encryption and decryption schemes of CTR$[E, \mathsf{add}]$ are defined in the bottom panels of Fig. 10. They are essentially the same as the standard CTR mode, except that they use the add operation instead of the modular addition in mod 2^n.

THE SCHEME CAU-SIV. The scheme CAU-SIV$[E, G, \mathsf{add}]$ is described in Fig. 10. Informally, one first uses KD1 on the given nonce to derive subkeys $K_{\mathsf{in}} \in \{0,1\}^n$ and $K_{\mathsf{out}} \in \{0,1\}^k$. One then follows the classic SIV paradigm [41] in building a

$\underline{\text{Enc}(K, N, A, M)}$	$\underline{\text{Dec}(K, N, A, C)}$
$K_{\text{in}} \| K_{\text{out}} \leftarrow \text{KD1}[E, k + n](K, N)$	$K_{\text{in}} \| K_{\text{out}} \leftarrow \text{KD1}[E, k + n](K, N)$
$\text{IV} \leftarrow \text{Tag}(K_{\text{in}} \| K_{\text{out}}, N, A, M)$	$M \leftarrow \text{CTR}[E, \text{add}].\text{Dec}(K_{\text{out}}, C)$
$C \leftarrow \text{CTR}[E, \text{add}].\text{Enc}(K_{\text{out}}, M; \text{IV})$	$\text{IV} \leftarrow \text{Tag}(K_{\text{in}} \| K_{\text{out}}, N, A, M)$
Return C	If $\text{IV} \neq C[1 : n]$ then return $\perp$
	Return M

$\underline{\text{KD1}[E, \ell](K, N)}$
For $i \leftarrow 1$ to $2\ell/n$ do $Y_i \leftarrow E_K(N \| [i]_{n-r})[1 : n/2]$
Return $Y_1 \| \cdots \| Y_{2\ell/n}$

$\underline{\text{Tag}(K_{\text{in}} \| K_{\text{out}}, N, A, M)} \ // \text{ GMAC}^+ \text{ or } \boxed{\text{GMAC2}}$
$X \leftarrow N \boxplus G(K_{\text{in}}, M, A); \quad Y \leftarrow E(K_{\text{out}}, X); \quad \boxed{Y \leftarrow Y \oplus X}$
Return Y

$\underline{\text{CTR}[E, \text{add}].\text{Enc}(K, M; \text{IV})}$	$\underline{\text{CTR}[E, \text{add}].\text{Dec}(K, C)}$
$// \ 0 \leq |M_m| < m;$ other $|M_i| = n$	$// \ 0 \leq |C_m| < m;$ other $|C_i| = n$
$M_1 \cdots M_m \leftarrow M$	$\text{IV} \| C_1 \cdots C_m \leftarrow C$
For $i = 1$ to $m - 1$ do	For $i = 1$ to $m - 1$ do
$\quad C_i \leftarrow E_K(\text{add}(\text{IV}, i)) \oplus M_i$	$\quad M_i \leftarrow E_K(\text{add}(\text{IV}, i)) \oplus C_i$
$C_m \leftarrow E_K(\text{add}(\text{IV}, m))[1 : |M_m|] \oplus M_m$	$M_m \leftarrow E_K(\text{add}(\text{IV}, m))[1 : |C_m|] \oplus C_m$
Return $\text{IV} \| C_1 \cdots C_m$	Return $M_1 \cdots M_m$

Fig. 10. The schemes CAU-SIV and CAU-SIV-C1 whose encryption and decryption schemes are given in the top-left and top-right panels, respectively. Procedure Tag implements GMAC$^+$ (for CAU-SIV) or GMAC2 (for CAU-SIV-C1); the latter contains the highlighted code, but the former does not.

misuse-resistant AE scheme: first use the PRF GMAC$^+$ on the triple (N, A, M) to derive an initialization vector IV, and then run CTR with that particular IV to encrypt M. However, unlike the standard SIV with key separation, here both GMAC$^+$ and CTR use E on the same key K_{out}. There is, however, a domain separation in the use of the blockcipher: GMAC$^+$ will only run E on an input whose most significant bit is 0, whereas CTR runs E on inputs of most significant bit 1.

THE CAU-SIV-C1 SCHEME. We now show how to add CMT-1 security to CAU-SIV. Recall that CAU-SIV internally uses a PRF GMAC$^+$ that is based on an AXU, weakly regular hash function G. The scheme CAU-SIV-C1 introduces an extra xor in GMAC$^+$, resulting in a new PRF construction that we call GMAC2, and that is the only difference between the two AE schemes. In particular,

$$\text{GMAC}^+[E, G](K_{\text{in}} \| K_{\text{out}}, N, A, M) = E(K_{\text{out}}, X) \ ,$$

where $X \leftarrow N \boxplus G(K_{\text{in}}, M, A)$. In contrast, GMAC2 employs the Davies-Meyer construction to break the invertibility of E, namely,

$$\text{GMAC2}[E, G](K_{\text{in}} \| K_{\text{out}}, N, A, M) = E(K_{\text{out}}, X) \oplus X \ .$$

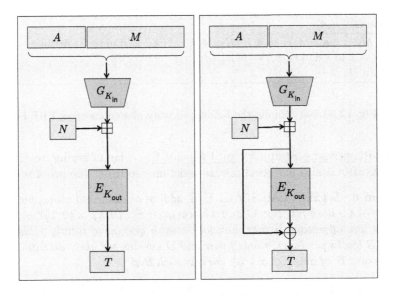

Fig. 11. The GMAC$^+$ construction (left) and its variant GMAC2 (right).

See Fig. 11 for a side-by-side pictorial comparison of GMAC$^+$ and GMAC2. The code of CAU-SIV-C1 is given in Fig. 10.

The difference of CAU-SIV-C1 and CAU-SIV is tiny, just a single xor. As a result, the speed and bandwidth costs of CAU-SIV-C1 are about the same as CAU-SIV for all message sizes. While one must intrusively modify CAU-SIV's code to obtain CAU-SIV-C1, since CAU-SIV is new, we anticipate that there will be very few legacy situations that one cannot adopt CAU-SIV-C1.

COMMITTING SECURITY OF CAU-SIV-C1. Theorem 5 below confirms that the extra xor indeed hardens CAU-SIV-C1, ensuring CMT-1 security. The proof is in [8]. Intuitively, the synthetic IV of CAU-SIV-C1 is obtained by a two-step chain of hashing: (i) first use the Iterative Truncated Permutation construction ITP$[E, r, n]$ to commit the master key K and the nonce N to the n-bit prefix of the blockcipher subkey K_{out}, and then (ii) use the Davies-Meyer construction DM$[E]$ to commit K_{out}. We show in [8] how this allows the CMT-1 security of CAU-SIV-C1 to reduce to the multi-collision resistance of ITP$[E, r, n]$ and DM$[E]$, both of which we justify with good bounds.

Theorem 5. *Let* SE = CAU-SIV-C1$[E, G, \text{add}]$ *be as described above, building on top of a blockcipher* $E : \{0,1\}^k \times \{0,1\}^n \to \{0,1\}^k$. *Let* $r < n$ *be the nonce length. Let* $s \geq 2$ *be an integer, and let* $t = \lceil \sqrt{s} \rceil$. *Then for any adversary* $\mathcal{A}$, *we can construct adversaries* $\mathcal{D}_0$ *and* $\mathcal{D}_1$ *such that*

$$\mathbf{Adv}_{\mathsf{SE},s}^{\mathrm{cmt\text{-}1}}(\mathcal{A}) \leq \max\{\mathbf{Adv}_{\mathsf{ITP}[E,r,n],t}^{\mathrm{coll}}(\mathcal{D}_0), \mathbf{Adv}_{\mathsf{DM}[E],t}^{\mathrm{coll}}(\mathcal{D}_1)\} .$$

Each of $\mathcal{D}_0$ *and* $\mathcal{D}_1$ *runs* $\mathcal{A}$ *and then makes at most* $6s$ *other blockcipher calls.*

Game $\mathbf{G}_{\mathsf{F},s}^{\mathrm{bind}}(\mathcal{A})$

$(K_1, M_1, \ldots, K_s, M_s) \leftarrow\!\!\$ \; \mathcal{A} \;/\!/\; (K_1, M_1), \ldots, (K_s, M_s)$ must be distinct

For $i \leftarrow 1$ to s do $(P_i, L_i) \leftarrow \mathsf{F}(K_i, M_i)$

Return $(P_1 = \cdots = P_s)$

Fig. 12. Game defining the binding security of a committing PRF F.

MISUSE-RESISTANCE SECURITY OF CAU-SIV-C1. The following result shows that CAU-SIV-C1 also has good misuse-resistance security; the proof is in [8].

Theorem 6. *Let* $\mathsf{SE} = \mathsf{CAU\text{-}SIV\text{-}C1}[E, G, \mathsf{add}]$ *be as described above, building on top of a c-AXU hash function G and a blockcipher $E : \{0,1\}^k \times \{0,1\}^n \to \{0,1\}^n$. Then for any adversary $\mathcal{A}$ that makes at most q queries of totally σ blocks with at most B blocks per (user, nonce) pair and D queries per user, we can construct an adversary $\mathcal{B}$ of $\max\{6q, \sigma + q\}$ queries such that*

$$\mathbf{Adv}_{\mathsf{SE}}^{\mathrm{mrae}}(\mathcal{A}) \leq 2 \cdot \mathbf{Adv}_{E}^{\mathrm{prp}}(\mathcal{B}) + \frac{6\sqrt{nDq}}{2^{3n/4}} + \frac{7\sigma B + (2c + 7)qB}{2^n} \; .$$

The running time of $\mathcal{B}$ is at most that of $\mathcal{A}$ plus the time to encrypt/decrypt the latter's queries.

CAU-SIV-C4 FOR CMT-4-SECURITY. Applying the HtE transform of Sect. 3, with a suitable choice of H, to CAU-SIV-C1, yields a CMT-4 and MRAE scheme that we call CAU-SIV-C4. There is no increase in ciphertext size. The computational overhead is independent of the message length.

7   Adding Key-Committing Security to Legacy AE

In this section, we describe two generic methods UNAE-then-Commit (UtC) and MRAE-then-Commit (RtC) that transform an AE scheme SE into a CMT-1-secure one. The former preserves unique-nonce security, whereas the latter preserves misuse-resistance security. As a stepping stone, we define a new primitive that we call *committing PRF*, which we will describe below.

COMMITTING PRFs. A *committing PRF* F is a deterministic algorithm, and associated with a message space $\mathcal{M}$ and key space $\{0,1\}^k$. It takes input a key $K \in \{0,1\}^k$ and a message $M \in \mathcal{M}$, and then produces $(P, L) \in \{0,1\}^\ell \times \{0,1\}^\lambda$. We refer to ℓ as the *commitment length* of F, and λ as the *mask length* of F.

We require that F be a good PRF, meaning that its outputs (P, L) are indistinguishable from $(P^*, L^*) \leftarrow\!\!\$ \; \{0,1\}^\ell \times \{0,1\}^\lambda$. In addition, for an adversary $\mathcal{A}$ and an integer $s \geq 2$, we define the advantage of $\mathcal{A}$ breaking the s-way binding security of F as $\mathbf{Adv}_{\mathsf{F},s}^{\mathrm{bind}}(\mathcal{A}) = \Pr[\mathbf{G}_{\mathsf{F},s}^{\mathrm{bind}}(\mathcal{A})]$, where game $\mathbf{G}_{\mathsf{F},s}^{\mathrm{bind}}(\mathcal{A})$ is defined in Fig. 12. Informally, a committing PRF is a combination of a PRF and a commitment scheme, where the string P is a commitment of the key K and the message M.

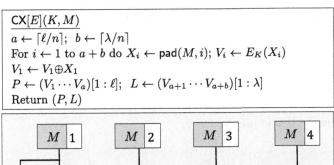

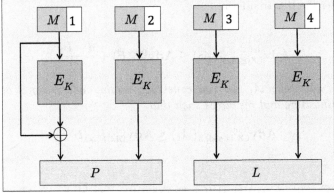

Fig. 13. The committing PRF scheme $\mathsf{CX}[E, \mathsf{pad}]$, illustrated for the case $\ell = \lambda = 2n$ and $\mathsf{pad}(M, i)$ is the concatenation of M and an $(n - m)$-bit encoding of i.

For $s = 2$, our notion of committing PRF can be viewed as a PRF counterpart of the notion of *right collision-resistant PRG* in [25]. We however will give practical instantiations via a blockcipher whereas the construction in [25] is theoretical, using hardcore predicates.

AN EFFICIENT COMMITTING PRF. We now describe an efficient committing PRF Counter-then-Xor (CX) that is built on top of a blockcipher $E : \{0,1\}^k \times \{0,1\}^n \to \{0,1\}^n$. Here the message space $\mathcal{M} = \{0,1\}^m$ and the key space is $\{0,1\}^k$, with $m < n$. Let pad denote a one-to-one encoding that turns a pair $(M, i) \in \{0,1\}^m \times \{1, \ldots, 2^{n-m}\}$ into an n-bit string. The commitment length $\ell \geq n$ and the mask length λ satisfy $\lceil \ell/n \rceil + \lceil \lambda/n \rceil \leq 2^{n-m}$. The construction $\mathsf{CX}[E, \mathsf{pad}]$ is shown in Fig. 13.

The following result shows that CX is a good committing PRF scheme. Part (a) is a straightforward application of the (multi-user) PRP/PRF Switching Lemma, with an observation that for each query that $\mathcal{A}_0$ makes to CX, it translates to $d = \lceil \ell/n \rceil + \lceil \lambda/n \rceil$ PRP queries on the blockcipher. For applications in this paper, $d \leq 5$. Part (b) is a direct corollary of Proposition 2, since the first block of P is obtained from the Davies-Meyer construction $\mathsf{DM}[E]$.

Proposition 5. *Let $\mathsf{CX}[E, \mathsf{pad}]$ be as above, and let $s \geq 2$ be an integer. Let $d = \lceil \ell/n \rceil + \lceil \lambda/n \rceil$.*
a) For any adversary $\mathcal{A}_0$ making q queries in total with at most B queries per user, we can construct an adversary $\mathcal{B}$ of about the same running time that makes at most dq queries such that

UtC[F, SE].Enc(K, N, A, M)	UtC[F, SE].Dec$(K, N, A, P^* \| C)$
$(P, L) \leftarrow F(K, N)$	$(P, L) \leftarrow F(K, N)$
$C \leftarrow$ SE.Enc(L, N, A, M)	If $P^* \neq P$ then return $\perp$
Return $P \| C$	Else return SE.Dec(L, N, A, C)

Fig. 14. The encryption (left) and decryption (right) schemes of the resulting AE scheme under the UtC transform.

$$\mathbf{Adv}^{\mathrm{prf}}_{\mathsf{CX}[E,\mathsf{pad}]}(\mathcal{A}_0) \leq \mathbf{Adv}^{\mathrm{prp}}_{E}(\mathcal{B}) + \frac{d^2 \cdot Bq}{2^n} \ .$$

b) For any adversary $\mathcal{A}_1$, we can construct another adversary $\mathcal{B}$ of about the same running time and resources such that

$$\mathbf{Adv}^{\mathrm{bind}}_{\mathsf{CX}[E,\mathsf{pad}],s}(\mathcal{A}_1) \leq \mathbf{Adv}^{\mathrm{coll}}_{\mathsf{DM}[E],s}(\mathcal{B}) \ .$$

THE UNAE-THEN-COMMIT (UtC) TRANSFORM. Let SE be an AE scheme with key space $\{0,1\}^k$ and nonce space $\mathcal{N}$. Let F be a committing PRF scheme of message space $\mathcal{N}$ and mask length k. The scheme UtC[F, SE] is shown in Fig. 14. Informally, under UtC, a ciphertext contains a commitment P of the master key K, ensuring CMT-1 security. The security of UtC[F, SE] is analyzed below; the proof is in [8].

Theorem 7. *Let SE and F be as above. Let $s \geq 2$ be an integer.*
a) For any adversary $\mathcal{A}_0$, we can construct an adversary $\mathcal{B}_0$ of about the same running time and using the same resources as $\mathcal{A}_0$ such that

$$\mathbf{Adv}^{\mathrm{cmt\text{-}1}}_{\mathsf{UtC}[F,\mathsf{SE}],s}(\mathcal{A}_0) \leq \mathbf{Adv}^{\mathrm{bind}}_{F,s}(\mathcal{B}_0) \ .$$

b) For any adversary $\mathcal{A}_1$ of at most B queries per (user, nonce) pair, we can construct an adversary $\mathcal{B}_1$ and $\mathcal{B}_2$ such that

$$\mathbf{Adv}^{\mathrm{unae}}_{\mathsf{UtC}[F,\mathsf{SE}]}(\mathcal{A}_1) \leq \mathbf{Adv}^{\mathrm{prf}}_{F}(\mathcal{B}_1) + \mathbf{Adv}^{\mathrm{unae}}_{\mathsf{SE}}(\mathcal{B}_2) \ .$$

The running time of $\mathcal{B}_1$ is about that of $\mathcal{A}_1$ plus the time to encrypt/decrypt the queries of $\mathcal{A}_1$ via SE, and its queries statistics is the same as $\mathcal{A}_1$. Adversary $\mathcal{B}_2$ has the same number of queries and the total query length as $\mathcal{A}_1$, but it makes at most B queries per user. It has about the same running time as $\mathcal{A}_1$.

DISCUSSION. Albertini et al. [4] also give a generic transform. (An instantiation of this transform is now deployed in the latest version of the AWS Encryption SDK, an open-source client-side encryption library [1].) It can be viewed as a specific instantiation of UtC, in which the committing PRF F is built on top of two collision-resistant PRFs. One of these two collision-resistant PRFs however

$\mathsf{RtC}[\mathsf{F},\mathsf{SE},H].\mathsf{Enc}(K,N,A,M)$	$\mathsf{RtC}[\mathsf{F},\mathsf{SE},H].\mathsf{Dec}(K,N,A,T\|C)$
$(P,L) \leftarrow \mathsf{F}(K,N)$	$(P,L) \leftarrow \mathsf{F}(K,N)$
$C \leftarrow \mathsf{SE}.\mathsf{Enc}(L,N,A,M)$	$T^* \leftarrow H(P,C[1\!:\!n])$
$T \leftarrow H(P,C[1:n])$	If $T \neq T^*$ then return $\perp$
Return $T\|C$	Return $\mathsf{SE}.\mathsf{Dec}(L,N,A,C)$

Fig. 15. The encryption (left) and decryption (right) algorithms of the scheme given by the RtC transform.

may have to provide up to 256-bit output (since this output is used as a key of the legacy SE), obstructing an obvious instantiation via Davies-Meyer on AES. As a result, Albertini et al. instantiate them via SHA-256. Not only is this instantiation slower than our Count-then-Xor construction, but using it in UtC also requires an additional primitive in addition to AES. In addition, we realize that UtC achieves CMT-1 security, whereas Albertini et al. only claim key-committing security.

THE MRAE-THEN-COMMIT (RtC) TRANSFORM. Let SE be an AE scheme with key space $\{0,1\}^\lambda$ and nonce space $\mathcal{N}$. Let F be a committing PRF scheme of message space $\mathcal{N}$, key space $\{0,1\}^k$, commitment length ℓ, and mask length λ (that is also the key length of SE). Assume that each ciphertext in SE is at least n-bit long. Let $H : \{0,1\}^\ell \times \{0,1\}^n \to \{0,1\}^n$ be a collision-resistant PRF. We can instantiate F via CX, and H via the Davies-Meyer construction. (The PRF security of this particular choice of H can be trivially obtained from Lemma 1.) The scheme $\mathsf{RtC}[\mathsf{F},\mathsf{SE},H]$ is shown in Fig. 15. Intuitively, RtC creates a two-step chain of commitments $K \to P \to T$, where K is the master key, P is the commitment generated by F, and T is the hash output, which is a part of the ciphertext. This leads to an underlying cascade of two hash functions whose collision resistance an adversary has to break in order to break the CMT-1 security of $\mathsf{RtC}[\mathsf{F},\mathsf{SE},H]$. Thus from Proposition 4, the CMT-1 security of $\mathsf{RtC}[\mathsf{F},\mathsf{SE},H]$ is reduced to the committing security of F and the collision resistance of H. The proof of the following is in [8].

Theorem 8. *Let* SE *and* F *be as above.*
a) Let $s \geq 2$ *be an integer, and let* $t = \lceil\sqrt{s}\rceil$. *For any adversary* $\mathcal{A}_0$, *we can construct adversaries* $\mathcal{B}_0$ *and* $\mathcal{B}_1$ *such that*

$$\mathbf{Adv}^{\mathrm{cmt\text{-}1}}_{\mathsf{RtC}[\mathsf{F},\mathsf{SE},H],s}(\mathcal{A}_0) \leq \max\left\{\mathbf{Adv}^{\mathrm{bind}}_{\mathsf{F},t}(\mathcal{B}_0), \mathbf{Adv}^{\mathrm{coll}}_{H,t}(\mathcal{B}_1)\right\} \ .$$

Each of $\mathcal{B}_0$ *and* $\mathcal{B}_1$ *runs* $\mathcal{A}_0$, *and then runs* $\mathsf{RtC}[\mathsf{F},\mathsf{SE},H]$ *to encrypt one out of the* s *messages that* $\mathcal{A}_0$ *outputs, and then evaluates* F *on* s *inputs.*

b) For any adversary $\mathcal{A}_1$ *of at most* B *queries per (user, nonce) pair and at most* q *queries, we can construct adversaries* $\mathcal{B}_2$, $\mathcal{B}_3$, *and* $\mathcal{B}_4$ *such that*

$$\mathbf{Adv}^{\mathrm{mrae}}_{\mathsf{RtC}[\mathsf{F},\mathsf{SE},H]}(\mathcal{A}_1) \leq \mathbf{Adv}^{\mathrm{prf}}_{\mathsf{F}}(\mathcal{B}_2) + \mathbf{Adv}^{\mathrm{mrae}}_{\mathsf{SE}}(\mathcal{B}_3) + \mathbf{Adv}^{\mathrm{prf}}_{H}(\mathcal{B}_4) + \frac{Bq}{2^n} \ .$$

Adversary $\mathcal{B}_2$ has the same query statistics as $\mathcal{A}_1$, and its running time is at most that of $\mathcal{A}_1$ plus the time to use RtC to encrypt/decrypt the latter's queries. Adversaries $\mathcal{B}_3$ and $\mathcal{B}_4$ have the same number of queries and the total query length as $\mathcal{A}_1$, but they make only B queries per user. The running time of $\mathcal{B}_3$ is about that of $\mathcal{A}_1$ plus the time to run H on q inputs, and $\mathcal{B}_4$ has about the same running time as $\mathcal{A}_1$.

CONNECTION TO LIBSODIUM'S APPROACH. The libsodium library [2] suggests the following transformation to add key-committing security to an AE scheme SE. Assume that a ciphertext of SE can be parsed as a concatenation of a tag T and a ciphertext core C^*. Let $H : \{0,1\}^* \to \{0,1\}^m$ be a cryptographic hash function. To encrypt (N, A, M) under key K, let $T\|C^* \leftarrow$ SE.Enc(K, N, A, M), let $T^* \leftarrow H(K\|N\|T)$, and output $T^*\|T\|C^*$. To decrypt $(N, A, T^*\|T\|C^*)$ with key K, first check if $T^* = H(K\|N\|T)$. If they agree then return SE.Dec$(K, N, A, T\|C^*)$, else return $\bot$.

The transform above works for the AE schemes in the libsodium libraries (namely GCM and ChaChaPoly1305) if we model (i) the hash function H as a random oracle, (ii) AES as an ideal cipher, and (iii) ChaCha20 permutation as an ideal permutation. The RtC transform can be viewed as a way to refine libsodium's approach to (i) work with a generic AE scheme and (ii) instantiate the hash function via the Davies-Meyer construction instead of SHA-256. While the libsodium's transform is suggested for unique-nonce security, we points out that RtC also works for misuse-resistance security.

Acknowledgments. We thank the EUROCRYPT 2022 reviewers for their careful reading and valuable comments. Mihir Bellare was supported in part by NSF grant CNS-1717640 and a gift from Microsoft. Viet Tung Hoang was supported in part by NSF grants CNS-2046540 (CAREER), CICI-1738912, and CRII-1755539.

References

1. AWS Encryption SDK 2.0 (2020). https://docs.aws.amazon.com/encryption-sdk/latest/developer-guide/introduction.html
2. The Sodium cryptography library (Libsodium) (2021). https://libsodium.gitbook.io/doc
3. Abdalla, M., Bellare, M., Neven, G.: Robust encryption. In: Micciancio, D. (ed.) TCC 2010. LNCS, vol. 5978, pp. 480–497. Springer, Heidelberg (2010). https://doi.org/10.1007/978-3-642-11799-2_28
4. Albertini, A., Duong, T., Gueron, S., Kölbl, S., Luykx, A., Schmieg, S.: How to abuse and fix authenticated encryption without key commitment. In: 31st USENIX Security Symposium (2022)
5. Bellare, M., Canetti, R., Krawczyk, H.: Keying hash functions for message authentication. In: Koblitz, N. (ed.) CRYPTO 1996. LNCS, vol. 1109, pp. 1–15. Springer, Heidelberg (1996). https://doi.org/10.1007/3-540-68697-5_1
6. Bellare, M., Canetti, R., Krawczyk, H.: Pseudorandom functions revisited: the cascade construction and its concrete security. In: 37th FOCS. IEEE (1996)

7. Bellare, M., Desai, A., Jokipii, E., Rogaway, P.: A concrete security treatment of symmetric encryption. In: 38th FOCS. IEEE (1997)

8. Bellare, M., Hoang, V.T.: Efficient schemes for committing authenticated encryption. Cryptology ePrint Archive (2022). https://ia.cr/2022/

9. Bellare, M., Kohno, T.: A theoretical treatment of related-key attacks: RKA-PRPs, RKA-PRFs, and applications. In: Biham, E. (ed.) EUROCRYPT 2003. LNCS, vol. 2656, pp. 491–506. Springer, Heidelberg (2003). https://doi.org/10.1007/3-540-39200-9_31

10. Bellare, M., Namprempre, C.: Authenticated encryption: relations among notions and analysis of the generic composition paradigm. In: Okamoto, T. (ed.) ASIACRYPT 2000. LNCS, vol. 1976, pp. 531–545. Springer, Heidelberg (2000). https://doi.org/10.1007/3-540-44448-3_41

11. Bellare, M., Ng, R., Tackmann, B.: Nonces are noticed: AEAD revisited. In: Boldyreva, A., Micciancio, D. (eds.) CRYPTO 2019. LNCS, vol. 11692, pp. 235–265. Springer, Cham (2019). https://doi.org/10.1007/978-3-030-26948-7_9

12. Bellare, M., Rogaway, P.: The security of triple encryption and a framework for code-based game-playing proofs. In: Vaudenay, S. (ed.) EUROCRYPT 2006. LNCS, vol. 4004, pp. 409–426. Springer, Heidelberg (2006). https://doi.org/10.1007/11761679_25

13. Bellare, M., Tackmann, B.: The multi-user security of authenticated encryption: AES-GCM in TLS 1.3. In: Robshaw, M., Katz, J. (eds.) CRYPTO 2016. LNCS, vol. 9814, pp. 247–276. Springer, Heidelberg (2016). https://doi.org/10.1007/978-3-662-53018-4_10

14. Bellare, M., Tackmann, B.: Nonce-based cryptography: retaining security when randomness fails. In: Fischlin, M., Coron, J.-S. (eds.) EUROCRYPT 2016. LNCS, vol. 9665, pp. 729–757. Springer, Heidelberg (2016). https://doi.org/10.1007/978-3-662-49890-3_28

15. Bernstein, D.: Chacha, a variant of salsa20. In: Workshop Record of SASC, vol. 8, pp. 3–5 (2008)

16. Bernstein, D.J.: The Salsa20 family of stream ciphers. In: Robshaw, M., Billet, O. (eds.) New Stream Cipher Designs. LNCS, vol. 4986, pp. 84–97. Springer, Heidelberg (2008). https://doi.org/10.1007/978-3-540-68351-3_8

17. Bernstein, D.J.: The Poly1305-AES message-authentication code. In: Gilbert, H., Handschuh, H. (eds.) FSE 2005. LNCS, vol. 3557, pp. 32–49. Springer, Heidelberg (2005). https://doi.org/10.1007/11502760_3

18. Black, J., Rogaway, P., Shrimpton, T.: Black-box analysis of the block-cipher-based hash-function constructions from PGV. In: Yung, M. (ed.) CRYPTO 2002. LNCS, vol. 2442, pp. 320–335. Springer, Heidelberg (2002). https://doi.org/10.1007/3-540-45708-9_21

19. Boneh, D., Di Crescenzo, G., Ostrovsky, R., Persiano, G.: Public key encryption with keyword search. In: Cachin, C., Camenisch, J.L. (eds.) EUROCRYPT 2004. LNCS, vol. 3027, pp. 506–522. Springer, Heidelberg (2004). https://doi.org/10.1007/978-3-540-24676-3_30

20. Bose, P., Hoang, V.T., Tessaro, S.: Revisiting AES-GCM-SIV: multi-user security, faster key derivation, and better bounds. In: Nielsen, J.B., Rijmen, V. (eds.) EUROCRYPT 2018. LNCS, vol. 10820, pp. 468–499. Springer, Cham (2018). https://doi.org/10.1007/978-3-319-78381-9_18

21. Coron, J.-S., Dodis, Y., Malinaud, C., Puniya, P.: Merkle-Damgård revisited: how to construct a hash function. In: Shoup, V. (ed.) CRYPTO 2005. LNCS, vol. 3621, pp. 430–448. Springer, Heidelberg (2005). https://doi.org/10.1007/11535218_26

22. Dodis, Y., Grubbs, P., Ristenpart, T., Woodage, J.: Fast message franking: from invisible salamanders to encryptment. In: Shacham, H., Boldyreva, A. (eds.) CRYPTO 2018. LNCS, vol. 10991, pp. 155–186. Springer, Cham (2018). https://doi.org/10.1007/978-3-319-96884-1_6

23. Dworkin, M.: Recommendation for block cipher modes of operation: Galois/Counter Mode (GCM) and GMAC. NIST Special Publication 800-38D (2007)

24. Farshim, P., Libert, B., Paterson, K.G., Quaglia, E.A.: Robust encryption, revisited. In: Kurosawa, K., Hanaoka, G. (eds.) PKC 2013. LNCS, vol. 7778, pp. 352–368. Springer, Heidelberg (2013). https://doi.org/10.1007/978-3-642-36362-7_22

25. Farshim, P., Orlandi, C., Roşie, R.: Security of symmetric primitives under incorrect usage of keys. IACR Trans. Symm. Cryptol. **2017**(1), 449–473 (2017)

26. Ferguson, N.: Authentication weaknesses in GCM. Manuscript, available in NIST webpage (2005)

27. Grubbs, P., Lu, J., Ristenpart, T.: Message franking via committing authenticated encryption. In: Katz, J., Shacham, H. (eds.) CRYPTO 2017. LNCS, vol. 10403, pp. 66–97. Springer, Cham (2017). https://doi.org/10.1007/978-3-319-63697-9_3

28. Gueron, S., Lindell, Y.: Better bounds for block cipher modes of operation via nonce-based key derivation. In: Thuraisingham, B.M., Evans, D., Malkin, T., Xu, D. (eds.) ACM CCS 2017 (2017)

29. Hoang, V.T., Tessaro, S., Thiruvengadam, A.: The multi-user security of GCM, revisited: Tight bounds for nonce randomization. In: Lie, D., Mannan, M., Backes, M., Wang, X. (eds.) ACM CCS 2018 (2018)

30. Jarecki, S., Krawczyk, H., Xu, J.: OPAQUE: an asymmetric PAKE protocol secure against pre-computation attacks. In: Nielsen, J.B., Rijmen, V. (eds.) EUROCRYPT 2018. LNCS, vol. 10822, pp. 456–486. Springer, Cham (2018). https://doi.org/10.1007/978-3-319-78372-7_15

31. Kaliski, B.: PKCS #5: Password-Based Cryptography Specification Version 2.0. RFC 2898 (2000). https://datatracker.ietf.org/doc/html/rfc2898

32. Katz, J., Yung, M.: Unforgeable encryption and chosen ciphertext secure modes of operation. In: Goos, G., Hartmanis, J., van Leeuwen, J., Schneier, B. (eds.) FSE 2000. LNCS, vol. 1978, pp. 284–299. Springer, Heidelberg (2001). https://doi.org/10.1007/3-540-44706-7_20

33. Lambæk, M.: Breaking and fixing private set intersection protocols. Cryptology ePrint Archive, Report 2016/665 (2016). https://eprint.iacr.org/2016/665

34. Len, J., Grubbs, P., Ristenpart, T.: Partitioning oracle attacks. In: Bailey, M., Greenstadt, R. (eds.) 30th USENIX Security Symposium. USENIX Association (2021)

35. Luykx, A., Mennink, B., Paterson, K.G.: Analyzing multi-key security degradation. In: Takagi, T., Peyrin, T. (eds.) ASIACRYPT 2017. LNCS, vol. 10625, pp. 575–605. Springer, Cham (2017). https://doi.org/10.1007/978-3-319-70697-9_20

36. McGrew, D.A., Viega, J.: The security and performance of the galois/counter mode (GCM) of operation. In: Canteaut, A., Viswanathan, K. (eds.) INDOCRYPT 2004. LNCS, vol. 3348, pp. 343–355. Springer, Heidelberg (2004). https://doi.org/10.1007/978-3-540-30556-9_27

37. Mouha, N., Luykx, A.: Multi-key security: the even-mansour construction revisited. In: Gennaro, R., Robshaw, M. (eds.) CRYPTO 2015. LNCS, vol. 9215, pp. 209–223. Springer, Heidelberg (2015). https://doi.org/10.1007/978-3-662-47989-6_10

38. Namprempre, C., Rogaway, P., Shrimpton, T.: Reconsidering generic composition. In: Nguyen, P.Q., Oswald, E. (eds.) EUROCRYPT 2014. LNCS, vol. 8441, pp.

257–274. Springer, Heidelberg (2014). https://doi.org/10.1007/978-3-642-55220-5_15

39. Rogaway, P.: Authenticated-encryption with associated-data. In: Atluri, V. (ed.) ACM CCS 2002 (2002)

40. Rogaway, P., Bellare, M., Black, J., Krovetz, T.: OCB: a block-cipher mode of operation for efficient authenticated encryption. In: Reiter, M.K., Samarati, P. (eds.) ACM CCS 2001 (2001)

41. Rogaway, P., Shrimpton, T.: A provable-security treatment of the key-wrap problem. In: Vaudenay, S. (ed.) EUROCRYPT 2006. LNCS, vol. 4004, pp. 373–390. Springer, Heidelberg (2006). https://doi.org/10.1007/11761679_23

42. Salowey, J., Choudhury, A., McGrew, D.: AES Galois Counter Mode (GCM) cipher suites for TLS. RFC 5288 (2008). https://datatracker.ietf.org/doc/html/rfc5288

43. Salowey, J., Choudury, A. McGrew, D.A.: AES Galois Counter Mode (GCM) cipher suites for TLS. RFC 5288 (2008)

On the Concrete Security
of TLS 1.3 PSK Mode

Hannah Davis[1], Denis Diemert[2(✉)], Felix Günther[3], and Tibor Jager[2]

[1] University of California San Diego, La Jolla, CA, USA
h3davis@eng.ucsd.edu
[2] Bergische Universität Wuppertal, Wuppertal, Germany
denis.diemert@uni-wuppertal.de, tibor.jager@uni-wuppertal.de
[3] ETH Zürich, Zürich, Switzerland
mail@felixguenther.info

Abstract. The pre-shared key (PSK) handshake modes of TLS 1.3 allow for the performant, low-latency resumption of previous connections and are widely used on the Web and by resource-constrained devices, e.g., in the Internet of Things. Taking advantage of these performance benefits with optimal and theoretically-sound parameters requires tight security proofs. We give the first tight security proofs for the TLS 1.3 PSK handshake modes.

Our main technical contribution is to address a gap in prior tight security proofs of TLS 1.3 which modeled either the entire key schedule or components thereof as independent random oracles to enable tight proof techniques. These approaches ignore existing interdependencies in TLS 1.3's key schedule, arising from the fact that the same cryptographic hash function is used in several components of the key schedule and the handshake more generally. We overcome this gap by proposing a new abstraction for the key schedule and carefully arguing its soundness via the indifferentiability framework. Interestingly, we observe that for one specific configuration, PSK-only mode with hash function SHA-384, it seems difficult to argue indifferentiability due to a lack of domain separation between the various hash function usages. We view this as an interesting insight for the design of protocols, such as future TLS versions.

For all other configurations however, our proofs significantly tighten the security of the TLS 1.3 PSK modes, confirming standardized parameters (for which prior bounds provided subpar or even void guarantees) and enabling a theoretically-sound deployment.

1 Introduction

The *Transport Layer Security* (TLS) protocol is probably the most widely-used cryptographic protocol. It provides a secure channel between two endpoints

Some of this work was done while Hannah Davis was visiting ETH Zurich. Felix Günther was supported in part by German Research Foundation (DFG) Research Fellowship grant GU 1859/1-1. Tibor Jager was supported by the European Research Council (ERC) under the European Union's Horizon 2020 research and innovation programme, grant agreement 802823.

O. Dunkelman and S. Dziembowski (Eds.): EUROCRYPT 2022, LNCS 13276, pp. 876–906, 2022.
https://doi.org/10.1007/978-3-031-07085-3_30

(*client* and *server*) for arbitrary higher-layer application protocols. Its most recent version, TLS 1.3 [48], specifies two different "modes" for the initial handshake establishing a secure session key: the main handshake mode based on a Diffie–Hellman key exchange and public-key authentication via digital signatures, and a *pre-shared key* (PSK) mode, which performs authentication based on symmetric keys. The latter is mainly used for two purposes:

Session resumption. Here, a prior TLS connection established a secure channel along with a pre-shared key PSK, usually via a full handshake. Subsequent TLS resumption sessions use this key for authentication and key derivation. For example, modern web browsers typically establish multiple TLS connections when loading a web site. Using public-key authentication only in an initial session and PSK-mode in subsequent ones minimizes the number of relatively expensive public-key computations and significantly improves performance for both clients and servers.

Out-of-band establishment. PSKs can also be established out-of-band, e.g., by manual configuration of devices or with a separate key establishment protocol. This enables secure communication in settings where a complex public-key infrastructure (PKI) is unsuitable, such as IoT applications.

TLS 1.3 provides two variants of the PSK handshake mode: *PSK-only* and *PSK-(EC)DHE*. The PSK-only mode is purely based on symmetric-key cryptography. This makes TLS accessible to resource-constrained low-cost devices, and other applications with strict performance requirements, but comes at the cost of not providing *forward secrecy* [29], since the latter is not achievable with static symmetric keys.[1] The PSK-(EC)DHE mode in turn achieves forward secrecy by additionally performing an (elliptic-curve) Diffie–Hellman key exchange, authenticated via the PSK (i.e., still avoiding inefficient public-key signatures). This compromise between performance and security is the suggested choice for TLS 1.3 session resumption on the Internet.

Concrete Security and Tightness. Classical, complexity-theoretic security proofs considered the security of cryptosystems *asymptotically*. They are satisfied with security reductions running in polynomial time and having non-negligible success probability. However, it is well-known that this only guarantees that a sufficiently large security parameter exists *asymptotically*, but it does not guarantee that a deployed real-world cryptosystem with standardized parameters—such as concrete key lengths, sizes of algebraic groups, moduli, etc.—can achieve a certain expected security level. In contrast, a *concrete security* approach makes all bounds on the running time and success probability of adversaries explicit, for example, with a bound of the form $\mathrm{Adv}(\mathcal{A}) \leq f(\mathcal{A}) \cdot \mathrm{Adv}(\mathcal{B})$, where f is a function of the adversary's resources and $\mathcal{B}$ is an adversary against some underlying cryptographic hardness assumption.

The concrete security approach makes it possible to determine concrete deployment parameters that are supported by a formal security proof. As an

---

[1] See [2,9] for recent work discussing symmetric key exchange and forward secrecy.

intuitive toy example, suppose we want to achieve "128-bit security", that is, we want a security proof that guarantees (for any $\mathcal{A}$ in a certain class of adversaries) that $\mathrm{Adv}(\mathcal{A}) \leq 2^{-128}$. Suppose we have a cryptosystem with a reduction that loses "40 bits of security" because we can only prove a bound of $f(\mathcal{A}) \leq 2^{40}$. This means that we have to instantiate the scheme with an underlying hardness assumption that achieves $\mathrm{Adv}(\mathcal{B}) \leq 2^{-168}$ for any $\mathcal{B}$ in order to upper bound $\mathrm{Adv}(\mathcal{A})$ by 2^{-128} as desired. Hence, the 40-bit security loss of the bound is compensated by larger parameters that provide "168-bit security".

This yields a theoretically-sound choice of deployment parameters, but it might incur a very significant performance loss, as it requires the choice of larger groups, moduli, or key lengths. For example, the size of an elliptic curve group scales quadratically with the expected bit security, so we would have to choose $|\mathbb{G}| \approx 2^{2 \cdot 168} = 2^{336}$ instead of the optimal $|\mathbb{G}| \approx 2^{2 \cdot 128} = 2^{256}$. The performance penalty is even more significant for finite field groups, RSA or discrete logarithms "modulo p". This could lead to parameters which are either too large for practical use, or too small to be supported by the formal security analysis of the cryptosystem. We demonstrate this below for security proofs of TLS.

Even worse, for a given security proof the concrete loss ℓ may not be a constant, as in the above example, but very often ℓ depends on other parameters, such as the number of users or protocol sessions, for example. This makes it difficult to choose theoretically-sound parameters when bounds on these other parameters are not exactly known at the time of deployment. If then a concrete value for ℓ is estimated too small (e.g., because the number of users is underestimated), then the derived parameters are not backed by the security analysis. If ℓ is chosen too large, then it incurs an unnecessary performance overhead.

Therefore we want to have *tight* security proofs, where ℓ is a small constant, independent of any parameters that are unknown when the cryptosystem is deployed. This holds in particular for cryptosystems and protocols that are designed to maximize performance, such as the PSK modes of TLS 1.3 for session resumption or resource-constrained devices.

Previous Analyses of the TLS Handshake Protocol and Their Tightness. TLS 1.3 is the first TLS version that was developed in a close collaboration between academia and industry. Early TLS 1.3 drafts were inspired by the OPTLS design by Krawczyk and Wee [42], and several draft revisions as well as the final TLS 1.3 standard in RFC 8446 [48] were analyzed by many different research groups, including computational/reductionist analyses of the full and PSK modes in [19–21, 25]. All reductions in these papers are however highly non-tight, having up to a quadratic security loss in the number of TLS sessions and adversary can interact with. For example, [17] explains that for "128-bit security" and plausible numbers of users and sessions, an RSA modulus of more than 10,000 bits would be necessary to compensate the loss of previous security proofs for TLS, even though 3072 bits are usually considered sufficient for "128-bit security" when the loss of reductions is not taken into account. Likewise, [14] argues that the tightness loss to the underlying Diffie–Hellman hardness assumption lets these bounds fail to meet the standardized elliptic curves' security target, and for large-scale adversary even yields completely vacuous bounds.

Recently, Davis and Günther [14] and Diemert and Jager [17] gave new, tight security proofs for the TLS 1.3 full handshake based on Diffie–Hellman key exchange and digital signatures (not PSKs). However, their results required very strong assumptions. One is that the underlying digital signature scheme is tightly secure in a multi-user setting with adaptive corruptions. While such signature schemes do exist [3,16,28,31], this is not known for any of the signature schemes standardized for TLS 1.3, which are subject to the tightness lower bounds of [4] as their public keys uniquely determine the matching secret key.

Even more importantly, both [14] and [17] modeled the TLS key schedule or components thereof as *independent* random oracles. This was done to overcome the technical challenge that the Diffie–Hellman secret and key shares need to be *combined* in the key derivation to apply their tight security proof strategy, following Cohn-Gordon et al. [11], yet in TLS 1.3 those values enter key derivation through *separate* function calls. But neither work provided formal justification for their modeling, and both neglected to address potential dependencies between the use of a hash function in the key schedule and elsewhere in the protocol.

Our Contributions. In this paper, we describe a new perspective on TLS 1.3, which enables a modular security analysis with tight security proofs.

New Abstraction of the TLS 1.3 Key Schedule. We first describe a new abstraction of the TLS 1.3 key schedule used in the PSK modes (in Sect. 2), where different steps of the key schedule are modeled as *independent* random oracles (12 random oracles in total). This makes it significantly easier to rigorously analyze the security of TLS 1.3, since it replaces a significant part of the complexity of the protocol with what the key schedule intuitively provides, namely "as-good-as-independent cryptographic keys", deterministically derived from pre-shared keys, Diffie–Hellman values (in PSK-(EC)DHE mode), protocol messages, and the randomness of communicating parties.

Most importantly, in contrast to prior works on TLS 1.3's tightness that abstracted (parts of or the entire) key schedule as random oracles [14,17] to enable the tight proof technique of Cohn-Gordon et al. [11], we support this new abstraction formally. Using the *indifferentiability* framework of Maurer et al. [46] in its recent adaptation by Bellare et al. [5] that treats *multiple* random oracles, in Section 4 we prove our abstraction *indifferentiable* from TLS 1.3 with *only* the underlying cryptographic hash function modeled as a random oracle, and this proof is *tight*. This accounts for possible interdependencies between the use of a hash function in multiple contexts, which were not considered in [14,17].

Identifying a Lack of Domain Separation. A noteworthy subtlety is that, to our surprise, we identify that for a certain choice of TLS 1.3 PSK mode and hash function (namely, PSK-only mode with SHA384), a lack of *domain separation* [5] in the protocol does *not* allow us to prove indifferentiability for this case. We discuss the details of why domain separation is achieved for all but this case in the full version of this paper [13].

This gap could be closed by more careful domain separation in the key schedule, which we consider an interesting insight for designers of future versions of TLS or other protocols. Concretely, the ideal domain separation method would be to add a unique prefix or suffix to each hash function call made by the protocol. However, existing standard primitives like HMAC and HKDF do not permit the use of such labels, so this advice is not practical for TLS 1.3 or similar protocols. For these, a combination of labels (where possible) and padding for domain separation seems advisable, where the padding ensures that the protocol's direct hash calls have strictly longer inputs than the internal hash calls in HMAC and HKDF. We outline this method in more detail in the full version.

Modularization of Record Layer Encryption. Like most of the prior computational TLS 1.3 analyses [17, 19, 21, 25], we use a *multi-stage key exchange* (MSKE) security model [24] to capture the complex and fine-grained security aspects of TLS 1.3. These aspects include cleverly distinguishing between "external" keys established in the handshake for subsequent use (by, e.g., application data encryption, resumption, etc.) and "internal" keys, used within the handshake itself (in TLS 1.3 for encrypting most of the handshake through the protocol's record layer) to avoid complex security models such as the ACCE model [33] which monolithically treat handshake and record-layer encryption.

As a generic simplification step for MSKE models, we show (in Sect. 5) that for a certain class of *transformations* using the internal keys, we can even avoid the somewhat involved handling of internal keys altogether. We use this to simplify our analysis of the TLS 1.3 handshake (treating the TLS 1.3 record-layer encryption as such transformation). The result itself however is not specific to TLS 1.3, but general and of independent interest; it furthermore is *tight*.

Tight Security of TLS 1.3 PSK Modes. We leverage the new perspective on the TLS 1.3 key schedule and the fact that we can ignore record-layer encryption to give our main results: the first *tight* security proofs for the PSK-only and PSK-(EC)DHE handshake modes of TLS 1.3.

Evaluation. Finally, we evaluate our new bounds and prior ones from [21] over a wide range of fully concrete resource parameters, following the approach of Davis and Günther [14]. Our bounds improve on previous analyses of the PSK-only handshake by between 15 and 53 bits of security, and those of the PSK-(EC)DHE handshake by 60 and 131 bits of security across all our parameters evaluated.

Further Related Work and Scope of Our Analysis. Several previous works gave security proofs for the previous protocol version TLS 1.2 [7, 27, 33, 40, 41, 44], including its PSK-modes [44]; all reductions in these works are highly non-tight.

Brzuska et al. [10] recently proposed a stand-alone security model for the TLS 1.3 key schedule, likewise aiming at a new abstraction perspective on the latter to support formal protocol analysis. While their treatment focuses solely on the key schedule and only briefly argues its application to a key exchange security result, it is more general and covers the negotiation of parameters [6, 22] and agile usage of various algorithms.

Our focus is on the TLS 1.3 PSK modes. Hence, our abstraction of the key schedule and the careful indifferentiability treatment is tailored to that mode and cannot be directly translated to the full handshake (without PSKs). We are confident that our approach can be adapted to achieve similar results for the full handshake, but leave revisiting the results in [14, 17] in that way to future work.

Like many previous cryptographic analyses [14, 17, 19–21, 25, 33, 40] of the TLS handshake, our work focuses on the "cryptographic core" of the TLS 1.3 PSK handshake modes (in particular, we consider fixed parameters like the Diffie–Hellman group, TLS ciphersuite, etc.). Our abstraction of the key schedule is designed for easy composition with our tight key exchange proof, and our indifferentiability treatment is important confirmation of that abstraction's soundness. We do not consider, e.g., ciphersuite and version negotiation [22] or backwards compatibility issues in settings where multiple TLS versions are used in parallel, such as [34]. We also do not treat the security of the TLS record layer; instead we explain how to avoid the necessity to do so in order to achieve more modular security analyses, and we refer to compositional results [17, 19, 21, 24, 30] treating the combined security when subsequent protocols use the session keys established in an MSKE protocol.

Numerous authenticated key exchange protocols [11, 28, 31, 32, 45] were recently proposed that can be proven (almost) tightly secure. However, these protocols were specifically designed to be tightly secure and none is standardized.

2   The TLS 1.3 Pre-shared Key Handshake Protocol

Overview. We consider the pre-shared key mode of TLS 1.3, used in a setting where both client and server already share a common secret, a so-called *pre-shared key* (PSK). A PSK is a cryptographic key which may either be manually configured, negotiated out-of-band, or (and most commonly) be obtained from a prior and possibly not PSK-based TLS session to enable fast *session resumption*. The TLS 1.3 PSK handshake comes in two flavors: PSK-only, where security is established from the pre-shared key alone, and PSK-(EC)DHE, which includes an (finite-field or elliptic-curve) Diffie–Hellman key exchange for added forward secrecy. Both PSK handshakes essentially consist of two phases (cf. Fig. 1).

1. The client sends a random nonce and a list of offered pre-shared keys to the server, where each key is identified by a (unique) identifier *pskid*.[2] The server then selects one *pskid* from the list, and responds with another random nonce

---

[2] In this work, we do not consider negotiation of pre-shared keys in situations where client and server share multiple keys, but focus on the case where client and server share only one PSK and the client therefore offers only a single *pskid*. However, we expect that our results extend to the general case as well.

and the selected *pskid*. In PSK-(EC)DHE mode, client and server additionally perform a Diffie–Hellman key exchange, sending group elements along
with the nonces and PSK identifiers. In both modes, the client also sends a
so-called binder value, which applies a *message authentication code* (MAC) to
the client's nonce and *pskid* (and the Diffie–Hellman share in PSK-(EC)DHE
mode) and binds the PSK handshake to the (potential) prior handshake in
which the used pre-shared key was established (see [12,39] for analysis ratio-
nale behind the binder value).

2. Then client and server derive *unauthenticated* cryptographic keys from the
   PSK and the established Diffie–Hellman key (the latter only in (EC)DHE
   mode, of course). This includes, for instance, the *client* and *server handshake
   traffic keys* (htk_C and htk_S) used to encrypt the subsequent handshake messages, as well as *finished keys* (fk_C and fk_S) used to compute and exchange
   finished messages. The finished messages are MAC tags over all previous
   messages, ensuring that client and server have received all previous messages
   exactly as they were sent.

   After verifying the finished messages, client and server "accept" *authenticated*
   cryptographic keys, including the *client* and *server application traffic secret*
   (CATS and SATS), the *exporter master secret* (EMS), and the *resumption
   master secret* (RMS) for future session resumptions.

Detailed Specification. For our proofs we will need fully-specified descriptions for
each of the TLS 1.3 PSK and PSK-(EC)DHE handshake protocols. Pseudocode
for these protocols can be found in Fig. 1, where we let $(\mathbb{G}, p, g)$ be a cyclic group
of prime order p such that $\mathbb{G} = \langle g \rangle$.

The two descriptions on the left and right in Fig. 1 show the same protocol,
but they use different abstractions to highlight how we capture the complex way
TLS 1.3 calls its hash function. This one hash function is used in some places
to condense transcripts, in others to help derive session keys, and in still others
as part of a message authentication code. We call this function **H**, and let its
output length be hl bits so that we have $\mathbf{H}\colon \{0,1\}^* \to \{0,1\}^{hl}$. Depending on
the choice of ciphersuite, TLS 1.3 instantiates **H** with either SHA256 or SHA384
[47]. In our security analysis, we will model **H** as a random oracle.

On the left-hand side of Fig. 1, we distinguish four named subroutines of
TLS 1.3 which use **H** for different purposes:

– A message authentication code $\mathbf{MAC}\colon \{0,1\}^{hl} \times \{0,1\}^* \to \{0,1\}^{hl}$, which
  calls **H** via the HMAC function $\mathbf{MAC}(K, M) := \mathsf{HMAC}[\mathbf{H}](K, M)$ where

$$\mathsf{HMAC}[\mathbf{H}](K, M) := \mathbf{H}((K \parallel 0^{bl-hl}) \oplus \mathsf{opad}) \parallel \mathbf{H}((K \parallel 0^{bl-hl} \oplus \mathsf{ipad}) \parallel M))$$

Here opad and ipad are bl-bit strings, where each byte of opad and ipad is set
to the hexadecimal value 0x5c, resp. 0x36. We have $bl = 512$ when SHA256
is used and $bl = 512$ for SHA384. When modeling SHA256 resp. SHA384 as a
random oracle, we keep the corresponding value of bl.

Left (detailed key schedule):

Client		Server

$r_C \xleftarrow{\$} \{0,1\}^{nl}$
$x \xleftarrow{\$} \mathbb{Z}_p, X \leftarrow g^x$
ClientHello: r_C
$[+ \text{ClientKeyShare: } X]^\dagger$
$ES \leftarrow \text{Extract}(0, PSK)$
$dES \leftarrow \text{Expand}(ES, \ell_3 \| H(\text{""}))$
$BK \leftarrow \text{Expand}(ES, \ell_0 \| H(\text{""}))$
$fk_b \leftarrow \text{Expand}(BK, \ell_6)$
$binder \leftarrow \text{MAC}(fk_b, H(CH^-))$
$+ \text{ClientPreSharedKey: } pskid, binder$

abort if $binder \neq \text{MAC}(fk_b, H(CH^-))$
accept $ETS \leftarrow \text{Expand}(ES, \ell_1 \| H(CH))$ 1
accept $EEMS \leftarrow \text{Expand}(ES, \ell_2 \| H(CH))$ 2

$r_S \xleftarrow{\$} \{0,1\}^{nl}$
$y \xleftarrow{\$} \mathbb{Z}_p, Y \leftarrow g^y$
ServerHello: r_S
$[+ \text{ServerKeyShare: } Y]^\dagger$
$+ \text{ServerPreSharedKey: } pskid$

$[DHE \leftarrow Y^x]^\dagger \quad [DHE \leftarrow 0]^\circ \quad [DHE \leftarrow X^y]^\dagger$
$HS \leftarrow \text{Extract}(dES, DHE)$
$CHTS \leftarrow \text{Expand}(HS, \ell_4 \| H(CH \| SH))$
$SHTS \leftarrow \text{Expand}(HS, \ell_5 \| H(CH \| SH))$
$dHS \leftarrow \text{Expand}(HS, \ell_3 \| H(\text{""}))$
accept $htk_C \leftarrow \text{DeriveTK}(CHTS)$ 3

accept $htk_S \leftarrow \text{DeriveTK}(SHTS)$ 4

$\{\text{EncryptedExtensions}\}$
$fk_S \leftarrow \text{Expand}(SHTS, \ell_6)$
$fin_S \leftarrow \text{MAC}(fk_S, H(CH \| \cdots \| EE))$
$\{\text{ServerFinished}\}: fin_S$

abort if $fin_S \neq \text{HMAC}(fk_S, H(CH \| \cdots \| EE))$
$MS \leftarrow \text{Extract}(dHS, 0)$
accept $CATS \leftarrow \text{Expand}(MS, \ell_7 \| H(CH \| \cdots \| SF))$ 5
accept $SATS \leftarrow \text{Expand}(MS, \ell_8 \| H(CH \| \cdots \| SF))$ 6
accept $EMS \leftarrow \text{Expand}(MS, \ell_9 \| H(CH \| \cdots \| SF))$ 7

$fk_C \leftarrow \text{Expand}(CHTS, \ell_6)$
$fin_C \leftarrow \text{MAC}(fk_C, H(CH \| \cdots \| SF))$
$\{\text{ClientFinished}\}: fin_C$

abort if $fin_C \neq \text{MAC}(fk_C, H(CH \| \cdots \| SF))$
accept $RMS \leftarrow \text{Expand}(MS, \ell_{10} \| H(CH \| \cdots \| CF))$ 8

Right (representation through TKDF_x functions):

Client		Server

$r_C \xleftarrow{\$} \{0,1\}^{nl}$
$x \xleftarrow{\$} \mathbb{Z}_p, X \leftarrow g^x$
ClientHello: r_C
$[+ \text{ClientKeyShare: } X]^\dagger$

$binder \leftarrow \text{TKDF}_{binder}(PSK, H(CH^-))$
$+ \text{ClientPreSharedKey: } pskid, binder$

abort if $binder \neq \text{TKDF}_{binder}(PSK, H(CH^-))$
accept $ETS \leftarrow \text{TKDF}_{ETS}(PSK, H(CH))$ 1
accept $EEMS \leftarrow \text{TKDF}_{EEMS}(PSK, H(CH))$ 2

$r_S \xleftarrow{\$} \{0,1\}^{nl}$
$y \xleftarrow{\$} \mathbb{Z}_p, Y \leftarrow g^y$
ServerHello: r_S
$[+ \text{ServerKeyShare: } Y]^\dagger$
$+ \text{ServerPreSharedKey: } pskid$

$[DHE \leftarrow Y^x]^\dagger \quad [DHE \leftarrow 0]^\circ \quad [DHE \leftarrow X^y]^\dagger$

accept $htk_C \leftarrow \text{TKDF}_{htk_C}(PSK, DHE, H(CH \| SH))$ 3
accept $htk_S \leftarrow \text{TKDF}_{htk_S}(PSK, DHE, H(CH \| SH))$ 4

$\{\text{EncryptedExtensions}\}$
$fin_S \leftarrow \text{TKDF}_{fin_S}(PSK, DHE, H(CH \| SH), H(CH \| \cdots \| EE))$
$\{\text{ServerFinished}\}: fin_S$

abort if $fin_S \neq \text{TKDF}_{fin_S}(PSK, DHE, H(CH \| SH), H(CH \| \cdots \| EE))$
accept $CATS \leftarrow \text{TKDF}_{CATS}(PSK, DHE, H(CH \| \cdots \| SF))$ 5
accept $SATS \leftarrow \text{TKDF}_{SATS}(PSK, DHE, H(CH \| \cdots \| SF))$ 6
accept $EMS \leftarrow \text{TKDF}_{EMS}(PSK, DHE, H(CH \| \cdots \| SF))$ 7

$fin_C \leftarrow \text{TKDF}_{fin_C}(PSK, DHE, H(CH \| SH), H(CH \| \cdots \| SF))$
$\{\text{ClientFinished}\}: fin_C$

abort if $fin_C \neq \text{TKDF}_{fin_C}(PSK, DHE, H(CH \| SH), H(CH \| \cdots \| SF))$
accept $RMS \leftarrow \text{TKDF}_{RMS}(PSK, DHE, H(CH \| \cdots \| CF))$ 8

Legend

MSG: Y message MSG sent, containing Y
$+$ MSG   extension sent within previous message
$\{$MSG$\}$ MSG sent AEAD-encrypted with htk_C / htk_S
$[\dots]^\dagger$ present only in PSK-(EC)DHE
$[\dots]^\circ$ present only in PSK
CH^- partial ClientHello up to (incl.) $pskid$
ℓ_x label value, distinct for distinct x

$\text{DeriveTK}(HTS) := \text{Expand}(HTS, \ell_{11} \| \text{Th}(\text{""}), hl) \| \text{Expand}(HTS, \ell_{12} \| \text{Th}(\text{""}), ivl)$
(traffic key computation, deriving a hl-bit key and a ivl-bit IV)

Fig. 1. TLS 1.3 PSK and PSK-(EC)DHE handshake modes with (optional) 0-RTT keys (stages 1 and 2), with detailed key schedule (left) and our representation of the key schedule through functions TKDF_x (right), explained in the text. Centered computations are executed by both client and server with their respective messages received, and possibly at different points in time. Dotted lines indicate the derivation of session (stage) keys together with their stage number. The labels ℓ_x are distinct for distinct index x, see the full version [13] for their definition.

$\text{TKDF}_{fin_S}(\text{PSK}, \text{DHE}, h_1, h_2)$:

1 $\text{ES} \leftarrow \textbf{Extract}(0, \text{PSK})$

2 $\text{dES} \leftarrow \textbf{Expand}(\text{ES}, \ell_3 \,\|\, \text{Th}(""))$

3 $\text{HS} \leftarrow \textbf{Extract}(\text{dES}, \text{DHE})$

4 $\text{SHTS} \leftarrow \textbf{Expand}(\text{HS}, \ell_5 \,\|\, h_1)$

5 $fk_S \leftarrow \textbf{Expand}(\text{SHTS}, \ell_6)$

6 $fin_S \leftarrow \textbf{MAC}(fk_S, h_2)$

7 return fin_S

Fig. 2. Definition of TKDF_{fin_S}, deriving the `ServerFinished` MAC.

- **Extract, Expand**: $\{0,1\}^{hl} \times \{0,1\}^* \rightarrow \{0,1\}^{hl}$, two subroutines for *extracting* and *expanding* key material in the key derivation paradigm of Krawczyk [36,38]. These functions are defined
  - $\textbf{Extract}(K, M) := \textsf{HKDF.Extract}(K, M) = \textbf{MAC}(K, M)$.
  - $\textbf{Expand}(K, M) := \textsf{HKDF.Expand}(K, M) = \textbf{MAC}(K, M \,\|\, \texttt{0x01})$.[3]

Despite the new naming conventions, this abstraction closely mimics the TLS 1.3 standard: **MAC**, **Extract**, and **Expand** can be read as more generic ways of referring to the HMAC, HKDF.Extract, and HKDF.Expand algorithms [35,36].

The right-hand side of Fig. 1 separates the key derivation functions for each first-class key as well as the binder and finished MAC values derived. This way of modeling TLS 1.3 makes it easier to establish key independence for the many keys computed in the key schedule, as we will see in Sect. 4. We introduce 11 functions TKDF_{binder}, TKDF_{ETS}, $\text{TKDF}_{\text{EEMS}}$, TKDF_{htk_C}, TKDF_{fin_C}, TKDF_{htk_S}, TKDF_{fin_S}, $\text{TKDF}_{\text{CATS}}$, $\text{TKDF}_{\text{SATS}}$, TKDF_{EMS}, and TKDF_{RMS} (indexed by the value they derive) and use them to abstract away many intermediate computations. Note that we are not changing the protocol, though: we define each TKDF function to capture the same steps it replaces.

Take as an example TKDF_{fin_S}, the function used to derive the MAC in the `ServerFinished` message. In the prior abstraction, a session would first use the key schedule to derive a finished key fk_S from the hashed transcript and the secrets PSK and DHE. It would then call **MAC**, keyed with fk_S, to generate the `ServerFinished` message authentication code on the hashed transcript and encrypted extensions. Accordingly, we define $\text{TKDF}_{fin_S} : \{0,1\}^{hl} \times \mathbb{G} \times \{0,1\}^{hl} \times \{0,1\}^{hl} \rightarrow \{0,1\}^{hl}$ as in Fig. 2. In the protocol, TKDF_{fin_S} takes inputs the pre-shared key PSK and Diffie–Hellman secret DHE and hash digests $h_1 = \textsf{Th}(\texttt{CH} \,\|\, \texttt{SH})$ and $h_2 = \textsf{Th}(\texttt{CH} \,\|\, \cdots \,\|\, \texttt{EE})$, and it outputs a MAC tag for the `ServerFinished` message. The remaining key derivation functions are defined the same way; we give their signatures in the full version [13].

Note that the definition of the 11 functions induces a lot of redundancy as we derive every value independently and therefore compute intermediate values (e.g., ES, dES, and HS) multiple times over the execution of the handshake. However, this is only conceptual. Since the computations of these intermediate values are deterministic, the intermediate values will be the same for the same inputs and could be cached.

---

[3] HKDF.Expand [36] is defined for any output length (given as third parameter). In TLS 1.3, **Expand** always derives at most hl bits, which can be trimmed from a hl-bit output; we hence in most places omit the output length parameter.

3   Code-based MSKE Model for PSK Modes

We formalize security of the TLS 1.3 PSK modes in a game-based multi-stage key exchange (MSKE) model, adapted primarily from that of Dowling et al. [21]. We fully specify our model in pseudocode in the full version [13]. We adopt the explicit authentication property from the model of Davis and Günther [14] and capture forward secrecy by following the model of Schwabe et al. [49].

3.1   Key Exchange Syntax

In our security model, the adversary interacts with *sessions* executing a key exchange protocol KE. For the definition of the security experiment it will be useful to have a unified, generic interface to the algorithms implementing KE, which can then be called from the various procedures defining the security experiment to run KE. Therefore, we first formalize a general syntax for protocols.

We assume that pairs of users share long-term symmetric keys (pre-shared keys), which are chosen uniformly at random from a set KE.PSKS.[4] We allow users to share multiple pre-shared keys, maintained in a list pskeys, and require that each user uses any key only in a fixed role (i.e., as client *or* server) to avoid the Selfie attack [23]. We do not cover PSK negotiation; each session will know at the start of the protocol which key it intends to use.

New sessions are created via the algorithm Activate. This algorithm takes as input the new session's own user, identified by some ID u, the user ID *peerid* of the intended communication partner, a pre-shared key PSK, and a role identifier—initiator (client) or responder (server)—that determines whether the session will send or receive the first protocol message. It returns the new session π_u^i, which is identified by its user ID u and a unique index i so that a single user can execute many sessions.

Existing sessions send and receive messages by executing the algorithm Run. The inputs to Run are an existing session π_u^i and a message m it has received. The algorithm processes the message, updates the state of π_u^i, and returns the next protocol message m' on behalf of the session. Run also maintains the status of π_u^i, which can have one of three values: running when it is awaiting the next protocol message, accepted when it has established a session key, and rejected if the protocol has terminated in failure.

In a multi-stage protocol, sessions accept multiple session keys while running; we identify each with a numbered *stage*. A protocol may accept several stages/keys while processing a single message, and TLS 1.3 does this. In order to handle each stage individually, our model adds artificial pauses after each acceptance to allow the adversary to interact with the sessions upon each stage accepting (beyond, as usual, each message exchanged). When a session π_u^i accepts in stage s while executing Run, we require Run to set the status of π_u^i to accepted_s and terminate. We then define a special "continue" message. When session π_u^i

---

[4] While our results can be generalized to any distribution on KE.PSKS (based on its min-entropy), for simplicity, we focus on the uniform distribution in this work.

in state $\mathsf{accepted}_s$, receives this message it calls Run again, updates its status to $\mathsf{running}_{s+1}$ and continues processing from the point where it left off.

3.2 Key Exchange Security

We define key exchange security via a real-or-random security game, a formalization of which can be found in the full version [13].

Game Oracles. In this security game, the adversary $\mathcal{A}$ has access to seven oracles: INITIALIZE, NEWSECRET, SEND, REVSESSIONKEY, REVLONGTERMKEY, TEST, and FINALIZE, as well as any random oracles the protocol defines. The game begins with a call to INITIALIZE, which samples a challenge bit b. It ends when the adversary calls FINALIZE with a guess b' at the challenge bit. We say the adversary "wins" the game if FINALIZE returns true.

The adversary can establish a random pre-shared key between two users by calling NEWSECRET.[5] It can corrupt existing users' pre-shared keys via the oracle REVLONGTERMKEY. The SEND oracle creates new protocol sessions and processes protocol messages on the behalf of existing sessions. The REVSESSIONKEY oracle reveals a session's accepted session key. Finally, the TEST oracle servers as the challenge oracle: it returns the real session key of a target session or an independent one sampled randomly from the session key space $\mathsf{KE.KS}[s]$ of the respective stage s, depending on the value of the challenge bit b.

Protocol Properties. Keys established in different stages possess different security attributes, which are defined as part of the key exchange protocol: replayability, forward secrecy level, and authentication level. Certain stages, whose indices are tracked in a list INT, produce "internal" keys intended for use only within the key exchange protocol; these keys may only be TESTed at the time of acceptance of this particular key, but not later. This is because otherwise such keys may be trivially distinguishable from random, e.g., via trial decryption, due to the fact that they are used within the protocol. To avoid a trivial distinguishing attack, we force the rest of the protocol execution to be consistent with the result of such a TEST. That is, a tested internal key is replaced in the protocol with whatever the TEST returns to the adversary (which is either the real internal key or an independent random key). The remaining stages produce "external" keys which may be tested at any time after acceptance.

For some protocols, it may be possible that a trivial replay attack can achieve that several sessions agree on the same session key for stage s, but this is not

---

[5] Our model stipulates that pre-shared keys are sampled uniformly random and honestly. One could additionally allow the registration of biased or malicious PSKs, akin to models treating, e.g., the certification of public keys [8]. While this would yield a theoretically stronger model, we consider a simpler model reasonable, because we expect most PSKs used in practice to be random keys established in prior protocol sessions. Furthermore, we consider tightness as particularly interesting when "good" PSKs are used, since low-entropy PSKs might decrease the security below what is achieved by (non)-tight security proofs, anyway.

considered an "attack". For example, in TLS 1.3 PSK an adversary can always replay the ClientHello message to multiple sessions of the same server, which then all derive the same ETS and EEMS keys (cf. Fig. 1). To specify that such a replay is not considered a protocol weakness, and thus should not be considered a valid "attack", the protocol specification may define REPLAY[s] to true for a stage s. REPLAY[s] is set to false by default.

As we focus on protocols which rely on (pre-authenticated) pre-shared keys, our model encodes that all protocol stages are at least *implicitly* mutually authenticated in the sense of Krawczyk [37], i.e., a session is guaranteed that any established key can only be known by the intended partner. Some stages will further be *explicitly* authenticated, either immediately upon acceptance or retroactively upon acceptance of a later state. Additionally, the stage at which explicit authentication is achieved may differ between the initiator and responder roles. For each stage s and role r, the key exchange protocol specification states in EAUTH[r, s] the stage t from whose acceptance stage s derives explicit authentication for the session in role r. Note that the stage-s key is not authenticated until both stages s and EAUTH[r, s] have been accepted. If the stage-s key will never be explicitly authenticated for role r, we set EAUTH[r, s] = ∞.

We use a predicate ExplicitAuth to require the existence of an honest partner for explicitly authenticated stages upon both parties' completion of the protocol, except when the session's pre-shared key was corrupted prior to accepting the explicitly-authenticating stage (as in that case, we anticipate the adversary can trivially forge any authentication mechanism).

Motivated by TLS 1.3, it might be the case that initiator and responder sessions achieve slightly different guarantees of authentication. While responders in TLS 1.3 are guaranteed the existence of an honest partner in any explicitly authenticated stage, initiators cannot guarantee that their partner has received their final message. This issue was first raised by FGSW [26] and led to their definitions of "full" and "almost-full" key confirmation; it was then extended to "full" and "almost-full" explicit authentication by DFW [15]. Our definitions for responders and initiators respectively resemble the latter two notions most closely, but we rely on session identifiers instead of "key confirmation identifiers".

We consider three levels of forward secrecy inspired by the KEMTLS work of Schwabe, Stebila, and Wiggers [49]: no forward secrecy, weak forward secrecy 2 (wfs2), and full forward secrecy (fs). As for authentication, each stage may retroactively upgrade its level of forward secrecy upon the acceptance of later stages, and forward secrecy may be established at different stages for each role. For each stage s and role r, the stage at which wfs2, resp. fs, is achieved is stated in FS[$r, s, \mathsf{wfs2}$], resp. FS[r, s, fs], by the key exchange protocol.

The definition of weak forward secrecy 2 states that a session key with wfs2 should be indistinguishable as long as (1) that session has received the relevant messages from an honest partner (formalized via matching contributive identifiers below, we say: "has an honest contributive partner") or (2) the pre-shared key was never corrupted. Full forward secrecy relaxes condition (2) to forbid corruption of the pre-shared key only before acceptance of the stage that retroactively provides full forward secrecy. We capture these notions of forward secrecy in a predicate Fresh, which uses the log of events to check whether any tested session key is trivially distinguishable (e.g., through the session or its partnered being revealed, or forward secrecy requirements violated). With forward secrecy encoded in Fresh, our long-term key corruption oracle (REVLONGTERMKEY), unlike in the model of [21], handles all corruptions the same way, regardless of forward secrecy.

Session and Game Variables. Sessions π_u^i and the security game itself maintain several variables; we indicate the former in *italics*, the latter in sans-serif font.

The game uses a counter time, initialized to 0 and incremented with any oracle query the adversary makes, to order events in the game log for later analysis. When we say that an event happens at a certain "time", we mean the current value of the time counter. The list pskeys contains, as discussed above, all pre-shared keys, indexed by a tuple $(u, v, pskid)$ containing the two users' IDs (u using the key only in the initiator role, v only in the reponder role), and a unique string identifier. The list revpsk, indexed like pskeys, tracks the time of each pre-shared key corruption, initialized to $\mathsf{revpsk}_{(u,v,pskid)} \leftarrow \infty$. (In boolean expressions, we write $\mathsf{revpsk}_{(u,v,pskid)}$ as a shorthand for $\mathsf{revpsk}_{(u,v,pskid)} \neq \infty$.)

Each session π_u^i, identified by (adversarially chosen) user ID and a unique session ID, furthermore tracks the following variables:

- $status \in \{\mathsf{running}_s, \mathsf{accepted}_s, \mathsf{rejected}_s \mid s \in [1, \ldots, \mathsf{STAGES}]\}$, where STAGES is the total number of stages of the considered protocol. The status should be $\mathsf{accepted}_s$ immediately after the session accepts the stage-s key, $\mathsf{rejected}_s$ after it rejects stage s (but may continue running; e.g., rejecting 0-RTT data), and $\mathsf{running}_s$ for some stage s otherwise.
- *peerid*. The identity of the session's intended communication partner.
- *pskid*. The identifier of the session's pre-shared key.
- accepted[s]. For each stage s, the time (i.e., the value of the time counter) at which the stage s key was accepted. Initialized to ∞.
- revealed[s]. A boolean denoting whether the stage s key has been leaked through a REVSESSIONKEY query. Initialized to false.
- tested[s]. The time at which the stage s key was tested. Initialized to ∞ before any Test query occurs. (In boolean expressions, we write tested[s] as a shorthand for tested[s] $\neq \infty$.)
- sid[s]. The session identifier for each stage s, used to match honest communication partners within each stage.
- skey[s]. The key accepted at each stage.
- $cid_{\mathsf{initiator}}[s]$ and $cid_{\mathsf{responder}}[s]$. The contributive identifiers for each stage s, where $cid_{role}[s]$ identifies the communication part that a session in role *role* must have honestly received in order to be allowed to be tested in certain scenarios (cf. the freshness definition in the Fresh predicate). Unlike prior models, each session maintains a contributive identifiers for each role; one for itself and one for its intended partner. This enables more fine-grained testing of session stages in our model.

The predicate Sound captures that variables are properly assigned, in particular that session identifiers uniquely identify a partner session (except for replayable stages) and that partnering implies agreement on (distinct) roles, contributive identifiers, peer identities and the pre-shared key used, as well as the established session key.

Definition 1 (Multi-stage key exchange security). *Let* KE *be a key exchange protocol and* $G^{\mathsf{MSKE}}_{\mathsf{KE},\mathcal{A}}$ *be the key exchange security game defined above. We define*

$$\mathrm{Adv}^{\mathsf{MSKE}}_{\mathsf{KE}}(t, q_{\mathrm{NS}}, q_{\mathrm{S}}, q_{\mathrm{RS}}, q_{\mathrm{RL}}, q_{\mathrm{T}}, q_{\mathrm{RO}}) := 2 \cdot \max_{\mathcal{A}} \Pr \left[\mathsf{Game}^{\mathsf{MSKE}}_{\mathsf{KE},\mathcal{A}} \Rightarrow 1 \right] - 1,$$

where the maximum is taken over all adversaries, denoted $(t, q_{\mathrm{NS}}, q_{\mathrm{S}}, q_{\mathrm{RS}}, q_{\mathrm{RL}}, q_{\mathrm{T}}, q_{\mathrm{RO}})$-MSKE-*adversaries, running in time at most* t *and making at most* q_{NS}, q_{S}, q_{RS}, q_{RL}, q_{T}, *resp.* q_{RO} *queries to their respective oracles* NEWSECRET, SEND, REVSESSIONKEY, REVLONGTERMKEY, TEST, *and* RO.

4 Key-Schedule Indifferentiability

In this section we will argue that the key schedule of TLS 1.3 PSK modes, where the underlying cryptographic hash function is modeled as a random oracle (i.e., the left-hand side of Fig. 1 with the underlying hash function modeled as a random oracle), is *indifferentiable* [46] from a key schedule that uses *independent* random oracles for each step of the key derivation (i.e., the right-hand side of Fig. 1 with all TKDF$_x$ functions modeled as independent random oracles). We stress that this step not only makes our main security proof in Sect. 6 significantly simpler and cleaner, but also it puts the entire protocol security analysis on a firmer theoretical ground than previous works. For some background on the indifferentiability framework, see the full version [13].

In their proof of tight security, Diemert and Jager [17] previously modeled the TLS 1.3 key schedule as four independent random oracles. Davis and Günther [14] concurrently modeled the functions HKDF.Extract and HKDF.Expand used by the key schedule as two independent random oracles. Neither work provided formal justification for their modeling. Most importantly, both neglected potential dependencies between the use of the hash function in multiple contexts in the key schedule and elsewhere in the protocol. In particular, no construction of HKDF.Extract and HKDF.Expand as independent ROs from one hash function could be indifferentiable, because HKDF.Extract and HKDF.Expand both call HMAC directly on their inputs, with HKDF.Expand only adding a counter byte. Hence, the two functions are inextricably correlated by definition. We do not claim that the analyses of [14,17] are incorrect or invalid, but merely point out that their modeling of independent random oracles is currently not justified and might not be formally reachable if one only wants to treat the hash function itself as a random oracle. This is undesirable because the gap between an instantiated protocol and its abstraction in the random oracle model can camouflage serious attacks, as Bellare et al. [5] found for the NIST PQC KEMs. Their attacks exploited dependencies between functions that were also modeled as independent random oracles but instantiated with a single hash function.

In contrast, in this section we will show that our modeling of the TLS 1.3 key schedule is indifferentiable from the key schedule when the underlying cryptographic hash function is modeled as a random oracle. To this end, we will require that inputs to the hash function do not appear in multiple contexts. For instance, a protocol transcript might collide with a Diffie–Hellman group element or an internal key (i.e., both might be represented by exactly the same bit string, but in different contexts). For most parameter settings, we can rule out such collisions by exploiting serendipitous formatting, but for one choice of parameters (the PSK-only handshake using SHA384 as hash function), an adversary could conceivably force this type of collision to occur; see the full version [13] for a detailed discussion. While this does not lead to any known attack on the handshake, it precludes our indifferentiability approach for that case.

Insights for the Design of Cryptographic Protocols. One interesting insight for protocol designers that results from our attempt of closing this gap with a careful indifferentiability-based analysis is that proper domain separation might enable a cleaner and simpler analysis, whereas a lack of domain separation leads to uncertainty in the security analysis. No domain separation means stronger assumptions in the best case, and an insecure protocol in the worst case, due to the potential for overlooked attack vectors in the hash functions. A simple prefix can avoid this with hardly any performance loss.

Indifferentiability of the TLS 1.3 Key Schedule. Via the indifferentiability framework, we replace the complex key schedule of TLS 1.3 with 12 independent random oracles: one for each first-class key and MAC tag, and one more for computing transcript hashes. In short, we relate the security of TLS 1.3 as described in the left-hand side of Fig.,1 to that of the simplified protocol on the right side of Fig. 1 with the key derivation and MAC functions TKDF_x and modeled as independent random oracles. We prove the following theorem, which formally justifies our abstraction of the key exchange protocol by reducing its security to that of the original key exchange game.

Theorem 1. *Let* $\mathsf{RO_H} \colon \{0,1\}^* \to \{0,1\}^{hl}$ *be a random oracle. Let* KE *be the TLS 1.3 PSK-only or PSK-(EC)DHE handshake protocol described on the left hand side of Fig. 1 with* $\mathbf{H} := \mathsf{RO_H}$ *and* **MAC**, **Extract**, *and* **Expand** *defined from* $\mathbf{H}$ *as in Sect. 2. Let* KE' *be the corresponding (PSK-only or PSK-(EC)DHE) handshake protocol on the right hand side of Fig. 1, with* $\mathbf{H} := \mathsf{RO_{Th}}$ *and* $\mathsf{TKDF}_x := \mathsf{RO}_x$, *where* $\mathsf{RO_{Th}}$, RO_{binder}, ..., $\mathsf{RO_{RMS}}$ *are random oracles with the appropriate signatures (see the full version [13] for the signature details). Then,*

$$\mathsf{Adv}_{\mathsf{KE}}^{\mathsf{MSKE}}(t, q_{\mathsf{NS}}, q_{\mathsf{S}}, q_{\mathsf{RS}}, q_{\mathsf{RL}}, q_{\mathsf{T}}, q_{\mathsf{RO}}) \leq \mathsf{Adv}_{\mathsf{KE}'}^{\mathsf{MSKE}}(t, q_{\mathsf{NS}}, q_{\mathsf{S}}, q_{\mathsf{RS}}, q_{\mathsf{RL}}, q_{\mathsf{T}}, q_{\mathsf{RO}})$$
$$+ \frac{2(12 q_{\mathsf{S}} + q_{\mathsf{RO}})^2}{2^{hl}} + \frac{2 q_{\mathsf{RO}}^2}{2^{hl}} + \frac{8(q_{\mathsf{RO}} + 36 q_{\mathsf{S}})^2}{2^{hl}}.$$

We establish this result via three modular steps in the indifferentiability framework introduced by Maurer, Renner, and Holenstein [46]. More specifically we will leverage a recent generalization proposed by Bellare, Davis, and Günther (BDG) [5], which in particular formalizes indifferentiability for constructions of *multiple* random oracles.

4.1 Indifferentiability for the TLS 1.3 Key Schedule in Three Steps

We move from the left of Fig. 1 to the right via three steps. Each step introduces a new variant of the TLS 1.3 protocol with a different set of random oracles by changing how we implement **H**, **MAC**, **Expand**, **Extract**, and eventually the whole key schedule. Then we view the prior implementations of these functions as constructions of new, independent random oracles. We prove security for each intermediate protocol in two parts: first, we bound the indifferentiability advantage against that step's construction; then we apply the indifferentiability composition theorem based on [46] given in the full version [13] of this paper to bound the multi-stage key exchange (MSKE) security of the new protocol.

We give a brief description of each step; all details and formal theorem statements and proofs can be found in the full version [13].

From one random oracle to two. TLS 1.3 calls its hash function **H**, which we initially model as random oracle RO_{H}, for two purposes: to hash protocol transcripts, and as a component of **MAC**, **Extract**, and **Expand** which are implemented using HMAC[**H**]. Our eventual key exchange proof needs to make full use of the random oracle model for the latter category of hashes, but we require only collision resistance for transcript hashes.

Our first intermediate handshake variant, KE_1, replaces **H** with two new functions: Th for hashing transcripts, and Ch for use within **MAC**, **Extract**, or **Expand**. While KE uses the same random oracle RO_{H} to implement Th and Ch, the KE_1 protocol instead uses two independent random oracles $\mathsf{RO}_{\mathsf{Th}}$ and $\mathsf{RO}_{\mathsf{HMAC}}$. To accomplish this without loss in MSKE security, we exploit some possibly unintentional domain separation in how inputs to these functions are formatted in TLS 1.3 to define a so-called *cloning functor*, following BDG [5]. Effectively, we partition the domain $\{0,1\}^*$ of RO_{H} into two sets D_{Th} and D_{Ch} such that D_{Th} contains all valid transcripts and D_{Ch} contains all possible inputs to **H** from HMAC. We then leverage Theorem 1 of [5] that guarantees composition for any scheme that only queries $\mathsf{RO}_{\mathsf{Ch}}$ within the set D_{Ch} and $\mathsf{RO}_{\mathsf{Th}}$ within the set D_{Th}.

We defer details on the exact domain separation to the full version [13], but highlight that the PSK-only handshake with hash function SHA384 *fails* to achieve this domain separation and consequently this proof step cannot be applied and leaves a gap for that configuration of TLS 1.3.

From SHA to HMAC. Our second variant protocol, KE_2, rewrites the **MAC** function. Instead of computing $\mathsf{HMAC[RO_{Ch}]}$, **MAC** now directly queries a new random oracle $\mathsf{RO_{HMAC}}\colon \{0,1\}^{hl} \times \{0,1\}^* \to \{0,1\}^{hl}$. Since $\mathsf{RO_{Ch}}$ was only called by **MAC**, we drop it from the protocol, but we do continue to use $\mathsf{RO_{Th}}$, i.e., KE_2 uses two random oracles: $\mathsf{RO_{Th}}$ and $\mathsf{RO_{HMAC}}$. The security of this replacement follows directly from Theorem 4.3 of Dodis et al. [18], which proves the indifferentiability of HMAC with fixed-length keys.[6]

From two random oracles to 12. Finally, we apply a "big" indifferentiability step which yields 12 independent random oracles and moves us to the right-hand side of Fig. 1. The 12 ROs include the transcript-hash oracle $\mathsf{RO_{Th}}$ and 11 oracles that handle each key(-like) output in TLS 1.3's key derivation, named RO_{binder}, $\mathsf{RO_{ETS}}$, $\mathsf{RO_{EEMS}}$, RO_{htk_C}, $\mathsf{RO_{CF}}$, RO_{htk_S}, $\mathsf{RO_{SF}}$, $\mathsf{RO_{CATS}}$, $\mathsf{RO_{SATS}}$, $\mathsf{RO_{EMS}}$, and $\mathsf{RO_{RMS}}$. (The signatures for these oracles are given in the full version [13].) For this step, we view TKDF as a construction of 11 random oracles from a single underlying oracle ($\mathsf{RO_{HMAC}}$). We then give our a simulator in pseudocode and prove the indifferentiability of TKDF with respect to this simulator. Our simulator uses look-up tables to efficiently identify intermediate values in the key schedule and consistently program the final keys and MAC tags.

Combining these three steps yields the result in Theorem 1. In the remainder of the paper, we can therefore now work with the right-hand side of Fig. 1, modeling **H** and the TKDF functions as 12 independent random oracles.

5   Modularizing Handshake Encryption

Next will argue that using "internal" keys to encrypt handshake messages on the TLS 1.3 record-layer does not impact the security of other keys established by the handshake. In the full version [13], we give a theorem that formulates our argument in a general way, applicable to any multi-stage key exchange protocol, so that future analyses of similar protocols might take advantage of this modularity as well.

Intuitively, we argue as follows. Let KE_2 be a protocol that provides multiple different stages with different external keys (i.e., none of the keys is used in the protocol, e.g., to encrypt messages), and let KE_1 be the same protocol, except that some keys are "internal" and used, e.g., to encrypt certain protocol messages. We argue that either using "internal" keys in KE_1 does not harm the security of *other* keys of KE_1, or KE_2 cannot be secure in the first place. This will establish that we can prove security of a variant TLS 1.3 *without* handshake encryption (in an accordingly simpler model), and then lift this result to the actual TLS 1.3 protocol *with* handshake encryption and the handshake traffic keys treated as "internal" keys.

---

[6] This requires PSKs to be elements of $\{0,1\}^{hl}$, which is true of resumption keys but possibly not for out-of-band PSKs.

Theorem 2. *Let* KE_1 *be the TLS 1.3 PSK-only resp. PSK-(EC)DHE mode with handshake encryption (i.e., with internal stages* $\mathsf{KE}_1.\mathsf{INT} = \{3, 4\}$*) as specified on the right-hand side in Fig. 1. Let* KE_2 *be the same mode without handshake encryption (i.e.,* $\mathsf{KE}_1.\mathsf{INT} = \emptyset$ *and AEAD-encryption/decryption of messages is omitted). Let* $\mathsf{Transform}_{\mathsf{Send}}$ *and* $\mathsf{Transform}_{\mathsf{Recv}}$ *be the AEAD encryption resp. decryption algorithms deployed in TLS 1.3 and* $\mathsf{K}_{\mathsf{Transform}} = \mathsf{KE}_1.\mathsf{INT} = \{3, 4\}$. *Then we have* $\mathrm{Adv}_{\mathsf{KE}_1}^{\mathsf{MSKE}}(t, q_{\mathrm{NS}}, q_{\mathrm{S}}, q_{\mathrm{RS}}, q_{\mathrm{RL}}, q_{\mathrm{T}}, q_{\mathrm{RO}}) \leq \mathrm{Adv}_{\mathsf{KE}_2}^{\mathsf{MSKE}}(t + t_{\mathrm{AEAD}} \cdot q_{\mathrm{S}}, q_{\mathrm{NS}}, q_{\mathrm{S}}, q_{\mathrm{RS}} + q_{\mathrm{S}}, q_{\mathrm{RL}}, q_{\mathrm{T}}, q_{\mathrm{RO}})$, *where* t_{AEAD} *is the maximum time required to execute AEAD encryption or decryption of TLS 1.3 messages.*

For TLS 1.3 this means that we will not consider any security guarantees provided by the additional encryption of handshake messages. We consider this as reasonable for PSK-mode ciphersuites, because the main purposes of handshake message encryption in TLS 1.3 is to hide the identities of communicating parties, e.g., in digital certificates, cf. [1]. In PSK mode there are no such identities. The *pskid* might be viewed as a string that could identify communicating parties, but it is sent unencrypted in the ClientHello message, anyway, the encryption of subsequent handshake messages would not contribute to its protection.

6 Tight Security of the TLS 1.3 PSK Modes

In this section, we apply the insights gained in Sects. 4 and 5 to obtain tight security bounds for both the PSK-only and the PSK-(EC)DHE mode of TLS 1.3. To that end, we first present the protocol-specific properties of the TLS 1.3 PSK-only and PSK-(EC)DHE modes such that they can be viewed as multi-stage key exchange (MSKE) protocols as defined in Sect. 3. Then, we prove tight security bounds in the MSKE model in Theorem 3 for the TLS 1.3 PSK-(EC)DHE mode and for the TLS 1.3 PSK-only mode in the full version [13].

6.1 TLS 1.3 PSK-only/PSK-(EC)DHE as a MSKE Protocol

We begin by capturing the TLS 1.3 PSK-only and PSK-(EC)DHE modes, specified in Fig. 1, formally as MSKE protocols. To this end, we must explicitly define the variables discussed in Sect. 3. In particular, we have to define the stages themselves, which stages are internal and which replayable, the session and contributive identifiers, when stages receive explicit authentication, and when stages become forward secret.

Stages. The TLS 1.3 PSK-only/PSK-(EC)DHE handshake protocol has eight stages (i.e., $\mathsf{STAGES} = 8$), corresponding to the keys ETS, EEMS, htk_S, htk_C, CATS, SATS, EMS, and RMS in that order. The set INT of internal keys contains htk_C and htk_S, the handshake traffic encryption keys. Stages ETS and EEMS are replayable: $\mathsf{REPLAY}[s]$ is true for $s \in \{1, 2\}$ and false for all others.

Session and Contributive Identifiers. The session and contributive identifiers for stages are tuples $(label_s, ctxt)$, where $label_s$ is a unique label identifying stage s, and $ctxt$ is the transcript that enters key's derivation. The session identifiers $(sid[s])_{s \in \{1,...,8\}}$ are defined as follows:[7]

$$sid[1]/sid[2] = (\text{"ETS"}/\text{"EEMS"}, (\text{CH}, \text{CKS}^\dagger, \text{CPSK})),$$

$$sid[3]/sid[4] = (\text{"}htk_C\text{"}/\text{"}htk_S\text{"}, (\text{CH}, \text{CKS}^\dagger, \text{CPSK}, \text{SH}, \text{SKS}^\dagger, \text{SPSK})),$$

$$sid[5]/sid[6]/sid[7] = (\text{"CATS"}/\text{"SATS"}/\text{"EMS"}, (\text{CH}, \ldots, \text{SPSK}, \text{EE}, \text{SF})), \text{ and}$$

$$sid[8] = (\text{"RMS"}, (\text{CH}, \text{CKS}^\dagger, \text{CPSK}, \text{SH}, \text{SKS}^\dagger, \text{SPSK}, \text{EE}, \text{SF}, \text{CF})).$$

To make sure that a server that received `ClientHello`, `ClientKeyShare`†, and `ClientPreSharedKey` untampered can be tested in stages 3 and 4, even if the sending client did not receive the server's answer, we set the contributive identifiers of stages 3 and 4 such that cid_{role} reflects the messages that a session in role *role* must have honestly received for testing to be allowed. Namely, we let clients (resp. servers) upon sending (resp. receving) the messages $(\text{CH}, \text{CKS}^\dagger, \text{CPSK})$ set $cid_{responder}[3] = (\text{"}htk_C\text{"}, (\text{CH}, \text{CKS}^\dagger, \text{CPSK}))$ and $cid_{responder}[4] = (\text{"}htk_S\text{"}, (\text{CH}, \text{CKS}^\dagger, \text{CPSK}))$. Further, when the client receives (resp. the server sends) the message $(\text{SH}, \text{SKS}^\dagger, \text{SPSK})$, they set $cid_{initiator}[3] = sid[3]$ and $cid_{initiator}[4] = sid[4]$. For all other stages $s \in \{1, 2, 5, 6, 7, 8\}$, $cid_{initiator}[s] = cid_{responder}[s] = sid[s]$ is set upon acceptance of the respective stage (i.e., when $sid[s]$ is set as well).

Explicit Authentication. For initiator sessions, all stages achieve explicit authentication when the `ServerFinished` message is verified successfully. This happens right before stage 5 (i.e., CATS) is accepted. That is, upon accepting stage 5 all previous stages receive explicit authentication retroactively and all following stages are explicitly authenticated upon acceptance. Formally, we set EAUTH[initiator, s] = 5 for all stages $s \in \{1, \ldots, 8\}$.

Analogously, responder sessions receive explicit authentication right before accepting stage 8 via the `ClientFinished` message; i.e., EAUTH[responder, s] = 8 for all stages $s \in \{1, \ldots, 8\}$.

Forward Secrecy. Only keys dependent on a Diffie–Hellman secret achieve forward secrecy, so all stages s of the PSK-only handshake have FS$[r, s, \text{fs}]$ = FS$[r, s, \text{wfs2}]$ = ∞ for both roles $r \in \{\text{initiator}, \text{responder}\}$. In the PSK-(EC)DHE handshake, full forward secrecy is achieved at the same stage as explicit authentication for all keys except ETS and EEMS, which are never forward secret. That is, for both roles r and stages $s \in \{3, \ldots, 8\}$ we have FS$[r, s, \text{fs}]$ = EAUTH$[r, s]$. All keys except ETS and EEMS possess weak forward secrecy 2 upon acceptance, so we set FS$[r, s, \text{wfs2}]$ = s for stages $s \in \{3, \ldots, 8\}$. Finally, as stages 1 and 2 (i.e., ETS and EEMS) never achieve forward secrecy we set FS$[r, s, \text{fs}]$ = FS$[r, s, \text{wfs2}]$ = ∞ for both roles r and stages $s \in \{1, 2\}$.

---

[7] Components marked with † are only part of the TLS 1.3 PSK-(EC)DHE handshake.

6.2 Tight Security Analysis of TLS 1.3 PSK-(EC)DHE

We now come to the tight MSKE security result for the TLS 1.3 PSK-(EC)DHE handshake.

Theorem 3. *Let* TLS1.3-PSK-(EC)DHE *be the TLS 1.3 PSK-(EC)DHE handshake protocol (with optional 0-RTT) as specified on the right-hand side in Fig. 1 without handshake encryption. Let* $\mathbb{G}$ *be the Diffie–Hellman group of order* p. *Let* nl *be the length in bits of the nonce, let* hl *be the output length in bits of* $\mathbf{H}$, *and let the pre-shared key space be* KE.PSKS $= \{0,1\}^{hl}$. *We model the functions* $\mathbf{H}$ *and* TKDF$_x$ *for each* $x \in \{binder, \ldots, \mathrm{RMS}\}$ *as 12 independent random oracles* RO$_\mathsf{Th}$, RO$_{binder}$, $\ldots$, RO$_\mathsf{RMS}$. *Then,*

$$\mathrm{Adv}^{\mathsf{MSKE}}_{\mathsf{TLS1.3\text{-}PSK\text{-}(EC)DHE}}(t, q_\mathrm{NS}, q_\mathrm{S}, q_\mathrm{RS}, q_\mathrm{RL}, q_\mathrm{T}, q_\mathrm{RO}) \leq \frac{2q_\mathrm{S}^2}{2^{nl} \cdot p}$$

$$+ \frac{(q_\mathrm{RO} + q_\mathrm{S})^2 + q_\mathrm{NS}^2 + (q_\mathrm{RO} + 6q_\mathrm{S})^2 + q_\mathrm{RO} \cdot q_\mathrm{NS} + q_\mathrm{S}}{2^{hl}} + \frac{4(t + 4\log(p) \cdot q_\mathrm{RO})^2}{p}.$$

Remark 1. Our MSKE model from Sect. 3 assumes pre-shared keys to be uniformly random sampled from KE.PSKS, where here KE.PSKS $= \{0,1\}^{hl}$. This matches how pre-shared keys are derived for session resumption, as well as our analysis of domain separation, which assumes pre-shared keys to be of length hl.

Remark 2. Our bound is easily adapted to any distribution on $\{0,1\}^{hl}$ in order to accommodate out-of-band pre-shared keys that satisfy the length requirement but do not have full entropy. Expectedly, lower-entropy PSK distributions result in weaker bounds, due to the increased chance for collisions between PSKs as well as the adversary guessing a PSK.

Remark 3. In order to deal with small subgroup attacks, note that we assume that implementations properly validate received key shares by checking for membership in the appropriate prime-order group. This has to be done explicitly for NIST curves (secp256r1, secp384r1, and secp521r1 in TLS 1.3 [48, Sect. 4.2.8.2]). Curves like x25519 and x448 rule out small subgroup attacks implicitly, with a mechanism called "clamping". In our proof we treat Diffie–Hellman groups as prime-order groups with uniform exponents in $\mathbb{Z}_p$, as common in the cryptographic literature. However, we stress that clamping as in [43] makes exponents non-uniform over $\mathbb{Z}_p$. Hence, we implicitly assume that this difference in the DH key generation is indistinguishable for the adversary.

6.3 Proof overview

The proof proceeds via a sequence of games in three phases, corresponding to the three ways for an adversary to win the MSKE security game. We begin with Game$_0$, the original MSKE game for protocol TLS1.3-PSK-(EC)DHE described above. In the first phase, we establish that the adversary cannot violate the Sound predicate. In the second phase, we establish the same for the ExplicitAuth predicate. In the third phase, we ensure that all TEST queries return random keys regardless of the value of the challenge bit b, so long as the Fresh predicate is not violated. After that, the adversary cannot win the game with probability better than guessing, rendering its advantage to be 0. We bound the advantage difference introduced by each game hop; collecting these intermediate bounds yields the overall bound. For space reasons, we only provide a summary of the proof in the following and refer to the full version [13] for the full details.

Phase 1: Ensuring Sound

The Sound predicate checks that no more than two sessions can be partnered in a non-replayable stage, and that any two partnered sessions must agree on the stage, pre-shared key identifier, the stage-s key, and each others' identities and roles. We defined our session identifiers so that the stage-s session identifier contains (1) a label unique to that stage, (2) a unique ClientHello and ServerHello message, (3) the $binder$ message: a MAC tag authenticating the ClientHello and pre-shared key, and (4) sufficient information to fix the stage-s key. (This does not mean the key is computable from the sid; it is not.)

We then perform three incremental game hops that cause the FINALIZE oracle to return 0 in the event of a collision between two Hello messages, $binder$ tags, or pre-shared keys. We bound the difference in advantage in the first two game hops via a birthday bound over the number of potentially colliding values (i.e., pairs of nonces and KeyShares in $\mathbb{G}$ for Hello message collisions, and sampled PSK keys for pre-shared key collisions), and the third hop by a reduction to the collision resistance of the RO_{binder} random oracle whose advantage in turn is upper bounded by a birthday bound $\mathrm{Adv}^{\mathsf{CR}}_{\mathrm{RO}_{binder}}(q_{\mathrm{RO}} + q_{\mathrm{S}}) \leq \frac{(q_{\mathrm{RO}} + q_{\mathrm{S}})^2}{2^{hl}}$. The resulting bounds are, in this order: $\Pr[\mathrm{Game}_0] - \Pr[\mathrm{Game}_3] \leq \frac{2q_{\mathrm{S}}^2}{2^{nl \cdot p}} + \frac{q_{\mathrm{NS}}^2}{2^{hl}} + \frac{(q_{\mathrm{RO}} + q_{\mathrm{S}})^2}{2^{hl}}$. As long as no such collisions occur, each stage-s session identifier uniquely determines one client session, one server session (for non-replayable stages), one pre-shared key (and therefore one peer and identifier owning that key), and one stage-s session key. At this point, the Sound predicate will always be true unless FINALIZE would return 0, so the adversary cannot win by violating Sound.

Phase 2: Ensuring ExplicitAuth

In the second phase of the proof, we change the key-derivation process to avoid sampling pre-shared keys wherever possible, instead replacing keys and MAC tags derived from those pre-shared key by uniformly random strings. We then make the adversary lose if it makes queries that would allow him to detect these changes and bound that probability; in particular we ensure that the adversary does not correctly guess a now-random ClientFinished or ServerFinished MAC tag. Sessions achieve explicit authentication just after verifying their received Finished message; eliminating possible forgeries hence ensures that the ExplicitAuth predicate cannot be false without FINALIZE returning 0. All changes in this phase apply only to sessions whose pre-shared key has not been corrupted.

Game 4. Our first of six game hops eliminates collisions in the "transcript hash" function RO_{Th}. We reduce to the collision resistance of RO_{Th} and bound this advantage with a birthday bound: $\Pr[\mathsf{Game}_3] - \Pr[\mathsf{Game}_4] \leq \frac{q_{RO}+6q_S}{2^{hl}}$. (The factor 6 comes from the up to 6 transcript hashes computed in any SEND query.)

Game 5. Our next game forces FINALIZE to return 0 if the adversary guesses any uncorrupted pre-shared key in any random oracle query. Since we assume pre-shared keys are uniformly random, $\Pr[\mathsf{Game}_4] - \Pr[\mathsf{Game}_5] \leq \frac{q_{RO} \cdot q_{NS}}{2^{hl}}$.

Games 6 and 7. In our third game hop, we ask log the stage s key computed in any session in a look-up table SKEYS under its session identifier. Sessions whose partners have logged a key can then, in a fourth game hop, copy the key from SKEYS instead of deriving it. Partnered sessions will always derive the same key as guaranteed by the Sound predicate, so the adversary cannot detect the copying and its advantage does not change. In addition to logging and copying keys, we also log and copy the three MAC tags: *binder*, *fin$_S$*, and *fin$_C$* using another look-up table TAGS. Since MAC tags do not have associated session identifiers, they are logged under the inputs to RO_{binder}, RO_{SF}, resp. RO_{CF}. This technique is inspired by the work of Cohn-Gordon et al. [11].

Game 8. In preparation for the final step in this phase, our fifth game hop eliminates uncorrupted pre-shared keys altogether. We postpone the sampling of the pre-shared key to the REVLONGTERMKEY oracle so that only corrupted sessions hold pre-shared keys. As a consequence of this change, we can no longer compute session keys and MAC tags using the random oracles. Sessions will instead sample these uniformly at random from their respective range. In another look-up table, they log the RO queries they would have made so that these queries can be programmed later if the pre-shared key gets corrupted. Queries to RO before corruption cannot contain the pre-shared key thanks to the previous game, so we do not have to worry about consistency with past queries. We also cannot implement the previous games' check for guessed pre-shared keys in RO queries until these keys are sampled, so we sample new pre-shared keys for all uncorrupted identifiers at the end of the game in the FINALIZE oracle, then perform the check. The programming of the random oracles is perfectly consistent with their responses in earlier games, so the adversary cannot detect when pre-shared keys are chosen in the game and its advantage does not change.

Game 9. The final game in this phase ensures that either ExplicitAuth = true or FINALIZE returns 0. In this game, we return 0 from FINALIZE if any honest session would accept the first explicitly-authenticated stage (stage 5 (CATS) for initiators and stage 8 (RMS) for responders) with an uncorrupted pre-shared key and no honest partner. By the previous game, we established that sessions with uncorrupted pre-shared keys randomly sample their MAC tags, unless they copy a cached result in which case the same computation was made by another session. Thanks to the way we defined our session identifiers, no unpartnered session will copy their MAC tags: the computation of the `ServerFinished` MAC tag contains the hash of the stage-5 *sid* (excluding fin_S); likewise the `ClientFinished` tag contains the hash of the stage-8 *sid*. Since we ruled out hash collisions in the first game of the phase, any two sessions computing the same `ServerFinished` message are stage-5 partners and any two sessions computing the same `ClientFinished` message are stage-8 partners. So any unpartnered session with an uncorrupted pre-shared key has a random MAC tag, and the odds of the adversary guessing such a tag is bounded by $\frac{q_S}{2^{hl}}$. With the prior two games not changing the adversary's advantage, we have $\Pr[\mathsf{Game}_5] - \Pr[\mathsf{Game}_9] \leq \frac{q_S}{2^{hl}}$.

We are now guaranteed that any session accepting the stage that achieves explicit authentication without a corrupted pre-shared key has a partner in that stage. The Sound predicate guarantees that the partner agrees on the peer and pre-shared key identities, which is sufficient to guarantee explicit authentication for all responder sessions. For initiator sessions, we must also note that a partner in stage 5 will become, upon their acceptance, a partner in stages 6 (SATS) and 7 (EMS), whose *sids* are identical to that of stage 5 apart from their labels. An initiator's stage-5 partner will only accept a `ClientFinished` message identical to the one sent by the initiator, at which point they will become a partner also in stage 8. This ensures that the ExplicitAuth predicate can never be false unless one of the flags introduced in this phase causes FINALIZE to return 0.

Phase 3: Ensuring the Challenge Bit is Random and Independent

Our goal in the third and last phase is to ensure that all session keys targeted by a TEST query are uniformly random and independent of the challenge bit b whenever the Fresh predicate is true. Freshness ensures that no session key can be tested twice or tested and revealed in the same stage either by targeting the same session twice or two partnered sessions. It also handles our three levels of forward secrecy.

We can already establish this for TEST queries to sessions in non-forward secret stages 1 (ETS) and 2 (EEMS). These queries violate Fresh unless the sessions' pre-shared keys are never corrupted. Since Game_8, all sessions with uncorrupted pre-shared keys either randomly sample their session keys, or copy random keys from a partner session. If one of these session keys is tested, it cannot have been output by another TEST or REVSESSIONKEY query without violating Fresh. Therefore the response to the TEST query is a uniformly random string, independent of all other oracle responses and the challenge bit b.

The remaining stages (3–8) have weak forward secrecy 2 until explicit authentication is achieved, then they have full forward secrecy. These stages' keys may be tested even if the session's pre-shared key has been corrupted, so long as there is a contributive partner (or, in the case of full forward secrecy, that the corruption occurred after forward secrecy was achieved). We use one last game hop to ensure these keys are uniformly random when they are tested.

Game 10. In Game_{10}, we cause the FINALIZE oracle to return 0 if the adversary should ever make a random oracle query containing the Diffie–Hellman secret

DHE of an honest partnered session whose pre-shared key was corrupted. Without such a query, all keys derived from a Diffie–Hellman secret sampled uniformly at random by the random oracles.

We bound the probability of this event via a reduction $\mathcal{B}_{DHE}$ to the strong Diffie–Hellman problem in group $\mathbb{G}$. (Recall that $\mathbb{G}$ has order p and generator g.) In this problem, the adversary $\mathcal{B}_{DHE}$ gets as input a strong DH challenge $(A = g^a, B = g^b)$ as well as access to an oracle $stDH_a$ for the decisional Diffie–Hellman (DDH) problem with the first argument fixed. Given inputs $C \leftarrow g^c$ and W for any $c \in \mathbb{Z}_p$, $stDH_a(C, W)$ returns true if and only if $W = g^{ac} = C^a$. The goal of $\mathcal{B}_{DHE}$ is to submit Z to its FINALIZE oracle such that $Z = g^{ab}$.

The reduction $\mathcal{B}_{DHE}$ simulates $Game_{10}$ for the MSKE adversary $\mathcal{A}$. At a high level, it uses rerandomization to embed its strong DH challenge A, resp. B, into the key shares of every initiator session, resp. every partnered responder session. To embed a challenge A in its key share, a session samples a "randomizer" $\tau \xleftarrow{\$} \mathbb{Z}_p$, and sets its key share to $X \leftarrow A \cdot g^\tau$. If $\mathcal{A}$ should make an RO query containing the Diffie–Hellman secret associated with two embedded key shares, the reduction can detect this query with its DDH oracle. It then extracts the solution to its strong DH challenge from the query's DH secret, calls the FINALIZE oracle, and wins its own game.

There are a few subtleties to the reduction, which requires us to extend the technique of CCGJJ [11]. Unlike honest executions of the protocol, the reduction's simulated sessions with embedded key shares do not know their own secret Diffie–Hellman exponents. If their pre-shared keys are never corrupted, this does not matter because session keys and MAC tags are randomly sampled. Corrupted sessions, however, cannot use the random oracles to compute these values as they would in $Game_{10}$. Instead, $\mathcal{B}_{DHE}$ samples session keys and MAC tags uniformly at random and uses several look-up tables to program random oracle queries and maintain consistency between sessions.

With this infrastructure in place, the reduction proceeds in the following way. Whenever a partnered session with embedded key share would need its Diffie–Hellman secret, it searches all past RO queries for this secret. It looks up the initiator's stored randomizer τ and the responder's randomizer τ'. Then for each guess $\mathbb{Z}$ in a past RO query, the reduction queries the strong Diffie–Hellman oracle on the responder's key share SKS and $C \leftarrow \mathbb{Z} \cdot g^{-\tau}$. This query will return true if the adversary correctly guessed the Diffie–Hellman secret; in this case the reduction calls $FINALIZE(Z \cdot g^{-\tau} \cdot g^{-\tau'})$ and solves its strong DH challenge. Unpartnered sessions do the same thing, except that the responder has no randomizer; in response to the strong DH oracle answering true they hence merely program their session keys instead of calling FINALIZE. We emphasize that for tightness, it is crucial to maintain efficiency during this process. We do so by only checking RO queries whose context matches the hashed protocol transcript; this ensures $\mathcal{B}_{DHE}$ makes at most 2 $stDH_a$ queries for each RO query.

After a session chooses its session key or MAC tag, it stores the chosen value, its transcript, and all known randomizers in a table RndList. When the reduction answers future RO queries, it will use this table to check if a query contains the

Diffie–Hellman secret of an accepted session using the strong DH oracle as above; if so, they program or call FINALIZE in the same way.

This reduction solves the strong Diffie–Hellman problem whenever the adversary makes an RO query containing a partnered session's Diffie–Hellman secret, so for reduction $\mathcal{B}_{DHE}$ with runtime $t_{\mathcal{B}_{DHE}}$, we have $\Pr[\mathsf{Game}_9] - \Pr[\mathsf{Game}_{10}] \leq \mathsf{Adv}_{\mathbb{G}}^{\mathsf{stDH}}(t_{\mathcal{B}_{DHE}}, 2q_{RO})$. Davis and Günther gave a bound in the generic group model for the strong DH problem; applying their Theorem 3.3 [14] results in $\Pr[\mathsf{Game}_9] - \Pr[\mathsf{Game}_{10}] \leq \frac{t_{\mathcal{B}_{DHE}}^2}{p}$.

At this point in the proof, the adversary $\mathcal{A}$ cannot possibly make a RO query that outputs any tested session key of a forward secret (full or wfs2) stage s. If the tested session's pre-shared key is uncorrupted, $\mathcal{A}$ cannot make the query because of Game_5. If the session has a contributive partner in stage s, then from Game_{10}, $\mathcal{A}$ cannot make the query because it contains the Diffie–Hellman secret of a partnered session. If it has accepted with no contributive partner and a corrupted pre-shared key, then by the guarantees we established in Phase 2, the corruption must have occurred before forward secrecy and explicit authentication were achieved.

As a result, the output of any TEST query (that does not violate Fresh) is a random string, sampled by either a session or the RO oracle independently of all other game variables including the challenge bit b. The adversary therefore has a probability no greater than $\frac{1}{2}$ of winning Game_{10}. Collecting this probability with the other bounds between games in our sequence gives the proof.   □

6.4   Full Security Bound for TLS 1.3 PSK-(EC)DHE and PSK-only

We can finally combine the results of Sects. 4, 5, and our key exchange bound above to produce fully concrete bounds for the TLS 1.3 PSK-(EC)DHE and PSK-only handshake protocols as specified on the left-hand side of Figure 1. This bound applies to the protocol *with handshake traffic encryption* and *internal keys* when *only modeling as random oracle* $\mathsf{RO_H}$ the hash function **H**.

First, we define three variants of the TLS 1.3 PSK handshake:

- KE_0, as defined in Theorem 1 with handshake traffic encryption and one random oracle $\mathsf{RO_H}$. (This is the variant we want to obtain our overall result for.)
- KE_1, as defined in Theorem 1 with handshake traffic encryption and 12 random oracles $\mathsf{RO_{Th}}$, RO_{binder}, ..., $\mathsf{RO_{RMS}}$.
- KE_2: as defined in Theorem 2, with no handshake traffic encryption and 12 random oracles $\mathsf{RO_{Th}}$, RO_{binder}, ..., $\mathsf{RO_{RMS}}$.

Theorem 1 grants that $\mathsf{Adv}_{\mathsf{KE}_0}^{\mathsf{MSKE}}(t, q_{NS}, q_S, q_{RS}, q_{RL}, q_T, q_{RO}) \leq \mathsf{Adv}_{\mathsf{KE}_1}^{\mathsf{MSKE}}(t, q_{NS}, q_S, q_{RS}, q_{RL}, q_T, q_{RO}) + \frac{2(12q_S + q_{RO})^2}{2^{hl}} + \frac{2q_{RO}^2}{2^{hl}} + \frac{8(q_{RO} + 36q_S)^2}{2^{hl}}$.

Next, we apply Theorem 2, yielding the bound $\mathsf{Adv}_{\mathsf{KE}_1}^{\mathsf{MSKE}}(t, q_{NS}, q_S, q_{RS}, q_{RL}, q_T, q_{RO}) \leq \mathsf{Adv}_{\mathsf{KE}_2}^{\mathsf{MSKE}}(t + t_{AEAD} \cdot q_S, q_{NS}, q_S, q_{RS} + q_S, q_{RL}, q_T, q_{RO})$, where t_{AEAD} is the maximum time required to execute AEAD encryption or decryption of TLS 1.3 messages.

Theorem 3 then finally and entirely bounds the advantage against the MSKE security of KE_2. Collecting these bounds yields the following overall result for the MSKE security of the TLS 1.3 PSK-(EC)DHE handshake protocol.

Corollary 1. *Let* TLS1.3-PSK-(EC)DHE *be the TLS 1.3 PSK-(EC)DHE handshake protocol as specified on the left-hand side in Fig. 1. Let* $\mathbb{G}$ *be the Diffie–Hellman group of order* p. *Let* nl *be the length in bits of the nonce, let* hl *be the output length in bits of* $\mathbf{H}$, *and let the pre-shared key space be* KE.PSKS $= \{0,1\}^{hl}$. *Let* $\mathbf{H}$ *be modeled as a random oracle* $\mathsf{RO_H}$. *Then,*

$$\mathrm{Adv}^{\mathsf{MSKE}}_{\text{TLS1.3-PSK-(EC)DHE}}(t, q_{\mathrm{NS}}, q_{\mathrm{S}}, q_{\mathrm{RS}}, q_{\mathrm{RL}}, q_{\mathrm{T}}, q_{\mathrm{RO}})$$

$$\leq \frac{2q_{\mathrm{S}}^2}{2^{nl} \cdot p} + \frac{(q_{\mathrm{RO}} + q_{\mathrm{S}})^2 + q_{\mathrm{NS}}^2 + (q_{\mathrm{RO}} + 6q_{\mathrm{S}})^2 + q_{\mathrm{RO}} \cdot q_{\mathrm{NS}} + q_{\mathrm{S}}}{2^{hl}}$$

$$+ \frac{4(t + t_{\mathrm{AEAD}} \cdot q_{\mathrm{S}} + 4\log(p) \cdot q_{\mathrm{RO}})^2}{p}$$

$$+ \frac{2(12q_{\mathrm{S}} + q_{\mathrm{RO}})^2 + 2q_{\mathrm{RO}}^2 + 8(q_{\mathrm{RO}} + 36q_{\mathrm{S}})^2}{2^{hl}}.$$

Table 1. Exemplary concrete advantages of a key exchange adversary with given resources t (running time), $\#N$ (number of pre-shared keys), $\#S$ (number of sessions), and $\#RO$ (number of random oracle queries) in breaking the security of the TLS 1.3 PSK handshake protocols. Numbers based on the prior bounds by Dowling et al. [21] and our bounds for PSK-(EC)DHE and PSK-only (in Corollaries 1 resp. 2). "Target" indicates the maximal advantage $t/2^b$ tolerable for a given bound on t when aiming for the respective curve's (or hash function's, in case of PSK-only mode) bit security level b; entries in green -shaded cells meet that target. Mode indicates PSK-only mode (with SHA384) or otherwise PSK-(EC)DHE mode with the given curve secp256r1, x25519 (with SHA256), or secp384r1, x448, secp521r1 (with SHA384).

	Adversary resources						Security bound	
b	t	$\#N$	$\#S$	$\#RO$	Target	Mode	DFGS [21]	Us (Cor. 1, 2)
128	2^{60}	2^{25}	2^{35}	2^{50}	2^{-68}	PSK-only	$\approx 2^{-119}$	$\approx 2^{-152}$
128	2^{80}	2^{35}	2^{55}	2^{70}	2^{-48}	PSK-only	$\approx 2^{-59}$	$\approx 2^{-112}$
128	2^{60}	2^{25}	2^{35}	2^{50}	2^{-68}	secp256r1	$\approx 2^{-61}$	$\approx 2^{-132}$
128	2^{80}	2^{35}	2^{55}	2^{70}	2^{-48}	secp256r1	1	$\approx 2^{-92}$
128	2^{60}	2^{25}	2^{35}	2^{50}	2^{-68}	x25519	$\approx 2^{-57}$	$\approx 2^{-128}$
128	2^{80}	2^{35}	2^{55}	2^{70}	2^{-48}	x25519	1	$\approx 2^{-88}$
192	2^{60}	2^{25}	2^{35}	2^{50}	2^{-132}	secp384r1	$\approx 2^{-189}$	$\approx 2^{-259}$
192	2^{80}	2^{35}	2^{55}	2^{70}	2^{-112}	secp384r1	$\approx 2^{-108}$	$\approx 2^{-219}$
224	2^{60}	2^{25}	2^{35}	2^{50}	2^{-164}	x448	$\approx 2^{-200}$	$\approx 2^{-280}$
224	2^{80}	2^{35}	2^{55}	2^{70}	2^{-144}	x448	$\approx 2^{-110}$	$\approx 2^{-240}$
256	2^{60}	2^{25}	2^{35}	2^{50}	2^{-196}	secp521r1	$\approx 2^{-200}$	$\approx 2^{-280}$
256	2^{80}	2^{35}	2^{55}	2^{70}	2^{-176}	secp521r1	$\approx 2^{-110}$	$\approx 2^{-240}$

For the PSK-only mode, we obtain a similar bound, naturally omitting the strong Diffie–Hellman and group-element collision terms. Due to space restrictions, we only state the final PSK-only bound here and defer further details to the full version [13].

Corollary 2. *Let* TLS1.3-PSK *be the TLS 1.3 PSK-only handshake protocol as specified on the left-hand side in Fig. 1. Let nl be the length in bits of the nonce, let hl be the output length in bits of* **H**, *and let the pre-shared key space be* KE.PSKS $= \{0,1\}^{hl}$. *Let* **H** *be modeled as a random oracle* $\mathsf{RO_H}$. *Then,*

$$
\mathrm{Adv}^{\mathsf{MSKE}}_{\mathsf{TLS1.3\text{-}PSK}}(t, q_{\mathsf{NS}}, q_{\mathsf{S}}, q_{\mathsf{RS}}, q_{\mathsf{RL}}, q_{\mathsf{T}}, q_{\mathsf{RO}})
$$

$$
\leq \frac{2q_{\mathsf{S}}^2}{2^{nl}} + \frac{(q_{\mathsf{RO}} + q_{\mathsf{S}})^2 + q_{\mathsf{NS}}^2 + (q_{\mathsf{RO}} + 6q_{\mathsf{S}})^2 + q_{\mathsf{RO}} \cdot q_{\mathsf{NS}} + q_{\mathsf{S}}}{2^{hl}}
$$

$$
+ \frac{2(12q_{\mathsf{S}} + q_{\mathsf{RO}})^2 + 2q_{\mathsf{RO}}^2 + 8(q_{\mathsf{RO}} + 36q_{\mathsf{S}})^2}{2^{hl}}.
$$

7 Evaluation

Asymptotically, our tighter security bounds improve on prior analysis of TLS 1.3 by a quadratic factor. We evaluate ours and prior bounds over a wide range of fully concrete resource parameters, following the approach of Davis and Günther [14]. Table 1 shows exemplary concrete advantages; the full range of evaluated parameters is given in extended tables in the full version [13], along with reasoning for how we chose the various ranges of resource parameters. The tables show that while the prior PSK-(EC)DHE bound by Dowling et al. [21] meets the target security goals in a number of configurations, there are at least some settings for all elliptic-curve groups in which the targeted security is not met. Our bounds do significantly better than the target in all configurations we considered. The gap for the PSK-only handshake is less significant as the loosest prior reduction for TLS 1.3 was to the Diffie–Hellman problem.

Overall, our bounds improve on previous analyses of the PSK-only handshake by 15 to 53 bits of security, and those of the PSK-(EC)DHE handshake by 60 to 131 bits of security, across all our parameters evaluated.

References

1. Arfaoui, G., Bultel, X., Fouque, P.A., Nedelcu, A., Onete, C.: The privacy of the TLS 1.3 protocol. PoPETs **2019**(4), 190–210 (2019). https://doi.org/10.2478/popets-2019-0065
2. Avoine, G., Canard, S., Ferreira, L.: Symmetric-key authenticated key exchange (SAKE) with perfect forward secrecy. In: Jarecki, S. (ed.) CT-RSA 2020. LNCS, vol. 12006, pp. 199–224. Springer, Cham (2020). https://doi.org/10.1007/978-3-030-40186-3_10
3. Bader, C., Hofheinz, D., Jager, T., Kiltz, E., Li, Y.: Tightly-secure authenticated key exchange. In: Dodis, Y., Nielsen, J.B. (eds.) TCC 2015. LNCS, vol. 9014, pp. 629–658. Springer, Heidelberg (2015). https://doi.org/10.1007/978-3-662-46494-6_26

4. Bader, C., Jager, T., Li, Y., Schäge, S.: On the impossibility of tight cryptographic reductions. In: Fischlin, M., Coron, J.-S. (eds.) EUROCRYPT 2016. LNCS, vol. 9666, pp. 273–304. Springer, Heidelberg (2016). https://doi.org/10.1007/978-3-662-49896-5_10

5. Bellare, M., Davis, H., Günther, F.: Separate your domains: NIST PQC KEMs, oracle cloning and read-only indifferentiability. In: Canteaut, A., Ishai, Y. (eds.) EUROCRYPT 2020. LNCS, vol. 12106, pp. 3–32. Springer, Cham (2020). https://doi.org/10.1007/978-3-030-45724-2_1

6. Bhargavan, K., Brzuska, C., Fournet, C., Green, M., Kohlweiss, M., Zanella-Béguelin, S.: Downgrade resilience in key-exchange protocols. In: 2016 IEEE Symposium on Security and Privacy, pp. 506–525. IEEE Computer Society Press (2016). https://doi.org/10.1109/SP.2016.37

7. Bhargavan, K., Fournet, C., Kohlweiss, M., Pironti, A., Strub, P.-Y., Zanella-Béguelin, S.: Proving the TLS handshake secure (as it is). In: Garay, J.A., Gennaro, R. (eds.) CRYPTO 2014. LNCS, vol. 8617, pp. 235–255. Springer, Heidelberg (2014). https://doi.org/10.1007/978-3-662-44381-1_14

8. Boyd, C., Cremers, C., Feltz, M., Paterson, K.G., Poettering, B., Stebila, D.: ASICS: authenticated key exchange security incorporating certification systems. In: Crampton, J., Jajodia, S., Mayes, K. (eds.) ESORICS 2013. LNCS, vol. 8134, pp. 381–399. Springer, Heidelberg (2013). https://doi.org/10.1007/978-3-642-40203-6_22

9. Boyd, C., Davies, G.T., de Kock, B., Gellert, K., Jager, T., Millerjord, L.: Symmetric key exchange with full forward security and robust synchronization. In: ASIACRYPT 2021 (2021). To appear. Available as Cryptology ePrint Archive, Report 2021/702. https://ia.cr/2021/702

10. Brzuska, C., Delignat-Lavaud, A., Egger, C., Fournet, C., Kohbrok, K., Kohlweiss, M.: Key-schedule security for the TLS 1.3 standard. Cryptology ePrint Archive, Report 2021/467 (2021). https://eprint.iacr.org/2021/467

11. Cohn-Gordon, K., Cremers, C., Gjøsteen, K., Jacobsen, H., Jager, T.: Highly efficient key exchange protocols with optimal tightness. In: Boldyreva, A., Micciancio, D. (eds.) CRYPTO 2019. LNCS, vol. 11694, pp. 767–797. Springer, Cham (2019). https://doi.org/10.1007/978-3-030-26954-8_25

12. Cremers, C., Horvat, M., Scott, S., van der Merwe, T.: Automated analysis and verification of TLS 1.3: 0-RTT, resumption and delayed authentication. In: 2016 IEEE Symposium on Security and Privacy, pp. 470–485. IEEE Computer Society Press (2016). https://doi.org/10.1109/SP.2016.35

13. Davis, H., Diemert, D., Günther, F., Jager, T.: On the Concrete Security of TLS 1.3 PSK Mode. Cryptology ePrint Archive (2022). https://eprint.iacr.org/2022/246

14. Davis, H., Günther, F.: Tighter proofs for the SIGMA and TLS 1.3 key exchange protocols. In: Sako, K., Tippenhauer, N.O. (eds.) ACNS 2021. LNCS, vol. 12727, pp. 448–479. Springer, Cham (2021). https://doi.org/10.1007/978-3-030-78375-4_18

15. de Saint Guilhem, C., Fischlin, M., Warinschi, B.: Authentication in key-exchange: definitions, relations and composition. In: Jia, L., Küsters, R. (eds.) CSF 2020 Computer Security Foundations Symposium, pp. 288–303. IEEE Computer Society Press (2020). https://doi.org/10.1109/CSF49147.2020.00028

16. Diemert, D., Gellert, K., Jager, T., Lyu, L.: More efficient digital signatures with tight multi-user security. In: Garay, J.A. (ed.) PKC 2021. LNCS, vol. 12711, pp. 1–31. Springer, Cham (2021). https://doi.org/10.1007/978-3-030-75248-4_1

17. Diemert, D., Jager, T.: On the tight security of TLS 1.3: theoretically sound cryptographic parameters for real-world deployments. J. Cryptol. **34**(3), 1–57 (2021). https://doi.org/10.1007/s00145-021-09388-x
18. Dodis, Y., Ristenpart, T., Steinberger, J., Tessaro, S.: To hash or not to hash again? (in)differentiability results for H^2 and HMAC. In: Safavi-Naini, R., Canetti, R. (eds.) CRYPTO 2012. LNCS, vol. 7417, pp. 348–366. Springer, Heidelberg (2012). https://doi.org/10.1007/978-3-642-32009-5_21
19. Dowling, B., Fischlin, M., Günther, F., Stebila, D.: A cryptographic analysis of the TLS 1.3 handshake protocol candidates. In: Ray, I., Li, N., Kruegel, C. (eds.) ACM CCS 2015, pp. 1197–1210. ACM Press (2015). https://doi.org/10.1145/2810103.2813653
20. Dowling, B., Fischlin, M., Günther, F., Stebila, D.: A cryptographic analysis of the TLS 1.3 draft-10 full and pre-shared key handshake protocol. Cryptology ePrint Archive, Report 2016/081 (2016). https://eprint.iacr.org/2016/081
21. Dowling, B., Fischlin, M., Günther, F., Stebila, D.: A cryptographic analysis of the TLS 1.3 handshake protocol. J. Cryptol. **34**(4), 1–69 (2021). https://doi.org/10.1007/s00145-021-09384-1
22. Dowling, B., Stebila, D.: Modelling ciphersuite and version negotiation in the TLS protocol. In: Foo, E., Stebila, D. (eds.) ACISP 2015. LNCS, vol. 9144, pp. 270–288. Springer, Cham (2015). https://doi.org/10.1007/978-3-319-19962-7_16
23. Drucker, N., Gueron, S.: Selfie: reflections on TLS 1.3 with PSK. J. Cryptol. **34**(3), 1–18 (2021). https://doi.org/10.1007/s00145-021-09387-y
24. Fischlin, M., Günther, F.: Multi-stage key exchange and the case of Google's QUIC protocol. In: Ahn, G.J., Yung, M., Li, N. (eds.) ACM CCS 2014, pp. 1193–1204. ACM Press (2014). https://doi.org/10.1145/2660267.2660308
25. Fischlin, M., Günther, F.: Replay attacks on zero round-trip time: the case of the TLS 1.3 handshake candidates. In: 2017 IEEE European Symposium on Security and Privacy, EuroS&P 2017, pp. 60–75. IEEE (2017)
26. Fischlin, M., Günther, F., Schmidt, B., Warinschi, B.: Key confirmation in key exchange: a formal treatment and implications for TLS 1.3. In: 2016 IEEE Symposium on Security and Privacy, pp. 452–469. IEEE Computer Society Press (2016). https://doi.org/10.1109/SP.2016.34
27. Giesen, F., Kohlar, F., Stebila, D.: On the security of TLS renegotiation. In: Sadeghi, A.R., Gligor, V.D., Yung, M. (eds.) ACM CCS 2013, pp. 387–398. ACM Press (2013). https://doi.org/10.1145/2508859.2516694
28. Gjøsteen, K., Jager, T.: Practical and tightly-secure digital signatures and authenticated key exchange. In: Shacham, H., Boldyreva, A. (eds.) CRYPTO 2018. LNCS, vol. 10992, pp. 95–125. Springer, Cham (2018). https://doi.org/10.1007/978-3-319-96881-0_4
29. Günther, C.G.: An identity-based key-exchange protocol. In: Quisquater, J.-J., Vandewalle, J. (eds.) EUROCRYPT 1989. LNCS, vol. 434, pp. 29–37. Springer, Heidelberg (1990). https://doi.org/10.1007/3-540-46885-4_5
30. Günther, F.: Modeling Advanced Security Aspects of Key Exchange and Secure Channel Protocols. Ph.D. thesis, Technische Universität Darmstadt, Darmstadt, Germany (2018). http://tuprints.ulb.tu-darmstadt.de/7162/
31. Han, S., Jager, T., Kiltz, E., Liu, S., Pan, J., Riepel, D., Schäge, S.: Authenticated key exchange and signatures with tight security in the standard model. In: Malkin, T., Peikert, C. (eds.) CRYPTO 2021. LNCS, vol. 12828, pp. 670–700. Springer, Cham (2021). https://doi.org/10.1007/978-3-030-84259-8_23

32. Jager, T., Kiltz, E., Riepel, D., Schäge, S.: Tightly-secure authenticated key exchange, revisited. In: Canteaut, A., Standaert, F.-X. (eds.) EUROCRYPT 2021. LNCS, vol. 12696, pp. 117–146. Springer, Cham (2021). https://doi.org/10.1007/978-3-030-77870-5_5

33. Jager, T., Kohlar, F., Schäge, S., Schwenk, J.: On the security of TLS-DHE in the standard model. In: Safavi-Naini, R., Canetti, R. (eds.) CRYPTO 2012. LNCS, vol. 7417, pp. 273–293. Springer, Heidelberg (2012). https://doi.org/10.1007/978-3-642-32009-5_17

34. Jager, T., Schwenk, J., Somorovsky, J.: On the security of TLS 1.3 and QUIC against weaknesses in PKCS#1 v1.5 encryption. In: Ray, I., Li, N., Kruegel, C. (eds.) ACM CCS 2015, pp. 1185–1196. ACM Press (2015). https://doi.org/10.1145/2810103.2813657

35. Krawczyk, H., Bellare, M., Canetti, R.: HMAC: Keyed-Hashing for Message Authentication. RFC 2104 (Informational) (1997). https://doi.org/10.17487/RFC2104, https://www.rfc-editor.org/rfc/rfc2104.txt, updated by RFC 6151

36. Krawczyk, H., Eronen, P.: HMAC-based Extract-and-Expand Key Derivation Function (HKDF). RFC 5869 (Informational) (2010). https://doi.org/10.17487/RFC5869, https://www.rfc-editor.org/rfc/rfc5869.txt

37. Krawczyk, H.: HMQV: A high-performance secure Diffie-Hellman protocol. Cryptology ePrint Archive, Report 2005/176 (2005). https://eprint.iacr.org/2005/176

38. Krawczyk, H.: Cryptographic extraction and key derivation: the HKDF scheme. In: Rabin, T. (ed.) CRYPTO 2010. LNCS, vol. 6223, pp. 631–648. Springer, Heidelberg (2010). https://doi.org/10.1007/978-3-642-14623-7_34

39. Krawczyk, H.: A unilateral-to-mutual authentication compiler for key exchange (with applications to client authentication in TLS 1.3). In: Weippl, E.R., Katzenbeisser, S., Kruegel, C., Myers, A.C., Halevi, S. (eds.) ACM CCS 2016, pp. 1438–1450. ACM Press (2016). https://doi.org/10.1145/2976749.2978325

40. Krawczyk, H., Paterson, K.G., Wee, H.: On the security of the TLS protocol: a systematic analysis. In: Canetti, R., Garay, J.A. (eds.) CRYPTO 2013. LNCS, vol. 8042, pp. 429–448. Springer, Heidelberg (2013). https://doi.org/10.1007/978-3-642-40041-4_24

41. Krawczyk, H., Paterson, K.G., Wee, H.: On the security of the TLS protocol: a systematic analysis. Cryptology ePrint Archive, Report 2013/339 (2013). https://eprint.iacr.org/2013/339

42. Krawczyk, H., Wee, H.: The OPTLS protocol and TLS 1.3. In: 2016 IEEE European Symposium on Security and Privacy, pp. 81–96. IEEE (2016). https://doi.org/10.1109/EuroSP.2016.18

43. Langley, A., Hamburg, M., Turner, S.: Elliptic Curves for Security. RFC 7748 (Informational) (2016). https://doi.org/10.17487/RFC7748, https://www.rfc-editor.org/rfc/rfc7748.txt

44. Li, Y., Schäge, S., Yang, Z., Kohlar, F., Schwenk, J.: On the security of the pre-shared key ciphersuites of TLS. In: Krawczyk, H. (ed.) PKC 2014. LNCS, vol. 8383, pp. 669–684. Springer, Heidelberg (2014). https://doi.org/10.1007/978-3-642-54631-0_38

45. Liu, X., Liu, S., Gu, D., Weng, J.: Two-pass authenticated key exchange with explicit authentication and tight security. In: Moriai, S., Wang, H. (eds.) ASIACRYPT 2020. LNCS, vol. 12492, pp. 785–814. Springer, Cham (2020). https://doi.org/10.1007/978-3-030-64834-3_27

46. Maurer, U., Renner, R., Holenstein, C.: Indifferentiability, impossibility results on reductions, and applications to the random oracle methodology. In: Naor, M. (ed.) TCC 2004. LNCS, vol. 2951, pp. 21–39. Springer, Heidelberg (2004). https://doi.org/10.1007/978-3-540-24638-1_2

47. National Institute of Standards and Technology: FIPS PUB 180–4: Secure Hash Standard (SHS) (2012)

48. Rescorla, E.: The Transport Layer Security (TLS) Protocol Version 1.3. RFC 8446 (Proposed Standard) (2018). https://doi.org/10.17487/RFC8446, https://www.rfc-editor.org/rfc/rfc8446.txt

49. Schwabe, P., Stebila, D., Wiggers, T.: Post-quantum TLS without handshake signatures. In: Ligatti, J., Ou, X., Katz, J., Vigna, G. (eds.) ACM CCS 2020, pp. 1461–1480. ACM Press (2020). https://doi.org/10.1145/3372297.3423350

Correction to: Non-Interactive Zero-Knowledge Proofs with Fine-Grained Security

Yuyu Wang[ID] and Jiaxin Pan[ID]

Correction to:
Chapter "Non-Interactive Zero-Knowledge Proofs with Fine-Grained Security" in:
O. Dunkelman and S. Dziembowski (Eds.): *Advances in Cryptology – EUROCRYPT 2022*, LNCS 13276, https://doi.org/10.1007/978-3-031-07085-3_11

In an older version of this paper, there was an erroneous insertion of an equation on page 315. This has been removed.

The updated version of this chapter can be found at
https://doi.org/10.1007/978-3-031-07085-3_11

O. Dunkelman and S. Dziembowski (Eds.): EUROCRYPT 2022, LNCS 13276, p. C1, 2022.
https://doi.org/10.1007/978-3-031-07085-3_31

Author Index

Printed in the United States
by Baker & Taylor Publisher Services